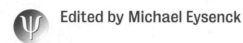
Edited by Michael Eysenck

Psychology

an integrated approach

Longman

Addison Wesley Longman Limited,
Edinburgh Gate, Harlow,
Essex CM20 2JE, England
and Associated Companies throughout the world.

*Published in the United States of America
by Addison Wesley Longman Inc., New York*

© Addison Wesley Longman Limited 1998

First published 1998

ISBN 0 582 29884 9

British Library Cataloguing-in-Publication Data

A catalogue record for this book is
available from the British Library

**Library of Congress Cataloging-in-Publication Data
are available**

*The publisher has made every attempt to obtain permission to reproduce
material in this book from the appropriate source. If there are any errors
or omissions please contact the publisher who will make suitable
acknowledgment in the reprint.*

Set in 10.5/11.5 Perpetua by 30

Produced by Addison Wesley Longman Singapore Pte Ltd
Printed in Singapore

Contents

Ψ Full contents

Contents

Ψ Preface

In recent years there has been a marked increase in the number of psychology students in universities throughout Europe. In the United Kingdom, for example, psychology is now the fifth most popular subject at university level, and it attracts far more students than any other science. Despite these encouraging statistics and the many excellent American texts around, there have been surprisingly few attempts to provide students with a genuinely European alternative, a need which this book seeks to address.

What have we tried to achieve in this book? First, we have attempted to combine the accessibility and good production values of American texts with more sophisticated coverage and an approach that encourages students to think for themselves. Second, whereas American textbooks tend to ignore the work of non-American psychologists, we have ensured that the best European psychology is fully represented in our textbook. Third, we have benefited enormously from the fact that the psychologists who have contributed chapters to this textbook are leading experts in their respective fields. Fourth, we have responded to the growing emphasis on the practical and professional applications of psychology in the teaching of undergraduate psychology. This has been done, for example, by including chapters on health and organizational psychology.

The production of this book has made use of the skills and expertise of many people, and I would would like to express my thanks and gratitude to all of them for the efforts they have put in. The authors of the various chapters have (at least for the most part!) responded well to the challenge of organizing their chapters in a common format for the benefit of readers, and have produced excellent accounts of their respective areas of expertise. The efforts of several people at Addison Wesley Longman have also been absolutely invaluable. Among those who have worked tirelessly and effectively on this project are the following: Christian Turner, Jane Toettcher, Claire Baumforth, Lynn Brandon, Maggie Wells, Lynette Miller and Christine Firth. However, special thanks should go to Sarah Caro, the Senior Commissioning Editor, whose enthusiasm and charm played a major role in ensuring that the contributors did what they were supposed to do when they were supposed to do it.

All of us who have been involved with this project believe that we have been successful in producing a textbook of great usefulness to all psychology students. However, it is of course ultimately up to you, the readers of this book, to decide whether our beliefs are justified or not.

Michael W. Eysenck

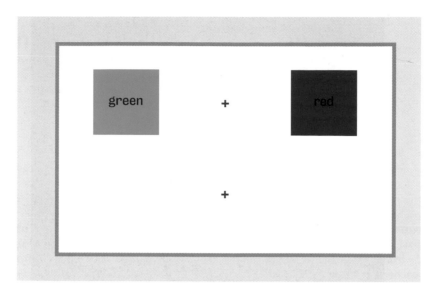

Colour Plate 3 Stare at the top cross for a minute or two under a bright light and then transfer your gaze to the bottom cross. You should see a coloured object appear for a while. This is an illusion because the paper is pure white. How is this explained? See Chapter 4.

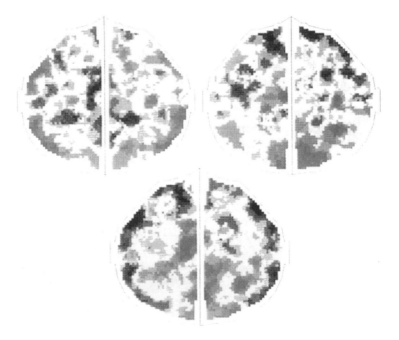

Colour Plate 4 Regional cerebral bloodflow patterns. The pattern at the top right was obtained while the subject silently recollected personal events that had happened many years ago. The pattern at the top left was obtained while the subject was silently thinking about a particular topic of general (semantic) information, initially acquired many years previously. In these patterns the yellow colours indicate the level of bloodflow near the mean of the hemisphere, the red colours indicate relatively higher levels of activation, and the green colours relatively lower levels. The bottom figure shows the difference between episodic and semantic patterns. Here yellows indicate little difference between the two kinds of mental activity, the reds show relatively greater activation of the region during episodic retrieval, and two greens show relatively greater activation during semantic retrieval.

A special characteristic of the discipline of psychology is that the study of the 'mind' is necessarily self-reflective. Whether we examine observable behaviour or develop theoretical models about the 'mind', we employ consciousness to investigate the products of consciousness. The psychologist is self-confronted: the mind observes and attempts to understand the mind.

Nazanin Derakshan

CHAPTER 1

Introduction and study skills
Michael Eysenck

KEY CONCEPTS • nature of psychology • history of psychology •
contemporary perspectives in psychology • ethical issues in psychology

❏ Chapter preview

When you have read this chapter, you should be able to

- have some understanding of the subject matter and scope of psychology
- appreciate the role played by other disciplines in the development of
  psychology as a scientific discipline
- summarize the major contemporary perspectives on psychology
- express some of the major ethical issues involved in conducting research
  on humans and the members of other species

Nature of psychology

Why study psychology? There are many answers to that question, but the best one is that psychology covers almost everything which is of interest to human beings. The great majority of people are more interested in what drives them and others than in just about anything else, and that is precisely what psychology is all about. You can see something of the enormous extent of contemporary psychology by considering the following (almost random) selection of issues which have been addressed by psychologists:

- Does telepathy exist?
- What happens when we dream?
- What are the similarities and differences between loving and liking?
- Why are some people cleverer than others?
- How does human memory work?
- How does therapy cure mental disorders?
- Are women better drivers than men?
- How do friendships form?

As might be expected from the great range of psychology, it has numerous applications in everyday life (see box). Other areas in which psychologists work are advertising and marketing, where a knowledge of psychology is of great value.

Before proceeding further, we need to consider how we are going to define psychology. According to the authors of most textbooks, psychology is the science of behaviour. This definition has some merit, because it is true that most psychologists do attach considerable importance to observing and measuring the behaviour of participants in their studies. However, psychology is not just the science of behaviour. Many psychologists accept that participants' accounts of their own conscious experience (often known as **introspection**) provide valuable information when trying to understand human behaviour. This led Sternberg (1995: 4) to define psychology as 'the study of the mind and of behaviour' and to argue that psychologists 'seek to understand how we think, learn, perceive, feel, act, interact with others, and even understand ourselves'.

There is another reason for not regarding psychology simply as the science of behaviour. Most psychologists are not in fact *directly* interested in behaviour itself. What they are attempting to do is to use information about behaviour in order to draw inferences about internal processes and motives. Thus, psychology is the science which uses introspective and behavioural evidence to understand the internal processes which lead people to think and to behave in the ways they do.

Psychology vs common sense

We are all psychologists in the sense that we spend much of our time trying to understand the motives and behaviour of other people. Perhaps it is for this reason that many people doubt the achievements of scientific psy-

---

Psychology as a profession

Psychology as a university subject is steadily increasing in popularity. With a psychology degree, graduates can choose from a wide range of possible careers.

- Clinical psychologists – from working with children with learning difficulties to counselling people with HIV/AIDS, clinical psychologists use a wide variety of techniques to diagnose and treat emotional and behavioural problems, often working as part of a team within the community or in hospital settings.

- Counselling psychologists – may work with individuals or groups, using psychological theories to enable people to overcome their problems and take control of their lives. They may be employed by general medical practitioners, large organizations or businesses or may work privately.

- Educational psychologists – employed in schools, colleges, nurseries and special units to diagnose and solve learning difficulties, social or emotional problems. They can work independently or through local authorities.

- Health psychologists – using psychological principles to promote healthier living. Employed in hospitals, academic health research units, health authorities and university departments.

- Occupational or industrial psychologists – work within industry, helping in selesting suitable candidates for employment, developing training programmes, ergonomics and the development of health and safety strategies and procedures.

chology. In particular, it is often argued that psychology represents only a modest advance on common sense. This argument does not stand up to scrutiny. For one reason, common sense does not include a coherent body of knowledge about human behaviour. This can be seen if we consider common sense in the form of proverbs. As is well known, there are several pairs of proverbs which are almost exactly opposite in meaning. For example, 'He who hesitates is lost' can be contrasted with 'Look before you leap', and 'Out of sight, out of mind' with 'Absence makes the heart grow fonder'. These examples are all taken from English, but similar pairs of contrasting proverbs are also found in many other languages.

Another reason why psychology is not just common sense is that the findings of many psychological studies are very different from what most people would have predicted. For example, Milgram (1974) carried out a series of studies in which an experimenter divided his participants into pairs to play the role of teacher and learner in a learning task. The teacher was instructed to administer electric shocks to the learner every time he made a mistake, and to increase the intensity of the shock each time. By the time that the shock reached 180 volts, the learner shouted 'I can't stand the pain', and at 270 volts he produced an agonized scream. How many people do you think would be willing to give the maximum (and potentially lethal) 450-volt shock? Milgram found that psychiatrists at a major medical school predicted that approximately one person in a thousand would do this, and non-experts produced similar estimates. In actual fact, Milgram (1974) found that about half of all participants gave the maximum shock. Thus, there was a 500-fold difference between what happened and what common sense would predict!

There are numerous other instances in which the findings of psychologists disprove commonly held views, but we will mention only two here. It is often thought that it is possible to assess people's personalities by asking them to describe what they can see in essentially meaningless inkblots; this is the well-known Rorschach Inkblot test. In fact, this test provides very little useful information about personality (see Chapter 14). In similar fashion, many people think that graphology, or the study of handwriting, is an effective way of assessing personality. The evidence accumulated by psychologists indicates that graphology has practically no value.

Hindsight bias

One of the reasons why non-psychologists claim that the findings of psychologists are commonsensical and unsur-

prising is because of what is known as **hindsight bias**. This is the tendency to be wise after the event. Fischhoff and Beyth (1975) reported evidence of hindsight bias. They asked American students to estimate the probabilities of various possible outcomes immediately prior to President Nixon's trips to China and the former Soviet Union. After the trips were over, the students were asked to do the same task, but they were explicitly told to pay no attention to their knowledge of what had actually happened. In spite of these instructions, the participants thought that the probability of events that had actually happened was considerably greater than they had done before the events had occurred. It seemed that the participants simply could not ignore their knowledge of what had happened, and could no longer remember how uncertain things had looked before the trips took place.

Hindsight bias is very difficult to eliminate. Fischhoff (1977) told his participants all about hindsight bias, and did his best to persuade them to avoid this bias. However, strong hindsight bias was still obtained in spite of these efforts. If you find yourself being unimpressed by some of the findings reported in this book, ask yourself whether this could have anything to do with hindsight bias!

Ψ Section summary

Psychology is the science which uses introspective and behavioural evidence to understand the internal processes which lead people to think and to behave as they do. Psychology is not just common sense, because many of the findings of psychologists differ greatly from what most people would have predicted. One reason why people think psychological findings are commonsensical is hindsight bias, which involves being wise after the event.

1 What is psychology? How does it differ from common sense?

History of psychology

Psychologists disagree among themselves on the origins of psychology. However, there is reasonable agreement that important psychological issues were first considered systematically by the ancient Greeks. Some psychologists argue that the true origins of psychology lie in the first application of the scientific method to psychological issues. In other words, they claim that psychology as a scientific discipline emerged only when proper experiments were conducted on human participants. What are proper experiments? They are experiments carried out under well-controlled conditions so that there is a good chance that the findings obtained can be repeated or replicated by other researchers. As we will see, the origins of experimental psychology were in Germany in the middle of the nineteenth century.

Philosophy

Plato and Aristotle were two of the greatest thinkers in ancient Greece during the fifth and fourth centuries BC. They were both interested in **philosophy**, a discipline which involves seeking after knowledge or wisdom. Plato (427–347 BC) was not convinced of the value of science. He dismissed it as nothing but 'a game and a recreation', and a 'presumptious prying of man into the divine order of nature.' The main reason why Plato did not have a high opinion of science was because he believed that scientific observations provide limited and sometimes misleading information. In contrast, thought allows true knowledge to be attained.

Plato tended to dismiss the scientific approach, but he had a number of important psychological insights. One example is the value he attached to 'mental health'. He argued that mental health depends on the body and on the mind: *mens sana in corpore sano* (a sound mind in a sound body). Gymnastic training is valuable to ensure that the body is healthy, whereas a study of the arts, mathematics and philosophy is useful for a healthy mind. These notions still seem reasonable over two thousand years later.

In spite of his views on mental health, Plato nevertheless drew an important distinction between the soul or mind and the body. In contrast, Aristotle (384–322 BC) argued that there is an intimate relationship between the soul and the body, with the soul effectively corresponding to the body in action. According to this point of view, there is a close link between biology (which is concerned with the body) and psychology (which is concerned with the soul or mind). This is very much in line with many contemporary theories.

Unlike Plato, Aristotle was very sympathetic to the scientific approach. Among his many scientific contributions was his pioneering work on embryology. He opened up hens' eggs at different points during the incubation process, and observed the ways in which the

Plate 1.1 Plato (427–347 BC) thought true knowledge was attained by thought, not science, but, with Aristotle, was one of the first philosophers to have an impact on psychological inquiry. His psychological insights included the idea that mental health depended on the body and the mind

embryo developed. Aristotle argued (as scientists continue to do) that scientific theories should influence the observations that are made, and that observations should influence and produce changes in theories. This argument comes across in his discussion of animal movement: 'We must grasp this not only generally in theory, but also by reference to individuals in the world of sense, for with these in view we seek general theories, and with these we believe that general theories ought to harmonise.'

Aristotle made many contributions to psychology. However, his most famous contribution is probably the notion that patterns of thought depend on three laws of association, those of contiguity, similarity and contrast. According to the law of contiguity or closeness, thinking of one thing can make us think of something else that we have encountered at the same time. For example, thinking of a refrigerator may make us think of an oven, because they are found together in many kitchens. According to the law of similarity, thinking of one thing (e.g. apples) may lead us to think of something similar (e.g. oranges). According to the law of contrast, thinking of one thing (e.g. God) may make us think of something very different (e.g. the devil). Plato had previously proposed that contiguity and similarity are important factors in determining thought patterns, but it was left to Aristotle to develop the proposal.

After the intellectual excitement of ancient Greece, philosophy and psychology (and other sciences) went into decline for a very long period of time. Perhaps the next philosopher who had a major impact on the development of psychology was René Descartes (1596–1650). He is best known for his view that there is a radical difference in humans between the body and the soul or mind, by which he seems to have meant consciousness. In contrast, animals do not have a soul or mind. As a result, animals can be regarded as machines which behave in predictable ways.

Plate 1.2 René Descartes (1596–1650) differentiated between the body and the soul or mind, by which he seems to have meant consciousness. He claimed that animals did not have a soul or mind, and could therefore be regarded as machines

The views of Descartes had a negative effect on the development of human psychology. Why is that so? He claimed that the soul or mind is the key part of a human being, and so to understand human thinking and behaviour we need to understand the workings of the soul. However, the soul does not have any biological reality, and so it is not possible to study it by using scientific methods. The implication of this point of view is that human psychology cannot be a scientific discipline, which is why Hearnshaw (1987) argued that Descartes led psychology down a cul-de-sac.

Baruch Spinoza (1632–77) put forward a philosophical position which is much more in tune with contemporary views. However, it was only a long time after his death that Spinoza became an influential figure. Spinoza's main contribution was to propose double aspect theory, according to which the mental and the physical are both part of the same underlying reality. In the words of Spinoza, 'The order and connection of ideas is the same as the order and connection of things.' Double aspect theory has the disadvantage that it is rather vague, but it has the strong advantage that it provides a philosophical underpinning for scientific psychology.

Psychophysics

We turn now to the first proper experiments in psychology, which were carried out in Germany by Ernst Weber (1834) and Gustav Fechner (1860). They were interested in the relationship between the mental and physical realms, or what they called **psychophysics**. For example, suppose we double the intensity of a sound. Will it sound twice as loud as the original sound? What Weber and Fechner discovered from a series of careful experiments is that the relationship between physical intensity and subjective intensity is not quite that simple. In fact, the physical intensity of a sound needs to be increased approximately eight-fold in order to double its perceived loudness. The relationship between physical and perceived intensity varies with different stimuli. For example, the physical intensity of electric shock does not even need to be doubled in order for the perceived intensity to double.

What is striking about the research of Weber and Fechner is that they found that there are reasonably straightforward relationships between the physical and perceived intensities of stimuli. However, it should be noted that these relationships tend to become more complex when the physical intensity of a stimulus is very high or very low. In spite of these complexities, Weber and Fechner demonstrated clearly that scientific experiments can play a valuable role in the development of psychology. That was an enormous contribution, which has influenced psychology through to the present day.

Physiology

At around the same time as Weber and Fechner were carrying out their studies, there were other important developments in Germany. Johannes Muller (1801–58) and Hermann von Helmholtz (1821–94) were both physiologists who played a crucial role in showing the potential value of physiology to psychology. Muller published a major three-volume textbook of physiology between 1833 and 1840. He was interested in the fact that visual perception is very different from auditory perception, and both differ considerably from the perception of taste or smell. He argued that this could be explained in part by assuming that there are some nerves which are specialized for vision, whereas others are specialized for hearing, taste and smell. It occurred to him that different parts of the brain might be specialized for each of the sense modalities, but he decided wrongly that this was unlikely.

Helmholtz argued that it is important to study perception, because it represents a meeting point between the disciplines of physiology and psychology. In his own words, 'The physiology of the senses is a border land in which the two great divisions of human knowledge, natural and mental science, encroach on one another's domain; in which problems arise which are important to both, and which only the combined labour of both can solve.'

Helmholtz's greatest contribution to physiological psychology may well have been his theory of colour vision. He argued that there are three basic colours (red, blue and green), each of which has its own receptor mechanisms in the eye. This theory is essentially correct as far as it goes, but more recent evidence indicates that information from the three receptor mechanisms is combined in a more complex fashion than was assumed by Helmholtz (Sekuler and Blake 1994; see Chapter 4).

Around the beginning of the twentieth century, Pavlov carried out important physiological research on salivary conditioning in dogs (see Chapter 3). This research played an important role in the development of behaviourism, which is discussed a little later in the chapter. For reasons that are not clear, there was a decline in physiological psychology in the period between the two world wars. According to Thomson (1968: 285), 'In spite of much admirable work in physi-

ology during this period, there was not much which could directly throw light on behaviour. At the same time, psychologists were inclined to be less concerned with physiology than in earlier, and later, periods'.

Biology

So far we have seen how the origins of psychology owed much to the disciplines of philosophy and physiology. However, biology played an equally important role, especially through the contributions of Charles Darwin (1809–82). Previous theorists had argued that the human species evolved from other species, but it was only in 1859 with the publication of Darwin's book

Plate 1.3 Charles Darwin's (1809–1882) book *Origin of Species* held several major implications for psychology, with its assertion that human psychology could be advanced by studying the behaviour of other species, and that the study of genetics would help to understand human nature

Origin of Species that most people became aware of the theory of evolution. This book had several major implications for psychology. One obvious implication was that there are important similarities between the human species and other species such as apes, and so much of relevance to human psychology can be learned by studying the behaviour of other species.

Another implication for psychology followed from Darwin's emphasis on heredity and on the notion that offspring usually resemble their parents. If heredity is as important in the human species as in other species, then a study of genetics will be of value in the task of predicting and understanding human behaviour.

Finally, Darwin's theory of evolution attached significance to individual differences. He argued that there is survival of the fittest, meaning that some members of a species are better equipped than others to cope with the demands of the environment in which they are living. This line of thinking led Francis Galton (1822–1911), a cousin of Charles Darwin, to embark on the study of individual differences in intelligence and to develop the first primitive test of intelligence. Galton's book, *Hereditary Genius*, was published in 1869, and represented the first systematic study of individual differences within psychology. The significance of this book was noted by Murphy and Kovach (1972: 138): 'Individual differences had not been seriously treated before as part of the subject matter of psychology. . . . It was Darwinism, rather than the previous history of psychology, which brought about an interest in the problem'.

Darwin's theory of evolution also influenced psychology through the work of John Dewey (1859–1952). He was an American philosopher and psychologist who was instrumental in developing the functionalist school of psychology. The functionalists were influenced by Darwin's ideas about survival of the fittest, which led them to focus on the functional value of thoughts and behaviour in allowing the individual animal or human to adapt to its environment. For example, what is the value of consciousness? According to the functionalists, it is of most use in complex situations in which habitual ways of responding are not appropriate.

One of the effects that biology had on psychology was to increase interest in the nature–nurture controversy. Galton argued strongly that individual differences in intelligence were due very largely to heredity, but others argued strongly that environmental factors were of more importance (see Chapter 13). The nature–nurture controversy continues to this day, and it is of importance in various areas of psychology (e.g. personality: see Chapter 14).

Psychoanalysis

The next major development in the history of psychology was the psychoanalytic approach of Sigmund Freud (1856–1939). In order to understand the revolutionary nature of his views on abnormal behaviour, it is necessary to consider the views which were common before his time. It was generally believed that abnormal behaviour was caused by demons, and that appropriate forms of treatment involved making life as unpleasant as possible for the demon. This viewpoint justified all kinds of barbaric acts, such as starving or flogging patients, or immersing them in boiling water. Freud argued that abnormal behaviour should be regarded as mental illness, i.e. it is caused by disturbed functioning of the mind. According to this perspective, psychology is of vital importance in the task of understanding and treating patients with mental disorders.

Psychoanalysis developed out of these ideas. There are really two separate, but interrelated, aspects to psychoanalysis. One aspect consists of a range of theories about human emotional development, whereas the other aspect consists of a form of treatment for mental disorders which is based in part on those theories. Freud was the first person to develop a systematic psychological approach to therapy. This approach was very influential; it led to the subsequent development of several other forms of psychotherapy (see Chapter 18).

Freud's psychoanalytic approach has also been influential in a more general way. Before Freud, psychology was relatively limited in terms of those aspects of thinking and behaviour it covered. For example, some of the main topics in psychology were in the area of cognition (e.g. sensation, perception, associative thinking and memory). Freud played a major role in extending psychology to include developmental processes, social processes, motivation, personality and sexual behaviour. Without any doubt, he is more responsible than anyone else for the contemporary richness and diversity of psychology.

Behaviourism

The next major development was the growth of **behaviourism** in the United States from about 1912 onwards. One of the main concerns of the behaviourists was that too much of psychology was subjective and unscientific. Many psychologists at that time relied on individuals' reports of their own experience, which is generally known as the introspective approach. John Watson (1878–1958), the founder of behaviourism, disapproved of introspective evidence because there is no way of establishing the accuracy or otherwise of introsopective reports. Watson (1913) expressed his preferred alternative in the following terms: 'Psychology as the behaviourist views it is a purely objective, experimental branch of natural science. Its theoretical goal is the prediction and control of behaviour. Introspection forms no essential part of its method.' In other words, Watson was an advocate of experimental psychology, with measures of behaviour being obtained under well-controlled conditions.

The behaviourists' emphasis on a scientific approach to psychology based on the precise observation and measurement of behaviour is still accepted nowadays by most (though not all) psychologists. However, the behaviourists also put forward a theory of behaviour. According to this theory, learning mainly involves simple stimulus–response associations formed by conditioning. Nearly all human behaviour depends on environmental factors, because heredity is of little or no importance. In the words of Watson (1924), 'There is no such thing as an inheritance of capacity, talent, temperament, mental constitution and characteristics. These things depend on training that goes on mainly in the cradle.' It is now generally accepted that this behaviourist theory is a substantial oversimplification.

Other approaches

During the course of the twentieth century, numerous different approaches to psychology (e.g. feminist psychology; cross-cultural psychology; social constructionism) became influential. However, many of these approaches are of sufficiently recent origin that it is difficult at present to assess their long-term significance. This is not the case with the two approaches that will be the central focus of this section: Gestalt psychology and humanism.

The Gestalt approach to psychology started in Germany in about 1912. It was developed by Max Wertheimer, Kurt Koffka and Wolfgang Köhler, all of whom were at the University of Frankfurt. The Gestalt psychologists were mainly interested in perception (see Chapter 5) and in problem solving and thinking (see Chapter 8). Their approach was very different in many ways from that of the behaviourists. For example, the Gestaltists made extensive use of **phenomenology**, which involves the direct description of conscious experience. In contrast, the behaviourists tended to reject such subjective evidence, preferring to rely on observable behaviour.

The Gestalt approach to psychology was very influential during the first half of the twentieth century, but thereafter its influence declined markedly. Why is this? In a nutshell, the Gestalt psychologists discovered several interesting and important phenomena in perception and problem solving, but their theoretical explanations of these phenomena have not stood the test of time.

Humanistic psychology is very different from the Gestalt approach in most respects, but the two approaches are similar in that they are both based on phenomenology. Humanistic psychology was developed by Carl Rogers and Abraham Maslow during the 1950s (see Chapter 14). A key notion in the humanistic approach is that people can be seen as striving for personal growth. In the terms used by humanistic psychologists, people have a need for **self-actualization**, which involves fulfilling one's potential and accepting oneself. Many people, including those suffering from mental disorders, find it hard to achieve a state of self-actualization. Accordingly, Rogers developed **client-centred therapy**. In this form of therapy, the therapist provides a very positive and encouraging environment designed to foster personal growth and to facilitate self-actualization.

Key figures

It should be clear that much of importance has necessarily been left out of the account of the history of psychology given above. A different way of trying to identify the highlights in the history of psychology is to identify the most outstanding psychologists. Korn *et al.* (1991) did precisely that. They asked historians of psychology to indicate the most eminent psychologists in the history of psychology. Below are the names of the ten most eminent psychologists identified by this procedure; they are arranged in descending order of rated eminence.

(1) Wilhelm Wundt (1832–1920): the founder of the world's first psychology laboratory at Leipzig, Germany, in 1879, and the writer of numerous books on different areas of psychology.

(2) William James (1842–1910): a US psychologist who made many contributions to our understanding of attention, memory and other topics, and helped to establish scientific psychology in North America.

(3) Sigmund Freud (1856–1939): an Austrian psychologist who was the founder of psychoanalysis, and a central figure in the development of psychological forms of treatment for mental disorders; he extended enormously the range of psychology.

(4) John Watson (1878–1958): the US founder of behaviourism, who was very influential in persuading American and other psychologists to focus on the principles of conditioning.

(5) Ivan Pavlov (1849–1936): a Russian physiologist who made systematic studies of classical conditioning in dogs, and who won the Nobel Prize for his research on the digestive tract.

(6) Hermann Ebbinghaus (1850–1909): a German psychologist who was the first person to carry out detailed experimental studies into human memory, using himself as a subject.

(7) Jean Piaget (1896–1980): a Swiss psychologist who was enormously influential in establishing developmental psychology and showing how cognition and intelligence develop during the years of childhood.

(8) Burrhus Frederic Skinner (1904–90): a US psychologist whose work on operant conditioning had a great impact on education (e.g. programmed learning) and on clinical psychology (e.g. behaviour modification).

(9) Alfred Binet (1857–1911): a French psychologist who constructed the first proper intelligence test (with Théodore Simon) in 1905; most subsequent intelligence tests resemble Binet's to some extent.

(10) Gustav Fechner (1801–87): a German scientist whose psychophysical studies on the relationship between the actual and the perceived intensities of stimuli were among the first proper experimental studies in psychology; it could be argued that he was the first experimental psychologist, although several other psychologists also have claims to that title.

There are a number of interesting features of the above list. Seven of these eminent psychologists were European, and only three were American. This suggests (accurately, I think) that psychology basically started in Europe, although it has of course been developed enormously in the United States. Indeed, it has been the case for several decades that there are more psychologists in the United States than in the rest of the world put together. Another feature of the list which you may have noticed is that all of the psychologists listed were men. Why is there this gender bias? The overwhelming reason for this is simply that there were very few women psychologists during the time that psychology was developing as a scientific discipline. Since then the position has changed for the better, and there are now very large numbers of women psychologists making outstanding contributions. It should also be borne in mind that lists of eminent people in any field are problematic, since they typically focus on the uncontroversial and the long dead.

Ψ Section summary

The ancient Greeks, especially Aristotle and Plato, contributed numerous ideas of relevance to psychology. Descartes argued that there is a radical difference in humans between the body and the soul or the mind, an approach which undermined psychology as a scientific discipline. Spinoza put forward double aspect theory, according to which the mental and the physical are both part of the same underlying reality. The work of Weber and Fechner on psychophysics represented the start of experimental psychology. The physiological approach to psychology owes much to the work of pioneers such as Helmholtz and Pavlov. Darwin had a major impact via his emphasis on heredity and the evolution of species. Other major developments were psychoanalysis (started by Freud) and behaviourism (started by Watson).

1 What were some of the key developments in the history of psychology?

Contemporary perspectives in psychology

In the previous section, we saw how the emergence of psychology as a scientific discipline was influenced by several other disciplines such as philosophy, physiology and biology. The notion that psychology is a complex, multidisciplinary subject is of central importance within contemporary psychology.

We can illustrate the breadth of psychology by considering various psychological approaches to an understanding of divorce. From the social psychological approach, it is important to focus on factors such as failed interpersonal relationships, differences in attitudes, and so on. From the developmental psychological approach, the focus is on experiences in childhood and adolescence which may influence the ability to be happily married. From the individual differences approach, it is important to consider the possibility that married

people with certain types of personality may find it difficult to relate well to their spouses. From the abnormal
psychological approach, it is important to consider
whether divorce has long-lasting effects on children,
such as increasing the probability of mental disorder in
adult life.

We have already seen that the emergence of psychology as a scientific discipline owed much to other disciplines such as physiology and biology. The influences of
these other disciplines are still clearly visible in modern
psychology. Thus, biological psychology and physiological psychology are both important contemporary perspectives. However, there are other major contemporary
perspectives which emerged only relatively recently in
the history of psychology, or which changed considerably during the course of the twentieth century. These
perspectives are discussed below.

Social psychology

Human beings are social animals. The most important
experiences we have in life involve our relationships
with other people, and how happy we are depends to a
large extent on having satisfactory intimate relationships
(M.W. Eysenck 1990). In view of the obvious importance of the social dimension in human psychology, it is
surprising that social psychology developed later than
most other branches of psychology. In the words of
Thomson (1968: 370), 'Social psychology did not
become sufficiently coherent and technically advanced
to receive much recognition until after the Second
World War'.

One of the key findings in social psychology is that
our behaviour is even more affected by other people than
we believe it to be (see Chapters 11 and 12). For example, we know that we sometimes modify our behaviour
to conform to the expectations or behaviour of others,
but most people are unaware of the strength of such
pressures to conform. The fact that we are so influenced
by other people makes it all the more important for psychologists to consider social processes in detail.

It is perhaps natural to assume that a scientific discipline such as psychology proceeds in a very similar way
in different countries. However, that is not the case with
social psychology. More specifically, there are important
differences between the American and European
approaches to social psychology. American social psychologists tend to study social processes within the individual, and to de-emphasize much of the external social
and cultural context. European social psychologists tend
to be more interested than their American counterparts
in such context. For example, they focus on factors such
as power, ideology and relative status.

Developmental psychology

Nearly everyone accepts that the experiences of childhood help to shape adult thinking and behaviour. That
is one of the main reasons why it is important to
include the developmental approach within psychology.
However, the prevailing views about the relationship
between childhood and adulthood were markedly different in earlier times. For example, it was often
believed that children were like smaller versions of
adults, which implied that there is no real process of
development as children become adults.

Sigmund Freud was perhaps the first psychologist to
appreciate the full significance of childhood as a determinant of adult behaviour. According to him, the origins
of adult mental disorder lie in problems and conflict
experienced during childhood. In other words, major
conflicts in childhood produce long-term vulnerability
to mental disorder. Evidence supporting this general
view has been reported by G.W. Brown (1989), in a
study of 400 women. He discovered that 64 per cent of
the women with panic disorder and 39 per cent of those
suffering from depression had experienced major adversity in childhood (e.g. through parental indifference
or abuse). These percentages are much higher than the
17 per cent of women free from disorder who had experienced childhood adversity.

The importance of a developmental approach to
psychology was also emphasized by Jean Piaget
(1896–1980). He focused on the development of thinking and intelligence during childhood and adolescence,
whereas Freud had concentrated on the development of
emotion and personality. According to Piaget, intelligence develops through a series of stages. Each stage
needs to be completed successfully before the child can
move on to the next stage. One of the major implications of this theoretical approach is that the emergence
of adult intelligence can be understood only by considering the preceding stages of intellectual development.

Developmental psychology has expanded greatly
since the innovative work of Freud and Piaget (see
Chapters 9 and 10). For example, there has been a considerable amount of work on language acquisition,
which happens surprisingly rapidly in the overwhelming
majority of young children. Another major area of
research is social development, in which the processes
involved in socialization are considered.

Individual differences

As our everyday experience makes clear, there are great individual differences in thinking, attitudes and behaviour. We saw earlier in the chapter that Francis Galton was the first psychologist to study individual differences in intelligence, and that he devised the world's first intelligence test. However, his test consisted of very simple tasks (e.g. reaction time) and failed to measure intelligence properly. At the beginning of the twentieth century, Alfred Binet devised the first adequate test of intelligence. He was asked by the French Ministry of Public Instruction to construct a test which would allow mentally retarded children to be identified at an early age so that they could be given special teaching. The key difference between Binet's intelligence test and that of Galton was that Binet focused much more than Galton on items which required the use of complex thought processes for their solution. Binet's approach has been followed by nearly all those who have developed intelligence tests in the years since his test first appeared (see Chapter 13).

There are, of course, numerous different kinds of important individual differences. However, psychologists have focused mainly on individual differences in intelligence and personality. The main way in which individual differences in personality have been assessed is by means of self-report questionnaires. J.P. Guilford (e.g. 1936) was a key figure in the development of such questionnaires, followed by personality theorists such as Cattell and H.J. Eysenck (see Chapter 14).

In view of the apparent importance of individual differences, it might be imagined that most psychologists would include a systematic investigation of individual differences in their research. In fact, this is not the case at all, since most researchers compare groups of participants and ignore individual differences. One reason put forward for this neglect of individual differences is that behaviour depends far more on the situation than on personality. This issue was studied by Sarason *et al.* (1975). They considered the role of personality and of the situation in determining behaviour in a total of 138 experiments which had been carried out by numerous different researchers on various issues. On average, personality and the situation had approximately the same impact on behaviour, but that of the situation was slightly greater than that of personality. In view of these findings, it is wrong to argue that behaviour depends very little on individual differences in personality.

Evolutionary psychology

Evolutionary psychology (also known as human psychobiology) is an approach to psychology which emphasizes the importance of biological factors. As might be expected, evolutionary psychology is based very much on Darwin's theory of evolution. A key assumption of evolutionary psychology is that 'individuals should act to maximise their inclusive fitness. Inclusive fitness refers to the number of descendants left in future generations, including those of relatives as well as direct descendants' (P.K. Smith 1983: 224). According to evolutionary psychologists, the goal of gene survival is involved when people decide on the benefits and costs of different forms of social behaviour.

Many psychologists are willing to assume that there is some validity in the claims made by evolutionary psychologists or psychobiologists. However, the great majority of psychologists believe that human social behaviour is determined much more by cultural and environmental factors than by purely biological ones. In the words of Smith, 'It seems likely that "naive" human sociobiology has most relevance to earlier phases of human evolution, and to less complex societies, and has a much more limited application in its unmodified form to modern industrial societies' (1983: 240).

Cognitive psychology

Cognitive psychology is concerned with several mental processes, including those involved in perception, attention, learning, memory, problem solving, decision making and the use of language (see Chapters 3, 5, 6, 7 and 8). Thus, cognitive psychology is very extensive, and is of great relevance to other areas of psychology. For example, what happens during social interactions depends in part on people's perceptions of each other, the information about each other they have stored in long-term memory, and so on. As a consequence, cognitive psychology can be regarded as being of central importance within social psychology

Cognitive psychology is also of importance in the clinical area (see Chapters 17 and 18). Many of the symptoms exhibited by anxious and depressed patients depend on distorted cognitive processes. For example, panic disorder patients often misinterpret their bodily sensations to mean that they are about to collapse or have a heart attack.

There are various different ways of studying cognitive processes. The first, and the traditional, approach is to carry out studies on cognition with normal individuals under laboratory conditions. This approach, called **experimental cognitive psychology** by M.W. Eysenck and Keane (1995), has contributed substantially to our understanding of human cognition. In recent years, however, this approach has been supplemented by two other approaches: cognitive neuropsychology and cognitive science. These two approaches are discussed below.

Cognitive neuropsychology involves studying cognitive processes in brain-damaged patients. It is not immediately obvious that this approach will tell us much about cognitive processes in normal individuals, but in fact it has done. Suppose that someone argued that we have only a single memory system, and this system is involved in short-term memory (e.g. remembering telephone numbers for a few seconds) and in long-term memory (e.g. remembering the events of our lives). It follows from this theory that brain-damaged patients with memory impairments must have suffered damage to this memory system. As a consequence, they should have poor short-term memory and poor long-term memory. In fact, as is discussed fully in Chapter 6, many patients have poor long-term memory but good short-term memory, whereas others display the opposite pattern. It is hard to escape the conclusion that normal individuals have somewhat separate short-term and long-term memory systems, and that brain damage can affect one system with little or no damage to the other one.

Cognitive science involves making use of computers in the attempt to understand cognitive processes. The goal of many cognitive scientists is to program computers to mimic the cognitive processes of humans, whereas other cognitive scientists are more concerned to produce computer programs which work effectively. The computer experts who constructed the computer program (Deep Blue) that played chess against Gary Kasparov in 1996 were clearly using the latter approach. It nearly beat Kasparov on that occasion, and defeated him in a re-match in 1997. However, Deep Blue does not mimic at all the thought processes of chess grandmasters. Chess grandmasters study a few possible moves in great depth, whereas the computer program considers approximately 2 million moves per second.

Those cognitive scientists who try to devise computer programs which will mimic human cognitive functioning have had many successes. In particular, these computer programs are more precise and detailed than most of the theories put forward by experimental cognitive psychologists, and so they provide a fuller account of cognitive processes. However, it remains a matter of

controversy whether computer functioning does resemble that of the human brain. The general feeling is that recent computer programs are much more similar to human cognitive processes than previous ones. For example, the brain tends to function as a parallel processing system (handling more than one thing at a time), and it is only since the mid-1980s that computers have begun to do the same.

As we will see in this book, cognitive psychology has benefited greatly from the coming together of experimental cognitive psychology, cognitive neuropsychology, and cognitive science. Studies on normal individuals, studies on brain-damaged patients, and computer simulations can all be used to provide thorough tests of major cognitive theories.

Abnormal psychology

Abnormal psychology owes its origins to the work of Franz Mesmer (1734–1815). He tried to treat mentally ill people by getting them to sit around a tub which contained iron filings. Mesmer attributed any cures that were produced to 'animal magnetism'. What was actually responsible was the hypnotic state into which the patients were put, which made them open to Mesmer's suggestions. This work was of great importance, because it showed that mental illness could be cured by psychological rather than medical means. At that time, most people who were mentally ill were simply locked up in asylums known popularly as 'madhouses'.

The greatest impetus to the development of abnormal psychology came from Sigmund Freud. He was the first person to develop systematic forms of treatment for mental illness based entirely on psychological principles; his approach is known as **psychoanalysis**. He emphasized the role played by childhood experiences in leading to adult neuroses, and used dream analysis in order to bring to light traumatic experiences which the patient may have suffered. The neo-Freudians (e.g. Alfred Adler, Erich Fromm, Anna Freud) expanded the Freudian approach to therapy, but they focused more on the social factors involved in the development of neurosis than had Freud.

Another major development in the history of abnormal psychology was **behaviour therapy**, which is based very much on the principles of behaviourism (see Chapters 17 and 18). Behaviour therapy is based on the assumption that conditioning plays an important part in the development of mental illness, and that conditioning can be used in order to alter the patient's behaviour in desirable ways. Even though behaviourism was introduced into psychology by John Watson in the early years of the twentieth century, it was only in the early 1960s that behaviour therapy became an influential form of treatment.

In spite of the introduction of psychological methods such as psychoanalysis and behaviour therapy, there are other approaches within abnormal psychology which are less psychological in outlook. For example, there is **drug therapy**. Clinical anxiety is often treated by means of drugs such as Valium and Librium, and the symptoms of clinical depression can be greatly reduced by administering Prozac and other similar drugs. However, it is important to note that all these drugs sometimes have unfortunate side-effects, and their prolonged use cannot be recommended.

More recently, there has been the development of **cognitive therapy**. Prominent theorists such as Aaron Beck and Albert Ellis argued that many of the problems of anxious and depressed patients revolve around their irrational thoughts and beliefs. For example, anxious patients may believe that they will be ridiculed by other people unless they are constantly successful in all their activities. It follows that a central focus in cognitive therapy is on challenging such irrational beliefs and trying to replace them with more accurate and less extreme beliefs.

Therapy is provided by clinical psychologists and by psychiatrists. The key difference between them is that psychiatrists have a medical degree, whereas clinical psychologists do not. In general, clinical psychologists tend to prefer more psychological forms of treatment such as cognitive therapy, whereas psychiatrists prefer other forms of treatment such as drug therapy, but there are numerous exceptions.

Health psychology

Health psychology emerged as an important area in its own right only during the 1970s. However, in the years since then it has grown remarkably rapidly, and is now accepted as one of the major areas within psychology (see Chapter 19).

In order to understand the nature of health psychology, it is important to draw a distinction between the biomedical model of health and the biopsychosocial model (Engel 1977). According to the biomedical model, illness is due to biological malfunction, and treatment should involve physical methods such as medication or surgery. This was very much the dominant approach within medicine until the mid-1980s.

It is assumed within the biopsychosocial model advocated by health psychologists that illness is determined by a range of biological, psychological and social processes interacting with each other. Within this model, psychological methods (e.g. following an appropriate lifestyle) are important in the prevention of illness and in treatment. In addition, psychological factors help to determine the effectiveness of physical methods of treatment. Finally, it is argued within the biopsychosocial approach that the success of medical treatment depends on psychological and social outcomes such as coping and quality of life as well as on the reduction of physical symptoms of disease.

One of the major emphases within health psychology is on the role of stress in disease. As Weinman (1994) pointed out, it has been recognized for several decades that stress has direct and indirect effects on disease. It has indirect effects by leading to increases in risk behaviour (e.g. smoking, drinking) and it has direct effects on health by producing physiological changes (e.g. increased blood pressure).

Occupational psychology

What is commonly known as occupational psychology was originally known as industrial psychology during the first part of the twentieth century. In general terms, **occupational psychology** is concerned with all of the ways in which psychology can be applied in personnel selection, increasing productivity of the individual and of the group, improving decision making, improving morale, coping with stress and conflict, and so on (see Chapter 20). A distinction is sometimes drawn between occupational psychology, which has as its primary focus the individual workers, and **organizational psychology**, which is more concerned with larger units within the workplace.

It is important to note that occupational psychology is closely linked to several other areas within psychology. For example, personnel selection relies heavily on the personality and intelligence tests developed within the individual differences approach to psychology. Another example is the way in which research on emotion and on clinical anxiety has been used to provide an understanding of occupational stress and the steps that might be taken to reduce it.

Ψ Section summary

Contemporary psychology has developed in several ways over the past 100 years. Social psychology, which developed later than other major perspectives, has more of a cultural and social emphasis in Europe than in the United States. Developmental psychologists such as Piaget and Freud argued that children proceed through a series of developmental stages. The individual differences approach has focused mainly on intelligence and personality. Evolutionary psychologists have argued that biological factors are of importance in explaining human behaviour. Cognitive psychologists have studied human cognition via experiments on normal and brain-damaged individuals, and by computer simulations. Abnormal or clinical psychology has seen the development of various types of therapy, including psychoanalysis, behaviour therapy, drug therapy and cognitive therapy. More recently, applied areas of psychology such as health psychology and occupational psychology have developed.

1   Discuss some of the major perspectives within contemporary psychology.

Ethical issues in psychology

When non-psychologists think of the kinds of experiments carried out by psychologists, what comes to mind tends to be thoughts of rats and other animals being given intense electric shocks. What is less well known is that the human participants in psychological experiments were also treated very badly on occasion. Striking examples of this are available in the research programme of Berkun *et al.* (1962). In one study, the participants were in a military plane when one of the engines failed. They were then told that the plane would shortly ditch in the sea, and that they had to fill in a complex 'emergency procedure' form for insurance purposes before that happened. Unsurprisingly, Berkun *et al.* (1962) discovered that these events (which had been set up deliberately by the experimenters) caused the participants to become extremely anxious.

Berkun *et al.* (1962) also arranged that soldiers on their own in the field could communicate with base only by means of a radio transmitter. Some of them were exposed to a series of explosions simulating a barrage of artillery shells, whereas others were informed that there was a dangerous fall-out from an accident with radioactive material. When the solders attempted to contact base, they found with dismay that the radio transmitter would not work. These terrifying situations were also produced deliberately by Berkun *et al.* (1962) in order to observe the effects on the soldiers' anxiety levels.

A better known example of poor treatment of participants is the research programme carried out by Stanley Milgram (1974) and discussed earlier in the chapter. The participants were told to administer progressively more intense electric shocks to a learner when he made a mistake, and the experimenter told them they must continue even if they wanted to stop. The effects of this experiment can be seen from this report by an observer on a 46-year-old encyclopedia salesman, who was a participant:

I observed a mature and initially poised businessman enter the laboratory smiling and confident. Within 20 minutes he was reduced to a twitching, stuttering wreck, who was rapidly approaching a point of nervous collapse. He constantly pulled on his earlobe, and twisted his hands. At one point, he pushed his fist into his forehead and muttered 'Oh God, let's stop it'.

(Milgram 1974)

Important ethical issues are also raised in clinical therapy (see Chapter 18). Patients may be persuaded to receive forms of therapy about which they have considerable doubts because of their exaggerated respect for the views of the therapist. There can also be complex ethical issues raised when patients who may endanger either themselves or others are very reluctant to receive treatment. Therapists can also face ethical issues if patients reveal certain kinds of information to them (e.g. their intention to kill someone). In such circumstances, therapists have to decide between respecting confidentiality and informing the appropriate authorities about possible dangers to others. Other ethical issues relating to clinical therapy are discussed below.

Since the late 1970s, there has been increasing agreement that the indignities heaped on participants in experiments and on clinical patients are simply unacceptable. This led to a systematic consideration of the principles that need to be followed in order to ensure that psychological research is ethical. The single most important principle is that of **voluntary informed consent**, meaning that participants are provided with full information about what they will be required to do before agreeing to take part in an experiment. This principle was disregarded in the research of Berkun *et al.* (1962) and Milgram (1974). However, many people agree that voluntary informed consent is not always needed. For example, some psychologists want to study incidental learning, which is learning in the absence of intention to learn. Incidental learning can be studied only by deceiving the participants about the purpose of the experiment, but most people would accept that the deception is innocuous.

Another important principle of ethical psychological research is that participants should have the **right to withdraw** from the experiment at any point without providing a reason. This principle was flagrantly ignored by Milgram (1974), who told his participants that they had to proceed with the experiment even if they were very reluctant to do so.

Two other important aspects of ethical research are **debriefing** and **confidentiality**. Debriefing involves providing participants with detailed information at the end of the experiment. It also involves systematic attempts to eliminate any distress that may have been caused by having taken part in the experiment. Confidentiality involves making sure that information about individual participants is not disclosed by the experimenter. The customary procedure is for published accounts of research findings to focus on group means, and not to reveal the performance of individuals within any given group.

In 1990, the British Psychological Society published its guidelines for ethical research, which referred to voluntary informed consent, right to withdraw, debriefing and confidentiality. According to these guidelines, the essential principle 'is that the investigation should be considered from the standpoint of all participants: foreseeable threats to their psychological well-being, health, values or dignity should be eliminated.'

Clinical therapy

There is general agreement that the principles for ethical research discussed above provide reasonably adequate safeguards for the participants in experimental research. However, clinical psychologists providing therapy can be faced by more difficult ethical issues than experimental researchers. For example, consider the provision of therapy for homosexuals. It could be argued that therapy should be given to homosexuals who indicate that they want to change their sexual orientation, because they have provided voluntary informed consent for treatment. However, such an argument is oversimplified. The true complexity of the situation was revealed by Silverstein (1972):

To suggest that a person comes voluntarily to change his sexual orientation is to ignore the powerful environmental stress, oppression if you will, that has been telling him for years that he should change. To grow up in a family where the word 'homosexual' was whispered, to play in a playground and hear the words 'faggot' and 'queer', to go . . . to college and hear of 'illness' . . . is hardly [to live in] an environment of freedom and voluntary choice.

(Silverstein 1972: 4)

What, then, should be the reaction of a clinical psychologist when a homosexual person seeks therapy? M.W. Eysenck (1994a) proposed the following answer:

A reasonable position is to regard treatment for homosexuality only as a last resort. It should be provided only for those homosexuals who are very distressed by their sexual orientation, and only when it appears no other solution is feasible. Every effort must be made to eliminate the idea that homosexuality should be thought of as a mental disorder.

(M.W. Eysenck 1994a: 150)

Animal research

Many of the ethical principles underpinning human research are simply not applicable to research with other species. Animals cannot provide voluntary informed consent, they cannot be given the right to withdraw from the experiment, and they cannot be debriefed after the experiment is over. One of the difficulties with devising appropriate ethical principles for animal research is that people have such different views about its acceptability. Some argue that all animal research is immoral, whereas others claim that research in which animals suffer a considerable amount of pain is justified if the research is likely to lead to reduced human suffering.

In spite of differences of opinion, the majority viewpoint is that the acceptability of any proposed research on animals depends in part on the benefits that are likely to follow from it. This general notion was embodied in a document issued in 1991 by the American Psychological Association Committee on Ethical Standards in Psychological Research: 'The general ethical question always is whether there is a negative effect upon the dignity and welfare of the participants that the importance of the research does not warrant.' This is a reasonable principle, but it can be hard to apply in practice. For example, it is often not possible to determine the importance of a research study until after it has been completed. In addition, the amount of suffering inflicted on animals by a given experimental procedure may not be easy to determine.

The issue of what kinds of experiments can ethically be carried out on animals has proved very controversial. At one extreme, some argue that animals should never be used in research, regardless of the potential benefits of the research. At the other extreme, it is argued that any animal research offering the prospect of benefiting humans is acceptable, regardless of the suffering of the animals involved. However, some research is so beneficial and involves so little discomfort that nearly everyone would favour it being carried out. For example, Simmons (1981) trained pigeons over a period of time to detect liferafts floating on the sea. Pigeons have much greater visual acuity than humans, and so they became superior to humans at this detection task. Helicopter crews detected 50 per cent of the liferafts, but the pigeons detected about 85 per cent of them.

A crucial consideration in deciding what can be done ethically with other species is the similarity between humans and the members of other species. If other species are very similar to us, then it could be argued that it is especially important to minimize any suffering they experience. There is no clear answer to the question of the similarity between humans and other species. However, Darwin (1872) carried out important research on the emotions of various species. He was impressed by the similarities in the expression of emotional states in humans and other species. These findings led him to conclude that many species probably experience emotional states resembling those experienced by humans.

What should be done in future? One useful strategy would be to try to discover as much as possible about the characteristics of each species. This would make it easier to decide whether it was justifiable to administer a particular procedure to the members of a given species.

It is useful to consider ethical issues of experimentation on animals in the broader context of the ways in which animals are treated by non-psychologists. There is growing concern that animals are being poorly treated in several ways. As M.W. Eysenck (1994a) pointed out,

There are three main areas of concern: meat production; ill-treatment of pets; and animals kept in captivity in zoos and circuses. . . . So far as meat production is concerned, it seems cruel and immoral to many people that animals such as calves and chickens are kept in severely restricted conditions so that they can scarcely move. There is also growing concern that the methods of slaughtering used in abattoirs may involve much more suffering than is generally admitted by those involved in meat production .

(M.W. Eysenck 1994a: 153)

Ψ Section summary

The key ingredient in ethical research is voluntary informed consent. Other important ingredients are the right to withdraw, debriefing and confidentiality. Special issues are often raised in clinical therapy. Most of the principles governing human research cannot be applied to animal research. The key consideration is that the importance of the research should be sufficient to justify whatever discomfort or pain is suffered by the animals involved.

1   What should psychologists do to ensure that their research is ethical?

Ψ Chapter summary

● Nature of psychology

Psychology is often regarded as the science of behaviour. In fact, psychology is more accurately defined as the science which uses information about behaviour and self-reported experience to understand the internal processes which lead individuals to think and behave in the ways they do. It is often argued that psychology is just common sense. However, it is often not clear what would be expected on the basis of common sense. There

is a tendency for people to be wise after the event (hindsight bias), and this helps to explain why they can mistakenly regard psychologists' findings as obvious.

● History of psychology

There were numerous different influences on psychology during its emergence as a science. The earliest influences were from philosophy over 2,000 years ago. Probably the first proper experimental studies in psychology were

Box continued

carried out by Weber and by Fechner in Germany during the nineteenth century in their work on psychophysics. Other major influences on the early history of psychology were physiology, biology, psychoanalysis, behaviourism, Gestalt psychology and humanism.

● Contemporary perspectives in psychology

Current psychology is characterized by a range of different perspectives, many of which initially became prominent early in the history of psychology. Several other contemporary perspectives have emerged recently, or changed dramatically during the course of the twentieth century. These perspectives include the following: social psychology; developmental psychology; individual differences; cognitive psychology; abnormal psychology; and applied psychology.

● Ethical issues in psychology

Ethical issues have become increasingly important in psychology. The key feature of ethical research with humans is voluntary informed consent, but other important features are the right to withdraw, debriefing and confidentiality. Special ethical issues are raised by clinical therapy, and it can be very difficult to know whether a specific form of treatment should be given to a particular individual. Animal research raises other problems, mainly because notions such as voluntary informed consent and right to withdraw are not applicable. In general terms, it is important that the likely benefits of any proposed animal research clearly outweigh the costs to the animal participants. However, it can be hard in practice to predict ahead of time what the benefits and costs of a study are likely to be.

Further reading

● Eysenck, M.W. (1994b) *Perspectives on Psychology*. Hove: Lawrence Erlbaum. Chapters 1, 2 and 6 of this book deal with most of the issues which are discussed in this chapter.

● Colman, A.M. (1988) *What is Psychology? The inside story*. London: Hutchinson. The nature of psychology is dealt with at length in a very accessible way in this book. It succeeds in giving the reader a clear idea of what current psychology is all about.

● Hearnshaw, L.S. (1987) *The Shaping of Modern Psychology: An historical introduction*. London: Routledge and Kegan Paul. There are numerous books on the history of psychology, but this book provides especially good coverage of the major developments in psychology during the twentieth century.

● Slovic, P. and Fischhoff, B. (1977) On the psychology of experimental surprises. *Journal of Experimental Psychology: Human Perception and Performance* **3**: 544–51. There are some examples of hindsight bias or being wise after the event in this article; these examples are of particular interest because they relate to the findings of scientific experiments.

● British Psychological Society (1990) Ethical principles for conducting research with human participants. **The Psychologist 3**: 270–2. The ethical issues which need to be considered by anyone carrying out research on human participants are discussed clearly and coherently.

Study skills
Michael Eysenck

KEY CONCEPTS • motivational factors • effective reading • time management

☐ Appendix preview

When you have read this appendix, you should be able to

- understand some of the main motivational factors relevant to studying
- know the processes involved in effective reading and remembering
- plan your time more efficiently

Introduction

There is no magic formula which can effortlessly turn you (or anyone else) into an outstanding student. However, there are numerous practical steps which can be taken in order to ensure that you use your study time more productively and efficiently. You are studying psychology, and most of the ingredients in a successful approach to study skills are based on psychological principles in one way or another. For example, effective reading involves good language comprehension skills (discussed in Chapter 7); it also requires good long-term memory for the information which has been read (see Chapter 6). Successful achievement of almost any kind depends very much on a suitably high level of motivation (see Chapter 16).

What is attempted in this chapter is to discuss some of the main factors associated with effective study skills. There is a major focus on motivation, because very little can be accomplished in the absence of a good level of motivation. There is additional relevant information in Chapter 21, especially with respect to writing essays and reports. Other aspects of study skills are covered in the references listed under Further Reading.

Motivational factors

It has sometimes been argued that some people are 'naturally' well motivated, whereas other people are 'naturally' lazy. It is possible that there is some truth in that argument, but it carries with it the unwarrantable assumption that little can be done to make people more motivated. In fact, nothing could be further from the truth. Much of what is important in motivation depends on the workings of the cognitive system, and cognitive processes can easily change over time.

One of the first systematic cognitive theories of motivation was put forward by Locke (1968). According to his goal-setting theory, human behaviour is purposeful, because individuals devote their energies to attaining various goals (e.g. passing an examination). Goals possess two key characteristics: goal difficulty, or the standard of performance which is regarded as acceptable; and goal commitment, which refers to the individual's level of determination to achieve a given goal. According to Locke (1968), both goal difficulty and goal commitment contribute towards determining the level of performance.

The evidence indicates that Locke's (1968) theory is on the right lines. Wood *et al.* (1987) reviewed the relevant literature. They found that 175 out of 192 laboratory and experimental field studies obtained support for the prediction that task performance is positively related to goal difficulty. This relationship was especially clear when there was a relatively high level of goal commitment.

The evidence that has accumulated from testing goal-setting theory (Locke and Latham 1990) and from related research indicates that there are various ingredients which are needed in order for goal setting to lead to successful performance:

- the goal needs to be difficult, but within your capabilities
- the goal needs to be clearly specified (e.g. obtaining 70 per cent for a given essay is a better goal than simply trying to do well)
- you must commit yourself fully to attaining that goal; if you tell one or two close friends about your goal, that may help you to become committed to it
- goals which are short or medium term are likely to be more effective than those that are long term (e.g. mastering a given topic in psychology over the next week is a better goal than focusing on obtaining a given class of degree in two years' time)
- there needs to be regular feedback; in other words, you need to have information about your progress towards any goal you have set yourself
- you should reward yourself for achieving a goal, and use it as the basis for setting more difficult goals in future
- you need to be realistic about the reasons for any failure to attain a given goal; there is a tendency (known as the self-serving bias) for people to attribute failure to external factors (e.g. bad luck) rather than internal factors (e.g. insufficient work), but you can improve your future chances of success only by being honest with yourself.

It is important to note that you really need to take ALL of the above points into account. If, for example, you set yourself a clear, medium-term goal, but do not obtain feedback on your progress, then it is unlikely that you will succeed.

Ψ Section summary

Motivation depends on cognitive factors such as goal difficulty and goal commitment. Goal-setting is most effective when the goals are short or medium term, when there is regular feedback, and when goal attainment is rewarded.

1 Describe the factors involved in producing the necessary motivation for effective learning.

Effective reading

One of the main skills which students need to acquire is the ability to learn and remember the information contained in books and in journals. Some useful strategies were discussed by P.E. Morris (1979), who focused on what is known as the SQ3R approach. SQ3R stands for Survey, Question, Read, Recite, Review. As this implies, the basic notion is that effective reading involves five successive stages, each of which will be discussed in turn.

(1) Survey stage: the major goal of this stage is to construct a framework or organization for the material to be read (e.g. a chapter from a textbook). In practical terms, this can be done by skimming fairly rapidly through the material, noting the main topics and the order in which they are discussed. If you are reading a chapter with a summary at the end of it, then this provides the easiest way of understanding the underlying structure of the material.

(2) Question stage: this stage (and the following two stages) should be applied to manageable-sized chunks of text. Most of the chapters in this book are approximately 20,000 words in length, which is far too long to qualify as a manageable chunk. Each major section within a chapter tends to be between 2,000 and 4,000 words long, and forms a chunk of manageable size. During the Question stage, readers should be asking themselves questions based on the headings within the major section. This serves the valuable function of helping to ensure that reading is purposeful.

(3) Read stage: this stage involves thorough reading of the major section or other manageable chunk. This reading should be focused, in that an important task at this stage is to attempt to use the text to obtain answers to the questions that were raised during the previous stage. In addition, learners in the Read stage should be trying to relate the information in the text to the knowledge they already possess.

(4) Recite stage: this stage involves the learner trying to describe to himself or herself the major ideas or essential information encountered during the Read stage. If you find that there are several important omissions or errors in your recall of the material, then you will need to go back and reread some or all of the material which you have just been reading.

(5) Review stage: the key task at this stage is to try to recall and to review all of the material which has been processed through the four previous stages. One of the main functions of the Review stage is to allow you to check whether you can still remember the key ideas contained within the text. The other major function is to provide an opportunity to integrate and make meaningful sense of the information contained in different parts of the text.

Why has the SQ3R approach proved so successful in promoting effective learning? Probably the main reason for its success is the emphasis on the reader as an active participant in the learning process. The least effective way of reading is to adopt a passive and uninvolved approach, which generally leads to very low levels of learning and memory. Readers who follow the SQ3R approach are not just active; more specifically, they are active in a focused way which facilitates understanding.

There is a further related advantage of the SQ3R approach. If you sit an examination in psychology, it will probably require you to provide essay-type answers to various questions. In order to succeed on such an examination, you will need to be able to recall relevant theories and experimental findings from long-term memory. What is required is very similar to the processes involved in the Recite and Review stages, and so the SQ3R approach provides practice in some of the key skills required for examination success. In contrast, many students stop reading the chapter of a textbook when they recognize as familiar the information contained in it. This can produce a nasty shock on the subsequent examination, because we can very often recognize information that we cannot recall (see Chapter 6).

Ψ Section summary

Effective reading requires an active involvement with the reading material. This can be achieved by using a five-stage approach based on surveying, questioning, reading, reciting and reviewing (SQ3R). It is important to practise recalling information if preparing for a written examination.

1 Discuss the ways in which reading can be made effective.

Time management

Assume that you sleep 8 hours a day on average. Since there are 168 hours in a week, that leaves 112 waking hours every week. Where does all that time go? Most people feel that there is not enough time to do everything they want to do, but they are usually fairly vague about how they actually spend their time. Time is such a valuable resource, that it makes sense to create a weekly timetable in order to maximize the chances that you will be able to do all of the things that matter to you.

Manageable chunks

McBride (1994) argued that the following old joke is relevant to time management: 'How do you eat an elephant?' 'One chunk at a time.' In other words, if you have a lot of work to do, it is important to break it down into manageable chunks. For example, all research postgraduate students in psychology have to write a thesis of about 70,000 words, in which they describe the findings from the research they have carried out. Some of them find it such a daunting prospect that they delay starting on it. My advice to them is to start writing a short part of the thesis which is easy for them to do (e.g. describing two of the leading theories in the area in which they have been working). When this has been done, they can move onto another small part of the thesis, and so on. In similar fashion, writing a long essay or revising for an examination can be broken down into small parts.

Timetabling

How much time needs to be allocated to study? You may need to start keeping track of just how long various work activities take. For example, suppose you need to produce a number of 1,500-word essays on your course. Keep a record of how much time you spent doing background reading, producing a first draft, producing a final draft, and so on, so you know the total amount of time that you require to produce an essay. Then you can ensure that your timetable includes adequate time for all of the work activities involved in producing future essays.

There are important individual differences in terms of the length of time that people can study effectively with good concentration. Organize your timetable with that in mind. If you can concentrate for only 40 or 50 minutes at a time, build frequent breaks into your schedule. If you can concentrate well for two or three hours at a time, then your timetable should reflect this ability. What you may find difficult to do is to avoid getting involved in other activities during the time that is meant to be devoted to studying. If that happens, then you need to reschedule your subsequent activities to catch up on the study time which has been lost.

Pie chart

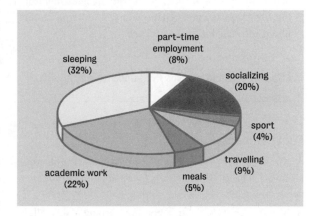

Figure 1.1 Illustrative pie chart showing the percentage of time devoted to different activities

Most students accept that there are advantages in devising weekly timetables and then trying to keep to them. However, many of them find it too much trouble to construct such timetables. Perhaps the simplest way of using time more efficiently is to construct a pie chart (see Figure 1.1). All you need to do is to take a typical week. At the end of each day, simply note down the amount of time devoted to different activities such as the following: travelling; studying; part-time employment; social life; leisure activities (e.g. watching television); others. Then work out the percentage of your time devoted to each activity, and fill in the pie chart accordingly. Finally, ask yourself whether you are devoting too much time to some non-academic activity; if so, you could reallocate that time to the benefit of your studies.

ψ Section summary

A weekly timetable can be constructed to assist the best use of time. Work should be divided into manageable chunks. Work timetables should be organized with frequent breaks. A pie chart may prove useful.

1 What are some of the factors involved in good time management?

ψ Appendix summary

- **Motivational factors**

Motivation for studying depends on setting goals which are hard, clear and realistic. It also involves monitoring progress towards those goals, and being honest about the reasons for any failures

- **Effective reading**

Effective reading involves five successive stages as follows: survey, question, read, recite and review. This approach works because the reader is actively involved in the reading material at all stages.

- **Time management**

Time is a valuable resource. Careful planning helps to ensure that you have adequate time for socializing and other activities as well as for your studies.

Further reading

- McBride, P. (1994) *Study Skills for Success*. Cambridge: Hobsons. This book goes into a considerable amount of detail on the best ways of developing good study skills.

- Morris, P.E. (1979) Strategies for learning and recall, in M.M. Gruneberg and P.E. Morris (eds) *Applied Problems in Memory*. London: Academic Press. This chapter reviews the evidence on approaches to effective reading and learning and on ways of enhancing long-term memory.

- Coles, M. and White, C. (1985) *Strategies for Studying*. London: Collins Educational. All of the key ingredients in successful studying are covered in this book.

CHAPTER 2

Biological bases of behaviour

Fred Toates

KEY CONCEPTS ● causation – the physiology of the body ● genes, environment and evolution ● plasticity ● targeting the brain when things go wrong ● pain ● emotions and stress ● consciousness

❑ Chapter preview

When you have read this chapter, you should be able to

- describe the basics of the organization of the nervous system, in terms of individual neurons, central and peripheral nervous systems, brain, spinal cord, somatic and autonomic nervous systems
- give some examples of how the control of behaviour can be understood in terms both of neurons forming systems and of other physiological events within the body
- explain the difference between a causal and functional explanation of behaviour, giving examples of each
- give some examples of the controversy and pitfalls that await the unwary in the application of biology to understanding behaviour
- explain what is meant by the mind–body problem and the relevance of biology to it

Introduction

Biology is the science of living things, the study of animals and plants and how they function in the natural world. Why then, you might be wondering, so soon into an introduction to psychology, are you being asked to study another discipline? The approach adopted here is that psychologists need to study biology in order to identify bridges that can be constructed between the two disciplines. Crucial insight into behaviour can be gained in this way.

To some theorists, the study of biology by psychologists would be termed **reductionism**, a process of trying to explain events at one level (e.g. behaviour) by looking at a lower level (e.g. the nervous system). In the extreme, reductionism suggests that all psychology can be reduced to biology. This is not the claim being made here. Rather, the present discussion reflects only a modest use of biology: to gain *some* insight by viewing behaviour in a biological context. Whatever information we can glean from biology will need to be understood within a context of psychology. The deliberate priority of starting this book in this way is not to suggest that *only* biology can provide a reliable basis for psychology.

The chapter will discuss three fundamental strands of the application of biology to understanding behaviour. The first is to consider how things work in the 'here and now', i.e. the immediate *causation* of behaviour. Consider a few examples. A person treads on a thorn (cause) and yells shortly afterwards (effect). Events within our bodies (causes), such as a low temperature, trigger the exertion of action on the external world as behaviour (effect). Thus, we can be motivated to seek food, water and often also a source of warmth to sustain our bodies. We are a biologically reproducing species who, as a reaction to a combination of internal and external events, is attracted to others. Thus, behaviour is an integral part of our biological being and one strand of investigation consists of looking at behaviour and seeing how it arises in relation to the body's biology and environment. Of course, not all behaviour can be understood in terms of causes as simple as treading on a thorn or hypothermia. Much of our behaviour has complex hidden causes. Here the role of biology in the explanation is more subtle.

The second strand to be considered is genetics. We inherit genes from our parents and they play a role in determining the structure of our bodies. Through this structure, primarily that of our nervous system, they also play a role in behaviour. The third strand of a biological approach arises from the theory that, over millions of years, we have evolved from a simpler form. This assumption, rooted in Darwin's theory of evolution, has something to say not only about how the physical structure of our bodies has arisen but also about our behaviour. We can gain insights into behaviour by considering how it has been shaped by evolution.

The most complete picture of behaviour can involve a parallel consideration of (1) here-and-now questions of what is causing a particular behaviour, as opposed to doing something else, (2) how genetics has contributed to a body that produces the behaviour and (3) how the behaviour might have arisen as a result of evolutionary processes and how it has been to the advantage of animals to exhibit it. The following three sections will introduce the fundamentals of each of these levels of explanation. Then the knowledge gained will be used in considering in more detail some examples of behaviour and showing where each perspective has something to contribute.

> ψ **Section summary**
>
> There are three fundamental strands to a biological perspective on psychology: causation, genetics and evolution.
> 1 Why is it important for psychologists to have an understanding of biology?

Causation – the physiology of the body

The branch of biology that is concerned with the structure and working of the body is physiology. Physiologists study how the organs of the body, such as the liver, heart and kidneys, work. As a simplification for explanation, there are various ways of conceptually dividing the body. One is in terms of systems defined by the role that they play, though this is a pragmatic convenience only and, of course, life requires interaction between systems. Thus, the circulatory system is responsible for moving blood around the body and consists of the heart and blood vessels. As psychologists, the nervous system will be our principal focus, though we will not lose sight of the other systems.

Another way of dividing the body for explanation is to consider that it is made up of cells, e.g. liver, kidney and brain cells. Each organ (e.g. heart, stomach) is made up of millions of cells. Cells are the fundamental building blocks of an organ and thereby the body. See Figure 2.1 (but note that some cells, e.g. red blood cells, are mobile). Each cell is to some extent 'self-contained'. It has a membrane around itself and the chemical environment on the inside is different from that on the outside. However, like an individual person within a society, the cell can survive only by its interaction with its immediate environment. Thus, nutrients are brought to the cell and waste materials are carried away from the cell by the blood.

All cells, whether in the brain, kidney or wherever, have features in common, e.g. the existence of a membrane and a difference in chemical composition on the two sides of it. However, cells also differ, in both their structure and role. As well as the general properties, cells are (again, rather like people) specialists, serving particular roles according to where they are located and to which organ they belong. For instance, red blood cells are specialists at carrying oxygen in the blood to be delivered to cells throughout the body. Nerve cells (termed **neurons**) are specialized at transmitting and processing information.

Maintaining the condition of the internal 'environment' of the body is crucial. Thus the working of each cell requires a supply of nutrients, which are obtained from outside the body with the help of behaviour. Body temperature is regulated within close limits. When internal conditions deviate from their optimal values,

action is usually taken to restore normality, a process termed **homeostasis**. Homeostasis involves **negative feedback**: deviations from the optimum value tend to cause action that returns the system to its optimum. In other words, deviations from optimum tend to be *self-eliminating*, hence the adjective 'negative' before feedback. This involves not only intrinsic processes like shivering and sweating but also behaviour such as emigrating to Florida. We are *motivated* to seek sources of nutrients, water and heat/cold (see Chapter 16).

The brain is informed of both the internal state of the body and events in the external world. For instance, a depletion of nutrients or water or a low body temperature is signalled to the brain. Information on the external world (e.g. presence of a source of warmth or food) is also signalled. Based upon this information, decisions are made and priorities of behaviour are established. Similarly, in organizing mating, internal signals from the body (e.g. those arising from hormone levels) and external signals from prospective mates are integrated in the brain and decisions on courtship made. Decision-making involves establishing priorities. During, say, feeding, the sight of a predator might cause prioritization to be instantly switched to fleeing. We shall later discuss how such information processing occurs.

Linking physiology and behaviour

Biologically oriented psychologists try to link behaviour to immediately preceding physiological events. For example, a hormone is injected and its effect on, say, mating or aggression noted. A drug said to improve memory might be injected and any effects on learning carefully measured. Whether the behaviour being studied is feeding, sex or anything else, the goal of researchers is to see how internal (e.g. hormones) and external (e.g. presence of a partner) events act together to determine behaviour.

In conducting such investigation, researchers can try to fit their observations into a theoretical structure in terms of the **function** of behaviour in a natural context. This is seen as being to maximize the chances of producing successful offspring (discussed in detail on pp. 47–50). For example, during the mating season, hormones excite sexual motivation. This can be understood in terms of the action of hormones on the brain and it also makes sense from the point of view of function. The chances of engaging in sexual behaviour at a time when the female can be fertilized and thereby reproduce are maximized. Similarly, drinking following a period of prior water deprivation makes sense in terms

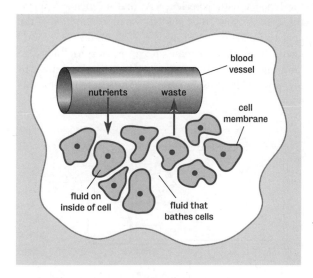

Figure 2.1 A group of cells that form part of an organ; note the fluid-filled spaces between the cells

of both its immediate consequences (to lower thirst) and function (to maintain the physical integrity of the body and hence allow reproduction).

Some behaviour is still difficult to interpret in terms of either its function or even short-term consequences. For example, animals, particularly in intensive agricultural systems, often perform apparently pointless behaviour, such as endless rituals of chewing or pacing, termed **stereotypies** (Ellinwood and Kilbey 1975). These sometimes involve self-mutilation. Is this simply a pathological aberration of behaviour, shown by an animal in an abnormal environment? Although such behaviour is difficult to interpret in rational terms, behavioural scientists still try asking the combined question: what internal and external events trigger behaviour and what (if any) consequence does it achieve? It might be that stereotypies provide, say, a source of stimulation or lower the level of stress in a way that is still unclear. Since the environment in which stereotypies are observed is so different from that in which animals evolved, it might prove misleading to suggest that they serve any function, in the sense just defined.

There is a central faith of biological psychology, which is as follows. Behaviour is determined by many external and internal factors acting in complex interaction upon the nervous system. Ultimately, whatever its initial causes and whether it is describable in rational terms (e.g. drinking following a period of water deprivation) or seemingly irrational (e.g. self-mutilation), behaviour reflects the activity of identifiable processes within the nervous system. Biological psychologists believe that in principle, by close analysis, these processes can be understood. One useful tool for looking at some aspects of behaviour is described in the next section.

Regulation

In some cases, behaviour can be better understood in terms of the principles of homeostasis and negative feedback. For example, if an animal is deprived of water for a period of time, it will continue to lose water from its body and the amount that it subsequently drinks reflects the magnitude of the loss. **Control theory**, a body of knowledge on how systems operate, and analogies between control systems, can be useful in understanding the control of behaviour. For example, regulating the temperature of a room with the help of a thermostat can be understood in such terms. A temperature is set on the dial and room temperature is automati-

cally compared against this. If room temperature falls below that set, heating is automatically activated until temperature is regained. However, such analogies should not be pushed too far. Rats and humans are not exactly like central heating systems but seeing the features in common can prove insightful.

Suppose that the cells of the body become depleted of water. Information on the dehydrated state of representative cells is conveyed to decision-making regions of the brain. If water becomes available, drinking restores hydration to the cells. This is termed **regulatory behaviour** (or homeostatic behaviour) since it regulates the internal environment, keeping it within safe limits. Such behaviour can be understood in terms of both its consequences and the function that it serves. Behaviour 'makes sense' in that the animal is seen to be constructed in such a way as to achieve an end-point by its behaviour, in this case equilibrium of hydration level and thereby survival.

A water-deprived rat can be trained to perform a task to earn water; it is *motivated* to do so (Chapter 16). For example, it can be taught to negotiate a maze for such reward; this can be viewed as **goal-directed behaviour**, since the animal achieves a goal (reaching water) by behaving in this way. It can be taught to press a lever in a **Skinner box** (Figure 2.2) for small units of water (Chapter 3). In acting in this way regulation of the internal environment is achieved.

Mazes and Skinner boxes are valuable instruments for looking at the controls underlying behaviour and how they change with experience. At first, in such an apparatus, the rat seems to be guided by a representation of the goal to be achieved. However, with extensive experience, the skilled rat seems to go on to something like 'autopilot control', reacting in an automatic fashion to the physically present stimuli. The evidence for this

Figure 2.2 Skinner box

claim is as follows. At first, a rat pressing a lever for food in a Skinner box is sensitive to the quality of the food. Suppose that the food becomes devalued by being paired with aversive after-effects (see p. 51 and also Chapter 3). After this experience, the devaluation is reflected in a lowering of the rate at which the rat presses the lever for such food. However, with extensive experience, rats go into autopilot control where they tend to press the lever irrespective of whether the food is one that they will eat or not (Adams 1982).

Not all behaviour is regulatory and we should not expect it to be so. For example, homeostasis does not lie at the biological basis of sexual behaviour, though this behaviour depends upon internal and external factors and it exhibits a form of negative feedback. This again draws attention to the consequences served by behaviour. Reproduction does not serve the consequence of restoration of optimal bodily conditions, whereas feeding and drinking do. However, sexual behaviour still, of course, makes sense in terms of its function: propagation of genes by means often described as pleasurable!

Non-regulatory ingestive behaviour

When an instance of feeding or drinking cannot be understood in terms of regulation, it is described as **non-regulatory behaviour**. A striking example of non-regulatory drinking was discovered by Falk (1961) and has occupied very many columns of print since then. To better understand Falk's discovery, it is useful, first, to consider a related example of regulatory behaviour.

Suppose a rat is deprived of food (but not water) for a period of time and then given access to food. It will tend to drink in association with eating. This drinking is regulatory since feeding tends to pull water from the blood into the gut and thereby creates a *need*, the amount drunk being commensurate with this need. But suppose rats are food deprived and allowed to receive only small morsels of food at a rate of, say, one 45 milligram pellet a minute. They are not water deprived and water is freely available from a spout adjacent to the platform where food pellets arrive. In this situation, rats gradually come to drink enormous quantities of water, a phenomenon termed **schedule-induced polydipsia** (Falk 1969) and an example of non-regulatory behaviour (non-homeostatic drinking).

You might find it bizarre that psychologists spend their time doing something as unnatural as giving tiny portions of food to hungry rats and observing how much they drink. Isn't this ammunition for those who claim that academics are often divorced from the problems of the real world? There is an important counter-argument to this. On reflection, much human behaviour seems no less irrational and compulsive than that of the polydipsic rat (Robbins and Koob 1980) and we desperately need new insights into the processes underlying such behaviour. For instance, placed in stressful situations, humans occasionally engage in self-mutilation, finger chewing or hair pulling. Especially in the case of humans with severe mental retardation, there is an increased tendency for stereotyped behaviour (e.g. body rocking) to occur when exposed to a schedule similar to the one just described for rats (Emerson and Howard 1992).

Although schedule-induced polydipsia remains something of a puzzle, none the less researchers into such diverse human behavioural phenomena as the repetitive motor sequences of autistic children (M.H. Lewis *et al.* 1987) and human drug-taking (Falk *et al.* 1983) frequently refer to it. Thus, a seemingly obscure phenomenon might just give some insight into broader issues of what controls behaviour and serve as a kind of model system or animal model. Researchers are somewhat like detectives, trying to pick up clues and seeing links between them. Based upon a collection of such clues, a theory can be proposed.

Why do rats sometimes act in a bizarre way, e.g. when exposed to such a food schedule? Does the rat occasionally become a philosophical existentialist, showing behaviour that is forever beyond the scope of rational analysis (Falk 1971)? If not, how might we try to understand this behaviour? Although the rat is not responding to a loss of water, the experimental psychologist's assumption would be that it is responding to some internal signal acting together with the environment. We need to try to identify how this combination works.

Drinking is an activity that naturally follows feeding in rats and so, in association with feeding, drinking might be the activity that is second in priority. There is nothing surprising in the fact that rats drink when on this schedule. It is the excessive amounts ingested that are surprising. A theory that might explain polydipsia will be developed in this chapter but before we can go far in this direction we shall need to address our central topic, the nervous system and how it organizes behaviour.

Research update

Schedule-induced polydipsia

This section brings together some old and some new clues that might offer, if not a solution, then at least a slightly better understanding of schedule-induced polydipsia. There are several interesting aspects of this behaviour, e.g. its similarity with some other forms of behaviour and a switch in the basis of the control of the behaviour as a function of the length of time of exposure to the schedule. Each of these will be looked at.

Each presentation of a small food pellet to a hungry rat might create a kind of anticipatory excitation of the feeding control system but this excitation is not discharged fully in feeding because of the size of pellets. The consequence might be an excitation of processes in the brain that are common to the control of a number of different behaviours (Ikemoto and Panksepp 1994; Killeen 1975; Salamone 1988; Wayner 1970). If the environmental supports are available, it therefore might tend to trigger behaviour other than feeding, e.g. drinking.

Suppose a water spout is not available in the spaced feeding situation. If a running wheel is present, rats will run in it. If paper towels are available, they will shred them. In the case of pigeons, one bird will attack another (Falk 1971). Again, it seems as if a carry-over effect of the excitation of feeding is present and this 'locks into' the control of another behaviour. Any such locking-in induces a strong effect; once established, it is difficult to deter drinking by means of making the taste unpalatable (Riley and Wetherington 1989). Thus, suppose that on one occasion the available liquid is paired with an aversive consequence, termed taste-aversion learning (see p. 51). This procedure strongly inhibits normal regulatory drinking, but there is only a relatively small effect on schedule-induced polydipsia (Riley and Wetherington 1989).

Suppose, however, that accompanying this schedule, a running wheel is also made available. Rats will spend time running and less time drinking. Why should the presence of a running wheel deter drinking more effectively than pairing the taste of the fluid with an aversive consequence? The result suggests that schedule-induced polydipsia is something like an addiction in that, with little else to do, drinking can create the conditions for promoting further drinking. The pull of the spout becomes irresistible. However, if an alternative activity

is available, the rat can engage in this and spend less time at the spout. This is a feature shared with both rat and human drug-taking. The tendency to addiction is less if the environment offers possibilities for engaging in non-drug-related activities (Riley and Wetherington 1989; Wolffgramm and Heyne 1995).

Suppose that a water spout is not available immediately but only after some days of exposure to the feeding schedule. When water becomes available, the development of drinking is relatively slow compared to when water is available from the start (Toates 1971). This suggests the possibility that, prior to the appearance of the spout, the animal found some other outlet for its behaviour.

Why is established schedule-induced polydipsia relatively difficult to suppress as compared to normal drinking? When offered under conventional conditions, fluids can be shown to be aversive to the same rat that ingests them under the schedule conditions. It would seem that behaviour derives its strength from an after-effect of the pellet and an over-excited feeding/approach system. In the rat's perceptual and memory systems, this excitation somehow gets associated with the water spout.

How does schedule-induced polydipsia compare with other behaviour? Behaviour such as feeding and drinking can be elicited by artificial electrical stimulation of certain brain regions through implanted electrodes, e.g. the hypothalamus (see p. 42) (Ikemoto and Panksepp 1994; Mittleman et al. 1986) (see pp. 43–4 and Chapter 16). A process similar to that just proposed for schedule-induced polydipsia is evoked in order to explain this behaviour (Berridge and Valenstein 1991). Damage to the hypothalamus eliminates schedule-induced polydipsia (Falk 1969).

For the rat eating in response to electrical brain stimulation, if the food is removed and water is available, electrically elicited drinking will sometimes slowly emerge (Valenstein et al. 1970). This is rather like the gradual appearance of schedule-induced polydipsia and suggests a common basis. Comparing different rats, there are differences in the strength of tendency to show electrically stimulated behaviour. Rats that have a strong tendency to show electrically elicited behaviour also have a strong tendency to show schedule-

Box continued

induced polydipsia. This suggests that there are differences in the brains of different rats corresponding to different strength of tendency to both schedule-induced polydipsia and electrically induced behaviour.

Once schedule-induced polydipsia has been established, it is more difficult to disrupt than when it was being acquired (Riley and Wetherington 1987; 1989; Robbins *et al.* 1983; Yoburn and Glusman 1982), a characteristic shared with stereotypies (Kennes *et al.* 1988). It appears that the basis of control shifts with experience. One might say that the behaviour is voluntary at the outset and becomes compulsive with experience (cf. Wolffgram and Heyne 1995). The pull of the spout appears to become addictive. Could this have parallels in other aspects of behaviour?

There is a general principle that appears to apply to many instances of human and non-human behaviour, as illustrated by the earlier discussion of mazes and Skinner boxes (Toates 1998). With extensive experience of performing the same task, the relative weighting of the control of behaviour shifts. Behaviour starts out being goal-directed (i.e. oriented to the achievement of a future goal) and with experience moves to being more automatic and more strongly under the control of immediately present stimuli (Schneider and Shiffrin 1977; Toates 1998).

We are surely all familiar with some such shifts. For instance, at first, driving a car is done with full concentration and attention to detail. After some experience, particularly in familiar territory, the same behaviour is performed in a more automatic mode. People come under the influence of familiar stimuli and react to them in a more automatic way. With drug addicts, self-administration becomes more stereotyped and robot-like after repeated experience (Tomie 1996). It is now possible that we are near to a more integrative view which sees at least some common features in a wide variety of behaviours from humans driving cars and taking drugs to rats running mazes and showing schedule-induced polydipsia.

Neurons and the nervous system

The principal focus of this chapter is how behaviour is determined by the nervous system. Therefore, we shall be concerned with the constituent cells of the system, the nerve cells, or neurons. The nervous system is made up of millions of neurons. Neurons come in many shapes and sizes, only a few of which look like the cells in Figure 2.1. Two types of neuron that we shall discuss are shown in Figure 2.3, both consisting of a long **axon** (sometimes termed a 'process' or 'fibre') and a cell body. Information is transmitted along the length of the axon as pulses of electricity rather like such pulses in a wire.

One logical way of dividing up the nervous system is shown in Figure 2.4, which also shows a few of the neurons that comprise the system in humans. The **central nervous system** (CNS), defined as the brain and spinal cord, is shown in white. The spinal cord passes along the middle of the back bone. By definition, all of the nervous system outside the central nervous system constitutes the **peripheral nervous system**, shown in blue. (The terms **neural** and **neuronal** are adjectives to refer to neurons, e.g. neural pathways.)

A neuron communicates and processes information. For example, information concerning events in the external world (e.g. sounds, chemical odours) is communicated via neurons to the brain (Chapter 4) where decisions are made. The embodiment of decision-making in the brain is further collections of neurons. If action is required, then information is conveyed via neurons to the muscles where it is effected. Also information arising within the body (e.g. concerning a stomach full of water) is conveyed to the brain by neurons.

The expression **nerve** describes a collection of axons, which are located (a) in the peripheral nervous system and (b) alongside each other such that they extend over a particular distance. They are similar to a

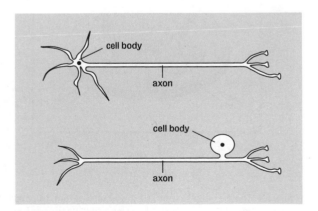

Figure 2.3 Neuron types

bundle of wires in a cable, e.g. as in the enlarged view in Figure 2.4b. Within a particular nerve, an individual axon is constructed so that it can convey information either *to* or *from* the CNS but not both. In Figure 2.4b the dark blue axons carry information from the CNS and the light blue axons carry information to the CNS. A given nerve is usually made up of a mixture of two sorts of axon, some carrying information to and others from the CNS. Some of the axons shown in Figure 2.4b would convey to the spinal cord information on specific events at a bodily region, in this case the hand. For example, one might convey information about tissue damage at the skin of a finger whereas a neighbour might signal an innocuous touch at this same area of skin. A third might signal information on temperature at the skin of the finger.

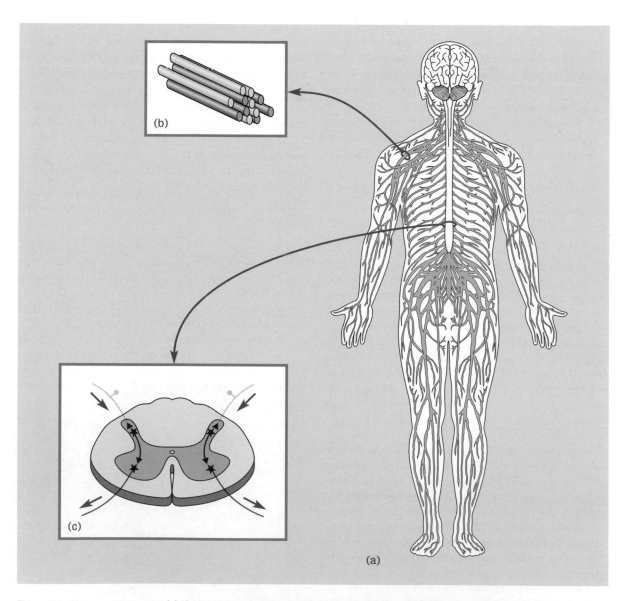

Figure 2.4 The nervous system (a) the whole system, (b) enlagement of part of a nerve showing four individual neurons, (c) a cross-section of the spinal cord showing a few incoming and outgoing neurons; arrows indicate direction of information flow

Take, for example, treading on a thorn. The reaction to this consists of two components: (1) the **reflex** of removing the foot from the thorn and (2) the perception of a traumatic event involving a conscious sensation of pain. For both components, the central nervous system is involved, as shown in Figure 2.5. (This is a simplified representation. In practice many neurons in parallel would be involved.) Both components rely upon specialized neurons (e.g. neuron 1), known as **nociceptive neurons**, which detect tissue damage at their tips. Electrical signals arise at the tip and are conveyed along the length of the axon of neuron 1.

Considering the reflex component, at the spinal cord, the nociceptive neuron communicates with neuron 2, which carries the message further to make contact with neuron 3. Neuron 3 conveys the information to neuron 4, which then transmits signals to a muscle and hence action is effected. When the information arrives at the muscle, contraction of the muscle occurs and the foot is removed from the offending object. In relation to the axons, note the different position of the cell body of neuron 1 as compared to the others, which can be compared with the neurons in Figure 2.3.

This is a reflex and information from tissue damage to the muscle does not pass through the brain. The distance that information travels is therefore relatively short and the reaction fast. Note however that the nociceptive neuron also communicates with neuron 5, which

projects up the spinal cord to the brain. Information conveyed by this route plays a part in the creation of the conscious sensation of pain with its negative emotional connotations. Such an experience can form a memory for thorns as noxious objects to be avoided.

In biological psychology, the term 'electrical signal' is used to mean a series of pulses of electricity, each travelling along the length of the neuron. Each pulse is termed an **action potential**. The action potential is one of the principal 'languages' of the nervous system, whatever the information being carried.

Figure 2.6 shows how information is conveyed by this means, in the *frequency* with which action potentials occur. For example, suppose that a neuron detects temperature, i.e. is sensitive to the temperature at its tip (part a). Action potentials travel along the neuron's length and come to an end at the terminals. Further neurons carry the message on. Part b shows the response to a mild temperature. In response to increasing temperature, an increasing frequency of action potentials arises at the tip of the neuron (part c). In part d, temperature is increased still more and the frequency correspondingly increases. In a given neuron, any action potential is just like any other and they travel at the same speed. What encodes information is first, which neuron is active, e.g. a temperature-sensitive neuron (Figure 2.6) or a tissue-damage-sensitive neuron (Figure 2.5), and second, how many action potentials occur in a unit of time in the particular neuron.

The nociceptive neuron and heat-sensitive neuron are examples of **sensory neurons**, i.e. neurons that convey sensory information to the CNS. Neuron 4 of Figure 2.5 is a **motor neuron**, i.e. one that conveys information from the CNS, which, in this case, activates a muscle. An **interneuron** is a neuron that is neither sensory nor motor but which lies somewhere in between. In Figure 2.5, neurons 2, 3 and 5 are interneurons. Our thinking, perceiving and feeling are the result of the activity of millions of interneurons in the brain, in part acting upon incoming sensory information.

The nociceptive neuron (Figure 2.5) and the temperature-sensitive neuron (Figure 2.6) involve sensory information that gets to the brain via the spinal cord. Much information is routed this way (Figure 2.4). However, above the level of the neck, information transfer between the brain and the body outside the brain is not via the spinal cord. It is via **cranial nerves**. For instance, a cranial nerve, the optic nerve, conveys visual information from the eyes to the brain. The auditory nerve conveys auditory information from the ears to the brain (see Chapter 4).

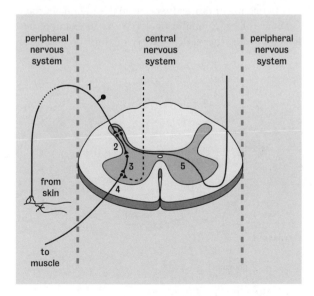

Figure 2.5 Slice of the spinal cord, showing neurons involved in detecting tissue damage and effecting action

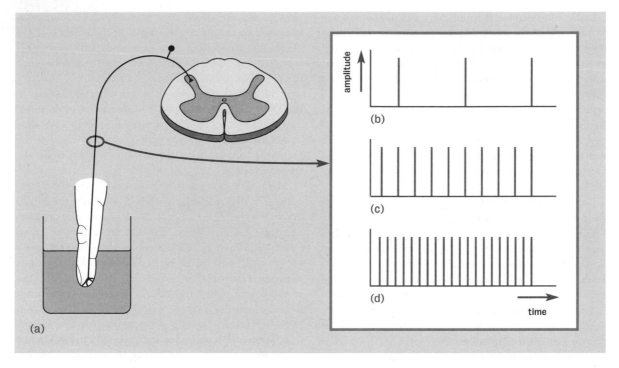

Figure 2.6 (a) A neuron that is sensitive to temperature at its tip, (b–d) the responses to increasing temperature; each vertical line represents one action potential

Communication between neurons

Neurotransmitters and synapses

Figure 2.7 shows in more detail an example of communication between neurons. Signals in neuron 1 convey information to neuron 2 and signals in 2 convey information to 3. The point of communication between neurons is known as a **synapse**. (Synapses come in many different forms, only one form being shown in Figure 2.7.) What exactly is meant by one neuron 'communicating' with another at a synapse? It means that action potentials arriving at the terminal of one neuron (e.g. neuron 1 in Figure 2.7) influence electrical events in the second neuron (neuron 2).

The way in which one neuron influences another depends upon the synapse in question. Suppose that an action potential arriving at the terminal of one neuron *increases* the chances that an action potential will occur in the second neuron. This would be termed an **excitatory synapse**. In Figure 2.5, the synapses between the neurons described so far are excitatory: a series of action potentials in neuron 1 triggers action potentials in subsequent neurons and then activity in the muscle. In other

cases, there are **inhibitory synapses** meaning that activity in one neuron *decreases* the chances that an action potential will occur in the second neuron. It inhibits activity that might otherwise occur in the second neuron.

What role does inhibition serve? As an example, let us reconsider the reflex involving limb withdrawal

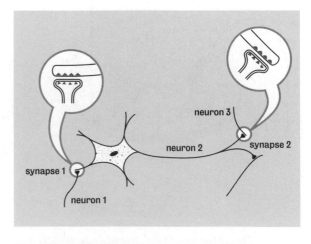

Figure 2.7 Communication between neurons at synapses

(Figure 2.5). Imagine that a bare-footed person has just secured a tenuous foothold on a ledge of a cliff, which the person cannot afford to lose. Yet on the ledge there are some thorns. To withdraw the foot would be to court disaster. In certain situations, the brain is able to exert inhibition upon the signals such that even though nociceptive neurons are excited, their ability to trigger the muscle is inhibited. Although the reflexive sequence normally bypasses the brain, none the less factors outside the reflex can sometimes inhibit it. Imagine that the neuron shown dotted exerts inhibition in this way.

For another example, consider an animal that has a deficit of water within the cells of its body, represented by the rectangle in Figure 2.8a. The brain extracts a signal corresponding to this deficit (see the trace drawn alongside the rectangle). Drinking is motivated by means of excitatory synapses (+) on a neuron that is marked 'motivation'. (For simplicity, only one such excitatory neuron and synapse is shown.) Note the inhibitory connection made by neurons sensitive to water in the stomach (marked −). At the start the stomach is empty. When an amount commensurate with the deficit is drunk, the animal stops drinking. Yet most of the water drunk is still in the stomach and intestine (part b). It appears that water passing the mouth and in the stomach can *inhibit* the tendency to drink. In part c some rehydration has taken place, hence the reduced activity of the neuron that detects cell hydration. Some water is still in the stomach. Still excitatory and inhibitory effects cancel.

How does electrical activity in one neuron either excite or inhibit the activity of another? To understand this, we need to look more closely at the synapse. One neuron does not quite make physical contact with another at the synapse. There is a minute gap between them. This is shown more clearly in the blown-up view of the synapse in Figure 2.7. In the terminal of the neuron, chemical **transmitter** (also termed neurotransmitter) is stored. When an action potential arrives at the terminal, the transmitter is released. The transmitter very rapidly moves across the gap between the two neurons and attaches itself to **receptors** at the second neuron. In attaching to receptors, the transmitter causes the second neuron either to be excited or inhibited. Which effect it has depends upon the nature of the transmitter and the receptors. A given synapse will always be either excitatory or inhibitory in response to the arrival of an action potential releasing neurotransmitter.

A neuron is characterized by the transmitter that it stores at its terminal and releases in response to the arrival of an action potential at the terminal. For example, a neuron might be described as 'serotonergic'. This means that the neuron synthesizes serotonin, stores it at the terminal and releases it when an action potential arrives. If the neuron makes a functioning synapse with another neuron, then there must be specific serotonin receptors at the membrane of the second neuron. Such a synapse would also be termed serotonergic.

Synapses and their neurotransmitters are fundamental to the study of psychology. For example, the emotions that we experience, e.g. depression and elation, depend to a large extent upon the activity of circuits of neurons in our central nervous systems. This activity depends upon synapses between neurons. It is possible to manipulate artificially the activity of populations of such neurons by targeting synapses. The branch of behavioural science concerned with this is termed **psychopharmacology**. It is occupied with developing drugs that can change mood and behaviour, e.g. anti-depressant and anti-anxiety medication.

The fact that mood can be altered by drugs is indicative of the close interdependence between mental states and such physical events as levels of chemical in the body. It points to the necessity for co-operation between researchers in psychology and biology. For instance a drug might boost levels of activity at serotonergic synapses throughout the body and thereby affect mood, Prozac being of this kind. The rationale of much of the pharmaceutical and psychiatric profession is to enable us, with official approval, to change radically our brains' neurochemistry. On a somewhat less professional level, people manipulate the functioning of their nervous systems by such well-known means as smoking, drinking alcohol and taking illegal drugs such as Ecstasy and heroin.

How do chemicals affect the functioning of circuits of neurons and thereby our mental states? Certain chemicals either boost or lower the efficacy of the body's natural neurotransmitters or mimic these natural chemicals. A chemical that has a similar effect to a particular natural transmitter is known as an **agonist**. For example, morphine and heroin are agonists to the natural morphine-like substances that the body produces. An inert substance that occupies receptors normally occupied by a natural transmitter and thereby blocks the effect of the natural substance is termed an **antagonist**. See Figure 2.9, which refers to an excitatory synapse.

Figure 2.10 shows another means by which chemicals can affect the functioning of the nervous system. After a neurotransmitter is released, it is normally rapidly removed from the synaptic region, either by being chem-

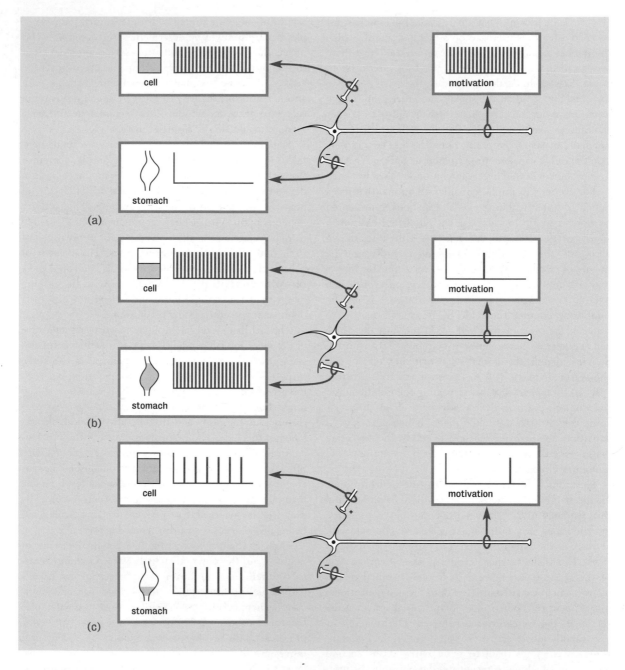

Figure 2.8 The tendency to drink as a function of excitatory and inhibitory influences (a) dehydrated animal (dotted rectangle, optimal cell hydration; full rectangle, actual), (b) at termination of drinking, (c) time after completion of drinking

ically broken down or by being taken back into the neuron from which it was released. In Figure 2.10b, a substance is introduced into the body that blocks reuptake of a specific neurotransmitter. Note the boost in level of transmitter at the receptors. As an example,

cocaine has this effect on the natural transmitter, dopamine. In regular cocaine users, the changes induced by the elevation of dopamine levels (in interaction with the rest of the nervous system) is experienced as a subjective 'high' and a craving for more (Volkow *et al.* 1997).

Agonists and antagonists are one of the means by which scientists can manipulate levels of activity within certain pathways of neurons. For example, a dopamine antagonist can be injected and the dopamine system temporarily inactivated. Subsequent changes in behaviour can give clues as to the normal role of dopamine (DA) in the organization of behaviour.

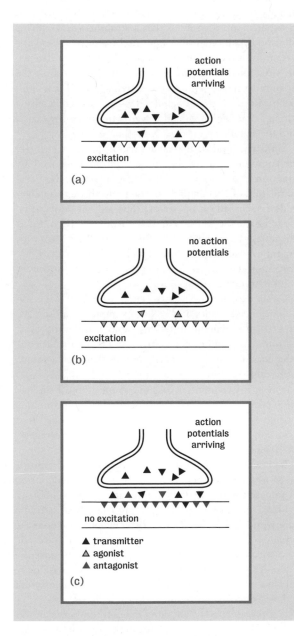

Figure 2.9 Manipulating a synapse (a) normal, (b) addition of an agonist, (c) addition of an antagonist

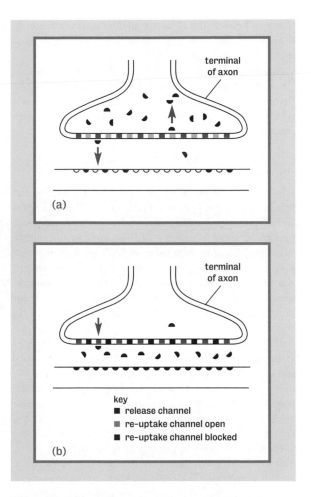

Figure 2.10 Manipulation of neurotransmitter levels by a chemical that blocks re-uptake. Blue channels = site of release, grey channels = site of re-uptake (a) normal situation, (b) addition of chemical (black represents blocked re-uptake channels)

Behaviour is a complex function of all of the neurons of the nervous system acting in interaction. Therefore, one neurotransmitter and its associated neurons cannot be said to be more important than another. If we ask a question like 'Is transmitter X involved in musical ability?', then the answer probably has to be 'yes' since this is an integrated body and mind activity. A trivial example will illustrate the point. Suppose we ask 'Is acetylcholine involved in musical ability?' The answer must be 'yes', since acetylcholine provides a crucial link between the nervous system and the body's muscles. Without it, there can be no performing of music nor any other behaviour. So we need to ask more refined questions such as where and how does transmitter X exert an effect on behaviour Y? Has the artificial manipulation of X an especially powerful effect upon behaviour Y as opposed to other behaviour?

Since space precludes a discussion of all the neurotransmitters, we must be selective and dopamine will be examined in detail, since a number of well-known behavioural abnormalities appear to be associated with abnormal levels of dopamine.

Dopamine as an example

Advances in understanding require both pursuing the details of a single phenomenon and looking broadly at several phenomena simultaneously. By comparing data on such diverse examples of behaviour as polydipsic rats, cats showing repetitive behaviour, human drug addicts and schizophrenics, we might get important insights, since abnormalities in certain dopaminergic neuronal pathways seem to be crucially involved in them all (Blackburn et al. 1992; LeDuc and Mittleman 1995; Mittleman et al. 1994).

Dopamine serves multiple roles as a neurotransmitter in various parts of the brain, some nearer the sensory and some nearer the motor side (Panksepp 1982). We shall focus upon effects at the level of sensory and motivational processes. As just noted, in human cocaine users, increasing dopamine levels is associated with a feeling of 'high' and also craving.

Rats lose interest in gaining such normally attractive things as food when drugs are injected that lower their level of dopamine (Wise 1982). There are various theories to explain this. In keeping with the reports of human cocaine users, Wise (1982) suggested that dopamine mediates the pleasure that comes from behaviour such as feeding and so dopamine-depleted rats find food to be without its normal hedonic appeal. Others have suggested that the dopamine-depleted brain exhibits a loss of attention (Solomon and Crider 1982) or an unwillingness to exert effort (Neill 1982). Much of the experimental evidence derived from dopamine depletion was equally compatible with each theory but more recent evidence has suggested something of a rethink.

More refined techniques now available enable us to note the rat's 'hedonic' reaction to food actually placed in minute controlled samples onto the tongue, which is found to be the same in dopamine-depleted rats as in normals (Berridge et al. 1989). This result has important implications. If dopamine does not help to mediate the pleasures of life as in food tasting good, why does dopamine depletion cause loss of interest in food and related stimuli? Conversely, we need to explain how elevated dopamine levels are associated with euphoria

in cocaine addicts. Cocaine might exert its *euphoric* effect through the activation of dopamine pathways that subserve pleasures other than those of feeding and sex, e.g. those associated with attaining a goal. Alternatively, it might stimulate pleasure through a route other than dopamine but mediate *craving* through a dopaminergic route.

Evidence suggests that dopamine has a role in the capacity of stimuli to attract. For example, suppose that an experimenter arranges that a stimulus (e.g. light) is followed by a biologically significant event (e.g. food at a certain location or finding a place of safety in a dangerous situation). When this is done, the light acquires the capacity to trigger dopamine activity (Blackburn et al. 1992; Mirenowicz and Schultz 1996). This might play a role in attracting an animal towards the place associated with the significant event, e.g. food or safety.

Similarly, suppose that an animal is placed in a certain environment and its dopamine system triggered by injection of a drug (a dopamine agonist) or electrical stimulation of certain parts of the brain through an electrode (discussed on pp. 43–4). The animal tends to be attracted to the particular region of its environment where it was present when the artificial activation of dopamine happened (Ellinwood and Kilbey 1975). Dopamine seems then to tag certain locations as attractive, i.e. to be pursued.

Other evidence points in a similar direction (Solomon and Crider 1982). For example, suppose that, rather than signalling something biologically important, a stimulus is applied repeatedly with no significant consequences. The animal normally learns that such a stimulus heralds nothing of consequence and so ignores it. However, if dopamine is injected at the time of the initial exposure, the animal has difficulty learning 'stimulus is of no consequence'; a stimulus exposed under these conditions still commands attention and the capacity to elicit behaviour.

Increasing levels of dopamine can also give stimuli the power to elicit repetitive stereotyped behaviour. A rat injected with the drug amphetamine, which boosts levels of dopamine, will show high levels of activity (Ellinwood and Kilbey 1975). Later when it is returned to the environment in which amphetamine was injected, the environment will arouse activity even in the absence of the drug. Again it seems that what are otherwise neutral cues become converted to cues for action as a result of their association with high dopamine levels.

Is it possible to see anything in common between the various effects associated with high dopamine levels? Can a theory or even a general summary statement start to be developed?

Research update

The role of dopamine

Among the spectrum of different stimuli that impinge on an animal's sense organs, some might be registered but not engage behaviour. Others have the capacity to engage attention, conscious awareness (in the case of humans) and behaviour. Some stimuli will have this capacity as a result of their intensity and others because of what, by learning, they have come to signal. Comparing different results and theories on the effects of elevated dopamine (Berridge and Robinson 1997; Ellinwood and Kilbey 1975; Robbins 1975; Schultz *et al.* 1997), in each case the power of stimuli to engage behaviour seems to be increased. Behaviour here means attention, attraction and repetitive responses.

Rhesus monkeys brought up under conditions of sensory deprivation have elevated levels of dopamine activity in certain brain regions. They attend even to stimuli that carry no information and engage in stereotyped behaviour at a relatively high frequency (Beauchamp *et al.* 1991). Similarly, schizophrenia (Chapter 16) is associated with disturbances to the dopamine system. Among other aspects of schizophrenia there are two that seem most appropriate in the present context. First, there are stimuli, which would be ignored by non-schizophrenic subjects (neutral or 'indifferent' events), but which repeatedly engage the attention of the schizophrenic. Second, schizophrenics show increased levels of apparently pointless repetitive behaviour (Robbins 1975).

The earlier discussion on a shift of the basis of control with experience seems to apply also to the role of dopamine (Ljungberg *et al.* 1992). Suppose that a stimulus is presented repeatedly and an animal comes to behave in a predictable way in response to it. Under these conditions, activation of dopaminergic neurons in response to this stimulus declines with repetition (Ljungberg *et al.* 1992). However, the capacity of the stimulus to engage behaviour is not lost. After a stimulus becomes familiar, it retains its capacity to trigger behaviour even if dopamine levels are artificially depleted (Hoffman and Beninger 1986). This suggests that dopamine activation labels stimuli as motivationally relevant, to be acted upon. Presumably, as the size of the dopamine activation declines with repetition, some other means of control takes over. This suggests that dopamine activation is necessary for the phase of recruiting behavioural action.

That dopamine is triggered by cues predictive of important events might be relevant to understanding schedule-induced polydipsia. As noted, rats subjected to a schedule of regular food drink excessive amounts. If a water spout is not present but a running wheel is, then rats will run in the interval between obtaining food pellets. On this schedule, both drinking (Keehn *et al.* 1976; Robbins and Koob 1980) and locomotor activity (Salamone 1988) are reduced by blocking dopamine, though the rat still eats the pellets. We might expect that a depletion of dopamine would be especially disruptive early in the acquisition of polydipsia, which is indeed the case (Robbins and Koob 1980; Robbins *et al.* 1983). Regulatory drinking in a familiar location is affected little, if at all, by the disruption to dopamine.

During schedule-induced polydipsia, the rat is subjected to cues predictive of food (e.g. sound of delivery apparatus and food pellet falling) and yet each morsel of food is very small and is rapidly eaten. Presumably, at least in the early stages of acquisition, dopamine is repeatedly activated in this situation. Feeding tends naturally to be followed by drinking and this might well coincide with dopamine activation, which would, it is suggested, make the spout attractive.

Excessive drinking does not appear immediately but takes time to develop. Could this be while a link between moving to the water spout and elevated dopamine levels is formed? Suppose the rat is exposed to the schedule of food delivery first and water is then introduced only after some days. It is predicted that the rat will be retarded in its acquisition of polydipsia since in the period prior to water available it might have found some other activity to perform. Time will be taken if it is to form a link between any elevated dopamine and the perception of the water spout. As noted earlier, polydipsia is acquired more slowly than if water was available from the outset (Toates 1971).

Earlier feeding induced by implanted electrodes was discussed and it was noted that rats vary in the strength of their tendency to show this behaviour. Animals that show such a tendency to electrically induced behaviour have a relatively high utilization of dopamine (Mittleman *et al.* 1986). Rats that have a strong tendency to show electrically elicited behaviour also have a strong tendency to show both schedule-induced polydipsia (see pp. 28–9) and active responding to a cue predictive of shock. This suggests that differences between animals might reflect intrinsic differences in the dopamine reactivity of a process underlying the control of each of these behaviours.

Hormones

Communication within the body is by means of **hormones** as well as neurotransmitters. Hormones and their actions constitute the **endocrine system**, which has interactions with the nervous system. What is the difference between a hormone and a neurotransmitter? A particular chemical is acting as a hormone if it is released at a site some distance from its target and is carried in the blood to its target. It is acting as a neurotransmitter if it is released from one neuron and attaches itself to receptors at an adjacent cell, i.e. neuron or muscle. The chemical that constitutes a hormone can be identical to a neurotransmitter. As with neurotransmission, where communication occurs by means of a hormone, there are receptors at an organ that are sensitive to the hormone. When the hormone attaches itself to these receptors, the target organ is affected and control exerted. For example, sex hormones released at the sex organs are transported in the blood to the brain, where they influence neurons underlying sexual motivation.

Adrenalin and noradrenalin can act as either hormones or as neurotransmitters. It depends upon where the substance is exerting its effect and its mode of transport from site of release to site of action. For example, at the heart muscle there are receptors to which adrenalin, arriving in the blood stream, attaches itself. When adrenalin attaches, the activity of the muscle is changed, a hormonal action. There are also adrenalin receptors within the CNS. These are on the membrane of neurons, to which adrenalin released from an adjacent neuron attaches itself, i.e. a neurotransmitter action. Figure 2.11 compares the action of (a) neurotransmitters at neurons and muscles and (b) hormones.

A hormone usually serves as a means of 'general' transmission of information throughout the body. It normally (though not always) involves several or many targets in different locations. By contrast, a neurotransmitter's action can be more localized. For example, by means of a neurotransmitter, a neuron is able to transmit information to a site no broader than a second adjacent neuron. For the transmission of information over relatively large distances, an advantage that neurons have over hormones is speed. It takes more time for a hormone to be released, circulate in the blood stream and influence a distant location.

Looking at the brain

To understand how the brain works it is necessary to build a description of its structure, a map. This enables researchers to locate reliably the various regions of the brain and the connections between them. Knowledge is built up about the neurons in different regions and their neurotransmitters. If neurons in one region are identified as, say, mainly serotonergic, it is possible to trace where such serotonergic neurons project their axons. Thus, a picture of the connections between brain regions can be formed.

Careful extrapolation from non-humans can sometimes give insight into the human brain. Also the misfortunes of war, accidents and disease provide patients with damaged brains, in whom any behavioural abnormalities can be investigated.

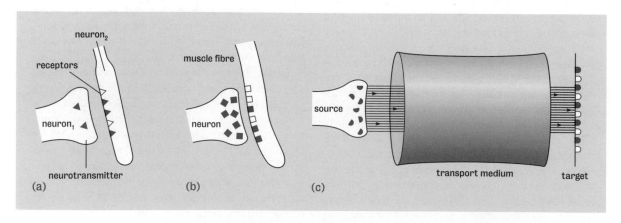

Figure 2.11 Communication by neurotransmitters and hormones (a) neurotransmitter at the junction between a neuron and another neuron, (b) neurotransmitter at the junction between a neuron and a muscle, (c) hormone

The hemispheres and the cortex

Figure 2.12 shows the human brain. Most of it is divided into two halves, known as hemispheres, along the midline. This gives a classification into left-half and right-half brains. There is a bundle of axons known as the *corpus callosum* that link the left and right hemispheres (see Figure 2.13). They convey information from one half of the brain to the other.

As Figure 2.12 shows, the outside of the brain has a wrinkled appearance, similar to a walnut. This reflects the fact that the **cerebral cortex**, the outer layer of the brain, is folded (Figure 2.14). Seen in terms of evolution, folding allows a large amount of cerebral cortex to be 'squeezed' into the skull. 'Cortex' is the Latin word for bark, the outer layer of a tree. The cortex is the outer layer of the brain. Some anatomical landmarks of the cortex, such as different lobes, are shown in Figure 2.14.

In processing information and controlling behaviour, different regions of cortex can be attributed with serving different specialized roles (Figure 2.14). For example, the visual cortex processes visual information, which is derived, via the optic nerve, from the eyes. The somatosensory cortex analyses information on touch, the responsibility of its different regions depending upon the region of body from which the information derives (see Figure 2.15). A mapping of the body across the surface of the somatosensory cortex according to the responsibility of each brain region is termed a **sensory**

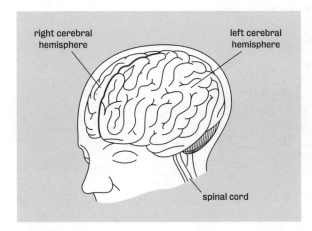

Figure 2.12 External view of the brain showing its division into two hemispheres

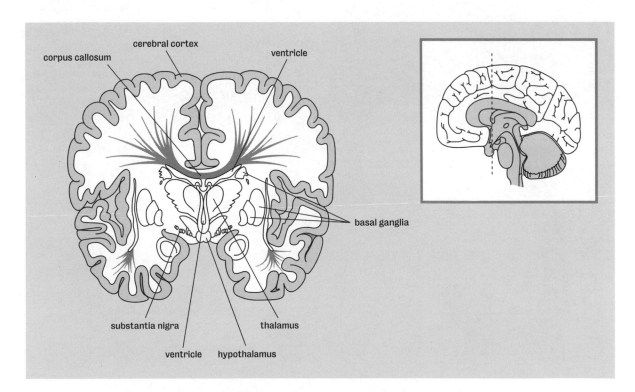

Figure 2.13 Cross-section through brain, location of which is indicated by broken line

homunculus. Some regions of the body surface are associated with relatively large areas of somatosensory cortex whereas other areas have a relatively smaller area. This variation corresponds to differences in the ability to resolve detail in these areas. Thus, for example, the fingers are associated with a relatively large area of cortex, which enables them to discriminate detail, whereas the back has little area of cortex and is relatively insensitive.

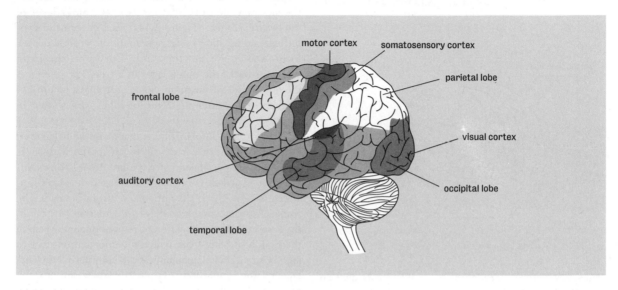

Figure 2.14 A view of the brain showing the lobes and different regions of cortex

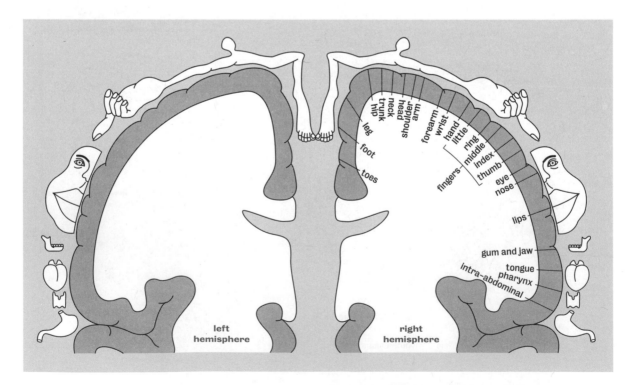

Figure 2.15 The somatosensory cortex and the associated sensory homunculus; neural pathways which start at the body parts represented by the homunculus terminate at the associated region of cortex

Figure 2.16 shows the motor cortex and again there is an homunculus. In this case, it represents the regions of the body over which motor control is exerted by each corresponding brain region. You can see that, as with the sensory homunculus, certain regions of the body are associated with a relatively large amount of cortex. This corresponds to the fine resolution of our motor abilities in controlling these areas, e.g. the fingers. Artificial electrical stimulation of the motor cortex at the points indicated in Figure 2.16 (e.g. arm) results in a muscular response at the associated body region.

Movement

Movements in relation to the outside world occur because of activity in motor neurons that innervate (meaning 'make a neural supply to') the muscles associated with the skeleton, termed **skeletal muscles**. This is true whether the instigation of movement results from a stimulus impinging and causing a reflex or because of a voluntary movement initiated in the brain.

Let us reconsider the analogy with a temperature regulating system. The value set on the dial is termed the **set-point** and the system defends this value against disturbances. If we change this setting, the system automatically takes action so as to achieve the new value. By comparing features of the control of the movement with thermostatic control, we might better understand movement.

The brain sets goals (analogous to the set-point) to be achieved by the body and the nervous system computes the difference between actual bodily state and the goal. The difference guides action in reaching the goal, i.e. such as to eliminate the difference. For animal and thermostat alike, this involves feedback. Something like changing the set-point of the thermostat, living systems change their goals, e.g. move from here to there. Local disturbances can be corrected without our conscious intervention, e.g. challenges to our physical stability, as in a sudden gust of wind, trigger automatic corrective action by realigning our limbs.

In the control of movement, current feedback to the central nervous system not only guides action in the here-and-now but also plays a role in future behaviour. Actions and their consequences are remembered and this memory used in the control of future actions. Information fed back derives from various sources, for example, through the eyes watching the effect of an

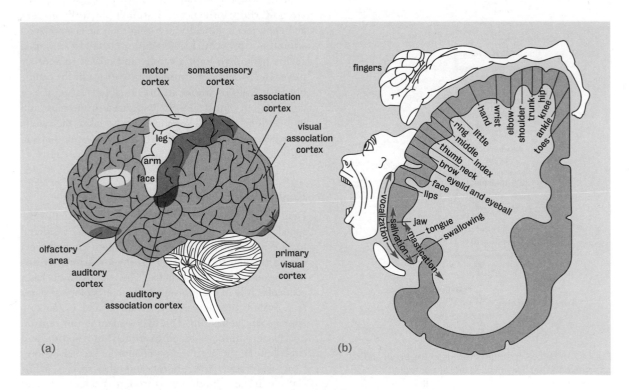

Figure 2.16 (a) The brain, showing the location of the motor cortex, (b) the motor homunculus

action. There is also feedback from the muscles. Sensory neurons whose tips are embedded in the muscles send information in the form of action potentials that inform on the magnitude of stretch.

Brain and spinal cord processes act in an integrated way to produce movement. Whether voluntary behaviour or reflexes, the final common route for effecting activity by muscles is motor neurons. The cell bodies of motor neurons that activate the skeletal muscles are located in the brain stem and in the spinal cord. Those in the brain stem are associated with axons that form part of the cranial nerves and innervate the muscles of the head. The muscles of the remainder of the body are innervated by motor neurons whose cell bodies are in the spinal cord. See the dark blue neurons shown in Figure 2.4c, which shows a slice of spinal cord and neuron 4 of Figure 2.5. The axons of such motor neurons leave the spinal cord and cover the distance to the muscle. Inputs that derive from local sensory neurons, i.e. reflex aspects, and from the brain, e.g. voluntary control (via neurons that descend in the spinal cord), both serve to activate such motor neurons.

The control of movement involves large amounts of information being transmitted between different regions

of the body and within the brain. This is represented in Figure 2.17. Some organization is carried at the level of the spinal cord (termed 'local level'). It is here that the cell bodies of motor neurons are situated. Where in the brain is the initial voluntary command to move initiated? In Figure 2.17, this corresponds to the box marked 'highest level'. We do not know the answer but it probably involves a number of different regions of the brain.

Frontal lobes – planning

Compared to other species, in humans relatively little of the cortex is either sensory or motor. Rather a large percentage is described as 'non-specific cortex'. In other words, large areas of the human brain are concerned directly neither with analysing incoming information nor with organizing motor output. We suppose that, among other things, these areas give us the facility for abstract thinking.

One such non-specific region, the frontal lobes, play a role in planning for future behaviour. To attain future goals, the brain needs the capacity to exploit knowledge on events that are not yet present. Damage to the frontal lobes disrupts this capacity. Patients are more strongly dependent upon the here-and-now. That is to say, they are powerfully influenced by stimuli physically present and experience difficulty in basing their behaviour upon stimuli not present. For example, Luria (1973) asked such a patient to light a candle and take it to another place. The patient with frontal lobe damage lit the candle but then tried to smoke it, presumably treating it as a cigarette, an object closely associated in the here-and now with lighting and smoking. To have taken the candle elsewhere would have required an extrapolation beyond current sensory information, to that 'somewhere else'.

Regulation, motivation and emotion

Figure 2.18 is another view of the brain and part of the spinal cord. Note the *thalamus*, which will be considered further in Chapter 4. Below the thalamus you will see a region termed the *hypothalamus* (hypothalamus means the region below the thalamus). The hypothalamus has a particular role in monitoring internal physiological states (e.g. water, temperature, hormones) and organizing appropriate behaviour. The hypothalamus and septum process emotional and motivational information and contribute to the organization of appropriate behaviour.

As was noted earlier, in rats and other species, artificial electrical stimulation (through an electrode and

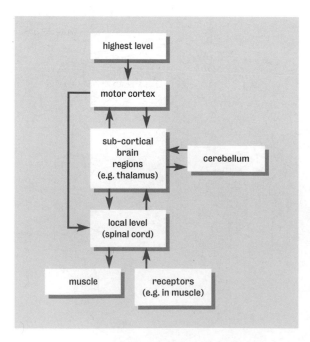

Figure 2.17 Some important regions of the brain and pathways that are involved in motor control
Source: modified from Vander *et al.* (1994: 351)

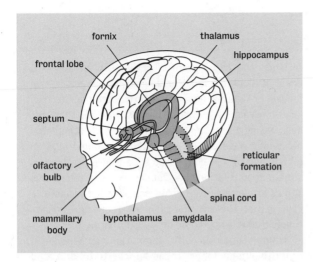

Figure 2.18 Imaginary view of the brain

under the control of the experimenter) of parts of the hypothalamus can result in feeding or drinking. However, in the absence of such things as food or water, it can also result in behaviour suggestive of rewarding (attractive) or aversive effects, depending upon the exact site and nature of the stimulation given.

Suppose that an electrode is implanted in a part of the hypothalamus and electric current applied when the rat is in a particular location within its environment. The rat will tend to return to that part of the environment. The location becomes a goal and the animal shows goal-directed behaviour in returning there. Olds (1958) also discovered that rats would learn to press a lever in a Skinner box in order to apply electrical stimulation to this same brain region. Thus, electric shock to such regions serves as what is called a **positive reinforcer**, the stimulation strengthens the tendency to engage in a particular behaviour. Indeed, rats seem to be addicted to this behaviour.

To have located regions of the brain having this significance was doubtless a discovery of major importance, 'a landmark in the history of the behavioural and neurosciences' (Atrens 1984). However, in the hands of popular writers the facts became exaggerated with unrealistic scenarios of mind control promised for the immediate future (see Valenstein 1973 for a critique). For example, factory workers could be persuaded to perform tiring tasks but with smiles on their faces as a result of stimulating their brains while they work.

The term 'positive reinforcer' can be objectively defined in terms of strengthening behaviour and experimental psychology likes objective terms. However, the

regions of the brain involved became known as 'pleasure areas'. This involves a *theory* of behaviour rather than simply a description as in 'positive reinforcement'. In such terms, the reinforcement effect is to be understood in terms of a particular consequence of the stimulation, which animals are subsequently motivated to attain. See Figure 2.19a. Whether rats really received pleasure or not, we shall never know but they acted *as if* they did.

Although electrical self-stimulation as an example of positive reinforcement is a robust phenomenon, there is evidence that the rat is not simply stimulating a pleasure area. Pleasure, if indeed the notion applies to rats, would seem to be a more complex property of the brain than can be tapped with a single electrode. For instance, suppose that a recording is made of the electrical stimulation that a rat freely delivers to its brain by lever pressing. Then in the absence of the lever, exactly the same electrical stimulation is applied to the brain by the experimenter. Rats attempt to escape from such a situation (Steiner *et al.* 1969). This suggests that any hedonic or even attractive consequence of responding for shock is a function not simply of activating a region of the brain but a combination of stimulation *and* the behaviour of the rat actively responding for this stimulation.

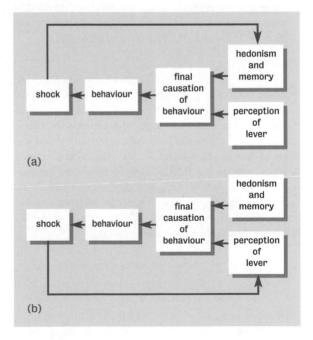

Figure 2.19 Models of electrical brain stimulation (a) a hedonic theory, (b) model based on the ideas of Robinson and Berridge (1993)

Research update

Electrical brain stimulation

Insight into this important effect might be provided by considering electrical brain stimulation in a broader context of behaviour that shares some similar properties. In a review looking at addictive drugs, Robinson and Berridge (1993) suggested that electrical stimulation might be activating a process of 'pulling' the animal to engage in this activity. In other words, as a result of the electrical current, the lever becomes an attractive incentive stimulus; it acquires *salience* (Figure 2.19b). It could be useful to consider some similarities between (a) electrical brain stimulation, (b) drug-taking and (c) animals engaging in stereotypies (described on p. 26). The similarities suggest the possibility of common underlying processes.

In electrical brain self-stimulation (Olds 1958), performing stereotypies (Dantzer 1986), schedule-induced polydipsia (Falk 1969) and working for drug infusion (Meisch and Carroll 1987), the intensity of behaviour is often increased by food deprivation. In the case of electrical brain stimulation and drugs, animals will return to an area associated with stimulation or the drug and there is some suggestion that animals are attracted to locations at which they have performed stereotypies (Cooper and Nicol 1993; Ellinwood and Kilbey 1975).

When the experimenter stimulates an animal's brain at a certain location so that it engages in, say, feeding or fighting, animals are attracted back to that location (Valenstein 1969). There is evidence that animals having a tendency to such electrically stimulated behaviour have a highly reactive dopamine system (Mittleman *et al.* 1986). Could it be that in each case, dopamine activation that occurs at a site labels this site as attractive? That is not necessarily the same as saying that the rat enjoys being there but rather simply that it is attracted or 'pulled' there.

Animals injected with amphetamines engage in repetitive behaviours. These appear to be of a kind where particular stimuli have the capacity to elicit particular behaviours, e.g. an animal will pursue another for hours (Ellinwood and Kilbey 1975). Animals self-administering drugs engage in activities, e.g. chewing and gnawing, directed towards a particular stimulus such as a light that is also triggered by drug-reinforced lever pressing (Tomie 1996). Viewed in such a context ESB (electrical stimulation of the brain) might be seen as a kind of compulsion, not driven by a hedonic consequence. By looking within a broad behavioural context, more insights into this behaviour might be gained.

Some authors (e.g. Atrens 1984) suggest that electrical brain stimulation produces a *forcement* effect. This means that the predominant effect is one that compels the animal to act, though there might also be a secondary hedonic effect of doing so. It was argued that stimulation is exciting neuronal systems that directly instigate behaviour. But then the counter-argument was given that rats will voluntarily seek out an environment associated with such brain stimulation, the goal-directed aspect. That sounds more like hedonism. How might the issue be resolved?

Ψ Section summary

Neurons are cells specialized for the transmission and processing of information. All of the neurons of the body constitute the nervous system. The central nervous system consists of the brain and spinal cord.

Neurons convey information by means of pulses of electricity termed 'action potentials'. Communication between neurons occurs at synapses. At synapses, neurotransmitter stored in one neuron is released and attaches itself to another. Different neurotransmitters serve different roles in controlling behaviour. To some extent, it is possible to associate different brain regions with particular roles in terms of behaviour and mental life.

1 'Drinking in response to dehydration is an example of negative feedback whereas schedule-induced polydipsia appears not to be explicable in these terms'. What is meant by this claim?
2 What is the difference in the role served by sensory neurons, motor neurons and interneurons?
3 What is meant by describing as 'dopaminergic' (a) a neuron and (b) a synapse?

❑ Genes, environment and evolution

Genes and reproduction

As noted earlier, the cells of the body, whether neurons or not, have certain features in common. Each cell contains a nucleus (not to be confused with the word nucleus when used to refer to a collection of neurons in the brain), a kind of executive control centre for organizing processes within the cell. With the exception of sperm cells in the male and egg cells in the female, the human nucleus contains 46 structures termed chromosomes. Chromosomes are the physical base for our **genes**. Sperm cells contain only 23 chromosomes as do egg cells. At conception these two sets of 23 chromosomes come together to give 46 (see Figure 2.20). From the moment of conception, the genes act in complex interaction with first their physical (within the womb) and later both the physical and social environment to determine the course of development of the individual. Genes act in teams, and together with the environment, influence body structure and working, e.g. height and hair colour.

At one time genes were commonly called 'blueprints' for development but this term is out of favour now. Blueprint, as in the design of an aircraft, suggests a fixed and predetermined plan that is followed faithfully. This analogy detracts from the important role of the environment acting in complex interaction with the genes in determining the outcome of development. It might be more accurate to describe the gene as a 'source of information' for development.

Figure 2.20 represents two important processes: replication and reproduction. Consider that an egg has been fertilized to produce a cell with 46 chromosomes. Yes – that is how you and I started out, as just a single cell! The fact that we are now somewhat more sophisticated and larger is due to a process of replication. The initial cell divides into two. These two then divide to give four cells and so on until we are fully developed. Each time a cell divides, the genetic material in its nucleus is copied, so that both cells have the same genetic information as that contained in their precursor cell. No matter what the role served by the cell is, e.g. a neuron or a cell in the kidney, it will contain a full copy of all of the original genetic material. Replication is then a process that is intrinsic to a given individual organism. Reproduction is a process involving two individuals, whereby a sperm and an egg come together to produce a new individual.

In replication, the genetic material of each cell is an exact replica of that of the precursor cell. However,

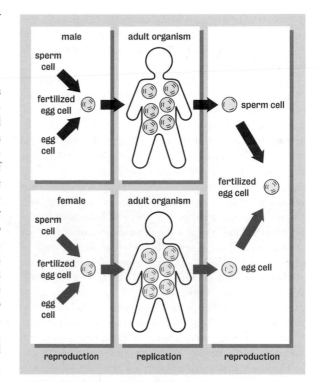

Figure 2.20 Replication and reproduction

after reproduction, the genetic material of the new cell is not an exact replica of either that of the mother or the father. Bringing together genetic material from mother and father yields a novel combination. Of course, the novelty is somewhat relative since the offspring often bear an uncanny resemblance to one or other parent and yet they are not identical. Following formation of the novel combination of genetic material in a new cell and then a long process of replication deriving from this single cell, we arrive at the you or me of the present.

Why is understanding of such a process important for psychologists? Nervous systems are made up of cells whose structure and role depends upon a history of interaction between genes and environment, i.e. development. In turn, behaviour is determined by the nervous system acting in complex interaction with an environment. Behaviour is executed by muscles whose activity is determined by activity within the nervous system.

Genes and environment

Unless we are very careful, the language that we commonly use can invite misunderstanding of the issue of genes and environment. Alas, discussions are commonly premised on statements of the kind – 'Is it genes or environment?' or 'Is aggression all in the genes?' Political considerations on both sides often serve to bring more heat than light to the discussion.

The gene carries information for the formation of complex chemical structures termed proteins that are physical constituents of the body. Without genes we would have no body. Similarly, without an environment, first in the womb and then out of it, an individual could not exist (see Figure 2.21). Thus, the structure of our nervous system depends upon genes and environment and, of course, behaviour depends upon the nervous system in interaction with an environment. Therefore, when discussing a particular piece of behaviour, questions of the kind 'What is the most important – genes or environment?' are essentially meaningless. They are as naive as asking 'What is the most important determinant of the area of a rectangle, its height or its length?' Without either a height or a length, a rectangle cannot exist. Another analogy that can prove useful is that of baking a cake. Without ingredients there can be no cake. Without cooking, there can be no cake. The notion of a cake necessarily implies both acting in interaction.

However, it is meaningful to ask whether differences between individuals are due to differences in their genes or differences in the environments to which they have been exposed. To pursue the analogy, if two rectangles are different in area, it is meaningful to ask whether this is due to differences in their height or length, or both. If two cakes are different, this could be due to differences in ingredients or cooking, or both. The degree to which differences between two individuals in a characteristic are due to genetic differences is called the **heritability** of that characteristic.

Discussions on this issue came into sharp focus in the 1960s and 1970s with arguments about the genetic contribution to differences in intelligence between people. A possible pitfall in the argument needs to be avoided. Suppose that, within a certain population, heritability of a characteristic is high. That is, differences between individuals are largely due to differences in genes. Consider now a second population within which heritability is also high. Now suppose that populations 1 and 2 are found to differ in the characteristic in question. It is tempting to suppose that this is due to genetic differences between them. This assumption is not necessarily justified, as an analogy can show.

A person puts her hand into a sack of seeds and takes out a random handful, which she puts into one plot of soil. She takes a second handful and puts into a different plot. The patch of soil to the left is uniformly rich and that to the right is uniformly poor. Therefore, differences in plants *within* a plot must be due to genetic differences since the soil is uniform in a given plot. However, differences *between* plots must be due to environmental differences since the seeds were taken at random.

It is not simply in the highly charged world of politics that misunderstandings on the issue of genes and environment can arise. Scientists studying animals occasionally make some imprecise statements in this area. Behaviours were sometimes said to be either innate (i.e. genetically determined) or learned (i.e. environmentally determined). It is not difficult to see why. Watching a bird effortlessly constructing a nest characteristic of its species in its first breeding season does rather logically lead to the assumption that the behaviour is innate (or 'instinctive'). The bird has not gone through a laborious trial-and-error process, neither is it imitating another

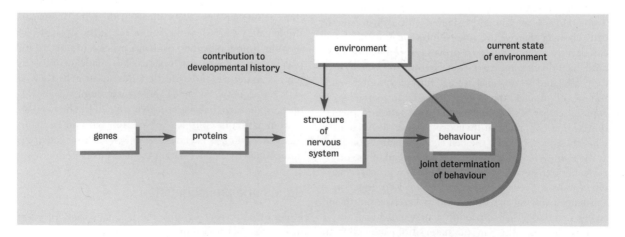

Figure 2.21 The determinants of behaviour

bird. A rat freezing (holding itself motionless) the first time it detects a predator also suggests an innate process. Conversely, an animal learning circus tricks would seem unambiguously to be acting as a result of learning, rather than any circus-trick instinct.

This particular linguistic distinction will probably not go away. However, it needs careful qualification. No behaviour is purely innate since from the time of conception an animal is reacting to events in its environment and thereby almost surely learning something relevant to that behaviour. The skills of a bird in constructing a nest doubtless owe much to earlier experiences gained with manipulating objects in its beak. Perceptual systems have a developmental history (see Chapter 4). Similarly, an animal exhibiting learning is employing nervous system structures that are partly coded genetically. In other words, the ability to learn is in part genetically determined.

A possible way of resolving this is to describe some behaviour as **species-specific behaviour** or 'species-typical behaviour', e.g. the 'freezing' response of the rat (Bolles 1970). This means that it is exhibited by most, if not all, members of a particular species, given a normal developmental history and the later presence of trigger cues. The animal's genes are such as to code for a nervous system that has a high probability of producing such behaviour, given the right cues. We cannot say that learning is irrelevant to the production of this behaviour since an animal's whole life will have involved learning and we cannot create a viable but non-learning animal. However, we can claim that the performance of such behaviour does not slowly emerge after trial-and-error experience in similar situations. Indeed, for defensive behaviour, one can see the advantage in having a behaviour ready to perform on the first appearance of a threat. The opportunity to learn by trial-and-error would seem to be limited since the first error might well also be the last! It is probably best to consider behaviours to be on a continuum of more or less species-specific rather than either/or.

Genes and evolution

The theory of evolution states that complex life-forms evolved from simpler precursor forms as a result of a process of evolution. How does this happen? The explanation is best taken in stages. First consider that, for a given species, the potential to reproduce is usually greater than the actual number of offspring that can survive. This is due to such things as predation, limited food and competition for resources, such as food, water and

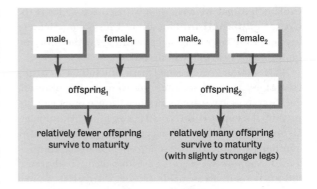

Figure 2.22 Inheritance and the consequences of mutation

shelter. Some individuals will be better equipped than others in their ability to survive and reproduce.

In coming together at fertilization new combinations of genes are produced and then, in effect, tested in the environment. Some combinations will be more successful than others. Some combinations will be unsuccessful. A change in frequency of different forms of animal, i.e. evolution, will occur by this means. Also, occasionally, in the process of producing either an egg or a sperm, a **mutation** occurs. This means that the genes contributed to reproduction by one sex are changed slightly. Now suppose that the change is such that the modified gene carries information that improves the offspring's chances of survival and reproduction. It might code for extra height so that taller trees can be exploited for food or it might code for a nervous system having a faster than normal capacity to learn. This particular offspring will have an advantage over others without the mutation. The mutant form of gene will tend to be copied in future generations and it will increase in frequency relative to other forms. The argument is that, over long time periods, such a process has contributed to the evolution of forms from the simple to the complex (see Figure 2.22), which might apply, say, to skill at hunting. Suppose that $male_1$ and $female_1$ mate to produce $offspring_1$. $Male_2$ and $female_2$ produce $offspring_2$. $Offspring_2$ has a slightly faster speed of chase than $offspring_1$ and so is at an advantage. It is descendants of $offspring_2$ that will tend to increase in frequency in the population relative to those of $offspring_1$.

Causal and functional explanations

When we consider an aspect of behaviour, we can bring two different forms of explanation to it. These are not competitive forms but complementary. The type of explanation that we have mainly discussed so far is the **causal explanation**. One event causes something to happen a bit later, e.g. a thorn sticks in the foot and causes a reflex of limb withdrawal.

This section is concerned with function. The **functional explanation** attempts to answer a different question: how has a particular behaviour contributed to an animal's **reproductive success** in its evolutionary history? Reproductive success is measured by the number of viable reproducing offspring that are produced. Suppose we were to ask this of the withdrawal reflex. It seems reasonable to suggest that an animal with such a reflex is at an advantage in that it reduces the chances of sustaining injury. Injury could lead to infection and illness which would of course be damaging to its chances of reproduction.

Take another example. When a jungle fowl is incubating its eggs, it lets its weight fall by not eating. How could this increase its chances of reproductive success? To leave the eggs to obtain food increases the chances of their cooling or being eaten by predators, so there is a clear advantage in staying. The example allows us to illustrate a number of features of a functional explanation, as follows.

First, it is not to the female's bodily advantage to stay on the eggs. Her individual survival might be best assured by leaving them to obtain food for herself. However, the chances of her genetic representation in future generations is presumably increased by incubation since she might have several eggs, each containing copies of her genes underneath her.

Second, we should not suppose that the jungle fowl has any knowledge of the situation or conscious intention to endow posterity with her genes. She just acts this way. Jungle fowl that did so have tended to be successful and so their descendants are around today. Their genes have been favoured by evolution. Evolution is said to be blind in this regard.

Third, and related to the second point, in asking the causal question of *how* such behaviour is organized, we must be careful not to confuse causal and functional explanations. Claims of the kind that the bird acts this way because she *needs* to reproduce are inherently misleading and lead to claims of a conscious intention on the part of the bird. On a causal level, we would simply speak of motivational systems of incubation and feeding, with there being an inhibitory link from incubation to feeding.

Sociobiology

One of the claims of sociobiology is that many features of human social life (e.g. worship in church, showing altruism) which might have been thought to be due to cultural influences are really to be explained biologically. This is sometimes expressed rather uncritically as 'a gene for adultery' or 'a gene for being religious'. In such terms, genes might be said to code for, say, religious worship since by so doing they have thereby been placed at an advantage; their possessors have been more successful in evolution. An immediate qualification is needed. Genes code only for bodily structures. However, one such is the nervous system and, in principle, genes might code for a nervous system having a bias towards even a complex piece of social behaviour. Such discussion has some important social messages. One of the reasons why sociobiology is controversial is that it seems to suggest a rigid determinism. If it is 'in the genes', there is little we can do about it. Another aspect that has fired the popular imagination is because of what sociobiology has to say about such things as differences in behaviour between the sexes.

Social scientists often discuss such things as that males make more use of prostitutes and pornography than do females. One might have supposed that this is a reflection of cultural norms and prohibitions deeply engrained in our institutions. Change society, give enough time, and behaviour might change correspondingly. On the contrary, sociobiologists would suggest that such differences between the sexes reflect different biologically determined strategies of mating. The optimal strategy for a male to perpetuate his genes is different from that of a female. An instant and relatively indiscriminate sexual arousal accompanied by promiscuity might be to the advantage of the male's genetic perpetuation since it maximizes his reproductive chances. There is relatively little to lose. Some female coyness and reserve might be to her genetic advantage since in this way she can select the optimal male with whom to tie up her reproductive capacity for nine months or so.

Of course, few if any males visit prostitutes with the conscious intention of perpetuating their genes but no one is supposing that conscious intentions have had much to do with the evolution of sexuality. All that is being claimed is that genes tend to code for those strategies which *in general* have served their own 'selfish' interests. In evolution, a combination of genes that tended to promote male promiscuity has been a successful combination. Not all males are promiscuous. Sociobiologists do not suggest that they should be, just as they do not suggest that all females should show coyness and fidelity. Genes are not blueprints. It is simply that one can see a biological basis in there being a difference between the sexes in this direction.

Sociobiology makes some predictions that can be tested and one of these concerns jealousy. Consider this in the human case. What is the cost to an individual if his or her partner exhibits infidelity? The cost to a male could be large since it could mean that his partner produces offspring bearing another male's genes, hence missing his own opportunity of genetic transmission. The male might even be fooled into helping to bring up someone else's offspring. Thus, male jealousy might involve a strong imperative against the sexual infidelity of his mate. For the female, the cost of a partner's infidelity seems to be much less. The female can at least be sure that the offspring she produces are in part genetically hers! The male can recover his sexual potency relatively quickly and with it his capacity to contribute genes to reproduction with the established female. However, there is a threat from other females and that comes from the risk of being abandoned. The danger of this might be signalled by the male showing an abnormally large interest in the emotional well-being of another female, i.e. emotional warmth and empathy. If that were to happen, the female might be put at a serious disadvantage in terms of raising offspring. Therefore, one might expect some asymmetry in the trigger stimuli to jealousy, with

 ## Research update

Sexual jealousy

In comparing human males and females, Buss *et al.* (1992) argue that the difference in situations that evoke jealousy is a species-typical characteristic. Hence one might expect it to be apparent in different cultures. Buunk *et al.* (1996) tested attitudes in Germany, the Netherlands and the USA. In the Netherlands, perhaps more than in any other country, sexual equality is emphasized. Subjects were asked to imagine the scenario of contact between their partner and someone else, specifically as follows:

SET 1

A Imagining your partner forming a deep emotional attachment to that person.

B Imagining your partner enjoying passionate sexual intercourse with that other person.

The results are shown in Figure 2.23a for the per centage of subjects reporting more distress caused by sexual infidelity as compared to emotional infidelity.

Scenarios were also suggested as follows:

SET 2

A Imagining your partner trying different sexual positions with that other person.

B Imagining your partner falling in love with that other person.

Figure 2.23b shows the results. Interestingly the same differences are evident in all three cultures. Of course, postulating that these results reveal a species-typical effect is not to deny a role of culture. The nature of the interaction between genetic and environmental determinants is doubtless a complex one here as elsewhere. However, theorists of a sociobiological persuasion feel that they can now make some sense of the phenomena in terms of biology.

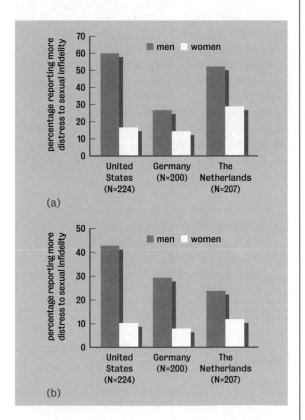

Figure 2.23 (a) Responses to set 1, (b) responses to set 2
Source: Buunk *et al.* (1996)

males triggered more strongly by sexual infidelity *per se* and females by 'emotional infidelity'.

A test of this was devised by Buss *et al.* (1992). These researchers posed questions to subjects, inviting them to imagine various scenarios and to estimate the magnitude of the negative feelings that were evoked. These scenarios were of your mate (1) having sexual intercourse with another and (2) forming a deep emotional attachment to another. While 85 per cent of the women found the second to arouse the most negative emotions, 60 per cent of the males found the first to do so. Sociobiology predicts a difference in this direction.

This completes the account of the three basic strands to a biological approach. Subsequent sections will look at some examples of behaviour and although the emphasis is upon causal mechanisms, where possible, the information on the different strands of explanation will be used in order to give an integrated perspective.

Ψ Section summary

Genes act in complex interaction with the physical and social environment to determine the course of development of an individual. According to the theory of evolution, complex animals evolved from more simple ancestors. Evolution occurs since some genes are more successful than others in coding for their own perpetuation. The functional level of explanation attempts to answer the question as to how a behaviour contributes to an animal's reproductive success.

1 Why it is misleading to attempt to divide behaviour into such distinct classes as 'genetically determined' and 'environmentally determined'?

2 What is meant by saying that causal and functional levels of explanation of behaviour are complementary rather than competitive?

3 In what sense is the expression 'selfish gene' a simplification?

❏ Plasticity

Nervous systems have the property of exhibiting some **plasticity**. This means that connections between neurons are not always fixed and immutable but can change as a function of development and learning. Corresponding to the plasticity of its biological bases, behaviour can change.

As part of development, certain synaptic connections are strengthened whereas other pre-existing connections weaken or may even be lost. Functioning synaptic connections can exert a self-reinforcing effect whereas silent synapses might become ineffective (see Figure 2.24). For example, visual stimulation from a rich environment can activate and strengthen synapses in the

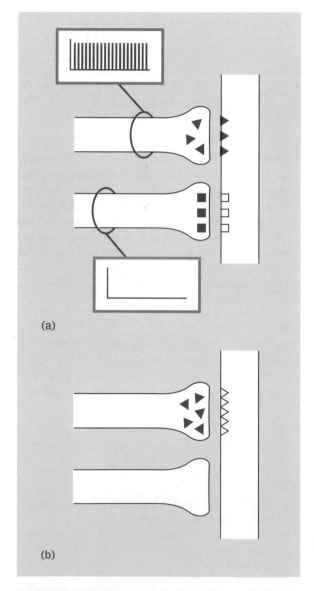

(a)

(b)

Figure 2.24 Plasticity in neural connections (a) initial connections, showing typical inputs, (b) following experience there is strengthening of top connection (note proliferation of receptors) and weakening of bottom (note loss of transmitter and receptors)

Ψ Case study

A psychologist with an aversion

The Cambridge psychologist Anthony Dickinson presents an interesting case study on taste-aversion learning (Dickinson and Balleine 1992). While on holiday in Sicily as a youth, he had his first experience of eating water-melon. This was followed by the ingestion of rather too much wine, which led to him feeling ill. Recovering from the hangover, he returned to the water-melon stall. However, on taking a bite, he discovered that he had formed an aversion to water-melon. From the days of youth to becoming a well-known experimental psychologist, no trace of water-melon has since passed Dr Dickinson's lips.

This experience shows that the water-melon aversion was latent and was manifest in behaviour and awareness only after actually coming into the presence of the fruit again. The true culprit was the wine but one can only suppose that the young Anthony had earlier benign experiences with wine which did not make this such a strong candidate as the novel water-melon taste. The fact that he knew perfectly well on a cognitive (intellectual) level that the wine was the guilty object was not sufficiently strong to overcome the more basic learning that related the aversion to the innocuous water-melon.

visual system (see Chapter 4), with implications for subsequent perception.

Learning represents an example of plasticity (see Chapter 3). The reaction to situations changes as a result of the organism's experience, Pavlov's famous study being a good example of this. Due to the properties of their nervous system, all dogs tend to salivate to the presence of food in the mouth. A bell was paired with the presentation of food a number of times and then the dog salivated when the bell was presented alone. Translated to a natural context, the functional value of this capacity is not difficult to understand. Suppose that a cue such as capture of prey precedes reliably food in the mouth. The animal that salivates and produces gastric juices in response to the stimulus of capture of prey would prepare its digestive tract for the arrival of food and thereby assist digestion.

How might this be explained in neural terms? Imagine that a neuron is activated by food in the mouth and tends to trigger salivation. Suppose that another neuron is activated by the bell but normally fails to trigger salivation. There might be a link formed as a result of the parallel activation of this pair of neurons such that the bell comes to trigger salivation.

Animals learn about food and the consequences of its ingestion (Garcia 1989). A taste has the potential to elicit either ingestion or a disgust/rejection reaction. Any ingestion has consequences for the subsequent rating given to a taste. If consequences are favourable (e.g. nutrient gain, no sickness), the tendency to ingest and approach will be strengthened. The taste is valued.

If a distinctive and novel taste is ingested and sometime later gastrointestinal illness experienced, food having this taste will tend subsequently to be rejected and to evoke a disgust reaction. Humans commonly report disgust even to the thought of a devalued food. This is termed **taste-aversion learning** or the **Garcia effect**. This clearly has a functional value since food with such taste might well be contaminated and harmful. To avoid it in future would aid survival. However, paradoxically, animals (including the occasional psychologist – see the case study!) sometimes still approach cues associated with a devalued taste even though the reactivity to the taste has changed such that, when encountered, it evokes disgust. Only following the encounter with the devalued taste, are the cues avoided.

Ψ Section summary

Not all of the connections between neurons are fixed but some can change as a result of development and learning. This gives the nervous system, and thereby behaviour, the capacity for flexibility. Taste-aversion learning is an example of where the reaction to a food changes as a function of an aversive experience with it.

1 Suppose over a period of time a particular synapse could be observed to change, in that both the amount of transmitter stored in the one neuron and the number of receptors at the other increase. Would this be described as strengthening the synaptic connection?
2 In what way was the behaviour of Pavlov's dog evidence for plasticity in the nervous system?

❏ Targeting the brain when things go wrong

More and more evidence is accumulating to indicate a relationship between abnormalities in the brain and abnormalities of behaviour. This section considers some examples of where the brain is targeted when things go wrong in our mental lives. The examples include that done by professionals and that represented by self-medication.

Depression

The term depression covers a number of somewhat different disorders. Of course, most people feel low at various times in their lives. This is considered normal and we would not want to classify such people as clinically depressed. Among the serious disorders, there is both unipolar depression, in which mood varies between neutral and a negative state and bipolar disorder, in which mood swings between depression and elation (Drevets *et al.* 1997).

Depression is characterized by a feeling of negative **affect**, powerlessness and inability to influence events. Possible symptoms include early morning waking and withdrawal from social contact. Memory recall tends to be biased towards negative events. In some cases unipolar depression appears to be a clear consequence of life events, e.g. marital breakdown. This is sometimes termed reactive depression. In other cases, there is no obvious change in the external world and one is lead to suppose that some internal change (e.g. abnormal neurotransmitter) triggers it. Either way, it is safest to assume that depression depends upon a complex interdependence between (1) activity in basic neural systems that underlie emotions and (2) external events and the way in which they are interpreted. (See also Chapters 17 and 18).

Treatments include cognitive therapy (targeting how the patient construes events in the external world) and drugs. The latter target certain populations of synapses in the CNS (e.g. serotonergic) and are assumed to change the operating characteristics of the synapses. Anti-depressant medication typically changes the level of a particular neurotransmitter by altering the rate at which it leaves the synaptic junction. Some anti-depressants block the re-uptake process shown in Figure 2.10. This increases the amount of transmitter available to occupy receptors.

Estimates vary as to the size of the genetic contribution to depression, depending in part upon the particular type of depression. Exactly how the genetic contribution is mediated is uncertain. Genes might code for an abnormally low or high population of receptors at certain synapses. From the work of Drevets *et al.* (1997) the possibility of abnormalities in brain structure is raised. Even though there might be a strong genetic contribution to depression, this does not mean that each instance of depression is simply 'written in the genes'. For an analogy, knowing that a piece of glass is brittle does not mean it will necessarily break. Rather it means that, given an external 'stressor', the brittle glass has a higher probability of breaking.

How might psychologists determine whether there is a genetic factor in depression? Knowing that there is a tendency for depression to 'run in families' is suggestive of this but is not sufficient. There could be a cultural transmission of this way of reacting. One way of investigating this is to compare identical twins (who are genetically identical) and fraternal twins. The term **concordance** refers to the closeness in tendency to depression and this is higher in identical twins than in fraternal twins.

Is it possible to make sense of depression from a functional perspective? One should not necessarily expect to be able to do so. By analogy, we would not ask what is the biological advantage of having a broken leg, though

---

 Research update

A picture of a depressed brain

There are now refined techniques available by which the structure of a living brain may be examined and estimates made of the neural activity of different regions of the brain. In the hands of Drevets *et al.* (1997), these techniques have given important insights into the brain of depressed patients.

Like other cells of the body, neurons require energy and oxygen in order to function. As they become more active, so their demand for these increases. Energy and oxygen are brought to the cells in the blood and, as local demand at a particular brain region increases, so local blood flow normally increases in response. Energy is brought to the neurons in the form of energy-bearing substances, specifically sugars.

The technique of **positron emission tomography (PET)** enables us to gain a profile of the activity of

Box continued

neurons in different regions of the brain. In this technique, researchers are able to exploit the property of a particular type of artificial sugar that enters cells normally but once inside simply accumulates within those that are most active. Suppose that a patient is injected with a small amount of this type of sugar that has been labelled radioactively. The sugar is eventually broken down and the procedure is without risk. It follows logically that any difference from normal in the amount of this sugar found in a brain region indicates abnormal energy demands and is strongly suggestive of abnormalities in the processing of information by the neurons located there.

The patient's head is placed inside a scanner which detects the location and density of the radioactive sugar in the brain. With the help of a computer, the apparatus can construct a profile of activity over each brain region (see Colour Plate 1). A patient can then be compared to a control subject.

Using this technique with depressed subjects, Drevets et al. (1997) found that there is a specific area of the frontal cortex that has an abnormal activity level. The area has been established as having a role in the processing of information of an emotional nature and is known also to be a target area for antidepressant medication. In subjects with a bipolar disorder, periods of depression were associated with a low activity in the area but the period of elation was accompanied by activity that was higher than normal. This suggests that changes in activity in this brain region are an important part of the physical basis of the changes in mood.

Since the results with the PET scan indicated abnormality in brain function, Drevets et al. also asked whether there were structural abnormalities in the brains of depressed patients. To do this, they utilized a technique known as **magnetic resonance imaging (MRI)**. This consists of exposing the patient's head to a strong magnetic field. Different tissues of the body interact with the magnetic field in different ways, depending upon their composition. Using this technique, abnormalities were found in the structure of brain tissue in the region implicated by the PET scans. In this way, the two results reinforced the conclusion that an important physiological basis for depression had been found. Of course, no one would suggest that depression can be simply explained in terms of an abnormality at one brain region. Depression, like normal mood, depends upon the whole brain acting within an environment. However, the results encourage the idea that we now have a better understanding of the part of the complex picture. The development of new therapeutic techniques might be helped by the discovery.

we might want to discuss the evolutionary significance of constructing bones from material that is able to break. However, depression could be a *maladaptive exaggeration* of something that has served a useful function in evolution. In the case of unipolar depression, one possibility is that quiet withdrawal from activity could be an appropriate temporary reaction to impossible circumstances. This would enable energy to be conserved, might deflect aggression and, in certain social creatures such as advanced primates, solicit help from kin.

Psychosurgery

In extreme cases, lesions are made to parts of the brain (e.g. frontal lobes) in an attempt to alleviate mental suffering. The logic is that disruption of certain regions might disrupt negative emotion. In recent years this has tended to be done only for such things as the most extreme and debilitating cases of depression and obsessive-compulsive disorder, where all else has failed.

Psychosurgery is an emotive and controversial topic (Valenstein 1973). It is sometimes argued that the effects are not specific and that the patient simply becomes unresponsive to everything. To some, psychosurgery is seen as a misguided application of a reductionist approach to a problem. For example, following riots in US ghettos in the 1960s, it was suggested by some eminent neuroscientists that there are intrinsic differences in the biological structures of the brains of the individuals involved (Mark and Ervin 1970). In this case, insight would be gained by looking at their biology. It might not be too far removed from this to suggest that if one could catch the rioters and lesion their brains this would make them more placid and less likely to riot. Of course, this might well be true. Similarly, if one removed their legs they might be less likely to riot. At this point the argument enters politics rather than science but the message is that behavioural science cannot always remain aloof from social and political debate.

ψ **Case study**

The tragedy of Tom

Tom was 19 years old, from an unhappy family and suffered severe obsessive-compulsive disorder (OCD), consisting of checking and handwashing (Solyom *et al.* 1987). Tom had earlier tried to commit suicide on several occasions. He complained to his mother about how unhappy he was. One day, the long-suffering mother replied 'Go and shoot yourself'. Tom went out, pointed a .22 calibre rifle in his mouth and did just that. The bullet damaged his brain's left frontal lobe but Tom survived and received neurosurgery. Almost immediately after the attempted suicide, Tom's OCD symptoms improved considerably. Tom had inadvertently performed a self-inflicted leucotomy in precisely the brain region that has been targeted by neurosurgeons. We cannot be sure that all of Tom's recovery was due to the leucotomy. Other people might have started to treat him differently, but the authors believe that in large part the loss of this neural tissue was the underlying cause.

Drug addiction

The so-called 'psychoactive drugs' such as alcohol, cocaine and heroin have their effects by acting upon the central nervous system. They either occupy receptors or they change neuronal activity in some other way. Therefore an understanding of drug-related behaviour will need to consider activity of drugs within the CNS. Therapy can usefully focus upon how to change these effects.

Compulsive drug-taking would seem to defy any functional explanation and appears to be maladaptive. However, two points need to be made, as follows. First, drug-taking might have originally served an adaptive function by, for example, relieving depression or anxiety. Only later might it have become maladaptive. Second, such things as hypodermic syringes were not around as part of our evolutionary history to play any part. They are a modern invention that enables the user to tap artificially into processes of natural reward that do serve an adaptive function. Of course, natural mechanisms of attraction to objects and pleasure as a result of interaction with them are an integral part of such things as feeding and mating (Chapter 15).

To explain the craving that can follow regular drug use, there have traditionally been two theories proposed, as follows. It has been argued that the pleasure is so intense that the addict is powerfully driven to repeat the experience, i.e. craving is a function of anticipated pleasure. Cues that in the past had been paired with drug-taking come to elicit reminders of the pleasure and the addict is moved to maximize the feeling. This might indeed be part of the story. However, the evidence suggests that it is not the major part. For example, it would not explain a result found with a group of people whose lives had been disrupted by an addiction to heroin or alcohol and who also smoked cigarettes. A majority of them claimed that, compared to their 'problem' drug, it would be *more* difficult to give up cigarettes in spite of the fact that they gave them less pleasure (Kozlowski *et al.* 1989). Repeated use of heroin commonly results in increased craving for the drug but less pleasure when it is actually taken (Robinson and Berridge 1993). The first contact with heroin commonly has aversive effects and yet a person can still desire it. Amphetamine users can experience acute psychotic terror and yet do not stop their habit (Ellinwood and Escalante 1970). Some drugs that are self-administered do not have hedonic effects (Atrens 1984). Therefore hedonism on its own seems a weak candidate.

In some cases, particularly after extensive use, there are negative effects of not having drugs, so-called withdrawal effects. Stimuli that in the past had been paired with withdrawal come to elicit signs of withdrawal even in the chemically drug-free individual (Siegel *et al.* 1987). Some addicts are said to apply self-medication by taking the drug to remove the negative effects arising from not having it. This and the hedonic theory are not mutually exclusive; a given individual might be driven by both anticipated hedonism (even though the reality might not live up to the expectation) and a desire to eliminate negative effects. However, not all addicts experience negative after-effects. For those that do, subjective withdrawal effects often show little correlation with physical signs of withdrawal (Henningfield *et al.* 1987). Animals can be trained to self-administer drugs in the absence of any signs of withdrawal. So how, given that both hedonic and withdrawal models seem inadequate, do we explain the increased craving with repeated exposure?

A theory of craving

A radical new theory was proposed by Robinson and Berridge (1993). Its central and novel assumption is a distinction between two neural processes, those subserving craving and pleasure. With taking the drug into the body repeatedly, the pleasure process adapts but a craving process is sensitized. Dopaminergic neurons are thought to play a crucial role in mediating craving. Paradoxically, over weeks or months, craving can increase while pleasure decreases.

A representation of this that could prove to have a broad application to behaviour is shown in Figure 2.25. A wanting/craving mechanism is linked to a pleasure mechanism but not one-to-one. What is strongly pleasurable promotes wanting/craving. A pleasure process is activated and wanting is strengthened as consequences of behaviour. However, wanting/craving is also sensitized simply as a function of drug use.

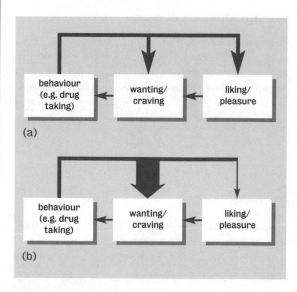

(a)

(b)

Figure 2.25 Model based upon the ideas of Robinson and Berridge (1993) (a) initial state, (b) following substantial drug intake

If rats are pressing a lever for injections of drug and the drug quantity is reduced they tend to press harder; this is termed 'hedonic regulation'. It appears that animals monitor such consequences of behaviour (e.g. hedonic effect) and compare this with the effect that they have come to expect in the situation. This result is of interest if we consider again electrical self stimulation of the brain. Rats do not show such compensation in response to a lowering of current threshold (Atrens 1984; Trowill *et al.* 1969). If current is lowered, response rate is lowered. If current is increased, response rate is increased. This suggests that electrical brain stimulation is tapping primarily into the wanting mechanism. On this account drugs are tapping into both the wanting and the liking mechanisms. However, with repeated use, the liking activation declines but the wanting increases.

Further evidence to suggest that electrical stimulation of the brain taps into a wanting mechanism is given by comparing this with working for drug reward. As just noted, when they are working for drugs a compensation process is shown. By contrast, giving a drug such as cocaine *increases* the rate at which rats press for electrical brain stimulation (Markou and Koob 1991). On withdrawal from drugs they work *less* hard for electrical stimulation of the brain. If electrical brain stimulation were tapping a pleasure area, one would expect compensation to apply, i.e. they would *increase* activity during drug withdrawal.

Suppose that dopamine mediates a wanting but not a liking mechanism. The prediction from Figure 2.25 is that injecting dopamine antagonists will immediately lower wanting and hence the intensity of behaviour, e.g. to obtain a drug. We would not expect to see a compensatory increase in activity, as would be expected if dopamine mediated pleasure. The evidence is still controversial (Ettenberg 1982; Koob 1982; Wise 1982) but under active consideration by researchers.

Section summary

Depression can be associated with abnormal activity at particular regions of the brain. Brain lesions have sometimes been prescribed for mental disorder, though their use raises profound scientific and ethical issues. Recent theorizing postulates a distinction between craving for drugs and the pleasure arising from them.

1 In what way might the issues of causation, genetics and evolution be relevant to understanding depression?
2 Why is psychosurgery an emotive topic?
3 In terms of drug-taking, how would you distinguish between craving and pleasure? Why might the distinction prove important?

Pain

Evolution has found two complementary means to defend the body against damage. First, as was discussed earlier, there are reflexes. These are fast, organized locally at the level of the spinal cord and they move a part of the body from a potentially damaging stimulus, e.g. moving a foot from a thorn. These reflexes are 'hard-wired' by genetics, meaning that they are largely fixed; we come into the world with, to a considerable extent, these reflexes in place. They are fairly stereotyped, i.e. similar for all people. They consist of nociceptive neurons (see p. 31) and interneurons which trigger activity in appropriate motor neurons, so as to distance the body region from the noxious stimulation. This reaction precedes the conscious perception of pain.

The second line of defence is the pain system, with its unmistakable emotional and motivational aspects. These aspects are organized centrally in the brain. The pain system opens up the possibilities for action; there can be flexible solutions to tissue damage. In response to the negative emotion, the animal can find solutions involving its whole body, their form being selected on the basis of whether they diminish pain. For example, you might be suffering from a back pain and find that pain is reduced by assuming one particular position. Since most of us have the common experience of pain, it can also play a role in soliciting help: others might sympathize with us and bring comfort. Also, as a result of this information being processed in the brain, a memory is formed, we learn and thereby might avoid pain in the future.

Functional value of pain

In functional terms, pain is of crucial value. An excruciating pain will counterbalance if not kill most positively inspired motivation for action. For example, if we have an injured limb, by resting we increase the recovery chances of the limb. Similarly, if we go to bed with the pain of a headache caused by, say, influenza, we help our

Case study

What the life of Miss C. taught us

The functional value of pain can be illustrated by the rare individual who has an inherited or congenital inability to experience it (Melzack and Wall 1982). A well-documented case is that of Miss C., a student at McGill University, Canada. Miss C. showed high intelligence and appeared to be normal in all other respects.

Miss C.'s life was fraught with hazards against which a pain system would have provided a good defence. As a young child, Miss C. bit off the tip of her tongue. She suffered severe burns from a hot radiator on which she kneeled to look out of the window. When examined in the laboratory and subjected to normally noxious stimuli, Miss C. reported no pain. Miss C. suffered from serious medical problems. Her joints and spine were damaged as a result of not making the normal compensatory moves to the threat of tissue damage, such as shifting her weight around when standing. Similarly, Miss C. failed to turn over in bed.

Tragically, Miss C. died at the young age of 29, in large part as a result of damage inflicted on her body by her inability to experience pain. One could only speculate that Miss C. might have died earlier if she had suffered, say, appendicitis with little or no associated discomfort.

recovery. Behavioural processes protect the body by not only reacting to damage but also pre-empting it, as when we change our body position. Pain's adaptive value is shown by the occasional individual who is born without the processes necessary for this sensation. They fail to make the normal pain-motivated reactions, e.g. to change body sides in bed and to move body weight around when standing.

The other aspect of the argument on functional value is that debilitating pain often more commonly appears in later years (e.g. cancer pains). By then, we might normally be past the age at which reproduction takes place. Viewed in functional terms, pains at such an age might not have been a disadvantage. They would be irrelevant to evolutionary processes and hence would not be selected against. In functional terms, some pains would even appear to be inadequate, an example being that associated with a hangover headache. Such pains often seem to do little to deter over-drinking.

Neural mechanisms of pain

Nociceptive neurons convey information from the periphery to the spinal cord (or to the brain in the case of those forming part of a cranial nerve). In Figure 2.5, note neuron 5, which conveys the message to the brain as part of a tract in the spinal cord. Throughout most of the body the tips of nociceptive neurons are located. Tissue damage, either of the tip itself or in tissue near to the tip, is the stimulus for this type of neuron.

Guided by functional considerations, we might suppose that activity in nociceptive neurons is both necessary and sufficient for pain. We hurt when our body is damaged and this has clear survival value. Activity in nociceptive neurons does indeed often correlate with pain. However, life is rarely so simple and there are some striking examples of pain that do not fit with this.

Logically, the way to cure an intractable pain would be to make a surgical cut through the axons in a particular pathway. By comparison, we would be confident that the sensation of vision would be lost by cutting the axons that form the optic nerve. Historically, much surgery for chronic pain consisted of cutting a specific pathway. Alas, in many cases the pain later returned (Melzack 1993).

There are pains with no evidence of tissue damage and, conversely, there can be tissue damage with little pain. What is termed a placebo response (discussed shortly) refers to a relief of pain caused by nothing more than taking medicine of completely arbitrary quality.

What is crucial to the placebo is that taking the medicine is done in association with a beliefs that it will be effective. Such phenomena need a radical revision of simple ideas and one such revision was provided by the gate theory.

The gate theory of pain

A simplified version of the **gate theory** of pain is shown in Figure 2.26, its assumptions being as follows (Melzack 1993):

(1) Nociceptive neurons synapse on neurons in the spinal cord, termed **T-cells**, but their capacity to excite T-cells is not constant.
(2) There is, metaphorically speaking, a gate in the spinal cord at the point where each nociceptor makes synaptic contact.
(3) The gate controls the ability of nociceptive neurons to excite T-cells.
(4) When action potentials in the nociceptive neurons are able to instigate action potentials in T-cells, the gate is said to be open. If the nociceptive neurons are active but this fails to activate the T-cells, the gate is said to be closed.
(5) Activity in a pathway from the brain can close the gate.
(6) In the brain, there are cognitive processes which exert some control over the opening and closing of the gate.
(7) Normally, when T-cell activity reaches a threshold, pain is felt.

The activity within neuron (S) in the spinal cord determines the opening and closing of the gate (Figure 2.27), the negative sign indicating that activity inhibits the synapse. Activity in a descending pathway from the brain excites neuron S. The exact nature of the inhibition exerted by neuron S is not known but it is thought that an **opioid** substance termed enkephalin is the chemical released by neuron S (Figure 2.27). The chemical occupies opioid receptors at either the terminal of the nociceptive neuron or the cell body of the T-cell or, as represented, at both.

What is the functional value of an inhibitory pathway from the brain? At times it might be useful to inhibit the effect of nociceptive messages, e.g. when fleeing injured from a predator, it would be maladaptive to attend to wounds. In the human context, even serious injury suffered, for example, in war is not always associated with pain until the soldier is away from the battle zone.

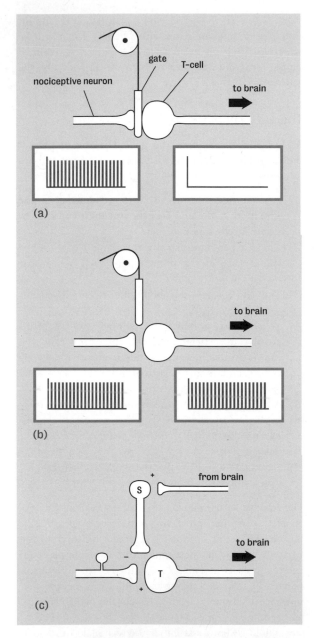

(a)

(b)

(c)

Figure 2.26 The gate theory of pain (a) gate closed, (b) gate open, (c) biologically realistic representation, showing neurons involved

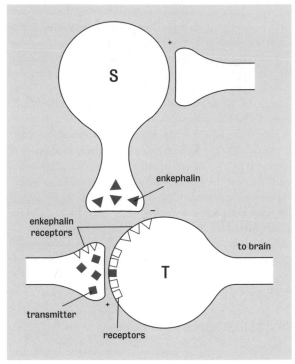

Figure 2.27 Representation of the possible mode of action of enkephalin released from neuron S

treatments for pain could function. For example, the Chinese technique of acupuncture might tap into the body's endogenous opioid system and thereby close the gate (Filshie and Morrison 1988).

Anomalies of pain

Commonly, people who have lost a limb still feel pain that appears to arise in the missing limb, so-called **phantom limb pain**. In some cases, the phantom pain feels like pains that were experienced earlier when the limb was still intact. This suggests that specific memories are implicated. Based upon the evidence of phantom limbs, the brain seems not to be a passive receiver of sensory information but more an active processor of it. Furthermore, the brain has the intrinsic capacity to generate the pain experience even in the absence of the corresponding sensory information.

The **placebo effect** tells a similar story to that of phantom limb pain. Suppose that there is a specific cause (A) of an effect (B); A causes B by means that depend, at least in part, upon the specific known properties of A, in the present context this usually means physiological

The theory that the pain system involves a gate that is controlled in part by psychological factors has had a profound influence. It provided a rationale for integrating different types of evidence, thereby bridging physiology and psychology. In clinical research, the notion of a gate provided a focus for thinking about how even unusual

Ψ Case study

The power of belief

Surgery provides examples of placebo effects (Wall 1993). An inadequate supply of blood to the muscle of the heart causes pain and is termed angina. One surgical intervention consisted of tying certain arteries that passed near to the heart. This was done in the hope that the disturbance to local blood flow would stimulate a growth of new blood vessels to supply the heart muscle. Many patients received the operation and were happy with its outcome. However, investigators were unable to find any growth of new blood vessels.

Researchers therefore carried out a **double-blind study**, involving two groups of patients. The patients and the clinicians assessing them were not informed as to which patient was in which group. Only other 'more distant' investigators had this knowledge. Both groups were told that their arteries had been tied during the operation. In reality, an experimental group of patients received the same operation as before. However, a control group simply received surgery that revealed the arteries. This was a trick designed to give the patient the impression that a conventional operation had been done, though there was no tying of arteries for this group. Both groups of patients said that they experienced significantly less pain.

properties of A. As examples, motor instability can be caused (B) by alcohol (A) and pain is reduced (B) by exploiting the known properties of morphine in closing the gate (A), just described.

The term 'placebo' refers to an effect that is similar to B but is caused by a non-specific process that involves the patient's belief or past experience, and is seen even without the specific cause (A) being present. For example, patients who expect to receive morphine but are injected with a neutral substance often report a significant reduction in pain. This shows that pain does not depend in a simple one-to-one way on tissue damage. Rather, although nociceptive input is a factor, so too are psychological expectations.

Ψ Section summary

The pain system serves in a flexible way to protect us from tissue damage. The gate theory suggests that nociceptive input is gated at the spinal cord. Psychological factors can serve to close the gate. Sometimes pain can be reduced by means of a placebo effect.

1 What insight into understanding pain is offered by a functional perspective?

2 What do the phenomena of phantom limb pain and the placebo effect tell us about the factors that determine pain?

❏ Emotions and stress

The emotions include such things as joy, elation and fear. They involve brain regions that organize behavioural reactions to certain stimuli, e.g. fleeing in response to a threatening stimulus. Emotions play a role in both controlling behaviour and changing the internal physiology of the body. They are also intimately related to the functioning of the body outside the nervous system. Evidence is accumulating that mental health has an important role to play in determining the well-being of the whole body. This section looks at this complex interdependence.

The organization of certain internal processes, such as the beating of the heart and the activity of the digestive tract, involves control by the nervous system and endocrine system. A good demonstration of the close interaction between psychological states and the physiological functioning of the body is provided by what happens during emotional experiences. In order to understand the reaction to emotion, it is necessary to consider a broad division within the classification of how action is effected.

Somatic and autonomic nervous systems

Earlier sections looked at the movement of limbs activated by skeletal muscles and such action concerns what is termed the **somatic nervous system**. The muscles with which it is associated exert action on the external world, e.g. to lift a weight. Another division of the nervous system, termed the **autonomic nervous system** (ANS), effects action within the body.

The ANS effects the so-called involuntary activities of the body, e.g. beating of the heart, digestive activity of the stomach and production of saliva. Figure 2.28 represents a neural influence on the heart. Information is conveyed from the CNS to the heart by neurons of the ANS. The activity of these ANS neurons is one of the factors that determine the activity of the heart muscle.

Such involuntary activities of the body are concerned with its internal working, sometimes thought of as the 'housekeeping functions' of the body. The beating heart serves to bring oxygen and nutrients to the body tissues and the churning of the stomach facilitates digestion. These activities of the body proceed when we are awake or asleep, without the necessity for conscious intervention.

Although by definition the ANS is autonomous, commands to action by the ANS can arise within the CNS.

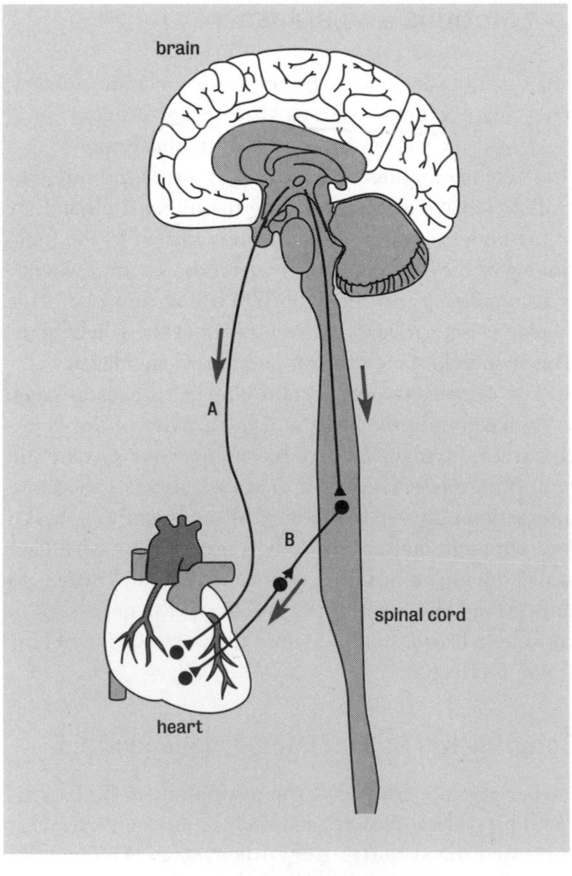

Mediated via the ANS, there are two different ways in which action can be exerted, summarized in Figure 2.29:

- Activity of neurons alters the tension of muscles (distinct from the skeletal muscles that effect action on the outside world). For example, ANS neurons can either excite or inhibit heart muscle. This makes the heart work more or less hard. Also, there are muscles in the walls of vessels of the circulation and their diameter depends in part upon the tension of the muscle. Tension in turn depends in part upon the activity of neurons of the ANS.
- Neurons cause the secretion of hormones or juices. For example, activity within ANS neurons triggers the release of adrenalin and noradrenalin from the adrenal gland (situated just above the kidney). These hormones affect multiple targets that are distant from the adrenal gland, e.g. the heart. In response to the presence of food in the mouth, neurons trigger the release of saliva.

The ANS is composed of what is termed sympathetic and parasympathetic branches, which, in general, exert opposite effects. Different types of neurotransmitter are released by neurons of the two branches and thereby exert different effects. For example, increased activity by the sympathetic branch causes the heart to increase its pumping activity. Conversely, increased parasympathetic activation tends to slow it down. Either branch of the system can dominate according to circumstances. At times of emergency when the body is activated, such as in fleeing an enemy or fighting, the sympathetic branch tends to be excited and the parasympathetic inhibited. This increases blood flow to the skeletal muscles. Conversely, at a time of rest, the parasympathetic tends to dominate over the sympathetic. Blood is diverted

Figure 2.28 Simplification showing neural influence on the heart

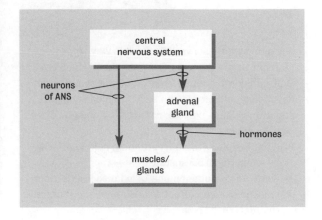

Figure 2.29 Mode of action of ANS

from the skeletal muscles to the gut and assists digestion. The heart beats less energetically since blood does not need to be circulated so rapidly.

What exactly is 'autonomic' about the ANS? It is called this because it has some intrinsic self-organization and therefore, to some extent, is autonomous from the rest of the nervous system. Such things as changes in heart rate at times of emotion and the secretion of saliva in response to the presentation of food occur without the need for a conscious intention that they should happen. However, although the ANS *can* perform certain actions without our conscious will, the CNS and ANS normally act in an integrated way. For example, when we perceive a threat, the CNS influences the ANS, among other things the sympathetic branch excites the heart.

A threat is also associated with another sequence of actions: acting via other hormones, the brain triggers the secretion of hormones termed corticosteroids from the adrenal glands. These are then transported in the blood stream where they effect a variety of processes throughout the body. Corticosteroids, together with adrenalin and noradrenalin, are responsible for preparing the body for action. The heart pumps vigorously, blood vessels are dilated to permit a high blood flow to the skeletal muscles and fuel is recruited from energy stores in the body. This again shows the close interdependence between nervous and endocrine systems.

The somatic nervous system and the autonomic nervous system normally work in harmony to achieve a goal. Take the example of the perception of a charging bull, where people generally instigate rapidly the most appropriate response, usually running. The functional value hardly needs mentioning! So the perception of a threat through the sensory channels is quickly translated into a central emotional state of fear and appropriate behaviour. The various aspects of emotion work as an integrated whole: specific thoughts ('cognitions'), subjectively felt emotions, autonomic manifestations and behaviour are all closely linked.

The biology of stress

Systems that organize reactions to threat clearly serve a vital function. However, they can be stretched to beyond their optimal range. Sapolsky (1994) draws an analogy: some electrical goods commonly have a disclaimer attached to them, pointing out that the manufacturer is not responsible for malfunction outside the designed range of use. We can sometimes exert agency over the potentially aversive events in our lives. If we are unable to do so, what are normally adaptive behavioural mechanisms can be stretched to beyond their adaptive range, a condition termed **stress** (Toates 1995). Stress is a chronic failure of coping mechanisms to function optimally.

The environment brings us **stressors**, e.g. regular confrontation with hostile elements or wild animals or, perhaps more often these days in western Europe, the challenge of traffic jams, unreasonable bosses and editors impatient for authors' words of wisdom. Thus stress might be defined in broad cognitive terms as a failure of perceived capacity for action to meet perceived demands. Such a definition is useful in that it points to features in common between a wide variety of different stressors.

In our evolution, in response to certain stressors, e.g. confrontation with dangerous animals, we have been able to recruit the appropriate defence mechanisms of fighting or running, which have apparently functioned well. We are prepared for action by the ANS and by corticosteroids: ready for 'fight or flight'. However, if there is no available coping strategy, we can be stretched by the stressors too much and over long periods of time. Pathological stress can result. For example, there is little we can do in response to the daily stressor of being confronted by an over-demanding boss or a traffic jam – neither fight nor flight are usually either possible or adaptive.

Physiological changes in stress

Stress is associated with pathology (e.g. putting a strain on the circulation, gastric ulcers, irritable bowel syndrome). When looking at the damage done by stress, lipids (fats) in the blood stream are important. When a threat is perceived, lipids are recruited from stores throughout the body and transported in the blood stream. If we are physically active, lipids can be utilized as a fuel. However, chronic elevation of lipid levels, particularly where they remain unused as in stressful inactivity, is a risk to the health of the circulatory system. In this state, lipids tend to gather on the artery walls, termed arteriosclerosis.

Personality, behaviour and attitude have a role in circulatory responses (Chapter 19). Hostility and anger appear to be damaging to our circulatory system. Some argue that being competitive and in a hurry are not in themselves dangerous, except where they trigger anger and hostility (R. Williams 1989).

Not only the nervous and endocrine system but also the immune systems are in complex interaction. A disturbance in any of them can have an influence in the other two. Since, as far as we know, emotions and stress arise in the CNS, we are particularly concerned with effects of the nervous system upon the endocrine and immune systems. A rise in corticosteroid level tends to suppress the immune system. Thus, stresses, which increase the levels of corticosteroids, can have a negative effect upon the immune system.

Countering stress

There are aspects of biology and behaviour that contribute to positive emotional health and act to counterbalance stress. Devotees of energetic sports such as jogging and aerobics report that mood is elevated (Johnsgard 1989; Morgan 1981). Endorphins (natural chemicals similar to morphine) are released into the blood at times of physical exertion and their arrival at the CNS might well play a crucial role in the elevation of mood (Harte *et al.* 1995).

Another contributor to good health is **belonging**, i.e. living in harmony with others such that we have a common purpose in life, as part of a social network. We can achieve socially acceptable goals and have some control and coping capacity.

Socially isolated people are at greater risk of a number of disorders than those who are harmoniously socially integrated (House *et al.* 1988; Williams 1991). There are psychobiological theories on how social isolation and contact might mediate such effects (Bovard 1985; Williams 1989, 1991). Seen in terms of evolution, we are social creatures who are born dependent upon other humans for our survival. This suggests that there are brain processes which are largely genetically determined and which are the basis of our social motivation

How can social interaction affect the physiology of the body? How do positive social bonds affect, say, the health of the circulatory system? As noted earlier, there are links from the CNS to the ANS and then to the body outside the nervous system. When in social bonds, there appears to be less activation from the sympathetic branch of the ANS to the circulatory system. A combination of effects upon heart muscle, coronary arteries and lipid levels act in the same direction as protection against arteriosclerosis. Conditioning (Chapter 3) doubtless also plays a role. From the time of birth, the presence of other humans might usually be associated with benefits, e.g. milk from the breast and tactile stimulation. The presence of friendly others might be able later to exert some beneficial conditioned psychological effects.

The immune system and stress

Social harmony appears to offer some protection even against cancer. Cancer patients with social support have an increased survival time. The mechanism for this seems to be an interaction between psychological state (as embodied in the CNS) and immune function, the immune system having a role in defence against cancerous cells (Maier *et al.* 1994). See Figure 2.30. As part of the indirect link, cells of the immune system have receptors for corticosteroids. Their occupation by corticosteroids tends to inhibit immune cell activity. Such things as student examinations, war, divorce, depression and bereavement lower immune response in humans (Maier *et al.* 1994). There is also a reciprocal link: the nervous system is influenced by events in the immune system.

The link from the nervous system to the immune system also involves conditioning. Suppose, as part of therapy, a drug is injected which, as a side-effect, suppresses the immune system. Cues paired with the drug (e.g. sight of needle, feel of injection) can come to mimic some of the drug's effects, a **conditioned immune suppressive effect**. This effect can be of practical significance in treatment (Maier *et al.* 1994). Chemotherapeutic drugs given for cancer are intended to target cancer cells but they tend also to inhibit healthy cells, e.g. cells of the immune system. Chemotherapy might well be given repeatedly in a particular context, e.g. a hospital building. This creates the possibility that cues paired with this context (e.g. approaching the hospital) might acquire a conditioned immune suppressive capacity.

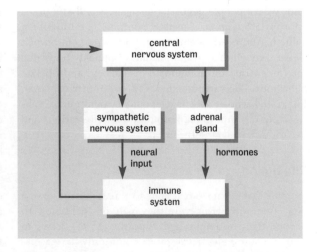

Figure 2.30 Links from nervous system to immune system. These are both direct (nervous system → immune system) and medicated via hormones (nervous system → hormones → immune system)

ψ Section summary

The autonomic nervous system is responsible for effecting action within the body, e.g. controlling heart rate and digestive activity. In general, the sympathetic and parasympathetic branches of the autonomic nervous system exert opposite effects. The sympathetic nervous system prepares the body for exertion, as in fighting or fleeing. Chronic and inappropriate activation of this system is associated with stress.

1 What would be the expected effect on the heart of injecting an antagonist to the neurotransmitter that neurons of the sympathetic branch release at the heart muscle?
2 In what way do emotions and stress illustrate the interactions between the nervous, endocrine and immune systems?

☐ Consciousness

At various points in the chapter, consciousness made a brief appearance, e.g. the conscious sensation of pain and conscious intention. Of course, the contents of consciousness are subjective. They cannot be inspected by others and measured objectively. However, as pain illustrated, we implicitly or explicitly make the assumption that our fellow humans share a conscious experience much like our own.

What is the nature of the relationship between the conscious mind and the physical brain? Philosophers have discussed this issue for centuries. One of the best known was the seventeenth-century French philosopher, René Descartes, who is associated with **dualism**. To Descartes, the physical brain observed the same laws as are applicable to matter in the rest of the physical universe and was therefore a viable target for scientific investigation. However, according to him, in addition to the physical brain, humans are in possession of a unique 'state' (finding the right class noun is part of the problem), variously termed mind, spirit or consciousness, which does not exist in a physical dimension. Rather, it has an existence distinct from the physical brain and can survive physical death. Within contemporary behavioural science, dualism is an idea that is out of favour except in the hands of a few 'mavericks' (Eccles 1991).

Yet Descartes served a vital function in focusing our minds (brains?) on the key issues.

Each individual would probably agree that there is something uniquely *me* about his or her own conscious mind, which involves at its core an awareness of one's self. Within our conscious mind, we can generate our own idiosyncratic and private ideas on such things as the conscious states of other people's minds. These ideas can be formed with respect to our own consciousness, e.g. 'He must be feeling sorry because now he knows how I must feel'. Yet, although it has this personal and idiosyncratic feel and is not directly observable to others, to most behavioural scientists the universal properties of consciousness form a viable target for scientific scrutiny. By comparison, our speech is idiosyncratic (most of your utterances are probably unique) and varies from culture to culture and yet there is a common biological basis for this faculty (cf. Stevens 1990). A focus for trying to understand consciousness is the brain. (See also Chapter 5).

Brain mechanisms

From a biological perspective, in terms of the processes underlying consciousness, we might start by posing two fundamental questions.

What is the relationship between conscious experience and the physical brain?

To most behavioural scientists, Descartes's dualism was wrong and conscious experience is always dependent upon the activity of the physical brain. They would probably ask somewhat indignantly 'How could consciousness possibly be other than a product of the physical brain?' In other words, for each conscious experience, there is a corresponding pattern of neural activity in the brain. This neural activity constitutes the necessary physical base of the conscious experience, i.e. no physical base then no conscious experience. A disembodied consciousness is impossible. Perhaps the simplest claim is that brain activity *causes* conscious experience.

However, the consensus view is not without its problems: we simply do not know how the physical brain gives rise to consciousness, if indeed it does. The fact that drugs, alcohol and brain damage can so radically change conscious experience is evidence that, at the very least, consciousness has much to do with the physical brain.

The body is made up of cells and their components, atoms and molecules. Looking closely at the nervous system and its components reveals nothing suggestive of a special property of this matter that might give rise to (or be identical to) conscious experience. For example, certain neurotransmitters and hormones are activated on occasions that we describe as emotional but how does their activation contribute to the subjective colouring of emotion? On looking at the chemical structure of these substances, they seem much like any other chemical that could attach itself to specific receptors. In principle, a wide variety of different chemicals could act as neurotransmitters and perform this role equally well. Neither does considering the properties of whole neurons give us insight and the circuits that they form can often be best understood by modelling on computers. So the physical brain yields none of its secrets in searching for insights into consciousness.

Some would suggest that consciousness is an **emergent property** of the brain, i.e. when brain complexity reaches a certain level, consciousness *emerges* from it. When grappling with something as daunting as this, we can appeal to analogies. Thus, by comparison, the property of negative feedback emerges from a combination of some components such as a thermostat and heater etc. For another analogy, when two gases, hydrogen and oxygen, combine we get the liquid, water. This liquidity is not evident in either component molecule but it emerges from their combination. To pursue the analogy, consciousness is not partly evident in any given neuron but becomes evident when millions of them are connected together in a certain way. I guess that this does not give you that 'now I see it' feeling and you would be forgiven for not feeling it. Whereas we know something about the rules of combination that yield liquids from gases, we remain ignorant of the analogous principles that relate to consciousness. However, analogies like these might be part of an initial first stage of gaining insight. The implications of different models of consciousness can be explored with the help of analogies. For example, suppose that the mind is analogous to the program being run on a computer (software) and the brain is analogous to the computer (hardware). If a particular computer is destroyed then so too is its software (unless, of course, back-up copies are made). If this analogy is useful, a disembodied consciousness is not possible.

Another way of viewing the relationship between mind and brain is in terms of **identity theory** (Gray 1971), which suggests that brain language and mind language are different ways of discussing the same underlying reality. By analogy, 'the table' and 'der Tisch'

are words in two different languages for describing the same normally four-legged piece of reality. It is not that one has 'a table' and somehow over and above this, there exists 'ein Tisch'.

However, exactly how an activity by millions of neurons gives rise to, or can be identical to (the exact language to use is intrinsically problematic), mental phenomena and a unitary state of conscious experience still escapes our imagination. It is difficult to envisage, let alone devise, experiments to investigate this issue and therefore one's image of the nature of the brain–mind relationship often seems to be more a matter of faith than scientifically observable truth.

Depending upon the answer to the first question, are there parts of the brain that have a particular relationship to consciousness?

If consciousness is a product of the physical brain, are all brain processes involved in conscious experience? A subset of processes might constitute the physical base of consciousness.

Functional explanations

From a functional perspective, a question that we can ask is: 'What evolutionary advantage does consciousness confer?' If consciousness is a product of the brain, why has a brain evolved that has the capacity to generate it?

You might feel that consciousness confers such obvious advantages that things could hardly be otherwise. However, as is revealed by our capacity to behave on 'autopilot', we can carry on many roles (e.g. brushing teeth, negotiating a familiar path) perfectly well at an unconscious level (Baars 1988; Reason 1979, 1984; Shallice 1972). Of course, if we find our familiar path flooded we will soon switch from autopilot to full conscious control. So, perhaps consciousness is something that switches in when autopilot processes fail. Suppose that consciousness is the product of a sophisticated brain and that such a brain evolved because consciousness gave its possessor an advantage. Understood in such terms, any advantage is probably considerable in order to offset the disadvantages of the large amounts of metabolic fuel that are required by such a brain and the difficulties of giving birth to a child with such a large head.

Some theorists argue that consciousness is to be understood in terms of its role in social communication.

We are social creatures; much of our social commerce depends upon the assumption that others share a similar experience of conscious awareness. When their skin is damaged, others hurt just as we do. They are deserving of sympathy because of what is happening to their conscious awareness. These others might well be our descendants and so by showing them help we are perpetuating our own genes. Also we can recruit the help of others. By extrapolating on the basis of our own consciousness, we can anticipate the moves of others, e.g. they are likely to shake our hand when pleased, attack when in pain or freeze when afraid. Thereby, we are able to engage in a rich and productive social dialogue with them.

One way of gaining some insight into consciousness is to look at brains that are damaged in some way and the next section considers an example of this.

Consciousness and the split-brain

Looking at the anatomy of the brain, can we get any insight into how consciousness and a feeling of a uni-fied self might emerge from it? Given its complexity, any destruction of brain regions might be expected to have a devastating effect on consciousness. Some damage does have serious effects. However, what is surprising about consciousness is how there can be extensive brain damage in some regions with little apparent effect, only detectable after subtle psychological tests. Removal by surgery of one of the brain's hemispheres does not destroy consciousness (MacKay 1987). Consciousness appears therefore to arise as a complex property of activity in both hemispheres in such a way that, if one hemisphere is lacking, in some way the other can compensate.

Ironically, considering the unity of consciousness, perhaps the most remarkable thing about the human brain is the division of most of it into two halves along the midline (see Figures 2.12 and 2.13). Of course, as you doubtless experience, in spite of this division of much of the brain into two halves, the world outside normally has a quality of unity about it. (Well, for at least much of the time, it does!) Furthermore, we nor-

---

ψ Case study

Can consciousness be split?

By surgery, can we create two people in one head? On the notion of 'two people', MacKay writes:

Each would have, at a minimum, to be a centre of conscious awareness and, at least in principle, a terminal of dialogue – someone who could be met, interrogated, informed, argued with and so forth. Moreover, each must be not just a receiver of sensory information and a generator of bodily movements but an evaluator of both. Evaluation is a crucial ingredient of personal agency.

Persons, however, are autonomous and conscious evaluators, in the sense that at least to some extent they are able to set and readjust their own norms and criteria according to changing circumstances, in the light of long-range plans. Most significantly for our purpose, talk of 'two persons' implies the possibility in principle of *dialogue between them.*

(MacKay 1987: 8)

Sperry (1967) and MacKay (1987) and their associates tested some split-brain subjects, attempting to introduce one half person to the other. Would it be possible to generate a dialogue between the two halves? It appeared that one hemisphere could pose a question of the other and would then wait to get an answer. Evidence was found for different sensory and motor coordinations and even different evaluations of a given stimulus in the two hemispheres. However, MacKay reported:

despite all encouragements we found no sign at all of recognition of the other 'half' as a separate person, nor of independence at the normative level where priorities and criteria of evaluation are themselves evaluated – the characteristic human activity with which we associate the term 'will'.

One subject's question to the experimenters would seem to be particularly relevant to the present discussion:

Are you guys trying to make two people out of me?

MacKay's argument is that independent sensory-motor action and even independent goal pursuit between the two hemispheres does not constitute two conscious beings. The notion of indivisibility of the subject's consciousness seemed to survive even the split brain procedure.

mally feel ourselves to be executing a unified consistent plan of action involving holistic control over muscular coordination.

Sometimes the bundle of fibres that link the two hemispheres, the corpus callosum, is surgically cut in an attempt to alleviate epilepsy (Figure 2.13), i.e. to stop epilepsy that arises from abnormal electrical activity in one hemisphere from influencing the other (Sperry 1967). Such patients are termed 'split-brain' patients. Using them as volunteers and employing specially designed tests involving a very brief exposure to visual stimuli (see Chapter 4), it is possible to send information to just one hemisphere (Sperry 1967). It is found that each hemisphere can perform a range of operations on its own but the subject cannot perform tasks that require inter-hemispheric communication. Does this mean that the operation has created two independent conscious 'selves' within the one brain?

Ψ **Section summary**

Contemporary psychologists and neuroscientists generally see the mind and consciousness as being a property of the physical brain. In so doing, they reject a dualistic view of brain and mind. Identity theory suggests that the language of brain and mind are two different ways of discussing the same underlying reality. Suggestions for understanding the functional value of consciousness include that it is a system that facilitates social communication.

1 In what way does identity theory differ from dualism?
2 What kinds of analogies might give useful insight into consciousness?

Ψ **Chapter summary**

● **Causation – the physiology of the body**

Physiology is the study of the working of the body, which can be divided into conceptual parts, i.e. systems. The maintenance of stability within the body is crucial to survival and the process of maintaining this stability is termed 'homeostasis'. The body is made up of millions of cells; the most important for the present study are those of the nervous system, termed neurons.

Communication along neurons is by means of action potentials, which are electrical signals. Neurons serve various roles. For example, sensory neurons are the class that detect events. Motor neurons effect action via muscles. The point of contact between a neuron and another cell is termed a synapse and communication across a synapse is by means of a chemical transmitter. Another means of communication is by hormones. These are also chemicals and they mediate communication over relatively long distances.

Scientists attempt to map regions of the brain and identify the roles that they serve. The outer layer of the brain is termed the cerebral cortex. It is possible to associate the lobes of the brain with different roles. For example, the frontal lobes are involved in planning behaviour. A brain region termed the hypothalamus is

concerned with regulation and motivation. Electrical stimulation of this region constitutes positive reinforcement, which refers to a procedure whereby behaviour is strengthened as a result of its consequences.

● **Genes, environment and evolution**

Genes are structures that convey information from parents to offspring. Together with the environment, genes determine, among other things, the structure of the nervous system. Behaviour is always a function of both genes and environment.

A causal explanation refers to why an individual animal does something, in terms of the here-and-now events within its nervous system. A functional explanation refers to how a particular behaviour has contributed to the evolutionary success of an animal's ancestors. A complete explanation of behaviour involves considering both causal and functional explanations. Sociobiology attempts to explain complex features of human behaviour in terms of their evolutionary value.

● **Plasticity**

The term 'plasticity' refers to the ability of the nervous system to change its properties as a result of experience and learning. As its biological basis within the

Box continued

nervous system, plasticity is thought to be a result of changes in synaptic connections between neurons. Connections can be either strengthened or weakened.

● Targeting the brain when things go wrong

When behaviour is abnormal, attention is often directed to the brain in a search for underlying malfunction. For example, depression is thought to have a neural base in the form of abnormalities at certain CNS synapses. Intervention can involve drugs or surgery. Psychosurgery refers to brain lesions prompted by a need to change mental states and behaviour. Researchers are seeking the biological bases of addictions by looking at processes within the brain. A recent theory suggests a distinction between the brain processes that underlie the craving for drugs and the pleasure derived from drugs.

● Pain

Pain serves the function of protecting the body tissues from damage. Nociceptive neurons are sensitive to tissue damage and often pain shows a one-to-one dependence upon their activity. However, this is not always the case and the gate theory suggests that the signal from nociceptive neurons is gated at its arrival in the CNS. Phantom limb pain and the placebo effect are examples of where pain perception does not relate simply to nociceptive neuron activity.

● Emotions and stress

In situations of threat, the emotions play a role in organizing both behaviour and the body's physiology. The somatic nervous system organizes skeletal muscle activity that performs work on the external environment. The autonomic nervous system organizes reactions within the body, e.g. heart rate elevation. In our evolution, these emotional reactions probably served a vital survival function. However, now their chronic activation is associated with stress. Stress refers to a stretching of defensive reactions to beyond their optimal range of activity. Nervous, endocrine and immune systems interact and these interactions are especially evident at times of emotional activation.

● Consciousness

Dualism suggests two fundamentally different domains of reality, the physical (brain) and the non-physical (mental). By contrast, identity theory suggests that there is just one domain of reality. In terms of identity theory, brain language and mind language are two different language systems for describing the same domain. An emergent property is something that emerges by virtue of the connections between components and is not evident in the performance of a component. It is sometimes said that mental events and consciousness are emergent properties from the physical brain.

Further reading

● Carlson, N.R. (1994) *Physiology of Behaviour*. Boston, MA: Allyn & Bacon; Kolb, B. and Whishaw, I.Q. (1990) *Fundamentals of Human Neuropsychology*. New York: W.H. Freeman. These are good basic textbooks on biological psychology.

● Rosenzweig, M.R., Leiman, A.L. and Breedlove, S.M. (1996) *Biological Psychology*. Sunderland, MA: Sinauer. This is especially accessible.

● Kandel, E.R., Schwartz, J.H. and Jessell, T.M. (1991) *Principles of Neural Science*, 3rd edn. New York: Elsevier. This can be recommended for reading at a more advanced level.

● *Journal of Consciousness Studies*. Good readable reviews on consciousness in relation to biology.

● Oatley, N. and Jenkins, J.M. (1966) *Understanding Emotions*. Oxford: Blackwell. An account of emotions that relates to biology.

● Toates, F. (1995) *Stress: Conceptual and biological aspects*, Chichester: Wiley. This reviews stress.

● Cabanac, M. (1995) *La Quête du plaisir*. Montreal: Liber. A philosophical work in French linking biology, psychology and pleasure.

● Buss, D.M. (1994) *The Evolution of Desire: Strategies of human mating*. New York: Basic Book. This discusses sociobiology.

CHAPTER 3

Learning and conditioning

Helena Matute

KEY CONCEPTS • developing a theory of learning • stimulus–stimulus associations • response–outcome associations • 'special' types of learning

❏ Chapter preview

When you have read this chapter, you should be able to

- understand what is a theory of learning, and why you should be interested in developing a good theory
- understand how humans and animals learn about the relationships between the events in their environment
- detect instances of Pavlovian and instrumental conditioning in everyday life
- evaluate the strengths and weaknesses of some of the major learning theories
- understand that many different types of learning, such as Pavlovian and instrumental conditioning, acquisition of causal and predictive relations, categorization, and spatial learning, appear to be subject to the same learning principles

❏ Developing a theory of learning

You probably have some ideas about what learning is. You may think of the many years spent at school and the many hours you have spent reading books and learning things. But think not only about how you acquired your school knowledge, but also about how you first learned to walk, to find your way back home when on an unknown street or in an unknown city, to predict a potentially dangerous situation, to relate with other people, to show emotions when it is appropriate to show them and to hide them otherwise. You might also think about how we learn our phobias and our preferences, how we learn the value of money, or how we learn appropriate behaviour for different situations (and inappropriate behaviour as well).

How does learning take place? Answering this question has motivated psychologists to study the learning process, to conduct experiments and to develop theories that should help us understand how we learn. That is, no matter how distinct the many things that we learn are, there must be something fundamental to all of these situations that allows learning to take place. Running experiments on learning and developing a theory of learning is simply trying to answer that question. If you are curious about it, as many psychologists have been, you should try to run your own experiments and to develop a theory of learning that could improve the current ones. You can start by imagining a simple theory that could explain the basic learning experiments which will be described below. Once you have your own theory, compare it with that developed by your classmates, find the pros and cons of each of those theories, and try to reach an agreement on one or two theories that appear to explain the examples of learning that are provided here as well as any other example of learning that you could think of. Then, compare your theory with those that other psychologists have developed. You will probably find that you arrived at many of the ideas that psychologists have proposed; you will also find that some of those ideas have been found problematic, and that many of those 'faulty' theories are still a matter for discussion at the present time. If possible, when you finish the chapter, try to find out ways in which you could improve the theories presented here, find further readings that will help you improve your theory, and run experiments that would test whether or not you are correct. Trying to solve the riddle of learning can be fun.

While trying to develop a simple theory of learning, you may want to think not only about how people learn but also about how other animals learn. You have probably heard about Pavlov's dog, which salivated upon hearing a tone that had previously been presented as a signal for food, or about Thorndike's cats, which learned how to escape from the puzzle boxes that Thorndike constructed to study how they did this. These are good instances of animal learning, but non-human animals also learn a great deal of other things. Finding their way home, relating with people and with other animals, differentiating friends from strangers, asking for a walk, differentiating eatable from non-eatable foods, how (and where) to obtain food, how to predict danger and how to escape from it, and so on. These things that animals learn are not too different from the ones that we learn. Admittedly, we learn more. But the basic idea that most learning theorists have entertained is that it is just a matter of quantity, not quality. You may or may not agree on this assumption, but that again is part of the excitement of studying learning. If you do not agree with the idea that the basic learning principles are general principles that apply across species, you should try to run experiments and find good arguments to challenge this general view, and develop a more satisfactory one. You must know that even though the psychology of learning has made great improvements over the years, and even though we know a lot more now than such pioneers as Pavlov and Thorndike knew when they started the experimental study of learning about 100 years ago, there is still much room for improvement, new knowledge, ideas, experiments and new and better theories.

Associative theories

Even if you do not agree with the idea of a general learning process that can suffice to explain all forms of animal and human learning, let us agree, at least for the time being, that there must exist a very simple mechanism underlying most types of learning, something that allows learning to occur in different situations and species — something that simply allows learning to take place.

Many of the psychologists who study learning have agreed that the most basic learning mechanism which underlies most types of learning must be an associative mechanism. That is, something that allows the animal (or human) to associate the mental representation of one event with the mental representation of another event (see Dickinson 1980). These two events could be two environmental stimuli (S) which occur close in time and space, such as when Stimulus 1 (S1) is immediately followed by Stimulus 2 (S2). For example, children usually learn to associate black sky (S1) with a storm (S2) after they experience some pairings of black skies followed by storms. In this case, the children learn an association between their mental representation of these two stimuli, and the adaptive value of such learning is that once they have formed such S1→S2 association, they will be able to predict when a storm is about to occur. But of course, such learning of **S–S associations** would not be of much help if it were not complemented by an additional type of learning that would allow us to learn what we should do after we have made the prediction (e.g. how to protect ourselves from the storm). Thus, not only do we need to form associations between environmental stimuli, but also we need to form associations between our behaviour and its consequences. For example, if we see a black sky and we remain outdoors, we will associate the black sky (S1) with the storm (S2) but we will also learn to associate our behaviour (staying outdoors) with a rather unpleasant outcome (getting wet and cold in the storm). In addition, we can also learn that a different behaviour (e.g. going indoors) produces a nicer outcome (staying dry and warm). When we learn an association between the representation of our own response (R) and that of the outcome (O) that it produces, we speak of having acquired an **R–O association**.

Thus, after acquiring many of those simple associations, we are able to better adapt and adjust our behaviour to our changing environment. Learning S–S associations allows us to predict our environment, and learning of R–O associations allows us to better adapt our behaviour to our environment. The main purpose of research in learning has been to analyse how those associations are acquired and used. The rest of this chapter presents a summary of some of the research which has been conducted on S–S and R–O associations.

❑ Stimulus–stimulus associations

Pavlovian or classical conditioning

Let us start by a very well known experiment. A hungry dog receives food from time to time and every single presentation of the food is preceded by a tone that signals that the food is about to be presented. After several trials in which the dog is exposed to the tone–food relation, the dog will salivate upon hearing the tone even if the food is not presented. This was demonstrated by Ivan Pavlov (1927) and has become the best known example

of **classical (or Pavlovian) conditioning**, which is a form of stimulus–stimulus (S-S) learning.

Note that what the dog learned here is very similar to our storm example above, in which children learned to predict storms after being exposed to several trials in which a black sky was followed by a storm. In Pavlov's experiment, the dog can easily learn to predict when food will be available, if it pays attention to the tone–food relationship. Interestingly, once the dog has learned that the tone predicts food, the dog will salivate upon hearing the tone. This is what Pavlov called the **conditioned response (CR)**. Why? Because it was a response that was conditional on learning that the tone would be followed by food. No dog would salivate upon hearing the tone unless it had previously learned that the tone would be followed by food. Thus, such salivary responding to the tone was conditioned (i.e. learned).

Although in the storm example above we did not mention the occurrence of a conditioned response (CR), acquisition of a black sky–storm association also produces CRs when we see a black sky. In that case, the CRs do not take the form of salivary responses, of course, but may take the form of fear responses. The child who has already learned to predict storms may feel fear upon observing a black sky (S1). Thus, CRs can take very different forms (e.g. salivation, fear, sexual arousal, and many others); they occur when the organism perceives S1, and S1 predicts the occurrence of an S2 which is biologically significant (e.g. food, storm, sex, water, sources of pain, drugs, illness). By contrast, if S1 predicts an S2 which is biologically irrelevant, conditioned responses will not be observed even though this does not mean that an S1–S2 association has not been learned. For example, if we hear a sequence of two numbers, S1 and S2, a few times (e.g. 2-5, 2-5, 2-5, 2-5, 2-5) we can perfectly predict S2 (5) upon hearing S1 (2) but we will not give a conditioned response. Similarly, we can learn an association between the name of a person (S1) and a phone number (S2), but this association will not normally produce a conditioned response. Thus, it is important to remember that although the occurrence of a CR indicates that an association has been acquired (as in the dog's example above), the absence of a CR does not mean that learning has not taken place: there are many S–S associations that are not ordinarily expressed in conditioned responses.

The term classical or Pavlovian conditioning should be reserved, therefore, for a certain type of S–S learning. In particular, the type of S–S learning that involves stimuli which are biologically significant. According to

Pavlov (1927), in order to obtain a conditioned response, S2 must be a biologically significant stimulus. For example, food, sex, water, electric shock or any other stimuli that would elicit responses unconditionally, that is, without any prior learning, are biologically significant stimuli. For this reason, in Pavlovian conditioning, S2 is generally called the **unconditioned stimulus (US)**, because it does not require any special conditions in order to produce a response. For example, food produces salivation without any prior learning, or, if the US were an electric shock, it would produce, among other responses, a leg flexion reflex. These responses that are produced unconditionally in all members of the same species by a US are called the **unconditioned response (UR)**.

S1 is called in Pavlovian conditioning the **conditioned stimulus (CS)**, because it produces the response (e.g. salivation) conditional on learning having taken place. The CS is usually a tone, a light, a colour, an odour or a taste, initially of low biological significance. The CS does not elicit the CR in all members of the same species, but only in those individuals that have undergone training with the same or similar USs (e.g. only dogs exposed to tone–food pairings will end up salivating at tones).

Figure 3.1 illustrates the different steps that take place during classical conditioning and may help you better remember the different terms that we are using. Before the CS becomes conditioned (see panel A of Figure 3.1), the CS is still a neutral stimulus which does not produce the CR, but which does produce an **orienting response (OR)**, when it is first presented. The orienting response consists of paying attention to the stimulus and noticing that something unexpected has occurred. Pavlov called it the 'what is that?' reflex. If we observe that a particular CS does not produce an OR when it is first presented, that means that we had better use a different stimulus for our conditioning experiment because a stimulus which does not command the attention of the organism will not become conditioned.

Panel B of Figure 3.1 shows the conditioning stage. During conditioning, the CS is presented immediately before the US. That is, the tone sounds and the food follows. It is important that the food follows the sound immediately or at most after a very short delay because contiguity between the CS and the US helps the animal to associate the two stimuli. The salivation that is produced during conditioning is produced solely by the food during the early tone–food pairings (thus, salivation is a UR during the early stages of conditioning) and it gradu-

ally begins being produced also by the CS as learning proceeds (thus, salivation gradually becomes a CR).

Panel C of Figure 3.1 shows that after conditioning has taken place, if we present only the tone (that is, the CS but not the US), the dog salivates to the tone. Only when salivation occurs on presentation of the CS alone (either on CS-alone trials, or in the presence of the CS before the US is presented on CS→US trials) can we say that the salivation observed is a CR. The CR serves the purpose of preparing the organism for the occurrence of the US (e.g.

Figure 3.1 Before conditioning (Panel A), the tone (CS) does not produce salivation (CR). However, it does produce an orienting response (OR) or, in Pavlov's terms, the 'what is that?' reflex. During conditioning (Panel B), the food (US) is presented immediately after the CS. Salivation is an unconditioned response (UR) at first and gradually also becomes a conditioned response (CR). After conditioning has taken place (Panel C), the CS produces a salivary response (CR)

salivation prepares the gastric system to receive food). Moreover, the CR can be used as an index of learning because its occurrence means that the dog has now learned to anticipate food in the presence of the tone.

Non-salivary Pavlovian conditioning

It should be clear by now that not all forms of Pavlovian or classical conditioning involve salivary responses. By simply looking at TV for a short while, we can discover many more examples of Pavlovian conditioning because it is widely used in advertising. For example, food commercials generally try to produce salivary conditioning; decaffeinated coffee advertisements generally involve associations that are aimed at producing relaxation CRs; the way in which perfumes are advertised almost always includes the establishment of an association between a given trade mark, which is an initially neutral stimulus (i.e. a CS, as the tone was in Pavlov's experiment) and an attractive person of the opposite sex, who is a biologically significant stimulus (i.e. the US, as was the food in Pavlov's work). The establishment of such associations is of course aimed at producing an appetitive reaction when we see the advertised brand at the store. Moreover, some governmental prevention campaigns make use of fear conditioning by associating, for example, alcohol with a fatal accident. The purpose is to produce relevant fear responses that might help prevent traffic accidents. We shall now look at some forms of Pavlovian conditioning that have been extensively studied in the laboratory: fear conditioning and taste aversions. The case study on p. 73 also shows how drug addictions can be explained as an example of Pavlovian conditioning.

Fear conditioning

A dog hears a tone, but this tone does not signal food. Instead, this tone (CS) is always followed by a footshock (US). The UR produced by the footshock US is, among others, a suppression of any ongoing behaviour. For example, if the animal is pressing a lever to obtain food, its lever-pressing behaviour will be suppressed if we shock the animal. Instead of lever pressing, the animal behaves defensively by freezing. As in the preceding examples, these pairings of a relatively neutral event (the tone) with a biologically significant event (in this case a painful stimulus) generally occur over several trials, but this time the CR elicited by the tone will be a fear reaction! The fear CR can be easily assessed through the behavioural suppression that it produces (Annau and

Kamin 1961; Estes and Skinner 1941). That is, if we present a CS (such as a light or other) that tells the animal that a footshock will be forthcoming, the animal experiences fear of footshock and will suppress any ongoing behavior motivated by a positive outcome such as food (e.g. lever pressing). It is not that the animal can escape shock by suppressing lever pressing or other behaviours when the tone is presented. It is simply that when animals (and humans) feel fear, they frequently suppress other behaviours (see Figure 3.2), probably because, in the past evolutionary history of many species, freezing was an effective way of avoiding being detected by sources of harm such as a hunting carnivore. In this way, we can assess whether the animal is expecting the footshock to occur after the CS. If the animal feels fear, its ongoing behaviour will be suppressed. The index of

Figure 3.2 Conditioned suppression is now a common way of assessing Pavlovian conditioning. In this case, instead of assessing the number of drops of saliva, as in Figure 3.1, we can assess the degree to which the rat freezes upon observation of the light (CS). Before conditioning, the rat in the figure was not afraid of lights and did not freeze when we turned the light on. However, if the rat has learned that the light (CS) will be followed by an electric shock (US), the rat will freeze when we present the light. This shows that fear conditioning has been acquired (i.e. the rat has learned the CS–US association). If we have a computer recording the rat's activity, such as, for example, the number of times that the rat presses a lever to obtain food, and the rat freezes when we present the light, the computer will record a suppression of lever-pressing behaviour when the light is turned on. Thus, suppression of ongoing behaviour can be used to assess whether animals have learned a CS–US association. This technique is more convenient than assessing salivary conditioning, and hence is now more frequently used

learning (the CR), in this case, is the degree to which an ongoing behaviour such as lever pressing is suppressed.

Thus, we have here a procedure which is very similar to the tone–food procedure, but the effect of the tone–footshock pairings is now the conditioning of a fear response. This raises new and interesting questions that go beyond salivary responding. For example, if fear is the result of conditioning because a neutral event is paired with a painful event, does this mean that we can reduce fear if we do the opposite type of conditioning (e.g. would pairing the tone with an appetitive event after it has been paired with shock reduce the fear reaction)? The answer to this question is yes. This technique is called *counterconditioning*. In brief, once a CS has been paired with a US which is aversive (such as footshock – or a scolding by a parent), we can perform countercondition-

ing which consists of pairing that CS with a US which is of the opposite valence (i.e. appetitive), such as food. A clear application of counterconditioning is the treatment of fears in clinical psychology. Alternatively, we can also countercondition an appetitive stimulus by pairing it with an aversive stimulus. This is sometimes used in the treatment of alcoholics by clinical psychologists. Thus, counterconditioning can either be used to give appetitive valence to a previously aversive stimulus or vice versa.

Taste aversion learning

Imagine now a person who eats a certain food and relatively soon feels sick. You have probably experienced something similar yourself. Conditioning here is said to occur because a person (or another animal) that experi-

---

 Case study

Drug addiction learning: tolerance and overdose effects

Like food or footshock, drugs (e.g. heroin) are also USs that produce URs. Thus, when they are taken, they become associated to the CSs that are present (e.g. group of friends or a certain location) and those CSs will end up producing CRs. However, whereas the UR produced by food (salivation) is very similar to the CR produce by a CS which has become associated with food (i.e. the tone also produces salivation after conditioning has taken place), the CRs produced by CSs which are associated with drugs are generally just the opposite reaction (opponent response) to that produced by the drug itself (e.g. alcohol produces hypothermia but the CSs associated with alcohol produce hyperthermia). Like in the case of food, in which the salivary CR served the purpose of preparing the organism to receive food, the opponent CR that produces the CSs associated with drugs also serves the purpose of preparing the organism to receive the drug by compensating for the effect that the drug will produce. In that way, the organism compensates for the effect of the drug, so that, when conditioning has taken place (when one has become a drug addict), the CSs will prepare the organism to receive the drug so that it will be less harmful. However, this opponent reaction produced by the CSs also produces the need to take

the drug in order to compensate for that opponent reaction. Therefore, the initial dose no longer produces the effect the drug addict was seeking because the UR effect is now being compensated for by the opposite CR. This compensation normally results in drug tolerance. As a consequence, drug addicts tend to increase the dose of the drug that they take (see Siegel 1983 for a review on drug tolerance and drug dependence).

One of the most dramatic effects of this process can be seen when, one day, the drug addict takes the drug in a new context (e.g. in a different location or with very different and unfamiliar people). In that new context, the CSs that produce the opponent CR are not present. Hence, the drug addict's body is not prepared to receive the dose that the addict is taking. Interviews with people who have survived after an 'overdose' (Siegel 1984) as well as studies with animals (Siegel *et al.* 1982) suggest that what is commonly known as death by overdose is not always due to an overdose (i.e. the doses are generally not larger than those to which the person is used to). Instead, it is sometimes due to taking the drug in an unfamiliar context. That is, in a context which does not produce the opponent CRs that should have prepared the organism to receive the drug. Thus, death by 'overdose' is sometimes due to taking a regular dose in a new context which does not produce the CRs that should compensate for the effect of the drug.

ences such food–illness relation will probably develop an aversion to that particular food and the mere odour or taste of that food may become a CS which will produce a CR of nausea in the future. If you have been sick after eating a certain food, it is likely that you developed an aversion to that food and avoided eating it again on subsequent occasions. Just thinking of eating it may produce a rather unpleasant CR. Of special interest in this type of conditioning is why you attribute the illness to *that* particular food among the many things that you ate that day. Moreover, why did you attribute it to the food instead of to, say, the people with whom you were eating (or the conversation that you had with them)?

The phenomenon of conditioned taste aversion was first studied by Garcia and Koelling (1966). They gave rats water to which they had added two CSs: a flavour CS and an audio-visual CS. That is, the water was flavoured and the apparatus from which the rats had to lick in order to obtain water produced a flashing light and a sound whenever the rats licked. The primary question was whether the flavour or the audio-visual stimulus would better serve as a CS. The US was either a drug that made the rats feel sick in their stomach or an electric shock to their feet. Thus, the question was, would the rats equally associate illness with a flavour and an audio-visual cue? And would they equally associate the footshock with the flavour and the audio-visual stimulus? In order to test this question, Garcia and Koelling later gave some test trials to the rats with either the flavoured water (and no audio-visual CS present) or the audio-visual water (with no flavour CS present). Garcia and Koelling found that the rats that had been given the drug which made them feel sick refused to drink the flavoured water but not the audio-visual water. Conversely, the rats that had been given the shock US refused to drink the audio-visual water but not the flavoured water. This means that rats tend to associate gastric illnesses more readily with flavours than with audio-visual stimuli; and that, by contrast, flavours do not work very well as cues for pain on the skin such as that produced by footshock (the flavour–shock associations were weaker than the associations formed between the audio-visual cues and the shock). Thus, contrary to what Pavlov thought, not all types of CSs can be equally associated with all types of USs. According to Garcia and Koelling, there is a predisposition which makes us (and other animals) better associate some CSs with some USs. This associative predisposition probably reflects both genetically coded information and prior experience of the human or animal.

Note that this does not mean that we (or rats) cannot associate illness with audio-visual cues. It only means that flavours are more readily associated with illness than are other cues. Indeed, other research has shown that although Garcia and Koelling were correct in concluding that illness is more readily associated with flavours than with other types of CSs, animals do also associate illness with other CSs (P.J. Best *et al*. 1977; Boakes *et al*. 1997; Loy *et al*. 1993). As an example, if you should feel sick after having eaten in a new restaurant, you will probably acquire a conditioned taste aversion to what you ate, but you will also probably acquire an aversive reaction toward the restaurant.

An important clinical application of taste aversion learning can be found in cancer patients who are exposed to chemotherapy (Bernstein 1978, 1991). Because chemotherapy often produces nausea and vomiting, the patient may come to associate that sickness with the CSs that occur close in time (e.g. the flavour of the food that they ate that day), and after some sessions of chemotherapy, many stimuli (flavours of lots of different foods) can become conditioned and will produce CRs of nausea and sickness, which creates a very serious eating problem for the patient. Although important progress has been made concerning how those taste aversions are produced, there is still a need for more research on how taste aversions can be treated. One possibility that researchers are exploring is presenting patients with unusual tastes immediately before chemotherapy so that the taste aversions get conditioned to those unusual flavours rather than interfere with the normal diet. (See also p. 51)

S–S associations between stimuli that are biologically neutral

So far we have seen that in Pavlovian conditioning, organisms associate the mental representations of two stimuli (S1 and S2) and S2 is generally a biologically significant stimulus (a US) which produces URs in the absence of any prior learning. However, as previously mentioned, stimulus–stimulus (S–S) associations can also occur between stimuli that are biologically irrelevant (such as, for example, the learning of an S–S association when these stimuli are both numbers). This type of S–S learning is not called classical conditioning and does not produce CRs (but it is also a form of learning).

Because the learning of associations between representations of neutral stimuli does not produce CRs, its study with animals has been more difficult than with humans. Thus, whereas much of the research on classical conditioning has been performed with non-human animals, much of the research on associations between neutral events has been conducted with humans (but see the case study to learn about studies with neutral events with animals).

Another difference between experiments on Pavlovian conditioning and experiments on associations between biologically neutral events has to do with whether the scientist is interested in the development of the CRs *per se* (e.g. how taste aversions are developed or extinguished in chemotherapy patients) or whether the researcher is interested in how learning occurs. Whereas in the past researchers were primarily con-

cerned with the development of CRs (such as in Pavlov's experiments), many of the current researchers are more concerned with the underlying learning process. In this later case, the CRs, or other types of responses, are used as a mere index to assess whether learning has occurred. Thus, if the researcher is interested, not in the development of a CR, but in whether or not the organism is acquiring an association between the mental representation of two events, such association can be equally assessed through a CR, through a verbal response, or through other means. The generalized use of computers allows present-day researchers to design computer programs in which S1 and S2 are biologically neutral stimuli that are presented through the

---

ψ Case study

How can we know if animals acquire associations between neutral stimuli ?

For many years, scientists believed that learning could not occur if conditioned responses (CRs) were not developed. Thus, because the acquisition of associations between the mental representations of neutral stimuli do not result in the development of CRs, researchers thought that animals could not learn such associations. But how could we even test if animals were able to learn such associations between neutral events? If the experimental subjects were humans, it would be easy: we could simply ask them whether they expect Stimulus 2 (S2) to occur after Stimulus 1 (S1). But how do we ask a rat if it believes that S1 will be followed by S2? Of course, if S2 were a US, the rat would 'answer' by showing a CR when we present S1. But when S2 is a neutral event rather than a US, the rat will not give a CR. Thus, how can we know if the rat has learned? Any ideas?

Scientists have developed an ingenious method for assessing whether animals have learned an S–S association between neutral stimuli. It is called sensory preconditioning (Brogden 1939; Rizley and Rescorla 1972). In a typical sensory preconditioning experiment, there are two groups of rats: the experimental group and the control group. The experimental group is the group that will be allowed to learn that S1 (e.g. a light) predicts S2 (e.g. a tone). Thus, during the first phase of the study, these rats will be exposed to several trials in

which S1 is immediately followed by S2. The control rats, by contrast, will receive unpaired presentations of S1 and S2 during that first phase. If the experimental rats learn the relationship between S1 and S2, they should be able to predict that S2 will occur if we present S1 in a subsequent test phase. However, they will not tell us that they can make such prediction. Thus, what we can do is to add a second training phase which occurs after the rats have experienced the S1→S2 pairings but before testing. In this second phase of the study, we show the two groups that S2 predicts a US (for example, a footshock) by exposing them to several S2→US pairings. Now, we can present S1 at test and see what happens. If the experimental rat has learned that S1 predicts S2, then, when we present S1 at test, the rat will expect it to be followed by S2. And because S2 predicts footshock, a CR will be observed. This is the CR that we need in order to assess whether the learning of the S1→S2 association has occurred. Note that S1 had never been paired with the US, and thus, such CR to S1 would not occur unless the rat had been able to predict that S2 would occur after S1. Rats in the control group, which had not experienced the S1–S2 pairings during Phase 1, do not show a CR when they are exposed to S1 at test. This shows that the CR observed in the experimental group was due to genuine learning of an association between the two neutral stimuli, S1 and S2. Thus, animals, as well as humans, can learn S–S associations between events that do not produce CRs.

computer's screen or speakers, and the keyboard responses (not CRs) of the human volunteers are automatically recorded in a data file in the computer. Thus researchers can easily assess how the learning process takes place under different neutral conditions. This has produced an enormous increase in the amount of research that is being conducted with neutral stimuli and humans subjects. Today, if a researcher wants to know about how learning occurs rather than about the formation of a CR, the experiment can often be simpler with humans than with animals.

One very common type of S–S experiment with humans consists of learning causal relations between two events (e.g. Allan and Jenkins 1983; Matute *et al.* 1996; Shanks and Dickinson 1987; Wasserman 1990a, 1990b). This may sound strange because we have not yet mentioned any relationship between conditioning and causal learning, but conditioning experiments with animals have also been frequently viewed as the animal's learning causal relations between events (e.g. Mackintosh 1977; Tolman and Brunswik 1935). Moreover, we know that the conditions that govern the acquisition of causal relations in humans are similar to those that govern the acquisition of conditioned responses (Shanks 1987). Although the details vary from one experiment to another, the following example illustrates how one of these experiments on human causal learning can be constructed.

Participants are seated in a room with a computer and given instructions on the computer's screen. These instructions tell the participants that they should imagine that they are an allergist who is going to see the medical records of several patients that have developed allergic reactions after taking certain medicines. The task of the participant will be to learn which medicines caused which reactions. Once the participants have read the instructions, the experiment begins. The screen then shows the records of fictitious patients, one at a time. It first shows the medicine that Patient 1 has taken (S1), and then it shows the allergic reaction that this patient has developed (S2). This process will be repeated for Patients 2, 3 and so on. Thus, in this example, each S1–S2 trial is represented by one fictitious patient which has taken one medicine (S1) and has developed a reaction (S2). After the participants have seen a series of trials (i.e. patients), we can ask them to which degree they think that each of the medicines was the cause of the allergic reaction. They normally respond by giving their judgement on a numerical scale (e.g. from 0 to 100) provided by the experimenter. The number that they give is called their causal judgement and it is the index that is

used in these experiments to assess whether learning has taken place. Thus, as you can see, using this index is different from assessing CRs, but serves the same purpose of assessing whether learning has taken place.

But not all experiments involve medicines and allergic reactions, or even test questions and causal judgements. Other experiments may use video games in which S2 is a tank which explodes if it enters a mine filed (S1) in the computer screen (Shanks 1985), yet other experiments use a Martians' invasion (S2) which is predicted by some cues (S1) in the screen (Arcediano *et al.* 1996). In this later case, the acquisition of the association is not necessarily assessed through a causal judgement. Instead, the computer ordinarily records the keys that the participant presses throughout the experiment, and a behavioural change is usually observed when the participant is expecting a Martians' invasion. This behavioural change is not observed in the early trials in which S1 predicts the Martians' invasion but it is gradually observed as learning proceeds. This produces a learning curve similar to that observed in Pavlovian conditioning (see Figure 3.3).

The interesting point when comparing the research on associations between neutral events and the research on associations between biologically significant events is that the same type of results are generally being observed in both cases. That is, even though some studies are more frequently conducted with animals and the other ones with humans, even though some studies produce CRs and the others do not, and even though there are many other important differences in the way that these two types of experiments are being conducted, in both cases, we can see that learning proceeds in a similar way and is similarly sensitive to various experimental manipulations. Thus, in the remainder of this chapter, we will indistinctly refer to either conditioning data or causal judgment data; to animal data or to human data. It must be noted, however, that as this trend to compare these two situations is increasing, some differences between the two situations are starting to show up. The research update on p. 85 shows one of such differences observed between experiments that use biologically significant USs versus those that use biologically neutral stimuli.

Learning to predict that S2 will not occur

So far, we have only considered conditions in which Stimulus 1 (S1) predicted Stimulus 2 (S2). But can we also learn the opposite relation? That is, can we learn that S1 predicts the absence of S2?

Consider, for example, the following experiment with humans using the causal judgement preparation described above. Student subjects are shown the medical records of fictitious patients who have developed allergic reactions after taking some medicines, and are told to figure out which medicines caused the allergic reactions in those patients. The students see the following types of patients: on the one hand, they see many patients that have taken medicine A and have developed the allergic reaction (we can represent this as A+). On the other hand, they also see many patients that have taken medicines A and X simultaneously and these patients have not developed the allergic reaction (represented as AX−). Now, if you were one of the students taking part in such an experiment and were then asked to give your causal judgement about the likelihood of medicines A and X causing the allergic reaction, what would you say ? The rating scale in these cases goes from +100 to −100, with +100 meaning that you are absolutely certain that the medicine produced the allergic reactions, 0 meaning that there is no relation between the medicine and the allergic reaction, and −100 meaning that you are certain that the medicine absolutely prevents (or *inhibits*) the occurrence of the allergic reaction. Most students give a rating close to +100 for medicine A (i.e. they attribute the allergic reaction to A) and a rating close to −100 for medicine X (i.e. they attribute to medicine X inhibitory or preventive properties with respect to the allergic reaction). Thus, this shows not only that we can learn when one stimulus (e.g. A) predicts S2 (the allergic reaction), but also that we can learn when another stimulus (e.g. X) predicts that S2 will not occur.

This has been demonstrated with human subjects (e.g. Chapman 1991; Chapman and Robins 1990; though their procedure was slightly different from the one described here) as well as with animals. With animal subjects, this was demonstrated long ago by Pavlov (1927) and has been generally called Pavlovian Conditioned Inhibition. When this type of experiment is run with animals, A and X are usually lights and tones, S2 (the allergic reaction in our example) is usually food or footshock, and the index of learning is the degree to which the CR is inhibited when X is presented (e.g. inhibition of a salivary or a fear CR) rather than a causal judgement. Otherwise, the experiment works much the same way, and animals also learn to predict when the US will not be presented, and show it by inhibiting the CR in the presence of X that should otherwise have been observed (see also Rescorla 1969).

One important factor in the development of these inhibitory reactions is that they can be acquired only if the context in which they are learned is a context which has been associated to S2. That is, imagine a dog that is given X→no shock training. Unless the dog had any reason for expecting the shock to occur in such a context (i.e. unless the context were associated with shock), the dog would not interpret such X→no shock pairings as X→no shock, but simply as X. The same is true for our medicine example above. If participants judge medicine X as preventing the development of an allergic reaction it is because they had a reason to expect the allergic reaction (i.e. medicine X was taken in compound with medicine A, which was a medicine strongly associated with the development of the allergic reaction, and hence, A played the role of the context which should produce the allergic reaction unless X prevented its occurrence).

Extinction and spontaneous recovery

One of the things that Pavlov noted in his classical conditioning experiments was that, after conditioning had occurred, if the CS was repeatedly presented alone (i.e. without the US), the CR would gradually disappear. This is called *extinction* of the CR. You have probably experienced a similar process many times in the past. For example, you may have associated a given perfume or music (CS) with a given person (US) and this may have produced some emotional CRs after several pairings. Moreover, even if you had not listened to that music or smelled that perfume again in many years, the CRs would still occur if you were now exposed to the CS again. That is, CRs are generally not 'forgotten' by the mere passage of time (although there may be some decrease in the magnitude of the CR). However, if you continue exposing yourself to the CS when the US is not present (you listen to that music over and over in the absence of the US), the CRs will eventually extinguish (i.e. become successively smaller and finally vanish).

This is shown in Figure 3.3, which first shows (Panel A) how the responses are gradually acquired in most learning situations, and then shows (Panel B) how the responses are gradually extinguished. Moreover, we also know that extinction does not imply unlearning or forgetting (Bouton 1993; Pavlov 1927; Rescorla 1996). For example, once extinction has taken place, if the subject is not exposed to either the CS or the US for some time (Panel C), and then we present again the CS in order to test whether it would produce a response (Panel D), it does produce a response. This restoration of responding

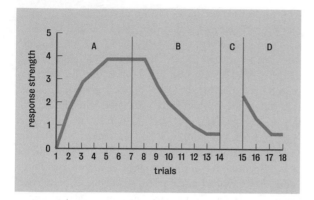

Figure 3.3 Hypothetical data from a learning experiment. Panel A shows how the response strength increases during each of the acquisition trials in which the CS is followed by the US. Panel B shows how the response strength is reduced during each of the extinction trials in which the CS alone is presented. Panel C shows a rest period in which no CSs or USs are presented. In Panel D, only the CS is presented. Note that the response is spontaneously recovered in this example when the CS is again presented in trial 15 after the rest period. However, it is then extinguished again as a result of further repeated presentations of the CS alone.

is called *spontaneous recovery* because the response is spontaneously recovered (by the mere passage of time) after it had been extinguished. Once a response has been recovered, it can either be re-conditioned or re-extinguished, and this time, either process will usually be easier than the first time. This has important implications in clinical psychology. After therapists have been able to extinguish a problematic response in a patient (e.g. a fear response), they must be aware that the response is potentially subject to spontaneous recovery over time. Thus, the patient will need to be monitored for future possible re-treatments, after the response is extinguished.

Generalization and discrimination

Another process of which we have to be aware is generalization. If subjects learn an association between two stimuli, S1 and S2, they will probably transfer what they learned to other stimuli that are similar to S1. Thus, if a dog has learned that a tone is followed by food, it will probably salivate not only at the sound of that particular tone, but also at other tones which are relatively similar to the original S1. The greater the similarity between the original S1 and the probe stimulus, the greater the transfer will be. This process allows us and other animals to efficiently use previous knowledge in new situations.

Otherwise, we would have to undergo the whole process of new learning every time that we encountered a situation which was not exactly the same one in which our learning had taken place. And in practice exactly the same situation never arises twice.

But there might be situations in which we do not want the CR (or the causal judgement or the predictive behaviour) to generalize to other similar situations. In this case, we must use a discrimination procedure to teach the subject to discriminate between those stimuli that are followed by S2, and those that are not followed by S2. For example, learning that a given medicine produces an allergic reaction could produce the generalized belief that all medicines produce the allergic reaction. Thus, in order to discriminate, the subject must also be exposed to medicines that do not produce the allergic reaction (e.g. Matute *et al.* 1996). The way in which Pavlov used to do this with his dogs was by exposing them to some CSs that were followed by food, and also to CSs that were followed by the absence of food. In that way, the animals were able to discriminate between the CSs that produced food and those that did not. In consequence, the CR tended to concentrate only around the CSs that produced the food. Similarly, in a human experiment using the Martians video game mentioned above, college students were trained to predict that colour blue would be followed by a Martians' invasion, whereas colour yellow would not (Arcediano *et al.* 1996). But in order to learn this, subjects needed to be exposed to both conditions. If they were exposed only to the blue→invasion relation, then they would also expect the invasion in the presence of other colours that we might test after learning had occurred (i.e. generalization).

This discrimination training procedure is also known as differential inhibition, because, presumably, inhibition is acquired with respect to the stimulus that signals the absence of S2, but not with respect to the stimulus that signals the presence of S2. The stimulus that signals that S2 will occur is called the excitatory stimulus (or S+) and the stimulus that signals that S2 will not occur is called the inhibitory stimulus (or S−).

Theories of S–S learning

S–R versus S–S theories

Many psychologists believed that the important association going on in classical conditioning was the one that become established between the CS and the response (e.g. Hull 1943), that is, the **S–R association**. For example, after several trials in which the tone was followed by food (and thus by salivation), the dog came to associate, according to S–R theories, the tone with the salivary response. And this was the reason why the tone ended up eliciting salivation. If you think carefully about the implications of this view, you will notice that S–R theory does not assume that the dog has learned to predict when food will be available. It simply assumes that the tone will produce salivation because tone and salivation have occurred together many times. This theory was more mechanical than current theories, and did not assume the existence of any cognitive processes in the mind of the dog or the human which had been conditioned (see Rescorla 1988 for further elaboration on differences between this view and today's view).

Instead, according to current stimulus–stimulus (S–S) theories, the important association is the one formed between the mental representations of the two stimuli, that is, the one that allows the animal to predict Stimulus 2 (S2) on the presence of Stimulus 1 (S1). Modern psychology has shown that there are many cases in which CRs do not occur (and therefore, S–R associations cannot be formed) and even so, organisms are able to learn that one stimulus predicts another. As an example, consider sensory preconditioning (see case study on p. 75). In sensory preconditioning experiments, animals are able to learn an association between two stimuli that are biologically irrelevant, and which do not produce URs or CRs. Thus, those experiments cannot be explained by assuming that an S–R association is what the animal acquires. Moreover, S–R theories would not be able to account for any of the examples of learning of causal or predictive relations between neutral stimuli in humans. Although modern psychology assumes that S–R associations are formed in many situations (Dickinson 1989), it also assumes that S–S associations, rather than S–R associations, are necessary to explain the vast majority of findings in learning research (Dickinson 1980).

Contiguity theory

Temporal and spatial contiguity is one of the most important conditions that modulate the establishment of associations (Pavlov 1927). As an example, consider an experiment in which there are several groups of subjects. All of them are exposed to the same CSs and USs (same intensity, etc.) and for the same number of trials. However, in one group the US always occurs immediately after the CS, whereas in other groups we vary the interval between the CS and the US. The longer the

CS–US interval (onset to onset), the weaker the CR that will be observed. Even in situations such as taste aversion learning, in which the delay between the CS and the US can be relatively long, the effect of varying the CS–US interval can also be detrimental in the formation of associations (e.g. if we feel sick one day at 6 p.m. we will probably associate our illness with something that we ate for lunch a few hours earlier, but not with something that we ate the day before). Thus, contiguity between S1 and S2 modulates the acquisition of associations.

But Pavlov's theory stated that contiguity was the only important factor which determined the formation of associations. According to Pavlov, when a CS and a US occurred contiguous in time, a connection was formed between the CS centre and the US centre in the brain and, in that way, the CS gradually came to substitute for the US in eliciting the response. Pavlov's contiguity theory has been challenged by the results of several experiments that showed that contiguity was not the only condition that enabled the formation of associations. Some of those experiments are described next.

Some problems with contiguity theory

Contingency
Rescorla (1968) conducted an interesting experiment that showed that contiguity between two events was not the only important factor that affects associative learning. He used several groups of animals that he exposed to several pairings of CS–US (tone–shock). However, he also inserted trials in which the US was presented in the absence of the CS. For some animals, there were few of those US-alone trials, for other animals there were as many USs in the absence as in the presence of the CS. Now, what would you think if you were exposed to those conditions? For example, consider the case in which the probability of the US when the CS is presented, p(US | CS), equals the probability that the US will occur when the CS is not present, p(US | noCS). That is, a footshock (US) occurs with the same probability when a tone (CS) is on or when the tone is off (noCS). Do you think that the animal should acquire any special fear reaction to the tone? Surely not. The tone has no informative value. It does not help the animal predict when a footshock is about to occur.

Thus, what Rescorla observed was that, despite all subjects being exposed to the same number of CS–US pairings and to the identical CS–US contiguity, reducing the informative value (i.e. contingency) of the CS by inserting several US-alone trials, produced a dramatic decrease in the magnitude of the CR. The strongest CRs were observed when the positive contingency was strongest. That is, when the probability of the US in the presence of the CS was much larger than the probability of the US in the absence of the CS. In those cases, the occurrence of the US was contingent (depended) on the occurrence of the CS. Thus, the CS had a great predictive value, and subjects learned that the CS was an accurate signal of when the US would be presented. According to Pavlov, all groups should have acquired a similar fear response because all of them had been exposed to the identical contiguity during the identical number of CS–US pairings. Thus, this effect shows that, in addition to contiguity, the informative value of the CS (or, in other words, the contingency between the CS and the US) is also an important factor. Note, however, that contingency alone is also unable to explain learning because it cannot explain how the learning curve occurs in a trial-by-trial basis. That is, if contingency were the only important factor, we should expect a flat learning curve, with subjects detecting the degree of contingency in the same way in any learning trial. However, the learning curve typically observed in learning situations (see Figure 3.3) suggests a gradual process in which the acquired associations are strengthened or weakened over the learning trials.

Overshadowing

Imagine now a situation in which two CSs are presented in compound as signals of a US. For example, two different tones are presented simultaneously and followed by food. Would the two tones acquire the capacity to elicit a CR? According to contiguity theory, if the two tones are equally contiguous to the food, the two of them should acquire a CR of similar magnitude. However, many experiments have shown that one of the two CSs frequently acquires greater response potential and overshadows the other CS. The weaker CS elicits a response if trained individually, but becomes overshadowed if trained in compound with the strongest CS. Apparently, the stronger CS *competes* with the weaker one. This was first observed by Pavlov (1927) and has been later demonstrated in many different situations. Contiguity theory cannot explain why this occurs.

Forward blocking

Another experiment that was critical in showing that Pavlov's contiguity theory did not suffice to explain learning was Kamin's (1968) blocking experiment. (The word 'blocking', unless otherwise stated, normally refers to forward blocking; later in this chapter you will see some examples of a different type of blocking which has been demonstrated more recently and which is ordinarily called backward blocking.) Kamin exposed an experimental group of animals to several pairings of CS1 followed by a US during the first phase of the study (i.e. CS1→US). Then in Phase 2, he continued using the CS1→US pairings but he added a new CS (CS2) which was presented in compound with CS1. Thus, during Phase 2, both CS1 and CS2 were potential predictors of the US (i.e. CS1–CS2→US). According to Pavlov, both CSs should become associated with the US because both of them were contiguous with the US. To test this expectation, Kamin then presented CS2 alone during a subsequent test phase. If it had become associated to the US, it should produce the CR. But it did not! Moreover, this failure to respond to CS2 did not occur in a control group that had not been exposed to the initial CS1→US pairings during Phase 1 but that had received the identical CS1–CS2→US treatment during Phase 2. Thus, the control group demonstrated that the number of CS2→US pairings had been sufficient because good responding was observed in the control group. Then why was responding to CS2 *blocked* in the experimental group? According to Kamin, the experimental subjects had previously learned that CS1 produced the US, and thus the subsequent introduction of CS2 as a predictor was absolutely redundant. The animals did not need an additional predictor to know when the US was going to occur. Animals were already responding to CS1 and the occurrences of the US were not surprising at all. As a consequence, according to Kamin, the association between CS2 and the US could not be acquired. This suggests that only USs that are surprising can become associated to CSs.

For an example of how blocking works in humans, consider the medicines and allergies experiments previously described. Imagine that you are taking part in one of those experiments and you see many patients who have developed the allergic reaction after taking medicine A, and that later, you see patients who have taken medicines A and X simultaneously and they also develop the allergic reaction. Would you attribute the allergic reaction to medicine X? Why not? If contiguity theory were correct, seeing a sufficient number of patients that have developed the allergic reaction after they had taken A and X (thus allowing for contiguity between X and the reaction) should produce good learning. However, we tend to attribute the allergic reaction to medicine A rather than X if we have previously learned that A alone is sufficient to produce the effect and it is present on the subsequent training trials with X.

Note that the effect of forward blocking can also be regarded as the effect of previous knowledge. For example, you may develop an allergic reaction after having eaten shrimps (A) and potatoes (X). But despite the allergic reaction being equally contingent and contiguous with both the shrimps and the potatoes you will probably attribute the allergic reaction to the shrimps, and will probably discount the potential causal role of the potatoes, correct? Why? You probably have some previous knowledge that shrimps may produce allergic reactions. Previous knowledge comes from a previously established association between shrimps and allergic reactions. And this association *competes* with the association between potatoes and allergic reactions.

Thus we now know that, in addition to contiguity (Pavlov 1927) and contingency (Rescorla 1968), it is also important that there are no competing associations in order to observe a CR or a causal or a predictive judgement. Note, however, that the concept of contingency can be regarded as showing the importance of an absence of competing associations. That is, contingency refers to whether S2 occurs in the absence of S1 (as well as contiguously with it), but this can be regarded as the formation of competing associations because when the S2-alone trials occur, S2 necessarily becomes associated to other cues (e.g. background cues that are present in the experimental context). Thus, in addition to contiguity, most current associative theories have emphasized the importance of an absence of competing associations for the occurrence of a CR or a causal judgement (e.g. Rescorla and Wagner 1972).

Inhibitory learning

Consider also the examples on inhibitory learning described above in which a subject (human or animal) learned to predict that S2 would not occur (e.g. when subjects attributed to medicine X preventive or inhibitory properties with respect to the allergic reaction). If S2 (e.g. an allergic reaction) does not occur when S1 is presented (medicine X), S2 is not contiguous to S1. Thus, contiguity theory cannot explain such learning. Then, how does inhibitory learning occur?

The concept of contingency could perhaps provide an explanation for inhibitory learning because, in these cases, S2 (the allergic reaction) is occurring with greater frequency in the absence than in the presence of S1 (medicine X). Indeed, if you recall the examples of inhibitory learning described above, the allergic reac-

tion occurred when medicine A was taken but not when medicine X was taken. Thus, the probability of the reaction (S2) was greater in the absence than in the presence of S1 (medicine X). This is a negative contingency situation in which S2 is contingent (depends) on the non-occurrence of S1. These negative contingency situations result in the inhibition rather than elicitation of the CR or the causal judgement. Also, if you think about this, you will note that this probably occurs because the allergic reaction (S2) was associated with medicine A rather than with our critical S1 (medicine X). Thus, we could also say that inhibitory learning occurs because S2 is associated with a competing stimulus (such as medicine A or background contextual cues), during the trials in which S2 occurred in the absence of S1. This could explain inhibitory learning as a type of competition by the CSs (or contextual cues) that are present in the experimental situation. Several other possibilities have also been considered and it is not yet clear how we should best explain inhibitory learning. What appears clear is that learning to predict the absence of an event implies that such event was in some way expected (e.g. because it was associated to something in that context) and its absence when the CS was presented was noticed (see Mackintosh 1983 for further elaboration of these issues).

CS-pre-exposure and US-pre-exposure effects

Now imagine that one day you feel sick after having eaten bread. You will probably attribute your illness to some other thing that you ate rather than to the bread. Moreover, if you ate something new that day you will almost certainly attribute your illness to that new food. The reason is that you have probably eaten bread many times in the past and those experiences have never been followed by illness. Thus, even though you now felt sick after eating bread, you probably would not associate your illness with bread. In this case, we say that you were pre-exposed to the CS (bread) in the absence of the US and this made the formation of a CS–US association unlikely. That is, novelty is one more factor that influences conditioning.

Once again we can see that contiguity between the CS and the US is not sufficient for the establishment of an association. If subjects receive exposure to either the CS alone or the US alone before the CS is paired to the US in a conventional conditioning paradigm, conditioning becomes retarded (e.g. Lubow and Moore 1959; Randich and LoLordo 1979). For example, a dog that has heard a tone several times before conditioning will later have difficulties in associating that particular tone with food during the conditioning stage. The same occurs when the subjects are exposed to the US alone before conditioning. If contiguity between a CS and a US during the conditioning stage were the only necessary condition for the formation of associations, pre-exposure to either the CS or the US alone should be irrelevant. But it is not. Why? There are several potential explanations. On the one hand, we could assume that if a subject is exposed to either the CS alone or the US alone, the subject will learn that the CS or the US is unrelated to anything significant. Thus, subjects should later have difficulties in associating that stimulus to another one (e.g. Baker and Mackintosh 1977). Another potential explanation is that the pre-exposed stimulus becomes associated to the context in which it is being presented, and thus, its potential to become associated to another stimulus during the conditioning stage becomes reduced (e.g. Wagner 1981).

Current theories

Psychologists have developed several associative theories that improve on Pavlov's view concerning how the associations are acquired and strengthened in a trial by trial basis (e.g. Mackintosh 1975; Pearce and Hall 1980; Rescorla and Wagner 1972). Most current associative theories are formalized by a mathematical equation which captures the basic assumptions that these theories make about how the learning process occurs during each learning trial. At first, it may sound strange to see that a learning theory can be summarized as an equation. Note, however, that qualitative theories are generally imprecise. That is, they do not allow us to make specific predictions for specific situations. For example, so far we have seen that for learning to occur, S2 must be surprising (i.e. the degree to which a CS will be blocked is directly related to the extent to which the US is predicted by another CS). But what we do exactly mean, for example, by *being predicted*; or when exactly can we say that the US is *surprising*? Formalizing these ideas into a mathematical model allows researchers to better know what the specific predictions of each theory are. Moreover, this allows researchers to write the theories into computer programs that should be able to 'learn' in the way predicted by the theory (e.g. see Mercier 1996 for a computer simulation of Rescorla and Wagner's and Pearce and Hall's theories).

By writing computer simulations of learning theories, the data from experiments can be more easily contrasted with the predictions of each of the different theories and a better assessment of these theories is possible as a function of how well each computer simulation fits the experimental data. Perhaps the most widely known of these theories is the one developed by Rescorla and Wagner (1972). Although the Rescorla-Wagner model is not a perfect theory of learning, it is probably the theory that has generated more experiments than any other model (see R.R. Miller *et al.* 1995, for a detailed assessment of the successes and failures of this theory). Interestingly, this theory is very similar to the 'delta' rule, commonly used in cognitive science as well as in the construction of machine learning programs by computer scientists (see Gluck and Bower 1988; Lieberman 1990). This similarity between current learning theories and the delta rule is another factor which has contributed to the current interest in associative theories, which are now no longer restricted to the psychology of learning, but are being explored in many different areas of scientific research.

The Rescorla and Wagner Model

Without going into the details of the equation (see Rescorla and Wagner 1972 and Mercier 1996 if you would like to know more about it), according to the Rescorla-Wagner model, when a CS and a US occur contiguous in time during a learning trial, the association between them will be strengthened only if the US was unexpected. Consider for example the learning curve in Panel A of Figure 3.3. During the early trials, the US is unexpected (there are no previous associations to the US); thus, it becomes more and more strongly associated to the CS. Note also that the increment of the associative strength during each of the early learning trials is large, and certainly much larger than the increase that occurs during each of the later trials (see Panel A of Figure 3.3). This is because the discrepancy between what the subject is expecting to occur after the CS and what actually occurs is large during the early trials (at first the subject does not expect the US to occur after the CS). However, this discrepancy between the subject's expectations and what actually occurs becomes gradually reduced as learning proceeds and the subject learns to predict the US after the CS. Thus, for each trial, the equation captures the difference between what the organism is expecting and what actually occurs, and this produces the typical learning curve.

If you now look at the extinction curve in Panel B of Figure 3.3, this process works symmetrically. During the first extinction trials, the subject is fully expecting the US to occur, but it does not occur. Thus, its absence is surprising and much learning (in this case, unlearning) can be accomplished. Gradually, the subject comes to expect that the US will no longer occur, and thus, its absence is not surprising anymore. At this point, no more extinction can take place. Thus, this model can explain the shape of the acquisition curve (Panel A), and superficially it also explains the shape of the extinction curve (panel B). But does it really explain extinction? The Rescorla-Wagner model fails because it explains extinction as if it were unlearning. Recall that the phenomenon of spontaneous recovery – and several other findings – show that extinction is not unlearning (see Bouton 1993; Pavlov 1927; Rescorla 1996). Although the phenomena of extinction and spontaneous recovery have been known since Pavlov's days, their explanation has remained elusive. Indeed, they are still a matter of research (e.g. Bouton 1993; Rescorla 1996).

Consider now a blocking experiment. During Phase 1, the subjects learn to fully predict the US any time that CS1 is presented. Thus, when in Phase 2 we introduce CS2 in compound with CS1 (i.e. CS1–CS2→US), the US is by then fully predicted by CS1 and thus, no more learning can occur. The CS2→US association cannot be acquired according to the Rescorla-Wagner model. Thus, according to this model, blocking is a failure to learn the CS2→US association that occurs because the companion stimuli of CS2 (i.e. CS1) fully predicts the US when CS2 is first presented.

If you think of other phenomena described so far, you will notice that this same process can also explain the US-pre-exposure effect (but not the CS-pre-exposure effect). That is, when the US is pre-exposed before conditioning, it becomes associated to the context in which it is being pre-exposed. Thus, the pre-exposure phase can be regarded as a CS1–US training, with CS1 being the experimental context. Then, when we present our target CS (let us call it CS2) followed by the US during the conditioning stage, the context is also present and can play the role of a blocking CS that blocks responding to our target CS (i.e. CS2). Similarly, contingency experiments can also be explained by assuming that when we present the US in the absence of the CS, what we are actually doing is pairing the experimental context with the US. Thus, by the same reasoning as above, the context–US association will again compete with the association between the target CS and the US.

In summary, the association between a CS and a US that are present in a given learning trial will be strengthened only if the CS is not yet fully predicting the US, and also, if there are no other CSs present that are fully predicting the US because they have strong associations to the same US. If other CSs that are associated to the same US were present (including background contextual CSs) and these CSs were already fully predicting the US, then the US would not surprise the subject and thus, would not become associated with the target CS.

Problems with the Rescorla-Wagner model

Apart from the extinction and spontaneous recovery problems mentioned above, there are several other phenomena that are problematic for the Rescorla-Wagner model (see R.R. Miller *et al.* 1995 for a detailed review). One of these problems is the CS-pre-exposure effect. The Rescorla-Wagner model assumes that learning depends on variations on the effectiveness of the US: as conditioning proceeds and the US becomes being predicted by the CSs present in the situation, the ability of the US to enter into associations becomes reduced. Thus, this model cannot explain why presentations of the CS alone before conditioning should affect subsequent learning of a CS–US association (Baker and Mackintosh 1977). Indeed, explaining the CS-pre-exposure effect is problematic. One possibility is that during the pre-exposure stage subjects learn that the CS does not predict anything important. Then at the conditioning stage they should learn that the CS predicts a US but their initial expectation that the CS predicts nothing makes the new learning difficult (Mackintosh 1975). Several other possibilities have also been suggested (e.g. Pearce and Hall 1980; Wagner 1981) but it is not yet clear how we should best explain this effect.

One of the major problems for associative theories such as that of Rescorla and Wagner (1972; see also Mackintosh 1975; Pearce and Hall 1980) has been the observation of *backward blocking* and other retrospective revaluation effects. If you recall the *forward blocking* effect previously described, it referred to a situation in which the subjects had *previous* knowledge that, for example, medicine A produced an allergic reaction, and this made them discount the potential causal role of a second medicine, say medicine X, that the patients had taken in compound with medicine A. The interesting point for our present purposes is that blocking has also been observed in situations in which the medicine A→allergic reaction association is acquired *subsequently*. That is, imagine that you have taken two medicines, A and X, and have developed an allergic reaction. You might well attribute your allergic reaction to both A and X. However, if you *later* learn that medicine A, taken alone, frequently produces allergic reactions, you will probably *retrospectively* discount the potential causal role that you might had initially attributed to medicine X. This is called a backward blocking effect because it is the result of subsequent rather than previous knowledge. This has been demonstrated using several different procedures with either human (Chapman 1991; Shanks 1985) or non-human animals (Denniston *et al.* 1996; Miller and Matute 1996). In addition to backward blocking, several other types of retrospective revaluation effects, showing that organisms re-evaluate their initial attributions, have also been reported (Baker and Mercier 1989; Miller and Matzel 1988). Backward blocking and retrospective revaluation effects are something that traditional associative theories (e.g. Rescorla and Wagner 1972) cannot explain because they assume that only stimuli that actually occur during a given learning trial can be learned about (only the stimuli that are present in a given learning trial enter into the equation for that trial). That is, those models cannot explain learning about a stimulus (medicine X) which is presented neither during or after acquisition of the competing A–US association. Thus, the subsequent learning about A cannot affect what subjects had already learned about X, because X is no longer present at the time in which subjects are learning about A. According to Rescorla and Wagner, what we learn about X cannot be retrospectively revaluated once we have learned it.

One possibility to explain backward blocking and retrospective revaluation effects is the so-called Comparator Hypothesis, suggested by Miller and Matzel (1988). According to these authors, blocking is not a failure to acquire associations as it is regarded to be by the Rescorla and Wagner model. Instead, they suggest, like Pavlov did, that contiguity between a CS and a US is sufficient for the formation of associations. Thus, even the 'blocked' CSs are learned about if they have occurred contiguously with a US, regardless of whether or not other CSs are present. Thus, in a typical forward blocking experiment, subjects would learn about both medicines, A and X, despite the allergic reaction being fully predicted by A by the time that X is initially presented. However, they also point out that some associations are stronger than others. Thus, after learning has

taken place, if the associative strength of A (i.e. the strength of its association with the allergic reaction) is stronger than the associative strength of X (and X and A are themselves strongly associated because they have occurred in compound), this will result in our discounting the potential role of X in producing the allergic reaction. The same would also be true for an animal discounting the potential role of a light in predicting the US, if the light had been trained in compound with a tone and the strength of the tone→US association were stronger than the light→US association. Thus, according to these authors, a comparison between the strength of the different associations *after* learning has taken place (not during learning) is what determines our favouring some CSs and blocking other CSs as potential causes of S2. This allows this theory to predict both traditional (forward) blocking and backward blocking, because, if the comparison that leads to blocking occurs once learning has proceeded, then the order in which we encounter the information (either previously or subsequently) should be irrelevant (see also Baker and Mercier 1989 for a related account).

But there is also a different possibility that several researchers have considered. Imagine, for example, a backward blocking experiment in which subjects first are exposed to the CS1–CS2→US pairings and then are exposed to the CS1→US pairings. We could assume that what the subjects learn during Phase 2 is not only that CS1 produces the US, but also that CS2 does not produce the US. Thus, each of the CS1→US pairings that occur during Phase 2 will strengthen the CS1→US association but will weaken the CS2→US association because CS2 is not presented when the US occurs during Phase 2. Several researchers have suggested that this assumption can be incorporated into the Rescorla-Wagner model by making a very slight modification in the original Rescorla-Wagner equation. This consists of assuming that when a stimulus is expected to occur in a given trial but it does not occur (e.g. when subjects have been experiencing compound presentations of CS1 and CS2 during the first phase of a study, and then only CS1 occurs during Phase 2), the representation of the absent stimulus (CS2) becomes negatively activated in the trials in which it is not presented. Representing the stimuli that are absent (such as CS2 in this case) with a negative activation value in the equation produces a decrease in the strength of its association to the US (Dickinson and Burke 1996; Markman 1989; Tassoni

Research update

Biologically significant stimuli appear to be resistant to backward blocking

In the past, experiments on learning used to be conducted almost exclusively with animals. Moreover, they used to be almost exclusively conditioning experiments with biologically significant outcomes (i.e. USs). Since the mid-1980s, however, there has been an enormous increase in the amount of research that is being conducted with human subjects as well as in the amount of research that is not primarily concerned with the development of CRs (e.g. pure S1–S2 learning research with S2, not being biologically significant). The clearest finding of this recent trend is that much of the major learning phenomena can be observed with either animal or human subjects; as well as with CS–US, cause–effect tasks, or absolutely neutral S1–S2 situations. For example, Kamin's (1968) forward blocking effect was initially demonstrated in animal conditioning but has now also been shown in human Pavlovian conditioning (Martin and Levey 1991), as well as in human causal judgement situations (Shanks 1985).

However, the phenomenon called backward blocking was initially demonstrated in human causal judgement (Shanks 1985) but could not be demonstrated in animals during many years (see R.R Miller *et al.* 1990). Backward blocking implies retrospective revaluation of initial attributions (see text), and thus, it appeared possible that perhaps humans were able to retrospectively re-evaluate their initial attributions, but animals were not able to do so. It could also mean that perhaps causal judgement is subject to retrospective re-evaluation,

but Pavlovian conditioning is not. However, recent experiments have shown that backward blocking can occur in rats, as long as rats are exposed to S1–S2 pairings in which S1 and S2 are neutral stimuli rather than S2 being a biologically significant US (Denniston *et al.* 1996; Miller and Matute 1996). Thus, we now know that rats, as well as humans, are able to retrospectively re-evaluate their initial attributions. In consequence, the theories that explained these effects in humans (e.g. Dickinson and Burke 1996; Miller and Matzel 1988) can also be applied to animal learning. However, these experiments also suggest that backward blocking can occur only in neutral S1–S2 learning situations. This is at variance with the general view stated through this chapter that Pavlovian conditioning is equivalent to S1–S2 learning, where S1 and S2 are neutral stimuli. Thus, even though conditioning and the acquisition of associations between neutral events generally work in the same way, and even though most learning phenomena can be observed in both situations, there appear to be some exceptions. Some phenomena, like backward blocking, can be observed in neutral S1–S2 learning with either humans or animals, but has not yet been observed in conditioning situations with either humans or animals. For some yet unknown reason, stimuli that are inherently biologically significant (such as food, water and sex, i.e. USs), or stimuli which have previously acquired biological significance by means of their pairings with a US, appear to be resistant to backward and forward blocking (Denniston *et al.* 1996; Hall *et al.* 1977; LoLordo *et al.* 1982; Miller and Matute 1996).

1995; Van Hamme and Wasserman 1994). In this way, each of the CS1→US pairings of Phase 2 results in some unlearning of the association between the absent CS (CS2) and the US. Thus, this particular revision of the Rescorla-Wagner model can also explain backward blocking and other retrospective revaluation effects. At the present time, either this negative activation view or the comparator view mentioned in the above paragraph (Baker and Mercier 1989; Miller and Matzel 1988)

appear to be equally able to explain most of the data available on retrospective revaluation effects. The main difference between these two views is that the negative activation view assumes that backward blocking is due to unlearning whereas the comparator view assumes that it is the result of a post-learning comparison of the strength with which each of the CSs is associated with the US. Further research is needed to better discriminate between these two views.

ψ Section summary

We generally speak of stimulus–stimulus (S–S) learning when an association is formed between the mental representation of two stimuli. The acquisition of these associations allows us to predict that the second stimulus will occur upon observation of the occurrence of the first one. Pavlovian (or classical) conditioning is an example of this type of learning. In this case, an initially neutral stimulus (the CS) becomes associated to a biologically significant US such as food or a painful event. Fear conditioning, taste aversions and drug addictions are some examples of classical conditioning. The S–S learning that occurs in classical conditioning frequently results in the elicitation of a conditioned response (CR). But S–S learning can also occur in situations in which no USs are involved and no CRs are elicited (as in the learning of associations between neutral events by humans or animals). The learning of causal relations is an example of S–S learning which does not necessarily involve USs and CRs. In S–S learning, contiguity between the two stimuli is an important factor in the formation of associations, but not the only one. Current theories of associative learning, such as that of Rescorla and Wagner, take into account, not only contiguity, but also the degree to which the second stimulus is surprising. This theory can explain many of the learning phenomena described in this section but it also presents several problems which have not yet been fully solved (see text).

1   How many examples of Pavlovian conditioning can you think of?
2   What does the learning of causal relations have to do with Pavlovian conditioning?
3   How does the Rescorla-Wagner model explain blocking? Which are the strengths and weakness of this theory?

◻ Response–outcome associations

So far, we have seen many examples of stimulus–stimulus (S–S) learning, but you have probably noted that what we call S–S learning does not cover all types of learning. One important feature of S–S learning is that it enables us and other animals to predict our environment (e.g. to predict a dangerous situation). However, it does not allow us to control our environment (for example, it does not allow us to avoid danger once we have predicted that a harmful event is about to occur). To use a different example, imagine a dog which is exposed to tone–food pairings. The animal can learn to predict when the food is about to be presented and will learn to react accordingly (e.g. the dog will salivate when the tone is presented). However, S–S learning alone does not allow the animal to control its environment. That is, the dog could not obtain more food if its only way of learning and responding were Pavlovian (i.e. S–S learning). This is because, in classical conditioning, the food and the tone are contingent (i.e. the presence of the food depends upon the tone), whereas the food and the dog's behaviour are not contingent.

Thus, there are other forms of learning in which, instead of learning about the relationship between environmental events (e.g. tone and food), organisms can also learn about relationships between their own behaviour and environmental events. For example, a rat may learn to predict when a shock is about to occur, but it may also learn that pressing a lever prevents the shock from occurring. In such cases, we say that the rat has learned a relationship between its response (in this case, lever pressing) and an environmental outcome (no shock).

The learning of response–outcome (R–O) associations can be said to occur in much the same way as does the learning of S–S associations, although it raises some additional and interesting issues because the first event in the association is not an environmental event such as a CS, but is our own behaviour. Thus, how does our future behaviour change when our own behaviour, rather than a CS, is followed by a reinforcer such as food? Consider the rat in Figure 3.4. If the rat presses the lever, it will obtain food. Moreover, the occurrence of the food is now contingent on the lever-pressing response rather than on the occurrence of a CS. Of course the rat will also salivate in this situation, much the same as Pavlov's dog did. However, we can also observe how the rat's lever-pressing behaviour changes as it learns how to obtain the reinforcer (e.g. food). Once the rat has learned the relationship between the food and lever pressing, it will press the lever anytime that it is hungry. This process is called instrumental conditioning (or learning). Tolman (1932) defined instrumental behavior as *purposive behaviour*, because, unlike Pavlovian responding, instrumental responding occurs with the purpose of obtaining something or avoiding something (but not all psychologists agreed on this definition; see e.g. Skinner 1953). Thus, the responses that are acquired or maintained in this way are generally referred to as **instrumental responses** because they serve as instruments to obtain certain outcomes. Instrumental conditioning refers to how such instrumental responses are acquired and maintained; the learning of R–O associations is a more theoretical term which refers to the underlying learning which presumably takes place.

The learning of an R–O association may or may not be always reflected in an instrumental response. For example, a rat may have learned that pressing a lever produces a certain outcome, but the rat will ordinarily not press the lever unless it wants to obtain that outcome (e.g. Dickinson and Balleine 1994). Thus, the observation of instrumental responses implies that the R–O association has been acquired, just as much as the occurrence of a CR during Pavlovian conditioning indicated that the CS–US association had been acquired. However, like in Pavlovian conditioning, an absence of an instrumental (or Pavlovian) response does not necessarily mean that the organism has not learned the R–O (or the CS–US) association. As an additional example, if you learn an instrumental response that will produce money, such as accepting a baby-sitting job, you will probably be inclined to exhibit this response when you need money but not otherwise.

Edward Thorndike, who was the first scientist to study this type of learning in the laboratory, used cats and some ingenious puzzle boxes that he constructed to study instrumental learning (Thorndike 1898). His experiments consisted of putting a cat inside the box, and the food reinforcer nearby outside the box (see Panel A of Figure 3.5). If the cat wanted to get out of the box, it had to open the door by pressing a pedal that was located inside the box. In the mean time, Thorndike would assess how much time the cat took to get out of the box during successive learning trials. As you can imagine, a cat takes a long time to get out of such a box when it is first placed inside it. Then seemingly by accident, the cat presses the pedal by chance, the door opens and the cat gets out and then eats the food (see Panel B of Figure 3.5). The next trial would look much the same as the first one, though maybe a bit shorter. Gradually, the cat learns how to get out of the box. Once the cat has learned the relationship between the pedal and the escaping from the box, it will get out in just a few seconds. In this way, Thorndike was able to draw many

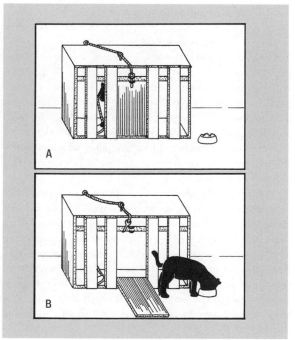

Figure 3.5 Thorndike's puzzle box. Panel A shows the cat inside the box and the food outside. Pressing the pedal becomes reinforced by the opening of the door and access to food (Panel B). A learning curve is evident if we assess the time that the cat needs to get out of the door in the successive learning trials.

Figure 3.4 Schematic representation of the Skinner box. In the front wall, there is a lever that the rat can press. Lever presses are the instrumental response through which we assess learning in this box. Next to the lever, there is a cup where food pellets are delivered. This provides reinforcement for lever-pressing behaviour. The floor is constructed of metal rods, through which an electric current can be applied if the experiment deals with the effects of aversive stimuli (e.g. punishing the rat for lever pressing).

learning curves and, most importantly, developed the law of effect, which is the law that basically defines the way in which instrumental responding works. When a given response is followed by a pleasant consequence, this response will become more firmly connected to the environmental situation in which it occurred so that, in the future, the organism will tend to repeat the same response when in the same environmental situation. Conversely, when a given response is followed by an unpleasant consequence, the connection between the environmental stimuli and the response becomes weaker, and this reduces the probability that the response be repeated the next time that the subject is in the same environmental situation (Thorndike 1911).

Thorndike's work has been continued by B.F. Skinner (1953) and many other psychologists over the years. Skinner preferred to work with rats and pigeons, rather than cats, and he constructed a new experimental apparatus which became very popular and is probably the most widely used apparatus in animal research even today. He called it the Operant Chamber, but most people call it the 'Skinner box'. A schematic representation of it is shown in Figure 3.4. The front wall generally has a lever protruding from it that the rat has to press down to obtain food (or a plastic disc that the pigeon has to peck), as well as a cup where the food pellets (reinforcers) are delivered when lever presses occur. If the experiment is to study the consequences of aversive stimulation on the rat's behaviour (e.g. the effect of punishment on the rat's lever-pressing behaviour), an electric current can be applied through the floor of the box, which is made of metal rods. In present-day laboratories, the box is connected to a computer which presents the stimuli and reinforcers, as well as records the animal's responses.

What type of experiments are generally conducted in instrumental learning? In instrumental learning we can study several phenomena that are highly analogous to those that were described with respect to S–S learning. That is, we can study acquisition, extinction, generalization, discrimination, contingency, blocking, overshadowing, and many other phenomena. In general, they work in much the same way, although there are also some specific aspects of R–O learning about which you should know.

Aspects of R–O learning that are similar to those observed in S–S learning

Extinction, generalization, discrimination, blocking, contiguity and contingency were described with regard to stimulus-stimulus (S-S) learning but also work in a similar way in response–outcome (R-O) learning.

After an instrumental response has been acquired, it will become extinguished if it no longer is followed by the outcome. In S–S learning, extinction occurred when Stimulus 1 (S1) no longer predicted Stimulus 2 (S2); in instrumental learning the process is similar but now it is the instrumental response (e.g. lever pressing) that is extinguished because it no longer is followed by the outcome. For example, the rat in Figure 3.4 would stop lever pressing if lever pressing no longer produced food. Similarly, when children try to obtain the attention of their parents by making a noise, that instrumental response could be extinguished if the parents did not produce the outcome for which the child is looking (i.e. giving the child their attention).

Generalization can also be observed in instrumental learning. If we teach the rat that food will be available only when a light is on, the rat will learn to press the lever with greater frequency when the light is on. However, if we test generalization by presenting a slightly different light, the rat will probably generalize the response and will press the lever in the presence of this second light, although probably somewhat less vigorously than in the presence of the original light. If we want the rat to press the lever only in the presence of one specific light, we have to use a discrimination training procedure similar to that shown with respect to S–S learning. That is, we must teach the rat that pressing the lever in the presence of one light (S+) will produce food, whereas pressing the lever in the presence of the other light (S−) will not produce food. Once this discrimination is acquired, we speak of stimulus control because the response is only produced in the presence of S+ (Skinner 1953).

Instrumental responses can also result blocked in both animal (Pearce and Hall 1978) and human subjects (Hammerl 1993; Shanks 1985) if there exists a more valid predictor of the reinforcer. Recall that blocking in S–S learning occurred when there were two potential causes of S2 (e.g. CS1–CS2→US). If subjects had previous knowledge that CS1 produced the US, they tended to discount the potential causal role of the other stimulus (CS2) in producing the US. Thus, if you now imagine a situation in which both CS1 (an environmental event) and your own response (R) are potential causes or predictors of an outcome, and you have previous knowledge that CS1 can produce the outcome, you will probably discount (i.e. block) the potential causal role of your own response in producing the outcome.

For example, Shanks (1985) demonstrated this effect in an experiment with college students who played a video game. The students were supposed to fire shells (R) at tanks that passed through a minefield (CS1) in the computer's screen. The reinforcer was the explosion of the tank that occurred during some of the trials. But of course, it was not easy to know whether the explosion had occurred because the shot had been accurate or because the tank had hit a mine. Some of the students were allowed an observational phase before they tried to destroy the tanks. During the observational phase they did not perform any responses, and thus, they were able to observe the probability of the tanks exploding if they hit a mine. Thus, when the game started, these students already had formed the mine→explosion association (i.e. they had acquired some previous knowledge of the mine–explosion relation). What Shanks observed was that the attribution of causality that these students made with regard to the effectiveness of their own responses when they played the game was weak (i.e. was blocked) in comparison to the attribution that had been made by the students who had not been given the observational period (i.e. they had no previous knowledge of the mine→explosion association). Moreover, blocking occurred regardless of whether the observational period was given before (i.e. forward blocking) or after (i.e. backward blocking) the phase in which both the response and the minefield were paired with the outcome. This demonstrates that blocking of R–O associations can occur, just as blocking of S–S associations.

Contiguity and contingency also affect R–O associations in a way similar to S–S associations. For example, Wasserman (1990b) and Shanks and Dickinson (1987, 1991) have reported numerous experiments in which human participants were sensitive to the response–outcome contingency and contiguity under very different conditions. The response could be pressing a telegraph key, in some of the experiments (Wasserman), or shooting at tanks in a video game in other experiments (Shanks and Dickinson). The outcome could be, for example, a flashing light, or a tank exploding. In all conditions, the greater the R–O contiguity and contingency, the greater the attribution of causality that the subjects made concerning their response. If the outcome occurred with greater probability in the presence than in the absence of a response, the subjects would conclude that there was positive contingency between the response and the outcome (i.e. they concluded that the response produced the outcome). If the outcome occurred with greater probability in the absence than in the presence of a response, the subjects concluded that the contingency was negative (i.e. they concluded that the response prevented the outcome from occurring). If the two probabilities were alike, the students were also able to learn that the outcome was independent of their behaviour. Thus, the effect of contingency is similar in R–O and in S–S learning.

Finally, there is an issue which we have not yet mentioned, but that you may have missed. What about reinforcers such as money or social praise? Why do these stimuli reinforce our behaviour? They are what we call conditioned reinforcers or second-order reinforcers. That is, they have become reinforcers because they have been associated with primary reinforcers such as food or sources of pain. In human instrumental behaviour, conditioned reinforcers are often more important than primary reinforcers. And the same is true for Pavlovian conditioning. Second-order CSs can be conditioned if we first pair a CS (e.g. a light) with a US (e.g. food) and then we use that CS to reinforce another CS (e.g. tone–light). The second-order CS (in this case the tone) will also come to produce a conditioned response by means of its having been associated with a first-order CS.

Effects of reinforcement and punishment on instrumental responses

The process by which we increase the probability of an instrumental response by pairing it with a pleasant outcome is called **reinforcement**, and the process by which we reduce the probability of an instrumental response by pairing it with an unpleasant outcome is called **punishment**. Thus, although both types of learning involve the learning of response–outcome (R–O) associations, the effect on the response will be diametrically opposite, depending on whether the response is reinforced or punished.

There are two different types of reinforcement. For example, if we want to reinforce the rat in Figure 3.4 for pressing the lever, we can give the rat a positive reinforcer (e.g. food) for pressing the lever. However, we could also reinforce the rat with a negative reinforcer. Consider a rat in the Skinner box receiving shocks from time to time. If pressing the lever stops or prevents the shock from occurring, the lever-pressing behaviour will be reinforced. In this case, we speak of negative rather than positive reinforcement because it is the omission of the second event in the association (the shock) that reinforces the subject. Note that both positive and negative reinforcement can be seen as cases in which the response produces a pleasant outcome. The effect of both types of reinforcement is an increase in the probability of the instrumental response. In the case of negative reinforcement we can subdivide it into escape behaviour (when the behaviour terminates the aversive stimulation, but does not prevent it from occurring) and avoidance behaviour (when the behaviour avoids or prevents the aversive stimulation from occurring). Thus, in summary, an instrumental response can be positively reinforced when its outcome is the occurrence of an appetitive event (e.g. money) and it can be negatively reinforced when the outcome of the response is either the termination (escape) or the avoidance (non-occurrence) of an aversive situation.

Similarly, we do not always need to give a shock to the rat in order to reduce its lever-pressing behaviour (punishment). We can also use omission training, which consists of omitting the presentation of food if the rat presses the lever and this should also reduce the probability of the response. You can probably think of many other examples of omission training, as when, for example, a child is being kept from watching TV after having done something that the parents want to prevent from happening in the future.

Interval schedules of reinforcement

In most real-life situations, reinforcement is not provided for every single response that the subject performs. Consider, for example, a parent who is not always present to provide reinforcement every time that the child produces a certain behaviour. Or consider a supervisor who provides feedback on a fixed weekly interval schedule (e.g. every Friday). Or consider also rain reinforcement for farmers, which occurs on a variable interval schedule. What type of behaviour can we expect when reinforcement occurs according to interval schedules?

Imagine two rats pressing a lever in the Skinner box to obtain food. For one of these rats, food is available on a *fixed interval schedule*. For example, one food pellet will be available every minute. This means that, regardless of how many responses the rat gives, these responses will not be reinforced until after that minute has elapsed and one food pellet is ready to be delivered. At this point, the first response that occurs once reinforcement is available will be reinforced. Thus, once the rat has learned how this schedule works, it will probably concentrate its responses around the last part of the interval, which is when food can be

expected. The other rat is exposed to a *variable interval schedule*. For this rat, one pellet per minute will be available on *average*. However, the rat will never be able to know when exactly food is available because the schedule is a variable one. That is, sometimes food will be available after 30 seconds, sometimes after 2 minutes. Thus, even though the average is also 1 minute, the rat needs to respond more often and more regularly than under the fixed interval schedule because in the variable schedule, the rat cannot know when food will be available. Thus, many laboratory experiments have shown that rats learn to press the lever more often if they are given food on variable rather than fixed interval schedules, even though getting the food does not depend on how many times they press the lever (Ferster and Skinner 1957). As an additional example, consider the effects that may be produced in students' behaviour with a variable as opposed to a fixed interval schedule for examinations in a particular course. Studying habits would of course be more regular if the examinations were delivered on a variable rather than fixed interval schedule.

Ratio schedules of reinforcement

Now consider a company which does not pay their employees for work based on some time interval, but on the basis of 'the number of responses' that they give, for example, the number of cars that they sell, or the number of letters that they send out during a mailing campaign. Or consider a rat that has to emit a certain number of lever-pressing responses in order to obtain a food pellet. If reinforcement is given on a *fixed ratio schedule* (e.g. payment is given after the mailing is complete for each of 1,000 customers), the person will probably work very hard in order to obtain payment and will probably then take a break before starting on the mailing for the next 1,000 customers. However, if reinforcers were given on a *variable ratio interval* (e.g. also 1,000 customers on average, but randomly distributed, so that sometimes takes more and sometimes takes less than 1,000 letters), these people cannot be certain of when reinforcement is going to occur, and thus, they tend to be more regular in their behaviour. Many animal experiments have shown that a much more regular rate of responding can be obtained if subjects are reinforced according to a variable, rather than fixed, ratio interval. This is a well-known principle in companies that make their profits out of gambling machines. Variable ratio schedules induce very high and regular response rates

ψ Case study

Superstitious behaviour

Reinforcers are not always contingent (dependent) on the subject's behaviour. Sometimes, they occur non-contingently (i.e. regardless of whether or not the subject responds). For example, in ancient civilizations, people invented rain dances that they thought would produce rain, but of course rain was response-independent. Even so, many people acquired response-outcome (R–O) associations between the dances and the rain if their dancing behaviour was accidentally followed by rain from time to time (e.g. variable ratio schedule).

The first laboratory experiment on superstitious behaviour was conducted by Skinner in 1948. He gave 'free' food to pigeons every 15 seconds. That is, the pigeons did not have to peck any key or do any other type of job to obtain food. However, he observed that each pigeon developed a specific pattern of responding,

as if it 'thought' that that was the way to obtain food. According to Skinner, this could allow us to explain human superstition. That is, perhaps humans develop superstitious behaviour in the same way that pigeons do. In brief, the first time that the food reinforcer occurred, the pigeon must have been doing something, for example, R1. Thus, R1 become reinforced and in consequence, its probability of occurring again in the near future was increased. This also augmented the probability of the next reinforcer occurring again in the presence of R1 and in turn, of R1 being reinforced again. According to Skinner, human superstitious behaviours are established in a similar way when they become accidentally reinforced (see Herrnstein 1966; Skinner 1948, for a more detailed elaboration of this view; see the main text to learn about some potential problems of this view as well as to know about related research conducted with humans).

(Ferster and Skinner 1957). Moreover, the behaviour reinforced under variable ratio schedules becomes highly resistant to extinction because the subject knows that reinforcement depends on the number of responses, but does not know how many responses are needed to obtain it.

Superstitious behaviour and illusion of control

You can probably think of many examples of superstitious behaviour. Some of them are acquired through social learning. For example, someone tells us that 13 is a bad-luck number, and most people try to avoid it, 'just in case'. As a result, many hotels avoid labelling floor 13 as such in their lifts and simply label floor 14 after floor 12. This is a social superstition which is transmitted by social interaction and we cannot be certain about how it came to be established many years ago. But there are also many personal superstitions and the establishment of these can be studied in the laboratory. Perhaps you and your friends have developed some of these personal superstitions that you may use when you are going to take an exam or when playing football or tennis. Some students like to wear black (or blue) when they are going to take

an exam; others, in contrast, are more preoccupied by the route they take when they go to school; yet others think that the necklace that they wear is a good-luck amulet. Among football, tennis or golf players, these types of personal superstitions are also well known.

Skinner (1948) showed that pigeons, as well as humans, developed superstitious behaviours if non-contingent reinforcers occurred from time to time which accidentally reinforced what they were doing (see case study). Skinner's experiment, however, presented some problems of interpretation (Staddon and Simmelhag 1971). One of the problems was that Skinner's data could be interpreted as the result of classical conditioning rather than superstitious conditioning. That is, Skinner had been giving food to the pigeons every 15 seconds, and thus the 15 seconds interval could have played the role of a classically conditioned CS which predicted food. If this were true, we should expect Pavlovian CRs to occur every 15 seconds or so. According to Staddon and Simmelhag, what Skinner had observed in his pigeons were not superstitious instrumental behaviours but Pavlovian CRs. The responses were not arbitrary responses, as would be expected from Skinner's view, but were responses appropriate to the nature of the anticipated US and timing of that US.

Nevertheless, many researchers have reported superstitious behaviours in human experiments which cannot be interpreted as classical conditioning (see case study). For example, Wright (1962) reported an experiment in which college students tended to develop different sequences of key presses despite none of them being related to the production of reinforcement. Reinforcement was simply given at different random intervals, but students tended to believe that the sequence of key presses that they were developing was what produced the reinforcers. Moreover, several researchers have shown that human subjects tend to perceive reinforcers that occur independently of their behaviour ('free reinforcers') as if they had produced them (e.g. Alloy and Abramson 1979; Langer 1975; Wortman 1975). For instance, Alloy and Abramson (1979) performed a study with college students who were pressing keys and obtaining different types of reinforcers under different R–O contingencies. Under some contingencies, the reinforcer was absolutely independent of the subject's behaviour (it was pre-programmed to occur with the same probability regardless of whether or not the student responded). However, students tended to believe that they were producing the reinforcers. This is called the *illusion of control*, because the subjects not only behave superstitiously, but also believe that they are controlling an outcome which is uncontrollable. More recently, Matute (1994, 1995) also observed superstitious behaviour and illusion of control in college students who were exposed to an uncontrollable negative reinforcer. The students were told that their task was to find the way to stop the noises that would be produced by a computer from time to time. Thus, the negative reinforcer was the termination of noises. But it was actually uncontrollable. That is, noise duration was pre-programmed for each trial and the student's responses did not have any effect on it. However, most students developed illusions of control. Very few students noticed that their responses were not controlling noise termination.

Thus, apparently, we can sometimes form R–O associations even when reinforcers are independent of the response. The probability of the occurrence of the reinforcer is one of the factors that affect this result. That is, the students who received a larger number of free reinforcers developed higher illusions of control than the students who received a smaller number of free reinforcers. But this is surely not the only factor affecting the illusion of control. For example, Alloy and Abramson also showed that non-depressed subjects developed stronger illusions of control than did depressed subjects, and that in normal subjects, receiving uncontrollable reinforcers produced stronger illusions of control than receiving uncontrollable punishment (see also research update on p. 93 to learn more about this).

Nevertheless, it is important to note that despite the many experiments demonstrating superstitions and illusions of control, there are also many experiments that have shown that when reinforcers are uncontrollable, animals (e.g. Killeen 1981) and people (e.g. Shanks and Dickinson 1987; Wasserman 1990b) are able to realize that they are not controlling the reinforcers. For example, Killeen (1981) performed an experiment to test whether pigeons would discriminate between an outcome produced by their own behaviour and an outcome produced by a computer. The pigeons could peck at three different keys in a row. Pecking at the central key sometimes produced the effect of turning off the light. However, from time to time, the light was also turned off by the computer. The pigeon's task was to learn whether the light had turned off because of its pecking or because the computer had turned it off. If the computer had turned off the light, the pigeon had to 'say' this by pecking at the left-side key, and if it was true, the pigeon was reinforced with food. By contrast, pecking at the right-side key meant 'I turned the light off', and this response was followed by food if it was true that the pigeon, rather than the computer, had turned the light off. The pigeons were incredibly accurate in their responses. Thus, if an accurate detection of non-contingency is possible, why, then, do people and animals sometimes behave superstitiously? The research update addresses this problem.

Learned helplessness

The term *learned helplessness* refers both to an experimental effect and to one of the theories that attempts to explain that effect. Moreover, it also refers to a model of human depression which was later developed as an extension of the theories and data that were developed in the animal and human laboratories.

The *learned helplessness effect* was first demonstrated by Overmier and Seligman (1967) and has been extensively investigated in animal and human research (e.g. Hiroto

Research update

Illusion of control and superstitious behaviour versus accurate judgements of R–O independence and learned helplessness

When we are exposed to uncontrollable reinforcers, do we learn that reinforcers are independent of our behaviour, or do we, by contrast, behave superstitiously and develop illusions of control? As we have seen, the experimental results are quite mixed. Some experiments show that we notice that we do not have control; others show that we do not notice. Why?

One potential explanation is that in order to learn that an outcome occurs independently of our behaviour, we have to test both what happens when we perform the response and what happens when we do not, and this is something that we do not always do. For example, Matute (1996) observed that student subjects who were trying to turn off uncontrollable noises produced by a computer tended to respond at every opportunity. In consequence, although the noise termination was always controlled by the computer, the subjects did not notice that the noises would have equally stopped even if they had done nothing. Because uncontrollable reinforcers occur with the same probability regardless of whether we respond or not, if we respond at every opportunity they will always become associated to our own behaviour rather than to other causes. Indeed, when a different group of subjects was explicitly instructed that they should refrain from responding from time to time in order to test how much control they had over noise termination, the uncontrollable reinforcers (noise termination) occurred both in the presence and in the absence of the response, and these subjects were able to learn that they had no control. Possibly, in this later group, the reinforcers become associated to causes different from the subject behaviour (e.g. the computer program) and hence, S–O associations were formed that competed with the R–O association, thus reducing the illusion of control.

Similar processes can also be found outside the laboratory. For example, a person who has been diag-nosed with an incurable illness has several courses of action. One is to do nothing and acknowledge that reinforcers do not depend on her or his behaviour; this may produce depression and helplessness. Another possible course of action may be to try all types of therapies, including the most superstitious ones (e.g. witchcraft). If transient recoveries occur, they will be associated with those 'therapies'. This will produce an illusion of control and a superstition, but note that it might also be preventing a depression. Indeed, in cases in which the outcome is uncontrollable, letting patients keep their illusions and superstitions, or even favouring the development of new ones, can sometimes have prophylactic effects against helplessness, depression and other problems (see Alloy and Abramson 1988; Alloy and Clements 1992).

Note also that there are many factors which reduce the tendency to respond and which, therefore, should tend to reduce the illusion of control (e.g. fatigue, extinction, punishment, depression and many others). For example, the finding by Alloy and Abramson (1979) that depressed people are less prone to develop illusions of control than non-depressed people could be due to depressed people being generally more passive than non-depressed people. As noted by E.A. Skinner (1985), the low rate of responding probably prevents the development of R–O associations in depressed patients because uncontrollable reinforcers are more likely to occur in the absence than in the presence of their responding (see Matute 1996; Skinner 1985, for further elaboration of this view). Of course, this is not to say that the rate of responding is the only factor affecting the development of the illusion of control versus accurate judgements of response–outcome independence. The important point for our present purposes is that even though helplessness and super-stition, and accurate versus illusory acquisition of R–O relations, may seem to be contradictory experimental results in the scientific literature, they all appear to occur also in real life, and are, probably, opposite ends of the same continuum.

and Seligman 1975; Maier and Seligman 1976; Seligman and Maier 1967). In brief, many experiments have shown that dogs can be trained to escape shocks by jumping over a barrier that leads to a safety compartment or by performing other types of instrumental responses. However, if the dogs are previously given shocks that are unpredictable and uncontrollable (i.e. shock termination does not depend on the dog's behaviour), dogs will later be less able to escape shocks when given the opportunity to do so. Moreover, the consequences of being exposed to uncontrollable and unpredictable shock were not limited to the subsequent failure to escape from shocks that were escapable. The dogs also developed several other deficits which have been described as emotional deficits (which are presumably similar to the sad and depressed state that a person feels after learning that reinforcers are uncontrollable), motivational deficits (the dogs did not even try to escape the shocks when they were later given the opportunity to do so), and cognitive deficits (the dogs were unable to learn that the shocks were controllable during the last phase of the studies).

These effects could in principle be explained in several different ways. For example, perhaps all of the dog's responses were extinguished because none of them was followed by the reinforcer (shock termination). Or perhaps a passive behaviour became superstitiously associated with shock termination (e.g. Balleine and Job 1991). Another potential explanation, and the one that has become most popular, is the so-called *learned helplessness theory* (Abramson *et al.* 1978; Seligman 1975). According to this theory, the reason that the dogs showed those deficits was because they had learned to be helpless during Phase 1 of the study. That is, they learned that nothing that they could do allowed them to control the reinforcer (shock termination). In each trial, shock termination was controlled by the experimenters, and the dogs were able to learn that they had no control on shock termination. It is important to note that, according to learned helplessness theory, it is the lack of control over reinforcers, rather than the absence of reinforcers, that produces the deficits (see Abramson *et al.* 1978; Seligman 1975). The dogs in the control condition had been exposed to the identical reinforcers (shock termination occurred with the same probability and identical parameters), but these dogs were not helpless because they, rather than the experimenter, were the ones that were controlling shock termination. If the effect were due to an absence of reinforcers, the effect could be explained by the extinction of all voluntary responses. However, because the effect appeared to be due to a lack of control over reinforcement, Seligman

and his colleagues concluded that subjects had actually learned that reinforcers were uncontrollable, and that this was what produced the helplessness effect.

The learned helplessness theory has become very popular as a model of human depression and of several other human disorders (e.g. school failure). According to the *learned helplessness model of depression* (Abramson *et al.* 1978), a person who is exposed to uncontrollable outcomes will learn that no one response can control those outcomes and thus this person may develop the expectancy that the desired outcomes will remain uncontrollable in the future. If this occurs, this person will become depressed. As in the animal learned helplessness experiments, human depression frequently includes an emotional deficit (being sad and anxious), a motivational deficit (a depressed person frequently says: 'nothing will work, so why try?') and a cognitive deficit (according to this theory, depressed persons frequently have problems in learning that an event is controllable).

But can subjects really perceive the lack of relation between their responses and the outcome? Learned helplessness research has not tested this question (see Matute 1994). However, if we look at the superstition and the illusion of control literature, they suggest that subjects receiving uncontrollable reinforcers frequently (not always) perceive them as controllable (see above). According to learned helplessness theory, learned helplessness effects could not take place if subjects do not detect that reinforcers are uncontrollable. Of course, if reinforcers never occur, subjects would perceive such absence of reinforcers and would stop responding, but that would be extinction rather than helplessness. Thus, learned helplessness theory needs to specify under which conditions animals and humans can detect that reinforcers are uncontrollable, because only under those conditions can they become helpless (Maier and Seligman, 1976). The study of the illusions of control (see pp. 91–2 and also the research update) can probably shed some light on the question of when can uncontrollable reinforcers be perceived as uncontrollable.

S–R versus R–O associations

As previously mentioned, according to Thorndike's (1911) law of effect, whenever a response was followed by a pleasant consequence, this strengthened the stimulus–response (S–R) connection between the environmental stimuli (S) present in that situation and the response (R) that the subject had performed. In this way, the probability that under the same environmental situation (same S), the same response would be repeated in the future was increased. Thus, Thorndike, as well as many other psychologists, thought that instrumental behaviour was due to S–R associations that were acquired by contiguity. However, modern psychology has shown that organisms also learn response–outcome (R–O) associations and that these associations are important in determining their instrumental performance (Colwill and Rescorla 1986; Dickinson and Shanks 1995). Moreover, we also know now that, as in stimulus–stimulus (S–S) learning, contiguity is not the only important factor determining the learning of R–O associations and instrumental performance. As in Pavlovian conditioning, contingency and blocking effects also show that instrumental learning is more complex than the initial contiguity theories had assumed. But how do we really know that organisms can acquire R–O associations rather than simply strengthening the S–R connections? Some of the experiments that demonstrated the existence of R–O associations are described next.

Figure 3.6 shows a rat in a T-shaped maze, which is a very commonly used apparatus in instrumental learning. Generally, there is food in a box which is located at the end of one arm of the maze and there is no food at the end of the other arm. S–R theorists believed that although the rat at first chose at random (represented in Figure 3.6 by the rat tossing a coin), the finding of food in one of the end-boxes served to reinforce the response that the rat had just performed (e.g. turn left), so that, in the future, the probability that that response would occur when the rat is in the T-maze was increased. The rat would no longer chose which way to turn in a random manner.

One experiment by Tolman and Gleitman (1949) demonstrated that the rat's behaviour was not that

Figure 3.6 'Tossing a coin to decide which way to go in a T-maze? Man, you must be the new subject that just got started.'

simple. They used a maze with a distinctive box at the end of each arm (one was white, the other one was black). During Phase 1 of the study, food could be obtained in either box. Thus, according to the S–R view, both responses should have become equally reinforced and the rat should have kept choosing at random which way to go. And this was true. The rats kept 'tossing a coin' in deciding to go right or left because food could be obtained in either direction. However, during Phase 2 of the study, the rats were put into each box by hand during several trials. In one box, say the white box, they were shocked. In the other one they found food. Then in Phase 3, the rats were allowed to run the maze again. Which way would they go? According to S–R theory, both responses, right and left, had been equally reinforced and thus rats should keep on choosing at random. However, if they had learned an R–O association (left leads to white) and an S–S association (white leads to shock), then rats should certainly chose right. And of course, that is what they did!

Another study that showed the importance of R–O associations in instrumental learning was reported by Adams and Dickinson (1981). They trained hungry rats to press a lever to obtain food pellets in an operant chamber. Later, they conditioned a taste aversion to the pellets. This was accomplished by injecting the rats with a drug that made them feel sick after they ate some pellets, but the lever was not present at this stage and the rats were simply given the pellets without the requirement of any instrumental response. After this aversion to pellets was acquired, the rats were again given the opportunity to lever press in the operant chamber. No pellets were provided during this test. But would the rats press the lever? According to S–R theory, the acquired taste aversion should not affect the lever-pressing behaviour. That is, if the reason why they lever press is simply that such a response has been strengthened by reinforcement during the first stage of the study, rats should again lever press when given the opportunity to do so. However, if rats had really learned an R–O association (i.e. lever pressing produces pellets), they should not show much interest in lever pressing once they feel nausea for pellets. And this is just what the results showed. Rats no longer pressed the lever after they had acquired a taste aversion to the pellets. Thus, this study also demonstrated that an R–O association was what had been acquired and that it was governing the rat's behaviour (see also Colwill and Rescorla 1985 for further evidence of this). Now we may ask, how are these R–O associations acquired? We do not yet have a complete theory of R–O learning, but many researchers assume that, at least in principle, the same theories that explain the acquisition of S–S associations can explain the acquisition of R–O associations (see e.g. Mackintosh 1983).

ψ Section summary

We generally speak of response–outcome (R–O) learning when the events in the association are an instrumental response and the outcome that it produces. This type of learning is presumably responsible for the behavioural changes that are often observed in instrumental learning. In general, organisms will tend to perform those responses that they expect to be reinforced (either positively or negatively reinforced) and will not perform those responses that they expect to be punished. Although older theories did not speak of R–O associations, we now know that rats (and humans) will not perform an instrumental response (no matter how strongly that response has been reinforced), if they expect that response to produce an outcome that they do not want. Thus apparently organisms acquire a mental representation of the outcome produced by their response and this allows them to decide whether or not they want to perform the response. Although R–O associations generally reflect an accurate causal relation between the response and the outcome, superstitious behaviours and illusions of control can also be sometimes acquired in situations in which the outcome does not depend on the response. Extinction, generalization, discrimination, blocking and many other phenomena that were described with regard to S–S learning have also been reported in R–O learning situations.

1 What is the difference between Pavlovian and instrumental conditioning?

2 How do we know that animals acquire R–O associations?

3 What does superstitious behaviour have to do with the learning of R–O associations?

❑ 'Special' types of learning

There are many other types of learning that we have not yet discussed. Imitative learning, category learning and spatial learning are some examples of situations that have traditionally been thought of as 'special' forms of learning that could not be explained by associative theories. But this was in part due to the old theories of learning not being able to explain those effects. For example, imitative learning occurs when we observe someone doing something and being reinforced for it, and then we tend to imitate that behaviour (Bandura 1977). Of course, the old stimulus–response (S–R) theories could not explain such learning because the subject was not performing any response while learning was taking part through observation of the model's behaviour. That is, not one of the subject's responses could be reinforced because the subject was not performing any response. However, current learning theories could explain imitative learning as a form of associative learning. Throughout this chapter, we have seen evidence suggesting that associations are formed between mental representations of events and that responses are not necessary for learning to occur. For example, in sensory preconditioning the animals were able to associate the representation of two neutral events. And in response–outcome (R–O) learning the animals were able to associate a response with an outcome and to refrain from producing the response if the outcome had been devalued (as in the cases in which the outcome 'food pellets' was paired with nausea after the R–O association had been acquired). Thus, we know that rats (or people) would perform a response if they have learned that that response produces a desirable outcome and would not perform the response if they know that it leads to an undesirable outcome. Thus, if we observe a person performing a response and obtaining a given outcome, we can form an association between that response and that outcome, just as we can associate any other type of events that we observe. Once we have acquired such R–O association we can later imitate or not the response as a function of whether we wish to obtain that particular outcome. Similarly, spatial learning and category learning are also being found to be explicable in terms of associative learning. Some examples of this are described below.

Spatial learning

Many researchers have been curious about the way we learn spatial relations. How do we find our way through a new city, for example? Or to use a laboratory example, how does a rat find its way through a new maze? Tolman (1948) suggested that rats, and humans, build up cognitive maps of spatial locations such as mazes and cities while they learn, and they later use these maps when they need them (see Figure 3.7). This seems a reasonable explanation with which many scientists agree. But it has the problem of being rather vague. That is, what exactly is a mental map? Moreover, this explanation presents the problem of explaining spatial learning as a type of learning which is different from other types of learning; that is, spatial learning is treated as an exception to the general rules of learning. In consequence, many researchers have tried to determine if spatial learning is really an exception. The principle of parsimony in science tells us that, if we can have one simple explanation that can explain all forms of learning, such an explanation should be preferred over the use of different explanations for each individual situation. Thus, researchers have tried to determine if spatial learning could be explained by our already well tested associative mechanisms and have apparently found one such way. Seemingly, rats (and people) use cues in their mazes (and cities) that help them find their way to their goal (see Figure 3.8). These cues can play the role of S1 in an S1–S2 learning and become associated with the goal (S2). Moreover, they can also play the role of discriminative stimuli which indicate to the subjects when an instrumental response will be reinforced (as when a certain light in the Skinner box indicated that food was available and a different light indicated that food was not available). In this way, the subject can learn in a maze which cues indicate that a particular response (e.g. turn left) will be reinforced or punished.

In an experiment which illustrates this point, Rodrigo *et al*. (1997) used a circular swimming pool to study spatial learning in rats. The pool was full of water, but there was an underwater platform in a certain location. The rats had to swim through the pool and their goal was to reach the platform which would allow them to step on it and take a rest. These researchers also added a few cues through the pool that would help the rats find where the platform was located. Indeed, the only way by which this problem could be solved was by learning about those cues because the platform was consistently located in relation to them. The rats had no trouble in getting to the platform after they had learned where it was located in relation to the cues (which can be regarded as several S1s which became associated to the platform, i.e. S2). However, when a new (and redundant) cue was added during Phase 2 of the study, the rats did not learn to use it. Apparently, they had already learned to predict where the platform was by using the other cues, and thus the

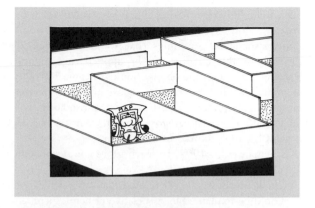

Figure 3.7 'Let's see what my cognitive map says now.'

Figure 3.8 'Hey, these signals look pretty clear! I don't think I need a map.'

learning about the cue which was added during Phase 2 was blocked. This shows that the learning of spatial relations can also be blocked by using a procedure which was known to produce blocking in S–S and in R–O associative learning. This suggests that spatial learning is probably just one more instance of associative learning rather than a special case of learning.

Category learning

Consider now when in your childhood you were learning to categorize items as furniture as opposed to non-furniture or as games versus non-games. Consider how medical students learn to categorize symptoms under disease categories. Moreover, consider how pigeons may learn to distinguish the concept of fish from that of non-fish by pecking only at pictures that show fish on them (Herrnstein and deVilliers 1980). Category learning has been frequently classified as a 'non-associative' form of learning. However, researchers are now finding that the same associative principles that we have described throughout this chapter can be applied to category learning. Moreover, the observation of category learning in animals, such as the example above of pigeons learning to classify pictures as fish versus non-fish adds support to the idea that category learning is not a special type of learning limited to the human species (see also Wasserman *et al*. 1992, to learn more about concept learning in animals).

Gluck and Bower (1988) noted that category learning could be explained by associative principles similar to those used to explain conditioning experiments. They described a simple computer simulation that was able to learn to categorize items using the Rescorla-Wagner model as its learning equation. After this, many other computer programs have been written that have improved upon the initial simple program described by Gluck and Bower, and that have contributed to a current renewed interest in associative theories, not only with regard to the psychology of learning, but also within other areas of psychology. The new programs can learn to categorize new items with great accuracy (e.g. Kruschke 1992). Moreover, the results provided by these programs are similar (both in successes and in errors) to those produced by human and animal subjects who are trained to perform the equivalent categorization tasks. Thus, we can now also explain category learning through associative principles.

As a final exercise, consider writing a learning equation (e.g. Rescorla and Wagner 1972; see Mercier 1996) in your computer. By doing so, you would be telling your computer how the associations between S1 and S2 should be strengthened every time that S1 and S2 occur together. Once your program is finished, you can start the learning stage by introducing several S1–S2 pairings. For example, describing a particular chair (S1) followed by the label 'furniture' (S2) will be an example of an S1-S2 pairing. When you present each new S1, your computer should give a response by telling which S2 is it expecting (e.g. furniture or non furniture). Then, you can provide feedback on whether the computer's response was correct, just as you would do with a child or a pigeon, in order to allow learning to take place. In this way, the system will start acquiring associations between S1s and S2s and those associations will be strengthened or weakened according to the learning rule that you have implemented in your equation. Of course, as in any other learning situation, there will be many failures during the earlier phases of learning. But as learning proceeds, the responses should be more and more accurate, assuming that the theory that your equation represented was a good theory. Once you have introduced a sufficient number of different S1–S2 pairings, the system should have learned to categorize those items. That is, the system should be able to recognize each S1 as a member of its corresponding S2 category. Moreover, responding to new items that the system has never 'seen' before can be accomplished by generalization (the more similar a new item is to those stored under the category representation, the greater the probability that the new item will be classified as a member of that category).

Thus, like spatial learning, category learning does not appear to be a 'special' type of learning. Whether other forms of learning which currently may still appear to be outside of the domain of associative learning will someday be integrated within the same body of associative knowledge that applies to most forms of learning is something that will be decided by the research performed by future generations of psychological researchers, or, in other words, by you and your colleagues.

Ψ Section summary

Several types of learning have been traditionally regarded as exceptions to the laws of learning because the older stimulus–response (S–R) theories were not able to provide a satisfactory explanation of how they occurred. Examples of these are imitative learning, spatial learning and category learning. Current theories, however, assume that responses are not necessary for learning to occur, and that learning consists of the acquisition of associations between mental representations of events (be they responses or environmental stimuli). As a consequence, current developments are showing that many of those 'special cases' no longer need to be regarded as exceptions to the laws of learning. Current associative theories, such as that of Rescorla and Wagner, can provide a reasonable explanation of these types of learning.

1 Are cognitive maps always necessary to explain spatial learning? Why?
2 How can we explain category learning as an instance of associative learning?

Ψ Chapter summary

● Developing a theory of learning

If you are curious about how we learn, developing a theory of learning is no more than trying to solve that question. Most current theories explain learning as the process through which we acquire associations between the mental representations of events. In this chapter, the strengths and weakness of major theories are described, along with critical human and animal experiments that help us assess the contributions of each theory.

● Stimulus–stimulus associations

We generally speak of stimulus–stimulus (S–S) learning when an association is formed between the mental representation of two stimuli. Pavlovian conditioning is a type of S–S learning in which an initially neutral stimulus (the conditioned stimulus or CS) becomes associated to a biologically significant stimulus (the conditioned stimulus or US). As a result of this learning, a conditioned response (CR) is often observed. But S–S learning can also occur in situations in which no USs are involved and no CRs are elicited, such as, for example, in many human causal learning situations.

● Response–outcome associations

We generally speak of response–outcome (R–O) associations when the events in the association are an instrumental response and the outcome that it produces. This type of learning is presumably responsible for the behavioural changes that are often observed in instrumental learning. Current research suggests that organisms acquire a mental representation of the outcome produced by their response and this allows them to decide whether or not they want to perform the instrumental response.

● Special types of learning

Several types of learning have been traditionally regarded as exceptions to the law of learning because older theories were not able to provide a satisfactory explanation of how they occurred. Examples of these are imitative learning, spatial learning and categorization learning. Current developments, however, are showing that many of those 'special cases' no longer need to be regarded as exceptions to the laws of learning.

Further reading

● Domjan, M. (1998) *The Principles of Learning and Behavior*, 4th edn. Pacific Grove, CA: Brooks/Cole. This is a good textbook which reviews much of the major findings in learning research. Provides good and balanced coverage of different types of theories.

● Tarpy, R.M. (1997) *Contemporary Learning Theory and Research*. New York: McGraw-Hill. Like Domjan (1998) this is also a nice textbook which should help you understand the principles of learning theory and research before you read more specialized material.

● Dickinson, A. (1980) *Contemporary Animal Learning Theory*. Cambridge: Cambridge University Press. This book provides excellent discussions on current learning theories and on the type of learning research that psychologists are conducting today. It is worth reading it after you have read a more introductory textbook (e.g. Domjan or Tarpy.)

● Pavlov, I. (1927) *Conditioned Reflexes*. London: Clarendon Press. This is a classical book on learning which has inspired generations of psychologists. Even though many of Pavlov's views have been challenged by later discoveries, many are still of great value and you should read this book to form your own opinion on learning and conditioning.

● Skinner, B.F. (1953) *Science and Human Behavior*. New York: Macmillan. Like Pavlov's, Skinner's book is another classic. It has often been challenged by later discoveries but has had a profound influence in the psychology of learning and in the development of applications of learning theory. A must-read book.

Acknowledgements

This chapter was written under support of grants PB95-0440 and PI96-006 from Dirección General de Enseñanza Superior (Spain) and from Departamento de Educación, Universidades e Investigación (Basque Government), respectively. I would like to thank Lourdes Albóniga, Victoria D. Chamizo, Ralph R. Miller, Oskar Pineño and Pedro Villegas for their highly valuable comments on an earlier version of this chapter. Special thanks are due to Martha Escobar for the excellent art work that she has contributed to this chapter.

Sensory systems

Fred Toates

☐ Chapter preview

When you have read this chapter, you should be able to

- describe some of the features of the sensory systems of hearing, vision, touch, taste and smell, in such a way that similarities and differences between them are clear
- show how some features of the processing of information can be understood in terms of the properties of neurons and the systems that they form
- relate the structure of sensory systems to the function that they serve
- show the relevance of an understanding of sensory systems to such processes as motivation, emotion, memory and development.

Introduction

The process of detecting sensory information is described in this chapter and perception is described in Chapter 5. Our perception of the world depends upon both sensory information and our memories and expectations about the world. Sometimes perception is described as being dependent upon both a bottom-up factor, the sensory information, and a top-down factor, the memories and expectations etc. You met an example of this in Chapter 2: the experience of pain was described as dependent upon both sensory information on tissue damage (bottom-up) and expectations of pain (top-down). Although this chapter concerns the bottom-up factor, it will be necessary to refer to the top-down factor in order to place the discussion in context.

Sensory systems involve the eyes, ears, nose, skin and tongue and are responsible for (1) detecting the presence of physical events in the external world, (2) conveying information on the detection to the brain and (3) processing the information as it is conducted towards the brain. The information from the external environment contributes to visual, auditory, smell, tactile, temperature and taste sensations. (A specialized tactile system, involving pain, was introduced in Chapter 2.)

Each sensory system detects events in the world and the initial stage of detection is done by **sensory receptors**. The physical events that carry information to which our sensory systems are responsive consist of such things as lights, odours and pressure waves in the air (normally termed sounds). Our brains are not sensitive to these physical events as such. Rather, the language that brains utilize is that of action potentials in neurons (see Chapter 2). Therefore, the first stage of processing is common to all the systems we shall study: the sensory receptor performs a *translation* from physical events in a form other than electrical (e.g. a chemical in the air or on the tongue, a noxious stimulus at the skin) to an electrical signal. This process performed by the sensory receptor is termed **sensory transduction**.

Each sensory quality is associated with specialized receptors. For example, as you saw in Chapter 2, nociceptive neurons transduce between tissue damage and action potentials. In this case the sensory receptor is the tip of the nociceptive neuron. In other cases, the whole cell is described as the receptor. For example, in the retina there are specialized receptor cells that transduce between light and electrical signals. Of course, the sensory receptors of the eye and ear are not in immediate contact with the external environment but are within an organ.

The fundamental difference between sensory channels, e.g. the auditory and visual nerves, lies not in the means by which information is carried since in both cases it is by action potentials. Rather the difference is in terms of the particular nerves that carry the information and the parts of the brain at which these nerves arrive. We see lights because the optic nerve is activated and hear sounds because the auditory nerve is active. The retina is sensitive to light and not to sound. However, if mechanical pressure is applied to the eye, we can sometimes see flashes that appear to be light. Objectively, there is no such light but activity in this particular input channel is interpreted as light. Activity within the auditory nerve is interpreted as sound.

Action potentials within a particular neuron of a sensory system encode the presence of a physical event in the world. However, apart from their all-or-none presence, events have duration and intensity. Pressure waves in the air also have such qualities as pitch. How are these qualities encoded, given that the nervous system has only a series of action potentials available as its means? There are basically two different means of conveying information about different qualities: which neurons are active and the pattern of action potentials within neurons. As you have seen, differences *between* sensory systems, say, auditory information and visual information correspond to different nerves. Similarly *within* a given sensory system, differences can be conveyed by differences in activity between neurons. For example, sugar tastes sweet and a lemon tastes bitter because of different patterns of activity within different neurons, as triggered by those two different chemical qualities. Different neurons within the auditory nerve are triggered by high and low frequency sounds.

As was discussed in Chapter 2, the frequency of action potentials can code for intensity, e.g. as the intensity of the physical stimulus increases, so does the frequency of action potentials, an example of **frequency coding**. Information can also be carried by means of the population of neurons that is activated by a stimulus, termed **population coding**. A fine pointed gentle stimulus on the skin might trigger few sensory neurons, whereas a heavy stimulus might trigger a larger population. Thus, increasing frequency of action potentials in individual neurons and an increasing population of active neurons together encode increasing stimulus intensity.

Figures 4.1a and 4.1b show one means of coding information in a sensory neuron. In the absence of a stimulus, there is no activity in this neuron. The duration

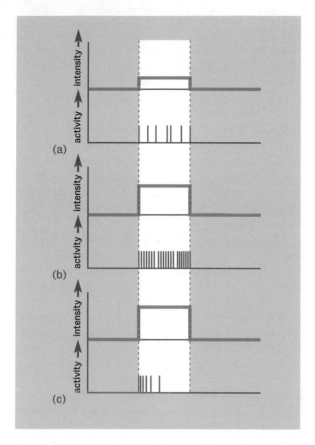

Figure 4.1 How information on a stimulus can be encoded (a) weak stimulus, (b) strong stimulus, (c) receptor that adapts to constant levels of stimulation

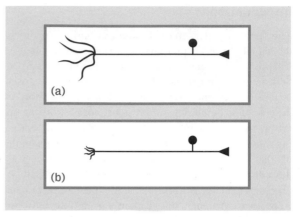

Figure 4.2 Nociceptive neurons, with (a) large and (b) small receptive fields

tion. As will be discussed later, the notion of receptive field is one that can be applied also to vision.

This completes the discussion of general principles and we now turn to considering each particular system. Through the following discussion you need to be alert to where the principles illustrate common features and where they are peculiar to a given system. As is traditional, vision will dominate the discussion. This is because most information on perception gained by psychologists has been by using visual stimuli.

of the stimulus is encoded by the duration of time over which action potentials occur. The frequency of action potentials codes for the intensity of the stimulus. Figure 4.1c shows a neuron that is sensitive only to the onset of a stimulus. It is unresponsive to the steady value, a property termed **adaptation**.

Another feature of some sensory systems can be illustrated by reconsidering the nociceptive neuron, as shown in Figure 4.2. If you compare Figures 4.2a and 4.2b, you will see that the extent of branching of the tip is different in the two cases. A consequence of this is that the neuron of Figure 4.2a is influenced by tissue damage over a wider area than that of Figure 4.2b. The area over which the nociceptive neuron detects tissue damage is termed the **receptive field** of the neuron. A receptive field is that area of sensory surface which, when stimulated, will influence the activity of the neuron in ques-

---

ψ Section summary

Sensory receptors detect events in the outside world. By means of action potentials, sensory systems convey to the brain information on these events. The difference between sensory systems is in terms of which nerves are activated and their location of arrival at the brain. Neurons within some sensory systems can be characterized by their receptive fields, i.e. the region of sensory surface, which, when stimulated, influences the activity of the neuron.

1 How can the frequency of action potentials in neurons be said to represent information on events in the environment?
2 How can mechanical pressure on the eye result in the perception of light flashes?

Hearing

The physical stimulus

The physical stimulus that we perceive as sound consists of changes in the pressure of the air, a special case of which is illustrated by Figure 4.3a. The tuning fork is hit and it starts to vibrate. The vibration produces waves of compression (relatively high pressure) and rarefaction (low pressure) in the air, which we perceive as sound. Figure 4.3b shows a graph of these changes in pressure, which takes a form described as a sinewave. Note two characteristics of it: wavelength and amplitude. The wavelength is the period of time that the wave takes to complete one cycle, in this case, say, 1/50th of a second. This means that the wave completes 50 cycles in 1 second. This is a measure of the frequency of the wave. Cycles per second are usually expressed in the units of Hertz. Amplitude is a measure of the size of the waves of pressure and rarefaction. Figure 4.3c shows a different tuning fork. When this one is struck it has the characteristic of vibrating at a different frequency, say, 100 Hertz. See Figure 4.3d. Note that, in this case, the amplitude is the same as in b. Part e shows what happens if this tuning fork is struck harder; there is an increase in amplitude but the frequency remains the same.

The ear serves the function of converting such changes in pressure in the air to changes in the electrical activity of neurons. This involves more than one stage of transduction. The human ear, shown in Figure 4.4, is sensitive to frequencies between 30 and 20,000 Hertz (abbreviated to Hz). Other animals can have a different range of sensitivity.

The outer ear channels air pressure changes to the middle ear. Changes in pressure in the air are transduced into changes in mechanical oscillation of the tympanic membrane or eardrum. If it is exposed to changes in pressure, such as those shown in Figure 4.3, the ear drum will vibrate at the same frequency as the air. So, movements of the ear drum are the initial transduction, representing changes in air pressure. This representation in the form of ear drum movements will then cause other changes that will be described in a moment.

Of course, outside the laboratory, most of the sounds that we hear do not normally consist of pure oscillations of the kind shown in Figure 4.3. Rather, they are more complex. However, it is a property of complex pressure changes that they can be represented by a sum of component parts of the kind shown in Figure 4.3. This is illustrated in Figure 4.5. A complex sound is equivalent to the sum of a series of sinewaves added together.

Imagine the infinite variety of complex waves that we are able to perceive. How does our sensory system start to categorize all of these? The ear *analyses* pressure waves

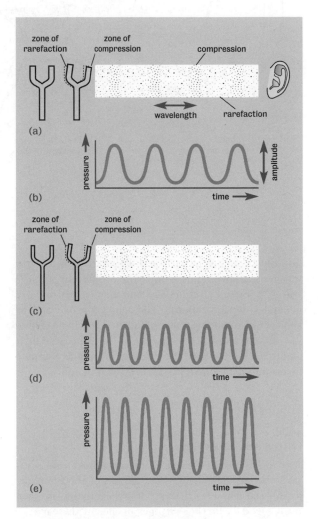

Figure 4.3 The generation of sound (a) tuning fork after being struck, (b) changes in pressure in the air recorded in the vicinity of the tuning fork, (c) a different tuning fork being struck, (d) changes in pressure, (e) the result of the second tuning fork being struck harder
Source: Based upon Vander *et al.* (1994)

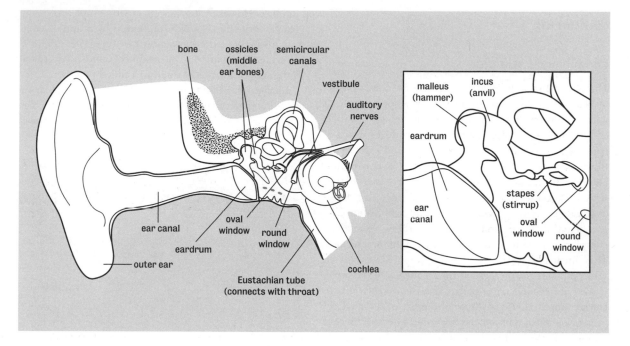

Figure 4.4 The ear
Source: Carlson (1994: 183)

into their component parts at different frequencies. Just imagine the horrendous complexity of different pressure waves at various frequencies and amplitudes that are generated by an orchestra. The conductor, or even the audience, will not hear chaos. Rather they will be able to identify the individual instruments. This is because their auditory systems have the capacity to analyse complex forms into component parts. How is this done?

From pressure to neural activity

Outer and middle ears

As you saw, the first stage of transduction is from pressure changes in the air to oscillations of the tympanic membrane. These oscillations of the membrane are then transduced to further changes deeper in the ear (see Figure 4.4). Within the middle ear, there are three bones, which are caused to oscillate by oscillations of the tympanic membrane. The bones communicate oscillations to a fluid-filled coiled structure termed the cochlea at the oval window. The membrane that forms the oval window vibrates back and forth in sympathy

with the tympanic membrane. At the oval window, movements of a bone are transduced into pressure changes in the fluid that fills the cochlea. This probably seems like a tortuous process and it is not over yet! Tortuous it may be but it is incredibly effective. We now look more closely at the cochlea to see how changes in pressure within a fluid can cause changes in the pattern of activity in neurons.

Inner ear

Figure 4.6 is a simplification of part of the auditory system, showing how vibrations of the tympanic membrane are transduced into vibrations of the basilar membrane. When pressure waves occur in the cochlea, the basilar membrane is caused to move back and forth at a particular location. This location depends upon the frequency of the vibrations, a relationship that is termed a **place code** (see Figure 4.7). For high frequency vibrations, the displacements in the basilar membrane occur near to the end at which it is secured, i.e. the oval window end. Lower frequency vibrations cause movements at points far from the oval window. In other

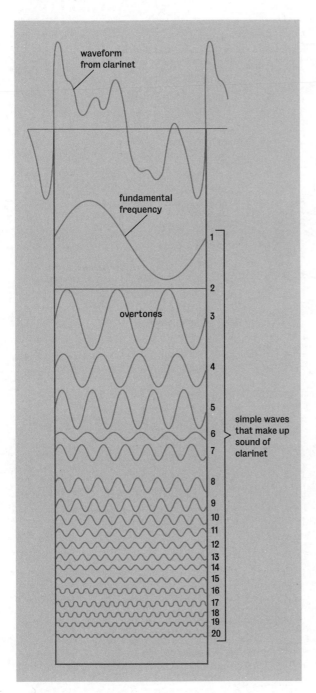

Figure 4.5 A complex wave shown to be the sum of simpler waves
Source: Carlson (1994: 194)

words, there is a transduction process such that frequencies of air pressure are represented by locations on the basilar membrane. Amplitude of changes in air pressure are represented by amplitude of displacements of the basilar membrane.

At the basilar membrane there are fine hair cells. These cells communicate with neurons that project to the brain. When these hair cells are displaced during vibration of the basilar membrane, electrical changes occur in them. This gives rise to action potentials which are transmitted to the brain (see Figure 4.8). Thus, to summarize the sequence, changes in air pressure at different frequencies are transduced into different locations of vibration at the basilar membrane, which are then transduced into different neurons that are activated. (At very low frequencies, such coding can also be in terms of activity in certain neurons being in synchrony with the oscillations of the air pressure.)

Neural mechanisms

A series of neurons conveys information from the ear, through various brain regions to the auditory cortex. Intensity of pressure waves is coded by the rate at which action potentials occur in a particular neuron. The code that frequency is represented by location at the basilar membrane is preserved at the auditory cortex. In other words, at the auditory cortex particular neurons are responsive to particular sound frequencies, corresponding to particular basilar membrane locations. This is known as a **tonotopic representation** (from 'tonos', meaning tone and 'topos', meaning place).

Our auditory system is able not only to discriminate the frequency and intensity of sounds but also the location of their source, whether to the left or the right. How is this achieved? A source of sound to one side will arrive at one ear slightly sooner than the other. This means that action potentials are initiated in one ear slightly sooner than in the other. Among other processes, the brain can exploit differences in arrival times to determine the direction of a sound's source. Neurons carrying information from each ear feed into other neurons in the brain that perform **feature detection** on the incoming information. In this case, the feature is the side from which the sound arrives, as derived from which ear is the source of the first input.

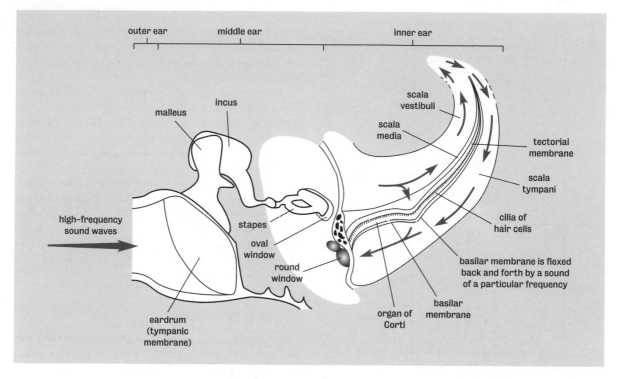

Figure 4.6 Transduction between vibrations of the tympanic membrane and vibrations of the basilar membrane
Source: Carlson (1994: 186)

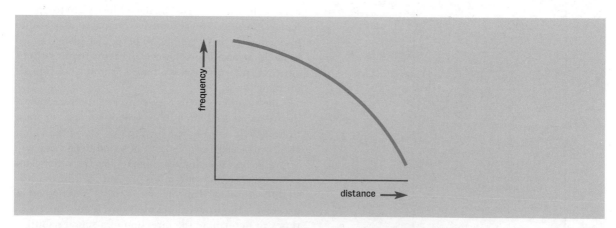

Figure 4.7 Relationship between frequency of sound and location on the basilar membrane (distance from oval window) that responds maximally to it

Another means that the auditory system can exploit is differences in intensity between the two ears. If a source of sound is to the left, then the left ear not only will receive stimulation slightly sooner than the right ear, but it will be more intensely stimulated. The right ear is in a *sonic shadow* cast by the head. Certain neurons in the brain are sensitive to differences in intensity, another example of feature detectors.

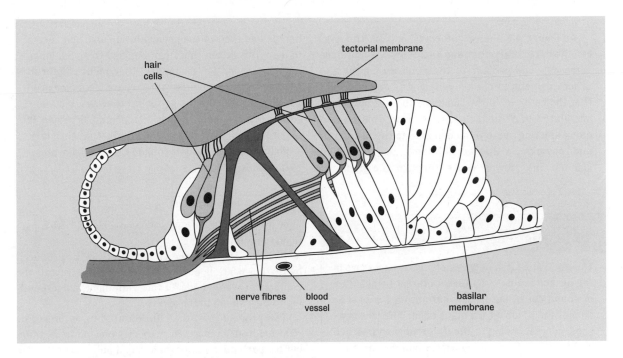

Figure 4.8 Basilar membrane and associated neuron endings
Source: Vander *et al.* (1994: 262)

 Research update

The routes taken by auditory information

Le Doux (1994, 1995) suggested that, at least for emotional information, two memories may be established in parallel, a more basic one in the amygdala and a more complex one in the cortex. This doubtless has important implications for therapies designed to help a patient to overcome fears, such as post-traumatic stress disorders and phobias.

Information on the auditory system and the pathways that auditory information takes has been crucial in the development of Le Doux's model. This is a good example of where we need to take a holistic view of brain and behaviour. That is, knowledge gained in one area of investigation is relevant to a broader area of study. Although for convenience drawing boundaries around systems (e.g. sensory, perceptual, emotional) is sometimes necessary, we also need to be able to stand back and view the system as part of a bigger whole.

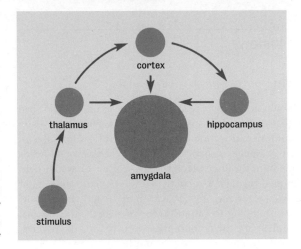

Figure 4.9 Routes that auditory information takes to the brain
Source: Le Doux (1994: 36)

Box continued

As Figure 4.9 shows, information from the ears reaches the thalamus (see Chapter 2). From here some neurons project to the auditory cortex and others project to the amygdala. Le Doux suggests that the route from the thalamus to the amygdala is implicated in a rapid arousal of fear. This gives a quick alerting system in response to the receipt of auditory signals that herald danger, e.g. very loud signals. The slower route through the auditory cortex and then to the amygdala can also play a role in fear. This latter route can be used to give a more refined perception of danger. This might reinforce the fear activated by the faster route, if further processing confirms its danger value. However, if on further processing the signal is interpreted as benign, it might act to inhibit fear activation by the amygdala. A similar dual pathway is found in the visual system, to be discussed next.

Ψ Section summary

The ear transduces between changes in pressure in the air and action potentials. Different frequencies of sound cause different locations on the basilar membrane to vibrate, a place code. Different neurons, corresponding to the different locations, are activated. At the auditory cortex different neurons respond to different sound frequencies.

1 What would be the expected effect of damage at a particular location on the basilar membrane?
2 How do we know from which side of our head a sound originates?

Vision

Light

The physics of light is more difficult to understand than is that of sound. However, light has certain features in common with sound and the topic is best introduced after grasping the basics of sound. Whereas sound needs a medium through which to pass, e.g. air or water, light can pass through a vacuum. However, like sound, light is characterized by a wavelength and frequency. Corresponding to variations in wavelength (the physical stimulus) are the colours that we perceive (the psychological dimension). For example, we describe light having a wavelength of 690 nanometers (nm) as red light. To be more precise, we mean that, given a human's colour vision, light of such a wavelength is normally perceived as red. Strictly speaking then, red is a psychological quality, albeit one usually associated with a particular physical stimulus.

Figure 4.10 shows the visible spectrum, as produced by passing white light through a prism. This reveals the component wavelengths of the white light, corresponding to the colours of the spectrum.

The properties of the light emitted by an object or reflected from an object in part determine our perception but the perception can be understood only by considering the physical stimulus within a context. For example, the hair of a blond person will tend to look light in a wide variety of different conditions of illumination, from sunlight to moonlight. However, the quality of blondness is not intrinsic within the intensity of the light that is reflected from the hair and arrives in the viewer's eyes; blond people cannot be classified as those who reflect high levels of illumination. More light will be reflected from a person with black hair viewed in sunlight than a blond in moonlight. What characterizes the blond person is that, relative to a surround (e.g. standing next to a dark-haired person), the blond person's hair tends to reflect more light. What is said to be *invariant* is the hair's property of a high reflectance. Similarly, a robin's breast tends to look red because it reflects a large proportion of red light relative to other objects, such as its wings (Zeki 1993).

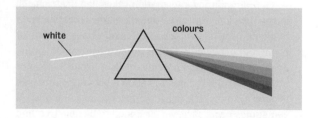

Figure 4.10 The visible spectrum (see colour plate 2)

From eye to brain

Optics of the eye

See Figure 4.11: the optics of the eye forms an image of the outside world at the retina, i.e. the cornea and lens normally bring rays of light to a focus there. The image on the retina is upside down and reversed left to right with respect to the external world. Of course, the fact that the world is upside down on the retina has no particular significance for our vision since the image has always been upside down. Thus, there is a consistency between a particular pattern of image and the signals produced in neurons.

Following Stratton's lead, other investigators also tried inverting their visual worlds by wearing optical instruments (see Gregory 1973). From surveying such accounts, Gregory suggests that there is something very odd about the perceived world, even though the investigators cannot articulate exactly what it is. He suggests that rather than the world starting to appear normal, they might simply cease to notice how odd it is until their attention is drawn to a particular feature of it.

Returning now to consider normal non-inverted worlds, the external world is not static and the objects

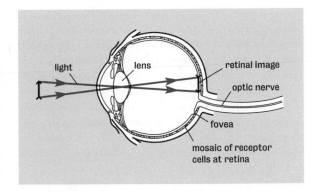

Figure 4.11 The eye

of our attention tend to move relative to our eyes. Also, even when viewing a static world, the object of our attention can vary. When this object does not coincide with an optimal location on the retina, movements of the eyes in space are necessary. Such movement can arise from movement of the head or whole body or from movements of the eyes relative to the head.

The eyes rotate in their sockets as a result of the activity of special oculomotor muscles attached to the eyeballs. Oculomotor nerves (examples of cranial

---

Ψ Case study

A scientist wearing inverting spectacles

Researchers into vision have sometimes gallantly experimented upon themselves in order to gain knowledge of the underlying processes. A classic case was that of George Stratton of the University of California. In the latter part of the nineteenth century, Stratton wore an optical instrument in order to invert the images on his retina (Stratton 1897). This meant that the image was now the 'right' way up relative to the external world. When Stratton was not wearing this apparatus, he was blindfolded. He was interested in discovering how the visual system adapted, if at all, to the new conditions. He walked around, sometimes through his village, for a period of eight days wearing the apparatus.

At first Stratton experienced a complete inversion of the external world: 'Almost all movements performed under the direct guidance of sight were laborious and embarrassed', he reported.

An important role of memory and of integration between sensory channels in determining perception was evident:

As regards the parts of the body, their pre-experimental representation often invaded the region directly in sight. Arms and legs in full view were given a double position. Beside the position and relation in which they were actually seen, there was always in the mental background, in intimate connection with muscular and tactual sensations, the older representation of these parts.

(Stratton 1897: 344–5)

Towards the end of the period, Stratton experienced some adaptation to the new condition. Movements came to be made with respect to the new perceived position and without a conscious readjustment. This shows some capacity for the nervous system to adapt to something even as fundamental as a complete inversion of the visual image.

nerves) contain neurons that activate these muscles. Some eye movements are smooth, as when we track a smoothly moving target. Other movements are sudden and jerky, known as **saccadic eye movements**. Such saccadic eye movements can be involuntary ('automatic'), as in the case of a sudden movement of the object of attention, corresponding to a move of the image from one retinal location to another. Saccadic movements can also be voluntary, as when we decide to move our object of attention suddenly from one location to another.

A neural pathway

Considering the details more closely, Figure 4.12 shows a much simplified cross-section through part of the retina. A mosaic of receptor cells of two kinds, rods and cones, forms a layer within the retina. These receptor cells are sensitive to light, meaning that when they absorb light they change their electrical state (explained on p. 31). Note that, curiously, the eye is 'inside-out'. Light must pass through layers of other cells before reaching the receptor cells.

When light is absorbed by a receptor cell, a sensitive instrument would be able to detect a slight change in electrical activity at the cell. This is not an action potential but a less abrupt change than that. On absorbing light, the rods and cones then pass on a message, via synapses, to other neurons, the bipolar cells (see Figure 4.12). This message conveys information about the light absorbed by the receptors. Again via synapses and something like in a relay-race, the bipolar cells relay the information to ganglion cells which then convey the

information to the brain as a pattern of action potentials. The bundle of millions of the axons of the ganglion cells constitutes the optic nerve, one of the cranial nerves (see Figures 4.11 and 4.12).

The eye is sometimes compared to a camera but, although the analogy has some validity, it is misleading to pursue it too far. Like the camera, there is an apparatus for forming an image and there is photosensitive material (film or receptors). Where the analogy breaks down is that vision is an active dynamic construction based only in part upon information at the retina and also, in part, upon memories, expectancies, and so on.

The fact that the wavelengths shown as different colours in Figure 4.10 constitute the visual stimuli to which our eyes are responsive is explained by the properties of the chemicals contained within the receptors. The rods come in just one variety and Figure 4.13 shows an absorption curve of the chemical contained within a rod. As far as the rods' contribution to vision is concerned, we are sensitive to light of a particular wavelength to the extent that it is absorbed by the chemical contained within the rods. Note that the rod is maximally sensitive to a wavelength of 498 nm, sensitivity falling to either side.

Cones come in three forms corresponding to three different chemicals contained within them. The absorption characteristics of the three kinds of cones are also shown in Figure 4.13; the significance of these for colour vision is explored on pp. 116–17. The three types of cones are commonly termed red, blue and green but immediately caution is in order in using these expres-

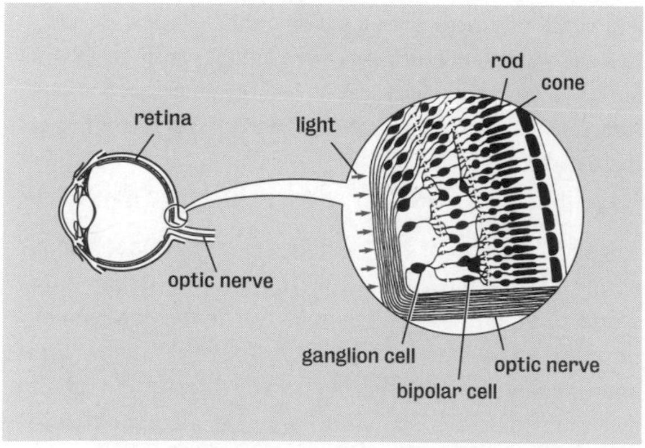

Figure 4.12 Cross-section through a part of the retina

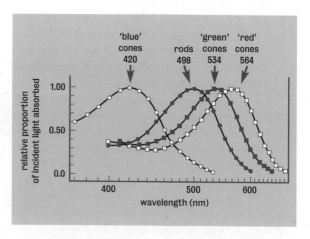

Figure 4.13 The absorption characteristic of the chemical contained within rods and the three types of cones

sions. The terms derive from the wavelengths of light to which the cone is maximally sensitive. Note though that, say, a green cone is not simply sensitive to green light but is also sensitive (though less so) to a range of other wavelengths including those corresponding to blue and red. The other caution is in thinking that because a cone is labelled as a 'green cone', the psychological perception of green is simply associated one-to-one to the absorption of light by such a cone. Complex processing is involved in the psychological perception of green, of which the absorption of light of a particular wavelength by cones is only one part.

Figure 4.14 shows a view of the visual system. The optic nerve, one of the cranial nerves, is made up of the axons of all the ganglion cells. Imagine that the absorption of light by a number of receptors leads to a burst of activity, i.e. action potentials, in a particular ganglion cell. These action potentials are transmitted along the length of the axon of the ganglion cell. Ganglion cells have various destinations, one of which is a nucleus of the thalamus, known as the lateral geniculate nucleus (LGN). As shown in Figure 4.14, some ganglion cells go to another brain region, termed the superior colliculus.

Consider for a moment the pathway to the LGN and beyond. The ganglion cells make synapses in the lateral geniculate nucleus. Information leaves the LGN neurons by the axons of LGN neurons. This information is still specific to a given eye. Thus any LGN neuron is driven by either the left or right eye but not by both. The LGN neurons arrive at the visual cortex, where they form synapses with cortical neurons.

The external world as viewed by the eyes is termed 'the visual field' (Figure 4.14). Consider the visual field to the right of the midline of each eye. Light arising from the right half of the visual field arrives at the left half of each retina. Light from the left visual field arrives at the right half of each retina. Neural pathways run from the left half of each eye to the left half of the brain. Pathways from the right side of each eye run to the right side of the brain. This involves a cross-over of half the pathway from each eye to the other side, at the optic chiasm.

Processing in the pathway

In stating that information is *conveyed* from the retina to the brain, an important qualification needs to be added. The information carried in the visual image is not simply converted one-to-one into the form of a faithful electrical signal that conveys exactly the same information.

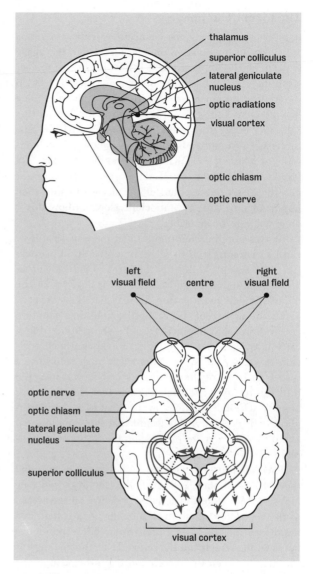

Figure 4.14 Imaginary view of the visual system; this view is from above but shows the visual pathway, which is actually hidden below the cerebral cortex

Rather, in the process of conveying information, some information is discarded and other signals are accentuated. The brain receives information already predigested as far as importance is concerned. Systems of connections between the neurons within the visual pathways are such that certain types of information are either valued or devalued. This section gives some examples of the kind of information processing that occurs at the level of the retina.

The form of an image

In a variety of species, the connections within the retina are such that information on contours within the image is particularly emphasized. It is not difficult to understand the value of this process. Imagine yourself to be on the African savannah with an enraged elephant bearing down on you. Your survival is best guaranteed by putting a distance between you and the elephant. To achieve this, the visual system needs to place weight upon the contours of where the elephant stops and the clear blue sky starts. Neither the exact shade of grey of the elephant nor the exact hue of blue of the sky is of quite such importance to you! An important aspect of how this is done will now be described.

As was noted earlier, neurons in the visual pathway can be characterized by their receptive field properties. The receptive field is that area of retina which, when stimulated by light, affects the activity of the neuron under investigation. Researchers have investigated the nature of the receptive field of a ganglion cell (i.e. neuron) in a cat's visual system. To do this, a cat was anaesthetized and its head held in a fixed position. A very small spot of light was projected onto a screen in front of the cat. An electrode was inserted into the optic nerve such as to detect the electrical activity within a single axon, i.e. that of a single ganglion cell. Typically, it is found that the ganglion cell exhibits some activity even when the retina is in complete darkness.

Then the retina is explored with the spot of light and the activity of the ganglion cell again observed (see Figure 4.15). Note the activity as shown on the screen of the recording apparatus. Since the head is held in a fixed location, there is a one-to-one correspondence between the screen and the retina. Thus, the investigator can map between the screen and the retina assuming a constant relationship.

First, consider that the spot is applied at the location marked 1 on the screen, as represented in Figure 4.16a. Suppose that there is no change in frequency of action potentials from when the eye is in complete darkness. This means that, by definition, location 1 is outside the receptive field of the neuron, i.e. stimulation with light at this site does not affect the neuron. Therefore, a zero (0) is indicated on the figure. Similarly, light falling at location 2 has no effect and a 0 is placed there also. At location 3, the ganglion cell is observed to reduce its frequency of action potentials relative to darkness. This means that light falling here *is* within the receptive field, since it influences the frequency of action potentials of

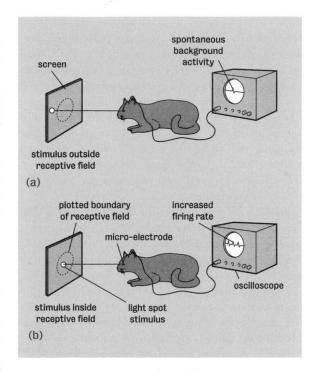

Figure 4.15 Procedure for recording the electrical activity of ganglion cell, shown when light is (a) outside receptive field, (b) inside excitatory area of receptive field

the cell. Specifically, it is within the inhibitory region of the receptive field and so a minus sign is placed at 3. Similarly a minus sign is placed at 4. When light is projected to 5, the ganglion cell now *increases* its rate of action potentials as compared to darkness. Therefore a plus is placed at 5. The same effect is found at 6. Illumination at 7 yields no reaction and so a zero is placed there.

Suppose that we explore all of the retina with the small spot of light, while still recording from the same ganglion cell. Typically we might find the effect shown in Figure 4.16b. If we join together all of the pluses and all of the minuses, we obtain the shape shown. This defines the receptive field of the ganglion cell, consisting of an excitatory centre (termed ON region) and an inhibitory surround (termed OFF region).

Let us now consider some light stimuli and see what the reaction of the ganglion cell is. What is the optimal stimulus to trigger activity in this ganglion cell? It is a spot of light that is large enough to fill the excitatory centre region but not sufficiently large as to encroach upon the inhibitory surround, as shown in Figure 4.17a. Note the excitation when the light is switched on.

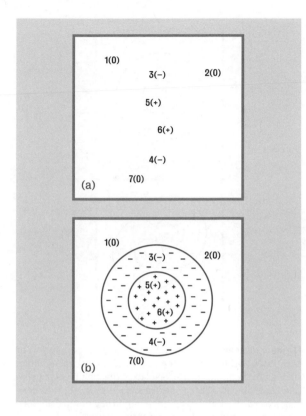

Figure 4.16 Results obtained from stimulating retina (a) some points, (b) complete pattern of points joined together

There are other ganglion cells that have precisely the opposite characteristic: light falling on the centre region of the receptive field inhibits the ganglion cell whereas light falling on the outer area excites it (see Figure 4.18). What kind of stimulus might trigger such activity? One possibility is a polar bear's black nose surrounded by pristine white fur. As it approaches you, it will at some point correspond to the trigger stimulus. The adaptive value of being informed of such a stimulus hardly needs mentioning!

The type of ganglion cell that has just been described is one which has a particular receptive field organization. Light of *any* wavelength falling within the ON area of the receptive field tends to excite the ganglion and light of any wavelength in the OFF area tends to inhibit it. This is the property of **lateral inhibition**, i.e. inhibition across the retina from one location to another. An analogous inhibition exists in other sensory systems (Latto 1995). The ganglion cell under consideration is

What is the optimal stimulus to inhibit activity in the cell? An annulus of light that fills the surround region but does not encroach upon the centre (see Figure 4.17b).

Suppose a large light stimulus is applied that covers both the centre and surround regions. Can you work out for yourself what its effect might be? It depends upon the relative weightings of the two regions of the receptive field but the effect of light in one region will cancel the effect of light in the other. Typically, there might be no response at all from the ganglion cell (see Figure 4.17c).

As you can see, the ganglion cell has performed feature detection. By an increase in action potential frequency to above baseline, it indicates the presence of a spot of light at the centre region but not encroaching into the surround. What kind of stimulus might trigger such activity? The light from a small star at night might just fill the ON region with no light falling in the OFF region. By contrast a bright sky would produce light falling on all of the receptive field and therefore trigger no activity in the ganglion.

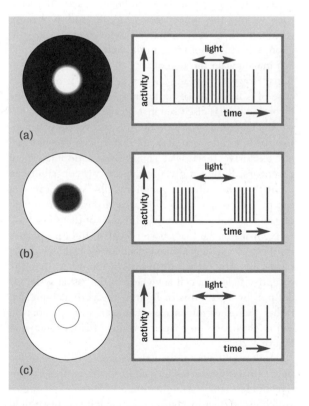

Figure 4.17 Responses of a ganglion cell to various light stimuli (a) light spot in centre region of receptive field, (b) light annulus in outer region, (c) illumination of all of the receptive field

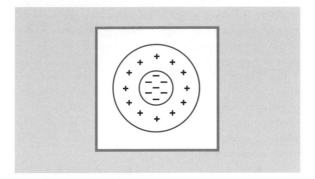

Figure 4.18 An OFF centre/ON surround characteristic of a ganglion cell's receptive field

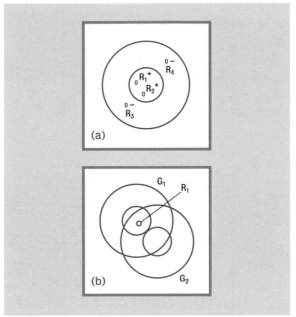

Figure 4.19 Receptive field properties (a) a population of receptors within the centre region of the receptive field, such as R_1, R_2, make excitatory links (through bipolar cells) to a ganglion cell; other receptors, such as R_3, R_4, that correspond to the OFF area, make inhibitory connections to the ganglion, (b) overlapping receptive fields

unable to signal information on the wavelength of light. It simply signals the presence or absence of lights of any wavelength within the sub-regions of its receptive field. Based upon this property, it is possible to speculate what kind of neural connections cells at the retina form with such a ganglion cell, as shown in Figure 4.19a. All receptors within the inner area (e.g. R_1 and R_2) make (through other cells) excitatory connections to the ganglion, whereas all of those in the outer area (e.g. R_3 and R_4) make (again through other cells) inhibitory connections. However, not all ganglion cells are of this type. A type of cell that signals differences in wavelength of the incoming light is discussed in a later section.

As Figure 4.19b shows, there is an overlap of receptive fields at the retina. It is not that a given ganglion cell has exclusive territorial rights over a population of receptors. Rather a given receptor can contribute an input to many different ganglion cells. As you can see, receptor R_1 is within the ON area of the receptive field of ganglion cell G_1 but in the OFF area of that of G_2.

Neurons in the LGN have receptive field properties similar to those of ganglion cells. However, those of cortical cells are rather different. Remember that the receptive field of a cell anywhere in the visual system is defined by a stimulus of light at the retina. Typically, rather than the concentric form seen so far, a cortical cell might have a slit-shaped receptive field, as shown in Figure 4.20a.

How might we explain the form of this receptive field? Imagine a series of ganglion cells whose receptive fields form a straight line at the retina, some of which are shown in Figure 4.20b. Each receptive field is made up from an ON centre and an OFF surround. Now imagine that these ganglion cells feed into a series of LGN cells. The LGN cells all feed into a single

cortical cell. What will be the optimal stimulus to trigger activity in this cortical cell? Activity in all of the LGN cells that feed it. Such activity will derive from activity in all of the ganglion cells that feed the LGN cells. What light stimulus will maximize the activity in this series of ganglion cells? A slit of light as shown in Figure 4.20c.

The sensitivity of cortical cells to the orientation of a stimulus (e.g. the particular orientation of the receptive field shown in Figure 4.20) provides a particularly good example of the subtle interdependence between genetics and environment in the development of the visual system. In general, genetics and a normal early exposure to visual stimulation yield a pattern of orientation sensitivity of the cells of the visual cortex such that all orientations are well represented and each eye has roughly equal amount of strength of input to excite these cells (Zeki 1993).

However, an equal representation of all angles and each eye arises only if the condition of a history of *normal* visual stimulation is met. Suppose vision is defective in one eye. In that case, the intact eye will tend to

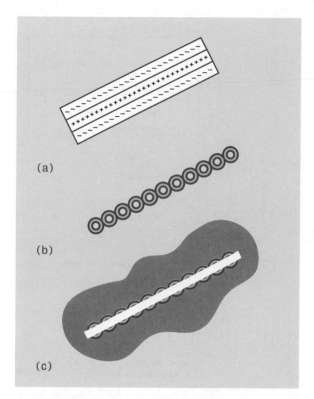

Figure 4.20 The properties of a cortical cell (a) receptive field of cortical cell, made up of excitatory inner slit and inhibitory surround, (b) receptive fields of a series of ganglion cells that provide the excitatory input to the cortical cell, (c) optimal stimulus to trigger the cortical cell

Detailed features or a coarse perception?

Depending upon the visual stimulus, sometimes an animal needs to resolve fine detail (e.g. a flying hawk distinguishing the movements of a mouse in a corn-field) and at other times less detailed analysis will suffice (e.g. a mouse detecting the presence of a large shadow). The ability of the visual system to resolve detail varies depending upon the region of retina on which the image falls.

There are many more receptors at the retina than there are ganglion cells. In humans, there are something like 106 million receptors for 'only' 1 million ganglion cells. This means that there is a considerable convergence of the outputs from receptors on to ganglion cells. The extent of this convergence varies from one part of the retina to another. At the region called the fovea (Figure 4.11), there is rather little convergence. In some cases, individual cones have private links to the brain. By contrast, in the periphery, very many rods all feed their inputs into a single ganglion cell.

The implications of this variation in convergence are considerable since the kind of visual processing that the regions of retina can perform are a function of it. Where there is little convergence, i.e. at, or near, the fovea, the ability to resolve fine detail is high, described as a high **acuity**. At the periphery of the retina, there is a large convergence of inputs to ganglion cells. In contrast to the fovea, here the ability to resolve detail is poor since there is a pooling of output from receptors. However, as a result of this pooling, the ability to detect the presence or absence of weak lights is relatively good.

An analogy can help here. Suppose that we are interested in producing a profile of the rainfall at a series of streets of terraced houses. To do so, we inspect the flow of water down the drainpipes. Suppose that all of the houses within a long street have one single communal drainpipe. Monitoring flow within it would give us a sensitive measure of even light drizzles falling somewhere in the street since the roofs are pooling what falls on all of them to give the single flow. However, we would not be able to resolve the detail of where exactly in the street the rain was falling. Suppose instead that each house has its own individual drainpipe. It might be difficult to detect the presence of a light shower since only a little flow would be generated from what is caught by a single roof. If, however, it was pouring down at number 12 but dry at number 22 we would be aware of this from monitoring individual drainpipes. As you can see, two different sorts of information are derived from the communal and the individual drainpipes.

seize control of more cortical cells at the expense of the eye that is not functioning normally. This suggests that although the input connections are coded genetically, they are not rigidly fixed. Similarly, if an animal is raised in a world of only vertical stripes, the number of cortical cells sensitive to vertical lines will be relatively high. Genetics and early development provide a 'provisional plan' which is then normally consolidated by visual experience. As discussed in Chapter 2, it suggests that there is competition for control of the cortical cell. Active synapses are strengthened and inactive ones are eliminated. This illustrates a case of the plasticity of the nervous system.

When the response properties of neurons in the visual cortex are examined there is an orderly relationship between the retina and the cortex. Adjacent regions of retina are associated with adjacent neurons in the visual cortex, something described as a **topographical map** (Zeki 1993).

By analogy with the drainpipes, the eye has the benefit of both systems. When you resolve fine detail as in watchmaking, by means of eye movements the image is brought to the fovea. When you want to detect the presence of a weak light stimulating a relatively large area of retina, the eyes will move such as to bring the image away from the fovea. You can experiment with this yourself. Find a faint distant star and stare in a focused way at it. You might well find that it will then disappear. Staring corresponds to bringing its image to a focus at the fovea.

Colour

So far we have mainly considered the detection of images in terms of light–dark. How do we perceive colour? Before we look briefly at what a knowledge of sensory systems can contribute to answering this question, it can be useful to consider a related theme: how things might have been otherwise. For instance, imagine an eye that had only rods and was lacking cones. Could such an eye extract information on the wavelength of light? You have seen that rods are differentially sensitive to wavelength (Figure 4.13), which might have suggested that they are able to do this. However, it is easily demonstrated that it is not possible for the rods to exploit this differential sensitivity to encode information on wavelength.

As shown in Figure 4.21, suppose that a light of wavelength X (498 nm) and intensity 100 units were to fall on the rods. Suppose also that this generates action potentials at a frequency of 100 per second in the ganglion cell to which the stimulated rods provide an input. Now keeping the light intensity at 100 units, suppose that the wavelength is changed to Y, to which the rods are less sensitive. The action potential frequency falls to, say, 50 per second. You might have supposed that the frequency of action potentials in the ganglion cell would therefore give a measure of wavelength. In a sense you would be right and this might work provided that the light intensity always stayed the same. But, of course, the world is not usually made up of lights having a constant intensity. As you can imagine from inspecting Figure 4.21, there would be no way that the rods and thereby the ganglion could distinguish between a light of 100 units intensity at wavelength X and one of 200 units intensity at wavelength Y. Of course, we are able to make such distinctions. Blue looks blue whether it is an intense blue light or a faint one. So how is this done?

The trick is that, by employing more than one type of cone, the visual system can *in effect* compare the responses of one cone with that of another. If the light is

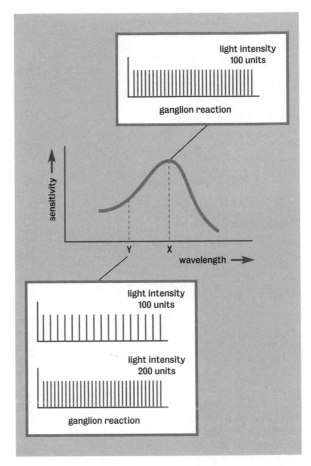

Figure 4.21 Sensitivity of a population of rods to light of various wavelengths and associated activity in a ganglion cell

of wavelength 534 nm, the green cone will always be more strongly stimulated than the red or blue, irrespective of the intensity of the light falling on the eye, as Figure 4.13 represents.

One possible mode of connections to a ganglion cell is that the output from, say, green cones excites the cell whereas the output from red cones inhibits it. Thus, an increase in firing above the spontaneous level indicates the presence of green light and a suppression to below this level indicates a red light. This is an example of **opponent-process coding**. For some ganglion cells, there is a red ON region and a green OFF region, or vice versa, as illustrated in Figure 4.22 (Rose 1995). You can demonstrate the existence of opponent-process coding for yourself with the help of Figure 4.23. Stare at the top cross for a minute or two in a bright light and then transfer your gaze to the bottom

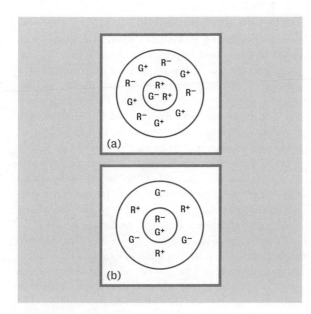

Figure 4.22 Ganglion cells with colour-specific sub-regions of receptive field (a) cell with centre red+, green– and periphery green+, red–, (b) cell with centre green+, red– and periphery red+, green–

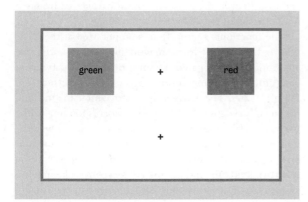

Figure 4.23 Illusion which demonstrates colour opponency (see colour plate 3)

cross. You should see coloured objects appear for a while. They should be rather different from those at which you stared. This is an illusion since the paper is pure white. How is it to be explained?

As a result of exposure to light, cones fatigue and thereby, after a period of stimulation, signal the light's presence less strongly. Cones that are relatively unstimulated will not be fatigued. When light first falls on them, they will tend to give a strong response. Consider the green object. While you stare at the cross, the green object will be fatiguing your green cones within an area of retina but your red cones within this same area will be relatively unfatigued. When you divert your gaze to the bottom cross, the light that is stimulating this retinal area is white. As we have seen (Figure 4.10), white light is made up of all the colours of the spectrum, including both green and red. So the red component of the white light will stimulate preferentially a population of red cones that are not fatigued and therefore they give a strong response. The green component of the white light stimulates a fatigued population of green cones, which respond weakly. It is therefore as if the eye were being stimulated with red light and indeed that is exactly what you perceive. Within a short time the red cones will be as fatigued as the green, there is no differential fatigue and so the perception is of white. (A similar logic applies to the red object.)

Stereopsis

Because of their physical separation in space the two eyes have slightly different views of an object. The information from the two eyes first comes together at the cortex. There are cells in the cortex which are driven by both eyes and which are sensitive to differences in the image. This enables us to estimate the distance of objects.

Parallel processing within the visual system

When you reflect upon your psychological perception of the world, it doubtless has a sense of unity to it. It might come as some surprise to you to know how this is achieved. In fact, perception depends upon a number of distinct processes acting in parallel, encoding different aspects of the visual image. That, at some level, this all comes together to give a unified perception represents a daunting achievement.

This section looks at two types of parallel processing of information. In one classification system, the ganglion cells form the input to two different systems of information processing. In humans, these systems are sometimes termed the **primary visual system** and **secondary visual system** (Bronson 1974). However, more recent classifications have made this neat dichotomy somewhat less clear. Some neurons from the lateral geniculate nucleus of the thalamus do not go to the visual cortex but go to the amygdala (Le Doux 1994). This gives vision a pathway corresponding to that described for the auditory system (see research update 'The routes taken by auditory information'). Indeed, Le Doux describes a very vivid example of how fear can be aroused by visual information arriving at the amygdala: a person perceives that she is about to step on a snake.

Not only can the visual system be categorized between primary and secondary systems but also there is a distinct categorization within the primary system. This is the second topic of this section.

Primary and secondary visual systems

So far we have focused upon the primary visual system, i.e. the sequence ganglion cell $\rightarrow$ LGN $\rightarrow$ visual cortex. However, in humans, some 100,000 ganglion cell axons provide information outside the (LGN) $\rightarrow$ (visual cortex) route (Weiskrantz 1986). This is more than the number of axons in all of the auditory nerve. Thus, a significant segregation of information already starts at the retina. A number of ganglion cells make synaptic connections in the superior colliculi (see Figure 4.14). It is somewhat unfortunate that this system is termed the secondary visual system, since in evolutionary terms it is the older system (Bronson 1974). For so-called lower animals this is probably the most important visual system. The system of projection to the cortex is a more recent evolutionary development.

The primary and secondary systems serve different functions. Whereas the primary system evolved in the service of fine-grained discriminations of the image, the secondary system is specialized for more coarse 'rough and ready' analysis (Schiller 1985). This enables the superior colliculus to direct quick reflex responses to strong and easily identified stimuli. Examples include prey capture or predator avoidance where there is a premium upon a quick reaction. Another example of such a rapid reaction is the role of the superior colliculus in producing eye movements. The secondary system is particularly sensitive to stimuli falling on the periphery of the retina. At least in primates, it appears to be unable to resolve the fine detail of complex patterns, which is performed by the primary system (Bronson 1974). The functions of the superior colliculus include that of moving the direction of gaze of the eyes towards a target that is stimulating the periphery of the retina. An output from the superior colliculus goes to neurons that control the neck muscles (Schneider 1969). Trevarthan (1968) refers to *ambient vision* as that mediated by the secondary system and *focal vision* as that mediated by the primary visual system. As another way of looking at this and a first approximation, the secondary system is responsible for detection and localization of objects, whereas the primary system is responsible for their identification and fine-grained analysis (Schneider 1969; Weiskrantz 1986).

Within the primary system

Parallel processing also occurs within the route from retina to the cortex. Consider again two things about visual perception. (1) Events that we perceive fall on a population of receptors at the retina. (2) We see the world as a unitary integrated whole. Therefore, given 1 and 2, it might seem surprising to you that qualities such as colour, movement and depth are, to a large extent, processed separately. The unitary nature of perception doubtless led researchers for many years to reject the idea of separate parallel channels (Zeki 1993). However, in reality, the component computations are combined only at a relatively late stage of perception to give the wholeness that we experience (Livingstone and Hubel 1995).

The division of labour starts at the retina. The evidence suggests that two different types of ganglion cells correspond to the start of separate channels of processing. These two types of ganglion cells are termed magno and parvo cells (Livingstone and Hubel 1995; Rose 1995). The magno cells are especially sensitive to fast-moving stimuli and to differences in illumination in the image. They seem to provide an input to the brain from which movement is calculated. However, they are insensitive to differences in colour. The parvo cells are sensitive to stationary images and to colour, in that they are strongly triggered by, say, a border between red and green in the image.

The functional segregation is emphasized at the LGN where the inputs from magno and parvo cells are anatomically segregated, in spite of these two types of ganglion cells being intermingled at the retina (see Figure 4.24). The LGN cells onto which magno and parvo cells synapse show responses corresponding to the magno and parvo properties of ganglion cells. Hence the information that is sent to the cortex remains functionally segregated constituting what might be termed a **magno system** and a **parvo system**. The magno system is particularly tuned for changes in the image. Images that are visible with the help of only this system disappear within a few seconds if fixated (Livingstone and Hubel 1995). Thus, it is tuned for the detection of moving objects. The parvo system is specialized for the analysis of the details of the world, a process that can take time and involve exploiting differences in colour. The magno system appears to be older in the sense of its emergence in evolution, with the parvo system being a more recent acquisition (Livingstone and Hubel 1995).

At the primary visual cortex there remains some segregation but also some combination of information occurs (Livingstone and Hubel 1995). That is to say, there are cortical neurons that have both magno and

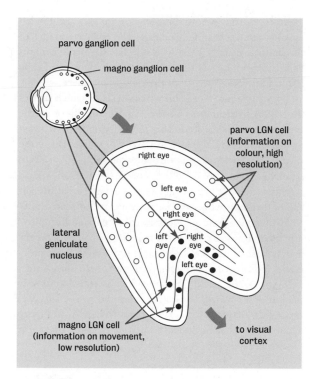

parvo ganglion cell

magno ganglion cell

parvo LGN cell (information on colour, high resolution)

right eye

left eye

right eye

left eye

right eye

lateral geniculate nucleus

left eye

magno LGN cell (information on movement, low resolution)

to visual cortex

Figure 4.24 Segregation of parvo and magno cells at the LGN

parvo inputs. Beyond the primary visual cortex other distinct cortical regions are each responsible for analysis of a particular quality of the visual image: form, colour and motion. This is the theory of *functional specialization* in the visual cortex, proposed by Zeki (1993).

That brain damage can make a subject blind for just one quality of vision is evidence for functional specialization of processing. When this blindness is just for colour, the condition is termed **achromatopsia** (Zeki 1993). Colour perception involves both the primary visual cortex *and* other cortical regions that are specific for the processing of information on colour.

Grandmother cells?

Consider the sequence of information from light impacting upon the retinal receptors, to ganglion cells, then LGN cells, to cells in the primary visual area of the cortex and then to functionally distinct regions of the cortex. Successively further features are 'extracted' from the information originally at the image.

How we perceive, say, a red Volkswagen is still something of a mystery. Do we have a specific 'red Volkswagen' neuron? That we can identify red Volkswagens in so many different orientations suggests that we might even have a series of such neurons. The theory that we have a specific neuron for the perception of each object is generally summed up in the expression **grandmother cell**, meaning that, following this line of theorizing, we would have a neuron specific to a particular grandmother. Usually when such a notion was discussed it was done so in the context of rejection of the idea. It seemed implausible that we should have a single neuron for each perception. If one could remove this single neuron would we then fail to identify our grandmother? Only a slight accident or a lowered blood supply to the specific brain region might easily kill this particular cell and then one

 Case study

Madame R.'s visual deficit

In 1888, Dr L. Verrey, an ophthalmic surgeon working in Neuchâtel, Switzerland, reported a case of a patient, Madame R., 60 years of age, who experienced a loss of colour sensation in the right part of the visual field (Verrey 1888). Coloured objects appeared to be grey. Verrey noted that earlier cases of such loss were accompanied by loss of other faculties such as reading. However, Madame R. seemed to represent a pure case of loss of colour sensation with all other abilities remaining functional, albeit with slight impairment. This suggested that there exists a specific brain region

serving the function of colour analysis. Verrey noted that this was a notion that several authors had resisted. It was one which continued to be resisted even after Verrey provided his evidence (Zeki 1993).

Verrey noted at the autopsy of his patient that she had a discrete lesion in the left occipital lobe. Nowhere else was there damage to be seen. The case of Madame R. is a good example of where valuable insight can be gained from the misfortune of brain damage. Her case also reminds us that evidence that does not fit the current fashion still needs to be given serious consideration and not rejected.

might have a selective blindness for one of our two grandmothers (Zeki 1993)! In spite of the rejection of the idea of grandmother cells as being naive, scientists have been less clear as to how to explain the biological basis of the later stages of perception. Also an increasing amount of evidence has been accumulated enabling us to locate particular neurons having particular responsibility for certain key perceptions, such as human faces (Perrett *et al.* 1995).

So where does this leave us regarding the existence of red Volkswagen cells and grandmother cells? Presumably no one would suggest that we have inborn neural systems common to all people for recognizing red Volkswagens! The existence of certain preferential perception processes such as those underlying face perception does not really illuminate the issue of how the multitude of different perceptions arise.

The visual system in context

Having introduced the details, this section looks at the visual system in a broader context, among other things considering the way in which some visual systems differ from the normal intact adult human variety. To do so, it considers these systems within the contexts of abnormality and development. Brains can be damaged by accidents and disease. Pathology requires the removal of brain regions or lesioning of neural pathways. How the visual system performs following such events can give valuable insights into its normal function. Also it is possible to compare visual systems asking whether damage to an adult system creates changes that make it more like an undeveloped system or more like that of another species. Of course, the human visual system does not come into the world in its adult form 'ready made' and 'hard-wired' to go. It has a developmental history, involving growth of cells and changing the connections between them. Developmental changes are a source of valuable insight.

Damaged brains

This section will, first, look again at split-brain patients, introduced in Chapter 2, and then will consider the phenomenon of blindsight.

Sometimes the corpus callosum is surgically cut (Figure 4.25) in an attempt to alleviate epilepsy, i.e. to stop epilepsy that arises from abnormal electrical activity in one hemisphere from influencing the other (Sperry 1967). Such patients are termed 'split-brain' patients.

Figure 4.25 shows how some responsibilities are divided up between the two hemispheres. The language centre of the brain is usually located in the left hemisphere. This hemisphere controls the activity of the right hand. The left hand is controlled from the right hemisphere.

Look at Figure 4.25. Information from which half of the visual field arrives in the same hemisphere as the speech centre is located? This information is first transformed from light to electric activity in which half of the retina? Try to work this out for yourself. Information from the right visual field is converted into electrical activity at the left half of each retina and arrives at the left half of the brain where the language centre is located.

Using split-brain patients as volunteers and employing specially designed tests in which images are very briefly flashed on to a screen, it is possible to send information to just one hemisphere. Figure 4.26 shows this. In Figure 4.26a, the information 'key' is available to only the left hemisphere. The subject can both verbalize 'key' and select a key with the right hand. When, as in Figure 4.26b, the information is available to only the right

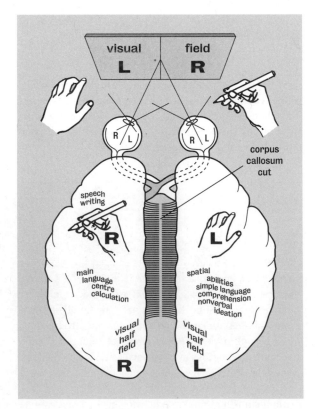

Figure 4.25 A split brain

hemisphere the subject can neither select the correct object with the left hand nor verbalize 'key'.

If the right hand were touching the objects or they were projected to the right visual field, then the subject could verbally articulate them. Subjects could select with their left hand an object corresponding to the word projected onto the left visual field (e.g. a knife in response to the word knife). Each hemisphere could function on its own but could not perform tasks that required inter-hemispheric communication.

Figure 4.26 Projecting information to just one hemisphere and setting a task that requires just the one hemisphere (a) task for left hemisphere, (b) task for right hemisphere; note that the right hand is controlled by the left hemisphere and vice versa
Source: Metcalfe (1992, Figure 6.8)

The second phenomenon to be considered here is that of **blindsight**. To explain this, it is useful to consider some background information. It used to be believed that in humans a lesion in the visual cortex causes total blindness corresponding to a region of the visual field. Thus, its effect would be comparable to that of a lesion in the retina, which is indeed one of total blindness corresponding to the affected region. However, there was the occasional dissenting voice suggesting that patients were sensitive to moving objects within the so-called blind region of the visual field (Zeki 1993). Also there is a paradox here, as follows (Weiskrantz 1986). As noted earlier, some 100,000 ganglion cell axons convey information outside the (LGN) → (visual cortex) route. What are these 100,000 axons doing? In the 1970s, scientific evidence emerged showing that patients did indeed retain a certain visual capacity corresponding to the affected areas.

D.B. is the most famous blindsight patient but he is by no means alone. A syndrome of blindsight has now been established and the study of these patients has contributed a valuable understanding not only to the visual system but to theories on the nature of conscious and unconscious determinants of behaviour (Moscovitch 1995).

In blindsight, where is the unconscious processing taking place? There are some neurons that pass from the LGN to cortical regions other than the primary visual cortex and these could play a role (Zeki 1993). Some regions of cortex appear to be activated even when light stimuli are applied corresponding to the 'blind' region of retina. Also, as noted there are routes involving the superior colliculus and these might also play a role.

D.B. illustrates a profoundly important issue: that humans are not necessarily aware consciously of all the determinants of their behaviour. If we are able to generalize from D.B. to intact subjects, humans can identify and behave on the basis of certain events without having any conscious awareness of doing so. Traditionally, the world of human sensory and perceptual systems has been studied on the basis of the subject's own report of what he or she perceives. D.B. serves as a warning that such reports might need careful qualification. The verbal report of the patient is fundamental to clinical assessment. Yet, as Weiskrantz (1986: 118) notes: 'an "unexpected" revelation of a capacity may occur when one uses an unusual method of testing for it.'

Development

The primary visual system acquires an increased weighting as it matures, reflecting the general principle that the human cortex is immature at birth and the control of behaviour is dominated by sub-cortical mechanisms (McGraw 1943). In the human neonate the secondary system brings the fovea into alignment with salient stimuli in the image, even though the primary visual system

---

 Case study

Blindsight in D.B.

A subject known as D.B. provided Weiskrantz (1986) and his fellow researchers with invaluable knowledge about a phenomenon that came to be termed blindsight. D.B. was born in 1940 in a small market town in England. Life was normal for D.B. until the age of 14 when he reported headaches on the right side of his head. These were usually preceded by the appearance of a phantom flashing light. When D.B. reached his twenties, he noticed that there was a blank region in the left of his visual field. An abnormality in the tissue of the visual cortex was identified. In 1973, D.B. received brain surgery to remove the abnormality. The surgery greatly improved D.B.'s state of well-being. He was largely free of headaches and the phantom flashes of light. However, most of DB's left visual field was blind.

What attracted researchers to D.B. was the observation by his ophthalmic surgeon that D.B. retained a capacity to locate objects in what was apparently a blind left visual field at an accuracy much better than chance. For example, in terms of his own account, D.B. was not able to see an outstretched hand but none the less could reach for it with some accuracy. D.B. was able to point to objects while denying that he could see them. He could even discriminate a pattern of stripes from a uniform grey. There was a separation between D.B.'s actual ability and conscious awareness of this ability. Certain perceptual and motor skills that he exhibited were unavailable to DB's consciousness and he denied that they existed.

is still relatively undeveloped in its ability to process the information (Bronson 1974).

In neither cats, monkeys nor humans does cutting of the corpus callosum impair basic locomotion in space (Trevarthan 1968). Reaching with a hand is still accurate. Trevarthan suggests that this is because sub-cortical mechanisms, undivided by the operation, are responsible, i.e. the secondary visual system.

The central regions (fovea and near) of the human retina are especially undeveloped at birth as compared to more peripheral areas. Looking at the pattern of neural development of the visual system reveals differences in the rate of maturation (Bronson 1974). Maturity occurs earlier in the lateral geniculate nucleus and superior colliculus than in the cortex. However, there are 'islands of cortical functioning' (Johnson 1990) even in new-born humans. By three months, the cortex is in a state of rapid development. In other words, the primary visual system, deriving its input from foveal regions of the retina, is less developed at birth than is the secondary visual system, deriving its input from more peripheral retinal regions.

Normal adult vision involving movements of the eyes to direct attention at various parts of the image is determined by a combination of sensory-driven and memory-driven aspects (Paillard 1987). We are able voluntarily to direct attention to what is normally a less salient feature of an image. By contrast, the reaction of a new-born infant can be predicted largely on the basis of the stimulus qualities. There is an 'obligatory attention', involving long periods of fixation and a difficulty in disengaging from a target (Johnson 1990). When an image moves in a regular pattern, saccadic eye movements of a 5-week-old human lag behind movements of the image (Johnson 1990). Eye movements are a *response* to movements of the image rather than (as in older infants) an *anticipation* of such movements. This would appear to correspond to maturation of cortical brain regions involved in eye movement control.

As development proceeds, a history of stimulation (visual memory) is acquired. After the second month, it is necessary to consider both current stimulation and this history to predict eye movement reactions. The reaction is different depending upon whether the object has been viewed before. Presented with a choice of targets simultaneously and depending upon the amount of exposure to them, sometimes the infant will prefer a familiar object and sometimes a novel one. Satiation to a very familiar object and a preference for novelty is seen.

What is involved in encoding the complete features of a stimulus into memory? Attention needs to be directed to the various parts of the object, including both attractive and less attractive components. There must be *inhibition* upon those processes that tend to direct attention to what are intrinsically the most salient features, e.g. large extents of sharply defined contours (Bronson 1974). At about 3–4 months this capacity is clearly evident.

Thus, with the development of the foveal region of the retina and the associated region of the cortex, by about the second month the child is able to (1) focus attention upon features of the image that coincide with the fovea and (2) start to encode these features into memory. However, the child's attention will still be subject to some capture by the most salient features of the stimulus. As memories are built up and consolidated, so the capacity to direct attention on the basis of memories increases. This is the acquisition of voluntary control. Bronson (1974: 879) suggests that 'all neonatal reactions can satisfactorily be explained by reference to automatic mechanisms, hence it is not necessary to assume volitional control in the new-born infant'.

It is insightful to compare the visual systems of various vertebrate types. This suggests that in primates the primary visual system augments but does not supersede the evolutionarily older secondary system (Trevarthan 1968). The end product is a closely integrated visual system, where component parts share responsibility.

To understand broader issues of development and perception one needs some understanding of how sensory systems work. The idea that development is associated with a shift in weight of sensory and perceptual systems has interesting implications for face recognition. Human infants appear to be born with some kind of innate recognition process for the features of a face. They possess information that directs their gaze towards a face (Morton and Johnson 1991). This gives an initial attentional bias towards the later assimilation of information on faces.

Morton and Johnson suggest that there are two distinct processes that mediate attention to faces: one that is present from birth and which loses its capacity to exert control as the infant matures, and one that develops with experience and which takes over control from the first. They argue that the first process is organized sub-cortically, the superior colliculus being a prime candidate (Johnson 1990) whereas the second is organized in large part in the cortex. Sub-cortical pathways mature earlier than cortical pathways.

Research update

A step towards integration

It is now possible to relate observations on both the development of vision and brain damage to a broader model, designed to represent the relationship between stimuli and cognitions as determinants of behaviour (Toates 1998). Using a wide variety of evidence from humans and non-humans, Toates proposed a model of two sets of processes that are jointly responsible for the control of behaviour: cognitive (memory) processes and stimulus-driven process. The weighting of these processes as determinants of behaviour changes as a function of development, disease and learning.

The changes with development and learning reflect adaptive considerations. The stimulus-driven processes provide relatively simple but inflexible solutions in a situation where behaviour can be specified on the basis of sensory input. In the case of certain reactions to visual stimuli (e.g. eye movements, attentional mechanisms), the reaction of the human infant is heavily dependent upon sensory input, organized largely sub-cortically. Development corresponds to acquisition of an increased weighting of cognition. Cognitive control offers flexibility but at a high cost in terms of processing capacity. It corresponds to maturation of the cortex. Cognitive control offers the possibility of inhibiting the automatic reactions that might otherwise arise as a result of the stimuli that impinge. This is generally what we mean by the emergence of voluntary control.

In general, development corresponds to a move towards a greater cognitive control. However, life is not simply a move in one direction. In some situations, there is some loss of cognitive control and an increased relative weighting of stimulus-driven control. This is seen in pathological states (e.g. damage to the cortex means that the subject is more at the mercy of current visual stimuli as far as attentional mechanisms are concerned). A move to a more automatic mode of control is not always synonymous with pathology. As Chapter 2 discussed, whether it is rats running mazes or motorists making turns off a motorway exit, when behaviour becomes predictable there is an increased weighting attached to automatic processes (the subject shifts into 'autopilot'). It seems that, with repetition of a task, the adult reverts to a more undeveloped mode of control with a consequent sparing of cognitive processing capacity for other tasks.

An examination of the control of eye movements shows that infants start out under what Johnson (1995) terms 'exogenous' control (i.e. stimulus-driven). Development corresponds to the acquisition of what he terms 'endogenous' control (i.e. memory driven). Infants as young as 4 months old have acquired the ability to suppress automatic saccadic eye movements that would otherwise be triggered exogenously by a stimulus.

In adults, damage to certain regions of the frontal cortex (e.g. lesions for intractable epilepsy) disrupts eye movements (Guitton *et al.* 1985). There is an inability to suppress automatic saccades and difficulty in initiating eye movements where the goal is known but not yet visible. An individual can find it difficult to unlock voluntarily the gaze from what is currently the object of attention (Bronson 1974; Trevarthan 1968). The capacity to follow a moving target remains intact. Similarly, damage to the occipital lobe can result in the subject's gaze being diverted to a highly salient part of the image and away from the intended focus of attention.

Ψ Section summary

The optics of the eye form an image on the retina. Light is detected by receptors, i.e. rods and cones, at the retina. Electrical signals are conveyed from receptors, via bipolar cells to ganglion cells. The axons of ganglion cells constitute the optic nerve. Cones are of three different types, each having a different sensitivity to wavelength. A receptive field of a neuron in the visual pathway is the area of retina, which when stimulated changes the activity of the neuron. A retinal ganglion cell has a receptive field made up of ON and OFF areas. The fovea is a region of retina specialized for detecting fine detail. Researchers have identified a primary visual system and a secondary visual system. There is parallel

Box continued

processing of information (e.g. on colour and movement) within the primary visual system. Using so-called split-brain subjects and projecting visual information to just one hemisphere, researchers can investigate specializations of each hemisphere. Subjects with brain damage can sometimes react to visual stimuli but without having conscious awareness of their presence, a phenomenon termed blindsight. Different regions of the visual system mature at different rates.

1 What is meant by saying that the receptive field of a retinal ganglion cell is made up of ON and OFF regions?

2 Why is a topographical map so called?

3 What is the significance of the fovea and the receptors located there as far as (a) resolving fine detail and (b) detecting the presence of weak lights are concerned?

4 What is the evidence for there being more than one 'system' within the visual system?

5 What is a grandmother cell? What is the problem raised by suggesting its existence?

6 What can damaged brains tell us about vision?

7 What is meant by an endogenous control of eye movements?

❏ Touch

It is obviously of crucial importance to an animal's survival that it can gain information on tactile stimuli that come into physical contact with the skin. For example, an object that impacts upon the skin might represent an event that requires defensive action. Also our successful manipulation of objects depends upon an ability to resolve fine detail with our fingers. The tactile sense is clearly important from a developmental perspective; infants learn about their self-generated movements, resultant contact with objects and the tactile consequences of their manipulation of objects. The first stage of this process of extracting tactile information consists in the activation of specialized receptors at the skin by external objects. Each such receptor has a receptive field at the skin.

You have already met part of the system involved in processing tactile information: the somatosensory cortex and the mapping of the body, which constitutes the sensory homunculus (Figure 2.15, p. 40). You should recall that different regions of the body are represented in different regions of the somatosensory cortex. What does 'represented' mean here? It means that there is a correspondence between (1) neurons with tips in the region of the body indicated by the sensory homunculus and (2) the activity of cortical neurons at points alongside the homunculus. The receptive fields at the skin are such that tactile stimulation triggers activity in a cortical cell located at the point indicated by the homunculus. In human subjects, electrical stimulation of such cortical neurons evokes the sensation of tactile stimulation at the region of skin corresponding to the particular point of the homunculus.

Can you recall a feature of the relationship between area of body and area of homunculus in terms of relative magnitudes? Regions of skin where the ability to resolve fine detail is high (e.g. finger tips) are represented by relatively large amounts of cortex. Regions where this ability is lower (e.g. back) have relatively small areas of cortex. (You might find it interesting to speculate as to the functional value of the relatively large amount of cortex devoted to the lips!)

The next section looks in more detail at the neurons that form the first stage of processing in this system.

Receptive neurons

Over the surface of the body, there are located the tips of neurons that are sensitive to different qualities of tactile stimulation, termed **somatosensory neurons**. Some examples are shown in Figure 4.27. You have already met one example of a somatosensory neuron in Chapter 2, the nociceptive neuron, which is specifically sensitive to tissue damage in the vicinity of its tip. Another type of neuron is especially sensitive to vibration at its tip. As you can see, in Figure 4.27, for one type of somatosensory neuron, the ending of the neuron wraps itself around the root of a hair, so that displacements of the hair trigger action potentials in the neuron.

In Figure 4.28, note the receptive field of a touch-sensitive neuron, the area of sensory surface whose stimulation affects the activity of the neuron. Note also that the density of receptor branches is greatest at the centre of the receptive field, which means a greater sensitivity to tactile stimulation there. In principle then by exploiting the properties of such a neuron, some information might be transmitted on the location of a stimulus within the receptive field by means of the frequency of

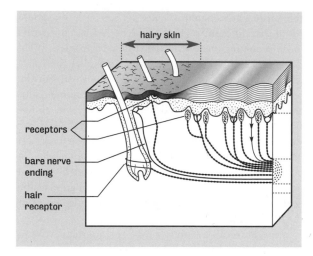

Figure 4.27 Types of somatosensory neurons

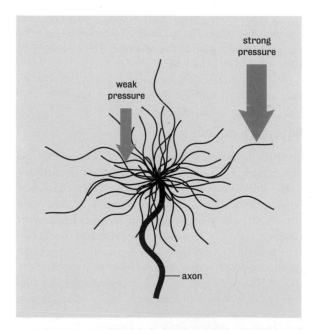

Figure 4.28 A somatosensory neuron and tactile stimulation within its receptive field; a low pressure, slight indentation at the centre of the receptive field and a high pressure, deep indentation at the periphery

action potentials. A high frequency could signal a stimulus near the centre and a lower frequency a stimulus nearer the periphery. However, you will probably see an analogy here with the visual system and the detection of wavelength. How could a single neuron generate a signal that discriminates between a weak indentation at the centre of a receptive field and a strong indentation at the periphery? It couldn't. How the problem might be solved is, as with vision, by employing a population of neurons and comparing their levels of activity.

As another similarity with vision, somatosensory neurons have receptive fields that are large or small, as was shown in Figure 4.2. The smaller receptive fields (e.g. at the finger tips) are associated with greater tactile acuity, analogous to foveal vision. The back is associated with larger receptive fields. These differences in acuity correspond also to comparable differences in the relative proportions of somatosensory cortex devoted to analysing information from these body regions.

Some somatosensory neurons rapidly adapt to tactile stimulation (see Figure 4.1c). They signal only the onset of a stimulus, which often carries the most information. You will doubtless have noticed that you become unaware of much of the tactile stimulation of the body, such as the pressure of the top of a sock or the pressure of your rear against the chair on which you are sitting. Usually, it is *changes* in stimulation that are the most important. The constant pressure of the substrate as you lie on the ground does not need to command attention but any changes, as in the ground shifting, are of crucial importance. Other receptors adapt slowly, if at all. Nociceptive neurons detecting real or threatened tissue damage are an example of a neuron type which adapts rather little (how often we must have wished it were otherwise).

Somatosenory pathways

Figure 4.29 shows an example of the route taken by somatosensory information from the periphery to the somatosensory cortex. Note the synapse formed in the thalamus, comparable to the visual pathway. Note also the cross-over of information from one side of the body to the opposite side of the brain.

Researchers are able to place the tips of fine electrodes within sensory neurons that convey information from the skin to the spinal cord, including in human subjects (Vallbo 1995: see Figure 4.30). With the help of these electrodes, they can then stimulate the neuron electrically and record the response or simply record electrical activity in the neuron in response to mechanical stimuli at the skin. When they are recording, they can look at the relationship between three crucial events: (a) the tactile stimulus at the skin, (b) activity in the form of action potentials in the sensory neuron, (c) the subject's verbal

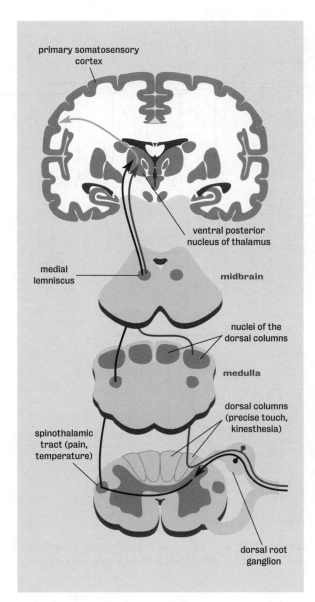

Figure 4.29 Pathway of tactile information from skin to brain.
Source: Carlson (1994: 205)

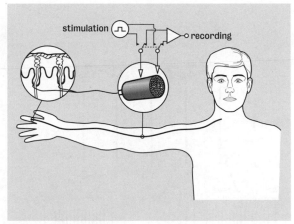

Figure 4.30 Stimulation of sensory neuron
Source: Vallbo (1995: 240)

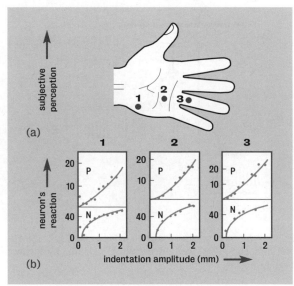

Figure 4.31 Responses to pressure (indentation) at three points on the hand, 1, 2 and 3 (a) neural response of sensory neuron, (b) subject's estimate of pressure
Source: Vallbo (1995: 246)

report of what they are feeling. Also neurons can be stimulated artificially by the electrode and again the subjective reports noted. Figure 4.31 shows a result of this kind. As you can see, the activity of the neuron increases as pressure (indentation) increases, though there is a levelling off. However, this levelling off is not reflected in the psychological perception of intensity. By recording, we can see that some neurons are sensitive only to *changes* in tactile stimulation, as shown in Figure 4.1c. Others are

active for as long as the deformation at the skin lasts, as shown in Figures 4.1a and 4.1b (Vallbo 1995).

It is possible to identify neurons, which, when stimulated, evoke the sensation of painless mechanical touch (as in Figure 4.31), rather than, say, pain or temperature. The extent of the sensation at the skin is reported as around 2–3 mm, corresponding to the size

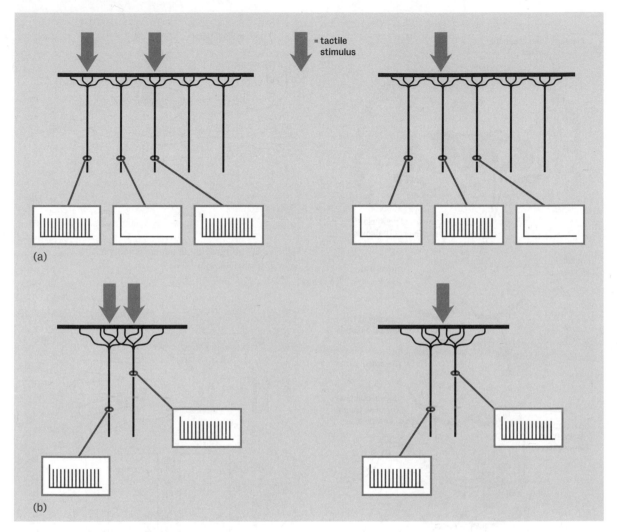

Figure 4.32 Skin where receptive fields of sensory neurons are (a) small and non-overlapping, (b) large and overlapping. Left of each figure: two tactile stimuli, indicated by arrows; right of each figure: one stimulus. Graphs show action potentials in sensory neurons

of the receptive field at this location. Situated alongside such neurons are others that convey information on temperature and tissue damage. If the intensity of applied stimulation is increased, subjects do sometimes report pain. This suggests that adjacent neurons that would normally carry information on tissue damage are being simultaneously excited.

The receptive field of somatosensory neurons is made up simply of an excitatory region (comparable to that of retinal receptors). However, there is further processing of this information so that neurons (e.g. in the thalamus) whose activity depends upon activity in sensory neurons have receptive field properties that are more complex, comparable to that of ganglion cells in the visual system. That is to say, within such a pathway, there are processes of lateral inhibition, entirely comparable to that of the visual system (discussed on p. 113).

Resolution of detail

Not only do we register the presence of a stimulus at the skin but also we can be aware of details in the stimulus, an ability closely analogous to that of acuity in the visual system. Our ability to discriminate detail varies with different regions of skin. One measure of this is the ability to discriminate between one and two points applied to the skin, as shown in Figure 4.32. You can see that in Figure 4.32a, comparing one and two tactile stimuli, the profile of activity in the sensory neurons can discriminate the situations. This represents a region of high acuity, e.g. the finger tips. By contrast, comparing the sensory neurons shown in Figure 4.32b, you can see that the profile in activity does not give a different signal as conditions are changed between one and two points of stimulation.

The ability to discriminate one and two points does vary; the back is poor at this and the fingers are good at it. With the help of a good friend, you can easily try the experiment for yourselves.

Information from somatosensory neurons is processed at the thalamus. Figure 4.33a represents an example of a neuron in a part of the thalamus concerned with process-

ing tactile information and a representative three of the sensory neurons that influence it. At the skin, the receptive field of the thalamic neuron is made up of an excitatory (ON) region, surrounded by an inhibitory (OFF) region. What then is the optimal tactile stimulus to trigger activity in this thalamic neuron? A tactile stimulus that fills the centre region but does not encroach upon the inhibitory surround, as shown in Figure 4.33b. This is closely analogous to the ON centre/OFF surround ganglion cell shown in Figure 4.16.

Top-down modulation

So far we have spoken of the flow of information from the periphery to the CNS. However, there is also a modulation of the information carried in these pathways. There is evidence that pathways arising in the brain are used to modulate the activity of the sensory pathway, amplifying some information and inhibiting other information. The gate control theory of pain (Chapter 2) is a good example of such modulation.

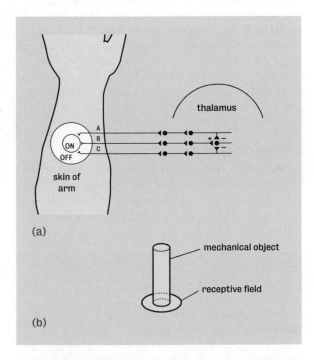

Figure 4.33 A touch sensitive neuron in the thalamus and its receptive field at the skin (a) the tip of neuron B is within the excitatory (ON) area; the tips of neurons A and C are within the inhibitory (OFF) area. Note that neurons such as B exert an excitatory influence and neurons such as A and C an inhibitory influence on this particular thalamic neuron; it is therefore excited by tactile stimuli within the inner area but not encroaching upon the outer area and thereby resolves detail, (b) optimal stimulus

Ψ Section summary

Somatosensory neurons are sensitive to tactile stimulation. Differences in the size of receptive fields of somatosensory neurons at different parts of the body correspond inversely to differences in the ability to resolve fine detail. Within the thalamus there are neurons with receptive field properties made up of ON and OFF regions at the skin, analogous to the property of retinal ganglion cells.

1 How do we explain that the ability to resolve fine detail varies from one region of the body to another?
2 Suppose that you record from a neuron in the thalamus with a receptive field made up of ON and OFF regions at the skin. What is the effect of a tactile stimulus within each region of receptive field?

❏ Chemical senses

This section looks at two sensory systems that are sensitive to the presence of chemicals, i.e. taste and smell. In each case, activity in sensory neurons arises as a result of the detection of specific chemicals by chemoreceptors. (There are also **chemoreceptors** that are sensitive to particular chemical qualities inside the body but discussion of this topic is beyond our scope.)

The senses of taste and smell serve different but related functions. Both inform an animal of the nature of various chemicals physically present at the sensory detector, respectively the tongue and nose. However, the significance of this information is different between the two systems. The nose can provide information on physical objects located some distance away, such as the pheromones (airborne chemicals used in communication concerning mating) emitted by another animal or the odour of a potential food. For taste to provide information, the object in question must already be in the mouth.

The systems of taste and smell usually act in close cooperation. For example, the perception of the flavour of food depends upon an interaction between information derived from the two sensory channels. You will probably have experienced that, when a cold impairs your sense of smell, food does not taste as it should. Some common foods, especially garlic, coffee and chocolate, are very difficult to identify without the assistance of smell (Coren *et al.* 1994). We will deal first with taste and then with smell, noting similarities and differences.

Taste

It is generally agreed that there are four primary tastes, these being sweet, salty, sour and bitter (Coren *et al.* 1994). These are *psychological* perceptions that correspond to different *physical* stimuli, that is broad classes of chemical molecules (note the analogous distinction in the visual and auditory systems between psychological

and physical dimensions). A sensation of sweetness is generally produced by sugars, signalling the availability of nutrients that can be ingested. A sensation of saltiness signals the presence of a substance like sodium chloride (common table salt). In nature, sourness is commonly an indicator that a potential food has decayed and is something to be avoided. In our evolutionary history, a bitter taste is commonly indicative of poisonous plants and is, of course, to be avoided.

It is important to distinguish between the two successive processes of the sensory detection of a chemical quality and the motivational significance that can then be attached to this detection. Sourness and bitterness are normally associated with rejection and avoidance irrespective of the circumstances. However, the reaction to sweetness and saltiness depends to a large extent upon the physiological state of the body (see Chapter 15). For example, suppose we detect the presence of sodium chloride. At a later stage of processing in the nervous system, this might evoke either acceptance or rejection as a function of the body's state of salt depletion or repletion. In our evolution, we imagine that at times of salt deficiency it would be adaptive for us to be able to ingest salt. Thus, to understand the functional value of chemical sensory detection, it should be considered in the context of homeostasis (see Chapter 2) and motivation (see Chapter 15).

Sensory detection

On the surface of the tongue is a mosaic of small organs, known as **taste buds**, each of which is made up of receptors for chemicals that make contact with the tongue (see Figure 4.34). Taste buds are also in regions of the mouth

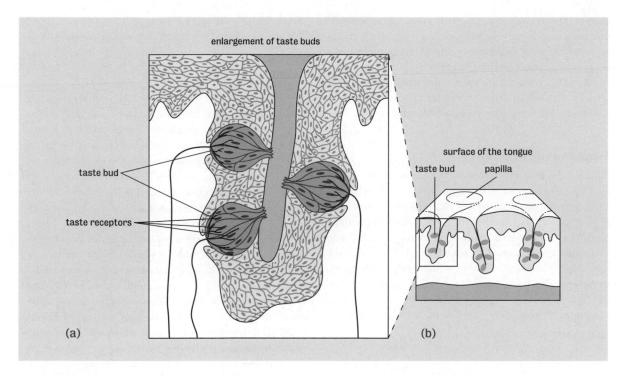

enlargement of taste buds

surface of the tongue

taste bud

taste bud   papilla

taste receptors

(a)   (b)

Figure 4.34 Taste buds
Source: Carlson (1994: 214)

other than the tongue. The tips of sensory neurons make contact with these receptors. When specific chemicals are detected by the receptors of the taste buds, action potentials arise in the associated sensory neurons.

At one time it was believed that each specific taste cell and associated neuron would respond only to a specific chemical quality such as the presence of a sugar. This would then constitute a quality-specific private line to the brain. Indeed, depending upon the species, there might well be a certain number of neurons showing this property and hence providing a labelled-line coding (Dodd and Castellucci 1991). However, it is probably more common that the taste receptors of each taste bud and the associated neuron respond to some extent to each of the chemical qualities. Different taste buds respond differently to them, as shown in Figure 4.35. Thus, the information carried in a given neuron could not discriminate between a low concentration of a chemical to which it is highly sensitive and a high concentration of a chemical to which it is less sensitive. The fact that tastes can be resolved implies a comparison between signals carried by different neurons. This comparison is done in the brain where there is an integration of infor-

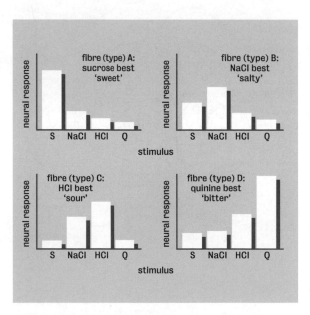

Figure 4.35 Responses of different types of taste buds to different taste stimuli. S = sucrose, NaCl = sodium chloride, HCl = mild acid and Q = quinine
Source: Coren *et al.* (1994: 259)

mation. This is analogous to colour vision where a particular cone (e.g. a red cone) responds preferentially to one wavelength but is sensitive to some extent to other wavelengths (e.g. corresponding to green). The further processing that is necessary on the information from the sensory neurons in order to extract taste information is something like opponent-process coding for colour.

From tongue to brain

Figure 4.36 shows the pathway of taste information carried by neurons from the tongue to the brain. The sensory neurons travel as part of a cranial nerve to a brain region known as the medulla, where they terminate. Synaptic connection is made with further neurons that carry the information to a specific region of the thalamus. Note the similarity here with visual, auditory and somatosensory information each of which also projects to its own specific region of thalamus. The similarity continues in that after the thalamus further neurons

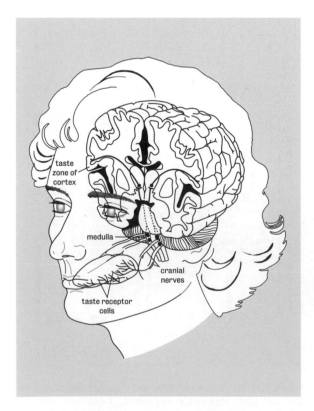

Figure 4.36 Pathways taken by gustatory information from taste receptor cells, to taste zone of cortex
Source: Rosenzweig *et al.* (1996)

convey taste information to specific regions of cortex that are specialized for processing within this modality.

Smell

The chemicals to which our noses are responsive in triggering the sense of smell (olfaction) are described as volatile. A similar principle applies to olfactory stimuli as to taste stimuli: there is a distinction between the detection of chemical qualities and the motivational significance attached to them. Whereas certain odours will always evoke a rejection and avoidance reaction, others can evoke pleasantness/approach or unpleasantness/avoidance depending upon internal physiological state. In a hungry person with a benign history of associations, the smell of a vegetable vindaloo might well evoke approach but, following a taste-aversion experience (Chapters 2 and 3), the same smell would be expected to evoke avoidance. The difference lies not in any difference in the process of detection of the chemicals involved but in the context into which this detection is placed by further processing within the nervous system.

An odour can have a particularly strong capacity to evoke a memory of a related event that is emotionally coloured. Most people probably have a story to tell about an odour that is especially powerful in its capacity to revive a childhood memory, whether pleasant or unpleasant.

Sensory detection

The process of sensory detection of volatile chemicals by the nose has some similarities to that of the detection of chemicals by the tongue. The nose contains specific receptors that are sensitive to the physical presence of particular chemicals. In humans there are some 50 million such **olfactory receptors**. They are located as shown in Figure 4.37. By sniffing we increase the flow of air into the nose and hence increase the contact of volatile chemicals with these olfactory receptors. Olfactory receptors are parts of neurons which not only transduce the chemical information but also, in the form of action potentials, convey the information away from the site of detection and towards the brain. However, whereas there are a few basic types of taste quality and types of receptor, olfactory stimuli and receptors appear not to be able to be categorized into a few classes (Bartoshuk and Beauchamp 1994). Rather, there may well be hundreds of different types of receptors each specialized for a particular olfactory quality.

According to the 'lock and key theory', the action of volatile chemicals in triggering these receptors is somewhat analogous to neurotransmitters attaching themselves to receptors at a synapse (Chapter 2). In each case, there is a chemical specificity like a key and lock. Similarly, in each case occupation of the 'lock' by the 'key' triggers further events within the cell and is normally short-lived as there are processes that remove the 'key' shortly after its attachment (Coren *et al.* 1994).

There are many odours that we can readily identify as belonging to specific objects in our environment (e.g. frying eggs, vegetable vindaloo, cigar smoke) and each of these is made up of very many different chemicals. This implies that the outputs of numerous different olfactory receptor types is combined to form our psychological perception of a particular odour. In other words, olfaction is a *synthetic* sense, i.e. one that puts together component bits of information to yield a combined perception (Carlson 1994). In this sense, it is like vision. However, suppose three smells of familiar objects are present simultaneously, as in smoking a cigarette,

while a curry is being served in the presence of someone wearing a strong perfume. We can still resolve the familiar components, so in this regard olfaction is *analytic*, something like hearing.

From nose to brain

The axons of olfactory receptors form synapses at the brain region termed the olfactory bulb (see Figure 4.37). Further neurons then convey olfactory information from the olfactory bulb to other brain regions, e.g. the olfactory cortex and hypothalamus. Unlike the other sensory systems, e.g. vision and touch (see pp. 111 and 129), information getting to the cortex does not do so via the thalamus. There are also fibres which carry information 'top-down' to make synapses in the olfactory bulb. It is still unclear exactly what their role is in the processing of information.

Recordings from parts of the cortex show that particular neurons located there are responsive to particular odours.

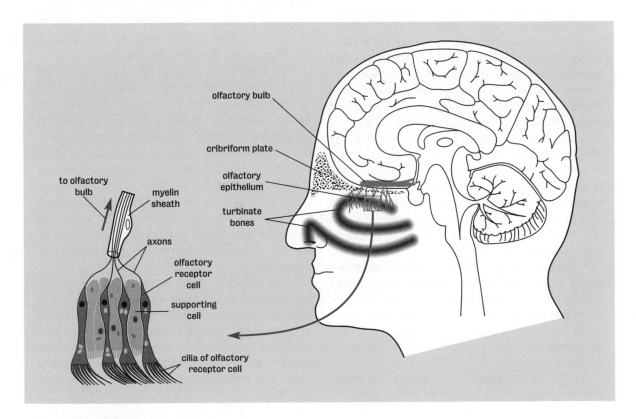

Figure 4.37 Sensory system of olfaction
Source: Carlson (1994: 220)

Pheromones

In the case of a number of animal species, there is a distinct olfactory system whose detectors are also in the nasal cavity and is known as the **vomeronasal system** (Bartoshuk and Beauchamp 1994). Distinct vomeronasal nerves made up of sensory neurons form synapses in the olfactory bulb. From the olfactory bulb, information is conveyed to brain regions concerned with reproduction. This system specializes in the detection of **pheromones**, which are airborne particles used in communication, analogous to hormones used for communication within the body. They have been studied closely in non-human species who, in secreting them, advertise their state of

sexual arousal. The ability of a male to detect their presence means that he can discriminate a potentially sexually receptive female from a sexually unreceptive female.

Evidence suggests the existence of at least the rudiments of a vomeronasal system also in humans, which operates at a level below conscious awareness (Bartoshuk and Beauchamp 1994; Monti-Bloch *et al.*1994). Through this system, stimulation by airborne particles can influence the activity of the autonomic nervous system (see Chapter 2). The attraction of perfumes in humans suggests the possibility that these might be simulating something of the pheromones that could play a part in human sexual attraction (Rosenzweig *et al.* 1996).

 Research update

Odour and mood

For a long time there have been anecdotal reports that, in humans, odour can influence mood, contributing to psychological well-being (Martin 1996). Practitioners of aromatherapy have expressed the belief that it is possible to gain a therapeutic effect of odour in treating such conditions as depression. This presents something of a dilemma to psychology. On the one hand, such 'experiential' reports are worth taking seriously, since they would seem to have some ecological validity, being gained from people in a 'real life', non-laboratory situation. In principle, any effects might be most evident in such situations rather than in the sterility of the laboratory. On the other hand, therein lies a fundamental problem that is endemic to psychology. Much of the evidence has been gathered in a non-scientific way from observers who have a strong interest in the success of any such treatment.

There has been a growing interest in testing such claims under rigorously controlled conditions and relating the evidence to biological structure and functional considerations. Some scientifically based evidence suggests that human mood, cognitive skills and social reactivity can be significantly influenced by odours (Martin 1996).

Martin (1996) suggests that, from functional considerations, it would appear to make good sense for

certain unpleasant odours to be associated with negative moods. An odour such as that of rotting food is a sign of danger. It might well be to a subject's advantage to be motivated to change such a situation by moving elsewhere and negative mood could play a role here. It is not so clear as to what might be the biological advantage in, say, lavender improving mood.

The results obtained so far need to be interpreted with some caution (Martin 1996). There is an indication of such mood elevation as a function of exposure to certain odours. There is also reason to suggest that in some cases a placebo effect (Chapter 2) could be at work. That is to say, beliefs about the odour rather than the intrinsic chemical properties of it could be implicated, at least in part. Thus, in one experiment, subjects tended to give an olfactory rating of pleasant even when sampling odourless water. This consideration is important if we apply scientific principles to therapy, where subjects arrive with some expectation of success.

Theorists have tended to associate any odour-induced mood elevations with evolutionary old neural pathways from sensory receptors to such brain regions as the amygdala. However, Martin suggests that the evidence of sophisticated cognition involved in a placebo effect would tend to implicate also the evolutionary newer area of the cortex. Electrical recordings support such an involvement.

ψ Section summary

The senses of taste and smell are initiated by the detection of specific chemicals by chemoreceptors. The four primary tastes, sweet, salty, sour and bitter, are psychological perceptions corresponding to a broad class of molecules at the tongue. Taste buds at the tongue detect the presence of chemicals. Olfactory receptors in the nose are sensitive to volatile chemicals. The vomeronasal system is specialized for the detection of pheromones.

1 In what way can the reaction to a taste or smell depend upon the physiological state of the body?
2 What are some similarities and differences between the senses of taste and smell?

❑ Overview

This chapter has spanned the sensory systems of hearing, vision, touch, taste and smell. This final section takes a brief overview, looking at similarities and differences in these systems. It also considers briefly the point that there is an integration of information from different sensory systems in obtaining a perception of the world.

Ambient vision mediated via the secondary visual system has a close interdependence with measures of space as detected by other sensory channels (Trevarthan 1968). Thus, a unified and stable representation of space is constructed and used as a frame of reference for action. Stratton's (1897) perception of the world through inverting spectacles depended upon information from other sensory channels integrated with that from vision and from memories as to how the visual world used to appear.

As a general principle, the amount of cortex devoted to analysis of the signals from different regions within a sensory system reflects the importance attached to the regions in terms of the ability to resolve detail. Thus, the fingers are associated with a relatively large area of somatosensory cortex and the fovea with a relatively large area of visual cortex. This is termed a **magnification factor**. It can be quantified, for example, in the case of the visual system, by the amount of cortex in square millimetres associated with each degree of visual space (Zeki 1993).

There is also some plasticity in cortical representation. If a visual input from one eye is lacking, LGN neu-

rons that would normally derive their input from that eye will be relatively ineffective in establishing synaptic links in the visual cortex. This is also true of the input to the somatosensory cortex from different regions of the body. If the input from a region is lacking then that from other regions will expand to occupy the missing space (Zeki 1993).

Vision has dominated the discussion. In terms of cortical connections, the structure of the visual cortex appears to be much like that of cortical regions not involved with vision (Zeki 1993). This suggests that important general principles of information processing might be gained by looking at vision.

The visual system employs just four types of receptors, from which information on the whole range of the visual spectrum is extracted. In other words, there is not a one-to-one receptor to physical stimulus relationship. A similar set of a few receptors is responsible for the many tastes to which we are responsive. By contrast, it would seem that something much nearer to a one-to-one relationship exists in the olfactory system. An odour might be uniquely specified by a particular chemical and associated receptor type, necessitating a vast number of different receptor types (Zeki 1993).

It is sometimes said that the task of the visual system is to analyse the image or to analyse the external world. The word 'analyse' means to break down into component parts. A good example is when a chemist analyses a complex chemical into the simpler chemicals of which it is composed. To some extent the structure of parts of the visual system suggests a similar process. Thus, colour is processed by different brain regions from movement and form. However, in some respects the word 'analyse' is inherently misleading (Zeki 1993). A moving red Volkswagen is perceived as just that, a unified perception. So clearly part of the task of the visual system is to synthesize as well as analyse. Also its task is to *categorize*. A wide variety of different light stimulations of different intensities and wavelengths are all classified as a robin's breast. This is not a process of breaking up into bits but rather a top-down classification.

The world that we perceive is an active construction based in part upon sensory information. Abnormal activity within the brain can simulate the condition of a particular sensory input even in its physical absence. As Chapter 2 described, there is the experience of phantom limb pain, where the brain's activity is interpreted as arising from a limb that no longer exists or might even never have existed. Similarly, in the case of vision, there is the phenomenon of phantom chromatopsia (Zeki

1993) in which a particular colour impresses itself upon perception and invades the person's consciousness as if the whole world were radiating this colour. It appears to arise from abnormal activity in regions of the visual processing system of the brain. To use the term 'illusion' to describe such phenomena is correct in one respect: the conscious perception does not correspond to a consensus view of what is in the world. However, the notion of illusion might carry connotations of delusion or deception, whereas to the sufferer this is a pressing reality (Zeki 1993).

Whichever sensory system and its corresponding conscious perception we consider, we encounter a philosophical problem regarding the nature of conscious experience. How is it that the activity of neurons gives rise to conscious experience (Chapter 2)? For instance, suppose that we are led to postulate a grandmother cell sensitive to all of the features of a grandmother. How

can activity in this cell translate into the conscious perception 'grandmother'? It might seem to require still more processing in order to look at this electrical activity but that is a cul-de-sac to be avoided. We cannot solve our problem by proliferating ill-defined processes. Or consider the issue of parallel processing of features such as colour and speed. The fact that we perceive a red Volkswagen at speed suggests that all of the independent computations must be brought together. Certainly at some level component bits of information are integrated in order to yield a unified perception. However, should we suppose that separate red, form and speed neurons all feed into a red, fast Volkswagen neuron? To do so leaves us with the same dilemma as that of the grandmother cell. New ways of looking at perception, consciousness and the brain are needed and the challenge of the future is to find them. A knowledge of sensory systems will be central to this quest.

Ψ Chapter summary

• Introduction

Sensory information is detected by sensory receptors, a process termed sensory transduction. Different sensations (e.g. visual and auditory) correspond to different pathways being stimulated. The means by which information is transmitted (patterns of activity in neurons) is similar in any pathway. Coding of information by the frequency of action potentials is known as frequency coding. The receptive field of a particular neuron is that area of sensory surface which, when stimulated, changes the pattern of activity of the neuron. The minimum level of stimulation that can be detected is known as the threshold.

• Hearing

Changes of pressure in the air are the physical stimulus that triggers the psychological sensation of sound. Such changes of pressure can be characterized by oscillations of a particular frequency and amplitude. The auditory system is sensitive to a range of frequencies. Pressure changes in the air are converted to vibrations of the tympanic membrane. In turn, oscillations of the tympanic membrane are associated with vibrations of the basilar membrane. Frequency is

coded by means of the location on the basilar membrane which vibrates at the maximum extent.

• Vision

The colours that we perceive correspond to differences in the wavelength of light. The retina contains a mosaic of receptor cells, known as rods and cones. Receptor cells influence bipolar cells, which in turn influence ganglion cells, the optic nerve consisting of the axons of retinal ganglion cells. The primary visual system consists of the route from the retina, through the lateral geniculate nucleus to the visual cortex. The secondary visual system consists of the superior colliculus and a population of ganglion cells that are routed to it.

At the fovea there is little convergence between receptors and ganglion cells and hence high acuity. At the periphery there is much convergence and a low acuity. The visual system is particularly sensitive to contrast. The receptive field of a retinal ganglion cell is made up of excitatory (ON) and inhibitory (OFF) areas. Some ganglion cells are sensitive to wavelength, light of one wavelength will excite the ganglion and light of another will inhibit it. This is known as opponent-

Box continued

process coding. Cells in the visual cortex typically have slit-shaped receptive fields. There is parallel process-ing of information in the ganglion–LGN–cortex pathway, corresponding to magno and parvo systems.

The idea that there exists a neuron corresponding to each perception is generally described by the expression 'grandmother cell'. It is a concept that is usually dismissed.

In so-called 'split-brain' subjects, where the corpus callosum is cut, it is possible to target visual stimuli to just one hemisphere. In blindsight, a subject can per-form behaviour that depends upon processing visual information but be unaware consciously of having such an ability. Human development is associated with an increased role of the primary visual system relative to that of the secondary visual system.

● **Touch**

Somatosensory neurons are sensitive to tactile stimu-lation. From region to region of the skin, their receptive fields vary in size, a reflection of a varying ability to resolve detail. A process of lateral inhibition is found in the somatosensory system.

● **Chemical senses**

Chemoreceptors detect the presence of particular chemicals and thereby instigate events that lead to taste and smell. There are four primary tastes: sweet, salty, sour and bitter. Sour and bitter are associated with an avoidance reaction. The olfactory system is sensitive to volatile chemicals. The attachment of a chemical to its receptor in the olfactory system is analogous to a key and a lock.

Further reading

● Coren, S., Ward, L.M. and Enns, J.T. (1994) *Sensation and Perception*. Fort Worth, TX: Harcourt Brace. For devel-oping further any of the information contained in this chapter, this book is recommended.

● Rosenzweig, M.R., Leiman, A.L. and Breedlove, S.M. (1996) *Biological Psychology*. Sunderland, MA: Sinauer. This is especially accessible.

● Vander, A.J. Sherman, J.H. and Luciano, D.S. (1994) *Human Physiology: The mechanisms of body function*. New York: McGraw-Hill. For the physiology of sensory systems, this can be recommended.

● Yost, W.A. (1994) *Fundamentals of Hearing*. San Diego, CA: Academic Press. For the details of hearing.

● Zeki, S. (1993) *A Vision of the Brain*. Oxford: Blackwell. A stimulating and amusing review of vision.

● Bartoshuk, L.M. and Beauchamp, G.K. (1994) Chemical senses. *Annual Review of Psychology* **45**: 419–49. This article can be recommended for its review of taste and smell.

● Schaal, B. and Porter, R.H. (1991) 'Microsmatic humans' revisited: the generation and perception of chemical signals, in P.J. Slater, J.S. Rosenblatt, C. Beer and M. Milinski (eds) *Advances in the Study of Behaviour*, vol. 20. San Diego CA: Academic Press. A good review of human olfaction.

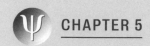

CHAPTER 5

Perception and attention

Michael Eysenck

KEY CONCEPTS • organization in visual perception • pattern recognition • depth perception • object recognition • colour perception • constructivism and the ecological approach • visual systems and the brain • attention • focused auditory attention • focused visual attention • divided attention • automaticity

☐ Chapter preview

When you have read this chapter, you should be able to

- understand the basic organizational processes involved in visual perception
- evaluate theoretical approaches to pattern recognition
- describe the main factors involved in depth perception
- evaluate major approaches to object recognition
- discuss the processes underlying colour perception
- compare and contrast the constructivist and ecological approaches to perception
- describe some of the main brain areas involved in visual perception
- discuss the factors associated with focused auditory and visual attention
- evaluate the role played by automaticity in studies of divided attention

Introduction

Most people feel that there are at least two things they know about our ability to see and to hear. First, they are precious abilities. Second, they are straightforward; for example, we rarely have to think hard in order to understand what we are seeing or hearing. The first belief is well founded, as is shown by the fact that people who are blind or deaf experience substantial difficulties in coping with everyday life or with other people's attitude to them. However, the second belief is incorrect. Our ability to see and to understand what we see is actually a major achievement. It has proved surprisingly difficult to produce adequate theoretical accounts of this ability, as will become clear later in the chapter.

This part of the chapter is concerned with the ways in which we make use of the information presented to our eyes. This is generally known as visual perception. According to Roth (1986: 81), the term **perception** 'refers to the means by which information acquired from the environment via the sense organs is transformed into experiences of objects, events, sounds, tastes, etc.'. A distinction can be drawn between sensation and perception. **Sensation** is the basic, uninterpreted information which is presented to our sense organs, whereas perception is organized and involves interpreting and attaching meaning to sensations. In general terms, sensation is followed by perception, but it is important to note that the processes underlying sensation and perception frequently overlap in time.

The following part of this chapter is concerned with **attention**. The most obvious characteristic of attention is that it generally involves selective processing of some aspects of the environment at the expense of others. William James (1890) conveyed the importance of selective attention in the following words:

Millions of items of the outward order are present to my senses which never enter into my experience. Why? Because they have no interest for me. My experience is what I agree to attend to. Only those items which I notice shape my mind – without selective interests, experience is an utter chaos.

(James 1890: 381)

❑ Organization in visual perception

When you look at a given object (e.g. a female friend) in the visual environment on several different occasions, there is a reassuring tendency for it or her to appear much the same each time. This is more surprising than it seems, because the information in the retinal image changes considerably from one occasion to another. The size of your friend in the retinal image is much smaller when she is far away from you than when she is close by. The colour of her skin in the retinal image varies as a function of the lighting conditions, and her shape in the retinal image depends on the angle from which you are looking. The term **visual constancies** is used to refer to the tendency for objects to look the same size, colour, shape and so on in spite of great variations in the retinal image. Size constancy, colour constancy and shape constancy are examples of visual constancies.

The visual constancies serve the purpose of helping to allow us to perceive the world in an accurate and well-organized fashion. However, the visual constancies on their own would not permit us to see the world in an organized way. Information about the visual environment is transferred into a retinal image, where it forms a complex pattern of intensity variations. However, this is not how we see the world. Instead, we perceive people and objects occupying different positions within a three-dimensional environment. We will consider some of the factors responsible for depth perception a little later in the chapter. Before that, we will focus on the issue of **perceptual segregation**. This concerns the processes which allow us to divide up the visual information presented to the retina into a number of separate objects.

Gestaltist theory

The Gestaltists were a number of German psychologists who were very influential during the 1920s, 1930s and 1940s. The key Gestaltists were Max Wertheimer, Kurt Koffka and Wolfgang Köhler, and their major contributions were made in the areas of perception and problem solving. The German word 'Gestalt' means 'form', and the Gestaltists were especially interested in the organization of visual perception.

One of the notions emphasized by the Gestaltists was that 'the whole is more than the sum of its parts.' For example, suppose there is a song you know well because it has been recorded by one of your favourite groups. If you were to hear the same melody played in a different key, you would almost certainly still recognize the song. In terms of the Gestaltist position, the whole (i.e. the melody) can still be recognized even though all of its parts (i.e. the individual notes) have been changed.

Evidence that the whole can be more important than the parts was reported by Navon (1977). He showed his

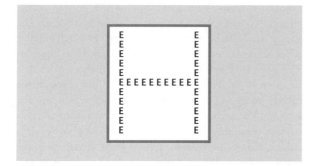

Figure 5.1 An example of the type of stimulus used by Navon (1977)

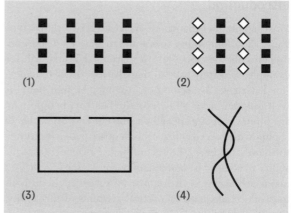

Figure 5.2 Four of the Gestalt laws of perceptual organization: (1) law of proximity, (2) law of similarity, (3) law of closure, (4) law of good continuation

participants visual stimuli such as the one in Figure 5.1. They sometimes had to decide as rapidly as possible whether the large letter was an H or an E. At other times they had to perform the same task with respect to the small letters. The time to decide whether the large letter was an H or an E did not depend at all on whether the small letters were the same as, or different from, the large letter. In contrast, the time to decide whether the small letters were Hs or Es was much longer when the large letter was different from the small letters than when it was the same. These findings suggest that visual processing starts with the whole and then moves on to its parts. That is why the whole can disrupt processing of the parts, but the parts do not disrupt processing of the whole. However, it should be noted that Kinchla and Wolfe (1979) obtained different findings from those of Navon (1977) when their large letters were much larger than those used by Navon. In those circumstances, the small letters seemed to be processed before the large one. They concluded that the whole is processed first only when it is small enough to be perceived in a single eye fixation.

The other key notion put forward by the Gestaltists was the **law of Prägnanz**. This law was perhaps most clearly described by Koffka (1935: 138): 'Of several geometrically possible organizations that one will actually occur which possesses the best, simplest and most stable shape'. The Gestaltists also put forward other, more specific laws, which indicated some of the ways in which the best and simplest shape was achieved. Some of these laws are as follows (see Figure 5.2 for illustrations):

(1) law of proximity: according to this law, parts of a visual display which are close together will tend to be perceived as belonging together

(2) law of similarity: according to Wertheimer (1923: 119), 'Other things being equal, if several stimuli are presented together, there is a tendency to see the form in such a way that the similar items are grouped together'

(3) law of closure: according to this law, small missing parts of a figure are filled in to complete it; thus, for example, a rectangle with a small gap in it is still seen as a rectangle

(4) law of good continuation: according to this law, parts of a display are grouped together so as as to involve the smallest number of interruptions in smooth lines

These various laws of organization all make sense. If you look around you, you will probably find that the parts of the visual scene which belong to a given object tend to be close together and to be similar. The law of closure is useful when we are looking at a distant object which is partially hidden by a closer object, and the law of good continuation is of value when we are looking at a complex scene with overlapping objects.

A final aspect of the Gestalt approach to visual perception was their emphasis on **figure-ground organization**. When we look at a visual scene, part of it stands out as a solid, well-defined object (the figure), whereas the rest of the scene seems less distinct and important (the ground). According to the Gestaltists, the various laws of perception we have discussed help to explain how figure-ground organization is achieved.

Views about the Gestalt approach

The greatest strength of the Gestaltist approach was that they discovered several important features associated with visual organization. However, their contribution extends beyond that. As Gordon (1989) pointed out,

the Gestalt psychologists were right about many things. Geometric illusions continue to fascinate theorists and experimenters alike; constancy in perception is undoubtedly one of its major achievements; we do seem to respond to relationships among stimuli rather than to their absolute values; context influences perception; wholes are more than the sum of their parts; stimuli become organized into patterns. The Gestaltists had undoubtedly chosen some important and reliable phenomena with which to support their claims.

(Gordon 1989: 63)

The greatest weakness is that they provided a *description* of certain phenomena, but they failed to go on to offer a good *explanation* of these phenomena. They tried to provide an explanation based on the doctrine of **isomorphism**. According to this doctrine, there is a very close correspondence between our organized visual experience and organized processes within the brain. They assumed that there are electrical 'field forces' in the brain which underlie our organized perceptual experience. This theory has never received convincing support. Lashley *et al.* (1951) tried to disrupt the electrical field forces of two chimpanzees by inserting gold foil in the visual cortex of one of them and gold pins in the cortex of the other one. Both chimpanzees had almost normal visual perception afterwards, suggesting that vision does not depend on electrical field forces.

Restle (1979) showed how the law of Prägnanz or good form could be made more precise. He considered in detail how people perceive and code information about three or more dots moving smoothly backwards and forwards across a display. If the dots were perceived to be entirely independent in their movements, then predicting their future movements would require an enormous amount of information processing. On the other hand, if the dots are perceived as belonging to groups, then there would be a substantial reduction in information processing. As the Gestaltists would have predicted, participants consistently perceived the dots as being grouped in a simple and coherent fashion. Restle's (1979) major contribution was that he was able to predict mathematically what the simplest way of perceiving the dots would be, and this corresponded to how the dots were seen.

ψ **Section summary**

Visual perception is generally organized, and exhibits figure-ground organization. There is evidence that the whole can be more than the sum of its parts, or at least that visual processing can start with the whole before moving on to the parts. The Gestaltists argued that perceptual organization depends on various laws, including those of Prägnanz, proximity, similarity, closure, and good continuation.

1   Describe some of the ways in which visual perception is organized.

Pattern recognition

When we are presented with a familiar two-dimensional pattern, we are often able to recognize it. This is often more of an achievement than it might seem to be. For example, we can read handwritten words written in different ways, and we can read text printed in several fonts or in different orientations. In other words, our visual system operates in a rather flexible fashion to make sense of the two-dimensional patterns we encounter every day. The central issue which has been addressed by theorists is how to account for this flexibility.

Template theories

One of the simplest approaches to pattern recognition is to assume that there is a **template** or miniature copy of each of the patterns we know stored within long-term memory. According to simple template theories, all that happens in pattern recognition is that a visual stimulus is matched with whichever template provides the best fit.

The main problem is that the basic template theory does not explain how we manage to recognize any given pattern in spite of great variability in the visual stimulus. There are at least two ways in which one might try to improve the basic theory. One way is to abandon the assumption that there is a single template for each pattern, and to replace it with the assumption that each pattern is represented by several templates. This would permit greater flexibility in pattern recognition, but would make the theory more cumbersome and difficult to test. Another way of modifying the basic theory is to assume that visual stimuli undergo a process of normalization before they are matched with templates. Normalization involves altering the internal representation of a stimulus so that it is in a standard orientation, of a standard size, and so on. There would need to be an enormous number of rules influencing the normalization process, and it would probably not work well in practice.

Feature theories

Visual stimuli can be thought of as consisting of a number of features. For example, the human body consists of two legs, two arms, a trunk and so on, and a face consists of hair, two eyes, two eyebrows, a nose, a mouth and a chin. According to feature theorists, pattern recognition involves identifying the features of a visual stimulus, and then deciding what the pattern is by comparing its features against those of patterns stored in long-term memory.

The potential value of a feature-based approach can be seen if we consider the fact that we can read letters written in many different ways. Feature theorists assume that the basic features remain the same regardless of handwriting style. For example, a capital letter A consists of two straight lines and a connecting cross-bar, and it can be identified correctly on the basis of these features.

Evidence that there are specialized cells within the brain for feature-like processing was obtained by Hubel and Wiesel (1962). They inserted micro-electrodes into the brains of cats. They found that some cells responded maximally to vertical lines, whereas other cells responded maximally to diagonal lines. They argued that cells in the visual system could be divided into slit detectors, line detectors and edge detectors but it has since been discovered that matters are much more complex than that. This evidence that many brain cells respond to specific aspects of visual stimuli seems to be consistent with a feature-based approach to pattern recognition, but is less supportive than used to be thought (see Bruce *et al.* 1996).

Selfridge (1959) put forward a version of feature theory known as the Pandemonium model, which was originally intended as a computer program to recognize Morse Code. According to this model, there is a hierarchical system of 'demons', with feature demons at the lowest level, cognitive demons at the intermediate level and a decision demon at the highest level. Each feature demon responds selectively to a specific feature (e.g. right angle; continuous curve), 'shouting' to the cognitive demons according to the extent to which its feature is present in the visual stimulus. The cognitive demons

represent individual letters, and they respond to the appropriate features. The cognitive demons 'shout' to the decision demon according to the number of the features of their letter which are present, and the decision demon decides which letter has been presented on the basis of which cognitive demon shouts the loudest.

Neisser (1964) tested feature theory in studies of visual search. The participants were presented with lists of letters (see Figure 5.3) and had to find a target letter as rapidly as possible. The time taken to detect the target depended on the similarity of features between the target and distractor letters. The participants found it harder to detect the letter Z when the distractor letters consisted of straight letters (e.g. M, W) than when they contained rounded features (e.g. Q, U). According to Neisser (1964), it was easier to find a target when its features were dissimilar to those of the distractors.

Harvey *et al.* (1983) obtained evidence that the perception of letters does not only depend on specific features such as those emphasized by Neisser (1964). They considered spatial frequency, which is high when alternating dark and light bars are far apart and low when they are close together. The task they used was naming letters that were presented very rapidly. Letters having similar spatial frequencies but few common features were often confused, whereas letters with several common features but differing in spatial frequency tended not to be confused. The implication is that spatial frequency plays an important role in letter identification.

Problems with feature theories

Feature detection often plays an important part in pattern recognition. However, feature theories provide only a partial account of the processes involved. In essence,

	LIST 1						LIST 2					
W	M	X	V	I	E	G	R	U	Q	O	D
V	M	W	E	V	X	O	D	Q	R	U	G
E	X	V	I	W	M	R	O	G	U	Q	D
E	W	V	X	M	I	U	D	G	O	U	Q
I	M	X	W	E	V	U	G	O	Q	D	R
W	V	Z	I	E	X	D	Q	Z	U	G	O
E	I	V	W	V	X	O	Q	D	R	G	U
V	M	X	E	W	I	G	U	O	Q	R	D
I	W	E	V	M	X	R	Q	D	O	G	U
I	X	M	E	W	V	U	O	R	G	D	Q

Figure 5.3 Lists of the type used by Neisser (1964); the target letter Z is easier to find in List 2 than in List 1

feature theories focus on some of the bottom-up processes underlying pattern recognition; however, top-down processes based on contextual information and expectations are ignored. Consider, for example, the central stimulus in Figure 5.4. If it is seen in the context of the letters above and below it, then it looks like the letter B. In contrast, it looks like a number 13 if seen with the numbers to the left and right of it. In this case, pattern recognition is influenced by context rather than solely by the features of the stimulus.

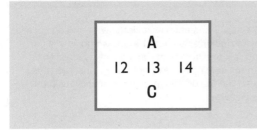

Figure 5.4 Perception of the central stimulus depends on the context (horizontal or vertical)

Performance on Neisser's visual search task also does not depend entirely on bottom-up processes. An important reason why the letter Z can be detected is because feature detectors for curves are 'switched off' (Duncan and Humphreys 1989). The decision to switch off these feature detectors involves top-down rather than bottom-up processes.

Structural descriptions

Bruce *et al.* (1996) argued that an approach to pattern recognition based on structural descriptions is more adequate than one based on templates or on features. A structural description 'consists of a set of propositions (which are symbolic, but not linguistic, although we describe them in words) about a particular configuration' (Bruce *et al.* 1996: 212). We can make this more concrete by considering a possible structural description of a capital letter L, which might consist of the following propositions: (1) there are two parts; (2) one part is a vertical line; (3) one part is a horizontal line; (4) the bottom of the vertical line joins the left end of the horizontal line.

One of the significant advantages of structural descriptions is that they focus on the most important aspects of visual stimuli. For example, the relative and absolute lengths of the vertical and horizontal lines in the letter L do not matter within fairly wide limits, and so information about their lengths is omitted from the structural description.

In order to have an adequate theory, we would need to know how structural descriptions are produced from visual stimuli, and also how such structural descriptions are matched with the relevant structural description in long-term memory. The approaches of Marr (1982) and of Biederman (1987) to object recognition are relevant in this connection, and are discussed in detail a little later in the chapter.

ψ Section summary

There are various theoretical accounts of our ability to recognize two-dimensional patterns. According to template theories, long-term memory contains a miniature copy or template of each pattern we know, and pattern recognition involves matching the visual stimulus with the best fitting template. According to feature theories, visual stimuli consist of various features. Pattern recognition involves comparing the features of a presented stimulus against those of patterns stored in long-term memory. Feature theories account for some of the bottom-up processes in pattern recognition, but de-emphasize top-down processes based on contextual information and expectations. An approach based on structural descriptions is potentially more adequate than those based on templates or features.

1   How do we recognize two-dimensional patterns?

❏ Depth perception

One of the most impressive achievements of visual perception is our ability to see a three-dimensional world even though the retinal image is two-dimensional. How is this done? There are several cues to depth, but they can be divided into **monocular cues** and **binocular cues**. Monocular cues are ones which need the use of only one eye, but which can still be used with two eyes. In contrast, binocular cues are ones which require both eyes to be used together.

Monocular cues

One of the most important of the monocular cues to depth perception is *interposition*. This cue is available when a nearer object obscures part of a more distant object. Some idea of the strength of this cue is given by Kanizsa's (1976) illusory square (see Figure 5.5). It looks as if there is a white square in front of four blue circles, even though most of the square is missing. In other words, the visual system 'invents' an interposed square to make sense of the missing parts of the blue circles.

Another important cue to depth is provided by *familiar size*. If we know the size of an object, then we can use information about its retinal size to work out how far away it is. In one study (Ittelson 1951), the participants had restricted monocular vision of three playing cards. One of these cards was of normal size, one was twice the normal size, and the last one was only half the normal size. Each playing card was presented on its own 7.5 feet away, and the participants were asked to estimate its distance. The estimated distance of the normal-sized card was 7.5 feet, compared to 15.0 feet for the half-sized card and 4.6 feet for the double-sized card. Thus, distance estimates were based almost entirely on the assumption that all the playing cards were of normal size.

There are some interesting exceptions to the general reliance on familiar size. For example, Ittelson (1952) made use of what is known as the Ames room. This room produces the same retinal images as a normal rectangular room when viewed from a particular point in the front wall, but it actually possesses a very unusual shape. One end of the rear wall is much further away from the observer than is the other end, but this is not clear because the floor slopes and the end of the wall which is further away is much higher than the end which is nearer. Someone standing in the corner further away from the observer looks much smaller than someone of

Plate 5.1 One phenomenon associated with motion parallax occurs when looking through the side windows of a car that is travelling fast; objects further away seem to be moving in the same direction as the car, whereas those closer than the fixation point seem to be moving in the opposite direction

the same size standing in the nearer corner, because the observer assumes they are the same distance away. In this case, our knowledge that most people are approximately the same size does not influence judgements of distance or of size.

Another monocular cue is **motion parallax**. This cue is based on the movement of an object's image on the retina. In general terms, the amount of movement of the image tends to be greater for moving objects that are close to the observer than for objects that are far away. Another phenomenon associated with motion parallax can be seen if you look through the side windows of a car that is travelling fast. Objects further away from you than the fixation point seem to be moving in the same direction as the car, whereas those closer than the fixation point seem to be moving in the opposite direction.

Rogers and Graham (1979) managed to set up a situation in which motion parallax was the only depth cue available to the participants. They used a display of 2,000 random dots, and produced relative movement or motion parallax in part of the display to mimic the movement of a three-dimensional object. The participants saw a three-dimensional object apparently standing out in front of the surrounding dots. This led Rogers and Graham to conclude that 'parallax information can be a subtle and powerful cue to the shape and relative depth of three-dimensional surfaces' (1979: 134).

There are further binocular cues to depth which are often used by artists when painting three-dimensional scenes. For example, parallel lines pointing away from

Figure 5.5 Illusory square (Kanizsa 1976)

us appear closer together as we look towards the horizon; this is known as **linear perspective**. You may have noticed, especially when the atmosphere is rather dusty, that more distant objects look rather hazy. The differences in colour and brightness between distant objects tend to look less than those between nearby objects, and this is known as a lack of contrast. This haziness and lack of contrast form the depth cue of aerial perspective. Fry *et al.* (1949) found that objects can be made to look further away by reducing the contrast between them.

Two final depth cues used by artists are *texture* and *shading*. The usefulness of texture as a cue can be seen if you look along a carpet which has a repeating pattern. The distance between successive patterns seems to become less as you look at the more distant parts of the carpet. Gibson (1979) described this as a texture gradient, meaning that there is an increased gradient or rate of change of texture density as you look from the nearby to the distant parts of an object that is slanting away from you. Shading is a useful cue to depth, because it is only three-dimensional objects that cast shadows.

Binocular cues

There are three main depth cues which can be used only by those looking at the world with both eyes together. First, there is **accommodation**. The curvature of the lens of the eye changes when we focus on nearby objects, and it is possible that we can use this in depth perception. However, accommodation can be used only with objects close to us, and even then it seems to be of limited value (Kunnapas 1968).

Second, there is **convergence**: there is more turning inwards of the eyes when looking at close objects than at more distant ones. Convergence can be used only with close objects. However, there is increasing evidence that it is never of much use. In the words of Logvinenko and Belopskii (1994: 216), 'Convergence does not supply sufficient information for the perception of distance'.

Third, there is **stereopsis**. There is a slight difference or disparity in the images projected on to the retinas of the two eyes, and this information can be used to form a three-dimensional representation of the external world. Wheatstone (1838) showed the importance of stereopsis. He devised a stereoscope, in which slightly different pictures of a scene are shown to each eye. The disparity in the retinal images creates a strong impression of depth. Stereopsis is a powerful cue to depth for objects which are close to us.

Some individuals suffer from stereoblindness, which is an inability to see depth properly using information about retinal disparity. The most common condition involving stereoblindness is strabismus, in which the two eyes look in somewhat different directions. This is a serious problem, leading either to double vision or to reliance on one eye only even when both eyes are open (see Sekuler and Blake 1994).

It has proved difficult to establish exactly how we are able to combine, or match up, the information from two separate images into a single percept. According to Marr and Poggio (1976), three main rules are used:

- compatibility constraint: in order for parts of the two retinal images to be matched up, they need to be compatible or similar in some way (e.g. shape, colour)
- continuity constraint: parts of the two retinal images are more likely to be matched up if the disparity between them is similar to the disparity for nearby parts of the retinal images which have already been matched up
- uniqueness constraint: each part of one retinal image is matched up only to one part of the other retinal image

Combining depth cues

In our discussion of depth cues, we have dealt with them one at a time. In the real world, however, there are usually numerous depth cues available. Thus, we need to consider how the information from different depth cues is combined to produce depth perception. Bruno and Cutting (1988) pointed out that one possible strategy is *additivity*, in which all the available information is added together. Another possible strategy is *selection*, in which the information from one depth cue is used to the exclusion of the information from other cues.

Bruno and Cutting (1988) carried out a series of studies to decide which strategy is used. Their participants looked with one eye at visual displays, and were provided with some or all of the following depth cues: interposition; motion parallax; relative size; and height in the projection plane. The findings indicated that the participants were using the additivity strategy. This strategy has some advantages over the selection strategy. Errors in depth perception are less likely to happen when all of the depth information is used than when total reliance is placed on a single depth cue.

What happens when two depth cues provide conflicting information about depth? This issue was studied by Rogers and Collett (1989). They set up a situation in which conflicting information was provided by binocular disparity and motion parallax. The additivity strategy was used: 'Given apparently contradictory disparity and parallax information about the structure of 3-D objects, it would appear that the visual system attempts to find a solution that is maximally consistent with the available information' (Rogers and Collett 1989: 716)

The additivity strategy is used most of the time, but there are some exceptions. In one study, described by Woodworth and Schlosberg (1954), participants looked monocularly at two playing cards attached vertically to stands. The nearer playing card had a corner clipped from it, and the two cards were arranged so that the edges of the more distant card fitted precisely into the cutout edges of the nearer card. It seemed to the participants that the more distant card was in front of, and partially obscuring, the nearer card. The participants focused entirely on the cue of interposition, and took no account of familiar size. In other words, they used the selection strategy rather than the additivity strategy. Presumably this happened because the cue of interposition nearly always provides very powerful and accurate information about depth.

ψ Section summary

Depth perception is based on a range of monocular and binocular cues. Monocular cues include interposition, familiar size, motion parallax, linear perspective, texture and shading. The main binocular cues are stereopsis, accommodation and convergence, but only stereopsis is of much value in depth perception. The information from different depth cues is usually combined, but there are occasions on which the information from one depth cue is used to the exclusion of other depth cues. For example, in the Ames room a person standing in the further corner can appear much shorter than someone of the same size standing in the nearer corner, because the observer assumes they are the same distance away (Ittelson 1952).

1 What are the main factors involved in depth perception?

❏ Object recognition

One of the main purposes of visual perception is to achieve **object recognition**, i.e. identifying the objects in the visual environment. As Humphreys and Bruce (1989) pointed out, there are various kinds of information which can be involved in object recognition.

Marr's theory

One of the most influential theories of visual perception generally and of object recognition in particular was put forward by Marr (1982). According to his computational theory, visual perception is considerably more complex than is often thought to be the case. More specifically, he argued that visual perception involves producing three increasingly detailed representations or descriptions of the visual environment:

* primal sketch: this representation is two-dimensional, and includes information about contours, edges and blobs; this information is obtained by making use of light-intensity changes in the visual scene
* $2\frac{1}{2}$-D sketch: this representation uses information from shading, binocular disparity, motion and so on to form a description of the relative depth and orientation of visible surfaces
* 3-D model representation: this representation is an advance on the $2\frac{1}{2}$-D sketch in two ways: it is three-dimensional, and it is independent of the observer's viewpoint.

It is the 3-D model representation which is of most relevance to an understanding of object recognition. Marr and Nishihara (1978) argued that objects within the 3-D model representation can be described as consisting of an assembly of connected generalized cylinders, each of which has a major axis. According to them, information about the major axis can usually be identified from all viewing positions, which makes it of particular importance. Other kinds of information (e.g. precise shape) cannot be established so readily from different viewing angles, and so are of less value in object recognition. Object recognition occurs when the 3-D model representation based on the major axes of the visual stimulus is matched against the large collection of 3-D model representations stored in long-term memory.

Marr and Nishihara (1978) applied their theoretical approach to the ways in which the human body and its parts are represented in the 3-D model representation:

First the overall form of the 'body' is given an axis. This . . . can then be used to specify the arrangements of the 'arms', 'legs', 'torso', and 'head'. The position of each of these is specified by an axis of its own. . . . The shapes are drawn as if they were cylindrical, but that is purely for convenience: it is the axes alone that stand for the volumetric qualities of the shape, much as pipecleaner models can serve to describe various animals.

(Marr and Nishihara 1978)

How are the major axes of an object detected? According to Marr and Nishihara (1978), concavities or parts of the contour pointing inwards are used to identify the main parts of an object, and then the major axis of each part is found. For example, each arm can be identified as a separate part because of the concave area where the underneath part of the upper arm joins the torsso.

Hoffman and Richards (1984) obtained evidence that concavities are important in recognition. They used the faces-goblet ambiguous figure. They found that the faces are seen when the focus is on the concavities associated with their noses, lips and chins, whereas the goblet is seen when the focus is on the concavities associated with its base, stem and bowl.

One of the implications of the Marr-Nishihara theory of object recognition is that brain-damaged patients who find it hard to identify the major axes of objects should be poor at object recognition. This implication was tested by Humphreys and Riddoch (1984), in a study based on brain-damaged patients having right posterior cerebral lesions. The patients were given the task of deciding which two out of three photographs were of the same object, or they were asked to identify the object presented in a photograph. The task was made more difficult by presenting unusual views of objects; these views were unusual either in the sense that a distinctive feature was hidden or because of foreshortening. Foreshortening should make it difficult to identify the major axis of the object. Humphreys and Riddoch (1984) found that the object recognition of a number of the patients was impaired by foreshortening but not by the lack of a distinctive feature, suggesting that identifying the major axis is important to object recognition.

Marr's achievements

Marr's (1982) theory has been extremely influential. One of its main achievements was to demonstrate that object recognition involves much more complex processes than had been assumed previously. The notion that there is a series of processes intervening between the presentation of an object and its recognition is still accepted, although many of the details of those processes are disputed by others. As we will see shortly, Biederman (1987) has developed Marr's (1982) general approach into a more adequate theory of object recognition.

Biederman's theory

There are approximately 500,000 words in the English language, and all of them consist of different combina-tions of only 26 letters. Biederman (1987, 1990) argued in his recognition-by-components theory that something similar is true of object recognition. He claimed that there are approximately 36 basic shapes or components, which he called 'geons' (geometric ions). Arcs, wedges, spheres, cylinders and blocks are examples of geons. Recognition of an object usually occurs when we have worked out its geons and their spatial relationships. For example, a cup and a bucket both consist of a cylinder and an arc; however, the arc is connected to the top of the bucket, whereas it is connected to the side of the cup.

As can be seen in Figure 5.6, information about the geons or components of an object in the visual environment is matched against object representations stored in long-term memory. Whichever stored object representation provides the best fit or match with the geons of the visual object determines what the visual object is perceived as being.

How does the observer decide the number and nature of geons of which an object consists? According to Biederman (1987, 1990), two main processes are involved. First, those parts of an object's contour which are concave generally provide very valuable information about how to divide up the object into its geons or components. For example, a wine glass has major concavities

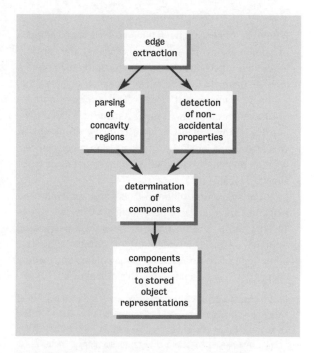

Figure 5.6 The key features of Biederman's (1987) recognition-by-components theory

where the base joins the stem and where the stem joins the bowl, and these concavities facilitate the task of segmenting the wine glass into its geons. Biederman (1987) discussed evidence showing the importance of concavities. His participants were shown degraded drawings of objects. They found it much harder to identify the objects when the drawings omitted information about concavities than when they omitted other information.

Second, it is important to detect what Biederman (1987) called the **non-accidental properties** from the edges of visual objects. Non-accidental properties are those that do not change as we look at an object from different angles. Such properties provide more useful information than properties which differ considerably as a function of viewing angle. Examples of non-accidental properties are symmetry, parallel lines and curvature. Apart from remaining invariant over different viewing angles, the non-accidental properties also have the advantage that they can be detected even when parts of the relevant edges are hidden from view.

When we are looking at a word, we can often decide what it is even if some of its letters are missing or hard to read. For example, you can probably work out that COMP*T*R is meant to be COMPUTER. In similar fashion, according to Biederman (1987), we can still recognize objects even when some of the geons are missing or obscured from sight. Biederman *et al.* (1985) presented their participants with drawings of objects possessing either six or nine geons. They were able to identify the objects correctly about 90 per cent of the time even when only three or four of the geons were present.

Problems with Biederman's approach

It is generally accepted that Biederman (1987, 1990) has made a significant contribution to our understanding of object recognition. However, his recognition-by-components theory is limited in some ways. First, relatively little account is taken of the influence of contextual information on object recognition. For example,

---

Ψ Case study

Visual agnosia: John

A number of researchers have studied **visual agnosia** in the attempt to understand visual perception. Brain-damaged patients with visual agnosia have a specific problem in recognizing common objects from vision. It is important to note that such patients do not have problems with most aspects of visual perception. They are often able to draw an object at which they are looking, and their vision is not blurred. What is missing is the ability to make sense of what they are looking at.

Humphreys and Riddoch (1987) studied John, who exhibited a particularly pure form of visual agnosia. In 1981, he had an emergency operation for a perforated appendix. After the operation, he suffered a stroke. Some idea of the nature of his problems with visual perception can be gained from his own account:

I have come to cope with recognising many common objects, if they are standing alone, and I can manage in the flat by trying to keep things in the same place – just as I were blind. When objects are placed together, though, I have more difficulties. To recognise one sausage on its own is far from picking one out

from a dish of cold foods in a salad. Since coming round I have never been able to recognise any person by sight alone. I cannot recognise my wife except by the sound of her voice, nor my grandchildren, nor family, nor friends.

(Humphreys and Riddoch 1987: 33–4)

In spite of his great problems with visual perception, John remained a very intelligent and articulate man. Extensive testing indicated that he had no impairment in his memory system. The evidence from John and other patients with visual agnosia indicates that there is very selective impairment of a few aspects of visual perception. It is consistent with the views of Biederman (1987) and others that object recognition consists of various different processes, and that it is possible for brain damage to spare most of those processes. Can we be more precise? According to Humphreys and Riddoch (1987), John perceived the elements or features of objects clearly, but had great difficulty in organizing these features to form meaningful objects. For example, consider his description of a paintbrush: 'It appears to be two things close together; a longish wooden stick and a shorter, darker object' (1987: 60).

Palmer (1975) found that the probability of recognizing a briefly presented picture of an object was significantly higher when it was preceded by an appropriate context (e.g. a loaf of bread preceded by a picture of a kitchen). Second, the theory is designed to account for object recognition at a relatively general level. For example, the theory explains how we identify an object such as a cup. However, it does not explain how we make more subtle discriminations (e.g. between our favourite cup and other cups).

ψ Section summary

According to Marr (1982), object recognition is achieved by forming three increasingly detailed representations: the primal sketch; the 2½-D sketch; and the 3-D model representation. Objects within the 3-D model representation are described in terms of cylinders having a major axis. The main parts of the object are identified by making use of concavities in its contour. Biederman (1987) developed these ideas in his recognition-by-components theory. He argued that there are approximately 36 basic shapes or components, which he called 'geons'. Object recognition occurs when its geons and their spatial relationships have been worked out. Information about concavities is used to identify an object's geons. Object recognition also depends on non-accidental properties which do not depend on the viewing angle. Biederman's theory has the limitations of de-emphasizing the importance of context and of not accounting for subtle discriminations among objects.

1 Describe and evaluate theories of object recognition.

☐ Colour perception

The main function of colour perception is to facilitate the detection of objects. As Sekuler and Blake (1994) pointed out, manufacturers produce yellow tennis balls because they are easier to see than white ones, and they produce orange golf balls because they are easy to find if your shots stray off into the rough. The existence of camouflage provides more evidence of the importance of colour perception: some species (e.g. praying mantises) are very similar in colour to their normal environment, and this makes it hard for predators to find them.

Colours differ from each other in terms of three different qualities. First, there is hue, which relates to our experience of reds, greens, yellows, and so on, and is largely determined by the light's wavelength. Second, there is brightness, which is determined by the amount of light present. Third, there is saturation, which is the quality that distinguishes between vivid and pale colours. Thus, to provide a complete account of the colour of some object, it is necessary to specify its hue, brightness and saturation.

Colour constancy

Earlier in the chapter we discussed some of the visual constancies, which involve the tendency for objects to look the same in spite of substantial changes in the retinal image. One of these constancies is colour constancy, which is the tendency for an object to look the same colour through changes in the light reflected from it. For example, most artificial lights are yellower than outdoor light, and so the light reflected from objects contains more yellow when viewed indoors than when viewed outdoors. However, this generally has little or no effect on their perceived colour.

There are various reasons for colour constancy. First, we are familiar with the colours of thousands of objects, and can use this information to work out its colour if seen under unusual lighting conditions. For example, people in Britain know that the postboxes are red, and so they still look red even in the dark. Throughout Europe, traffic lights are designed so that green means that motorists can go, and red means that they must stop.

Second, colour constancy often depends on distinguishing between the effects of the pigments in the surface of an object and the effects of the illumination striking that surface. As Dannemiller (1989) and others have pointed out, changes in illumination generally alter the light reflected from several objects, whereas changes in the pigment of an object (e.g. the colour of someone's cheeks when they blush) have much more restricted effects.

Third, prolonged exposure to any particular illumination produces adaptation, in which there is a reduction in the responsiveness of neurons. For example, when you come indoors after being out in bright sunshine, you may initially be struck by the yellowness of the artificial lights. After a while, however, the process of adaptation means that you respond less to the long-wavelength light indoors, and so it no longer looks yellow. The implication of adaptation for colour constancy is that any distorting effects of different kinds of illumination gradually decrease with increased exposure.

Young–Helmholtz theory

Young and Helmholtz independently argued that the eye contains three types of receptors, each of which is most sensitive to light of different wavelengths. According to this theory, human vision is trichromatic, meaning that all the hues we are able to perceive result from variable activity in these three types of receptors. It is now accepted that these receptors are in the form of cones within the eye. The three cone pigment types underlying colour vision are as follows:

- one cone type is most sensitive to light of short wavelength and underlies perception of blue
- a second cone type is especially sensitive to light of medium wavelength, and underlies perception of green
- a third cone type is most sensitive to light of long wavelength, and underlies perception of red.

Other colours involve two or all three cone types. For example, yellow is seen if there is activity of the second and third cone types, and white light is seen if all three cone types are active at the same time.

Striking evidence for the essential correctness of the Young–Helmholtz theory was reported by Dartnall *et al.* (1983). They made use of a technique known as **microspectrophotometry**. In essence, this technique involves shining a tiny spot of light onto a single cone in the eye, and measuring the amount of light absorbed at various wavelengths. The results are shown in schematic form in Figure 5.7. As can be seen, the three types of receptors or cones predicted by the Young–Helmholtz theory were found.

Subsequent research has revealed that we have under 1 million short-wavelength cones, over 4 million long-wavelength cones, and over 2 million medium-wavelength cones (Cicerone and Nerger 1989). All three types of cones are primarily found at the fovea or centre of the retina, or close to it. As a consequence, colour vision is virtually non-existent in the periphery of vision, as can be ascertained if you look out of the corner of your eye.

Hering's opponent process theory

In spite of the great success of the Young–Helmholtz theory, there are some findings which suggest that it is incomplete. For example, there are **afterimages**. If a patch of colour is fixated for several seconds and then removed, there is generally a positive afterimage followed by a negative afterimage (Woodworth and Schlosberg 1954). The positive afterimage is similar in hue and brightness to the original stimulus, whereas the negative afterimage is opposite in brightness and complementary in colour. Thus, for example, the negative afterimage of a blue stimulus is yellow, and the negative afterimage of a green stimulus is red.

Another interesting phenomenon is **colour contrast**, in which the differences in colour between two adjacent objects are exaggerated. Thus, for example, a small grey square looks blue on a yellow background, yellow on a blue background, red on a yellow background, and so on.

The phenomena of afterimages and colour contrast suggest that there may be some kind of opposition or conflict between complementary colours. This notion was contained within Hering's (1890) opponent process theory. According to this theory, there are three processes, each of which can function in opposite directions. One process is responsible for the perception of red at one extreme and green at the other, the second process produces the extremes of blue and yellow, and the third produces white and black.

Physiological evidence supporting Hering's general approach was reported by DeValois and DeValois

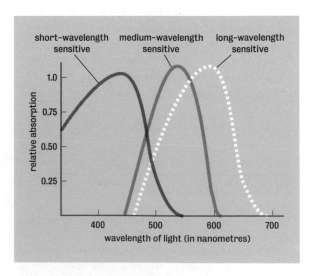

Figure 5.7 Three types of colour receptors or cones found by the use of microspectrophotometry
Source: Based on data in Dartnall *et al.* (1983)

(1975). They found opponent cells in the lateral genicu-late nucleus of monkeys. These cells showed increased responses to some wavelengths of light but decreased responses to others. For some of these cells the transi-tion between increased and decreased responsiveness occurred approximately at that part of the spectrum between green and red, and they were accordingly called red-green cells. For other cells, the transition occurred between the yellow and blue parts of the spec-trum; they were called blue-yellow cells. As Sekuler and Blake (1994) pointed out, there is some doubt as to whether matters are really this simple.

DeValois and DeValois (1975) also found non-opponent cells. Some of these cells increased their activ-ity to all wavelengths of light, whereas others decreased their activity to all wavelengths. Hering (1890) argued that there is an opponent process which produces perception of white and black, and it is possible that these non-opponent cells are involved in that process.

Synthesis

We have seen that there is convincing evidence in favour of the Young-Helmholtz theory, and also in favour of the rather different opponent process theory. How can this be so? Hurvich (1981) argued that the two theories should be combined into a two-stage theory, and a sim-plified version of his proposed theory is discussed by Atkinson et al. (1993).

Some of the basic ideas behind the two-stage theory are shown in Figure 5.8. The three cone types identified within the Young-Helmholtz theory send signals to the opponent cells identified within opponent process theory, and this determines what colour is seen. The short-wavelength cones send excitatory signals to the blue-yellow opponent cells, whereas the long-wave-length cones send inhibitory signals. Blue is perceived if the strength of the excitatory signals exceeds that of the inhibitory signals; otherwise, yellow is seen. In similar fashion, the green-red opponent cells receive excitatory signals from the medium-wavelength cones, and inhibitory signals from the long-wavelength cones. If the strength of the excitatory signals is greater than that of the inhibitory signals, then green is seen; otherwise, red is seen.

Individuals suffering from colour deficiency provide some support for this theory. There are several forms of colour deficiency, but the most common ones are due to a lack or insufficiency of medium- or long-wave-

length cones. In either case, the functioning of the green-red opponent cells is disrupted, and red-green deficiency results.

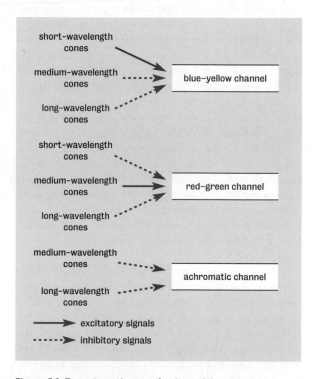

Figure 5.8 Two-stage theory of colour vision

Ψ Section summary

Colours differ in terms of hue, brightness and satu-ration. There are three cone pigment types underly-ing colour vision; these cone types differ in terms of the light wavelengths to which they are most sensi-tive. Their existence has been confirmed by means of microspectrophotometry. The phenomena of afterimages and colour contrast suggest that there is opposition or conflict between complementary colours. There are three opponent processes, one being responsible for red and green, one for blue and yellow, and one for white and black. It appears that the three cone types send signals to the oppo-nent cells responsible for opponent processes.

1   What are some of the main factors involved in colour perception?

☐ Constructivism and the ecological approach

In general terms, perception can be regarded as depending on a combination of bottom-up and top-down processing. **Bottom-up processing** is processing which depends directly on external stimuli, whereas **top-down processing** is processing which is influenced by expectations, stored knowledge, context and so on. Tulving *et al.* (1964) demonstrated the effects of both kinds of processing on the accuracy of word perception. The involvement of bottom-up processing was increased by lengthening the exposure time of the word, and the involvement of top-down processing was increased by providing more sentence context before the word was presented. Bottom-up and top-down processing both had significant effects on the accuracy of word identification. Top-down processing produced by the sentence context had less effect when exposure time for the word was relatively long.

Some theorists (e.g. Gregory 1980; Neisser 1967) have emphasized the role of top-down processes in perception. According to these theorists, perception is an active and constructive process that involves testing hypotheses (e.g. informed guesses; inferences) about the environment. As a consequence, we will refer to the approach favoured by these theorists as constructivism. This approach is discussed below. Other theorists have emphasized the importance of bottom-up processes. For example, Gibson (1950, 1966, 1979) argued that environmental stimuli are a rich source of information; indeed, this information is generally adequate for accurate visual perception. Gibson proposed an ecological approach, and this is also discussed below.

Constructivism

The basic assumption of constructivist theorists is that perception is influenced by hypotheses and expectations. There is convincing experimental support for this assumption. In one study (Bruner *et al.* 1951), the participants were presented briefly with playing cards, some of which were incongruous in colour (e.g. black hearts). When they were asked to indicate the colour, their responses were sometimes influenced by their expectations (e.g. black hearts would be reported as brown or purple). In other words, perception of colour was influenced by top-down as well as bottom-up processes.

Misapplied size-constancy theory

Gregory (1970, 1980) applied the constructivist approach to some of the best known visual illusions, such as the Muller-Lyer illusion (see Figure 5.9). He argued that some of the processes used to produce size constancy for three-dimensional objects are mistakenly used with two-dimensional drawings. Accordingly, Gregory described his approach as the **misapplied size-constancy theory**.

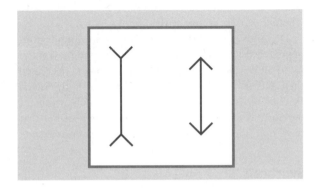

Figure 5.9 Muller–Lyer visual illusion

In order to understand the misapplied size-constancy theory, we will consider its explanation of the Muller-Lyer illusion. The two vertical lines are actually the same length, but the one on the left looks longer than the one on the right. According to Gregory (1970), the drawing on the left resembles the inside corner of a room, whereas the drawing on the right looks like the outside corner of a building. Thus, the vertical line on the left would be further away from us than the rest of the figure in three-dimensional space, but the vertical line on the right would be closer to us than the rest of the figure. Since the retinal images of the two vertical lines are the same size, the inference is made that the line further away (the left one) is actually longer than the closer line (the right one).

Misapplied size-constancy theory can also account for the Ponzo illusion (see Figure 5.10). The two circles are actually the same size, but the top one looks larger than the bottom one. According to the theory, the top circle would appear to be further away than the bottom circle in a three-dimensional representation (e.g. of a road receding into the distance). Since the retinal images of the two circles are the same size, the top circle must be larger than the bottom one.

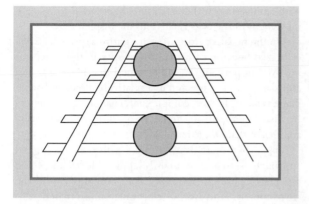

Figure 5.10 Ponzo illusion

One of the problems with misapplied size-constancy theory is that visual illusions such as the Muller-Lyer and the Ponzo appear flat and two-dimensional even though they are supposedly interpreted in some ways as three-dimensional representations. Gregory (1980) addressed this problem, claiming that depth cues can be used even when observers realize that they are looking at a two-dimensional drawing. He discussed research which seemed to support his theory. When observers are shown luminous or glowing two-dimensional Muller-Lyer figures in a dark room, most of them report that they look three-dimensional.

It seems reasonable to assume that the depth cues provided by two-dimensional drawings are less powerful than those provided by photographs. This assumption was tested by Leibowitz and colleagues (1969). They found that the Ponzo illusion was much greater with a photograph than with a line drawing.

Misapplied size-constancy theory provides a plausible account of many visual illusions. However, there is evidence that the Muller-Lyer illusion does not depend only on misapplied size-constancy. An illusory effect is found when the fins on both drawings are replaced by squares or circles (Gross 1992). It may be that one vertical line looks longer than the other because it is part of a larger object rather than because it appears to be further away.

Problems with the constructivist approach

On the positive side, there is no doubt that perception is often affected by the top-down processes emphasized by constructivist theorists. However, the influence of top-down processes is greater in artificial laboratory conditions than in everyday life. In the words of Gordon (1989: 144), studies supporting the constructivist posi-

tion involve 'the perception of patterns under conditions of brief exposure, drawings which could represent the corners of buildings, glowing objects in darkened corridors . . . none of these existed in the African grasslands where human perceptual systems reached their present state of evolutionary development'.

If everyday perception were heavily influenced by top-down processes, then it would be prone to errors. For example, the tendency to perceive what we expect to see would produce mistakes when our expectations are wrong. In fact, perception is essentially accurate nearly all the time, indicating that bottom-up processes usually supply adequate information about the environment. As Tulving *et al.* (1964) found in a study discussed earlier, top-down processes are more important when limited exposure time reduces the effectiveness of bottom-up processes.

Gibson's ecological approach

Gibson (1950, 1966, 1979) argued that theories of perception should focus on perception in the real world rather than under highly artificial laboratory conditions. Accordingly, he developed what he called an ecological approach to visual perception. One of the major assumptions of this approach is that there is a close relationship between perception and action. Another major assumption is that the information provided by the visual environment is much richer and more complete than is assumed by constructivist theorists. Indeed, Gibson assumed that members of all species use that information to move around their environment without needing to make use of internal hypotheses or thought processes. Gibson emphasized the role of bottom-up processes in perception, with his theoretical approach providing a sophisticated account of how this happens.

We can understand the ecological approach by considering a practical issue addressed by Gibson (1950). He wondered how pilots manage to land planes successfully. He discovered that they had available to them valuable information in the form of **optic flow patterns**. Within the optic flow pattern, the point towards which the plane is heading seems motionless, whereas everything else in the visual environment appears to be moving away from that point (known as the 'pole'). If the plane changes direction, then the location of the motionless part of the optic flow changes as well. As the plane moves closer to the landing strip, there is an increase in the speed at which parts of the visual environment seem to move away from the pole. A similar effect is created if the plane accelerates. In other words, optic flow patterns provide detailed information about a plane's direction, distance from the landing strip, and speed.

One of the theoretical implications which Gibson (1950) drew from his investigation of optic flow patterns was the importance of identifying those aspects of the visual environment which remain the same as people move around. They are known as invariants, and they provide very useful information about the layout of the environment. In the case of optic flow patterns, the pole is an invariant. Another invariant is the horizon ratio relation: the ratio of an object's height to the distance between its base and the horizon remains invariant when its distance from the observer changes.

There are two other important concepts put forward by Gibson: **resonance** and affordance. According to Gibson, resonance is the process which permits us to 'pick up' or detect invariant information in the visual environment. This process resembles the way in which a radio works. A radio needs to be properly tuned in order for the signal from a radio station to be received clearly. When that happens, the radio is said to resonate (or be attuned with) the information contained in the electromagnetic radiation. In similar fashion, we can detect invariants effortlessly if we are attuned to the visual environment.

The term **affordance** refers to those uses of an object which can be readily perceived. For example, a pen or pencil affords writing, and a book affords reading. According to Gibson (1979: 139), the concept of affordances is also applicable to postboxes: 'The postbox . . . affords letter-mailing to a letter-writing human in a community with a postal system'. Much of the meaning of objects relates to their potential uses, and so Gibson made the controversial assumption that object meaning can be perceived directly rather than that such information is stored in long-term memory (e.g. Biederman 1987).

Issues raised by the ecological approach

On the positive side, Gibson was correct in his assumption that the visual world generally contains all (or nearly all) of the information needed for basic perception. This is especially so when the observer is in motion, as was discussed earlier in connection with optic flow patterns. The richness of the information available in the everyday visual environment is generally much greater than that available in the laboratory. As M.W. Eysenck and Keane (1995: 79) pointed out, 'Traditional laboratory research generally involved static observers looking at impoverished visual displays, often

with chin rests or other restraints being used to prevent movement of the eyes relative to the display'.

On the negative side, Gibson's entire approach can be criticized because of his failure to specify the processes involved in perception. He assumed that invariants and affordances were detected in a relatively direct and automatic fashion. In fact, complex internal processes underlie visual perception, and Gibson did not adequately appreciate that fact (Marr 1982).

The other main limitation of Gibson's ecological approach is that it is mainly applicable to the basic aspects of perception involved in moving around the environment. However, there is much more than that to perception. Fodor and Pylyshyn (1981) argued that perception involves *seeing* and *seeing as*. They considered the hypothetical case of someone called Smith, who was lost at sea. If Smith looks at the Pole Star, then he sees a star, but he may or may not see it as the Pole Star. For his survival, it may be of crucial importance that Smith realizes that it is the Pole Star rather than any other star he is looking at. According to Fodor and Pylyshyn (1981), Gibson theory applies to *seeing* but not to *seeing as*. In other words, the complex significance or meaning attached to visual stimuli in the course of perception is largely ignored by the ecological approach.

Ψ Section summary

Perception depends on bottom-up and top-down processing. Constructivist theorists have emphasized top-down processes in the form of testing hypotheses about the environment. Gregory used the constructivist approach in his misapplied size-constancy theory, which provides an explanation of many two-dimensional visual illusions. Visual perception seems to be less prone to error than would be expected on the constructivist approach. According to Gibson's ecological approach, there is a close relationship between perception and action, and the visual environment generally provides rich and complete information. Resonance is the process allowing us to detect invariant information in the environment, and affordance refers to those uses of an object which can be readily perceived. Gibson's approach fails to specify the processes involved in perception, and it is mainly applicable to basic aspects of perception.

1   Compare and contrast the constructivist and ecological approaches to visual perception.

Research update

Perception of affordances

Gibson consistently argued that there are very close links between perception and action. However, research on affordances has not taken full account of this part of his approach. Affordances are the possibilities for action offered by the environment and the objects in it. For example, we decide whether a ladder 'affords' or allows ascent or descent by considering the gaps between successive rungs in relationship to the length of our legs. Does our perception of affordances depend on our own actions? For example, it could be argued that assessing the catchability of a moving ball (i.e. can I move rapidly enough to catch it before it falls to the ground?) depends not only on our visual perception of the ball in flight, but also on our movements towards it. If so, this would be entirely consistent with Gibson's emphasis on the notion that perception is often dependent on action.

Oudejans and colleagues (1996) studied the factors involved in perceiving catchability. In their first study, a machine shot tennis balls from behind a screen. The participants remained stationary and judged the catchability of each ball. Expert baseball outfielders and non-experts who had no baseball experience were equally poor at judging how possible it would be to catch the tennis balls.

In their second study, Oudejans et al. (1996) allowed their non-expert participants to see each ball moving for only one second. They were wearing liquid crystal display spectacles that shut at a predetermined time. The participants either started to run towards the ball during the one-second interval, or they remained standing. Judgements of catchability were significantly better when the participants were moving than when they were stationary. Indeed, simply running towards the ball for a very limited period of time reduced judgement errors by almost half.

What do these findings tell us about affordances? The key discovery is that it is often important for us to move around in order to make an accurate assessment of an affordance. Thus, Gibson was basically correct when he claimed that perception and action are interdependent.

Visual systems and the brain

So far we have paid very little attention to the brain systems involved in visual perception. Until the late 1980s, rather little was known about these brain systems. As a consequence, most theories of visual perception did not take into account the slowly accumulating knowledge about relevant brain functioning. However, there are indications that we are beginning to make significant progress in understanding the underlying brain systems. Zeki (1992, 1993) has provided an excellent account of most of this recent brain research.

The basic theoretical assumption made by Zeki (1992) is that there are several different parts of the brain which are involved in visual processing (see Figure 5.11). Each part tends to be specialized for only some aspects of visual perception. More specifically, he focused on the following areas of visual cortex:

- V1 and V2: these areas of the visual cortex are most involved early on in visual processing, and are mainly concerned with the processing of form and colour

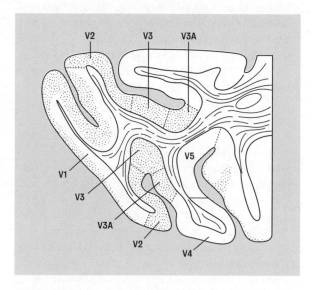

Figure 5.11 The visual cortex of the macaque monkey shown in cross-section
Source: Zeki (1992); reproduced by permission of Scientific American Inc. (Eysenck and Keane 1995: 43)

- V3 and V3A: these visual cortex areas are involved in processing information about an object's form but not about its colour
- V4: this area is mostly concerned with colour processing, but is also involved in processing line orientation; there is recent evidence that cells in this area respond to complex visual patterns (e.g. concentric circles, spirals)
- V5: this area of the visual cortex is involved in the processing of visual motion

Zeki (1992, 1993) reviewed a considerable body of evidence which supports his general theoretical position. Some of this research involved PET scans which provide information about which areas of the brain are most active when a given task is being performed. Haxby and colleagues (1991) found from PET scans that there was increased activity in the occipital cortex and the temporal lobe during a face-matching task. During a spatial task, there was increased activity in the occipital cortex and the parietal lobe. The implication is that the temporal lobe is involved in processing information about form, colour and the identity of objects, whereas the parietal lobe is involved in spatial processing.

Visual area V4 was especially active when human participants looked at an abstract colour painting (see Zeki 1992). In contrast, visual area V5 was most active when human participants looked at a pattern of moving black-and-white squares (see Zeki 1992).

According to Zeki's (1992, 1993) theoretical position, the various aspects of visual processing occur in different parts of the brain. It follows that there should be brain-damaged patients who exhibit very specific impairments in visual perception. There is considerable support for this prediction, and we will consider a few examples (see also case study). Zeki (1992) coined the term *chromatopsia* to describe patients who have essentially intact colour vision, but nearly all other visual

---

Ψ Case study

Colour processing in the brain

Lueck and colleagues (1989) achieved significant progress in our understanding of colour vision. They presented their participants with abstract displays of coloured squares and rectangles, or they presented the same displays with the rectangles various shades of grey. Lueck *et al.* (1989) used PET scans to measure increases in blood flow. They found that there was an increase of 12–14 per cent in blood flow in area V4, but not in other areas, suggesting that V4 is a specialized colour centre.

The notion that V4 is specialized for colour vision can be investigated by studying cases of *achromatopsia*, in which there is no colour vision as the result of central nervous system disease. This was done by Shuren *et al.* (1996). They studied an achromatopsic, E.H., who was a 63-year-old man working as an airport security guard. He suffered a stroke, after which he reported that everything looked grey and devoid of colour. He was given various tests of colour vision, all of which indicated that he had essentially no colour vision. However, he had normal visual acuity and his visual fields were normal. A magnetic resonance imaging (MRI) brain scan indicated that area V4 was among the parts of the brain which had been damaged by the stroke. This provides support for Zeki's (1992, 1993) theory.

Farah (1989) argued that forming an image of an object makes use of the same stored representations which are used in visual perception. This led him to conclude that patients with achromatopsia should have impaired colour imagery. Shuren *et al.* (1996) gave E.H. various tests of colour imagery. One test involved deciding which two out of three verbally described objects had the same colour, and another test required E.H. to decide which of two objects had more of a given colour (e.g. 'plum and eggplant, which has more red in it?'). His performance on these tests was normal, indicating that he had intact colour imagery in spite of the loss of colour perception.

How can we interpret these findings? According to Shuren *et al.* (1996), there is a single visual system involved in colour perception and colour imagery. E.H. probably had intact stored colour representations of objects, which allowed him to perform colour imagery tasks. However, the connections between visual input and the stored colour representations were destroyed or unusable, and this produced a total absence of colour perception. (See also p. 119).

processes are very impaired. Chromatopsia results from widespread brain damage caused by carbon monoxide poisoning. Another condition is *akinetopsia*, in which moving objects appear invisible, even though the same objects when stationary can be seen reasonably clearly. Akinetopsia involves damage to area V5.

Zeki (1992) argued that the available evidence strongly supports the notion that there are 'four parallel systems concerned with different attributes of vision – one for motion, one for colour, and two for form' (1992: 47). What remains rather unclear is how information from the different areas of the cortex concerned with visual perception is integrated and combined. This is known as the 'binding' problem, and the complex processes solving this problem are poorly understood.

ψ Section summary

PET scan studies have indicated that several parts of the brain are involved in visual processing, with each part tending to be specialized for only certain aspects of visual perception. For example, some areas are involved in the processing of visual motion, whereas others are involved in processing line orientation, form and colour. How information from these different areas is integrated in object perception is unclear.

1 Describe some of the major brain systems involved in visual perception.

Attention

'Attention' is a rather vague concept that has been used with a number of different meanings over the years. However, it is used most frequently to refer to a tendency to process selectively some stimuli at the expense of others. In the words of William James (1890: 403–4), attention 'is the taking possession of the mind, in clear and vivid form, of one out of what seem several simultaneously possible objects or trains of thought. ... It implies withdrawal from some things in order to deal effectively with others'.

There is a major distinction between **focused attention** and **divided attention**. Both forms of attention are studied by presenting people with two stimulus inputs at the same time. In studies of focused attention, the participants are told to process one input and to ignore the others. In studies of divided attention, they are told to do their best to process both inputs and to respond appropriately to both inputs. Thus, studies of focused and divided attention fulfil different functions. Investigating focused attention tells us the extent to which people can select one input while ignoring another, whereas investigating divided attention provides us with information about attentional and processing capacity.

Much theory and research have been based on the assumption that there is a single entity called attention. This is an oversimplification of reality. As Allport (1993) pointed out,

There is no uniform function, or mental operation . . . to which all so-called attentional phenomena can be attributed . . . It seems no more plausible that there should be one unique mechanism, or computational resource, as the causal basis of all attentional phenomena than that there should be a unitary causal basis of thought or perception.

(Allport 1993: 203–4)

Posner and Petersen (1990) made an impressive attempt to identify some of the components of visual attention. They argued that attention involves at least three rather separate processes: the disengagement of attention from a stimulus; the shifting of attention from one visual stimulus to another; and the engagement of attention to a new visual stimulus.

Much of the evidence supporting this theory of attention involves brain-damaged patients. It has proved possible to find patients with severe deficiencies in only one of the three attentional processes, suggesting that the processes are separate. For example, patients suffering from simultanagnosia seem to have particular problems with the disengagement of attention. These patients can attend to only one object at a time even when there are a number of objects close together in the visual field, presumably because they find it difficult to disengage attention from the object on which they initially focus (Ellis and Young 1988).

Attention and consciousness

Before proceeding to discuss research on attention, it is worth considering the relationship between attention and consciousness (see also pp. 63–6). It has often been argued that there is a substantial overlap (or even identity) between the two concepts. However, this argument was convincingly refuted by Baars (1997). According to him, we can gain some understanding of the distinction between attention and consciousness by considering sentences such as, 'We look in order to see' or 'We listen in order to hear.' In the words of Baars (1997: 364), 'The distinction is between selecting an experience and being conscious of the selected event. In everyday language, the first word of each pair involves attention; the second word involves consciousness'. In other words, attentional mechanisms control access to consciousness.

This distinction helps to identify the dissimilarities between attention and consciousness. Attention is typically active and controllable. In contrast, consciousness is more passive and less controllable, and occurs as a result of prior attentional processes. Baars (1997) illustrated this fundamental point by means of an analogy: attention is like selecting a television channel, and consciousness is like the visual display appearing on the screen.

The notion that attention and consciousness are conceptually distinct is supported by the fact that studies of attention and of conscious experience differ greatly in a number of ways. It is common in studies of selective attention for the participants to be given instructions to attend to certain stimuli and to ignore others, to avoid being distracted by non-task stimuli, and so on. The key dependent variable is generally some measure of performance, with the focus being on investigating the effects of attentional manipulations. In contrast, the key dependent variable in studies of conscious experience (e.g. perception studies) is on verbal reports of the participant's experience. More precisely, Baars (1997) argued that psychologists typically accept that their participants are providing evidence of a conscious experience under the following conditions:

- the experience is communicated by means of a voluntary signal (e.g. verbal report)
- there is some independent evidence that the conscious experience is genuine
- the reported experience is claimed to be conscious
- the conditions at the time of reporting are suitable (e.g. there is no pressure on the participants to be dishonest)

In practice, it is often difficult to assess the genuineness of other people's reports of their conscious experience. The main reason for this is that we cannot have direct access to anyone else's conscious experience. Wittgenstein (1958) expressed this major problem in terms of an analogy between each individual's conscious experience and the contents of a box:

No-one can look into anyone else's box, and everyone says he knows what a beetle is only by looking at his beetle . . . it would be quite possible for everyone to have something different in his box . . . the box might even be empty.

(Wittgenstein 1958: para. 293)

Focused auditory attention

Suppose that you are at a party, and there are several conversations going on around you. What most people find is that it is surprisingly easy to follow one conversation and ignore all of the others. Cherry (1953) investigated how we are able to do this. He found that what is of crucial importance is the existence of physical differences between the message we want to follow and the others. These physical differences can be based on the physical location of the speakers, on voice intensity, or on the sex of the speaker. In one study, Cherry eliminated these physical differences by presenting two messages in the same voice to both ears at once. The participants were very poor at following one message and ignoring the other purely on the basis of its meaning.

Cherry (1953) also studied selective attention by instructing his participants to shadow (repeat back out loud) the auditory message presented to one ear while ignoring the message presented to the other ear. When the participants were asked afterwards, they were usually unable to report anything about the unattended message. Even when the unattended message was in a foreign language, the participants typically failed to notice that there was anything unusual about it. However, they did notice when there were changes in the physical characteristics of the unattended message (e.g. the sudden introduction of a pure tone).

Filter theory

Broadbent (1958) put forward a filter theory of attention to account for Cherry's findings. According to this theory, a stimulus input needs to pass through a filter before it can be processed thoroughly. This filter selects one stimulus input on the basis of its physical characteristics, and it rejects all of the others presented at the same time.

Broadbent's filter theory explains Cherry's data, but it does not account for some of the findings reported by Allport et al. (1972). They presented pictures to their

Research update

Shifts in auditory attention

Cherry's (1953) studies on the cocktail party effect remain important and influential to the present day. It is now generally accepted that people will shift attention to the unattended channel when there is some dramatic change (e.g. loud noise) on that channel, while people will not shift attention to the unattended channel when there is a more subtle change (e.g. in language or meaning) on that channel. Suppose, however, that the change on the unattended channel is neither dramatic nor subtle. For example, Cherry (1953) found that some (but by no means all) of his participants noticed when the message on the unattended channel changed from normal English to English played backwards. However, he did not explain what was happening.

Why do some of the participants notice the shift to reversed speech? One possibility is that they shift their attention from the attended channel from time to time, and this attentional shift allows them to detect the reversed speech. In fact, Wood and Cowan (1995) found that that did not seem to be the case. They looked at the accuracy of shadowing or repeating back of the message on the attended channel before and after the shift to reversed speech on the unattended channel. If we assume that shifting attention to the unattended channel causes reduced accuracy on the shadowing task, then it might be predicted that those who noticed the switch to reversed speech would have had impaired shadowing either before the switch or shortly thereafter. In fact, shadowing errors peaked between 10 and 20 seconds after the onset of reversed speech.

What do these findings mean? According to Wood and Cowan (1995: 258), 'Automatically detected discrepancies in the irrelevant stimulus provoked attention shifts, rather than habitual sampling of the irrelevant channel leading some participants to notice the backward speech'. It is clear from the work of Wood and Cowan (1995) that more research is needed to explore the mechanisms underlying shifts in auditory attention.

Plate 5.2 Research on auditory attention includes Cherry's studies on the cocktail party effect, which measured shifts in the attention of participants when a message on the unattended channel changed from normal English to English played backwards

participants while they were shadowing an auditory message, and found that 90 per cent of the pictures were recognized subsequently. However, when shadowing was combined with auditorily presented words, there was very poor memory for the words. These findings pointed to an important conclusion: only one out of two stimulus inputs can be processed when the inputs are similar to each other (e.g. auditorily presented words), but both inputs can be processed when they are dissimilar to each other.

A different problem for filter theory was identified by Gray and Wedderburn (1960). They used what is known as the dichotic listening task, in which pairs of words are presented one to each ear, followed by free recall of what has been presented. The participants heard a series of words such as 'who five there' in one ear and 'eight goes four' in the other ear. According to filter theory, recall should have been ear by ear. In fact, most of the participants reported the words on the basis of their meaning, for example, 'who goes there' followed by 'eight five four'.

Attenuation theory

Some of the problems with Broadbent's filter theory were resolved by Treisman (1964), who put forward attenuation theory. According to attenuation theory, the initial analyses of a stimulus input focus on its physical characteristics (e.g. voice intensity, sex of speaker), whereas later analyses deal with meaning. If there is insufficient attentional capacity to process two simultaneous stimulus inputs thoroughly, then the less important will receive only the initial analyses.

Treisman's (1964) attenuation theory accounts for the fact that the unattended stimulus input is sometimes processed. It also accounts for the finding that the physical characteristics of an unattended stimulus input are more likely to be processed than the meaning. However, these findings can also be explained by a theory proposed by Johnston and Heinz (1978). They agreed with Treisman (1964) that the attentional system operates in a flexible fashion. More specifically, they argued that there are several stages of processing that can be applied to a stimulus input, and each of these processing stages uses up some of the available processing capacity. As a consequence, the unattended stimulus input receives only the minimum processing needed to carry out the current task.

Johnston and Heinz (1979) reported the findings of a study designed to test their theory. Their participants shadowed or repeated back one set of words while ignoring another set of words. In the easy condition, the to-be-shadowed words were presented in a male voice and the other words were presented in a female voice. In the difficult condition, both sets of words were spoken in the same male voice. Johnston and Heinz (1979) assumed that the participants would need to process the non-shadowed words more thoroughly in the difficult condition, because the shadowed and non-shadowed words could not be identified on the basis of physical characteristics. Two pieces of evidence supported this assumption. First, the non-shadowed words were recalled better on an unexpected test of free recall in the difficult condition than in the easy one. Second, more processing resources were used in the difficult than in the easy condition.

Ψ Section summary

When people attend to one conversation, they tend to be aware only of the physical characteristics of other conversations being held at the same time. According to Broadbent's filter theory, one stimulus input is selected on the basis of its physical characteristics, and all of the others presented at the same time are rejected. This theory is too inflexible, and was superseded by Treisman's theory. According to this, there is generally less thorough or attenuated processing of less important stimulus inputs than of the most important one. According to the theory of Johnston and Heinz (1978), the unattended stimulus input is processed only as much as is needed to perform the current task.

1 Evaluate theoretical approaches to focused auditory attention.

❏ Focused visual attention

When we look at a visual scene, part of it is in sharp focus, and the rest is blurred and unclear. This has suggested to various theorists that visual attention resembles a spotlight. For example, Eriksen (1990) put forward a zoom-lens theory, according to which the attentional spotlight has an adjustable beam. In other words, we are able to decide whether to focus on a relatively broad or narrow area.

LaBerge (1983) obtained findings which are consistent with the notion of an adjustable spotlight. His participants were presented with five-letter words, and given a task which involved focusing either on the entire word or on only the middle letter. The attentional spotlight was broad when the participants were performing the former task, and narrow when they carried out the latter task.

The zoom-lens theory is partially correct, but it is oversimplified in some ways. Consider, for example, a study by Neisser and Becklen (1975). Two visual scenes in motion were superimposed on each other, and the participants were instructed to attend to one scene and to ignore the other one. They were able to do this, indicating that visual attention can be directed to certain objects rather than to a particular area as is implied by the spotlight.

According to the zoom-lens theory, there should be very little processing of visual stimuli falling outside the spotlight. Such stimuli generally have little or no disruptive effect on the processing of stimuli within the spotlight, suggesting that they are hardly processed at all. Indeed, Johnston and Dark (1986: 56) used such evidence to conclude that 'stimuli outside the spatial focus of attention undergo little or no semantic processing'. However, this conclusion is not warranted. For example, Tipper and Driver (1988) found that the unattended visual stimulus on one trial had a disruptive effect on the processing of a related stimulus on the next trial. This finding indicates that the meaning of stimuli outside of the spotlight can be processed.

Treisman's feature integration theory

One of the limitations of the zoom-lens theory is that it does not specify the processes underlying focused visual attention. Treisman (1988) attempted to fill this gap with her feature integration theory. The starting point for this theory is the assumption that objects consist of various features such as size, shape and colour. There are two processes involved in focused visual attention. The first process involves rapid, parallel processing of the features of all the objects present in the visual environment. The second process operates in a slow, serial fashion and involves combining features to form objects (e.g. an object having redness, roundness and smallness

as its features might be identified as an apple). The second process usually involves focused attention, in which case features from the same object are combined to form an object. If focused attention is not involved, then features may be combined from different objects to produce 'illusory conjunctions'. For example, a red square surrounded by green circles might be seen as a green square. Treisman and Schmidt (1982) reported several illusory conjunctions when their participants distributed their attention over a number of stimuli rather than focusing on only one.

Evidence which is consistent with feature integration theory was reported by Treisman and Gelade (1980). They used a task in which the participants had to decide whether a target stimulus was present in a visual display consisting of between one and thirty stimuli. The crucial manipulation was the nature of the target: in one condition, it was defined by one feature (a blue letter; the letter S); in the other condition, it was defined by a combination of features (a green letter T). In the latter condition, all of the non-target stimuli shared one feature with the target, being either green Xs or brown letter Ts.

The findings are shown in Figure 5.12. Consider first the effects of target type on positive trials on which a target was presented. There was no effect of the number of items in the display on decision times when targets were defined by a single feature. However, display size had a large effect when targets were defined by a combination of features. According to feature integration

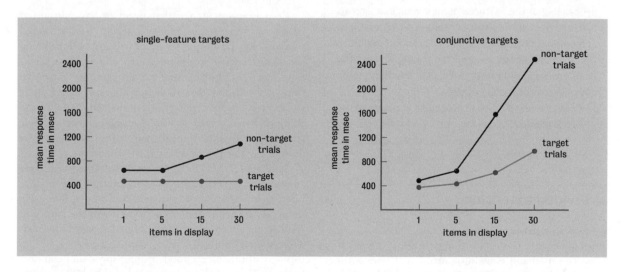

Figure 5.12 Time taken to decide that a target was present (positive trails) or absent (negative trials) as a function of target type (single-feature or conjunctive) and number of stimuli in the display
Source: data from Treisman and Gelade (1980)

theory, only rapid, parallel processing of features is needed to detect the former targets, whereas the slow, serial process is required to detect the latter targets. The findings were less clear on negative trials, but there was a much greater effect of display size when targets were defined by a combination of features.

Treisman and Gelade (1980) assumed that searching for a target defined by two features is slow because all of the stimuli in the display need to be processed. However, Treisman and Sato (1990) adopted a modified version of feature integration theory. They argued that searching for such targets involves processing stimuli sharing at least one feature with the target, but ignoring stimuli having no features in common with the target stimulus. As predicted by this modified theory, Treisman and Sato (1990) found that decision times were influenced by the similarity between the target stimulus and the non-target stimuli.

Ψ Section summary

Eriksen (1990) proposed a zoom-lens theory, according to which focused visual attention resembles a spotlight with an adjustable beam. There is evidence in support of this theory, but it appears that stimuli outside the spotlight can be processed more thoroughly than is implied by the theory. According to Treisman's feature integration theory, focused visual attention involves a rapid, parallel processing of the features of all stimuli in a display, followed by a slow, serial process in which features are combined to form objects. Treisman and Sato (1990) subsequently revised the theory, so that the first process is limited to stimuli sharing one or more features with the target.

1 Compare and contrast theoretical accounts of the processes involved in focused visual attention.

❏ Divided attention

We all know from personal experience that it is sometimes fairly easy to do two things at once (e.g. walking down the road and chewing gum), but it is sometimes very difficult or impossible (e.g. reading a book and holding a conversation). The term 'divided attention' is used to refer to those situations in which people try to per-

form two or more tasks at the same time. It has proved surprisingly difficult to provide a good theoretical account of the processes involved in divided attention. However, some of the main factors determining whether or not two tasks can be combined successfully have been identified: task difficulty, practice, and task similarity. Each of these factors is discussed in turn below.

It seems reasonable to assume that two easy tasks can be combined much more successfully than two difficult tasks. Sullivan (1976) manipulated task difficulty in a study in which the participants shadowed or repeated back aloud one message while at the same time trying to detect target words on a second message. The shadowing task was easy when the shadowed message contained many redundant words, and it was difficult when there was a substantial reduction in redundancy. Far fewer target words were detected when the shadowing task was difficult than when it was easy.

There is no doubt that task difficulty plays an important role in determining how successfully attention can be divided between two tasks. However, there are two major issues which need to be addressed. First, there are many different ways in which a task can be difficult, and it is very hard to measure task difficulty with any precision. Second, the difficulty of a task should not be considered in isolation from the other task being performed at the same time. A task may be relatively difficult when it is combined with another task which has conflicting demands, but the same task may be easy when its demands are compatible with those of the other task (Duncan 1979).

Convincing evidence that practice has substantial effects was reported by Spelke et al. (1976). They asked two students, Diane and John, to read and to understand short stories while writing down spoken words to dictation. When the students first tried to combine these two tasks, they found that their reading speed and their handwriting were both greatly impaired. After Diane and John had received 30 hours' training, however, their reading speed and comprehension were unaffected by performing the dictation task at the same time.

Spelke et al. (1976) discovered that Diane and John had practically no awareness of the meaning of the dictated words they wrote down. Accordingly, they gave them additional training in writing down the names of the categories to which the dictated words belonged. After several hours of training, Diane and John could do this and still maintain good reading speed and comprehension. These findings indicate that the ability to perform two complex tasks together improves considerably with practice. However, as Hirst and colleagues (1980) found in a related study, even extended practice does not permit people to perform two complex tasks together as well as each task can be performed on its own.

Task similarity is another important determinant of performance in studies of divided attention, with performance generally being better when two tasks are dissimilar rather than similar. There are various ways in which tasks can be similar: they can involve stimuli from the same sense modality (e.g. vision); they can involve the same internal processes (e.g. verbal rehearsal); or they can involve similar responses. There is evidence that all of these forms of similarity affect the extent to which two tasks interfere with each other (Wickens 1984). For example, McLeod (1977) found effects of response similarity. One of the tasks he used was a tracking task on which the responses were made with one hand. The other task involved identifying tones, with the responses being either spoken or made with the other hand. The tracking task was performed worse when manual responses were used for both tasks.

Ψ Section summary

Our ability to perform two tasks at the same time depends on various factors, including the difficulty of the tasks, practice, and task similarity. Tasks can be similar in terms of sense modality, internal processes, or response requirements. Do not attempt the question until you have read the next section.

1   What are the major factors determining whether two tasks can be performed successfully at the same time?

Automaticity

As has already been mentioned, people generally become much better at performing tasks as a result of practice. What may be happening is that practice may lead certain processes to become automatic. It has often been assumed that **automatic processes** do not require attention, they do not involve conscious awareness, and they are unavoidable, in the sense that they will always occur when an appropriate stimulus is presented. Unfortunately, it has proved difficult to find automatic processes which meet all of these criteria.

This suggests that many processes are partially rather than fully automatic.

Shiffrin and Schneider

Some of the best known studies on automaticity were reported by Shiffrin and Schneider (1977) and Schneider and Shiffrin (1977). Their starting point was that there is an important distinction between automatic and controlled processes. Automatic processes do not depend on attention, have no capacity limitations and are difficult to alter, whereas controlled processes depend on attention, are of limited capacity and can be used in a much more flexible way than automatic processes. The task used by Shiffrin and Schneider (1977) and Schneider and Shiffrin (1977) was as follows:

- the participants memorized between one and four items (the memory set)
- they were then shown a visual display consisting of between one and four items
- they decided as rapidly as possible whether one of the items in the visual display was the same as one of the items in the memory set

Two categories of items were used with the above task: consonants and numbers. In order to understand the findings, it is important to note that the crucial manipulation was consistent mapping versus varied mapping. Consistent mapping was involved when all of the items in the memory set belonged to one category, and all of the distractor items in the visual display belonged to the other category. As a consequence, all that the participants needed to do was to decide whether any of the items in the visual display belonged to the same category as the one used to form the memory set. In contrast, numbers and consonants were both used to form the memory set and to provide distractors for the visual display with varied mapping. Thus, varied mapping was much harder than consistent mapping.

The main findings are shown in Figure 5.13. With varied mapping, decision times were greatly affected by the number of items in the memory set and in the visual display. With consistent mapping, the effects of increasing the number of items were much smaller. How can these findings be explained? According to Shiffrin and Schneider (1977), the participants used automatic processes in the consistent mapping condition because of the many years' practice they had in distinguishing between numbers and letters. In contrast, controlled processes had to be used in the varied mapping condi-

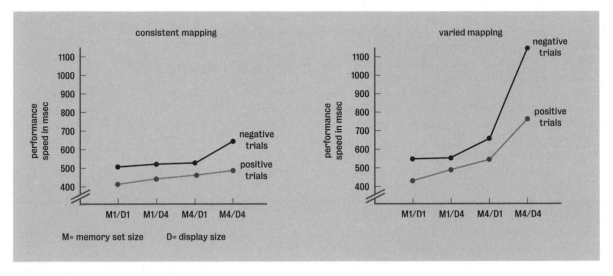

Figure 5.13 Performance speed as a function of memory set size, display size, and consistent versus varied mapping
Source: data from Shiffrin and Schneider (1977)

tion. More specifically, the participants had to compare each item in the memory set with each item in the visual display in turn, and this was time-consuming when there were several items.

From the findings discussed so far, it would seem that automatic processes are superior to controlled processes. However, a significant disadvantage with automatic processes was revealed in another study by Shiffrin and Schneider (1977). They used consistent mapping with two categories of letters, one of which consisted of the consonants between B and L, and the other of which consisted of the consonants between Q and Z. The evidence indicated that automatic processes had developed over the course of 2,100 trials. Throughout these trials, the items in the memory set always came from the same category and the distractors in the visual display always came from the other category. After that, there were 2,400 extra trials with consistent mapping, but with the two categories swapped over. The findings from these trials revealed the inflexibility of automatic processes. The participants performed very poorly with this reverse consistent mapping: they needed almost 1,000 trials before their performance improved to its level at the start of the experiment.

Limitations of the Shiffrin/Schneider approach

Shiffrin and Schneider (1977) and Schneider and Shiffrin (1977) provided convincing evidence for the existence of two kinds of processing, one of which is fast but inflexible, and the other of which is slower but flexible. However, there are at least three major limitations with their theoretical approach. First, they argued that automatic processes have no capacity limitations, which leads to the prediction that decision times in the consistent mapping condition should be unaffected by the number of items in the memory set or in the visual display. As can be seen in Figure 5.13, this was not what Shiffrin and Schneider (1977) found. The number of items had a small, but significant, effect on decision times.

Second, Shiffrin and Schneider (1977) claimed that practice can lead to the development of automatic processes, but they did not specify exactly what is involved. As Cheng (1985) noted, practice may lead to the same processes being used faster and faster, or it may lead to significant changes in the nature of the processes being used. It is not really clear which of these possibilities applies to the practice effects observed by Shiffrin and Schneider (1977).

Third, Shiffrin and Schneider (1977), in their notion of controlled processes, seemed to regard attention as a unitary process or function. As we saw earlier, there are powerful reasons for believing that attention is complex and multi-dimensional (Allport 1993; Posner and Petersen 1990).

Norman and Shallice

Norman and Shallice (1980, 1986) developed some of the theoretical ideas put forward by Shiffrin and Schneider (1977). The main difference between the two theories is that Norman and Shallice (1980, 1986) distinguished between two kinds of automatic processing. First, there is fully automatic processing, which occurs very largely in the absence of conscious awareness. Second, there is partially automatic processing based on what Norman and Shallice described as contention scheduling: this involves the relatively automatic resolution of conflicts among competing processes by selecting the one that is most appropriate in the circumstances. This partially automatic processing is usually associated with some conscious awareness.

In addition to the two kinds of automatic processing just described, Norman and Shallice (1980, 1986) identified a third form of processing resembling Shiffrin and Schneider's (1977) controlled processing. This form of processing is based on a supervisory attentional system, and involves controlling attention, thinking and behaviour. Most of the workings of the supervisory attentional system involve conscious awareness.

The theoretical approach of Norman and Shallice (1980, 1986) is an advance on that of Shiffrin and Schneider (1977). In particular, the notion that there is an important distinction between fully automatic processing and partially automatic processing is consistent with the evidence that different automatic processes do not all meet the same criteria for automaticity.

Ψ Section summary

According to a stringent definition, automatic processes do not require attention or conscious awareness, and they should be unavoidable. In practice, automatic processes tend to be only partially automatic in terms of this definition. Shiffrin and Schneider (1977) obtained evidence supporting a distinction between automatic and controlled processes. Automatic processes depend heavily on practice. According to Norman and Shallice (1980), we should distinguish between fully automatic processing and partially automatic processing based on contention scheduling. In addition, they argued that there is a supervisory attentional system, which controls attention, thinking, and behaviour.

1 What are automatic processes? How can they be accounted for?

Ψ Chapter summary

• Organization in visual perception

Visual perception is usually highly organized, with the visual world being divided up into a number of separate objects. According to the Gestaltists, the best and simplest perceptual organization is achieved; this involves parts of the visual scene which are similar or close to each other being perceived as belonging together. Their approach is descriptive rather than explanatory.

• Pattern recognition

Pattern recognition has been addressed by template and feature theories. According to template theories, a pattern is matched with whichever template or miniature copy stored in memory provides the best fit. According to feature theories, the features of a visual stimulus are identified and compared against those of stored patterns. Feature theories are more useful than template theories, but they leave top-down processes out of account.

• Depth perception

Depth perception depends on a range of monocular and binocular cues. Among the former are interposition, familiar size, motion parallax, and linear perspective; the latter consist of accommodation, convergence and stereopsis. Information from the various cues is usually, but not always, combined in an additive fashion.

• Object recognition

According to Marr (1982), object recognition involves forming an observer-independent 3-D model representation based on an object's major axes, and then matching it against the 3-D model representations stored in memory. According to Biederman (1987), the concavities in an object's contour and its non-accidental properties are used to work out its components or geons and their spatial relationships. These geons are

Box continued

matched against stored object representations to achieve object recognition. Neither theory accounts for contextual effects or subtle visual discriminations (e.g. between breeds of dog).

● Colour perception

Colours differ in their hue, brightness and saturation. Colour constancy depends on familiarity with the colours of objects and on adaptation. There are three types of cones which are responsive to light of different wavelengths. These three types of cones send signals to red-green cells, to blue-yellow cells and non-opponent cells which may play a role in the perception of black and white. Evidence that this theoretical approach is correct comes from individuals with various kinds of colour deficiency.

● Constructivism and the ecological approach

According to constructivist theorists, perception is influenced by hypotheses and expectations. The constructivist approach in the form of the misapplied size-constancy theory has been used to explain many visual illusions. The top-down processes emphasized by constructivist theorists are more important in artificial laboratory conditions than in everyday life. According to Gibson's ecological approach, the visual environment provides all of the information needed for visual perception in the form of optic flow patterns, the horizon ratio relation, and so on. Gibson's theory is more applicable to seeing than to seeing as.

● Visual systems and the brain

There is convincing evidence that different areas of the visual cortex are involved in the processing of information about motion, colour and form. The evidence comes in various forms (e.g. PET scans). It is still unclear how the brain solves the 'binding' problem, i.e. integrating the information from the different brain areas to produce coherent visual perception.

● Focused auditory and visual attention

Focused auditory attention often involves selecting one input on the basis of its physical characteristics. The amount of processing of the non-attended input is variable, and depends on task requirements and capacity limitations. Focused visual attention resembles an adjustable spotlight in some ways. However, stimuli outside the spotlight are sometimes processed for meaning, and visual attention can be directed at objects rather than at a specific area of the visual environment. According to Treisman's (1988) feature integration theory, rapid parallel processing of the features of all visible objects is followed by slow serial processing in which features are combined to form objects. This theory is oversimplified, and has subsequently been modified.

● Divided attention and automaticity

The success (or otherwise) of divided attention to two tasks depends on task difficulty, practice, and task similarity. According to Shiffrin and Schneider (1977), there is an important distinction between controlled (or attentional) processes and automatic processes. Practice can lead to the development of automatic processes, which do not depend on attention, have no capacity limitations, and are hard to change. Automatic processes can facilitate divided attention. Shiffrin and Schneider (1977) did not clarify the processes involved in the development of automatic processes. In a modified version of their theory, Norman and Shallice (1980) proposed a distinction between fully and partially automatic processes.

Further reading

● Sekuler, R. and Blake, R. (1994) *Perception*, 3rd edn. New York: McGraw-Hill. This book provides good accounts of most aspects of visual perception, including depth perception and colour perception.

● Bruce, B., Green, P.R. and Georgeson, M.A. (1996) *Visual Perception: Physiology, psychology, and ecology*, 3rd edn. Hove: Psychology Press. There is comprehensive coverage of key topics in visual perception in this book, and the underlying physiological processes are discussed in some detail.

● Eysenck, M.W. and Keane, M.T. (1995) *Cognitive Psychology: A student's handbook*. Hove: Lawrence Erlbaum. Some of the main topics in perception and attention are dealt with in Chapters 2–6 of this book.

● Kinchla, R.A. (1992) Attention, in M.R. Rosenzweig and L.W. Porter (eds) *Annual Review of Psychology*, vol. 43. Palo Alto, CA: Annual Reviews. There is good coverage of theory and research on visual attention in this chapter.

CHAPTER 6

Memory

Michael Eysenck

KEY CONCEPTS • multi-store models • working memory • learning processes • long-term memory • semantic memory • retrieval processes • forgetting • amnesia • memory for stories • eyewitness testimony

❏ Chapter preview

When you have read this chapter, you should be able to

- understand the importance of the distinction between short-term and long-term memory
- appreciate why conceptions of short-term and long-term memory have become more complex
- describe some of the main processes involved in learning
- understand the processes involved in retrieval and in forgetting
- describe the nature of amnesia, and understand its relevance to normal human memory
- describe what is typically remembered from stories, and relate this to schema theory
- understand some of the limitations of eyewitness testimony, and the ways in which these limitations can be overcome

Introduction

No one can deny the importance of memory. Without memory, everything would seem as novel and mysterious to us as it does to a newborn infant. Many (or even most) people feel that they have a bad memory. This does not just reflect a sense of modesty, because very few people will admit that they have a poor sense of humour or below-average intelligence! As we will see in this chapter, most people have fairly efficient memory systems. We can remember thousands of personal events, we have extensive knowledge about the world, and we remember how to perform large numbers of complex and skilled motor actions. Why then do we feel that our memories are poor? The most likely answer is that forgetting is often an embarrassing experience, as when we forget someone's name or birthday. It is a tribute to our memory systems that we tend to be very good at remembering such embarrassing events.

Learning and memory are obviously very closely related to each other. Memory can occur only when there has been previous learning, and learning can best be demonstrated by good performance on a memory test. It is often argued that learning and memory involve three successive stages in the following order:

(1) the encoding stage, during which the to-be-learned information is processed in various ways (e.g. in terms of its meaning)
(2) the storage stage, during which some of the information processed at the encoding stage is stored in the memory system
(3) the retrieval stage, during which some of the information stored within the memory system is recovered or remembered

Many researchers have focused on only one of the above stages. However, it is important to note that all three stages are closely related to each other. As Tulving and Thomson (1973: 359) argued, 'Only that can be retrieved that has been stored, and . . . how it can be retrieved depends on how it was stored'.

❏ Multi-store models

Short-term and long-term memory

One of the main issues which has concerned memory theorists over the years is to decide how many memory stores or systems we possess. William James (1890) made the influential suggestion that there is an important distinction between **primary memory** and **secondary memory**. Information that has been presented remains in primary memory for as long as it is still in consciousness. Information that is no longer in consciousness, but which is still stored in the memory system, is in secondary memory. In other words, information in primary memory may be said to form the psychological present, whereas information in secondary memory forms the psychological past.

Nowadays, we use the term 'short-term memory' to refer to primary memory, and the term 'long-term memory' to refer to secondary memory. It is assumed that only a limited amount of information can be held in short-term memory, and that this information is in a fragile state. It is important to note that short-term memory has been defined in two rather different ways. It has sometimes been defined as consisting of those items that are the current focus of attention, and sometimes as the information in long-term memory that is currently activated. As Cowan (1993) pointed out, these two definitions are not interchangeable, because the information which is the current focus of attention is usually only a subset of the long-term memory information which is active.

Miller (1956) argued that about seven items (plus or minus two) can be held in short-term memory. He based this figure on span studies, in which participants have to repeat in the correct order a series of items they have heard. For example, the participants in a digit-span study might hear the digits '2 7 8 3 6 5 9'. Most adults can repeat back about seven digits without error, but find it difficult or impossible to repeat back more than that.

According to Miller (1956), approximately seven **chunks** or meaningful units of information can be held in short-term memory. For example, the sentence, 'The cat and the dog fought frequently', consists of seven chunks in the form of words, whereas 'L P R S C V T' consists of seven chunks in the form of letters. The capacity of short-term memory has often been assessed by using span measures. In the case of digit span, a series of random digits is presented, and the participant has to repeat them back. Digit span is defined as the largest number of digits that can be recalled correctly in the right order. In normal adults, the digit span is typically about seven.

Simon (1974) tested Miller's chunking hypothesis by studying the memory span for words and phrases. The number of chunks that could be recalled was seven for one-syllable and two-syllable words, but it dropped to four for two-word phrases and to three for eight-word phrases. In contrast to Miller's hypothesis, it seemed that the number of chunks that could be recalled depended to some extent on the size of each chunk.

How long does information stay in short-term memory? Peterson and Peterson (1959) addressed this question. Their participants were presented with a three-letter stimulus, followed by a three-digit number. Their task was to remember the three-letter stimulus, while at the same time counting backwards by threes from the number they had been shown. After a few seconds of counting backwards, they were asked to recall the three-letter stimulus. As can be seen in Figure 6.1, their ability to remember the three-letter stimulus fell rapidly over time. The fact that their success rate was only approximately 50 per cent with six seconds of counting backwards indicates that information is lost quickly from short-term memory.

It is important to have ways of deciding whether any given information is in short-term or long-term memory. An influential attempt to do that was reported by Glanzer and Cunitz (1966). They carried out an experiment in which a list of words was presented. This was followed by **free recall**, in which the words could be recalled in any order. When the free recall occurred immediately after list presentation (0-sec. delay), there was evidence for a **primacy effect**, meaning that the first few words in the list were especially well remembered (see Figure 6.2). There was also a **recency effect**, meaning that the last few words in the list were also very well remembered.

The key assumption made by Glanzer and Cunitz (1966) was that information in the primacy effect was

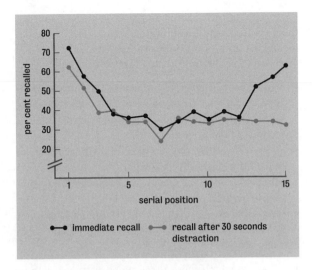

Figure 6.2 Free recall at each serial position as a function of duration of the interpolated task
Source: data from Glanzer and Cunitz (1966)

in long-term memory, whereas information in the recency effect was in short-term memory. They tested this assumption by further conditions, in one of which the participants counted backwards for 30 seconds before producing free recall. As can be seen in Figure 6.2, counting backwards eliminated the recency effect but hardly reduced the primacy effect or recall of the middle portion of the list. According to Glanzer and Cunitz (1966), information in short-term memory is in a fragile state, and so is easily disrupted by the counting backwards task. In contrast, information in long-term memory is less fragile, and so is not affected by the task.

Crowder (1993) argued that the recency effect may not actually reflect the contents of short-term memory. He pointed out that a similar recency effect is found in long-term memory. For example, when people were asked to recall the teams that had played against the local rugger team, their memory was best for recent opponents (Baddeley and Hitch 1977). According to Crowder (1993), all recency effects can be explained by assuming that the most recent items or events are more distinctive than earlier ones.

Atkinson and Shiffrin's model

During the 1960s, several psychologists used the growing understanding of short-term and long-term memory to propose theories or models of the structure of human memory. The most influential of these theories was the

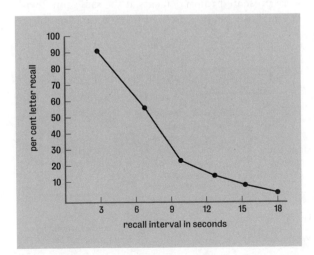

Figure 6.1 Short–term forgetting of a three–letter stimulus
Source: adapted from Peterson and Peterson (1959)

one proposed by Atkinson and Shiffrin (1968), and that theory will be the focus of our discussion. The fundamental assumption of their multi-store model was that there are three different types of memory store:

- sensory stores: there is a separate store for each sensory modality (e.g. vision, hearing), with each store holding information very briefly in a relatively uninterpreted fashion
- short-term store: this has very limited capacity, and holds information for a period of a few seconds via rehearsal (repeating words or other verbal information to oneself)
- long-term store: this has very large capacity, and holds information for long periods of time up to a lifetime

The ways in which these three types of store relate to each other are shown in Figure 6.3. Information from the outside world first of all reaches the sensory stores. A small fraction of that information is attended to and moves on to the short-term store. After that, information in the short-term store which is rehearsed is transferred to the long-term store. More specifically, it was assumed that there is a direct relationship between the amount of rehearsal that information receives in the short-term store and the strength of its representation in the long-term store. The way in which forgetting occurs was assumed to differ for each type of memory store. Information in the sensory stores simply decays fairly rapidly. Information in the short-term store is displaced by new information entering the store, and information in the long-term store is forgotten because of interference from other, related information.

Sensory stores

The most explored sensory stores are the iconic store and the echoic store. The **iconic store** is a memory store which holds visual information for about 500 milliseconds. Sperling (1960) studied its properties in studies in which visual displays were presented for 50 milliseconds. Each display consisted of three rows of four letters, and the participants were able to recall only four or five of the twelve letters. However, the participants were adamant that they had seen several more letters than they had been able to report. Sperling (1960) tested the accuracy of their reports as follows: after the presentation of each visual display, there was a tone indicating which one of the three rows of letters had to be reported. When the tone followed immediately after the visual display, the participants were able to report three of the letters in the specified row. Since there were three rows, this suggested that they had nine letters available. When the tone was presented 0.3 seconds after the visual display, the number of letters available fell to six, indicating that there was a very rapid decay of information from the iconic store.

The **echoic store** is a memory store which holds auditory information for a short period of time. If someone speaks to you while you are reading, you may initially think that you have not heard what they said. However, you then realize that you do know what they have said, because the information is still contained within the echoic store. The findings of a study by Treisman (1964) provide an estimate of the duration of information in the echoic store. Two auditory messages were presented to participants at the same time, with one message being presented to each ear. One of the

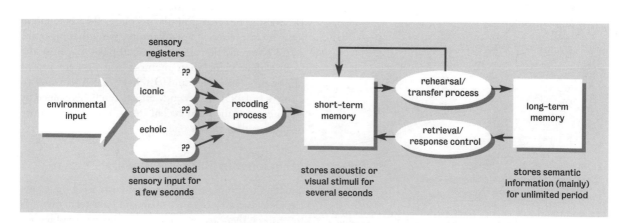

Figure 6.3 The key features of the Atkinson and Shiffrin (1968) multi-store model of memory

messages had to be shadowed or repeated back, and the participants were told to ignore the other one. When the two messages were the same, the participants realized this only when the message on the unattended ear was no more than two seconds in advance of the one on the attended ear. The implication of this finding is that information stays in the echoic store for approximately two seconds, but other researchers have argued that this is an underestimate (e.g. Darwin *et al.* 1972).

Short-term and long-term memory stores

The findings of Glanzer and Cunitz (1966) supporting the distinction between short-term and long-term memory stores have already been discussed. Some of the strongest evidence has been obtained from brain-damaged patients. Patients suffering from amnesia have very poor long-term memory but normal or almost normal short-term memory. This has been shown in studies of free recall (e.g. Baddeley and Warrington 1970). Amnesic patients have poor recall of the early and middle parts of the list, which involve long-term memory. However, they have the normal recency effect, and this involves short-term memory. In other studies (Butters and Cermak 1980), it has been found that amnesic patients have normal digit span. This provides additional evidence that they have relatively intact short-term memory.

In theory, it might also be possible to find brain-damaged patients who have poor short-term memory but essentially intact long-term memory. There are far fewer patients showing this pattern than the opposite, but some have been studied. Shallice and Warrington (1970) considered K.F., who suffered damage to the brain after a motorcycle accident. K.F. had a digit span of two items or less, and his recency effect was only one item in some circumstances. In contrast, K.F.'s long-term memory was good. However, it should be noted that K.F. showed poor short-term memory for verbal materials (e.g. words, letters, digits), but had good short-term memory for other meaningful sounds (e.g. telephones ringing, cats mewing).

According to Atkinson and Shiffrin (1968), the main way in which information is transferred from the short-term store to the long-term store is by means of rehearsal. The importance of rehearsal was shown by Rundus and Atkinson (1970). They presented a list of words followed by free recall. During list presentation, the participants were allowed to rehearse any words they wanted to, but were asked to rehearse out loud. They found the usual primacy effect in free recall, with

the first words in the list being better recalled than the others. They also found that the first words in the list were rehearsed far more often than most of the other words, suggesting that the primacy effect is due to extra rehearsal. However, this is true only up to a point. When steps are taken to equate the amount of rehearsal given to each word in the list, the primacy effect is reduced but not eliminated (Fischler *et al.* 1970).

According to Atkinson and Shiffrin (1968), one of the major distinctions between the short-term and long-term stores is in terms of the forgetting mechanism involved. Forgetting from the short-term store seems to occur because of diversion of attention away from the information within the store, and because of interference from other incoming information (Reitman 1974). For example, Glanzer and Cunitz (1966) found that counting backwards caused forgetting from the short-term store. That task prevented the participants from attending to the words in short-term memory, and it may also have caused some interference.

Forgetting from the long-term store is discussed in detail later in the chapter. Information which is forgotten in long-term memory is often still within the long-term memory store, but it is inaccessible or difficult to retrieve. For example, you might meet someone you know slightly, but realize you have forgotten her name. However, if you were told that her name was Christine, Mary, Clare or Jessica, you would very likely be able to select the correct one. This would demonstrate that the name had not been lost from the memory system.

Theoretical oversimplification

The greatest strength of the multi-store model is its assumption that there are three different kinds of memory store. In general terms, that assumption has stood the test of time. There is strong evidence that the sensory stores, short-term store and long-term store differ from each other in a number of important ways. Four of the major differences are as follows:

- temporal duration: information stays in the sensory stores for a fraction of a second (iconic store) or two to three seconds (echoic store); it stays in the short-term store for a few seconds; and it stays in the long-term store for months or years
- storage capacity: the sensory stores have rather limited capacity, the short-term store has a capacity of approximately seven items, and the long-term store has essentially unlimited capacity

- entering process: information enters the sensory stores without the individual engaging in any active processing; it enters the short-term store as a result of attention; and it enters the long-term store as a result of rehearsal
- forgetting mechanism: information is lost from the sensory stores through decay; it is lost from the short-term store via diversion of attention and interference; and it is forgotten from the long-term store mainly through inaccessibility

The greatest weakness of the multi-store model is that it provides a very oversimplified view of human memory. For example, it is assumed that there is a single short-term memory store and a single long-term memory store. Neither of these assumptions is warranted. So far as short-term memory is concerned, let us return to the case of K.F. He had impaired short-term memory for verbal materials, but not for other meaningful sounds. In addition, he had reasonably good short-term memory for visual stimuli. If there is only one short-term store, it is very difficult to understand why K.F. showed good short-term memory with some stimuli but very poor short-term memory with other stimuli.

So far as long-term memory is concerned, it is clear that it contains a huge amount of very diverse information and knowledge. For example, it contains information about our personal experiences over the years, all our general knowledge about the world, knowledge about how to perform all of the motor skills we possess, and so on. As we will see, it is no longer reasonable to argue that all of this knowledge is stored in a single long-term memory store.

ψ Section summary

According to the multi-store model, there are three types of memory store: sensory stores, in which information remains briefly; a short-term store of limited capacity, in which information typically remains for a few seconds; and a long-term store, in which information remains for long periods of time. These three types of stores differ in storage capacity, entering process and forgetting mechanism, as well as in terms of temporal duration. The multi-store model suffers from the disadvantage that it is oversimplified.

1 Describe and evaluate the multi-store model of memory.

Another major limitation of the multi-store model is its emphasis on rehearsal as the main process involved in the storage of information in long-term memory. Most of the research carried out by multi-store theorists was based on presenting word lists and then testing participants' ability to remember them. It is likely that rehearsal is important in such circumstances. In our everyday lives, however, we rarely make use of rehearsal. In spite of that, we are constantly acquiring new knowledge. Thus, rehearsal is very much less important to long-term memory than was claimed by the multi-store theorists.

☐ Working memory

It is generally agreed that short-term memory is much more complex than was allowed for in the multi-store approach. For example, Shiffrin (1993: 195) argued that the most favoured contemporary view of short-term memory 'contains three components: temporary activation, control processes, and capacity limitations. . . . The precise relationship between them . . . remains an area of active study'. In contrast to the multi-store model, it is assumed that the limited capacity of short-term memory depends on processing limitations rather than on storage limitations.

An influential attempt to provide a more adequate theory of short-term memory was proposed by Baddeley and Hitch (1974). According to them, the short-term store should be replaced by a working memory system consisting of the following three components:

- central executive: this is an attention-like system of limited capacity
- articulatory loop: this is a limited capacity system which contains information in a phonological (speech-based) form; it is used for verbal rehearsal; it is now known as the phonological loop
- visuo-spatial scratch-pad (later renamed sketch-pad): this is a limited capacity system which stores visual and/or spatial information

It is assumed that each of these components is relatively separate from the other two components in its functioning. This can be tested by finding two tasks which make use of different components of the working memory system. Since they are not competing for the same processing resources, each of the tasks should be performed as well together as when they are performed separately. This strategy was used by Hitch and Baddeley (1976).

They utilized a verbal reasoning task mainly involving the central executive; the other task required constant repetition of 'one-two-three-four-five-six' and made use of the articulatory loop. The two tasks were performed together successfully, with only a small adverse effect on performance of the verbal reasoning task (see Figure 6.4).

Hitch and Baddeley (1976) also combined the verbal reasoning task with the task of repeating out loud a random sequence of six digits. They assumed that this latter task would involve the resources of the central executive as well as of the articulatory loop, and so would interfere with performance of the verbal reasoning task. As can be seen in Figure 6.4, substantial interference effects were observed.

Articulatory or phonological loop

Much of our information about the articulatory or phonological loop was obtained by Baddeley *et al.* (1975). They studied the word-span task (immediate recall of a short list of words in the correct order), and assumed that rehearsal within the articulatory loop played an important role on this task. When the words were presented visually, they found that the participants' performance was better with short words than with long words (see Figure 6.5); this is known as the word-length effect. Of particular importance, Baddeley *et al.*

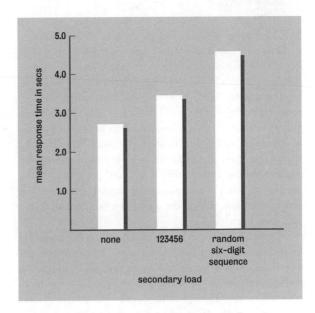

Figure 6.4 Performance on a verbal reasoning task performed on its own, together with saying '1 2 3 4 5 6' repeatedly, or together with repeating a random sequence of six digits
Source: adapted from Hitch and Baddeley (1976)

(1975) found that, for both short and long words, the participants recalled the number of words they could read out loud in approximately two seconds. The impli-

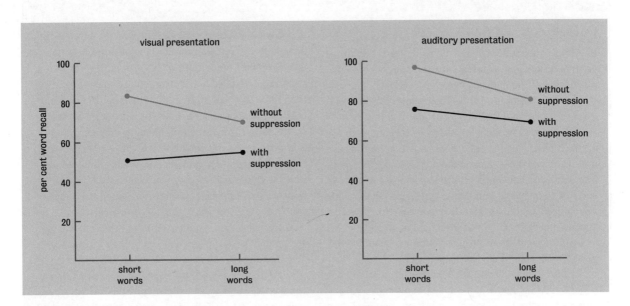

Figure 6.5 Percentage word recall for short and long words presented visually or auditorily with or without articulatory suppression
Source: data from Baddeley *et al.* (1975)

cation of this finding is that the articulatory loop can hold about two-seconds' worth of verbal information.

How do we know that the word-length effect depends on the articulatory loop? In one study, Baddeley *et al.* (1975) gave their participants the word-span task with visual presentation. They asked them to repeat the digits one to eight while the words were being presented (this is known as an articulatory suppression task). This was done on the assumption that the digit-repetition or suppression task would use up the capacity of the articulatory loop, and prevent it being used on the word-span task. As predicted, the use of the suppression task caused the word-length effect to disappear (see Figure 6.5).

Matters become more complex when we consider further findings from Baddeley *et al.* (1975). When the words on the word-span task were presented auditorily, the usual word-length effect was obtained. However, in contrast to the findings with visually presented words, the word-length effect was *not* abolished by having the participants perform a suppression task at the same time (see Figure 6.5). These findings suggest that the articulatory loop functions in a different way for visually presented words than for auditorily presented words.

In view of complications such as those discovered by Baddeley *et al.* (1975), Baddeley (1986, 1990) put forward a revised account of the articulatory loop, renaming it the **phonological loop**. As can be seen in Figure 6.6, the phonological loop consists of a phonological or speech-based store and an articulatory control process. When words are presented auditorily, they automatically enter the phonological store. However, when words are presented visually, they enter the

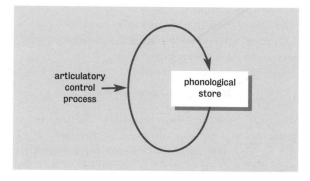

Figure 6.6 The phonological loop within the working memory system as envisaged by Baddeley (1990)

Ψ Case study

Patient G.B. with anarthria

It seems reasonable to assume that the articulatory control process associated with the phonological loop makes use of the muscles involved in speech. In order to test this assumption, Baddeley and Wilson (1985) studied an Oxford University student, G.B. G.B. suffered from **anarthria**, in which there is damage to the system controlling the speech musculature. In the case of G.B., he was able to produce only a single meaningless sound, which was a groan as he took a breath. In spite of this severe impairment, G.B. had essentially unimpaired language abilities. For example, he had good comprehension performance, and in spite of his inability to speak he could produce language effectively by using a keyboard device.

Baddeley and Wilson (1985) asked G.B. to carry out a range of tasks on which most people make extensive use of the articulatory control process. They found consistently that he seemed to be making use

of subvocal rehearsal or articulation in spite of not being able to use his speech musculature. G.B. had a fairly normal digit span of six items. He showed a normal word-length effect on span tasks, indicating that he was using subvocal rehearsal. On another task, he was asked to indicate whether two items would sound the same if spoken. In different conditions, these items were two words (e.g. key–quay), two non-words (e.g. frelame–phrelaim). G.B. did very well on this task. Finally, he was asked to decide whether non-words (e.g. oshun) sounded the same as any English words. Once again, he performed well.

What are the implications of these findings? According to Baddeley (1986: 107), they suggest that 'the loop and its rehearsal processes are operating at a much deeper level than might at first seem likely, apparently relying on central speech control codes which appear to be able to function in the absence of peripheral feedback'.

phonological store only indirectly via use of the articulatory control process. Performing a suppression task at the same time as being presented with words for learning prevents the articulatory control process from being used on the words. This stops visually presented words from entering the phonological store, but it does not stop auditorily presented words from doing so. If the phonological store underlies the word-length effect, this explains why suppression eliminates the effect with visually presented words, but not with auditorily presented words.

Evidence supporting the distinction between an articulatory control process and a short-term phonological store was reported by Longoni *et al.* (1993). They used articulatory suppression to eliminate use of the articulatory control process, and concluded that 'the encoding, maintenance, and retrieval of spoken material within the phonological store do not depend on a process of articulatory rehearsal' (1993: 11).

How is the phonological loop used in everyday life? It is likely that it plays a role in reading, especially if a text is difficult to understand. Some relevant evidence was reported by Baddeley and Lewis (1981). They presented their participants with a number of sentences, and asked them to decide whether each sentence was meaningful. On some trials, the participants' task was made more difficult, because they had to perform an articulatory suppression task at the same time. Suppression had a severe effect on the participants' performance only when it was important to remember the order in which the words in the sentence were presented. This suggests that information about word order is preserved in the phonological loop.

Visuo-spatial sketch-pad

In the same way that the articulatory or phonological loop is used for the temporary storage of verbal information, so the visuo-spatial sketch-pad is used to store visual and spatial information (see Smyth and Scholey 1994). Logie (1986) investigated the visuo-spatial sketch-pad in a study in which word lists were learned either with rote rehearsal or with the use of imagery. He assumed that the sketch-pad would be used more in the latter condition. To test this assumption, Logie (1986) presented irrelevant line drawings or speech during learning. The irrelevant pictures reduced memory performance only in the imagery condition, presumably because the pictures and the use of imagery competed for the limited capacity of the visuo-spatial sketch-pad.

Baddeley (1990) addressed the issue of the usefulness of the visuo-spatial sketch-pad in the real world:

It seems likely that the spatial system is important for geographical orientation, and for planning spatial tasks. Indeed, tasks involving visuo-spatial manipulation have long formed an important component of intelligence test batteries, and have tended to be used as selection tools for professions where visuo-spatial planning and manipulation are thought to be important, such as engineering and architecture.

(Baddeley 1990: 113–14)

Central executive

Baddeley (1986) argued that the central executive may resemble a supervisory attentional system. More specifically, he proposed that the central executive is involved in planning and decision-making, and is used to sort out problems that cannot be dealt with by lower systems such as the phonological loop or the visuo-spatial sketch-pad. Baddeley (1986) proposed that the central executive may be located in the frontal lobes. The thinking of patients with damage to the frontal lobes often seems to lack direction and control (Rylander 1939), and these are characteristics which are associated with the central executive.

Working memory vs short-term store

The greatest strength of the working memory model is that it represents a considerable advance over the short-term store proposed by Atkinson and Shiffrin (1968). The working memory model has been applied successfully to tasks such as verbal reasoning, mental arithmetic, and reading, as well as to memory tasks. In contrast, the short-term store was applied almost exclusively to memory tasks. Another advantage of the working memory model lies in its treatment of verbal rehearsal. Rehearsal plays a minor role in Baddeley's (1986, 1990) theory, occurring within only one out of three components of the working memory model. In contrast, rehearsal was accorded too much significance by Atkinson and Shiffrin (1968), being the major process occurring within the short-term store.

The greatest weakness of the working memory model is that limited progress has been made in understanding the central executive, which is the most important of the three components. For example, it is assumed that the central executive has limited capacity, but its capacity is not known with any precision. Baddeley (1986, 1990) argued that the central executive is a unitary system, meaning that it operates in a single, uniform fashion. However, there is increasing evidence that the central executive is not unitary. Consider the case of E.V.R., who had had a large cerebral tumour removed. In many ways he seemed to have an intact central executive: he had a high IQ, and did well on tests of hypothesis testing and reasoning. However, his decision-making and judgements were often poor, and he found it difficult to make even simple decisions such as where to eat (Eslinger and Damasio 1985). These findings suggest that parts of E.V.R.'s central executive was functioning normally but parts were severely damaged. This pattern is consistent with the notion that there are two or more central executives.

ψ Section summary

The working memory system consists of an attention-like central executive, an articulatory or phonological loop, and a visuo-spatial scratch (or sketch) pad. These three components function relatively separately from each other. The articulatory or phonological loop is used for the temporary storage of verbal information, whereas the visuo-spatial sketch-pad is used to store visual and spatial information. The working memory model has been applied successfully to verbal reasoning, mental arithmetic, and reading, in addition to various memory tasks. More remains to be discovered about the workings of the central executive.

1   What are the components of working memory? How successfully does the working memory model account for the evidence?
2   Compare and contrast the short-term store of the multi-store model with the working memory system.

❑ Learning processes

There is general agreement that the processes occurring at the time of learning have an important effect on subsequent long-term memory. Perhaps the first systematic theory to be based squarely on this notion was the levels-of-processing theory, which is discussed below. There are several learning processes which are impor-

tant, but we will consider only two of the most important ones: organization and imagery. It seems reasonable to assume that learning which is organized will lead to better long-term memory than is learning which is disorganized, and that the use of imagery can enhance memory. These assumptions are considered in the light of the evidence.

Levels-of-processing theory

One of the most influential theories of memory during the 1970s was proposed by Craik and Lockhart (1972). They argued that the information that is stored in long-term memory depends on the attentional and perceptual processes occurring at the time of learning. More specifically, they claimed that there are various different levels of processing. At the lowest level, there is shallow processing of the physical characteristics of stimuli, such as deciding whether words are printed in capitals or in lower case. At the highest level, there is deep processing, which involves processing the meaning of stimuli. According to Craik (1973: 48), ' "Depth" is defined in terms of the meaningfulness extracted from the stimulus rather than in terms of the number of analyses performed upon it'.

The key theoretical assumption made by Craik and Lockhart (1972) was that deep processing produces more elaborate, longer lasting, and stronger memory traces than does shallow processing. Relevant evidence was reported by Hyde and Jenkins (1973). They used several groups of participants, who were presented with a list of words. Each group was given a particular task to perform, with the tasks differing in terms of the depth of processing involved. One task involved rating the words for pleasantness, whereas another task was to detect the occurrence of the e's and g's in the list words. Some of the participants were told to remember the words (intentional learning), whereas the others were not told about the subsequent memory test (incidental learning).

After they had processed all the list words, the participants were asked to provide free recall. The findings are shown in Figure 6.7. As you can see, recall was much better when the task involved rating pleasantness than detecting specific letters. According to Hyde and Jenkins (1973), this occurred because rating pleasantness involves processing meaning, whereas the letter task did not. It is of interest that it made no difference whether learning was intentional or incidental. These findings suggest that long-term memory depends on the nature of processing rather than on the motivation to learn.

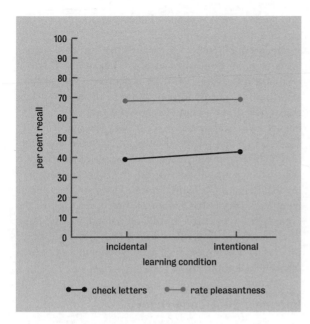

Figure 6.7 Free recall for associatively related and unrelated word lists as a function of orienting task
Source: data from Hyde and Jenkins (1973)

One of the contributions made by Craik and Lockhart (1972) was to our understanding of rehearsal. They distinguished between **maintenance rehearsal**, which involves repeating analyses which have already been carried out, and **elaborative rehearsal**, which involves deeper analysis of the stimulus. According to Craik and Lockhart (1972), elaborative rehearsal leads to improved long-term memory, but maintenance rehearsal does not. This view is in contrast to that of Atkinson and Shiffrin (1968), who claimed that all forms of rehearsal benefit long-term memory. It has been found that additional rehearsal time for maintenance rehearsal sometimes has surprisingly small effects on memory. Glenberg *et al.* (1977) found that a nine-fold increase in rehearsal time increased recall by 1.5 per cent. However, the same nine-fold increase in rehearsal time had more effect on recognition memory, improving performance from 65 per cent to 74 per cent.

It was found in subsequent research that long-term memory depends on elaboration (the amount of processing of any given kind) and distinctiveness (uniqueness or unusualness) as well as on the level of processing. Craik and Tulving (1975) studied elaboration of processing. Their participants had to decide whether words fitted into sentence frames which were either elaborate (e.g. 'The great bird swooped down and carried off the

struggling —— ') or non-elaborate (e.g. 'She cooked the —— '). Recall of the words was better with elaborate than with non-elaborate sentences.

Bransford and colleagues (1979) found that distinctiveness was an important factor. They presented sentences which were either distinctive ('A mosquito is like a doctor because they both draw blood') or non-distinctive ('A mosquito is like a raccoon because they both have heads, legs, jaws'). Recall was much better for the distinctive sentences even though they were less elaborate than the non-distinctive sentences.

Theoretical limitations

The central assumption of the levels-of-processing theory is that long-term memory depends to a large extent on the type of processing which occurs at the time of learning. The evidence indicates that this assumption is correct. However, the evidence indicates that long-term memory also depends on the relationship between the information stored at the time of learning and the nature of the retention test. This notion was proposed by Morris *et al.* (1977) in their transfer-appropriate processing theory. They claimed that we remember stored information only when that information is relevant to some subsequent memory test. In their study, participants processed some words in terms of their meaning and other words in terms of their sounds. They were then given a rhyming recognition test. On this test, words that rhymed with the list words were presented rather than the list words themselves, and the participants were told to select words rhyming with list words. Memory performance on this test was significantly higher for those words that had been processed in terms of their sounds (shallow processing) than for those processed in terms of meaning (deep processing). This finding indicates the importance of the relevance of initial learning to the requirements of a subsequent memory test, and also provides an experimental disproof of levels-of-processing theory.

It is often difficult to know whether a given processing task has involved deep or shallow processing. For example, Hyde and Jenkins (1973) argued that deciding on the part of speech of list words is a shallow processing task that does not involve processing meaning. However, as M.W. Eysenck (1978) pointed out, it has sometimes been suggested that this task does require meaning to be processed. We do not usually have any independent measure of processing depth, and so it is very difficult to know whether deep or shallow processing is involved.

Organizational processes

When people learn things, they seem to have a natural tendency to impose organization or structure on their learning. This can be shown very simply by using what is known as a categorized word list, which consists of words belonging to various categories (e.g. trees, sports, articles of furniture). The words from the categorized word list are presented in a random order, and this is followed by free recall. What nearly always happens is known as **categorical clustering**; that is, the words are recalled category by category rather than in the order in which they were presented.

The phenomenon of categorical clustering indicates that organizational processes are important. However, there are at least two possible ways in which organizational processes may be involved: our knowledge of categories may influence processes at the time of learning or at the time of retrieval. Important evidence that organizational processes are used at the time of learning was reported by Weist (1972). He presented categorized word lists in a random order, followed by free recall. In addition, he asked his participants to rehearse out loud during the presentation of the list. He found substantial evidence for categorical clustering in the pattern of rehearsal, indicating that organizational processes are involved at the time of learning.

It seems probable that the participants' rehearsal was organized because organization enhances long-term memory. Weist (1972) obtained evidence for this: those participants who showed the greatest amount of categorical clustering in their rehearsal and in their free recall recalled significantly more words than did those who showed less clustering.

Organizational processes are not only used when the organizational structure of the to-be-learned material is fairly obvious. Mandler (1967) showed the power of organization in studies in which he presented his participants with longish lists of words selected at random. They were asked to sort these words into between two and seven categories of their own devising. When they had reached the stage of sorting the words in a consistent fashion, they were asked to provide free recall of the entire list. Mandler (1967) found that there was an increase in recall of approximately four words per extra category used in the sorting task. The implication was that those participants who used several categories in sorting were imposing more organization on the list than were those who used only a few categories. In the words of Mandler (1967: 328), 'memory and organiza-

tion are not only correlated, but organization is a necessary condition for memory'.

Hodge and Otani (1996) argued that category sorting leads to good long-term memory because it involves relational processing, i.e. it leads people to see relationships among words. In order to test this assumption, they carried out a study using three tasks designed to involve relational processing: category sorting, narrative construction and relational imagery. Narrative construction involved creating a story relating the objects in each successive group of four words, and relational imagery involved creating a mental image based on the objects from each successive group. All three tasks led to the same high levels of free recall and recognition memory. These findings suggest (but do not prove) that relational processing was responsible for the good memory performance on all of the tasks.

Imagery: dual-code theory

Most of the research on the effects of imagery on memory has been based on Paivio's (1971, 1979) dual-code theory. According to this theory, there are separate verbal and imaginal coding systems, both of which are of importance in learning and memory. In the words of Paivio (1979),

The theory assumes that cognitive behaviour is mediated by two independent but richly interconnected symbolic systems, which are specialised for encoding, organising, transforming, storing, and retrieving information. One (the image system) is specialised for dealing with perceptual information concerning nonverbal objects and events. The other (the verbal system) is specialised for dealing with linguistic information.

(Paivio 1979)

Much of the evidence relating to the dual-code theory has involved concrete and abstract words. Concrete words (e.g. cow, radio, song) refer to objects that can be perceived by one or more of the sense modalities, whereas this is not the case with abstract words (e.g. faith, honour). According to Paivio (1971), concrete and abstract words can both be strongly processed by the verbal coding system, but concrete words can also be processed to a limited extent by the imaginal coding system. The fact that concrete words can be processed by two coding systems but abstract words are processed by only one coding system should give concrete words an advantage in long-term memory. Concrete words are much better remembered than abstract words in tests of free recall, cued recall and recognition memory (Paivio 1971).

According to dual-coding theory (Paivio 1971), pictures should generally be better remembered than either concrete words or abstract words. The reason is that pictures are strongly processed by the imaginal coding system, and are also often processed moderately strongly by the verbal coding system. The evidence indicates that pictures are usually better remembered than concrete or abstract words (Paivio 1971).

Some evidence for the existence of separate verbal and imaginal coding systems was reported by Watkins *et al.* (1984). Their participants were presented with picture–word pairs (e.g. a picture of a walrus accompanied by the word 'walrus'). Some of them were told to engage in verbal rehearsal, whereas others were told 'to try to maintain an image of the picture in your mind's eye.' Memory was then tested either by a word-fragment completion task (e.g. – A L – – S) or by a picture-fragment completion task (i.e. deciding what was pictured from a fragment). Verbal rehearsal improved memory performance on the word-fragment task, and imaginal rehearsal improved performance on the picture-fragment task. These findings suggest that there may be separate verbal and imaginal coding systems, and that both may enhance long-term memory in some circumstances.

Alternative theoretical views

Much of the available evidence is consistent with dual-coding theory. However, some of the evidence provides only indirect support for the theory. For example, the robust finding that concrete words are better remembered than abstract words indicates clearly that there is some important difference between the two types of words. However, that difference may not involve the greater use of imaginal coding with concrete than with abstract words. As a result of our experiences with the referents of concrete words, we may simply possess much more information about concrete words than abstract words. Thus, concrete words may receive more elaborate verbal coding than abstract words, and it may be this increased elaboration rather than the use of imaginal coding that produces the concrete-word superiority effect.

Nelson *et al.* (1977) put forward an alternative to the dual-coding theory which they called the sensory-semantic model. According to this model, pictures produce better sensory codes than words. Pictures also differ from words in the way that meaning is accessed. In order to access the name of a picture, it is necessary to process the meaning of the picture. However, the 'name' of a word is available simply by processing its phonemic characteristics. Some of the evidence supports the sensory-semantic model rather than the dual-coding theory (see Zechmeister and Nyberg 1982).

Ψ Section summary

According to levels-of-processing theory, deep or semantic processing produces better subsequent long-term memory than does shallow or non-semantic processing. The depth of processing is generally important, but elaboration and distinctiveness of processing also affect long-term memory. The relevance of initial learning to the requirements of a subsequent memory test is another important determinant of memory performance. There is reasonable evidence indicating that long-term memory depends on organization. This is the case, regardless of whether organizational processes depend on prior knowledge or are imposed on random lists of words. Some evidence indicates that there are separate verbal and imaginal coding systems, each of which can improve long-term memory.

1 Outline levels-of-processing theory. How successful has this theory been in accounting for the evidence?
2 Discuss different ways in which the processes operating at the time of learning affect long-term memory.

Long-term memory

One of the assumptions made by Atkinson and Shiffrin (1968) was that there is a single long-term memory store. This seems implausible if you consider the enormous variety of information which is stored in long-term memory. Accordingly, many psychologists have argued that there are two or more relatively separate long-term memory systems. Some of their suggestions will be discussed here, and other ideas are discussed later in the section on amnesia.

Episodic and semantic memory

Tulving (1972) argued that there is an important distinction between two kinds of long-term memory which he called episodic memory and semantic

Plate 6.1 Episodic memory is essentially autobiographical in nature, containing personal experiences associated with a particular time and place

memory. **Episodic memory** is essentially autobiographical in nature, containing personal experiences associated with a particular time and place. For example, memories of your last summer holiday would qualify as episodic memories. **Semantic memory** is concerned with our knowledge about the world and lacks the personal quality of episodic memory. According to Tulving (1972: 386), semantic memory 'is a mental thesaurus, organized knowledge a person possesses about words and other verbal symbols, their meanings and referents, about relations among them, and about rules, formulas, and algorithms for the manipulation of these symbols, concepts, and relations'. There is more detailed information about semantic memory in the next section of this chapter.

The distinction between episodic and semantic memory is a reasonable one. However, it is clear that episodic and semantic memory are highly interdependent in their functioning rather than separate. For example, if you think about the events of your last holiday, this involves episodic memory. However, semantic memory in terms of your knowledge of concepts and the world is involved if you think about beaches, sitting in the sun, swimming in the sea, and so on.

Wheeler et al. (1997) defined episodic memory in a somewhat different way from Tulving (1972). According to them, the major distinguishing characteristic of episodic memory is 'its dependence on a special kind of awareness that all healthy human adults can identify. It is

Ψ Case study

Endel Tulving

Endel Tulving (1989a) used himself as a 60-year-old participant in a study designed to show whether the distinction between episodic and semantic memory is an important one. The key assumption was as follows: if episodic and semantic memory are partially independent long-term memory systems, then they may well be located in different parts of the brain. This assumption was tested by injecting very small quantities of radioactive gold into Tulving's bloodstream. He then thought about episodic memories (e.g. the events of a summer 47 years previously), or he thought about semantic memories (e.g. the history of astronomy, and the work of Copernicus, Brahe and Kepler). Activity within the brain was recorded by a battery of 254 gamma-ray detectors that surrounded Tulving's head snugly.

Blood flow within the cortex was different for the two tasks (see colour plate 3). In essence, there was a higher level of activity in the front parts of the cortex (the frontal and temporal regions) during episodic memories than during semantic memories. In contrast, the back parts of the brain (the parietal and occipital regions) were more active with semantic memories. Tulving obtained similar findings with other participants, including his own wife. His findings suggest that episodic and semantic memories may be based in different parts of the brain, and that they may be partially independent systems. However, as Tulving (1989a: 21) himself pointed out, 'Because of the preliminary nature of the study, it would be inappropriate to read much theoretical significance into these data'.

Several similar studies on retrieval have been carried out since then using PET scans (see Wheeler et al. 1997 for a review). In these studies, the blood flow in the brain during a semantic memory task is subtracted from the blood flow during an episodic memory task. In 25 out of 26 studies, the right prefrontal cortex was more involved in the episodic task than in the

(case study continued)

semantic task. Further PET scan studies have been carried out during episodic and semantic encoding. The findings indicate that the left prefrontal cortex is involved in episodic encoding.

Studies on brain-damaged patients provide some support for the notion that the prefrontal cortex is of importance in episodic memory. According to Wheeler et al. (1997),

the overall pattern of results is broadly consistent with the hypothesis that damage localised to the prefrontal cortex causes a selective loss in the episodic memory system, but it also lends itself to other reasonable interpretations. The most obvious of the alternative explanations is that the frontal lobes play a critical role in the ability to select and execute complex mental operations.

(Wheeler et al. 1997: 338)

the type of awareness experienced when one thinks back to a specific moment in one's personal past and consciously recollects some prior episode or state as it was previously experienced' (Wheeler et al. 1997: 333). They used the term autonoetic consciousness to refer to this kind of recollection. In their own words,

The major distinction between episodic and semantic memory is no longer best described in terms of the type of information they work with. The distinction is now made in terms of the nature of subjective experience that accompanies the operations of the systems at encoding and retrieval.

(Wheeler et al. 1997: 348–9)

Explicit and implicit memory

There has been an enormous amount of interest in recent years in the distinction between **explicit memory** and **implicit memory**. These terms were defined by Graf and Schacter:

Explicit memory is revealed when performance on a task requires conscious recollection of previous experiences. . . . Implicit memory is revealed when performance on a task is facilitated in the absence of conscious recollection.

(Graf and Schachter 1985: 501)

When the participants in a study take part in tests of free recall, cued recall, or recognition memory, they make use of conscious recollection of information, and so explicit memory is involved.

What might a test of implicit memory involve? Tulving et al. (1982) first of all asked their participants to learn a list of words such as 'toboggan'. After a retention interval of one hour or one week, the participants completed word fragments (e.g. – O – O – G A –). Half of the word fragments could be completed with list words, whereas half could not, but the participants were not told that there was any link between the word list

and the word-fragment task. More of the word fragments were completed when they matched list words, thus demonstrating the existence of implicit memory.

Tulving et al. (1982) reported two additional findings suggesting that implicit memory differs substantially from explicit memory. First, the participants also performed a recognition-memory test on the list words. Implicit memory was the same for words that were recognized as for words that were not recognized, indicating that implicit memory was unrelated to explicit memory. The effects of retention interval were different on the word-fragment and recognition-memory tasks. Explicit memory was much worse after one week than after one hour, whereas there was no effect of retention interval on implicit memory.

There is substantial evidence that the distinction between explicit and implicit memory is an important one (Ashcraft 1994). However, the distinction has only limited explanatory value. As Schacter (1987: 501) argued, explicit and implicit memory 'are *descriptive* concepts that are primarily concerned with a person's psychological experience at the time of retrieval'. Roediger (1990) made an influential attempt to provide some theoretical understanding. He drew a distinction between data-driven processes and conceptually driven processes. **Data-driven processes** are those which are determined entirely by external stimuli, whereas **conceptually driven processes** are those started by the individual. Implicit memory tends to involve data-driven processes, whereas explicit memory tends to involve conceptually driven processes. Finally, Roediger (1990) assumed that either form of memory will be better when the type of processing needed on the memory test matches that used at the time of learning than when it does not. This notion closely resembles that of transfer-appropriate processing (Morris et al. 1977), which was discussed earlier in the chapter.

The findings of a study by Jacoby (1983) are consistent with Roediger's (1990) theory. We will consider part of his study here. The participants were given words to learn in three conditions, two of which were no context (e.g. XXX–black) and generate (white– ?). In the generate condition, the participants were told to generate the opposite of the word presented to them. It is reasonable to assume that the no context condition involved data-driven processing, whereas the generate condition involved conceptually driven processing. After that, they were given a test of recognition memory (explicit memory) and a test of perceptual identification involving identifying briefly exposed words (implicit memory). It can be assumed that perceptual identification depends largely on data-driven processing, whereas recognition memory makes much more use of conceptually driven processing.

The findings are shown in Figure 6.8. In line with Roediger's theory, memory performance was better when the same kind of processing was used at learning and at test than when different kinds of processing were required.

It is increasingly argued that there is more than one type of implicit memory. For example, Tulving and Schacter (1990) distinguished between perceptual implicit tests and conceptual implicit tests. On perceptual implicit tests, the information presented at the time of learning is generally presented at the time of test in an incomplete form (e.g. word-fragment completion). In contrast, conceptual implicit tests usually involve pre-senting information at the time of test which is only conceptually related to the information presented at the time of learning. Srinivas and Roediger (1990) found that performance on a conceptual implicit test was affected by the level of processing at learning, whereas performance on a perceptual implicit test was not. This suggests that it is important to distinguish between these two forms of implicit memory.

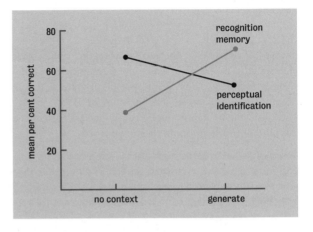

Figure 6.8 Recognition memory and perceptual identification as a function of encoding conditions (no context vs generate)
Source: data from Jacoby (1983)

 Research update

Conscious recollection

The distinction between explicit and implicit memory is based on the presence versus absence of conscious recollection. However, it is often very hard to know the extent to which the participants in a study are actually making use of conscious recollection. It has generally been assumed that conventional memory tests (e.g. free recall, cued recall, recognition) rely on conscious recollection and thus involve explicit memory, but that assumption is not easy to test. However, as we will see, Jacoby *et al.* (1993) came up with an interesting way of measuring the involvement of conscious recollection on cued recall.

Jacoby *et al.* (1993) presented a list of words, followed by two tests: first, an inclusion test, on which the participants were told to complete word stems (e.g. Cha____) with list words or with the first word that came to mind, thus resembling a typical cued recall test; second, an exclusion test, on which they were told to complete word stems with words that had not been presented on the list. A miniature example is shown below:

List words	Inclusion test	Exclusion test
Chair	Chair	Chain
Shoes	Shoot	Shoes
Floor	Floor	Flood
Books	Boats	Books
Rides	Rides	Rider
Boars	Boats	Boars

Box continued

The basic logic of this study was as follows: if the participants had no conscious recollection of the list words, then they would be as likely to produce list words on the exclusion test as on the inclusion test. On the other hand, if they had perfect conscious recollection of the list words, then the words produced on the inclusion test would all be list words, and none of the list words would be produced on the exclusion test. Thus, the difference between numbers of list words produced on each test provides a measure of the involvement of conscious recollection. In the example, three of the list words were produced on the exclusion test and three were produced on the inclusion test. This indicates that there was an absence of conscious recollection.

Jacoby *et al.* (1993) made use of full-attention and divided-attention conditions. In the full-attention condition, the participants were told that they should try to remember the list words for a future memory test. In the divided-attention condition, they performed a complex task while reading the list words, and they were not told that there would be a memory test. The findings are shown in Figure 6.9. They indicate that conscious recollection (and so explicit memory) played an important role in performance on the full-attention condition, but that performance in the divided-attention condition depended wholly on implicit memory. The major contribution of this study is that it provides a way of identifying the contribution of conscious recollection to memory performance.

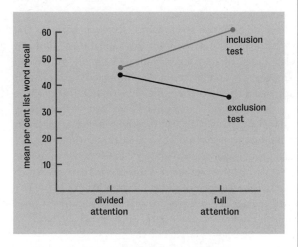

Figure 6.9 Inclusion and exclusion test performance as a function of attention condition (divided vs full)
Source: adapted from Jacob *et al.* (1993)

ψ Section summary

Tulving argued that there are two rather separate long-term memory systems: episodic or autobiographical memory and semantic memory. However, episodic and semantic memory are probably highly interdependent in their functioning. There is good evidence to support the distinction between explicit and implicit memory. Explicit memory tends to involve conceptually driven processes, whereas implicit memory tends to involve data-driven processes.

1 What are the advantages and disadvantages of assuming that there are separate episodic and semantic memory systems?
2 Discuss the distinction between explicit and implicit memory in the light of the evidence.

❏ Semantic memory

Semantic memory is general knowledge about the world and about language which we have stored in long-term memory. Probably the most obvious fact about semantic memory is that it is highly organized. This is shown by our ability to retrieve information from semantic memory very rapidly. For example, most people can think of the capital of France within a second or two, and within about the same time they can decide that a chair is an article of furniture or that a goat is a four-footed animal. It is improbable that we would be able to extract the relevant piece of information from among the millions stored in semantic memory unless the semantic memory system were organized.

Collins and Quillian

Collins and Quillian (1969) proposed the first systematic account of semantic memory. They assumed that semantic memory is organized into a large number of hierarchical networks. An example of an hierarchical network is shown in Figure 6.10. Major concepts such as animal, bird and canary are represented as nodes, and various properties or features (e.g. eats, has wings) are associated with each node.

You may be wondering why features such as eats and breathes are associated with the animal node, but not with the bird or canary nodes. After all, birds and canaries eat and breathe. An important notion that influenced the theorizing of Collins and Quillian (1969) was that of cognitive economy. They argued that having features such as eating and breathing stored at all levels of the hierarchy would go against this notion; instead, each property or feature is stored at the highest possible level within the hierarchy. Only those features which distinguish one species of bird from others (e.g. the fact that canaries are yellow) are stored at the lowest level of the hierarchy.

Collins and Quillian (1969) tested their theory by asking their participants to decide as rapidly as possible whether various sentences were true or false. These sentences were of the form, 'A canary can fly', or 'A canary is yellow.' It was predicted that the time taken to make each decision would depend on how far apart the subject and predicate were in the hierarchy. For example, the feature 'is yellow' is stored with the concept 'canary', and so it should take very little time to decide that a canary is yellow. In contrast, the feature 'can fly' is stored further up the hierarchy than 'canary', and so it should take longer to decide that a canary can fly. As predicted, decision times for true sentences were fastest when the subject and predicate were at the same level of the predicate were two levels apart.

Problems with the theory

Collins and Quillian (1969) claimed correctly that it is often necessary for us to make certain inferences when using semantic memory. For example, suppose that you were asked whether Mozart had a backbone. It seems highly improbable that this information is stored

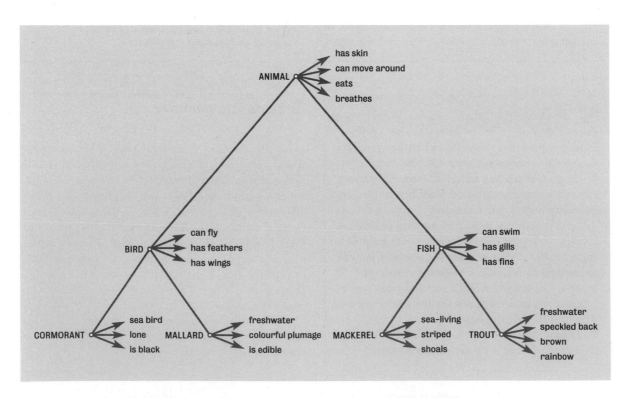

Figure 6.10 Part of the hierarchical semantic network proposed by Collins and Quillian (1969)

directly in your semantic memory. What you would do is work out that Mozart was a human being, and human beings have backbones, and so therefore Mozart had a backbone. This kind of inferential reasoning is precisely what Collins and Quillian (1969) assumed we do much of the time.

There are various problems with the theory proposed by Collins and Quillian (1969). Conrad (1972) pointed out that the sentences used by Collins and Quillian (1969) differed in familiarity as well as in the hierarchical distance between subject and predicate. For example, the sentence, 'A canary has skin', is very unfamiliar as well as involving considerable hierarchical distance. Conrad (1972) equated the various groups of sentences for familiarity, and found that the hierarchical distance between subject and predicate had very little effect on decision time. This finding has serious consequences for the theory, because it undermines the main evidence for the importance of hierarchical distance.

According to the theory, the time taken to make a decision about category membership should be the same for all members of the category. In fact, less time is needed for more typical members of a category than for less typical ones. For example, people decide more rapidly that a robin is a bird than they decide that a chicken is a bird. These findings indicate that the structure of semantic memory is more complex than was envisaged by Collins and Quillian (1969).

Spreading activation theory

Collins and Loftus (1975) pointed out that the hierarchical networks of Collins and Quillian (1969) were too inflexible, and made logical rather than psychological sense. They proposed spreading activation theory, according to which semantic memory is organized in terms of semantic relatedness. There are various ways in which semantic relatedness can be assessed. One way is simply to ask people to indicate how closely related they regard pairs of words as being. Another way is to ask people to provide lists of members of categories such as four-footed animals and trees. Those members listed most often (e.g. dog, cat) are more closely related to the category than are those listed least often (e.g. ocelot).

Collins and Loftus (1975) assumed that the corresponding node in semantic memory is activated whenever we think about a concept. This activation then spreads to other concepts, especially those which are closely related semantically. Spreading activation can speed up cognitive processes. For example, it is possible to decide rapidly that the sentence, 'A robin is a bird', is true because activation spreads from robin to bird, and facilitates the processing of the sentence.

Evidence for the importance of spreading activation has been obtained from studies on lexical decision, in which the participants have to decide rapidly whether a letter string is an English word. In a modified version of this task, Meyer and Schvaneveldt (1971) presented two letter strings at a time, and asked their participants to respond 'yes' if both letter strings were words, and 'no' otherwise. They found a strong effect of semantic relatedness on yes trials: decisions were made much faster when the two words were related (e.g. bread butter) than when they were not (e.g. nurse butter). This effect appears to depend on semantic activation spreading automatically between the two words rather than on more conscious processing (Neely 1977).

Beyond semantic relatedness

Spreading activation theory is much more realistic than the hierarchical networks proposed by Collins and Quillian (1969). There is no doubt that performance on many semantic memory tasks depends on semantic relatedness rather than on the location of concepts within hierarchies. In addition, there is strong evidence that thinking about a concept causes activation to spread to other, related concepts.

On the negative side, spreading activation theory is rather limited. Concepts are related to each other in a complex fashion, and the notion of semantic relatedness covers only one kind of relationship. We can think about the information in semantic memory in many ways, and spreading activation is one among many processes that are involved.

Concept instability

The approaches to semantic memory which have been considered so far have been based on the assumption that all concepts are stored in, and retrieved from, long-term memory in a stable and fixed fashion. However, Barsalou (1982 1989) argued that this assumption is incorrect. According to him, concepts are often represented differently in different contexts. For example, we usually think of a piano mainly as a musical instrument. However, we may think of the fact that pianos are heavy if we hear about someone lifting a piano. Barsalou (1982) used the term *context-dependent information* to refer to the notion that information relevant to the current context will be activated. In other words, the norm is concept instability rather than the concept stability assumed by previous theorists. However, Barsalou (1989) was more in line with other theorists in his view that concepts have a central core of context-independent information.

There are various ways in which concept instability reveals itself. For example, American participants in a study by Barsalou (1989) argued that a robin is a more typical member of the bird category than is a swan. However, when asked to adopt the perspective of the average Chinese citizen, most of them decided that a swan was a more typical bird than was a robin.

Barsalou (1983) pointed out that some of the concepts or categories that people use are formed in an ad-hoc way rather than being based entirely on organized information in long-term memory. For example, you might form a category of 'things to sell at a car-boot sale'.

Barsalou's approach has the advantage of emphasizing the flexible ways in which we construct and use concepts. However, it remains unclear whether this approach can be developed into a comprehensive theory of semantic memory.

Ψ Section summary

Collins and Quillian argued that semantic memory is organized into a large number of hierarchical networks. The support for this position is flawed. It appears that the assumed hierarchical networks are too inflexible, and based too much on logical rather than psychological principles. Spreading activation theory is based on the assumption that activation of a concept or node in semantic memory leads to the activation of semantically related concepts. This approach is more realistic than that of Collins and Quillian. Barsalou pointed out that concepts are less stable and rigid than has generally been assumed, in the sense that the information that we access about a concept depends in part on the current context.

1 Compare and contrast various theories of semantic memory.

❑ Retrieval processes

Recall and recognition are two of the main ways of testing people's memories for information stored in long-term memory. If you are asked to produce the name of the current Foreign Secretary, that is a test of recall. If you given a short list of prominent politicians and asked to indicate which one is the current Foreign Secretary, that is a test of recognition memory. As might be expected, recognition memory is usually much better than recall (Parkin 1993). Several explanations have been proposed, two of the best known of which are the two-process theory and the encoding specificity principle.

Two-process theory

Various theorists (e.g. Anderson and Bower 1972) have proposed slightly different versions of the two-process theory of recall and recognition. The reason that it is called two-process is because it is assumed that recall involves two separate processes. The first process is a retrieval process, in which possible items are produced from long-term memory. The second process is a decision or recognition process, and involves deciding whether the information produced by the retrieval process is appropriate. It is assumed within the theory that recognition memory involves only the decision or recognition process, and does not involve the retrieval process.

According to two-process theory, recall can never be better than recognition. Recognition fails if the decision process does not work effectively, whereas recall fails if either the retrieval process or the decision process is ineffective. Evidence supporting two-process theory was reported by Bahrick (1970). He presented his participants with a list of words followed by free recall. He then presented them with recall cues that were associated with the list words they had not been able to free recall. According to two-process theory, the probability of successful cued recall should equal the probability of correctly retrieving each list word multiplied by the probability of recognizing it after it has been retrieved. That is what Bahrick (1970) found, suggesting that recall involves the two processes identified by two-process theory.

Two-process theory is oversimplified, and some of its predictions have been disconfirmed. For example, consider the prediction that recall cannot be better than recognition memory. This prediction was tested by

Watkins (1973). His participants were presented with paired associates such as 'EXPLO-RE' and 'SPANI-EL'. After that, they were given a test of cued recall (e.g. 'EXPLO-?') or of recognition memory (e.g. 'RE'). Recall performance was at 67 per cent, compared to only 9 per cent for recognition.

In sum, two-process theory describes the processes which are sometimes involved in recall and recognition. However, it does not provide a generally adequate theory. For example, it is probably true that we some- times try to recall the name of an acquaintance by retrieving some possible names and choosing one of them. Suppose, however, that someone asked you the name of your boyfriend or girlfriend. It seems unlikely that you would think of several possible names before producing your answer! In other words, the theory is more applicable to recall when the recall task is difficult than when it is easy.

Encoding specificity principle

The most important contribution to our understanding of retrieval from long-term memory has come from Endel Tulving (e.g. 1979). His central view of what is involved is embodied in the **encoding specificity principle**, which is as follows:

> A to-be-remembered (TBR) item is encoded with respect to the context in which it is studied, producing a unique trace which incorporates information from target and context. For the TBR item to be retrieved, the cue information must appropriately match the trace of the item-in-context.
>
> (Wiseman and Tulving 1976: 349)

In other words, the information at the time of retrieval needs to overlap as much as possible with the informa- tion contained in the memory trace for retrieval to occur.

The encoding specificity principle is intended to apply to both recall and recognition memory. The reason why recognition memory is usually better than recall is because the information available on most recognition- memory tests provides greater overlap with the infor- mation stored in the memory trace. Consider, however, the study by Watkins (1973) discussed above, in which recall was superior to recognition. It is reasonable to argue that the retrieval cue 'EXPLO' provides more overlap with the relevant memory trace ('EXPLORE') than does 'RE'.

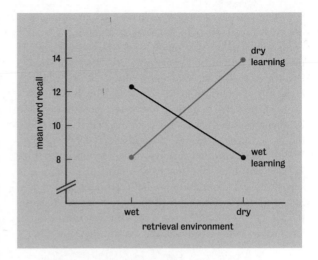

Figure 6.11 Mean recall as a function of learning and retrieval environments
Source: adapted from Godden and Baddeley (1975)

Evidence consistent with the encoding specificity principle was reported by Godden and Baddeley (1975). The participants in their study learned a word list either on land or 20 feet underwater, and this was followed by a test of free recall which was administered either on land or 20 feet underwater. As can be seen in Figure 6.11, free recall was considerably better when learning and recall took place in the same environment. These findings fit the encoding specificity principle in the fol- lowing way: information about the environment (land vs. underwater) was stored in the memory traces, and so testing in the same environment maximized the overlap between the information in the memory traces and the information available in the retrieval environment

The findings of Godden and Baddeley (1975) demon- strate that recall is better when the *external context* (i.e. environment) is the same at learning and at test. It fol- lows from the encoding specificity principle that memory performance should also be better when the *internal context* (e.g. mood state) is the same at learning and at test; this is known as **mood-state-dependent memory**. A review of the relevant studies by Ucros (1989) revealed that mood-state-dependent memory has been obtained several times, but the effects are often rather modest. She concluded that the effects are usually greater for positive moods than for negative moods, and they are greater when the learning material is personally relevant than when it is not.

There is a phenomenon known as recognition failure of recallable words which can be accounted for by the encoding specificity principle, but which is difficult to understand within two-process theory. There are several studies (e.g. Tulving and Thomson 1973) in which a recognition-memory test is followed by recall, with some of the items that could not be recognized nevertheless being recalled. This should not happen at all according to two-process theory, but is actually fairly common. The findings from the various studies were discussed by Tulving and Flexser (1992), who noted that there is a surprisingly weak relationship between recall and recognition memory. They argued that this happens because the information available on a recall test is almost unrelated to the information available on a recognition test.

Limitations of encoding specificity

The notion that memory depends on the relationship between the memory trace and the information available at the time of retrieval is a valuable one. Tulving was also right to emphasize the fact that contextual information is usually stored in the memory trace along with the to-be-remembered information. However, a problem with the encoding specificity principle is that it is difficult to test. According to the principle, what is important for memory is the overlap between the information in the memory trace and in the retrieval environment, but we usually do not know in detail what information is in the memory trace.

Another weakness of the encoding specificity principle is that it assumes that the processes involved in recall and recognition are essentially the same. However, Baddeley (1982) argued against that assumption. He drew a distinction between **intrinsic context**, which directly influences the meaning of to-be-learned material, and **extrinsic context**, which has no real impact on the meaning of such material. He then argued that intrinsic context affects both recall and recognition, whereas extrinsic context affects only recall. The study by Godden and Baddeley (1975), which was discussed above, demonstrates the impact of extrinsic context on recall. Godden and Baddeley (1980) repeated the experiment with recognition memory rather than recall, and found that extrinsic context in terms of on land versus underwater had no effect.

Another weakness of the encoding specificity principle can be seen if we consider the theoretical ideas of Jones (1982). He argued that there are two separate routes to recall. There is a direct route, in which the cues available in the retrieval environment match information in the memory trace, and so lead rapidly to retrieval of the appropriate information. There is also an indirect route, in which the cues in the retrieval environment do not match stored information, and in which recall is achieved only after a more complicated search through long-term memory. According to Tulving (1979), recall involves only the direct route. In fact, however, Jones (1982) obtained evidence that both routes are used. His participants learned word pairs such as 'regal-BEER'. All of them then tried to recall the second member of each pair when given the first as a cue word (e.g. regal– ?). In order to allow some of the participants to use the indirect route, they were informed that recall might be increased if they reversed the letters of the cue word (e.g. regal becomes lager). Those participants who used the indirect route as well as the direct one recalled approximately twice as many words as those who used only the direct route.

A final weakness of the encoding specificity principle is that retrieval often involves much more than simply matching the information in the retrieval environment with the information in the memory trace. As M.W. Eysenck and Keane (1995: 143) pointed out, people asked the question, 'What did you do six days ago?', typically respond by 'engaging in a rather complex problem-solving strategy which takes some time to reconstruct the relevant events'. The encoding specificity principle tells us little or nothing about such retrieval strategies.

Ψ Section summary

There have been various attempts to explain why recognition memory is usually better than recall. According to two-process theory, recall involves the two processes of retrieval and of decision or recognition, whereas recognition memory involves only the latter process. This theory is oversimplified, and its account of recall is more appropriate when recall is difficult than when it is easy. According to the encoding specificity principle, memory performance is most likely to be high when the information at the time of retrieval (including contextual information) overlaps considerably with that contained in the memory trace. The encoding specificity principle is important

Box continued

because of its emphasis on contextual information. However, retrieval often involves much more than simply matching information in the retrieval environment with information in the memory trace.

1 To what extent does the two-process theory provide an adequate account of recall and recognition?
2 What is the encoding specificity principle? Does it explain recall and recognition performance?

Forgetting

As we all know to our cost, our memory for specific events or pieces of information tends to become progressively worse over time. The first systematic evidence of the decline in memory over time was provided by Hermann Ebbinghaus (1885/1913). He used himself as the participant in his studies, in which he first of all learned a list of nonsense syllables (syllables possessing no meaning). He then tested his ability to recall the nonsense syllables at various retention intervals. In order to assess how much he had forgotten, he compared the number of trials it required for him to relearn the list perfectly against the number it had taken originally. This is known as the **savings method**: the greater the reduction or saving in the number of trials to perfect recall between original and second learning, the higher is the level of remembering of the material. As can be seen in Figure 6.12, there was a substantial increase in forgetting over the first hour after learning, followed by more gradual forgetting thereafter.

What causes forgetting? As we will see, it has proved rather difficult to provide an adequate answer to that question. As Baddeley (1990: 261) expressed it, 'The explanation of forgetting . . . remains an open question'. However, some of the most influential attempts to explain forgetting are discussed below.

Trace decay theory

One possible reason for forgetting is simply that memory traces decay or fade spontaneously over time, presumably because of basic processes operating within the brain. Ebbinghaus (1885/1913) argued that trace decay might be one of the factors behind forgetting: 'The persisting images suffer changes which more and more affect their nature.' It is very difficult to test trace

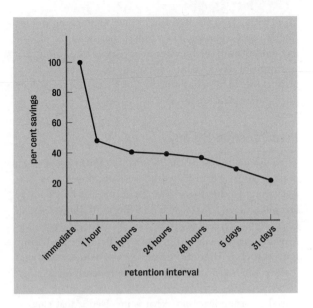

Figure 6.12 The course of forgetting as the retention interval increases
Source: based on Ebbinghaus (1885)

decay theory directly, but it can readily be tested in an indirect fashion. According to the theory, the time that has elapsed since learning is of crucial importance. As a consequence, what happens during the retention interval should be of secondary importance to the length of that interval in determining forgetting.

Jenkins and Dallenbach (1924) carried out a famous study to test trace decay theory. Two students were asked to recall lists of nonsense syllables at retention intervals varying between one and eight hours, and they were either awake or asleep during the period of time between learning and test. Jenkins and Dallenbach (1924) found that there was much less forgetting when the students were asleep during the retention interval, which is contrary to the prediction from trace decay theory. They interpreted the findings as indicating that there is much more interference with memory during the waking day than during sleep.

In spite of its fame, the study by Jenkins and Dallenbach (1924) was poorly designed. When the students slept during the retention interval, learning always took place in the evening. However, when they remained awake, learning generally took place in the morning. As a consequence, we cannot tell from their findings whether forgetting depends more on time of learning or on what happens during the retention interval. Clarification of these findings was reported by Hockey *et al.* (1972), who studied the effects of sleeping during the day on forgetting. They found that sleep during the day did not reduce the rate of forgetting, indicating that the time of day at which learning takes place is more important than whether the participants are asleep during the retention interval.

Interference theory

Throughout much of the twentieth century, the most popular approach to forgetting was interference theory. According to this theory, forgetting is caused by interference; there are two major kinds of interference. **Proactive interference** occurs when what was learned previously interferes with later learning. **Retroactive interference** occurs when what was learned previously is disrupted by later learning.

Most studies of interference theory have made use of paired-associate learning. What is involved is that pairs of words are presented to participants (e.g. animal–ball; leaf–book). The first word in each pair (e.g. animal; leaf) is known as the stimulus term, and the second word (e.g. ball; book) is the response term. After a list containing pairs of words has been presented on the first learning trial, there is a memory test. On this test, the participants are given the stimulus term, and asked to supply the matching response term. Memory for the paired associates increases as there are more learning trials, until finally the whole list has been learned.

Interference with paired associates can be shown when the participants start to learn a second list which is similar to the first list. The precise ways in which proactive and retroactive interference are demonstrated are shown in Figure 6.13. Both forms of interference are assessed by the extent to which the experimental group performs worse than the control group on the final memory test. What is of particular importance is that proactive and retroactive interference are both greatest when two different responses are associated with the same stimulus, and are small or non-existent when two different stimuli are involved (Underwood and Postman 1960).

The predictions of interference theory have generally been supported in the laboratory, but it is doubtful whether interference theory applies well to everyday life. For example, it is probably rare in everyday life for the same stimulus to be paired with two responses, although it does happen (e.g. many women adopt a different surname when they marry).

Proactive interference			
Group	Learn	Learn	Test
Experimental	A–B	A–C	A–C
Control	–	A–C	A–C

Retroactive interference			
Group	Learn	Learn	Test
Experimental	A–B	A–C	A–B
Control	A–B	–	A–B

Figure 6.13 Experimental designs for studying proactive and retroactive interference

According to interference theory, learning a second response to a stimulus word causes the first response to be unlearned. However, this simply does not happen when associations learned outside the laboratory are studied. Slamecka (1966) asked his participants to produce free associates to stimulus word (e.g. animal might produce 'dog'). He then paired the stimulus words with new responses (e.g. animal–goat), which should have caused unlearning of the free associations. Finally, he asked his participants to try to remember their free associations to the stimulus words. There was no evidence at all of retroactive interference. This indicated that pre-existing associations such as 'animal–dog' are unaffected by interference, and thus that the theory is very limited.

Cue-dependent forgetting

Tulving (1974) drew an important distinction between trace-dependent and cue-dependent forgetting. When information is forgotten, one possibility is that it has simply disappeared from the memory system; this is **trace-dependent forgetting**, and is the major source of forgetting according to trace decay theory. The other possibility is that the information is still in the memory system, but cannot be accessed. When this happens, it is known as **cue-dependent forgetting**.

Tulving and Pearlstone (1966) provided a clear demonstration of cue-dependent forgetting. The participants in their study were presented with a list of words belonging to various categories, and they were asked to learn the words. Some of the participants were then given the category names as they recalled the list words (cued recall), whereas others attempted recall without being given the category names (free recall). Those who were given the category names recalled many more words than those who were not. In other words, much of the forgetting shown by the free recall participants occurred because they did not have the retrieval cues given to the cued recall participants; this is what is meant by cue-dependent forgetting.

Tulving and Psotka (1971) showed the advantage of the cue-dependent approach to the interference theory approach. The participants learned between one and six word lists, with each list consisting of four words belonging to six categories. After the presentation of each list, the participants produced free recall of the words on that list (original learning). After they had learned their last list, they were asked to provide free recall of all the words from all of the lists (total free recall). Finally, they were given the names of all the categories in all the lists, and tried again to recall all the words (total cued recall).

As can be seen in Figure 6.14, the findings from total free recall show strong evidence of retroactive interfer-

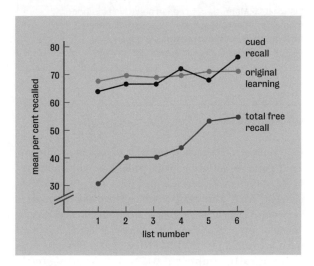

Figure 6.14 Effects of retroactive interference on original learning, total free recall, and cued recall
Source: adapted from Tulving and Psotka (1971)

ence, with the number of words being recalled from each list decreasing in line with the number of other lists intervening between learning and recall. According to interference theory, this retroactive interference reflects a process of unlearning. Consider, however, performance on cued recall. When the category names were available, there was no retroactive interference and no forgetting compared to the original learning. The forgetting observed in total free recall consisted almost entirely of cue-dependent forgetting, and was eliminated by the provision of retrieval cues in the form of category names.

It has proved easy to demonstrate powerful effects of cue-dependent forgetting inside and outside the laboratory. It seems probable that this is the main reason for forgetting in long-term memory.

Repression

One of the best known approaches to forgetting was the repression theory put forward by Freud. He argued that very threatening or traumatic information is often prevented from gaining access to consciousness, and he described this process as **repression**. Freud (1915: 86) claimed that 'The essence of repression lies simply in the function of rejecting and keeping something out of consciousness'. The 'something' referred to in the quotation was usually the anxiety-provoking memory itself. However, it was sometimes the emotion associated with the memory that was repressed rather than the memory itself (Madison 1956).

In most laboratory studies, the attempt has been made to create repression by making the participants anxious. This is then followed by removal of the anxiety in order to demonstrate that the repressed information is still in long-term memory. The participants are often given failure feedback for their performance on a task to produce anxiety, and are then told the failure feedback was fake to reduce anxiety. The anxiety created in the laboratory is probably much less than that experienced by Freud's clinical patients, and this may help to explain the disappointing findings. Holmes (1990) reviewed the relevant studies, and concluded as follows:

Warning. The concept of repression has not been validated with experimental research and its use may be hazardous to the accurate interpretation of clinical behaviour.

(Holmes 1990: 97)

Research update

Repressors

The view that repression cannot be demonstrated in the laboratory may be unduly pessimistic. Another way of looking at repression is to identify individuals who have a repressive coping style (see Chapter 14). These individuals are often called 'repressors', and they are usually defined as having low scores on the personality dimension of trait anxiety (susceptibility to anxiety) and high scores on the Marlowe-Crowne Social Desirability Scale, which is a measure of defensiveness. Repressors can be distinguished from the truly low-anxious (low on trait anxiety and on defensiveness), the high-anxious (high on trait anxiety and low on defensiveness) and the defensive high-anxious (high on trait anxiety and on defensiveness).

In a study by Myers and Brewin (1994), the female participants were asked to recall negative memories from childhood as rapidly as possible. As can be seen in Figure 6.15, the repressors took considerably more time than any of the other groups to do this. However, the repressors did not find it harder than members of the other groups to retrieve positive childhood memories, indicating that they did not have a generally poor ability to retrieve distant memories.

It could be argued that the repressors had happier childhoods than the other groups, and so had fewer negative childhood memories available for retrieval. However, Myers and Brewin (1994) found through detailed

questioning in a semi-structured interview that repressors had experienced greater indifference and hostility from their fathers than any of the other groups. Thus, the slow retrieval of negative childhood memories by repressors seems to be due to repression-like processes rather than to the small number of such memories.

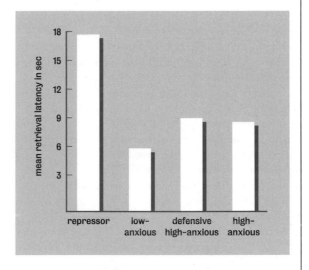

Figure 6.15 Mean time to recall negative childhood memories in repressor, low-anxious, defensive high-anxious and high-anxious groups
Source: data from Myers and Brewin (1994)

Ψ Section summary

Trace decay is a possible reason for forgetting. However, the available evidence does not suggest that it is an important factor in forgetting. Some forgetting is due to proactive and retroactive interference, but interference effects are easier to demonstrate in the laboratory than in everyday life. Cue-dependent forgetting is very important, and is almost certainly more important than trace decay or interference. Some forgetting is probably due to repression, but most of the evidence is rather controversial.

1 Why do we forget?

❏ Amnesia

One approach to human memory is to look at brain-damaged patients suffering from problems with memory. Most of the research in this area has focused on patients suffering from **amnesia**, of which the main symptom is very poor long-term memory. More specifically, several characteristics of the so-called 'amnesic syndrome' have been identified (see also Baddeley 1990). First, there is **anterograde amnesia**, which refers to a greatly reduced ability to remember new information learned after the onset of the amnesia. Second, there is **retrograde amnesia**, which refers to a reduced ability to remember events dating back to the period before the onset of the amnesia. Third, there is little or no impairment of short-term memory. Fourth, as we will see, patients with the amnesic syndrome usually possess some residual learning ability after the onset of the amnesia. Fifth, amnesic patients have a normal level of intelligence.

There are several ways in which someone can develop the amnesic syndrome, and somewhat different parts of the brain are most involved in different cases. Some of the relevant brain structures are shown in Figure 6.16. Chronic alcoholism produces Korsakoff's syndrome, and involves damage to the diencephalon (e.g. the mamillary bodies and dorsothalamic nucleus) and to the frontal cortex (Wilkinson and Carlen 1982). On the other hand, herpes simplex encephalitis typically involves damage to the lateral and medial temporal cortex, although other areas of the brain are also sometimes damaged as well.

There has been some controversy as to whether damage in these different areas of the brain really pro-

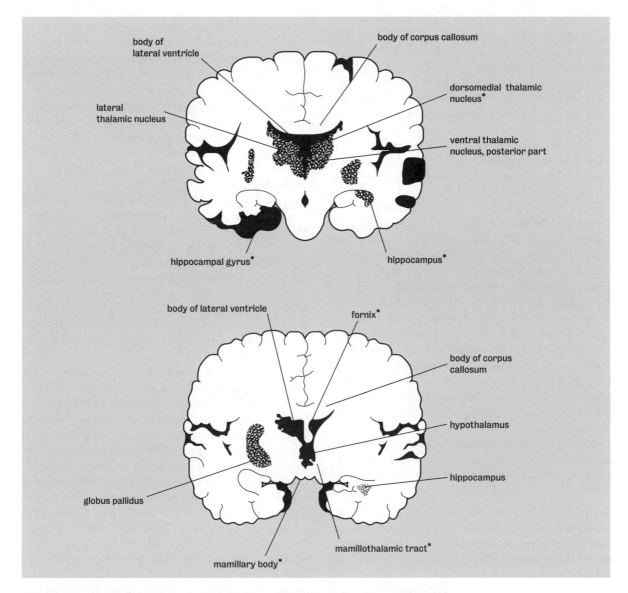

Figure 6.16 Some of the parts of the brain which are often damaged in amnesia (indicated by asterisks)
Source: adapted from Butters and Cermak (1980)

duces a single amnesic syndrome. There is some evidence that the precise details of memory impairment may depend on the particular parts of the brain that are damaged (Parkin 1990). However, many experts (e.g. Squire *et al.* 1993) argue strongly that the diencephalon and the temporal lobes are both parts of a single memory system. This is supported by much of the evidence, and makes sense in view of the fact that those parts of the brain are close to each other. In the rest of this section, it will be assumed that there is a single amnesic syndrome.

In recent years, many psychologists have argued that the study of brain-damaged patients suffering from amnesia provides a good way of testing theories of normal memory. That may sound like an unlikely argument, so it is worth considering it in a little detail. Atkinson and Shiffrin (1968) seem to have assumed that there is a single long-term memory store. If that assumption were correct, it would be expected that patients with amnesia would find it difficult to learn and to remember all kinds of information. Suppose, however, that there are two separate long-term memory systems (A and B), which are located in separate parts of the brain. It would follow that some patients might have damage to long-term memory system A but not B, so that some aspects of long-term memory were greatly impaired but others were intact. Other patients might have damage to long-term memory system B but not A. These patients would show the opposite pattern to the other patients in terms of which aspects of long-term memory were intact and impaired. Technically, finding both patterns is known as double dissociation. As we will see, there is evidence pointing to a double dissociation in amnesic patients. This has convincingly disproved the notion of a single long-term memory system, and allowed us to make some headway in developing a more adequate account of long-term memory.

Before proceeding to discuss research and theory on amnesic patients, it is worth pointing out that there are many inconsistencies in the literature. As Mayes and Downes (1997) pointed out,

very few detailed claims about the pattern of cognitive and memory deficit shown by patients or the lesions that cause their condition are universally accepted. There is a lack of universal agreement (and sometimes lack of any agreement at all!) in several theoretically important areas.

(Mayes and Downes 1997: 32)

Residual learning ability

Most amnesic patients have very poor long-term memory. This was described clearly by Korsakoff (1889) in his account of a male amnesic patient:

He does not remember whether he had his dinner, whether he was out of bed. On occasion the patient forgets what happened to him just an instant ago: you came in, conversed with him, and stepped out for one minute; then you come in again and the patient has absolutely no recollection that you had already been with him.

In spite of their generally very impaired long-term memory, amnesic patients are as good as normals at various kinds of learning. Two main categories of such learning will be discussed here: repetition-priming effects and motor skills. **Repetition-priming effects** are shown when performance in response to a stimulus is better the second time the stimulus is presented than the first time. Such effects occur because useful information is stored in memory from the first presentation of the stimulus. Repetition priming is an example of implicit memory, which was discussed earlier in the chapter.

Cermak *et al.* (1985) studied repetition-priming effects in amnesic patients and non-amnesic alcoholics. They presented both groups with a list of words, followed by a perceptual identification task. This task involved presenting words for progressively longer periods of time until the participants were able to identify them. A repetition-priming effect is shown if the identification time is significantly less for list words than for words that were not on the list. The amnesic patients showed as great a repetition-priming effect as the non-amnesic alcoholics.

Amnesic patients have been found to learn several motor skills as rapidly as normals (Parkin and Leng 1993). As M.W. Eysenck and Keane (1995: 160–1) pointed out, these skills include 'dressmaking; billiards; finger mazes; tracking a moving target on a pursuit rotor (involving a rotating turntable); jigsaw completions; reading mirror-reversed script; and mirror drawing'.

One of the relevant studies on motor skills' learning was carried out by Cohen and Squire (1980). They looked at the reading of mirror-reversed script, in which text reflected in a mirror has to be read as rapidly as possible. There are two kinds of learning which can occur with practice on this task: general improvement in the skills involved, which speeds up the reading of any mirror-reversed text; and specific improvement, which is limited

Case study

Patient W.J. with amnesia

Most research on amnesic patients has involved comparing a group of amnesic patients against a group of normal controls in order to assess the pattern of memory impairment in the amnesic patients. However, it is also possible to carry out revealing case studies of individual amnesic patients. Such a study was reported by Klein *et al.* (1996). The participant in their study was W.J., who was an 18-year-old female undergraduate student. About six months after starting university, she received a head injury after a fall, which resulted in concussion. This caused her to forget numerous events stretching back over a period of several months. However, this retrograde amnesia had largely disappeared eleven days after the accident.

Klein *et al.* (1996) conducted several memory tests on W.J. five days after the accident. When she was asked to think of personal or autobiographical memories from the past six months in response to cues, she could not think of any. However, her memory for general facts about her life (e.g. the classes she had attended) was largely intact, and she performed well on semantic memory. In other words, she showed impaired episodic memory but intact semantic memory.

It occurred to Klein *et al.* (1996: 250) that there were two interesting questions in personality research that could be addressed in W.J.: 'Does a person's knowledge of his or her traits depend on an ability to recall his or her own past behaviour? Is it possible for a person who cannot recall any personal experiences – and therefore cannot know how he or she behaved – to know what he or she is like?' They tried to answer these questions by giving W.J. a personality test once while she was still suffering from amnesia and then again four weeks later after the amnesia had gone. The same personality test was filled in by W.J.'s boyfriend, who filled it in as he thought she would have. W.J.'s personality profile while in an amnesic state was very similar to her personality profile when she completed the test four weeks later and to the profile produced by her boyfriend. There was also evidence that W.J.'s ability to assess her own personality accurately when amnesic did not depend solely on personal memories from pre-university years. Thus, it seems that the answers to the two questions addressed by Klein *et al.* (1996) are 'No' and 'Yes', respectively. In other words, a significant amount of information about our own personalities is stored in semantic memory.

to a speeding up in the reading of texts which have been read previously in mirror-reversed form. Amnesic patients showed both general and specific improvement, and some of this improvement was still present three months after the initial learning sessions. In subsequent research, Martone *et al.* (1984) also found that amnesics showed good general improvement in reading mirror-reversed, but specific improvement was less than in normals.

Theoretical accounts

Episodic and semantic memory

As discussed earlier, Tulving (1972) drew a distinction between episodic or autobiographical memory and semantic memory or memory for general knowledge, and the definition of episodic memory was subsequently revised by Wheeler *et al.* (1997). There are some reasons

for arguing that amnesic patients have severely impaired episodic memory but intact semantic memory. So far as episodic memory is concerned, such patients are very poor at remembering personal events that happen to them. So far as semantic memory is concerned, amnesic patients have good language skills and they possess sufficient general knowledge to perform at average levels on intelligence tests.

Some support for the above point of view is available in the case of an amnesic patient known as K.C. This case was discussed by Tulving (1989b):

K.C.'s case is remarkable in that he cannot remember, in the sense of bringing back to conscious awareness, a single thing that he has ever done or experienced in the past.... Those aspects of K.C.'s intellectual functioning that do not depend on remembering personal experiences are reasonably normal ... his understanding and use of language are unimpaired ... and his thought processes are intact.

(Tulving 1989b: 362)

In other words, K.C. totally lacks episodic memory but has reasonably intact semantic memory. Interesting differences between episodic and semantic memory were also shown by W.J. (see case study).

There is at least one great weakness with the view that amnesic patients have poor episodic memory but intact semantic memory. Those aspects of semantic memory which are largely intact (e.g. language skills; much general knowledge) were learned many years before the onset of the amnesia. What about semantic memories that were learned after the onset of the amnesia? Most amnesics are very poor at recognizing the faces of people who became famous after the onset of their amnesia. In addition, many of them are ignorant about what is going on in the world, such as the names of the current Prime Minister or President of the United States (Baddeley 1984). Thus, amnesic patients have poor episodic and semantic memory for information learned after the onset of the amnesia, and so the distinction does not really shed much light on the amnesic condition.

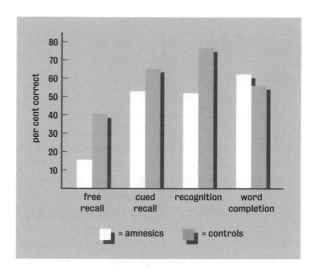

Figure 6.17 Explicit memory (free recall, cued recall and recognition memory) and implicit memory (word completion) in amnesic patients and controls
Source: adapted from Graf et al. (1984)

Explicit and implicit memory

Schacter (1987) argued that amnesic patients perform poorly on tests of explicit memory but reasonably well on tests of implicit memory, which do not involve conscious recollection. Some of the evidence we have already discussed is consistent with that point of view. Episodic and semantic memory both usually involve explicit memory, and we have just seen that both kinds of memory are poor in amnesic patients. So far as implicit memory is concerned, some of the evidence we have discussed can be regarded as involving it. More specifically, implicit memory is involved in most (or all) of the motor skills' tasks and repetition-priming effects on which the performance of amnesic patients has been found to be normal.

A study in which explicit and implicit memory were compared directly was reported by Graf et al. (1984). The participants in their experiment were presented with a list of words followed by a memory test. Three of the tests that were used were typical tests of explicit memory: free recall, cued recall and recognition memory. The fourth test was a word-completion test. On this test, the participants were given three-letter stems (e.g. CHA_____), and were told to think of a word starting with those letters. Implicit memory was shown by the tendency to think of list words as completions. As can be seen in Figure 6.17, amnesic patients did poorly on all three measures of explicit memory, but

performed as well as the control group on the test of implicit memory.

Ostergaard (1994) was not convinced that implicit memory is intact in amnesic patients. According to him, priming based on implicit memory is generally impaired in amnesics. However, a careful analysis of the findings suggests that he exaggerated the amount of impairment. According to Curran and Schacter (1997: 45), 'Implicit memory phenomena such as priming are normally spared in amnesia, but deficits may become apparent under conditions in which normal subjects are able to integrate different types of information that are associated with a target stimulus'.

In sum, amnesic patients usually seem to exhibit impaired explicit memory and intact implicit memory. However, that statement represents a description of what has been found rather than a theoretical explanation of the memory problems of amnesic patients. Accordingly, we turn now to a related approach that may offer more prospect of providing such an explanation.

Declarative and procedural knowledge

Ryle (1949) drew a distinction between knowing *that* and knowing *how*. We know that summer is warmer than winter, that Henry VIII had six wives, and that we went to a party last Saturday. We know how to ride a bicycle, how to play tennis, how to play netball, and so on.

Essentially this differentiation was used by Cohen and Squire (1980), who drew a distinction between **declarative knowledge** and **procedural knowledge**. Declarative knowledge involves knowing that, and includes episodic and semantic memory. In contrast, procedural knowledge involves knowing how, and includes motor and other skills.

Cohen (1984) made it clear that declarative knowledge usually involves explicit memory, whereas procedural knowledge involves implicit memory. According to him, declarative knowledge is represented 'in a system . . . in which information is . . . first processed or encoded, then stored in some explicitly accessible form for later use, and then ultimately retrieved upon demand'. In contrast, procedural knowledge is involved when 'experience serves to influence the organization of processes that guide performance without access to the knowledge that underlies the performance' (Cohen 1984: 96).

Cohen (1984) argued that the declarative system is damaged in amnesic patients, but the procedural system is intact. So far as the declarative system is concerned, the fact that amnesic patients find it difficult to form new episodic and semantic memories supports Cohen's contention. Motor skills' learning and priming effects can be regarded as involving procedural learning, and amnesics have essentially normal performance on tasks of motor learning and priming.

If there are separate brain systems underlying declarative and procedural knowledge, then some patients should have damage to the procedural system but not to the declarative system. There are indications that that may be the case. For example, Heindel et al. (1988) studied patients with Huntington's disease, which is a degenerative condition affecting the basal ganglia. These patients found it very difficult to acquire motor skills (based on procedural learning), but their performance on recognition-memory tests (based on declarative learning) was normal.

It is interesting to speculate on the reasons why humans possess two more or less separate memory systems. This issue was addressed by Squire et al. (1993):

One system . . . provides the basis for conscious recollections. This system is fast, phylogenetically [in terms of evolution] recent, and specialised for one-trial learning. . . . The system is fallible in the sense that it is sensitive to interference and prone to retrieval failure. It is also precious, giving rise to the capacity for personal autobiography and the possibility of cultural evolution. Other kinds of memory have also been identified . . . these forms of memory are phylogenetically early, they are reliable and consistent, and they provide for myriad, nonconscious ways of responding to the world . . . they create much of the mystery of human experience.

(Squire et al. 1993: 485–6)

ψ Section summary

Amnesic patients often suffer from anterograde amnesia and retrograde amnesia. Studying such patients has proved of value in testing theories of normal memory. It has been argued that amnesic patients have poor episodic but intact semantic memory. However, the evidence suggests that amnesic patients have poor semantic memory for information learned after the onset of the amnesia. Amnesic patients typically have an impaired declarative system, but an essentially intact procedural system. Some patients (e.g. those with Huntington's disease) have been found to have problems with procedural learning, but not with declarative learning.

1 What has the study of amnesic patients told us about normal human memory?

Memory for stories

Most of the research we have discussed in this chapter has been concerned with memory for small units of information (e.g. words). In everyday life, on the other hand, much of what we learn and remember involves considerably larger units of information (e.g. newspapers, books, lectures). It is of theoretical and practical interest to study the ways in which we remember such information, and that is the focus of this section of the chapter.

The most obvious feature of our memory for a large unit of information such as a story or a book is that it is very selective. Gomulicki (1956) studied the selective nature of story recall in an interesting study. Some of his participants recalled a story from memory, while others produced a précis or summary of the same story that was present in front of them. Finally, other participants were shown a mixture of the recalls and of the précis or summaries, and were asked to decide which were which. They were largely unsuccessful in doing this. This indicates that memory for stories is like a summary, in that the central themes are included and the minor details are omitted.

Bartlett's approach

An important approach to memory for stories was initiated by Bartlett (1932). His key assumption was that memory is influenced by an individual's past experience

Plate 6.2 Studies indicate that memory for stories is often like a summary, in that central themes are included and the minor details are omitted. Prior knowledge in the form of schemes often influences comprehension and retrieval processes

and knowledge as well as by the information presented to him or her. According to Bartlett (1932: 213), 'Remembering is not the re-excitation of innumerable fixed, lifeless and fragmentary traces. It is an imaginative reconstruction, or construction, built out of the relation of our attitude towards a whole active mass of organized past reactions or experiences'. He used the term 'schema' to refer to organized packets of knowledge stored in memory which are used in remembering.

Bartlett (1932) devised a clever way of testing whether prior knowledge in the form of schemas has a significant impact on memory for stories. He presented stories from other cultures (e.g. the North American Indian culture) to undergraduates at Cambridge University, and then asked them to recall these stories. The best known of these sto-ries was 'The War of the Ghosts'. Most of the story recalls distorted the content and style of the original story. The most common distortion was what Bartlett termed **rationalization**; it involves changing the story to make it read more like a conventional English story. For example, one student recalled that a dying Indian 'foamed at the mouth', whereas the original stated that 'something black came out of his mouth'. Other distortions included flattening (a failure to include unfamiliar details in the recall) and sharpening (elaboration of some details of the story).

One of the problems with Bartlett's research is that the instructions he gave to his participants was rather vague. In his own words, 'I thought it best, for the purposes of these experiments, to try to influence the subjects' procedure as little as possible' (1932: 78). The problem with this is that the distortions in recall may have been based on deliberate guesses, or attempts to make the recall coherent, rather than on genuine distortions in memory. This possibility was investigated by Gauld and Stephenson (1967) using 'The War of the Ghosts'. They discovered that about half of the distortions usually produced were eliminated when the participants were told to make sure that they recalled only information which had actually appeared in the story.

An important theoretical issue is whether past experience and knowledge influence processing at the time of comprehension or processing at the time of recall. According to Bartlett's (1932) reconstructive hypothesis, prior knowledge has its major impact at the time of retrieval. In contrast, Bransford (1979) proposed a constructive hypothesis, according to which prior knowledge influences comprehension rather than retrieval processes.

Some of the evidence supports Bartlett (1932). For example, the participants in a study by Dooling and Christiaansen (1977) read a paragraph about Carol Harris. This started 'Carol Harris was a problem child from birth. She was wild, stubborn, and violent'. One week later, the participants were asked whether the sentence, 'She was deaf, dumb, and blind,' had been included in the passage. Very few said 'Yes'. Other participants were asked the same question after being told that the paragraph they had read was really about Helen Keller (who was a famous deaf, dumb and blind person). Many of them mistakenly said 'Yes', because their prior knowledge of Helen Keller distorted their memory for the paragraph.

Evidence that prior knowledge can influence comprehension processes was reported by Bransford and Johnson (1972). They presented their participants with a difficult passage, which started like this:

The procedure is actually quite simple. First you arrange items into different groups. Of course one pile may be sufficient depending on how much there is to do. If you have to go somewhere else due to lack of facilities that is the next step, otherwise, you are pretty well set. It is important not to overdo things.

(Bransford and Johnson 1972: 722)

As you might imagine, those participants who heard this passage said that it was incomprehensible, and managed to recall only 2.8 idea units from it. Those participants who were given the title 'Washing clothes' after hearing the passage recalled only 2.6 idea units. In contrast, those who were given the title before hearing the passage rated it as easy to understand, and recalled an average of 5.8 idea units. Providing a title allowed the participants to make use of their relevant prior knowledge during the comprehension process, and this influenced comprehension and recall.

Schema theory

During the 1970s and 1980s, several schema theories were proposed (see Alba and Hasher 1983). It has increasingly been argued that there are various types of schema. For example, the term 'script' is used to refer to stored knowledge about expected sequences of actions (e.g. in a theatre or restaurant) and the term 'frame' is used for stored knowledge about common visual scenes (e.g. an office or farm). Schank (1978) put forward a fairly extreme form of schema theory:

We would claim that in natural language understanding, a simple rule is followed. Analysis proceeds in a top-down predictive manner. Understanding is expectation based. It is only when the expectations are useless or wrong that bottom-up processing begins.

(Schank 1978: 94)

One of the problems with notions such as schema, script and frame is that they tend to be rather vague. Bower et al. (1979) tried to clarify exactly what information is contained in, for example, the restaurant script and lecture-attending script. They asked students to indicate which activities they associated with these events. For the lecture script, they found that most of the students listed the following activities as part of the lecture-attending script: entering the lecture theatre, finding a seat, sitting down, taking out a notebook, listening to the lecturer, taking notes, checking the time, and leaving.

Bower et al. (1979) went on to test whether the information contained in scripts caused distortions in memory. They presented stories relating to various scripts, and found that parts of the script that were not mentioned in the story tended to occur in the participants' recall and recognition memory.

What happens to information that does not form part of the schema, script or frame being used during comprehension? One possibility is that such information is simply ignored because it is regarded as irrelevant. Another possibility is that we pay particular attention to unexpected information that does not fit the current schema, and so it is well remembered. Much of the evidence supports the latter position rather than the former. Friedman (1979) presented her participants with drawings of scenes (e.g. a kitchen, an office). Most of the objects in each drawing were those that would be expected in that setting, but some unexpected objects were also included. The first look at unexpected objects was twice as long as at expected objects, and recognition memory was considerably better for unexpected than for expected objects.

D.A. Smith and Graesser (1981) put forward the schema copy plus tag hypothesis. According to this hypothesis, what is stored in memory from an event or story is the underlying schema that is relevant to the event or story, plus the unexpected or atypical details which do not conform to the schema. They presented their participants with stories relating to various scripts (e.g. taking a dog to the vet) and included a mixture of typical and atypical actions within each story. An example of an atypical action was as follows: 'While waiting for the vet, Jack dropped his car keys'. Recall and recognition were better for typical than for atypical actions. However, the good performance on typical actions was due in part to guessing on the basis of script knowledge. When the influence of guessing was removed, memory performance was better for atypical actions than for typical ones. Overall, the study provided good support for the schema copy plus tag hypothesis.

Limitations of schema theories

The various schema theories that have developed from Bartlett's (1932) original schema approach have served a number of valuable functions. First, they have emphasized the fact that most of the knowledge stored in long-term memory is highly organized. Second, it is undoubtedly true that the processes involved in comprehension and retrieval are much influenced by prior knowledge. Third, many of the errors which occur in memory for events and stories are due to the distorting impact of prior knowledge.

There are two main problems with schema theories. First, it is usually easy to explain the findings of any study by assuming that the participants have certain kinds of schemas or scripts. However, there is usually little or no direct evidence that they do actually possess these schemas or scripts, and it is difficult to obtain such evidence. Second, schema theories are designed to account for errors and distortions in memory. As Alba and Hasher (1983) pointed out, our memory is usually reasonably accurate, and there is a danger that schema theories predict more memorial errors than are actually found. Much of the relevant evidence is discussed by Stangor and McMillan (1992).

ψ Section summary

Memory for stories is often like a summary, with the central themes included and the minor details excluded. Prior knowledge in the form of schemas often influences comprehension processes when reading a story, and it can also affect retrieval processes. Many of the errors found in story recall occur because of the distorting impact of schematic information.

1 Evaluate schema theories of story recall.

☐ Eyewitness testimony

Every year there are hundreds of criminal cases in which the only evidence against the defendant is in the form of eyewitness testimony. Unfortunately, as has been known for a long time, eyewitnesses often make mistakes when trying to remember the details of a crime. This is a serious matter, because large numbers of innocent people have been sent to prison on the basis of mistaken eyewitness testimony.

Eyewitnesses may make mistakes either because of what happens at the time of the event or incident or because of what happens after the event. There is no doubt that eyewitness testimony is sometimes inaccurate because the eyewitness was not attending fully to the incident or was not aware of its significance. Another important factor is whether or not the criminal or criminals use violence. Loftus and Burns (1982) made use of two filmed versions of a crime, in one of which a boy

was shot in the face as the criminals were making their escape. Those participants who saw this violent version had poorer memory for information presented during the previous two minutes than did those who saw the non-violent version.

Impressive evidence that what happens after the incident is also important was reported by Loftus and Palmer (1974). All of the participants were shown a film of a two-car accident. Afterwards, they were asked a number of questions about what they had seen. Some participants were asked how fast the cars were going when they smashed into each other, whereas others were asked the same question with the verb 'hit' replacing 'smashed into'. The former participants gave an average speed estimate of 40.8 m.p.h., whereas the latter ones estimated the speed at 34.0 m.p.h. A week later, the participants were asked whether they had seen any broken glass. In spite of the fact that there hadn't been any broken glass, 32 per cent of those who had been asked the question about speed with the verb 'smashed' being used said 'yes'. In contrast, of those who had been asked the question with the verb 'hit', only 14 per cent said they had seen broken glass. These findings suggest that the memory of an eyewitness is rather fragile and can easily be distorted by post-event questioning.

Loftus (1979) originally argued that post-event information caused a genuine alteration to the original memory traces of the incident. More recently, however, Loftus (1991) suggested that this probably happens only to a limited extent. More important is what she calls *misinformation acceptance*. Eyewitnesses are often willing to 'accept' misleading post-event information, later regarding it as part of their memory for the preceding incident. This tendency for eyewitnesses' memories to be influenced by misinformation acceptance increases as more and more time elapses since the original incident.

There is a considerable amount of evidence that the memory of eyewitnesses is often distorted by post-event information. However, it should be noted that the focus of most research has been on distorted memory for fairly trivial details, such as the presence or absence of broken glass. As one might expect, misleading post-event information has less effect on eyewitnesses' memory for crucial information (e.g. the type of weapon used) than for unimportant details (Fruzzetti *et al.* 1992).

Kassin *et al.* (1989) argued that the most important findings from research on eyewitness testimony are those which are reliable and contrary to common sense. Accordingly, they asked a group of experts to identify reliable findings, and to indicate whether or not each finding was commonsensical. The most counter-intuitive findings (with the percentage of experts claiming that each one was commonsensical) were as follows:

- the confidence of eyewitnesses does not predict the accuracy of their testimony (3 per cent)
- eyewitnesses usually overestimate the duration of events (5 per cent)
- eyewitnesses' testimony about an event depends in part on information obtained afterwards (7 per cent)
- eyewitnesses' memories for an event show a normal forgetting curve (24 per cent)
- eyewitnesses' testimony can be influenced by the way in which questions put to them are worded (27 per cent)
- there is an increased risk of misidentification when only one person is in an identification parade than when there are several (29 per cent)

Practical improvements

The various findings of laboratory research have several implications for the treatment of eyewitnesses in the real world. For example, when the police or detectives interview eyewitnesses, they need to ensure that their questions do not distort eyewitnesses' memory as happened in the study by Loftus and Palmer (1974). There are other problems. It used to be common in the UK for the police to interrupt eyewitnesses repeatedly as they tried to remember the details of an incident. It was difficult for an eyewitness to remember as much as possible because of the adverse effects of the interruptions on his or her ability to concentrate. The situation has now been rectified, with the Home Office advising police officers to start their interviews by asking eyewitnesses to provide free recall of the incident, with specific questions being asked only later on.

Geiselman et al. (1985) argued that it should be possible to use our knowledge of the workings of human memory to improve police interviews. They developed what they termed the **basic cognitive interview** on this basis. Two major assumptions were involved. First, memory traces usually consist of a number of different related pieces of information, and this means that various retrieval cues may allow us to gain access to any given memory trace. For example, some people might think of the name 'Mrs Thatcher' when given the retrieval cue 'won three consecutive general elections in the UK in the 1970s and 1980s' or the retrieval cue 'British Prime Minister during the Falklands War'. Other people might think of Mrs Thatcher only when given the retrieval cue 'first woman Prime Minister in the UK'.

Second, it was assumed that a retrieval cue will be effective only when the information it contains overlaps with information contained in the memory trace. This assumption is simply a restatement of the encoding specificity principle, which was discussed earlier in the chapter.

The basic cognitive interview, based on the two assumptions just described, has the following features:

- eyewitnesses should try to re-create the external and internal context present when the incident occurred, in order to maximize the overlap with the information in the memory traces; this can involve revisiting the scene of the incident and recreating the mood state at the time of the incident
- everything of any possible relevance to the incident is reported, even if it is in a very incomplete or fragmented form
- the events and details of the incident are reported from different perspectives (e.g. that of another eyewitness watching the incident from a different angle); this makes use of different retrieval cues
- the details of the incident are recalled in different orders; the first details recalled act as retrieval cues for the others

In order to assess the usefulness of the basic cognitive interview, Geiselman et al. (1985) compared it against the standard police interview and against interviewing under hypnosis. In a laboratory study, the basic cognitive interview proved much more successful than the standard police interview, producing 40 per cent more correctly remembered details. It also produced 12 per cent more correct details than did the interview under hypnosis.

Following the success of the basic cognitive interview, Fisher et al. (1987) added some extra ingredients to it, and came up with an **enhanced cognitive interview**. These additions were summarized in the following way by Roy (1991):

Investigators should minimise distractions, induce the eyewitness to speak slowly, allow a pause between the response and next question, tailor language to suit the individual eyewitness, follow up with interpretive comment, try to reduce eyewitness anxiety, avoid judgemental and personal comments, and always review the eyewitness's description of events or people under investigation.

(Roy 1991: 399)

Fisher et al. (1987) found in a laboratory study that the number of details of an incident correctly recalled was 45 per cent higher with the enhanced cognitive interview than with the basic cognitive interview. However, the disadvantage of the enhanced cognitive interview was that it produced 28 per cent more incorrectly remembered details than did the basic cognitive interview.

Research update

Eyewitness memory

The finding that the confidence which eyewitnesses have in their testimony does not predict its accuracy is a puzzling one. Perfect and Hollins (1996) decided to look at this effect in more detail. In order to see whether there is something special about eyewitness memory, they compared it against memory for general knowledge.

The participants were shown a short film about a girl who has been kidnapped. The next day they tried to answer several questions about the film, and were asked to indicate their level of confidence in their answers. Then they were given a test of recognition memory. The same procedure was followed with respect to general knowledge questions obtained from encyclopedias and trivial pursuits books.

As had been found before, Perfect and Hollins (1996) found that those individuals who were most confident in the accuracy of their eyewitness recall were not actually any more accurate than those who were least confident. However, this was not the case for general knowledge, where more confident individuals had superior recall to less confident ones. Why is there this difference? According to Perfect and Hollins (1996) the reason is as follows:

individuals have insight into their strengths and weaknesses in general knowledge, and tend to modify their use of the confi-

dence scale accordingly . . . general knowledge is a data base that is shared between individuals, with publicly agreed correct answers that subjects can calibrate themselves against. So, for example, individuals will know whether they tend to be better or worse than others at sports questions. However, eyewitnessed events are not amenable to such insight: subjects are unlikely to know whether they are better or worse, in general, than others at remembering the hair colour of a participant in an event, for example.

(Perfect and Hollins 1996: 379)

A possible implication of the above findings is that the confidence judgements of eyewitnesses have no predictive power at all. However, Perfect and Hollins (1996) obtained evidence that this implication is not justified. Most eyewitnesses had better recall for those items where their confidence was highest than for those items where their confidence was lowest. Indeed, the within-subjects correlation between recall accuracy and confidence level was +0.54, which was only slightly lower than the recall-confidence correlation (+0.65) for general knowledge. In other words, eyewitnesses have some idea about which of their memories are accurate and inaccurate, but do not know whether their memories of an event are likely to be more or less accurate than those of other people.

The finding that the enhanced cognitive interview is effective under laboratory conditions does not necessarily mean that it will be effective with eyewitnesses who have observed real crimes. This issue was addressed by Fisher *et al.* (1990). They gave training in the enhanced cognitive interview to detectives in the Metro-Dade Police Department in Miami, Florida. This training led to a 46 per cent increase in the number of details of incidents recalled by eyewitnesses.

Ψ Section summary

Eyewitness testimony is often distorted by post-event information because of misinformation

Box continued

acceptance. Eyewitness confidence often fails to predict the accuracy of their testimony, and eyewitnesses tend to overestimate the duration of events. The value of eyewitness testimony can be improved by means of the basic cognitive interview, which is based on the encoding specificity principle and the notion that memory traces contain numerous pieces of information. The enhanced cognitive interview incorporates the assumptions underlying the basic cognitive interview, with some added ingredients.

1 Why is eyewitness testimony often inaccurate?
2 How can eyewitnesses be treated so as to maximize the accuracy of their testimony?

Ψ Chapter summary

• Multi-store models

Learning and memory involve successive encoding, storage and retrieval stages. According to Atkinson and Shiffrin (1968), there are separate sensory stores, a short-term store and a long-term store. The sensory store in the visual modality is the iconic store, and in the auditory modality it is the echoic store. Information reaches the short-term store through attentional processes, and it reaches the long-term store through rehearsal. The sensory stores, the short-term store and the long-term store differ from each other in terms of their temporal duration, storage capacity, entering process and forgetting mechanism.

• Working memory

The working memory system consists of three components (central executive, articulatory or phonological loop, and visuo-spatial sketch-pad) working reasonably independently of each other. The phonological loop consists of a phonological or speech-based store and an articulatory control process.

• Learning processes

According to levels-of-processing theory, deep or semantic processing leads to better long-term memory than does shallow or non-semantic processing. There is evidence that elaborative rehearsal is more effective than maintenance rehearsal, and that long-term memory also depends on elaboration of processing and on distinctiveness. There is insufficient consideration of the relationship between what is learned and the nature of the memory test in levels-of-processing theory.

• Long-term memory

One distinction within long-term memory is between episodic or autobiographical memory and semantic memory or general knowledge. There is value in the distinction, but the two forms of memory are closely interdependent in their functioning. There is another distinction between explicit memory, which involves conscious recollection, and implicit memory, which does not. Explicit memory tends to involve conceptually driven processes, whereas implicit memory tends to involve data-driven processes.

• Semantic memory

Semantic memory is highly organized. It used to be thought that it was organized into hierarchical networks, but this approach now seems too inflexible. It seems that semantic memory is organized in terms of semantic relatedness, with activation spreading among related concepts.

• Retrieval processes

According to two-process theory, recall involves a retrieval process followed by a recognition process, whereas recognition memory involves only the latter process. This provides an explanation for the general superiority of recognition over recall, but is an over-simplified view of the processes involved. Recall and recognition are better understood within the framework of the encoding specificity principle, according to which memory performance depends on the degree of overlap between stored information and information available at the time of retrieval.

• Forgetting

According to interference theory, forgetting occurs because of proactive and retroactive interference. Interference is especially likely when two responses are associated with the same stimulus. There are strong interference effects under laboratory conditions, but it is not clear that interference causes much forgetting in everyday life. Cue-dependent forgetting is very important, and can be demonstrated by showing that information inaccessible with one cue can be retrieved with a different cue. Repression, or motivated forgetting of anxiety-provoking information, has proved hard to produce in the laboratory. However, it appears that some people have a repressive coping style which leads them to repress unpleasant memories.

• Amnesia

Amnesic patients have impaired long-term memory but essentially intact short-term memory. In spite of their poor long-term memory, they show normal repetition-priming effects and motor skills learning. Most of the evidence can be accounted for by assuming that amnesic patients have an intact procedural learning

Box continued

system (dealing with knowing how), but a severely deficient declarative learning system (dealing with knowing that and encompassing episodic and semantic memory).

● **Memory for stories**

Bartlett argued that distortions occur in our memory for stories because of the influence of past experience and knowledge. According to his reconstructive hypothesis, this influence occurs mainly at the time of retrieval. In contrast, Bransford put forward a constructive hypothesis, according to which prior knowledge has its main impact at the time of comprehension or learning. The evidence suggests that both hypotheses are partially correct. Some of Bartlett's ideas have been developed in more recent schema theories. However, it remains difficult to establish what information is contained in a schema, and there is a danger that schema theories predict too many errors and distortions in memory.

● **Eyewitness testimony**

Eyewitness testimony is often inaccurate because of the influence of post-event information or questioning. Much of this influence is due to misinformation acceptance by eyewitnesses; this is more likely to occur with trivial details than with event information of central significance. Eyewitness testimony can be improved through use of the basic cognitive interview and the enhanced cognitive interview. These interview techniques are based on the assumption that most memory traces are complex and contain several different pieces of information which can be accessed in a number of different ways (e.g. recalling an event in different orders).

Further reading

● Ashcraft, M.H. (1994) *Human Memory and Cognition*, 2nd edn. New York: HarperCollins. This book contains several chapters dealing with major issues in human memory.

● Baddeley, A.D. (1990) *Human Memory: Theory and practice*. Hove: Lawrence Erlbaum. Alan Baddeley is one of the leading memory researchers in the world, and he writes in an accessible way about theory and research in memory in this book.

● Eysenck, M.W. and Keane, M.T. (1995) *Cognitive Psychology: A student's handbook*. Hove: Lawrence Erlbaum. Chapters 6, 7 and 8 contain detailed accounts of numerous topics relating to those covered here.

● Groeger, J.A. (1997) *Memory and Remembering: Everyday memory in context*. Harlow: Longman.

● Squire, L.R., Knowlton, B. and Musen, G. (1993) The structure and organization of memory. *Annual Review of Psychology* 44: 453-95. This chapter is especially good for its account of recent theoretical views on amnesia and on long-term memory generally.

● Loftus, E.F. (1991) Made in memory: distortions in recall after misleading information, in G.H. Bower (ed.) *The Psychology of Learning and Motivation*, vol. 27. New York: Academic Press.

● Hanley, J.R. and Young, A.W. (1994) Cognitive neuropsychology of memory, in P. Morris and M. Gruneberg (eds) *Theoretical Aspects of Memory*. London: Routledge. This chapter provides a good review of different types of memory disorder following brain injury.

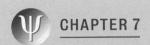

Language

Michael Eysenck

☐ Chapter preview

When you have read this chapter, you should be able to

- understand different approaches to reading
- discuss the basic processes involved in reading
- describe the main processes of speech perception
- indicate how syntactic and semantic information is extracted from text
- describe why and how inferences are drawn in reading
- understand the main processes of speech production

Introduction

How important is language to humans? Without a shadow of doubt, language is of extraordinary importance to us. Language is of vital significance in communication: think how hard it would be to convey our thoughts and feelings to other people without making use of language! Without language, our ability to learn would be considerably reduced. We learn from books, lectures, conversations, newspapers and television, all of which rely heavily (or exclusively) on language. Written language is of great importance in providing us with information about the past, and in giving us a sense of the historical development of our culture. Probably you are now convinced (if you weren't already) that language plays a major role in making us human.

There has been some controversy on the issue of whether language can be taught to other species, especially apes. Some experts (e.g. Savage-Rumbaugh *et al.* 1986) have argued that chimpanzees can master the essentials of language, but others (e.g. Terrace 1979) disagree. The consensual view is a compromise position. This was expressed in the following terms by Harley (1995: 28): 'Although there have been several attempts to teach non-human primates a human-like language, there is as yet no unequivocal [unambiguous] evidence that these have been successful'. What is clear is that any language abilities which have been taught to chimpanzees are considerably more limited than those acquired by most humans. Thus, full command of language is unique to members of the human species.

Plate 7.1 Some experts have argued that chimpanzees can master the essentials of language, although there is no unequivocal evidence that such attempts have been successful. However, it is clear that full command of language is unique to members of the human species.

There are several different language skills. It is convenient to divide these skills into **receptive language** and **productive language**. Receptive language involves comprehension, and involves either speech perception or reading. Productive language involves communication and is typically in the form of speech production or writing. Psychologists have devoted more attention to reading than to other language skills, and they have devoted the least attention to writing skills. Our coverage of language will take into account the fact that much more is known of the processes involved in reading than those involved in other aspects of language use.

Cognitive neuropsychology is concerned with understanding the patterns of cognitive performance exhibited by brain-damaged patients. The cognitive neuropsychological approach has been used extensively in language research, and so it is worthwhile at this stage to indicate some of its major assumptions. The first assumption is that of **modularity**: there are several modules or cognitive processors, each of which operates relatively independently of the rest of the cognitive system. These modules are assumed to be in different parts of the brain, so that brain damage will generally impair the functioning of some of these modules while leaving others intact. If we compare the cognitive performance of brain-damaged patients and normal individuals, this will help us to identify the main modules involved in cognition.

Another major assumption is that modules can be identified by discovering double dissociations. A **double dissociation** is defined in the following way: one patient has normal performance on task A coupled with impaired performance on task B, whereas another patient has impaired performance on task A coupled with normal performance on task B. It is assumed that double dissociations are found when two tasks involve two different modules, either of which can be affected by brain damage while leaving the other module intact.

A further major assumption made by many cognitive neuropsychologists is that the focus of research should be on single case studies rather than on groups of brain-damaged patients. This position is in marked contrast to the more traditional approach. In that approach, the emphasis was on identifying groups of patients suffering from the same **syndrome**, which involves a given set or collection of symptoms. For example, patients with severe impairments of long-term memory but essentially intact short-term memory were said to be suffering from the amnesic syndrome.

The key problem with the syndrome-based approach is that it exaggerates the similarities among patients who are allegedly suffering from the same syndrome. In reality, different patients rarely have precisely the same brain damage and pattern of impaired performance, and so there is an inevitable oversimplification involved in assigning them to the same syndrome. However, the alternative approach based on single case studies is not beyond reproach either. There are various reasons why a given patient might exhibit impaired performance, as was pointed out by Shallice (1991):

A selective impairment found in a particular task in some patient could just reflect: the patient's idiosyncratic strategy, the greater difficulty of that task compared with the others, a premorbid lacuna [gap] in that patient, or the way a reorganised system but not the original normal system operates.

(Shallice 1991: 433)

As we will see during the course of this chapter, the cognitive neuropsychological approach has greatly enhanced our understanding of language. The focus of cognitive neuropsychology has been very much on identifying the major components or modules involved in receptive and productive language. These components are generally shown as boxes in diagrams of the language system, and are connected together by arrows. However, what is relatively neglected is a detailed understanding of the processes occurring within the various boxes (Seidenberg 1988). In other words, cognitive neuropsychology has proved more successful at identifying the structure of the language system than at clarifying the processes operating within that structure.

Since the early 1980s, another approach to the study of language has become increasingly popular. This approach is known as **connectionism**, and it involves computer-based modelling of language processes. The models constructed by connectionists consist of large numbers of neuron-like units These units are strongly interconnected within a network. When one of the units is highly activated, activation spreads from that unit to the other units with which it is connected.

What are the advantages of the connectionist approach? Probably its greatest strength is that it compels theorists to be explicit about all of their detailed assumptions. In contrast, there is often a considerable amount of vagueness about theories of language expressed solely in words. Connectionism also has advantages over previous computer-based approaches, in that it seems to correspond more closely to the functioning of the human brain. The brain consists of huge numbers of interconnected neurons, and the same is true of connectionist networks. However, the complex-ity of brain functioning is dramatically greater than that of connectionist networks.

We will be discussing some connectionist models of language later in the chapter, including an evaluation of their strengths and weaknesses. Most of these models provide accounts of rather basic language processes rather than high-level ones. What is the reason for this? According to Baddeley (1990: 376), connectionist models 'may be appropriate for opaque processes, processes that operate relatively automatically, while models based on symbol processing will continue to provide a better account of those aspects of cognition that are . . . open to conscious manipulation'.

❑ Basic processes in reading

Reading involves a series of processes. In order to understand a text, it is necessary to identify and to make sense of individual words. However, there are also higher-level processes operating at the level of the phrase, the sentence, and the structure of the entire text. We will consider some of the basic processes involved in reading before dealing with higher-level processes.

Methods of study

Several methods have been used in the attempt to understand the basic processes involved in reading. Here we will focus on three of the most-used methods: word-identification techniques; subject-controlled presentation of text; and eye-movement recording.

As the name implies, *word-identification techniques* are used when we want to know how long it takes the reader to identify a single word. For example, there is the lexical decision task. This involves presenting a string of letters, and asking the participants to decide as rapidly as possible whether the string forms a word. Another word-identification technique is the naming task, which simply involves saying a word as quickly as possible. Both tasks have the advantage that they ensure that some basic processes have been applied to each word. However, they both have the disadvantage that they interfere with normal reading by requiring participants to do more than simply try to understand the text in front of them.

One way of trying to establish how long readers spend in processing different parts of a sentence is to make use of *subject-controlled presentation of text*. In essence, readers can see only one word or a small number of words at any given time, and they press a key when they want to move on to the next fragment of text. This technique is rather artificial, and it has the disadvantage that it disrupts the processes involved in normal reading. Indeed, Just *et al.* (1982) found that the speed of reading was considerably slower with subject-controlled presentation of text. However, those parts of the text that took the longest to read under normal reading conditions were the same as those that took the longest with subject-controlled presentation of text, suggesting that similar processes were being used in both cases.

Recording eye movements during reading is the most generally adequate way of studying the processes involved in reading. It has the great advantage over other methods that it allows the reader to read a text in the same way that he or she would if eye movements were not being recorded. It also has the advantage that it provides detailed information about the direction of attention during the entire reading process. The only real limitation of the eye-movement technique is that it can be difficult to decide what processing was occurring during each eye fixation.

Eye movements

As we are reading, it seems to us that our eyes are moving smoothly forwards over the text. However, what is actually happening is very different in two ways. First, the eyes move in **saccades** or rapid jerks lasting for approximately 15 milliseconds, each of which is followed by an eye fixation lasting for about 200–50 milliseconds. Second, approximately 10 per cent of saccades are **regressions**, meaning that the eyes move backwards through the text.

Saccades vary in length, but they average out at about eight letters or spaces (Rayner and Sereno 1994). According to cognitive guidance theory (O'Regan and Levy-Schoen 1987), eye fixations in reading tend to occur at those points in the text providing the most information. Thus, for example, fixations on spaces or punctuation marks are relatively rare. Fixations tend to occur near the centre of longer words, and such words are generally more informative than short words.

The central part of the retina is known as the fovea, and it is this area of the retina which is associated with precise vision. Since the fovea is small, it is reasonable to expect that the amount of text from which useful information can be obtained on any given fixation should be relatively limited. The available evidence indicates that the **perceptual span**, which is the total field of view, generally extends about three or four letters to the left of the fixation point and about fifteen letters to the right, and does not include the line below the one fixated (see Rayner and Sereno 1994 for a review).

 Research update

Eye fixation times

Much of what we know about the processes involved in reading has come from the study of eye movements. One of the key issues is to identify the factors determining the length of each eye fixation. There are two major competing hypotheses. According to one hypothesis, low-level factors are important. For example, fixations should be shorter when the middle of a word is fixated than when either end of the word is fixated. According to the other hypothesis, fixation times are determined by the processing complexities of language. For example, fixation times will be longer for words whose meaning is hard to assess.

Rayner *et al.* (1996) tested the above hypotheses. They measured fixation times on rare and common words which were embedded in passages of text. It should be mentioned that word frequency (which is measured in terms of the numbers of times different words appear in print) correlates highly with word familiarity (which is based on rated familiarity and resembles personal frequency). Gernsbacher (1984) argued that familiarity is more important than frequency, but that has not been shown clearly (Harley 1995).

Low-level factors were of limited importance. Initial fixation times on words were not affected by the place within the word which was fixated. However, readers were much more likely to re-fixate a word if the initial fixation was at either end of the word rather than in the middle. Processing complexities of language were of greatest importance: fixation times were much longer to rare words than to common ones.

In sum, readers spend longer fixating on complex or rare words than on common words, presumably because it takes longer to access the meaning of complex words. In addition, if the initial fixation on a word is not in the middle section, then there is often a second fixation on it in order to work out its meaning.

Word identification

It seems logical to assume that identifying a visually presented word occurs after the letters within the word have been identified. In fact, there is evidence that complete letter identification does not necessarily have to precede word identification. This was demonstrated in the so-called **word superiority effect** (e.g. Reicher 1969). What happens is that a letter string is presented rapidly, and then the participants have to decide which of two letters was presented in a given position within the letter string. Reicher (1969) found a word superiority effect, in that his participants did better on this task when the letter string formed a word than when it did not.

McClelland and Rumelhart (1981) put forward an interactive activation model, which was designed to account for the word superiority effect. The key features of the model are shown in Figure 7.1. It has three levels:

- the feature level, at which features of letters (e.g. diagonal line, curved line) are identified
- the letter level, at which the individual letters of a word are identified
- the word level, at which the word itself is identified

An important assumption of the theory is that there are excitatory and inhibitory processes operating throughout the system. For example, when a given letter in a given position within a word is identified, excitatory processes lead to the activation of all word units containing that letter in that position, with inhibitory processes being directed to all other words. These processes also operate in the opposite direction. Activation of a given word unit leads via excitatory processes to activation of all of its letter units at the letter level and to inhibitory processes to other letter units.

The interactive activation model is based on the assumption that there are bottom-up and top-down processes in letter identification and word recognition. Information at the feature and letter levels affects activation of word units via excitatory and inhibitory processes operating in a bottom-up fashion. In addition, information at the word level affects activation at the letter and feature levels via excitatory and inhibitory processes operating in a top-down fashion.

The word superiority effect is accounted for in terms of top-down processes. Brief presentation of a word (e.g. BELT) produces activation of the appropriate word unit, and this in turn increases the activation of all of its letters. This additional activation coming from the word level facilitates the task of deciding whether, for example, the second letter in the letter string was an E or an I. An alternative non-perceptual explanation is the sophisticated guessing hypothesis. According to this hypothesis, participants use their knowledge of English spelling to enhance performance on word trials. Prinzmetal and Lyon (1996) investigated this hypothesis with an effect resembling the word superiority effect, but found no evidence in its favour.

The interactive activation model has proved very successful, and it is generally accepted that word identification often involves a combination of bottom-up and top-down processes. The success of the model led McClelland and Elman (1986) to make use of similar ideas in their TRACE model of spoken word recognition, which is discussed later in this chapter. However, an important limitation of the interactive activation model is that it was explicitly designed to apply only to four-letter words, and would need additional theoretical assumptions to handle longer words.

Another possible limitation of the model is that it is assumed that word identification is based only on visual information and does not involve phonological information. One way of testing this assumption is to compare identification times for regular words (whose pronunciation corresponds to their spelling) and for irregular words (whose pronunciation does not correspond to their spelling). If word identification depends only on visual information, then irregular words should be identified as easily as regular ones. In fact, Seidenberg *et al.* (1984) found that rare irregular words took longer to name than did rare regular words, suggesting that the

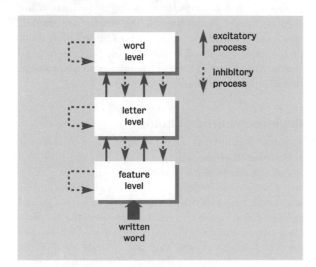

Figure 7.1 The interactive activation model for word identification put forward by McClelland and Rumelhart (1981)

identification of some rare words involves phonological information as well as visual information. However, there was no effect of word regularity on naming times for common words.

Word pronunciation

This section of the chapter is concerned with the processes involved in reading words in the sense of pronouncing them. We usually experience little or no difficulty in pronouncing words, but there is increasing evidence that a number of different processes are involved. For example, consider what is involved in pronouncing the following: 'yacht' and 'vore'. There are various spelling-to-sound correspondence rules (also known as **grapheme-phoneme correspondence rules**) which indicate how sets of letters are normally pronounced in the English language. There is some controversy about the number and nature of these grapheme-phoneme correspondence rules, but it is clear that we cannot use our knowledge of such rules to pronounce 'yacht' correctly. Presumably we know how to pronounce 'yacht' only because we have specific information about that word's pronunciation stored in long-term memory. On the other hand, 'vore' is not an English word, and so its pronunciation cannot be stored in long-term memory. It might be pronounced by making use of grapheme-phoneme correspondence rules, or it might be pronounced by analogy with similar real words (e.g. 'bore', 'more', 'sore').

Dual-route model

What was described in the previous paragraph is essentially the dual-route model of reading or pronunciation. This model, or more complex versions of it, has been endorsed by several theorists including Ellis and Young (1988) and Coltheart *et al.* (1993). According to this model, one of the routes (known as the direct or lexical route) involves the lexicon, which is a mental dictionary containing several different kinds of information about the words we know (e.g. their sounds and spellings) and providing access to their meaning. When we see an irregular word such as 'yacht', information about its pronunciation is obtained from the lexicon. The other route (known as the non-lexical route) involves grapheme-phoneme correspondence rules, and is used to read non-words.

How do we decide which route to use? One possibility is that we try to use the lexical route with every letter string we see, resorting to the non-lexical route only if no relevant information can be found in the lexi-

con. In fact, however, most theorists (e.g. Coltheart *et al.* 1979) assume that both routes are used at the same time. According to this view, the pronunciation of a word is determined by whichever route is the first to complete its processing.

Limitations of the dual-route model

As Harley (1995) pointed out, the version of the dual-route model which has been described so far is clearly too simple. For example, it cannot readily account for the findings obtained by Glushko (1979). He compared the speed with which different types of non-words were pronounced. Some of the non-words (e.g. 'fead') resembled real words having regular grapheme-phoneme correspondence (e.g. 'bead', 'read'), but also resembled irregular words (e.g. 'dead', 'head'). Other non-words (e.g. 'feal') resembled only regular real words (e.g. 'deal', 'real', 'seal', 'weal'). The key finding was that it took the participants significantly longer to pronounce non-words like 'fead' than non-words like 'feal'. The implication is that the pronunciation of non-words is affected by information in the lexicon, which is not meant to happen on the dual-route model.

Another one of Glushko's (1979) findings is also problematic for the dual-route model. He compared the pronunciation speed of regular words which either resembled (or did not resemble) other words which were irregular. For example, 'base' is a regular word but it resembles the irregular word 'vase'. Regular word related to one or more irregular words took longer to pronounce than did regular words related only to other regular words. According to the dual-route model, words are pronounced on the basis of information about their sounds contained in the lexicon. Thus, there is no reason why the regularity or irregularity of other words should influence pronunciation time.

Cognitive neuropsychology

In spite of problems with the dual-route model, the notion that there are different routes between print and sound remains popular. A triple-route model of reading was advocated by Morton and Patterson (1980) and by Ellis and Young (1988). The essentials of such a model are shown in Figure 7.2. As can be seen, the increase from two to three routes has been achieved by dividing the direct or lexical route into two separate routes. One of these routes goes via the semantic system, whereas the other one does not.

Much of the evidence for this triple-route model has come from patients suffering from various **acquired**

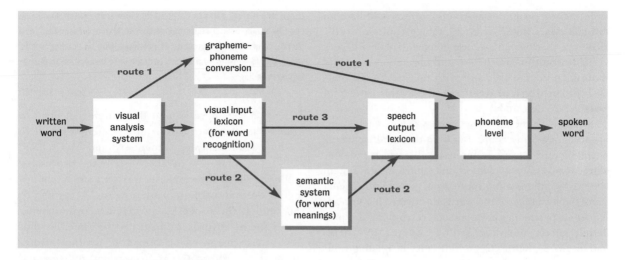

Figure 7.2 The triple-route model of reading
Source: adapted from Ellis and Young (1988)

dyslexias, which involve impairments in reading ability in adults produced by brain damage. The basic logic is that brain damage might impair two of the three routes, leaving only one intact. If some brain-damaged patients use only route 1, others use only route 2, and still others use only route 3, then this would greatly strengthen the triple-route model.

In theory, someone who could use only route 1 would be able to pronounce non-words and words having regular spelling-to-sound correspondences, but would find it very difficult to pronounce irregular words accurately. The closest approximation to that pattern of performance is found in patients with **surface dyslexia** (see case study).

Ψ Case study

Surface dyslexics J.C. and M.P.

Marshall and Newcombe (1973) introduced the term **surface dyslexia** to refer to a condition in which there is a selective impairment in the ability to read irregular words. One of the patients they studied was J.C. He was able to read 67 out of 130 regular words correctly, but he was able to read only 41 out of 130 irregular words. These findings indicate that there was a strong reliance on route 1, but that this was not the only route used. If J.C. had read all words by means of grapheme-phoneme conversion, then he would have mispronounced all irregular words. In fact, his success rate with irregular words was just over 30 per cent.

J.C., in common with other surface dyslexics, could understand all of the words he said correctly, and could indicate what they meant. This indicates that he did not have an impairment of the semantic system.

However, this is not true of all surface dyslexics. Bub *et al.* (1985) studied a surface dyslexic M.P. She resembled J.C., in that she found it much harder to pronounce irregular words than regular ones. She could read only 40 per cent of relatively rare words correctly, although her reading performance improved to 80 per cent on common irregular words. In contrast, her reading performance on regular words was excellent, and was very close to 100 per cent for fairly common words.

M.P. differed from J.C. in that she often could not understand words that she pronounced correctly. M.P. also differed from most surface dyslexics in that she was good at reading non-words. In view of the various differences among surface dyslexics, there is considerable doubt whether the category should be retained. However, what is clear is that a patient such as J.C. provides support for the triple-route model of reading.

In theory, people using route 2 only would have no difficulty in reading or pronouncing familiar words. However, their inability to use grapheme-phoneme conversion would mean they would have great difficulty with unfamiliar words and with non-words. Patients with **phonological dyslexia** display this pattern of reading (see case study).

In theory, someone using route 3 only would resemble someone using route 2 only in that familiar words would be read accurately, but unfamiliar words and non-words would not. In addition, since the semantic system is bypassed, those using route 3 only would not understand the meanings of the words they were able to read. A patient producing performance resembling the predicted pattern was discussed by Coslett (1991). This patient, W.T., had extreme difficulty in reading non-words. However, in spite of a severe semantic impairment, W.T. was good at reading familiar words.

Evaluation of the triple-route model

The triple-route model has proved very successful, especially in its ability to account for the findings from brain-damaged patients. However, it clearly needs to address the problems with the earlier dual-route model highlighted by the findings of Glushko (1979). These problems were summarized by Harley (1995) in the following way:

> there are lexical effects on reading nonwords, which should be read by a non-lexical route insensitive to lexical information, and there are effects of regularity of pronunciation on reading words, which should be read by a direct, lexical route insensitive to phonological recoding.
>
> (Harley 1995: 111)

Some theorists have argued that we do not need to assume that there are two or three different routes to reading. For example, Seidenberg and McClelland (1989) put forward a parallel-distributed processing model in which the emphasis was on a single phonological route in reading printed words. According to this model, the processes involved in pronouncing words and non-words are basically the same. In addition, they proposed a semantic reading route. However, this alternative route was not implemented in their model.

Seidenberg and McClelland (1989) tested their model on a set of 2,897 words. They claimed that regular words, irregular words and non-words were all read well by the model. If that claim is correct, then the more complex triple-route model would be in serious trouble. In fact, however, there is good evidence that the parallel-distributed processing model does not perform as well as claimed. According to Coltheart *et al.* (1993), that model can read only approximately 55 per cent of the non-words on which it has not been trained.

Ψ Case study

Phonological dyslexic A.M.

Phonological dyslexia involves a selective impairment in the ability to read non-words but little or no impairment in reading familiar words. Patterson (1982) studied a phonological dyslexic, A.M. He was a 62-year-old former supervisor from a printing firm. His language abilities were generally good. For example, he had very good comprehension of speech, and experienced only minor difficulties of speech production.

He could usually read out correctly over 90% of familiar content words, but he sometimes made slight errors (e.g. reading applaud as applause). In contrast, he was able to read aloud correctly only 8% of non-words. What generally happened was that he misread a non-word as a real word that looked like it (e.g. 'soof' was 'read' as 'soot'). In addition to his problems with non-words, he was also relatively unsuccessful when trying to read function words (e.g. 'with', 'yet').

The evidence from A.M. provides strong support for the triple-route model. His reading performance suggests that he had little or no ability to make use of grapheme-phoneme conversion, and this is why he was very poor at pronouncing non-words. Grapheme-phoneme conversion is not needed to pronounce familiar words, and so impairment to the system involved in grapheme-phoneme conversion did not affect significantly his ability to pronounce such words.

Coltheart *et al.* (1993) devised their own dual-route cascaded model, which is a computational model based on the approach shown in Figure 7.2. This model was able to read 90 per cent of non-words on which it had not been trained, which is considerably higher than the figure for the Seidenberg-McClelland model. Of particular interest, that figure of 90 per cent is remarkably close to the figure of 91.5 per cent obtained by human participants reading the same non-words.

In sum, it is probable that triple-route models will become more complex in the future. However, there is no doubt that existing dual- and triple-route models are on the right lines. As Coltheart *et al.* (1993) pointed out,

Our ability to deal with linguistic stimuli we have not previously encountered (. . . to read a non-word aloud) can only be explained by postulating that we have learned systems of general linguistic rules and our ability at the same time to deal correctly with exceptions to these rules (. . . to read an exception word aloud) can only be explained by postulating the existence of systems of word-specific lexical representations.

(Colheart *et al.* 1993: 606)

ψ Section summary

There are various techniques for studying reading. Recording eye movements is the most useful technique, because it is unobtrusive and provides a considerable amount of information. Fixation times are longer for words whose meaning is hard to assess. According to the dual-route model, reading or pronouncing words can involve either a direct lexical route, or it can involve an indirect route based on grapheme-phoneme correspondence rules. Some theorists favour a triple-route model, in which the direct or lexical route is divided into two separate routes. Evidence supporting this model has been obtained from surface dyslexics and from phonological dyslexics. Seidenberg and McClelland have proposed a rival parallel-distributed model of reading, but it has not been shown to be more adequate than the triple-route model.

1 What has been learned about reading from eye-movement data?
2 Discuss the possible ways in which written words are read or pronounced.

☐ Speech perception

The basic sounds of a language are known as phonemes, with the number and nature of phonemes varying from one language to another. There are about 46 phonemes in English, and in combination they generate all of the 500,000 words in the English language. So far as the production of phonemes is concerned, it is useful to distinguish between consonants and vowels. The pronunciation of consonants differs in terms of the following three factors:

- manner of articulation: there is either a partial or a total blockage of the airflow (e.g. the first consonant in 'fix' involves partial blockage; the second consonant in 'hat' involves total blockage)
- place of articulation: this is the place within the vocal tract at which the airflow is blocked; it can vary between the lips at one extreme and the glottis, which is part of the larynx; /b/ is articulated at the lips, whereas /h/ is articulated at the glottis
- voicing: the vocal chords either vibrate at the same time as the blockage of the airflow (e.g. /b/ in 'ban'), or they vibrate subsequently (e.g. /p/ in 'pan')

Somewhat different factors are involved in the pronunciation of vowels, because they do not involve any disruption of the airflow. The pronunciation of vowels varies in terms of placement in the mouth, and whether the tongue position is high, middle or low.

Listeners to speech exhibit what is known as categorical perception, meaning that slightly different physical sounds will nevertheless be perceived as the same phoneme. Evidence of categorical perception was reported by Liberman *et al.* (1957). They presented a series of 14 consonant sounds which were identified as b, d or g. There seemed to be clear phoneme boundaries: small changes in the physical stimulus had little or no effect on identification if they occurred within the confines of a phoneme boundary, but they had large effects if they crossed a phoneme boundary.

Complexities of speech perception

Accurate speech perception is much more of an achievement than might be thought. Some notion of its complexity can be gained by considering the evidence gained from spectrographs. What happens with a spectrograph is that sound enters through a microphone, is converted into an electrical signal, and this signal is then fed to a bank of filters. What emerges from the spectrograph is a **spectrogram**, which is a visible record of sound frequencies over time. The pattern of sounds does not look nearly as neat and tidy as our normal perception of speech would suggest.

One of the major difficulties with speech perception is known as the **segmentation problem**. It stems from the fact that speech usually consists of a relatively continuous stream of sound, and we have to decide how to divide it up into a series of words. It may seem hard to believe that there are very few periods of silence between spoken words. However, if you have listened to someone speaking a foreign language with which you have some familiarity, you may well have noticed that there were very few gaps in the stream of sound.

Another major difficulty with speech perception is the **non-invariance problem**. This refers to the fact that the sound pattern for any given phoneme varies as a function of the phonemes preceding and following it. The non-invariance problem is greater for consonants than for vowels, because the sound pattern for consonants is often affected by the characteristics of the following vowel. Why does the invariance problem exist? Speech is produced at up to about ten phonemes per second (Liberman *et al.* 1967); as a result more than one sound needs to be articulated at the same time. This is known as co-articulation, and it is responsible for much of the variability in the production of phonemes.

One of the ways in which we deal with the problems of segmentation and non-invariance is by making use of contextual information. Pollack and Pickett (1964) found that only 47 per cent of tape-recorded words could be identified when they were presented on their own. However, performance was much better when longer segments of speech were played, presumably because this allowed the participants to make use of the semantic and syntactic context to assist in speech perception.

The complexities of speech perception as revealed by spectrograms were expressed rather neatly in an analogy by Hockett (1955):

Imagine a row of Easter eggs carried along a moving belt; the eggs are of various sizes, and variously coloured, but not boiled. At a certain point, the belt carries the row of eggs between the two rollers of a wringer, which quite effectively smash them and rub them more or less into each other. The flow of eggs before the wringer represents the series of impulses from the phoneme source; the mess that emerges from the wringer represents the output of the speech transmitter. At a subsequent point, we have an inspector whose task it is to examine the passing mess and decide, on the basis of the broken and unbroken yolks, the vari-ously spread-out albumen, and the variously coloured bits of shell, the nature of the flow of eggs which previously arrived at the wringer.

(Hockett 1955: 210)

Word identification

It has already been mentioned that we use sentence context to assist in the task of identifying spoken words. One of the best known studies on the effects of context was reported by Warren and Warren (1970). They presented sentences with a small part deleted and replaced by a meaningless sound. The actual sentences used are given below, with the asterisk indicating the point at which the meaningless sound was inserted:

(1) It was found that the *eel was on the axle
(2) It was found that the *eel was on the shoe
(3) It was found that the *eel was on the table
(4) It was found that the *eel was on the orange

The participants who listened to sentence (1) heard *eel as 'wheel', whereas those who listened to the other sentences heard exactly the same sound as 'heel', 'meal' and 'peel', respectively. They called this phenomenon the **phonemic restoration effect**. Perhaps surprisingly, none of the participants noticed that there was anything unusual about what they had heard. This is a very powerful context effect, made all the more impressive by the fact that the key context (the last word in the sentence) was presented some time after the ambiguous sound. Subsequent research by Samuel (1981) indicated that context does not have a direct influence on perceptual processing in the phonemic restoration effect; rather, it provides additional information which is taken into account when deciding what word was represented by the ambiguous sound.

People do not only rely on auditory information when listening to someone who is talking to them. Cotton (1935) obtained evidence that we also make use of visual information. The participants in his study listened to speech that was made harder to understand by the addition of a buzzing sound. When the participants could see the speaker's lips, they were able to understand what he was saying. When the speaker was not visible, however, they found that what he was saying was unintelligible.

A striking demonstration of the importance of visual information in speech perception was provided by McGurk and MacDonald (1976). They prepared a video-tape in which the participants saw someone saying 'ba' repeatedly, but what they heard on the sound track was 'ga' being said repeatedly in synchrony with the lip movements. The participants claimed that what they heard was neither 'ba' nor 'ga'. They reported hearing 'da', which is what is obtained by combining the visual and auditory information.

Theories of speech perception

Historically, one of the most important theories of speech perception was put forward by Liberman *et al.* (1967). They argued in their motor theory of speech perception that listeners tend to imitate the articulatory movements of the speaker, and by so doing produce a motor signal. However, this may be done in a covert way, and need not involve actual articulatory movements. The basic rationale for this theory was the notion that the motor signal produced by the listener is more reliable and consistent than the speech signal provided by the speaker. As a result, speech perception is more accurate when listeners rely on their own motor signal than when they make use only of the speech signal itself.

There are several severe problems with the motor theory, and it is no longer regarded as adequate. For example, the motor signal actually seems to be as variable and inconsistent as the speech signal (MacNeilage 1972), so that it is unlikely that speech perception is based on the information contained in the motor signal. In addition, as M.W. Eysenck and Keane (1995) pointed out, simultaneous translators are able to listen to speech in one language while at the same time using their speech musculature to talk fluently in another language. This would seem to be difficult or impossible on the motor theory of speech perception. It remains possible that the motor signal sometimes facilitates speech perception, but it does not play the central role assumed by Liberman *et al.* (1967).

Cohort theory

Marslen-Wilson and Tyler (1980) put forward the cohort theory of speech perception, which was designed to account for the perception of individual words. According to their theory, word perception involves a mixture of bottom-up and top-down processes. When the first part of a word is heard, all of those words which the listener knows starting with that sound sequence are activated in long-term memory. This set of words is called the 'word-initial cohort'. After that, members of this cohort are gradually eliminated for var-

ious reasons. They may fail to match later parts of the sound sequence (bottom-up processing) or they may fail to match the semantic or other context (top-down processing). At some point, only one word remains in the cohort, and that is the word the listener hears.

Marslen-Wilson and Tyler (1980) provided some experimental support for their theory. Their participants listened to sentences and were instructed to detect target words as rapidly as possible. The sentences ranged from normal to random sentences consisting of a series of unrelated words, and in one condition the targets were identical to a given word. It was predicted from the theory that target detection would be faster with the normal sentences than with the random sentences, because the contextual information contained in normal sentences should allow top-down processes to eliminate words from the word-initial cohort. The findings were in line with this prediction. In addition, the participants began to respond to the identical targets approximately 200 milliseconds after the onset of the target when they were presented in normal sentences. Since the spoken duration of the target words averaged out at 369 milliseconds, this confirms the assumption that contextual information is used at an early stage of processing.

The original version of cohort theory attached too much importance to the first phoneme of the word. For example, it predicts that word perception should not occur if the initial phoneme is ambiguous, but Connine *et al.* (1993) found that word recognition was reasonably good under those circumstances. Marslen-Wilson (1990) proposed a modified version of cohort theory, which had the advantage of being more flexible than the original version. According to the modified version, the word-initial cohort contains words having similar initial phonemes to the presented word, as well as those having the same initial phoneme. This modified version can accommodate findings such as those of Connine *et al.* (1993).

TRACE model

McClelland and Elman (1986) proposed a TRACE model of speech perception. This model is similar to cohort theory in that it emphasizes the notion that bottom-up and top-down processes interact in word recognition, but it differs in most other respects. According to the TRACE model, there are processing units or nodes at three different levels: features (e.g. voicing, place of articulation), phonemes, and words. These three levels are strongly interconnected. When a word is presented, this causes activation within the system. The word which is recognized is the one having the highest level of activation. The level of activation is determined by bottom-up activation proceeding upwards from the feature level and by top-down activation proceeding downwards from the word level.

Some of the studies already discussed (such as those of Warren and Warren 1970 and by Marslen-Wilson and Tyler 1980) provide support for the notion of top-down processing. More specific tests of the model were carried out by Elman and McClelland (1988). The TRACE model predicts that the activation of phoneme nodes or units by top-down processes from the word level is comparable to their activation by bottom-up processes from the feature level, and that is precisely what they found.

Trace model: top-down processing

The TRACE model is generally regarded as providing a good account of some of the processes involved in speech perception. However, as M.W. Eysenck and Keane (1995) pointed out, it has the disadvantage of exaggerating the importance of top-down processes. Top-down processes are often important when the quality of the speech sounds is poor (e.g. in the study by Warren and Warren 1970), but they tend to be less important when the sound quality is good. For example, Frauenfelder *et al.* (1990) gave their participants the task of detecting the occurrence of specific phonemes. On some trials, they presented a non-word that was very similar to an actual word, for example, 'vocabutaire' instead of 'vocabulaire'. According to the TRACE model, top-down effects from the word 'vocabulaire' should have made it hard to detect the 't' in the presented stimulus. In fact, this did not happen, indicating that top-down processes had no effect on phonemic processing.

ψ Section summary

All spoken words consist of phonemes, of which there are about 46 in the English language. Speech perception is a complex achievement, in part because of the segmentation and non-invariance problems. Word identification depends on a mixture of bottom-up and top-down processes (e.g. sentence context). Most people also make some use of lip-reading. The motor theory of speech perception is based on the

Box continued

---

assumption that listeners mimic the speaker's articulatory movements. The motor signal is more variable than was assumed by advocates of the motor theory, and the theory cannot readily account for simultaneous translation. According to the cohort theory, word identification involves using information from the presented word and from the context to reduce an initial set of possible words down to a single word. According to the TRACE model, there are three interconnected levels: feature, phoneme and word. The word which is recognized is the one having the highest level of activation.

1 What are some of the reasons why speech perception is a complex achievement?
2 Discuss theories of speech perception.

❑ Semantic categories

In this section, we will be concerned with the study of meaning or semantics. One of the key issues is to understand how the meanings of words are represented. Most words have a central core of meaning. However, the precise aspects of a word's meaning which are accessed depend on the sentence context in which it is presented. These issues are discussed below.

Several theorists have focused on the ways in which words are organized in semantic memory. For example, Collins and Quillian (1969) argued that words are represented within a semantic network. This theory and other views are discussed in Chapter 6.

Prototypes

Wittgenstein (1958) pointed out that there are only a few (or no) features which are common to all members of any given category. He illustrated his point with reference to the category of 'games':

What is common to them all . . . if you look at them you will not see something that is common to *all*, but similarities, relationships, and a whole series of them at that. . . . Look for example at board-games, with the multifarious relationships. Now pass to card-games; here you will find many correspondences with the first group, but many common features drop out, and others appear. When we pass next to ball-games, much that is common is retained, but much is lost. . . . Is there always winning and losing, or competition between players? Think of patience. In ball-games there is winning and losing; but when a child throws his ball at the wall and catches it again, this feature has disappeared.

(Wittgenstein 1958: 31–2)

The essence of Wittgenstein's (1958) position was that the members of a category share 'family resemblances.' In other words, different members of a category will always have some features in common, but no features will be common to all members. Evidence supporting Wittgenstein was reported by Rosch and Mervis (1975). They chose twenty members from each of six categories (vehicles, fruit, furniture, clothing, weapons, vegetables) and instructed their participants to list the features or attributes of each category member. For none of the six categories was there more than a single feature that was common to all of the twenty members of that category.

According to Rosch (1978), each category is organized around a **prototype**. A prototype is a set of characteristic features, with some features being more important or relevant than others. An object is regarded as being a member of a category if there is a sufficiently good match between its features and those of the category prototype.

One of the predictions that flows from prototype theory is that some members of a category should be

Plate 7.2 Ludwig Wittgenstein (1889–1951) posited a close, formal relationship between language, thought and the world. His work on semantic categories indicated that members of a category will always have features in common but no features will be common to all members.

'better' members than others. More specifically, the best members of a category are those sharing most features with the prototype, whereas the worst members share relatively few features with the prototype. For example, when we consider the bird category, it seems reasonable to argue that a robin is a better member of that category than is a chicken. Rosch and Mervis (1975) explored this issue by asking their participants to rate the typicality of various category members. The most typical members of a category were those sharing the most features with other members of the category, combined with sharing the fewest features with members of other categories.

Additional support for the notion that some members are better than others was reported by Rips et al. (1973). They asked their participants to decide whether sentences such as 'A robin is a bird' were true. Verification times were faster for more typical or representative category members than for relatively atypical ones.

According to prototype theory, there are often no features which are possessed by all members of a category. In other words, there are no defining features but rather a number of characteristic features. It follows that the boundaries of a category will tend to be rather imprecise. As a consequence, it is hard to tell whether an object possessing only a fraction of the characteristic features of a category should be regarded as a member of that category. Supporting evidence was reported by McCloskey and Glucksberg (1978). They found that 53 per cent of people thought that a 'stroke' is a disease, whereas 47 per cent did not. Precisely the same percentages were obtained when the same people were asked whether a 'pumpkin' is a fruit. Further evidence of the imprecise nature of category boundaries was obtained one month later. Over one-third of the participants had changed their minds about a stroke being a disease, and almost one-third had changed their minds about a pumpkin being a fruit.

Basic level categories

Most of the objects we encounter in our everyday lives can be categorized at three different levels. For example, the same creature on a lead can be described as a 'labrador', a 'dog' or a 'four-footed animal'. We may use all of these categories sometimes. However, most of the time we avoid the most specific category (e.g. labrador) and the most general one (e.g. four-footed animal), preferring the category in the middle (e.g. dog). Presumably this intermediate-level category (often referred to as the **basic level category**) is used more often than the other levels because it is generally of most value for perception, thought and action.

Rosch *et al.* (1976) investigated the three levels of categorization we have described. They asked their participants to list all the features that applied to objects at each level. Very few features were listed for the most general categories (e.g. four-footed animal), presumably because these categories tended to be abstract. Many more features were listed at the basic level (e.g. dog) and at the most specific level (e.g. labrador). However, at the lowest level, very similar features were listed for different members of the same basic level category (e.g. labrador, poodle, dachshund). Rosch *et al.* (1976) concluded that the basic level categories are of most value because they offer the best combination of informativeness and economy. General categories lack informativeness, whereas specific categories lack economy. Another way of expressing the point is to argue that the basic level of categorization provides maximal within-category similarity relative to between-category similarity.

There is other evidence supporting the notion that the basic level of categorization is more important than the other levels. Rosch *et al.* (1976) also found that it is the level of categorization used most often by adults when asked to describe objects. In addition, Jolicoeur *et al.* (1984) found that objects can be named faster at the basic level than at the other levels.

Evaluation of prototype theory

As Harley (1995: 195) pointed out, 'the prototype is now generally considered to be the best approach to the representation of meaning that we have'. The notion that categories can be thought of as prototypes with a large number of characteristic features has proved valuable, as has the associated view that categories or concepts are fuzzy rather than well defined. Finally, there is strong evidence that we use the basic level of categorization much more often than more general or specific levels.

On the negative side, it is not always the case that the basic level of categorization is preferred to the other levels. People possessing special expertise (e.g. birdwatchers) have almost as much knowledge at the most specific level as they do at the basic level (Tanaka and Taylor 1991). Thus, basic level categories may be of more use to those lacking specialized knowledge than to experts.

Another limitation of prototype theory was discovered by Hampton (1981) in a study of abstract categories. Some abstract categories (e.g. 'a science', 'a work of art') seemed to have prototypes in the same way as concrete categories. However, other abstract categories (e.g. 'a belief', 'a rule') did not have prototypes. There

are almost limitless numbers of possible beliefs and rules, and this may help to explain why these categories lack the structure of concrete categories.

Cognitive neuropsychology

One of the main issues in the area of semantics is that of deciding whether or not there is a single semantic system. For example, Paivio (1971) proposed a dual-code theory (see Chapter 6). According to this theory, there are two separate but interconnected semantic systems. There is a verbal system which processes linguistic information, and there is a non-verbal system which is involved in perceptual and imaginal processing. This theory can be tested by cognitive neuropsychologists looking for patients who appear to have impairments to only one of these two systems.

Controversial evidence apparently supporting Paivio's general theoretical approach is based on **optic aphasia**. This is a condition in which patients cannot name objects presented visually, but are able to name them when they have been handled. However, patients know what visually presented objects are in the sense that they can gesture their use. Beauvois (1982) studied the optic aphasic J.F., and argued that his visual semantic system had become disconnected from his verbal semantic system. However, Riddoch and Humphreys (1987) came to a rather different conclusion from their study of another optic aphasic patient. According to them, there is only one semantic system, and optic aphasics have difficulty in gaining access to that system through visual processing.

Other evidence favouring the notion of two semantic systems was reported by Bub *et al.* (1988). Their patient, M.P., had extremely poor comprehension of material presented verbally, but reasonable comprehension of material presented in the form of pictures.

There are other ways in which the semantic system might be divided up. Various theorists have argued that there are separate animate and inanimate object categories within the semantic system for distinguishing between living creatures and lifeless objects. For example, a patient, J.B.R., had much better naming and comprehension performance for inanimate objects than for living things (Warrington and Shallice 1984). While this evidence is consistent with the notion that there are separate animate and inanimate categories, there are other possibilities. For example, we tend to distinguish among living things in terms of their perceptual characteristics or physical properties, whereas we distinguish among inanimate objects in terms of their functions or uses. It is of interest to note that J.B.R. had difficulty in naming inanimate objects (e.g. precious stones, musical instruments) which are distinguished mainly on the basis of their perceptual characteristics.

Further support for the distinction between animate and inanimate categories was provided by Warrington and McCarthy (1983, 1987). They studied patients who exhibited better performance with living things than with inanimate objects. However, there were some complexities in the data. For example, one patient (Y.O.T.) was good at identifying large inanimate objects, and seemed to have a problem mainly with small objects.

The fact that some patients perform better on inanimate objects than on living things (e.g. J.B.R.), whereas others show the opposite pattern, provides suggestive evidence that the organization of the semantic system is based in part on the animate–inanimate distinction. However, it has proved hard to avoid methodological problems in this area of research. For example, Funnell and Sheridan (1992) studied a patient, S.L., who seemed to have greater difficulties with naming pictures for living than for non-living things. However, this difference was no longer present when stimulus familiarity was controlled.

In sum, it is very important to try to establish the organization of the semantic system. However, progress so far has been relatively slow. As we have seen, many of the findings are open to a number of different interpretations. In spite of the problems, psychologists will almost certainly use the cognitive neuropsychological approach more and more in the attempt to unravel the mysteries of the semantic system.

Context effects

As was mentioned earlier, the precise meaning that is assigned to a word depends on the context in which it is presented. Halff et al. (1976) provided a simple demonstration of such context effects. They constructed several sentences containing the word 'red'. These sentences were presented two at a time to the participants, who had to decide whether the red object in one sentence was definitely redder than the red object in the other sentence. The main finding was that the degree of redness associated with the word 'red' varied considerably from sentence to sentence. In addition, the word 'red' was thought to cover a wider range of redness in some sentences (e.g. 'The boy with red hair stood out in the crowd') than in others (e.g. 'As the sun set the sky turned red').

Barclay et al. (1974) obtained evidence that sentence context can determine which features of a word's meaning are processed. They presented sentences such as 'The student picked up the ink' or 'The student spilled the ink'. These sentences were followed by phrases as cues to prompt recall of the object nouns. 'Something in a bottle' was a better cue than 'Something that can be messy' for the former sentence, whereas the opposite was the case for the latter sentence. If we assume that the effectiveness of a phrase cue depends upon how the to-be-remembered information was comprehended, then these findings indicate that sentence context influences which semantic features of a word are processed during comprehension. However, it is possible that the findings of Barclay et al. (1974) depended on processes occurring at retrieval rather than during comprehension.

Some of the clearest evidence that the meaning assigned to a word can be influenced by context comes from studies on ambiguous words. Homographs and homophones are examples of ambiguous words. Homographs (e.g. bank, socks) are words which have the same spelling but separate meanings. Homophones are words of different meanings which have the same pronunciation but different spellings (e.g. pain and pane; pair, pear and pare), so that they are ambiguous only when presented auditorily.

What processes are involved in selecting the appropriate meaning of a homograph or homophone? Harley (1995) argued that there are three main theoretical answers to that question:

- according to the context-guided single reading lexical access model, the context somehow restricts processing so that only the appropriate meaning is accessed
- according to the ordered access model, the most common meaning of the word is accessed and related to the sentence context, if that meaning is not appropriate, then the next most common meaning is accessed and checked against the context, and so on
- according to the multiple access model, all of the meanings of an ambiguous word are activated when it is presented, and the appropriate meaning is selected on the basis of contextual information

The relevant experimental findings are rather inconsistent (see Simpson 1994 for a review) and only a few of the more important findings will be discussed here. Moss and Marslen-Wilson (1993) presented sentences auditorily. They obtained evidence that all meanings of ambiguous words were accessed regardless of the sentence, which is consistent with the multiple access model. They also investigated access to particular semantic properties of words. For example, lemons possess the properties of sourness and edibility, and which property is more relevant depends on the sentence context. Moss and Marslen-Wilson (1993) found that mainly relevant semantic properties seemed to be accessed, which is consistent with the context-guided single reading lexical access model.

The ways in which meaning is accessed for homographs during reading has been studied by recording eye movements (see Simpson 1994 for a review). Somewhat different findings have been obtained from balanced homographs (in which the meanings are equally frequent) than from unbalanced homographs (in which one meaning is much more common than any other). When the disambiguating context comes after the homograph, then readers spend longer looking at balanced homographs than unbalanced ones, which are fixated only for as long as ordinary words. The implication is that both meanings of balanced homographs are accessed for balanced homographs, but only the dominant meaning for unbalanced homographs. These findings provide only partial support for the multiple access and the context-guiding single reading lexical access models.

When the disambiguating context comes before the homograph, there is no difference in fixation time between balanced and unbalanced homographs provided that the dominant meaning is relevant. If the less frequent meaning is relevant, then the fixation time is longer for unbalanced homographs. These findings suggest that the dominant meaning of unbalanced homographs is accessed regardless of the preceding context, which is consistent with the ordered access model.

In sum, there is some support for all three of the theoretical models we have been considering. However, there is probably rather more support for the multiple access model than the others. It is clear that all the meanings of homographs and homophones are often accessed, but this is more likely to happen with balanced than unbalanced homographs and homophones, and when the disambiguating context follows the ambiguous word.

Ψ Section summary

According to Rosch (1978) each category is organized around a prototype or set of characteristic features, some of which are more important than

Box continued

---

others. According to prototype theory, the boundaries of most categories are rather imprecise. One problem for prototype theory is that some abstract categories do not seem to have prototypes. Categories at the intermediate or basic level are generally of most value for perception, thought and action. Evidence from brain-damaged patients suggests that there may be an important distinction between animate and inanimate categories. The precise meaning given to a word is often affected by the surrounding sentence context.

1 Describe and evaluate prototype theory.
2 Discuss some of the ways in which a word's meaning is affected by sentence context.

Parsing and syntax

Most of our discussion of language processing has focused on individual words. However, we nearly always encounter language in the form of complete sentences or sets of sentences. Therefore, it is important to consider the processes required to understand sentences. Some of the processes involve parsing, which is working out the syntactic or grammatical structure of sentences. Parsing involves taking account of word order and other information to work out the subject and object of each sentence, as well as the action relating subject and object. It also involves assigning each word in the sentence to its appropriate grammatical category (e.g. noun, verb, adjective, adverb).

The processes involved in parsing are probably rather similar whether a sentence is read or spoken. However, speakers sometimes provide useful cues to syntactic structure (known as **prosodic cues**) based on variations in their pitch, intonation, stress and timing. For example, suppose someone says, 'The old men and women walked to the community centre.' If this ambiguous sentence is intended to imply that the women were not old, then the spoken duration of the word 'men' will tend to be long, and the stressed syllable in the word 'women' will typically have a steep rise in pitch contour. Both of these features will usually be missing if the speaker wants to imply that the women were old.

It has often been suggested in the research literature that speakers generally produce sufficient prosodic cues to resolve syntactic ambiguities. However, as Allbritton *et al.* (1996) pointed out, most of the research has made use of trained speakers. They found that most untrained speakers did not produce disambiguating prosodic cues when reading ambiguous sentences. Thus, these cues may be less available to listeners than has been assumed in the past.

One of the key issues concerns the relationship between syntactic processing and semantic processing. Various different theoretical positions have been advanced (see Mitchell 1994 for a review). One view is that syntactic processing normally occurs before any semantic processing. Another view is that semantic processing occurs before syntactic processing, with the processing of meaning influencing syntactic processing. Another possibility is that syntactic and semantic processing occur independently of each other. The evidence relevant to these various theoretical views is discussed in the next section.

Syntactic ambiguity

Much of the research on parsing has made use of ambiguous sentences known as garden-path sentences. These are sentences which tend to be misinterpreted initially, but which are then reinterpreted in the light of subsequent evidence. For example, consider the sentence, 'The old man the boats.' It is natural to interpret 'man' as being a noun, but the rest of the sentence indicates that it is being used as a verb in that sentence.

Frazier and Rayner (1982) were theorists who argued that the *initial* syntactic structure which readers or listeners construct for a sentence is not influenced by the meaning of that sentence. However, initial syntactic decisions can be overridden by semantic factors According to their garden-path model, there are two basic general principles which guide the construction of the initial syntactic structure. First, there is the principle of minimal attachment, which involves favouring the simplest syntactic structure. Second, there is the principle of late closure, which involves attaching new words to the current phrase or clause if this is possible.

The principle of late closure can be illustrated by an example provided by Rayner and Pollatsek (1989). Suppose that someone reads or hears the sentence, 'Since Jay always jogs a mile seems like a short distance.' According to the principle of late closure, people should initially attach the words 'a mile' to the preceding phrase, and this mistaken syntactic processing then has to be changed. In contrast, the principle of late closure leads to a correct syntactic structure for a slightly different sentence such as 'Since Jay always jogs a mile this seems like a short distance to him.'

According to the garden-path model, readers will persist with a single grammatical structure until there is evidence that it is wrong. Frazier and Rayner (1982) used eye-movement data to test this prediction, arguing that readers should have long eye fixations at the point where the favoured grammatical structure proves inadequate. In the sentence 'Since Jay always jogs a mile seems like a short distance', this occurs at the word 'seems'. As predicted, most readers had very long fixations on the word 'seems', presumably because they were producing an alternative grammatical or syntactic structure for the sentence.

One of the major assumptions of the garden-path model is that meaning plays no role in the initial construction of a syntactic structure for a sentence. This assumption may sound implausible, but evidence for it was reported by Rayner *et al.* (1983). They presented their participants with sentences such as 'The performer sent the flowers was very pleased with herself' and 'The florist sent the flowers was very pleased with herself.' They found that the participants took the same length of time to read both sentences. However, if meaning were used to work out the grammatical structure, then the former sentence should have been easier to read than the latter sentence. The reason for that is that it seems more likely that a performer would be sent flowers than that a florist would.

Various theorists (e.g. Crain and Steedman 1985; Taraban and McClelland 1988) have opposed the garden-path model, claiming that semantic factors normally influence decisions about syntactic structure. Crain and Steedman (1985) used pairs of sentences which had the same syntactic structure but differed in meaning. For example, one pair of sentences consisted of 'The teachers taught by the Berlitz method passed the test' and 'The children taught by the Berlitz method passed the test.' Many more participants judged the former than the latter sentence to be ungrammatical. These findings suggest that the processes involved in assigning a grammatical structure to a sentence are influenced by the meanings of the words in that sentence.

Taraban and McClelland (1988) proposed a content-guided processing theory, according to which meaning helps to determine the construction of grammatical structure. The meaning of the early part of a sentence sets up certain expectations about the rest of the sentence, and these expectations influence the assignment of grammatical structure. They tested their theory against the garden-path model of Frazier and Rayner (1982). Taraban and McClelland (1988) measured the processing time on the final word of sentences such as 'The reporter exposed corruption in the government' and 'The reporter exposed corruption in the article.' They argued that the grammatical structure of the former sentence is more consistent with the readers' expectations than is the grammatical structure of the latter sentence, and so its final word should be processed more rapidly. In contrast, Frazier and Rayner (1982) would predict precisely the opposite, because only the grammatical structure of the latter sentence is in agreement with the principle of minimal attachment. The findings supported the content-guided processing theory, thus demonstrating that meaning can be more important than grammatical principles such as that of minimal attachment.

Syntax and meaning

The evidence indicates that readers and listeners typically construct only one initial syntactic structure for a sentence. As Mitchell (1994) pointed out, this happens even with ambiguous sentences for which

the parser has a tendency to make structural commitments some-what prematurely ... there seems to be an unevenness of support for the various potential readings of any ambiguous structure, and this bias often appears to manifest itself well in advance of the appearance of any material that would licence a decision one way or the other.

(Mitchell 1994: 388)

The key issue is whether meaning influences the construction of this initial syntactic structure. The evidence appears somewhat inconsistent. However, it is generally the case that meaning has little effect when one particular grammatical structure is strongly implied by a sentence. In contrast, meaning can have a substantial effect when no such strong implication is present.

Ψ Section summary

Speakers often provide useful cues to syntactic structure in the form of intonation, pitch, stress and timing. Readers and listeners typically construct only one initial syntactic structure for a sentence. Meaning is most likely to influence the construction of this initial syntactic structure of a sentence when no particular grammatical structure is strongly implied.

1 Discuss the relationship between the syntactic and semantic processing of sentences.

❏ Inference drawing

There is general agreement that the process of drawing inferences or filling in gaps in spoken or written language is of major importance in language comprehension. Indeed, Schank (1976: 168) argued that the drawing of inferences is 'the core of the understanding process'. Everyday evidence of the importance of inferences can be obtained if you overhear a conversation between two friends. As a result of their shared experiences and knowledge, they will often not feel the need to spell things out in detail. Since you do not have the same experiences and knowledge, it may be difficult for you to make the appropriate inferences.

As Harley (1995) pointed out, there are three major kinds of inferences:

- logical inferences: these are inferences which depend solely on the meanings of words; for example, the sentence 'The librarian is a spinster' permits the logical inference that the librarian is female.
- bridging inferences: these are used to relate new information to previous information; for example, we can make sense of the two sentences, 'It was Fred's birthday. A fishing rod was his best present', by assuming that the fishing rod was a birthday present.
- elaborative inferences: these involve adding to the text by making use of our knowledge of the world; for example, from the sentence, 'The Queen was concerned about her children', we might draw the inference that it was their broken marriages and the associated publicity that concerned her.

Much of the evidence indicates not only that inferences are drawn, but also that people often mistakenly believe that the inference was actually presented to them. Bransford *et al.* (1972) presented their participants with sentences such as, 'Three turtles rested on a floating log, and a fish swam beneath them.' This sentence permits the inference that the fish swam beneath the log. On a subsequent recognition memory test, the participants were as confident that they had heard the inferences as the sentences that were presented. It is unclear in this study whether the inferences were drawn at the time of presentation or during the memory test.

O'Brien *et al.* (1988) studied inference drawing by presenting their participants with the following passage:

All the mugger wanted was to steal the woman's money. But when she screamed, he assaulted her with his weapon in an attempt to quiet her. He looked to see if anyone had seen him. He threw the knife into the bushes, took her money, and ran away.

O'Brien *et al*. (1988) argued that the inference that the weapon referred to in the second sentence was a knife might have been made immediately, or it might have been made only after coming upon the word 'knife' in the last sentence. The participants took a long time to read the last sentence, suggesting that the inference that the weapon was a knife was made while the last sentence was being read.

O'Brien *et al*. (1988) also used another condition in which the second sentence was reworded so as to make it clearer that the weapon was a knife: 'But when she screamed, he stabbed her with his weapon in an attempt to quiet her.' In this condition, the last sentence was read more rapidly, suggesting that the inference that the weapon was a knife had been made earlier on.

Inference drawing in conversations

Inference drawing is very important when we read a text, but it may be even more important when we are listening to someone with whom we are having a conversation. For example, we often draw inferences about the speaker's motives and about his or her personality as well as the standard logical, bridging and elaborative inferences already discussed. There is often a distinction between the literal meaning of an utterance and its intended meaning. For example, the sentence, 'Can you pass the salt?', is asking at the literal level whether the listener has the ability to pass the salt, but its intended meaning is a request for the salt to be passed. According to Gibbs (1986), over 90 per cent of requests in English are expressed in this kind of indirect way.

Searle (1979) argued that listeners work out the literal meaning first. If that meaning seems inappropriate in the context, then the intended meaning is calculated. Keysar (1989) favoured an alternative theoretical posi-

tion, according to which listeners work out the intended meaning at the same time as, or instead of, the literal meaning. The fact that the intended meaning is understood at least as rapidly as the literal meaning (Taylor and Taylor 1990) suggests that Keysar's (1989) one-stage model is preferable to Searle's (1979) two-stage model.

Theories of inference

There has been a theoretical controversy as to the frequency with which inferences are drawn. According to the constructionist theory advocated by Bransford *et al*. (1972) and others, the comprehension process typically involves drawing numerous elaborative inferences in order to achieve a full understanding of the events described in a text. In contrast, McKoon and Ratcliff (1992: 440) put forward the minimalist hypothesis: 'In the absence of specific, goal-directed strategic processes, inferences of only two kinds are constructed: those that establish locally coherent representations of the parts of a text that are processed concurrently and those that rely on information that is quickly and easily available'.

The key assumption put forward by McKoon and Ratcliff (1992) was that inferences are drawn mainly when they need to be to achieve the reader's goals. In contrast, it is assumed within constructionist theories that inferences are drawn whenever they will increase understanding. A study by Dosher and Corbett (1982) seems to provide support for the minimalist hypothesis rather than for the constructionist theory. Their participants were presented with sentences permitting instrumental inferences; for example, 'spoon' is the instrumental inference from the sentence 'Mary stirred her coffee.' The participants did not seem to make instrumental inferences unless they were specifically instructed to guess what the instrument was in each sentence.

 Research update

Search-after-meaning theory

Graesser *et al*. (1994) proposed a theory that is to some extent a compromise between the constructionist and minimalist approaches. According to their search-after-meaning theory, there are three factors which determine whether or not specific inferences are drawn:

- inferences which relate to the reader's goals tend to be drawn
- inferences which are needed to construct a coherent meaning of the text tend to be drawn
- inferences which allow the reader to explain the actions and events contained in the text tend to be drawn.

Box continued

Graesser *et al.* (1994) gave an example of the way in which the reader's goals influence the number of inferences drawn. If someone is engaged in proofreading, and so is not interested in extracting full meaning from a text, then few or no inferences will be drawn. In contrast, someone who is reading a murder mystery is likely to draw numerous inferences about the motives of the various characters.

Graesser *et al.* (1994) considered the predictions of the constructionist, search-after-meaning and minimalist theories for nine types of inferences. As can be seen in Figure 7.3, they argued that the constructionist approach predicts that all nine types of inferences will normally be drawn, the search-after-meaning theory that six will be drawn, and the minimalist theory that three will be drawn. In fact, the evidence indicates that five or six types of inferences are normally drawn. This is more consistent with the predictions of the search-after-meaning theory than either of the competing theories.

	Inference type									Inference types
	1	2	3	4	5	6	7	8	9	
Experimental evidence	✓	✓	✓	✓	?	✓	✗	✗	✗	1 = Referential (what does this refer to?)
Minimalist hypothesis	✓	✓	✓	✗	✗	✗	✗	✗	✗	2 = Case structure role assignment (what role is played by this man?)
Search-after-meaning theory	✓	✓	✓	✓	✓	✓	✗	✗	✗	3 = Causal antecedent (why did this happen?)
Full constructionist theory	✓	✓	✓	✓	✓	✓	✓	✓	✓	4 = Supraordinate goal (what is the central goal?)

Inference types:
1 = Referential (what does this refer to?)
2 = Case structure role assignment (what role is played by this man?)
3 = Causal antecedent (why did this happen?)
4 = Supraordinate goal (what is the central goal?)
5 = Thematic (what is the main theme?)
6 = Character reaction (why is the person feeling?)
7 = Causal sequence (what is the next event?)
8 = Instrument (what instrument was used to achieve this?)
9 = Subordinate goal action (how was the action produced?)

Figure 7.3 The types of inferences which are normally drawn according to different theories
Source: adapted from Graesser *et al.* (1974)

Evaluation of inference theories

If one compares the constructionist and minimalist theories of inference, then the constructionist theory is the least satisfactory one, in that it fails to specify clearly which inferences will and will not be drawn. In addition, the constructionist theory appears to predict that more inferences will be drawn than is actually the case. The minimalist hypothesis is at the opposite extreme, in that it appears to predict that too few inferences will be drawn. For example, readers tend to draw inferences so that they can understand why the characters in a story are behaving as they are (see research update). However, these inferences should not be drawn according to the minimalist hypothesis. What is needed is a theoretical position which is somewhere between the constructionist and minimalist hypotheses (see research update).

 Section summary

Inference drawing is of major importance in language comprehension. The inferences that can be drawn include logical, bridging and elaborative inferences. According to the minimalist hypothesis, inferences are drawn mainly when they need to be to achieve the reader's goals. According to the constructionist theory, numerous inferences are drawn to achieve full understanding. The search-after-meaning theory of Graesser *et al.* (1994) represents a reasonable compromise between the other two theoretical approaches.

1 Which kinds of inferences do readers tend to make? Which theoretical approach provides the most adequate account of inference drawing?

❑ Discourse processing

So far we have focused mainly on the processes involved in understanding single sentences or short passages. However, it is also important to consider larger linguistic communications. The term 'discourse' is often used to refer to complete texts or spoken communications, and the emphasis in this section will be on the processes involved in understanding and remembering discourse.

Probably the most striking finding from studies of memory for discourse is the way in which important information is remembered and unimportant information is forgotten. This was shown in a neat study by Gomulicki (1956). One group of participants recalled a story from memory, and another group wrote a summary of the same story while they looked at it. Afterwards, a third group of participants was asked to discriminate between story recalls and story summaries. They were largely unable to do this. These findings indicate that story memory closely resembles a summary, presumably because both involve a focus on the key ingredients of the story.

A possible reason why important information is remembered and details are forgotten is simply because more time is spent processing important information. Eye-movement studies indicate that more important parts of a text are fixated for longer than less important ones (Harley 1995). However, this does not really explain the memory findings. Britton et al. (1986) controlled processing time so that it was the same for more and less important information, but they still found that the important information was remembered the best.

Some theorists (e.g. Rumelhart 1975; Thorndyke 1977) have argued that every story possesses a hierarchical structure which can be expressed in terms of a **story grammar**. For example, Rumelhart (1975) argued that a story generally consists of a setting, a theme, a plot and a resolution. Further down the hierarchy, the setting involves characters, one or more locations, and time, whereas the theme involves one or more events and a goal.

Evidence apparently supporting the story grammar approach was reported by Thorndyke (1977). Some of his participants heard stories presented in their normal form so that the underlying hierarchical structure was easy to identify. Other participants heard versions of the same stories in which the sentences were presented in such a way that the underlying structure was very difficult to work out. Recall of the jumbled stories was considerably worse than recall of the normal versions of the stories. Thorndyke (1977) argued that the poor recall of the jumbled stories occurred because their structure had been destroyed. However, jumbling stories has other damaging effects, such as making it difficult to know who is being referred to in sentences containing words such as 'he', 'she' and 'they'. This is known as loss of referential continuity. Much of the poor recall of jumbled stories is due to loss of referential continuity rather than to loss of story structure (Garnham et al. 1982).

It is now generally accepted that story grammars do not provide a convincing account of the ways in which stories are processed and remembered. Some of the reasons why the story grammar approach has fallen into disfavour were identified by Harley:

There is no agreement on story structure: virtually every story grammatician has proposed a different grammar. Current story grammars only provide a limited account of a subset of all possible stories.

(Harley 1995: 233)

Kintsch's construction–integration model

Kintsch (1988, 1994) put forward a construction-integration model of discourse processing. This model is designed to explain how information contained in a text or other form of discourse is combined with stored knowledge in order to form an overall representation of its meaning. Some of the main ingredients in the theory are shown in Figure 7.4. Information in the text is turned into a linguistic representation in the form of propositions, which are the smallest units of meaning to which a truth value can be assigned. A number of propositions from the text are put into a propositional net, which is a short-term store.

The processing up to this point has all been bottom-up, meaning that it is triggered directly by the text itself. Top-down processes now enter the picture. Propositions related to textual propositions, including inferences, are added on the basis of information stored in long-term memory. The various propositions produced from bottom-up and top-down processes are all entered into the elaborated propositional net. This is the construction stage, and it suffers from the limitation that many unimportant or irrelevant propositions are contained within the elaborated propositional net.

There is then an integration process, which is designed to ensure that the most important propositions are incorporated into the text representation. This is

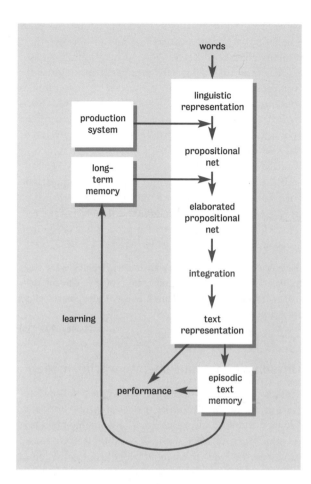

Figure 7.4 Kintsch's (1988, 1994) construction–integration model
Source: adapted from Kintsch (1992)

achieved by means of a spreading activation process, in which the probability of including propositions in the text representation is determined largely by their level of activation. Those propositions which are closely linked to other propositions are the most highly activated, and such propositions are likely to be of central importance to the meaning of the text.

One of the key features of the construction–integration model is the way in which different levels of representation are formed during discourse processing. There are three levels of representation, as follows:

(1) surface representation: the actual text
(2) propositional representation: the propositions formed from the text
(3) situational representation: a coherent model of the situation described in the text

Experimental evidence

Evidence that propositions play an important role in reading was obtained by Kintsch and Keenan (1973). They compared the time taken to read sentences having the same number of words but varying in terms of the number of propositions they contained. For example, consider the following two sentences: 'Cleopatra's downfall lay in her foolish trust of the fickle political figures of the Roman world' and 'Romulus, the legendary founder of Rome, took the women of the Sabine by force.' The first sentence contains eight propositions, whereas the second one contains only four propositions. It took the participants in this study approximately four seconds longer to read the first sentence than the second one.

Kintsch *et al.* (1990) tested the assumption of the construction-integration model that long-term memory is best for the situational representation and worst for the surface representation. They found that memory for surface information was extremely poor at a retention interval of 40 minutes, and was completely lost after four days (see Figure 7.5). In contrast, situational information was well remembered, and there was no evidence of any forgetting even after four days. Long-term memory for propositional information was intermediate between that for surface and for situational information.

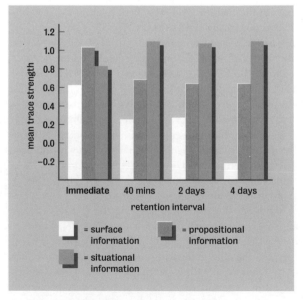

Figure 7.5 Memory for surface, propositional and situational information
Source: adapted from Kintsch *et al.* (1990)

Usefulness of the construction-integration model

The greatest strength of the construction-integration model of discourse processing is that it specifies in more detail than other theories the processes involved. As a result, Kintsch (1988) was able to carry out computer simulations of parts of the model. These simulations provided support for some of the processes proposed in the theory.

Another strength of the model is the notion that those propositions selected for inclusion in the text representation are selected on the basis of spreading activation levels. As Kintsch *et al.* (1990: 136) pointed out, the approach adopted within most other theories is very different, being based on 'strong, "smart" rules, which, guided by schemata, arrive at just the right interpretations, activate just the right knowledge, and generate just the right inferences'. The problem with this approach is that such strong rules would need to be extremely complex, and it would be very difficult to construct rules that would apply equally well in all circumstances. In contrast, the notion of spreading activation is simple and avoids the inflexibility associated with strong rules.

The greatest weakness of the construction-integration model is that important parts of it have not been tested properly as yet. For example, it is assumed that several inferences and other propositions are included in the elaborated propositional net, but are then discarded and left out of the subsequent text representation. This sounds like an inefficient procedure, and there is very little evidence that several propositions are discarded in this way. In general terms, most of the experimental tests of the model have been piecemeal, focusing on only a small fraction of the complete construction-integration model. What is needed is more evidence that the various processes and structures within the model actually relate to each other in the ways specified in the model.

ψ Section summary

Studies of memory for discourse indicate that important information tends to be remembered, whereas unimportant information is forgotten. The notion that every story possesses a hierarchical structure which can be expressed in terms of a story grammar

Box continued

---

has not proved very useful. According to Kintsch's construction-integration model, propositions from a text are put into a propositional net. These propositions, together with propositions related to textual propositions (e.g. inferences) are entered into an elaborated propositional net. The most important of these propositions are incorporated into the text representation. Parts of the construction-integration model have not been tested fully.

1 What are the main processes involved in processing of, and memory for, discourse?

❑ Speech production

When we speak, it is nearly always because we are trying to communicate with others. In order for us to communicate effectively, it is necessary that what we say should conform to certain basic rules or conventions. According to Grice (1967), it is especially important for speakers and listeners to follow the Co-operative Principle. This principle states that speakers and listeners should do what they can to be co-operative.

Grice (1967) went on to suggest four further maxims or principles which should be taken into account by speakers. First, there is the maxim of quantity, which states that the speaker should provide as much information as necessary, but no more. Second, there is the maxim of quality, namely, that the speaker should tell the truth. Third, there is the maxim of relation, which states that the speaker should focus on saying things which are relevant to the ongoing situation. Fourth, there is the maxim of manner, namely, that the speaker should endeavour to make what he or she says easy to understand.

How do speakers try to make sure that they adhere to the maxim of quantity? As Olson (1970) pointed out, context is a relevant factor. For example, someone might say, 'That's my son over there', if there is only one boy in the direction indicated. However, if there are several boys close together, it would be necessary to say something like 'That's my son with the red sweater and the baseball cap', in order for the listener to be able to identify the speaker's son.

Another factor which is relevant to the maxim of quantity is what Clark and Carlson (1981) referred to as the 'common ground'. This common ground consists of shared knowledge and beliefs between speaker and listener. In general, two people who are close friends will have much more common ground than people who are casual acquaintances. As a result, it is not necessary to spell things out in as much detail to a close friend as to a casual acquaintance.

Clark and Haviland (1977) argued that there is an important distinction between given information and new information. Given information is information which the speaker assumes is already known to the listener, whereas new information is information which the speaker assumes that the listener does not know. Speakers generally try to adhere to what Clark and Haviland called the given-new contract:

Try to construct the given and the new information of each utterance in context: (a) so that the listener is able to compute from memory the unique antecedent that was intended for the given information, and (b) so that he [sic] will not already have the new information attached to that antecedent.

(Clark and Havilland 1977: 9)

Given information usually occurs earlier in a sentence than new information.

Clark and Haviland (1977) predicted that comprehension would be slowed down if the given-new contract were violated. Here is an example of such a violation:

- Ed wanted an alligator for his birthday.
- The alligator was his favourite present.

Since the listener has not been told that Ed was given an alligator for his birthday, he or she will take some time to understand the second sentence. As predicted, the listeners took longer to understand the second sentence than when it was preceded by a sentence which provided all the necessary background information ('Ed was given an alligator for his birthday').

Theoretical approaches

Several theories of speech production have been proposed, including those of Garrett (1975, 1976), Dell (1986) and Bock and Levelt (1994). All of these theories share many features, and we will discuss these common features before considering Dell's (1986) theory in more detail. In the first place, it is assumed within all of the above theories that speakers generally plan what they are going to say before saying it. Speakers tend to produce about six words between successive pauses (H.H. Clark 1994), suggesting that the forward planning of speech covers approximately six words.

A second common feature of most theories is the notion that the processes of speech production proceed from the general (the meaning the speaker wishes to convey) down to the specific (the precise sounds produced by the speaker). In general terms, the processes involved in speech production operate in the opposite direction to those involved in comprehension, since comprehension starts with the physical message (visual or auditory) and proceeds towards an understanding of its meaning.

A third common feature is that there is reasonable agreement on the number and nature of the processes involved in speech production. Most theories assume that there are four processing stages, with the first stage concerned with the speaker's intended meaning, and the second stage concerned with grammatical structure.

A fourth common feature is that most of the support for the various theories has come from evidence about speech errors. As we will see later, the kinds of errors made by speakers can tell us much about the underlying processes involved in speech production.

Dell's theory

Dell (1986) and Dell and O'Seaghdha (1991) put forward a spreading-activation theory of speech production. According to this theory, there are four different processing stages or levels involved in the planning of speech, with a different representation being formed at each level. Processing can occur at all four levels at the same time, but generally proceeds most rapidly at the semantic level and most slowly at the phonological level:

(1) semantic level: it is at this level that the speaker works out the meaning to be expressed
(2) syntactic level: at this level, the grammatical structure of the planned utterance is organized
(3) morphological level: at this level, the morphemes (basic units of meaning) are added to the grammatical structure
(4) phonological level: at this level, the phonemes (basic units of sound) are added to the planned utterance

There are two other key features of Dell's spreading-activation theory which need to be mentioned before we consider the relevant evidence. First, it is assumed that there are categorical rules at each level of processing. These rules indicate which categories of items are and are not acceptable at any point in the planned utterance. For example, the categorical rules at the syntactic level

ψ Case study

Anomia in E.S.T.

Anomia involves impaired naming of objects and pictures of objects. E.S.T. was a male patient suffering from anomia who was studied by Kay and Ellis (1987). An indication of his problems with speech production can be seen from the following attempt to describe a picture:

Er . . . two children, one girl one male . . . the . . . the girl, they're in a . . . and their, their mother was behind them in in, they're in the kitchen . . . the boy is trying to get . . . a . . . er, a part of a cooking . . . jar. . . . He's standing on . . . the lad is standing on a . . . standing on a . . . standing on a . . . I'm calling it a seat, I can't . . . I forget what it's, what the name of it is. . . . It is er a higher, it's a seat, standing on that, 'e's standing on that . . . this boy is standing on this, seat . . . getting some of this stuff to . . . biscuit to eat.

E.S.T. did not seem to have particular problems at the syntactic level, because his speech was reasonably grammatical. There are at least two possible reasons for his inability to find many of the words he was looking for. First, there may have been problems at the semantic level, in that he found it hard to gain access to words possessing a given meaning. Second, there may have been problems at the phonological level, in that he found it very hard to access the phonemes of some of the words he wanted to say.

Other evidence indicated that his problems did not centre on the semantic system. When he was asked to select the picture that matched a word he had just heard, his performance was perfect. He also performed very well on a task in which he was asked to choose which of two pictures had the closer associations to a heard word. Thus, it would appear that E.S.T.'s problems occurred at the fourth or phonological level within Dell's (1986) model, although it is also possible that he had a problem in accessing lexical representations.

specify the syntactic categories (e.g. nouns, verbs) to be used. Second, there are insertion rules, which also operate at different levels within the speech-production system. These rules select for inclusion in a representation those relevant items which are the most highly activated. According to the theory, several items will generally be activated at the same time. For example, if you think of the concept 'dog', then activation will spread from that concept to other related concepts (e.g. cat, horse). Finally, it is assumed that the activation level of any item that is selected for inclusion in a planned utterance falls to zero as soon as it has been selected. This assumption is included to prevent any given item from being selected over and over again.

Evidence from speech errors

According to the theory, speech errors occur when an incorrect item is more activated than the correct one. Several of the more common types of speech errors can be predicted from the spreading-activation theory. One example is what is known as anticipation errors, in which a word appears too early in an utterance (e.g. 'I must let the cage out of the cage'). Anticipation errors occur because all the words in a planned utterance are activated at an early stage, so that a later word can be more activated than the word that should be spoken.

Anticipation errors often turn into word-exchange errors, in which two words in an utterance are swapped (e.g. 'I must let the cage out of the hamster'). These errors occur in part because the activation level of a selected word falls to zero. In the example, the premature use of the word 'cage' can prevent its activation level returning to a high enough level for it to be used in its appropriate place at the end of the sentence. It is of interest that the two words involved in word-exchange errors practically always belong to the same part of speech. This follows from the theory, because of its emphasis on categorical rules.

According to spreading-activation theory, the processing of grammatical structure and of morphemes or basic units of meaning takes place at different levels. Some support for this view comes from the existence of morpheme-exchange errors. These errors involve morphemes from two different words being swapped even though the associated suffixes or inflections remain in place. Here is an example of a morpheme-exchange error: 'He has tested two fails.'

Analyses of speech errors have proved very useful for testing theories of speech production. However, some doubts about the value of speech errors have been expressed. First, most collections of speech errors (e.g. those of Garrett 1975 and Stemberger 1982) are based on errors heard by the researchers themselves. It is possible that they were more likely to notice some kinds of errors than others. If so, little faith can be had in the relative frequencies of different categories of errors.

Second, several categories of speech errors occur very rarely in normal speech. In some cases, the incidence is approximately only 1 in 10,000. It may be unwise to use such evidence to support or to refute theories of speech production.

Third, it would be agreed by most researchers that there should not be sole reliance on speech errors. As Levelt et al. (1991: 615) pointed out, 'an exclusively error-based approach to . . . speech production is as ill-conceived as an exclusively illusion-based approach in vision research'.

Cognitive neuropsychology: aphasia

The theories we have considered assume that there are a number of separate processing stages or levels involved in speech production. If this assumption is correct, then it would be expected that some brain-damaged patients would have impairments of one or more processing stages with the other processing stages remaining intact. In this section, we will consider the cognitive neuropsychological evidence for selective impairments in speech production. The general term **aphasia** is used to refer to impaired speech production which is caused by brain damage. For the purposes of understanding the processes involved in speech production, however, it is more valuable to focus on specific forms of aphasia.

Some brain-damaged patients suffer from what is sometimes referred to as **agrammatism**. Such patients are poor at sentence construction, tending to speak the words in a sentence in the wrong order. In addition, they tend to leave out function words (e.g. 'a', 'the', 'and', 'for') and word endings, both of which are important to the grammatical structure of speech. Finally, there is good evidence that patients with agrammatism are poor at syntactic comprehension. For example, Linebarger et al. (1983) found that agrammatic aphasics found it difficult to decide whether a string of words formed a grammatical sentence. The type of speech produced by agrammatics can be seen in this following example from

Saffran et al. (1980): 'The kiss . . . the lady kissed . . . the lady is . . . the lady and the man and the lady . . . kissing.'

Many of the findings from patients with agrammatism can be accounted for by Dell's (1986) theory. Presumably there is a problem in moving from the semantic level to the syntactic level, and this is why agrammatic aphasics produce such ungrammatical speech. However, this is only a partial explanation. It does not account for the comprehension problems experienced by agrammatic aphasics, which are due to damage elsewhere in the language-processing system.

Miyake et al. (1994) proposed an interesting explanation of agrammatism based on the notion that it results from an impairment of working memory (see Chapter 6). They found that some of the symptoms of agrammatism could be produced in normals by reducing their working memory capacity. It remains to be seen whether this approach can account for agrammatism.

According to Dell's (1986) theory, there should be other kinds of aphasic patients. For example, some patients might have no problems at the syntactic level, but might find it hard to find the appropriate words because of impairments at the morphological and/or phonological level. This pattern of impairment is found in patients with **jargon aphasia**, which is characterized by use of the wrong words and by made-up words which are not in the dictionary. In spite of these speech errors, the speech of jargon aphasics is reasonably grammatical.

Ellis et al. (1983) provided a transcript of the description of a picture of a scout camp provided by the jargon aphasic R.D. In this transcript, the words which R.D. was assumed to have been looking for are given in parentheses:

A b-boy is swi'ing (SWINGING) on the bank with his hand (FEET) in the stringt (STREAM). A table with orstrum (SAUCEPAN?) and . . . I don't know . . . and a three-legged stroe (STOOL) and a strane (PAIL) . . . table, table . . . near the water. . . . A man is knocking a paper . . . paper with notist (NOTICE) by the er t-tent, tent er tet (TENT) er tent.

The findings from patients with agrammatism, jargon aphasia, and anomia are generally consistent with theoretical approaches such as the one proposed by Dell (1986). However, the data are more complex than has been indicated here (see Harley 1995). It is also important to note that many experts are sceptical about the existence of syndromes such as agrammatism and jargon aphasia. As Harley (1995: 276) pointed out, 'The status of these patterns of impairments as syndromes is highly controversial'.

Ψ Section summary

Speakers generally plan what they are going to say before saying it. The processes of speech production proceed from considerations of meaning to considerations of the precise sounds that need to be uttered. According to Dell, there are four processing stages or levels involved in the planning of speech: semantic; syntactic; morphological; and phonological. Evidence supporting this general approach has been obtained from brain-damaged patients and from speech errors produced by normal individuals.

1   Describe the main stages involved in speech production. What evidence supports this stage-based account?

☐ Structure of language system

We have discussed reading, speech perception and speech production in some detail. The other major language-based activity, writing, has not been discussed because relatively little is known about it as yet (but see Eysenck and Keane 1995 for a review). It is of importance to ascertain the extent to which these different language functions make use of the same structures and processes. For example, Harley (1995) asked whether or not the same lexicon or mental dictionary is used for all language functions. As he pointed out, there are various possibilities:

The most parsimonious arrangement is that there is only one lexicon, used for the four tasks of writing, reading, speaking, and listening. Then there are two plausible intermediate positions where there are two lexicons. The first two-lexicon arrangement is separate lexicons for written (visual) language and spoken (verbal) language (each covering input and output tasks), the second is separate lexicons for input and output (each covering written and spoken language).

(Harley 1995: 281)

Some of the most relevant research has been carried out on brain-damaged patients. For example, S.E. Kohn and Friedman (1986) studied a patient suffering from pure word deafness. This patient could read, speak and write normally, but was unable to understand speech. However, the patient was able to repeat speech back. These findings suggest (but do not prove) that there is a separate speech input lexicon. Beauvois and Derouesne (1981) found a patient who could read words satisfactorily, but was very poor at spelling. This could be taken as evidence that different lexicons are involved in reading and writing.

There are many other studies on brain-damaged patients which suggest that different lexicons may be used for different kinds of language activities, but we will consider only one more here. Ellis *et al.* (1983) studied a patient, R.D., whose ability to spell was generally very good. However, as we saw earlier, his speech was greatly impaired: he called a screwdriver a 'kistro', a penguin a 'senstenz', and so on. These findings could be taken as suggestive evidence for separate speech output and graphemic output lexicons.

There are two main reasons for not drawing sweeping conclusions from studies such as those considered here. First, as Harley (1995: 286) pointed out, there is a plausible alternative explanation of the findings: 'Suppose we have one lexicon, but four different methods of gaining access to it. In this case what is lost in the neuropsychological dissociations are not the lexical stores, but the access routes'. It is very difficult (or impossible) to distinguish between that explanation and the multiple-lexicon explanation on the basis of currently available data. Second, there are relatively few patients who exhibit one or more greatly impaired language functions combined with one or more essentially intact ones. It may be unwise to attach considerable significance to the findings from so few patients.

Ψ Section summary

It is important to consider the relationships between reading, speech perception, speech production, and writing. For example, it could be argued that there is only one lexicon, or two lexicons, or four lexicons. This issue has been examined with brain-damaged patients. The evidence suggests that there may be four separate lexicons, one for each of the major language functions. However, it remains entirely possible that there is only one lexicon with multiple access routes, any of which can be affected by brain damage.

1   Discuss the interrelationships of the four main language functions.

Ψ Chapter summary

- ### Basic processes in reading

Eye-movement recordings can be taken to understand some of the processes involved in reading. Fixations are generally on those points in the text providing the most information. The identification of words in reading involves top-down as well as bottom-up processes. Words can be read aloud either by use of a direct or lexical route (involving or not involving the semantic system), or by use of an indirect route based on grapheme–phoneme correspondence rules. Many brain-damaged patients (e.g. surface dyslexics, phonological dyslexics) have selective damage to one route.

- ### Speech perception

Listeners to speech have to contend with the segmentation and non- invariance problems. Word identification is facilitated by taking account of the sentence context and by lip-reading. According to the motor theory, listeners mimic the articulatory movements of the speaker. This theory is inadequate. According to cohort theory, word perception depends on bottom-up and top-down processes. According to the TRACE model, there are processing units or nodes at the feature, phoneme and word levels. These three levels are strongly interconnected, with the amount of activation of word nodes determining word identification.

- ### Semantic categories

It is often argued that categories are organized around prototypes, with a prototype being a set of characteristic features of varying levels of importance. Members of a category may share few or no features, as a result of which the boundaries of a category are often imprecise. Categories differ in their generality. Categories at an intermediate level of generality (often known as base level categories) are most used in everyday life.

- ### Parsing and syntax

Readers and listeners need to work out the syntactic or grammatical structure of sentences, and they need to work out the meaning of the text. Does meaning influence the construction of the initial syntactic structure?

The evidence is rather inconsistent. However, meaning usually has little or no effect when a given grammatical structure is strongly implied by a sentence. Meaning often has a marked effect when that is not the case.

- ### Inference drawing

We often draw inferences (logical, bridging, elaborative) in order to make sense of what we are reading or listening to. We are most likely to draw inferences which relate to our goals in reading or listening, which are needed to construct a coherent meaning of the text or speech, or which allow us to explain the actions or events being described.

- ### Discourse processing

There is evidence that discourse processing leads to the formation of three types of representation. First, there is the representation of the text itself. Second, there is the propositional representation, based on the propositions formed from the text. Third, there is the situational representation, which is a coherent model of the situation described in the text.

- ### Speech production

Much has been learned about the processes involved in speech production from the study of speech errors. Speakers generally plan what they are going to say before saying it. Such planning proceeds from the general (the meaning the speaker wishes to convey) down to the specific (the precise words and sounds produced by the speaker). Various theorists have argued that there are four processing stages involved in speech production.

- ### Structure of language system

There are four main language functions: reading; speech perception; speech production; and writing. Evidence from brain-damaged patients suggests that there may be separate lexicons for each of these functions. However, the findings can also be accounted for in terms of damage to one or more of the access routes to a single lexicon.

Further reading

● Harley, T.A. (1995) *The Psychology of Language: From data to theory*. Hove: Lawrence Erlbaum. This is an excellent book. It covers virtually all of the major topics in language in detail and in an accessible way.

● Rayner, K. and Pollatsek, A. (1989) *The Psychology of Reading*. Englewood Cliffs, NJ: Prentice Hall. The processes involved in reading are discussed very thoroughly. The book is especially good in terms of its coverage of the use of eye-movement recordings to understand reading.

● Eysenck, M.W. and Keane, M.T. (1995) *Cognitive Psychology: A student's handbook*, 3rd. Edn. Hove: Lawrence Erlbaum. Chapters 10, 12, 13 and 14 deal with various topics in the psychology of language in greater detail than has been possible here.

● Mitchell, D. (1994) Sentence parsing, in M.A. Gernsbacher (ed.) *Handbook of Psycholinguistics*. London: Academic Press. The various theoretical positions with respect to parsing are considered in depth in the light of the available evidence.

● Bock, K. and Levelt, W. (1994) Language production: grammatical encoding, in M.A. Gernsbacher (ed.) *Handbook of Psycholinguistics*. London: Academic Press. This chapter provides an up-to-date and well-informed account of theory and research on speech production.

CHAPTER 8

Thinking and reasoning

Michael Eysenck

KEY CONCEPTS • problem solving • expertise • conditional reasoning • syllogistic reasoning • mental models • probabilistic reasoning • human rationality

☐ Chapter preview

When you have read this chapter, you should be able to

- understand some of the major historical and contemporary approaches to problem solving
- account for some of the ways in which expertise affects problem solving
- have a good knowledge of research and theory on syllogistic reasoning
- appreciate the mental-model approach to human reasoning
- understand some of the main ways in which we make judgements under uncertainty
- assess the extent to which human thinking and reasoning are rational

Introduction

Human beings spend a lot of their time making use of what are sometimes termed 'higher mental processes'. These are the processes used in complex cognitive tasks involving thinking and reasoning. If you are playing a game of chess, trying to solve a crossword puzzle, considering the probabilities of different events in the absence of definite information, trying to decide what follows from certain assumptions, or planning your future, then you are almost certainly using higher mental processes.

It is often assumed that there are close links between thinking and problem solving. For example, Humphrey (1951) defined thinking as 'what happens in experience when an organism, human or animal, recognises and solves a problem'. The processes involved in reasoning are similar to those involved in problem solving. Drever (1964: 241) defined reasoning as 'a process of thinking involving inference, or of solving problems by employing general principles'.

It may have occurred to you that there should be close links between the study of the higher mental processes in thinking and reasoning on the one hand, and the study of intelligence on the other hand (see Chapter 13). The reason why there should be close links is because both fields of research are concerned with complex cognitive skills. In practice, however, there has been less cross-fertilization than might have been expected. As Sternberg and Frensch (1990) pointed out, this is due in part to the fact that researchers in the two fields have had different emphases. Researchers on thinking and reasoning have been especially concerned with examining the details of cognitive processing by using a variety of similar cognitive tasks, and then comparing performance on each task. In contrast, researchers on intelligence have focused on individual differences in intellectual ability. They have typically used factor analysis to analyse the data from a wide range of different tasks, and have tended historically not to investigate cognitive processes with any precision.

❏ Problem solving

According to Mayer (1990: 284), problem solving is 'cognitive processing directed at transforming a given situation into a goal situation when no obvious method of solution is available to the problem solver'. In other words, it involves cognitive rather than automatic pro-

cessing; it involves directed or purposeful activity; and it is personal in the sense that what is a problem for one person may not be so for someone who possesses much more relevant knowledge. For example, driving a car can be a major problem for a learner driver. However, it is not a problem at all for an experienced driver.

Problems can be divided into **well-defined problems** and **ill-defined problems**. In a well-defined problem, the initial state or situation, the goal state or solution, and the permissible moves or operators are all clearly specified. Playing chess is an example of a well-defined problem. The starting position is clear, the ways in which each piece may be moved are clear, and the goal state is clear (i.e. capturing the opponent's king). In an ill-defined problem, there is a general lack of clarity. For example, suppose that you are locked in a building late at night. The desired goal state is to be outside the building, but the only rapid way of reaching this goal state may involve damaging or breaking doors and windows. The problem is ill defined in the sense that it is not clear how much damage to the building will be regarded as acceptable.

Even with well-defined problems, there can be alternative ways of structuring or representing the problem, and it can be difficult to find the best representation. Consider, for example, the mutilated chessboard problem (see Figure 8.1). The diagonally opposite corners of a chessboard are cut out and removed, thus leaving 62 squares. You have 31 dominoes, each of which can cover two squares. Is it possible to arrange the dominoes so that all 62 squares are covered? The key to solving this problem is to focus on the colours of the squares, and to realize that each domino will cover one white and one black square. Since two diagonally opposite corners

Figure 8.1 The mutilated chessboard problem

must be the same colour, it follows that there is no possible arrangement of the dominoes that leads to all of the squares being covered.

Most laboratory studies of problem solving have used well-defined problems, whereas the problems of everyday life tend to be ill defined. The processes and skills appropriate to well-defined problems probably differ from those appropriate to ill-defined problems, so it is important to bear in mind the distinction between the two types of problems in what follows.

Gestaltist approach

Some of the earliest systematic research on problem solving was carried out by Thorndike (1898). Hungry cats were put in a cage and could see food on the outside. In order to escape from the cage, they had to make an arbitrary response (e.g. hitting a pole, pulling on a loop of string). Thorndike was unimpressed by the problem-solving behaviour of the cats he studied: they ran around the cage, squeezed the bars, and so on, and only slowly increased the speed with which they escaped from the cage. He described their apparently random behaviour as **trial-and-error learning**.

Several years later, Gestalt psychologists (especially Wolfgang Köhler 1925) argued that other species are better able to solve problems than was suggested by Thorndike (1898). They drew a distinction between productive thinking, in which a problem is restructured to permit a novel solution to a problem, and reproductive thinking, in which previous experience is used to apply an already existing approach to a new problem. Köhler (1925) claimed that apes are capable of productive thinking. In one of his studies, an ape was placed in a cage with some sticks, none of which was long enough to reach a banana outside the cage. After a while, the ape seemed to restructure the problem. He rapidly joined two sticks together, and used this elongated stick to obtain the banana. Köhler used the term **insight** to refer to this restructuring, which is also sometimes known as the 'aha experience'.

The early experiences of Köhler's ape were not known. As a result, it is possible that its ability to join two sticks together depended on previous learning rather than on sudden insight. Birch (1945) studied apes who had been raised in captivity, and found very little evidence of insightful problem solving among them.

Maier (1931) carried out a study of restructuring in humans. They were given the 'pendulum problem', which involves tying together two strings hanging from

the ceiling. The reason why it is a problem is because the two strings are sufficiently far apart that they cannot both be grasped at the same time (see Figure 8.2). The best solution to this problem is to tie a pair of pliers to the end of one string, and to swing that string until it comes within grasping range while the other string is being held. Very few of the participants solved the problem without help. However, when the experimenter 'accidentally' brushed against one string and made it swing, many of the participants restructured the problem and produced the pendulum solution. Most of them claimed that their problem-solving behaviour had not been influenced by the experimenter's actions. This suggests that they had very limited conscious awareness of the processes involved in problem solution.

The unconscious cue effect reported by Maier (1931) does not seem to have been replicated. According to J. Evans (pers. comm.), his methodology 'would not pass for a modern undergraduate project let alone a classic journal article'. Battersby et al. (1953) studied the string problem. Some of the participants (the 'restricted' group) were told that they could use only objects provided by the experimenter to solve the problem. The experimenter then placed a pair of scissors, a clothes peg, a small pulley, a yo-yo, and a fishing-line sinker in front of the participant. Other participants (the 'unrestricted' group) found these objects in the room when they arrived, and they were simply instructed to use any object in the room. The restricted participants solved the string problem in under $2\frac{1}{2}$ minutes on average, whereas the unrestricted participants averaged over 15 minutes. Thus, problem solving was greatly facilitated by highlighting objects that were relevant to the problem.

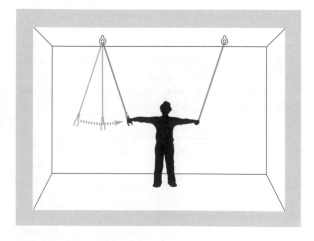

Figure 8.2 The solution to Maier's (1931) pendulum problem

Support for the notion of insight was reported by Metcalfe (e.g. 1986). She found that her participants could often predict accurately whether they knew the solution to a memory question they could not answer, suggesting that relevant information was available prior to solution. However, their predictions on insight problems were inaccurate, suggesting that these problems were solved by sudden insight rather than by the accumulation of information.

Other Gestalt psychologists studied reproductive thinking. We generally assume that past experience will have a beneficial effect on problem solving, but the Gestaltists argued that past experience is often disruptive. For example, Duncker (1945) studied **functional fixedness**, which involves assuming from past experience that objects have only a small number of possible functions or uses. The task was to mount a candle on a vertical screen; among the objects available were a box full of nails and a book of matches. The correct solution was to use the nail-box as a candle holder by nailing it to the wall. However, very few of the participants found the solution, presumably because they perceived the nail-box as a container rather than as a platform. As expected, the participants' performance was better when the container function of the box was de-emphasized by having the box empty from the outset.

There is an important limitation with Duncker's (1945) study. He did not know what past experiences his participants had had with boxes. From a scientific viewpoint, it is preferable to control the participants' relevant past experience by providing it during the course of the experiment. Luchins (1942) did precisely that in his experiments on water-jar problems. In each problem, there were three jars of different capacity. The task was to pour water from one jar to another in order to obtain a specified amount in one jar. In one experiment, one of the final problems involved obtaining 25 quarts of water from three jars having capacities of 28, 76 and 3 quarts. It is not difficult to see that filling the 28-quart jar and then using some of its contents to fill the 3-quart jar will leave 25 quarts in it. Of those participants who had already been given similar problems, 95 per cent solved this problem. In contrast, only 36 per cent of those who had been given a series of problems having the same complex three-jar solutions managed to solve it. What is going on here? According to Luchins (1942), people tend to adopt a problem-solving set or fixed approach when several problems can be solved in the same routine fashion, and they find it hard to abandon this set when it is inappropriate. In the words of

Luchins (1942: 15), 'Einstellung – habituation – creates a mechanized state of mind, a blind attitude towards problems; one does not look at the problem on its own merits but is led by a mechanical application of a used method'. As a footnote to this research, it would be very hard to lift a jar containing 28 quarts of water, and it would probably be impossible for most people to lift one containing 76 quarts of water!

Problems with Gestalt approach

The Gestalt approach to problem solving was successful in various ways. The Gestaltists showed the importance of the distinction between productive and reproductive thinking. They also showed convincingly that previous experience can have adverse effects on problem solving as well as beneficial ones. Finally, they demonstrated that problem solving is often facilitated when a restructuring of the problem takes place, and the concept of insight is probably of value.

On the negative side, some of the studies carried out by the Gestaltists were poorly designed and the findings have proved hard to replicate. In addition, while it is true that past experience can make our thinking blinkered and ineffective, it far more often has beneficial effects. Thus, phenomena such as functional fixedness or problem-solving set may not be very common in everyday life. At the theoretical level, the processes responsible for restructuring and insight were not specified by the Gestaltists, and the terms themselves are vague and difficult to measure. However, Ohlsson (1992) made some progress in that direction. He argued that there are three ways in which restructuring can occur:

- elaboration or adding information about the problem (e.g. brushing against a string in the pendulum problem)
- constraint relaxation, adopting a broader view of what would be an acceptable goal or solution
- re-encoding or re-categorizing (e.g. perceiving the nail-box as a platform in the candle problem).

Each of these forms of restructuring facilitates retrieval of the relevant operator or operators from long-term memory.

Computational approach

One of the greatest breakthroughs in our understanding of problem solving came in the theory and research of Allen Newell and Herb Simon (1972), who argued that it would be useful to produce a theory that was applicable to numerous different problems. As a result, they applied their General Problem Solver to eleven different problems, including the Tower of Hanoi, letter-series completion, and the missionaries and cannibals problem. What is common to all of these problems is that they can be thought of as involving a problem space; this consists of the initial state of the problem, the goal state, all the legitimate operators or moves, and all the intermediate states of the problem. In the course of solving a problem, people move through a series of knowledge states, with the movements from one knowledge state to the next being produced by the use of operators.

The approach pursued by Newell and Simon (1972) is known as the computational approach, because systematic computer simulations of problem solving were incorporated into the General Problem Solver. Newell and Simon (1972) assumed that the human cognitive system has limited short-term storage capacity, processes information in a serial fashion, and can access information contained in long-term memory. Accordingly, the General Problem Solver was equipped with these characteristics.

Some of the above ideas will become clearer if we consider a concrete example. In the initial state of the simplest version of the Tower of Hanoi problem, there are three pegs, and three discs piled on the first peg, with the largest at the bottom and the smallest at the bottom (see Figure 8.3). The goal state involves having these three discs in the same order on the last peg. The rules allow only one disc to be moved at a time, and forbid a larger disc to be placed on top of a smaller one.

According to Newell and Simon (1972) people trying to solve the Tower of Hanoi problem (and other problems) make much use of **heuristic methods**, which are rules of thumb used in problem solving. Heuristic methods can be contrasted with **algorithmic methods**,

which are specific procedures which are certain to produce the correct answer. The procedures used to solve mathematical problems are examples of algorithms. Algorithmic methods have the advantage over heuristic methods of being more accurate. However, they have the severe disadvantage that they are often extremely time-consuming.

The most important of the heuristic methods is known as **means-ends analysis**. This involves finding the difference between the current state of the problem and the goal state, producing a sub-goal that will reduce that difference, and finally selecting an operator that will allow the sub-goal to be reached. For example, suppose that someone doing the Tower of Hanoi problem has the choice between putting the largest disk on the last peg or the middle peg. If he or she is using means-ends analysis, the disc will be put on the last peg, because that is more effective in reducing the difference between the current and goal states.

An important prediction that follows from this approach is that people should have particular difficulties when the best move in a problem involves increasing the difference between the current state and the goal state. This prediction was tested by Thomas (1974). He used a version of the missionaries and cannibals problem in which three hobbits and three orcs had to be taken across a river using a boat that could hold only two creatures. The orcs wanted to eat the hobbits, and so the number of orcs must not exceed the number of hobbits on either bank of the river. One move in the middle of the problem involves one orc and one hobbit returning to the starting point. This move is inconsistent with means-ends analysis, and most of the participants had great difficulties at this point in the problem.

Unfortunately for the General Problem Solver, the places in the missionaries and cannibals problem at which it experiences difficulties are not always the same as those at which human problem solvers have difficulties. Greeno (1974) directly compared human problem solvers and the General Problem Solver, and found that the General Problem Solver had no particular difficulty at that point in the problem at which means-ends analysis fails to provide the best move. In contrast, consider the position very shortly before the solution is reached. All three missionaries, two of the cannibals, and the boat are on the destination side, and the remaining cannibal is on the starting side. Most people realize very rapidly that all that is needed is to send one person (a missionary or a cannibal) to the start side to collect the final cannibal. However, the General Problem Solver finds it hard to do this.

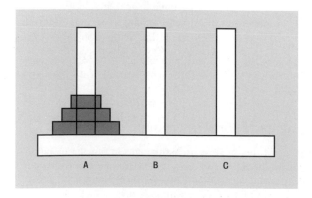

Figure 8.3 The Tower of Hanoi problem

Computational approach: ill-defined problems

Perhaps the greatest achievement of Newell and Simon (e.g. 1972) was to provide convincing evidence that human cognitive processes can be simulated by computer programs. That is now generally accepted, but it was a revolutionary view in the 1960s and early 1970s. In addition, their notion that much problem solving is based on heuristic methods rather than algorithmic methods is essentially correct, and has been confirmed numerous times over the years.

On the negative side, the computational approach is much better suited to well-defined problems such as the Tower of Hanoi and missionaries and cannibals problems than it is to the ill-defined problems of everyday life. In general terms, people trying to solve well-defined problems usually have relatively little relevant knowledge available, and so they have to rely on heuristic methods such as means-ends analysis. In contrast, successful solving of the ill-defined problems that confront us in our lives typically depends on possessing appropriate knowledge rather than on using heuristic methods.

Analogical problem solving

One common way in which problems are solved is by drawing an analogy (noticing important similarities) between the current problem and some other related problem. There are numerous examples of analogical reasoning in the history of science, including the hydraulic model of the blood circulation system and the computer model of human cognitive functioning. The importance of analogical thinking was demonstrated by Spearman (1927), who used problems of the form 'A is to B as C is to D' (e.g. 'Hand is to foot as finger is to ?'). He found that performance on analogy problems correlated approximately +0. 8 with IQ.

Sternberg (1977) carried out a detailed investigation of analogy problems (e.g. 'Hand is to foot as finger is to toe'). He did this by presenting only part of the problem first, and then the rest when the participant was ready for it. He argued that six processing components are involved in solving analogy problems:

(1) Encoding of the terms A and B (e.g. hand and foot)
(2) Inference: discover the rule relating A to B
(3) Mapping: discover the rule relating A to C (e.g. hand and finger)
(4) Application: decide what the fourth term should be and compare against the fourth term provided (e.g. toe)

(5) Justification: test the accuracy of the previous operations (this component is optional)
(6) Preparation-response: prepare and produce the answer

Sternberg (1977) obtained evidence that all five of the necessary components were used in three different types of analogy problems. This suggests that these components have some generality. Sternberg (1977) claimed that participants with differing levels of ability all used the same basic processes of analogical reasoning. However, Heller (1979) pointed out that Sternberg's (1977) research was carried out on highly intelligent students. She used participants having a wider range of ability, and found that there were clear differences in strategy. None of her good problem solvers failed to reason in an analogical way, whereas 50 per cent of her poor problem solvers did (e.g. looking for a relation between the A and D terms). Thus, Sternberg's (1977) six component model may be fully applicable only to those of high ability.

Gick and Holyoak (1980) were interested in the issue of how readily people make use of analogies when confronted by complex problems. They presented their participants with what is known as Duncker's radiation problem:

Suppose you are a doctor faced with a patient who has a malignant tumour in his stomach. It is impossible to operate on the patient, but unless the tumour is destroyed the patient will die. There is a kind of ray that can be used to destroy the tumour. If the rays reach the tumour all at once at a sufficiently high intensity, the tumour will be destroyed. Unfortunately, at this intensity the healthy tissue that the rays pass through on the way to the tumour will also be destroyed. At lower intensities the rays are harmless to healthy tissue, but they will not affect the tumour either. What types of procedure might be used to destroy the tumour with the rays, and at the same time avoid destroying the healthy tissue?

(Gick and Holyoak 1980: 307-8)

What do you think is the solution to this problem? The answer is to use several low-intensity rays which reach the tumour from different directions. Gick and Holyoak (1980) found that only approximately 10 per cent of the participants given this problem managed to solve it. The ability to use analogical reasoning was studied by presenting other participants with a relevant story about a general who wanted to capture a fortress. The general could not mount a full-scale attack, because all the roads leading away from the fortress had been mined. However, small groups of men could proceed safely along any given

Plate 8.1 Duncker's radiation problem was used to see how readily people make use of analogies when confronted by complex problems

road. The general decided that the best plan of action was to divide his army into small groups who would converge on the fortress at the same time along different roads. When the participants were told that one of the stories might be relevant to solving the radiation problem, about 80 per cent of them solved it. More interestingly, only about 40 per cent of those given the story about the general and the fortress, but not specifically informed that it might be relevant, managed to solve the problem.

Perhaps the participants in the above study failed to make spontaneous use of the story because there are so many superficial differences between the story and the problem. Keane (1987) tested this notion. He presented different groups of participants with one of the following relevant stories a few days ahead of being given the radiation problem:

- a story about a surgeon using rays on a cancer
- a story about a general using rays to destroy a missile
- the story about the general and the fortress

He found that about 90 per cent of the participants given the first story retrieved it spontaneously when given the radiation problem, compared to 60 per cent given the second story, and 10 per cent given the third story. In other words, the superficial similarities between the story and the problem greatly influenced the likelihood of the story being applied to the problem.

It follows from Keane's (1987) approach that people should tend to retrieve information that is superficially related to a current problem, even if that information does not provide a useful analogy. For example, participants who are trying to solve the radiation problem might retrieve a story about doctors using rays, even if

the story contains no useful information. Precisely that finding was reported by Gentner *et al.* (1992).

How can we train people to make more use of appropriate analogies? One answer was proposed by Cummins (1992). She made use of a series of algebra word problems, followed by some additional problems. When the participants were told to focus on one problem at a time, they mostly failed to draw analogies between the initial problems and the later ones. However, when they were instructed to compare the training problems to each other, they were much more likely to use these problems as a basis for drawing analogies on the later problems. In the latter condition, the participants were more likely to identify the underlying structures of the problems rather than attending mainly to their superficial characteristics.

Ψ Section summary

Laboratory studies generally make use of well-defined problems, but everyday problems are mostly ill defined. The behaviourists studied trial-and-error learning, whereas the Gestaltists focused on insight and on the ways in which past experience can disrupt present problem solving. Newell and Simon (1972) proposed a computational approach to problem solving with their General Problem Solver. According to their theoretical approach, people make much use of heuristic methods or rules of thumb when engaged in problem solving. Analogical problem solving has often proved useful in the history of science, and tests of analogical thinking correlate highly with IQ. People often fail to find the most appropriate analogy with a current problem, retrieving inappropriate information that is only superficially relevant.

1 Compare and contrast different approaches to problem solving.

Expertise

Most of the studies of problem solving we have discussed so far have involved participants who possessed only limited knowledge about the problems they were asked to solve. One way of trying to understand in more detail the processes involved in problem solving is to compare the performance of experts and novices.

Experts have much more relevant knowledge than novices, and this additional knowledge contributes to their superior problem-solving performance. However, the extent to which experts possess other advantages over novices is a matter of some controversy. We will consider this issue in the context of chess-playing expertise. One of the advantages of studying chess expertise is that chess generally involves dozens of moves, and these moves allow us to make inferences about the strategies being followed by the players.

De Groot (1966) carried out some of the earliest research in this area. In one of his studies, he presented grandmasters and less expert players with board positions taken from different games. They were then asked to reconstruct these positions from memory. Grandmasters did this successfully 91 per cent of the time, compared to only 41 per cent for the less expert players. This difference was not due to the fact that the grandmasters had generally better memories. When the players were asked to reconstruct random board positions from memory, the grandmasters had no advantage over the less expert players. Presumably the reason the grandmasters were so good at reconstructing actual board positions is because they were able to relate these board positions to the large amount of information about past games they have stored in long-term memory.

Chase and Simon (1973) argued that chess players memorize board positions by dividing the pieces into a small number of familiar or meaningful units or chunks. They predicted that more expert players would be able to form larger chunks than less expert ones as a result of the relevant knowledge they have acquired over the years. Three players were given the task of reconstructing the board position on one chessboard on a second chessboard, with the first chessboard still in view. They assessed the size of the chunks being formed on the basis of the number of pieces placed after each glance. The strongest player formed chunks averaging 2.5 pieces, whereas the weakest player had chunks averaging 1.9 pieces. In addition, the strongest player had shorter glances than the other players at the first board, suggesting that he was able to identify chunks faster than less able players.

Chase and Simon (1973) used the findings from their reconstruction task to work out the number of chess patterns that chess masters have stored in long-term memory. They estimated the total at somewhere between 10,000 and 100,000 patterns. This number was so high because Chase and Simon (1973) assumed that the locations of the pieces on the board were included in the knowledge stored in chunks.

We should not draw the conclusion from the evidence discussed so far that storing thousands of chess positions in memory is the only secret in becoming a grandmaster. Holding and Reynolds (1982) repeated de Groot's (1966) finding that expert players are no better than less expert ones in reconstructing random board positions, suggesting that none of them had relevant chess positions stored in memory. The players were then asked to think of the best move from each of the random board positions. The expert players thought of better moves than the less expert players, indicating that they have superior strategic processing skills as well as more detailed knowledge of chess positions.

De Groot (1966) asked grandmasters and expert players to think aloud before they made each move in games of chess. He found that both groups of players considered relatively few different moves, and did not differ in terms of the number considered. They also did not differ in terms of how many moves ahead they thought, but later evidence indicates that stronger players think further ahead than weaker ones (Charness 1991).

It is perhaps worth mentioning that we are unlikely to learn much about the processes humans use when playing chess by studying chess programs. Deep Blue beat the world champion Gary Kasparov in 1997, but it did so by adopting a radically different approach from human players. For example, it considered approximately 2 million moves a second, whereas grandmasters consider only one or two.

Acquiring expertise

Anderson (1983, 1993) has tried to identify some of the processes involved in the acquisition of expertise. His ACT (Adaptive Control of Thought) model consists of three interconnected systems (see Figure 8.4; see also Chapter 6):

- declarative memory, which contains a network of interconnected concepts; the information in declarative memory can be reported
- procedural memory, which contains IF . . . THEN production rules (e.g. if someone greets you, then you return the greeting); these rules are applied automatically in appropriate situations
- working memory, which contains information which is currently active or being processed

According to Anderson (1983, 1993), skill or expertise acquisition typically involves knowledge compilation. What happens in knowledge compilation is that there is a

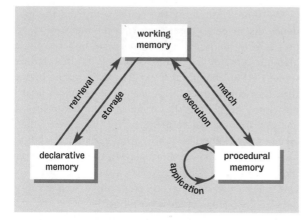

Figure 8.4 Anderson's (1993) ACT (Adaptive Control of Thought) model

shift from a reliance on declarative knowledge to a reliance on procedural knowledge. The acquisition of touchtyping is a good example of the process of knowledge compilation. In the early stages of learning to touchtype, typing is very slow and there is a heavy reliance on information in declarative memory (e.g. 'The letter H is just to the left of the home key for the right index finger'). After a considerable amount of practice, typing becomes an essentially automatic skill based on production rules. Indeed, highly skilled typists often rely so much on automatic skills that they find it hard to describe where individual letters are on the keyboard.

Anderson (1983, 1993) argued that there are two key processes involved in knowledge compilation:

- proceduralization: this is the process which changes declarative knowledge into production knowledge
- composition: this process involves eliminating any production rules which are not needed to achieve the desired pattern of behaviour

Composition is a way of making fairly large changes to the production rules used in the course of skill acquisition. Minor changes involve what is known as *production tuning*. For example, any production rule becomes stronger whenever it is used successfully, and this increases the probability that it will be used in similar situations in the future.

Anderson's (1983, 1993) ACT model has proved reasonably successful in accounting for several aspects of skill acquisition. The model has been used to produce computer simulations of human skill acquisition in a number of different areas, including the learning of geometry (Anderson *et al.* 1981) and computer programming (Pirolli and Anderson 1985). What are the limitations of the ACT model? The model is basically designed to reveal the processes involved in developing expertise of a routine nature, in which flexibility of approach is not of major importance. It is not equipped to provide an understanding of the development of more creative and adaptive forms of expertise, such as those involved in scientific theory construction.

 Research update

Selecting chess moves

Robbins and colleagues (1996) argued that a complex task such as selecting chess moves involves the working memory system. This system (which is discussed in more detail in Chapter 6) has three components: a central executive resembling attention; an articulatory or phonological loop used for verbal rehearsal; and a visuo-spatial sketch-pad used for visual and spatial processing. Selecting chess moves might make use of all components, since we can think about chess either visuo-spatially or in more verbal ways.

In essence, Robbins *et al.* (1996) asked two questions: (1) What is the involvement of each of the components of working memory in chess? (2) Do expert players differ from less expert players in their use of any of these components? They answered these questions by requiring their participants to suggest continuation moves from various chess positions under four conditions, which differed in terms of the secondary task they had to perform at the same time as solving the chess problems:

- control: repetitive tapping
- central executive suppression: random numbers had to be generated in order to make use of the central executive
- visuo-spatial sketch-pad suppression: the eight peripheral keys of a 3 × 3 keypad had to be pressed

Box continued

in a repetitive, clockwise fashion to make use of the visuo-spatial sketch-pad

- articulatory loop suppression: the word see-saw had to be repeated rapidly to make use of the articulatory loop

The findings are shown in Figure 8.5. As can be seen, the participants performed worse on the move selection task when the secondary task made use of the central executive or the visuo-spatial sketch-pad, but not when it made use of the articulatory loop. One strong implication of these findings is that thinking about possible chess moves requires the attention-like central executive and visuo-spatial processing, but does not require verbal rehearsal. The other strong implication was expressed as follows by Robbins *et al.* (1996: 91): 'there was little evidence . . . in this study to suggest that differences in chess skill depend either qualitatively or quantitatively on differences in the operation of working memory'. Presumably stronger chess players process information about chess more efficiently than weaker ones while using the same processing mechanisms.

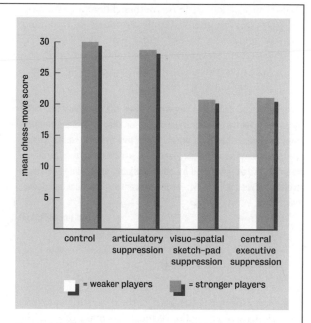

Figure 8.5 Chess move selection in stronger and weaker players with various secondary tasks
Source: adapted from Robbins *et al.* (1996)

Ψ Section summary

A valuable approach to developing an understanding of problem solving is to compare the performance of experts with that of novices. In studies of chess playing, it has been found that experts seem to have many more chess patterns stored in memory than do less skilled players. However, expert chess players also have superior strategic processing skills, even when confronted by a random board position. Anderson produced an Adaptive Control of Thought model, in which expertise acquisition involves a shift from declarative knowledge to procedural knowledge. This model has proved successful, but does not account for creative forms of expertise.

1 What has been learned about expertise from the study of chess players?

☐ Reasoning

Researchers on reasoning have often distinguished between **deductive reasoning** and **inductive reasoning**. Deductive reasoning involves drawing certain conclusions which follow necessarily provided that certain statements are assumed to be true. For example, from the statements 'If I can see a boy, then it is my son' and 'I can see a boy' it follows by deductive reasoning that I can see my son. In contrast, inductive reasoning involves drawing a general conclusion from specific information; this conclusion is not necessarily true. For example, a scientist may decide that his or her findings confirm a general theory, but it is always possible that future research will produce different findings and disprove the theory.

The distinction between deductive reasoning and inductive reasoning is a valuable one so far as logicians are concerned, but it is less clear that it is of use to psychologists. The key issue is whether different psychological processes are involved in the two kinds of reasoning, but the evidence is not clear cut. Bolton (1972) reviewed the relevant evidence, and concluded that there was much overlap in the processes involved in deductive and inductive reasoning:

Experiments on deductive reasoning show that subjects are influenced sufficiently by their experience for their reasoning to differ from that described by a purely deductive system, whilst experiments on inductive reasoning lead to the view that an understanding of the strategies used by adult subjects in attaining concepts involves reference to higher-order concepts of a logical and deductive nature.

(Bolton 1972: 154)

Conditional reasoning

It is of interest to many psychologists to decide whether human reasoning is basically logical or illogical. One way of investigating this issue is to make use of the propositional calculus which forms an important part of formal logic. Propositional calculus is based on logical operators (not; and; if . . . then; or; if and only if) which are incorporated into propositions. Within the system of propositional calculus, propositions are true or false on the basis of logic rather than on the basis of our knowledge of the world.

The type of problem generated by propositional calculus can be illustrated by considering conditional reasoning. Here is an example of a problem in conditional reasoning:

Premises
If it is cold, then Aristotle was a woman
It is cold

Conclusion
Aristotle was a woman

The conclusion is valid or true in logical terms, even though it is untrue in terms of our knowledge of Aristotle. However, the conclusion 'Aristotle was a man' would not follow logically from the two premises.

The above syllogism illustrates the rule of inference known as **modus ponens**: given the premise, 'If A, then B', and given A, it is valid to infer B. The great majority of people find it easy to decide whether a conclusion is valid or invalid with modus ponens; in studies by Marcus and Rips (1979) and by Evans *et al.* (1995), the figure was close to 100 per cent. However, many more errors,

exceeding 40 per cent in the Marcus and Rips (1979) study, are made with another rule of inference known as modus tollens. **Modus tollens** involves the following reasoning: given the premises, 'If A, then B', and. 'B is false', then the conclusion 'A is false' follows logically. Here is an example of this rule of inference:

Premises
If it is Wednesday, then it is sunny
It is not sunny

Conclusion
It is not Wednesday

Another inference which causes errors involves *affirmation of the consequent* and can be illustrated as follows:

Premises
If it is Wednesday, then it is sunny
It is sunny

Conclusion
Therefore, it is Wednesday

In the Evans *et al.* (1995) study, 21 per cent of the participants drew the affirmation of the consequent inference when presented with abstract versions of the above. The conclusion may seem valid, but in fact it is not. The premises do not rule out the possibility that it can be sunny on other days of the week, and so it is not necessarily Wednesday.

Finally, there is the inference based on denial of the antecedent. Here is an example:

Premises
If it is Wednesday, then it is sunny
It is not Wednesday

Conclusion
Therefore, it is not sunny

In the Evans *et al.* (1995) study, the participants received abstract versions of this inference. More than 60 per cent of them accepted the denial of the antecedent inference even though it is false.

Evans *et al.* (1995) obtained clear evidence of what has been called negative conclusion bias. This is the tendency to be more willing to draw inferences with negative conclusions than with positive ones. However, this bias was mostly restricted to denial of the antecedent and modus tollens inferences, and was not generally found with modus ponens and affirmation of the consequent inferences. These findings led Evans *et al.* (1995) to argue as follows:

Clearly we have a robust bias, but it is not a 'negative conclusion bias' in the sense of a general tendency to do something (endorse a negative conclusion) than a failure to do something (deny a negative proposition in order to draw an affirmative conclusion). We are tempted to call it a 'double negation effect'.

(Evans *et al.* 1995: 663)

Theories

The fact that numerous errors are made with modus tollens and with affirmation of the consequent suggests that many people do not think or reason in a logical fashion. However, Braine (1978) and Braine and O'Brien (1991) have proposed an abstract-rule theory. This is essentially a theory of propositional reasoning based on the notion that people apply a mental logic to reasoning tasks, and it has been used to explain performance on conditional reasoning problems. The mental logic identified by Braine (1978) involves the use of various abstract reasoning rules. One of these rules corresponds to modus ponens, which explains why this form of inference is used so accurately. Why, then, are so many mistakes made on conditional reasoning problems? There are three main reasons why valid conclusions are rejected or invalid ones accepted:

* comprehension failure, in which one or more of the statements or premises are misinterpreted
* heuristic inadequacy, in which the various abstract reasoning rules applied to the premises are not properly co-ordinated with each other
* processing errors, in which there is a failure to hold all of the necessary information in working memory

Comprehension failure is important because the way we interpret statements in everyday life is often different from the way they should be interpreted on a conditional reasoning task. For example, consider the following task involving *denial of the antecedent*:

Premises
If you mow the lawn, I will give you one pound
You do not mow the lawn

Conclusion
Therefore, I will not give you one pound

In terms of strict logic, the conclusion is not valid, because there could be other reasons why I will give you one pound. However, in everyday conversation, the statement 'If you mow the lawn, I will give you one pound' clearly suggests the inference 'If you don't mow the lawn, I will not give you one pound' (Geis and

Zwicky 1971). If one interprets the first premise in this way, then the conclusion becomes valid.

Some of the most impressive support for the abstract-rule theory was reported by Braine *et al.* (1984). They used a series of reasoning problems, each of which could theoretically be solved simply by applying one of the abstract reasoning rules contained within the theory. As predicted, the participants did very well on these simple problems. More complex reasoning problems, involving the use of two or more of the abstract rules, were also used. Performance on these problems was well predicted on the basis of the number and complexity of abstract rules which needed to be used to solve them.

There is no doubt that people do make mistakes on syllogistic reasoning problems for the reasons proposed by the abstract-rule theory. However, as M.W. Eysenck and Keane (1995) pointed out, the theory is limited in some ways. In particular, there is inadequate specification of the processes involved in the misinterpretation of premises by the comprehension system. Another limitation is that the theory is well designed to account for the findings on propositional reasoning, but it would require a number of modifications to be applicable to other kinds of reasoning problems. Some of the findings accounted for by the abstract-rule theory can also be explained by rather different theoretical approaches. One such approach is based on mental models (Johnson-Laird 1983) and is discussed later in the chapter.

Wason selection task

One of the most useful ways of studying conditional reasoning is the Wason selection task, named after its inventor Peter Wason. There are four cards lying on a table, and each card has a number on one side and a letter on the other side. The participants are told that there is a rule which applies to the four cards. In one version of the task, the four cards are as shown in Figure 8.6, and the rule is 'If there is an R on one side of the card, then there is a 2 on the other side of the card'. The partici-

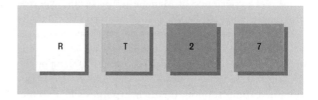

Figure 8.6 Wason selection task

pants' task is to select those cards that need to be turned over to decide whether or not the rule is correct.

What do you think the answer is to this problem? Only about 5 per cent of university students get the answer right (Wason 1968), so it is clearly a very difficult problem. The most popular choices are to select the R card or the R and 2 cards. In fact, the 2 card does not need to be selected. If it has an R on the other side, then this means that the rule may be true. If it has anything else on the other side, then it has no relevance to the rule. The correct answer is R and 7. Why does the 7 card need to be selected? If the 7 card has an R on the other side, then it disproves the rule.

Performance on the selection task can be related to our earlier discussion of conditional reasoning. Someone who understands modus ponens but not modus tollens will turn over the R card and fail to turn over the 7 card. This is precisely what was done by 33 per cent of Wason's (1968) participants. However, 46 per cent of participants turned over the R and 2 cards, and this cannot simply be due to a misunderstanding of modus tollens.

There are various reasons why most people might experience difficulty with the Wason selection task. One possible reason is because the problem is presented in an abstract fashion. Wason and Shapiro (1971) compared performance with the abstract version of the Wason task against performance on a concrete version. In the concrete version, the four cards had Manchester, Leeds, car and train printed on them, and the rule was 'Every time I go to Manchester I travel by car'. Only 12 per cent of the participants produced the correct answer with the abstract version, compared to 62 per cent with the concrete version.

Subsequent research showed that it is not simply the case that reasoning is always better when the Wason task is presented in a concrete and meaningful version. Griggs and Cox (1982) utilized the same concrete and abstract versions of the task as those used by Wason and Shapiro (1971). Their American participants did no better with the concrete version than with the abstract one. According to Griggs and Cox (1982), the difference in findings occurred because their participants had no direct experience of Manchester or Leeds, whereas the participants in the Wason and Shapiro (1971) study were English, and so had more relevant experience.

Griggs and Cox (1982) proposed a memory cueing hypothesis, according to which successful reasoning on the Wason task requires relevant specific experiences. They obtained some support for their hypothesis in a second experiment. Students in Florida were given a version of the Wason task, in which the rule was based on the Florida law relating to under-age drinking: 'If a person is drinking beer, then the person must be over 19 years of age'.

The memory cueing hypothesis did not emerge very well from a later study by Griggs and Cox (1983). Their participants were asked to imagine that they were store managers, and had the responsibility of checking sales receipts. The rule used in this version of the Wason task was as follows: 'If a purchase exceeds $30, then the receipt must be approved by the departmental manager'. Even though the participants had no personal experience of checking sales receipts, 70 per cent of them produced the correct solution.

Cheng and Holyoak (1985) tried to explain the findings of Griggs and Cox (1983) in their pragmatic reasoning theory. According to this theory, we have learned pragmatic reasoning schemas or rules relating to permission and obligation situations. For example, permission schemas are of the form 'If an action is to be taken, then a precondition must be satisfied'. Use of these pragmatic reasoning schemas will generally lead to successful reasoning, as in the study by Griggs and Cox (1983). In contrast, reasoning performance will often be poor if these reasoning schemas are not used.

Cheng and Holyoak (1985) provided fairly convincing support for their pragmatic reasoning theory. They compared the standard abstract version of the Wason task against another abstract version based on a permission situation: if one is to take action A, then one must satisfy precondition P. Only 19 per cent of the participants given the standard version found the solution, compared to 61 per cent of those given the abstract-permission version. These findings indicate that relevant pragmatic reasoning schemas are more important than the use of concrete material in producing effective reasoning performance.

Is the selection task realistic?

Literally dozens of studies on Wason's selection task have been reported in the literature, and several ingenious theories have been put forward to account for the relatively poor performance shown by most participants. A key issue with respect to evaluating this research is whether it enhances our understanding of the ways in which human beings typically think and draw inferences. There are grounds for arguing that it does not. Most human reasoning involves uncertain and plausible inferences, whereas the reasoning required on Wason's selection task is certain and logical. Thus, the

ψ Case study

Unilateral brain lesions

Golding (1981) argued that one of the reasons why people make errors on the Wason selection task is because its visual aspects (i.e. the sight of the cards) interfere with verbal reasoning. She also argued that the visual processing which disrupts performance on the selection task occurs primarily in the right hemisphere. She investigated these hypotheses by studying three groups of people: patients with right-hemisphere lesions; patients with left-hemisphere lesions; and normal controls.

The performance of each participant was classified as completely correct, partially correct or incorrect. The findings were striking. As can be seen in Figure 8.7, the patients with right-hemisphere damage performed significantly better than either of the other two groups. These findings suggest that reasoning on the Wason task can be adversely affected by right-hemisphere visual processes. This conclusion was strengthened by findings from a test of visual perception on which the participants had to identify photographs of objects shown from unconventional angles. Those right-hemisphere patients who performed best on the selection task did much worse on the unconventional angles test than did right-hemisphere patients whose answers on the selection task were incorrect. In other words, a relative inability to use certain processes of visual perception effectively was associated with good reasoning performance.

What do these various findings indicate? According to Golding (1981: 39–40), they provide 'strong support

for the hypothesis that control subjects fail to solve the problem [selection task] because of the dominating effects of the perceptual aspects of the task cards at the expense of verbal reasoning'.

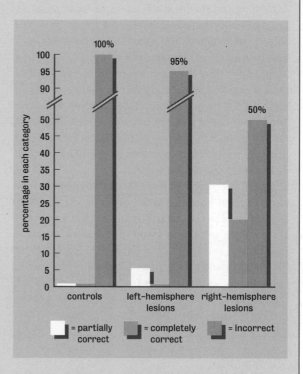

Figure 8.7 Performance on the Wason selection task by patients with left-hemisphere or right-hemisphere lesions
Source: data from Golding (1981)

poor performance typically observed on the selection task may occur because people apply non-logical ways of reasoning which work well in everyday life to an artificial task which requires a different form of reasoning.

Oaksford (1997) developed this line of argument. He proposed that people select cards on the selection task so as to gain the maximum amount of information. He illustrated the point by considering how people might test the rule 'All swans are white'. According to Wason's approach, people should search for swans (equivalent to the R card) and for non-white birds (equivalent to the 7

card), the argument being that finding a non-white bird that is a swan would be very informative. That argument is correct. However, in the real world, relatively few birds are swans, and few birds are white. Thus, it is likely to prove extremely time-consuming to try to find a non-white swan. In the circumstances, it is more informative to search for white birds (equivalent to the 2 card) and see whether they are swans.

The main implication of Oaksford's (1997) position is that the selection of the R and 2 cards by many participants in studies on the selection task should not

Research update

Cheating detection theory

Numerous theories have been put forward to account for performance on Wason's selection task. An interesting new theory was proposed by Cosmides (1989) and developed by Gigerenzer and Hug (1992). According to this cheating detection theory, people are more likely to produce the correct solution on the Wason selection task when the task content relates to cheating, and they are encouraged to adopt a cheating perspective. Why is this? In essence, the participants need to think about falsifying the rule rather than verifying it if they are to produce the correct answer. Those who cheat can be regarded as rule breakers, and so cheating versions of the Wason task should increase participants' focus on rule falsification, and so improve their performance.

How Gigerenzer and Hug (1992) tested their theory can be seen if we describe two of the tasks they used. Both were based on the information that the elders of the Kulumae tribe have made the following rule: 'If a man eats cassava root, then he must have a tattoo on his face'. Among the Kalumae tribe, a married man is indicated by a tattoo on his face. The four cards are 'has a tattoo'; 'has no tattoo'; 'eats cassava root'; and 'eats molo nuts'. In the cheating version of this task, the participants were told that the cassava root was a tasty, nutritious and rare aphrodisiac. They were also told that the rule was in force in order to ration the rare cassava root for the married, and so prevent premarital sex. In the non-cheating version, the participants were told to adopt the perspective of an anthropologist.

What did Gigerenzer and Hug (1992) find? They discovered that 80–90 per cent of the participants had correct performance with the cheating versions of the Wason task compared to only 40 per cent with the non-cheating versions of the task. A few years later, Liberman and Klar (1996) pointed out that the study by Gigerenzer and Hug (1992) contained some problems of experimental design. For example, the nature of the rule to be tested was clearer in the cheating versions of the task than in the non-cheating ones. They observed that some of the differences between the cheating and non-cheating versions found by Gigernezer and Hug (1992) were due to these design problems. However, Liberman and Klar (1996: 147) concluded as follows: 'The cheating situation is usually an efficient way to produce interpretation of the task situation that coincides with formal logic, but it does not necessarily have this property, and is by no means the only way to do so'.

---

simply be dismissed as illogical. What happens is rather that the artificial nature of the selection task requires ways of thinking that are not normally needed in the real world.

Syllogistic reasoning

Syllogistic reasoning has been of interest to philosophers and psychologists since the time of Aristotle. A syllogism consists of two statements or premises followed by a conclusion, and the participant's task is to decide whether the conclusion is valid. There are many kinds of syllogism, but here is an example of a categorical syllogism:

Premises
All politicians are clever
All Members of the European Parliament are politicians

Conclusion
Therefore, all Members of the European Parliament are clever

The conclusion of this syllogism is valid, because it follows logically from the premises. It should be noted that the truth of the premises in the real world is irrelevant to the task. Thus, for example, the conclusion is valid logically even if you do not agree that all politicians are clever.

The premises in the above example are both universal affirmative premises with the form 'All A are B'. Syllogistic reasoning can also involve particular affirmative premises (Some A are B) universal negative premises (No A are B) or particular negative premises (Some A are not B).

One of the most powerful findings in studies of syllogistic reasoning is what is known as belief bias. **Belief bias** is the tendency to accept believable conclusions and to reject unbelievable conclusions regardless of whether the conclusions are actually valid. Evans *et al.* (1983) obtained clear evidence of belief bias, and they also found that this bias was greater on invalid syllogisms than on valid ones (see Figure 8.8).

How can we account for belief bias? Evans *et al.* (1983) favoured a response bias account. According to this account, the participants start by examining the conclusion. If it is believable, they simply accept it. If it is not believable, then they study the premises and try to reason logically. These assumptions can be applied to the findings shown in Figure 8.8. The tendency to accept valid conclusions and to reject invalid ones is much greater with unbelievable conclusions than with believable ones, because it is only in the latter case that logic is applied to the problem.

Evans *et al.* (1983) reported additional evidence supporting their response bias account. About 40 per cent of the participants reported that they had focused only on the conclusions, and a further 30 per cent focused on the conclusions before considering the premises.

Subsequent research by Newstead *et al.* (1992) showed that the response bias account was incorrect. They pointed out that invalid conclusions can be either determinately false (definitely wrong) or indeterminately false (possibly wrong and possibly right). All of the invalid syllogisms used by Evans *et al.* (1983) were indeterminately false. Newstead *et al.* (1992) replicated the finding of Evans *et al.* (1983) of an interaction between the believability of the conclusion and its validity when conclusions were indeterminately false, but the interaction disappeared when the conclusions were determinately false. According to the response bias account, there should be an interaction regardless of whether the conclusions are determinately or indeterminately false.

Newstead *et al.* (1992) put forward an alternative explanation based on the mental model approach of Johnson-Laird (1983) and of Johnson-Laird and Byrne (1991). A **mental model** is a representation of the information contained in the premises of a reasoning problem. Mental models are 'structural analogues of the world' (Johnson-Laird 1983: 165), having 'a structure that corresponds directly to the structure of the state of affairs that the discourse describes' (Johnson-Laird 1983: 125). This approach is discussed in more detail below, but in essence the notion is that people construct one or more mental models or representations of the information presented in a reasoning problem. These mental models are then used to decide on the validity of the conclusion. Newstead *et al.* (1992) applied the mental model approach to syllogistic reasoning, arguing that people will be more likely to construct more than one mental model when the first model leads to an unbelievable conclusion. Only one mental model will be constructed if the initial conclusion is believable.

According to the mental model account, the number of possible mental models that can be constructed from the premises of a syllogism is an important factor in determining reasoning performance. More specifically, an interaction between the validity of the conclusion and its believability of the type shown in Figure 8.8 should be found when multiple models can be constructed, but should not be found when only one model is possible. With multiple models, syllogisms with believable and unbelievable conclusions are treated very differently: only one model is constructed in the former case and multiple ones in the latter case. As a result, the logical validity or otherwise of the conclusion has more impact when the conclusion is unbelievable. This difference in processing associated with believable and unbelievable conclusions is not found when only one mental model can be constructed.

Newstead *et al.* (1992) tested the above predictions. The findings are shown in Figure 8.9. As can be seen, they provide good support for the mental model approach. As Newstead *et al.* (1992: 282) concluded, 'it would appear that the mental models approach provides the best explanation of belief bias effects'.

Ford (1995) carried out a study of syllogistic reasoning using a wide range of syllogisms. She asked her par-

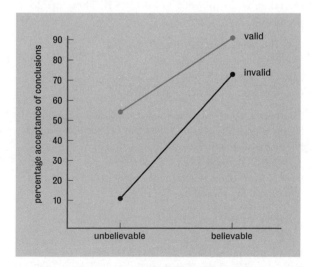

Figure 8.8 Belief bias for valid and invalid syllogisms
Source: based on data in Evans *et al.* (1983)

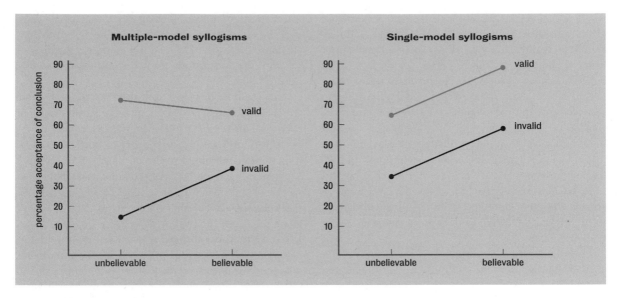

Figure 8.9 Belief bias for valid and invalid syllogisms in multiple-model and single-model syllogisms
Source: based on data in Newstead *et al.* (1992)

ticipants to say aloud what they were thinking while trying to solve each syllogism, and then to use pencil and paper to explain how they reached their conclusion. Her main finding was that there were two major strategies that were used in syllogistic reasoning, with most of the participants favouring one or the other. Spatial reasoning was used by 40 per cent of the participants, whereas 35 per cent favoured verbal reasoning. Spatial reasoners 'used shapes in different spatial relationships to represent different classes and their relationships' (Ford 1995: 41). Verbal reasoners 'manipulated the verbal form of the syllogisms as though doing algebraic problems' (p. 19).

Ford's (1995) findings seem to have relevance for the mental models approach:

Neither the spatial nor the verbal reasoners could be said to provide evidence of developing mental models that are structural analogues of the world. . . . The spatial reasoners could be said to provide evidence of developing a model and reasoning by manipulating the model, but the nature of the representation they use is one specifically rejected by Johnson-Laird – it is a model where the class itself and not the finite members of the class is represented. The verbal subjects give no evidence of reasoning by the manipulation of mental models. Their reasoning processes . . . are equivalent to the well known inference rules of logic – modus ponens and modus tollens.

(Ford 1995: 69)

Mental models

As has already been pointed out, Johnson-Laird (1983) and Johnson-Laird and Byrne (1991) argued that mental models play a key role in human reasoning. Among the forms of reasoning covered by their theory are conditional reasoning and syllogistic reasoning.

In order to clarify what is involved in the construction of a mental model, consider the following example taken from Johnson-Laird (1983). There are four premises:

(1) The lamp is on the right of the pad
(2) The book is on the left of the pad
(3) The clock is in front of the book
(4) The vase is in front of the lamp

The task is to decide whether the following conclusion follows from those four premises: 'The clock is to the left of the vase'.

Johnson-Laird (1983) argued that people use the information from the four premises to form a mental model looking something like this:

book   pad   lamp
clock   vase

When this mental model has been constructed, it is clear that the conclusion that the clock is to the left of the vase is valid.

As we have seen, people form mental models during the process of comprehending the basic information presented on a reasoning task. They then combine the various models that have been formed in order to arrive at an integrated model and to reach some conclusion. Finally, they validate or check the accuracy of the conclusion by seeing whether they can construct an alternative model based on the information provided. If they can construct a model that makes the conclusion incorrect, then they reject the conclusion. Otherwise, they accept the conclusion.

If people construct the appropriate mental model or models, then their reasoning performance will be accurate. However, there are various reasons why errors are made. One reason is because it is sometimes possible to construct two or more models from a set of premises, but people do not always construct the complete set of models. Consider, for example, the following set of premises:

(1) The lamp is on the right of the pad
(2) The book is on the left of the lamp
(3) The clock is in front of the book
(4) The vase is in front of the pad

The task is to decide whether the conclusion that 'The clock is to the left of the vase' is valid.

The above premises are consistent with two different mental models:

book	pad	lamp
clock	vase	

and

pad	book	lamp
vase	clock	

An individual who constructed only the first mental model would mistakenly decide that the conclusion was valid, whereas someone who constructed both models would decide correctly that we do not know whether the conclusion is valid.

Another related reason why people who construct mental models may make mistakes in reasoning is because of the limited capacity of working memory (see Chapter 6). In general terms, it is expected that the demands on working memory will increase in line with the number of different mental models that can be formed. In one study, Johnson-Laird (1983) found that 78 per cent of the participants produced a valid conclusion when only one mental model could be formed from the premises, but this declined to only 13 per cent when three mental models could be formed.

Legrenzi *et al.* (1994) tested the mental model approach on a problem involving modus tollens. Some of the participants received the following problem, having been told that each card had one geometrical shape at the top and another at the bottom:

Alberto put some of the cards in a box, on the basis of the following rule:

> **If there is a circle at the top of the card, then there is a square at the bottom.**

Vittorio, who doesn't know what Alberto has done, has taken one of the cards from the box, but he can see only the bottom part, where there is a triangle. Is it possible to draw a conclusion about the upper part (the concealed part) of the card from the box by Vittorio? If so, what is the conclusion?

Legrenzi *et al.* (1994) found that only 40 per cent of participants drew the correct conclusion that there wasn't a circle at the top of the card. They argued that this happened because the initial mental model that is formed does not include the possibility of anything other than a square appearing at the bottom of the card. Accordingly, Legrenzi *et al.* (1994) used another condition, in which the information that there was a triangle on the bottom part of the card was presented before the information about the rule. Theoretically, this should make it easier for people to form the appropriate mental model. As predicted, the correct conclusion was found by significantly more participants (69 per cent) in this condition.

How are mental models formed?

The mental model approach to reasoning is superior in most ways to previous theories. The notion that comprehension processes are of central importance in reasoning is plausible and in line with most of the evidence, as is the view that people construct one or more mental models when carrying out a reasoning task.

On the negative side, there is a certain amount of vagueness about various parts of the theory. For example, Johnson-Laird and Byrne (1991) argued that background knowledge is used by people when they form mental models, but they failed to specify in detail the processes involved. As Garnham (1993) pointed out, it is not always easy to work out how many mental models would be appropriate for complex reasoning tasks. It is also not always clear how many mental models people actually construct. However, some headway was made by Byrne and Johnson-Laird (1990). They argued that some evidence about the mental models constructed could be obtained by using tests of recognition memory.

People form conclusions from the mental models they construct, and these conclusions are stored in memory even if they are rejected later. These rejected conclusions were falsely recognised by the participants as being the conclusions they had finally drawn, indicating that the associated mental models had been constructed.

Inductive reasoning

One of the most interesting inductive reasoning tasks was devised by Wason (1960). His participants were told that the experimenter had a rule in mind which applied to sets of three whole numbers. They were also told that '2 4 6' was an example of a set of numbers conforming to the rule. Their task was to discover the rule by generating sets of numbers and having the experimenter inform them each time whether the set conformed or did not conform to the rule.

The rule used by Wason (1960) would seem to be simple: 'three numbers in ascending order of magnitude'. However, most of the participants had great difficulty in discovering the rule. Even though they were told to announce the rule when they were very sure that they knew it, only 21 per cent of the participants announced the actual rule at their first attempt.

Why did the participants perform so poorly on Wason's inductive reasoning task? Most of them started by thinking of a rule that was too specific (e.g. the third number is the sum of the first two numbers). Having thought of a specific rule, they then generated sets of numbers that were consistent with that rule (e.g. 3 10 13; 66 97 163). This tendency to gather evidence consistent with the current rule or hypothesis is known as *confirmation bias*. Every time the participants produced a set of numbers based on a rule that was too specific, the experimenter told them that the set conformed to the rule. This led them to the mistaken conclusion that their specific rule was the correct one.

In fact, as Wason (1960) pointed out, the best approach is to look for sets of numbers that will *disconfirm* the rule being considered rather than for sets of numbers that will *confirm* it. For example, participants who thought the rule was that the third number equals the sum of the first two might have generated a disconfirming set of numbers such as 45 60 200. When they discovered that this set of numbers also conformed to the rule, they would have abandoned their incorrect rule or hypothesis.

Further evidence of confirmation bias was reported by Wason (1968) using the same inductive reasoning task as Wason (1960). He asked his participants to indicate what they believed the rule or hypothesis to be. After that, he instructed them to indicate what could be done in order to decide whether their hypotheses were incorrect. Over half of the participants said that they would simply generate more sets of numbers consistent with their hypothesis, and almost 20 per cent insisted that their hypothesis was definitely correct. Only 25 per cent of the participants argued correctly that what needed to be done was to generate sets of numbers that were inconsistent with their hypothesis.

Wason (1960, 1968) argued that his research on inductive reasoning was relevant to the conduct of scientific research. He argued that scientists typically design experiments to confirm some existing hypothesis or theory rather than to disconfirm it. In other words, they are also guilty of confirmation bias. According to Wason, this is not a satisfactory approach to research. As Popper (1968) pointed out, hypotheses can be falsified or disconfirmed, but it is not possible to confirm a hypothesis.

What can be done to dissuade people from showing confirmation bias? Tweney *et al.* (1980) used Wason's inductive reasoning task, and discovered a very effective way of achieving this goal. They told their participants that the experimenter had two rules in mind, one of which generated DAX triples and the other of which generated MED triples. They were instructed that 2-4-6 was a DAX triple. The DAX rule was any three numbers in an ascending sequence, and the MED rule was the rule that generated any other set of three numbers. On each trial, the participants were told that their set of numbers was DAX or MED. This way of conducting the experiment led over 50 per cent of the participants to produce the correct rule on their first attempt. This happened because the participants could work out the DAX rule by seeking to confirm the MED rule rather than by actively trying to disconfirm the DAX rule.

Hypothesis confirmation

As Evans (1995) pointed out, studies on the 2-4-6 problem do not prove that the participants were trying to confirm their hypotheses. It is possible that they were actually trying to produce positive tests of their hypotheses. For example, Evans (1995) considers the example of a scientist who wants to test the hypothesis that all metals expand when heated. The obvious way of doing this would be to carry out positive tests in which one metal after another is heated to observe the effects. It would not make much sense to heat non-metal objects to test the hypothesis. The crucial point is that the participants trying to solve the 2-4-6 problem were not aware that positive tests could not allow them to work out the rule.

An implication of the above points is that people may have a bias towards positive testing rather than towards confirmation. Another implication is that performance on the 2-4-6 problem may be much less informative about the nature of scientific reasoning than Wason assumed.

ψ Section summary

Conditional reasoning is usually accurate with modus ponens inferences, but is often poor with other inferences such as modus tollens and affirmation of the consequent. According to Braine's abstract-rule theory, errors can occur through comprehension failure, heuristic inadequacy, or processing errors. There have been several attempts to account for the generally poor performance on the Wason selection task. Among the theories proposed are the memory cueing hypothesis, the pragmatic reasoning theory and the cheating detection theory. The selection task may put too much emphasis on logic to be applicable to everyday life. There is evidence for belief bias in syllogistic reasoning, and there is an interaction between the believability of the conclusion and its validity in some circumstances. Most of the findings on belief bias can be explained by the mental model approach. However, this approach is less able to account for the finding that some people use verbal reasoning on syllogistic reasoning tasks, whereas others use spatial reasoning. There is reasonable support for the mental model approach to understanding reasoning, but it often fails to specify in detail the processes involved. Wason assumed that performance on his 2-4-6 inductive reasoning task provided evidence of confirmation bias, and that it was of relevance to scientific reasoning. These assumptions are dubious.

1   Discuss the major reasons why errors are made on Wason's selection task.
2   What has been learned about human reasoning from studies of syllogistic reasoning?
3   Discuss some of the findings from Wason's 2-4-6 problem, and their relevance to an understanding of inductive reasoning.

☐ Probabilistic reasoning

Many of the decisions we make in everyday life are simple and relatively automatic. One of the reasons why this is so is because the same or rather similar issues tend to keep recurring during the daily routine. However, there are many occasions in life in which we have to make judgements or decisions on the basis of somewhat limited information. Such judgements involve us making use of the available evidence and trying to draw sensible conclusions from it.

The important area of judgement or probabilistic reasoning was opened up by Kahneman and Tversky (1973). They argued that the judgements we make are often very inaccurate because we fail to take account of all of the relevant evidence. For example, consider the following problem that was used by Casscells et al. (1978):

If a test to detect a disease whose prevalence is 1/1,000 has a false positive rate of 5%, what is the chance that a person found to have a positive result actually has the disease, assuming that you know nothing about the person's symptoms or signs?

When this problem was given to staff and students at Harvard Medical School, 45 per cent gave the answer '95%'. In fact, the correct answer is '2%', but this was given by only 18 per cent of the participants.

According to Kahneman and Tversky (1973), people's judgements of probability are often inaccurate because they fail to take account of what they termed **base-rate information**, which has been defined as 'the relative frequency with which an event occurs or an attribute is present in the population' (Koehler 1996: 16). In this case, the base-rate information is that 999 out of 1,000 people do not have the disease. The fact that there are substantially more non-sufferers than sufferers from the disease means that even someone who tests positive is still unlikely to have the disease. More specifically, if 1,000 people were given the test, 5 per cent or 50 would give a false positive result and 1 would give a true positive result. Thus, there is 1 chance in 51 or 2 per cent that someone testing positive has the disease.

Tversky and Kahneman (1980) reported another study in which people ignore base-rate information. The participants were told that a taxi was involved in a hit-and-run accident. They were also told that 85 per cent of the taxis in the city belong to the Green taxi company and the remaining 15 per cent belong to the Blue taxi company. An eyewitness identified the taxi as belonging to the Blue taxi company. However, when she was tested under appropriate visibility conditions with equal numbers of Green and Blue taxis, she correctly identified whether the taxis belonged to the Green or Blue companies only 80 per cent of the time. The participants' task was to decide the probability that the accident had been caused by a Green taxi. If there had been no eyewitness, then clearly there would be an 85 per cent probability that a Green taxi was responsible. However, most of the participants ignored the base-rate information that most of the taxis in the city belonged to the Green taxi company, arguing that there was an 80 per cent probability that the taxi was Blue. When this base-rate information is taken into account, the true probability is 41 per cent, which is radically different from the participants' estimates.

Tversky and Kahneman (1980) then asked themselves what needed to be done to persuade people to make use of the base-rate information. The answer they came up with is that base-rate information is more likely to be used if its *causal significance* is made more explicit. Accordingly, they used another version of the problem, as follows: 'Although the two companies are roughly equal in size, 85 per cent of cab accidents in the city involve Green cabs, and 15 per cent involve Blue cabs'. With this rewording, they found that the estimated probability that the accident involved a Blue taxi dropped to 60 per cent, indicating that the base-rate information was having some effect.

Kahneman and Tversky (1973) also found that base-rate information is sometimes used and sometimes ignored. The participants were told that 5 descriptions of individuals had been selected at random from a total of 100 descriptions. Half of the participants were told that there were descriptions of 70 engineers and 30 lawyers, whereas the other half were informed that there were 70 lawyers and 30 engineers. When the participants were asked to estimate the probability that an individual chosen at random (about whom they had no information) was an engineer, they produced a figure of 0.7 or 0.3, precisely in line with the base-rate information. The findings were very different when they were provided with an uninformative description: 'Dick is a 30-year-old man. He is married with no children. A man of high ability and high motivation, he promises to be quite successful in his field. He is well liked by his colleagues'. The participants who read this description typically ignored the base-rate information, and rated the probability that Dick was an engineer at 0.5.

What is going on here? Holland *et al.* (1986) argued that people have a preference for 'specific-level evidence'. When specific information is provided about an individual (even if the information is almost worthless), then that information is used and the underlying base rate is ignored. Only when there is no specific information available do people consider base rates.

Representativeness and availability heuristics

Tversky and Kahneman have found numerous other situations in which people make inaccurate judgements. In most cases, the errors occur because of a reliance on heuristics, which are informal rules of thumb or educated guesses.

An example of how people use heuristics comes in a study by Kahneman and Tversky (1971). They gave their participants the following problem:

All the families having exactly six children in a particular city were surveyed. In 72 of the families, the exact order of births of boys (B) and girls (G) was G B G B B G. What is your estimate of the number of families surveyed in which the exact order of births was B G B B B B?

Most of the participants came up with an estimate that was a little or a lot less than 72, although in fact 72 is the best estimate. The reason why 72 is the best estimate is that the probability of having a boy or a girl is the same at 0.5. As a consequence, all sequences of six children, including G G G G G G and B B B B B B, are equally likely.

According to Kahneman and Tversky (1971), their participants made use of the **representativeness heuristic**, in which the judged likelihood of an event is based on how representative that event appears to be of the larger group or population from which it came. The birth order G B G B B G seems more likely than the birth order B G B B B B because it is more representative of the number of males and females in the population, and because it looks more random.

Tversky and Kahneman (1983) obtained more evidence of the inappropriate use of the representativeness heuristic in a study on the conjunction fallacy. Some of the participants were told that Linda is a former student activist, single, very intelligent, and a philosophy graduate. After that, they estimated the probabilities that Linda is a bank teller, a feminist, or a feminist bank teller. The judged probability that she is a feminist bank teller was much higher than the probability that she is a bank teller. This is clearly wrong, because the category of bank tellers includes all feminist bank tellers.

Tversky and Kahneman (1973) studied the **availability heuristic**, which involves making judgements on the basis of how easily apparently relevant information can be brought to mind. They gave their participants five seconds to estimate the product of one of the following sets of numbers: $8 \times 7 \times 6 \times 5 \times 4 \times 3 \times 2 \times 1$, or $1 \times 2 \times 3 \times 4 \times 5 \times 6 \times 7 \times 8$. The median estimate for the first set of numbers was 2,250, and it was only 512 for the second set. The actual products must be the same in both cases, but the estimate was greater for the first set because multiplying the first few numbers together gives a much higher total with the first set than the second. As a matter of interest, the correct answer is 40,320, so most of the answers were substantial underestimates!

There is evidence that the availability heuristic is used in everyday life. For example, Lichtenstein *et al.* (1978) considered our judgements about the probabilities of different kinds of lethal events. They argued that these judgements are influenced by the availability heuristic, and that this in turn is influenced by the amount of publicity given to different lethal events. As they predicted, causes of death (e.g. murder) which attract considerable publicity are judged to be more common than those

(e.g. suicide) which attract less publicity, even when this is exactly the opposite of the true state of affairs.

Undue reliance on the availability heuristic can lead people to behave in irrational ways. If there are a few well-publicized terrorist incidents in Europe in which US citizens are the victims, then many Americans decide to take a holiday in the United States rather than Europe. However, an inspection of the evidence would probably suggest that they are five or ten times more likely to be murdered in the United States than in Europe!

Theoretical limitations

There is no doubt that judgemental reasoning in the real world is often fallible in the same kinds of ways as those identified by Kahneman and Tversky. In particular, most people's thinking is strongly influenced by various heuristics or rules of thumb such as the representativeness and availability heuristics. It is striking that even highly intelligent people often think irrationally, completely ignoring some of the relevant evidence. However, as we will see shortly, it is not clear that base-rate information is ignored nearly as often as was suggested by Kahneman and Tversky.

 Research update

Base-rate information

It is generally assumed that findings in the area of judgemental reasoning are straightforward, with the key phenomena having been demonstrated numerous times. However, the notion that base-rate information is nearly always ignored has been challenged. It will be remembered that Casscells *et al.* (1978) found that most staff and students at Harvard Medical School seemed to ignore base-rate information when given a medical diagnosis problem. Cosmides and Tooby (1996) used a very similar problem, but expressed it in a way that emphasized the frequencies of individuals falling into different categories, and encouraged the participants to construct a visual representation of the information in the problem. What they found was that 92 per cent took full account of the base-rate information, and produced the correct answer.

Koehler (1996: 1) has reviewed the literature on judgemental reasoning and the use of base-rate information. According to him, this literature 'does not support the conventional wisdom that people routinely

ignore base rates. Quite the contrary, the literature shows that base rates are almost always used and that their degree of use depends on task structure and representation'.

What is going on here? There are three major problems with the assumption that base-rate information is always ignored. First, as Koehler (1996) pointed out, it is simply not true that most studies indicate that base-rate information is totally ignored. It is much more common for people to attach less weight than they should to base-rate information, but that is not the same as ignoring such information.

Second, it is customary in laboratory studies to provide the participants with full information about underlying base rates. In the real world, however, base-rate information may be hard to obtain or of less value than it is in the laboratory. As a result, probability judgements in the laboratory may be very different from those made in the real world. As Koehler expressed it,

Box continued

When base rates in the natural environment are ambiguous, unreliable, or unstable, simple normative rules for their use do not exist. In such cases, the diagnostic value of base rates may be substantially less than that associated with many laboratory experiments.

(Koehler 1996: 14)

Third, we often learn about base rates in the real world through personal experience rather than through being provided immediately with such information in the way that happens in the laboratory. Some of the evidence suggests that base-rate information acquired through direct experience has more effect on probability judgements than does the same information acquired in other ways. Christensen-Szalanski and Bushyhead (1981) studied doctors who had learned that there is a low base rate for pneumonia from their clinical experience. They found that these doctors relied heavily on this base-rate information when making diagnoses.

In sum, the most important implication of Koehler's (1996) analysis is that most studies of base-rate information are so artificial and unrealistic that they do not tell us much about what normally happens in everyday life.

The greatest weakness of research is that it has failed to lead to the development of a well-specified theoretical account. For example, consider the availability heuristic. As we have seen, availability of information can be based on media publicity or on partial calculations, and different processes are probably involved in each case. In general terms, use of the availability heuristic involves retrieving information from long-term memory, but no detailed theoretical account of the retrieval processes involved has been forthcoming.

Ψ Section summary

Judgements of probability often do not take base-rate information sufficiently into account. However, base-rate information acquired through direct experience may have more effect on probability judgements than the same information presented in the laboratory. Inaccurate judgements also arise because of reliance on rules of thumb such as the representativeness heuristic and the availability heuristic.

1   What are some of the main reasons for errors in probability judgements in laboratory studies? What is the relevance of this research for everyday life?

Human rationality

Many of the findings discussed in this chapter shed an unflattering light on human reasoning. For example, even highly intelligent people make numerous errors in studies of conditional reasoning and the Wason selection task, and seem to have particular problems with the modus tollens rule of inference. Numerous errors are also found in studies of syllogistic reasoning, in part because of systematic biases in thinking (e.g. belief bias). Systematic errors are also very common in studies of judgemental reasoning. In the words of Kahneman and Tversky (1973: 237), 'In making predictions and judgements under uncertainty, people . . . rely on a limited number of heuristics which sometimes yield reasonable judgements and sometimes lead to severe and systematic errors'.

In spite of the evidence that people reason in an irrational way, the tendency to make errors can sometimes be markedly reduced by changing the wording of a problem. Fiedler (1988) provided a clear example of this in a study on the conjunction fallacy based closely on a study by Kahneman and Tversky (1983), which was discussed earlier. All of the participants were given information about Linda, who was single, outspoken, very bright, and a former student activist. Fiedler (1988) found that about 75 per cent of participants who were asked to decide whether it was more likely that she was a bank teller or a feminist bank teller mistakenly chose the latter option, and so committed the conjunction fallacy. Other participants were asked to estimate how many out of a hundred people like Linda would be bank tellers and how many would be feminist bank tellers. About 75 per cent of the participants argued correctly that more would be bank tellers than would be feminist bank tellers.

The fact that substantial changes in the percentage of people making reasoning errors can be produced by apparently minor alterations in the wording of a reasoning problem suggests caution in drawing sweeping conclusions on the basis of limited evidence. Many of the studies that have been carried out on human reasoning can also be criticized for their artificiality and remoteness from the forms of reasoning typically found in everyday life. As Oaksford (1997) pointed out, human reasoning is generally based on uncertain and incomplete evidence. As a result, we normally make plausible rather than logical inferences. In contrast, many types of reasoning problems studied in the laboratory (e.g. the Wason selection task, syllogistic reasoning, conditional reasoning) involve certain or completely reliable information. Such problems require logical rather than plausible inferences to be drawn.

The artificiality of many of the reasoning problems studied in the laboratory probably makes human reasoning seem less rational than is actually the case. Why is this so? The key point was expressed as follows by Oaksford (1997: 260): 'Many of the errors and biases seen in people's reasoning are likely to be the result of importing their everyday probabilistic strategies in to the lab'. In other words, human reasoning strategies are rational and successful in the everyday settings for which they have evolved. However, these reasoning strategies can appear irrational and error-prone when applied to the very different demands of reasoning problems in the laboratory.

Evans *et al.* (1994) argued along similar lines. According to them, there is an important distinction between two kinds of rationality. Rationality$_1$ involves reasoning which leads to achievement of one's goals, whereas rationality$_2$ involves reasoning which conforms to a system such as logic. In general terms, most of the evidence suggesting that people's thinking is irrational has been based on logic-type problems designed to assess rationality$_2$ rather than rationality$_1$. However, according to Evans *et al.* (1994: 184), 'The notion of rationality which really matters to people is rationality$_1$. People in general do have this to a fair degree, as they do tend to be reasonably good at achieving most of their goals'.

Some of the most convincing evidence that rationality$_1$ is generally more developed than rationality$_2$ in humans comes from research on the Wason selection task. As we saw earlier in the chapter, most people find it fairly easy to solve the selection task when it is phrased so as to refer to permission, obligation or cheating situations (e.g. Cheng and Holyoak 1985; Gigerenzer and Hug 1992), but very difficult when it is presented in an abstract form (e.g. Wason 1968). It can be argued that using permission, obligation or cheating situations allows people to use the practical reasoning strategies associated with rationality$_1$, whereas the abstract version of the selection task forces them to rely much more on rationality$_2$.

Plate 8.2 Using permission, obligation or cheating situations arguably allows people to use the practical reasoning strategies associated with rationality$_1$

Evans *et al.* (1994) argued that humans show good evidence of rationality$_1$, but they also made it clear that our goal-directed reasoning is often imperfect. They argued that our rationality is limited by our processing capacity and ability. As a result of our cognitive limitations, we often achieve our goals by finding an adequate solution (this is known as satisficing) rather than by persevering until we produce the optimal solution.

ψ Section summary

Human performance on a variety of reasoning tasks (syllogistic reasoning, conditional reasoning, probabilistic reasoning) is often surprisingly poor. One way of interpreting these findings is by assuming that human thinking is essentially irrational. However, the fact that small changes in reasoning problems can produce large changes in performance suggests caution in interpreting the evidence. It seems that the forms of thinking which are generally fairly effective in everyday life are often applied inappropriately to reasoning problems in the laboratory. We can distinguish between rationality$_1$ involving goal-directed reasoning and rationality$_2$ involving logic-based reasoning. In general terms, humans perform better on tasks requiring rationality$_1$ than on those requiring rationality$_2$, but there are limitations on our ability to use goal-directed reasoning effectively.

1   Is human reasoning rational or irrational?

Ψ Chapter summary

• Problem solving

Thorndike argued that much problem solving is apparently random, whereas the Gestaltists emphasized the notion of sudden insight leading to problem solution. The Gestaltists also argued that past experience can disrupt current problem solving via functional fixedness and problem-solving set. According to Newell and Simon (1972), people trying to solve well-defined problems make extensive use of heuristic methods, especially means-ends analysis. Many problems can be solved by using analogies. However, people tend to think of superficially similar analogies even if they are inappropriate, but tend not to think of appropriate analogies which share only a deep similarity to the problem.

• Expertise

One of the advantages chess experts have over non-experts is that they possess much more relevant knowledge, and so can structure chess information into larger chunks. They also possess superior strategic processing skills.

• Conditional reasoning

Some of the mistakes made on syllogistic reasoning problems are due to belief bias. However, as Braine argued in his abstract-rule theory, many errors are made in conditional reasoning because the processes are used in the same way as in ordinary conversation. Performance is generally very poor on abstract versions of Wason's selection task. According to the memory cueing hypothesis, successful reasoning on the task requires relevant specific experiences. However, a superior account is provided by pragmatic reasoning theory, according to which performance is high when pragmatic reasoning rules or schemas relating to permission or obligation situations can be used. There is also cheating detection theory.

• Syllogistic reasoning

Syllogistic reasoning is often inaccurate, especially with certain kinds of inferences such as modus tollens and acceptance of the consequent. Some errors are due to belief bias, which is influenced by how many mental models are constructed. Some people use mainly verbal reasoning with syllogisms, whereas others use mainly spatial reasoning.

• Mental models

According to Johnson-Laird, reasoning involves the construction of mental models, which are representations of the information contained in a problem. Errors in reasoning occur if the complete set of models is not constructed, for example, because of the limited capacity of working memory.

• Probabilistic reasoning

Judgements under uncertainty are often inaccurate because we make use of a range of heuristics, such as the representativeness and availability heuristics. However, the precise processes underlying these heuristics are not known, and the artificial nature of much of the research limits its applicability to the real world.

• Human rationality

Human reasoning appears irrational on a wide range of tasks such as conditional reasoning and probabilistic reasoning. However, dramatic improvements in performance can sometimes be produced by apparently minor changes in the way in which a problem is presented. There is an important distinction between rationality$_1$, which is based on goal-directed reasoning, and rationality$_2$, which involves logic-based reasoning. Humans tend to perform better on tasks requiring the former type of rationality. Evidence for this is the much improved performance on conditional reasoning tasks when the problem facilitates the use of rationality$_1$.

Further reading

- Gilhooly, K.J. (1995) *Thinking: Directed, undirected and creative*, 3rd edn. London: Academic Press. This book explores many of the topics dealt with in this chapter in more detail than has been possible here.

- Eysenck, M.W. and Keane, M.T. (1995) *Cognitive Psychology: A student's handbook*, 3rd edn. Hove: Lawrence Erlbaum. Some of the topics discussed in this chapter are dealt with in more detail in Chapters 15, 16 and 17 of this book.

- Johnson-Laird, P.N. and Byrne, R.M.J. (1991) *Deduction*. Hove: Lawrence Erlbaum. The mental model approach is discussed fully in the light of the relevant experimental evidence.

- Keane, M.T. and Gilhooly, K.J. (eds) (1992) *Advances in Thinking Research*. London: Harvester Wheatsheaf. Several different areas of research on thinking are reviewed in depth.

- Evans, J. St. B., Newstead, S.E. and Byrne, R.M.J. (1993) *Human Reasoning: The psychology of deduction*. Hove: Lawrence Erlbaum. Major areas of reasoning research are reviewed in a comprehensive fashion.

CHAPTER 9

Cognitive development

Peter Bryant

KEY CONCEPTS • one line or several lines of intellectual development? • domain-general development • domain-specific development: innate abilities • domain-specific approach: independent abilities • question of cultural transmission • the transition problem

☐ Chapter preview

When you have read this chapter, you should be able to

- know the central questions about children's cognitive development
- have a good idea of the basic features of the main theories about children's cognition, such as Piaget's and Vygotsky's
- understand the distinction between domain-general and domain-specific approaches to development, and have an understanding of how both kinds of theories deal with evidence for abilities which are present at birth and with evidence for abilities which children acquire subsequently
- evaluate the significance of cultural tools such as reading and writing and systems for counting and measuring in children's intellectual development
- understand how developmental psychologists test theories about the causes of developmental change

Introduction

As children grow older, their understanding of the world around them and the people in it changes time and again, and so does the way that they solve intellectual problems. Ask a 7-year-old European child what happens to a ball when someone drops it in Australia and the child will probably tell you that it will plummet into space (Figure 9.1); two years later that child will almost certainly know better (Nunes 1995; Vosniadou and Brewer 1992). Tell a 6-year-old child that you have six hats but your brother has eight, and then ask how many more your brother has, and the answer you will get is usually eight; a 9 year old will make the right calculation (Nunes and Bryant 1996). Put a toy duck in your hand and put your hand under a cushion and leave the toy there, and then remove your hand: the interested 12 month old will look for the duck in your hand but won't bother about the cushion; six months later the child will upturn the cushion as soon as he or she finds your hand empty (Piaget 1954). Ask a 3 year old, a 7 year old and a 9 year old to draw a person and you will reliably be given three vastly different portraits of the kinds that you can see in Figure 9.2 (Cox 1993, 1997).

In each of these cases and in many others there is a striking change in the child's intellectual abilities and in each case the advent of an entirely new way of doing things. Change and the arrival of new intellectual strategies are the subject matter of cognitive development. We want to explain how children add new intellectual strategies and reorganize this repertoire over and over again from the time that they are born right through their childhood.

The topic is a large one because it covers many different aspects of children's behaviour, such as their understanding of their physical and also of their social environment, their ability to remember, to classify, to be logical and to solve problems. Nevertheless there are three basic issues about cognitive development which are easy to grasp and which dominate all discussions about the nature of this development. These are

- the debate between domain-general and domain-specific theories
- the question of the role of culture in intellectual development
- the problem (often called the transition problem) of what causes developmental change and what makes it possible for children to behave in radically new ways as they grow older.

The first issue is about the unity or disunity of the child's cognitive development: the question is whether there is one underlying line of development which accounts for all the apparently disparate changes (in understanding the properties of objects in causal reason-

Figure 9.2 How children's drawings change as they grow older
Source: Cox (1993)

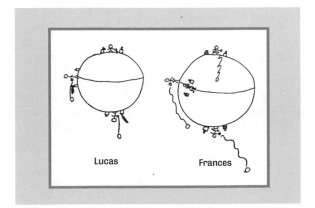

Figure 9.1 Depictions by a 6 year old (Lucas) and an 8 year old (Frances) of what would happen if someone drops a ball at different points on the globe
Source: Nunes (1995)

ing, in making inferences about other people's knowledge, in logic, in mathematics, in reading and writing) that happen in childhood. The second is whether the pattern or patterns of intellectual development are universal or whether they depend at all on the culture that the child happens to be born into. The third issue is the most contentious and the most difficult of the three. We need to explain the causes of cognitive development and in particular we are faced with the problem of explaining how it is that children apparently acquire from time to time entirely new ways of thinking or solving problems.

One line or several lines of intellectual development?

The question here is whether cognitive development is all of a piece or not. Some developmental psychologists take the *domain-general approach* (Case 1992; Halford 1993; Inhelder and Piaget 1958; Piaget and Garcia 1987) and argue that there is one line of development which determines all other changes in the child's intellectual repertoire. Others adopt the *domain-specific approach* (Gopnik and Meltzoff 1997; Karmiloff-Smith 1992; Leslie 1994) and claim that there are several completely different lines of cognitive development which have very little to do with each other.

A domain-general theorist would argue, to take two of the examples mentioned above, that the changes in a child's understanding of gravity and in his or her ability to compare two numbers, though on the surface as different from each other as chalk from cheese, are in fact both determined by exactly the same underlying changes in the child's cognitive skills. To a domain-specific theorist these two developmental changes – in understanding gravity and in comparing numbers – probably have nothing to do with each other and are governed by quite independent mechanisms.

The most famous developmental psychologist of all, Jean Piaget, produced a domain-general theory. He argued that the fundamental change which determines the shape of all other intellectual development is in the child's ability to be logical: all other intellectual changes during childhood are either the direct or indirect result of these logical changes. For example, he claimed that young children have difficulty in measuring or in understanding the whole idea of measurement (Piaget *et al.* 1960); measurement is taught at school, of course, but in Piaget's view the initial and the only significant stumbling block is the child's inability to use the correct

logic. In order to understand how to use a ruler, you have to appreciate that two quantities can be compared through another quantity, such as a ruler, and Piaget and Inhelder argued that this is exactly the kind of logical inference which is impossible for children below the age of roughly 8 years.

Many psychologists agree with Piaget's general idea of one underlying line of developmental changes which accounts for all of intellectual development, but they do not share his view that this development is in logic. Most notably several 'neo-Piagetian' (Case 1992; Halford 1993) developmental psychologists have insisted that the underlying development is in the amount of information that the child can handle at any one time; these psychologists tend not to dispute the importance of logic but they argue that a child's success with logical problems is an offshoot of his or her information processing ability.

Domain-specific theorists argue that development is more heterogeneous than this. Their actual hypotheses are quite varied. One common idea is of a series of modules which are determined innately and which come into play at different periods in a child's life (Leslie 1994). Leslie argues for one module which deals with physical causality and another which deals with psychological causality. Others have argued for a specialized module for learning to speak and to understand speech (Pinker 1994). The initial power of these modules is a matter of some disagreement. For example Karmiloff-Smith (1992) argues that they provide the basis for learning, and this learning allows children to become explicitly aware of what they are doing and hence more in control. Leslie (1992), however, gives less priority to learning and more to innately fixed mechanisms in his account of independent modules.

Evidence for domain–general development

Any domain-general approach must go further than just to claim that different aspects of development stick together: it must say what the glue is. The most coherent idea that we have on that is Piaget's theory about logic. Logic is truly general in that it affects virtually every aspect of intellectual behaviour, since so much of that behaviour depends on our ability to make inferences and to organize the world into logical categories. So Piaget's empirical task was to demonstrate that children's logical abilities do change radically with age, and that these changes affect a very wide range of their intellectual abilities.

The huge body of work by Piaget and his colleagues was in many ways a remarkable attempt to achieve this aim. Piaget argued that there were three main **development stages** in a child's intellectual life. In the first three years or so children go through *the sensory-motor period* when they learn the basic rules of space and time and causality, but do so only at the level of action; Piaget often described the kind of intelligence being acquired in these years as 'practical intelligence'. Children learn how to get around and how to solve various practical problems by making logical inferences, but they are never aware of the rules that they are using. They are learning what to do, not how to think.

Next, between the ages of 4 and roughly 11 years, children go through the *concrete operations period* in which they begin to think their way through problems. The essential ingredient of this thinking, according to Piaget, was the ability to manipulate internal images. Piaget had the idea that children begin to be able to anticipate what could happen by transforming mental images. This means that they can begin to consider different possible future scenarios.

The third period in Piaget's scheme, which lasts from roughly 11 years to the end of adolescence, is the *formal operations period*. During this time children eventually begin to reflect logically on their own thought processes; this makes it possible for them to reason scientifically, and also to solve more complex mathematical problems than before.

In this section we will concentrate on the middle of these three periods. It is in the concrete operations period that the child, according to Piaget's ideas, makes the most obvious strides in logic. Most of the important changes in this period, it should be noted, take place roughly between the ages of 7 and 9 years.

Piaget claimed that children advance in logic during the concrete operations period because they begin to be able to manipulate their own perceptual input. They eventually become able when shown a row of counters to imagine what this row would look like if it were bunched up or stretched out: if they see it being stretched out they can work out what the row would look like if this change were cancelled out. They also develop the ability to take someone else's point of view: for example, when they sit opposite someone they begin to be able to understand what this person will be able to see. Piaget called the ability to make such internal manoeuvres '*reversibility*' (see Flavell 1963; Gold 1987) and he used it to explain the increasing success

that children have with a wide variety of logical problems as they grow older.

Conservation

One example is the famous **conservation** experiment which was originally devised by Piaget and his colleagues to investigate children's understanding of the principle of invariance (which is that a quantity does not change unless it is added to or subtracted from). The most commonly used version of the conservation task involves number (Piaget 1952a). The child is shown two equal rows of counters or sweets lined up alongside each other like two ranks of soldiers and is asked whether the sets have the same number. The child usually answers that they do, whereupon the experimenter changes the appearance of one of the rows by spreading it out or bunching it up, and then asks the child whether the two rows are still equal in number (see Figure 9.3).

Piaget found, and it has very often been confirmed, that younger children (in this case younger than roughly 7 years) give the wrong answer, usually affirming that the longer of the two rows has more in it than the other row. Older children rightly insist that though the rows now look different, they still have the same number of objects as each other.

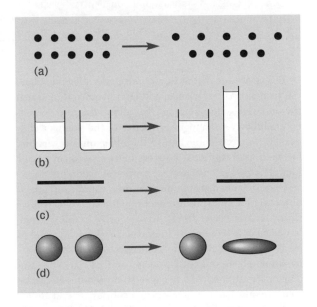

Figure 9.3 The two parts of the conservation task: number, liquid, length and matter

ψ Case study

Conservation studies

Piaget applied the idea of **conservation** very widely and to many kinds of quantities. As Figure 9.3 shows, he also did experiments with liquid poured from different containers, with two rods of equal length (length conservation) and with balls of plasticine (conservation of matter. These are the commonest forms of the conservation task but there are others. One quite difficult form of conservation is conservation of weight, in which children are given two identical balls of plasticine and asked to predict what would happen if they were put on either side of a balance scale. Nearly every child judges rightly that the scale would balance, and they are shown that this judgement was right. Then the experimenter transforms one ball into a sausage and the child is asked essentially the same question: 'Will the scales balance if the ball is put on one side and the sausage on the other?' Usually children up to the age of roughly 10 years answer incorrectly that the scale will no longer balance and they usually claim that the sausage will be the heavier of the two. An even more difficult version of the conservation task is called conservation of volume. In this task children are given two identical balls of plasticine and two identical glasses of water, both half full. The child is asked to imagine what would happen if each ball was put in one of the glasses: will the level of liquid rise to the same extent in the two containers? This question hardly ever causes children any difficulty. But then the experimenter reshapes one of the balls, again into a sausage, and asks the same question about the displacement of the liquid in the two containers. Children under the age of 13 years very rarely get the answer to this second question right, and the task causes difficulty to many children older than that and even to some adults.

The fact that children solve different conservation problems at different ages (number at roughly 7 years, liquid, length and matter about a year later, weight at approximately 10 years and volume three or more years after that) is something of a difficulty for Piaget's theory, for these problems all pose the same underlying logical problem about invariance. If, therefore, logic is the only driving force here children should learn to solve all the conservation problems at the same time, as soon as they have mastered the principle of invariance. Piaget's way of dealing with this problem was to give it a name – 'horizontal décalage' – which meant that there were delays within his major developmental stages. But this is a way of describing the problem rather than of solving it.

Piaget argued that at first children do not understand the principle of invariance, and later acquire it, and that the underlying development that allows them to do so is reversibility. The thought processes of the younger children were irreversible and of the older ones reversible. He then used this idea of reversibility to explain a large number of other changes that happen at around this age.

Piaget claimed that young children cannot categorize objects in a logical hierarchy without reversibility (Inhelder and Piaget 1964). To categorize in this way one has to be able to think of a major class as a whole and to be able to divide it up into subclasses at the same time – to think of the class of flowers and of daffodils and daisies simultaneously, because to do so one has to be able to conceive of a division in a subclass (i.e. daffodils vs roses) and at the same time to cancel this division out and form a major class (i.e. flowers). For very similar reasons, Piaget argued that younger children are incapable of understanding the relation of part to whole, and therefore of appreciating proportions or fractions. Young children can treat a quantity as a whole or they can take in its component parts, but they cannot deal with the whole and its parts at the same time.

Piaget also claimed that younger children cannot even form an ordinal series – A>B>C>D – again because they think in an irreversible way. If they think of B as being smaller than A, then they cannot at the same time think of it as bigger than D: it takes reversible thought processes, according to Piaget, to work out that a value can simultaneously be both larger than one other value and smaller than a third. This difficulty with ordered series led Piaget to argue that young children cannot solve the inferential problem: if A>B, and B>C, how does A compare to C? In fact his first experiments apparently showed that young children have very great difficulty with such inferences, and Piaget then claimed that this showed that they were unable to compare two separated quantities on the basis of an intervening measure, on the grounds that he had shown that they could not relate A and C through the common measure B.

Finally Piaget argued that the lack of reversibility meant that young children are egocentric: for example they cannot work out another person's viewpoint (Piaget and Inhelder 1963). To work out what a person sitting opposite you is actually seeing, you have to be able to rotate your own visual scene in your head, according to Piaget and Inhelder (1963), and this was precisely the kind of mental manipulation which he called **reversibility**. In fact Piaget extended his claim about this kind of egocentrism (not being able to work out someone else's spatial viewpoint) to egocentrism in social life generally: he argued that young children simply cannot work out what other people think and believe and know when these thoughts, etc., are different from the child's.

All these negative claims are counterbalanced by positive ones: during the concrete operation period (usually between the ages of 7 and 9 years) children begin to be able to manage all the tasks that have just been mentioned. They come to understand the invariance principle, they begin to form hierarchical categories, they solve part–whole problems, they form ordered series, they begin to measure, and they become much less egocentric. The bulk of Piaget's empirical research was designed to show that there are considerable cognitive changes during this period.

Piaget's conclusions are all still highly controversial. The most effective criticism of Piaget's claim that young children do not understand invariance has been made by a number of different authors (Donaldson 1978; Light et al. 1979; Rose and Blank 1974). They argued that young children often fail the conservation task for an entirely different reason. The child, it will be recalled, first makes a judgement about two quantities which look identical, and then sees one quantity transformed, and finally is asked to compare the two quantities. According to Donaldson and others, children are unwittingly pressured into giving the wrong answer by this procedure: they know that they have said that the two quantities are the same, they see the experimenter changing a quantity whereupon they are asked the same question again; they conclude that, since there has been a change, they should now change their answer, and they do so even though they do understand the principle of invariance.

To show that this might be so, McGarrigle and Donaldson (1974) reported an experiment with a new version of the conservation experiment in which the transformation of the quantity happened as though by accident. Half of the trials in this experiment were called Accidental: the children made the first comparison in the normal way, and then the experimenters produced a naughty teddy bear which marauded around the table and incidentally managed to disturb the appearance of one of the rows, spreading it out. The teddy bear was then removed and the experimenter asked the child again about the two rows. In the rest of the trials, which were called Intentional, the children were given the conservation task in the usual way, i.e. the experimenter intentionally changed the appearance of one of the quantities. Donaldson found that 4 and 6 year olds made the conservation error in the Intentional trials more often than in the Accidental ones, and concluded that many children give the wrong answer in the traditional conservation task because they have misconstrued the experimenter's intentions.

Several other experiments have produced similar results (Light et al. 1979; Rose and Blank 1974), but it would be too hasty to dismiss the conservation experiment as a clumsy manoeuvre whose results are based on a compete misunderstanding between adult experimenters and the children whom they test. For one thing, in the Donaldson experiment and in others, the children in the favourable condition did not always get it right: there was still an appreciable number of conservation failures and these need explaining. For another, there is a considerable possibility of false positive in the experiments of these researchers who themselves regard failures in the traditional conservation experiments as false positives. The marauding teddy bear for example could have so captured the child's attention that the child may not have noticed what had happened to the two quantities and may not have realized that one now looked different from the other. Indeed there is some evidence for this: Moore and Frye (1986) ran the Accidental and the Intentional tasks but now including a different transformation. One transformation was as before – the length of the row was changed. The other transformation was quite different: the experimenter added a counter to one of the rows of counters, thus actually changing the number so that the correct answer to the question after the transformation would be that the rows were now unequal. Moore and Frye found that the teddy bear procedure got in the way in the addition trials: the children were more likely to say that the two rows were still the same and that nothing had changed in the addition trials when the teddy bear produced the transformation than when the experimenter did. Apparently they paid less attention to what happened to the quantity when the teddy bear was around. It would be wrong, therefore, to dismiss Piaget's claims about the development of invariance out of hand.

Transitive inferences

Piaget also argued that the lack of reversibility prevented children from understanding relationships between quantities. If an adult is told that A>B (premise 1) and that B>C (premise 2) the adult can readily infer that A must also be greater than C. In fact in his first empirical research on children, Piaget (1921) dealt with this form of understanding. In this study he asked children questions like 'Jane is fairer than Sue, Sue is fairer than Ellen. Who is fairer, Jane or Ellen?' and he was struck by a very different thought when he saw the way young children react to such problems. He found, as Burt (1919) had found before him, that these particular inferences – they are called transitive inferences because they involve transitive relations along a quantity continuum – are strikingly difficult for young children to make. Yet, they involve a form of reasoning which lies at the heart of some fundamental forms of intellectual understanding.

If you cannot make a transitive inference, Piaget argued, then you cannot really work out the ordinal relations in any continuum: so you will not understand that if 3 is more than 2 and 2 more than 1 then 3 must be more than 1. Nor can you understand how measurement works, for both transitive inferences and measurement involve taking a common measure (B) to compare two or more quantities (A and C) which cannot be directly compared with each other (Piaget *et al.* 1960). If children of 6, 7 and 8 years really cannot make or understand transitive inferences, as Piaget immediately claimed, there will be much that is obscure for them in their initial maths lessons. This logical gap should also lead to difficulties with spatial relationships, according to Piaget. He argued quite convincingly that, in order to understand spatial dimensions like horizontality and verticality, we have to be able to link separate spatial comparisons (the water level in a tilted glass is parallel to the table; the table top is parallel to the floor; the floor is parallel to the water level; therefore they are all in the same orientation), and to co-ordinate comparisons in this way is in effect to make a series of transitive inferences (Piaget and Inhelder 1963).

This conclusion is also controversial. The strongest objection to it was raised by Tom Trabasso and myself (Bryant and Trabasso 1971; Bryant 1974). We argued that children may fail this task not for logical reasons but simply because they cannot remember the premises, and we introduced a task in which we ensured that children did remember these premises reasonably well. We found that under these conditions even 4-year-old children made the transitive inference correctly and that the few failures that they made could be readily attributed to these few memory failures. But this conclusion is itself quite controversial (see research update).

 Research update

Transitivity

The question of children's ability to make transitive inferences is one of the most vexed in the field of cognitive development. The controversy began with the Bryant and Trabasso (1971) study, which was based on the argument that the traditional Piagetian method of measuring transitivity in children was plagued by two great weaknesses. The first was that young children might fail for reasons which have nothing to do with logic; the second was that children might succeed for reasons which have nothing to do with logic. The first point has been made already: if children forget the premises they will have no chance to put them together logically: a memory failure is not a failure in logic. The second point is a bit more complex. Our worry was that children might be parroting a response that they made when they were given the A>B and the B>C premises. The trouble here is that the correct answer to the inferential A?C question is that A is the larger and C the smaller of the two: but when A is originally compared to B (A>B) and when C is originally compared to B (B>C), A is the larger and C the smaller one. So the children could produce the correct answer

Box continued

to the A?C inferential question simply by remembering what they called A or C when they first saw them.

The solution to the problem of memory, it seemed to us, was to make the children very familiar with the premises before asking the inferential question and also to test the children's memory for the premises at the same time as asking the inferential question. The solution to the problem about parroting was to increase the number of quantities involved from three to five, and thus to have four premises – A>B, B>C, C>D, and D>E. Now the quantities B, C and D are equally often the larger and the smaller one in the original premises. This means that any inference formed on the basis of these three quantities cannot be based on

parroting. One inferential question, B>D, fits this bill and the main discovery of the Bryant and Trabasso (1971) study was that even 4-year-old children make this inference reasonably successfully.

There are many people who argue that the precautions that we took to make sure that the children remember the premises might have had the quite unintended effect of training them how to make inferences (Perner and Mansbridge 1983). The question is still unresolved although later work of ours (Pears and Bryant 1991) appears to show that 4-year-old children can make transitive inferences about spatial position even when there is no great memory load and therefore no memory training was involved.

Reversible thought and part–whole distinctions

One of Piaget's main contributions was to point out in many different ways the importance of being able to relate parts to the whole. In order to understand a proportion or a fraction you have to understand the relation of a part (e.g. one-third of a cake) to the whole, and therefore have to think about a part of the cake and the whole of it simultaneously. This is a problem about multiplication and division, but the need to think about part and whole simultaneously is also present in addition and subtraction problems. As Piaget pointed out, children have to learn about the additive composition of number which means that they have to understand that if $4 + 3 = 7$ then it follows that $7 - 3 = 4$, and this plainly means being able to think of the whole (7) in relation to its parts (4 and 3).

Piaget made the interesting argument that one needs reversible thought to be able to deal with the whole and its parts at the same time: if you divide the whole into its parts, you need to be able to reverse the process and reassemble the parts into wholes in order to think of the whole and its parts at the same time.

In several experiments Piaget did demonstrate that young children have a great deal of difficulty with understanding and using proportions. Some of these experiments (Piaget and Inhelder 1975) involved probability: the children had to work out from which container they were more likely to pull out a particular ball in comparison where the absolute number of this kind of ball and its proportions to other balls in each of the

containers were pitted against each other. Younger children were much more likely to be swayed by the absolute number and much less likely to attend to its relation to the total number of balls in each of the boxes than older children were. Other experiments on the understanding of proportions involved judgements about shadows and about weight and distance in a balance beam problem (Inhelder and Piaget 1958). All of these tasks proved extremely difficult for young children, and Piaget's claim that young children do have great difficulty with proportional problems is probably the least controversial that he has made.

More recent data (Spinillo and Bryant 1991) support the idea that children's difficulties with proportional problems are due to their inability to relate parts to wholes. Young children are quite good at making simple relational judgements like 'larger' and 'more' and so can easily judge whether, for example, a rectangular box containing bricks which are divided vertically into a blue and a white section, has more blue than white bricks or vice versa. This means, in effect, that they can judge whether more than half the bricks, or less than half, or half, are blue. But though this sounds like a proportional judgement it is not, because it involves comparing only part to part – a part–part judgement not a part–whole one.

Spinillo and Bryant (1991) showed 6 to 8 year olds two such boxes with different blue and white ratios and gave them a much smaller picture in which the blue–white relation was the same as in one of the boxes although the spatial arrangement was different (Figure 9.4). They found that the children could make this

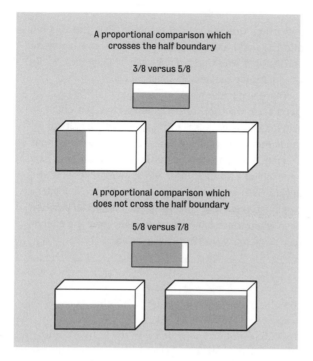

Figure 9.4 Easy comparisons which crossed the half boundary and difficult ones which did not cross that boundary in Spinillo and Bryant's (1991) test of children's understanding of proportions

judgement if there were more blue than white (e.g. 5/8 blue) in one box and more white than blue (e.g. 5/8 white) in the other – in other words if the judgement crossed the half boundary. However, if more than half the bricks were blue in both boxes (e.g. 5/8 blue in one and 7/8 blue in the other) then the children were confused. In this latter case simple 'larger than' relations are not enough and the child has to pay attention to the relation between the two parts and the whole box and this proved too difficult for most of the children.

Drawing

Piaget's theory may seem tailor-made to account for children's reactions to logical and mathematical problems, but he easily extended it to much more informal aspects of children's lives. His analysis of children's drawings provides us with a very good example of the way in which a domain-general theory can draw together a set of apparently heterogeneous developmental changes. Piaget was interested in two aspects of children's drawings. One of his interests was in the amount of information that they conveyed in their drawings and

the other was in the way that they drew spatial relations.

The first of these interests was triggered by a distinction originally made by Luquet (1927) between **visually realistic** drawings in which artists correctly represent what they see and leave out what they cannot see, and **intellectually realistic** ones in which artists incorrectly represent what they know to be true as well as what they can see at the moment and thus include details which they do not actually see from the position in which they are drawing. So a visually realistic picture of a train drawn from its side will depict the wheels on one side and an intellectually realistic picture on both sides (Figure 9.5). Piaget claimed that children's drawings are likely to be intellectually realistic at first, because lack of reversible thought processes makes it impossible for them to understand that different people looking at the same scene from different viewpoints see different things. The child is therefore egocentric and this egocentrism shows itself in intellectually realistic pictures in which no attempt is made to represent the scene from one viewpoint only.

There is some impressive evidence that young children do indeed draw intellectually realistic pictures. We live in a cluttered world and most objects that we see are partly hidden by other objects. At the moment I can see the front of my keyboard, but only part of it because

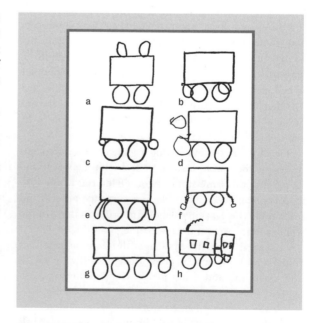

Figure 9.5 Children's intellectually realistic depictions of the wheels on a train
Source: Goodnow (1977)

my hands cut out the rest. One piece of paper to the side partly covers another piece and itself is partly hidden by a pen. So an accurate picture of this scene would include only parts of each of these objects – part of the keyboard and the sheets of paper. Artists have to leave out parts that they know to be there, and there is strong evidence that young children are not good at this sort of omission. They draw what they know rather than what they see.

In 1897 Clark showed 6–16 year olds an apple with a hatpin stuck through it and asked them to draw it. Most of the younger children, and all of the 6 year olds, drew all the pin. In a more recent study Freeman et al. (1977) showed 5–10 year olds two apples, one in front of and partially obscuring the other. The younger children (up to roughly 7 years) represented the apples as separate on the page. This mistake in younger children was confirmed by Light and McIntosh (1980) with 6 year olds. This was almost certainly an intellectually realistic error, since children are drawing a spatial relation (spatial separation) which they know to be true. Freeman and Janikoun (1972) gave 5–9 year olds a cup to draw with (1) its handle turned away and thus not visible and (2) a flower painted on the visible side. Most of the younger children drew the handle and some drew both the handle and the flower – an impossibility. Older children drew visually realistic pictures with the flower but without the handle.

The most striking demonstration of intellectual realism is young children's tendency to try to draw all sides of a 3-D cube. Phillips et al. (1978) gave 7 and 9 year olds two pictures of a cube to copy, one with dots like a die and one blank, and also two 2-D looking designs. They also had to draw a cube from memory. In the 3-D cube drawing conditions most of the errors were intellectually realistic i.e. the children drew flattened out cubes sometimes with five sides. These errors occurred more in the younger group, and did not occur in the 2-D conditions (Figure 9.6).

It is just possible that some of the intellectually realistic drawings are due to difficulties in production rather than to a desire to draw what one knows rather than what one sees. Light and MacIntosh (1980) investigated this possibility in an experiment in which they showed children a small toy house which was placed inside a transparent jug in one condition and behind it in another. In the behind condition several children produced the usual intellectually realistic error – drawing the jug and the house as separate entities – but in the inside condition they all drew the house as encircled by

the perimeter of the jug. This is good evidence that children who make the intellectually realistic error do so because they are producing a literal representation of spatial relations that they know to be true.

Is intellectual realism a conceptual failure, as Piaget and Inhelder (1963) suggested, or simply a misunderstanding of the conventions of drawing? If children make the mistake only because they don't understand what they're meant to do when drawing, they should be helped in a condition which makes the need for visual realism obvious. A.M. Davis (1984; 1986) gave 4, 5 and 6 year olds the cup (hidden handle) task in two conditions. In one (paired cup) the children had to draw two cups, one with the handle invisible and the other with it visible. In the other (single cup) they drew one cup with a hidden handle. She found that some children (17 out of 96) made the intellectually realistic error in the single but not in the paired condition, which shows that they could be visually realistic when it was made more obvious that visual realism was needed. However 23 out of 96 children made the error in both conditions, and the remaining 56 of the children didn't make the error at all. So it seems that intellectual realism is deeply rooted in many young children.

It is certainly hard to teach children to abandon intellectual realism. Light and Simmons (1983) devised a communication condition in which children were shown a red and blue ball, one in front of the other, on a table and were asked to draw a picture so that the next child to come in could work out from the drawing where the

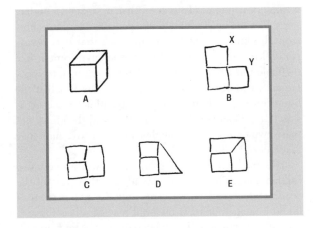

Figure 9.6 Intellectually realistic drawings of a cube: the figure to be copied is A and all the other figures are children's attempts to copy it
Source: Pratt (1985)

first child had been sitting. Other children (control condition) were simply asked to draw the two balls. The children were divided into three age groups: 5 and 6 years, 7 and 8 years, 9 and 10 years. The experimenters found no difference between conditions in the youngest group, most of whom made the intellectually realistic error (no partial occlusion) in both conditions. In the middle group 8 out of 18 children depicted partial occlusion in the communication condition and only 1 out of 18 in the control condition. In the oldest group, there was no difference between the conditions, and the majority of children in both conditions did produce visually realistic pictures, i.e. with partial occlusion. Thus only the 7–8 year olds were helped by the communication game, and not all of them succeeded even in this condition. So it seems reasonable to conclude that the intellectually realistic mistakes made by children are due to a fundamental conceptual difficulty. There is a degree of misunderstanding in 7–8 year olds of the conventions of drawing as the Light and Simmons study shows. But for the most part, and certainly in the case of children younger than that the error cannot be explained in this way.

Piaget *et al.* (1960) also claimed that young children have no idea of horizontality or verticality, and the result is that the spatial relations in the children's pictures are all over the place. The main evidence for this is in their drawing of the water level in tilted containers and chimneys on roofs which tend to be drawn at right angles to the base line rather than as horizontal or vertical (Figure 9.7). Again he attributed these errors, and children's lack of any idea of horizontality and verticality, to a weakness in logic. He argued that in order to understand that the level of liquid in a container is always horizontal when still, the child must see that it is always parallel to some stable feature of the environment like the table top whichever way and however much the container is tilted. The child must take in the fact that the liquid level and the table top are parallel on one occasion (L1 = T) and on another (L2 = T) and then must put these two comparisons together in a transitive inference that L1 = L2 = T.

This is an interesting idea on which we have very few further data. There is some evidence that part of the reason why children misrepresent the orientation of liquid in a glass or trees on a hill may be a bias towards drawing perpendicular lines (Ibbotson and Bryant 1976); but this discovery does not eliminate Piaget's interesting hypothesis that children's failure to represent vertical and horizontal features properly is fundamentally a logical failure.

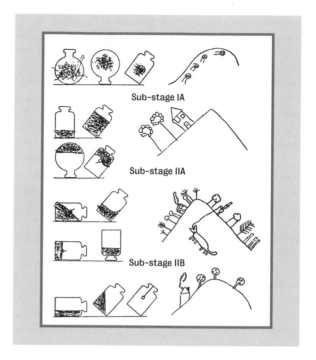

Figure 9.7 The errors that children of different ages make in drawing vertical and horizontal surfaces when these have a tilted baseline
Source: Piaget and Inhelder (1963)

Conclusion about Piaget's theory

Piaget's ambitious notion of a central, unitary line of development which affects virtually the whole of cognitive behaviour still has to be taken seriously. If this domain-general notion is right, children cannot understand the nature of number or any other quantity, cannot form categories, cannot measure or understand proportions or fractions, cannot obey the conventions of drawing and cannot even work out what other people perceive and know until they have through the concrete operations period and have developed reversible thought processes. The evidence that we have reviewed suggests that this is still a viable idea. Despite many attempts to dislodge the theory, it is still quite possible, though not certain, that the developmental changes that we have discussed in all these aspects of the children's intellectual life can be traced back to the underlying logical changes which Piaget claims take place.

Although Piaget's theory has been strikingly resilient in the face of some determined opposition, I should like to sound two notes of caution. One is that the theory is remarkably silent about the possibility of changes between the ages of 2 and 5 years. It may be true, but it seems implausible, that children's intellectual mechanisms undergo no great changes during that time. The other is that Piaget had very little truck with human inventions, such as counting systems, measuring systems and reading and writing. Yet very early on children have to come to grips with these, and it seems unlikely that they are an insignificant part of children's intellectual growth. We shall return to this question in a later section.

Evidence for domain-specific development: innate abilities

Understanding of the nature of objects

The two approaches that we are discussing – domain-specific and domain-general – are based on different sets of data. Domain-general theories are based for the most part on children's initial failures in various cognitive tasks – failures which are surprising and which persist into middle childhood. Domain-specific theories concentrate for the most part on the equally surprising success on the part of quite young babies.

It has been claimed, for example, that babies are born with the ability to compare (Antell and Keating 1983; Starkey and Cooper 1980; Starkey *et al.* 1983, 1990) and even to add numbers (Wynn 1992), that they have a considerable understanding of the physical nature of the objects around them (their permanence, their solidity, the effects of gravity) (Baillargeon 1987; Baillargeon and Hanko-Summers 1990; Baillargeon *et al.* 1985, 1992; Kim and Spelke 1992) and that they are immediately able to tell people apart and to remember their appearance (Bushnell *et al.* 1989). If these innate skills do exist, it would be quite easy to account for them as based on a set of disparate and specific psychological mechanisms and quite difficult to explain them as the product on general developmental system. Specific mechanisms do not have to be innate, but innate intellectual mechanisms are more likely to be specific ones.

Piaget's view (1952b, 1954) was that babies know and understand very little indeed at the start, and that they learn about the nature of the environment quite slowly during their first two years. In fact the baby's first main problem, according to Piaget, is to work out the boundary between herself and the rest of the world: she does not at first realize that one of the objects that she often sees moving across her field of vision is her own hand and therefore part of her, while another is the family pet and thus not part of her at all. The baby even-

Plate 9.1 The psychologist Piaget (1896–1980) thought that babies know and understand very little at the start and learn about the nature of the environment by conducting experiments during their first two years. It has been claimed more recently that babies are born with a considerable understanding of the physical nature of objects around them

tually makes this basic distinction as a result of co-ordinating of perception and movement and thus being able to realize that she can move her hand when she wants to simply by making the appropriate motor command, but she cannot move the cat. When the child understands this (roughly by the age of 5 months) she still has a lot to learn about the cat and also about inanimate objects in her environment, according to Piaget, for he argued that children do not understand that objects (animate or inanimate) go on existing when they can no longer see or hear them. His main evidence for this came from observations that he made of his own three children's reactions when they saw objects disappear from view. A typical example was when, with his 7-month-old daughter looking on, he put a toy duck that the child liked, under a cushion. The child lost interest straight-away, and Piaget argued that the child thought that the act of covering the toy had actually obliterated it: the child thought that the object no longer existed. This empirical observation is reliable: it has often been repeated.

However, Piaget's interpretation is still controversial. Other work seems to show that quite young children do understand the continued existence of objects which they can no longer see. The most famous series of experiments of this sort were conducted by Rene Baillargeon, a French psychologist working in USA. She and her colleagues (Baillargeon 1986; Baillargeon *et al.* 1985) showed 4-month-old children a drawbridge on the table and demonstrated how it could be lifted and turn backwards through a 180° angle until it was flat again (Figure 9.8). Then they placed a wooden block immediately behind the drawbridge. After a while they raised the drawbridge so that it concealed the block from the baby completely. They pulled the drawbridge through an angle of 120° and in the normal course of events its path would have been impeded by the block at that point. But the experimenters arranged matters so that half the time the drawbridge went through a full 180° semicircle (impossible event); the other half of the time it stopped where it should have, after turning 120° (possible event).

Baillargeon and her colleagues' measure was the amount of time that babies would look at these different events. On the whole babies look longer at new and surprising scenes, and Baillargeon argued that if they understood anything about the existence and the solidity of the block of wood – now hidden behind the drawbridge – they ought to be more surprised and thus look longer at the impossible event (drawbridge goes through 180°) than at the possible one (drawbridge goes through 120°). This was what she found and in later experiments she produced evidence that children of 6 months even took into account the height of the hidden block, being more surprised when the drawbridge went through 140° with a high block (impossible event) than with a low one (possible event). These results suggest not only that young children do realize that an object is hidden from view but also that they can take into account and remember information about its physical characteristics such as its height and its solidity.

Baillargeon's conclusions are supported by the results of a study reported by Thomas Bower (1971; 1982) in which he monitored 4-month-old babies' heart rate. He did this to see what surprised the babies, whose heart rate usually changes when they are faced with some novel or surprising turn of events. Bower placed an object in front of each baby and then placed a screen in front of the object, so that the baby could no longer see it. Soon afterwards, he removed the screen; half the time the object was still there, as it should have been, while on other trials it was no longer there (it had been removed by trickery). Bower reported that the babies' heart rate changed, and thus that they may have been surprised, much more when the object was no longer there than when it was. He concluded that the babies expected the object to be there and thus understood its continued existence.

These are impressive results, but then why did the babies fail in Piaget's simple task? The difference may lie in the fact that to solve Piaget's problem the baby would have had to pick the cushion up to uncover the object. As Piaget pointed out 6-month-old babies can pick things up, but it is still quite possible that they may not understand that this is the solution – that you have to uncover covered up objects if you want to see them again. If this is right, young babies understand the permanence of objects but do not know what to do about them when they disappear from view.

Baillargeon's discoveries about the understanding of permanence are echoed in several similar experiments which she and others have conducted on other properties of physical objects. For example, 6-month-old babies seem to be more surprised when a drawbridge apparently crushes a hard block of wood than when it crushes a sponge. They are also surprised when unsupported objects stay suspended, but not when they fall.

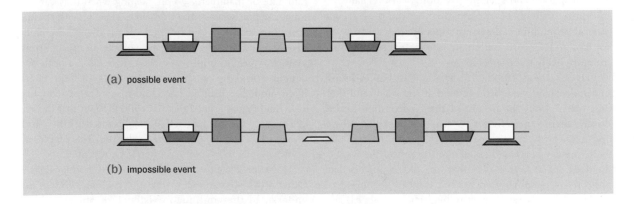

(a) possible event

(b) impossible event

Figure 9.8 The possible and impossible events in the experiment by Baillargeon *et al.* (1985)

All in all, these experiments show that very young babies indeed have a considerable understanding of the physical properties of their environment. The results largely disagree with Piaget's theory about the early stages of the development, and they are consistent with the domain-specific approach.

Understanding number

Babies and number

Given the importance that Piaget ascribed to logic, the apparently negative results of the experiments on objects that we have reviewed may not be so serious. There is no particular reason why knowledge about solidity and permanence and gravity should depend on logic. But there are other dimensions which are more closely related to logic and one of these is number. Some psychologists have claimed that babies also have an innately determined understanding of some aspects of number. Several experiments (Antell and Keating 1983; Cooper 1984; Starkey and Cooper 1980; Starkey et al. 1983, 1990; Strauss and Curtis 1981, 1984) have shown that when babies get used to seeing a card with for example three things on it over and over again in successive trials they are quite surprised to see (i.e. they look longer at) a card which has two objects on it, or vice versa, even when the position of the objects and the actual objects on the cards vary from trial to trial. In other words they appear to discriminate numbers, at any rate when the numbers are small; it should be noted that these experiments have never worked with numbers greater than three.

Even more surprisingly, young babies appear to have some understanding of addition and subtraction. Wynn (1992), for example, showed children one object and put it behind a screen: then in full view of the baby she took another object and placed that too behind the screen, so that there now were two there, though the baby had never seen them together. Then she lifted the screen; some of the time there were indeed two objects there, while on other trials there was a different number – again an impossible event. The babies looked more at, and therefore were probably more surprised by, the impossible event (Figure 9.9).

Older children and number
The work on babies which suggests that they have a good understanding of number is in strong conflict with Piaget's idea that they do not grasp the nature of number until they understand conservation. But other people have tried to show that children at this later age do have a good understanding of the number system.

This is the conclusion reached by Gelman and Gallistel in their 1978 book on young children's counting and by Gelman and Meck (1983) in a later study of children's judgements of the correctness of a puppet's counting. Gelman and her colleagues argued that children must grasp certain basic principles in order to understand what they are doing when they count. These principles apply to any counting system in the world: they are counting universals. What Gelman calls the 'how to count' principles are

- *one to one*, which means knowing that one must count all the objects in a set and count each object once and once only
- *stable order*, which is that one produces count words in a stable order, i.e. always 1-2-3 and not 1-2-3 on one occasion and 2–3–1 on another
- *cardinality*, which is that the last number counted gives you the number of the set: '1-2-3-4-5-6 – there are 6'.

The main conclusion of her research is that children as young as 2 and 3 years do understand these principles even though they make many mistakes when they count. The name that Gelman gives to this theoretical position is **principles before skills**. Children understand the basic principles of counting right from the start, she argues: their mistakes are merely failures to put these principles into practice all the time, and this rests on skills which it takes them some time to acquire.

The main aim of Gelman's research on counting was to show that even very young children understand these principles at the time that they begin to count, and therefore know from the start what counting means. Gelman and Gallistel (1978) observed young children counting sets of objects and recorded whether the children always counted the same order and always counted each object once, and also whether they seemed to recognize that the last number counted signified the number of the set. Gelman and Meck (1983) also asked children to make judgements about a puppet which they saw counting: this puppet occasionally violated the one-to-one principle and the cardinal principle, and the aim of these experiments was to see whether the children could spot these violations. By and large the results of these studies supported Gelman's contention that the children did have some understanding of the three 'how to count' principles as these were set out in her model.

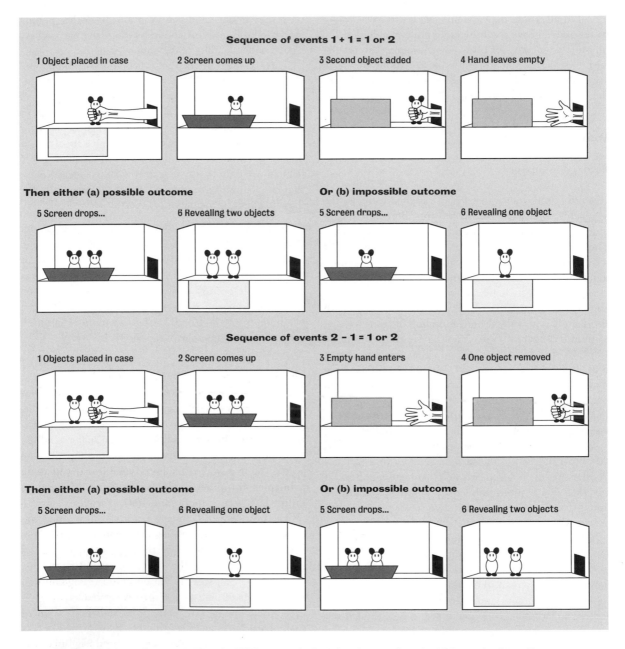

Figure 9.9 The sequence of events in Wynn's (1992) study of infants' understanding of addition and subtraction

However, there is some striking evidence which fits well with Piaget's ideas and not with Gelman's, that young children who count quite proficiently still do not know how to use numbers to compare two different sets. Both Michie (1984) and Saxe (1979) have reported a remarkable reluctance in young children who have been asked to compare two sets of objects quantitatively

to count the two sets. They knew the number sequence and so they were in principle capable of counting the objects and it would have been the right thing to have done, but they did not do so.

This reluctance to use number as a comparative measure was also demonstrated by Sophian (1988) who asked 3 and 4 year olds to judge whether a puppet who counted was doing the right thing. This puppet was given two sets of objects and was told in some trials to compare the two sets and in others to find out how many objects there were in front of it altogether. So in the first kind of trial the right thing to do was to count the two sets separately while in the second it was to count them together. Sometimes the puppet got it right but at other times it mistakenly counted all the objects together when it was asked to compare the two sets and counted them separately when it was asked how many objects there were altogether.

The results of this experiment were largely negative. The younger children did particularly badly (below chance) in the trials in which the puppet was asked to compare two different sets. They clearly had no idea that one must count two rows separately in order to compare them, and this suggests that they had not yet grasped the cardinal properties of the numbers that they counted.

This evidence suggests that Gelman's requirement for the understanding of cardinality was too undemanding. It is in principle possible for a child to understand that the last number counted is important and still have no idea about its quantitative significance. In fact one of the most obvious differences between the two approaches is that Piaget is concerned above all with relations between sets while Gelman concentrates on children counting one set at a time.

My conclusions on this controversy about children's understanding of counting are simple. Of the two sets of requirements Piaget's are better than Gelman's. Children will understand the quantitative significance of the number words that they learn only when they have grasped both the cardinal and the ordinal properties of the number sequence. Most of the evidence suggests that children at first do not understand cardinality and Gelman's own work on the cardinal principle, as she defines it, throws no doubt on this suggestion. Our knowledge about children's understanding of ordinality is much less advanced, but again Gelman's work on the stable order principle does not in any way show that children understand the ordinal relations in the number sequence. There are good reasons for thinking that at first children are practising little more than a verbal routine when they begin to count.

Causal reasoning

Babies

Another aspect of cognition where logic must play a part is in causal reasoning. Much of our understanding of events must depend on causal inferences. The cup fell on the floor because the dog must have pushed it off the table; the car stopped because it ran out of petrol. Some of the experiments with babies that we have mentioned already seem to involve some inferences of this kind — inferences, for example, about a solid block stopping the drawbridge or about support being necessary for objects to stay suspended.

There are also some direct experiments on causal reasoning. One of these is by Leslie and Keeble (1987) who showed 6-month-old babies an abstract scene with two objects (A and B). Then babies saw A move towards and eventually collide with B: what happened then varied. One group of babies saw object B move on directly, while the other saw B move after a 5 second delay. Leslie and Keeble (1987) argued that if babies of this age take in causal relations in the same way as adults do, the first group should judge that the first object launched the movement of the second, whereas the second should see no causal connection between the movement of the two objects. To test this they reversed the sequence, and all the babies saw B moving towards and colliding with A and then A moving immediately. Leslie and Keeble found that the first group of babies (who had seen the apparent immediate launching of B by A previously) were surprised (i.e. looked longer) when B now apparently launched A whereas other babies did not show this effect. The experimenters concluded that the first group had definitely concluded that the first group of babies had justifiably concluded that the relationship between A and B's movements was a causal one on the basis of the temporal sequence of events and that the second group, also justifiably, had not reached this conclusion. The experiment shows that very young children indeed are able to infer casual relationships in a rational way on the basis of temporal events.

An even more remarkable experiment establishes that young babies can actually reason causally about intentions. Gergely et al. (1996), a group of Hungarian psychologists, showed children two temporal sequences with abstract figures. The first scene that the children saw was of a circle moving across a screen towards a square which was on the other side of the screen, but halfway there was a straight vertical line which gave the appearance of a barrier. When the circle reached the barrier it apparently jumped over it: it moved in a semi circle over the line to the other side and then went on to reach the square. Next the infants saw the same scene except that now the barrier was no longer there. Half the children saw the circle move in a straight line directly towards the square: the other half saw the circle make the same semicircular jump half way there, only this time over nothing.

The experimenters reasoned that if the child had inferred that the intention of the circle was to visit the square as directly as possible, and had jumped only to avoid the barrier the first time round, then those who saw the circle making the same jump in the second scene would be genuinely surprised. On the other hand if they simply looked at the scene as a mechanical series of movements, the semicircular trajectory would be no surprise, for they had seen it before. In fact the experiment showed that the children who saw the circle jump for the second scene were apparently surprised: they looked at the scene much longer than those who saw the circle take the direct route. They concluded that the children can read intentions and explain movements rationally and do so even with the most abstract of scenes.

The ability of rather older babies to reason about intentions has been confirmed in a remarkable series of experiments by Meltzoff (1985, 1988a, 1988b, 1988c). In these studies 18-month-old babies saw adults attempting to perform some fairly simple action, like putting beads into a container or putting a loop of string over a hook. Some of the infants saw the adult trying but failing to do these things (i.e. dropping some beads outside the container or undershooting the hook); the rest saw the adult complete the action perfectly. Then the infants were left to carry out the action themselves and the two groups managed to do well and as well as each other. Apparently the first of the two groups had worked out the adult's intentions and were trying to fulfil those (and succeeding) rather than merely imitating the unsuccessful actions they had seen before. The children were able to infer the adults' intentions.

There is no doubt that recent ingenious and exciting research done on babies' cognitive abilities has on the whole provided support for the idea of some impressive innate abilities, and that in turn is support for the idea of domain-specific abilities. However, just to show that some abilities are innate is not enough to justify this hypothesis. You should also demonstrate that they are independent. For example the previous section dealt with babies' understanding of physical causes and of human intentions. Human intentions are of course one of the main causes of human behaviour, and are not to be found in objects: objects do not have intentions. So are we dealing with one module for causal understanding, or with two – one for understanding of physical causes and the other for the understanding of psychological causes? Leslie (1994) argues for two separate mod-

ules, one for dealing with mechanical causality and the other with theory of mind (which in effect is about psychological causes), but there is no evidence at all that the reasoning shown so successfully in experiments on babies' understanding of physical causes and in experiments dealing with human intentions are the same or not. We need direct evidence of this.

Older children

If it is true that babies have a considerable understanding of physical causes from the start, then older children should also be able to understand causes and as soon as they begin to learn the appropriate words should be able to express their causal reasoning coherently. Piaget did not think so. In his early work he tried to show that children have considerable difficulties with the word 'because' and do not treat it as a causal connective. When asked to complete unfinished sentences they say things like 'The man fell off his bicycle because he broke his arm'. Piaget also claimed from his conversations with children that it is a long time before they think in terms of mechanical causality and tend to use animistic explanations instead such as 'The rope is untwisting because it wants to'. These conclusions are at odds with those drawn from the experiments with babies which we have just looked at. However, other psychologists have tried to show that there is no conflict and that older children too show considerable understanding of the physical causes.

There are several necessary components to this understanding. One is that the children must understand the temporal relations between cause and effect. Causes can come before effects but they cannot follow effects: people who reason that the police cause traffic jams on the grounds that wherever there are huge traffic jams, you can always find a police officer have forgotten this principle: the fact that the police come after the traffic jam has occurred and not before does not seem to be part of their reasoning, and it should be. Young children on the whole do better. Bullock and Gelman (1979), for example, showed that 3, 4 and 5 years old did rather well in a task in which they had to judge which of two marbles that they dropped into a piece of apparatus was responsible for a jack-in-the-box emerging. One of these was dropped before and one after the jack's appearance; for the most part even the youngest children judged that the earlier marble was the causal agent.

Another aspect of causal understanding is about co-variation: if A causes B then B should always be preceded by A and should not occur without A. Schultz and Mendelson (1975) showed 3 and 4 years olds an apparatus in which there were two levers and a light: switching one of the levers caused the light to go on but the position of the other lever did not affect the light one way or another. These experimenters found that most of the children worked out which lever caused the light to go on without much difficulty, and they confirmed young children's understanding of co-variation in other studies as well (Siegler and Liebert 1974).

Finally causal inferences are an essential part of causal reasoning, and there is still much debate about young children's ability to make causal inferences. Gelman *et al.* (1980) claimed that even 3 year olds can make respectable inferences about what has been the cause of an event. In one task they showed children a picture of an object, such as a cup, and then another picture of the same object but transformed, so that it was now, for example, an broken cup. They also showed the child a picture of three other objects and asked which of these had caused the change: in this example one of the pictures was of a hammer and this was the correct choice. Even 3 year olds were able to solve this problem and other variants of it (see Figure 9.10).

But this is insufficient evidence for proper causal inferences, because the children could have solved the problem by association (knives are associated with cut things) without ever working out that the difference between the beginning and end-state is due to cutting by the knife. More recently, das Gupta and Bryant (1989) carried out another version of this test in which the beginning state was unusual. It was for example a broken cup. In this case the end-state was a broken cup; when the children had to choose instruments they were given a water tap as one possible agent and a hammer as the other. In another version the cup started as a wet cup and finished again as a wet cup but now broken as well. So the end-state (wet, broken cup) was the same in the two cases (see Figure 9.10). The question was whether the children could choose the tap in the first case and the hammer in the second: das Gupta and Bryant found that 3 year olds simply could not manage this task and therefore probably did not take into account the difference between the beginning and end states when making causal inferences. However, 4-year-old children did quite well in this task. It seems that

Figure 9.10 The sequence of events in the experiment by das Gupta and Bryant (1989)

Psychology

children's ability to make causal inferences increases sharply at around this time.

Conclusions about children's causal reasoning

The fact that babies seem to use some elements of causal reasoning is impressive, but it does not mean that there is a separate and independent ability which determines causal reasoning about physical objects. The evidence of considerable changes in children's ability to make causal inferences later on suggests that one constraint in their thinking about causes is logical, as Piaget claimed. For the moment we have no way of deciding whether or not there is a separate module for causal reasoning.

Children's theory of mind

The strongest claims made for an independent developmental module have been for one that determines children's ability to work out what other people think and know and believe. The best known hypothesis about this ability is Leslie's (1994): he claims that there is a point in childhood around the child's fourth year when the module which is innately determined is switched on relatively suddenly. Leslie's own hypothesis is based largely on experimental work with autistic children: he and others have produced a great deal of evidence supporting the idea that most autistic children either lack this particular ability or possess it to a very limited degree. As we shall see, however, the evidence on children's understanding of other people's minds does not give a great deal of support to the idea that this is an independent module and there is a domain-general alternative account of the children's acquisition of a theory of mind.

This alternative, not surprisingly, is Piaget's, who also argued that children acquire the ability to work out what someone else thinks, and know when those thoughts and pieces of knowledge are different from the child's. However, Piaget argued that children originally cannot manage to get into another person's psychological shoes because they are egocentric, and this is because of the absence of reversible thought processes. *Mutatis mutandis* children eventually acquire a workable **theory of mind** according to Piaget (the actual term 'theory of mind' post-dates Piaget but the idea does not) through reversibility.

Piaget's own work on this topic mainly took the form of conversations between children, which plainly showed that they were not taking account the different viewpoint of the other child. More recent research has involved experiments. The most famous of these are two tasks devised by Wimmer and Perner. In the first

Wimmer and Perner (1983) told children a story, which they enacted with dolls, about a boy called Maxi, who saved some chocolate which he put in a green container in the kitchen and then leaves the room (Figure 9.11). While he was out his mother took some of the chocolate for cooking and put the rest in another container, a blue container. Then Maxi came back to look for his chocolate and the experimenter asked the child being told the story where Maxi will look for the chocolate. Younger children had a great deal of difficulty in answering this question even though they could recall the whole sequence up till then quite well: they tended to say that Maxi would look in the blue container, i.e. they seemed to think that Maxi's belief and their own about the position of the chocolate will be the same. (This is precisely what Piaget meant when he talked about 'egocentrism'.)

This result has often been confirmed and in its commonest form (a task in which children are told about one girl hiding something by moving it from one container to another while the other is out of the room)

Figure 9.11 The two scenes in Wimmer and Perner's (1983) false belief task
Source: copied from Mitchell (1997)

children of 3 years give the wrong answer: 4 year olds get it right on the whole. The developmental change may be universal: Avis and Harris (1991) managed to show a similar developmental pattern with a version of the hiding task with young Baka children, who live in a remote part of the Cameroon jungle. Such results have led many psychologists to claim that there is a fairly abrupt developmental change from not having to having a theory of mind at around the age of 4 years.

The hiding task is quite complex, and so Perner *et al.* (1987) devised another task in which they showed each child a tube of Smarties (chocolate buttons) and asked him or her what was in it. When the child answered that there were Smarties inside, they opened it up and showed the child that the tube contained pencils. Then they closed the box up and asked the child what the next child whom they were gong to interview would say was in the tube. Most 3 year olds said 'pencils'; most 4 and 5 year olds said 'Smarties'. Perner *et al.* claimed this as support for the idea of a major developmental change between 3 and 4 years. Subsequently Gopnik and Astington (1988) showed that the 3 year olds who got it wrong often couldn't even remember their original belief – that there were Smarties in the container. Here then is support for the idea of a relatively sudden developmental change.

However, 3 year olds can be helped to do this particular task: Lewis and Osborne (1990) improved the 3 year olds' performance markedly when they asked the children 'What will she [the next child] think is in the box *before* she opens the lid?' This suggests that part of the younger children's problem was in imagining what would be the sequence of events when the next child was brought in.

More recently psychologists have turned to the child's ability to lie and deceive others successfully because they take the view that deception is a sign that children understand that other people can have different beliefs from their own. To deceive someone intentionally is to make that person have a **false belief**. Therefore if children show that they understand what to do in order to deceive someone, they must have some understanding of how other people's beliefs can be different from their own. Chandler *et al.* (1989) set up a task which involved a doll going to hide some treasure and leaving lots of footprints (washable ink on a plastic surface) on the way. The children were then asked what they should do to conceal where the treasure was hidden from someone outside the room at the time. Most children wiped away the footsteps, and then the experimenter asked if there

was anything else they could do to deceive the other person (Figure 9.12). Many children including 2 and 3 year olds then planted footprints to a different container. Chandler *et al.* argued that their removing and fabricating evidence showed that they knew about false beliefs and presented the study as evidence against the modular view that a theory of mind module suddenly starts operation in the child's fourth year. However, this appears to be a pretty fragile result: other research workers (e.g. Sodian *et al.* 1991) have not been able to repeat it with 2 and 3 year olds.

Put together, there are strong signs of a developmental change in theory of mind task though there is some disagreement about how suddenly the change takes place. Chandler *et al.* (1989) argue that the change is relatively gradual and begins long before the fourth year; Leslie (1994) argues for a much more sudden change. However, these data do not allow any clear claim one way or the other about domain-specificity. We need experiments which contrast the way in which children make inferences about other people's beliefs with their success in making very similar inferences which are not about beliefs. If the specific modular approach is right, there should be very little developmental connection between the two.

In fact the little evidence that we have suggests the opposite conclusion. Zaitchik (1990) gave 3- and 4-year-old children a task very like the theory of mind tasks

Figure 9.12 The deception task devised by Chandler, Fritz and Hala (1989): the doll leaves tracks and the question is whether the child will wipe out these tracks and create false tracks instead
Source: copied from Mitchell (1997)

that we have just considered, but this time the child had to think about the workings of a camera and not of someone else's mind. Zaitchik put a doll on a mat and then took a photograph of it with a Polaroid camera. In the short interval while the camera was producing the photograph she moved the doll from the mat onto the top of a box, and then she asked the child where the doll would be in the photo – on the mat or on top of the box (Figure 9.13). Most of the 3-year-old children answered incorrectly that the photo would show the doll on top of the box; 4 year olds mainly answered correctly that the doll would be on the mat in the picture. The young children's mistakes in this task and the sharp developmental change between the ages of 3 and 4 years mirror the theory of mind tasks exactly, and yet the children are no longer working out what is going on in other people's minds. So it seems unlikely that the development that we are considering is due to the switching on of a module precisely set to work out what other people know. It is much more likely that the young children's difficulties lie in making a clear distinction between what was true in the past and what is true now.

Figure 9.13 The two scenes in Zaitchik's (1990) camera task
Source: copied from Mitchell (1997)

Further evidence for the domain–specific approach: independent abilities

The issue of domains raises another question of very great importance in work on children's intellectual development and that is about differences in the way in which children develop. We are used to the idea of some children being generally more intelligent than others, and the idea is of course promoted and reinforced by intelligence tests which are in effect domain-general measures. Children with high IQs are expected to do well in every intellectual task that they set their hands to, and children with low IQs to have rather general difficulties (M. Anderson 1992).

In fact IQ measures on their own are not strong evidence for domain-general intelligence. It is true that they are reasonably well related to children's performance in school, but that is precisely what they were originally designed to do. Even so there is a degree of specialization in the IQ–school performance relationship: different parts of intelligence tests predict particular aspects of development better than other parts do. For example, children's performance in verbal tasks in intelligence tests is closely related to their progress in reading (Bryant and Bradley 1985); their performance in non-verbal, spatial tasks is more strongly related to their mathematical achievements (Macfarlane Smith 1964).

To settle the domain-specific versus domain-general argument, we have to look at the particular developments in question; the trouble is that very few people have tried to see whether different aspects of development are independent of each other (the domain-specific hypothesis) or not. The most direct attempt to do so with the kinds of early ability that we have been discussing is to be found in the work of Gopnik and Meltzoff (1997). They have a version of the domain-specific theory which they call the theory-theory: it is that children build up a set of different and independent theories about specific aspects of their world. Initially each theory is inadequate and in some cases downright wrong, but children change their theories over time in the face of contradictory evidence. They behave, in effect, like scientists – producing hypotheses, testing these with empirical evidence, adjusting the hypotheses. These successive adjustments according to Gopnik and Meltzoff are the stuff of cognitive development.

These two researchers also have an interest in the relation between cognitive development and language acquisition; they argue that if there are specific domains then children's cognitive progress ought to be related to the kinds of words and linguistic structures that they are acquiring. Different kinds of cognitive development should be associated with different kinds of words.

In one study with children aged from 13 to 19 months, Gopnik and Meltzoff (1986) looked at two aspects of cognitive development. One was the babies' ability to search for hidden objects either when these had been visibly displaced (moved from one location to another with the child looking on) or – much harder – when they were invisibly displaced (moved from one place to another under a cover). The other was their success in tasks which were called 'means-ends' tasks: the babies had to use a string or a stick to pull or push an object towards them. Gopnik and Meltzoff also looked at particular aspects of their language. Babies of this age are in what is often called the one-word stage: most of their utterances consist of one word. Some of these words of course are nouns (e.g. 'dog', 'Mummy') but many are not. For example, quite early on children comment on the disappearance of objects, using words like 'gone' or occasionally two words like 'no dog'. They also produce words which are clearly comments on their successes and their failures – 'there', for example, for success and 'uh-oh' for failure.

Gopnik and Meltzoff (1986) claimed that infants have separate theories about the existence or non-existence of hidden objects and about means-end relationships; this led them to make two predictions. First, that there should not be a close relation between children's successes in one kind of task and in the other: children who do well in the hidden objects tasks should not necessarily do well in the means-end tasks and vice versa. Second, they predicted a close relationship between the children's performance in the hidden object task and their use of disappearance words on the one hand and between how they did in the means-ends task and their acquisition of success words. Both predictions were successful: there was very little relationship between children's performance in the two kinds of tasks and there were strong connections (1) between their use of disappearance words and their performance in the hidden object task, and (2) between their use of success/failure words and their performance in the means end task. However, the acquisition of disappearance words was not related to the means-end task scores, and the children's use of success words bore no relation to their performance in the hidden objects task.

In a later study Gopnik and Meltzoff (1992) showed a similar connection between children's knowledge and use of nouns and their success in sorting objects into categories (like boxes and balls). On the other hand there was no relationship at all between this aspect of language acquisition and the children's performance either in hidden object tasks or in means-end tasks.

Studies of this sort provide strong evidence for the domain-specific approach, but they are rare. We need more of them – particularly with very young children – if we are to continue to take this approach seriously. In fact, we have to look at work with much older children to find any strong evidence for the independence of different aspects of development. Almost invariably, however, these studies are about aspects of the world which are artificial in that they have been invented by human beings: they concern, for example, children's success in learning to read, in mastering music, in drawing. We shall deal with the question of human-made systems in a later section.

Ψ Section summary

The Piagetian hypothesis of developmental changes in logical ability which affect a wide range of intellectual activities is still a viable one. But this theory has little to say about changes in the 2–5 year period, although more recent research on causal reasoning and on theory of mind has shown some striking developmental changes during this period. Some of the arguments for domain-specific abilities are weak. It is not enough to say that two lines of development (e.g. the understanding of physical and of psychological causality) because they seem so, unless you can show the two developments to be independent empirically. Most of this evidence is from studies showing cognitive innate abilities in babies. The evidence for certain innate abilities, which affect children's behaviour from birth is now very strong, and these fit well with a modular theory. The strongest evidence for domain-specific developments comes from studies which also show a degree of independence in the development of different cognitive skills: but such studies are very rare.

1   What compelling auguments are there for underlying factors which govern aspects of children's development which are apparently quite different from each other, such as their mathematical understanding and their sensitivity to other people's knowledge and beliefs? What is the evidence for the opposite hypothesis – that different domains of development are determined by quite different factors?

2   What bearing does the demonstration of various innate cognitive skills have on the domain-general versus domain-specific debate?

☐ Question of cultural transmission

The question

Up till now we have concentrated on children's acquisition of abilities which are universal. Logic, for example, has always been with us and applies everywhere; there is therefore a reasonable case for thinking that all children might become logical in much the same way. All children in all cultures need in the end to make causal inferences and to be able to work out what other people know.

But there are aspects of intellectual development which are not universal. A great deal of children's intellectual life is taken up with human inventions (e.g. counting systems, written language, navigational systems, scientific methods) which vary widely from culture to culture but which undoubtedly are an important aspect of cognitive development.

So we also have to consider how children learn about these human-made systems. Take, for example, number systems. These were invented by people and they vary between different cultures. To understand number systems you certainly have to be logical; there are certain essential and universal features of all number systems, as Gelman and Gallistel (1978) pointed out. But there are other features which are not essential, not universal and which came late in human intellectual history. One is the decimal system (Nunes and Bryant 1996): we count in 10s, 100s, 1,000s, and so on, and this has the immense advantage that we do not have to remember a long series of numbers because we can generate them: we do not have to remember that 250 follows 249 because we know that we start a new decade after 9 and that the next decade after 40 (four 10s) is 50 (five 10s). Decimal systems are not universal since there are counting systems which do not contain them, and there are also considerable variations in the structure of the number words in different decimal systems: English-speaking children are, for example, plagued by the irregularities of some of the teen and decade words 'eleven, fifteen, twenty'; Japanese and Chinese children are blessed with a more predictable set of number words, so that the word for 11 is the equivalent of ten-one, for 23 two-ten-three (Figure 9.14).

The issue here is whether cognitive development is entirely a matter of children conquering the universal

Plate 9.2 Although some abilities, like logic, are universal, other aspects of intellectual development are not universal and human inventions such as counting systems and written language vary widely from culture to culture

Japanese			
	10 ju	20 niju	30 sanju
1 ichi	11 juichi	21 nijuichi	31 sanjuichi
2 ni	12 juni	22 nijuni	
3 san	13 jusan	23 nijusan	
4 shi			
5 go			
6 roku			
7 sichi			
8 hachi			
9 ku			

Chinese			
	10 shr	20 ershr	30 sanshr
1 yi	11 shryi	21 ershryi	31 sanshryi
2 er	12 shrer	22 ershrer	
3 san	13 shrsan	23 ershrsan	
4 sz			
5 wu			
6 lyou			
7 chi			
8 ba			
9 jyou			

Figure 9.14 The regularity of the Chinese and Japanese number words

aspects of intellectual functioning, such as being logical, remembering accurately, classifying and so on, or whether an important part of a child's intellectual development is being taught in one way or another about these cultural inventions (they have to be taught because the idea that each child has to reinvent for him or herself the decimal structure or the writing system is plainly preposterous).

There are two sharply different views on this topic. The most obvious proponent of one view was again Piaget (1952a), who argued that the essential element in development was in acquiring logic, which of course is a universal, and that children's understanding of cultural inventions is a mere offshoot of that more fundamental developmental change. But many of the domain-specific theories are as insistent on universal development as Piaget was: it is quite easy to suggest a module for acquiring spoken language, since all cultures speak, but the idea of a module for written language, or for trigonometry, which is quite a recent phenomenon, is completely implausible.

The starkest contrast to these universal approaches is to be found in the ideas of Lev Vygotsky (1978, 1986), a Russian developmental psychologist, and of his many followers (Cole 1985, 1996; Wertsch and Stone 1985; Wertsch and Tulviste 1992). Vygotsky claimed that in studying children's development one must always bear in mind humankind's intellectual development over centuries. He pointed out that over these centuries humans have invented a set of devices, such as number systems, navigational systems, writing systems, measurements, geometry, algebra, systems of communications, calculators and computers, which have transformed their intellectual powers. These **cultural tools**, as he called them, are an indispensable part of our cognition. It is impossible for children to function effectively in their schools or outside of them unless they learn to read and conquer the number system. But, Vygotsky argued, it is inconceivable for the child to reinvent these systems. It took millennia for the first alphabet to be devised, and that was probably because the idea of splitting words up into their component phonemes does not come naturally to humans. So it has to be passed on from generation to generation; this communication of skills is an essential part of cognitive development.

Reading and writing

If the transmission of cultural tools from one generation to the next is indeed an important part of cognitive development, one would expect to find two patterns. First, certain cognitive skills should depend on formal or informal teaching. Second, there should variations between children from different cultures. There is some striking evidence on both counts.

Let us turn to one of the most important of cultural tools – written language. There are several different kinds of scripts; the main difference between them is the way in which the written symbols represent sounds. Here we shall concentrate on alphabetic scripts. Alphabetic letters represent single phonemes for the most part. A **phoneme** is the smallest unit of sound that can affect the meaning of a word and that means that the alphabet is an economic and ingenious system for transcribing sounds. It took many centuries in the history of writing systems for this kind of writing system to be devised; there is some evidence that it was invented only once (Gelb 1963).

So it seems to have been difficult to think of a writing system based on phonemes in the first place; this difficulty is reflected in the problems that children have in getting to grips with breaking up words into phonemes. It does not come naturally to pre-school children, who fail in most tasks in which they have to make judgements about phonemes. Most of the evidence demonstrates that children cannot cope with such tasks until they have learned to read, which suggests that they might only become aware of phonemes as a result of learning to read. Some strong further support for this idea comes from studies of adults (Morais et al. 1979, 1986) who have been illiterate for most of their lives. These people also have great difficulties with phoneme judgement tasks, unless they take literacy courses and learn to read; then they too become better at making judgements about phonemes. Furthermore there is some evidence that people who learn to read non-alphabetic scripts are not so good at making judgements about phonemes. Read et al. (1986) showed that Chinese adults who had learned only the traditional Chinese script, which does not represent phonemes, made many more mistakes in phoneme tasks than others who had also learned an alphabetic version of Chinese. Mann (1986) found that Japanese children whose script does not represent phonemes either were worse than American children of the same age at phoneme tasks, but were as good as them in syllable tasks.

It seems therefore that awareness of phonemes is a specialized achievement which depends heavily on the experience of being taught an alphabetic script. Since there is compelling evidence that children must become aware of phonemes in order to learn to read (Goswami and Bryant 1990; Morais et al. 1987), we have an example here of a cultural tool, which was devised centuries ago and proved to be of very great value, and which has been handed on across generations ever since.

When Vygotsky (1978, 1986) considered written language as a cultural tool, he had the idea that becoming literate might have much wider effects than this. Olson (1994) has argued trenchantly that reading is an important in promoting logical and scientific thinking and is probably indispensable to it. However, there is a serious problem for researchers here. There is a direct relationship between literacy and schooling: the longer and more effective the teaching that children get, the more literate they are. It is therefore usually not possible to tell apart the direct and specific effects of learning to read and to write and the general effects of being at school.

Everything that we have said so far about children's awareness of sound and learning to read points to the importance of teaching and therefore of cultural transmission. But there is also evidence that children develop considerable phonological skills informally before they go to school and that these affect the progress that they make in reading and writing during their first years at school quite radically. Most children can detect whether words rhyme quite well by the time that they are 3 or 4 years old (Bryant *et al.* 1989, 1990). Several longitudinal studies have shown a close relation between children's ability to make such judgements before they learn to read and their success in reading years later on (Goswami and Bryant 1990). These early rhyming skills are also strongly related to

Plate 9.3 There is a direct relationship between literacy and schooling: the longer and more effective the teaching that children get, the more literate they are

children's ability to detect phonemes later on. It is also the case that increasing the experience that children with rhymes and making other phonological judgements before they go to school has a beneficial effect on their progress in reading when they get to school. Thus it is clear that children's early awareness of phonological distinctions, acquired long before they are taught about the alphabet, has a definite effect on their eventual ability to analyse words into phonemes and to learn to read. Another interesting point that has emerged about these early informally acquired phonological skills is that they are not at all related to children's eventual progress in learning mathematics. Scores on rhyming tasks predict reading but not mathematics. Here is an interesting example of domain-specificity in the context of educational knowledge, reading and mathematics, which undoubtedly has to be learned.

So we conclude that the phonological side of learning to read involves an interesting mixture of informally acquired and formally transmitted phonological knowledge. Children develop some phonological skills informally before they go to school and these undoubtedly affect their success in learning how to analyse sounds into phonemes. But they have to be taught about phonemes as well and that usually happens when they are being taught to read.

Numeracy and the decimal system

Another example that we have given of a cultural tool is the decimal structure of the number system. Two lines of research have show how well this fits the Vygotskian analysis. One is the work of Geoffrey Saxe (1991) with the Oksapmin, a remote people in Papua New Guinea. At the time that Saxe visited the Oksapmin, their number system had very little structure. Their names for numbers were based on body parts, presumably as an *aide-mémoire*. The word for 1 was also the word for the little finger on the right hand, for 2 the next index finger on the same hand and so on through the right elbow, right shoulder and on to the head, then down the left arm, ending up with the left little finger (Figure 9.15). Saxe found that the nature of this number system limited the Oksapmin's use of number and was particularly hard for children, who frequently muddled left with right and thus produced numbers wrongly and understood them wrongly.

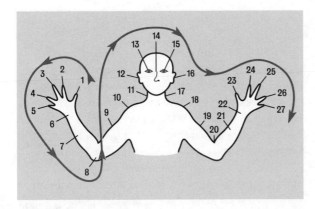

Figure 9.15 The counting system of the Oksapmin in Papua New Guinea observed by Saxe
Source: Saxe (1991)

Later Saxe and Posner (1983) also observed the effects of the introduction of money (the Australian pound) into the Oksapmin culture and observed that as a result they spontaneously began to adopt a base 20 system in their own counting (base 20 because there were 20 shillings to an Australian pound at the time).

These observations demonstrate that the child's experiences of number and of counting are heavily dependent on the nature of the counting system that children happen to be given. In a similar way there are notable variations even between different countries which do use the decimal system. As we have noted, one important difference between different languages is in the regularity of their number words; in some languages like Chinese and Japanese the nature of the decimal structure is absolutely transparent. This makes a very big contrast with English or French, where the words eleven/onze or twenty/vingt give nothing away about their relation to the decimal system. There is evidence that the transparency of the system is an important factor in the progress that children make in counting and perhaps in coping with multi-digit addition and subtraction as well. Miller and Stigler (1987) showed that American children are far worse than Chinese-speaking children at producing the right number names when they count, though there was no difference between the groups in one-to-one correspondence, another important aspect of counting. Fuson and Kwon (1992a, 1992b) have since found that Korean children (the Korean counting system is also highly regular as far as the decimal structure is concerned) fare extremely well with two and three digit

addition and subtraction sums. It is quite likely that their striking success is a direct result of their experiences with a counting system which gives them a clear picture of the decimal structure.

The effects of these linguistic differences go far beyond just counting. Miura and her colleagues (Miura *et al.* 1988, 1994) have shown that children from France, Sweden and North America, countries with irregular number words, are at a distinct disadvantage to Japanese, Chinese and Korean children in a task in which it is possible to use the decimal structure as a short cut. In this task children were given wooden blocks which were either single units or stuck together in blocks of 10s; they were asked to give the experimenter a certain number of blocks (e.g. 15, 27, 45). The quickest way to do so was to use the 10s as well as the units (thus making up 45 with four 10s and five units) and the most laborious was to count out the units. The experimenters found that the Asian children were far more likely to use the 10s than the European children were.

There are clear cultural variations here, and they surely give us good enough grounds for considering the effects of culture and of the transmission of cultural tools on cognitive development. However, it is worth noting that the nature of this transmission needs to be studied as well. With mathematics in particular there is growing evidence that informal experiences are important. For example, children often deal with money early on which gives them direct experience with the decimal structure. There is also often a gulf, as far as children are concerned, between the **street mathematics** which they use and almost certainly learn in informal circumstances and the mathematics that they learn at school. Terezinha Nunes and her colleagues (Nunes *et al.* 1993) worked with children who sold vegetables and other produce on their parents' stalls in street markets. The experimenters bought various things and recorded the details of the transactions, and particularly the calculations that the children made to work out the price and also the change. Later on the experimenter gave the children the same calculations to do as straight sums and as mathematical problems embedded in simple stories. The children made many more mistakes with these new problems, and particularly with the written sums, even though the mathematical calculations were exactly the same ones that they had made in the market. We certainly need to know more about how children learn about cultural tools and the circumstances under which they use them.

ψ **Case study**

Street mathematics

Saxe (1991), when working in north-east Brazil, confirmed the proficiency of youthful street (and beach) traders in addition, subtraction and also in proportional judgements (Brazil at the time had an inflationary economy). The Brazilian team of researchers (Nunes *et al.* 1993) later extended their work to adults who had very little schooling but now had responsible jobs which involved mathematical calculations. One group that they studied consisted of foremen working on building sites. They had never been taught about proportions at school but now they had to work from architects' scale plans, which meant that they had to understand the proportions of the lengths in the plans to the actual lengths in the building. Nunes *et al.* (1993) were able to show that the foremen were much better than students who had been given intensive teaching about

proportions in working out what the ratio between the lengths in new plans and the actual lengths in a building. The same research team showed a similar pattern with fishermen who have to make quick calculations about the relationship between the price of fresh and of dried fish: they too were expert in proportional judgements.

These striking demonstrations of the power of informal mathematics raise two highly important questions. One is about the way in which children and adults acquire these informal skills: are they taught about them by others in the informal economy or do they work it out for themselves? The second question is about the reason why children do not take advantage of their formidable powers in the formal setting of school. We need to know more about what it is that makes children think that their calculations outside school have little value inside it.

ψ **Section summary**

An important part of cognitive development is to learn how to use the intellectual inventions which have to be passed on from one generation to another (they cannot be reinvented by young children). These inventions are 'cultural' in that they differ from one culture to the next. Work on 'informal mathematics' suggests that the cultural tools are also transmitted informally and used in informal circumstances as well as being taught formally at school.

1 What is the importance of cultural inventions in the child's growing understanding of the world?

2 To what extent is cognitive development different in different cultures?

☐ The transition problem

The research that we have been discussing has established a great deal about what changes as children grow older, but not much about what causes these changes to happen when they do. This second problem is usually

known as the transition problem, and anyone trying to solve it has to do two things. One is to explain what prompts a child to adopt an entirely new intellectual strategy, and the other is to account for the fact that it often takes children a very long time to do so. In other words we have to consider not only why change happens but also why it takes so long to happen.

The transition problem is certainly the most difficult that developmental psychologists face. It is easy enough for them to establish how 4-year-old children manage a particular cognitive task differently in a different way from 3 year olds. It is much harder to study the changes as they happen, and that makes it particularly difficult to find out what actually causes these changes.

Because of this, most developmental psychologists, including Piaget and Vygotsky, tried to infer the causes of development from the nature of the developmental changes themselves. So although their causal hypotheses were interesting and immensely influential there is virtually no empirical support for them.

Empirical approaches

However, since the 1980s many developmental psychologists have adopted one or both of two promising empirical approaches to the transition problem.

Computer models

One approach is to turn to computer models. With such models one can mimic particular developmental changes and study directly what makes them happen at any rate in their modelled form. Since the late 1980s we have seen the rise of connectionist models which are specifically designed to model change and are therefore well suited to developmental psychology. Connectionist models consist of networks of units. The strengths of the connections between the units varies and changes over time. Networks typically contain three layers of units which are input units, hidden units and output units, and for the developmental psychologist the changes in the hidden units are usually the most important, for these changes determine the model's reactions to particular tasks. In fact this approach has been used quite successfully to model aspects of language acquisition (Elman *et al.* 1996; MacWinney *et al.* 1989; Plunkett and Sinha 1991), of the development of causal reasoning (Shultz *et al.*1995) and of problem solving (McClelland 1995; Shultz *et al.* 1995).

Microgenetic method

The second approach is to adopt the increasingly used microgenetic method. Developmental psychologists have begun to realize that it may not be all that impossible to study developmental changes as they happen. In **microgenetic studies** children are studied in several sessions spread over a relatively short period and are given much the same task in each session. So the experimenter is able to see how the child's behaviour changes over this period.

Piaget and the equilibration theory

Piaget's stage theory prompts a difficult causal question. What makes it possible for a child to acquire an entirely new way of thinking, such as **reversibility**? He answered this question in different ways as we shall see but his main answer was his theory about 'equilibration'. He argued that children 'construct' their own intelligence: they interact with their own physical and social environment and these interactions provide them with experiences which eventually lead to their changing their ideas about, and thus improving their understanding of, this environment. The experience most likely to lead to change, according to Piaget's theory, was 'disequilibrium': Piaget argued that children actively think about their world, and from time to time find that they

have two mutually incompatible ideas about the same topic. For different reasons a child may conclude for example that the area of a rectangle is determined entirely by its height, but also that it is entirely determined by its width, two ideas which would lead them into conflicting conclusions about relative area of different rectangles. This kind of conflict leads to cognitive disequilibrium, an unpleasant state of affairs which children eventually resolve by changing their views on the determinants of area – in this case by realizing that area is determined both by height and by width.

This causal theory does not place children entirely on their own. According to Piaget, they will benefit not only from physical but also from social interactions. They will learn from instruction and from being able to imitate others, particularly if they are able to understand the logical basis of other people's words and of their actions. Here, in fact, is the rub. Piaget often argued that it is no use simply to tell children the answer: this will have no effect at all unless they have already acquired the logical structures that they need to understand what they are being told. So it is no use to tell a child whose thinking is still irreversible about the solution to a transitive inference problem, but it is a lot of use to tell a child who can make transitive inferences about how to measure with a ruler. In Piaget's view all that was needed to learn how to use a ruler was the ability to make transitive inferences and a basic understanding of number.

This idea of children constructing their ideas about the world for themselves through conflict has had a great effect, particularly on people's views on education. It is highly original and appealing, but it has one serious weakness: it does not answer the most important question about how a child acquires an entirely new cognitive strategy. It is certainly true that the experiences of a conflict between two incompatible views which is said to spark off the process of change in the first place could very well be an effective signal to the child that something is wrong in his or her thinking. At least one of the two conflicting views must be wrong, but the trouble is that this is all the information that the child has. The conflict will not tell him or her which view is wrong, whether both are and, more worryingly, it cannot tell the child what is the right view to take. The conflict between judging a rectangle by its width and judging it by its height will not tell the child the height by width solution.

The solution to this problem might be found in one of Piaget's earlier books *The Origins of Intelligence* (Piaget 1952b). In this, he suggested another quite different possible cause of change: this was *co-ordination*. He claimed that children may acquire new strategies by combining two or more old ones. The interaction between them was enough, he claimed, to produce something different. An example is what happens when at the age of 4–5 months babies begin to reach for things which they can see. At this point, Piaget argues, they co-ordinate visual space with motor space, which till then had been quite separate as far as the child was concerned, and this leads to an entirely new conception of space and of their own position in it. Many would dispute this specific claim, but I mention it here as a causal argument which is completely different from conflict, and one that could be extended to a wide range of intellectual developments in order to explain the advent of new intellectual strategies. We will consider an example later.

Vygotsky and internalization

In Piaget's view children have to construct their knowledge for themselves: each child must reinvent logic. Vygotsky (1978, 1986), who gave such significance to children learning about cultural tools, naturally argued that children need help from others. He argued that children learn about these cultural tools and how to use them mainly by internalizing: he claimed that children first learn to use them with the help of adults and then eventually, by internalizing the adult's role in these interactions, children manage to do it on their own.

Any function in the child's cultural development appears twice. First it appears on the social plane, and then on the psychological plane. First it appears between people as an interpsychological category, and then within the child as an intrapsychological category. This is equally true with regard to voluntary attention, logical memory, the formation of concepts. . . . It goes without saying that internalization transforms the process itself and changes its structure and functions. Social relations . . . underly all higher functions.

(Vygotsky 1981: 81)

Vygotsky gave a striking name to the period when children progress from being able to do something only with an adult's help to being able to do it on their own: he called it the **zone of proximal development** (ZPD).

The zone of proximal development . . . is the distance between the actual developmental level as determined by independent problem solving and the level of potential development as determined through problem solving under adult guidance or in collaboration with more capable peers.

(Vygotsky 1981: 81; see also Cole 1986)

At the beginning of the ZPD children need help to solve some intellectual problem, but later, because of the help that they initially received, they will manage by themselves. What happens in between is that children make sense of what they are doing. Vygotsky described this as a revolutionary activity.

This emphasis on the transmission of intellectual skills from one generation to another goes automatically with a theory which emphasizes inventions like the alphabet and the decimal system because, as we have seen, it would be impossible to expect children to reinvent systems which took humankind millennia to produce in the first place. However, it is interesting that Vygotsky did not simply claim that intellectual development is a matter of direct instruction. The process of internalization has an element of construction in it: children must construct for themselves the actions of the adult. However, this construction through internalization is quite different from the conflict-driven construction for which Piaget argued. Children go through an period of apprenticeship when learning about a **cultural tool**: they learn from and copy adults and come to understand the nature of the tool by using it with help from others.

The main conceptual difficulty with this model is that it does not explain the constraints in development. It takes a very long time at school before children are able to deal with fractions and proportions, and they get there only after years of working with addition and subtraction problems. What is holding them back? Piaget provides a clear answer to this question; Vygotsky does not.

On the other hand, Vygotsky's ideas have no problem with the other main question about causes, which is how to explain the advent of entirely new intellectual strategies and which, as we have seen, is a real difficulty for Piaget's conflict theory (though not for his idea about co-ordination). According to Vygotsky, children adopt new ways of thinking because these are handed on to them.

Modules and Karmiloff-Smith's idea of representational redescription

If children change simply because innate modules get switched on, as Leslie (1994) claims, then there is no problem to solve, apart from how to find the physiological mechanism which does the switching on. However, another way to look at modules is to think of them as learning mechanisms. This is Karmiloff-Smith's (1992) view. She argues that different modules prompt children to learn about different aspects of their world, but that the nature of the learning is much the same in every case. There are different modules, according to her, for language, for notation (maps, writing), for mathematics and for theory of mind and for understanding of the physical environment. However, in each case the knowledge that the child acquires through these modules changes over time and always in the same direction. The knowledge is implicit at first and gradually becomes entirely explicit. Children learn to speak, but at first their knowledge of language is entirely implicit. Later they begin to be able to think about the rules of their language. This growing explicitness, which Karmiloff-Smith calls 'representational redescription', gives children much more control over what they do and allows them to manipulate their knowledge more effectively. Once they know the rules, they know how to break them.

Karmiloff-Smith's methods are mostly microgenetic. She studies not only what children do in particular sessions, but also how their behaviour changes across sessions. One good example is a study of the way children depict a route to be taken along a route with several turns. On the whole the children's initial drawings were full of details, most of which were actually irrelevant. But with repeated experience their representations became more economical and more restricted to the information that a person needed to know whether or not to take a particular turn (see Figure 9.16). According to Karmiloff-Smith the children's awareness of the structure of the task became more explicit, and they were as a result able to change their initial and almost automatic procedure of drawing almost everything to representing only the essential details.

Karmiloff-Smith took drawing as another example of children starting with rigid and unanalysed procedures for drawing houses and human figures, for example, and gradually becoming explicitly aware of the nature of drawing. In another study she gave 4 to 11 year olds the task of drawing a version of a house, a man and an animal 'which doesn't exist'. The changes introduced by young children (4–6 years) involved either deletions or overall changes in size and shape whereas the older children (8–11 years) tended to change the relations between elements and add elements from other conceptual categories (see Figure 9.17).

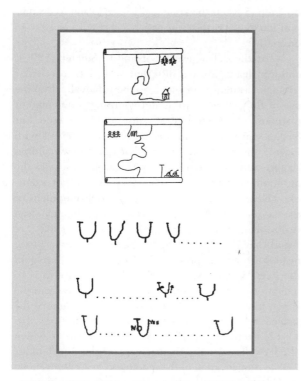

Figure 9.16 The mapping task devised by Karmiloff-Smith
Source: Karmiloff-Smith (1992)

Figure 9.17 Some attempts to draw figures that do not exist
Source: Karmiloff-Smith (1992)

Karmiloff-Smith (1992) concluded that the younger children produce drawings which are 'internal representations as a sequentially fixed list' and they simply cannot break into this sequence. So they make the changes round the edges of the sequence. But the older children are more aware of the sequence and can change it more radically.

Karmiloff-Smith argues that her idea of representational redescription is particularly suited to connectionist modelling, but she still has to produce a successful model of these developmental changes. Another way of looking at this idea about development is to turn to the distinction between developmental changes which may be universal (e.g. in logic) on the one hand and learning about cultural inventions on the other. The skills which all children acquire, such as learning to speak, or becoming logical or understanding spatial frameworks, may remain implicit as far as the child is concerned, until she is being taught about a cultural tool. Learning to read and to write is one example: as we have seen, children have to become explicitly aware of the structure of sounds in words of which they have had a good implicit knowledge for many years. Much the same argument could be applied to children's initially implicit understanding of space which has to become explicit when they learn about geometry and also when they struggle with drawing perspective (Willats 1977). Even logic may go through the same process as Piaget himself has pointed out in his work on children's scientific reasoning (Inhelder and Piaget 1958; see also Kuhn *et al.* 1988). In order to test a scientific hypothesis, Piaget argues, one has to be explicitly aware of one's own ways of reasoning.

Siegler and the microgenetic method

Another developmental psychologist who has used the microgenetic method to great effect is Siegler (1996). He argues that there are two ways to approach development. One is to look on cognitive development as a series of *successive* discrete steps from one way of thinking to another: the child has one way of understanding (usually incorrect) some aspect of the world, and then abandons it in favour of another which is usually a closer approximation to the truth, and still later on abandons this in favour of another even more accurate way of thinking, and so on. According to this approach, cognitive development consists of a series of discrete stages, each dominated by one way of thinking, and each preceded and followed by a completely different way.

The alternative approach is to assume that children may *simultaneously* have several very different views of the world around them and different ways of solving problems, and that they may adopt one on one occasion and another on a different occasion. In this view, developmental change is in the priorities children give to each way of solving problems. Psychologists who adopt this view naturally argue that children change as a result of directly comparing the results of the different alternative cognitive strategies that they have at their disposal.

Siegler (1996) endorses the second approach. He claims that, by using the microgenetic method (seeing the same children on several different occasions), one can demonstrate children typically have a choice from a 'multiplicity' of strategies when faced with difficult cognitive problems and that they use different strategies at different times. Many of the examples that Siegler gives of this variability are taken from the domain of mathematics. He produces quite convincing evidence that the same child will tackle addition problems or multiplication problems in quite different ways on two different occasions. With addition a child will use the fingers at one time, and will count at another; with multiplication the same child will take to repeated addition on one occasion (5×3 is the same as $5 + 5 + 5$) and to decomposition (5×3 is the same as $5 \times 2 + 5 \times 1$ i.e. $10 + 5$) on another.

What then changes? According to Siegler (1996), children learn to give different weight to particular strategies as they grow older. So they gradually drop the use of fingers in addition and counting problems but maintain other strategies. This could be true but Siegler's answer has one weakness which it shares with Piaget's theory. It does not really explain how children acquire new intellectual strategies. Siegler discusses the question, but without a satisfactory answer. For example, he has worked on the interesting development of the so-called 'MIN strategy'. At a certain time children realize that, when they are given addition sums like 9 + 3 and they don't immediately know the answer, they need not solve the problem by laboriously counting all the items in both sets. All that they need to do is to 'count on' from one of the sets, and preferably from the larger. In this case counting on would mean counting the smaller set starting with the next number after 9 i.e. 10-11-12. There is evidence that this is a strategy which children discover for themselves. Siegler and Jenkins (1989) studied some of them doing so in a microgenetic study lasting several sessions. These experimenters argue that the arrival of the new strategy is 'mediated' by the strategy of counting everything because they find that children stop using this strategy or use it much less at the time that they adopt the new one. But this does not explain where the new idea came from. It only documents the simultaneous adoption of one strategy and abandonment of another.

In fact, this particular development can plausibly be explained as the result of the kind of co-ordination between existing strategies which Piaget once suggested. It has been shown that 5- and 6-year-old children adopt the MIN strategy only if they have an understanding of the commutativity of addition – in other words if they understand that $3 + 2$ is the same as $2 + 3$ (Turner and Bryant 1998). Children usually realize that you need to count on from one quantity only if you know the number of each of the sets to be added. Co-ordinating these two pieces of knowledge could easily lead the child to see that it does not matter which set one chooses to count and which to count on from, and also that the quickest and most efficient solution is to count the set with least in it. This is just a hypothesis, but it shows that the idea of co-ordination as a cause of intellectual development is potentially a very powerful one.

ψ Section summary

The transition problem is about the causes of development change. It is a question of immense theoretical and practical importance, since a good understanding of the reasons for cognitive change would be of great help in education. Much of the research on this question has been provoked by two theories, Piaget's equilibration theory which stresses the effects of internal conflict as a spur to changes from one developmental stage to the next, and Vygotsky's theory about the importance of cultural transmission and the zone of proximal development. Other approaches to the transition problem have flourished since the 1970s. One is to use computer models to describe the nature of cognitive change, and here the most promising models have been connectionist in nature. A second approach, advocated by Karmiloff-Smith, is to attribute change to an increase in explicit awareness of particular skills. A third approach, put forward by Siegler, is to argue that cognitive change is more a matter of changing emphasis on particular intellectual strategies than of acquiring new strategies. There are many common strands in these various hypotheses about the nature of developmental transitions, and in the end the correct theory will probably draw on all of them.

1 What are the main causes of cognitive changes during childhood?
2 How has the use of computer models helped us understand the underlying mechanisms of cognitive change?

ψ Chapter summary

● **One line or several lines of intellectual development?**

There seems to be no more need to juxtapose the domain-general and the domain-specific approaches. Both are right. The case for a central development in logic which then affects a wide range of intellectual changes is still a strong one. However, it is also clear that children depend as well on specialized intellectual mechanisms. The strongest evidence for these lies in the impressive innate structures which are active from birth onwards. It is also clear that learning about cultural tools makes some specific demands. For example, children's ability to build up explicit knowledge of the sounds in words has a strong influence on the progress that they make in reading but not on how well they learns mathematics. However, the claims that have been made for other domain-specific skills which develop after birth and which are not geared to cul-

Box continued

tural tools (e.g. the distinction between understanding physical and psychological causes) are much less convincing, mainly because they rest more on assertions by psychologists rather than sound empirical evidence.

● Question of cultural transmission

In the past domain-general theorists and domain-specific theories which postulate innate modules have paid very little attention to learning about cultural tools, which have to be taught (because one could not expect each generation of children to reinvent them) and which play an important part in all our intellectual lives. There are good grounds for thinking that representational redescription plays a particularly important part in learning about these tools.

● The transition problem

The most difficult problem in the study of cognitive development is how to find out about the causes of developmental change, particularly when this involves the acquisition of a completely new way of thinking. Piaget's ideas about co-ordination and Vygotsky's about internalization seem the most promising ideas about the transition problem. Microgenetic methods are probably the most promising way to gather sound empirical data about the causes of cognitive development.

Further reading

● Siegler, R.S. (1996) *Emerging Minds*. New York: Oxford University Press. This short and clear book gives an up-to-date account of work on cognitive development and a detailed discussion of the advantages and disadvantages of the microgenetic method.

● Nunes, T. and Bryant, P. (1996) *Children Doing Mathematics*. Oxford: Blackwell. This gives a comprehensive account of children's mathematical development, together with a discussion of the relevance of Piaget's ideas about logical development and Vygotsky's about cultural tools.

● Gopnik, A. and Meltzoff, A. (1997) *Words, Thoughts and Theories*. Cambridge, MA: MIT Press. This book includes a stimulating discussion of the theory/theory approach to cognitive development, and of the domain general-specific distinction.

● Mitchell, P. (1997) *Introduction to Theory of Mind*. London: Arnold. Here is a very clear and exciting account of the latest work on children's theory of mind which also relates it to research with animals and with autistic children.

● Karmiloff-Smith, A. (1992) *Beyond Modularity: A developmental perspective on cognitive science*. Cambridge, MA: MIT Press. This book presents the author's theory about representational redescription, and it also has an interesting discussion of the question of domain-specific developmental modules.

CHAPTER 10

Social development

Peter Smith

Key concepts • social development in infancy • early peer relationships • friendship and sociometric status • aggression and bullying • prosocial and moral development • sex differences • ethnicity • adolescence: transition from child to adult • transition to parenting and caregiving • social development in adulthood • social aspects of ageing

❏ Chapter preview

When you have read this chapter, you should be able to

- understand the development of early social skills and attachment to caregivers in infancy
- understand the development of peer relationships in the school years, and the importance of friendship and sociometric status
- appreciate issues relating to sex, and ethnicity, in social behaviour
- know the main developmental features of social behaviour in adolescence
- appreciate the role of parenting on children's development, and factors affecting quality of parenting
- understand the significance of grandparenthood and the importance of social life in elderly people

Introduction

New-born babies cry, as they are born into a world of which as yet they know almost nothing. What will the future hold for them? What will have happened to these babies in 10 years, as schoolchildren? In 30 years, perhaps as parents? In 70 years, as grandparents, will they look back on their life with satisfaction, or sadness? And how much of this development will be their own responsibility, how much due to their parents, their teachers, their friends, their social environment? These are profound questions, often posed in novels and the creative arts, and which we will reflect on for our own lives. Developmental psychology tackles these questions too, through systematic study, and we are beginning to shape the answers to some of these questions.

In this chapter we will look at social development from a lifespan perspective, from birth through to old age. Most emphasis will be on infancy and childhood, since rapid, dramatic developments take place as the helpless infant, with only limited social abilities, develops in the space of a few years into a well-functioning social being, with attachment figures, friends, and a definite personality. Also, many developmental theorists believe that these early years set a pathway for future development which, while not irrevocable, may be quite difficult to change; these pathways may be healthy and socially well adjusted, or they may be more deviant. We will study adolescence, traditionally a period of relative social turmoil. And we will examine the time of choosing a partner and starting a family, and in this context, the influence of parents on their children. We conclude with a description of grandparenthood, and finally of social life in elderly people.

☐ Social development in infancy

During the years of infancy, social development takes place primarily with parents and adult caregivers. From birth and soon afterwards, babies possess reflexive abilities and learning capacities which assist the development of social interchanges with adults. They preferentially focus on the kinds of visual and auditory stimuli that adults typically provide when talking, and when putting their face close to an infant. Also, they enjoy the kinds of **contingent responsiveness** that are generally obtained from adults – for example, vocalizing when they coo or babble, cuddling them when they cry.

Some psychologists, such as Trevarthen (1977), strongly emphasize the early abilities of rhythm and intersubjectivity that the infant brings to these social interchanges. Others, such as Kaye (1984), rather emphasize the limited abilities of the infant in the first year of life, and the role of the adult caregiver in **scaffolding** the interactions by providing the right response to whatever the infant does, and timing responses appropriately to mesh in with the infant's timing. Certainly, the infant will be learning a great deal over the first 12 to 18 months, through observation and imitation.

Attachment in infancy

Infants will also be learning to discriminate between different adults and caregivers, and typically are becoming attached to a small number of these towards the end of the first year. Despite evidence for some discrimination much earlier, the obvious signs of preferring a familiar caregiver to a stranger, and being reassured by the former but not by the latter, usually appear from 7 months on. This process of **attachment** has been described in detail by Bowlby (1969); he argues that the attachment system functions to provide a secure base for the infant to explore the physical and social environment. If alarmed or stressed, the infant will return to seek the proximity and reassurance of the attachment figure.

Attachment theorists, such as Ainsworth *et al.* (1978) and Main (1991), distinguish between **secure attachment** and **insecure attachment**. A securely attached infant, when distressed, is reassured by the attachment figure. An insecurely attached infant, when distressed, will show some ambivalence to, or avoidance of, the attachment figure, or may show a disorganized response. These patterns of attachment (which measure a relationship between an infant and a particular caregiver) are summarized in Table 10.1. They are measured by a procedure called the **strange situation**, which re-enacts in miniature a situation involving an infant being mildly stressed by being left with a stranger, and assessing response to the caregiver on her or his return; behaviour at this reunion of infant and caregiver is crucial to the assessment (Ainsworth *et al.* 1978). The procedure is applicable to infants aged 1 to 3 years. Beyond that age, attachment theorists prefer to talk about **internal working models** of relationships (Main 1991), which can be assessed by different means in middle childhood (for example, asking children to respond to photographs of separation experiences, called the **Separation Anxiety Test**) and through to adulthood (as in the **Adult Attachment Interview**: see pp. 314–15).

Despite an earlier misplaced emphasis by Bowlby (1953) on the unique importance of mothers as attach-

Table 10.1 Main attachment types from the strange situation

Label	Description
A Insecure-avoidant	Child ignores or avoids caregiver on reunion
B Secure	Child responds positively to caregiver on reunion, and if upset is quickly reassured
C Insecure-ambivalent	Child often upset, but not quickly reassured on reunion; both seeks and resists comfort
D Disorganized	Child shows poorly organized, incoherent behaviour which is difficult to classify

ment figures, it is now generally accepted that attachment figures can include fathers, grandparents, older siblings and familiar non-family adults such as nannies or childminders. It is also possible for a child to be attached to several such persons, without any problems of emotional security. This recognition has to some extent defused the long-running controversy about whether infants can be left in non-family day-care situations without any adverse effects. Some uncertainty still remains

Plate 10.1 Contrary to earlier research which emphasized the unique importance of mothers as attachment figures, it is now generally accepted that attachment figures can include fathers, grandparents, older siblings and non-family members such as nannies

about the effects of intensive, early day-care on the quality of mother–infant attachment (Belsky 1988), but most reviews conclude that there are no necessary adverse effects consequent upon high-quality day-care (McGurk *et al.* 1993). However, it is the case that extreme shared care can lead to emotional problems; studies of children brought up in children's homes, who had experienced up to 50 caregivers, did reveal continuing emotional difficulties (Hodges and Tizard 1989).

Temperament

An importance aspect of infants' behaviour, and how they adapt to new and stressful situations, is called **temperament**. From birth and soon after, babies begin to assert their individuality. Some seem to be easy babies, seldom crying and adapting well to changes. Others are difficult babies, fretting a lot, and disliking changes to routine. Some babies are fearful, others are not.

Based on a longitudinal study in New York, mainly of mothers' reports, Thomas and Chess (1977) described nine aspects of temperament, shown in Table 10.2. Other researchers have developed similar schemes.

Table 10.2 Main dimensions of temperament, from the work of Thomas and Chess (1977)

Label	Description
Activity level	Amount of physical activity during sleep, feeding, play, dressing, etc.
Regularity	Of bodily functioning in sleep, hunger, bowel movements, etc.
Adaptability to changes in routine	Ease or difficulty with which initial response can be modified in socially desirable ways
Response to new situations	Initial reaction to new stimuli, food, places, people, toys or procedures
Level of sensory threshold	Amount of external stimulation (sounds, changes) necessary to produce a response
Intensity of response	Energy content of responses regardless of their quality
Positive or negative mood	Amount of pleasant or unpleasant behaviour
Distractibility	Effectiveness of external stimuli (sounds, toys) in interfering with ongoing behaviour
Persistence and attention span	Duration of maintaining specific activities with or without external obstacles

There is some controversy about the extent to which temperament is an individual characteristic of a baby or child, probably largely inherited, and the extent to which it is an aspect of a particular relationship, e.g. mother–child. This may partly depend on how temperament is measured. In any event, it is an important variable to consider when examining parenting skills and outcomes, as parents are certainly affected by a child's temperament.

Development of concepts of self and others

An important milestone in social development is the recognition by the infant that he or she exists as a person, separate from other people; in other words, having a sense of self, or achieving **self-concept**. This is generally thought to be closely linked to cognitive development, and in particular the development of person permanence (see Chapter 9), which is also an important precursor for attachment development.

One ingenious way of studying the early development of a sense of self has been to use mirror experiments. In this procedure, infants are placed in front of a mirror to see how they react. It is supposed that if they recognize that the person in the mirror is themself, then they have a sense of self; whereas in the absence of a sense of self, they would treat the image as being another child.

In order to clearly distinguish these two alternatives, the experimenter puts some distinguishing mark on the infant's face, while it is asleep; for example, lipstick or rouge, on the nose or brow. The infant is placed in front of the mirror when it wakes up. In a study by Lewis and Brooks-Gunn (1979), this procedure was carried out with infants aged 9 to 24 months. As can be seen, in a 'no rouge' control condition, very few infants touched their own nose. But if rouge had been put on the infant's nose before, then from 15 months on some infants started touching their own nose, and most infants did so by 21 months (see Table 10.3). This seems to date the origins of self-concept at around 18 months. This is also around the age when infants start to use verbal labels to label self, and others ('baby', 'mummy', 'daddy', etc.).

Table 10.3 Proportion of infants touching their own nose, in the mirror experiment of Lewis and Brooks-Gunn (1979)

Age (months)	9	12	15	18	21	24
Rouge	0	0	19	25	70	73
No rouge	0	0	0	6	7	7

Ψ Section summary

Parents and caregivers respond to the signals and reflex behaviours of the new-born infant, and scaffold early social interaction sequences. By around 7 months, infants direct proximity-maintaining behaviours preferentially to certain attachment figures. Security of attachment is assessed by means of the strange situation technique.

1 What is meant by secure and insecure attachment?
2 What are the main dimensions of temperament?
3 How can we measure self-concept in infancy?

❑ Early peer relationships

By the age of 2 years, peers – other children of about the same age – become increasing sources of interest. In fact, peers seem to be especially interesting to children even in the second year of life. In one study of 12–18-month-old infants, two mother–infant pairs who had not previously met shared a playroom together. The infants touched their mothers a lot (remaining in proximity to them, as we would expect from attachment theory), but *looked* most at the peer, who clearly interested them (Lewis *et al.* 1975). A study of French children at 11 months and at 23 months (Tremblay-Leveau and Nadel 1996) used an ingenious triadic situation to look at how these toddlers dealt with social exclusion. They put two toddlers together with a familiar experimenter in a playroom. Some social interaction did occur between the toddlers; but a toddler made much more effort to interact with the other toddler, if the latter was playing with the experimenter! This made the first toddler five times more likely (at 11 months) and eight times more likely (at 23 months) to try and get into interaction.

When left to themselves, the interactions between under-2s often consist of just looking at another child and perhaps smiling, or showing a toy, or making a noise. In ordinary toddler groups an infant might make such overtures to another child once every minute or so, and interactions are usually brief (Mueller and Brenner 1977). This rather low level of peer interaction is probably because infants have not yet learnt the skills of social interaction. Whereas adults can scaffold social interactions with infants, it takes young children some two or three years to become really competent at interacting socially with age-mates, knowing what are appropriate behaviours in certain situations, what behaviour to expect back, and waiting to take one's turn. There is some evidence that early peer experience (e.g. in toddler groups or day nurseries) can help this along. Some studies suggest that infants who are securely attached to their mothers are more confident and better able to explore both objects and peers, and to make new social relationships over the next few years (Bretherton and Waters 1985; P. Turner 1991).

Siblings

The majority of us have siblings – brothers or sisters. Usually, siblings differ in age by only a few years. Although not exactly peers, they are generally close enough in age, and similar enough in interests and developmental stages, to be important social partners for each other in the family. Older siblings can show great tolerance for younger ones, and can act as an important model for more competent behaviour. They can also show hostility and ambivalence; this has been observed in many different societies (Eibl-Eibesfeldt 1989).

Dunn and Kendrick (1982) made observations in the homes of 40 first-born children living with both parents in or near Cambridge, UK. At first visit, a new sibling was due in a month or so, and the first child was usually nearing his or her second birthday. After the birth of the sibling they made further visits, when the second child was about 1 month old, and again at 8 months and at 14 months.

They found that many first-borns showed some signs of jealousy when the new sibling arrived. Although they had previously been the centre of attention from mother, father or grandparents, the new brother or sister now got the most attention. Much of the jealousy and ambivalence of the first-born was directed towards parents. Not many first-borns showed much overt hostility to the infant, but some showed ambivalence or hostility, as the following extract of conversation shows:

Child: Baby, baby (caressing her). Monster. Monster.

Mother: She's not a monster.

Child: Monster.

However the great majority of the first-borns showed much interest and affection towards their new sibling; seeking to please them, or being concerned if they cried. Overall, Dunn and Kendrick (1982) felt that the sibling relationship was one in which considerable emotions may be aroused – both of love and of envy.

This close and emotionally powerful relationship may also be an optimal situation in which to learn how to understand others. Siblings seem to be learning how to frustrate, tease, placate, comfort or get their own way with their brother or sister. Dunn and Kendrick (1982) relate one incident in which 14-month-old Callum repeatedly reaches for and manipulates some magnetic letters which his 3-year-old sister Laura is playing with on a tray. Laura repeatedly says 'no' gently. Callum continues trying to reach the letters. Finally, Laura picks up the tray with the letters and takes it to a high table that Callum cannot reach. Callum is furious and starts to cry. He turns and goes straight to the sofa where Laura's comfort objects, a rag doll and a pacifier, are lying. He takes the doll and holds it tight, looking at Laura. Laura now gets very upset, starts crying, and runs to take the doll.

Callum seems to have calculated how to annoy Laura so as to get his own back on her. These are interesting observations to compare with ideas about children's **theory of mind**, as well as the critique of Piaget's ideas about egocentrism (see Chapter 9). But it is also worth bearing in mind that children can learn these social cognitive skills with adults and peers, as well as with siblings. Research on only children appears to suggest that they do well on achievement and intelligence scores, and show no deficits in sociability or adjustment (Falbo and Polit 1986).

Social participation

By 2 or 3 years of age a child is usually thought ready for nursery school. The period from 2 to 4 years does see a great increase in the skills that children have with peers. The increase in social behaviour in pre-school children was first documented by Parten (1932). She observed 2–4 year olds and described how they might be unoccupied, an onlooker on other's activities, or, if engaged in an activity, they could be solitary, in parallel activity with others or in associative or co-operative activity with others. **Parallel activity** is when children play near each other with the same materials, but do not interact much – playing independently at the same sandpit for example. **Associative activity** is when children interact together at an activity, doing similar things, perhaps each adding building blocks to the same tower. **Co-operative activity** is when children interact together in complementary ways; for example, one child gets blocks out of a box and hands them to another child, who builds the tower. Parten (1932) found that the first four categories declined with age, whereas associative and co-operative activity, the only ones involving much interaction with peers, increased with age.

Most group activity involves just two or three children playing together, though the size of groups tends to increase in older pre-schoolers and in the early school years. A study of more than 400 Israeli children in outdoor free play found that group activity predominated, while parallel activity became very infrequent; the number of groups comprised of more than five children increased from 12 to 16 per cent between 5 and 6 years of age (Hertz–Lazarowitz *et al.* 1981). The size of children's groups continues to increase through the middle school years, especially in boys, as team games such as football become more popular. The nature of children's groups changes again as adolescence is reached, when large same-sex cliques or gangs become common in early adolescence, changing as heterosexual relationships become more important in later adolescence.

Social play

A lot of the time that pre-school and infant school children are together, they spend playing. Play generally refers to enjoyable activities that are carried out for their own sake, without any obvious external goal. Play need not be social, but much of it is.

Smilansky (1968) postulated a four-sequence developmental model of play, shown in Table 10.4. This has been combined with Parten's scheme of social participation, referred to above, to create a **play hierarchy** (Rubin *et al.* 1978). This scheme is useful for coding children's activities, but it has two limitations. First, it implies a developmental progression which is not universally accepted; some solitary play can be quite mature for example; and constructive play seems to coexist with dramatic play rather than precede it. Second, it omits important kinds of play, particularly, **rough-and-tumble play** (friendly play-fighting with a partner) and language play.

Table 10.4 Smilansky's four-sequence developmental model of play

Label	Description
Functional	Simple body movements or actions with objects, e.g. banging bricks
Constructive	Making things with objects, e.g. building a tower with bricks
Dramatic	Acting out roles in a pretend game, e.g. pretending to be a doctor
Games with rules	Playing in a game with publicly accepted rules, e.g. football, hopscotch

Ψ Case study

Rough-and-tumble play

Rough-and-tumble play, or play-fighting, is quite common in middle childhood. Observations in school playgrounds suggest it can take up about 10 per cent of playground time. It involves wrestling, grappling, kicking, tumbling and rolling on the ground, and chasing. These activities could be mistaken as actual fighting; in fact, they sometimes are mistaken, by teachers and playtime supervisors, who may intervene to break up a 'fight' only to be told 'We're only playing, miss!'

Interviews with children, and careful observations, have shown that most of the time, rough-and-tumble does not lead to fighting (Schäfer and Smith 1996). Children enjoy it, especially boys. Playful fighting is characterized by laughter, self-handicapping and restraint (not hitting or kicking hard or even making contact at all), and reversals (taking it in turns to be on top). It is not yet clear what function this play may have; but it appears similar to the kinds of play-fighting seen in many species of mammals, kittens and puppies for example. Most likely, it helps develop physical strength for skills such as fighting, and maybe helps children realize their own strength and establish a dominance hierarchy.

Although the great majority of rough-and-tumble is really playful, occasionally things can go wrong and a fight develops or someone gets hurt. This may happen if a play signal such as a playful punch is misinterpreted (lack of social skills) or it may happen if one child deliberately abuses the play expectations of the other to inflict hurt while 'on top' (manipulation). The likelihood of this happening seems more common in sociometrically rejected children (Pellegrini 1994); indeed, this behaviour could contribute to their rejection. It may also become more common in adolescence. This research suggests that rough-and-tumble play may have particular importance for children's social and dominance relationships, especially in boys' peer groups (Pellegrini and Smith 1998).

Research update

Pretend play and theory of mind

In pretend play, a child makes a non-literal use of an object or action – that is, it does not mean what it usually means. Consider an example recorded by Piaget, of his daughter Jacqueline at the age of 15 months, when pretend often begins. She lay down with her head on a cloth, sucked her thumb, blinked her eyes – and laughed! Piaget interpreted this as Jacqueline pretending to go to sleep – especially as she did similar actions to her toy animals a month or so later. Another famous example, used by Leslie (1987), is of a child picking up a banana and putting it to his or her mouth and ear; not to eat, of course, but to pretend it is a telephone.

Some pretend play is solitary, but observations in the homes of children suggest that usually about 75 per cent of pretend play is social. Haight and Miller (1993) made videofilms of nine children playing at home, in a longitudinal study from 12 to 48 months; even early pretend play was usually social, with mothers; later, social play with peers became more common.

Howes and Matheson (1992) have described stages in the development of social pretence. Early pretend play appears to be largely imitative, supported by the mother or older partner, and following well-established 'scripts' or story lines, such as 'feeding the baby' or 'nursing the patient'. By around 3 to 4 years however, children are very aware of play con-ventions and competently negotiating roles within sociodramatic play sequences.

Leslie (1987) argued that pretend play might have a leading role in developing theory of mind abilities (see Chapter 9). He argued that pretend play demonstrated what he called **metarepresentation** (something represents something else, e.g. a banana represents a telephone), that metarepresentation was a key component of theory of mind, and that pretend play, starting at 15–18 months, emerged earlier than traditional theory of mind performance (at 3 to 4 years). However, this view has been challenged (Jarrold *et al.* 1994; Lillard 1993). The Howes and Matheson sequences show that early pretend play need not be metarepresentational; the toddler with the banana may be imitating someone else. Metarepresentation in social pretend seems to come in clearly at 3–4 years, which is concurrent with other theory of mind abilities.

Nevertheless, other theorists continue to argue for the possible role of pretend play in theory of mind. Meins and Russell (1996) found that 2 year olds who were securely attached in the strange situation were more able to make use of the suggestions of an adult in their pretend play. Fonagy *et al.* (1997: 35) argue that 'the experience of sharing a world of pretend may foster an understanding of the mental states of others and that this capacity is in turn facilitated by secure attachments in infancy'.

Ψ Section summary

Peer interactions develop slowly in the first two years, although sibling relationships can be intense at an early age. In the pre-school years, social play, particularly pretend play and rough-and-tumble play, becomes frequent, and social participation increases.

1 What kind of emotional relationship do siblings have?
2 What is the 'play hierarchy'?
3 How important are different kinds of play for children's development?

❏ Friendship and sociometric status

Usually we take friendship to mean some close association between two particular people, as indicated by their time spent together or their psychological attachment and trust. It is quite possible to interact a lot with others generally but not have any close friends.

Conceptions of friendship

Friendship relations do seem to have special qualities (Hartup 1996). In a review of a large number of studies, Newcomb and Bagwell (1995) concluded that, compared to interactions between non-friends, those between friends characteristically exhibit four features. First, not surprisingly, there is more intense social activity; friends play together more. Second, the quality of the interaction is different; specifically, there is more reciprocity and intimacy. Third, although there may be conflicts with friends (as with non-friends), there is more frequent conflict resolution between friends. Fourth, there is more effective task performance; in joint or co-operative tasks, friends seem to be able to help each other better and criticize each other more constructively.

How do children themselves conceive of friendship? Bigelow and La Gaipa (1980) asked Scottish and Canadian children, aged 6 to 14 years, to write an essay about their expectations of best friends. Based on a content analysis, Bigelow and La Gaipa suggested a three-stage model for friendship expectations. A reward-cost stage, based on common activities, living nearby and having similar expectations, was common up to 8 years. From 9 to 10 years, a normative stage emphasized shared values, rules and sanctions. At 11–12 years, an empathic stage showed a more mature conception of friendship based on understanding, and self-disclosure, as well as shared interests. These and other studies suggest a shift towards more psychologically complex and mutually reciprocal ideas of friendship during the middle school years, with intimacy and commitment becoming especially important later in adolescence.

The measurement of friendship: sociometry

It is possible to build up a picture of the social structure in a group of children using a technique called **sociometry**. This can be done by observation. A.H. Clark *et al.* (1969) observed nursery school children to record who was playing with whom, at intervals over a five-week period. They constructed **sociograms** (an example is shown in Figure 10.1). Each symbol represents a child; the number of lines joining two children represents the percentage of observations on which they were seen playing together. The concentric circles show the number of play partners a child has; if many, that child's symbol is towards the middle, if none, at the periphery. In this class there is one very popular girl who links two large subgroups; one boy and one girl have no clear partners.

Observation shows who associates with whom, but this may not be quite the same as friendship. An alternative is to ask each child 'Who are your best friends?' This nomination data can also be plotted on a sociogram. If John chooses Richard as a best friend, but Richard does not choose John, this can be indicated by an arrow from

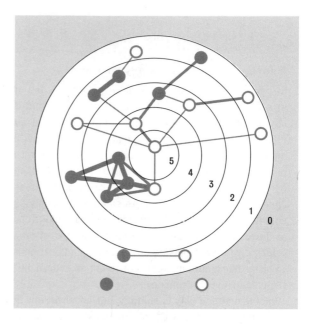

Figure 10.1 Sociogram of association networks in a class of pre-school children
Note: white circles represent girls, black circles represent boys
Source: adapted from A.H. Clark *et al.* (1969)

John to Richard; if the choice is reciprocated, the arrow would point both ways on the sociogram.

A common nomination method is to ask all the children to name their three best friends. Some investigators have also asked children to say whom they do not like. There may be ethical objections to this (for example, such questions actually might bring about increased negative behaviour to unliked peers) but so far ill-effects have not been found (Hayvren and Hymel 1984). Researchers who have obtained both positive and negative nominations have not constructed sociograms (which would then look very complicated), but have instead categorized children as popular, controversial, rejected, neglected or average, according to whether they are high or low on positive and on negative nominations (see Table 10.5).

Coie and Dodge (1983) looked at the stability of these **sociometric status** categories between 8 and 11 years. They found that stability was highest for rejected children; 30 per cent of those rejected at 8 years were still rejected four years later, and another 30 per cent were neglected. By contrast, those merely neglected at the start of the study tended to become average.

Rejected children do seem to differ in their behaviour from most other children, in what seem to be mal-

Table 10.5 Five types of sociometric status

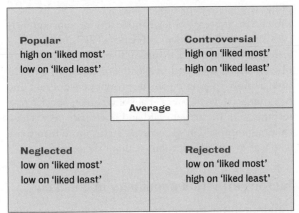

Popular high on 'liked most' low on 'liked least'	**Controversial** high on 'liked most' high on 'liked least'
Average	
Neglected low on 'liked most' low on 'liked least'	**Rejected** low on 'liked most' high on 'liked least'

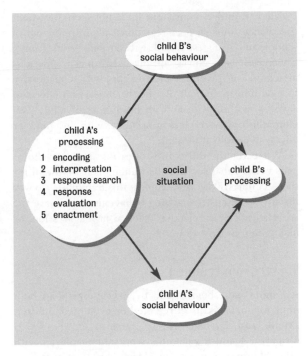

Figure 10.2 A model of social skills and social exchange in peer interaction
Source: adapted from Dodge *et al.* (1986)

adaptive ways. Ladd (1983) observed 8 and 9 year olds in playground breaks. Rejected children, compared to average or popular children, spent less time in co-operative play and social conversation, and more time arguing and fighting; they tended to play in smaller groups, and with younger or with less popular companions. Dodge *et al.* (1983) looked at how 5 year olds attempted to get into ongoing play between two other peers. Popular children first waited and watched, then gradually got themselves incorporated by making group-oriented statements; by contrast, neglected children tended to stay at the waiting and watching stage, while rejected children tended to escalate to disruptive actions such as interrupting the play.

Children who are rejected in the middle school years may be more in need of help even than those who simply keep a low profile and are ignored or neglected. The findings above suggest that rejected children are lacking in some social skills. This is a widely held view, and has been developed by Dodge *et al.* (1986). They suggest that the social skills of peer interaction can be envisaged as an exchange model (see Figure 10.2). Suppose child A is interacting with child B. According to this model child A has to (1) encode the incoming information – perceive what child B is doing, (2) interpret this information, (3) search for appropriate responses, (4) evaluate these responses and select the best, and (5) enact that response. Child B will be engaged in a similar process with respect to child A.

This model may be helpful in making the term social skills more explicit. If a child has a social skills deficit, where is this located? Does an over-aggressive child misinterpret others' behaviour (stage 2), or just too readily select aggressive responses (stage 4), for example?

Evidence relating to the model is reviewed by Crick and Dodge (1994).

However, not all behaviour labelled as maladjusted may be due to lack of social skills. Some aggressive children may be quite skilled at manipulating others. And some rejected children may be simply reacting to exclusion by the popular cliques and would not necessarily be rejected or lacking in social skills in other situations outside the classroom.

The importance of friendship

It seems likely that having friends is important for a child's development, but it is difficult to prove this. Parker and Asher (1987) reviewed many relevant studies, most carried out in the USA. They looked at three measures of peer relationships: peer acceptance/rejection (number and quality of friendships); aggressiveness to peers; and shyness or withdrawal from peers. They examined the relationship of these to three main kinds of later outcome: dropping out of school early; being involved in juvenile and adult crime; and adult psychopathology (mental health ratings, or needing psychiatric help of any kind).

They found a consistent link between low peer acceptance (or high peer rejection) and dropping out of school, and a suggestive link with juvenile/adult crime. There was also a consistent link between aggressiveness at school and juvenile/adult crime, with a suggestive link with dropping out of school. The data on effects of shyness/withdrawal, and on predictors of adult psychopathology, were less consistent, with any links or effects unproven at present.

Whatever the difficulties of proof, many psychologists believe that social skills training may be useful for those children who lack friends; this training is anyway usually directed to changing behaviours which are the correlates of peer rejection (such as high aggression, or high withdrawal).

Social skills training

Attempts have been made by psychologists to help improve social skills in rejected or neglected children (Malik and Furman 1993). Furman *et al.* (1979) observed 4 and 5 year olds who seldom played with other children. Some received special play sessions with a younger partner, to see if this might give them more confidence in social interaction. This did seem to help, more so than play sessions with a same-age peer or no intervention at all. Other researchers, working with middle school children, have used more direct means of encouraging social skills. A child might watch a film showing an initially withdrawn child engaged in a series of increasingly complex peer interactions. This has been shown to increase social interaction subsequently (O'Connor 1972). Oden and Asher (1977) used a more instructional approach, coaching 8 and 9 year olds identified as socially isolated (neglected or rejected) on skills such as how to participate in groups, co-operate and communicate with peers. They did this in special play sessions with the target child and one other peer. These children improved in sociometric status more than those who had special play sessions without the coaching.

Factors affecting popularity in children

Children differ in popularity and some less popular children may have less adequate social skills. But other factors are certainly at work. One such factor is physical attractiveness. Vaughn and Langlois (1983) obtained ratings of physical attractiveness for 59 preschool children, and found a high correlation with sociometric preference. Other studies have found that ratings of physical attractiveness correlate with sociometric status.

Popularity may also be influenced by the composition of the peer group a child is in. Children tend to pick as friends peers similar to themselves. A child might tend to appear sociometrically neglected or rejected simply because he or she differs in social class, or ethnicity, from most others in the class.

Ψ Case study

Self-esteem

How do you think of yourself? How would you describe yourself, if you had to write some statements about yourself? This is an easy test to do, and of course psychologists have done it! These self descriptions give an indication of what is called **self-esteem** or self-perception.

As children develop, they tend to move from concrete descriptors ('I am a boy. I love football') to more abstract descriptors ('I am kind hearted. I sometimes trust people too much'). However, another area of interest is whether children tend to describe themselves, or think that others see them, in positive or negative ways. This would correspond to high, or low, self-esteem, respectively.

Several questionnaires have been devised to measure self-esteem. One well-known instrument, the Harter Self-Perception Scale, gives a series of statements such as 'some kids find it hard to make friends BUT some kids find it pretty easy to make friends'. The children decide whether this is true, or untrue, of them; and then, whether this is so 'a little' or 'a lot'; effectively, a four-point rating scale. The statements give self-perception or self-esteem in five areas: physical appearance, social acceptance, behavioural conduct, scholastic competence, and athletic competence; as well as global self-worth.

The ten statements shown in Table 10.6 make up a scale called the Rosenberg Self-Esteem (RSE) Scale

(case study continued)

(Rosenberg 1986). There are 10 items scored 4, 3, 2 or 1 depending on strength of agreement (with reversed scoring for negative self-esteem items). Maximum score is 40; the average score in a large US sample was about 35, with a standard deviation of about 5. You could assess your own self-esteem on this scale, but remember there is a lot of variation even in normal samples.

Self-esteem is a useful indicator of psychological health and well-being in children. For example, self-esteem tends to be lower in victims of bullying (see research update p. 305). The onset of puberty tends to bring about important changes in self-perception, and self-esteem links closely to ideas of identity, thought to be a significant developmental phase in adolescence.

Table 10.6 Rosenberg Self-Esteem Scale

	Strongly agree	Agree	Disagree	Strongly disagree
1 On the whole, I am satisfied with myself				
2 At times I think that I am no good at all				
3 I feel that I have a number of good qualities				
4 I am able to do things as well as most people				
5 I feel I do not have much to be proud of				
6 I feel useless at times				
7 I feel that I am an okay person, at least as okay as others				
8 I wish I could have more respect for myself				
9 All in all I am inclined to feel that I am a failure				
10 I take a positive attitude towards myself				

Ψ Section summary

Friends are characterized by more intense social activity, intimacy and reciprocity, conflict resolution, and effective task performance. Friendship structure in a group is measured by sociometric techniques. Sociometric status types result from combinations of liked most and liked least nominations. Rejected (disliked) children are often aggressive and disruptive, and in some cases lack social skills.

1   What are the different methods used to measure friendship?
2   Is having friends important?
3   How can we help children who are sociometrically rejected, or lack friends?

❏ Aggression and bullying

It is not unusual for children to show aggression, and for young children this will often be shown in physical forms such as fighting, or in verbal taunts. Jersild and Markey (1935) observed conflicts in 54 children at three nursery schools, and described many kinds of conflict behaviour such as taking or grabbing toys or objects held or used by another child; and making unfavourable remarks about someone such as 'You're no good at it' or 'I don't like you'. Some decline in conflicts occurred with age, and boys took part in more conflicts than girls. Nine months later, conflicts had become more verbal, but individual differences between children tended to be maintained. Cummings *et al.* (1989) similarly reported that aggressive boys tended to stay aggressive between 2 and 5 years of age, even though the overall level of physical aggression declined over this period.

A number of researchers distinguish **instrumental aggression** and **hostile aggression** (based on whether the distress or harm is inferred to be the primary intent of the act) and individual and group aggression (depending on whether more than one child attacks another). Regarding the type of aggressive act, a traditional distinction is between *verbal* and *non-verbal* aggression (based on the presence or absence of verbal threats or insults); more recently, researchers in Finland (Bjorkqvist *et al.* 1992) and the USA (Crick and Grotpeter 1995) have distinguished **indirect or relational aggression** from **direct aggression**. Whereas direct aggression is done face-to-face (hitting or taunting someone), indirect or relational aggression is done via a third party, for example persuading others not to play with someone, or spreading nasty stories about someone. Indirect aggression is more subtle, and in some ways more socially acceptable than direct aggression; it becomes more important with age as direct aggression declines. Indirect aggression is also more characteristic of girls than of boys.

Causes of high aggression

A certain amount of aggressive and assertive behaviour is normal. However, some children show high levels of aggression, often of a hostile or harassing nature, which can be quite stable over time and for which some adult intervention seems justified. If not dealt with at the time, children who show persistent high aggressiveness through the school years are at increased risk for later delinquency, anti-social and violent behaviour (Farrington 1990).

There is considerable evidence that home circumstances can be important influences leading to aggressive and later anti-social behaviour. Patterson *et al.* (1989) suggest that certain key aspects of parenting are involved. Children who experience irritable and ineffective discipline at home, and poor parental monitoring of their activities, together with a lack of parental warmth, are particularly likely to become aggressive in peer groups and at school. Anti-social behaviour at school is likely to be linked to academic failure and peer rejection, they argue; and in adolescence, especially if parental monitoring is lax, these young people are likely to be involved in deviant and delinquent peer groups. Their hypothesis is shown in Figure 10.3.

This approach suggests that the social skills of parenting are very important in preventing anti-social behaviour; interventions can focus on helping parents improve their child-management skills, for example via manuals and videotaped materials.

Aggression, dominance, popularity and leadership

How does aggressive behaviour relate to popularity and leadership? One view is that aggressive children tend to be disliked and unpopular. Rejected children often show disruptive behaviour with peers, being disliked because of their unprovoked aggression. Some children, however, are quite aggressive but not clearly disliked. These

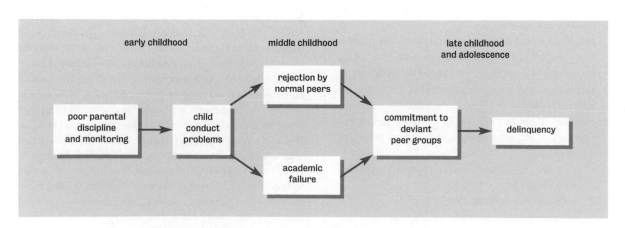

Figure 10.3 A developmental progression for anti-social behaviour
Source: adapted from Patterson *et al.* (1989)

Research update

Bullying in schools

Bullying in schools is one kind of persistent aggressive behaviour which can cause great distress to victims (Olweus 1993). It can be carried out by one child, or a group, and is usually repeated against a particular victim. The victim usually cannot retaliate effectively, because they are physically weaker, psychologically less confident, or simply outnumbered. While some bullying takes the form of hitting, pushing or taking money, it can also involve teasing, telling stories and social exclusion.

Research in western Europe, including the UK, Ireland, Norway, Netherlands, Germany, Spain, Portugal and Italy, as well as other countries such as Canada, Australia and Japan, suggests that bullying is quite pervasive in schools, probably to a greater extent than most teachers and parents realize, since many victims keep quiet about it (e.g. Genta *et al.* 1996). However, victims are lower in self-esteem (Boulton and Smith 1994) and long-term victimization can lead to depression and even suicide (Olweus 1993).

Involvement in school bullying may be related to experiences in the home. Studies in Italy and England suggest that some victims come from over-protective family environments and perhaps have not learnt assertive skills (Berdondini and Smith 1995). Other studies show that children who persistently bully others may come from families where there is lack of warmth, harsh and inconsistent discipline, and lax parental monitoring of child behaviour (Olweus 1993).

However, schools can take action to reduce the problem, by having clearly written whole school policies on the issue, improving playground supervision, raising awareness through curricular activities, and working intensively with individuals and small groups who are affected. Studies in Norway (Olweus 1993) and in England (P.K. Smith and Sharp 1994), and in progress elsewhere, show that these methods can reduce bullying – as measured by confidential self-report questionnaire surveys – by up to 50 per cent; this is a substantial achievement in real-life settings.

are sociometrically controversial children. Peers describe them as good leaders, but also as tending to start fights – a pattern of behaviour that appeals to some peers but not to others. Thus, some children may use aggressive behaviour in quite a socially skilled way, to acquire status in the peer group.

Sluckin (1981) made a detailed study of playground behaviour in an Oxford first school. He describes how a boy called Neill was known by his peers as the 'boss' of the playground. Neill was seldom observed in actual fights (he was not physically strong), but he often tried to raise his prestige and manipulate social situations by verbal means. For example, in a race with Ginny, where they finished at the same time, Neill cried out 'Yes yes' (I'm the winner). Ginny called out 'Draw', to which Neill replied 'No, it wasn't, you're just trying to make trouble'. Or, playing football, Neill said 'I'm in goal, bagsee'. Nick replied 'No, I'm in goal'. Neill retorted 'No, John's in goal' and John went in the goal. Neill had kept the initiative, avoided a fight but given the impression of being in charge (even though he did

not get his own way entirely). Neill had a high dominance status in the playground, and was clearly a leader of sorts, but was not especially popular. His leadership was often disruptive, since he always insisted on winning games.

Playground observations by Sluckin and others suggest that school children can rank others for **dominance** or fighting strength in a consistent way, and experiments confirm this can be done reliably from about 4 or 5 years of age onwards (Sluckin and Smith 1977). Winning fights is one criterion of dominance, but more generally it is taken as getting one's one way or influencing others. Thus, the concept is close to that of leadership.

In general, some children are popular, and often leaders, because they are socially skilled and assertive but not gratuitously aggressive. Another way of being a leader, or achieving high dominance status, is to be a good fighter. This is a more controversial way, which may not bring true popularity with all one's peers. High aggression without the social skills to go with it, however, leads to unpopularity and rejection.

ψ Section summary

Various types of aggressive behaviour have been described, and pathways of aggressive behaviour have been delineated. Bullying refers to persistent aggressive behaviour against victims unable to defend themselves.

1 In what ways have aggressive behaviours been classified?

2 What can be done to reduce aggression and bullying in schools?

3 How can we distinguish between aggression, dominance, leadership and popularity?

Prosocial and moral development

Prosocial behaviour provides the other side of the coin to aggressive behaviour. In prosocial behaviour, a child helps someone else, for example by sharing something, or comforting a person who is hurt or distressed. If done at some cost to oneself, and for unselfish reasons, this would be called altruistic behaviour.

Prosocial behaviour emerges in the second year. In a now classic study, Zahn-Waxler and Radke-Yarrow (1982) asked 24 mothers to keep a diary account of episodes of prosocial behaviour by their children, from when they were 12 to 30 months of age. In particular, they were asked to focus on reactions of their child to someone else's distress. For younger children (up to 20 months) this often took the form of getting distressed themselves, but showing little prosocial behaviour beyond touching or patting the distressed person. After 20 months, however, prosocial behaviours such as reassurance, giving objects, getting help from a third party or attacking the person causing the distress, became quite common.

These researchers also found that the way a child reacted to distress was associated with how the mother reacted if the child caused distress to someone else. Those mothers who let their children know they were wrong to cause distress, but explained why, tended to have children who were prosocial themselves; mothers who used unexplained verbal prohibitions ('Don't do that!') had children who were less prosocial.

Many other factors affect the development of prosocial behaviour. These include responses of siblings, as well as parents, and perceptions of whether one is being

treated fairly with respect to siblings (Dunn 1995). The school environment can be important too, for example, the extent to which co-operative values are encouraged in the classroom and peer support systems are encouraged (Cowie and Sharp 1996).

Moral reasoning

Another factor which may affect moral behaviour, but is to some extent independent, is **moral reasoning**. This refers to how someone thinks about moral issues, such as whether it is ever right to steal, or to kill, or to have an abortion. Here, it is not so much the decision – after all, there can be deep and sincerely held beliefs both for and against issues like abortion – but the quality of the reasoning process used to justify the decision.

These reasoning processes were studied systematically by Piaget (1932) in *The Moral Judgement of the Child*. Based on both observations of games, and responses to short stories, Piaget argued that the child moved from a stage of moral realism, in which reasoning was based on damage done, to a more mature stage of moral subjectivism, in which account was taken of the intent of the person causing damage. Piaget thought that this transition occurred at around 9–10 years. However (as with Piaget's work in cognitive development, see Chapter 9), later researchers pointed to problems with Piaget's methodology and find evidence for awareness of intent in children at younger ages (Karniol 1978).

An American psychologist, Kohlberg (1969), took Piaget's approach further. He started a longitudinal study of 50 males initially aged 10 to 26 years, and gave them hypothetical dilemmas to reason about. On this basis, he delineated six stages broken down into three levels. The scheme was later revised by Colby *et al.* (1983) and now comprises five levels (see Table 10.7).

Kohlberg's (1969) scheme appears to hold true in different cultural settings, so far as the first two levels (four stages) are concerned; but the fifth stage is commonly found only in urban societies (Snarey 1983). There is controversy about whether this means that the scheme is culturally biased, or whether non-urban societies simply do not encourage the highest levels of moral reasoning. Kohlberg's scheme does have implications for moral education, as he believed that children would be attracted to reasoning just one level above their current reasoning; similar to Vygotsky's (1978) view of the **zone of proximal development (ZDP)** (Chapter 9), this suggests that a challenge, but not too much of a challenge, created by the social environment, optimally advances further development.

Table 10.7 The five stages in the revised version of Kohlberg's model of moral reasoning

Level	Stage	Description
1 Preconventional	1 Heteronomous morality	Obedience for own sake, avoiding physical damage or punishment
	2 Individualism, instrumental purpose and exchange	Following rules if in one's own interests, or as a fair exchange
2 Conventional	3 Mutual interpersonal expectations, relationships and interpersonal conformity	Concern for others, trust, living up to what is expected of you by people close to you
	4 Social system and conscience	Following rules and duties as expected by the group or society you are in
3 Postconventional	5 Social contract or utility and individual rights	Aware that rules are relative to your group, but that some may have universal validity

ψ Section summary

Prosocial behaviour emerges in the second year; it is influenced by various factors in the home environment. Researchers have also studied the development of moral reasoning, by means of observations of games, and use of short stories and dilemmas.

1 What factors affect the development of prosocial behaviour?

2 What levels of moral reasoning did Kohlberg describe, and how universally applicable are they?

❏ Sex differences

Many researchers have compared behaviour, and toy and activity preferences, in boys and girls, and have theorized about their explanation (Archer and Lloyd 1986; Golombok and Fivush 1994). Up to 2 years there are not many consistent differences between behaviour of boys and girls. The similarities certainly outweigh the dissimilarities; but girl infants may be more responsive to people, staying closer to adults, whereas boy infants may be more distressed by stressful situations which they cannot control. Girls also seem to talk earlier.

Observations of 2 year olds at home, and of 3 and 4 year olds in nursery classes, have found characteristic differences in choices of activity. Girls tend to prefer dolls, and dressing-up or domestic play. Boys tend to prefer transportation toys, blocks and activities involv-ing gross motor activity such as throwing or kicking balls, or rough-and-tumbling. Many activities, however, do not show a sex preference at this age.

In nursery school, children tend to select same-sex partners for play, and more so as they get older. By the time children are getting into team games from about 6 or 7 years onward, sex segregation in the playground is much greater. Girls prefer indoor, more sedentary activities, and often play in pairs. Girls tend to be more empathic, and remain more orientated towards adults (parents and teacher) longer into childhood. Boys tend to prefer outdoor play and, later, team games. Boys more frequently engage in both play-fighting and in actual aggressive behaviour.

Lever (1978), in a study of 10–11 year old children in American playgrounds, found that boys more often played in larger mixed-age groups, while girls were more often in smaller groups of same-age pairs. Boys liked playing competitive team games that were more complex in their rules and role-structure, and which seemed to emphasize 'political' skills of co-operation, competition and leadership in their social relations. Girls put more emphasis on intimacy and exclusiveness in their friendships.

Stereotypes of sex roles

Sex-role stereotypes are acquired early; these are beliefs about what is most appropriate for one sex, or the other. Kuhn *et al.* (1978) showed pre-school children a male doll and a female doll, and asked which doll would do each of 72 activities, such as cooking, sewing, playing with trains, talking a lot, giving kisses, fighting

Table 10.8 Beliefs about boys and girls, held by both boys and girls aged 2½ and 3½

Beliefs about girls	play with dolls like to help mother like to cook dinner like to clean house talk a lot never hit say 'I need some help'
Beliefs about boys	like to help father say 'I can hit you'

Note: Only results at or approaching statistical significance are recorded
Source: Kuhn *et al.* (1978)

or climbing trees. Even 2½ year olds had some knowledge of sex-role stereotypes (see Table 10.8). This sex-stereotyping increases with age and by the middle school years it is firmly established. In a study of 5 and 8 year olds in England, Ireland and the USA (D.L. Best *et al.* 1977), the majority of boys and girls agreed that females were soft-hearted whereas males were strong, aggressive, cruel and coarse. By 8 years of age children's stereotypes are very similar to those obtained with adults.

Explanations of sex differences

The sex differences in behaviour and sex-role stereotypes so far discussed apply to western urban societies such as the UK and the USA. Barry *et al.* (1957) made a survey of the anthropological literature on child-rearing in 110, mostly non-literate, societies. In more than 80 per cent of societies, girls more than boys were encouraged to be nurturant, whereas boys more than girls were subject to training for self-reliance and achievement. In many societies responsibility and obedience was also encouraged in girls more than boys. Pressure for sex-typing is especially strong in societies where male strength is important for hunting or herding; it is less strong in societies with small family groups, where sharing of tasks is inevitable.

Sex hormones may have some effect on behaviour (Collaer and Hines 1995). In normal foetal development male sex hormones perhaps predispose boys to become more physically active and interested in rough-and-tumble play (see case study on p. 298). This is consistent with evidence that such sex differences appear

early in life, and in most human societies. However, biological factors do not in themselves explain the process of sex-role identification, and the variations in sex-roles in different societies. Psychologists such as Bandura (1969b) argue that children are moulded into sex-roles by the behaviour of adults, especially parents and teachers – the social learning theory approach. The idea of reinforcement is particularly important in this theory, which postulates that parents and others reward or reinforce sex-appropriate behaviour in children, for example encouraging nurturant behaviour in girls, and discouraging it in boys. Children may also observe the behaviour of same-sex models, and imitate them; for example, boys might observe and imitate the behaviour of male figures in TV films, in their playful and aggressive behaviour.

Kohlberg (1969) initiated a cognitive-developmental approach in this area, arguing that the child's growing sense of **gender identity** – the awareness that one is a boy or a girl – is crucial to sex-role identification. Children attend to and imitate same-sex models, and follow sex-appropriate activities, because they realize that this is what a child of their own sex usually does. This process has been termed **self-socialization** by Maccoby and Jacklin (1974), since it does not depend directly on external reinforcement.

While reinforcement does seem to have some effect, it looks as though its effects are being modulated by other factors. Any complete understanding of sex-role development will require an integration of biological factors, reinforcement and social learning provided by others, with the cognitive-developmental view which provides an active role for the child himself or herself.

Ψ Section summary

Characteristic sex differences emerge in the pre-school years. These may be caused by a combination of hormonal influences, sex stereotypes influencing behaviour of adults, and self-socialization through children acquiring gender identity.

1 What sorts of sex differences are seen in young children's behaviour?
2 What is meant by self-socialization into sex-roles?

Ethnicity

Besides differing by gender, people differ in terms of their racial or ethnic group; both are usually obvious from physical characteristics such as hair and skin colour, and facial appearance. There is not universal agreement on how people should be classified by ethnic group. Besides country of origin, other important dimensions are language (e.g. English Canadian and French Canadian) and religion (e.g. Muslim Indian and Hindu Indian).

As a child grows up he or she will become aware that people differ by ethnic origin. By 4 or 5 years children seem able to make basic discriminations, for example between black and white, and during the next few years more difficult ones, such as Anglo and Hispanic. By around 8 or 9 years, children understand that **ethnic identity** remains constant despite changes in age, or superficial attributes such as clothing.

How do children react to, and evaluate, the ethnic differences which they become aware of from about 4 years? A number of studies of this kind have found that in a test situation where they can choose a doll, or photo, representing children of differing ethnicity, most white children choose or prefer the white doll (or photo) from 4 years, whereas black and other ethnic minority children are more divided, with (in some of the earlier studies) most of them choosing the white doll too. These preferences strengthen up to about 7 years. Beyond 7 years, black children tend to choose the black doll or photo more frequently. These studies were mostly carried out in North America or the UK, where whites form the dominant and more privileged social group; this probably influenced the results. The extent to which minority group children choose their own group has increased, at least among 7 to 11 year olds (Milner 1983), with the rise of ethnic minority group consciousness and pride in their own culture which has characterized recent decades in North America and the UK.

Another way of looking at ethnic preference is more naturalistic, observing whom children actually choose as play partners, in playgroup or playground situations. Children often segregate by race, as well as by gender. Finkelstein and Haskins (1983) observed black and white kindergarten children in the USA. They found that these 5 year olds showed marked segregation by race, which increased during a year in kindergarten.

However, neither black nor white children behaved differently to other-colour peers from same-colour peers.

In older children too, segregation by race is noticeable. However, segregation by race seems to be less marked than segregation by sex, by the middle school period, and is not so evident among boys as girls, perhaps because boys play in larger groups than girls; when playing football, for example, ethnic group may be ignored in order to fill up a team with the requisite number of good players.

Ethnic prejudice

Preference is not identical with prejudice. Prejudice implies a negative evaluation of another person, on the basis of some general attribute (which could be for example sex, race, or disability). Thus, **racial prejudice** means a negative evaluation of someone as a consequence of their being in a certain racial or ethnic group. If a white child dislikes a black child because of some individual attribute, this is not prejudice. But if a white child dislikes a black child (and black children) simply because of their colour, this is racial prejudice.

Prejudice can be measured by asking children to put photos of other children from different ethnic groups along a scale of liking (Aboud 1988), or to assign positive adjectives such as 'work hard' and 'truthful', or negative adjectives such as 'stupid' or 'dirty', to all, some, one or none of photos representing different ethnic groups (Davey 1983). The results are rather similar to those of ethnic identity; prejudice seems to increase from 4 to 7 years, mainly at the expense of minority ethnic groups. During middle childhood, white children tend to remain prejudiced against black or minority group children, while the latter show a more mixed pattern but often become more positive to their own group.

Aboud (1988) has argued that before about 3 or 4 years of age, ethnic awareness is largely absent and prejudice is not an issue; but that from 4 to 7 years, children perceive other ethnic groups as dissimilar to themselves, and because of this tend to have negative evaluations of them. From 8 years onward, children become able to think more flexibly about ethnic differences, and in terms of individuals rather than groups, so that their earlier prejudice can be modified.

Schools have been a focus for work to reduce racial prejudice in children. A multi-racial curriculum approach which emphasizes the diversity of racial and cultural beliefs and practices and gives them equal evaluation, may help in this process. Procedures such as **Co-operative Group Work** (Cowie *et al.* 1994) bring together children of different race (and sex) in common activities, and may thus reduce ethnic preference and prejudice in the classroom.

Ψ **Section summary**

Children acquire an ethnic identity. Children show characteristic ethnic preferences, and may show prejudice to other ethnic or racial groups. Prejudice can be influenced by school curricula.

1 What is the difference between ethnic identity and ethnic prejudice?

2 At what ages do ethnic identity, and ethnic prejudice, tend to appear?

Influences on social development in childhood: conclusions

The early important influences on the social development of the child are clearly parents or caregivers. Through caregiver–infant interactions the infant acquires basic social skills and develops social attachments.

As the child enters school and progresses to middle childhood, the influence of peers becomes more important. Social participation and friendships with peers, and sociometric status in the peer group, appear to relate in significant ways to later development. To some extent, the peer group is an autonomous world with different systems, customs and culture from the adult world (Sluckin 1981). Nevertheless, the family continues to exert an influence, through patterns of attachment, management practices of parents (including a direct influence on the out-of-school peer network) and the effects of siblings. The older child, too, is increasingly aware of, and influenced by, the expectations of society for someone of their age, gender, ethnicity and social background, as mediated by peers and by socializing influences such as schools, and the mass media. By adolescence, the separation from parents is becoming more complete, and the young person is moving toward a mature sense of identity and social being.

☐ Adolescence: transition from child to adult

Adolescence – the teenage years – has been described as a period of turmoil, anxiety, 'storm and stress'. It is also a transition to independence, from childhood to adulthood. It is marked not only by a biological phenomenon, the **adolescent growth spurt**, and the onset of **puberty**, but also by an increase in ability for logical and conceptual thought (see Chapter 9).

Adolescent growth spurt and puberty

Around 11 years (for girls) and 13 years (for boys), children experience the adolescent growth spurt. After a period of steady physical growth through middle childhood, height and weight gain accelerates for about a three-year period before levelling off toward adult height. This acceleration can help account for the awkward feelings some adolescents experience, as their bodies change and shoot up rapidly.

The body of the adolescent is changing in other ways as well, as they become sexually mature. Triggered by the hypothalamus, the body starts producing growth hormones and sex hormones. Besides growth in size, these result in the development of primary reproductive organs, and also coarser facial and body hair in males, breast development in females, and changes in body hair, skin texture, sweat gland activity and voice production.

The actual 'age of puberty' depends on the measure used, and also shows considerable individual variation. Nowadays, puberty often arrives at around 12 years for girls, 14 years for boys. Interestingly, in earlier times – in Europe at least – there is evidence for later onset of puberty. One study (Møller 1985) looked at when the voice change (breaking or deepening of the voice) occurred in Bach's choirboys in Leipzig during 1727–47. From the records, it was clear that this usually occurred around 17 years, compared to 14–16 years in the late twentieth century. Historical analysis of age of beard growth – from portraits, letters, and writings – suggest that this often started in the twenties, rather than around 17 years as at the present time (Møller 1987). Analysis of age of menarche in girls over the past 100–150 years in several European countries and the USA suggests a decrease of several years, from around 14–16 years in the nineteenth century, to around 13 years in the 1960s, a trend now levelling off

(Bullough 1981). Effects of poor diet during the period of the industrial revolution in these countries may help explain these long-term trends.

There are marked individual differences, too, in reaching puberty; at 12 or 13 years, for example, one girl may show no sexual development and not have started periods, another may have been having periods for some time and have well-developed breasts and more adult body shape. Psychologists have wondered whether early or late puberty has any psychological consequences. In general, early maturing boys tend to be more confident and popular; their increase in body size and strength can be an advantage in boys' peer groups, where sports and physical prowess is often a mark of status. Early maturing girls, however, do not have this advantage so much, and may initially feel awkward. Academically, there is some evidence that early maturers can score higher on school tests, though this finding is difficult to interpret; children from smaller families and higher social class groups tend to do better on school tests and also (perhaps because of better diet) reach puberty earlier.

A study in Sweden by Magnusson *et al.* (1985) showed that early maturation can have complex but long-lasting effects. These investigators followed the life histories of 466 girls from before puberty through to the age of 25 years. They found that early maturing girls were more likely to be involving in taking alcohol and other drugs, and breaking social norms; however, this was not true of all early maturers – only of those who associated with an older peer group. These effects were transient, since by 25 years there was no difference between the early and late maturers on these measures. But there was also a non-transient effect; early maturers engaged in sexual activity earlier, got married earlier, and by age 25 had more children and were less likely to have gone on to higher education.

Some writers, such as Elkind (1967), used Piaget's ideas to explain what were seen as typical adolescent preoccupations with how others viewed them, and their high degree of self-consciousness. The physical changes of adolescence might interact with the increased ability to think hypothetically and abstractly, to cause adolescents to think much more about how others might (hypothetically) be thinking about them. Also, this might explain the increased concern and idealism of many adolescents with moral and religious issues, as they start reasoning about what should be happening in the world, given certain belief systems or moral standards.

Identity in adolescence and Erikson's stages

Some theorists have proposed that the emergence of the sense of self and identity is a crucial development in the adolescent years. After all, in these years the young person is becoming sexually mature, and able to think in more abstract terms. In many societies, they are becoming able to marry, and to vote. And they have to decide what career to follow, and what religion or moral code to believe in. Erik Erikson described identity formation as the **normative crisis** of adolescence.

Erikson published his first major work, *Childhood and Society*, in 1950. In this he argued that the growing person moved through a sequence of eight psychosocial stages of ego development (see Table 10.9). He thought that at each stage there was a normative crisis in development – an aspect of development which most people would encounter then and which should be dealt with successfully if healthy development was to continue. The crisis can be described in terms of an interplay of opposites. For example, for the young child there is a contrast in the polarity of trust versus mistrust. Depending on how the infant resolved these two opposites, he or she would develop a quality of ego functioning which Erikson identified as hope, the capacity to view life with optimism.

Erikson had worked with Freud (see Chapter 14) and was influenced by his view of development; however, whereas Freud and the psychoanalysts thought that infancy and early childhood were the decisive periods for personality formation, Erikson did not agree. He had a more **lifespan perspective**, but in so far as he saw one period as particularly influential, it was adolescence, with its normative crisis of identity versus role confusion. This is set out in his next major work, *Identity, Youth and Crisis* (Erikson 1968). In this, he argued that

Table 10.9 Erikson's stages of lifespan development

Age (years)	Normative crisis
0–1	Trust vs mistrust
1–2	Autonomy vs shame and doubt
3–5	Initiative vs guilt
6–puberty	Industry vs inferiority
Adolescence	Identity vs role confusion
Early adult	Intimacy vs isolation
Midlife	Generativity vs stagnation
Old age	Integrity vs despair

adolescence could be thought of as a period of **psychosocial moratorium** – a time in which society allowed or sanctioned young people to try out different beliefs, whether sexual, religious or political, without undue pressure. Also, one could try out different career aspirations. Eventually, a choice was made after having worked through this **identity crisis**.

Erikson's theories were based on case studies and clinical experience rather than the more usual process of large samples and empirical study. In the area of identity development, James Marcia (1980) took Erikson's ideas further and put them in a testable form. He developed a semistructured interview to measure **identity status**. There are four identity statuses, shown in Table 10.10.

Marcia (1980), following Erikson's writings, felt that young people would start in confusion (or diffusion) about identity; as they started to think about moral, political and religious issues and matters of identity in adolescence, young people might first move into foreclosure, adopting family or community values unquestioningly, before moving into moratorium where they actively challenged conventional beliefs and worked through alternative ways of thinking and behaving; finally, they would reach achievement where a clear identity had at last been reached.

Research has found some support for this sequence of changes (Waterman 1988). However, others feel there are strong limitations to this work (Cote and Levine 1988). First, despite his commitment to thinking cross-culturally (and innovative as his ideas were in his day), from current perspectives Erikson's work may be seen as limited, culturally and historically. Was the psychosocial moratorium especially obvious in the late

1960s, when so many young people in western Europe and North America were, for a while, doing just this? Is it true in all cultures that we should expect adolescents to rebel against family or traditional values and experiment with strange ideas? In many societies this would not be appropriate, or would just not be tolerated. And how final is identity achievement? With high levels of unemployment, and of divorce, many people may face challenges to a previously established identity, even in adulthood. Probably, identity formation is indeed a strong feature of adolescence and early adulthood, but beyond that, some of the implications and developments of Erikson's ideas are certainly questionable.

Parent–child and peer relationships in adolescence

By and large, parent–child relationships do seem to get a bit more distant and tense during adolescence (Laursen and Collins 1994). It has been called a period of 'storm and stress'. It is possible to over-exaggerate this phenomenon; often, adolescents have good relationships with parents, and disagreements may be over minor matters such as time of coming in at night or types of clothes worn, rather than really major issues (Coleman and Hendry 1990). Rutter et al. (1976) looked at the experiences of 14–15 year olds on the Isle of Wight, off southern England. Compared to when these children were 10 years old, there was some increase in signs of depression and of conflict with parents; but these characterized only a minority of these adolescent children. The authors concluded that 'adolescent turmoil is a fact, not a fiction, but its psychiatric importance has probably been over-estimated in the past' (Rutter et al. 1976: 55). Nevertheless, parent–child relations are generally described as less close in adolescence than either in childhood, or later in adulthood (Rossi and Rossi 1991).

What causes this temporary distancing in adolescence? The possible explanations have been reviewed by Paikoff and Brooks-Gunn (1991). One factor may simply relate to the effects of puberty. Steinberg (1987) studied 204 families with 10 to 15 year olds and found that, irrespective of when puberty occurred, it was associated with increased behavioural autonomy, decreased emotional closeness towards parents, and increased conflict. Another factor may be changes in thinking processes, and thus in adolescents' expectations of parents and the attributions they make of their actions. Related to this may be changes in self-definition and how one views oneself, and a need to establish a separate identity as Erikson supposed.

Table 10.10 Marcia's four identity status types

Identity status type	Description
Diffusion	Has not started thinking about issue seriously, or made any commitment
Foreclosure	Has made commitment based on family or social expectations, without seriously considering alternatives
Moratorium	Going through a crisis; actively considering different alternatives
Achievement	Has been through crisis and reached a resolution based on considering alternatives

In addition, the peer group becomes more important in adolescence than in earlier childhood, and this might increase conflict with parents. Certainly, experimental studies of conformity to peer pressure suggest that this peaks around 15 years (Berndt 1979); anxieties about friendships are also very high at this age (Coleman 1980). Adolescents often associate in large gangs or 'crowds', and conformity of dress and interests is an important mark of belonging to a particular group. These groups will differ in outlook. Some may value educational achievement, others concerned with sporting success, yet others rebellious or anti-social with respect to adult norms (B.B. Brown *et al.* 1994). In some instances, peer pressure or desire to belong to a particular group may lead to conflicts with parents over such matters as academic work, dress style, or sexual behaviour.

Attitudes to sexual behaviour

Attitudes to sexual behaviour are an important challenge to the adolescent. They may provide an area of conflict with parents; and unprotected intercourse would be within the definition of reckless behaviour described by Arnett (see case study). Attitudes to sexual intercourse generally in young people liberalized during the 1960s and 1970s. For example in the UK, three large-scale surveys suggest a steady increase in the

Plate 10.2 The years between 10 and 15 are associated with increased behavioural autonomy, decreased emotional closeness towards parents and increased conflict

proportion of young people who have experienced sexual intercourse. Taking the figures for 17 year olds, the Schofield report (1965) reported an incidence of 25 per cent for males and 11 per cent for females. The Farrell report (1978) reported figures of 50 per cent for males and 39 per cent for females. Breakwell and Fife-Schaw (1992) reported an incidence of around 60 per cent for both sexes. There are similar changes from North American data. Noticeable here is not only the

---

ψ Case study

Delinquency and risk-taking in adolescence

Statistics in western societies show clearly that there is a peak in criminal offences at adolescence. In the UK, Home Office statistics show a peak at 14–16 years of age, followed by 17–20 years. The great majority of these offences are for crimes such as house-breaking, shop-lifting and car burglaries. Most are committed by young males, but there is a similar age trend for offences by females.

Arnett (1992: 339) hypothesizes that 'adolescents are overrepresented statistically in virtually every category of reckless behavior'. In such behaviour, besides delinquency and crime, he includes driving at high speeds and while drunk; having sex without contraception; and illegal drug use. He explains this overrepre-

sentation in terms of the usual cluster of influences at adolescence – hormonal changes associated with puberty; cognitive changes; and peer influences.

Arnett argues that this trend to reckless behaviour can be strongly influenced by socialization practices. In what he calls 'narrow socialization', typical of traditional societies, there are firm expectations and clear restrictions, and strong community pressures on young people. This reduces independence and creativity, and also reckless behaviour. By contrast, in what he calls 'broad socialization' typical of modern western societies, there are few restrictions on adolescents, which encourages self-expression and autonomy, but at the price of more reckless behaviour, including crime and delinquency.

increase in incidence of sexual intercourse, but also the decrease in the double standard which advocated less permissive behaviour for females than for males.

Ψ Section summary

Adolescence is characterized by a growth spurt and the onset of puberty. Time of maturation has psychological consequences. Erikson considered identity to be a crucial part of adolescent development. In addition, parent–child distance increases, and adolescents tend to show more reckless behaviour.

1 What factors cause variations in the age of puberty?

2 How did Erikson describe identity development in adolescence?

3 Why do parent–child relationships change during adolescence?

☐ Transition to parenting and caregiving

Erikson viewed the adolescent years as one of identity formation (Table 10.9); certainly, it is a period of learning and adjustment while the young person typically leaves the birth family, and starts thinking about a future career, and developing intimate and sexual relationships. With the period of young adulthood – usually in the twenties – comes the need to develop the capacity for intimacy, the ability to be committed to other people through friendship, sexual relationship and love, often enhanced and deepened through the experience of caring for children.

It is the mother who will actually give birth to the child and (with the historically recent exception of bottle-feeding in urban societies) will breastfeed the infant. It is usually the mother rather than the father who carries most of the responsibility for the care of the young child. Research suggests that fathers can fulfil a parenting role just as much as mothers, for example in lone-parent father families; but that typically fathers do not play such a large part in child-rearing and domestic tasks as do mothers (Lamb 1987). Even in egalitarian

societies such as Sweden, mothers still do a larger share of childcare.

Parke and Tinsley (1987) found that mothers and fathers use a very similar repertoire of behaviours when interacting with their newly born children – bouncing, talking, cuddling – and that the same sort of mutual pleasure in the interaction is commonly seen. But with older children, fathers typically engage in a different set of behaviours from mothers. The father role includes more boisterous play activity and more games, in contrast to quieter interactions and routine caregiving on the part of the mother. One explanation of these differences is that these are part of the sex-role differentiation for men and women in our culture. An alternative explanation could be that these represent biologically determined differences in the ways in which men and women interact with young children.

Earlier in this chapter we described how the infant develops attachments to caregivers. In general infants prefer either the mother or the father to a stranger. However, where the child is frightened he or she is more likely to turn to the mother rather than the father (Lamb 1981). The more time that mothers, fathers, or any caregivers spend in playing, caregiving and becoming sensitively attuned to the baby's needs, then the stronger will be the child's attachment. Sensitive parenting involves the capacity to respond quickly to a child's needs; a secure attachment is then likely to develop. This forms the basis within the child for feelings of self-worth and self-confidence.

The mother's own experience of being mothered can, according to attachment theory, strongly influence her parenting style. Main and Goldwyn (1984) used the **Adult Attachment Interview (AAI)** to probe adults' memories of their own childhood experiences. Their work resulted in four major classifications (see Table 10.11). These classifications correspond with those of infant attachment shown in Table 10.1. A review of research using the AAI (van IJzendoorn 1995) shows that autonomous mothers (or parents) tend to have secure infants; dismissing mothers tend to have avoidant infants; and enmeshed mothers tend to have ambivalent infants.

Many autonomous mothers have had happy experiences of childhood and of being parented themselves; but not all. Some mothers, who had had very negative experiences with their own parents, seemed to have come to terms with this, and ascribed rational reasons to it (for example marital stress, or overwork). These mothers perhaps had succeeded in updating their own working models of attachment relationships, even in retrospect, to the benefit of their relationships with their own children (Fonagy 1994).

Table 10.11 Main adult attachment types from the AAI

Label	Description
Ds Dismissive	Dismisses early attachment relationships as of little concern, value or influence
F Autonomous	Can recall earlier attachment related experiences openly and objectively, even if they are not favourable
E Enmeshed	Preoccupied with dependency on own parents, still actively struggling to please them
U Unresolved	Has experienced a trauma, or early death of attachment figure, and has not yet come to terms with this

This research suggests that if adults have easily accessible memories of their relationship with their own parents and are able to talk openly about the positive and negative aspects of that relationship, then they are more likely to have a secure relationship with their own children. By contrast, if they find it difficult to get in touch with their feelings about their parents, or if they are still preoccupied with issues which were unresolved in their own childhood, then they are more likely to have an insecure attachment with their own children.

The social context of parenting

Attachment theorists place a great deal of emphasis on sensitive mothering. Phoenix *et al.* (1991) are critical of the emphasis on maternal availability and sensitivity implied in some models of effective parenting. They argue that the caring relationship and maternal availability said to be necessary for the healthy development of young children is offered at a price – the mother's self-esteem, career aspirations and adult relationships. A

 Research update

Good enough parenting

Scarr (1992) has suggested that by and large, parents need provide only a basically warm, supportive and nurturant environment, for their children to develop their innate potential. She supports her argument by reference to studies in **behaviour genetics**. Using twin and adoption studies, behaviour geneticists have shown that what is called the **shared family environment** – the aspects of the family environment common to all siblings – contribute very little to understanding individual differences. For example, children adopted into the same family, show very little similarity as they grow up (Plomin 1994). If this conclusion is accepted, then modest individual differences are due to heredity, plus **non-shared family environment**, the latter referring to the particular rearing environment each child has.

Even the non-shared family environment can be influenced by what are called **genotype-environment interaction**. In other words, to some extent children help to create their own rearing environment. A child's temperament for example (which appears to be strongly genetically influenced) influences the ways

parents behave to that child and expectations they have of the child.

Of course, no one denies that extremes of environment can adversely affect development; studies of children reared in profoundly non-stimulating environments, and studies of environmental enrichment, show that children can be held back if they do not receive a basic minimum of language, intellectual stimulation, and love and affection. Scarr accepts this, and says that children require this 'average expectable environment' for normal development; but that beyond this, individual variation in development is mainly due to inherited individual potential, finding expression in a reasonably good environment that is partly created by the person for themselves.

Scarr's views give greater prominence to genetic factors than some psychologists think is justified; they appear to downplay the importance of parenting, beyond the basic minimum of 'good enough parenting'. They also imply that many parent–child similarities are due to genetic rather than environmental factors. These issues are controversial and hotly debated (Baumrind 1993). For a good review of this fast-growing area of behaviour genetics, see Plomin *et al.* (1997).

study by Small *et al.* (1994) indicated that 10–20 per cent of mothers are depressed in the first year of childbirth – a significant minority. Reasons given varied from lack of social and emotional support, to being exhausted or unwell, and having no time for themselves. While not denying that childbirth and parenting are normally the source of great emotional well-being and satisfaction, Small *et al.* argued that it is crucial for healthcare workers and other professionals to be aware of the contexts in which mothers are most at risk and in need of support.

In western societies, it is usually expected that parents are responsible for the social and physical well-being of their children, whether from poor or wealthy families. In fact, many parents share this responsibility with other adults in the extended family or in the community. Many families rely on the active participation of grandparents who can act as babysitters while the parents are at work. The grandparents' role is especially important in the case of lone-parent families where the incidence of poverty is more likely to be a significant factor. Other forms of backup for parenting can come from the community, for example through nursery or playgroup provision or through childminders. The relationship between parents and their children is a developing and changing one throughout the lifespan, as we have already seen. For the most part, child-rearing is reported by parents themselves as a rewarding experience, but the task is achieved at some cost. Not surprisingly, the experience of parenting can place strain on the relationship between the parents themselves.

Divorce and step-parenting

Divorce has become more common in modern western societies; each year, between 1 per cent and 2 per cent of marriages end (Richards 1994). Thus, by the time a child is 16, there is something like a one-in-four chance that he or she will have experienced parental separation and divorce. Partners who go through the experience of divorce usually suffer a period of emotional crisis. For many couples it is stressful or even traumatic. What are the consequences of this for the child's development? As divorce has become more frequent since the 1960s, several studies have been made in an attempt to answer this question. Family reactions will vary depending on the ages of the children and on the stage at which the separation itself is at.

Wallerstein and colleagues (1988) describe the adjustment to parental divorce as a process which goes through three main phases. First is the acute phase, typically lasting about two years, in which the emotional and physical separation takes place. Second is a transitional phase, in which each parent experiences marked ups and downs while establishing separate lives. Third is a post-divorce phase, in which each parent has established a new lifestyle, either as a single parent or remarried. The impact on children varies through time as well; longitudinal studies are necessary to get any real understanding of the impact of divorce on children.

Remarriage and the presence of a stepfather seems to improve matters for sons who may respond well to a male figure to identify with; but the step-family situation may make matters worse for daughters, with the stepfather–stepdaughter relationship being a particularly difficult one. Step-parents are often seen as intruders by stepchildren, and find it difficult to strike a balance between discipline and disengagement. Ferri (1984) documented the difficulties facing step-families in a study in London, but pointed out that many such families had successfully met the challenge. While remarriage can increase life satisfaction for the adults involved, forming strong relationships with stepchildren is often a gradual and difficult process.

Richards (1994), in a review of recent research into divorce, points out that children whose parents divorce show consistent behaviour differences from those whose parents remain together, and as adults they tend to have different life courses. They achieve on average at a lower level academically; their self-esteem is lower and they have a higher incidence of conduct disorders; they seem to grow up more quickly; they are more likely to leave home early, to enter into sexual relationships early, to marry and bear children early. Their relationships with parents are more likely to be distant when they reach adulthood; they are more likely to be depressed.

These findings are based on averages and there is wide variation in the reactions of children to divorce due to differences in quality of life, poverty, arrangements for access, feelings of the adults involved, and relationships among members of the reconstituted family itself. Material conditions play a part, as do legislation and the provision of social and emotional support for families in distress. Table 10.12 shows a summary of some of the factors which may affect the impact of divorce on children, from Richards's (1994) review. Children who report the most emotional damage are those whose parents were unable or unwilling to talk about the separation with them in a rational way; those

Table 10.12 Factors which may affect the impact of divorce on children, from Richards (1994)

Divorce-prone couples
Couples prone to divorce may have different styles of child-rearing
Relationship with parents
The change from two parents to a single residential parent, and/or changes in contact and styles of parenting after separation
Conflict
Conflict between parents can have negative consequences for children including lowered self-esteem
Economic factors
A frequent decline in income, especially for mother-headed families, can damage life chances
Life changes
Associated changes (move of house, change of school) are added stressors
Relationship with wider kin
Loss of relationships in wider kin network deprives child of social support

who took sides with one parent and continued to have a poor relationship with the other parent; and those who were unhappy with custody arrangements. Hetherington (1989) describes 'winners, losers and survivors' of parental divorce. Depending on circumstances, some children may continue to be damaged and insecure through to adulthood; others recover and 'survive'; yet others may develop particularly caring and competent ways of behaving as a result of coping with the experience.

Child abuse

Usually, parents love and care for their children. No parent is perfect, but most provide 'good enough' parenting. Some conflict between parents and their offspring is inevitable but generally such disagreements are kept within reasonable bounds.

In some cases, however, parents or other caregivers may neglect a child, failing to give him or her the love, care and attention necessary for normal healthy development. Even more drastically, some may subject a child or children to physical or sexual abuse. Since the mid-1970s, violence against children within the family has been identified as a major social problem in industrialized countries. Abuse can result in severe injuries, long-lasting psychological trauma, and even death.

Physical abuse has been defined as the intentional, non-accidental use of force on the part of the parent or other caretaker interacting with a child in his or her care aimed at hurting, injuring or destroying that child (Gil 1970). **Sexual abuse** has been defined as the involvement of dependent, sexually immature children and adolescents in sexual activities that they do not fully comprehend, to which they are unable to give informed consent or that violate the social taboos of family roles (Kempe 1980).

What leads a parent to abuse a child? Abusing parents have been found very often to have insecure attachment relationships with their children; this in turn may relate back to their own experiences of having been parented. Browne (1989) found that 70 per cent of maltreated infants had insecure attachments to their caregivers, compared to only 26 per cent of infants with no record of maltreatment. Crittenden (1988) examined the representations of relationships in abusing parents, using the idea of internal working models discussed earlier. She interviewed 124 mothers in Virginia, USA, many of whom had abused or maltreated their children. She reported that adequate mothers generally had warm and secure relationships with both their children and their partner. By contrast, abusing mothers appeared to conceptualize relationships in terms of power struggles. They tended to be controlling and hostile with anxiously attached children, and to have angry and unstable adult relationships. Another group, of neglecting mothers, appeared to conceive of relationships as emotionally empty. They were unresponsive to their anxiously attached children, and were involved in stable but affectionless relationships with partners. These findings have implications for working with these families.

Sexual abuse has been a particularly controversial area of social policy. The difficulties of evidence have been compounded by the suggestions of **false memory syndrome**, in which it is supposed that allegations of earlier abuse may arise from memory distortions and even indoctrination. Causes of abuse are also debated. Whereas attachment theorists emphasize intergenerational transmission of parenting, feminist explanations of child sexual abuse see it as an abuse of male power, consequent on the nature of power inequalities between men, women and children in society (Sarraga 1993). Biological explanations point to the relatively higher risks of abuse in step-parent families, where ties of biological relatedness are absent (Daly and Wilson 1996).

A model of parenting

Belsky (1984) has advocated a model of parental functioning which distinguishes three main influences on the quality of parental functioning. In order of suggested importance, these are:

(1) personal psychological resources of the parent: this will include parental mental health, the quality of internal representations of relationships and their developmental history

(2) contextual sources of support: including the social network of support from partner, relatives and friends, and job conditions and financial circumstances

(3) characteristics of the child: in particular easy or difficult temperament.

Belsky's actual process model of factors influencing parenting is illustrated in Figure 10.4. It clearly brings out the importance of a variety of factors, which in combination can make child abuse much more likely than the presence of any single factor alone. While useful for conceptualizing abuse and neglect in the family, the model is also useful more generally for understanding how variations in family functioning, satisfactory as well as unsatisfactory, may come about.

ψ Section summary

Becoming a parent is an important transition. Parenting is influenced by one's own experience of being parented; in addition, the social support and context of parenting is important. Divorce and step-parenting have important consequences for children. Physical and sexual abuse are extreme negative consequences of parenting. Belsky has proposed a model of factors influencing parenting.

1 What is meant by 'good enough parenting'?
2 What are typical effects of divorce on children?
3 How useful is Belsky's model of parenting?

Social development in adulthood

Erikson's seventh stage – maturity – describes the need to be concerned to guide the next generation, whether through parenthood or through the process of passing on skills and knowledge to others. The polarities here are

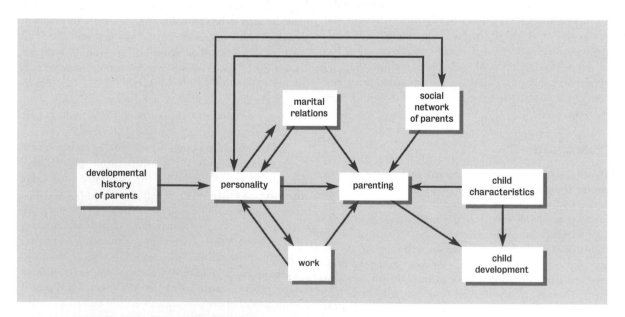

Figure 10.4 Belsky's process model of the determinants of parenting
Source: adapted from Belsky (1984)

generativity and stagnation (see Table 10.9). In his final stage – old age – the individual encounters the polarities of ego integrity and despair. Ego integrity involves the calm acceptance of one's life as it has been lived and a recognition of its richness; by contrast, despair is the anguished regret for all that was not done or experienced and a terror of impending death. However, Erikson did not write so much about these later stages as he did about adolescence.

Levinson: the seasons of a person's life

Daniel Levinson and his colleagues built on Erikson's work to make a more systematic investigation of the subjective experience of adult life (Levinson 1978, 1990). They originally studied a sample of 40 men; more recently they reported a comparable study of women's lives. Levinson's research methods incorporated biographical interviews, projective tests and interviews with participants' partners and colleagues; his aim was to tap both conscious and unconscious processes in adult life. He aimed to discover answers to questions like 'What does it mean to be an adult?' and 'What are the key issues in adult life?' Levinson's concept of the life cycle incorporated the metaphor of seasons. He noted that this metaphor can take many forms – spring, summer, autumn, winter in the year; daybreak, noon, dusk and night within a single day; phases in a relationship. The metaphor is one which is meaningful to many people when contemplating the nature of the course of life.

On the basis of his empirical work, Levinson suggested that adult life can be viewed as a sequence of four overlapping developmental eras (see Table 10.13). The first era, that of childhood and adolescence, provides a base for the new kinds of development which will be required in the next era. The Early Adult Transition is a developmental period in which pre-adulthood draws to a close and the era of Early Adulthood approaches; a bridge between adolescence and adulthood which was not fully a part of either. In the second era, Early Adulthood, the person begins to create a new life structure. Biologically the person is at the peak of his or her life cycle. This is the time to identify and pursue important aspirations, to find a place in society, to form close relationships, probably to establish a family, and to attain a more responsible position in the world of adults. It is a time of energy and creativity; at the same time there are great stresses.

The Midlife Transition ends Early Adulthood and marks the shift to Middle Adulthood. Levinson's findings suggested that, at around this age, many people report the experience of a **midlife crisis**, a phenomenon which can take a whole range of forms. Adults in this age group may feel trapped between the generations, with children growing up and leaving home on the one hand and ageing parents requiring extra support on the other. Earlier aspirations may not have been realized and a growing sense of discontent may develop. At this point, the adult may, uncharacteristically, embark on an intense affair or abruptly seek out a new career direction. The midlife crisis may be expressed in less dramatic ways but, nevertheless, it is a common experience to many adults at this point in the lifespan.

Table 10.13 Levinson's stages of lifespan development

Late Adulthood (65+)		Late adulthood
		Late Adult Transition (60–65)
		Culmination of middle adulthood
Middle Adulthood (45–60)		Age 50 transition
		Entering middle adulthood
	Midlife Transition (40–45)	
	Settling down	
Early Adulthood (22–40)	Age 30 transition	
	Entering the adult world	
	Early Adult Transition (17–22)	
	Childhood and adolescence	
Birth to Adolescence	Birth	

The process of change, which begins during the Midlife Transition, continues throughout the third era, Middle Adulthood. Although the person's biological abilities are less during this era than they were, they are usually sufficient to permit the person to live an energetic and useful life, with responsibility and a concern for the next generation. This is a time when many adults become senior members of their own world. This may be in the domain of work through responsibility or promotion, in the domain of voluntary or community work, or within the family. Levinson's studies suggested that, if some sense of recognition or of self-worth is not evident at this stage, the person's life becomes increasingly trivial and stagnant.

The Late Adult Transition links Middle and Late Adulthood and is part of both. In the fourth era – Late Adulthood – men and women who have been in employment will usually have retired, but many continue to lead active lives and to remain physically fit. Levinson found that at this stage adults are likely to become even more inward looking; the prospect of death and separation from loved ones is an aspect of the broader individuation process of self-review and evaluation. However, Levinson says relatively little about this part of the life cycle since his sample was not representative of this older age group.

Bühler's studies of lifespan development

In Germany, Charlotte Bühler and her colleagues carried out a systematic analysis of over 400 biographies written by individuals from a range of backgrounds, including a sub-set of highly creative people. Bühler and Massarik (1968) proposed that there are five distinct stages of human development, three of which focus on adult life. Between 25 and 50 years of age, individuals are typically engaged in the process of identifying goals in their personal and professional lives and working towards achieving them. Between 45 and 60 years, they are still active and energetic, despite some waning of physical powers, but there emerges a need to evaluate life and reflect on its meaning; in later stages, there was also a need to come to terms with changes such as retirement, the 'empty nest', significant losses of close partners and decreasing physical powers. Bühler and her colleagues found wide differences among adults in the age group of 65 years and over. Some people were very active; the highly creative sub-set in the sample, for example, continued to grow and develop in their work. Others in this age group adjusted to a more restricted range of activities.

There are similarities in the findings of Bühler and of Erikson. However, unlike Erikson, Bühler and her colleagues did not find open despair among their sample but rather a resignation to a sense that life was less fulfilling than before, and that it will end.

Becoming a grandparent

The average age of becoming a grandparent, in western societies, is approximately 50 years for women, and a couple of years older for men (Rossi and Rossi 1990). About 70 per cent of people become grandparents. Grandparenthood is thus an important part of the life cycle for most people. For many, the role is very much a positive one.

A few earlier studies on grandparenting were based mainly on impressions and case studies. Grandparents were sometimes portrayed as older people who were likely to be frail and cantankerous (as a function of their age), and to interfere in the raising of grandchildren, being inflexible, and variously either too lenient and indulgent, or too strict and old-fashioned in their views. There is some evidence that grandmothers in the 1950s were indeed stricter than mothers. Staples and Smith

Plate 10.3 In the west, the average age of becoming a grandparent is 50 years for women, 52 for men and about 70 per cent of people will become grandparents. Today's grandparents will have had a fuller education and will have quite frequent contact of a positive nature with their grandchildren

(1954) interviewed 87 grandmother–mother pairs, and found the grandmothers to have stricter and more authoritarian views than the mothers did. These gaps between the views of grandparents and parents might have been especially large in the 1950s, as a function of rapidly changing child-rearing opinions over the previous decades. Such differences in views may have lessened. In the 1990s grandparents, at least the younger ones, will have had a much fuller education; also probably fewer live directly with the grandchild. More recent evidence does not strongly support the notion of very strict grandparents (P.K. Smith 1991), but reports on it in a predominantly positive light. Grandparents are seen as having quite frequent contacts of a positive nature with their grandchildren, and acting as important support agents in certain circumstances.

Grandparents can influence their grandchildren's behaviour both directly and indirectly (Tinsley and Parke 1984). Indirect influence is mediated by some other person or agency, without necessitating any direct interaction. For example, grandparents can continue to provide emotional and financial support for parents. Also, the parent–child interaction will be influenced by the way the parent has been brought up and the experiences of child-rearing which the parent has had modelled by his or her parent i.e. the grandparent. Such influences can of course be positive or negative. Huesmann et al. (1984) found that the severity of discipline received from parents when their subjects were 8 years old, predicted both to their subjects' levels of aggression at 30, and to their children's aggression at 8 years; that is, grandparents' disciplinary practices 22 years earlier predicted the aggression of their grandchildren.

The most obvious forms of grandparent influence are nevertheless direct, face-to-face ones. Some grandparents act as a surrogate parent when the child is young (for example in a single parent family, or teenage pregnancy, or as a caregiver while both parents work). Radin et al. (1991) reported that grandfathers can have a positive direct influence on the social and cognitive development of their grandchildren, in the context of young (1 to 2 year old) grandchildren of teen mothers.

Even if not acting as a surrogate parent, a grandparent who has contact with a grandchild can act as a companion and be an important part of the child's social network. 'When we go fishing with Grandpa, we talk. We tell each other about ourselves'. 'With Grandma I can talk about my problems' (Tyszkowa 1991). They can also act as a source of emotional support, acting as a 'buffer' in cases where a grandchild is in conflict with

the parents for example, or where the parents are in conflict with each other or in process of divorce.

ψ Section summary

Like Erikson, Levinson proposed a stage model of lifespan development, but with more emphasis on adult development. He highlighted the midlife crisis which may occur as the parenting role comes to an end. Another model was proposed by Bühler. Most people are grandparents for about one-third of their lifespan. Grandparents can have both direct and indirect effects on their grandchildren, usually positive although sometimes negative.

1 How compatible are the stage models of Erikson, Levinson, and Bühler?
2 Are grandparents important for grandchildren?

Social aspects of ageing

Ageing is a gradual but inevitable process, marked by physical, mental and social changes. Although some aspects of ageing start much earlier, in terms of the general view of ageing in western society, people over about 65 years of age are seen as 'older'. This is generally the age of retirement from work, and one which Levinson (Table 10.13) saw as the transition to later adulthood.

Older people are often seen as losing interest in social interaction. Indeed a prominent theory, called **disengagement theory** by Cumming and Henry (1961), held that old age involved a natural withdrawal from social activities and societal obligations. In contrast to this, Neugarten et al. (1968) proposed an **activity theory**, that health and life satisfaction are maintained through continuing social activity and involvement, and that any decrease tends to be brought about by societal discrimination.

Research findings tend to favour activity theory over disengagement theory (Pratt and Norris 1994). For example Dolen and Bearison (1982) looked at the lives of 122 generally healthy adults aged 65 to 89 years, living in New York. Neither social participation, nor scores on social cognition tasks, showed any pronounced decline with age. Nevertheless, social participation and social cognition scores did correlate significantly, indicating that those who remained socially active and involved also stayed cognitively alert and socially understanding. A study of elderly people in England, aged 85 or over, by Grundy (1994) found that those who kept in touch with family and friends had a lower risk of death (even allowing for differences in state of health). And social support generally provides a buffer against stress, including the age-related stresses of retirement and bereavement .

To some extent, modern societies may discriminate against older people; for example by forcing retirement at an arbitrary age, or by perpetuating, in the mass media and elsewhere, negative stereotypes of elderly people and the ageing process. Neugarten *et al.*(1968) labelled this **ageism**. Birren (1969) proposed that, rather than use chronological age as a societal indicator, we might use **functional age** – an individual's actual capacities, irrespective of chronological age. A consequence of this view would be that retirement age might be determined by functional age, rather than by chronological age, for example. So far, this view has not held sway widely; but in some domains, such as politics, quite elderly people

have achieved or stayed in very influential positions. An acclaimed example is that of Nelson Mandela becoming President of the new South Africa at the age of 75. Not all elderly leaders are acclaimed, but older persons do accumulate knowledge and wisdom; in some circumstances, these can be important assets.

Ψ Section summary

After nominal retirement age, most elderly people are still socially active. Disengagement theory proposed that elderly people experience a natural withdrawal from social activities, but evidence tends to favour activity theory, which proposes that continued social involvement is natural in older people and helps to maintain health and life satisfaction.

1 What is the evidence in favour of activity theory?
2 What is meant by 'ageism'?

Ψ Chapter summary

● **Social development in infancy**

Parents and caregivers respond to the signals and reflex behaviours of the new-born infant, and scaffold early social interaction sequences; by around 7 months, infants direct proximity-maintaining behaviours preferentially to certain attachment figures; security of attachment is assessed by means of the strange situation technique.

● **Early peer relationships**

Peer interactions develop slowly in the first two years, although sibling relationships can be intense at an early age; in the pre-school years, social play, particularly pretend play and rough-and-tumble play, becomes frequent, and social participation increases.

● **Friendship and sociometric status**

Friends are characterized by more intense social activity, intimacy and reciprocity, conflict resolution, and effective task performance. Friendship structure in a group is measured by sociometric techniques. Sociometric status types result from combinations of

liked most and liked least nominations. Rejected (disliked) children are often aggressive and disruptive, and in some cases lack social skills.

● **Aggression and bullying**

Various types of aggressive behaviour have been described, and pathways of aggressive behaviour have been delineated. Bullying refers to persistent aggressive behaviour against victims unable to defend themselves.

● **Prosocial and moral development**

Prosocial behaviour emerges in the second year; it is influenced by various factors in the home environment. Researchers have also studied the development of moral reasoning, by means of observations of games, and use of short stories and dilemmas.

● **Sex differences**

Characteristic sex differences emerge in the pre-school years. These may be caused by a combination of hormonal influences, sex stereotypes influencing

Box continued

behaviour of adults, and self-socialization through children acquiring gender identity.

● Ethnicity

Children acquire an ethnic identity. Children show characteristic ethnic preferences, and may show prejudice to other ethnic or racial groups. Prejudice can be influenced by school curricula.

● Adolescence: transition from child to adult

Adolescence is characterized by a growth spurt and the onset of puberty. Time of maturation has psychological consequences. Erikson considered identity to be a crucial part of adolescent development. In addition, parent–child distance increases, and adolescents tend to show more reckless behaviour.

● Transition to parenting and caregiving

Becoming a parent is an important transition. Parenting is influenced by one's own experience of being parented; in addition, the social support and context of parenting is important. Divorce and stepparenting have important consequences for children.

Physical and sexual abuse are extreme negative consequences of parenting. Belsky has proposed a model of factors influencing parenting.

● Social development in adulthood

Like Erikson, Levinson proposed a stage model of lifespan development, but with more emphasis on adult development. He highlighted the midlife crisis which may occur as the parenting role comes to an end. Another model was proposed by Bühler. Most people are grandparents for about one-third of their lifespan. Grandparents can have both direct and indirect effects on their grandchildren, usually positive although sometimes negative.

● Social aspects of ageing

After nominal retirement age, most elderly people are still socially active. Disengagement theory proposed that elderly people experience a natural withdrawal from social activities, but evidence tends to favour activity theory, which proposes that continued social involvement is natural in older people and helps to maintain health and life satisfaction.

Further reading

● McGurk, H. (ed.) (1992) *Childhood Social Development: Contemporary perspectives*. Hove: Lawrence Erlbaum. A wide-ranging collection from a range of experts.

● Bowlby, J. (1988) *A Secure Base: Clinical applications of attachment theory*. London: Tavistock. An advanced text on attachment theory by the founder of the field.

● Dunn, J. (1988) *The Beginnings of Social Understanding*. Oxford: Basil Blackwell. An authoritative review of early social development, sibling relationships, and how understanding of others develops.

● Coleman, J.C. and Hendry, L. (1990) *The Nature of Adolescence*. London: Routledge. An excellent review of current work on adolescence.

● Reder, P. and Lucey, C. (eds) (1995) *Assessment of parenting*. London: Routledge. A collection about issues related to parenting, particularly strong on problem areas such as child abuse.

● Pratt, M.W. and Norris, J.E. (1994) *The Social Psychology of Ageing*. Cambridge, MA and Oxford: Blackwell. A useful review of social life in older people.

CHAPTER 11

Social psychology 1

Evanthia Lyons

KEY CONCEPTS • epistemological perspectives and levels of analysis • self and identity • symbolic interactionism • social identity theory • social cognition • self-categorization theory • attitudes • attribution theory

❏ Chapter preview

When you have read this chapter, you should be able to

- define what is social psychology
- describe different ways of producing social psychological knowledge and of the assumptions underlying these different approaches
- understand different levels of explanation of social psychological phenomena
- understand the role of the concept of identity in explaining social behaviour and thought
- discuss the relationship between attitudes and behaviour and the factors that influence this relationship
- understand the way we attribute social events and behaviour to specific causes

Introduction

Social psychological research is concerned with developing an understanding of how we make sense of our world, how we interact and communicate with each other and the social processes that shape our cognitions and social interaction. How do we make sense of and judgements about ourselves and others? How do we relate to each other? How can we explain social behaviour? How do other people and social structures influence the way we think and act?

Social psychologists adopted different approaches to the study of these phenomena. Underlying these approaches are different ways of theorizing the relationship between the individual and society, different assumptions about the status of social reality and the nature of social psychology as a science.

This chapter introduces the student to some of these debates. First, we focus on different approaches to the production of social psychological knowledge and illustrate the different methods by social psychologists. Second, we discuss some of the ways of conceptualizing self and identity and thus begin to address one of the major issues that has challenged social psychologists over the years, that is, the relationship between the individual and society. Third, we focus on the concept of attitude and its relationship to behaviour, and finally, we discuss theories which describe how people process information in order to make causal inferences about particular events or behaviour. These two topics dominate the field of social psychological investigation with respect to intra-individual functioning, perhaps because they have important implications for, and direct applicability to, real life.

☐ Epistemological perspectives and levels of analysis

Brief historical background

Social psychology is often thought to have the same ancestral roots as sociology, particularly with respect to the preoccupation with understanding the interface between the individual and society (Farr 1996; McGarty and Haslam 1997). For example, the work of Berger and Luckmann (1966) on *The Social Construction of Reality* contributed in a substantial way to the thinking of both social psychologists and sociologists about how social reality is constructed and the individual's place therein. Farr (1996) reports, however, that social

psychology seemed to mutate into two separate research streams, one sociologically oriented and the other psychologically oriented. The sociological branch associated itself with the study of social interaction and the construction of meaning in social life (e.g. Blumer 1937) in the symbolic interaction tradition. According to Farr (1996) this field is still 'a vital and versatile tradition of social psychology within American sociology'. The psychological branch of social psychology was assimilated into mainstream experimental psychology in the positivist scientific tradition. The two types of social psychology thus became differentiated. Sociological social psychology focused on the study of social interaction, social communication and the construction of social life through language, a largely **inter-individual** and cultural concern. In contrast, psychological social psychology focused on the study of people's cognition and perception with respect to social life, a largely **intra-individual** and arguably 'non-social' concern (Semin 1997). Each of these traditions evolved from a different set of **epistemological** assumptions and developed different methods of investigation most suited to their respective tasks (e.g. qualitative techniques like participant observation and interviews versus quantitative techniques involving experimentation and statistical analysis).

Social psychology in Europe has none the less attempted to bridge the gap, by fashioning its own set of epistemological assumptions derived from both sociological and psychological social psychology (Doise 1997). Before we move on to explain the epistemological foundations of social psychology, we will examine how social psychological knowledge is produced.

Prevailing ideologies in the production of social psychological knowledge

The prevailing epistemology within social psychology, particularly North American social psychology, is called logical **empiricism**. This prescribes the so-called 'scientific method' (i.e. experimentalism) as the way to proceed in the production of social psychological knowledge. Radical criticisms of the appropriateness of the experimental method for studying social psychological phenomena began to be voiced in the 1970s when Tajfel (1972a) wrote his piece on 'experiments in a vacuum'. Since then, there have been many European theorists on the issue including Moscovici (1976), Potter and Wetherell (1987) and Shotter (1984). These and many other theorists have questioned the way in which social reality is construed by logical empiricists. They argue that social reality is not an objective phenomenon 'out there' to be tested and measured. On the contrary, it is represented and negotiated via the shared environment of language. Shotter (1984) proposed that what we perceive as social reality is very much created in joint action. These and related arguments dramatically shift the focus of psychology and social science away from the individual as the originator of social realities and behaviour, to focusing upon the constructive aspects of relations between individuals. This has led to a **paradigm** challenge within social psychology leading some to say that social psychology is in 'crisis'. However, logical empiricism is still very much alive and well.

Logical empiricism

Logical empiricism has been the prevailing ideology or 'paradigm' within the social sciences for almost as long as the history of social psychology. Logical empiricism has also been called 'positivism' because of the major influence of the work of Karl Popper on scientific thinking. **Positivism** prescribes a hypothetico-deductive approach to investigation and the identification of precise causal links. This involves producing a testable hypothesis from a precisely defined theory that is then subject to experimental test. The theory can be either confirmed or disconfirmed. Reality is defined as something 'out there' waiting to be observed. With the right tools and techniques, objective reality can be causally mapped and precisely represented such that universal laws and propositions can be formed.

These assumptions about the systematic conduct of science predominate both the natural and the social sciences. The illusion of impartiality and a value-free scientific enterprise still holds strong in many quarters, perpetuated by scientific elitism. It is these kinds of assumptions that contributed to the dualism inherent in thinking about the individual relative to society (see Farr 1996) and which has come under severe attack by some social psychologists. There is now a significant force within contemporary social psychology in disagreement with the positivist belief in a hypothetical reality that is ultimately knowable from the application of conventional 'scientific' method. The underlying theme bringing protagonists together is the supposition that psychological realities are largely socially constructed through the shared environment of language.

Constructionist approaches

Constructionist approaches are many and varied but they all derive from the same assumption that reality is socially constructed. Shotter (1975) argues vehemently against the view of people as social objects who can be observed and studied in the same way as phenomena in the physical world. The box describes some of the approaches branching out of constructionism and highlights their preferred method of study. The taxonomy is by no means exhaustive nor are the categories of constructionism described indicative of distinct and autonomous forms.

Constructionist approaches within social psychology

Discourse analysis
Discourse analysis (DA) presupposes that discourses are the building blocks of social reality. The focus of investigation is on how social reality is 'linguistically constructed' aiming for a better understanding of social life and social interaction from the study of social texts (Potter and Wetherell 1987: 7). DA assumes that people use a range of linguistic resources to create a version of events and that their discourses are action-oriented and purposive. DA requires the detailed qualitative analysis of written and verbal text

derived from conversational forums. There is also a finer-grained version of DA called conversation analysis (e.g. Wooffitt 1992) focusing on the linguistic as opposed to social organization of talk.

Deconstructionism
Kitzinger (1992) is a major proponent of a form of discursive psychology involving the deconstruction of the taken-for-granted categories used by social scientists with view to unpacking their political, moral and social uses. For example, Burman (1994) 'decon-

Box continued

structs' all of developmental psychology to highlight the gender and cultural assumptions built into research on child development and parenting. She argues that development psychology has been hived off from the historical and sociopolitical conditions of childhood and child-raising.

Dialogic theory

Sampson (1993) in *Celebrating the Other* advocates a form of social psychology derived from dialogic theory and a post-modern critique of the prevailing monologic view. The monologic view presents a picture of a self-contained, individualistic and monologic Self and its fearful suppression of all that is Other — all that is different from the self-affirming, white, male, ethnocentric standard. Denying the Other (i.e. cultural diversity and the multiplicity of meaning) creates a world secured on behalf of dominant groups' interests. The realities constructed for Others are created to serve and service the desires of the dominant group. Sampson rejects this approach advocating a dialogic alternative and focusing on the conversational quality of human nature. This involved the observation and analysis of interactions and conversations between people (i.e. dialogue).

Social representations theory

Social representations theory (SRT) advocates study of cultural and social processes via communication practices (Moscovici 1976). Proponents of SRT typically use qualitative methods to investigate their subject; however, some researchers have conducted experiments as well (see Doise 1997).

Grounded theory

Glaser and Strauss (1967) proposed an approach to the development of theory 'grounded' in interviews, observations and textual material. Grounded theory assumes an inextricable link between subjectivity and objectivity in research, and the construction of scientific knowledge. It advocates the close inspection and analysis of qualitative material including documentary evidence, fieldwork observation and interview transcripts, to generate theory that can then be further tested and elaborated through more qualitative analysis. More recently, discursive ori-

ented social psychologists have started developing grounded theory more explicitly within the constructionist epistemological tradition (e.g. Henwood and Pidgeon 1995).

Feminism

Griffin (1995) cites a definition of feminism as 'the political theory and practice that struggles to free all women'. Feminism is committed to collective action, valuing personal experience and consciousness raising. It does not represent a coherent set of assumptions, beliefs or propositions, being a 'contested space' under continual dispute and negotiation (Griffin 1995: 119). A key area of dislocation between traditional research and feminism is in the critique of the positivist emphasis on experimentation as 'political' and perpetuating inequality and differential power relationships. Feminism thus advocates a qualitative approach to data collection and analysis.

Rhetorical approach

Billig (1991) revisits sociological insights into the rhetorical nature of argumentation as a means of exploring contemporary issues of ideology and opinion. He argues that holding opinions is an essentially rhetorical and argumentative matter, and also deeply ideological. No one set of empirical tools is advised although the flavour of the research approach is distinctively qualitative.

Ethnomethodology

Ethnomethodology is concerned with cultural description. An emphasis is laid on actors' understandings and theorizing about their actions. Goetz and LeCompte (1984: 2) defined ethnography as the 'analytic descriptions or reconstructions of intact cultural scenes and groups. Ethnographies recreate for the reader the shared beliefs, practices, artefacts, folk knowledge, and behaviours of some groups of people'. The methods used aims to do four things: elicit phenomenological data or the world-views of individuals or groups, they are employed in naturalistic settings, aim to represent the totality of the phenomenon under investigation and aim to be multi-method (see Uzzell 1995).

You will note from the box the emergence of a discursive theme in social psychology (Edwards and Potter 1992; Harré and Gillett 1994) that has gathered much momentum since the mid-1970s. This was largely spawned by the work of Berger and Luckmann (1966) and also Harré and Secord (1972). Of central interest is how we talk about the world, how we represent it to one another via discourse, how we describe and explain social phenomena and how this in turn shapes social reality. Within the evolution of this new paradigm is a view of the nature of truth as a malleable narrative. Gergen (1985) for instance, advocates that all psychological knowledge is socially constructed and thus relative to an historical, cultural and linguistic context. This view is indicated by the term post-modernism. Recognition of the relative nature of social knowledge calls for a completely different conceptual and methodological framework than hitherto the case. Focus on the ever changing narratives of life implicates a qualitative approach using interviews and focus groups to elicit people's verbal accounts of their actions — as exemplified by discourse analysts (Potter and Wetherell 1987).

The role of values in the science of social psychology

Values not only are an object of study within social psychology, but also permeate everything we do, our choice of research topic, the issues that preoccupy us, the way we investigate them, analyse and present them. As you will see in Chapter 12, the study of prejudice prevailed during the 1940s during the fascist reign in Europe. The 1970s brought with it a wave of research on gender and sexism, corresponding with the rise of feminism. In the 1980s and 1990s the issue of how people respond to multicultural diversity came into prominence, reflecting the social concerns of the time. To this extent, social psychology is a reflection of social history and by no means value free.

Another perhaps more subtle influence of values is via the preconceptions held by social psychologists about the nature of social reality and our place in it. Unless they are explicitly uncovered and challenged, we often take our values and assumptions for granted, particularly if they are shared. During the 1970s and 1980s feminists highlighted the workings of many unexamined sexist assumptions or biases within psychological and social psychological thinking. For instance, psychologists have tended to favour biological explanations of gender differences rather than social explanations reflecting an under-

lying ideology of political conservatism (e.g. the role and behaviour of women is determined by their biological make-up — a belief that preserves and perpetuates the status quo with respect to women's place in society: Unger 1985). Of course, feminists have their own values and agendas at stake. The point is that these need to be clearly spelled out and open to debate. Feminist psychology has begun to legitimize the debate about whose social reality we are talking about — male or female.

Values also underpin our concepts. The terms **prejudice** and social discrimination have very negatively valued connotations. Many social psychologists have devoted their life's work to describing, explaining and trying to develop interventions to get rid of prejudice and discriminatory attitudes and behaviours (e.g. R. Brown 1995; Tajfel 1978). The concept of **personal identity** reflects the western concern with the supremacy of the individual over the collective. In collectivist society such individualistic terms are often not part of the vocabulary (Kavolis 1984). These kinds of implicit values are not wrong, they simply need to be recognized. They will be present in the way we generate our data, the way we handle it and interpret what we have 'found'. Scientific interpretation is no less prone to subjectivity than everyday non-scientific interpretation. The analysis of social representations in this chapter will highlight the social and cultural processes involved in conducting science and generating scientific thought (Moscovici 1976).

Levels of analysis in social psychological thinking

Social behaviour can be explained by using theoretical constructs reflecting different levels of analysis. We can explain, for example, somebody's expression of sadness in terms of physiological factors, interpersonal communication processes or cultural representations of the particular emotion (Parkinson 1995).

In response to criticisms levelled against social psychology as being too **reductionist** in its explanations (see e.g. Moscovici 1972; Pepitone 1981), it has been argued that 'articulating analyses of different levels is an essential aspect of social psychologists scientific endeavour' (Doise 1997: 72). Doise differentiates between four levels of analysis: intra-individual, inter-individual and situational, power and status relations, and systems of social belief, representation, evaluations and norms (see box). These different levels of analysis are not mutually exclusive: any one piece of research may address more than one level of analysis.

Aggression

- *Intra-individual*
  This level focuses on intra-individual processes, i.e. the way individuals organize their experiences of the environment. Examples of this approach are studies of social categorization, social judgement and perception.
- *Inter-individual*
  This level focuses on inter-individual and situational processes whereby individuals are conceived of as interchangeable. Interest is in observing, documenting and analysing interactional systems. Examples of this approach are studies of group processes in the Lewin (1948) and Sherif (1966) tradition.
- *Power and status relations*
  This level focuses on the different positions occupied by individuals in society as exemplified by the work of Lorenzi-Cioldi (1988).
- *Social beliefs, social representations and norms*
  This level focuses on the cultural and ideological productions of society and groups as exemplified by work on group dynamics and inter-group relations.

To illustrate these distinctions between levels of analysis the topic of aggression will be used, referring to the work of Mummendey (1996). Traditional theories of aggression began from the intra-individual level of analysis with the intention of identifying aggressive instincts (e.g. McDougall 1908) and uncovering their mechanisms. In 1939 Dollard *et al.* initiated research on the so-called frustration-aggression model that proposed frustration arising from the blocking of goal attainment is the cause of aggression. This gave rise to research examining 'readiness for aggression' and 'the environmental cues' for aggression (e.g. Berkowitz 1964). Thus an extension to the intra-individual focus to include an inter-individual focus was also contemplated in so far as the role of 'situational' cues in aggressive behaviour were explored. More recently, the social construction of aggression has become of interest, the argument being that aggression is an interpretive construct (Mummendey 1996). Research is thus focused on identifying the particular social-normative context embedding the use of the label 'aggression' (e.g. norm violation). One way to investigate this is by deploying attribution theory to examine how people infer intent from action performed by another person. This presupposes that attributions of causes play a critical role in determining the interpretation and evaluation of an action as aggressive. These interests bring the topic of aggression into a different research level – the level of social beliefs, representations and norms. Mummendey (1996) also describes research on aggression in the context of conditions of power. In Chapter 12 you will see that aggression can be looked at in the context of inter-group behaviour and collective action.

> ## Ψ Section summary
>
> This section discussed different approaches to the production of social psychological knowledge and the different methods used by social psychologists. It described the historical background and the divergence of social psychology into two streams, the sociological branch and the psychological branch. It looked at logical empiricism, the experimental approach to research that it prescribes and some criticisms of the paradigm. Constructionist approaches were then discussed. This section highlighted the importance of recognizing the values held by social psychologists and their effect on research and the different levels of social psychological analysis that exist.
>
> 1 What are the differences between sociological social psychology and psychologica social psychology?
>
> 2 What are the underlying assumptions of logical empiricism and what criticisims have been made against this paradigm?
>
> 3 'All constructionist approaches derive from the assumption that reality is socially constructed.' Explain what this statement means, then describe two constructionist approaches and the methods of research they use.
>
> 4 Why is the concept of values important in social psychology?

❏ Self and identity

Within social psychology, the relationship between the individual and the society is typically tackled via theories of self and identity. To quote Stryker (1997):

if the point of social psychology is to deal with the reciprocal relationship of society and person, then social psychology must incorporate a concept of self, or the equivalent of self, to get very far; for it is the set of self-conceptions, or self-definitions that make up self, that mediate the relation of society to behaviour and of behaviour to society.

(Stryker 1997: 321)

What drives this statement is the belief that people's definitions and interpretations are critical to organized life. To behave in an organized and coherent way, argues Stryker (1997), one must define the scene (e.g. classroom, work), who are the others in the scene (students, employees) and who one is his or herself (e.g. teacher, manager). Definitions of self relative to others within a particular scene, or in Stryker's (1997: 322) words 'the actor's reflexive response to him or herself as an object', are fundamental to behaviour. He argues that there are elements of both social control and personal control in the way people behave and that these elements are built into **self-conception**. Social control pertains to instances where the individual acts in line with the demands of the situation (as construed by the actor) while personal control pertains to instances where the individual acts in line with his or her own idiosyncratic motives and values. Describing and explaining the processes involved in these two aspects of control provide the seeds of a theoretical account of the way society impacts on the person and vice versa. The concepts of self and identity are central to this analysis.

One of the first people to tackle the interface issue using the concepts of self and identity was George Herbert Mead (1934) – an approach to social reality now known as symbolic interactionism. After examining the propositions of Mead, we will move on to look at role theories. While heavily interlinked with the symbolic interactionist approach, role theories have also evolved a distinctive face of their own within social psychological thinking.

Symbolic interactionism and role theories

Symbolic interactionism refers to a group of theories originating from the work of George Herbert Mead (1934), a social psychologist at the University of Chicago. The term was introduced by Blumer, who was a sociologist and succeeded Mead in delivering social psychology lectures at Chicago (Farr 1996). Mead was influenced by the work of Darwin, who saw the development of the mind and self as embedded in evolution-

ary processes (Farr 1996).

Mead believed that the mind, self-consciousness, and the self developed through social interaction. Society is based on meanings and symbols which are constructed during continuous social activity. He saw these activities as having an adaptive function, reflecting the influence of the writings of William James (1912) on his thinking (Burkitt 1991). Humans continuously adapt and change their behaviour as a reaction to how others react to their behaviour. It is through this continuous social activity, communication and adaptation, that the self is developed. At first, communication is based on gestures. People treat an infant as an object. The infant will react to these actions and these reactions will be seen as a stimulus for the other person's response. In this way behaviour changes and adapts to the requirements of the social group the self is part of. As infants become aware that their actions can stimulate responses of others, they begin a process of self-reflection which allows them to adapt their behaviour in order to get the required response. Thus meaning is generated by interpreting the effect that actions have on the responses of others. At the moment when the person realizes that activities have meanings, self-consciousness emerges. Central to this conceptualization is the notion that the self is both an object and a reflexive subject. As an object, the self ('me') is seen as a product of the social communication and adaptation processes and to that extent the self reflects society. As a reflexive subject ('I'), the self reflects on the self as an object in order to adapt her actions to produce the desired responses from others. In this sense, the agentic nature of the self is developed.

According to Mead, language also becomes very important for the development of self-consciousness. As an advanced form of symbolic interchange, language becomes the medium through which the self can reflect on not only other people's immediate and 'objective' responses but also their own actions and words. For Mead,

The self which consciously stands over other selves thus becomes an object, an other to himself, through the very fact that he hears himself talk, and replies. The mechanism of introspection is therefore given in the social attitude which man necessarily assumes towards himself, and the mechanism of thought, insofar as thought uses symbols which are used in social intercourse, is but an inner conversation.

(Mead 1913: 146)

The development of language also allows the self to engage in an inner conversation with the 'generalized other', a cognitive entity reflecting the values and morals of the group and the person's expectations and reactions of others who are significant to her. In this way, self-consciousness is said to depend not only on interpersonal social interaction but on 'thinking' as well.

Although Mead saw society as pre-existing the individual, he does not distinguish between collective and individual levels of analysis. Instead, he argues that the self emerges through social interaction processes but at the same time the self is involved in constituting society through its participation in social interaction. The self and society are thus described as being dialectically interrelated. These propositions formed the basis of contemporary role theories, which we shall now discuss.

Role theories

Based on symbolic interactionism, role theories presuppose a reciprocal relationship between the society and the self. Identities are construed as internalized sets of role expectations and society is seen as a network of social relationships (Stryker 1980) or a network of social roles (Heiss 1981) or as a network of organizations (Aldrich 1982). It is via the content, structure and dynamics of self that the organization of society is seen to be reflected (Stryker 1987). The content of the self comprises those roles that a person performs, has performed, aspires to perform or has considered performing in the past. The structure of the self reflects the structure of the society in three ways:

- the size of the identity set of an individual reflects the degree to which society distinguishes between different roles
- the composition of the set of role identities a person has reflects the way these roles cluster and link with each other in society.
- the person's hierarchical valuation of the role identities he or she holds reflects the relative value society attaches to these roles.

The reciprocal relationship between the self and society is conceptualized in identity dynamics – the way a person negotiates an identity across situations (Alexander and Wiley 1981), different roles (Broadhead 1980) and in the acquisition, transformation and phasing out of particular role-identities (Gordon 1976; Zurcher 1983). As Stryker (1987: 135) claimed 'It is this key dynamic of identity negotiation, then, that reciprocity – not merely as mirroring but in the deeper sense of mutual shaping – is to be found between self and society'.

One criticism is that role theory is vague about the mechanisms involved in the social interchange process. A way in which this criticism has been addressed within social psychology is to elucidate the cognitive and perceptual basis of role assimilation and accommodation. We shall now look at one particular arm of social psychology that has concentrated its efforts on doing exactly this – the field of social cognition.

Social cognition and self

Social cognition is primarily concerned with how people perceive and make judgements about themselves and others and the theories they produce in order to justify their judgements (Leyens and Codol 1989). Social cognition pertains to the notion that people actively process the information they receive from their social context in order to construct their own social world – they do not just passively receive external information (Markus and Zajonc 1985). In short, research in social cognition is focused on those cognitive processes involved in the 'acquisition, organization and use of knowledge' (Neisser 1976: 1). Concern thus tends to be centred on intra-individual functioning rather than issues to do with how processes interface with society. This contrasts with the symbolic interactionist approach to social knowledge which sees it as being the result of social interaction. It likewise contrasts with the propositions of social representations theory that views social objects and knowledge as being constructed through communication between individuals and the interaction of the individual with the physical world. Instead, the social cognition model is concerned with how social knowledge is processed, rather than how social knowledge comes about and is deployed.

We might therefore ask, what then is 'social' in social cognition? Leyens and Codol (1988) and Leyens and Dardenne (1996) argue that cognition is social because it deals with social objects such as the processing of information about the self (e.g Codol 1986; Linville and Carlston 1994; Markus 1977), other people (e.g. Fiske and Neuberg 1990), groups (e.g. Leyens et al. 1994) and so on. Moreover, cognition is believed to be influenced by the social context and can therefore be seen as having social origins. Markus and Kitayama (1991) showed that people from different cultures tend to think about people in different ways. For instance, describing people by traits is apparently not a universally preferred way even though it is the dominant one in western cultures.

Plate 11.1 Markus and Kitayama (1991) showed that people from different cultures tend to think about people in different ways. Describing people by traits is not a universally preferred way even though it is the dominant one in western cultures

Finally, social cognitions are deemed 'social' in so far as they often shared by members of a particular group or society. Leyens and Dardenne (1996: 119–20) argue, 'cognition is a mental reconstruction of that which is real, based on an individual's past experience, needs, desires and intentions'.

Self is one of the objects studied within the social cognition perspective largely within the North American paradigm. This approach models the self as a body of knowledge in the individual's head or as content-free, focusing rather on how the self mediates information processing (Deaux 1992). Within this paradigm, self has been conceptualized as a schema and researchers have studied how people process information about the self, how they regulate their behaviour and interact with other people and the motivations that are likely to guide these processes.

The concept of **schema** refers to a cognitive structure of a particular stimulus domain such as social roles, events, and other people. It comprises our knowledge and expectations about the stimulus. Schemata are said not only to represent social information in memory, but also to have an impact on the way we process and select new information (Taylor and Crocker 1981).

Self-schemata are defined as 'cognitive generalisations about the self, derived from past experience, that organise and guide the processing of self-related information contained in the individual's social experiences' (Markus 1977: 64). That is, self-schema is a cognitive structure of all the information and attributes the people have about themselves. Furthermore, individuals have clear conceptions of themselves on some attributes and no particular conception of themselves on others. For example, you may know very well that you are a hard-working, conscientious student but not have a clear idea as to whether you are frivolous. That is, you have a schema about hard work but not about being frivolous. Whether individuals are schematic or aschematic on a particular dimension of their self-concept is believed to depend on three criteria: whether the particular dimension is very important to them, whether they think of themselves as being extreme on that dimension and whether they know that the opposite pole of the dimension does not apply to them (Markus 1977).

Self-schemata affect the way people process information about themselves. Research has shown that if a person is schematic in a particular domain, he or she is likely to process information about the self more efficiently in that domain (see e.g. Bargh 1982) and remember more information in that domain (e.g. Sweeney and Moreland 1980). If, for example, you are schematic on conscientiousness, you are likely to judge yourself on this trait rapidly and remember many examples of past conscientious behaviour. In addition, a person who is schematic on a particular dimension will be able to better predict self-initiated actions in that domain (Markus 1977), resist new information that is counter to one's self-concept in that domain (Cacioppo et al. 1982) and better evaluate the relevance of new information to that domain (Fiske and Dyer 1985; Sentis and Burnstein 1979).

This discussion of the concept of self-schema and its relationship to information processing exemplifies much of the work carried out within the field of social cognition. It also models a relationship between the individual and society as follows: individuals are information processors and the way they process information will be influenced by the social context. Through these processes they also gather and store knowledge. This knowledge in turn guides the way they perceive and understand their social world. Next we move on to look at cognitive-perceptual approaches to self and identity that as you will see are none the less heavily influenced by the positivist paradigm. These approaches are termed 'social identity theory' and 'self-categorization theory'. While these two theoretical approaches are interlinked, they will be dealt with separately since they have different aims and have led to different research foci.

Social identity theory

Tajfel (1972a: 31) defined **social identity** as 'the individual's knowledge that he/she belongs to certain social groups together with some emotional and value significance to him/her of the group membership'. It is via an identification process that the individual is said to become attached to, and invested in the particular social groups to which they belong. As defined by Tajfel (1972a) the concept of social identity provided the hinge for the evolution of social identity theory (Tajfel 1978), borne primarily from a concern to explain the largely ethnocentric character of inter-group behaviour. Here is not the place to enter into a discussion about inter-group behaviour *per se*: this is dealt with in Chapter 12. For now it is merely important to note the broader context in which considerations of social identity are derived. The important thing to note is that the concept of social identity was proposed not only as a means of explaining **ethnocentrism** but also as a means of understanding how collective concerns can become individual concerns, and vice versa.

Tajfel (1978) argued that social identity is a product of the workings of two cognitive-social processes – social categorization and social comparison processes – and a motivational principle, known as the drive for **positive distinctiveness**. **Social categorization** refers to a fundamental cognitive process which allows the individual to adapt to their social world by structuring the infinite stimuli in the environment and thereby simplifying perception. An early experiment by Tajfel and Wilkes (1963) showed that when subjects were asked to judge the length of individual lines from a continuous series where the four shorter lines were labelled A and the four longer lines were labelled B, they tended to exaggerate the differences in length between the set of lines A and B. This so-called accentuation effect was also found to hold true for social stimuli. For example, in a set of experiments white subjects were shown a series of photographs of faces ranging from pure Caucasian to pure Negro and were asked to rate the degree of physiognomic and psychological 'negroness'. The subjects divided the pictures into white and black and tended to exaggerate similarities within and differences between those faces falling in the two categories (Secord 1959; Secord *et al.* 1956). This basic accentuation effect has since been robustly demonstrated in many studies and extends also to the categorization of attitude statements as social stimuli (Doise 1978; Eiser 1980; Eiser and van der Pligt 1984).

Social comparison processes are said to be the mechanism through which social categorization processes derive clarity and meaning, and for the working of the positive distinctiveness principle that satisfies the fundamental individual motivation to achieve positive self-esteem. Social comparison processes within the social identity model are similar to those proposed by Festinger (1954), but that are operational at the inter-group (i.e. comparisons between groups) rather than interpersonal (i.e. comparisons between individuals) level of analysis. As for interpersonal comparisons, inter-group comparisons are fuelled by the need for positive self-esteem at work via the positive distinctiveness principle. Thus, in making inter-group social comparisons, we are inclined to accentuate differences between groups along the dimensions on which the ingroup will be more positively evaluated. The result of this are asymmetrical evaluations and behaviours in favour of the groups to which individuals perceive themselves to belong – i.e. in which they have invested themselves cognitively, emotionally and behaviourally.

Social identity researchers have argued that important cognitive-perceptual and motivational processes are at work in the determination of what makes group life possible. However, as you will see in Chapter 12, there are limits to the explanatory power of social identity theory with respect to the identity concept. The concept of social identity remains unelaborated within classic social identity theory research, serving merely as a hypothetical explanatory concept. This has led to the criticism that the social identity concept is little more than a black box construct (e.g. Millward 1995; see also Chapter 12). Integral to this criticism is a recognition of the need to elucidate the workings of social identity processes in more detail and in particular to examine identification mechanisms. Until fairly recently it has been largely unclear how social identity interrelates with the many other concepts of identity afforded by the social psychology literature (e.g. personal identity, role identity, self identity). We shall now look at how these kinds of issues have been tackled.

Self-categorization theory

Personal and social identity

The terms personal and social identity are derived from the ideas of Gergen (1971) writing on the topic of self-concept. Personal identity refers to personal identifications or self-descriptions 'that usually denote specific attributes of the individual' (Gergen 1971: 62) or idiosyncratic self-referents mostly grounded in relationships with specific individuals or objects (Hogg and Abrams 1988). Social identity however refers to social identifications or self-descriptions that derive from membership in social categories – race, sex, occupation, nationality, team and other such group memberships.

Turner (1982: 1885) elaborated on this distinction by assuming that personal and social identity represent different levels of self-categorization. This argument rests on two assumptions: one originates from the belief that the basis of behaviour is cognitive-perceptual and the second originates from the realization that social categorizations are overwhelmingly used with reference to self. Self-categories are groupings of some class of stimuli as identical and different from some other class. Personal identity refers to self-categories that define the individual as a unique person in terms of their individual differences from others. Social identity refers to social categorizations of self and others. Social self-categories define the individual in terms of his or her shared similarities with members of certain social categories in contrast to other social categories. Social identity more formally then pertains to the shared social categorical self (us versus them, ingroup versus outgroup).

The theory says that when we think of and perceive ourselves as we and us (social identity) as opposed to I and me (personal identity) this is a normal self-experience in which the self is defined in terms of others who exist outside of the individual person doing the experiencing and therefore cannot be reduced to personal identity. Thus at certain times the self is defined and experienced as identical, equivalent or similar to a social class of people in contrast to some other class. Effectively then, it is proposed that the self can be defined and experienced subjectively as a social collectivity.

The difference between personal and social identity is not a matter of the attributes which define the categories nor of the abstract level of inclusiveness of the categories used to define the self. Someone can define herself as caring as an individual compared with other individuals (to enhance her individuality) and as in ingroup member (nurses) compared to outgroup members (doctors). What matters is how the self is actually experienced in a specific instance. These perceptions of self are said to be relative and highly context-dependent.

Plate 11.2 Social identity, as distinct from personal identity, refers to social identifications or self-descriptions that derive from membership in social categories, such as sex, race, occupation, nationality and team memberships

Social identification as a depersonalization process

The theory proposes that as shared social identity becomes salient, self-perception tends to become depersonalized. That is, individuals tend to define and see themselves less as differing individuals and more as the interchangeable representative of some shared social category membership. For example, when someone categorizes herself as a woman, she will subjectively tend to accentuate perceptually her similarities with other women (and reduce her idiosyncratic personal differences from other women) and enhance perceptually her stereotypical differences from men (Hogg and Turner 1987). In short, when social identity is salient, a change in level and content of self-perception and behaviour occurs that depersonalizes the experience of self with respect to others. It should be noted that **depersonalization** does not mean de-individuation or loss of identity, but a change in the level of inclusiveness of the self-concept (Turner and Oakes 1986). Moreover the distinction between personal and social identity is said to be purely for theoretical convenience. Empirically speaking, identity comprises both personal (idiosyncratic) and social (group level) components in varying combinations depending on social context (Oakes *et al.* 1994).

Identification salience

In order to predict when people would define themselves in terms of social and personal identity, an analysis of the general principles governing the use of self-categories was developed. Turner and colleagues argued that variation in how people categorize themselves is the rule rather than the exception and that the collective self arises as part of this normal variation. Following Bruner, the theory explains variation as a function of an interaction between the 'readiness' of a perceiver to use a particular self-category (its relative accessibility) and the 'fit' between category specifications and the stimulus reality to be represented (Oakes 1987). Fit has two aspects: comparative and normative.

Relative accessibility
Relative accessibility reflects a person's past experience, present expectations and current motives, values, goals and needs. It reflects the active selectivity of the perceiver in being ready to use categories that are central, relevant, useful or likely to be confirmed by the evidence of reality.

Comparative fit
Comparative fit is defined by the principle of meta-contrast (Turner *et al.* 1987) which states that a collection of stimuli is more likely to be categorized as an entity to the degree that the average differences between them is less than the average differences perceived between them and the remaining stimuli which comprise the frame of reference. The principle defines fit in terms of the emergence of a focal category against a contrasting background. For example, it can also be used to define fit for the salience of a dichotomous classification. For example, any collection of people will tend to be categorized into distinct groups to the degree that intra-group differences are perceived to be smaller on average than inter-group differences within the relevant comparative context.

 Case study

A test of the 'fit' hypothesis
To test the fit idea, Oakes *et al.* (1991) had subjects watch a video of a group discussion between six students, three of whom were arts and three science students. In the 'conflict' conditions, the arts and science students disagreed with each other but agreed within each of these categories. In other conditions either all six students agreed with each other (consensus) or one arts student disagreed with the other five students (deviance) (comparative fit manipulations). In half of all these conditions, a target arts student expressed views consistent with stereotypes of arts students and in the other half, expressed views consistent with stereotypes of science students (normative fit manipulation). The students' social identities became most salient in the consistent condition where there was both comparative and normative fit. Oakes *et al.* (1991) argued that there must be a systematic and meaningful correlation between perceived intra-group and inter-group differences and the relevant social categorization before individuals will be perceived in terms of that social categorization and their category identity accentuated.

Normative fit

Normative fit refers to the content aspect of the match between category specifications and the instances being represented. For example, to categorize people as Catholics as opposed to Protestants, not only must they differ (in attitudes, actions, etc.) from Protestants more than from each other (comparative fit), but also they must do so in the right direction on specific content dimensions of comparison. Their similarities and differences must be consistent with our normative beliefs and theories about the substantive social meaning of the social category.

The context dependence of self-categorization

Research testing the fit hypothesis has identified several important ways in which self-categories vary with the social context of comparison (Oakes *et al.* 1994; Spears *et al.* 1997). The meta-contrast principle is explicit that categorization is inherently comparative and hence is intrinsically variable, fluid, and relative to a frame of reference. It is always context-dependent. They are not fixed entities that can be 'switched on' like light bulbs contrary to the original analogy used by Turner (1982). Four important forms of variation can be derived from the fit hypothesis:

- A critical form of variation is the salient level of self-categorization. When do people define themselves and others at the group or individual level of analysis? Social identity tends to become salient in inter-group contexts while personal identity tends to become salient in intra-group/interpersonal contexts (Haslam and Turner 1992; Hogg and Turner 1987).

- Which specific self-category tends to become salient at any given level? Self-categories must match the relations between self and others in terms of normative fit and content. We know what particular social categories are like or are supposed to be like, and we employ social categorizations that are consistent with our background knowledge and implicit theories. This is as yet a relatively unresearched area of the theory.

- It is not only that categorizations should match in terms of the specific content dimensions of comparison, but also proposed that the meaning of the salient social category will reflect the content of the diagnostic differences between groups in specific contexts. The content of categories is selectively varied to match what is being represented in terms of out implicit theories. In other words, there is not a fixed category content being applied: the category content is selectively defined by what it represents.

- The internal structure of self-categories (i.e. relative prototypicality of members) varies with the context within which the category is defined. Categories are not defined by a fixed prototype (nor a fixed set of exemplars) but vary in the relative prototypicality of their members as a function of context. What the typical psychologist is like will vary depending on whether the comparison is made with sociologists, physiologists, engineers or whatever. Change the basis for comparison and the meaning of the category will change as will the way the most prototypical member is defined.

Ψ **Case study**

Constructing meaning for self-categories

The relative and context-dependent way in which the content of self-categories is constructed is demonstrated by a study conducted by Haslam *et al.* (1992a) showing that the content of the stereotype of Americans (what Americans are like) varied significantly from the beginning to the end of the Gulf War, with the groups comprising the frame of reference. For example, compared to the Soviet Union during the war, Americans were seen as aggressive; compared to Iraq they were seen as less aggressive. At the beginning of the war, Americans were seen as more ambitious compared with British and Australians than when compared with Iraq; at the end of the war, this pattern was completely reversed. At one time, compared to one group, being American meant one thing; at another time or compared to other groups, being American meant something else. In a related study, Australians judged on their own (by Australians) are seen as happy-go-lucky, straightforward, and sportsmanlike; judged in the context of Americans (where perceived ingroup homogeneity increases) they are seen as even more sportsmanlike but less happy-go-lucky, and a new trait also made its appearance called pleasure-loving (Haslam *et al.* 1992b).

Research update

Social variability of self

Recent developments within self-categorization theory make points about the self experience and the nature of social reality (Oakes *et al.* 1994; Spears *et al.* 1997):

- The variability in self-categorization is not arbitrary or chaotic but is systematic and lawfully related to variation in social contexts (the principle of fit).

- Self-categories are social definitions of the individual; they represent the perceiver in social terms, in terms of social relationships of similarities and differences to others in relation to a social context. Self-categories are social representations of the individual-in-context in that they change with that context not just with the attributes of an individual. They are not representations of enduring individual attributes somehow adjusted or displaced by context. In fact, it is more accurate to say that they are social contextual definitions of the perceiver; definitions of the individual in terms of his or her contextual properties. The meaning and form of the self-category derives from the relationship of the perceiver to the social context.

- Self-categories are veridical in that their variation is systematically related to changes in social reality. The variability of self-categorization is not a sign of a true identity of the person being distorted by external circumstances. On the contrary, variability is necessary if self-perception is to be veridical, accurate and useful, if it is to get right the changing contextual properties of people. Identity varies in order to represent the perceiver's changing relationship to reality.

A self-categorization is comparative, inherently variable and context-dependent, then the interface is that the self is not a fixed mental structure, but the expression of a dynamic process of social judgement.

Identity process theory

Identity process theory was proposed by Glynis Breakwell (1986) and is fundamentally a theory of identity rather than a theory of group and inter-group processes.

Within identity process theory (Breakwell 1986, 1992), identity is seen as the outcome of an interaction between the biological characteristics of memory, consciousness and organized construal and physical and societal structure and process along a temporal dimension. Identities are said to be articulated through thought, affect and action in a context of personal and social power relationships. It is proposed that the structure of identity has two dimensions: the content and value dimensions. The content dimension comprises information about the person that makes him or her unique. This includes attitudes and belief systems, behavioural styles, self-ascribed attributes and belief systems, as well as group memberships. The value dimension comprises the values attached to each element of the identity.

Identity is also conceptualized in terms of two processes: assimilation-accommodation and evaluation. The assimilation-accommodation process refers to the absorption of new information and restructuring of the existing identity structure to accommodate such information. The evaluation process refers to the apportionment of value to the new information assimilated into the identity. The processes of identity are guided by four main principles that determine which endstates are desirable for the structure of identity, i.e. self-esteem, continuity, distinctiveness, and self-efficacy. **Self-esteem** signifies the desire to be evaluated positively. Continuity signals the desire to give a consistent account of self-conception over time. Distinctiveness signals the desire to be unique. Self-efficacy signals an individual's striving to be competent. It is proposed that these principles are historically and socially defined.

One of the main elements of the theory is to explain how people adopt different strategies for coping with threatened identities. An identity is threatened when the 'processes of identity, assimilation-accommodation and evaluation, are, for some reason, unable to comply with the principles of continuity, distinctiveness and self-esteem, which habitually guide their operation' (Breakwell 1986: 47). A threat can originate either externally from a change in the social context (for example, from becoming unemployed) or internally from an individual's attempt to change his or her position in relation to their social network. There are a range of intrapersonal, interpersonal and inter-group strategies that an individual can adopt in order to cope with threats to their identity.

Such a conceptualization of identity is useful because it encompasses both concepts of identity as a structure and process, is succinct in describing identity as the product of social forces and has built into it the temporal dimension which is very important in understanding the development of identity processes and yet is very often omitted from social psychological theorizing on identity.

Cultural specificity of the individuated self and the social construction of the self in linguistic practices

'There is no universal, transhistorical self, only local selves; no universal theory about the self, only local theories' (Cushman 1990). It has been argued that social psychological theories of the self and identity have in common the conceptualization of the individual as a coherent and bounded entity. Furthermore, it has been argued that this notion of the individuated self is a reflection of cultural assumptions contingent in a specific historical time rather than a reflection of the 'true nature' of the individual (see e.g. Henriques *et al.* 1984;

 ## Research update

Incorporating place into identity process theory

Proponents of identity process theory have argued that places are important sources of identity elements (Twigger-Ross *et al.* 1998). Places embody social symbols and are invested with social meanings and importance. These meanings arise because places represent personal memories and are located in the sociohistorical matrix of inter-group relations.

For identity process theory (IPT) a number of studies apply its principles to environmental changes, and include the importance of place for identity dynamics and development.

Twigger-Ross and Uzzell (1996) examined the relationship between place and identity processes in the context of the redevelopment of Surrey Docks, an area in London. Their study showed that for people who were attached to their local area that attachment was used in order to develop and maintain identity principles. In this sense they provide evidence for the function of place attachment to identity.

Devine-Wright and Lyons (1996) investigated how four places representing different historical eras were represented by people involved in Irish traditional activities and those who were not; the study examined the perceived significance of these places for maintaining a positive evaluation of Irish national identities. Places were seen 'as repositories of specific meanings, memories' (1996: 9). They found that the two groups

represented only two of the places in different ways; giving some support to the hypothesis that the social memories were different for the two groups and that they may construct Irish history in different ways. In a similar way different places were important to each of the groups in maintaining a positive evaluation of an Irish national identity.

Speller *et al.* (1996), adopting Breakwell's identity process model, studied the self-evaluations of residents before and after a forced relocation from an old mining village in England to a new site. The aim was to study links between threats to identity and evaluation of the environmental change; as well as to show the role of place identity in maintaining principles of identity. Residents evaluated the environmental change, of relocation differently depending on whether it was seen as a threat to the identity and depending on which principle was threatened. On the whole, residents' comments suggest that whenever a threat to their identity is perceived, they responded to it exhibiting distress. Such threats pertained three of the four principles postulated by IPT: that is, discontinuity to their assumptions, reduced self-esteem, and reduced self-efficacy. On the contrary, distinctiveness was conceived as neither a positive nor a negative attribute: the lack of threat to distinctiveness was interpreted on the basis of the culture of strong solidarity of the community, which would be valued above distinctiveness.

Kitzinger 1992; Potter *et al.* 1984; Sampson 1983). It is therefore more appropriate to examine the way self is constructed at different historical times and across different social situations in order to understand the social and interpersonal functions of different self constructions. Attempting to produce universal theories of self or to understand the true nature of individuals is seen as a futile task and a cultural artefact.

There is some empirical evidence which shows both that different conceptions of the individual exist in different cultures as well as at different historical times within the same culture (Elias 1978,1982; Hayes 1993). For example, J. Smith (1981) and Harré (1983) present such evidence in their description of the Maori culture in New Zealand. One of the characteristics of Maori culture is that individuals are not seen as the origin of their actions. Emotions are not considered to be experiences of the individual; they are seen as visitations of external powers.

The Maori individual was amalgam of various independent organs of experience, and it would appear from the description of these . . . that to a significant extent these organs reacted to external stimuli independently of the 'self'. Thus Maori experience compared with our own was impersonal and objective. Because the 'self' was not in control of experience, a man's experience was not felt to be integral to him; it happened *in* him but not *of* him. A Maori individual was not so much the experiencer of his experience as the observer of it.

(J. Smith 1981: 152)

Kitzinger (1992) also reviewed some of the studies which illustrated that in many cultures the individual is not seen as an autonomous unit whose rights have priority over those of the society or the social group (see e.g. Dumont 1970; G.R. Taylor 1972; Tuan 1982). Kitzinger pointed out the basic unit of such societies is not always the same (it could be either class, or kinship, the tribe or the community); nevertheless it is never the individual.

Conceptions of self do not only differ across cultures. Examining the concept of self across historical time, Logan (1987) and Elias (1978, 1982) illustrated that prior to the late Middle Ages, the self was more likely to be defined in terms of group identities rather than individual traits. Individualism is thought to have emerged with the increasing centralization of the state under aristocracy. During this time, behaviour was controlled by abstract and regular rules and punishments. However this external control of behaviour was gradually replaced by self-control as these abstract rules were internalized by people (Widdicombe and Wooffitt 1995).

Sampson (1988) described the historical process of individuation rather vividly: 'The introduction of the private chair to replace the bench and specialized eating utensils for the meal, for example, as well as the emergence of private spaces and rooms within the house, marked a movement toward the self-contained individual to match the similarly individualized quality of the other structures of life.' Furthermore, different emotions seem to be relevant in different historical times (Harré 1986) and individual moral worth shifted from resulting from adherence to external rules to stemming from within the self as notions of 'sincerity' or 'authenticity' became significant (Berger and Kellner 1973).

Acknowledging the historical and cultural specificity of the self, social constructivists argue that self is fluid and continually constructed through talk. According to Potter and Wetherell (1987: 102) 'There is not "one" self waiting to be discovered or uncovered but a multitude of selves found in the different kinds of linguistic practices articulated now, in the past, historically and cross-culturally'. The task of social psychologists should therefore be the study of how self is represented in different discourses and the functions that these different constructions serve. This is in accordance with strong social constructionism concerns of 'how the language we use, and the taken-for-granted categories we employ about the world, construct our experience in ways which we then reify as "natural", "universal", and "the way things have to be" (Kitzinger 1992: 224).

For example, social constructivists have argued that the categories of 'men' and 'women' are seen as 'natural' even though they are fundamentally ideological and political categories rather than biological (Kitzinger 1989; Unger 1988). The category 'woman' is seen by French feminist writers as biologizing a historical situation of domination (Wittig 1981).

Within the broad umbrella of social constructivism, there have been different approaches to theorizing about and studying the self (Potter and Wetherell 1987). These range from examining how the grammar of the language allows for certain ways of expressing selfhood (Harré 1985) to examining the functions served by different constructions of selfhood (Gergen 1989) and how uses of particular discourses about the self maintains power relationships in society (Parker 1989).

Harré (1985) argued that self-experience is formed as children learn the grammar of the language and acquire the linguistic resources with which they can express themselves in a way that appears credible in different situations. The striving to be credible and accountable and the linguistic resources available to us will constrain our self-expression and sustains a socially shared organization of self-experience. He also argued that certain social psychological conceptualizations of the self reflect features of the grammar of the language rather than 'real' cognitive processes or structures. For instance, concepts such as the private versus public self reflects the ability afforded to us by grammar to talk about the person both as a subject and an object (e.g. 'You are deceiving yourself' or 'I made myself do it' or 'I talked myself into it').

Gergen (1989) focused on the social functions served by certain constructions of the self. In particular, he claimed that people strive to have their constructions of events prevail against competing versions Because of this desire to maximize one's 'warrant' to be heard, certain self-constructions will dominate. An example of this is provided by Coyle (1995) who analysed the discourse used by a facilitator at a workshop which attempted to challenge the traditional Christian discourse on homosexuality. He showed how self-constructions as a scholar, 'benign teacher or guide' and an honest person were used by the facilitator to establish warrant.

We have now toured very briefly through the social constructionist approaches to self and identity, and merely skimmed the surface of this growing and ever popular literature within social psychology.

truly social because the dialectic between the individual and society is reduced to an information processing mechanism.

Another arm of the cognitive approach emphasizing more perceptual basis of identity processes and examining how this provides the means for understanding the origin of collective processes. This approach is reflected in the social identity and self-categorization theories. Identity process theory presents a more integrative conceptualization of identity, encompassing both the social and individual elements of the identity system. Social contructionist approaches construe language as having pride of place in the way social reality comes about, arguing that social reality is culturally and historically relative.

1 How is self developed according to symbolic interactionism?

2 What is personal and social identity? How useful is it to distinguish between the two concepts? To what extent are identities just ways of talking about ourselves?

3 What are the principles of identities according to identity process theory? What are the potential threats to immigrant identities?

ψ Section summary

We have tackled the individual/society interface issue via theories of self and identity from a number of different epistemological perspectives. We began with the work of George Herbert Mead whose work on the self and the evolution of the mind has permeated much social psychological thinking. The notion that society is internalized by the individual and actively articulated in the self is also taken up by role theories, although some would argue that the angle these have taken is too deterministic, neglecting consideration of how creatively the self is articulated and expressed. The social cognition approach evolved to address the creative side of the equation, modelling the self as a cognitive schema and detailing the way social knowledge is assimilated and accommodated therein. Critiques of this approach argue that social cognition is not

Box continued

☐ Attitudes

One of the main theoretical constructs used by social psychologists to understand how we make sense of the world and behave is the concept of attitudes. It is a common-sense assumption as well as a persistent assumption in social psychology that attitudes towards an object are related to behaviour. We expect that if we knew somebody's attitudes towards a political party we would be able to predict how they would vote. We expect that attitudes towards health issues would be linked to health-related behaviours such as diet or taking exercise. Similarly public campaigns wishing to change the public's behaviour such as smoking or sexual behaviour start with trying to change public attitudes towards for example smoking or safe sex.

Attitudes and attitude models

The concept of attitudes has a long history and has had a central place in social psychology. Allport (1935) noted that 'Attitude is the most distinctive and indispensable concept in contemporary social psychology' and Eagly and Chaiken's (1993) review of attitude research showed that this held true up to now. Although there are numerous definitions of the concept, most researchers would agree that **attitudes** refer to a general and rather stable orientation towards an object. An **attitude object** refers to an entity to which one can respond positively or negatively; for example, social groups, individuals, inanimate objects, concepts, social issues, social and individual actions and so on.

There are two main models of attitudes – the **tripartite model** and **unidimensional model**. The first comprises a three-component model. According to this, an attitude is a theoretical construct which can be accessed only via three distinguishable reactions to an object; cognitive, affective and behavioural responses (Rosenberg and Hovland 1960). Similarly Eagly and Chaiken (1993: 155) define attitudes as 'tendencies to evaluate an entity into some degree of favor or disfavor, ordinarily expressed in cognitive, affective, and behavioural responses'. Cognitive responses refer to our opinions and beliefs about the object, affective responses refer to emotions, our like or dislike of the attitude object and behavioural responses refer to behavioural intentions or action tendencies. These three components of attitude are supposed to be related but separate. Therefore only a moderate correlation between the three components of attitudes is predicted.

An example of the three-component model is provided by attitudes towards smoking. Smoking comprises the attitude object. Cognitive responses may include beliefs about the association between smoking and lung cancer, beliefs about the secondary effects of smoking, opinions about the tobacco as a substance and and any images and associations arising with respect to smoking (e.g. 'smoking is cool', 'smoking stops me eating too much', 'smoking relaxes me and helps me chill out'). Affective responses may include whether we find it pleasurable to smoke or to experience the secondary effects of smoking, whether we feel good about smoking (e.g. peer group associations, self-image maintenance), and whether we feel that it has positive (e.g. relaxation, aids dieting) or negative effects (e.g. coughing a lot, smelling of smoke). Behavioural responses would refer to our intentions for example, to continue, to cut down, to stop smoking or to never smoke at all, and to our actual behaviours (e.g. whether we smoke or not, how many we smoke and when). The three-component model would assume that it is quite possible for thoughts about smoking to be inconsistent with feelings and/or behav-

iours (e.g. 'smoking is bad for my health, but it makes me feel good, so I still smoke').

Unidimensional models of attitude stem from the recognition that the three components of attitudes described above are not always highly correlated if at all. Clearly, individuals do not always act in ways consistent either with their beliefs or their emotions. Unidimensional models regard the affective component as the only reliable indicator of the orientation towards the attitude object and use the terms emotion and evaluation interchangeably. Thus Petty and Cacioppo (1981: 7) argued that 'the term attitude should be used to refer to a general, enduring positive or negative feeling about some person, object or issue'. McGuire (1985) regards attitudes as responses that locate 'objects of thought' on 'dimensions of judgement', while Zanna and Rempel (1988) define attitudes as the categorization of the attitude object along an evaluative dimension.

Reviews of empirical studies carried out by Chaiken and Stangor (1987) and Eagly and Chaiken (1993) showed that there is no conclusive evidence to support either of the two models. **Factor analytic** studies showed that it is difficult to distinguish between the three proposed components of attitudes (McGuire 1985) whereas other studies showed that when measured by different scales, each of the three components of attitude correlated highly with itself but not with the other two (Kothandapani 1971). Other research suggests that the issue of the dimensionality of attitudes may be more complicated, depending on the attitude object and the individual who holds the attitude. It was shown that where the beliefs about an attitude object are multiple and contradictory, the structure of the attitude is unlikely to be reflected in a single affective response (Schlegel 1975; Schlegel and DiTecco 1982). Moreover, it has been argued that the complexity of the attitude structure is also likely to be related to individual differences variables such as cognitive complexity and tolerance of ambiguity.

Functions of attitudes

Katz (1960) argued that attitudes could fulfil the following four functions.

Knowledge function

Attitudes help us to understand the social world we live in by structuring and organizing information we encounter. When they are well established, attitudes have also been shown to guide information processing (Fazio 1989; Shavitt 1990).

Utilitarian function

Attitudes help us to achieve goals and rewards and to avoid punishment. So we tend to hold positive attitudes towards attitude objects that are consistent with our goals and negative attitudes towards objects that are likely to lead to frustration of our goals and needs. Also by expressing particular attitudes in specific situations we are likely to gain others' approval.

Value-expressive function

Attitudes also make a statement of who we are. It is assumed that it is important for people to demonstrate and maintain their central values, and long-term standards and orientations. By expressing attitudes towards issues or people one feels strongly about, one validates their own self-concept.

Ego-defensive function

Using psychoanalytic concepts such as defence mechanisms and projection, Katz (1967) postulated that individuals may hold attitudes towards certain attitude objects in order to hide their feelings about themselves or their own situation.

Relationship between attitudes and behaviour

One of the prime concerns of attitude researchers is the relationship between attitudes and behaviour. This question is crucial both for theoretical and pragmatic reasons. Given the emphasis given to changing attitudes by public campaigners in a variety of fields such as health, politics, and consumer behaviour, it is crucial that we understand how and the extent to which attitudes are related to behaviour. The theoretical basis for expecting a close relationship between attitudes and behaviour comes first from the very definitions of attitude and second from theories of consistency. The three-component model of attitude postulates that behavioural responses as well as evaluative and affective responses toward an attitude object are indicators of a favourable or unfavourable attitude. One would therefore expect that there will be a certain degree of consistency between evaluative and behavioural responses.

The consistency principle permeates a lot of social-psychological thinking (Frey and Gaska 1993; Heider 1946). Perhaps one of the most influential of such theories is **cognitive dissonance** theory (Festinger 1954).

The theory is based on the assumption that humans need to maintain consistency between their cognitions, that is, between different pieces of information about their environment or about themselves. When individuals perceive inconsistencies between their cognitions, they will be motivated to change their attitudes in order to reduce or eliminate the cognitive dissonance she experience. Similarly, the theory predicts that if there is a discrepancy between individual attitudes and behaviour, attitudes will change in line with behaviour. It is therefore clear that cognitive dissonance theory leads to the expectation that there will be a drive towards maintaining consistency between attitudes and behaviour.

One of the earliest and most often cited study examining the relationship between attitudes and behaviour was carried out by La Piere in the USA during the 1930s. The study was conducted in the context of anti-Asian attitudes which were prevalent at that time. La Piere (1935) travelled around the USA with a Chinese couple, visiting a number of hotels and restaurants. Despite expectations, he found that only 1 out of 251 places refused to provide accommodation. After six months, he wrote to all the establishments asking them whether they would accept Chinese guests. The vast majority of these establishments (92 per cent) claimed that they would not. La Piere's study was taken to suggest that there is no relationship between attitudes and behaviour.

La Piere's study has been criticized on various grounds, for example that there was no evidence that the people who actually returned the questionnaires were the same people who accepted him and the Chinese couple six months earlier. It could also be argued that the weak relationship between attitudes and behaviour may be due to the long time that elapsed between the time of the behaviour (i.e. the visits) and attitude measurement (i.e. the letters). None the less, further evidence suggesting that there is only a weak link between attitudes and behaviour was produced by Wicker (1969, 1971). Wicker (1969) summarized 45 studies which looked at this issue and reported that the correlation between measures of attitude and direct behaviour rarely exceeded 0.30. In other words, only about 10 per cent of the variance of behaviour was found to be explained by attitude measures. Wicker concluded that

Taken as a whole, these studies suggest that it is considerably more likely that attitudes will be unrelated or only slightly related to overt behaviours than that attitudes will be strongly related to actions.

(Wicker 1969: 65)

As a response to these earlier findings, since the 1970s research has focused on the factors that are likely to influence the strength of the link between attitudes and behaviour rather than the extent to which there is a link at all. A number of studies have looked at the effect of methodological issues, attitude characteristics, personality factors and contextual factors which are likely to frame and affect the relationship between attitude and behaviour.

Methodological issues in attitude–behaviour research

It has been argued that much of the research, especially earlier research, on the attitude–behaviour link suffered from two major weaknesses concerned with the measurement of the two concepts (Ajzen and Fishbein 1977; Manstead 1996). First, many studies used single item measures of either attitude (La Piere 1935) or behaviour (DeFreur and Westie 1958). Second, there has often been a lack of compatibility between attitude and behaviour measures either in terms of their discrepancy in the degree of specificity of attitude and behaviour measures or the function of attitudes and behaviour or the relative cognitive and affective focus of the two measures.

It is now generally agreed that attitudes, and behaviours, are more reliably measured by multiple items rather than single items. Responses to single items may reflect other factors rather than individuals' attitude. For example if you were to use a single item, such as 'Do you recycle your glass bottles?' to measure environmental behaviour, some individuals' negative responses may reflect the fact that there is no bottle bank close to them rather than that they do not care about the environment. However, if individuals said that they did not recycle bottles or paper and did not try to conserve energy and did not buy recycled paper, a more reliable pattern of anti-environmental behaviour would emerge. It would therefore seem reasonable to expect that multi-item measures of attitude and behaviour will be more highly correlated than single item measures. Indeed Weigel and Newman (1976) have reported a correlation of 0.62 between an aggregate measure of pro-environmental behaviour and a general measure of attitude towards environmental protection.

Another criticism levelled against this area of research is that not enough attention is paid in measuring attitudes and behaviour with the same level of specificity. Ajzen and Fishbein (1977) advocated four ways in which behaviour can vary: the action performed, the object at which the action is directed, the context in which the action takes place and the time at which it takes place. It is therefore argued that one could expect that if the attitude is measured at a general level and the behaviour is specific to a particular action, object, context, and time the correlation between the two would be rather poor. Similarly, if attitude measurement is compatible with behaviour measurement in terms of these four elements then the correlation between the two measures is likely to be high.

Indeed in reviewing studies examining the attitude–behaviour relationship, Ajzen and Fishbein (1977) have found empirical evidence which strongly supports the notion that compatibility between levels of specificity of attitudinal and behavioural measures are likely to produce high correlations between them. For example, Davidson and Jaccard (1979) studied the relationship between attitude towards contraception and use of oral contraceptives over a period of two years. The attitude was measured with varying degrees of specificity, ranging from a general attitude to contraception to attitude to using oral contraceptives and attitude to using oral contraceptives during the next two years. The correlation between these attitudinal measures and behaviour increased as the compatibility of the specificity of the attitude measure and behaviour increased. Thus the correlation between the general attitude measure to contraception and behaviour was 0.08 while the correlation between attitude to using oral contraceptives during the next two years and behaviour was 0.57. This is not to argue that general attitudes cannot be good predictors of behaviour. If behaviour is also measured at a general level then a strong attitude–behaviour link would be expected.

More recent research has shown that compatibility in the functions of attitude and behaviour is also likely to strengthen the relationship between attitude and behavioural intention. Shavitt and Fazio (1991) conducted an experiment in which they examined the relationship between attitude and behavioural intention toward two beverages, '7-Up' and 'Perrier' water, which were assumed to differ in terms of the attributions along which they would be evaluated. It was assumed that '7-Up' would be evaluated in terms of taste whereas 'Perrier' water would be evaluated in terms of social impression. Before measuring the attitudes towards the two beverages, the experimenters manipulated the salience of the taste and social impression attributes by administering questionnaires, asking the subjects to evaluate either a list of goods in terms of taste or a list of actions in terms of the social impression they may create. Shavitt and Fazio's (1991) findings showed that the correlation between attitude and behavioural intention was higher in the conditions where the functions of attitudes and behavioural intentions were compatible. The correlation between attitude towards '7-Up' and the intention of buying or drinking '7-Up' was higher in the 'taste' salient condition than that obtained in the 'social impression' salient condition. The reverse pattern was found in the case of 'Perrier' water.

Correspondence between the relative focus of affective and cognitive aspects of attitude and behaviour has also been shown to strengthen the link between the two measures. In an experiment carried out by Millar and Tesser (1989), subjects were asked either to think about how they felt about some puzzles which were allegedly designed to improve analytic ability or to think about

Plate 11.3 Shavitt and Fazio (1991) conducted an experiment in which they examined the relationship between attitude and behavioural intention toward two beverages, Perrier and 7-Up. The correlation between attitude and buying intention for 7-Up was higher in the 'taste' salient condition, while for Perrier it was higher in the 'social impression' salient condition

why they felt the way they did about the puzzles. Thus in the first condition, the affective aspect of the attitude was made salient while the cognitive aspect of the attitude was emphasized in the second condition. Subjects' attitudes were measured immediately after this manipulation. The focus of the behavioural choice was manipulated by presenting working on the puzzles either as an end in itself (affective) or as being instrumental in improving the subjects' performance on a later test (cognitive). Millar and Tesser (1989) found that in the conditions where there was compatibility between the focus of the attitude and that of behavioural choice, the relationship between the two elements was stronger than that obtained in the condition where the foci of the two elements were incompatible.

Attitude characteristics and the attitude–behaviour relationship

Another set of factors identified as potentially affecting the relationship between attitudes and behaviour are related to the special characteristics of attitudes. It has been shown, for instance, that attitudes formed through direct experience are more strongly linked to behaviour than those who are not based on any direct experience (Regan and Fazio 1977; but see also Schlegel and DiTecco 1982). A number of mechanisms mediating this relationship have been hypothesized and tested. It was found that attitudes based on direct experience are more strongly related to behaviour that those who are not formed through direct experience because they are held with more clarity (Fazio and Zanna 1981) and commitment, and are more stable. Furthermore, such attitudes are also better predictors of behaviour because they are more easily available (Fazio *et al.* 1982, 1986).

Personality factors and the attitude–behaviour relationship

It has also been suggested that characteristics of the individual who holds the attitude may also affect the degree of strength of the attitude behaviour link. Two of such characteristics are level of self-awareness and self-monitoring. Self-awareness refers to the extent to which a person's attention is directed at self rather than other people or the environment (Duval and Wicklund 1972; Wicklund 1975). Those people who have high levels of self-awareness, which could be seen as a trait or a variable internal state, were found to exhibit a higher correlation of attitude and behaviour (Gibbons 1978).

Also, those people who are low self-monitors are likely to show high attitude–behaviour consistency (Snyder and Swann 1976; Zanna *et al*. 1980). **Self-monitoring** refers to the degree to which individuals act to comply with situation demands rather than act on the demands imposed by their own internal selves (Snyder 1974; Snyder and Tanke 1976). High self-monitors who are more concerned with behaving consistently with the social norms of a given situation show more variability in their behaviour across situations which may explain the weak link found between their attitudes and behaviour. Another explanation for the difference between low and high self-monitors may be that those individuals of low self-monitoring seem to have more accessible attitudes which suggests that they may have stronger object-evaluation associations (Kardes *et al*. 1986).

Contextual factors and the attitude–behaviour relationship

It has been suggested that the above-mentioned approaches to understanding the rather weak relation-ship between attitude and behaviour evinced by earlier research are rather individualistic. Specifically, they seem to ignore the context in which the attitude–behaviour relationship is likely to be embedded. In particular, they tend to ignore the impact that others' expectations may have on an individual's behaviour. In response to these kinds of criticisms, the theory of reasoned action was developed by Fishbein and Ajzen (1975). This theoretical framework was based on two main tenets. First, it was based on the principle of compatibility of specificity of attitude and behaviour measures in terms of the action, object context and time elements of behaviour. Second, the theory postulated that attitude was only one of likely determinants of behaviour, with behavioural intention rather than attitude being the immediate determinant of behaviour.

Figure 11.1 represents the network of causal relationships in which the attitude–behaviour relationship is embedded. The theory has as its focus those behaviours which are volitional. It is concerned with behaviours that individuals have a choice whether to perform or not; for instance, researchers applied this theory to areas

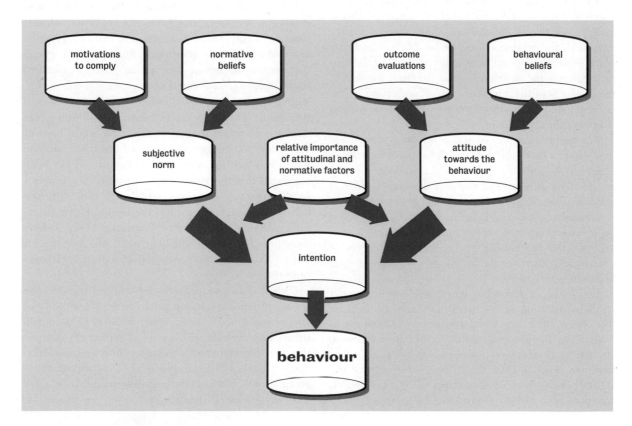

Figure 11.1 The attitude–behaviour relationship

such as abortion (Smetana and Adler 1980), smoking marijuana (Ajzen *et al.* 1982) or mothers' intentions to limit children's sugar intake (Beale and Manstead 1991). Such behaviours, it is argued, are directly influenced by behavioural intention which in turn is influenced by the attitude towards the behaviour (the individual's evaluation of the behaviour), the subjective norms (that is the extent to which the individual believes that significant others expect her to perform the particular behaviour) and the relative importance of the attitude and the subjective norm in determining behaviour. The theory also claims that behavioural beliefs (the individual's beliefs about the consequences of the target behaviour) and outcome evaluations (the individual's evaluations of these consequences) are the two determinants of the attitude towards the target behaviour. Subjective norms are determined not only by normative beliefs (the individual's beliefs that each of the significant others would expect them to perform the behaviour) but also by the individual's motivation to comply with these expectations. Furthermore, this model specifies that each of the pairs of the determinants of attitude and those of subjective norm are combined together in a multiplicative manner. Each behavioural belief is multiplied by the evaluation rating of the corresponding outcome and the sum of all the products of behavioural beliefs and outcome evaluations provide an indirect index of the attitude towards the target behaviour. Similarly the sum of the products of the normative beliefs multiplied by the corresponding motivation to comply provide an indirect index of subjective norm.

The theory of reasoned action was later revised and extended to form the theory of planned behaviour in order to explain not only volitional behaviours but also behaviours which may not be under the direct control of the individual (Azjen 1991; Ajzen and Madden 1986). A new variable, perceived behavioural control, was added as a determinant of behavioural intention. It was assumed that individuals' perception of the degree of control they have over the behaviour will influence their behavioural intention.

Empirical evidence has lent considerable support to the predictions of the theory of planned behaviour (see Ajzen 1991; Eagly and Chaiken 1993) and meta-analytic studies showed that the correlations between attitudes and subjective norms and behavioural intention are much higher than those reported for the attitude–behaviour relationship (see Wicker 1969). Sheppard *et al.* (1988) showed that the average correla-

tions between these measures ranged from 0.53 to 0.68, while correlations between behavioural intentions and behaviour were just above 0.50. Also, in summarizing the results of 88 studies which examined the relationship between attitudes and future behaviour, Kraus (1995) found that 52 per cent of the correlations were above 0.30, and 25 per cent were 0.50 or greater.

Despite the empirical support enjoyed by the theory of reasoned action and its extension, the theory of planned behaviour, a number of criticisms were levelled against them. First, it was argued that there are a number of factors which can influence behaviour which are not mediated by attitudes or social norms. Habits (Bentler and Speckart 1979), personal and behavioural norms (Schwartz and Tessler 1972), experienced moral obligation to perform a particular behaviour (Gorsuch and Ortberg 1983), commitment to perform a particular behaviour (Breakwell *et al.* 1994) and the importance of the particular behaviour for self-identity outcomes (Granberg and Holmberg 1990) were also found to substantially influence behaviour.

Second, the underlying assumption of the theory that behavioural decisions are based on a rational decision-making model (involving elaborate cognitive calculations of likelihoods of behavioural outcomes, benefits and costs) have been questioned. Simon (1981) argued that because of human information processing limitations, people's behavioural choices are guided by subjective levels of aspiration rather than optimization of the benefit. People are likely to be satisfied with a particular outcome if it exceeds their subjective level of aspiration rather than strive to achieve the outcome with the maximum utility. Furthermore, it has been suggested that the assumption of intense deliberations of the benefits and costs associated with different behavioural outcomes renders the theory inappropriate for explaining either routine, habitual everyday behaviours or behaviours in situations where the individual is not motivated to engage in intense cognitive elaborations (Frey *et al.* 1993).

Third, it has been suggested that contrary to the theory of reasoned action predictions, accessibility of attitudes will be the main determinant of behaviour in situations where the individual has neither the motivation nor the opportunity to engage in reasonable decisions (Fazio 1990). In such circumstances, those attitudes which are highly accessible are likely to automatically guide behaviour.

ψ Case study

Applying socio-cognitive models of attitude–behaviour relationship in preventing health behaviours

Promoting changes in sex behaviour has become one of the main challenges facing applied social psychologists. It has been estimated that 13 million people have been infected by the human immunodeficiency virus (HIV) throughout the world (World Health Organization 1993). Since there is no known cure for Aids, it is very important that risky practices such as unprotected sex and needle sharing are limited if we are to control the extent of an Aids epidemic.

Adolescents have been one of the groups which have been targeted by Aids prevention campaigns. Such campaigns have usually been based on giving more information about Aids but had no theoretical basis (Fisher and Fisher 1992). However, intervention strategies based on empirically validated theories are likely to be much more effective. One model used to describe and predict adolescent sexual behaviour is Ajzen's theory of planned behaviour (TPB: Ajzen 1985, 1991).

Richard et al. (1995) have argued that models such as TPB neglect the importance played by emotions in engaging in safe sex behaviours. In particular they have argued that if anticipated, post-behavioural, affective reactions to unsafe sexual behaviours are incorporated into the TPB models, the predictive ability of such models is likely to be increased. Richard et al. (1995) elicited data on young Dutch people's

- behavioural expectations: subjects were asked to consider each of three different situations (e.g. suppose the following weekend you meet a nice person and both of you want to make love) and give the likelihood of the following three behavioural alternatives: making love without having sexual intercourse, having sexual intercourse and using a condom, having sexual intercourse without using a condom
- anticipated affective reactions: subjects were asked to evaluate the feelings they would have after each of the three alternative courses of action described above in terms of how worried, how much regret and how tense or relaxed they felt
- subjective norms: subjects were asked to indicate how important others (e.g. parents, best friends and individually selected others) would find it if they performed each of the behaviours described above

Richard et al. (1995) found that anticipated affective reactions such as worry and regret predicted behavioural expections over and above the components of the theory of planned behaviour. This study has important implications for Aids prevention campaigns. It highlights that people do not always make rational decisions based on systematic use of information that is available to them. Emotions seem to play an important role in this process. Campaigns should therefore also focus on inviting adolescents to think what they may feel after they engage in unsafe sexual behaviour.

ψ Section summary

This section discussed the concept of attitudes. It looked at two different models of attitudes – the tripartite and unidimensional models. It discussed the functions that attitudes fulfil and examined theories that describe the relationship between attitudes and behaviour. This section presented evidence which showed that the relationship between attitudes and behaviour is not always very strong. Some of the methodological, personality and contextual factors that may influence the strength of this relationship are also discussed.

1 What is an attitude? What are the functions of attitudes?

2 If you are to design a study to examine whether attitudes towards a particular health behaviour, what factors would you take into consideration in developing or choosing measures of attitudes and behaviour?

3 What aspects of the social context in which the relationship between attitudes and behaviour is embedded are particularly important for understanding this relationship?

Attribution theory

It is a basic premise of attribution theory that we believe that what happens in the world does not occur at random: events must be caused by one or more factors. Moreover if we are to feel in control and able to predict what is likely to happen around us we need to make inferences about the likely causes of particular events or behaviour. Why did I fail my English exam? Why did my friend suddenly stop talking to me? Why did my football team lose the last match? Why were the fans of my football club violent towards the fans of the opposite team? How people go about answering these questions is the focus of attribution theories and the large body of empirical research they have inspired. Attribution theories are concerned with what information social perceivers use and how they process it when they make **causal attributions**, that is when they attribute social events and behaviour to specific causes. We begin this section by examining the origins of attribution theories.

Heider's theory of naïve psychologist

People behave like naïve scientists, argues Heider (1944, 1958). In order to anticipate and influence what will happen to them and others, people need to make inferences about what causes particular events and behaviours. Lay persons therefore try, in a common-sense way, to infer unobservable causes from observable social events and behaviour. Heider (1958) postulated three principles said to guide causal inferences. First, people are assumed to see the cause and effect as a perceptual unit. Two factors, temporal proximity and similarity, would determine whether two particular events or objects are likely to be perceived as causal units. So, two events temporarily proximal and similar to each other are more likely to be linked in causal relationship than if they were distal or dissimilar. Second, people are more likely to attribute behaviour to single rather than to multiple causes. Third, causes can either be seen to reside in the actor (**internal attribution**) or in the environment (**external attribution**). Internal causes refer to the motivation and ability of the actor to achieve the action whereas the external causes refer to situational factors such as luck, task difficulty and so on. Thus the social perceiver will use information about the motivation, ability and situational factors which are likely to affect the outcome of an action available to them to arrive at a causal attribution of an event. Furthermore,

Heider (1958) claimed that the more the social perceiver favoured an internal attribution, the less that person would favour an external attribution and vice versa. So if by taking into consideration whether you tried to prepare diligently for the exam or not, whether you had the skills required to take the exam, the degree of difficulty of the exam paper and whether you felt ill the day you took the exam or not, you decide that you failed the exam because you did not work hard enough to prepare; you would be unlikely to also favour strongly the idea that you failed the exam because the paper was too hard.

Correspondent inference theory

Following Heider's pioneering work, E.E. Jones and Davis (1965) developed a model of attributional processes based on the assumption that people try to make sense of others' behaviour in a way that will enable them to draw conclusions about the actors' stable characteristics. In other words, people seek to obtain meaningful information about others' dispositions from observed behaviour in order to be able to predict how they might act in the future. For example, if somebody behaved in an outgoing and loud manner during a serious meeting, it may be attributed to the fact that he or she is an extravert.

Correspondent inference theory is specifically concerned with how we make judgements about an actor's underlying traits, beliefs or attitudes from observed behaviour and also some of the factors that are likely to bias such judgements. The process by which a behaviour is attributed, or judged to correspond to an actor's trait, is called correspondent inference and has two stages. At the first stage, the social perceiver considers whether the actor knew before acting what the consequences of the particular behaviour would be and whether the actor had the ability to accomplish that action. If the answer is yes to both questions, then the perceiver attributes intention to the actor. At the second stage, a dispositional attribution is made. The perceiver has to infer which of the actor's stable qualities or characteristics made that person perform the action.

To arrive at a dispositional attribution, the perceiver adopts different strategies. First, in cases where more than one courses of action are available to an individual, the perceiver can compare the consequences of the chosen and non-chosen actions and make a correspondent inference by identifying the distinctive consequences of a chosen course of action. In addition if the chosen course of action can have more negative consequences than the non-chosen actions, then the perceiver can infer that the distinctive consequences of the chosen course of action must be particularly important to the actor.

Second, the perceiver also considers what other people would do in the same situation. Only when the actor behaves in a non-normative way, a correspondent inference can be made. Whether a behaviour is normative or not (according to E.E. Jones and Davis 1965) will depend on the social desirability of the consequences of the particular behaviour. It is assumed that the more socially desirable the consequences of the behaviour, the more likely it is that people would attempt to achieve it. Therefore, correspondent inference will be more likely to occur when the actor's behaviour is socially undesirable.

Third, the social perceiver will consider whether the actor's behaviour is part of a social role. If the behaviour is seen as being part of the actor's social role, it will not be very helpful in making a correspondent inference. The perceiver cannot infer that the behaviour is caused by one or other of the actor's underlying qualities. However, in cases where the actor has a well-defined role and acts out-of-role, the perceiver can attribute the behaviour to an underlying disposition.

Fourth, the perceiver will use prior expectations of the actor's behaviour to help arrive at a dispositional inference, when such information is available. In addition to expectations based on beliefs about what would be normative behaviour in a given situation which have been discussed above, the perceiver's expectations may be based on the actor's category membership (e.g. she is a woman so of course she will be emotional) or on knowledge about previous behaviours of the target individual (e.g. she has always acted emotionally so she will be emotional).

According to E.E. Jones and Davis (1965), there are two biases that may affect the accuracy of the perceiver's judgement of the actor's dispositional qualities. The first, called **hedonic relevance**, concerns the effect that the behaviour has on the perceiver. If the behaviour is seen as harming or benefiting the perceiver, then it is likely to produce a correspondent inference. The second bias is called **personalism** and refers to the perceiver's beliefs not only that the behaviour has an impact on the perceiver but also that the actor intended to benefit or harm the perceiver.

Correspondent inference theory focuses on the attributional process which imputes single instances of behaviour to the actor's dispositions. However, people also make attributions of causality in situations where they have information about multiple instances of behaviour or events. Furthermore, people attribute behaviour not only to other people's dispositions but also to situational factors. We now turn to analysis of such attributional processes developed by Kelley (1967, 1972).

The covariation model

Kelley (1967, 1972) forwarded the covariation or ANOVA model to describe the attributional process made on the basis of information of multiple instances of the same or similar observed behaviours. He also developed the notion of **causal schema** to account for attributions made on the basis of information about a single behaviour or event. According to the covariation model, in circumstances where the perceiver has information about multiple instances of behaviour (e.g. 'how my business partner behaves with different clients'), the perceiver will employ the principle of covariation (i.e. co-occurrence of two events) to decide which effects are attributed to which of several factors. The model is based on the same principle that underlies the statistical technique of analysis of variance, ANOVA, which investigates how a dependent variable (i.e. the effect) changes as the independent factors (i.e. the conditions) vary.

In contexts where the perceiver attributes causality to a person's behaviour towards a particular stimulus at a particular time (e.g. Why was David angry with his client?), the perceiver will process the available information in terms of three dimensions: consensus, distinctiveness and consistency. Consensus refers to the extent to which the perceiver believes that not only the actor but also other people would respond to the stimulus in the same way (e.g. Is it only David or would other people be angry with his client?). Consistency refers to whether the behaviour is generalizable to other situations as well (e.g. Does David always get angry with this client?). Distinctiveness refers to the extent to which the perceiver believes that the behaviour is a response only to the particular stimulus and not to other stimuli (e.g. Does David get angry with all his clients?).

According to Kelley, people tend to answer these questions in a dichotomous way giving either a high or a low value to each of the three dimensions. Given that there are three dimensions and two possible responses there are potentially eight different patterns of information. Different patterns of information lead the perceiver to different attributions. For instance if the perceiver believes that all people would respond to the stimulus in the same way (e.g. Not only David but other people would be angry with that client) (high consensus), that the behaviour is generalizable to other situations (e.g. David has got angry with this client in the past) (high consistency), and that the behaviour is a response to the particular stimulus (e.g. David gets angry with only this client) (high distinctiveness), then the perceiver will attribute causality to the situation (e.g. David was angry with his client because of something about this client). If on the other hand the perceiver had available a pattern of information which showed low consensus, low distinctiveness and high consistency, the perceiver would attribute the behaviour to the actor. These two patterns of information are likely to lead the perceiver to certain attributions with confidence. Other patterns however may make the perceiver more cautious in attributing a behaviour to particular causes. For example if consensus and distinctiveness are high but consistency is low (e.g. David does not always get angry with his client), the perceiver would probably arrive at a situational attribution (e.g. there must be something about the client that made David get angry) but it could also be something about the context in which the interaction took place.

Empirical evidence has lent some support to Kelley's covariation model. McArthur (1972) conducted a study where subjects were given twelve different events such as 'John laughs at the comedian' and additional information with respect to consensus, consistency and distinctiveness for each of the events. All possible patterns of information were included in the design. The subjects were then asked to make situational or personal attributions for the twelve events. The findings of the study supported Kelley's predictions with regard to the effect of different combinations of information about consensus, consistency and distinctiveness on attributions of causality. Other studies with similar designs have produced similar findings (Chen et al. 1988; Ferguson and Wells 1980; McArthur 1976; Zuckerman 1978).

Despite the supporting evidence produced by studies using the above experimental design, Kelley's attribution model can be criticized on a number of grounds. First, it seems that people are not very skilled at assessing covariation. Spears et al. (1986) showed that subjects tend to perceive different sets of stimuli to be correlated when they think that they ought to be causally related and fail to see covariation between sets of stimuli when a relationship is unexpected. An earlier study by Chapman and Chapman (1969) also showed that subjects' expectations of the relationship between responses on psychological diagnostic tests and patient symptoms had a greater effect on perceptions of covariation than the information given to the subjects. Furthermore, it seems that in naturalistic situations people may neither look for the kind of information nor look for the information in the systematic way postulated by the covariation model. Garland et al. (1975), for example, showed that people often choose to seek out information about the personality of the actor or various situational constraints rather than information on consensus, consistency and distinctiveness.

Second, studies have shown that people utilize the three types of information differently. People tend to use consensus information less than the other two types of information while they tend to use consistency information more than distinctiveness information (Kruglanski 1977; Kruglanski et al. 1978; Olson et al. 1983). Third, the covariation principle may be limited as a basis for attributing causality since correlation does not necessarily mean causality.

Fourth, it is unlikely that people engage in the systematic and rather complex information processing that is required by the covariation model (Nisbett and Ross 1980). The cognitive processes involved in attributional judgements is the focus of more recent work. It has also been suggested that attributions are 'often more influenced by people's own theories and expectations than by a careful consideration of various types of information' (Eiser and van der Pligt 1988: 57).

Causal schemas

To address criticisms of the covariation model, Kelley (1972) developed the notion of causal schemas and the principles of discounting and augmenting to describe the attributional process when the perceiver does not have the types of information required by the covariation principle. In a case where perceivers have information only about a single event, it is expected that they will use a causal schema – an implicit theory of how certain causes relate to certain effects – in order to decide which of the effects relate to which of the causes. According to Kelley (1972: 151), 'A causal schema is a general conception the person has about how certain kinds of causes interact to produce a specific kind of effect'. People are said to acquire these schemas through their experiences of how different causes produce specific effects in the real world. So in cases when social perceivers have unclear and limited information, they will make causal attributions by comparing and integrating the available information to one of the schemata.

Two of the schemata described by Kelley (1972) are the multiple sufficient causes schema and the multiple necessary causes schema. The multiple necessary causes schema refers to cases where an extreme effect is considered to be caused by the combination of a number of different causes while the multiple sufficient causes schema assumes that any one of a number of causes can produce a specific effect. For example, if David wins a trial in court, his success could be attributed to his advocacy skills or to lack of evidence against his client or to lack of skill of his opposing counsel and so on. Any one of these causes could explain the event equally well. The perceiver can then employ another principle, the *discounting principle*, described by Kelley, to help him make the attribution. According to this principle, in cases where any one of a number of different causes can produce a particular effect, the perceiver will discount other possible causes if a potential cause is present (Cunningham and Kelley 1975). In the example given above, if the perceiver has information about David's advocacy skill, she will discount any of the other potential causes and attribute his success to his high level of advocacy skill.

The augmenting principle is another device that the perceiver could employ when the multiple sufficient causes schema is utilized. According to this principle, the perceiver will put more emphasis on causes which facilitate the production of the effect rather than on causes which inhibit the occurrence of the event. Returning again to our earlier example, if David won his trial despite strong evidence against his client, the perceiver should infer that his success is due to especially high advocacy skills.

The notion of causal schemata has been criticized on both empirical (see e.g. Surber 1981) and conceptual grounds (Fiedler 1982). Causal schemata are unlikely to be content free, rather they should comprise organized knowledge based on cultural experiences. However, Fiske and Taylor (1991) argued that causal schemas are important because they help people to make causal attributions when information is incomplete and enable the perceiver to make causal judgements speedily and easily by providing a 'causal shorthand'.

Attributional biases

Underlying attribution theories has been the assumption that the attributional process is a rational one. The perceiver, like a scientist, seeks to find out the causes of what is happening around them in a systematic and logi-cal way. However, research has shown that although these theories have some value as 'as if' models of the attributional process, they do not describe adequately what people actually do when they attribute events to causes (Hewstone and Fincham 1996). They are prescriptive rather than descriptive models. Researchers have therefore focused on examining how people actually make causal inferences. This research led to the realization that causal inferences deviate from the normative, prescriptive, model because the perceiver either does something wrong (attribution error) or systematically overuses or underuses some of the stipulated procedures (attribution bias) (Fiske and Taylor 1991). These biases could be either the result of cognitive limitations or motivational reasons or both cognitive and motivational.

We shall now discuss four of these biases:

- fundamental attribution error: perceivers tend to underestimate the impact of situational factors and overestimate the importance of internal factors
- actor–observer bias: actors tend to attribute their own actions to external situational causes, whereas observers tend to attribute the same actions to stable internal characteristics of the actors
- false consensus bias: people tend to see their own attitudes and behavioural choices as shared with most other people
- self-serving bias: perceivers tend to attribute desirable actions to internal psychological causes in themselves and undesirable actions to external, environmental aspects.

Fundamental attribution error

One of the most frequently cited biases of the attribution process is the tendency of people to ignore likely situational determinants and overestimate a person's dispositional qualities as causing behaviour (Ross 1977). Empirical evidence for this bias comes from research stemming from the correspondent inference theory which showed that even when situational factors such as constraints imposed by the actor's social role or whether the actor chooses to act in a particular way or not, the perceiver tends to attribute behaviour to the actor's attitudes or personality traits (E.E. Jones and Harris 1967; A.G. Miller *et al.* 1981; Ross *et al.* 1977a; Schuman 1983). However, the hypothesis of a fundamental attribution error has not gained universal support. Studies have shown that this bias is more evident when the behaviour is overt and visible rather than covert and implied, when the performance is skilful rather than unskilful (Reeder and Fulks 1980) and when behaviour is consistent rather than inconsistent with expectations (Ajzen *et al.* 1979; Kulik 1983).

There is evidence to suggest that both cognitive and cultural factors may account for this bias. It may be that the bias is a result of differential attention being paid to the actor performing the particular behaviour rather than the situational factors surrounding the event (Kassin and Pryor 1985; S.E. Taylor and Fiske 1978). Another cognitive factor likely to affect the fundamental attribution bias is people's tendency to remember dispositional causes better than situational causes (see e.g. Peterson 1980). Support for cultural explanations comes from research which shows that people increasingly attribute behaviour to dispositional rather than situational causes as they grow older (see White 1988 for a review) and that these trends are culturally specific (J.G. Miller 1984). Semin and Fiedler (1991) have argued that people may be led to make dispositional attributions because of linguistic reasons, i.e. dispositional inferences may be triggered by different types of verbs (Hewstone and Fincham 1996).

Actor–observer bias

People tend to explain other's behaviours in terms of dispositional factors whereas they tend to attribute their own behaviour to situational factors (E.E. Jones and Nisbett 1972). For example, we are more likely to attribute our bad temper to the lack of sufficient time to do all we want to do while we may attribute somebody else's bad temper to the fact that person is surly. There is ample empirical evidence demonstrating the validity of this bias (E.E. Jones and Nisbett 1972; Kelley and Michela 1980; Monson and Snyder 1977; see also D. Watson 1982 for a review of relevant studies) though it has also been shown that the effect could be reversed depending on the type of behaviour an explanation is sought for and on the orientation of the observer (Fiske and Taylor 1991). For example, it was shown that in cases where the outcomes of the behaviour are positive, the actor may attribute the behaviour more to dispositional factors than the observers (e.g. Chen *et al.* 1988). Also, if actors are encouraged to pretend to see themselves as another person or the observer they are more likely to make internal attributions. Similarly, if observers are asked to empathize with the actor they are likely to make more external attributions (e.g. Frank and Gilovich 1989; Gould and Sigall 1977).

These latter studies point to one of the most important explanations for the actor–observer bias which is based on the claim that actors and observers have different foci of attention. While the actor is looking outwardly to the situation, the observer's attention is likely to focus on the person behaving. In a classic experiment, Storms (1973) attempted to test the hypothesis that visual salience will have an effect on the type of attributions made by the actor and the observer. Storms got two strangers to have a conversation for five minutes (Actors A and B). Two observers were also there (Observers A and B) each observing one of the actors. The conversation was also video-recorded by two cameras, each focusing on one of the actors. The design of the experiment allowed for comparisons across three visual orientations. In the first condition (control), the subjects were showed no video at all. In the second condition (same orientation), subjects were replayed the videotape, repeating the subject's original orientation while in the third condition (new orientation) the videotape was replayed to the subjects, reversing the orientations of the actors and observers. Subjects then had to rate the actor's talkativeness, dominance, friendliness and nervousness during the conversation they had. They were also asked to what extent they thought that the behaviour exhibited during the conversation was due to personality traits, attitudes and so on and to what extent it was due to situational factors. Storms's findings indeed showed that when the orientation was reversed, the actor–observer bias was reversed; actors attributed their behaviour more to dispositional causes and observers attributed behaviour more to situational causes.

Other factors accounting for the actor–observer bias are the differential amount of information actors and observers have about the actor (E.E. Jones and Nisbett 1972; White and Younger 1988); the salience of the actor (the more salient the actor the more the dispositional attributions made by the observers: McArthur and Post 1977) and the tendency of actors and observers to use different linguistic devices in making attributions (Semin and Fiedler 1989).

False consensus bias

We often believe that our preferences are shared with most other people. If I like listening to jazz then I am likely to overestimate the number of other people who like jazz. People tend to overestimate the number of people likely to vote for their preferred party and so on. This tendency of people to overestimate the number of people who share the preference for a particular behaviour or attitude that they prefer has been called the false consensus bias. Empirical research has shown it to be a robust phenomenon. For instance, Ross et al. (1977b) demonstrated the effect in the case of students walking around the campus wearing a sandwich board with the message 'Eat at Joe's', van der Pligt and Eiser (1984) with energy conservation, Ross et al. (1977b) with playing tennis once a week and van der Pligt et al. (1983) with attitude towards building more nuclear power plants (see also Mullen et al. 1985 for a review).

Fiske and Taylor (1991: 77) have found that the following factors may influence the extent of the false consensus bias. False consensus effect is stronger when

- external attributions are stronger than internal attributions (Marks and Miller 1987)
- the behaviour or issue at hand is important to the person (Granberg 1987)
- the person is certain about his or her opinion (Marks and Miller 1985)
- the person's position is threatened (Sherman et al. 1984)
- positive qualities are involved (van der Pligt and Eiser 1984)
- the person perceives others as similar to himself or herself (Sherman et al. 1984)

The false consensus bias has been explained both in motivational and cognitive terms. A motivational explanation is based on the assumption that people need to feel that other people share their beliefs and preferences in order to feel rational, normal and appropriate (Ross et al. 1977b; Sherman et al. 1984). Alternatively, the bias could be a perceptual distortion. For instance, it was argued that false consensus bias may reflect the person's selective exposure to other people who think and behave in a similar way to them. Thus their inference is based on this distorted available information. Alternatively, as a person's own opinions may be particularly salient, when they are asked to make a social inference about a particular opinion, theirs is the only one available in consciousness (Marks and Miller 1987; Wetzel and Walton 1985).

Attempts to disentangle the relative importance of the motivational and cognitive explanations have been inconclusive (Eiser and van der Pligt 1988). None the less, Mullen et al. (1985) carried out a meta-analysis of 115 relevant studies and concluded that cognitive explanations seem to be more consistent with their findings than motivational explanations.

Self-serving bias

We tend to take credit for what we succeed in and deny responsibility for our failures. We often attribute our success in an exam to our effort or skill or intelligence and our failures to how difficult the exam paper was and what bad luck it was that the questions we prepared did not come up and what about the poor lecturer who taught the subject. If we win in a competition it is because we are good at the particular task; if we lose it was bad luck or something in the situation. This tendency to accept credit for our successes and deny responsibility for our failures is known as the self-serving bias. This is found to be evident not only in our culture but in others as well (Fletcher and Ward 1988; Kashima and Triandis 1986; Zuckerman 1979).

There are two biases involved in this phenomenon – a self-enhancing and a self-protection bias. In general, there is empirical support that self-enhancing bias is more often evident than self-protection (D.T. Miller and Ross 1975). People tend to take credit for their successes but do not always deny responsibility for their failures especially if the failure can be attributed to a cause that one can have some control over it in the future (Weiner et al. 1971). It was also found that level of self-esteem may have an effect on the kind of attributions made. For instance, both those people who have high self-esteem and those who have low self-esteem attribute their success to internal causes. However, those with high self-esteem tend to attribute failure to external causes while those with low self-esteem tend to attribute failure to internal causes (Campbell and Fairey 1985; Maracek and Metee 1972; Shrauger 1975).

Two types of explanations have been put forward to explain self-serving bias – motivational and cognitive. Those who favour the motivational explanation claim that the asymmetry reflects people's motivation to enhance or protect their self-esteem (McFarland and Ross 1982; Zuckerman 1979). Other researchers have also argued that for self-presentation reasons and for gaining the approval of others the actor may have to accept a moderate credit for their success and accept responsibility for their failures (Schlenker and Oleary 1982; Schlenker et al. 1990; Weary 1980). However, D.T. Miller and Ross (1975) argued that this asymmetry can reflect cognitive factors. People's general expectations to succeed rather than fail, their experience of putting effort into succeeding and by overusing instances in which they had been successful in the past more than those in which they failed may have an effect on their perceptions of covariation between effort and success and on the amount of control they feel they have over their successes. How far one can distinguish between the two explanations has been doubted (Hewstone and Fincham 1996; Tetlock and Manstead 1985). Both explanations seem to be involved. Motivational factors seem to have an effect on information processing and cognitive explanations seem to have motivational elements in them (Zuckerman 1979). Much of this work has also been criticized on methodological grounds. Studies often require subjects to solve puzzles or play games. Failure to solve a puzzle may not be seen by people as their own failure, however in more realistic settings such as being unsuccessful at an interview for a job may be experienced differently (Markus and Zajonc 1985).

Ψ Section summary

In the course of our everyday lives we continuously make inferences about the likely causes of particular events or behaviour. Attribution theories seek to describe how we process information in order to make such inferences. Research in this area shows that individuals' causal attributions reflect a number of different biases and that such inferences are not automatic.

1 To what extent do people use information from the social context in a systematic way in order to make inferences about causes of particular events or behaviour?

2 Is the distinction between internal and external attributions justified and useful?

3 What are the biases reflected in people's causal attributions? How useful it is to describe these phenomena as biases?

Ψ Chapter summary

- **Epistemological perspectives and levels of analysis**

Social psychology involves understanding how we make sense of our world, interact and communicate with others and the processes which shape and form our cognitive and social interactions. Two traditions can be distinguished within social psychology, each deriving from a different set of epistemological assumptions and favouring different methods of investigation. The sociologically oriented branch focuses on social interaction and the construction of meaning in social life at inter-individual and cultural levels. The psychological branch concentrates on issues such as cognition and perception with respect to social life, and operates at the intra-individual level. Logical empiricism, or positivism, has been the prevailing paradigm within social psychology, particularly in North America. It assumes that objective reality can be causally mapped and precisely represented and, by using quantitive methods, universal laws established. However, the appropriateness of the experimental method for investigating social psychological phenomena has been heavily criticized.

Constructionist approaches, including discourse analysis and ethnomethodology, derive from the assumption that reality is socially constructed and use qualitative methods. Social psychologists must be aware of their own values and the influence these have on the research they undertake, and also that any social behaviour can be explained at different levels of analysis: intra-individual; inter-individual; power and status relations, and social belief, representations and norms.

- **Self and identity**

Self and identity theories are used to explain the relationship between the individual and society. Symbolic interactionist theories view society as based on meanings and symbols which are constructed during continuous social activity. The self emerges through social interaction processes and is also involved in constitut-

Box continued

ing society through participation in social interaction. Based on this, role theories assume a reciprocal relationship between the society and the self. Social cognition concerns how people perceive and make judgements about themselves and others and the theories they produce in order to justify their judgements. In contrast to symbolic interactionist approaches, the focus is on how social knowledge is processed and intra-individual functioning. It neglects the issue of how these processes interface with society.

● Attitudes

The concept of attitudes is one of the main theoretical constructs used by social psychologists to understand how we make sense of the world and behave. Attitudes refer to a general and stable orientation towards an attitude object, e.g. social group or individual. They help us structure and organize information and thus understand our social world. The relationship between attitudes and behaviour is a prime concern for researchers. Recent research has focused on the factors that influence the strength of the link between attitudes and behaviour. It has been suggested that characteristics such as level of self-awareness and self-monitoring affect the degree of the strength of the attitude–behaviour link.

● Attribution theory

Attribution theory assumes that what happens in the world does not occur at random. It is concerned with the information that social perceivers use and how they process it when they attribute events and behaviour to specific causes. Correspondent inference theory focuses on the attributional process which imputes single instances of behaviour on the actor's disposition. The covariation model incorporates the idea that people attribute behaviour to situational factors as well as dispositions. Attribution theory assumes that the attributional process is a rational one. However, research has shown that individuals' causal attributions can reflect different biases. These include the tendency to ignore likely situational determinants and overestimate dispositional qualities as causing behaviour, cultural factors, actor–observer bias and false consensus bias.

Further reading

● Breakwell, G.M. (ed.) (1992) *Social Psychology of Identity and the Self-Concept*. London: Academic Press. A book of readings which includes chapters on major approaches to the study of self and identity such as social identity theory, identity process theory and social constructionist approaches.

● Eagly, A.H. and Chaiken, S. (1993) *The Psychology of Attitudes*. San Diego, CA: Harcourt Brace Jovanovich. A complete overview of research on attitudes.

● Fiske, S.T. and Taylor, S.E. (1991) *Social Cognition*, 2nd edn. New York: McGraw-Hill. This is perhaps the most comprehensive book on social cognition.

● Hewstone, M. (1989) *Causal Attribution: From cognitive processes to collective beliefs*. Oxford: Blackwell. It provides a comprehensive review of a number of different areas of research.

● Oakes, P.J., Haslam, S.A. and Turner, J.C. (1994) *Stereotyping and Social Reality*. Oxford: Blackwell. An account of self-categorization theory and a review of research on stereotyping.

● Purkhardt, S.C. (1993) *Transforming Social Representations: A social psychology of common sense and science*. London: Routledge. An interesting account of social representations theory.

CHAPTER 12

Social psychology 2

Lynne Millward

KEY CONCEPTS • interpersonal and inter-group behaviour • what is a group? • group formation: intra-group behaviour • group formation: role of similarity and attraction • social influence processes • referential informational influence • group polarization • false consensus or 'group-think' • minority versus majority influence • obedience to authority • inter-group conflict • the self-esteem proposition • is social discrimination the same as prejudice? • inter-group co-operation • inter-group perceptions • collective action

❏ Chapter preview

When you have read this chapter, you should be able to

- describe and explain the importance of different levels of analysis as a starting point for understanding how people behave in group, inter-group and collective contexts
- debate the concept of group as both a sociological and psychological entity
- describe and explain the distinct character of group, inter-group and collective behaviour
- critically discuss two contrasting explanations of group formation against the evidence
- describe and explain processes of social influence in both majority and minority contexts
- link different processes of social influence to differences in outcome
- compare and contrast various proposals about the mechanisms of social influence
- debate the relative viability of various explanations of inter-group conflict
- trace the patterns in group and inter-group perception and discuss alternative ways in which this might be explained
- debate the meaning and explanation of action in collective contexts from different theoretical angles

Introduction

Groups are inextricably linked with who we are and how we behave. We are born into them in one form or another (e.g family groups, ethnic/racial groups, socio-economic groups, community groups, cultural and sub-cultural groups), we move in and out of them (e.g. peer groups, class groups, interest groups, work or project groups, etc.) throughout the life course and effectively we come to live and breathe them. Hence, groups are taken-for-granted aspects of our social existence. But what exactly is a **group**? Can it be characterized simply as the sum of all who comprise it? Or is it more than the sum of its parts? How are groups formed? What functions do group memberships serve? How do our group memberships influence how we think, feel and behave?

More often than not, group memberships are given a bad press, seen as having a largely corrupting influence on our personality and behaviour. Is this necessarily so? Might this not depend on the nature of the group, its goals, norms and functions in society? What is a crowd and how does this differ, if at all, from a group? Can we talk about collective behaviour in the same way that we talk about group behaviour? How is group or collective behaviour distinct from individual behaviour? These are some of the fundamental questions that have challenged the minds of social psychologists (also sociologists and social anthropologists) since its inception during the early twentieth century. They are questions that hinge on an understanding of the relationship between the individual and society. In this chapter the literature on groups and group behaviour is examined by taking a distinctly European stance on the question of how the individual and the group interrelate. This presupposes that the group experience is a valid topic in and of itself, and strives to describe and explain the uniquely psychological aspects of this experience in all its facets. In particular it attempts to address the issue of what makes social life possible. This is not to deny the contributions of sociology and social anthropological disciplines, merely to complement them.

Group behaviour as a fundamentally psychological experience

This journey into the realm of the group experience begins with the work of Stephen Reicher (1984) whose detailed study of 'The St Paul's Riots' of April 1980 demonstrated that, contrary to popular belief, collective behaviour has a clear and socially meaningful form (see quotes).

'Just everybody came out of their houses, just everybody local'

'I think it was quite honestly a case of us against them. Us, the oppressed section of society, if you like, against the police, against authority, basically'

'All the atmosphere was against the police. It wasn't like the papers say. This absolute mob. Everyone was together. They were looking at each other the whole time. It was black and white and all ages and that was fantastic.'

'It was due to police harassment. Everybody seems to be bound together against it in some way.'

This analysis of **collective action** challenged the long-held idea that the group has a negative impact on individuals, making them behave in irrational and ani-malistic ways (Le Bon 1947). So-called **group-mind theory** asserts that individuals revert to a primitive unconscious state in crowd situations, thereby accounting for why collective action is often barbaric. This depiction of the crowd presupposes two things: first, that the only valid psychological reality is that of the rational individual and second, that crowd behaviour is caused by biological forces beyond rational control.

In contrast, Reicher (1984) argues that group-mind theory denies the social basis of crowd behaviour, in terms of both causes and consequences. His case study of the St Paul's riots illustrates that there are socially determined limits to crowd action: limits to participation in terms of who does and who does not take part in the events, and limits to content in terms of which actions occur and which do not. For example, crowd action was limited to the St Paul's community (the ingroup, defined in opposition to the police, who were the outgroup). Collective participation was limited to these two groups and was clearly targeted. In particular, Reicher shows how these social limits originated from an ideology in the form of a social identification. In his words 'the social identity of "St Paul's community member" adopted by crowd members, provides the criteria for legitimate action' (Reicher 1984: 18). Evidence of the strong ingroup cohesion displayed by the community, he says, is indicative of crowd members reacting to each other on the basis of social rather than individual factors. In short, crowd action has rational rather than irrational form, and this rationality is prescribed by the limits of social identification.

The case study also raises a critical point about the tone (i.e. positive/negative) of crowd action. If crowd action does indeed have a rational and socially meaningful form (in terms of both what it does, as well as how it goes about achieving this) it would mean that its tone is just as much likely to be positive (i.e. quiet, calm, pro-social) as negative (i.e. hostile, riotous, anti-social). Witness the public reaction to the death of Diana, Princess of Wales, on 31 August 1997. Crowd action was described by many as bordering on 'hysteria'. This cast it in a largely negative light (i.e. uncontrolled, irrational, melodramatic, tearful, noisy, violent), yet the crowd response to Diana's death was not of this kind. A powerful behavioural **norm** evolved from the moment the death of the Princess had been announced, which created a social imperative among people to place flowers and letters of love and condolence outside many institutions connected with Diana's life. This norm might be said to be **prototypical** of a grief reaction demonstrated by those who were first to make a public, but also inherently very private, declaration of their sadness at the death of the Princess they loved and identified with.

From then on, the norm spread rapidly (facilitated by the media) across not only the UK but also the entire world. Witness too the socially meaningful form of this behaviour. Typecast as the Princess of Hearts (consistent with Diana's own wishes) and also the Princess of the People, it was not surprising to observe grief reactions permeated with the discourse of 'love'. The grief reaction was extreme (i.e. prototypical) but highly patterned and controlled. Perhaps even more of a challenge yet to

animalistic metaphors of crowd action is the behaviour of the crowd at the Princess of Wales's funeral. The funeral was described as a funeral for the People's Princess, and 'the people' responded with dignity, calmness and a high degree of respect. Millions of people travelled to London to take part in the event, yet no violence or anti-social behaviour of any kind was reported. Indeed, the event united Royalists and Republicans alike.

Thus, the crowd 'behaved'. It behaved despite a strong police presence, and despite the 'crowded' character of the event physically speaking. How can it be said then, that crowd action is necessarily barbaric and instinct driven? Crowd action in this instance was normatively contained and prototypical of a grief reaction. Identification was with the Princess and with those to whom she was closest. As the Princess of the People, someone described as basically 'classless', the identification process operated at its most superordinate level, crossing all of the usual kinds of differences (i.e. in beliefs and values) and boundaries (i.e. national, ethnic, political, etc.) that ordinarily keep people apart. While the experience of grief is fundamentally a private one, the behaviour demonstrated during this event was fundamentally social in character and form. It is left to you, the reader, to decide on the level of analysis you think to be the most appropriate.

Plate 12.1 The grief reaction of the crowd during Princess Diana's funeral was extreme but highly patterned and controlled, with a high degree of respect and no violence or anti-social behaviour

The social psychological analysis of collective action provided by Reicher (1984), and also the more anecdotal one describing the crowd reaction to the death of the Princess of Wales, frames the content of this chapter. It reflects a distinctly social level of explanation and highlights the explanatory significance of the concept of social identity – both of which contribute to the makings of a European social psychology (see also Turner 1996). What is meant by a distinctly social level of analysis? To answer this, a distinction made by Tajfel (1978) between interpersonal and group/inter-group behaviour is next described and discussed.

Interpersonal and inter-group behaviour

Tajfel (1978) said that **interpersonal behaviour** describes instances where people act as individuals, in terms of their idiosyncratic profiles of personal attributes, values, abilities and other such characteristics. **Inter-group behaviour**, however, describes instances where people act as group members, adopting a uniform stance in the way they behave. Employees on strike because of an inadequate pay deal are acting in terms of their group membership for example, whereas the employee who refuses to take strike action for fear of job loss or personal reasons is more likely to be operating as a unique individual. For this person, membership in a social category of financially deprived 'employees' *vis-à-vis* the social category of 'financially well-off' employer is perhaps less salient than the sense of personal security and possibility of promotion obtained from opting to continue working. For those on strike, the act of collective opposition may be symbolic of something more important to them (e.g. employee rights, worker rule), than their personal job security and promotion prospects.

Critical to the distinction between interpersonal and inter-group behaviour is the assumption that interpersonal and inter-group behaviours require a different level of explanation and analysis. Tajfel (1978) argued that these assumptions are critical to the way we think about and explain behaviour from a social psychological standpoint. It also means that explanations addressing interpersonal level phenomena (e.g. interpersonal conflict) cannot be extrapolated to explain inter-group level phenomena (e.g. inter-group conflict).

Tajfel noted that behaviour of all kinds can be located somewhere along the interpersonal–inter-group continuum, anchored by the two extremes described above. He proposed three main factors as a means of understanding where exactly on the continuum a particular behaviour can be located:

- the clarity and salience of membership categories and the divisions between them
- the relative variability or uniformity of the perceptions and attitudes of individuals
- the relative variability or uniformity of the behaviour exhibited by individuals.

In short, interpersonal attitudes, perceptions and behaviours are likely to be highly variable as typified by the normal range of individual differences obtained by psychometric measures used to assess the individual. By contrast, inter-group attitudes, perceptions and behaviours are likely to be highly stereotypical and uniform.

Brown and Turner (1981) noted that behaviour within a group (i.e. **intra-group behaviour**) is also often characterized by stereotypical perception, uniformity of attitudes and behaviour, and awareness of category boundaries. This led them to propose an amendment to the behavioural continuum proposed by Tajfel (1978), substituting 'group' for 'inter-group', resulting in the interpersonal–group continuum. Group behaviour can thus refer to intra-group and/or inter-group phenomena. More contentiously, the continuum has since been employed by Turner and colleagues (Hogg 1993; Oakes *et al.* 1994; Turner 1982a, 1985; Turner and Oakes 1986; Turner *et al.* 1986) to refer to the difference between personal and social forms of identity. Personal identity pertains to the interpersonal end of the bipolar continuum while social identity pertains to the group/inter-group end of the analytical pole.

If you recall from Chapter 11, the terms personal and social identity are derived from the ideas of Gergen (1971). To recap, personal identity refers to self-descriptions 'that usually denote specific attributes of the individual' (Gergen 1971: 62) while social identity self-descriptions derive from membership in social categories (race, sex, occupation, nationality, team and other such group memberships).

The conceptual correspondence between cognitive-perceptual criteria and behavioural criteria has been subject to some debate. The problem is more to do with the assumption made about how social identity is manifested and that this is not necessarily confined to group and inter-group contexts.

Ψ Section summary

Group behaviour, including crowd behaviour, has a socially meaningful character and form. The notion of social identity is critical to understanding how this can be. Behaviour can be described and explained at different levels of analysis. At the interpersonal extreme, behaviour is governed by uniquely individual concerns, is inherently variable and open to explanation by drawing on theories of individual difference. At the group/inter-group extreme, behaviour is governed by distinctly group-oriented concerns, and is highly stereotypical and uniform in character. Attitudes and perceptions, including self-perceptions, are said to be different in character at group as opposed to individual levels of analysis. Identity is believed to be inextricably linked with the transformation in thoughts, feelings and behaviours that occur when group memberships come into salience.

1 How far can you detect differences in how you think, feel and behave as a function of your group memberships? Do you think, feel and behave differently in group as opposed to individual contexts? How exactly might you be able to characterize these differences?

2 Is your behaviour in a group context positive, negative or both? How far does this depend on the particular type of group to which you belong?

3 To what extent would you say that your identity is intimately bound up with the group or groups to which you belong?

❑ What is a group?

Chase (1995) notes that definitions of 'group' within psychology are often contradictory. While many groups are defined in terms of observable (i.e. socio-demographic and sometimes structural and geographical) criteria, others are not. Those groups without concrete form may exist merely as representations in the mind of observers. The representational or 'psychological group' may or may not have socio-demographic or structural form. At one end of the continuum are those groups that

exist purely as representations (e.g. Martians, family ancestors, future generations). At the other end are those groups that are physically present and have some concrete form on a day-to-day basis – 'sociological groups' (e.g. family groups, peer groups, friendship groups, sports groups, committee memberships, project groups). There are thus two forms in which a group can be said to exist. It can exist in the form of people regularly interacting together on a face-to-face basis: the sociological group. However, it can also exist in the form of a representational or category membership: the psychological group. For example, a teacher, a lecturer or a psychologist represents categories of 'professional'. A student or client is also a category member.

Psychological groups have more of an abstract than concrete presence. None the less, membership of psychological groups can have an extremely powerful influence on the way people see themselves and how they think and behave in relation to others. To this extent you will find that as well as providing a means of information exchange and communication they espouse a particular group identity involving a set of norms, values and assumptions about how the member is expected to think, feel and behave. For instance, a teacher will do more than just teach, he or she will operate with various values, assumptions and beliefs about student capability and learning style, and will be expected to use the teaching models and techniques 'legitimized' by the profession. Those using iconoclastic (i.e. non-mainstream) principles and methods will usually be considered 'illegitimate' and subject to intense criticism by other teachers (Day *et al.* 1993).

Many psychological groups can also have sociological form, but this is not necessary for the existence and reality of a group. For example, national identity is not necessarily rooted in a particular country, geographical location or social structure (e.g. the European Union). The sociological form of a psychological group may be expressed in some kind of common currency like language, economic, business and defence policies for example. Psychological groups are significant at the macro as well as micro levels of analysis, including national groups, racial and ethnic groups, political parties, gender, community and class-based systems of societal classification. The European Union, for instance, has highlighted the issue of national identification in the European context. Barrett and Lyons (1998) studied the national group identifications of English, Scottish, Italian and Spanish children. Many nations are also multi-ethnic, each ethnic group having its own distinctive sense of category membership and identification (e.g. Indian, Chinese, Vietnamese and Afro-Caribbean communities in Europe and North America).

Sociological groups have some psychological significance to members (and also non-members). While the family is a largely socio-demographic entity, it also has psychological meaning and significance for family members. Moreover, family members may hold representations of their family in the past (ancestral history) and the future (future generations) that no longer or do not yet have any concrete presence and form. In groups that have concrete day-to-day presence (e.g. family group, project group, work group, seminar group) members regularly interact with each other to achieve a specific function or goal, or to complete a particular task. Each member of the group contributes something distinctive towards goal or task accomplishment.

The sociological group may be organized formally into a particular structure (e.g. a status hierarchy) or set of roles (e.g. team leader, secretary, senior and junior personnel). Informal groups – i.e. 'friendship' groups which spring up voluntarily – are likely to be more fluid in the way they are organized. They are also likely to be composed of individuals who are similar to each other in some way, or who have some common interest that voluntarily brings them together. Formal groups are usually comprised of people who might not otherwise volunteer to work together. This difference in group composition – by personal choice or not – will make a critical difference to the way it functions. Members of a project team, of a primary healthcare team, of a tutorial or seminar group, clients in group therapy, or a sports team, will work in a different way together than members of an informal friendship group. For example, group members may evolve into informal cliques or sub-groups by discipline or professional background, by age, or by gender, sometimes creating conflict or problems of communication. The bigger the group the more likely this is to happen (Makin *et al.* 1989). Sometimes the group exists only temporarily in concrete form. Members of a tutorial or seminar group, for example, come together for a particular purpose, at a particular time and then split up.

In contemporary society – nearing the millennium – many groups that once existed in concrete form now exist merely as representations. The ever-expanding world of electronic communication has meant that many people now work from home, working with others via the various electronic media available to them (e-mail, voice-mail, internet, video-conference facilities, and so on). More and more people are now operating in virtual environments, are members of virtual organizations, groups and teams, with these collective entities existing and generating social realities only through the minds of the beholders. Thus representational or psychological groups are rapidly obtaining prominence and social significance in the world of work.

R. Brown (1988) cautions us to be careful not to argue that groups can exist *only* in the minds of the beholders. Hogg (1993) describes a group as a 'collection of individuals who classify, define and evaluate themselves in terms of a common social category membership.' However, this implies that groups have no socio-demographic or sociological form yet many of them do. Brown (1988: 2–3) thus says that a group exists if two or more members define themselves as group members and where its existence is recognized by at least one other.

Some basic assumptions about groups

Any one person can be a member of several groups. A student, for example, may belong to a year group, a tutorial group, a friendship group, a professional group, a sports team, an interest group, a religious group, a family group and a national group. A psychologist may belong to a departmental team, a research team, a teaching team, a professional committee, an administrative committee, a sub-discipline (e.g. clinical psychology, occupational psychology) as well as the category of 'psychologist'. A junior doctor as a member of a 'medical firm' (a group in itself) may also belong to several ward and/or clinical teams. These memberships will vary in relative importance for an individual and therefore in how much influence they have on personal attitudes and behaviour. Thus, central to the description and explanation of group behaviour is an understanding of how and in what ways group memberships can influence individual attitudes and behaviour.

Festinger (1954) argues that group memberships satisfy five sets of psychological needs:

- the need for affiliation – the need to be with others
- the need for a sense of self-identity and self-esteem; who we are, and our personal value and standing, is determined by our membership of various groups
- the need to test out and establish social reality – groups develop beliefs about the way things are and how things work

- the need for a feeling of security and mutual support to manage anxiety and reduce uncertainty
- the group may also act as a problem solver for its members

Ψ **Section summary**

A distinction can be made between the group as a sociological and the group as a psychological entity. Groups exist in both forms. In this chapter, it is the psychological reality of the group experience that is of interest. This brings to bear an angle on the group that highlights the importance of cognition and perception, and more specifically, the role of social categorization processes. Groups fulfil social and psychological needs of various kinds. The importance of group memberships to identity and self-esteem can in particular be emphasized. An understanding of the kinds of needs fulfilled by group membership provides a starting point for explaining how group life, from the social psychological point of view, becomes possible.

1 In what form of reality can the family as an instance of a social group be said to exist?

2 How might the family group be described as both a sociological (i.e. a socio-demographic and sub-cultural entity) and psychological (i.e. having a psychological presence over and above its concrete and structural form) reality?

3 What kinds of needs do your own group memberships fulfil? To what extent do these needs bind you to the group, and influence how you think, feel and behave?

☐ Group formation: intra-group behaviour

What are the causes and consequences of group formation at both the 'group' and 'individual' level? The European answer to this is heavily reliant on the concept of 'psychological group' described earlier.

However despite various attempts to systematically distinguish the group from the individual level of analysis (e.g. Asch 1952; McDougall 1921) the prevailing view – in the US literature at least – is that the term 'group' is little more than a linguistic device used to describe a collection of individuals who are in some way bound together in time and space (Allport 1924; Cartwright 1968; Shaw 1976). In short, group-based phenomena are regarded as merely extensions of inter-individual phenomena. From this standpoint groups are sociological entities and have little if any psychological significance in and of themselves.

An inter-individual analysis of the social group

The prevailing North American view embraces a distinctive model of the social group as comprising a set of individuals bonded together like atoms by the forces of interpersonal attraction. The set of assumptions implicit to the model have since been developed into a perspective labelled **social cohesion theory** (Hogg 1987, 1992, 1993) see Table 12.1. Social cohesion theory argues that a collection of individuals will form a group (either spontaneously or deliberately) to the extent that they have needs capable of mutual satisfaction as a result of their association. Group formation and maintenance arises out of inter-individual interaction via which individual needs are fulfilled. Successful need fulfilment is said to bring about feelings of mutual personal attraction (Hogg 1987: 91). The social cohesion model of the group is elaborated in Table 12.1.

Criticisms of the social cohesion theory perspective on group formation have been voiced on both conceptual and empirical grounds. From an empirical standpoint, there is substantial evidence that personal attraction may not be necessary to group formation. Studies from sports psychology demonstrate that sociometric measures of interpersonal valence within the group can be inversely related to team success (e.g. Landers and Luschen 1974; McGrath 1962). Instances of group behaviour have been documented where members actually dislike each other on an interpersonal level (e.g. Hogg and Turner 1985a; Turner *et al.* 1983). Findings show that one does not necessarily have to feel attracted to or like everyone in the group(s) one belongs to, to succeed as a group.

Table 12.1 Social cohesion model of the group

(1) The social group comprises a collection of individuals specifiable in time and space – such as a tutorial or seminar group (e.g. Deutsch 1949; Homans 1968; Shaw 1976; Sherif 1966)

(2) The social group is defined by its cohesiveness: bonds of interpersonal attraction confer cohesiveness on an aggregate and cause it to become a group (e.g. Cartwright 1968; Lott and Lott 1965). Without cohesiveness the group ceases to exist. This means, for example, that for the tutorial group to be considered a true group, everyone who is a member should feel positive about each other, and bonded in some way to one another.

(3) Cohesiveness is merely interpersonal attraction by another name (e.g. Back 1951; Deutsch 1949; Newcomb 1953; Schacter et al. 1951). In the words of Lott (1961: 279) cohesiveness is 'that group property which is inferred from the number and strength of mutual positive attitudes among members of a group'. Pursuing our tutorial group theme, this means that the more attracted individual members feel towards one another, the greater their cohesiveness and therefore the more likely they are to operate together as a 'group'.

(4) Interpersonal attraction evolves over time as individuals needs are mutually satisfied – thus groups take time to form. The 'primary condition for the development of mutual positive attitudes among group members will be seen to be the attainment of goals or the receipt of rewards in one anothers presence' (Lott 1961: 279). In short, so long as group members co-operate with each other their fundamental needs will be satisfied and they will come to feel good about each other accordingly.

Group formation relies on patterns of inter-individual interaction becoming stabilized in terms of shared norms, values, and rules of conduct in action towards some motivationally significant task (e.g. a social cause, completing assignments, passing exams, helping a client). According to the social cohesion model, this process can take as little as a week of continuous and co-ordinated interaction. Cohesiveness, then, can be studied only once personal relations have stabilized such that 'it is possible just by counting interactions to map out a group' (Homans 1950: 84; see also Sherif 1966).

(5) Cohesiveness (i.e. interpersonal attraction) is facilitated by relatively voluntary interaction, co-operative or interdependent task relationships, acceptance by others, small group size, status congruence, externally imposed shared threat or frustration, similarities/compatibility's relevant to group existence and unpleasant initiation rites (see Hogg 1992; Lott and Lott 1965 for comprehensive and critical reviews).

(6) All group behaviour can be explained in terms of cohesiveness: the generation of group behaviour depends on the dynamics of interpersonal attraction and the determinants of attraction. Evidence shows that ingroup cohesiveness as traditionally defined can enhance productivity and performance (Goodacre 1951; Schacter et al. 1951), increase conformity to group norms (e.g. Festinger et al. 1951), improve morale and job satisfaction (Exline 1957; Gross 1954), facilitate intra-group communication (Knowles and Brickner 1981) and reduce intra-group hostility and direct it towards relevant outgroups (Pepitone and Reichling 1955).

Moreover, factors that create liking do not elevate cohesiveness if there is an emotionally charged or salient category boundary dividing individuals (Lott and Lott 1965). Cohesiveness is elevated through the opportunity to interact, but only within the confines of an already established category membership (Brewer and Silver 1978; Brown and Turner 1981). Also, groups that suffer failure in the sense of not mediating rewards for its members, can none the less bounce back with enhanced cohesiveness (Hogg 1992 for a review of pertinent studies derived from the sports context; Turner et al. 1984).

Perhaps most challenging to the social cohesion theory model is the fact that group behaviour (e.g. ingroup favouritism, inter-group discrimination, **conformity** to ingroup norms) (Levine and Campbell 1972) can be obtained in the absence of all so-called traditional determinants of group formation (Tajfel 1978; Tajfel and Turner 1979; Tajfel et al. 1971). How can we explain the uniform behaviour of large collectives like nations at war in terms of interpersonal attraction? Were all of the St Paul's community in the Bristol riots (Reicher 1984) attracted to one another? Were all of those millions present at Diana's funeral attracted to each other? Even if they were, could this explain the socially meaningful character of the behaviour observed?

A social categorization analysis of the social group

The minimal group experiments

In Chapter 11 it was noted that the mere awareness of belonging to a group can strongly influence our perceptions, attitudes and behaviours. Evidence for this is furnished by the so-called **minimal group** experiments (Tajfel *et al.* 1971) much replicated since (see B. Mullen *et al.* 1992 for a meta-analytic review of the findings). Mere awareness of group membership – a cognitive and perceptual construct – came to be known as the 'minimal conditions' of group behaviour. Even arbitrary allocation to a simple and largely meaningless form of category membership was sufficient to engender group-oriented perception and behaviour. This suggests that all it requires for individuals to become a group is a collective recognition of their membership unity. For example, although there are thousands of nurses the vast majority of them have never and will never meet on a one-to-one basis, yet bringing their category status into relief (e.g. by making salient what they have in common) will be enough for them to act as group (Millward 1991).

The cognitive-perceptual basis of group membership

The **self-categorization** analysis of group formation requires two major shifts in focus. The first involves a redefinition of the group from one emphasizing its concrete and physical presence in time and space (the so-called 'sociological group') to one which refers to the group as a subjective or psychological entity (the so-called 'psychological group') which may or may not have any here and now form (Hogg 1992: 66; Turner and Bourhis 1996: 28). Even those aligned with the social cohesion model acknowledge the distinctive psychological reality of group life and behaviour (Deutsch 1949; Homans 1968; Shaw 1976; Sherif 1966). Moreover, Allport (1924) – from a standpoint of ardent individualism – recognized that people can and do act in terms of supra-individual realities. 'Although', Allport (1924: 20) noted, 'we may never know whether [groups] are independently real, it does make considerable difference in

our thinking and living if we act as though they are real', adding later that the 'extension of awareness of self to include the group . . . can have a strong controlling force on the individual' (Allport 1924: 278). The patterns and regularities discernible in group-oriented behaviour led Allport and other writers on the subject of group processes to propose that this might be traced to the operation of some kind of irreducible logic of its own (e.g. Asch 1952).

The issue then is one of reconceptualizing the group not as something that comprises individuals, but that which is represented by them (Hogg 1993: 97). The self-involving nature of these representations of the group were summarized by Asch (1952: 257) who noted that 'group conditions penetrate to the very centre of individuals and transforms their character'. This indeed, is the crux of self-categorization theory (Tajfel 1978; Turner 1982a, 1985; Turner and Bourhis 1996; Turner and Oakes 1986; Turner *et al.* 1987). Building on the ideas of Asch (1952: 253) and his notion of the 'socially structured field within the individual', self-categorization theory explains how shared aspects of society mediate and are, in turn, mediated by psychological representation (Turner and Oakes 1986).

The second shift in focus concerns the proposed causal antecedents of group formation. The **social cohesion** model sees interpersonal attraction as the primary determinant of group formation. Yet the evidence suggests otherwise: mere categorization as a group member in the absence of interpersonal familiarity and attraction is sufficient to engender group behaviour (i.e. shared collective reactions) indicative of psychological group formation (Hogg 1987). In this case it might well be claimed that attraction is a product, rather than a cause, of group formation. As put by Turner (1982a: 17) 'we may not . . . tend to join people we like so much as like the people we perceive ourselves joined to'; the psychological reality of group membership having a primarily cognitive-perceptual basis rather than an interpersonal one. Recognition that group formation can evolve from categorization processes is not new (e.g. Cartwright 1968) but it is only recently that this possibility has been systematically researched. This is the starting point for the self-categorization theory model of the group and group formation processes (Turner 1982a, 1985; Turner *et al.* 1987).

ψ Section summary

The analysis of group formation has until recently been dominated by a perspective on the group that assumes it is little more than the sum of its parts. This perspective, called social cohesion theory, describes group cohesion as a form of interpersonal attraction borne of intensive interaction among group members, proximal to each other in both time and space, and having certain attitudes in common. Group formation is thus said to be the product of interpersonal attraction, and is a largely physical (i.e. in time and space) and sociological (i.e. certain clearly discernible sociometric patterns of interaction evolve) event. There is evidence to suggest however that group formation can be explained as a largely cognitive–perceptual event, neither dependent on a particular time, space, or sociometric structure or levels of interpersonal attraction within the group. This is not to say that groups do not ever form in the way described by social cohesion theory, but that the way it is explained does not take into consideration the transformation in thinking, feeling and behaving that occurs upon identification with a cognitive–perceptual category, nor the possibility that groups might not exist at all in any physical or concrete sociometric form. This argument paves the way for a self-categorization analysis of group formation.

1 Think of a group to which you belong and in which you also invest in heavily. How cohesive is this group? How might you describe and explain this level of cohesiveness?

2 Is a group built out of interpersonal attraction among group members? Or is the relationship between group members something fundamentally different from this?

🗅 Group formation: role of similarity and attraction

According to self-categorization theory, interpersonal similarity and attraction lead to group formation only to the extent that they act as criteria for category assignment (Hogg 1987: 50; Turner *et al.* 1987: 27–30). Cognitive-perceptual unit formation is cued by factors like 'proximity', 'common fate', 'shared threat' (Turner 1982a: 27; see also Campbell 1968; Heider 1958) – all of which are empirical correlates of interpersonal attraction (Lott and Lott 1965). However they lead to group formation by enhancing the salience of social similarities and differences or the clarity of existing categorical designations (Hogg 1987: 102–3; Hogg and Turner 1985a: 54; 1985b: 280; Turner *et al.* 1983: 236).

Re-examination of some of the classic cohesiveness-group formation experiments involving anonymous co-participants indicates that 'cohesiveness' was manipulated by instructions as general as 'people that you would like and who will like you' (e.g. Pepitone and Reichling 1955). While clearly the intention was to manipulate the personal attractiveness of other group members, no truly individuating information was ever made available in these experiments. In many cases, subjects were pre-categorized as members of an 'extremely congenial group' (Bovard 1951; Downing 1958; Exline 1957; Schacter *et al.* 1951). Research may therefore have unwittingly induced a 'social' rather than 'personal' form of attraction (Hogg and Abrams 1988: 109; Hogg and Turner 1985a; 1985b). The social attraction hypothesis states that under conditions of minimal individuating information an assumption of common category membership will prevail which activates an identification process (Hogg and Turner 1985a: 62; Turner *et al.* 1987: 109). These conditions are similar to those arising during the early stages of a relationship (Duck 1977) or at a first encounter between strangers (Hogg and Abrams 1988: 109).

Personal and social attraction

Hogg (1987: 112) argues that traditional conceptualizations of cohesiveness as interpersonal attraction fail to deal with the qualitatively different types of relationships made possible by processes of group identification. Although both types of attraction are subjectively experienced as inter-individual attitudes, they differ at the level of generative process: the object of personal attraction is the unique individual, while the object of social attraction is the ingroup prototype. Support for this assumption is derived from work on interpersonal relationship formation. Duck (1977), for example, has

Research update

Ethnocentrism in dating preferences

According to Lui *et al.* (1995) inter-ethnic marriage rates are on the increase. This, they argue, affords the unique opportunity to examine the interplay between inter-group (e.g. inter-group differentiation processes) and interpersonal (e.g. perceived similarity, physical attractiveness) factors. They begin with the question of to what extent do the established indicators of interpersonal attraction operate within an inter-group context? Their research shows that ethnocentrism is firmly the rule in partner preferences and perceptions of similarity operate within the accepted (i.e. ethnocentric) range. This finding provides independent verification of the distinction proposed by Hogg (1993) between personal and social attraction. In short, the factors which determine interpersonal attraction (like perceived similarity) operate within a group context and are arguably operating at the level of social rather than personal attraction. Support for this interpretation is also obtained from the finding that normative approval (or disapproval) from family and close friends strongly predicted ethnocentrism in dating preferences. However, the one factor which does appear to cross ethnic boundaries, operating at a fundamentally personal level of attraction, is physical attractiveness. Lui *et al.* (1995) argue from their findings that physical attractiveness is also connected stereotypically to a number of desirable traits that may increase the possibility of long-term relations (see also Eagly *et al.* 1991 for a review).

Plate 12.2 One factor which does appear to cross ethnic boundaries, operating at a fundamental personal level of attraction, is physical attractiveness

shown that people are largely 'stimulus objects' to each other at first encounter and become personalized only later on in the relationship. Stereotypes are then no longer applied. Duck distinguishes between short-term attraction based on the assumption that one shares certain beliefs and attitudes (i.e. common value similarity) and long-term attraction based on knowledge of a person as a deeper more idiosyncratic level – a distinction which resonates with that maintained by the self-categorization perspective.

Evidence for the qualitative distinction between personal and social attraction pertaining to the group context can also be cited. Sherif (1966), for example, allowed close interpersonal relations to form among boys during their first days at summer camp then assigned best friends to opposing groups. Ingroup loyalty and outgroup hostility was generated immediately thus reversing the pattern of interpersonal relationships developed earlier. By the end of the summer camp, 90 per cent of the boys nominated an ingroup members as their 'best friend' (see also Boyanowsky and Allen 1975). More directly, others have found that interpersonal factors bear little relationship to group behaviours (e.g. Dion 1973). Evidence from sports psychology has also shown how interpersonal relationships are inversely related to group cohesiveness under conditions of group success (e.g. Fielder 1954 *vis-à-vis* football).

More direct evidence is provided by a series of experiments conducted by Hogg and colleagues in a systematic programme of research concerned with elucidating the character and process of group formation. In one of the earliest studies in this programme, Hogg and Turner (1985b) manipulated interpersonal attitudes (i.e. idiosyncratically likeable or dislikeable) independently of group/inter-group ones (i.e. commonly likeable/dislikeable). They also asked subjects to provide their impressions of individual members as well as the group as a whole. Consistent with expectation, they found that 'personal likeableness' affected the valence of interpersonal but not group/inter-group attitudes: subjects expressed a positive orientation towards likeable rather than unlikeable individuals irrespective of their group membership. Interpersonal attraction had no effect on group behaviour. By contrast, explicitly categorized subjects expressed discriminatory inter-group behaviour irrespective of the personal likeableness of the individuals within each of the two groups. These findings substantiate previous ones comparing the relative explanatory power of categorization and interpersonal attraction in producing group behaviour using the minimal group paradigm (Hogg and Turner 1985a; Turner *et al.* 1983).

While in the absence of explicit categorization, Turner *et al.* (1983) found that people discriminated more in favour of those whom they and others 'liked' (i.e. people on the whole that you will like) categorization enhanced the effect. The act of categorization transformed the meaning of the attraction information from interpersonal to intra-group. Moreover, discrimination was obtained even when the categorization criterion was explicitly negative (i.e. people on the whole that you will not like). Negatively categorized subjects felt as much part of their group as those who were positively categorized. The absence or presence of explicit categorization thus appeared to be more important than the valence of the attraction information. Similarly, Hogg

and Turner (1985a) found that 'interpersonally unattractive' ingroup members are favoured over 'interpersonally attractive' outgroup members. Both studies provide evidence to show how interpersonal effects can be transformed by the categorization process. Although 'attractive' individuals are favoured over 'unattractive' ones, the effect is stronger when the valence of members is critical of group membership.

The core idea that social self-categorization depersonalizes the basis of inter-individual attraction suggests that ingroup members should be liked in proportion to their perceived prototypicality (Turner *et al.* 1987: 60). Some support for this is derived from the review of Lott and Lott (1965) who describe how the attractiveness of individual group members is related to how relevant, important or normative their characteristics are to the group. For example, Hare (1962) provides evidence for a systematic relationship between popularity and the extent to which the individual represents the group ideal. More direct evidence for this is provided by a number of experiments showing that social attraction is based on group prototypes (Hogg 1993; Hogg and Hardie 1991, 1992; Hogg *et al.* 1991, 1992).

In a field study involving an Australian football team, Hogg and Hardie (1991) issued questionnaires during a team practice session designed to elicit subjective perceptions of the prototypicality of team members and ratings of self-prototypicality. The group prototype was significantly more closely related to social attraction and social popularity than personal attraction and personal popularity. Members who identified more strongly with the team employed prototypicality as a stronger basis of social attraction: members who were most socially and prototypically popular were also those who themselves were identified most strongly with the team and defined themselves as most prototypical.

As Hogg and McCarty (1991) recognize, more work is needed to elucidate the processes of accessibility and fit in predicting the content and use of self-categories (see also Oakes *et al.* 1993). However self-categorization may be only one of many factors contributing to unit formation: others may include 'perceived interdependence, proximity, a shared territory, similar preferences and shared labels, shared threat, the anticipation of actual intragroup interaction, and inter-group competition' (Rabbie *et al.* 1989: 179).

Ψ Case study

Study of group formation

Brown and Millward (1993) used a quasi-experimental design involving a cohort of novice nurses on entry to training school, followed up after a one-year period. Within minutes of entry to the school, novice nurses have donned a new uniform, must wear other group identifying insignia, and are subject to explicit labelling by nurse tutors. In this study, labelling took the form of the following public statement: 'Each of you is now a nurse; you have a professional identity'. These novice nurses are of particular theoretical interest since their initial knowledge of other ingroup members and the various outgroups within the interdependent network of professional groups is very limited – most often zero. Here lies the crux of the quasi-experimental approach. Field research is often accompanied by a switch in emphasis away from causes to the consideration of 'effects' from which potential causes can be inferred (Brewer and Kramer 1985). Thus, while the antecedents of group formation predicted by contrasting models of group formation (i.e. categorization versus interpersonal familiarity) could not be directly manipulated in this study, they were plotted by examining the consequences of categorization in conditions analogous to the minimal group paradigm, prior to the opportunity to interact. This then served as a baseline against which to trace any subsequent changes. Empirically, it is the time factor that allows test of the validity of contrasting models.

Immediate to categorization, novice nurses provided estimates of ingroup and outgroup variability on various dimensions both relevant and irrelevant to the categorization criterion. If group formation is immediate to categorization we would expect perceptions of the ingroup and outgroup to be relatively stereotypical (i.e. minimal variability) from the start and to exhibit little if any change over time. If, on the other hand, group formation depends on interpersonal familiarity and interaction, then we might expect perceptions of the ingroup to become stereotypical over time. This means that at the outset of

training the ingroup will be perceived as more internally heterogeneous than the outgroup.

Most striking of all the findings – which are too lengthy and complex to describe in full here – was how little perceptions of ingroup variability changes. Only on the irrelevant criteria were there any discernible changes and this was reflected in an increase in perceptions of ingroup heterogeneity. Both findings are consistent with the self-categorization model of group formation. Self-categorization predicts selectivity in the use of criteria on which to express social identification. The increase in perception of heterogeneity observed on relevant criteria is not surprising, since these were designed to elicit interpersonal rather than group level effects. With the increased availability of individuating information of each other, group members used personal/interpersonal level criteria to emphasize individual differences rather than similarities – hence the increase in perceptions of heterogeneity obtained. However, on consideration of the relative pattern of changes over time in perceptions of group variability, there were signs of substantial increase in perceptions of ingroup homogeneity over time in the way predicted by the social cohesion model. This increase in perceptions of ingroup homogeneity was caused mainly by shifts in the perception of other groups as more internally heterogeneous. Indeed there was substantial evidence of change, the nature of which is not completely reconcilable with either model of group formation. Brown and Millward (1993) suggested that the role of categorization in ingroup formation, though clearly important, needs to be supplemented with consideration of how exactly factors like face-to-face interaction interact with this in the group formation process. It is quite feasible to assume that cohesion initially derived from a categorization process can develop a realistic basis with time. Expectations may be fulfilled and/or interpersonal comparison with 'similar' others may actually engender true rather than inferred similarities (Eiser 1985; Festinger 1954).

Ψ Section summary

Self-categorization theory affords a radically differ-ent explanation for group formation than that pro-vided by social cohesion theory. The former hinges on the assumption that groups have a cognitive-per-ceptual reality that arise from a self-categorization process. A qualitative shift in self-categorization from a personal (i.e. individual) to a social (i.e. collec-tive) level is said to be 'causal' basis from which the psychological reality of the group is borne. While both social cohesion and self-categorization theory agree that attraction between group members is indeed part of what it means for a group to experi-ence cohesion, there is disagreement on not only the focus, direction and meaning of attraction between group members but also its causal status with respect to group formation processes. Specifically, self-categorization theory advocates that attraction between group members is contingent upon group formation as opposed to being responsible for it, the stance taken by social cohesion theory. Moreover, attraction at the group level of analysis (i.e. social attraction) is said to be of a qualitatively different kind (i.e. attraction towards others as group mem-bers, rather than unique individuals) than that char-acterizing interpersonal attraction. Interpersonal attractiveness may be important to group formation only to the extent that it represents or raises the salience of group boundaries. In the final analysis, group formation is said to be caused by a cognitive-perceptual shift in level and scope of psychological orientation. Shifts in self-categorization and identity are context bound and depend on variations in cate-gory salience, and also the relative diagnostic power of one particular category over another. A critical test of these two competing explanations of group formation is provided by research investigating groups and their formation over time. The extent to which cognitive-perceptual relative to sociometric factors are involved can be ascertained. Research to this effect has afforded the conclusion that the two sets of explanations might in fact be more appropri-ately seen as complementary perspectives on the issue of group formation.

Box continued

1   What kinds of processes underpin group form-ation? To what extent might interpersonal attraction be involved? Might this be only one of many other factors that provide a cue for self-categorization processes to be set in train? What might these other factors be?

2   To what extent do you think that it is feasible to attribute a causal role to self-categorization in the group formation process?

3   How would you provide a critical test of the two competing explanations of group formation?

❑ Social influence processes

Group formation processes exemplify a concern with examining the influence of social factors on behaviour. Typically though, the concept of **social influence** is defined in a much more delimited way as the change in judgements, opinions and attitudes of an individual as a consequence of exposure to the judgements, opinions and attitudes of another (Van Avermaet 1996). Before venturing into this literature we need to make clear that the influence of social factors on behaviour can have dif-ferent consequences depending on what type of influence mechanisms are at work. We can, for example, differenti-ate between an outcome of **behavioural compliance** (i.e. acting in the ways expected by others though not consistent with one's attitudes and beliefs) and one that involves **internalization** (i.e. changing attitudes and beliefs consistent with those being proposed).

Internalization versus compliance

The minimal group experiment (Tajfel *et al*. 1971) is typical of research conducted in the tradition of creating miniature 'group worlds' enabling close observations to be made of the way groups operate (Asch 1952). In one of the earliest experiments on norm formation in small groups, Sherif (1935) exposed subjects to a static pin-point of light amidst complete darkness. These condi-tions create the **autokinetic effect** – a perceptual illusion whereby the light appears to move about erra-tically in absence of a stable reference point. Either alone or in groups of two or three, subjects were required to provide verbal estimates of the extent of movement of the light. Over a series of trials, individual judgements tended to converge on a group norm. Later, group members gave their estimates in solo. These estimates deviated very little from the original group norm thus indicating that it had endured. The norm had been internalized. These findings were confirmed by Bovard (1948). Using the same paradigm, he found the responses of solo individuals to be still aligned with those of the original group 28 days later. In more natural settings, group norms may become deeply ingrained within individuals. Newcomb showed in a longitudinal study how girls with conservative values were strongly influenced by the liberalism prevalent in their college. Twenty years after leaving the college, this liberalism still held sway (Newcomb 1953).

Mead (1934: 219) wrote of internalization as a sense of being identified with the group, as a result of which individuals assume its values as their own. These values then become independent of their original source. In short, they become deeply harnessed within the individual's own motivational system such that their actions and beliefs fully coincide. Holzner and Roberts (1980) describe this as a 'genuine' integration of the intrinsic interests of the individual with those of the group. It is this which is believed to be the hallmark of 'group identification' (Tajfel 1978).

Kelman (1958, 1971) sees internalization as one of three qualitatively distinct ways in which the individual can be tied to the group. The other two ways – compliance and identification – are based on different kinds of motives. **Compliance**, for example, denotes circumstances where the individual behaves in line with group obligations to attain a favourable reaction from its agents (i.e. for approval and reward, or merely to avoid punishment). The values signified are not integral to the individual's own. Instances of this are seen among professional trainees in so far as their behaviour is geared towards receiving the approval of superiors (e.g. Light 1979). They might 'act professional' but as yet do not feel that the identity is true or congruent with their own identity. This indicates that a public (i.e. overt) but not private (i.e. covert) type of attitude change has occurred (Kiesler and Kiesler 1969).

By contrast, **identification** occurs where individuals accept influence from others whom they find attractive in some way and model themselves accordingly. This in itself provides them with a satisfying self-definition. The difference between this and compliance is that private attitude change does occur. The aim is to 'be' (i.e. think, feel) like the attractive model, not just behave in line with them to seek approval. So professional trainees

might select out for modelling purposes those whom they perceive as 'attractive', i.e. fit their conceptions of the professional prototype or ideal (Millward 1991). Where this differs from internalization is that attitudes and behaviours are believed to remain anchored to the model. If contact with the model were to end, then the effect would disappear, unless of course there were other role models available who resemble the ideal figure and to whom the individual can transfer their attachment. Unlike internalization, changes in attitude are said not to become integrated with (therefore disassociated from the model) the value system of the actor.

Normative and informational influence processes

The distinction between different kinds of social influence phenomena is based on the assumption that each serves a different motivational goal. There is dependency of some kind on the group for need fulfilment (Moscovici 1976). The notion of dependency is fundamental to traditional explanations of conformity phenomena. Hogg and Turner (1987) suggests that the issue can be addressed in terms of two influence mechanisms – normative and informational (Deutsch and Gerard 1955). These will each be considered in turn.

Normative influence

Normative influence is defined as 'influence to conform to the positive expectations of another' (Deutsch and Gerard 1955: 629). It is concerned with how the individual might depend on the group for instrumental reasons (i.e. for acceptance and social approval and/or to avoid censure). This leads to behavioural compliance with the view to maximizing positive outcomes but no underlying attitude change (see also Kiesler and Kiesler 1969).

Normative influence is expected to occur in conditions of group surveillance and where certain members are granted the power to deliver rewards (e.g. praise) and sanctions (e.g. criticism). The group may be one that the individual does not yet belong to, one none the less aspired to as a source of self-reference. This is the case for trainees in the professions who report to more qualified members of the profession. By virtue of this, the latter might be invested with 'referent power' (French and Raven 1959; Raven and Kruglanski 1970). In most professions those who have the authority to impose sanctions do tend to lay a forceful emphasis on trainees attaining high standards of 'professional behaviour' (e.g.

Kramer 1974). Those who wish to improve their relative standing in the group would need to maximize the positive and minimize the negative consequences of their behaviour in the eyes of authority (Dittes and Kelley 1955). Low status and/or new members who are unsure of how to act may be especially keen to behave in line with expectation (e.g. Buss 1983).

Informational influence

Informational influence, by contrast, is defined as 'influence to accept information obtained from another as evidence of reality' (Deutsch and Gerard 1955: 629). This is concerned with how the individual can depend on the group for information and where group members are believed to have a more 'accurate' view of reality upon which to rely. The power of reference (i.e. non-membership) groups might therefore also arise from its members possessing a certain specialist knowledge or expertise which the individual wishes to acquire. This is especially true for aspiring members of groups. New entrants are especially likely to be susceptible to informational influence (Weiss 1977). This may be due to the fact of uncertainty regarding the nature of reality and their ability to deal with it (Louis 1980). They are likely to be highly dependent on others for guidance as to norms for appropriate behaviour as well as for learning relevant skills and abilities. Information is thereby sought to reduce the uncertainty felt.

The mechanism of informational influence stems from Festinger's (1950, 1954) **social comparison** theory. Fundamental to this is the assumption that people have an innate need for self-evaluation. For this, they require a stable source of self-reference against which to assess their opinions and abilities. If 'objective' (physical/non-social) sources are not available, stability is undermined. This can engender uncertainty as to the nature of reality. The solution, then, is to fall back on other people as 'bench-marks' for judging the validity of their attitudes and action (Jones and Gerard 1967). It leads to the hypothesis that the greater the uncertainty the greater the need for interpersonal comparison with others similar to oneself (Suls and Miller 1977).

Uncertainty may arise from lack of confidence concerning some aspect of self (e.g. ability) and/or objective ambiguities in the environment (e.g. lack of structure) (Deutsch and Gerard 1955). Both tend to increase the degree of informational dependence exhibited in the group situation (e.g. Asch 1956; Blake *et al.* 1957; DiVesta 1959). It must be more than coincidence that new entrants to a group are usually preoccupied with seeking out as much information as they can about appropriate behaviour from existing group members (e.g. Moreland and Levine 1982).

The power of normative influence: the Asch experiments

Hundreds of people experienced the dilemma described in the case study (p. 372) during Asch's perceptual judgement experiments. What would you do? Conform or stick to the evidence of your own eyes? Overall, 37 per cent of them committed errors (i.e. conformed) relative to 0.7 per cent in the control group: they said what everyone else said was the right answer even though it was blatantly wrong. They had no idea that all of their peers had been coached by the researcher to give identical wrong answers. An error of 37 per cent may not seem like a very big percentage but the fact that even some, to quote Asch (1955), 'reasonably intelligent and well-meaning people are willing to call white black' was enough to suggest the normative power of the group to influence individual behaviour. In the Asch experiment there was no obvious pressure to conform – displays of independence were not penalized and there were no rewards for 'team play' – yet group conformity occurred. Even those who resisted conformity became obviously uncomfortable and hesitant, beginning to doubt the evidence of their own eyes.

Most would now agree that the Asch paradigm elicits public compliance, but not necessarily private attitude change or internalization of the social reality presented by the group (Van Avermaet 1996). Thus, individuals are aware that the group is wrong but they suppress their disagreement at the time. If one of the psychological needs fulfilled by group membership is the need to test out and establish social reality (Festinger 1954: see p. 362), when social reality is ambiguous, it is highly probable that the individual will rely on the group to tell them what is going on. In this case, the 'right' (and of course 'safest') answer is what the group says it is. This basic conformity effect has been much replicated since, using different subject populations and different judgemental tasks (see Van Avermaet 1996 for a commentary on these results).

Hogg and Abrams (1988) point out that in most circumstances normative and informational influence mechanisms may operate in tandem to initiate confor-

Ψ Case study

Conformity

A classic example of the power of normative influence processes to elicit conformity – even in instances where normative reality blatantly contradicts otherwise unambiguous information – is provided by the work of Asch (1952). In the Asch experiments, a unanimous majority in relation to a lone individual exemplifies normative pressures. Imagine partaking in one of the Asch experiments, allegedly an exercise on 'visual discrimination'. You are sixth in the row of seven people around a table taking part in a study of perceptual judgement. The researcher asks each member of the group to say which of three lines matches the standard line. All five people before you in the row answer in the way you expect them to: line 2 matches

the standard one. Isn't the answer obvious? The next set of lines is also easy to match. How tedious!

However, in the next trial, although the answer seems just as obvious, the first person gives the 'wrong' answer and says, for example, that line 1 matches the standard one. When the second person in the row gives the same 'wrong' answer you sit bolt upright and check the line lengths again. The third, fourth and fifth person in the row also provide the 'wrong' answer and you start to wonder whether they or you are blind. When it comes to your turn what do you say? 'What is the right answer – I'm now no longer sure?' 'Is the right answer the one fellow group members are telling me or what my eyes are telling me?'

---

mity. Indeed, according to Kelley (1952) most groups perform a normative as well as informational function for their members. This can be applied to our example of 'professional groups'. Here, pressures are exerted in association with norms of conduct embodied in formal codes of practice. These are prescriptive so deviations are cited as examples of 'professional misconduct'. The actions of all professionals are also open to public scrutiny, the issue of 'accountability' being a salient issue for most professionals these days. For many professional trainees, the major concern is to 'get through' training as a result of which they tend to become preoccupied with successful performance. This makes them particularly vulnerable to normative pressures and highly dependent on the outcome of their actions for self-esteem (Martin and Greenstein 1983; Millward 1991).

One line of research revolves on the topic of self-doubt as a mediator of conformity (e.g. Campbell and Tesser 1986; Tesser *et al*. 1983). Campbell and Tesser's (1986) findings are particularly interesting. Their research took as its point of departure the fact that self-doubt increases focus of attention to the point of becoming more 'scrupulous in observing and comparing' (Asch 1952: 463). Whether this renders individuals susceptible to influence might vary depending on how secure they are within the group. To demonstrate this, two processes of influence were compared for their

relative power over a long-term series of trials: self-doubt (informational influence) and group pressure (normative influence). Influence became progressively more difficult with time. Initially either one or the other type of influence was sufficient to facilitate conformity. At this stage, individuals were simply concerned with 'getting on'. Later both types of influence were necessary – a stage where individuals were involved in a more detailed negotiation of their roles.

It would appear from these findings that subjective uncertainty in its various forms (e.g. self-doubt, situational ambiguity, and so on) is the condition under which both normative and informational processes of influence are optimally at work. This presupposes that individuals are in some ways vulnerable (due to lack of information and/or confidence) and therefore dependent on the group for normative and informational support.

The conditions of social influence: subjective uncertainty and social-psychological dependency

The uncertainty hypothesis as a condition for influence has much in common with the notion of 'cognitive dissonance' (Festinger 1957), the assumption that all action is directed towards reduction or removal of subjective discomfort. Cognitive dissonance theory claims the existence of a basic need in people for consistency in their thoughts. If one thought were to imply the opposite of another, Festinger reasoned that it would result in an unpleasant state of arousal or dissonance, which people would be motivated to reduce. It is often by means of attitude change that dissonance is said to be managed (e.g. Festinger and Carlsmith 1959).

What if individuals found themselves acting in contradiction with their self-perception? If they feel 'forced' to do so, the resultant inconsistency could be attributed to the fact of them having to 'act against their will'. However, if they chose to act this way (i.e. could be held responsible for doing so), dissonance is likely to arise. One way it can be rid is by altering self-perception in a direction consistent with the otherwise dissonant action (Festinger and Carlsmith 1959). There are, of course, many other ways of reducing dissonance. For instance one might engage in a compensatory form of action in line with one's existing self-image. This would 'boost' those aspects of self-image undermined by the counter-attitudinal behaviour (e.g. Steel and Liu 1983). The concern here, however, is with the impetus for change.

Sherif et al. (1961: 13) linked dissonance explicitly with the experience of uncertainty in relation to attitude change and self-perception. They noted that 'to the extent an individual's attitude is intimately related to his self-picture, the confrontation of views, events, situations, discrepant from his attitude arouses uncertainty, disturbance or dissonance.' In short, inconsistency bearing on self-perception is believed to be especially likely to facilitate attitude change. Evidence for this is quite substantial (e.g. Chaiken and Stangor 1987).

One line of research that is particularly relevant to this issue has looked at the effects of 'role-play' on attitude change (e.g. Axsom and Cooper 1981; Janis and King 1954). Here individuals actively engage themselves through role-play in support of an issue that requires them to espouse opinions contrary to their own. As such, a lot of personal investment is entailed. This induces dissonance and results in attitude change because of the need to justify the efforts made (see also Zanna and Cooper 1974).

None the less dissonance does not explain all attitude change. Many questions still remain (see Eiser and Van der Pligt 1984) and alternative explanations have been offered (e.g. Schlenker 1982). Much depends on clarifying the exact meaning of dissonance. It is not clear whether a link can be made between this and the experience of uncertainty. Uncertainty may be due more to the need for cognitive clarity than consistency – although the two may not in fact be so different. Where

differences do occur is in what is believed to happen as a result. Uncertainty is seen as giving rise to dependency on others in the group for information or self-evaluation, whereas dissonance can lead to cognitive adjustment. The former concerns outcomes in terms of altered behaviour in relation to others (i.e. an intra-group perspective), while the latter is concerned with altered behaviour in relation to merely oneself (i.e. intra-individual perspective). It is our belief that both perspectives are probably necessary.

Chaiken and Stangor (1987: 616) have called for a consideration of attitude change in the context of 'real groups with real attitudes in real settings', due to what they see as an impoverished paradigm of laboratory research. Hitherto, they believe there has been an underestimation of the 'extent to which group norms, social roles and social interaction affect social influence' (Chaiken and Stangor 1987: 616). Does subjective uncertainty underpin susceptibility to influence? For example, Sherif et al. (1961: 185) note that 'Whether a discrepant communication will produce personal feelings of uncertainty . . . is not a foregone conclusion'. Only Moscovici (1976) has taken up the issue in any real detail, declaring that uncertainty arises from an awareness of disagreement between people among whom agreement is otherwise expected. From this angle, conformity (and attitude change) are said to be a result of a need for consistency – not of personal attitudes, but of attitudes between people. This is the starting point for the hypothesis of referential informational influence. Its merit lies in the attempt to integrate two theoretical considerations: intra-individual and intra-group.

ψ Section summary

Social Influence processes have been traditionally conceptualized using a two-process model involving normative and informational aspects. Normative influence presupposes that the individuals will comply with group expectations and norms in return for some kind of instrumental gain like social approval. Information influence on the other hand presupposes that we are influenced by those who provide us with a basis for testing the nature of reality and who provide us with a source of social

Box continued

comparison and self-evaluation. Subjective uncertainty (e.g. about the nature of social reality and one's place in it) is said to be a precondition for social influence to occur in both normative and informational forms. An example of these processes at work in the instance of conformity to a group is provided. A distinction is drawn between attitude and behaviour change, which are said to be underpinned by different kinds of mechanisms (i.e. compliance versus internalization). It is argued that most instances of social influence will more than likely involve both normative and informational types of social influence.

1   Think of an example where you have been influenced into behaving in a way contrary to the way you would ordinarily be inclined (i.e. on the basis of your attitudes), and explain what kinds of processes you think may have been involved.

2   Think of an instance where you have experienced change at both attitude and behavioural levels. Again, explain what kinds of processes you think might have been involved and in particular why in this instance you changed your attitude as well as your behaviour.

❑ Referential information influence

Turner *et al.* (1987) maintain that there is redundancy in the two-process formulation (i.e. informational and normative influence). They maintain that influence processes involve both influences in synchrony. Normative processes are required to ensure that the informational content of others' responses is a 'correct' picture of reality. Turner *et al.* (1987: 71) argue that the very possibility of social influence depends on shared category membership. It is assumed that identification with a group can occur even in the absence of familiarity with another of its members. This involves a 'process by which one defines oneself as a category member, forms a group stereotype on the basis of other category members behaviour and applies the stereotype to oneself' (Turner 1982a: 32). As a result of this **self-stereotyping** process, internalization of all pertinent group attributes is said to have occurred.

The self–stereotyping hypothesis

To account for how this process of self-stereotyping might operate, Turner (1982a) proposed a mechanism which is specific to and governed by group membership, termed **referential informational influence**. Three stages are proposed:

(1)   Individuals must first acknowledge their membership of a distinct social category and define themselves accordingly.

(2)   Individuals learn the stereotypical norms appropriate to this category membership and the prescribed modes of behaviour. These modes of behaviour are definitive (i.e. 'criterial') of category membership and distinguish it from other groups.

(3)   When this category membership becomes psychologically salient, individuals assign these stereotypical norms to themselves as guidance for their own attitudes and behaviour. Their behaviour is correspondingly likely to become normative (i.e. in conformity with the group stereotype).

(Turner 1982a: 31)

The validation hypothesis

Turner *et al.* (1987) link referential informational influence processes with the precondition of uncertainty. It is proposed that once identification has occurred, similarly categorized members will assume that they have something in common with each other and that mutual agreement will therefore prevail. If, given the same stimulus situation, there are discrepancies or a lack of agreement between group members, individuals experience uncertainty (Turner *et al.* 1987: 73). This can occur in situations where group norms and values are unclear and/or ready made normative responses are not yet available – as in the case of new entrants to a group. This in turn leads to efforts to reduce discomfort. One method is to generate agreement through mutual social influence. Mutual social influence entails trying to deduce the criterial norms and attributes of the group as exemplified by representative (i.e. prototypical) group members. As such the basis for self-stereotyping is formed.

Social influence is thus seen to originate from the need to reach agreement with others who they perceive as interchangeable group members – i.e. interchangeable in respect to relevant attributes (Turner *et al.* 1987: 72). Informational content *per se* is not as important as the fact that it is validated through intra-group consensus. In this respect, the informational advantage of the group lies in its ability to provide consensus information that validates the responses of its members as correct, appropriate or desirable (cf. Moscovici's (1976) validation hypothesis). Through this process, members are able to ensure that their perceptions of group social reality are veridical (appear to be confirmed by subsequent events). This proposition reads very much like the model of social influence originally developed by Festinger (1950), who reasoned that levels of aspiration for good performance might be derived from the standards of the group to which individuals belonged. By definition, shared group membership signifies that individuals therein are in some way alike. Conversely, those who do not belong to the group may represent opinions and/or abilities that diverge too greatly for valid comparisons to be made.

Like Festinger (1950) then, the referential informational influence approach sees social influence processes as being contained within the group and influence attempts are credible or meaningful only in so far as they exemplify group norms. Influence occurs within normative limits: outside these limits influence attempts are said to have little or no credibility. At best the individual will comply with non-ingroup member demands but conformity (via the vehicles of identification and internalization) will not occur. According to Turner (1982a), conformity is an intra-group process and refers to (i.e. it is 'referential') ingroup information.

Selectivity in social comparison processes

Major and Forcey (1985) illustrate how selectivity in social comparison processes of the kind described above might operate. They found that both men and women emphasized the importance of similarity in wage comparisons. The majority chose to look first at the pay of those who were the same sex and in the same jobs as themselves. Only a small minority of those in jobs dominated by the opposite sex first compared their wages across sexes rather than within (see also Crosby 1982). Where the referential informational influence approach differs from Festinger's is in its view of the object of conformity. For the former, it is the cognitive representation of the group and its stereotypical characteristics (the 'psychological group'), not necessarily the overt form of their behaviour, that is the source of influence. The role of interaction and interpersonal communication (the 'sociological' or generative form of the psychological group) is merely to elaborate upon the group stereotype already internalized. Influence is expected to be effective only to the extent that the attributes, experience, role or

position of its source is perceived to be prototypical of the group as a whole (Turner et al. 1987: 74).

This means that there is also a difference between mechanisms, in that common category members need not be interpersonally similar or attractive to each other. The basis for informational influence is ingroup or social similarity, rather than interpersonal similarity, as Festinger's (1954) analysis would claim. Thus, social comparisons are said to be intra-group rather than interpersonal in form. It predicts that individuals will compare themselves with ingroup members even if they are dissimilar to themselves on an interpersonal level (similar only on a criterial or group membership basis) and that they will refrain from interpersonal comparisons across group boundaries (or at least not pay heed to the information derived from these comparisons) (Hogg et al. 1995).

Consistent with this is research that demonstrates a preference of individuals to compare themselves with those who are much higher in ability than they. Feldman and Ruble (1981) found that people select for comparison those of highest ability in order to maximize the amount and quality of information derived. Those of highest ability may be perceived as 'standard setters' because they best exemplify what is expected of group members in the long term. Monteil and Michinov (1996) found that the social value of the dimension of comparison (socially valued or inferior) was an important determinant of social comparison strategies (i.e. upward or downward). These findings are not dissimilar from the idea that comparison is motivated by a 'unidirectional drive upward' (Festinger 1954: 125), meaning that individuals will select for observation those who actually display the abilities and opinions they aspire to. However, Festinger did not spell out exactly how far the degree of interpersonal discrepancy could go before it would signify non-comparability. His theory would lead us to expect that individuals aspire to adopt attitudes and behaviours not too divergent from their own, whereas in Turner's theory comparability is given by the categorization criterion (i.e. ingroup versus non-ingroup/outgroup). Thus nurses are more likely to compare themselves on a personal level with other nurses (ingroup members) than with doctors (non-ingroup or outgroup members); students are more likely to compare themselves with other students rather than with their lecturers.

Another difference between theories lies in the interpretation of the origins of uncertainty. Traditionally, it has been seen to arise from the objective ambiguity of the stimulus situation yet uncertainty can arise even when circumstances are totally non-ambiguous (Hogg and Abrams 1988). For Turner, uncertainty stems from an awareness of disagreement between those among whom mutual agreement is expected. If disagreement exists between members of different groups, there is less cause for uncertainty and therefore less inclination to conform (Hogg and Abrams 1988).

Relatively 'automatic' psychological impact of social categories

The referential informational influence analysis presupposes that the influence process occurs automatically upon category assignment. Evidence for this can be derived from studies demonstrating conformity (i.e. behaviour becomes more normative) as a function of mere reference group salience (e.g. Hogg and Abrams 1987; Reicher 1984). This is likely to be situation-specific (see also Boyanowsky and Allen 1973). For example, referential informational influence explains the immediate almost transformational impact of role assignment on attitudes and behaviour consistent with the associated stereotype (Zimbardo 1971, 1972).

Zimbardo's study illustrates what Turner (1982a: 33; Turner et al. 1987: 53) would describe as internalization of a 'preformed' social category – a category which is already 'culturally available'. Studies of career choice

and socialization process are consistent with this idea. Van Maanan (1976), for example, defines the group entry process as 'anticipatory': people enter groups – especially professional groups – whose values they perceive to be congruent with their self-concepts (see e.g. Kelman 1974; West and Nicholson 1989). To this extent it might be argued that people 'precategorize' themselves according to culturally available and historically originated prototypes: a form of self-stereotyping par excellence. Indeed there is some support for this in the idea of 'self-to-prototype-matching' (Niendenthal *et al.* 1985; Setterland and Niendenthal 1993) and the finding that social situations are cognitively represented in terms of the typical person who would be found in them (Cantor and Mischel 1979).

Anticipatory self-categorization processes

Specifically, Niendenthal and colleagues have shown that individuals seek out situations they believe to be self-defining and in which they receive self-verifying feedback. From their findings they claim that

individuals imagine the typical person who would be found in each of the situation options . . . then compares the defining traits of the prototypes with those of him or herself and selects the product, situation or institution associated with the greatest similarity between self and the prototypic person-in-situation.

(Setterland and Niendenthal 1993: 269–70)

Ψ Case study

Potency of roles in a simulated prison

To examine the extent to which personal and situational factors influence individuals, Philip Zimbardo (1972) constructed a simulated prison in the basement of Stanford University Psychology Department. Half the group of male volunteers he randomly designated as 'guards'. He gave them uniforms and whistles and instructed them to enforce certain 'prison' rules. The other half were assigned to the role of 'prisoner' and were made to wear degrading shirts and locked up in cells. It took only a day for all involved, including the experimenters, to become completely absorbed in the exercise. The guards started behaving cruelly and with hostility, devising rigorous and debilitating routines for the prisoners. The prisoners either broke down, became apa-

thetic or actively rebelled. In the words of Zimbardo (1972) there emerged 'a growing confusion between reality and illusion, between role-playing and self-identity'. Although the exercise was originally planned to run for two weeks, it had to be closed down 'because what we saw was frightening. It was no longer apparent to us or most of our subjects where they ended and their roles began. The majority had indeed become "prisoners" and "guards", no longer able to clearly differentiate between role-playing and self' (Zimbardo 1971: 3). This highly controversial simulation exercise demonstrated above all that a simple and hypothetical role could very quickly evolve into a social reality for individuals, whose identities got caught up and could not be distinguished from the roles they were playing.

ψ Case study

Assimilation of 'new' into 'old'

There is some evidence that trainees see themselves as constituting a different group from that of their qualified colleagues. In Moreland's (1985) experiment, existing members were perceived and treated by new recruits as an outgroup. Only after a series of interactions between them during scheduled meetings, did assimilation of the ingroup with the so-called 'outgroup' (in this instance an aspired-to category) occur. This also helps to explain why compliance-based concerns tend to prevail during the training period.

Self-to-prototype matching is likely to be used when the choices that people make have implications for others beliefs about their identity – especially choices laden with personal and social meaning as in the career context. It is quite feasible to expect that categorization on entry to a group will therefore have fairly immediate and profound consequences for group behaviour.

There is also much evidence from work on trainees to indicate that individuals select their role models according to whom they perceive as relevant to their image of what is required of them. Preconceived ideas operate as filters of information that seems to fit or is perceived as being appropriate (e.g. Shuval and Adler 1980). The important point to note is that these preconceived ideas of information relevance in the training process are shared, which suggests that group stereotypes may indeed be at work (e.g. Sherlock and Morris 1967). Other findings by Ellemers and colleagues (1986) show that aspiring members will try to 'simulate' the defining characteristics of the superior category. Consistent with this is the finding that professional organizations tend to recruit trainees who already conform to or espouse norms and values considered central to the profession (Moreland and Levine 1982). Also pertinent is the fact that recruits may see themselves as similar to other group members on some dimensions by sheer virtue of having been selected as suitable for membership (e.g. Brim and Wheeler 1971).

ψ Section summary

Self-categorization theory argues that normative and informational influence processes are subordinate to a more overarching mechanism called 'referential informational influence'. This mechanism presupposes that the very possibility of influence depends on perceptions of shared group membership. Once self-categorization processes are set in play, an imperative to agree and be seen to agree with other group members is created. Perceptions of disagreement between self and other ingroup members produces discomfort or 'dissonance' which is believed to be resolved via a self-stereotyping process whereby an individual takes on the characteristics and attributes prototypical of the group membership. Evidence for this is provided by the transformational and often automatic effect that taking on a particular 'social role' can have on the attitudes and behaviours of an individual. Additional evidence is afforded by the selective nature of the social comparisons that individuals are inclined to engage in, and also the often anticipatory effect that self-categorization can have in instances where individuals aspire to membership of, and/or are shortly to become members of, a particular group.

1 How far do you think that group membership delimits and proscribes the social influence process in the way assumed by self-categorization process?

2 Are there instances where social influence can occur independent of actual or aspired to group memberships?

3 How does the self-stereotyping explanation fare relative to traditional explanations, as provided for example by cognitive dissonance theory?

Group polarization

Another influence of the group on individual attitudes and behaviour is 'polarization' (Wetherell 1987). It might be expected that a group decision will correspond to the average of the decisions of its individual members. Consequently we would expect the group decision to be fairly middle of the road. However, intuition proves completely wrong. A series of experiments conducted during the 1960s showed that the group decision was not at all middle of the road: quite the opposite. The classic experiment conducted by Stoner (1961) involved making judgements about a number of social dilemmas. These dilemmas required individuals to make a choice between two courses of action, one involving taking a higher degree of risk than the other. The complication was that the higher risk decision was posed as the more desirable option. For example,

Mr B, a 45 year old accountant, has recently been informed by his physician that he has developed a severe heart ailment. The disease would be sufficiently serious to force Mr B to change many of his strongest life habits – reducing his workload, drastically changing his diet, giving up his favourite leisure-time pursuits. The physician suggests that a delicate medical operation could be attempted which, if successful, would completely relieve the heart condition. But its success could not be assured, and in fact, the operation might prove fatal. Imagine that you are advising Mr B. Listed below are several probabilities that the operation will prove successful. Please indicate the lowest probability that you would consider acceptable for the operation to be performed.

(From the Choice-Dilemmas Questionnaire developed from Stoner's work by Kogan and Wallach 1964)

After making an individual decision, groups were formed and asked to reach a unanimous decision on each dilemma. Stoner found that these group decisions were nearly always riskier than the average of the individual decisions made privately before discussion. Hence the phenomenon known as the Risky Shift Effect was proposed: the risky shift was not particular to a type of group or culture.

Hundreds of later studies have demonstrated that the group shift is not necessarily towards a riskier decision. For choice dilemmas involving a large stake a 'cautious' shift is observed. A cautious shift also occurs when individual decisions already err on the side of caution (e.g. Moscovici and Zavalloni 1969). In short, discussing decisions seems to polarize the initial decision tendency. Risky decisions become more risky and cautious decisions become more cautious; the more

extreme the initial judgement the more extreme the shift. The shift phenomenon was renamed **group polarization**, meaning the enhancement of an initially dominant position as a result of group discussion (Myers 1982). Also group polarization is not found to be limited to decisions involving risks. Group discussion tends to polarize the attitudes of its members too. Indeed, the group polarization phenomenon has been documented in a wide variety of social contexts – stereotyping, prosocial and anti-social behaviour, jury decisions, and interpersonal impressions – to name but a few (Lamm and Myers 1976).

How can group polarization be explained? There are three main classes of explanation for the group polarization effect: normative-influence, informational influence and referential informational or self-categorization theory.

Normative influence explanation

The normative influence standpoint builds on social comparison theory (Festinger 1954). Sanders and Baron (1977) argue that there are a number of social values associated with decision-making (e.g. not risking health) and that group discussion heightens the salience of these social values. Social comparison theory predicts that people are motivated to compare themselves favourably with similar others – e.g. other ingroup members. To this extent they will change their stance to fit the most socially desirable position within the group in order to present themselves in a favourable light. The joint effect of these individual social comparison tendencies is to 'polarize' the group position. Some support for this interpretation has been derived from Sanders and Baron's (1977) work (see also Myers 1978) but others have not found that the social comparison hypothesis bears up when tested against explanations from an informational influence model (Burnstein and Vinokur 1977; Isenberg 1986).

Informational influence explanation

One such explanation from the informational influence tradition stems from persuasive arguments theory (Burnstein and Vinokur 1977). This view – focusing on the content rather than the process of group discussions – holds that the main factor underlying group polarization is the exchange of information and arguments. At first individuals will not have access to all of these arguments. Discussion, however, brings all this information out into the open and a mutual persuasion process is said to occur. Myers (1982) argues that the extent of the shift in viewpoints is a function of the proportion of the arguments favouring one side as opposed to another, their cogency and novelty. The arguments *per se*, and as such not the process of mutual persuasion, are said to be fundamental to group polarization effects.

Burnstein and Vinokur (1973) tested this proposition by creating a situation in which subjects had no knowledge of each other's position. Subjects were each informed that they would be instructed as to what position to defend, such that they could never be clear whose position was what. Half were in fact instructed to argue for their own position (ambiguous-for), while the other half were instructed to argue against it (ambiguous-against). They reasoned that those who were able to argue in line with their own views would generate more and stronger arguments in favour of their position than those whose views were contrary to what they had to argue. Thus, significant shifts were predicted in the ambiguous-for (in either a risky or cautious direction depending on the items) but not in the ambiguous-against condition. These expectations were strongly supported.

Referential informational influence explanation

While persuasive-arguments theory tends to fare better than social comparison theory as an explanation of group polarization, neither can explain the finding that group polarization can occur even when holding position information and persuasive arguments constant (Wetherell 1987). Self-categorization theory offers the key to explaining this, and also other findings in the group polarization literature (Turner *et al.* 1987). J. Turner (1991) notes that the group norm is not simply a reflection of the average of all positions therein, but a symbol of the prototypical position of the group. The prototype is the position that corresponds best to what the group has in common, and also what differentiates it from other groups. The prototype (according to self-categorization theory) is the normative reference point for the group and refers to an ideal self-categorization. The definition of the prototype will also vary with the social context – i.e. the distribution of positions within the group – and the differences between these positions and those of the other groups. Wetherell (1987) argues that what is happening when the group polarizes is that group members are conforming more closely to the position they see as normative (most prototypical) of the group. Individuals categorize themselves as group members and internalize group norms. When a situation makes a group identity salient (i.e. in the presence of a relevant outgroup),

the relevant ingroup norms come to the fore and individuals shift towards this in their thinking and behaving (see Hogg *et al.* 1990).

If the outcome of conformity in groups is unanimity and cohesion, a group may be prone to '**groupthink**', described as 'the psychological drive for consensus at any cost that suppresses dissent and appraisal of alternatives in cohesive decision-making groups' (Janis 1972: 8).

ψ Section summary

Group polarization describes an instance whereby a group takes on a more extreme position than would ordinarily be predicted from considerations of individuals' pre-existing attitudes. At one time the phenomenon was known as the risky shift effect, but in later research it transpired that shifts towards the more conservative extreme are also possible depending on the bias or direction of pre-existing individual attitudes. Explanations of group polarization draw upon the social influence literature reviewed earlier. Recent work suggests that referential informational influence processes might be at work in the way predicted by self-categorization theory, in so far as the extreme position adopted by group members upon discussion of an issue reflects the most prototypical position as proscribed by the group's identity. The validity of this explanation is yet to be fully established empirically.

1 What processes are at work in group polarization?
2 Why might it be that individuals change their position into one much more extreme upon discussion of an issue within a group context?
3 To what extent do you think that self-categorization and self-stereotyping processes are at play?

☐ False consensus or 'groupthink'

Janis (1972) analysed US foreign policy decisions made between 1940 and 1970 (e.g. the decision to invade Cuba and the escalation of the Vietnam War) and identified why they turned out badly for the decision-makers (i.e. American interests were damaged). He argues that the decision process could be characterized as 'drifting along'. This drift builds false consensus in the group – i.e. decisions are couched in such broad terms that a number of interpretations are possible so each person will end up with a different understanding of what was agreed. Also, individuals who disagree with the group rarely voice their opinion.

Janis (1972) argues that groupthink is marked by five features:

- the group making the decision is very cohesive
- it was typically insulated from information outside the group
- decision-makers rarely searched systematically through alternative policy options to appraise their relative merits
- the group was often under some stress caused by the need to reach a decision urgently
- the group was nearly always dominated by a very directive leader.

Janis (1972) reckoned that these five conditions generated strong conformity pressures and that it is these 'concurrence seeking tendencies' that lead to defective decision-making called 'groupthink'. The groupthink profile painted by Janis is aptly described by Brown (1988: 159) as one of a tightly knit group isolated from outside influences, converging rapidly onto one 'normatively correct' point of view and thereafter being convinced of its own rectitude and of the inferiority of all the other competing opinions (or groups) (see box). Group members often provide powerful sources of reality construction. If all members give the appearance of total agreement on some issue one may be led to the conclusion that this is the only valid viewpoint. This can inhibit the search for creative solutions and may even lead to a positive rejection and ridiculing of other opinions and their sources.

Similar cases of groupthink have been presented by Hensley and Griffin (1986).

The findings of Griffiths and Luker (1994) in the case study and Janis's (1972) findings would suggest that there is a negative side to group cohesiveness or 'collegiality'. However, Brown (1988) argues that group cohesiveness *per se* is not the cause of groupthink. He believes that leadership style is central to groupthink. Only groups with leaders seeking to manufacture unity become prone to concurrence seeking. Brown reviews evidence showing that tight-knit groups are just as able to make effective decisions as fragmented ones, so long as decision-making procedures still permit a proper appraisal of all the relevant ideas. Vinokur *et al.* (1985) cited in Brown (1988), for example, studied the process and outcomes of discussions at the National Institute of Health conferences in which a panel of experts and consumers meet to evaluate new medical technologies. From participation in six conferences,

Symptoms of groupthink

- The group feels invulnerable. It displays excessive optimism and risk-taking.
- The rationalizing away of non-preferred solutions: warnings that things might be going awry are discounted by group members in the name of rationality.
- Unquestioned belief in the group's morality. It will ignore questionable stances on moral or ethical issues.
- Those who dare to oppose the group are labelled evil, weak or stupid (i.e. stereotyping of opponents in negative terms).
- There is direct pressure on anyone who opposes the prevailing mood of the group to conform.
- Individuals in the group censor if they feel they are deviating from group norms: self-censorship.
- There is an illusion of unanimity. Silence is seen as consent.

- There are self-appointed people or 'mindguards' in the group who censor undesirable information and opinions.

Preventing groupthink

How might groupthink be prevented? Brown (1988) concludes from a review of many studies that groupthink lies in the style of the group leader. If leaders adopt a neutral role and avoid stating their opinions too explicitly, ingratiation by group members can be avoided. The leader should encourage expression of views from minority and deviant standpoints so that a wide range of views is available for consideration. This may involve appointing someone to play a devil's advocate role whose responsibility is to provide a critical appraisal of the groups preferred solution (so long as this person is not used by the group to legitimize preferred decisions).

ᴪ Case study

Groupthink among district nurses

A concrete example of groupthink is provided by a report published in the *Journal of Advanced Nursing* (Griffiths and Luker 1994). The investigation involved observations of and interviews with 16 district nurses (DNs) working in two primary healthcare centres in north-west England. The DNs operated as caseload managers being authorized to carry out patient assessment and make decisions about treatment. Griffiths and Luker found that DN practice was underpinned by 'unspoken' group rules that preserved team harmony and cohesion at the expense of client needs and interests.

The main 'rule' they uncovered declared that it was unacceptable to commit a colleague to anything when carrying out a first assessment visit on their behalf. They could cover for a colleague's absence but were unable to interfere by offering opinions, question their nursing decisions or provide nursing input. The culture in which these invisible rules had become deeply entrenched was one of 'collegiality' (Friedson 1975), i.e. intra-professional respect and mutual support. This resulted in the evolution of a protective norm making it unacceptable to either appraise or criticize one's peers. In the words of Griffiths and Luker (1994: 1042) 'the reason for not challenging a colleague's treatment decisions become an excuse for evasion when faced with the uncomfortable prospect of creating friction between colleagues'. Thus intra-group relationships are smoothly managed but to what effect? Griffiths and Luker (1994) found that the DN culture inhibited the possibility of patient involvement and choice in care decisions. The DN culture had evolved with a model of the patient as passive and unable to cope with the potentially contradictory opinions of more than one nurse.

Vinokur obtained various measures of the decision-making process, ratings of the chairperson, assessments of the amount and quality of information exchanged and lastly an evaluation of the quality of final policy statements. Quality of outcomes was positively associated with the facilitative style of the chairperson who encouraged full participation. Contrary to expectation, level of cohesiveness was not associated with the quality of decisions made.

Most of what we have discussed so far refers to the influence of a majority on individual perception, attitudes and behaviour. Largely the picture created is one of a passive individual exposed to, and in the main successfully influenced by, the majority rule. This assumes that either conformity or resistance are the only behavioural options open to the individual in responding to majority influence. Are there any instances where individuals can actively influence the majority to change its standpoint? Van Amermaet (1996) argues that a **minority influence** scenario is one that is much closer to reality than the Asch paradigm. It is most likely to be the active minority that challenges the reality we live and breathe on a day-to-day basis. Yet how can this be? The minority group is little in number, it does not have normative control over the majority, and it and its members are more often subject to ridicule than taken seriously.

ᴪ Section summary

Groupthink is an instance of extreme conformity to the group, for the sake of conformity alone. Group members become fearful of going against the grain of thinking and behaving within the group, and the situation can self-perpetuate to the point of dysfunction. Explanations of groupthink focus on the role of the leader in creating such an extreme climate (i.e. where the leader seeks consensus at all odds).

1 What are the symptoms of groupthink? How can this come about?

2 What might be the consequences of groupthink for group functioning?

3 What can be done to prevent groupthink?

Minority versus majority influence

Moscovici (1976) in his book *Social Influence and Social Change* argues that the key to the influencing power of a minority group is their behavioural style of consistency. He claims that minority impact lies in the clarity and strength of their conviction, i.e. the minority position is clearly advocated and consistently defended, despite pressures from the majority.

The consistency hypothesis

Consistency can be broken down into two types: inter-individual (or consistency of agreement among members of the minority group) and intra-individual (or consistency of the position presented by individuals over time). Thus a minority group can influence the majority group (i.e. by promoting questioning and rendering their position insecure) in so far as its members agree among themselves on what they are advocating and continue to do so over time.

A seminal experiment demonstrating the impact of consistency was reported by Moscovici *et al.* (1969) using a variation of the Asch paradigm (1952). After passing a test for colour blindness, subjects participated in a colour perception task in groups of six. The task required them to judge the colour of 36 blue slides, differing only in intensity. Subjects had to name the colour aloud. Two of the six subjects were confederates of the experimenter. In the consistent condition, these two subjects answered 'green' on all trials (intra-individual and inter-individual consistency). In the inconsistent condition, they answered 'green' 24 times and 'blue' 12 times. In the control condition no confederates were involved. Only 0.25 per cent of the control group incorrectly judged the slides to be 'green'. The results however demonstrated the power of the consistent (8.42 per cent of the majority gave a minority response) over the inconsistent minority (only 1.25 per cent of the majority gave a minority response) to impact majority judgements. It is important none the less to note that the 8.42 per cent of incorrect responses on the part of the majority group could be attributable only to a small number of people. There were some members of the majority group who were not influenced at all.

Consistency coupled with flexibility and compromise

Later findings lent some qualification to the consistency proposition. Nemeth *et al.* (1974) found, unlike Moscovici *et al.* (1969), that consistent minorities do not significantly influence majority responses. They argued that consistency is a double-edged sword: in some circumstances minority consistency might be perceived as rigid and unrealistic, thereby undermining its impact. The discussion of opinion statements, for instance, may call for a degree of flexibility and compromise. Mugny and Papastamou (1980) cite direct evidence in support of this point. In their experiment minority proposals presented in written form were far less effective in inducing change when they were slogan-like and uncompromising than when articulated in more moderate terms. 'Rigid' and 'flexible' messages were perceived as equally consistent, yet the latter had far more impact. Mugny and Papastamou (1980) concluded that consistency might be a necessary condition for influence to occur, but whether influence does actually occur may depend on how the consistency is interpreted and the image formed of the minority group. If the image formed is of a minority group that consistently affords a distinct and alternative perspective on reality yet is willing to compromise, then influence is likely to occur. Consistency beyond a certain point is otherwise at risk of generating an image of minority dogmatism and thus a substantially reduced impact of their viewpoint (see also J. Turner 1991).

Why is consistency so important?

Many experiments can be cited demonstrating the validity of the consistency proposition as a description of how a minority achieves its impact. Comprehensive and critical review of these experiments can be found in Maass and Clark (1984) and Wood *et al.* (1994). Little progress has yet been made, however, towards explaining why it is that consistency has the effect it does. One suggestion has been that the impact of a minority depends on how their 'unexpected behaviour' is explained by the majority (i.e. the attributions they make for why it might be that the minority is proposing a non-normative viewpoint) (e.g. Maass and Clark 1984). There is some evidence that if the majority can explain minority behaviour in terms of the psychological characteristics (e.g. crazy, weird, dogmatic) of its members, as opposed to their position on reality, then minority impact is substantially lessened (Mugny and Papastamou 1980). This finding suggests that if the minority position is held to be a viable one (there is high agreement on what constitutes reality by minority members, members are consistent in their advocacy of this position and distinctive in no other respect than their advocacy of this position) then the minority stands a fair chance of success in its influence attempts (Chaiken and Stangor 1987). However, the conclusions of Wood *et al.* (1994), derived from a comprehensive statistical meta-analysis of the minority influence literature, are less optimistic. They note that while consistency is indeed a significant mediator of minority influence, no proposed mediators (e.g. attribution processes) have yet been found to have a systematic effect on the power of minority influence.

The snowball effect

One qualifier to the largely static picture of how minority influence operates is the finding that typically the minority effect begins to show only after a certain period (Nemeth 1982). This has led to the suggestion of a snowball effect at work (Van Avermaet 1996), whereby the potential correctness of the minority stance is consolidated by public acknowledgement that some majority group members have taken up the minority viewpoint. For example, Kieser and Pallak (1975) informed subjects that one majority member had either moved even further away from the minority viewpoint (reactionary), or towards the minority position (compromise) or completely defected towards the minority position (defection). Results showed that the compromise condition produced the most subsequent influence while defection produced the least. If the majority, however, is firmly committed to its existing standpoint (Paicheler 1976), and/or consistently refuses to give in the minority view (Doms and Van Avermaet 1985), the minority influence effect is likely to disappear.

Two-process theory

More recent thinking about minority relative to majority influence processes is reflected in the proposition that they are qualitatively different in the type of influence they bring in to effect (Moscovici 1980). According to two-process theory, majority influence is typified by the conformity paradigm involving normative pressure and public compliance (the individual makes a public judgement about normative reality in the presence of a majority audience). Moscovici argues that this will invoke an interpersonal social comparison process such that rather than pay attention to the issue itself the individual is more concerned with the self-evaluative consequences of presenting a non-normative viewpoint. Once freed from the presence of an audience the individual will probably revert back to his or her prior position. In short, compliance but not internalization might be said to have occurred.

Minority influence, by contrast, is said to evoke a cognitive validation process aimed at understanding why the minority consistently holds onto its position. The focus of attention is on the position itself, such that the majority may begin to see things through the eyes of the minority. This could lead to opinion conversion – at least privately, such that the majority in effect converts to the minority stance. Normative pressures, however, tend to prevent individuals from making their conversion obvious. Moscovici (1980) presents an intriguing set of experiments providing support for this model of influence (see also Personnaz 1981).

Some cautionary notes

A major point arising from the social impact approach is its focus on social influence as a mutual and dynamic process, contrasting with the rather unidirectional and static picture derived from the minority influence literature to date. In the words of Van Avermaet (1996: 508) 'either the majority or minority is essentially a group of frozen confederates [thus] a lot could be gained by paying more attention, not only theoretically but also empirically, to reciprocal influence effects'. Van Avermaet also advocates caution in evaluating the relative validity of dual compared with unitary process approach (see J. Turner 1991 for a unitary process approach to social influence). He notes that research has tended to yield widely discrepant operationalizations of the majority and minority status of the source (e.g. absolute size, relative status) making it difficult to justify making comparisons across studies (see also Perez *et al.* 1995). Van Avermaet (1996) notes that there are as yet no commonly agreed criteria for differentiating between a dual or unitary process model at the empirical level. Finally, it is still not clear that minority and majority influence processes differ (see also Kruglanski and Mackie 1996).

It has been proposed, for example, that minorities elicit a differential amount of cognitive activity and involvement among the majority than majorities do, a proposition that resonates with the distinction between central and peripheral processing advocated by Petty and Cacioppo (1986). Cognitive activity appears to mediate influence effects, but there is little difference between majority and minority sources in the amount of cognitive activity they evoke. Wood *et al.* (1994) found that majorities and minorities could produce influence at both public and private levels. On the other hand, they did find that minority influence did evoke more private than public level effects than majority influence under certain conditions (e.g. where majority and minority identity was defined in terms of group membership). These and other findings (e.g. Kruglanski and Mackie 1996) suggest that there is no reason to believe that there is an exclusive relationship between the source and the kind of influence effect produced. Van Avermaet concludes that any relationship that does arise can be attributed in the main to other characteristics that tend naturally to correlate with the source (e.g. perceived status, power, meaning of minority group membership) and/or the influence setting itself (e.g. intra-group, inter-group), rather than majority/minority status *per se*.

Do minorities facilitate creating thinking?

Nemeth (1986) has proposed an alternative definition of influence to refer to any change in thought processes, opinions and decisions, irrespective of the direction of these changes. In line with Moscovici, Nemeth assumes that minorities evoke more cognitive effort in their targets than majorities do. Unlike Moscovici though, she proposes that this is because thought processes become issue-oriented rather than position-oriented. Issue-oriented thinking, she claims, is likely to induce a more divergent than convergent style of thinking involving the

consideration of multiple alternative viewpoints, even viewpoints not explicitly stated by the minority in advancing its case. Majorities, by contrast, elicit more convergent and restricted thinking and the mere imitation of contrary viewpoints.

Nemeth and Wachtler (1983) offer support for this view of minority influence from an experiment involving subjects in groups of six in a figure detection task. Subjects were shown slides featuring a standard figure and a set of comparison figures. They were required to detect the standard figure in as many of the comparison figures as possible. Two or four confederates named two of the comparison figures — one hard and one easy, either correctly or incorrectly. The results showed that irrespective of the correctness of confederate responses, subjects exposed to a majority of four were more likely to imitate responses than those exposed to a minority of two. Moreover, those exposed to the minority viewpoint produced substantially more novel responses and a higher percentage of correct responses. Nemeth and Wachtler claim that this demonstrates that minorities stimulated a more active and differentiated consideration of the data, affording the detection of more correct and also novel solutions. Since then, Nemeth and colleagues (1990; see also Martin 1995) have argued for the positive contribution of minority viewpoints to creative thinking and problem solving. The impact of

---

 Research update

Dissociation model of minority influence

Mugny and Perez (1991) and Perez et al. (1995) argue that minority groups influence majority group members through a process of social cryptoamnesia (Mugny and Perez 1989), meaning that minority ideas are assimilated into the majority viewpoint without acknowledgement or memory of their source. In short, the content and the source of the ideas become dissociated. The dissociation model presupposes that minority ideas are often so strongly associated with their source that to adopt the message is to assume a negative identity in allowing oneself to be influenced by an illegitimate (i.e. non-normative) source. If, on the other hand, the ideas can be dissociated from their source the majority 'ingroup' members can resist overt identification with the 'outgroup' while drawing inspiration at the latent, indirect or private level. This

'dissociation' process may account for why the conversion effect generated by minority groups, discussed by Moscovici (1976) and Moscovici and Personnaz (1980), is so often delayed. The process of assimilation of ideas is slow because initially they may have been vigorously resisted purely because of their source. Over time, these ideas will have become detached from their source, and can thus reappear in the individual's mind as his or her own.

This perspective on minority influence requires a more dynamic approach to investigation than is traditionally the case in one-shot experimentation. If minority influence operates via a slow and indirect infusion of ideas in the way described here, we can now see how it is possible for *zeitgeists* to be actively created by minority groups despite the overt and strong resistance they most often encounter.

minority status coupled with the originality of minority proposals (so long as they cannot be attributed to dogmatism or minority madness) is also indicated by the findings of Mucchi-Faina *et al.* (1991).

Ψ Section summary

Explanations for the influence of a minority group on a majority centre on the notion of consistency. Evidence is weighted heavily in favour of the fact that a minority group which is consistent in its standpoint (i.e. agreement within the group and also within the group across time), yet willing to enter into a constructive discussion and even to compromise, is significantly more influential than one that is either inconsistent or consistent yet dogmatic in its approach. The influence of a consistent but flexible minority group is also said to be more powerful to the extent that its position on reality cannot be attributed to anything intrinsically negative and perceived to be bound up with the character of the group (e.g. weirdos). Critics have noted that the influence of a minority group is more dynamic than these explanations presuppose, being more appropriately conceptualized as a 'snowballing' process occurring over time. Two-process theory of minority influence argues that minority influence is qualitatively different from that of majority influence: it gives rise to opinion conversion in the truest and deepest sense (i.e. identification and internalization), while majority influence is more likely to be superficial opinion change (i.e. public compliance). At first, normative pressures within the majority group are likely to prevent individuals from displaying the fact that their opinion has been changed by a minority group. The referential informational influence model requires that we note the fact that most influence occurs within groups not between them. Either the minority group is influential because in some ways it is still part of the majority group (only appearing to be different because of its more polarized standpoint) or we need to account for the fact that   influence is indeed taking place across group boundaries, in which case an alternative explanation is required which takes this into consideration. The idea that minorities are influential to the extent they are part of the normative majority is a paradoxical and unsatisfactory explanation,

Box continued

which leaves us with the more probable instance of having to explain how influence across group boundaries is possible. To this end, the notion of opinion conversion as advocated by two-process theory is said to provide the most befitting analogy. On the other hand, there is little evidence for the idea that majority and minority influence processes do differ qualitatively in the way proposed. Some preliminary findings suggest that it is not minority or majority status *per se* that is important, but other characteristics which are correlated with the influence source like the influence setting and the exact nature of what is being advocated. It can be concluded, at the most general level, that minority influence tends to show up on indirect, private and delayed public measures while majority influence is more likely to reflect in overt, public and immediate measures of influence, the minority message tends to generate more cognitive informational processing than the majority message, and that some form of dual-process rather than unitary model of influence is probably necessary to explain these findings (but see Clark 1995 who argues that we should not totally reject the unitary process model).

1 How do minority groups exert their influence? To what extent do you think that minority and majority influence processes differ and in what ways exactly? To what extent do you feel that time is an important factor in the explanation of minority influence process?

2 Compare and contrast unitary approaches (consistency theory, referential information influence theory, and social impact theory) with two-process theory as explanations of minority influence.

3 What other factors might be at work to facilitate the minority influence process?

☐ Obedience to authority

So far we have assumed that influence occurs between parties of equal status, and that influence occurs in a subtle non-directive way. In real life, however, an entirely different influence scenario is created when the source of influence is higher in status, gives explicit orders to behave in a way that contravenes personal moral and ethical principles, and who continually checks whether orders have been enacted.

Ψ Case study

Unquestioning obedience

Milgram (1974) identified four factors that created 'obedience' among individuals in his experiments:

- 'emotional' distance: least compassion was demonstrated when the 'learner' could not be seen. Compliance dropped from nearly 100 per cent to 30 per cent when the 'teacher' was in close contact with the 'learner'. Few soldiers would disobey an order to drop a bomb on a helpless village in a situation of war (a depersonalized situation) but faced with having to kill a single villager many would not fire or even aim the gun at them. People act more compassionately when the circumstances are personalized.

- closeness and legitimacy of authority: when the person making a request is physically close, compliance increases. In Milgram's experiment, compliance dropped to 21 per cent when the request was made by telephone. The authority figure must however be perceived as legitimate.

- institutional authority: the reputation and prestige of the institution backing someone's authority (e.g. Royal College of Nursing or British Medical Association).

- liberating effects of group influence: if one or two others defy authority then it is easier for someone else to do so too.

In Milgram's (1974) classic experiment, 65 per cent of individuals (in the 'teacher' role) administered the maximum severity electric shock (450 volts) to their pupils to 'punish' them for a wrong answer. They did this even when the pupils screamed audibly with pain or when they entered a state of ominous silence. When pressed to continue by the researcher, most of those who did showed signs of stress and anxiety like trembling or nervous laughter. They carried on none the less. At the end of the experiment all volunteers were told the true nature of the research and that no electric shocks were actually administered. None the less, what the experiment clearly showed was that many people will *without question* follow the directions of authority figures even in the case of obvious pain being inflicted on another individual.

For ethical reasons experiments like the one in the case study are not conducted nowadays so there is no other research to back up Milgram's findings. None the less there are many real-life instances of mass atrocity, such as the Nazi treatment of Jews in the Second World War, which provide Milgram's findings with much warrant. In the words of Milgram (1974: 6) 'ordinary people simply doing their jobs, and without any particular hostility on their part can become agents in a terrible destructive process.' In other words, good people can sometimes do bad things when they are in group situations.

Compliance with legitimate authority is common in organizations structured by a status hierarchy. The hospital pecking order is one such organization where some have more authority than others to issue orders. For example, an unknown physician orders you to administer an obvious overdose of a drug to a patient. What would you do? Would you obey? Or would you question

the order? Hofling *et al.* (1966) posed this question to a group of nurses and nursing students. Most of them said that they would refuse to administer the medication as prescribed. None the less when 22 nurses were actually faced with this order, all except one obeyed without question or delay (until they were intercepted on their way to the patient). Hofling *et al.* argued that nurses were following an ingrained script: a doctor orders (a legitimate authority) and a nurse obeys. While Rank and Jacobson (1977) were unable to reproduce these findings another example is provided by the case of 'rectal ear-ache' (Cohen and Davis 1981, cited by Cialdini 1988). A physician prescribed eardrops for a patient suffering from infection in the right ear. 'Place in right ear' was abbreviated to 'place in R ear' on the prescription. The nurse read the order and dutifully put the required number of drops into the compliant patient's rectum: sometimes compliance can take precedence over common sense!

Ψ Section summary

Obedience to authority describes a response to a unidirectional type of influence that exploits a position of high status or power. Generally speaking when obeying, one is complying with orders rather than experiencing attitude change. Evidence shows that people are apt to comply to orders, even when they feel that what they are being required to do is morally or ethically unacceptable.

1 What characterizes obedience to authority? How can obedience to authority be explained?
2 Why might people be prone to obedience even when being required to do something they believe to be wrong or inappropriate?

❑ Inter-group conflict

In-group bias and inter-group discrimination

The largely ethnocentric character of group behaviour was first documented as far back as 1906 by Sumner (Levine and Campbell 1972: 8). Sumner defined **ethnocentrism** as a

view of things in which one's own group is the centre of everything, and all others are scaled and rated with reference to it . . . each group nourishes its pride and vanity, boasts itself superior, exalts its own divinities, and looks with contempt at outsiders. Each group thinks its own folkways are the right ones, and if it observes that other groups have other folkways, these excite its scorn.

(Sumner 1906)

Ethnocentrism is a robust phenomenon evident in the reactions and responses of adults and children alike (see Tajfel and Turner 1986 for a review of adult studies; see Verkuyten et al. 1995 for a review of studies involving children).

Tajfel (1972) argued that discriminatory attitudes and behaviours are rooted in the dynamics of group membership. In short, he construed ethnocentrism as group prejudice by another name. This has since been mostly taken for granted in social psychology. In the words of Hogg (1987: 105) 'ingroup favouritism or discrimination in favour of one's group ... is a reliable and characteristic expression of group formation.' Almost

the entire edifice of social psychology has since arisen out of Tajfel's concern with determining how exactly ethnocentrism comes about and why (see Turner 1996 for a historical review of Tajfel's influence on European social psychology).

Realistic conflict theory

One of the first attempts to locate prejudice in an inter-group model is represented by the classic work on **realistic conflict** of Sherif and colleagues during the late 1950s and early 1960s. Sherif (1966) argued that inter-group attitudes and behaviours will reflect the objective interests of one group vis-à-vis the others. If group goals are incompatible such that what one group seeks is at the expense of the other a competitive orientation is likely to result, thereby predisposing the groups towards prejudicial attitudes and mutual hostility. If, on the other hand, group goals are compatible such that both groups are effectively working towards the same objective (and who may even need each other for successful goal attainment), then it is more functional for groups to adopt a mutually friendly and co-operate relationship with each other. An example of competitive interdependence is given by instances of strike, whereby workers demand wage increases at the expense of reducing the employer's profit margin. An example of co-operative interdependence is provided by different groups of healthcare workers with respect to the mutually held goal of quality patient care.

Sherif's experiments demonstrated the impact of objective inter-group relations (e.g. negative interdependence of fate) in determining inter-group attitudes and behaviours (see also Brown et al. 1986). However, it was still unclear whether negative interdependence of fate was a necessary or sufficient condition of hostile inter-group relations. Moreover, Sherif's work focused on objective interdependence of fate rather than subjective or perceived interdependence of fate. Extending this argument, Rabbie and Horowitz (1969) proposed that the necessary or essential condition for the arousal of group feelings was the perception of interdependence of fate (following Lewin 1948). In their experiment children were randomly allocated to two groups comprising four people each. Members of the two groups were identifiable with either green or blue badges, and were seated so that at first they could see only members of their own group. All but the control group then experienced a 'common fate' manipulation involving being given or deprived of a prize. The screens were removed

Ψ Case study

Realistic conflict

Sherif and colleagues pursued three longitudinal studies said to demonstrate the viability of this analysis of inter-group relations (Sherif and Sherif 1953; Sherif *et al.* 1955, 1961). All of the research was conducted in a boys' summer camp, all boys (aged around 12) were strangers to each other on arrival and had been carefully screened to ensure they were 'psychologically well-adjusted'. This was to ensure that all behaviour exhibited during the camp experience could not be attributed to prior friendship history or psychological dysfunction. In the first two experiments, the boys were split into two experimental groups after the first few days. Best friends, formed during these first few days of camp, were split up so that the majority of each boy's best friends were assigned to the out-group. Each group engaged itself in various activities without having much to do with the other. In the second phase of the experiment, a series of inter-group contests was announced (e.g. tug-of-war), for an overall prize of a group cup and personal penknife for each of the winning group members. Losers would receive nothing. This intervention was designed to introduce negative interdependence. As Brown (1996: 538) describes, 'whereas in the first stage group members had coexisted more or less peacefully, they were now transformed into two hostile factions, never losing the opportunity to deride

the outgroup and, in some instances, physically attack it.' Consistent ingroup favouritism was also exhibited in sociometric preferences, irrespective of the initial bonds of friendship forged in the first few days of camp. Clearly, the inter-group relationship was powerful enough to overshadow interpersonal level (i.e. 'friendship') considerations.

In a variation of this design (third phase), boys were assigned to groups in different but nearby camps. Neither group knew of each other's existence until strategically informed. In this instance, several of the boys spontaneously offered to challenge the other group in a sporting contest. The same kinds of biased and discriminatory attitudes and behaviour exhibited by boys in the first two experiments were then observed. All three experiments have been much cited in support of Sherif's (1966) theory of inter-group behaviour. The behaviour of the boys varied systematically with the changing level and character of their relationships with each other. Their attitudes and behaviour exhibited homogeneity in the way described by the group/inter-group pole of the behavioural continuum, and could thus not be attributed to personality dysfunction or a particular set of psychological traits. The findings therefore raised severe challenge to the idea that prejudice phenomena are rooted in intrapsychic disorders of personality.

---

and each person had to read aloud some personal details about him or herself. Meanwhile, all the other children rated the speaker on various evaluative scales. The results showed clear and consistent evidence of ingroup favouritism on evaluative rating criteria In the control condition, little significant ingroup favouritism was said to have occurred (but see Horowitz and Rabbie 1982). Rabbie and Horowitz (1969) concluded that classification into groups must correlate with a common experience of deprivation or reward, for inter-group attitudes and perceptions to arise.

Much controversy has since arisen from the point made by Rabbie and Horowitz (1969, 1988) that the prerequisite factor for inter-group behaviour is the sub-

jective experience of common fate (Rabbie *et al.* 1989; Turner and Bourhis 1996).

Social identity as the basis for ethnocentric attitudes and behaviours

Social identity theory begins from the premise that the self is intimately bound up with social categorization processes in three principal but interrelated ways. First, upon identifying with a group, the individual takes on its defining attributes – a process labelled 'self-stereotyping' (Turner 1982a) – as described in some detail earlier. Second, individuals derive a sense of self-worth from their group affiliations; they evaluate themselves in terms of the group. The evaluative significance of the group as a whole is likely to reflect on, and therefore have crucial implications for, self-esteem. Third, group memberships hold affective value for individuals – i.e. membership of groups gives rise to certain emotions either positive or negative, leading individuals to have particular feelings about their group membership.

Tajfel (1972: 31) defined social identity as 'the individual's knowledge that he/she belongs to certain social groups together with some emotional and value significance to him/her of the group membership'. It is via an identification process that the individual is said to become attached to, and invested in the particular social groups to which they belong. It is this process that is also said to make it possible for an individual to become socially oriented to, while at the same time contributing to the creation of collective forms of life.

Tajfel (1978) argued that social identity is a product of the workings of two cognitive-social processes – social categorization and social comparison processes – and a motivational principle, known as the drive for **positive distinctiveness**. Each of these processes will be described in turn.

Social categorization

Social categorization refers to a fundamental cognitive process which allows the individual to adapt to their social world by structuring the infinite stimuli in the environment and thereby simplifying perception. An early experiment by Tajfel and Wilkes (1963) showed that when subjects were asked to judge the length of individual lines from a continuous series where the four shorter lines were labelled A and the four longer lines were labelled B, they tended to exaggerate the differences in length between the set of lines A and B. This *accentuation effect* was also found to hold true for social stimuli. For example, in a set of experiments white subjects were shown a series of photographs of faces ranging from pure Caucasian to pure Negro and were asked to rate the degree of physiognomic and psychological 'Negro-ness'. The subjects divided the pictures into white and black and tended to exaggerate similarities within and differences between those faces falling in the two categories (Secord 1959; Secord *et al.* 1959). This basic accentuation effect has since been robustly demonstrated in many studies and extends also to the categorization of attitude statements as social stimuli (Doise 1978; Eiser 1985; Eiser and van

der Pligt 1984). One important qualifier however is that the accentuation effect occurs only on those perceptual dimensions believed to be correlated with the categorization criterion (Doise *et al.* 1978; Tajfel *et al.* 1964) and is most pronounced when the categorization is salient to the individual – i.e. important and meaningful (Tajfel 1959).

Social comparison

Social comparison processes are said to be the mechanism through which social categorization processes derive clarity and meaning, and for the working of the positive distinctiveness principle that satisfies the fundamental individual motivation to achieve positive self-esteem. Social comparison processes within the social identity model are similar to those proposed by Festinger (1954), but are operational at the inter-group (i.e. comparisons between groups) rather than interpersonal (i.e. comparisons between individuals) level of analysis. As for interpersonal comparisons, inter-group comparisons are fuelled by the need for positive self-esteem at work via the positive distinctiveness principle. Thus, in making inter-group social comparisons, we are inclined to accentuate differences between groups along the dimensions on which the ingroup will be more positively evaluated. The result of this are assymmetrical evaluations and behaviours in favour of the groups to which individuals perceive themselves to belong, i.e. in which they have invested themselves cognitively, emotionally and behaviourally.

The positive distinctiveness proposition

Social identity theory is further built on the assumption that all behaviour, whether interpersonal or group derived, is motivated by a fundamental need for self-enhancement. This proposition is not new (e.g. Cooley 1902; James 1890) and is now considered crucial to the construction and maintenance of identity (e.g. Lancaster and Foddy 1988; Schlenker 1982). Since self-esteem at the level of social identity is believed to be mediated by group membership, social identity theory considers it necessary for members to distinguish themselves from others in a superior way to achieve a satisfactory self-esteem (as defined by Fleming and Watts 1980 as a sense of personal worth). Accordingly, the drive for self-enhancement via group membership should motivate individuals to actively differentiate themselves from other group members along criteria that are particularly relevant to the circumstances of mutual inter-group comparison. This presupposes that groups are led into a social contest with a view to carving out a favourable identity for themselves (Tajfel 1978; Turner 1975). This proposition is formalized in the principle of positive distinctiveness.

Social identity theory thus proposes that individuals will favour their group (the ingroup) over and above other groups to which they do not belong (outgroups) and that inter-group differentiation is activated by the search for positive social identity and self-esteem. This can occur sometimes to the extent of outgroup prejudice, inter-group conflict and hostility (Brown 1996).

Much research conducted within the social identity tradition – using minimal group and field work type methods – has since confirmed the strength of the finding that mere category assignment (a cognitive group) is sufficient to engender competition for superior ingroup identity, despite the absence of any true con-

flict of interest (B. Mullen *et al.* 1992). B. Mullen *et al.* (1992) used the results from 42 minimal group studies reported over the previous 15 years to produce an overall effect picture of the minimal group findings. They concluded that 'people tend to see the ingroup in more positive terms than they do the outgroup' and that the 'effect, on average, is of moderate magnitude' (B. Mullen *et al.* 1992: 117). Even nurses, for whom co-operation is an important part of caring practices, show evidence of ingroup bias and inter-group conflict – especially in terms of status differentials (Brown and Wade 1987; Oaker and Brown 1986; Van Knippenberg and Van Oers 1984).

Social competition as the basis for inter-group conflict

Social competition between groups is particularly likely to engender conflict to the extent that the legitimacy of respective status claims is not accepted (Brown and Ross

---

 Research update

Other patterns of ingroup bias

There are several strong indications in the literature that ingroup bias is not confined to measures of evaluation, and that it is revealed in many different often very subtle forms (e.g. Haslam *et al.* 1992b). Examples of this include the 'ingroup over-exclusion effect' (Yzerbyt *et al.* 1995), 'the black sheep effect' (Marques *et al.* 1988), 'ingroup overestimation effect' (Blanz *et al.* 1995) and 'subtle prejudice' (Pettigrew and Meertons 1995). The ingroup over-exclusion effect refers to the finding that people tend to reject ingroup members who are not totally in line with the requirements for ingroup membership. Protection of ingroup membership lends to tougher and more stringent criteria of acceptance to be applied to potential members. An illustration of this is provided by the movie *The Snake*, where Henry Fonda, in the role of director of the CIA, takes numerous and very sophisticated steps to ensure that a Soviet transfuge (played by Yul Brynner) is a genuine friend of the US as opposed to a smart pretender serving the Empire of Evil (cf. Yzerbyt *et al.* 1995). The argument is that people will be especially cautious about accepting someone as a member of their group because of the risk of possible misidentification (and potential threat

to social identity because it may suffer from association with the undesirable qualities of bad ingroup members) (Branscombe *et al.* 1993). Support for this argument is derived from findings pertaining to the black sheep effect, suggesting that people derogate bad ingroup members more than bad outgroup members despite their tendency to favour the ingroup over the outgroup (Marques *et al.* 1988). The ingroup overestimation effect similarly refers to the tendency of people to overestimate the status and size of the ingroup relative to the outgroup in the absence of status and size information (Blanz *et al.* 1995). Pettigrew and Meerton's (1995) concept of subtle prejudice hinges on 'socially acceptable' forms of rejection whereby people comply with the prevailing equalitarian norm, yet express their negative inter-group views under the carpet in ostensibly non-prejudiced ways. So, for example, Dovidio *et al.* (1989) found little difference in ratings made of ingroup and outgroup members on negative attributes (e.g. lazy) yet strong and systematic bias in favour of the ingroup on positive attributes (e.g. ambitious). Dovidio *et al.* (1989: 88) concluded that evidence is obtained for the kind of attitude that states 'blacks are not worse, but whites are better'.

1982). For example, in the nursing context, nurses faced opposition from the medical profession with respect to both current and proposed future changes towards professionalism (Coyle *et al.* 1998). Nurses are seeking to become more like doctors (i.e. an established profession) by advancing claims to autonomy in clinical decision-making in their own sphere of care. They are thus striving for recognition using ordinary 'medical criteria'. The British Medical Association (BMA) responded (to this form of social competition) by voicing its concern that nurses are making a power play in an attempt to create their own social empire (e.g. Burns 1982; Miller 1985). According to some, doctors have a vested interest in blocking the progress of nurses in view of their claims to a higher status 'and the establishment of a well-defined territory for nursing' (e.g Pepper 1977: 30; see also Muff 1982). Pepper (1977: 30) adds that this had led to the doctors guarding 'their power and status in the system jealously.'

Non-competitive inter-group strategies

Tajfel (1978) describes social competition as only one of three means of self-enhancement via group membership. The others are: positive re-evaluation of existing characteristics, and 'social creativity' (Tajfel 1978). Taking the nursing example further (Millward 1991), we can see how nurses are attempting to re-evaluate the existing nature of their role by heightening the value of their 'caring' practices as holistic and personalized, a necessary complement to the technical, less humanistic role of the medical profession. The nursing profession has also been 'creative' in its elaboration of new 'valued' group criteria (Millward 1995). For instance, the 'nursing process' is a method of cared delivery installed for the purpose of making it into a research-based professional science. It was Merton (1960) who pointed out that occupations seeking professional status tend to assert claims to a special kind of expertise in the realm of a 'needed' competence, i.e. one that serves vital functions for society. For nurses this is strongly represented by the ideology of 'professional care' (Millward 1995; Robinson and Strong 1987).

Role of 'aggravating variables'

The aggravation hypothesis is derived from the assumption that when social identity is threatened in some way, the tendency to display ingroup bias and to discriminate negatively against the outgroup will substantially increase (Brown 1984; Mummendey and Schreiber 1984). Threats to identity could come about via low socio-structural or psychological status and societal power, perceived similarity between groups (which threatens positive distinctiveness) and numerical status (e.g. minority versus majority). For example, in their meta-analysis of findings yielded from the minimal group paradigm, B. Mullen *et al.* (1992) examined the moderating effects of proportionate ingroup size and status. In line with the aggravation hypothesis, they found that ingroup bias increases as the proportionate ingroup size decreases, for both real-life and artificial group categorizations. This suggests that minority status (in the numerical sense) is linked with increased tendency towards ingroup favouritism. However, contrary to prediction ingroup favouritism did not increase with disadvantaged status, at least in laboratory contexts (e.g. see also Sachdev and Bourhis 1984, 1987).

Blanz *et al.* (1995) showed that in the presence of aggravating conditions (numerical minority, perceived similarity between groups) group members tend to exhibit ingroup favouritism even on negatively valenced indices, which is something they are often more reluctant to display in the absence of threats to identity (see also Mummendey *et al.* 1992). Consistent with the aggravation hypothesis Harmon-Jones *et al.* (1996) found that raising the salience of mortality among undergraduate psychology students was sufficient to 'threaten identity' and increase the motivation for intergroup differentiation and bias.

To explore the threatened identity hypothesis, Echabe and Castro (1996) investigated images of immigrants as a function of the perceived permeability of ingroup boundaries (i.e. Frontiers Policy). They found that anticipation of open borders led to more negative descriptions of immigrants from Third World countries and that these descriptions could be interpreted as negative reactions due to threatened insecurity. The impermeability of inter-group boundaries (thereby obstructing mass mobility of lower status outgroup members) eliminates feelings of negative insecurity and produces changes towards a more positive representation of the immigrant. Thus support was found for the threat hypothesis.

Can self-interest be ruled out?

The minimal group paradigm has been criticized for not taking into consideration the degree to which self-interest is at work as opposed to cognitive categorization and

Table 12.2 The problem with norms as an explanation of the findings in the minimal group paradigm

Problem 1 The circular nature of the explanation
- Need to be able to predict in advance which of the many different kinds of norms are likely to be operative in the minimal group situation (competitive, fairness, reciprocity); and
- No theory of norm salience at our fingertips to enable us to do this.

Problem 2 Reference to norms is too general
- Norms cannot predict systematic variations in the results obtained from minimal group experiments that could be observed within even one culture (Brown 1996); and
- Exactly what is a norm and how does it work?

identification processes (e.g. Rabbie *et al.* 1989). Rabbie *et al.* (1989) note that although the minimal group paradigm is designed to eliminate the possibility of direct displays of self-interest, self-interest considerations operate at a more subtle and indirect level. They believe that individuals will act according to a reciprocity norm (see Table 12.2), predicting that ingroup members will favour each other. By favouring each other, self-interest is preserved. Rabbie *et al.* (1989) tested this explanation of

ingroup favouritism in two variations of the minimal group experiment. In one condition it was specified that subjects would get only what other ingroup members gave them. In the other condition, subjects were led to believe that they would get only what outgroup members allocated them. This manipulation altered subjects' perceived dependence on each other. Results showed that this had the expected influence on subjects' matrix allocations. Ingroup favouritism was particularly high among those who perceived themselves to be dependent solely on the ingroup for personal rewards. Those dependent on the outgroup, however, demonstrated little ingroup favouritism, and if anything were more inclined to favour the outgroup in their allocation strategies.

Diehl (1989) is hesitant in assuming that the relationship between reciprocity expectations and actual behaviour is as straightforward as Rabbie *et al.* (1989) maintain. His own work has provided some support for the idea that self-interest motives are at work in the minimal group paradigm, but that this was not the sole determinant of subjects' behavioural strategies. For instance, no behavioural differences were observed between those who expected the outgroup to be fair, relative to those who anticipated them to be discriminatory. This suggested to Diehl that there is more to intergroup discriminatory practices than reciprocity norms

 Research update

Complexity of real-world group categorizations

Harstone and Augustinos (1995) argue that social categorizations in the real world are more complex than that represented by the minimal group experiment. Typically, the minimal group experiment imposes a dichotomous categorization that they believe predisposes individuals to adopt an oppositional (us versus them) orientation. Although some researchers have looked at the influence of two (A/B, X/Y) criss-crossed categorizations yielding four groups (AX, BX, AY, BY) (e.g. Deschamps and Doise 1978; Diehl 1989), no one has yet examined the influence of three distinct independent groups. Criss-crossed categorization is typically found to reduce the display of ingroup bias (but not eliminate it altogether), and is attributed to the reduced salience of

any one particular categorization (Brown and Turner 1981). Harstone and Augustinos (1995) replicated the basic minimal group experiment but with the introduction of a third categorization. They found that the three group condition did not elicit bias in the majority of subjects. Lowering the status of one of the groups did not influence the pattern of responding. Harstone and Augustinos (1995) do not claim that this finding is automatically generalizable to the real world, where inter-group discrimination and prejudice is largely a fact of life, even when there are more than two social categories involved (e.g. the Balkans War involving Serbs, Croats and Muslims). What their results suggest is that we need to understand the ways in which individuals perceive, interpret and construct the group context before we can make predictions about how they will behave.

and perceived interdependence. Moreover, as Turner and Bourhis (1996) point out, there is actually very little difference between the propositions made by Rabbie *et al.* (1989) and those advocated by a social identity explanation. Turner and Bourhis (1996) agree that 'perceived interdependence' is relevant to group and inter-group behaviour, but as a categorization criterion rather than a causal factor. It might also be added that if 'self' is inextricably bound up with categorization processes, then self-interest is always at work whether at the interpersonal or inter-group level of analysis. The difference is that at the inter-group level of analysis, self-interest operates via ingroup favouritism rather than at a more personalized level. If 'self' is perceived to be interdependent with the outgroup (the individual subjectively recasts him or her self as a member of the outgroup) then it is not surprising to find that outgroup favouritism is the result (cf. Gaertner *et al.* 1990).

Ψ Section summary

The largely ethnocentric character of group and inter-group behaviour is now well established. Ethnocentrism is characterized by ingroup bias and outgroup discrimination. Explanations for this began with the idea of differences in objective interest between groups, thereby creating competition for resources. This led to the idea that negative interdependence of fate is the cause of ethnocentrism and inter-group conflict. Later it was found that it is not negative interdependence *per se* that is important but how negative interdependence is perceived. This was criticized however as merely redescribing the group situation rather than explaining it. It was argued that inter-group behaviour is underpinned by three sets of processes: social categorization, social comparison and the drive to attain positive distinctiveness. These processes were described as largely cognitive-perceptual in mechanism, but motivational in spirit. It was argued that groups effectively comprise categories against which individuals anchor themselves and their identities. A group in which individuals invest provide them with a social identity. Due to an innate need to secure a positive self-esteem, group members are thus

Box continued

driven to compare themselves with members of other groups, in relation to whom they strive to be better or 'positively distinct'. Thus social identity theory was born. Evidence for these ideas was also substantial since it was clear that mere category assignment was all that was required (in the absence of any objective differences in interest and also self-interes), to engender ingroup bias and inter-group discrimination. The ideas have generated a vast literature ever since, although have not been without controversy (e.g. concerning the role of self-interest in the inter-group scenario).

1 Describe ethnocentrism in a group and inter-group context. How might ethnocentrism come about?

2 What role might perception play in the explanation of ethnocentrism? What role might motivation play in the explanation of ethnocentrism?

3 Compare and contrast two different explanations for ethnocentrism relative to the evidence available. Why has the social identity explanation spawned controversy?

The self-esteem proposition

Hyman and Singer (1968: 13–25) declared that 'the individual chooses a normative reference group so that in fantasy, or ultimately in fact, he can feel himself to be a part of a more favoured group . . . for social comparisons he chooses a group so as to enhance his self-regard.' The point that individuals derive positive self-esteem from their group affiliations is less open to challenge than the proposition that all group behaviour is motivated by the need for self-enhancement. Most problematic is that despite much evidence for ingroup bias and inter-group differentiation along the lines of the positive distinctiveness principle, this has never actually been directly related to the self-esteem of individual members. Social identity theory is in fact not clear exactly how self-esteem and group behaviour are supposed to interrelate. In an attempt to clarify this, Abrams and Hogg (1990) identify two threads to the argument: causal process and outcome content. In a nutshell, low self-esteem should motivate (cause) group members to restore it by seeking positive distinctiveness (outcome).

Most of the research has concentrated on the latter, i.e. the hypothesis that the achievement of positive distinctiveness will reflect favourably on self-esteem (e.g. Lemyre and Smith 1985; Oakes and Turner 1980; Turner and Spriggs 1982). The findings of Lemyre and Smith (1985) are particularly telling. Given categorization, subjects who discriminated (or who sought positive distinctiveness) on the point allocation task scored significantly higher on self-esteem than those who had completed the measures before the opportunity to discriminate. However, self-esteem in the 'no-categoriza-tion/no-discrimination' condition was equivalent to that of the former (also therefore higher than in the categorization-only condition) suggesting that the achievement of positive distinctiveness has a 'restoring effect' on self-esteem. The effect of categorization was therefore to lower individual self-esteem unless given the opportunity to achieve positive distinctiveness in terms of it. This is consistent with the self-esteem hypothesis.

None the less, the effect of categorization has also to be explained. Lemyre and Smith (1985) attribute it to the 'cognitive ambiguity' attached to belonging. Possibly,

---

 Research update

Global self-esteem: a problematic concept

Much of the problem arising from **self-esteem** as a concept stems from the absence of a comprehensive theory that would otherwise facilitate clarification. Most research has adopted the 'everybody knows what self-esteem is' approach, yet this has led to different usages and thus different and sometimes contradictory findings (Wells and Marwell 1976). This of course, indicates problems of measurement. Another confusion is of whether self-esteem is an outcome of, and/or an explanation for, certain behaviours. The former is an observable product (i.e. self-evaluation) while the other is an unobservable motive. The latter may be gauged by considering what behaviours it might be manifest yet this is apt to be circular (see Rosenberg 1979). If self-esteem is supposed to have some substance beyond the techniques used to measure it, what might that be? This is a question beyond the scope of this chapter. However, it is not to say that social identity theory would not profit from consideration of this kind of issue. For now, what does need to be clearer is the type of self-esteem (i.e. global or specific) to be dealt with in group research.

Tajfel and Turner (1979) refer to self-esteem in terms of the specific self-images that arise, this being apt to fluctuate depending on the situation. This assumes that self-esteem is differentiated, i.e. manifest in specific ways. It is context dependent and thus likely to vary. This contrasts with the view of self-esteem as a global entity characterized by stability as opposed to change (e.g. Rosenberg 1979), although it

has been said that both views are relevant (e.g. Fleming and Watts 1980). The Rosenberg Self-Esteem Scale was constructed to measure self-esteem as a global concept while the evaluative component of the semantic differential is believed to tap self-esteem more specifically in connection with, say, a particular group identity. Curiously, in the experiment conducted by Oakes and Turner (1980) on the relationship between inter-group discrimination and self-esteem, effects were obtained on the specific measure but not the global one. This suggests that there is some validity to the distinction being made (see Kelly 1989a).

Hunter *et al.* (1996) argue from their findings that the role of self-esteem in group and inter-group behaviour cannot be undermined, and that the concept is a necessary one in a thorough and comprehensive analysis of the psychological factors involved in inter-group relations. This is not to deny the importance of other psychological, socio-structural and wider contextual factors involved in the evolution of conflict between groups (Hunter *et al.* 1996: 644). In their research, several distinct aspects of the self-concept were assessed before and after real (i.e. non-minimal) group members evaluated each other. The results showed that when Protestant and Catholic adolescents engaged in bias against one another, the esteem in which they held specific self-images was substantially enhanced. However, global self-esteem was not affected by discriminatory practices. These results suggest that the distinction between specific and global measures of self-esteem in the context of group evaluation is a viable one.

they are referring to the inherent lack of meaning associated with arbitrary category assignment. If so, then an alternative explanation of the findings can be offered. Subjects may regain self-esteem not as a result of discriminatory action but the meaning it affords social identity in an otherwise quite meaningless situation. Thus whether discriminatory inter-group behaviour is the necessary and sufficient condition to restore (or enhance) self-esteem remains to be seen.

Research examining the causal relevance of self-esteem is similarly inconclusive. Some have used low status as an indicator of low self-esteem but have not found it to be a significant predictor of discriminatory inter-group behaviour. On the contrary, low status subjects in Sachdev and Bourhis's (1987) experiment discriminated less than those whose status was high (see also Sachdev and Bourhis 1985). It is of course questionable whether low status does reflect in low self-esteem. Looking at self-esteem directly, Crocker *et al.* (1987) found too that those individuals for whom self-esteem was low discriminated less than those (in the same group) for whom it was high. This result is completely contrary to the predictions of social identity theory.

Thus, two issues are raised in connection with self-esteem research in group psychology. First, it seems that positive distinctiveness may be only one vehicle through which self-esteem is gained (therefore meaning for social identity) in contexts otherwise devoid of meaning and/or where no other, less discriminatory route is available (as typical in laboratory conditions) (see also Mummendey and Schreiber 1984). Second, though not unrelated to this, is the possibility of behaviour being guided by a need for consistency or coherence (Tajfel 1969: 92) as opposed to, or in addition to self-esteem (e.g. Breakwell 1986). The finding of high not low self-esteem (or status) antecedent to discriminatory inter-group behaviour can be explained if we assume it to be motivated by a need to align the evaluative significance of the ingroup with existing self-esteem (Festinger 1957; see also Breakwell 1986). In short the self-stereotyping process may automatically gear the individual to align the ingroup with self-perceptions and vice versa. This also avoids the trap of assuming that group behaviour is always in the service of self-esteem needs.

This search for consistency may involve not only bringing self and ingroup into evaluative (as well as cognitive) balance, but also an 'effort after meaning' (Bartlett 1932) or the search for coherence (Tajfel and Wilkes 1963). This suggests that there are likely to be 'many other avenues' from which the group member can derive meaning other than discriminatory behaviour, as well as many other outcomes for the search than positive self-esteem (Abrams and Hogg 1990: 329; Millward 1995). Abrams and Hogg also indicate that the options available will depend very heavily on social context. Thus a broadened view of social identity and its motivational underpinnings is clearly required.

One possibility is that the search for meaning (or coherence) is geared by a general need for self-preservation. This could be looked at in two forms: defensive and assertive (Abrams 1984). The former implies that protective mechanisms of some sort are at work (e.g. Cooley 1902). Indeed, the likelihood is well supported by research showing how influences that might deflate self-esteem are, if unavoidable, rejected because either the message or its source is deemed invalid (e.g. Burns 1982; Kaplan 1982). So, although the group may compare unfavourably with others (e.g. status wise) it need not reflect negatively in self-esteem. For example, Simpson (1967) found that despite low status, psychiatric nurses enjoyed a strongly positive sense of self-worth derived from the successful fulfilment of group goals (i.e. patient care). Here, patient care was enhanced in value as a source of self-esteem while that of relative group status was minimized.

Assertive forms of self-preservation might also be employed. These depend on group members making themselves felt in relation to others. Some kind of recognition or appreciation is sought in order to do so, one way of which is to claim positive distinctiveness in terms of relevant criteria as predicted by social identity theory. Though, as Mead (1934: 208) said, while there exists some 'demand to realise one's self in some sort of superiority over those about us . . . superiority is not an end in view. It is a means of self-preservation.' Thus, positive distinctiveness is merely one route among many enabling recognition or appreciation to be gained. Other routes may include publicizing an affiliation with a more successful group – for instance, nurses could 'bask in the reflected glory' of the medical profession by the mere fact of affiliation (Cialdini *et al.* 1992). Another route to self-preservation may involve intra-group as opposed to inter-group comparisons, whereby individuals assert themselves in relation to others within the group and/or from the fulfilment of group goals *per se*. Either way the desire for recognition and appreciation is addressed.

Research update

Concept of collective self-esteem

Crocker *et al.* (1993) differentiated between personal and collective forms of self-esteem and moreover, they proposed that people differ in their degree of need for self-enhancement and self-protection at both personal and group levels of analysis. They argue that these differences may help to explain why there are contradictory findings with respect to issues of self-esteem in the inter-group literature. Collective self-esteem, they propose, is fundamentally linked with group memberships. Crocker *et al.* (1993) predicted that people with high collective self-esteem will be pri-

marily concerned with enhancing the self via positive ingroup evaluation as opposed to via the derogation of outgroups. People with low collective self-esteem, on the other hand, are said to be primarily concerned with protecting the self, thereby making it more likely that they will engage in outgroup derogatory practices. Verkuyten (1997) tested and confirmed these propositions with a sample of Dutch youth with respect to various ethnic minority groups (see also Long *et al.* 1994). These results suggest the complex nature of the relationship between self-esteem and group evaluations.

Support for these arguments is obtained from findings demonstrating that front-line nurses (as opposed to those in positions of leadership and power) do not necessarily regard the ideology of professionalism to be very meaningful to their sense of identity. They derive self-esteem not from claims to clinical autonomy (i.e. a positive distinctiveness strategy) but from their relationship with clients (e.g. Millward 1995; Perry 1982). Thus it might be clients who represent the vital reference group for nurses, not doctors. These considerations follow from the views of Williams (1984) who argues that there is a distinction between men and women in the meaning of group identity. She suggests that women, unlike men, define themselves in terms of relational criteria like 'co-operation', 'reciprocity', and 'closeness' — a communal style. Men, however, relate to the group in terms of largely instrumental criteria like 'competition' and 'distance from others' — a more agentic style (following Bakan 1966). Thus for women, especially those in the caring professions, 'identity can be given meaning by . . . the activities of care and service' and 'self-esteem can be derived from the group's ability to fulfil its functions or vocation' (Williams 1984: 324).

In a direct test of these ideas with nurses, Skevington and Baker (1989) found that, indeed, two different styles of relating to the group could be discerned, which matched those of the 'communal' and 'agentic' type proposed by Williams (1984). As predicted, the former was more predominant than the latter. They also noted how male as well as female nurses were inclined to characterize themselves in a communal way. This was attributed

to the communal nature of the group which thus determined how individuals will refer to it, regardless of sex. It should be noted too that some females as well as males defined themselves in agentic ways which gives credibility to this interpretation (the findings of Millward 1995 are consistent with this interpretation; see Lindeman and Sundvik 1995 for a detailed discussion of the social identity theory and gender issue).

Recognition of the communal style of relating to groups, and also 'communal-type' groups, acknowledges that there are likely to be instances where group behaviour occurs out of an inter-group context. In this case there may not be a pertinent outgroup available against which to compare the ingroup, or even if there were it might none the less not be used for bench-marking purposes. Brown and Williams (1984) developed these ideas by arguing for the need to consider identity in the context of a broader range of meanings. They argue that a straightforward index of group identification does not do justice to the 'variety of social interpretations or ideologies' provided to the individual by the group (see also Brown 1988: 29-30). Membership of a particular group could hence afford a number of different meanings, all leading to an equally strong sense of group-level or social identification.

While the idea of social identity as a group replicant shows how members might come to adopt its frame of reference as their own, it assumes that there is only one way to be a group member and that is prescribed within the confines of a stereotype. Moreover, it implies that group members will all be party to the same kinds of interpretations of their membership. Yet it is possible that there will arise several different interpretations of the same objective group reality because of the wide repertoire of meanings available to members of even the same social group (Hogg and Abrams 1988; Skevington and Baker 1989). In his work on Jewish identity Herman (1977) maintains an empirical distinction between the identity of the group and that reflected in individual members. What, for them, he asks, is the meaning of being a Jew? It further requires that a separation be made of 'abstract conceptual formulations of identity [from the] subjectively experienced sense of self-in-relation-to-reality' (Robertson 1980: 151). Theoretically, then, it might be more profitable to address the notion of social identity as an issue of meaning (Kelly 1989).

ψ Section summary

The idea that all group behaviour is driven by a need for positive self-esteem has generated much debate. It is clear that we actually know very little about how self-esteem and group behaviour interrelate. Is self-esteem a cause or consequence of ethnocentrism? This question cannot be definitively answered. Research suggests that self-esteem may be only one of many other motivational factors involved in group behaviour. For example, the need for meaning, or search for ingroup coherence, may be at work. The concept of self-esteem can in itself be shown to be problematic and not readily transported into the group literature in the way pursued by social identity theory. Moreover, we have to reckon with the idea of collective self-esteem in association with group status, as opposed to self-esteem in the classic intra-individual sense. It is suggested that collective self-esteem might be interrelated with the meaning of group membership, and that different groups might have different types of ideological orientation that in turn promote different types of inter-group coping strategies. In short, positive distinctiveness might not be the only way in which groups achieve self-esteem, and moreover, a different kind of self-esteem might be at work than originally presupposed. In addition, group behaviour might be driven by needs other than self-

esteem, like the search for meaning. The self-esteem issue prompts a need for reconsideration of how intra-individual and group processes interrelate. Evidence demonstrating that contrary to the predictions of social identity theory, group identification is not always a strong predictor of ethnocentric attitudes and behaviours, suggests that other as yet unexplained factors are at work.

1   Is all group behaviour a function of the need for positive self-esteem? What other kinds of motivation or need might drive a group to behave ethnocentrically?

2   To what extent is it possible for group members to attain self-esteem via non-ethnocentric routes? What is the relationship between individual and collective self-esteem, and between individual and group identity? Might self-esteem (collective or individual) be merely a product, rather than a cause of, ethnocentrism? What is the expected relationship relative to the actual relationship between group identification and ethnocentric attitudes and behaviour?

Box continued

🔲 Is social discrimination the same as prejudice?

Mummendey (1995) argues that social discrimination prompted by the need for positive distinctiveness is not the same as prejudice. He notes that prejudice often involves hostility to the point of extreme violence (persecutions, oppressions and other such emotional and physical injuries). The kind of social discrimination invoked in the laboratory context is clearly and obviously not on a par with the kinds of maltreatments observed in real life in association with ethnocentric attitudes and actions. So how far does the minimal group experiment go with helping us to explain ethnocentric 'atrocities'? Mummendey (1995) answers: not very far at all. For one thing, positive distinctiveness does not necessarily lead to social discrimination within the laboratory context, let alone atrocity. On the basis of much empirical evidence he advocates that this 'old couple' (positive distinctiveness and social discrimination) – functionally linked constructs within social identity theory – should now contemplate becoming more 'independent' of each other.

Mummendey (1995) further argues that categorization and social identity effects do not extrapolate to inter-group behaviour involving aversive stimuli, i.e. a positive–negative asymmetry is observed in social discrimination tendencies. While people do not hesitate to favour the ingroup on positively evaluated criteria (e.g. allocate more money to ingroup members than to outgroup members), they do not do so on negatively evaluated criteria (e.g. imposing negative burdens) – instead 'fairness' prevails. This suggests that the minimal group experiment is not able to explain the more profound forms of social discrimination evident in everyday life. Only under additional stress on social identity (extremely aggravating conditions) will outgroup discrimination arise in the negative domain where the threshold for discrimination seems to be much higher. Mummendey advocates that we look more closely at the 'aggravating' conditions that do prompt inter-group conflict and hostility beyond the kind of social discrimination observed in the laboratory context.

Ψ Section summary

Critics have argued that social identity theory cannot explain real atrocities or real-life conflict between groups, and that the kind of discriminatory behaviour displayed in a laboratory context is not the same as that evidenced for real. In support of this, evidence is cited for people's reluctance to discriminate openly between groups (at least in laboratory settings or research settings) using negative stimuli (e.g. imposing negative burdens). Critics thus conclude that social identity theory needs to undergo a reality check and that it would be profitable to seek alternative or complementary explanations for inter-group conflict of the real, often highly atrocious kind.

1 How far does social identity theory explain real life ethnocentrism?

2 To what extent do we need to contemplate alternative or complementary explanations for inter-group conflict, particularly of the extremely hostile and atrocious kind?

☐ Inter-group co-operation

Much research has been conducted in the attempt to identify the conditions of inter-group co-operation rather than conflict. This of course is an especially pertinent issue in collaborative healthcare. One suggestion is that inter-group conflict and rivalry can be minimized by reducing the salience of ingroup boundaries and increasing the salience of interpersonal ones (Hewstone and Brown 1986). This can occur when members of different groups have contact with each other on a regular basis. However, this is found to be successful only to the extent that group members are of equal status and where there is institutional or organizational support (external context) for co-operation (Brown 1988). More recently, this approach has been directed by the re-categorization model of integrated working. In other words, group members within, say, a team might be encouraged to re-categorize themselves in the broader terms required of effective teamwork (Gaertner et al. 1990).

A related line of inquiry is based on the idea of increasing the salience of superordinate shared goals (Brown and Wade 1987; Oaker and Brown 1986). Research shows that it is important that the outcomes of collaborative endeavours are positive. If shared goals are not achieved, 'blame' may be cast on the outgroup (nurses may blame doctors and doctors may blame nurses). A way to prevent this occurring is to increase the salience of distinctive group contributions to inter-group (e.g. multidisciplinary) ventures so that identities are not threatened by blurred group boundaries. Brown (1988: 211) writes 'groups which have a common interest in uniting or even just working together more closely may be well-advised to think carefully about how to allow each group to retain something of its identity in the joint operation.' Research reported by Van Oudenhoven et al. (1996) involving Dutch secondary school children confirms that outgroup attitudes are more likely to become positive in conditions where ethnic categorizations are increased in salience during positive interaction experiences with a single member of the outgroup category. They cite the following quotation from work conducted in the early 1940s reaching the same conclusions 'only if a psychological linkage is made between the image of specific individuals and the stereotype of a certain group, only when the individuals can be perceived as "typical representatives" of that group, is the experience with individuals likely to affect the stereotype' (Lewin 1943: 58).

ψ Section summary

Considerable effort has been made to identify the conditions of inter-group co-operation rather than conflict. Explanations and solutions vary. All however build on the assumption that the main block to co-operation is the inclination to self-categorize and identify with one group rather than another. Solutions involve reducing the salience of inter-group boundaries by promoting interpersonal contact, and/or creating a superordinate category with which two or more groups can identify thereby minimizing the salience of subordinate group boundaries.

1   How can inter-group co-operation be facilitated? What role is played by enhancing opportunities for contact between members of different groups?
2   Will contact minimize the salience of category boundaries or enhance them?
3   How can superordinate groups be created? To what extent can the creation of superordinate groups encourage inter-group co-operation?

☐ Inter-group perceptions

Many studies have examined how membership in a group influences people's perceptions and judgements of others. Group membership is found to influence evaluations such that people tend to attribute positive attributes and favourable task outcomes to members of their own group yet negative attributes and outcomes to members of other groups (Brewer and Kramer 1985; Hewstone 1990; B. Mullen *et al.* 1992). Attribution research has also demonstrated how attributions can maintain group stereotypes and other category-based perceptions and judgements (Pettigrew 1979; see also Chapter 11). This kind of research highlights the often motivated basis of group perception and judgement. Here we focus on asymmetry in perception as a means of exploring the motivational basis of group perception and perceptual bias.

Asymmetrical perceptions

Self-categorization theory (Turner *et al.* 1987) leads us to predict that people will typically accentuate similarities among stimuli falling within the same category and accentuate differences between stimuli falling in different categories – especially on dimensions subjectively perceived to be correlated with the categorization criterion (e.g. Doise 1978; Eiser 1985; Tajfel and Wilkes 1963). In other words, categorization of self and others, at the level of ingroup and outgroup, accentuates group stereotypicality or homogeneity (Turner 1982a, 1985). Both ingroup and outgroup members are thus 'depersonalized' (no longer perceived as unique individuals but as psychologically interchangeable with other ingroup or outgroup members). On this basis we can then expect that ingroup and outgroup homogeneity perceptions will be fairly equal, particularly on criterial dimensions. However an extensive literature is now available demonstrating that, to the contrary, group homogeneity perceptions are most typically asymmetrical (e.g. Brown 1996; Lorenzi-Cioldi 1993).

Two types of perceptual asymmetry have been documented. The first type of asymmetry has been labelled the outgroup homogeneity effect (Ryan and Judd 1992). In this instance the finding is that, irrespective of the type of group (ad hoc or real life) and the varying procedures used to elicit perceptions, individuals tend to perceive less variability among members of outgroups than among members of ingroups (Linville and Jones 1980; Linville *et al.* 1986; Park and Rothbart 1982; Quattrone and Jones 1980). The second type of asymmetry has been labelled the ingroup homogeneity effect (Brown and Millward 1993; Simon 1992a, 1992b; Simon and Brown 1987; Simon and Pettigrew 1990). In this instance, the finding is that under particular circumstances (e.g. of ingroup perceived vulnerability or threat), individuals tend to attribute less variability among members of ingroups than among members of outgroups (see Brown 1996, for a review).

Information availability and focus

Both types of asymmetry are said to be equally valid given the group and inter-group circumstances underpinning them (Brown 1996; Brown and Millward 1993). How can asymmetries be explained? Historically, most theoretical work on this issue was focused on explaining the outgroup rather than the ingroup homogeneity effect (Judo and Park 1988; Linville *et al.* 1989). The argument begins with a simple observation about self-alignment. Alignment to one category rather than another will determine not only cognitive orientation but also the type of information available to ingroup relative to outgroup members. Judd and Park (1988), for example, note that being a member of a particular category presupposes the availability of information about particular group members (exemplar-level information) whereas orientation to the non-membership category presupposes the availability of only group-level information or stereotypical abstractions. They point out that from this standpoint it is inevitable that judgements of intra group variability will highlight the heterogeneity of the ingroup relative to the outgroup.

On the same lines Linville et al. (1989) argued that interactions with ingroup members will take place more frequently and in a greater variety of contexts than interactions with outgroup members. Hence, greater familiarity with the ingroup should lead to more complex and differentiated category representations (i.e. to less perceived or assumed homogeneity) for ingroup members than for outgroup members. Linville and colleagues reported four studies, three of which provided support for this familiarity model. In the fourth experiment (a rare longitudinal study) there was evidence that this perceived ingroup heterogeneity increased over time consistent with the development of greater acquaintanceship with fellow ingroup members. However, a computer simulation designed to explain the results suggested a qualification to the straightforward familiarity hypothesis. The findings from this implied that ingroup variability effects would be greatest when ingroup members have been exposed to many exemplars of their group relative to exemplars of the outgroup. If, on the other hand, ingroup and outgroup members are both highly familiar with members of each respective group, then it is unlikely that asymmetry in homogeneity perceptions will be demonstrated.

The effects of cross-categorization

Cross-cutting membership status has only recently received systematic research attention (Marcus-Newhall et al. 1993). One suggestion is that cross-cutting status poses a threat to group distinctiveness and social identity (Brown and Smith 1987; Deschamps and Brown 1983). When social identity is threatened, group members will be increasingly motivated to positively differentiate their group from others in the inter-group matrix. Cross-categorized group members may therefore search for or

construct unique ways of positively differentiating themselves *vis-à-vis* their two parent groups. Effectively then, cross-categorized group members are induced to form inter-group comparisons (Tajfel 1978; Turner 1978). Cross-cutting in addition to minority status might in this case signify a double-dose of threat to group members, suggesting that they may be motivated to heighten their perceived homogeneity relative to their primary reference groups over time in order to carve out a strong and distinct social identity.

However, others argue that cross-categorized group status can reduce the salience of social categorization thereby promoting a more personalized basis for interaction (Marcus-Newhall et al. 1993). Personalized, rather than category-based, perceptions of others within the cross-categorized inter-group matrix will imply a reduction in perceived similarity of ingroup members and an increase in perceived similarity between members of different categories. Effectively, then, group members are induced by circumstances to form interpersonal rather than inter-group comparisons, and to thus ignore category boundaries. The findings of Brettencourt et al. (1992) show that the likelihood of inter-group competition and social identity driven group behaviour is considerably minimized under conditions of personalization.

Marcus-Newhall et al. (1993) assessed the relative validity of each of these two sets of predictions in an experiment designed to simulate conditions of cross-categorization. Their findings showed that cross-categorization will minimize the salience of group boundaries in conditions that afford the opportunity for personalization and individuation. Under these conditions ingroup members are significantly less inclined to display inter-group differentiation tendencies. In instances of cross-categorization without the opportunity for individuation, group boundaries become more rather than less salient, thus prompting social identity driven evaluative differentiation processes (Marcus-Newhall et al. 1993). It would appear from this that the critical determinant of whether the cross-categorized group will become preoccupied with carving out a distinct identity of its own is whether its members have the opportunity to interact in a personalized fashion. Thus an alternative prediction is that in addition to the likelihood of heightened cognitive-familiarity of ingroup members over time, cross-categorized status will not only reduce the salience of category boundaries and therefore the inter-group level of comparison but also heighten possibilities for individuation and personalization across group boundaries.

Section summary

Studies of inter-group perception find that typically this is characterized by asymmetry. Asymmetry is particularly evident in the extent to which groups attribute homogeneity to each other. Both ingroup homogeneity (i.e. attribute more homogeneity to the ingroup than the outgroup) and outgroup homogeneity (i.e. attribute more homogeneity to the outgroup than the ingroup) effects have been documented. Various explanations have been sought for how asymmetry comes about including the relative availability of information about ingroup and outgroup members, threatened identities and the relative salience of group level self-categorizations. The self-categorization explanation provides the most parsimonious explanation for both ingroup and outgroup homogeneity effects, while the other explanations are most appropriate for one or other kind of homogeneity effect. It is possible that all three explanations have a part to play in explaining asymmetry effects.

Box continued

1 What kinds of perceptual asymmetries have been observed in an inter-group context? How can these asymmetries be explained?
2 What kinds of weaknesses can be identified in each of the explanations offered?

❏ Collective action

Strategies of social change

Most real world inter-group processes are predicated on differential status and power relations: 'society comprises social categories which stand in power and status relations to one another' (Hogg and Abrams 1988: 14). Here status refers to the outcome of an inter-group comparison and as such is a relative concept. What are the consequences for self-esteem and social identity for a group in a position of subordinate status and power? Low status does not necessarily imply low self-esteem. According to social identity theory, subordinate groups should be more motivated to carve out a positively distinct identity than groups of superior status. However

Ψ Case study

Individualistic strategies of social change

Tajfel (1978) notes that one way in which an individual can achieve a positive self-esteem is by leaving the subordinate group. The term used for this kind of strategy is disidentification with the ingroup. In this case, individuals distance themselves not only physically but also psychologically from the ingroup. The classic studies by Clark and Clark (1947) demonstrated that black children in the USA were more strongly identified with white children, and a preference for the dominant white group. This finding has since been replicated with other ethnic minority groups (Aboud 1988). Ellemers et al. (1986) studied disidentification phenomena experimentally by creating high status and low status groups between which movement was either permitted (Permeable) or not (Impermeable). The permeability condition had greater effects on low status group members who took the chance to move out of a position

of inferiority to a position of superiority. Under these conditions, group identification was significantly decreased. Mobility across group boundaries was particularly evident among the most able group members, perhaps because they were more confident of their chances to move up the social scale. Hogg and Abrams (1988) point out that this strategy is convenient for dominant groups because it leaves power and status relations basically unchanged. Lui et al. (1995) provide an example of this in their work on dating practices crossing inter-group ethnic boundaries. They found that 'physical attractiveness' was the key to individual mobility strategies via dating and marriage. To the extent that some individuals do 'marry into' the dominant group, the basic power relations between ethnic groups is still fundamentally maintained thereby reinforcing the stability of multi-ethnic social hierarchies (Sidanius 1993).

the reverse effect is ordinarily found: high status groups are more likely to discriminate in favour of the ingroup than low status groups (Sachdev and Bourhis 1985, 1987). According to Tajfel and Turner's (1986) model of individual and social change strategies, group members may not necessarily choose to use discriminatory strategies as their means of achieving enhanced status and self-esteem. They may restrict the comparisons they make to other groups similar in status, such that the outcome of their inter-group comparisons are more favourable to ingroup esteem (i.e. positive re-evaluation of existing characteristics), or they may create new dimensions of comparison against which to evaluate themselves (i.e. social creativity). Both these strategies were described earlier when discussing the ways in which group members can construct a positive identity for themselves.

Alternatively group members may choose to be instrumental in creating social change. The efforts of many feminist groups can be seen as exemplars of this kind of strategy in action (Kelly and Breinlinger 1996) – collective action par excellence. Wright *et al.* (1990: 995) define collective action as an instance where 'a group member engages in collective action anytime that he or she is acting as a representative of the group and the action is directed at improving the conditions of the entire group'. Kelly and Breinlinger (1996) note from their analysis of social movements within Britain during the 1990s that collective action is commonly seen as inappropriate, and that common perceptions of society activists are largely unfavourable. They attribute this in part to the *zeitgeist* of individualism in contemporary British society.

Relative deprivation theory

Runciman (1966) claimed that social unrest among subordinate groups is generated by a sense of relative deprivation, i.e. perceived inequality in what one has and what one feels entitled to. Perceived discrepancy can arise from comparisons with other groups or with one's own group in the past when conditions were better. Runciman (1966) proposes that people will perceive themselves to be relatively deprived of a valued object if they do not have it, they see other people having it (which may include self in the past), they want it, and consider it feasible that they should have it and/or that they are entitled to have it (Crosby 1976). Walker and Pettigrew (1984) distinguish between personal and collective feelings of deprivation. They argue that if a gap is revealed between personal-level achievements and aspirations, individuals are likely to feel motivated to move away from this

Plate 12.3   When deprivation is attributed to collective fate, rather than personal reasons, the probability of collective agitation or social unrest is much more likely

position to pursue change for and by themselves. If, rather, the deprivation is attributed to collective fate (rather than attributed to personal reasons) then the probability of collective agitation or social unrest is much more likely. Research has confirmed that it is a collective perception of inequity and discontent as a result of disadvantaged inter-group comparison that is most often (although not necessarily strongly) tied to participation in collective action (see Kelly and Breinlinger 1996 for a review of this work).

It has been suggested that perceptions of deprivation are alone not necessarily sufficient to produce discontent; people must feel strongly – even passionately – about doing something with regard to the inequalities they experience (Petta and Walker 1992). In the words of Martin and Murray (1983) this passion may arise, for example, out of 'deep anger'. Kelly and Breinlinger (1996) point out that these kinds of feelings originate from group memberships with which an individual is strongly identified – cognitively, behaviourally and emotionally.

Relevance of social identities in the collective process

Kelly and Breinlinger (1996) conclude, from their detailed consideration of research identifying what prompts individuals to take collective action, that collective action to improve the position of the group tends to occur as a last resort, particularly when personal mobility is not possible. They further argue that people will pursue those strategies that are most likely to succeed in a specific context, guided more by the feasibility of the different strategies available to them

Ψ Case study

Self-categorization

Reicher and Hopkins (1996) argue that any account of the salience and definition of collective self-categories needs to consider the ways in which both are defined in discourse and settled through argument. To illustrate their argument, Reicher and Hopkins (1996) examined the ways in which different political speakers (Margaret Thatcher and Neil Kinnock) construed the context and categories involved in a single event (the British miners' strike of 1984–5). The analysis showed very clearly that both speakers construed the nature of the event such that their party was representative of an ingroup encompassing the entire population, and such that their policies with respect to the strike were consistent with this definition of ingroup identity. Thatcher constructed a frame of 'democracy against terrorism' wherein the inclusive category is British and anti-strike, represented by the conservatives and the working miners who are defending themselves against the exclusive category of the National Union of Miners' (NUM) executive. Kinnock constructed a frame of 'Thatcherism against society' wherein the inclusive category is the people, is pro-strike, represented by the Labour party and the striking

miners, and defended against the exclusive category of Margaret Thatcher (Reicher and Hopkins 1996: 369).

Moreover, the two political leaders invoked different values as guides for mass action. Thatcher's 'national community' is mobilized with respect to the values of resoluteness, courage and order. Kinnock's 'people' are mobilized with respect to the values of care, compassion and solidarity. It is argued that the category constructions of these political leaders mirrored the ways in which they respectively sought to mobilize the electorate during the strike. Both speakers built up the ingroup in their rhetoric so as to include as much of the social field as possible, hiving off only a restricted membership (e.g. NUM, Thatcher) to serve as the outgroup. This reflects their respective aim of mass mobilization. Reicher and Hopkins (1996) note that much more research needs to be done with a view to exploring how political rhetoric gains effect (e.g. in this context, mass mobilization). The theoretical approach advocated here thus rejects the assumption that mass action is an expression of collective irrationality in the Le Bon tradition (1895, trans. 1947). Instead, the rational and ideational basis of collective action is emphasized (see also Reicher 1996 on *The Crowd Century*).

(see also Lalonde and Sliverman 1994). Moghadden and Perreault (1992) are none the less critical of the assumption that individuals will always give priority to personal rather than group means of mobility. Kelly and Breinlinger (1996: 49) address this criticism by arguing that 'the desire for self-advancement will be most strongly felt where personal rather than social identity is salient.' Personal identity is associated with intra-group comparison while social identity is associated with inter-group comparisons.

Kelly and Breinlinger (1996) found from their sample of feminine activists that the initial trigger for these activists was the feeling of injustice that they then interpreted as discriminatory. This afforded the development of a feminist consciousness coupled with the realization that this experience is shared with other women. Interestingly, the strongest correlate of subsequent behaviour was the extent to which the individual saw herself as an 'activist'. Not 'standing up to be counted' would be contrary to this very important aspect of their identity. The strong sense of gender

identification of feminist activists is also not surprising. 'For strong identifiers, participation in collective action – doing something positive – is central to their social identity, as activists and as women' (Kelly and Breinlinger 1996: 174–5).

Ψ Section summary

Collective action is defined as an instance where 'a group member engages in collective action anytime that he or she is acting as a representative of the group and the action is directed at improving the conditions of the entire group.' In western society collective action can be seen as inappropriate, attributable in part to the *zeitgeist* of individualism. Collective action is one way of securing social change, but there are also others, choice of which will depend on the possibilities presented by society

Box continued

and the prevailing social climate. Collective action tends only to be used as a point of last resort when personal escape or mobility is not possible. For social change to be contemplated group members need to perceive inter-group relations as unstable and illegitimate. These perceptions may stem from feelings of relative deprivation, a collective perception of inequity and discontent as a result of disadvantaged inter-group comparison. Perceptions of deprivation are alone not necessarily sufficient to produce discontent, they must be coupled with feelings of anger, and intimately associated with a group to which an individual is strongly identified. The particular strategies used will depend on which are perceived to be the most likely to succeed in a particular context. The meaning of a group's identity is also critical to whether collective action is pursued (e.g. identity as activists). Recent approaches to collective action include the way collective self-categories are defined in discourse and settled through argument.

1 What is collective action? What other kinds of strategies for social change can be identified?
2 What makes one group more likely than another to pursue a collective route to change?

ψ Chapter summary

- ### Interpersonal and inter-group behaviour

Group behaviour is far from chaotic and animalistic, it has pattern and meaning. The concept of social identity can help us to understand how this pattern and meaning can come about. People, Tajfel noted, display behaviour that can be described along an interpersonal–inter-group continuum. Where people act as group members, adopting a uniform stance in the way they behave, they are displaying inter-group behaviour. When they act as individuals, with their own attributes, abilities and values, they are displaying interpersonal behaviour. Interpersonal attitudes are likely to be highly variable, inter-group attitudes highly stereotypical and uniform.

- ### What is a group?

Groups exist at two levels – psychological (as representations without demographic form, e.g. Martians, ancestors, future generations) and sociological (physical and concrete, such as family groups, peer groups, sports groups, organizational groups). Despite their abstract presence, psychological groups are as powerful shapers of our thoughts and behaviour as sociological groups. Virtual groups, for example, exist only in the ether, yet no one can deny the influence that e-mail, internet and telephone communications and communicators have on us. You can also belong to more than one group at any one time – student, parent, friend, sibling, sports team member, employee, e-mail correspondent, newsgroup contributor.

- ### Group formation

While the North American view on groups embraces a more 'individuals bonded together by the forces of personal attraction' perspective (an intra-individual, sociological perspective called social cohesion theory by Hogg, Turner and colleagues), European social psychology draws heavily on Henri Tajfel's work in proclaiming the importance of the psychological group (social identity theory). Turner's self-categorization theory, a development of social identity theory, has helped further elaborate how and why groups form. Influences include proximity; shared values, similarities and differences; ideas about a common fate or shared threat. Indeed, interpersonal attraction may well be missing at times of group formation, but groups will form none the less. The pivotal role of social and self-categorization processes is discussed. Factors such as perceived interdependence and inter-group competition can also play vital roles in enhancing the salience of self-categorizations at the group level of analysis.

- ### Social influence processes

Social influence processes can be described as the way a person's opinions, attitudes and judgements are changed as a consequence of exposure to the opin-

Box continued

ions, attitudes and judgements of another. As a result, a person can change their behaviour but not attitude, or they can change their attitude but not their behaviour, or they can change both. They might wish to conform to social norms, or they might wish to become more iconoclastic.

• Group polarization

When in a group individuals appear to become even more polarized in their attitudes and opinions. Three theories – normative influence, informational influence and self-categorization – provide the three main types of explanations.

• False consensus or 'groupthink'

Derived from Janis's key work on foreign policy decision-making, 'groupthink' drives individuals to a consensus position that suppresses dissent and the consideration of alternative viewpoints. Factors such as group cohesiveness (or collegiality) and group leadership style play significant roles in the suppression or encouragement of groupthink. Open, encouraging leaders who welcome devil's advocates into their group, while fostering a forum of trust and acceptance of alternative viewpoints, appear to dampen the prospects of ingratiation and submission.

• Minority versus majority influence

The minority is able to influence the majority in many situations. Whereas 'majority' decisions and rules are made quickly, publicly and overtly, 'minority' influence is more likely to be found in delayed, private and indirect public measures. A government might not make a major sea-change in policy, but it may well introduce minority amendments quietly, through the back door once the fuss has died down. Similarly, a majority group may not change its position on a matter of minority interest, but individual members within the majority group may quietly move towards the minority position. Many doctors would publicly agree with the BMA stance that nurses are not qualified to prescribe medicine, but may privately hold views more conciliatory or even contrary to that. The temporal consistency of a minority message may play a significant part in forcing a majority group to both consider and appreciate the minority's message.

• Obedience to authority

The laying down of the individual's own values and beliefs and the taking up of behaviours ordered by figures of authority that are seemingly contrary to these values is well documented. Compliance can take precedence over common sense. It would appear that good people can do bad things when they are in group situations. It seems to depend on the amount of distance from the recipient of the behaviour they are; the closeness of the authority figure; the status of the authority figure; and how many others are also doing the same bad things. While many people would say that they would never do bad things, very often they do because they are following a deeply ingrained emotional and behavioural script – they order, I do.

• Inter-group conflict

Ethnocentrism, or the view that one's own group is the centre of everything and that all things are scaled and rated with reference to it, has been noted to be a fundamental part of group behaviour as far back as 1906. Ingroup favouritism and outgroup discrimination are reliable indicators of the formation of a group. Two different explanations of inter-group conflict are compared and contrasted: competitive interdependence and social identity theory. Social identity theory explanations predominate in the contemporary inter-group literature, hinging on the workings of social categorization and social comparison processes coupled with a motivational drive to secure positive distinctiveness and positive self-esteem. The empirical viability of this theory is critically discussed taking into consideration both the criticisms and the way in which they are being addressed by contemporary developments.

• Inter-group perceptions

'I am sparkling; you are unusually talkative; she is drunk'. 'I am righteously indignant; you are annoyed; he is making a fuss about nothing'. Whereas much research has shown the consistency of ingroup favouritism and outgroup discrimination, new research is showing that such categorization is not as general as previously believed, but is sometimes situation-specific. The degree to which group members know and are familiar with both in- and outgroup others affects the

Box continued

amount to which in- and outgroups are perceived to be 'all alike'. It would appear that internalizing the attributes of one's group leads to a perception that all others in the ingroup are relatively the same as you. Research into group members who cross other groups' membership boundaries suggests that, in such situations, interpersonal rather than inter-group categorizations and comparisons are made. It would appear that perceptions of other groups are more context-driven than simply being cognitive universals.

• Collective action

Social action can occur at two levels – individual and group. An individual, for example, may simply disidentify with a group and leave. At a group level, however, the common *zeitgeist* of the day may rule what behaviours are admissible or inadmissible. Often a sense of relative deprivation – a perceived inequality between what one has and what one feels entitled to – is the motivation behind collective action. But such a sense is not enough. A group needs to have an identity of 'action' before its individual members are able to feel 'permitted' to engage in social activity. Often this identity is drawn from its discourse. On top of this, group members need to strongly, emotionally and cognitively identify with the group before they will engage behaviourally in a manner consistent with the group's identity. The salience to the individual of the context and the group are, some feel, key to whether someone will engage in collective action.

Further reading

● Abrams, D. and Hogg, M. (1990) *Social Identity Theory: Contructive and critical advances*. Hemel Hempstead: Harvester.

● Brown, R.J. (1988) *Group Processes: Dynamics within and between groups*. Oxford: Blackwell.

● Brown, R.J. (1995) *Prejudice: Its social psychology*. Oxford: Blackwell.

● Janis, F.E. (1972) *Victims of Groupthink*. Boston, MA: Houghton Mifflin.

● McGarty, C. and Haslam, S.A. (eds) (1997) *The Message of Social Psychology*. Oxford: Blackwell.

● Oakes, P.J., Haslam, S.A. and Turner J. (1994) *Stereotyping and Social Reality*. Oxford: Blackwell.

● Robinson, W.P. (1996) *Social Groups and Identities*. London: Butterworth Heinemann.

● Spears, R., Oakes, P.J., Ellemers, N. and Haslam, S.A. (1997) *The Social Psychology of Stereotyping and Group Life*. Oxford: Blackwell.

● Tajfel, H. (1981) *Human Groups and Social Categories: Studies in social psychology*. Cambridge: Cambridge University.

● Turner, J.C. (1991) *Social Influence*. Milton Keynes: Open University Press.

CHAPTER 13

Intelligence
Michael Eysenck

KEY CONCEPTS ● concept of intelligence ● intelligence testing ● heredity and environment ● factor theories of intelligence ● systems theories of intelligence

❏ Chapter preview

When you have read this chapter, you should be able to

- discuss various meanings of the concept of intelligence
- understand how intelligence tests are constructed
- evaluate the roles played by heredity and environment in determining intelligence
- describe and evaluate factor theories of intelligence
- understand contemporary systems theories of intelligence

Concept of intelligence

Few areas of psychology have attracted as much controversy as that of intelligence. Some experts argue that intelligence is the most important aspect of individual differences, whereas others doubt its value as a concept (see below). There has also been much controversy about intelligence tests, especially whether they assess all aspects of intelligence and are equally applicable to all sections of the community. Yet another controversy concerns the roles played by heredity and environment in producing individual differences in intelligence. At one extreme, some psychologists claim that individual differences in intelligence depend almost entirely on genetic factors. At the opposite extreme, other psychologists argue that environmental factors account for nearly all individual differences in intelligence. All of these controversies (and some others) are discussed at length in this chapter.

Most people probably feel that they understand the meaning of **intelligence**. However, it is actually rather difficult to provide a good definition. Thorndike (1911) argued in the early years of the twentieth century that intelligence is 'the quality of mind . . . in respect to which Aristotle, Plato, Thucydides, and the like differed most from Athenian idiots of their day.' It was suggested by several psychologists in the 1920s that intelligence is what is measured by intelligence tests. Of more value are definitions which stress that intelligence involves the capacity to learn from experience, and to engage successfully in problem solving and abstract reasoning.

There are real problems with most of the definitions of intelligence which have been proposed. However, a definition which is very much in line with the opinions of most experts was offered by Sternberg (1985: 45) 'Mental activity directed toward purposive adaptation to, and selection and shaping of, real-world environments relevant to one's life'.

One of the most difficult issues relating to the concept of intelligence is to decide how broad it should be. In the early years of the twentieth century, psychologists typically defined intelligence as consisting of thinking, reasoning and problem-solving ability. Since the 1970s, many psychologists have argued that the concept of intelligence should include many other skills and abilities which are important for success in any given culture. For example, intelligence may include the skills associated with being 'street-wise' or being cunning in one's dealings with other people. If you refer back to Sternberg's (1985) definition of intelligence, you will see that it would appear to include street-wisdom.

Explanatory value

Some theorists have argued that the concept of 'intelligence' possesses little or no value. This was the position adopted by Howe (1990a, 1990b).

For the important task of helping to discover the underlying causes of differing levels of performance, there is no convincing evidence that the concept of intelligence can play a major role. So far as explanatory theories are concerned, the construct seems to be obsolete.

(Howe 1990b: 499)

For example, suppose that we claim that Jane is better at problem solving than Jim because she is more intelligent. It could be argued that this is simply describing what we have found, and does not provide any kind of explanation.

Plate 13.1 Some individuals have a high level of general capacity or intelligence, and are generally good across a wide range of abilities, whereas others are not. The level of an ability, such as a musical one, does not therefore depend simply on the time devoted to this ability

Ψ Case study

J.C.A. and other experts

According to most definitions of intelligence, the ability to perform tasks which are cognitively complex depends on the possession of a high level of intelligence or general intellectual capacity as measured by IQ (intelligence quotient). Evidence that this assumption may be wrong was provided by Ceci and Liker (1986). In their study, they were interested in the characteristics of expertise among long-time patrons at a harness racetrack in North Wilmington, Delaware. (Harness racing is between horses pulling a light two-wheeled cart (a sulky) holding one person.) Initial investigation of a large number of these patrons led to the identification of 14 experts and 16 non-experts. The IQs of the experts ranged from 81 to 128, and those of the non-experts from 80 to 130. The overall mean IQ of the two groups was 100. Of particular importance in this study, four of the experts had IQs in the low to mid-80s. One of them, J.C.A., was a construction worker who had an IQ in the mid-80s. These low-IQ experts provide the case study element in the study.

The experts and non-experts were given a complex task to perform. They were provided with information about 50 unnamed horses and an unnamed standard horse. This information was in the form of 14 variables (e.g. the horse's lifetime speed; claiming price; race driver's ability; track size). They were then told to assign the probable odds for 50 comparisons involving each horse in turn being pitted against the standard horse. Ceci and Liker (1986) argued that a high level of performance on this task required very complex cognitive processing, since the performance of the experts indicated that they were considering interac-

tions among up to 7 variables at the same time. As expected, the overall performance of the experts was far superior to that of the non-experts.

The key finding was that the level of expertise shown on this complex task was almost totally unrelated to IQ. Thus, experts with low IQs (such as J.C.A.) performed as well as those with high IQs. Even more surprisingly, the low-IQ experts were using more complex cognitive models to process the information than were the high-IQ non-experts. This happened in spite of the fact that nearly all of the experts and non-experts attended horse races nearly every day of the year.

What is the significance of the findings? According to Ceci and Liker, the findings mean that 'IQ is unrelated to real-world forms of cognitive complexity that would appear to conform to some of those that scientists regard as the hallmarks of intelligent behaviour' (1986: 255).

Ceci and Liker (1986) argued that their findings were inconsistent with the notion that general intelligence or IQ sets major limitations on the development of cognitive skills. Indeed, they wondered whether it makes much sense to talk in terms of general intelligence. Their findings provide only partial support for this view. They did demonstrate that very prolonged and well-motivated practice on highly specific skills can overcome some of the limitations of low IQs. However, it is indisputable that highly intelligent people are typically able to develop complex cognitive skills much faster and with much less effort than those of less intelligence. That suggests that it would be unwise to dispense with the concept of intelligence.

There are various reasons for not accepting Howe's argument that intelligence lacks explanatory value. First, tests of intelligence have often been used to predict how successful individuals will be in the future when studying subjects about which they knew nothing at the time of testing (Kline 1991). Second, consider the range of abilities shown by any given individual. Suppose that the level of these abilities depended solely on the amount of time devoted to developing them. That would mean that individuals who devoted a considerable amount of time to developing some abilities to a very high level would have little or no time to develop other abilities. In other words, individuals who were very good at some abilities would tend to be very poor at others. In fact, however, individuals are generally either good or poor across a wide range of abilities (Kline 1991). This suggests that some individuals have a high level of general capacity or intelligence, whereas others do not.

Ψ Section summary

Intelligence involves skills such as problem solving and reasoning, but it can also be regarded as covering skills relating to street-wisdom. It has been argued that the concept of intelligence has little or no explanatory value, but this is incorrect. Individuals with low IQs can develop very specific cognitive skills as a result of prolonged and well-motivated practice.

1 Discuss possible definitions of the term 'intelligence'.

Intelligence testing

The first primitive test of intelligence was devised by Sir Francis Galton (1822–1911) towards the end of the nineteenth century. However, most of the tests he devised were simple measures of sensory abilities or reaction time, and he failed to measure higher-level cognitive abilities such as reasoning and problem solving. The first intelligence test resembling those used nowadays was devised by the Frenchman Alfred Binet (1857–1911). He and his colleague produced an intelligence test in 1905 which included measures of memory, comprehension, and other cognitive processes. It was followed by numerous other tests. These included the Stanford-Binet test developed at Stanford University in the United States in 1916, the Wechsler Intelligence Scale for Children, the Wechsler Adult Intelligence Scale and the British Ability Scales.

The great majority of intelligence tests are designed to assess several different aspects of intelligence. A few examples of the kinds of items to be found on intelligence tests are given below. Vocabulary can be measured by providing a word and asking people to select its synonym from five or six other words (e.g. DISSEMBLE: assemble; fight; pretend; boast; disappear). Comprehension can be assessed by asking people to indicate the meanings of proverbs (e.g. 'A stitch in time saves nine'). Mathematical ability can be measured by means of simple problems (e.g. 'I have £5 more than Tim. How much money do I need to give him so that we have the same amount of money?') Visual ability can be assessed by a picture-completion task, in which people have to indicate what is missing from pictures.

Characteristics of good tests

Any good test of intelligence has the following three characteristics associated with it:

- it possesses **reliability**, meaning that it provides consistent and replicable measurement
- it possesses **validity**, meaning that the test measures what it claims to measure (i.e. intelligence)
- it is a **standardized** test, meaning that it has been given to large, representative samples so that the meaning of any individual's score can be assessed by comparing it against the scores of others

Reliability

One of the key assumptions about intelligence is that it is reasonably constant over time. Thus, we would expect an intelligence test to provide reliable or consistent measurement of intelligence. The most common way of assessing reliability is by means of the *test-retest method*. Several people all take the same intelligence test on two different occasions, usually separated by a few weeks or months. Their test scores on the two occasions are then correlated with each other. If the test is a reliable one, individuals should obtain similar scores each time, and the correlation coefficient will be high.

There are two other ways of assessing reliability which should be mentioned briefly: the *equivalent-forms method* and the *split-half method*. The equivalent-forms method involves giving two equivalent or comparable forms of a test (e.g. forms L and M of the Stanford-Binet intelligence test) to a large group of people. The scores obtained from these versions of the test are then correlated, with a high correlation coefficient indicating a high level of reliability. Finally, the split-half method involves dividing a test into two halves, and then correlating performance on the two halves.

All of the above methods of assessing reliability have their limitations. The main problem with the test-retest method is that there may be a practice effect, with scores improving on the second testing occasion because of familiarity with the test. Another possible problem is that test-retest reliability may be very high simply because individuals taking a test for the second time remember many of the answers they gave on the first occasion. The main problem with the equivalent-forms method is that it requires considerable time and effort to construct two equivalent forms of an intelligence test (see Chapter 21).

In practice, nearly all of the well-known intelligence tests possess good or very good reliability. Reliability correlation coefficients of about +0.85 to +0.90 are generally reported for all three methods of assessing reliability. There is one important exception to that generalization. When there are several years between successive administrations of a test, there is reduced reliability. This presumably reflects genuine changes in intelligence over long periods of time.

Validity

There are at least three main ways in which we could assess the validity of an intelligence test.

Content validity

The first of these is known as content validity, which can be divided into *face validity* and *factorial validity*. Face validity is the simplest form of validity. It involves scrutinizing a test to see whether the items within it seem to be relevant. Factorial validity is based on **factor analysis**, which is a complex statistical procedure designed to identify the various factors contained within a test. Suppose that an intelligence test contains twelve items which are claimed to measure mathematical ability, plus numerous other items designed to measure other abilities. There would be good factorial validity if the twelve items relating to mathematical ability were found through factor analysis to form a factor which did not include the other items in the test.

Empirical validity

The second and most direct way of deciding whether a test is actually measuring intelligence is by assessing empirical validity. It is reasonable to expect that students who do well in their examinations or who manage to obtain a university degree will be more intelligent than those who have a poor academic record. The assessment of empirical validity involves correlating performance on an intelligence test against some external criterion such as examination performance. There are two forms of empirical validity: *concurrent validity* and *predictive validity*. When information about the criterion is available at the time that the test is administered, we are concerned with concurrent validity. When the criterion measure is obtained some time after the test is given, then we are dealing with predictive validity.

The main problem with empirical validity is that there is no perfect criterion against which to evaluate intelligence tests. Academic performance depends on the student's level of intelligence, but it also depends on

several other factors (e.g. his or her level of motivation; parental encouragement or discouragement; the non-academic interests of the student). These considerations suggest that intelligence-test scores should correlate moderately (but not very highly) with academic performance. That is, indeed, what is usually found, with correlations of +0.5 or +0.6 typically being reported (Sternberg 1985).

There have been several studies in which the impact of non-cognitive factors on intelligent behaviour has been considered. For example, it seems reasonable to assume that the conscientiousness factor of the NEO Personality Inventory (McCrae and Costa 1985; see Chapter 14) should predict performance. Barnick and Mount (1991) reviewed studies on conscientiousness and job performance, and then carried out a meta-analysis based on data from these studies. They found that conscientiousness was a consistent predictor of job performance ratings. Digman and Takemoto-Chock (1981) found that personality characteristics directly related to conscientiousness (purposeful, persistent, well-organized) were associated with higher academic achievement.

Other non-cognitive factors which reduce the empirical validity of intelligence tests were identified by Terman in his long-term study of gifted individuals (see Renzulli and Delcourt 1986). The 150 most successful and the 150 least successful of these individuals did not differ in intelligence. However, the two groups did differ in various ways. The successful individuals were more persistent in the accomplishment of ends, had greater integration towards goals, greater self-confidence, and more freedom from feelings of inferiority.

Construct validity

The third way of deciding whether an intelligence test actually measures intelligence is by means of construct validity. Theories of intelligence generally contain predictions about differences in performance between those high and low in intelligence. For example, it might be predicted that speed of performance on a simple task is determined by the level of intelligence. If that prediction were confirmed, it would suggest that the test used to assess intelligence possessed some validity. Thus, construct validity involves using an intelligence test to test predictions from some theory of intelligence. The main problem with the construct-validity approach is how to interpret the findings if the predicted effects of intelligence on performance fail to materialize. Either the theory is wrong, or the intelligence test is a poor measure of intelligence, or both. However, it is often not clear which of these interpretations is correct.

Standardized test

As was mentioned earlier, standardization of a test involves administering it to thousands of individuals chosen to be representative of the population at large. The information so obtained is analysed so that it is possible to compare the test performance of any individual against the performance of others. The measure that is typically calculated is the well-known **intelligence quotient** or IQ. IQ is a global measure of intellectual ability based on an individual's performance on all of the various sub-tests within an intelligence test.

In order to assess a given child's IQ, his or her performance on an intelligence test is compared against that of a representative sample of children of the same age. Intelligence tests are usually designed so that they produce a normal distribution of IQs. As can be seen in Figure 13.1, the normal distribution is in the shape of a bell-shaped curve with an equal number of scores above and below the mean. Most individuals have IQs reason-

ably close to the mean, with a progressive reduction in numbers as one moves further away from the mean.

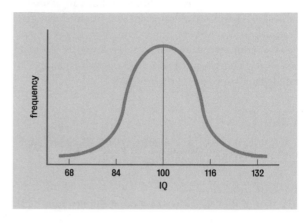

Figure 13.1 Normal distribution or bell-shaped curve of intelligence or IQ

Ψ Case study

Francis Galton

It is interesting to consider the lives of famous people in order to form an opinion of their level of intelligence. This approach (which admittedly is not very scientific) was used by Terman (1917) to assess the IQ of Francis Galton, who as we have seen devised the first basic intelligence test. Terman focused on Galton's early life (he had a very privileged background) and found that Galton was able to read a small book called *Cobwebs to Catch Flies* when he was only 2½ years old. One of his most impressive early achievements was to write the following letter to his sister at the age of 4:

> My dear Adele,
>   I am four years old and can read any English book. I can say all the Latin Substantives and adjectives and active verbs besides 52 lines of Latin poetry. I can cast up any sum in addition and multiply by
>   2, 3, 4, 5, 6, 7, 8, (9), 10, (11)
> I can also say the pence table, I read French a little and I know the Clock.
>
>   Francis Galton

There were no spelling mistakes in the letter. The numbers 9 and 11 were obliterated, presumably because

Francis Galton realized that he did not actually know the relevant tables.

There are numerous other examples of Galton's outstanding intelligence at an early age, but we will consider only one more. According to his father, the following conversation took place when Francis was 8:

I read him an extract about locusts in Peru and Violetta [his mother] said she'd seen lots at Ramsgate. Francis: 'Oh, those were cockchafers.' 'Well,' said Violetta, 'they are the same things.' Francis: 'Oh, no, they're quite different, for the cockchafer belongs to the order Coleoptera but the locust belongs to the order Neuroptera.'

Terman (1917) was particularly impressed that Francis Galton could tell the time, and knew his pence and multiplication tables at the age of 4, whereas most children are about 8 years old before they acquire those skills. Since Galton's abilities seemed to be about double those of the average child, Terman concluded that his IQ was about 200. However, Galton wrote the letter to Adele only one day before his fifth birthday, whereas Terman assumed he was several months younger. Thus, the estimated IQ should have been more like 160–170 than 200. In any case, Galton was clearly an extraordinarily intelligent child.

One of the features of normal distributions is that the spread of scores can be described accurately by a statistic known as the *standard deviation*. Within a normal distribution, 68 per cent of the scores lie within one standard deviation of the mean, 95 per cent lie within two standard deviations of the mean, and 99.73 per cent lie within three standard deviations of the mean. It is possible to describe an individual's performance by means of a *standard score*, which indicates his or her intelligence in terms of the number of standard deviations above or below the mean.

All intelligence tests are designed to produce a mean IQ of 100, and the standard deviation is usually 16 or close to 16 (see Figure 13.1). In terms of the standard score, an IQ of 116 is equivalent to a standard score of

+1.0. Since 50 per cent of the population have IQs below 100, and a further 34 per cent have IQs between 100 and 116, it follows that an individual with an IQ of 116 is more intelligent than 84 per cent of the population.

One of the limitations of the IQ measure is that it is very general. It does not provide information about individual variability in different aspects of intelligence. For example, someone with an IQ of 100 may be well above average on some sub-tests but well below average on others. It is possible with most standardized intelligence tests to extract more specific measures on aspects of intelligence such as numerical ability, perceptual speed, reasoning ability and spatial ability. It is often useful to focus on an individual's specific abilities rather than simply on his or her overall level of intelligence.

 Research update

Inspection-time task

Galton (1883) argued that people who are highly intelligent generally process information faster than those of low intelligence. In order to test this notion, he made use of simple measures of reaction time. However, as we have seen, these measures did not assess intelligence very well. Since the 1970s, interest has revived in the notion that intelligence could be assessed by speed of simple processing rather than by conventional tests of intelligence. Much of the relevant research has used the **inspection-time task**. This task measures the lowest exposure duration at which an individual can accurately make a simple perceptual discrimination in the visual modality.

It has generally been found that there is a moderate negative correlation between inspection time and intelligence. In other words, individuals with high IQs require less inspection time than those with low IQs. Kranzler and Jensen (1989) reviewed the relevant research. They reported that the mean correlation between inspection time and IQ was −0.55 when account was taken of the unreliability of measurement. The size of this correlation indicates that simple processing speed is clearly associated with intelligence.

Egan (1994) pointed out that there was a potential problem with most of the studies. Many participants performing inspection-time tasks report making use of

information about apparent motion in the display. He studied this phenomenon using a display in which the participants had to decide whether the vertical line on the left-hand side was longer or shorter than the vertical line on the right-hand side. Those participants who reported using information about apparent motion had significantly faster inspection times than did those who did not use this information. If more intelligent participants are more likely to use motion cues, then the correlation between inspection time and IQ may be due to differences in strategy between high and low IQ scorers rather than to differences in basic processing speed. However, Egan (1994) found there was no tendency for those of high IQ to make more use of motion cues than those of low IQ. He found an overall correlation of −0.41 between inspection time and non-verbal IQ, and came to the following conclusion: 'Despite motion cues enhancing performance on an IT [inspection time] task, the perception of these cues neither causes, nor reduces, the correlation between IT and IQ' (1994: 305).

Egan's (1994) study strengthens the argument that an important part of intelligence involves speed of simple processing. However, more needs to be discovered about the precise processes used on inspection-time tasks. In addition, we still lack an adequate theoretical account of the role played by simple processing speed in intelligent thought.

Ψ Section summary

Good tests of intelligence have high reliability and validity, and they have been standardized on large and representative samples. Intelligence tests assess IQ, and are designed so that the mean IQ is 100 and the standard deviation is about 16. The IQ measure is very general, and it is generally valuable to consider also more specific aspects of intelligence such as numerical ability, spatial ability and reasoning ability. There is evidence from the inspection-time task and elsewhere that speed of simple processing is of relevance to intelligence.

1 How can we decide on the usefulness of any given intelligence test?

☐ Heredity and environment

There has been a considerable amount of controversy about the relative importance of heredity and environment in determining intelligence and IQ. Unfortunately, many of those who have become involved in the controversy have assumed from the outset that intelligence is determined almost entirely by either heredity or environment (see the debate between H.J. Eysenck and Kamin 1981). As a result, there is a danger that the large literature on this issue has generated more heat than light.

Some psychologists (e.g. Donald Hebb) have argued that the issue of the relative roles of heredity and environment in determining intelligence is essentially meaningless. Hebb drew an analogy between addressing that issue and asking whether the area of a field is determined more by its length or by its width. Obviously, the area of a field depends crucially on both length and width, and it is very important to recognize that intelligence depends crucially on both heredity and environment. However, it is still meaningful to ask whether different fields vary in area more because of variations in their lengths or in their widths. In similar fashion, we can inquire whether individual differences in intelligence are caused more by variations in genetic endowment or by variations in environmental factors. Eventually, what is needed is a detailed account of the ways in which genes and environmental factors combine to determine the level of intelligence.

There is an important distinction between genotype and phenotype in research on individual differences in intelligence. The **genotype** is the individual's genetic potential, whereas the **phenotype** represents his or her observable characteristics. When we administer an intelligence test to someone, all we can hope to assess is that individual's phenotype, since the genotype itself is not directly measurable.

There are other difficulties which the researcher in this area has to confront. The commonest way of measuring intelligence is by calculating IQ on the basis of the results from an intelligence test. The assumption is that the IQ provides a good measure of an individual's intelligence. Since most intelligence tests assesses a relatively restricted range of cognitive abilities, this assumption may well not be warranted. Another difficulty is that we do not know in detail which aspects of the environment have the most impact on intelligence. Factors such as the type and length of schooling and aspects of the family environment are clearly important, but there are probably several other environmental factors about which little is known as yet.

Those who believe that intelligence depends mainly on heredity often make a number of predictions. However, it is important to note that each prediction is quite separate from the others. As a result, it is entirely possible for the evidence to support one or two of them without supporting the other(s). First, they predict that individual differences in intelligence within a group (e.g. white British people) are caused by heredity rather than by environment. Second, they predict that group differences in intelligence (e.g. between white and black groups) are due to heredity. Third, they predict that it should be possible to identify some of the basic processes and mechanisms underlying intelligence; this is sometimes referred to as 'biological intelligence'. Each of these predictions will be considered in turn.

Individual differences

In general terms, individuals who are similar in terms of heredity also tend to be similar in terms of the environment to which they are exposed. For example, the members of a family are generally similar genetically and in terms of environment (e.g. living in the same house). This makes it difficult to know whether similar levels of intelligence shown by the members of a family are due more to heredity or to environment. However, there are two kinds of studies which allow us to make some headway in investigating the roles of heredity and environment on intelligence. First, there are *twin studies*, in which twins differing in their level of genetic similarity are compared. Second, there are *adoption studies*, in which biologically unrelated children growing up in the same family are compared.

Before considering twin studies and adoption studies, it is important to consider the concept of heritability. **Heritability** can be defined as the ratio of genetically caused variation to total variation (environmental and genetic) within a population. It is concerned with what causes individual differences in intelligence or some other characteristic. Heritability is assessed in most twin and adoption studies, and it is often mistakenly assumed that it means the same as genetic determination. That this is not the case can be seen if we consider an example given by N. Block (1995). The number of fingers that human beings possess is overwhelmingly determined by genetic factors. However, individual differences in the number of fingers depend on environmental factors such as industrial accidents and problems in foetal development. As a result, the heritability of number of fingers is probably very low even though there is a very high level of genetic determination!

We have seen that heritability is not the same as genetic determination. There are other limitations of heritability as a measure. It does not apply to individuals directly, but only to differences among individuals. In addition, measures of heritability tend to depend on the amount of environmental similarity within the population being studied: high environmental similarity is often associated with high heritability and low environmental similarity with low heritability. People in western societies probably experience more similar environments than do those living in some other parts of the world. For example, there are societies in which many or most children receive practically no schooling. In such societies, heritability may well be lower than in western ones. In sum, it is incorrect to assume that there is a fixed value for the heritability of intelligence.

Twin studies

Several studies of intelligence have compared monozygotic or identical twins with dizygotic or fraternal twins. **Monozygotic twins** derive from the same fertilized ovum, and as a result they possess essentially identical genotypes. **Dizygotic twins** derive from two different fertilized ova, so their genotypes are no more similar than those of ordinary siblings. It would be expected that monozygotic twins would be much more similar in intelligence than dizygotic twins if heredity is

of major importance, whereas they would be no more alike in intelligence if environment is all-important.

Several reviews of the evidence have been published. Erlenmeyer-Kimling and Jarvik (1963) considered over 50 studies. The mean correlation coefficient for monozygotic twins was +0.87, whereas it was +0.53 for dizygotic twins. On the face of it, the fact that monozygotic twins were much more similar in IQ indicates that heredity plays a major role.

However, there is a complicating factor. Loehlin and Nichols (1976) discovered that monozygotic twins were treated in a more similar way than dizygotic twins. This was found with respect to the way they were dressed, parents trying to treat both twins in the same way, playing together, spending time together, and having the same teachers at school. Kamin (in H.J. Eysenck and Kamin 1981) analysed the data of Loehlin and Nichols (1976). He found evidence that similarity of treatment affected similarity of IQ. Thus, the greater similarity of IQ between monozygotic than dizygotic twins may be due in part to environmental factors rather than to heredity.

There is another point that needs to be made at this point. Plomin (1988) discussed findings which had been reported after the review by Erlenmeyer-Kimling and Jarvik (1963). In the newer studies, the correlation for monozygotic twins was about the same as in the earlier studies, +0.86 and +0.87, respectively. However, the

Plate 13.2 Monozygotic twins are treated in a more similar way than dizygotic twins, in the way they are dressed and with regard to their schooling. This similarity of treatment found in monozygotic twins, indicates that greater similarity in IQ may be due to environmental factors rather than to hereditary ones

mean correlation coefficient for dizygotic twins in the newer studies was +0.62, which is appreciably higher than the mean of +0.53 in the older studies. As Plomin (1988) pointed out, this narrowing of the gap between monozygotic and dizygotic twins indicates a smaller contribution of heredity to intelligence than was suggested by the earlier findings. Plomin (1988: 8) took all the twin data into account, and argued as follows: 'Leaving aside the differences between the older and newer data, the results converge on the conclusion that as much as half of the variance in IQ scores is due to genetic differences among individuals'. It is important to note that there is no fixed value for the contribution of genetic factors to individual differences in intelligence. The value which is obtained in any given study depends on the prevailing environmental influences in society, and is likely to change when those influences change.

So far we have considered only twin pairs brought up together. However, some monozygotic twins have been found who were separated at an early age and brought up apart. In principle, such twins provide an almost perfect test of the contributions of heredity and environment to intelligence. If heredity is the key factor, then monozygotic twins brought up apart should resemble each other very closely in intelligence. If environment is the main factor, then these twins should not have similar levels of intelligence. In fact, the review by Erlenmeyer-Kimling and Jarvik (1963) indicated that the mean correlation coefficient is +0.75. However, this figure includes the findings of Burt (1955), which are generally regarded as dubious. If one omits those findings, the correlation coefficient becomes somewhat lower than +0.75.

The fact that monozygotic twins brought up apart tend to be less similar in intelligence than monozygotic twins brought up together suggests that environmental factors are of importance. The finding that such twins are fairly similar in intelligence seems more difficult to account for in environmental terms. However, there is substantial evidence that many monozygotic twins reared apart were actually brought up in rather similar environments. For example, two-thirds of the pairs in one large study were brought up in different branches of the same family, and some of the twins actually attended the same school. In addition, many other pairs spent several years of childhood living together before being separated. Even when monozygotic twins are genuinely brought up in separate environments, there is still the issue of *selective placement*. Adoption agencies often have an explicit policy of placing children in circumstances which match as closely as possible those of their biological parents. All of these considerations suggest that monozygotic twins brought up apart may resemble each other in intelligence in part because of environmental factors.

Adoption studies

One of the largest adoption studies was the Texas Adoption Project, which was based on a total of 469 adopted children. On average, the correlation between the children and their biological mothers was +0.28, whereas it was only +0.15 for the children and their adoptive mothers (Horn 1983). These findings suggest that heredity is important. However, both correlations are so low, that it is not possible to identify the determinants of the adopted children's IQs with any precision.

Rather different findings were obtained when the children were re-tested ten years later. Loehlin *et al.* (1989) found that shared family environment had less effect than it had had earlier, and that heredity was now a more important determinant of IQ than it had been ten years previously.

Plomin (1988) reviewed the literature on adopted children. His review indicated that the correlation for IQ between genetically unrelated children reared together in adoptive families was about +0.30 when they were children, but it dropped to zero in adolescence and adulthood. This is in line with the findings of Loehlin *et al.* (1989) in showing the decreasing influence of shared family environment over time.

The above findings suggest that heredity is a major factor in the determination of children's level of intelligence. However, the finding that biologically unrelated children brought up together show some similarity in intelligence during childhood suggests that environmental factors are also important. As discussed earlier, a complicating factor is that adoption agencies tend to make use of selective placement. The implication is that at least part of the correlation between adopted children and their biological parents is due to the fact that adopted children tend to be placed in an environment which resembles that provided by the biological parents.

One of the most important adoption studies was reported by Capron and Duyne (1989). They managed to identify four groups of adopted children: those whose biological and adoptive parents had high socio-economic status; those whose biological and adoptive parents had low socio-economic status; those whose biological parents had high socio-economic status but whose adoptive parents had low socio-economic status; and those whose biological parents had low socio-economic status but whose adoptive parents had high socio-economic status. If heredity is the main factor determining intelligence, then the socio-economic status of the biological parents should predict the adopted child's IQ. If environment is of key importance, then the socio-economic status of the adoptive parents should predict its IQ.

The findings of Capron and Duyne (1989) strongly suggested that heredity and environment are both of comparable importance. When both sets of parents had low socio-economic status, the mean IQ of the adopted children was well below 100, whereas it was much higher when both sets of parents had high socio-economic status (see Figure 13.2). The other two groups of children had mean IQs intermediate between those two extremes. Adopted children with low status biological parents living with high status adoptive parents had a mean IQ of just over 100, and those with high status biological parents living with low status adoptive parents had a slightly higher mean IQ. Thus, favourable heredity or favourable environment both produced substantial improvements in IQ, with the contribution of favourable heredity being perhaps slightly greater than that of favourable environment.

It may be useful to interpret the above findings in the light of a distinction which Cattell (1963) made between knowledge-based or crystallized intelligence and fluid intelligence which is applied to new situations (see dis-

cussion on p. 422). It appears that Capron and Duyne (1989) assessed crystallized intelligence more than fluid intelligence, and so their findings may be mainly applicable to crystallized intelligence.

Relative contributions of heredity and environment

As we have seen, there are various problems of interpretation with twin studies and with adoption studies. However, it is very clear that heredity and environment both contribute in an important way to individual differences in intelligence. Much of the evidence is consistent with the notion that about 50 per cent of individual differences in intelligence are due to heredity and 50 per cent are due to environmental factors. However, it is important to note that these figures apply to the United States and some countries in western Europe. It is likely that the environments experienced by children and adults within those societies are more similar than are the environments experienced by those living in some other societies. If that is the case, then the contribution of environment to individual differences in intelligence would be greater in those other societies than it is in western societies. In other words, the contribution of heredity in producing individual differences in intelligence is greater in societies in which most people experience similar environments than in societies in which dissimilar environments are the norm.

Even within western societies, there is evidence that heritability of intelligence varies as a function of age. Acccording to Plomin (1990), the heritability of intelligence is about 30 per cent in childhood, 50 per cent in adolescence, and in excess of 50 per cent in adult life. How can this be? One explanation is that children are exposed to very different kinds of environments, whereas most adults are exposed to similar cultural forces. Another possible explanation is that adolescents and adults generally have more opportunity to select their own environments than have children.

Group differences

An area of great controversy has been that of group differences in intelligence, and how to interpret such differences. For example, blacks in the United States have an average IQ which is approximately 15 points lower than that of whites. In spite of this difference, however, about 20 per cent of blacks have an IQ which is higher than that of the average white. It has generally been

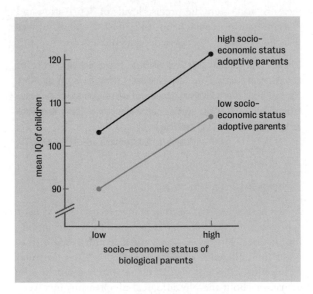

Figure 13.2 Children's IQ as a function of the socio-economic status of the biological and adoptive parents
Source: Based on data in Capron and Duyne (1989)

assumed that the group difference in measured IQ is due to environmental factors, especially the level of deprivation and discrimination suffered by black people in the United States. However, Arthur Jensen (1969) caused a major controversy by suggesting that the difference might be due to important genetic differences between whites and blacks.

This issue is of limited scientific interest, in that it is unlikely to increase our understanding of the processes involved in human intelligence. It is also somewhat meaningless, because considering group differences in intelligence seems to require the assumption that there are separate biological groups. Whites and blacks in the United States or in Europe do not form distinct biological groups, and this greatly complicates making sense of the data. Even if there were distinct biological groups, which differed in intelligence, it is unlikely that these groups would be adequately described by a crude black–white colour difference. Therefore, the finding of a mean IQ difference between blacks and whites cannot logically be attributed to a simple biological difference between these groups. However, much research has been addressed to the issue of group differences in intelligence, and we will consider some of it briefly.

One possible reason why blacks have lower average measured IQs than whites is because intelligence tests are culturally biased against them. Nearly all intelligence tests were devised by white, middle-class psychologists. As a result, the items on the tests might be worded in ways which are easier for whites than for blacks to understand. This argument sounds reasonable, but there is actually rather little evidence to support it. Quay (1971) reported a study in which the Stanford-Binet intelligence test was put into 'black English', which is the form of English spoken by a large number of black Americans. This version of the intelligence test was administered orally by black testers to black children, but their performance differed very little from that found on the standard form of the test.

Another reason why blacks tend to have lower measured IQs than whites is because they are far more likely to suffer from environmental deprivation during childhood. There is strong evidence that deprivation is a major factor. One way of considering the effects of deprivation is by comparing white and black individuals matched in terms of the conditions in which they live. For example, Mackintosh (1986) carried out two studies in which he matched white and West Indian children in England for father's employment status, number of brothers and sisters, family income, and so on. In the

first study, the 11-point difference in IQ which was found in unmatched groups reduced to only 5.2 points in the matched groups. In the second study, there was a 9-point difference in IQ between unmatched groups, but a very small difference of 2.6 points of IQ between the matched groups. Similar findings have been reported in the United States (see Loehlin *et al*. 1975).

Tizard *et al*. (1972) compared black, mixed and white children living in comparable circumstances in residential nurseries in the UK. Their average IQs were as follows: black children: 104; mixed children: 105; white children: 101. These findings suggest that group differences in IQ largely disappear when different groups are exposed to very similar environments.

Limitations in the evidence

Environmental factors (e.g. deprivation) may well account for most of the group differences in measured IQ, and it is possible that they account for all of such group differences. The general importance of environmental factors is shown by the Flynn effect. This is the finding that the average IQ in most countries has been increasing by about 3 points every 10 years during most of the twentieth century.

From a scientific point of view, it is not really possible to carry out definitive research. Many blacks suffer from environmental deprivation, but it is very hard to measure accurately the precise levels of deprivation and discrimination experienced. Even H.J. Eysenck admits that the evidence is necessarily inadequate:

Can we ... argue that genetic studies ... give direct support to the hereditarian position? The answer must, I think, be in the negative. The two populations involved (black and white) are separate populations, and none of the studies carried out on whites alone, such as twin studies, are [*sic*] feasible.

(Eysenck, in H.J. Eysenck and Kamin 1981: 79)

Biological intelligence

As we have seen, it is of importance to establish at least approximately the role played by heredity in determining intelligence. However, knowing that individual differences in intelligence are 50 per cent or 70 per cent due to heredity does not really tell us much about intelligence, or about the physiological mechanisms involved. Various attempts have been made to shed light on biological intelligence by studying *average evoked potentials*. In essence, a simple stimulus (e.g. light or tone) is presented several times, with the resultant brain activity being recorded each time. By averaging across the pattern of brain activity observed on a trial-by-trial basis, it is possible to identify the average evoked potential, indicating the average response of the brain to stimulation.

Hendrickson and Hendrickson (1980) in H.J. Eysenck's laboratory found that there was a substantial association between IQ and a measure based on the average evoked potentials to tones. Those with high IQs had more complex averaged evoked potentials containing more peaks and troughs (see Figure 13.3). The degree of complexity was assessed by using the 'string' measure, which was the length of a piece of string that was pinned down to follow the shape of each average evoked potential. This string measure correlated +0.72 with IQ. There was an even higher correlation of –0.83 between IQ and a different measure based on the average evoked potential. Even more strikingly, H.J. Eysenck and Barrett (1985) reported a correlation of +0.93 between average evoked potentials and factor loadings on the Wechsler Adult Intelligence Scale.

These findings seemed important and exciting for three reasons. First, it is usually difficult in psychology to obtain correlations above about +0.3 whenever two very different measures are correlated. The reported correlations between IQ and average evoked potentials of +0.7 and +0.8 are amazingly high. Second, they seemed to establish key aspects of the biological basis of intelligence. According to Eysenck:

There seems to be no doubt that we can now measure intelligence physiologically with an accuracy that compares favourably with the best IQ tests currently available. . . . We are, it seems, on the threshold of a revolution in the study of mental ability.

(H.J. Eysenck and M.W. Eysenck 1989: 112–13)

Third, as Hendrickson and Hendrickson (1980) argued, it is possible to use the findings to construct a biological theory of intelligence. According to them, the brain's processing of information is less prone to error in those of high intelligence. As a result, their processing of a stimulus is rather similar each time it is presented, and so there are plenty of peaks and troughs in their average evoked potentials. In contrast, those of low intelligence process a stimulus differently on each presentation, thus producing unclear average evoked potentials with short string length.

In spite of the initial enthusiasm for the use of average evoked potentials to measure intelligence, the biological basis of intelligence has not been discovered (see reviews by Barrett and H.J. Eysenck 1992; Caryl 1991). For example, Mackintosh (1986) used the same procedures as Hendrickson and Hendrickson (1982). He (Mackintosh) obtained a correlation of –0.33 between the string measure from the average evoked potential and performance on the Raven's Advanced Matrices, which is in the opposite direction to the earlier findings. Barrett and H.J. Eysenck (1992) used the same approach as Hendrickson and Hendrickson (1982), but found that IQ correlated up to –0.44 with the string measure based on average evoked potentials. This is also in the opposite direction to the earlier findings. Other failures to replicate findings led Barrett and H.J. Eysenck (1992) to the following conclusion:

With regard to the various studies of AEP [average evoked potential] correlates of IQ, there is very little that can be said other than that for every study that claims a 'significant' result, there is another study that claims the opposite . . . no confidence in correlations between AEP parameters and IQ can be expressed. Certainly, the production of theories, models, and detailed explanations of 'biological intelligence' is not warranted by the present state of the empirical evidence.

(Barrett and H.J. Eysenck 1992: 279)

In sum, there is either no true correlation between average evoked potentials and IQ, or there is a rather low and weak correlation. Whichever is the case, no progress has been made in uncovering the biological basis of intelligence. This failure perhaps suggests that intelligence is less exclusively dependent on heredity than some theorists have proposed. It remains a task for the future to identify the brain correlates of intelligence.

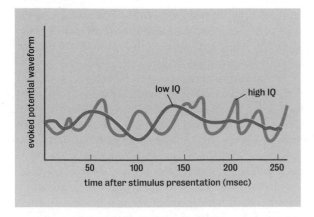

Figure 13.3 Average evoked potentials for individuals with high and low IQ
Source: Based on Hendrickson and Hendrickson (1980)

Ψ Section summary

The roles of heredity and environment in determining individual differences in intelligence within a group have been assessed in several twin and adoption studies. Monozygotic twins (even those brought up apart) tend to be more similar in measured intelligence than dizygotic twins. These findings, and those obtained from adoption studies, are consistent with the notion that genetic and environmental factors are of comparable importance in their influence on individual differences in intelligence within western society. Differences in measured intelligence between whites and blacks depend in large measure on the greater environmental deprivation experienced by blacks. Studies using average evoked potentials and other psychophysiological measures have been carried out in order to identify the biological basis of intelligence. These studies have been unsuccessful.

1   How can we study the roles of heredity and environment in producing individual differences in intelligence? What conclusions can be drawn from the relevant studies?
2   What has been discovered about the biological basis of intelligence?

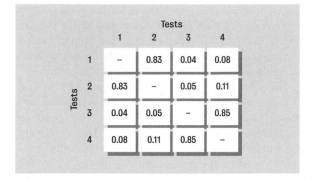

Figure 13.4 A correlation matrix in which the inter-correlations among four separate tests are shown

☐ Factor theories of intelligence

During the course of the twentieth century, several factor theories of intelligence were proposed. These theories differ in many important ways. However, what they have in common is the underlying notion that the structure of intelligence can be inferred by applying **factor analysis** to performance on intelligence tests. Factor analysis involves complex statistical procedures, but some indication of what it involves is given below.

What happens initially is that a battery of tests of various kinds (e.g. spatial, vocabulary and arithmetical) is given to a large group of individuals. The scores on these tests are inter-correlated, and these correlations are entered into a correlation matrix (see Figure 13.4). Correlations can range between −1.0 and +1.0, with 0.0 indicating that two tests do not correlate with each other. A high positive correlation between two tests occurs because those individuals who perform well on one test tend to perform well on the other test, whereas those who perform poorly on one test also perform poorly on the other test.

The information contained within the correlation matrix is of crucial importance in factor analysis. All forms of factor analysis are based on two key, related assumptions. First, the reason why two tests correlate highly with each other is because they are both measuring the same underlying intellectual ability or factor. Second, the reason why two tests do not correlate with each other is because they are measuring two different abilities or factors.

What is achieved by factor analysis is that numerous inter-correlations contained within the correlation matrix are reduced to a small number of factors. These factors are assumed to correspond to intellectual abilities, and are identified on the basis of those tests correlating most highly with each factor. For example, if the tests correlating best with a factor are all mathematical in nature, it might be assumed that the underlying factor is one of mathematical ability.

Factor analysis has proved to be useful, but it does suffer from a number of limitations. First, different methods of factor analysis often produce different sets of factors for any given correlation matrix. Second, factor analysis usually proceeds until all of the main factors have been extracted. However, there is a grey area between main and trivial factors, and some factor theorists include factors which other factor theorists would regard as too trivial to consider. Third, it is important to note that the results of a factor analysis depend on the particular tests entered into it in the first place. If the tests within an intelligence test battery exclude important intellectual abilities, then those abilities will also be excluded from the subsequent factor analysis.

Early factor theories

Spearman's two-factor theory

The British psychologist Charles Spearman (1904) was the inventor of factor analysis. In his 1923 book, *The Nature of 'Intelligence' and the Principles of Cognition*, he put forward the first factor theory of intelligence. This is generally known as the *two-factor theory*. According to this theory, there is a general factor of intelligence (which he termed '*g*'), which is involved in all of the tests included in an intelligence-test battery. There are also numerous specific factors, with a different specific factor associated with each test.

Spearman (1923) argued convincingly in favour of the notion of a general factor of intelligence. Of particular importance is the fact that virtually all of the tests in an intelligence-test battery correlate positively with each other. It is plausible to assume that these positive correlations occur because all of the tests rely to a greater or lesser extent on the general factor. However, the fact that most of these positive correlations are relatively low indicates that performance on the various tests does not depend solely on the general factor. According to Spearman (1923), it is necessary to assume the existence of specific factors in order to understand why the correlations are so low.

Thurstone's primary mental abilities

The American psychologist Louis Thurstone disagreed with Spearman's two-factor theory. He argued that factor analysis should be used to select a factor solution based on simple structure. Simple structure is achieved when each factor correlates highly with some of the tests, but fails to correlate at all with the other tests. Use of simple structure led Thurstone (1938) to identify seven factors, or what he called 'primary mental abilities'. These factors were as follows: numerical ability, verbal fluency, inductive reasoning, verbal meaning, perceptual speed, memory, and spatial ability.

Thurstone (1938) did not include a general factor of intelligence among his factors. However, the seven primary mental abilities identified by Thurstone correlate with each other. When factor analyses are carried out on these seven factors, then a single general factor emerges (Sternberg 1985).

Guilford's structure-of-intellect model

Guilford (1967) proposed a very complex factor theory of intelligence. He argued that each factor of intelligence can be defined on the basis of its location on three dimensions:

- the operations or mental processes involved
- the contents or types of information being processed
- the products or types of responses required

Guilford (1982) assumed that there are five basic operations: thinking, remembering, divergent production (based on original thinking), convergent production (based on logical thinking) and evaluation. There are also five kinds of content: symbolic (e.g. numbers), semantic (e.g. words), behavioural (e.g. the actions of others), auditory, and visual. Finally, there are six types of products: units (e.g. single words), classes (i.e. hierarchies), relations, systems, transformations, and implications. Since Guilford argued that each factor of intelligence involves one particular operation, type of content, and product, it follows that in principle there could be 5 (operations) × 5 (contents) × 6 (products) = 150 factors of intelligence.

In practice, Guilford was not able to identify 150 factors of intelligence. However, he did claim to have evidence for the existence of about 100 factors. In fact, Guilford did not have adequate evidence that his various factors are actually independent of each other. Moreover, he tended to de-emphasize the fact that nearly all of his tests of intelligence correlated positively with each other. The existence of these positive correlations suggests that far fewer than 150 factors are needed to explain the data.

Most damagingly, Horn and Knapp (1973) focused on the statistical approach (technically known as Procrustean rotation of a factorial solution) used by Guilford to support his structure-of-intellect model. They argued that this statistical approach is flawed, and exaggerates the true level of support for the model. More specifically, they discovered that Procrustean rotation provided as much support for randomly determined theories which they made up as it did for the structure-of-intellect model.

In sum, Guilford's structure-of-intellect model is unduly complex, and appears to be less useful than the hierarchical models proposed by other factor theorists. The main advantage of Guilford's approach is that it focuses attention on the processes and knowledge structures involved in successful completion of intelligence-test items.

Cattell's theory of crystallized and fluid intelligence

A rather different theory of intelligence was proposed by Cattell (1963). He argued that there are two conceptually distinct but correlated forms of intelligence: *crystallized intelligence* and *fluid intelligence*. Crystallized intelligence is involved when a task depends on the use of previously learned knowledge and skills. Vocabulary tests and reading-comprehension tests are good measures of crystallized intelligence. In contrast, fluid intelligence is involved when a task requires novel processes and ways of thinking. Tests involving analogies (e.g. 'Hand is to arm as foot is to ?') or completing a series (e.g. 1 4 9 16 25 ?? ??) are good ways of assessing fluid intelligence.

Crystallized and fluid intelligence show a different pattern over the lifespan. Crystallized intelligence reaches its maximum later in life than does fluid intelligence, and it declines much later. According to Cattell (1963), fluid intelligence starts to fall before the age of 40, whereas crystallized intelligence is often maintained at a high level into old age. In the case of a test of crystallized intelligence such as vocabulary, it has been found that healthy 85 year olds obtain approximately the same scores as middle-aged people and young adults (Blum *et al.* 1970).

Hierarchical approach

As we have seen, factor theorists differ enormously among themselves in terms of the number and nature of factors they favour. However, it is possible to reconcile some of these differences by assuming that intelligence possesses a hierarchical structure (e.g. Carroll 1986; Vernon 1971). In broad terms, theorists advocating a hierarchical approach assume that the hierarchy consists of three levels. At the highest level, there is general intelligence, or the *g* factor identified by Spearman. At the second level, there are various group factors or primary mental abilities (e.g. those identified by Thurstone). At the third level, there are rather specific factors associated with no more than a small number of tests; these resemble the specific factors discussed by Spearman.

Carroll's (1986) proposed hierarchical model of intelligence is shown in Figure 13.5. He identified a total of seven factors at the intermediate level of the hierarchy: fluid ability, general fluency, general visual perception, general speed, general auditory perception, general memory capacity, and crystallized intelligence. Some of these factors derive from the work of Thurstone, whereas others stem from the work of Cattell.

Ψ Section summary

Several theorists have used factor analysis in the attempt to identify the structure of intelligence. Spearman argued that there is a general factor of intelligence and numerous specific factors. Thurstone proposed seven factors or primary mental abilities, and Guilford claimed that there are 150 factors of intelligence based on the possible combinations of operations, contents, and products. Most of the evidence is consistent with a synthesis involving a three-level hierarchy. General intelligence is at the highest level, several less general factors are at the intermediate level, and numerous specific factors are at the bottom level.

1   What is factor analysis, and how has it been used to investigate the structure of intelligence?
2   Compare and contrast some of the main factor theories of intelligence.

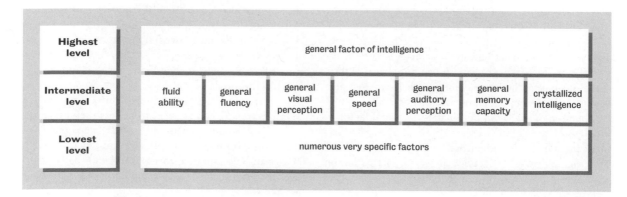

Figure 13.5 Hierarchical model of intelligence put forward by Carroll (1986)

☐ Systems theories of intelligence

Since the early 1980s, some psychologists have tried to develop theories of intelligence that are more comprehensive than the factor theories we have discussed, and in which intelligence is viewed as a complex system. Two of the most prominent systems theorists are Howard Gardner and Bob Sternberg. Gardner (1983) proposed a theory of multiple intelligences, and Sternberg (1985, 1988) put forward a triarchic theory of intelligence. These two influential systems theories are considered in detail in the rest of this section.

Gardner's theory of multiple intelligences

According to Gardner (1983), intelligence is complex and multidimensional. Accordingly, it is more fruitful to identify a number of conceptually separate intelligences rather than focusing on a general factor of intelligence. In his terminology, an intelligence is defined as 'an ability or set of abilities that permits an individual to solve problems or fashion products that are of consequence in a particular cultural setting' (Walters and Gardner 1986: 165).

Gardner (1983) proposed seven different intelligences. Each one is described below, with the names of two famous people excelling in that intelligence being given in parentheses.

- spatial intelligence: this form of intelligence is used in navigation or moving around the environment; it is also used in reading a map and in painting (Pablo Picasso; Berthe Morisot)
- musical intelligence: this form of intelligence is important whether playing a musical instrument, singing, or listening to music (Igor Stravinsky; Jacqueline du Pré)
- linguistic intelligence: this form of intelligence is used in all language abilities, including the comprehension of spoken and written language and the production of spoken and written language (T.S. Eliot; Jane Austen)
- logical-mathematical intelligence: this is of particular importance in solving abstract problems of a logical and/or mathematical nature and in logical reasoning (Albert Einstein; Marie Curie)
- interpersonal intelligence: this form of intelligence is used to interact in a sensitive and sympathetic way with other people and to understand their behaviour (Mahatma Gandhi; Mother Teresa)
- intrapersonal intelligence: this involves a high level of sensitivity to one's own inner states and abilities (Sigmund Freud; Diana, Princess of Wales)
- bodily-kinaesthetic intelligence: this involves precise control of bodily movements (e.g. in dancing or sport) (Martha Graham; Steffi Graf)

When deciding how many different intelligences to identify, Gardner (1983) argued that it was inadequate to rely solely on standard intelligence tests. Accordingly, he took into account a range of factors. For example, he argued that each intelligence should have its own symbol system (e.g. numbers, language), and there should be evidence from brain-damaged patients that each intelligence can be impaired without damaging the other intelligences. In addition, there should be evidence that each intelligence makes use of a specifiable set of major operations or functions, and information should be available about individuals possessing exceptional amounts of each intelligence.

Plate 13.3 Gandhi used interpersonal intelligence to interact in a sensitive way with other people and to understand their behaviour

One of the greatest differences between Gardner's theory of multiple intelligences and traditional approaches to intelligence is the greater range of abilities included within his theory. Traditional approaches have usually identified spatial, logical-mathematical and linguistic intelligence, but the four other intelligences identified by Gardner have typically been omitted.

More recently, Gardner (1993) has used his theory of multiple intelligences to study creativity. His basic approach was to identify seven individuals who displayed outstanding ability in one of the seven intelligences during the early years of the twentieth century. The individuals are the first of the pairs of names in parentheses beside the descriptions of the various intelligences.

Gardner (1993) was surprised to discover several similarities among these individuals who had succeeded in very different fields from each other. Freud, Gandhi, Eliot, Einstein, Picasso and Stravinsky did not face much adversity in childhood, but their families imposed high moral demands and insisted that they meet standards of excellence. They were all hard-driving and very ambitious individuals, who were willing to make considerable sacrifices for their work, and who caused much damage to those close to them. They needed much cognitive and emotional support at the time of their greatest achievement. They exhibited a number of childlike qualities, often behaving like a 'wonder-filled child' (Gardner 1993: 32). Perhaps surprisingly, Picasso was the only one of the seven who show any clear talent at an early age; indeed, it was totally unclear what would happen to the other six even at the age of 20.

Limitations of Gardner's theory

One of the strengths of Gardner's (1983) theory of multiple intelligences is that it is a much richer conceptualization of intelligence than is to be found in most factor theories of intelligence. Another strength is that there are several different kinds of evidence confirming the existence of all seven intelligences. In addition, Gardner's (1993) study of creativity indicates that individuals can display outstanding ability or intelligence in many very different ways.

On the negative side, it is not at all clear that all of the seven intelligences identified by Gardner are of equal importance. In many ways, musical intelligence and bodily-kinaesthetic intelligence seem less important than most of the others within western societies. Many individuals who are poorly co-ordinated and tone-deaf lead very successful lives, provided that they excel in one or more of the other intelligences.

Another problem for Gardner's theory is that the seven intelligences tend to be positively correlated with each other, whereas he seems to have assumed that they were all independent of each other. This raises the issue of whether an overarching general intelligence should be identified in addition to the more specific intelligences proposed by Gardner.

The theory of multiple intelligences is descriptive rather than explanatory. That is to say, the theory provides a descriptive account of the structure of human intelligence, but fails to indicate in detail how each intelligence actually works. For example, what are the precise processes involved that lead some individuals to have much higher levels of interpersonal intelligence than others?

Gardner's (1993) attempt to understand some of the factors related to outstanding creativity in each of the seven intelligences is relatively uninformative. There is a suspicion that what is true of the seven outstanding individuals studied by Gardner may not be true of other equally outstanding individuals. For example, Gardner (1993) was impressed by the fact that the seven individuals he studied did not suffer adversity during childhood. However, many outstanding people had very difficult childhoods. Leonardo da Vinci was illegitimate, and scarcely knew his mother. Linus Pauling, who won two Nobel Prizes, lost his father when he was 7; he subsequently became an orphan. Michelangelo's father was a failure, and so he had to embark on an apprenticeship at the age of 13. Edith Piaf had an impoverished childhood and began her career as a chanteuse by singing in the streets of Paris at the age of 15.

Sternberg's triarchic theory

Gardner (1983, 1993) has emphasized the notion that the different forms of intelligence are relatively independent of each other. In contrast, Sternberg (1985, 1988) focused on the ways in which the different components of intelligence combine and work together in his *triarchic theory of intelligence*. According to Sternberg, an adequate theory would include a consideration of the relationship of intelligence to the internal world, to the external world, and to experience. His triarchic theory consists of three subtheories. The *componential subtheory* deals with the individual's internal world, and indicates the cognitive processes and structures used in intelligent behaviour. The *contextual subtheory* deals with the individual's external world, and focuses on the processes used to handle environmental demands. Finally, the *experiential subtheory* deals with the effects of experience on intelligence, and on the relationship between the internal and external worlds.

Componential subtheory

Sternberg (1985) argued that performing cognitive tasks involves the use of various components or processes. He defined a *component* as 'an elementary information process that operates upon internal representations of objects or symbols' (1985: 97). Some idea of the nature of these components can be obtained by considering Sternberg's (1977) analysis of analogical reasoning. The participants are given analogies such as 'Kitten is to cat as baby is to adult', and have to decide whether each analogy is true or false. On the basis of several experiments, Sternberg (1977) claimed that successful performance on such a task involves the use of five or six components (one component is optional). For example, one component involves working out the rule relating the first two terms (e.g. kitten and cat) and another component involves working out the relationship between the first and third terms (e.g. kitten and baby).

Contextual subtheory

One of the weaknesses of the traditional approach to intelligence and intelligence testing was the assumption that intelligence does not depend on the cultural environment in which people live. This assumption is simply wrong. In western cultures, language skills tend to be very important for successful adaptation to the environment. In contrast, there are many other cultures in which seamanship and navigational skills are of vital importance. In other words, intelligence is a relativistic concept, with different components of intelligence being of most value from one culture to another.

Wagner and Sternberg (1986) investigated some of the ways in which contextual knowledge is of use. They argued that career success depends on possessing certain kinds of job-relevant knowledge which are rarely talked about. For example, it may be useful for British academic psychologists to publish their research in American journals as well as British ones. Wagner and Sternberg (1986) called this tacit knowledge, and devised various tests to measure it. Tacit knowledge did not correlate with IQ, but it did correlate approximately +0.4 with the career success of academic psychologists and business managers.

Experiential subtheory

Sternberg (1985) argued that intelligence can be assessed either when a task is relatively novel or when familiarity with a task has led many of the processes involved to become automatized. This distinction between the ability to handle relatively novel situations and the ability to develop automatic processes is similar to Cattell's (1963) distinction between fluid intelligence and crystallized intelligence. In other words, tests of fluid intelligence tend to involve relatively novel tasks, whereas tests of crystallized intelligence involve well-learned skills.

Creativity

There is an important distinction between **originality** and **creativity**. Originality is the tendency to produce several unusual solutions to a problem. For example, people can be asked to think of as many uses as possible for a brick, and the number of uses they think of that are different from those produced by other people can be taken as a measure of originality. In contrast, creativity refers to unusual or insightful solutions which are of real value. Creativity is more important than originality, but unfortunately it is much more difficult to assess.

Creativity often involves an insight or sudden understanding that occurs shortly before a creative solution is reached. Sternberg and Davidson (1982) proposed that there are at least three different ways in which insight or illumination can occur:

- selective encoding: the most important information is extracted from that available
- selective combination: the best way of combining the relevant information is perceived
- selective comparison: the information for the current problem is related by analogy to some previous relevant problem

Sternberg (1985) argued that each of these types of insight has occurred several times in the history of science. Alexander Fleming's discovery of penicillin involved selective encoding. Charles Darwin, who combined most of the known facts about natural selection, used selective combination in developing his theory of evolution. Madame Curie also used selective combination in her discovery of radioactive elements. Friedrich Kekulé had a dream in which a snake curled back on itself and caught its own tail. When he woke up, he realized by a process of selective comparison that this image was an analogy with the molecular structure of benzine.

Problem with the triarchic theory

The triarchic theory provides a comprehensive account of intelligence. It represents a systematic attempt to indicate how internal mental processes interact with environmental and cultural factors to produce effective intelligence. Furthermore, Sternberg (1985) has tried to bridge the gap between theories of intelligence and research in cognitive psychology with his emphasis on the processing components involved in intelligent behaviour.

The main limitation of the triarchic theory is that it provides a framework rather than a detailed account of the processes and structures involved in intelligence. For example, it is not clear how the three subtheories of the triarchic theory relate to each other. In addition, the distinction between intelligence and personality is somewhat obscure in parts of the theories. As Sternberg (1985: 54–5) admitted, the triarchic theory 'includes within the realm of intelligence characteristics that typically might be placed in the realms of personality or motivation'.

Ψ Section summary

Gardner argued that there are seven conceptually separate intelligences, some of which are assessed by traditional intelligence tests and others of which are not. There is evidence confirming the existence of each of these intelligences, but it is not clear that they are equally important within western societies. Furthermore, Gardner's theory of multiple intelligences is descriptive rather than explanatory. Sternberg's triarchic theory consists of three subtheories dealing with the individual's internal world, the individual's external world, and the effects of experience on intelligence. Sternberg has also developed an investment theory of creativity, which is based on the assumption that creativity depends on six basic resources: intelligence; knowledge; intellectual style; personality; motivation; and environmental context.

1 Compare and contrast two major theories of intelligence put forward in the 1980s.

Research update

Sternberg and Lubart (1991) developed what they called an investment theory of creativity. It is a wide-ranging theory, which includes some of the ideas contained in Sternberg's (1985) triarchic theory and in Sternberg and Davidson's (1982) approach. In essence, it is assumed that there are six basic resources underlying creativity, some of which are cognitive in nature:

- processes of intelligence, including those identified within the triarchic theory
- knowledge, but a very high level of knowledge can lead to rigidity of thought
- intellectual styles: of use to creativity are a legislative style (in which individuals like to produce their own rules) and a progressive style (in which change and innovation are favoured)
- personality: of use to creativity are tolerance of ambiguity, a willingness to surmount obstacles and persevere, and an openness to new experience
- motivation, especially task-focused motivation
- environmental context: the environment may nourish or suppress creative ideas

It might be thought that these six resources have additive effects on creativity. If so, then an individual's level of creativity could be assessed by simply adding together his or her individual resources. However, Sternberg and Lubart (1991) argued that these resources are interactive rather than additive. For example, someone who scored highly on five resources, but had no motivation or no relevant knowledge, would not be creative.

Sternberg and Lubart (1991) tested their investment theory in a study in which the participants were asked to produce two drawings, two creative stories, two advertisements, and two scientific problem solutions. Creativity was predicted best by various measures of intelligence, including tests of fluid ability, and measures of selective encoding, combination, and comparison. It was also well predicted by knowledge. An intermediate level of motivation was associated with the highest level of creativity, and desire to grow was the personality dimension most associated with creative performance. Legislative and progressive intellectual styles did not predict creative performance.

Ψ Chapter summary

● Concept of intelligence

Intelligence involves purposeful adaptation to one's environment and the ability to shape that environment. Doubts have been expressed about the explanatory value of the concept of 'intelligence', but it has been found to have reasonably good predictive value.

● Intelligence testing

Intelligence is best measured by standardized tests having good reliability and validity. IQ is a general measure of intelligence obtained from intelligence tests; it has a mean of 100 and a standard deviation of about 16.

● Heredity and environment

Attempts to determine whether individual differences in intelligence are due more to heredity or to environment have often involved twin studies or adoption studies. Monozygotic twins (whether brought up together or apart) tend to be more similar in IQ than dizygotic twins, indicating that heredity is of importance. Heredity and environment both emerge as important determinants of intelligence in adoption studies. Group (e.g. racial) differences in intelligence depend to a large extent on environmental deprivation.

It is entirely possible that environmental deprivation accounts for all such differences. Attempts have been made to find the underlying biological mechanisms of intelligence, but they have failed.

● Factor theories of intelligence

Some factor theorists (e.g. Spearman) emphasized the general factor of intelligence, whereas others (e.g. Thurstone) focused on group factors. The evidence supports the notion that intelligence has a hierarchical structure: at the top level is general intelligence, at the second level are various group factors, and at the bottom level are rather specific factors.

● Systems theories of intelligence

Gardner argued that there are seven independent intelligences spanning a wider range of intellectual abilities than is usually found on intelligence tests. There is some support for his theory, but it is more descriptive than explanatory, and the seven intelligences are correlated rather than independent. Sternberg put forward a triarchic theory consisting of componential, contextual, and experiential subtheories. Some of the ideas contained in the triarchic theory have been applied to creativity in the investment theory.

Further reading

● Eysenck, M.W. (1994) *Individual Differences: Normal and abnormal*. Hove: Lawrence Erlbaum. Chapter 2 of this book covers several major topics on intelligence.

● Sternberg, R.J. (1985) *Beyond IQ: A triarchic theory of human intelligence*. Cambridge: Cambridge University Press. The theoretical approach to intelligence favoured by Sternberg is discussed at length in this book.

● Eysenck, H.J. and Kamin, L. (1981) *The Intelligence Controversy: H. J. Eysenck vs. Leon Kamin*. New York: Wiley. The extreme hereditarian and environmentalist positions are discussed in detail in this book.

● Plomin, R. (1988) The nature and nurture of cognitive abilities, in R.J. Sternberg (ed.) *Advances in the Psychology of Human Intelligence*, vol. 4. Hillsdale, NJ: Lawrence Erlbaum. This chapter provides a balanced and informative account of the respective roles of heredity and environment in determining individual differences in intelligence.

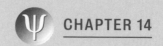

Personality

Michael Eysenck

KEY CONCEPTS • personality and its determinants • Freud's psychoanalytic theory • Freud's theory of psychosexual development • humanistic approach • personality assessment • factor theories of personality • five-factor model • social learning theory

❑ Chapter preview

When you have read this chapter, you should be able to

- understand some of the major theoretical approaches to personality
- assess the importance of early childhood, experiences throughout life, and heredity in determining adult personality, based in part on the evidence from twin studies
- understand the contributions made by Freud, the humanistic psychologists such as Maslow and Rogers, factor theorists such as Cattell and Eysenck, and social learning theorists such as Bandura and Rotter
- evaluate the strengths and weaknesses of the major theoretical approaches to personality
- evaluate the strengths and weaknesses of different kinds of personality tests and of other methods of assessing personality (e.g. case studies)

❏ Personality and its determinants

Think how dull life would be if everyone had exactly the same personality! Everyone we met would have the same entirely predictable approach to life, and there would be little point in building up a circle of friends. In fact, of course, real life is very different from that. All of us notice in our daily lives that there are marked differences between people. Some people seem to be cheerful and optimistic most of the time, whereas others are generally gloomy and depressed. Some people are very conscientious and hard-working, whereas others are lazy and unconcerned about work. The great puzzle (which forms a major part of this chapter) is to explain where all this exciting diversity comes from. As the Greek philosopher Theophrastus asked himself more than 2,000 years ago, 'Why is it that while all Greece lies under the same sky, and all the Greeks are educated alike, it has befallen to us to have characters variously constituted?'

Child (1968: 83) defined personality as the 'more or less stable, internal factors that make one person's behaviour consistent from one time to another, and different from the behaviour other people would manifest in comparable situations.' This definition is perhaps too broad, in that it includes intelligence as a component of personality. Some theorists (e.g. Cattell) regard intelligence as an aspect of personality, but most theorists agree that personality refers to individual differences at the emotional and motivational levels.

Hampson (1988) noted that there are four especially important words in Child's definition: 'stable', 'internal', 'consistent' and 'different'. When we speak of someone's personality, we assume it is reasonably stable and unvarying over time; short-lived emotional states are moods rather than aspects of personality. It is important to note that personality exists within individuals, and is not to be equated with their external behaviour. Of course, we make inferences about other people's personalities on the basis of their behaviour, but their behaviour is not the same as their personality. Behaviour provides only indirect evidence about personality. For example, someone may cry because he or she has a depressive personality, but people also cry because they have just been chopping up onions.

The notion that people's behaviour will be consistent over time follows from the assumptions that personality is stable, and that behaviour is determined in part by personality. Finally, the central focus of personality theorists is on explaining individual differences in behaviour. Nearly everyone walks along the pavement rather than in the middle of the road, and so this behaviour is of little or no interest to personality theorists. In contrast, individuals differ substantially in their behaviour in social groups, and it is such differences that help to define an individual's personality.

An important issue for personality theorists is to identify the main influences which determine adult personality. According to Freud, adult personality is determined mainly by childhood experiences, although he accepted that biological factors are also important. According to humanistic psychologists such as Carl Rogers and Abraham Maslow, personality is affected very much by the experiences that one has had throughout one's life. However, they regarded adult personality as much easier to change than did Freud. They linked the notion of personality to the self-concept, and argued that the self-concept can change considerably over time. Trait theorists such as Raymond Cattell and H.J. Eysenck argue that personality consists of a number of traits, and that these traits are determined mainly by heredity rather than by environmental factors. Finally, according to social-learning theorists such as Julian Rotter and Albert Bandura, what we are depends very much on the experiences we have had. In contrast to other theorists, however, they argued that experience generally has such specific effects on our behaviour that is doubtful whether personality as such really exists.

Something to ponder as you read about the various theories of personality is the following critical assessment by Singer and Kolligian (1987) of personality theory and research:

It is true that the lives and insights of Freud, Jung, Adler, Sullivan, Rogers, Maslow, etc. make extremely interesting reading, and their historical contributions highlight some of the issues of human relationships that must continue at the centre of personality research. But we may well ask why no one teaches cognition, social psychology, developmental psychology, or abnormal psychology by using the views of famous people as the centrepiece for the entire course.

(Singer and Kolligan 1987: 535)

As has been said by others, books on personality theory often resemble a walk through the graveyard. However, there are at least two good reasons for focusing on the contributions of major personality theorists. First, personality is a very broad area, and only a limited number of theorists have attempted the difficult task of producing theories designed to cover the whole of human personality. Second, personality theorists differ substantially among themselves in their basic assumptions about the

Multiple personalities

Most people seem to have a single, relatively stable, personality. However, there are a small number of individuals who suffer from what used to be called multiple personality disorder, but is now generally known as **dissociative identity disorder**. Probably the most famous case of dissociative identity disorder is Chris Sizemore, whose case was the central focus of the film, *The Three Faces of Eve*. Sometimes she was 'Eve White', a respectable and somewhat inhibited young woman. At other times, she was 'Eve Black', who was very different: she was promiscuous and very impulsive in her behaviour. Eve Black was aware of Eve White, but Eve White did not know of the existence of Eve Black. Finally, there was Jane. She was the most stable of the three personalities of Chris Sizemore. Jane knew about Eve White and Eve Black, and seemed to have a prefer-

ence for Eve Black. Even more bizarrely, she later claimed to have had 21 different personalities (Sizemore and Pittillo 1977). There is no convincing evidence for this claim.

So far, there have been very few detailed scientific studies carried out on sufferers from dissociative identity disorder. However, there is evidence that information which has been learned by one of the personalities of such individuals is often not remembered by their other personalities (Nissen *et al.* 1988). This strengthens the argument that people can genuinely possess several different personalities. It is possible that much could be learned about personality by focusing on the factors that lead those with dissociative identity disorder to switch from one personality to another. For example, does switching depend on the situation, on the individual's mood, or on other factors?

origins of human personality. The strengths and weaknesses of their basic assumptions will be examined by considering in detail the research which has been generated by their theories.

Personality refers to relatively stable, internal factors which produce consistent individual differences at the emotional and motivational levels. Adult personality may depend mainly on childhood experiences; this is the psychoanalytic approach, as in Freud's theories. It may depend on experiences throughout life, as studied in the humanistic approach, put forward by such psychologists as Carl Rogers and Abraham Maslow, or in the social learning theories of Julian Rotter and Albert Bandura. Alternatively, adult personality may depend mainly on genetic factors, as argued by trait theorists such as Raymond Cattell and H.J. Eysenck.

1 Discuss possible definitions of the term 'personality'.

Freud's psychoanalytic theory

Sigmund Freud (1856–1939) is probably the best known psychologist of all time. It is certainly true that his work is still referred to more often than that of any other psychologist in the world's psychological literature. He made numerous contributions to psychology, but is remembered mainly as the originator of **psychoanalysis**. Psychoanalysis refers to the theories of emotional development proposed by Freud, and it also refers to a form of treatment for mental disorders which is based to some extent on those theories. (See also chapters 17 and 18)

Our focus here is on the theories of personality put forward by Freud. The most distinctive feature of those theories is the importance attached to the first five years of life in determining adult personality. There are two main theories to be considered: the structural theory of personality, and the theory of psychosexual development. We will discuss them in turn.

Structural theory of personality

According to Freud, the mind is divided into three separate systems, the id, the ego and the superego. Newborn babies possess only an **id**, which consists mainly of unconscious sexual and aggressive instincts; the sexual instinct is usually known as **libido**. The id operates on the basis of the pleasure principle, in which the focus is on immediate personal satisfaction.

As young children develop, so they learn how to interact with the environment, and with the people in it. During the first two years of life, the **ego** is gradually differentiated from the id. The ego tries to satisfy the id, but it does so in ways which (unlike the id) take account of the realities of the situation. Thus, the ego is said to operate on the basis of the **reality principle**. For example, whereas hungry babies try to eat any food that is within reach, 2 year old children are less impulsive and less inclined to grab someone else's food.

Finally, there is the development of the **superego**, which occurs at about the age of 5. The superego incorporates society's values and standards, which have usually been communicated to the child by its parents. The superego consists of two parts: the conscience and the ego-ideal. The **conscience** is acquired through the use of punishment, and causes the child to feel guilty after behaving badly. The **ego-ideal** is acquired through the use of reward; it causes the child to feel proud after behaving well. These two components of the superego serve to inhibit the impulses of the id, and they also lead the ego to adopt high moral values.

In order to understand more fully the functioning of the id, ego and superego, it is necessary to consider another way in which Freud divided up the human mind. According to Freud, at any given moment some of our thoughts and information are in the conscious, others are in the preconscious, and still others are in the unconscious. The **conscious** consists of whatever thoughts are currently the focus of attention, whereas the **preconscious** consists of stored thoughts and information which could be retrieved and brought into consciousness without much difficulty. Finally, the **unconscious** consists of thoughts which are very difficult or impossible to bring into consciousness. For example, traumatic childhood experiences are often located in the unconscious mind.

It is reasonably easy to relate the above levels of awareness to Freud's structural model, even though these two aspects of Freud's theorizing were put forward more than two decades apart. According to Freud, the id operates almost entirely at the unconscious level, whereas the ego and the superego operate at all three levels (see Figure 14.1).

The reader may by now be rather bewildered by Freud's structural theory of personality, since it does not

	Id	Ego	Superego
Conscious		primary level of ego functioning	important level of superego functioning
Preconscious		important level of ego functioning	important level of superego functioning
Unconscious	primary level of id functioning	important level of ego functioning	important level of superego functioning

Figure 14.1 Freud's theory of the mind

seem to relate well to contemporary theories. However, this is not entirely true. As M.W. Eysenck (1994a) pointed out, the structural theory can be regarded as combining a theory of motivation, a cognitive theory, and a social psychological theory. The id, with its sexual and aggressive instincts, is essentially a motivational system. The ego is a cognitive system which represents the rational part of the mind. Finally, the superego internalizes the values which the child has been taught by the family and by society generally.

Another related way of regarding Freud's structural theory is as an account of the ways in which the growing child's behaviour is increasingly determined by multiple factors. Initially, the baby's behaviour is almost entirely determined by its basic needs. As it develops, however, there is a growing sense of self, which forms an important part of the ego. After a few years, the child learns that its parents and society generally want it to behave in certain ways, and that it needs to behave in certain ways to gain rewards and to avoid punishment.

Defence mechanisms

We have seen that Freud's structural model consists of the id, ego and superego. What has not been emphasized so far is that these three parts of the mind are often in conflict with each other. Conflicts between the id and the superego are especially frequent, because the id's demands for immediate gratification are often inconsistent with the moral standards of the superego. As a consequence, the ego devotes much of its time to resolving such conflicts. These conflicts, and the unreasonable demands of the id and the superego, create the unpleasant emotional state of *anxiety*. The ego will often defend itself unconsciously against anxiety by using various **defence mechanisms** which are designed to keep unacceptable thoughts and anxious feelings out of consciousness. Some of the main defence mechanisms are discussed below.

Repression

Freud (1938: 939) argued that 'the theory of repression is the cornerstone upon which the edifice of psychoanalysis rests' and repression is the most important of the defence mechanisms. He claimed that very threatening or anxiety-provoking thoughts cannot gain access to conscious awareness, and he used the term **repression** to describe this process. According to Freud (1915: 86), 'The essence of repression lies simply in the function of rejecting and keeping something out of consciousness.' In fact, as Madison (1956) pointed out, Freud used the term 'repression' in a number of different ways. On occasion he used it to refer to the inhibition of the capacity for emotional experience. According to this definition, repression could occur even when there was conscious awareness of threatening thoughts, provided that those thoughts did not produce an emotional reaction.

Suppression

Freud drew a distinction between repression and suppression. **Suppression** involves the conscious blocking of anxiety-provoking thoughts from awareness. In contrast, repression usually involves only unconscious processes.

Displacement

The essence of **displacement** is the unconscious shifting of impulses away from a threatening object and towards a non-threatening object. For example, someone who is made angry by their boss is probably ill advised to vent their anger on him or her. Instead, they let out their anger on someone else who is less threatening (e.g. boyfriend or girlfriend).

Denial

The defence mechanism of **denial** involves refusing to accept that some very threatening or unpleasant event has happened. For example, a widow or widower may refuse to accept that their spouse has died. At a slightly less extreme level, it has been found that patients with various life-threatening diseases seem to deny the impact of these diseases on their lives. They report the same level of satisfaction with their psychological and behavioural functioning as healthy individuals (Ogden 1996).

Intellectualization

Intellectualization is a defence mechanism in which individuals think about threatening information in such a

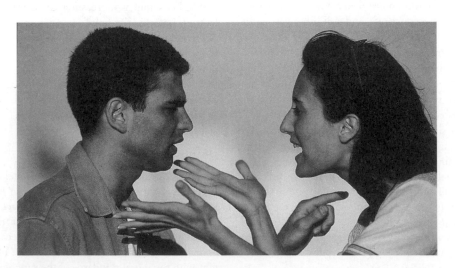

Plate 14.1 According to Freud's structural theory the ego defends itself against anxiety by using various defence mechanisms. Displacement involves shifting anger from a threatening object, such as a boss, to something less threatening like a boyfriend or girlfriend

way as to remove the emotion from it. For example, someone watching television coverage of people at a football match being injured or killed when a stand collapses might focus on structural defects in the stand rather than on the suffering of those injured.

Projection

The defence mechanism of **projection** is involved when someone attributes his or her undesirable characteristics to other people. For example, someone who is very hostile may refuse to accept the fact, and instead argue that it is others who are hostile. Thus, projection provides a way in which people can avoid facing up to their own inadequacies.

Reaction formation

Reaction formation is a defence mechanism in which people behave in a way which is the opposite to their unconscious thoughts and feelings. It is nearly always the case that the behaviour is much more socially desirable than the unconscious feelings. For example, a man who really hates his father may always be telling other people how much he loves him. In similar fashion, someone who is secretly fascinated by pornography may become involved in an anti-pornography campaign.

Experimental evidence and evaluation

There are real problems associated with investigating defence mechanisms under laboratory conditions. Freud obtained his evidence about the various defence mechanisms from therapy sessions with clinically anxious and depressed patients who had experienced a wide range of traumatic and highly threatening events. It would be totally unacceptable for ethical reasons to expose laboratory participants to the kind of threatening events which lead to the use of defence mechanisms. However, some relevant evidence has been obtained, especially in relationship to repression. One of Freud's theoretical assumptions was that the defence mechanisms are effective in reducing an individual's level of anxiety. As we will see, that assumption has been tested in some studies.

In many laboratory studies, failure feedback has been used in order to try to create anxiety and repression. Some of these studies suggest that repression can be created (see Holmes 1990 for a review). However, there are various reasons other than repression why failure feedback might lead to poor recall (e.g. subjects think about the failure feedback rather than concentrating on recall).

Rather stronger evidence for repression exists in studies of child sexual abuse. For example, L.M. Williams (1992) reported that 38 per cent of a group of African-American women who had been abused about 17 years earlier reported repressed memories of that abuse. It is usually hard to establish the accuracy of such repressed memories. However, Loftus (1993) discussed a convincing case of repressed memories. A 27 year old man managed to retrieve repressed memories of his mother attempting to commit suicide by hanging herself. His father confirmed that his son had witnessed his mother's attempted suicide when he was 3 years old.

Another promising way of studying repression is by identifying normal individuals possessing a repressive coping style. It has been found that such individuals find it difficult to retrieve negative childhood memories (Davis 1987; Myers and Brewin 1994). This evidence is discussed in more detail in Chapter 6.

Perhaps the greatest weakness of Freud's account of the various defence mechanisms is that we cannot predict ahead of time which defence mechanism will be used by a given individual. According to Freud, someone who is exposed to an extremely anxiety-provoking situation is likely to resort to a defence mechanism, but it is impossible to predict whether that defence mechanism will be repression, displacement, denial, intellectualization, projection or reaction formation. This greatly reduces the scientific usefulness of the theory.

In more general terms, there is some support for parts of Freud's structural theory of personality. In particular, there is convincing evidence that there are important non-conscious processes as well as conscious ones (see M.W. Eysenck and Keane 1995) and this is consistent with Freud's theoretical approach. However, his theory suffers from the fact that the key concepts (ego, superego, id) are all vaguely defined and underspecified. For example, the ego corresponds approximately to what is now known as the cognitive system. Freud's lack of detail about the functioning of the ego can be contrasted with the detailed knowledge of the workings of the cognitive system which has been achieved since about the mid-1960s by cognitive psychologists (see M.W. Eysenck and Keane 1995).

Ψ Section summary

Freud's structural theory was based on the notion that the mind consists of the ego, superego and id. New-born babies have an id, and this is followed in the course of development by the ego, and then finally by the superego. The ego defends itself against anxiety by using various defence mechanisms including repression, displacement, denial, intellectualization, projection and reaction formation. It is difficult to test this part of Freud's theory, in part because the theory does not allow us to predict which defence mechanism will be used by a given individual.

1 Describe and discuss Freud's structural theory of the mind.
2 Discuss some of the main defence mechanisms, and Freud's account of their functioning.

▢ Freud's theory of psychosexual development

It will be remembered that Freud argued that adult personality is determined to a large extent by the experiences of childhood. Most of his detailed views on this are contained in his theory of psychosexual development.

The five stages

According to this theory, nearly all children pass through five stages of psychosexual development in the following order: oral stage, anal stage, phallic stage, latency stage and genital stage. Ideally, the child should pass smoothly through these stages. However, what often happens is that the child experiences problems or excessive gratification at one or other of the stages. When this happens, it leads to **fixation**, in which basic energy or libido remains attached to that stage into adulthood. Fixation makes the individual vulnerable in later life. When adults are exposed to difficult and stressful conditions, they may show **regression**, in which their behaviour becomes less mature and more like the behaviour they displayed as children. Adults are especially likely to regress to a psychosexual stage at which they fixated as children.

Oral stage

The **oral stage** is the first stage, lasting for approximately the first 18 months of the child's life. During this stage, the young child derives considerable satisfaction from activities involving its mouth, lips and tongue. If there are problems at this stage (e.g. very rapid weaning), then the child may later develop an oral personality. Adults possessing an **oral receptive character** are unusually dependent on others, and very trusting. On the other hand, children whose parents have severely frustrated their needs at this stage may develop an **oral aggressive character**, becoming aggressive and dominating adults.

Anal stage

The **anal stage** follows the oral stage. It lasts approximately from 18 months of age to 36 months. During this stage, the anal region becomes the major source of satisfaction. This happens because this is the age at which toilet training occurs, and refusing to defecate when its parents want it to is an important way in which the child can exert its independence. Children who fixate at the anal stage sometimes develop an **anal retentive character**, consisting of meanness, orderliness and stubbornness. Other adults who develop an anal personality are unusually generous and giving as a result of their toilet-training experiences during the anal stage.

Phallic stage

The most important psychosexual stage is the **phallic stage**, which lasts between the ages of 3 and 6. It is during this stage that the main source of bodily satisfaction becomes the genitals (penis or clitoris). At about the age of 5, boys acquire the **Oedipus complex**, in which they develop sexual longings for their mother while at the same time becoming frightened that their fathers will cut off their penis (**castration anxiety**). The relevant case study of little Hans discusses this. Boys resolve the emotional problems associated with the Oedipus complex by identification with their fathers. In this process of **identification**, boys adopt many of the characteristics and attitudes of their fathers. Identification plays an important role in the development of the superego, since many of the moral values of the superego come from the same-sexed parent.

ψ **Case study**

Little Hans

One of the best known of Freud's case studies is that of little Hans. Hans was a 5 year old boy who was frightened of horses. This boy had shown much interest in his penis from the age of 3, and his mother had threatened to cut it off when he was about $3\frac{1}{2}$ years old. There was weak evidence that he had tried to 'seduce' his mother when he was 4 years old. About six months later, Hans went out for a walk with his nursemaid, and he saw a horse-drawn van tip over. After that, he developed a fear of horses, referring to 'black things around horses' mouths and the things in front of their eyes'. As a result of Hans's fear of horses, he refused to leave his home.

According to Freud, little Hans was suffering from the Oedipus complex. He was sexually attracted to his mother, but he was frightened that he would be punished for this by his father. The fear of his father was turned into a fear of horses, with the black muzzles and blinkers of horses standing for his father's moustache and glasses. This fear of horses had the beneficial effect of allowing Hans to spend more time at home with his mother, who was the source of his desires.

Some psychoanalysts have argued that this case study is an impressive demonstration of the powers of the Oedipus complex. However, there is very little evidence for most of Freud's interpretations. It is not at all clear that Hans really wanted sexual contact with his mother, or that he hated or feared his father. In addition, the notion that Hans's intense sexual excitement turned into anxiety seems doubtful at best. All in all, Freud's case-study approach as exemplified by the case of little Hans is unlikely to convince many sceptics of the value of psychoanalysis.

According to Freud, girls in the phallic stage develop penis envy when they discover that they lack the penis possessed by boys. Penis envy leads girls to resent their mothers for having brought them into the world without a penis. It also leads girls to desire their father because he possesses a penis; this is known as the **Electra complex**. The conflicts caused by girls' resentment of their mothers and their unrealistic longings for their fathers are resolved by identification with their mothers. Identification allows them to experience the sexual love of their fathers at second-hand, and reduces their resentment of their mothers.

Boys and girls who have problems at the phallic stage develop a **phallic character** later in life. In men, this phallic character involves great vanity, impulsiveness and self-assuredness. In women, it produces a constant striving for superiority over men.

Latency stage

After the Oedipus complex has been resolved, boys and girls enter the **latency stage**. During this stage, which lasts until the onset of puberty, sexual feelings are at a low ebb. An obvious feature of the latency stage is that boys and girls have very little to do with each other.

Plate 14.2 Boys and girls who have problems at the phallic stage develop a phallic character later in life. This can express itself in a variety of ways, including a passion for phallic symbols such as fast cars and skyscrapers

Genital stage

From the time of puberty onwards, children are in the **genital stage**. As with the phallic stage, the main source of sexual pleasure in the genital stage is in the genitals. The major difference is that the focus is now on sexual pleasure with another person rather than on one's own. Adults who have avoided severe problems and fixations during the earlier stages of psychosexual development are likely to develop a **genital character**. Such adults are mature and well adjusted, and have the ability to love and to be loved. Those with a genital character may engage in **sublimation**, in which sexual forces are channelled into the attainment of productive and creative goals.

Experimental evidence and evaluation

The main thrust of Freud's theory of psychosexual development is the notion that adult personality has its roots in childhood experiences, especially those occurring in the first five years of life. Unfortunately, it is very hard to test the specific predictions made by the theory. An important reason is that we can usually obtain only very limited and possibly distorted evidence about adults' childhood experiences when being fed or toilet trained. Even if it were possible to obtain fairly high correlations or associations between certain childhood experiences and a given adult personality type, this would still not demonstrate that the childhood experiences had determined the adult personality. This is because correlations cannot be used to establish causes. It is possible, for example, that heredity could lead a child to retain faeces during toilet training and then to develop an anal retentive character.

Some aspects of the theory can be tested in a limited way. Freud assumed that certain personality characteristics tend to be found together. For example, those with an anal retentive character are supposed to exhibit orderliness, parsimony or meanness, and obstinacy. There is some evidence that these three personal characteristics tend to cluster together (e.g. Pollack 1979). In similar fashion, Kline and Storey (1977) obtained evidence for two oral characters resembling Freud's oral receptive character and oral aggressive character. With respect to the oral aggressive character, there was a tendency for verbal aggression, ambition and hostility to be found together. With respect to the oral receptive character, there was a tendency for dependency, optimism and curiosity to cluster together.

Freud's account of the phallic stage, with his emphasis on the Oedipus complex and the Electra complex, is discredited. According to the theory, the development of identification depends on fear, and so boys should show more identification if their fathers are threatening than if they are warm and supportive. In fact, precisely the opposite is the case (Mussen and Rutherford 1963). Another weakness with Freud's theory is that he assumed that moral development depends very largely on the same-sexed parent. In fact, the other-sexed parent and other children usually make significant contributions to the development of the child's superego (Shaffer 1993). More generally, there is very little evidence for the existence of either the Oedipus complex or the Electra complex (Kline 1981).

Ψ Section summary

According to Freud, there are five stages of psycho-sexual development. The oral stage comes first, and is followed in order by the anal, phallic, latency and genital stages. Problems at any of these stages produces fixation, which can lead to regression to that stage in adult life. Freud assumed that childhood experiences in the various stages helped to determine adult personality. The fact that several years intervene between these experiences and the development of adult personality makes it very difficult to test the theory. However, Freud's notion that certain personality characteristics tend to be found together has received some empirical support.

1 What are the main stages of psychosexual development according to Freud?
2 Does the evidence support Freud's theory of psychosexual development? How testable is the theory?

❏ Humanistic approach

Historical background

The humanistic approach to psychology is associated particularly with two American psychologists, Carl Rogers and Abraham Maslow. However, the roots of this approach lie in existentialism. This is a position advocated by various European philosophers such as Jean-Paul Sartre, Sören Kierkegaard and Friedrich Nietzsche. Some of the central assumptions of existentialism were described by Ford and Urban (1963):

Man has the capacity for being aware of himself, of what he is doing, and what is happening to him. As a consequence, he is capable of making decisions about these things and of taking responsibility for himself. . . . He does not exist; he is not a being; rather, he is coming into being, emerging, becoming, evolving towards something. . . . His significance lies not in what he has been in the past, but in what he is now and the direction of his development, which is towards the fulfilment of his innate personality.

(Ford and Urban 1963: 448)

Some of the major themes which were later incorporated into the humanistic approach are mentioned in the above quotation. One such theme is the emphasis on personal responsibility and free will. A second theme is the importance of the here and now rather than the past. A third theme is that of personal growth and fulfilment.

Another major belief of the existentialist philosophers is also mentioned in the quotation from Ford and Urban (1963): the notion that we can understand ourselves by focusing on our own conscious experience. More specifically, the existentialists believed in the value of **phenomenology**, which requires individuals to provide accounts of their direct experience of themselves and of the world around them. It is important to distinguish between phenomenology, in which individuals freely communicate their conscious thoughts, and **analytical introspection**, in which individuals are instructed to focus on certain specified aspects of their experience.

Humanist psychology was developed in the United States in the 1950s and 1960s. It shared with existentialism a belief in the value of phenomenology. In more general terms, humanistic psychology is an approach which 'is concerned with topics that are meaningful to human beings, focussing especially upon subjective experience and the unique, unpredictable events in individual human lives' (Cartwright 1979: 5–6).

As you have probably gathered already, the existentialist and humanistic approaches differ radically from the mainstream scientific approach to psychology advocated initially by the behaviourists and later by cognitive psychologists. Neither of the major figures in the humanistic approach (Abraham Maslow and Carl Rogers) was at all apologetic about that state of affairs. According to Maslow (1968: 13), 'The uniqueness of the individual does not fit into what we know of science.

Then so much the worse for that conception of science. It, too, will have to endure re-creation.'

Rogers believed strongly that a reliance on phenomenology was preferable to use of the scientific method. As he expressed it in 1951:

To my way of thinking, this personal, phenomenological type of study – especially when one reads all of the responses – is far more valuable than the traditional 'hard-headed' empirical approach. This kind of study, often scorned by psychologists as being 'merely self-reports', actually gives the deepest insight into what the experience has meant.

(Rogers 1951: 133)

Abraham Maslow (1908–70)

The starting point for Maslow's humanistic approach to psychology was his interest in human motivation. As he noted in 1954, most psychologists at that time considered that people were mainly motivated by basic physiological needs such as those for food, water and sex, plus the needs to avoid pain and anxiety. According to Maslow, human motivation includes these needs, but it also encompasses several other important needs. Most of these needs are positive and desirable, as would be expected from someone who wrote the following:

Freud supplied to us the sick half of psychology, and we must now fill it out with the healthy half.

(Maslow 1954: 5)

The theory that Maslow (1954) proposed was based on a **hierarchy of needs** having five levels. The essence of this theory is shown in Figure 14.2, and is discussed in more detail in Chapter 16. At the bottom level of the hierarchy are physiological needs which are essential to survival (e.g. needs for food, water and sleep). At the next level of the hierarchy come safety needs, including a secure and predictable environment relatively free from physical and psychological anxiety. Above that level come belongingness and love needs, which are self-explanatory. At the fourth level, there is the need for esteem, which includes the respect of others and self-confidence. Finally, at the apex of the hierarchy, there is the need for **self-actualization**, which involves fulfilling one's own potential. It was defined in the following way by Maslow:

A musician must make music, an artist must paint, a poet must write, if he is to be ultimately at peace with himself. What a man *can* be, he *must* be. This need we may call self-actualization.

(Maslow 1970)

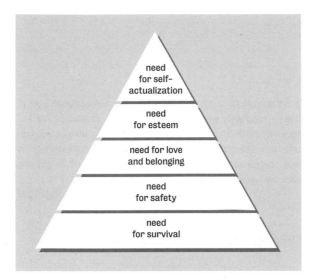

Figure 14.2 Maslow's hierarchy of needs

Limitations with Maslow's theory

The greatest strength of Maslow's theoretical approach is the fact that he produced a more comprehensive and realistic theory of human motivation than most earlier theories. He was right to insist that basic physiological needs are important, but not all-important, determinants of human behaviour. One of the weaknesses of Maslow's approach is his assumption that society tends to have negative effects on people's attempts to become self-actualized. For example, the pressures towards conformity may prevent self-actualization from occurring. While society sometimes hinders self-actualization, it is also true that society often assists in the process of self-actualization. Western societies provide considerable educational opportunities, training programmes for those with special abilities or skills, and so on. Thus, people often achieve self-actualization because of, rather than in spite of, the society in which they live.

Carl Rogers (1902–87)

Carl Rogers's approach to psychology was based on the notion of the **self-concept** . Each individual has a self-concept, which consists of his or her conscious thoughts and beliefs about himself or herself. This self-concept can be contrasted with the **ideal self**, which is essentially the self-concept that the individual would choose to have. Normal, well-adjusted people have much less of a discrepancy between their self-concept and ideal self than do those who are unhappy or maladjusted.

How can we assess an individual's self-concept and ideal self? Perhaps the most common method is to make use of the **Q-sort method.** The individual is given a pile of cards, each of which has on it a personal statement (e.g. 'I find life a constant struggle'; 'I am angry much of the time'). The individual then decides which statements best describe his or her own self, which statements are slightly less applicable, working through to those statements which are least descriptive. Then the procedure is repeated with the same statements, but this time the individual rates his or her ideal self.

Some evidence for the value of the above approach was reported by Gough *et al.* (1978). The Q-sort method was used to divide air force officers into those who had good agreement between their real and ideal selves, and those who had poor agreement. Those who had good agreement were described by others as being outgoing, efficient, co-operative and adaptable. In contrast, those who had poor agreement between their real and ideal selves were regarded as unfriendly, confused, awkward and slow.

Client-centred therapy

Rogers's most lasting achievement was the development of **client-centred therapy.** In order to understand this therapy, it is necessary to consider Rogers's views on the emotional problems that can occur in the course of development. According to Rogers, children as they grow up are increasingly affected by the opinions and values of other people (e.g. their parents). He identified the process of **introjection**, which is what happens when other people's values are incorporated into the child's own ways of thinking. These values produce **conditions of worth**, because they help to define the conditions which need to be fulfilled in order for us to experience positive self-regard. For example, children may feel pleased when they have done their homework conscientiously, because this is valued by their parents.

As children grow up, they will sometimes experience a state of incongruence, in which there is a discrepancy between their self-concept and their behaviour. For example, a child who bullies smaller children may think that he or she is kind-hearted. Such incongruence may lead to **distortion**, in which the experiences are reinterpreted (e.g. it wasn't really bullying at all). Alternatively, incongruence may lead to **denial** (i.e. the experiences never happened). In either case, incongruence can lead to anxiety and eventually to psychological maladjustment.

One of the basic assumptions of Rogers's client-centred therapy is that clients requesting therapy have incongruence between their self-concept on the one hand, and their experiences and the behaviour they display in some situations on the other hand. Some support for this assumption was obtained by Cartwright (1956), who presented his participants with a mixture of self-descriptive and non-self-descriptive words to learn. He argued that the processes of denial and distortion associated with incongruence would produce poor learning and recall of the words that were not self-descriptive. As predicted, those who had requested therapy or who had received unsuccessful therapy recalled fewer non-self-descriptive words than did well-adjusted individuals.

Rogers differed from the great majority of clinical psychologists in that he was relatively unconcerned about diagnosing or identifying the specific mental disorder from which a client was suffering. He was more interested in how his clients dealt with situations in which there was a mismatch between their experiences and their self-concepts. He identified a number of strategies, two of which were rationalization and fantasy. The essence of rationalization is that individuals distort their interpretation of their own behaviour to make it appear consistent with their self-concept. For example, a client may have been rude and unpleasant to someone, but claim unfairly that this was self-defence against the aggressiveness of the other person. Fantasy involves the creation of a new self-concept (e.g. 'I am Winston Churchill'), combined with denying experiences which do not fit this fantasized self-concept (e.g. 'No one else thinks I am Winston Churchill').

According to Rogers, therapists using client-centred therapy should display **unconditional positive regard** towards their clients. This positive response by the therapist encourages clients to express socially unacceptable thoughts and feelings without fear of rejection from the therapist. In practical terms, the therapist will often try to restate what the client is saying in more precise terms, and without offering any judgements on the desirability or undesirability of the client's statements. The flavour of client-centred therapy can be seen in the following exchange (Rogers 1947) between Carl Rogers and a female client called Mary Jane Tildon:

Client: I don't know what I'm looking for. It's just that I wonder if I'm insane sometimes. I think I'm nuts.
Rogers: It just gives you concern that you're as far from normal as you feel you are.

Client: That's right. It's silly to tell me not to worry because I do worry. It's my life . . . well, I don't know how I can change my concept of myself because that's the way I feel.
Rogers: You feel very different from others and you don't see how you can fix that.

(Rogers 1997: 138–9)

Apart from offering unconditional positive regard, successful therapists need to be *genuine*, in the sense that they really respect and value their clients rather than merely pretending to do so. Therapists also need to be *empathic*, that is, they need to have a good understanding of the feelings of others. When client-centred therapy is successful, clients come to see themselves as others do, and reduce incongruence by accepting who they are.

There has been some dispute about the importance to successful therapy of therapists showing unconditional positive regard, being genuine and being empathic. In one review of various methods of psychotherapy (Truax and Mitchell 1971), it was concluded that successful therapists generally possess those three characteristics. However, Beutler *et al.* (1986) reviewed later evidence, and concluded that unconditional positive regard, genuineness and empathy are less important in determining the success of therapy than was assumed by Rogers.

According to Rogers, one of the main changes that occurs during successful therapy is that the client's initially large discrepancy between self-concept and the ideal self is much reduced. This notion was tested by Rogers (1961), who gave client-centred therapy to a 40 year old woman with an unhappy marriage and guilt concerning the psychological problems of her daughter. Q-sorts carried out before the start of therapy indicated a low correlation of +0.21 between her real and ideal selves. In other words, she saw her real self or self-concept as being very different from what she wanted. After five and a half months of therapy, the correlation between her real and ideal selves had increased to +0.69, and there was a further increase to +0.79 at the one-year follow-up.

Strengths and weaknesses of Rogers's approach

One of the strengths of Rogers's approach was his emphasis on the self-concept, and on the discrepancy between the real and ideal selves as an indication of maladjustment. There is little doubt that the thoughts and feelings that individuals have about themselves are of importance in determining behaviour and adjustment.

A second strength of Rogers's approach was his development of client-centred therapy, which seems to be reasonably effective (Davison and Neale 1986). However, the evidence is less favourable to encounter groups, which are based on some of Rogers's ideas. The fundamental idea with encounter groups is that the participants should discuss their opinions and feelings openly with the rest of the group. Those taking part in encounter groups often feel that they have been valuable. However, encounter groups can have undesirable effects on those who have low self-esteem or are disturbed (Kaul and Bednar 1986).

On the negative side, Rogers focused too much on people's desire to become actualized or to realize their potential. As Rogers (1959) expressed it, 'this basic actualizing tendency is the only motive which is postulated in this theoretical system'. This ignores a large number of other motives (biological and psychological) which influence people's behaviour. There is also the problem that actualization is not defined with any precision. As Krause (1964: 70) pointed out, the notion of an actualizing tendency 'appears to explain too much too vaguely for any differential predictions to derive from it.'

Some of the available evidence indicates that Rogers's view that a small discrepancy between the real and ideal selves is a sign of maturity is oversimplified. For example, Katz and Zigler (1967) compared 11, 14 and 17 year old students, and found that the older students had greater discrepancies between their real and ideal selves than did the younger ones. They also found that the discrepancy was greater in more intelligent students. These findings suggest that increased maturity can make the individual more sensitive to differences between his or her behaviour and internal standards, thus producing findings which are exactly the opposite of those predicted by Rogers.

Evaluation of the humanistic approach

The humanistic approach possesses a number of significant strengths. For example, it provided a more comprehensive view of human motivation than that provided by other theorists. Many motivation theorists had focused on basic physiological needs, and had ignored powerful motivational forces such as those for self-esteem and self-actualization. The essential correctness of the humanistic approach is shown by the fact that millions of people whose physiological needs are met nevertheless feel dissatisfied and unfulfilled.

A second strength of humanistic psychology is its focus on issues which are of great importance to human beings. Most of us are concerned about our self-concept, our level of self-esteem and our success (or otherwise) in realizing our potential. In contrast, many theories in psychology seem to focus on relatively trivial issues.

A third strength of humanistic psychology is that some of its major ingredients have been incorporated into forms of therapy such as client-centred therapy. An evaluation of the success of client-centred therapy was provided by Davison and Neale (1986):

As a way to help unhappy but not severely disturbed people understand themselves better . . . client-centred therapy may very well be appropriate and effective . . . Rogerian therapy may not, however, be appropriate for a severe psychological disorder, as Rogers himself has warned.

(Davison and Neale 1986: 489)

Some of the major problems with humanistic psychology stem from its wholehearted reliance on phenomenology. If only things were that simple! It would mean that psychologists could obtain a very detailed understanding of other people simply by inviting them to talk about themselves. In fact, much valuable information lies below the level of conscious awareness, and so cannot be accessed by the use of phenomenology. People often report their experiences in a rather distorted fashion, and this also reduces the value of subjective experience.

An example of how unreliable conscious awareness can be was reported by Nisbett and Wilson (1977). They presented their participants with a horizontal array of very similar pairs of stockings, and asked them to select the best pair. When they were asked to justify their choice, most participants said that it was because the chosen pair was slightly better in colour or texture than the other pairs. In fact, most participants selected the right-most pair. This indicates that their choices were influenced by relative spatial position, a fact of which they were unaware.

The other major weakness of the humanistic approach is its relative neglect of some of the main determinants of personality. As Freud pointed out, adult personality is often influenced by the experiences of childhood, but there is very little consideration of such experiences within humanistic psychology. As we will see later in the chapter, there is considerable evidence that heredity plays an important role in the determination of personality. This contrasts with the view of Maslow and Rogers that we all inherit somewhat similar personalities.

Ψ Section summary

The humanist approach was developed by Maslow and Rogers in the United States. They emphasized the notions of personal responsibility, free will, personal growth and fulfilment. The humanist approach relies heavily on phenomenology rather than the scientific method. Maslow proposed a hierarchy of needs, with self-actualization at the top of the hierarchy. Rogers put forward client-centred therapy, which involves the attempt to reduce the client's discrepancy between his or her self-concept and ideal self. The therapist must display unconditional positive regard, and should be genuine and empathic. Client-centred therapy is fairly effective, especially in the treatment of relatively mild disorders. Humanistic psychologists focus on important issues, but their reliance on phenomenology limits its scope and scientific value. Humanistic psychologists de-emphasize the importance of childhood experiences and genetic factors as determinants of adult personality.

1 Describe and evaluate Maslow's theory of motivation.
2 What is client-centred therapy?
3 What are the main features of the humanistic approach? What are the strengths and weaknesses of this approach?

☐ Personality assessment

The approaches to personality which have been discussed so far have made relatively little use of personality tests. However, personality tests are of central importance to factor theories of personality. Before discussing factor theories in detail, we will consider some of the main types of personality tests which have been devised by psychologists.

Major types of tests

Personality tests can be regarded as falling into four major categories: questionnaires, ratings, projective tests and objective tests.

Questionnaires

Easily the most common method for measuring personality is by means of self-report questionnaire. This method involves individuals deciding whether certain statements do, or do not, apply to them. Sample questions are, 'Do you usually enjoy lively parties?' and 'Does your mood sometimes change for no apparent reason?' Self-report questionnaires are useful because the individual is likely to know more about his or her own personality than do other people. They are also useful because they are easy to administer.

Ratings

Another major method for assessing personality is via the use of ratings. Observers provide ratings about other people's personalities. For example, a rater might be supplied with a list of various forms of behaviour related to personality (e.g. 'tends to be aggressive'; 'smiles a lot'), and has to indicate whether the person being rated possesses these characteristics. In general terms, raters who have known someone for a long time produce ratings which are closer to that individual's own self-report questionnaire data than do raters who have had a short acquaintance with that individual.

Projective tests

Another approach to personality assessment is through the use of projective tests. Projective tests usually involve giving the subject some ambiguous stimuli and asking him or her to interpret or make sense of them. Consider, for example, the well-known Rorschach Inkblot Test, in which subjects have to decide what each inkblot suggests to them. The basic idea behind projective tests is that presenting people with an ambiguous or unstructured situation will allow their personality to manifest itself freely.

Objective tests

The final approach to personality assessment is based on objective tests. There is a very wide range of objective tests. What they have in common is that they measure behaviour relevant to personality in such a way that the subjects do not know what is being assessed. One example is the *fidgetometer*. This is a special chair with various electrical contacts that are closed by movement. The amount of movement over a fixed period of time is recorded, and it is assumed that this is a measure of anxiety. Another example is the task of blowing up a balloon until it bursts, which is regarded as a measure of timidity. Most objective tests have proved to be of rather limited value, because they do not provide consistent and valid measures of personality.

Reliability and validity

There are two main requirements of a satisfactory personality test. First, it should possess good **reliability**. In other words, it should provide consistent measurement of personality. Second, a personality test should possess good **validity**: it should measure those personality traits which it is supposed to measure. The reliability and validity of the different kinds of personality assessment are discussed below

Reliability

There are a number of ways in which the reliability of a personality test can be assessed. However, the most common method is by means of the *test-retest method*. Several individuals complete a personality test on two occasions, and the similarity between the scores obtained is calculated in the form of a correlation coefficient. Most of the major self-report questionnaires possess good reliability. For example, the test-retest reliability coefficient for tests such as the 16PF and the Eysenck Personality Questionnaire is normally in the range of +0.80 to +0.85 provided that the interval of time between test and retest is not too long. Not surprisingly, test-retest reliability falls well below +0.80 when several years intervene between test and retest (Conley 1984).

Validity

The various types of validity which were discussed in relationship to intelligence tests (see Chapter 13) are also applicable to personality tests. In particular, much of the focus with personality tests has been on **empirical validity** and **construct validity**. Empirical validity is involved when test performance is correlated with some appropriate external criterion. Construct validity is involved when performance on a personality test is used to test the predictions of some relevant theory.

Empirical validity can be illustrated in connection with the personality dimension of trait anxiety, which is often assessed by means of the State-Trait Anxiety Inventory (Spielberger *et al.* 1970). It would be expected that clinical patients who are diagnosed as suffering from generalized anxiety disorder would have high levels of trait anxiety. This prediction was tested by M.W. Eysenck *et al.* (1991). Generalized anxiety disorder patients had considerably higher trait anxiety scores than normal controls. Other approaches to empirical validity are discussed later in the chapter.

Construct validity of trait anxiety as assessed by Spielberger's State-Trait Anxiety Inventory was studied by MacLeod and Donnellan (1993). They were testing the hypothesis that anxiety reduces available working memory capacity (Eysenck and Calvo 1992). Subjects performed a reasoning task while at the same time trying to remember either several digits (high memory load) or a few digits (low memory load). It was predicted that high-anxious subjects would find it harder than low-anxious subjects to perform the reasoning task with the high memory load in working memory. As can be seen in Figure 14.3, that is precisely what was found. These findings support the theory relating anxiety to working memory and they also support the validity of the measure of trait anxiety.

When trying to assess the validity of either self-report questionnaires or personality ratings, it is possible to make use of **consensual validity**. All that is involved is that the participants' questionnaire responses are correlated with the ratings made by observers. It is assumed that the limitations of self-report questionnaires and rat-

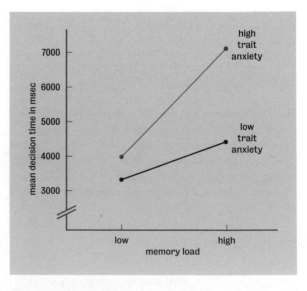

Figure 14.3 Performance on a reasoning task in high- and low-anxious groups as a function of memory load
Source: Macleod and Donnellan (1993)

ings are rather different. Self-report measures are liable to distortion because the individual gives an unduly favourable account of himself or herself, whereas ratings may be inaccurate because the observer or rater has only a limited knowledge of the person being rated. If a moderately high correlation between the self-report and rating measures is obtained in spite of the weaknesses of each measure, then we can have some confidence that both measures are reasonably valid.

Kenrich and Stringfield (1980) argued that personality traits differ in terms of *observability*. Relatively observable personality traits are those in which there is a fairly direct link between personality and behaviour, whereas relatively unobservable traits are those in which behaviour is a more indirect reflection of the underlying personality. They claimed that consensual validity is greater for more observable personality traits (e.g. extraversion) than for less observable ones (e.g. trait anxiety), and their evidence supported this claim.

Some of the most convincing evidence for consensual validity was reported by McCrae (1982). He correlated self-report measures of extraversion and neuroticism (a personality dimension resembling trait anxiety) with ratings provided by spouses. There was a correlation of +0.72 for extraversion, which was substantially greater than the correlation of +0.47 for neuroticism.

One of the major factors reducing the validity of self-report questionnaires is known as **social desirability response set**. This is the tendency to respond to questionnaire items in a socially desirable fashion, even if the answer given is not correct. One common way of assessing social desirability bias is to include items for which the correct answer is unlikely to be the same as the socially desirable answer. Sample items are 'Of all the people you know, are there some you definitely dislike?' and 'Do you ever talk about people behind their back?' If someone consistently answers such questions in the socially desirable direction, it is assumed that the person is lying.

Another way of trying to reduce or eliminate social desirability response set is used in some questionnaires such as the Edwards Personal Preference Schedule. Subjects completing this test are presented with several pairs of statements. They have to choose one out of each pair of statements, which were carefully constructed so that they are equally high or low in social desirability.

Another factor reducing the validity of self-report questionnaires is **acquiescence response set**. This is the tendency to respond 'yes' to all the items on a questionnaire regardless of item content. It is reasonably easy to assess acquiescence response set. Half of the items are constructed so that a 'yes' response indicates a high level of extraversion, hostility, or whatever, and the other half are written so that a 'no' response has the same meaning. Those individuals who mostly respond 'yes' to both sets of items are exhibiting acquiescence response set.

Sample tests

Self-report questionnaires

There are hundreds (or even thousands) of self-report questionnaires designed to measure personality. Two of the best known ones (Cattell's Sixteen Personality Factor Questionnaire and the Eysenck Personality Questionnaire) will be discussed later in the chapter. Another well-known questionnaire is the Minnesota Multiphasic Personality Inventory, which was produced in 1940. It was designed for diagnostic purposes, so that the precise nature of the psychiatric disorder from which someone was suffering could be ascertained. It contains a total of ten scales, nearly all of which have a rather psychiatric feel: *depression*, *neurosis*, *introversion*, *masculinity–femininity*, *hypomania* (over-excited and agitated), *hypochondria* (excessive health concerns), *schizophrenia* (involving loss of contact with reality), *paranoia* (involving delusions), *psychopathic deviate* (antisocial, aggressive) and *conversion hysteria* (with emotional outbursts).

There are hundreds of items in the Minnesota Multiphasic Personality Inventory. The decision as to which scale each item belongs was made on empirical rather than on theoretical grounds. More specifically, any item that was found to discriminate well between paranoid patients and patients with other diagnoses was included in the paranoia scale. This happened even if the relevance of the item to paranoia was totally unclear.

In addition to the ten scales already mentioned, the Minnesota Multiphasic Personality Inventory also includes scales designed to detect lying. One such scale contains items to detect social desirability response set resembling those discussed above. Lying was also detected by another scale containing strange statements along the lines of 'There are persons who are trying to steal my thoughts and ideas.' Very few patients endorse such statements, and so a tendency to agree with these statements is taken as evidence that the answers may be inaccurate.

In spite of its popularity, the Minnesota Multiphasic Personality Inventory suffers from two major problems.

First, the usefulness of the test depends crucially on the validity of psychiatric diagnoses, since such diagnoses formed the basis for allocating items to scales. In fact, psychiatric diagnoses are notoriously unreliable, and so do not form a solid foundation for test construction. Second, several of the scales are measuring rather similar things, and sometimes the same items appear in more than one scale. This issue was explored by Wakefield *et al.* (1974). They obtained evidence that the hysteria, depression, neurosis and conversion hysteria scales are all related to H.J. Eysenck's neuroticism dimension, whereas the paranoia, psychopathic deviate and schizophrenia scales are related to his psychoticism dimension.

Projective tests

Probably the best known projective test is the Rorschach Inkblot Test, which was published by the Swiss psychologist Hermann Rorschach in 1921. The basic test involves presenting ten inkblots to subjects, who are asked to make suggestions as to what might be represented by each inkblot. When this has been done, the subjects are asked to indicate the part or parts of the inkblot that were most influential in determining their responses.

It is difficult to interpret the responses produced by any given individual. In general terms, interpretations take into account information about content, location and determinants. Content is the object or objects reported by the individual, location is the part of the inkblot providing the basis of the response, and the determinants are those aspects of the inkblot, such as form or colour, which influence the choice of response. Most expert users of the Rorschach Inkblot Test argue that the location and the determinants are of more importance in interpretation than is content. Some of the general principles used in interpreting inkblots were described by Gleitman (1986):

> **Using the entire inkblot is said to indicate integrative conceptual thinking, whereas the use of a high proportion of small details suggests compulsive rigidity. A relatively frequent use of the white space . . . is supposed to be a sign of rebelliousness and negativism.**
> **(Gleitman 1986: 618)**

Another major projective test is the Thematic Apperception Test, which was developed by Henry Murray in the mid-1930s. Subjects are shown various pictures one at a time. Their task is to indicate what is happening in the picture, what preceded the situation shown, and what is likely to happen next. The responses of the subjects are then interpreted in an attempt to discover their underlying motives.

It has typically been found that most projective tests possess poor reliability and validity. People tend to respond rather differently to the same projective test on different occasions, perhaps because of their very unstructured nature. Much of the evidence on validity of projective techniques was discussed by Zubin *et al.* (1965). They concluded that the Rorschach test has generally poor validity. The presence of human movement responses to the inkblots is supposed to indicate creativity, but eminent artists fail to produce more of such responses than unselected groups of individuals. Any validity possessed by the Rorschach test seems to depend more on content than on location or determinants, which is precisely the opposite of what is claimed by Rorschach experts.

Figure 14.4 A meaningless shape resembling those in the Rorschach Inkblot Test

ψ Section summary

Personality can be assessed by means of questionnaires, ratings, projective tests and objective tests. Questionnaires are used most frequently, followed by ratings, with objective and projective tests being substantially less popular than they used to be. Satisfactory personality tests need to have good reliability and validity. The main self-report questionnaires have high reliability and moderate valid-

Box continued

ity. Among the factors reducing their validity are social desirability response set and acquiescence response set. Ratings also often have high reliability and moderate validity. Projective tests and objective tests generally have low reliability and validity.

1 Discuss the main requirements of a useful personality test, and how these requirements can be assessed.

2 Describe and evaluate some well-known personality tests.

Factor theories of personality

Several factor theories of personality have been proposed over the years. The basic assumption made by factor theorists is that factor analysis can be applied to the patterns of correlations among personality-test items to produce a reasonably small number of personality traits or factors. More specifically, questionnaire or rating items which correlate highly with each other are assumed to be measuring the same underlying personality trait, whereas those which do not correlate with each other reflect different traits.

Our coverage will focus on the factor theories of Raymond Cattell and H.J. Eysenck, as well as the more recent five-factor theory. Before discussing these theories in detail, we will consider some limitations of the factor analytic approach. Factor analysis has been compared to a sausage machine, in the sense that what you get out of it depends on what you put into it in the first place. For example, a factor or trait of conscientiousness will not emerge unless some items relating to conscientiousness are included in the original factor analysis. This limitation can be overcome if we include a sufficiently wide range of items in the factor analysis, but there is no satisfactory way of knowing whether we have achieved that goal.

Another limitation of factor analysis is that it is not guaranteed to identify important personality traits or factors. What factor analysis does is to provide guidelines or suggestions as to possible major personality traits. In order to confirm the importance of these traits or factors, it is necessary to obtain evidence that they are of consequence in everyday life.

A further limitation of factor analysis is that it operates at the descriptive rather than the explanatory level. Suppose for the sake of argument that factor theorists manage to identify all of the major personality traits. We would still need a theory which explained why those traits are important, and which explained the processes producing individual differences in these traits.

A final limitation of factor analysis is that there are a number of different factor analytic techniques, and a number of different ways of deciding how many factors to extract. For any given set of data, both the number and nature of the personality factors obtained will often vary dependent upon the precise factor-analytic approach which is used. A major difference between factor theorists is whether they regard it as acceptable for two personality factors to correlate with each other. Some theorists (e.g. H.J. Eysenck) favour independent or **orthogonal factors**, which must be uncorrelated with each other. In contrast, other theorists (e.g. Cattell) prefer **oblique factors** which are correlated with each other.

Is it preferable to focus on orthogonal or oblique factors? It is not reasonable to argue that one approach is in principle superior to the other. However, it is possible to decide between the two approaches in the light of the evidence. As we will see, theorists who have focused on orthogonal or uncorrelated factors have had more success in describing human personality than have theorists who prefer oblique factors.

Cattell's trait theory

The ultimate goal of most trait theorists is to discover all of the main personality traits. Raymond Cattell, who was born in 1905, tried to do precisely this. He used the term 'personality sphere' to refer to the total domain of personality traits, and argued that the best way to cover the entire personality sphere was by searching through all the words in the English language. According to what has been called the 'lexical hypothesis', every important aspect of human personality will be represented by one or more words in the language. This hypothesis is plausible, but there is no strong evidence that it is correct. In any case, Cattell (1943) based much of his approach to personality on the assumption that the lexical hypothesis is true.

Cattell embarked on his ambitious attempt to provide a comprehensive description of personality by making use of earlier work by Allport and Odbert (1936). They discovered a total of 18,000 words in the dictionary which were related to personality. Of these words, 4,500 were trait terms. These were reduced to 160 trait words by eliminating synonyms and unfamiliar words. After that, Cattell (1945) added a further 11 personality traits based on previous tests, finishing up with a total of 171 trait terms which allegedly covered the whole personality sphere.

Cattell (1945) then faced the problem that he still had a very large number of potential personality traits. To reduce the number, he used information from previous studies to find traits which seemed to be rather similar, and thus to be different measures of essentially the same trait. This enabled Cattell to reduce the number of personality traits to 35. These 35 traits he called surface traits, because they were readily observable. These surface traits were then examined in a number of rating studies, leading Cattell to the conclusion that there are approximately 16 basic or source traits underlying the 35 surface traits.

The findings which have been described so far were based very largely on rating data. Cattell referred to them as L data or life-record data. The major personality traits found in L data are not necessarily the same as those found in other kinds of data. Accordingly, Cattell decided to study the personality traits or factors to be found in questionnaire (Q) and objective test (T) data. He assumed at the outset that the same personality traits would emerge in L, Q and T data, but this assumption was not confirmed. Factor analyses of L and Q data produced broadly similar traits or factors, but there were major discrepancies between the factors found in objective test data and those found in the other two kinds of data.

The major measure of personality which emerged from Cattell's detailed exploration and accumulation of questionnaire, life-record and objective test data was a self-report questionnaire known as Cattell's Sixteen Personality Factor Questionnaire or 16PF. As its name indicates, the 16PF was designed to assess 16 different personality factors or traits (see below). Cattell adopted a rather broad definition of personality, and so his test includes measures of intelligence and social attitudes as well as more typical personality traits.

In spite of the enormous success of the 16PF, it is a seriously flawed test. Some of the initial evidence identifying its deficiencies was reported by Howarth and Browne (1971). They administered the 16PF to 567 subjects, and then carried out factor analysis of the data. They managed to identify only ten separate factors, leading them to the conclusion that 'the 16PF does not measure the factors which it purports to measure' (Howarth and Browne 1971: 117). Similar findings were reported by Barrett and Kline (1982), who gave the 16PF to 491 subjects. They analysed their data very thoroughly using five different methods of factor analysis to identify the factors contained in the 16PF.

Each analysis produced between seven and nine factors, and those factors bore little relation to those proposed by Cattell.

Why did Cattell claim that his test measures 16 different personality traits when the evidence indicates clearly that it measures only approximately half that number? An important part of the answer was provided by Howarth and Browne (1971). They pointed out that a fully adequate factor analysis of the 16PF requires the inclusion in the analysis of information about the answers given by every subject to every item. In contrast, Cattell initially placed information from several items into a 'parcel', and then proceeded to correlate each parcel of items with the other parcels. This arbitrary and subjective procedure of allocating items to parcels prior to factor analysis produced most of the distortions contained in the 16PF. Howarth and Browne (1971) were probably the first psychologists to carry out a full item analysis on the 16PF; this revealed that there are nothing like sixteen factors in the 16PF.

Strengths and weaknesses of Cattell's approach

Cattell's trait theory of personality possesses a number of significant strengths. Of particular importance is the general approach adopted by Cattell as he tried to discover the structure of human personality. He attempted to cover personality in a comprehensive fashion by starting with all the personality terms in the dictionary, and no superior way of achieving the goal of being comprehensive has been proposed by others. In addition, his argument that personality traits emerging in rating, questionnaire, and objective-test data are likely to be more important than those found in only one or two kinds of data is persuasive. The thorough way in which he studied personality based on all three kinds of data is indicative of the fact that Cattell has devoted more time and effort than anyone else to the systematic investigation of personality.

The greatest weakness of Cattell's approach is his focus on oblique or correlated factors of personality. This focus led to the development of the 16PF, but this test does not measure more than about eight factors. It might still be argued that the approach based on correlated factors is potentially superior to the one based on independent factors, because it can provide a richer description of human personality. However, psychologists have been trying for several decades to uncover 12–16 correlated personality factors, but without any great success (H.J. Eysenck and M.W. Eysenck 1985).

As with the case of the 16PF, what is generally found is that a smallish number of correlated factors is found, but even these factors are hard to replicate from one study to the next (H.J. Eysenck and M.W. Eysenck 1985).

Eysenck's trait theory

H.J. Eysenck shared with Cattell the view that factor analysis is a valuable way of identifying the structure of personality. However, there is a major disagreement between them in terms of the relative importance of specific first-order factors and more general second-order factors. Cattell focused mainly on first-order factors, which are also known as oblique or correlated factors. In contrast, Eysenck argued that second-order factors (also known as orthogonal or uncorrelated factors) are of more importance, because first-order factors are frequently weak and hard to find consistently.

Eysenck's (1944) first attempt to discover the main second-order factors in personality was based on a sample of 700 patients suffering from neurotic disorders. The ratings of psychiatrists on 39 rating scales were factor-analysed, and two second-order factors were found: **neuroticism** and **extraversion**. Those high in neuroticism tend to be tense, anxious and depressed. Subsequent research has established that neuroticism resembles trait anxiety, which is the predisposition or susceptibility to experience anxiety (H.J. Eysenck and M.W. Eysenck 1985). So far as extraversion is concerned, extraverts are more sociable and impulsive than introverts. These personality dimensions are measured by the Eysenck Personality Inventory.

H.J. Eysenck (1967) put forward theoretical accounts of the physiological bases of extraversion and neuroticism. According to him, introverts have a chronically higher level of cortical arousal (activity in the brain) than extraverts. The reason for this is that they have greater activity in a part of the brain known as the ascending reticular activating system. Those high in neuroticism were claimed to have greater activity than those low in neuroticism in the visceral brain. The visceral brain consists of the hippocampus, amgygdala, cingulum, septum and the hypothalamus. This hypothesis seems in line with the fact that those high in neuroticism report much more physiological activity and more physiological symptoms than do those low in neuroticism (Eysenck 1967).

Most subsequent research has confirmed that neuroticism and extraversion are important personality traits. H.J. Eysenck (1978) has added a third personality factor to his theoretical framework, and called it **psychoticism**. Those who score high on psychoticism are 'egocentric, aggressive, impulsive, impersonal, cold, lacking in empathy and concern for others, and generally unconcerned about the rights and welfare of other people' (H.J. Eysenck 1982: 11). Psychoticism has generally been measured by means of a self-report questionnaire known as the Eysenck Personality Questionnaire.

Eysenck (1978) argued that psychoticism assesses the predisposition to suffer psychotic breakdown, in which there is a partial or total loss of contact with reality. In fact, the evidence does not support this interpretation. Juvenile delinquents and prisoners generally obtain higher psychoticism scores than do psychotic groups such as schizophrenics (Zuckerman 1989). These findings led Zuckerman (1989) to argue that the psychoticism scale should be renamed a psychopathy scale, since psychopaths are aggressive criminals with an anti-social personality.

Experimental evidence

Behavioural studies

As we have seen, H.J. Eysenck (1967) argued that introverts are typically higher than extraverts in cortical arousal. This theoretical assumption has been tested under laboratory conditions by comparing the performance of introverts and extraverts on vigilance tasks. The essence of a vigilance task is that it is monotonous and long-lasting, with the subject only being required to respond occasionally. For example, Mackworth (1950) asked his subjects to observe a clock pointer, and to indicate whenever they detected an occasional double jump in the movements of this pointer.

There is considerable evidence that physiological arousal and vigilance performance both decline during the course of most vigilance tasks (Davies and Parasuraman 1982). It would thus be predicted that introverts, with their higher level of cortical arousal, should perform better than extraverts. M.W. Eysenck (1988) discussed twelve relevant studies. The performance of introverts was significantly better than that of extraverts in five studies, but the two groups did not differ in the other seven. In ten studies (overlapping considerably with those already discussed), the extent to which performance deteriorated over the course of the task was assessed. This so-called vigilance decrement was greater in extraverts than in introverts in four studies, but there were no effects of introversion–extraversion in the remaining six studies.

Physiological studies

Possible differences between introverts and extraverts in cortical arousal have been assessed in several psychophysiological studies (see H.J. Eysenck and M.W. Eysenck 1985 for a review). Some of the most relevant evidence has come from studies of electroencephalography or the EEG (brain-wave activity), since there is a pattern in the EEG which is characteristic of high arousal. Gale (1983) reviewed 33 studies containing a total of 38 comparisons between personality groups. Introverts were significantly more cortically aroused than extraverts in 22 comparisons, but introverts were significantly less aroused than extraverts in 5 comparisons. Thus, introverts tend to be slightly more cortically aroused than extraverts, but there are many situations in which this is not the case.

As we have seen, Eysenck (1967) claimed that individual differences in neuroticism depend on differences in the activity of the 'visceral brain'. It is not feasible to measure directly the level of activity in the visceral brain, but several indirect measures (e.g. heart rate, skin conductance, EEG) are available. There have been numerous studies considering a wide range of different physiological measures under stressful and non-stressful conditions. This evidence was discussed in detail by Fahrenberg (1992), who came to the following pessimistic conclusion:

> Over many decades research has failed to substantiate the physiological correlates that are assumed for emotionality and trait anxiety. There is virtually no distinct finding that has been reliably replicated across studies and laboratories.
>
> (Fahrenberg 1992: 212–13)

It is now clear why the predicted physiological differences between high and low scorers on neuroticism or trait anxiety are not found. There are essentially two groups of individuals who obtain low scores on neuroticism or trait anxiety: truly low-anxious individuals who are easy-going and enjoy life, and controlled individuals (known as 'repressors') who are controlled and who have a defensive coping style (Weinberger 1990). As was mentioned earlier in the chapter, truly low-anxious individuals obtain low scores on a measure of defensiveness such as the Marlowe-Crowne Social Desirability Scale, whereas repressors obtain high scores on the Marlowe-Crowne.

Weinberger et al. (1979) exposed truly low-anxious subjects, repressors and high-anxious subjects to a mod-erately stressful situation. They found that the repressors responded physiologically much more than the truly low-anxious; indeed, the repressors were more physiologically responsive than the high-anxious subjects on most of the measures, in spite of the fact that they typically report low levels of stress and anxiety. This pattern of results has been found in several other studies (see Weinberger 1990). The implication of these findings is that any relationship between neuroticism or trait anxiety and physiological responsiveness is obscured by the high responsiveness of repressors.

Role of heredity

According to Eysenck, individual differences in extraversion, neuroticism and psychoticism depend to a large extent on heredity. For example, he argued that 'the evidence suggests fairly strongly that something like 50 per cent of individual differences in neuroticism and extraversion … is accountable for in terms of hereditary influences' (H.J. Eysenck 1967: 210). Most of the relevant evidence has come from twin studies. If heredity is of major importance, then monozygotic or identical twins (who have very similar heredity) should be much more alike in personality than dizygotic or fraternal twins.

The earliest relevant twin study seemed to provide striking support for the importance of heredity. H.J. Eysenck and Prell (1951) measured neuroticism, and found that the correlation between identical twins was +0.85, whereas it was only +0.22 for dizygotic twins. These findings suggested that 80 per cent of individual differences in neuroticism are due to heredity.

Subsequent research has indicated that the findings of Eysenck and Prell (1951) were very anomalous, especially the remarkably high correlation for identical twins. Zuckerman (1987) reviewed the findings from eight twin studies of neuroticism. The highest correlation for monozygotic twins in any of those studies was +0.67, and the mean correlation was only +0.52. For dizygotic twins, the mean correlation was +0.24. The largest twin study to consider neuroticism was by Floderus-Myrhed et al. (1980). They studied over 12,000 twin pairs, and reported correlations of +0.50 and +0.23 for monozygotic and dizygotic twins, respectively.

Very similar findings have generally been reported for extraversion. However, in the first study (H.J. Eysenck 1956), anomalous findings were reported. The correlation for monozygotic twins was +0.50, whereas it was −0.33 for dizygotic twins. This suggested that 62 per cent of individual differences in extraversion are determined by heredity. More typical findings were reported in the Floderus-Myrhed *et al.* (1980) study. There was a correlation of +0.51 for monozygotic twins, and one of +0.21 for dizygotic twins. Zuckerman (1987) reviewed several twin studies, across which the mean correlation for monozygotic twins was +0.51, compared to +0.12 for dizygotic twins.

There is much less evidence on psychoticism, but the findings closely resemble those for neuroticism and extraversion. Zuckerman (1989) discussed four studies using psychoticism-type scales. The median correlation for monozygotic twins was +0.52, and that for dizygotic twins was +0.21. These figures suggest that approximately 40–50 per cent of individual differences in extraversion and neuroticism stem from heredity.

In principle, the most important evidence about the influence of heredity on personality can be obtained by considering monozygotic twins brought up apart. If heredity is of major importance, such twin pairs should be rather similar in personality. In contrast, if environment is of major importance, then they should show little similarity. The findings are somewhat inconsistent, in part because only a few pairs of twins were included in some studies.

The closest approach to a definitive twin study was reported by Pedersen *et al.* (1988). They used the Eysenck Personality Inventory to assess extraversion and neuroticism in 95 monozygotic pairs brought up apart, 150 monozygotic pairs brought up together, 220 pairs of dizygotic pairs brought up apart, and 204 dizygotic pairs brought up together. Of the twin pairs brought up apart 48 per cent were separated before their first birthday and 82 per cent were separated by the age of 5. For neuroticism, the correlations were as follows: +0.25 for monozygotic twins brought up apart, +0.41 for monozygotic twins brought up together, +0.28 for dizygotic twins brought up apart, and +0.24 for dizygotic twins brought up together. These figures indicated that 31 per cent of individual differences in neuroticism are due to heredity. For extraversion, the correlations were as follows: +0.30 for monozygotic twins brought up apart, +0.54 for monozygotic twins brought up together, +0.04 for dizygotic twins brought up apart, and +0.06 for dizygotic twins brought up together. Pedersen *et al.* (1988) argued from these data that 41 per cent of individual differences in extraversion are due to heredity.

In sum, the evidence suggests that somewhere between 30 per cent and 50 per cent of individual differences in neuroticism, extraversion and psychoticism are due to

heredity. However, there are ⬛ suggest that the true figure ⬛ gotic twins reared apart are o⬛ branches of the same family, a⬛ similar environments than ⬛ (Shields 1962). Second, the ⬛ heredity on personality are u⬛ tion that monozygotic and dizygotic twins have similar environments. However, monozygotic twins are treated more alike than dizygotic twins in terms of spending time together, having parents who try to treat them alike, in playing together, and in having the same teachers at school (Loehlin and Nichols 1976). This means that the greater similarity in personality of monozygotic than dizygotic twins may depend in part on greater environmental similarity rather than simply greater genetic similarity.

Strengths and limitations of Eysenck's approach

The main strengths of Eysenck's approach have been his high level of productivity, and his focus on two of the major factors of personality, i.e. extraversion and neuroticism. He identified these two factors during the 1940s, but several other psychologists had previously emphasized the importance of these two factors. For example, Guilford and Guilford (1936) carried out factor analyses of a personality questionnaire to identify three aspects of extraversion: shyness, emotionality and masculinity. Even earlier, Guilford (1934: 343) called attention to the 'very troublesome situation found by those who construct tests of I–E [introversion–extraversion] and of "neurotic tendency", a difficulty in keeping the two types of tests from correlating with one another'. In other words, several tests measuring factors resembling extraversion and neuroticism had been devised by the mid-1930s.

Eysenck's third factor of psychoticism possesses more originality. However, it seems that psychoticism is not really a major factor, and his psychoticism scale is probably more of a measure of psychopathy than of a predisposition to psychosis. His theory also contains some important omissions. As we will see shortly, his descriptive approach to personality has now been superseded by the more complete five-factor model.

The other strength of Eysenck's theoretical approach is his emphasis on the role of heredity as a determinant of adult personality, although other theorists had also done this many years earlier. For example, Guilford (1934: 335) argued that 'most writers

rded I–E [introversion–extraversion] as pri-
a matter of heredity'. Eysenck greatly exagger-
d the importance of heredity in some of his early
twin studies and in his theoretical statements. For
example, he argued that 'genetic factors contribute
something like two-thirds of the variance in major personality dimensions' (H.J. Eysenck 1982: 28). In fact,

it seems probable that only approximately 30 per cent
or 40 per cent of individual differences in neuroticism,
extraversion, and psychoticism are due to heredity.

The main weakness of Eysenck's trait theory is his
attempt to provide an explanatory theory of the physiological systems underlying the various personality dimensions. There is modest experimental support for the view

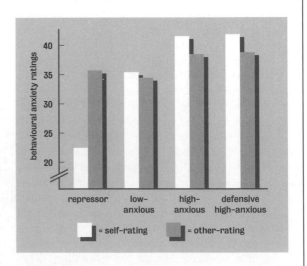

Research update

The cognitive approach

Since the early 1980s, there have been a number of
attempts to understand neuroticism or the closely
related personality dimension of trait anxiety from the
cognitive perspective. For example, M.W. Eysenck (1997)
has argued that there are important individual differences in cognitive biases. Individuals high in trait anxiety have a selective attentional bias (they generally
attend to threat-related rather than neutral stimuli)
and an interpretative bias (they tend to interpret
ambiguous stimuli in a threatening way). In contrast,
repressors (low in trait anxiety and high in social
desirability) have an opposite selective attentional bias
(they avoid attending to threat-related stimuli) and an
opposite interpretative bias (they tend to interpret
ambiguous stimuli in a non-threatening way).

Fox (1993) reported findings which fit this cognitive
theory. She assessed attentional focus when threat-
related and neutral stimuli were presented at the same
time. High-anxious participants showed selective attentional bias and repressors showed the opposite bias.

Other findings which fit the theory were obtained by
Nazanin Derakshan and M.W. Eysenck (1997) in a study
of interpretative bias. They made videotape recordings
of students giving a public talk in front of other students. The students then provided self-ratings of their
behavioural anxiety as revealed by the videotape.
Other-ratings based on the same videotapes were
obtained from two independent judges. Some of the key
findings are shown in Figure 14.5. High-anxious participants showed evidence of an interpretative bias,
because their self-ratings indicated greater behavioural anxiety than was found in the other-ratings. In
contrast, repressors showed evidence of an opposite
interpretative bias. Their self-ratings indicated lower
behavioural anxiety than did the other-ratings.

M.W. Eysenck's (1997) theory places much more emphasis on the importance of the cognitive system than previous trait theories. One of the advantages of his theory is
that it provides a way of explaining why there is practically no association between trait anxiety or neuroticism
and level of physiological activity, in spite of the fact that
those high in trait anxiety report many more physiological
symptoms. In essence, high-anxious individuals exaggerate the threateningness of their physiological symptoms
because of their cognitive biases. In contrast, repressors
minimize the threateningness of their physiological symptoms because of their different cognitive biases.

It is too early to evaluate fully the cognitive
approach. However, there is strong evidence for consistent individual differences in cognitive biases, and it is
likely that these cognitive biases are of importance in
accounting for individual differences in personality.

Figure 14.5 Self-rated and other-rated behavioural
anxiety in repressor, low-anxious, high-anxious and
defensive high-anxious groups
Source: Data from Derakshan and Eysenck (1997)

that individual differences in introversion– extraversion depend on levels of cortical arousal, but the physiological bases of neuroticism and of psychoticism remain obscure. At the theoretical level, Eysenck's claim that activity in the ascending reticular activating system underlies introversion–extraversion, whereas activity in the limbic system underlies neuroticism, does not make much physiological or anatomical sense. As Claridge (1986) pointed out, those two physiological systems are so closely interconnected that they should not be regarded as acting independently. Pervin (1993: 290) summarized Eysenck's contribution, referring to 'Eysenck's tendency to dismiss the contributions of others and exaggerate the empirical support for his own point of view'.

ψ Section summary

Prominent theories of personality based on factor analysis were proposed by Cattell and by H.J. Eysenck. Cattell made use of a very thorough and comprehensive approach, and collected extensive self-report, rating, and objective-test data. Cattell identified 16 correlated factors in self-report data. However, subsequent research has indicated that there are only about half that number of factors in Cattell's 16PF, and many of them do not resemble the factors identified by Cattell. H.J. Eysenck focused on three uncorrelated factors: extraversion, neuroticism and psychoticism. There is evidence that genetic factors play a role in accounting for individual differences in each of these three factors. H.J. Eysenck's attempts to identify the physiological bases for these personality dimensions proved rather unsuccessful.

1   How has factor analysis been used to investigate personality?

2   Compare the personality theories of Cattell and Eysenck.

Five-factor model

Since the early 1990s, several personality theorists have agreed among themselves that there are five major personality factors. There are some minor disagreements among them concerning the most appropriate names for these factors, but there are many more areas of agreement. The starting point for the five-factor model was the work of W.T. Norman (1963). He obtained rating data from students using Cattell's trait rating scales. In contrast to Cattell, Norman then looked for orthogonal or independent factors in his rating data. He obtained evidence for five personality factors:

- extraversion (e.g. sociable)
- agreeableness (e.g. co-operative)
- conscientiousness (e.g. responsible)
- emotional stability (e.g. calm)
- culture (e.g. imaginative)

Several other researchers have since reported similar findings. For example, McCrae and Costa (1985) obtained ratings on 80 scales, and identified five factors which they named extraversion, agreeableness, conscientiousness, neuroticism (the opposite of emotional stability) and openness (similar to culture). They produced a revised version of their NEO Personality Inventory incorporating these five factors (the letters NEO stand for neuroticism, extraversion and openness).

One of the criticisms that has been levelled at the five-factor model of personality is that the supporting evidence is rather narrow in scope. This criticism was addressed by Goldberg (1990). In his first study, he made use of 1,431 terms referring to aspects of personality. Student subjects provided self-descriptions using these terms, which were then formed into 75 categories. The data were finally analysed by means of ten different methods of factor analysis, and consistently produced the following five factors: surgency, agreeableness, conscientiousness, emotional stability and intellect. In a second study, Goldberg (1990) made use of 479 common trait terms grouped into 133 synonym clusters. The same five factors emerged in two sets of self-reports, and also in two sets of ratings. As he concluded,

It now seems reasonable to conclude that analyses of any reasonably large sample of English trait adjectives in either self- or peer-descriptions will elicit a variant of the Big-Five factor structure.

(Goldberg 1990: 1223)

Strengths and weaknesses of the five-factor model

The main strength of the five-factor model of personality is that it provides a good description of the structure of personality. It has been clear for a long time that the number of major personality factors is substantially less than Cattell's sixteen, and greater than Eysenck's three. There is impressive evidence supporting the view that there are five major personality factors, and they are at least approximately as described within the five-factor model.

The main weakness of the five-factor approach is that it is a descriptive model rather than an explanatory one. Suppose we ask the question, 'Why is it that surgency, agreeableness, conscientiousness, emotional stability and openness or intellect are the main factors of personality?' Most five-factor theorists would simply answer that that is how things are. In other words, they would not be able to provide any theoretical explanation of why these five, and only five, factors of personality are of importance.

Some attempt to provide the beginnings of a theoretical framework was made by Goldberg (1990). He argued that the factors relate to major themes in life. Surgency relates to power, agreeableness relates to love, conscientiousness relates to work, emotional stability to affect or emotion, and openness or intellect to intelligence.

It is assumed by advocates of the five-factor model of personality that the five factors are independent of each other. This is by no means always the case. For example, consider a rating study by Goldberg (1993). When those being rated included a number of disliked individuals, it was found that agreeableness, conscientiousness, emotional stability and intellect all inter-correlated with each other. What happened here was that the negative feelings towards some of those being rated led to them obtaining low ratings on those four personality factors.

Evaluation of the trait approach

The trait approach to personality has a number of major strengths. One of its strengths is the way in which this approach has made significant progress in identifying the major factors or dimensions of personality. It is a real achievement that different lines of research have converged on the same (or almost the same) five personality traits. Another strength is the strong evidence that heredity plays a role in producing individual differences in personality. This is predicted by trait theorists, but is inconsistent with the assumptions of humanistic psychologists and social learning psychologists (discussed later). A third strength of the trait approach is its adherence to the scientific method. As a consequence, this approach has developed over time in a way which has not happened with less scientifically based approaches such as the psychoanalytic or the humanistic.

On the negative side, it has proved very difficult for trait theorists to move from a descriptive to an explanatory account of personality. For example, the physiological and other processes underlying individual differences in personality remain unclear. Another important weakness relates to changes in personality over time. When personality questionnaires are used to measure personality, its consistency from one year to the next is +0.98 (Conley 1984). This indicates good consistency, but still means that fairly large changes in personality happen over a period of several years. Most trait theorists have not considered in detail the processes responsible for producing dynamic changes in personality.

Some critics of the trait approach (e.g. Mischel 1968) have argued that a central weakness of the trait approach stems from its assumption that any given person should behave in a reasonably similar or consistent fashion in different situations. This assumption is often known as **cross-situational consistency**. According to Mischel (1968), there is very little evidence of cross-situational consistency. He reviewed the evidence from several studies in which an attempt was made to predict people's behaviour in various situations on the basis of their personality scores. Mischel (1968) concluded that the correlation between personality and behaviour rarely exceeds +0.30. This suggests that personality traits do not account for more than 9 per cent of individual differences in behaviour, and thus that cross-situational consistency does not exist. These findings raise some fairly complex issues, which are discussed in the following section.

Situation versus trait controversy

One of the main conclusions which Mischel (1968) drew from his apparent discovery that cross-situational consistency does not exist is that people's behaviour is determined by the situation rather than by their personality. However, several studies published after Mischel's (1968) review reported high levels of cross-situational consistency. For example, Small et al. (1983) studied adolescents involved in a camping programme. Various measures of dominance and prosocial or co-operative behaviour were obtained while four groups of adolescents were camping, during mealtimes, and during free time. Correlations within each group were calculated separately for dominance and prosocial behaviour across pairs of situations. All of the correlations exceeded +0.30, and 75 per cent of them exceeded +0.70. In other words, the participants consistently behaved in a dominant or submissive way across situations, and the same consistency was observed for their prosocial behaviour.

One reason why cross-situation consistency is sometimes high and sometimes low was identified by S. Epstein (1977). He argued that consistency is more likely to be found if we combine or aggregate information about behaviour rather than considering one or two measures of behaviour. He found that sociability ratings from two one-day samples of behaviour correlated only +0.37. However, sociability ratings based on two 14-day samples of behaviour correlated +0.81. Thus, cross-situational consistency tends to increase when we take more extended and reliable behavioural measures.

There are other ways of testing Mischel's (1968) view that our behaviour is determined more by the situation than it is by our personality. Sarason *et al.* (1975) measured the percentage of the variance (differences in performance from one person to the next) accounted for by the situation and by personality. The higher the percentage of the variance (up to a maximum of 100 per cent) accounted for by a given factor, the greater the importance of that factor in determining behaviour. Across a total of 138 experiments, the situation accounted on average for 10.3 per cent of the variance, and personality accounted for 8.7 per cent of the variance. In other words, neither personality nor the situation predicted behaviour very well. The implication is that we need to consider both factors in order to predict how people will behave.

In spite of what has just been said, it is clear that there are some situations in which behaviour is determined almost entirely by the situation. For example, nearly everyone stops at a red light and arrives in time for an important examination. The notion that there are some situations in which individual differences in personality are not important was explored by Buss (1989). He argued that behaviour is determined by the situation rather than personality in the following laboratory situations:

- the situation is novel, formal, and public
- there are detailed and complete instructions
- subjects have little choice of behaviour
- the situation is of brief duration

In contrast, personality is important in the following situations:

- the situation is familiar, informal, and private
- there are general or no instructions
- there is considerable choice of behaviour
- the situation lasts for a long time

Several theorists (e.g. Bowers 1973; Endler and Edwards 1978) have argued that it is fruitless to argue that either personality or the situation is all-important. According to their interactionist approach, behaviour depends on the interaction between personality and sit-

Ψ Case study

Practical relevance

Tests such as the Eysenck Personality Questionnaire, the 16PF and the NEO Personality Inventory have been used extensively in personnel selection. If these tests have good empirical validity, then it might be expected that they would predict aspects of job performance. This issue was examined by Blinkhorn and Johnson (1990). They considered numerous studies in which the California Psychological Inventory, Cattell's 16PF or the Occupational Personality Questionnaire had been used to predict job performance. Fewer than 10 per cent of the correlations between personality traits and job performance were statistically significant, suggesting that these tests have poor empirical validity. Blinkhorn and Johnson (1990: 672) concluded as follows: 'We see precious little evidence that even the best personality tests predict job performance, and a good deal of evi-

dence of poorly understood statistical methods being pressed into service to buttress shaky claims'.

The general usefulness of the factor theory approach is limited if personality scores poorly predict real-world behaviour. However, Hough *et al.* (1990) reported greater success. They administered the Assessment of Background and Life Experiences to soldiers, some of whom were told that their responses might have an effect on their army careers, whereas others were not. The personality scores of the soldiers correlated reasonably well with the job ratings of other soldiers and supervisors, and this was equally the case for both groups. Hough *et al.* (1990) concluded that questionnaires can predict job performance if lie scales are used to detect distorted responses, and those being assessed are warned that distorted responses will be detected.

uation. Three forms which this interaction can take were discussed by Atkinson *et al*. (1993):

- reactive interaction: individuals behave differently in any given situation because they interpret and experience it in different ways
- evocative interaction: the behaviour of others towards us depends in part on the effect we have on them; for example, those who are aggressive are more likely to find that other people behave aggressively towards them (Atkinson *et al*. 1993)
- proactive interaction: the situations we find ourselves in are often those we have chosen to enter; for example, extraverts choose to spend more time than introverts in social situations (Furnham 1981)

Ψ Section summary

Cattell identified sixteen personality factors, while Eysenck identified three (extraversion, neuroticism and psychoticism), and argued that individual differences on all three factors are largely due to genetic components. The role of heredity seems to be less than was assumed by Eysenck, and it has proved difficult to find the predicted physiological differences between extraverts and introverts, or between those high and low on neuroticism. There is reasonable agreement that there are five major personality factors, but the five-factor model is descriptive rather than explanatory. Issues that arise in connection with factor theories of personality include that of cross-situational consistency and their practical relevance.

1 Are there sixteen, three or five personality factors?

☐ Social learning theory

Social learning theory, as proposed by theorists such as Julian Rotter (1954) and Albert Bandura (1977b, 1986), is one of the most important approaches to personality. Its origins owe much to behaviourism, and so key aspects of the behaviourist approach will be considered before turning to social learning theory.

Behaviourists such as Watson and Skinner emphasized the notion that behaviour is determined very largely by the environment. According to them, individual differences in behaviour can be explained on the basis that everyone has had a unique conditioning history. In general terms, people will spend their time engaged in activities which have been associated with reward or positive reinforcement in the past, whereas they will avoid activities which have been associated with punishment. This emphasis on the impact of the external environment on our behaviour led Watson (1924) to the following famous (or notorious) statement:

Give me a dozen healthy infants . . . and my own specialized world to bring them up in, and I'll guarantee to take any one at random and train him to become any type of specialist I might select – doctor, lawyer, . . . and yes, even beggarman and thief, regardless of his talents . . . tendencies, abilities . . . and race of his ancestors.

It is now accepted that the behaviourist approach is a very oversimplified one. For example, it is highly unlikely that an individual's behaviour is determined solely by the situation. As Rorer and Widiger (1983) argued,

If one really believes that situations determine behaviour, then there is no reason to test or interview prospective employees for jobs such as police officer; it is only necessary to structure the job situation properly. Picking a mate would simply be a matter of finding someone whose physical characteristics appeal to you. In a properly managed class all students would work to their abilities. Do you know anyone who believes these things? Obviously not.

Rotter's theory

Social learning theorists agree with the behaviourists that situational influences on behaviour are important, and that behaviour is influenced by rewards and punishments. However, they generally attach much more importance than the behaviourists to internal processes of various kinds. For example, Rotter (1954) put forward a social learning theory in which the emphasis was on **expectancies**. When we are rewarded or positively reinforced for a certain piece of behaviour, this increases our expectancy that that behaviour will be rewarded in the future. Rotter (1966) extended this approach, arguing that some people tend to believe that their actions will lead to rewards and punishments, whereas others feel that the rewards and punishments they receive depend relatively little on their own actions. Rotter (1966) devised a **locus of control** scale to measure these individual differences: those who believe that what happens to them depends on their own actions are said to have an internal locus of con-

Plate 14.3 Those with an internal locus of control are more likely to behave in ways that will keep them healthy

trol, whereas those who feel that what happens to them is the result of forces outside of their control have an external locus of control.

There is evidence that those with an internal locus of control tend to be physically healthier than those with an external locus of control (Strickland 1979). An important reason for this is that internals are more likely to behave in ways that will keep them healthy. For example, internals are more likely than externals to succeed in the task of giving up smoking (Shipley 1981), and obese internals are more successful than obese externals at losing weight (Balch and Ross 1975). Externals are relatively unsuccessful in pursuing a healthy lifestyle because they are not convinced that their behaviour will affect their later physical health.

Rotter (1954) also emphasized **reinforcement value**, which he defined as the extent to which we prefer one reinforcer over another when the probability of obtaining each of them is equal. Our behaviour is determined to some extent by the reinforcement value we associate with different activities, and reinforcement value in turn is determined by our past experiences. According to Rotter, an individual may devote exceptional time and effort to achieving a particular goal because he or she attaches considerable reinforcement value to it.

In sum, Rotter showed that the behaviourist or conditioning approach to human behaviour could be extended and improved by adding to it various internal processes (e.g. expectancies, reinforcement value). This general

approach was taken much further by Bandura (1977b, 1986); his contributions to social learning theory are discussed at length in the next section of the chapter.

Bandura's social cognitive theory

Albert Bandura, who was born in 1925, initially adopted a behaviourist position, arguing that behaviour is determined to a great extent by environmental influences. Subsequently, he put forward a more complex view known as **reciprocal determinism**. According to this view, environmental factors (e.g. reward, punishment), internal factors (e.g. beliefs, expectations) and behaviour all influence each other. Thus, the behaviourist emphasis on the influence of the environment on behaviour is regarded as merely one out of a number of influences.

Bandura also differs from behaviourists such as Skinner in his interpretation of the effects of reinforcement on behaviour. According to Skinner, reinforcement works in a rather automatic fashion, strengthening the response (e.g. lever pressing) which occurred immediately before the reinforcement was presented. In contrast, Bandura (1977b) argued as follows: 'Reinforcement serves principally as an informative and motivational operation rather than as a mechanical response strengthener.' In other words, reward has its effects by providing useful information about which responses are likely to be rewarded in future, and by providing the incentive or motivation to produce those responses in future. This is preferable to the behaviourist or Skinnerian position for the following reason: 'If actions were determined solely by external rewards and punishments, people would behave like weather vanes, constantly shifting in radically different directions to conform to the whims of others' (Bandura 1977b: 27).

There is another important way in which Bandura's theoretical position differs from that of most behaviourists. This difference was expressed clearly by Bandura:

Psychological theories have traditionally assumed that learning can occur only by performing responses and experiencing their effects. In actuality, virtually all learning phenomena resulting from direct experience occur on a vicarious [second-hand] basis by observing other people's behaviour and its consequences for them. The capacity to learn by observation enables people to acquire large, integrated patterns of behaviour without having to form them gradually by tedious trial and error.

(Bandura 1977b: 12)

Observation learning or modelling

We have just seen that Bandura emphasizes the importance of modelling or **observational learning**. Bandura *et al.* (1963) provided an early demonstration of the role of modelling in learning. One group of young children watched a film in which a female adult model behaved aggressively towards a large inflated clown known as a Bobo doll, punching it and sitting on it. (The Bobo doll is attached to a heavy base, so that it springs back upright when knocked down.) A second group of children watched a film in which the same adult behaved in a non-aggressive way towards the Bobo doll. After they had watched the film, the children were given the chance to play with the Bobo doll. The children who had observed the adult model behaving aggressively towards the Bobo doll were much more likely to attack it than those who had observed the adult model behaving non-aggressively.

Bandura later argued that an important aspect of modelling or observational learning is **vicarious reinforcement**. According to the notion of vicarious reinforcement, the extent to which we imitate the behaviour of models depends on whether the model's behaviour is rewarded or punished. Bandura (1965) considered vicarious reinforcement in a study in which young children watched a five-minute film of an adult model behaving aggressively towards a Bobo doll:

the model laid the Bobo doll on its side, sat on it, and punched it in the nose. . . . The model then raised the doll and pummelled it on the head with a mallet. . . . Following the mallet aggression, the model kicked the doll about the room.

(Bandura 1965: 590–1)

Some of the children saw only this film. Other children saw a second piece of film in which the model was either rewarded with soda pop and sweets or punished by being accused of being a coward and a bully and by being hit with a rolled-up newspaper.

The children were then allowed to play with the Bobo doll. Those children who had been exposed to the rewarded model exhibited the most aggression, whereas those who had seen the model being punished showed the least aggression. Bandura (1965) wondered whether these group differences in behaviour were matched by differences in learning. Accordingly, he then offered all of the children attractive prizes if they could imitate the behaviour of the model. All of the groups were equally successful at this task, indicating that differences in vicarious reinforcement affected performance rather than learning.

Bandura (1977b) identified a total of six regulatory mechanisms through which vicarious reinforcement can affect the behaviour of observers:

- informative: it provides information about the likely consequences of behaving in a certain way
- motivational: it can motivate the observer to imitate or to avoid the model's behaviour
- emotional learning: it can produce emotional arousal (e.g. fear) or a general increase in responsiveness
- influenceability: the observer's susceptibility to reinforcement may be increased by seeing the model's response to similar reinforcements
- modification of model status: the observer's perception of the model's social status can rise or fall depending on whether the model is rewarded or punished
- valuation: the observer's valuation of both the person administering reinforcement and of the model can be altered (e.g. seeing a model punished unjustly may make the observer think badly of the reinforcing agent and sympathetically towards the model)

Limitations of Bandura's approach

Bandura's research and theory on modelling or observational learning have been very influential. There is no doubt that such learning is important in everyday life, but previous theorists had paid relatively attention to it. However, observers by no means always show the strong tendencies to imitate the behaviour of a model found in many of Bandura's studies. For example, we have seen that children generally imitate the aggressive behaviour of an adult model towards a Bobo doll, but children tend not to imitate aggressive behaviour towards another child. There is also evidence that the novelty value of the Bobo doll is important. Children who had not seen such a doll before were five times more likely to imitate the aggressive behaviour of an adult model against it than were children who were familiar with it (Cumberbatch 1991).

Self-regulation

According to Bandura (e.g. 1986), much of our behaviour is self-governed by means of self-produced consequences for our own actions. More specifically, three different components are involved: *self-observation*, *judgemental process* or *personal standards*, and *self-response processes*.

People observe their own behaviour and relate it to their personal standards. These personal standards depend in part on the reactions of other people, but they also depend on our observations of various respected models. When an individual's behaviour exceeds his or her personal standards, then self-response processes such as self-satisfaction or self-pride will follow. When his or her behaviour falls short of his or her personal standards, then self-response processes will produce self-dissatisfaction or self-criticism.

Bandura and Kupers (1964) showed how self-reinforcement can influence behaviour. Children observed a model playing a miniature bowling game in which he rewarded himself with sweets either for superior performance only or for mediocre performance. The children then played the bowling game for themselves, and had access to a plentiful supply of sweets. In general, the self-reinforcement which the children gave themselves corresponded to the model's pattern of reinforcement.

In other words, children who had observed the model setting himself high standards for rewarding himself tended to adopt the same high standards for self-reinforcement.

Self-efficacy

Bandura (1977b, 1986) argued that many individual differences in behaviour depend on different levels of **self-efficacy**. Self-efficacy refers to an individual's assessment of his or her ability to cope satisfactorily with particular situations. According to Bandura (1977b: 391), self-efficacy judgements are concerned 'not with the skills one has but with judgements of what one can do with the skills one possesses.'

Bandura claims that self-efficacy has a key role in influencing people's behaviour:

> **Given appropriate skills and adequate incentives, . . . efficacy expectations are a major determinant of people's choice of activities, how much effort they will expend, and how long they will sustain effort in dealing with stressful situations.**
>
> **(Bandura 1977a: 194)**

Apart from self-efficacy, motivation depends on **outcome expectancies** and on **outcome value**. Outcome expectancies are expectations about whether the desired reward or reinforcement will be forthcoming if the person behaves appropriately. For example, will hard work at school lead to examination success? Outcome value refers to the perceived value of the reward or reinforcement to the individual.

Much evidence indicates that behaviour can be predicted on the basis of **efficacy expectations**, i.e. beliefs or convictions that the individual can produce certain outcomes or effects. For example, DiClemente *et al.* (1985) considering a group of people who were trying to give up smoking. They found that those high in self-efficacy were more likely to succeed than were those low in self-efficacy.

What determines an individual's sense of self-efficacy in any given situation? According to Bandura, there are four main factors involved:

- performance accomplishments: efficacy expectations depend mainly on what has happened in the past; previous success leads to high expectations, and previous failure leads to low efficacy expectations
- vicarious experiences: observing others succeed or fail can have similar (but smaller) effects on self-efficacy to those produced by one's own success or failure
- verbal persuasion: feelings of self-efficacy can be increased if someone you respect (e.g. parent, teacher) argues persuasively that you have the ability to cope successfully with a given situation
- emotional arousal: high levels of arousal can lead people to experience anxiety and tension, and to lower their feelings of self-efficacy

Clinical and health applications

Individuals who are generally low in feelings of self-efficacy are likely to experience feelings of distress, and to attempt relatively little appropriate coping behaviour.

As a result, it is not surprising that most clinical patients suffering from anxiety and depression have very low feelings of self-efficacy (Maddux 1991). Since this is correlational evidence, it is not clear whether the low self-efficacy plays a part in producing the clinical state, or whether the clinical state produces the low self-efficacy. However, creating low self-efficacy expectations has been found to be followed by low self-efficacy expectancies (Maddux 1991). This suggests that feelings of low self-efficacy can produce or increase feelings of depression.

Bandura (1986) argued that most clinical patients would benefit from an increase in their feelings of self-efficacy. He discussed several studies supporting this prediction. In one study, snake phobics were persuaded by models to have progressively more contact with boa constrictors or corn snakes. Eventually, influenced by the model's example, they were able to return the snake to its cage, and even allow it to crawl on their laps while they kept their hands by their sides. The phobics' efficacy expectations for doing these things were very low beforehand, but were much higher afterwards. In contrast, snake phobics who did not have the benefit of guided modelling had much lower efficacy expectations, and were not able to tolerate so much contact with the snake.

In other studies, Bandura (1986) considered vicarious experience, in which snake phobics simply observed models handling snakes and letting them crawl over them. Such vicarious experience increased efficacy expectations, reduced physiological arousal in the form of heart rate and blood pressure, and led to more contact with snakes than was found in control phobics who did not receive vicarious experience.

Evaluation of Bandura's theory

Bandura's social cognitive theory has had a considerable impact on personality research and on clinical practice. This is largely justified. Bandura has been especially successful in developing the views of Skinner and other advocates of operant conditioning so as to make them more realistic. More specifically, Bandura was absolutely correct to argue that cognitive processes of various kinds are very important in determining the effects of reward and punishment on behaviour. Although relatively ignored by other theorists, observational learning or modelling is of major significance in determining what we learn in our everyday lives.

Self-efficacy undoubtedly affects behaviour in many situations. However, this is probably mainly the case when the criteria for successful performance are clear

---

 Research update

Self-efficacy and health-related behaviour

Since the mid-1980s, some of Bandura's theoretical ideas have been applied successfully within health psychology. As an example, we will consider Schwarzer's (1992) health action process approach. According to this approach, health-related behaviour (e.g. giving up smoking) involves a motivational stage and an action stage. In the motivational stage, individuals decide whether or not to carry out a particular form of behaviour. Their level of motivation is determined by self-efficacy (e.g. 'I am very confident that I can stop smoking') and by outcome expectancies (e.g. 'Stopping smoking will improve my health'; 'If I stop smoking, I will gain the approval of others'). The level of motivation is very important in determining health-related behav-

iour. However, other factors are also important. For example, it is important to form adequate action plans (e.g. 'If someone offers me a cigarette, I will focus on the potential damage to my health') and social support from others can make it easier to persevere with health-related behaviour.

Schwarzer (1992) discussed a range of evidence on the factors influencing dental flossing, effective use of contraception, breast self-examination, drug addicts' intentions to use clean needles, intentions to stop smoking, and intentions to follow weight-loss programmes. In every case, self-efficacy was the main predictor of intentions and of behaviour. In other words, anyone who wishes to develop a healthier lifestyle should focus on increasing their level of self-efficacy.

and unambiguous, and when the required behaviour is under deliberate conscious control. In contrast, self-efficacy judgements may have little or no predictive value when these factors are not present (Brewin 1988).

Another potential problem for self-efficacy theory is that self-efficacy judgements are obtained by means of self-report measures which depend on the individual's conscious awareness of his or her internal processes. If individuals are unaware of some of the processes determining how confidently they will respond to a given situation, then such measures will be inadequate.

It is not altogether clear whether Bandura's social cognitive theory should be regarded as a theory of personality. Bandura has tried to predict and to understand people's behaviour in specific situations. This is very different from the approach of most personality theorists (e.g. trait theorists), who try to predict behaviour in a general sense. As M.W. Eysenck (1994a: 86) pointed out, 'It is arguable that Bandura is so far towards the specific end of the specificity-generality continuum, or line, that no general understanding of individual differences emerges'.

Finally, Bandura's social cognitive theory de-emphasizes the role of heredity in determining individual differences in personality. He has shown clearly how cognitive, behavioural, and environmental factors interact, but the biological reality underlying cognition and behaviour is not taken into account.

Ψ Section summary

Social learning theory has its origins in behaviourism. In Rotter's theory, there is an emphasis on expectancies and reinforcement value, and on the notion that there are individual differences in locus of control. Of special relevance for Rotter was the notion that being rewarded for behaving in a certain way increases the expectancy that the same will happen in the future. Bandura's social cognitive theory emphasizes the importance of observational learning or modelling, and the role of vicarious reinforcement. According to Bandura, self-regulation is based on self-observation, personal standards and self-response processes. Bandura also argued that motivation depends on self-efficacy, outcome expectancies and outcome value. Low levels of self-efficacy are found in many clinical patients. Studies in health psychology indicate that self-efficacy predicts intentions and behaviour of relevance to healthy and unhealthy lifestyles.

1 What are the main similarities and differences between the behaviourist and social learning approaches?
2 Discuss Bandura's theoretical approach. How successful has this approach been?

Ψ Chapter summary

• Personality and its determinants

Personality refers to relatively stable, internal factors which produce consistent individual differences at the emotional and motivational levels. Adult personality may depend mainly on childhood experiences (psychoanalytic approach), or it may depend on experiences throughout life (humanistic approach, social-learning approach). Alternatively, it may depend mainly on genetic factors (trait approach).

• Freud's psychoanalytic theory

According to Freud, the mind is divided into the id, the ego and the superego. The id operates at the unconscious level, whereas the ego and superego operate mainly at the conscious and preconscious levels. The id, ego and superego are often in conflict, and conflict produces anxiety. The ego protects itself against anxiety by using various defence mechanisms, which are designed to keep unacceptable thoughts and feelings out of consciousness. These defence mechanisms include repression, displacement and denial. There is reasonably strong evidence for repression.

• Freud's theory of psychosexual development

According to Freud's theory of psychosexual development, children pass through successive oral, anal, phallic, latency and genital stages. Problems or excessive gratification at any stage lead to fixation, in which basic energy or libido remains attached to that stage

Box continued

into adulthood and influences adult personality. A basic assumption of this theory is that adult personality depends mainly on experiences during the first five years of life. There is limited support for the types of personality described by Freud, but it has not been proved that childhood experiences influence personality development in the ways specified by Freud.

● **Humanistic approach**

The humanistic approach was proposed by Maslow and Rogers. This approach emphasizes personal responsibility, free will, the importance of the here and now, and the notion of personal growth and the need for self-actualization. Understanding is achieved by the use of phenomenology, in which individuals provide accounts of their direct experience. Maslow proposed a hierarchy of needs ranging from basic physiological needs at the bottom to the need for self-actualization at the top. Rogers distinguished between the self-concept and the ideal self, with those who are maladjusted having a large discrepancy between the two. He devised client-centred therapy, which makes use of unconditional positive regard by the therapist to produce changes in the self-concept.

The humanistic approach provides an unusually comprehensive account of human motivation, and it focuses on important issues. However, many of the concepts used by the humanists are very vague, and its anti-science stance has inhibited theoretical progress.

● **Personality assessment**

Personality can be assessed by means of self-report questionnaires (e.g. the MMPI), ratings, projective tests (e.g. the Rorschach Inkblot Test) and objective tests. Any good measure of personality should have high reliability and validity. Validity can be assessed by correlating self-report questionnaire scores with observers' ratings; this is known as consensual validity. Social desirability bias often reduces the validity of self-report questionnaires.

● **Factor theories of personality**

Cattell and H.J. Eysenck are leading factor theorists. Cattell tried to cover the entire personality sphere by using a dictionary to identify words relating to personality. He made use of life-record, questionnaire and objective-test data, but his main measure is the 16PF test. It is supposed to measure sixteen oblique factors

of personality, but actually measures about seven or eight. Eysenck identified the three independent factors of extraversion, neuroticism and psychoticism, and argued that all of these factors are mostly determined by heredity. Twin studies provide some support, but indicate that Eysenck exaggerated the role of genetic factors. His notion that introverts are higher than extraverts in cortical arousal has received some support, but little is known about the physiological systems underlying neuroticism and psychoticism. Subsequent research has confirmed the importance of extraversion and neuroticism, but failed to confirm that of psychoticism.

● **Five-factor model**

It is now generally accepted that there are five main independent factors of personality: extraversion, agreeableness, conscientiousness, emotional stability (the opposite of neuroticism) and culture or openness. The main weakness of this five-factor model is that it is descriptive rather than explanatory. Another weakness of the five-factor model, and one shared by the approaches of Cattell and Eysenck, is that cross-situational consistency of behaviour is less than predicted.

● **Social learning theory**

According to social learning theorists such as Rotter, Mischel and Bandura, individual differences in behaviour depend on our particular learning experiences rather than on inherited personality traits. For example, through observational learning we discover which forms of behaviour are likely to be rewarded or punished; this is termed vicarious reinforcement by Bandura. Bandura also emphasized the notion that behaviour is self-governed via self-produced consequences of our own actions. This self-regulation involves self-observation, personal standards and self-response processes. Bandura argued that the level of self-efficacy is especially important in predicting behaviour. The individual's level of self-efficacy depends on performance accomplishments, vicarious experiences, verbal persuasion and emotional arousal. Clinical patients typically have very low self-efficacy, and treatment designed to increase their feelings of self-efficacy have proved reasonably effective. Self-efficacy levels probably predict behaviour best when the criteria for successful performance are clear, and when the required behaviour is under conscious control.

Further reading

● Burger, J.M. (1993) *Personality*, 3rd edn. Pacific Grove, CA: Brooks-Cole. Nearly all of the theories discussed in this chapter are dealt with at length in this book, and there is good coverage of the relevant experimental findings.

● Eysenck, M.W. (1994) *Individual Differences: Normal and abnormal*. Hove: Lawrence Erlbaum. Chapters 3 and 4 in this book consider many of the personality theories discussed in this chapter.

● Pervin, L.A. (1996) *The Science of Personality*. New York: Wiley. This book provides coherent accounts of many issues in personality research, and is especially good in its coverage of the roles of heredity and environment in personality.

● Ryckman, R.M. (1993) *Theories of Personality*, 5th edn. Pacific Grove, CA: Brooks-Cole. This book contains readable accounts of most of the theories discussed in this chapter; towards the end of the book, there are interesting critical evaluations of the various approaches

● Block, J. (1995) A contrarian view of the five-factor approach to personality description. *Psychological Bulletin*, **117**: 187–215. This article provides a detailed account of the five-factor model, together with a range of damaging criticisms of it.

● Plomin, E. and Daniels, D. (1987) Why are children in the same family so different from each other? *Behavioral and Brain Sciences* **10**: 1–16. Some of the key environmental factors determining personality are dealt with in an impressive fashion in this article.

CHAPTER 15

Emotion

Tim Dalgleish

KEY CONCEPTS • defining emotion • number and type of emotions • development of emotions • biological aspects of emotion • cognitive aspects of emotion • social aspects of emotion • cultural and cross-cultural aspects of emotion

☐ Chapter preview

When you have read this chapter, you should be able to

- understand what psychologists take to be the components of emotional experience and the historical development of these ideas from Aristotle to the present day
- describe how we approach questions concerning the number of emotions and their interrelationship
- understand how emotions develop and change from infancy to adulthood
- describe which parts of the brain are involved in emotion, and the neurobiological theories of emotion
- assess the principal cognitive theories of emotion and their strengths and limitations
- discuss the role of emotions in social interactions and the social constructionist theories of emotion
- understand how emotions differ across cultures

Introduction

Emotions pervade every aspect of our lives. All our waking moments are characterized by nuances of feeling, surges of emotion, **mood** and **affect**. The world's literature, theatre and cinema is dominated by work that revolves around emotional issues and that explores the inner emotional life of its characters. Indeed, for most of us, the way in which we express and experience our emotions greatly defines who we are. It seems then that we must all know what emotions are. However, if we are put on the spot and asked to try and define emotion, the task proves remarkably difficult. Fehr and Russell (1984) found that, although people found it very easy to give examples of emotions, they found it difficult to say in any general, definitional way what emotions are. Emotions are paradoxical in this way. They are at once immediately obvious, yet frustratingly elusive. As it is, they present a major challenge to psychology and their study raises a number of thorny issues which are addressed in this chapter.

Despite these difficulties in trying to pin down exactly what emotions might be, the line taken here is that it is possible to provide at least a framework for understanding emotions – both what they are and why we have them. If you like, a point of view from which the various difficulties and contradictions and debates in emotion research can be critically examined. Briefly, the argument is that emotions are not just by-the-way experiences which serve little purpose and have even less meaning in our day-to-day lives; rather, they are important functional tools that have evolved to deal rapidly and efficiently with changes in the world. According to this view, negative emotions such as anger and fear are the emergency services of the mind – called up in a hurry when things do not go according to plan. Positive emotions, like joy, are signals that things are going well, that the person's goals are being realized and that things are being achieved. This approach to emotions is known as a **functionalist** one and it is probably the dominant idea in contemporary thinking about emotions among psychologists.

There are different ways in which emotions can be claimed to be functionalist. They can function at a very simple level, for instance by helping us to run faster or to react quickly. However, they can also function as complex forms of social communication. In this chapter we shall consider some of the different functional accounts of emotion on offer. Furthermore, there are a number of less well-subscribed, non-functionalist accounts of emotion and we shall touch on these also.

Another key to unlocking the mystery of emotions is to resist thinking of them as unitary phenomena. Instead, we shall suggest that emotions can be usefully thought of as comprising a number of key components, such as feeling, bodily change, and readiness to behave or interact in certain ways. So, how did contemporary psychology arrive at this functional, componential approach to emotions? In order to answer this question it is useful to take a quick trip through time and look at key historical thinkers on the emotions and to consider how their ideas have influenced the way we now think of emotions.

The debate about the nature of emotions dates back to the time of the ancient Greeks and is an integral part of the philosophical writings of authors such as Plato and Aristotle. Their work represents two different ways of approaching emotion that more or less persist to the present time. Plato's ideas were influential to a host of the most notable philosophers in history and Platonic thinking on emotions can be traced through the work of René Descartes (1596–1650), John Locke (1632–1704), David Hume (1711–76) and William James (1842–1910). Contrastingly, Aristotelian thinking on emotions proved relatively unpopular prior to the twentieth century, since when it has come to figure strongly in our current conceptualizations of the nature of emotion. Despite his unpopularity, shades of Aristotle's ideas can be found in the work of the Stoic philosophers, Seneca and Chryssipus (see Rist 1969 and the case study), Thomas Aquinas (1225–74) and Spinoza (1632–77).

So, how did these two giants of Greek philosophy – Plato and Aristotle – differ in their thinking about emotions? Plato viewed the emotions as wild, uncontrollable forces continually in opposition to the powers of reason. For Plato, the mind was a battlefield for the conflict between these unreasonable, wilful forces of emotion and the rational, calculating powers of reason. Furthermore, Plato himself was not an impartial observer of this battle; he strongly believed that the essence of civilization, the essence of a successful *Republic,* was the enslavement of emotion to the power of reason.

Plato's attitude to emotion is still broadly endorsed outside of the professional psychological community, and in some corners within it. Visit any bar on a Friday night and listen in to the conversations around you. It is clear that for most people emotions are viewed with some suspicion; they are frequently referred to as irrational and unhelpful, they cloud our judgement, prevent us from thinking clearly, and impede us from making

Ψ Case study

'That is not logical captain' – The case of Mr Spock, a futuristic Stoic?

By far the most popular character in the first series of the US television show *Star Trek* was that of Mr Spock. During the series' heyday, Leonard Nimoy, the actor who played Spock, was receiving mailsacks full of letters, week in, week out (Nimoy 1995). Unremarkable one might think for a big television star, except for the fact that Mr Spock was most famous for being half-alien and, as such, for not experiencing or expressing emotions – a character trait that, on first blush, does not seem to be the stuff that big audience figures are made of. However, rather than finding Mr Spock cold and unalluring, a considerable chunk of Nimoy's fan mail was from aspiring female companions who found Mr Spock highly attractive. In one case, Mr Nimoy was forced to escape from the roof of a building down a fire truck ladder because of his idolizing fans in the lobby. This surge of interest led Nimoy to publish a book in the 1970s entitled, somewhat defensively, *I am Not Spock*, aimed at trying to help his adoring public recognize the actor rather than the character. This move was met by uproar and condemnation by his fan base (Nimoy 1995): they were not interested in Leonard Nimoy, merely in his incarnation as Spock.

In a way, Spock is a modern-day (or even a futuristic) Stoic. The Stoic philosophers, as epitomized by Seneca, argued that expression of emotions such as anger was never acceptable in civilized society (see Seneca 1963). As Power and Dalgleish (1997) note,

Seneca's principal thesis was that no provocation adequately justifies anger, no situation permits it, and no benefit is ever gained by it. Once individuals allow themselves to become angry, that anger entirely consumes its possessors and prevents them from controlling their own behaviour, dulls their capacity for reasoning and sensible action, and harbours the potential to provoke people to terrible crimes.

(Power and Dalgleish 1997: 314)

You can almost hear Mr Spock politely expressing this message as Captain Kirk yet again loses his cool in the face of minor provocation from some alien life form.

Perhaps Seneca's suggestion that a calm and reserved surface should be presented to the world despite the internal battle to suppress strong feelings that is going on inside, is the clue to Mr Spock's popularity. Maybe Spock's fans do not really believe that he lacks emotions completely. Nimoy speculates on this in his second volume of autobiography. He wonders whether Spock's appeal to women is related to their desire to bring out his emotional side, to move him and attract him against the odds. This fact was cleverly exploited by the makers of *Star Trek*, who devised story lines to suggest that Spock's human, emotional side (he was half-human and half-Vulcan) was never far from the surface. Ironically then, it is perhaps Spock's latent emotionality rather than his lack of emotions that is attractive – in a way he is the epitome of the strong silent type.

sensible decisions. This is a very different view from the one we have considered at the beginning of the chapter where emotions carry out a useful functional role in our psychological life. For the origins of this latter approach to emotions we need to turn to the work of Plato's student, Aristotle.

Aristotle was the first to propose a functionalist theory of emotions and these days his ideas would also be described as a cognitive theory of emotions. Aristotle made two important contributions: the first was to propose that emotions are related to actions – they are somehow a function of the way we behave; second, emotions are responses to how we interpret the world. So, whereas for Plato anger was a boiling,

tumultuous force in the soul, waging a battle with the rational, reasoned part of the mind, for Aristotle, anger was an appropriate emotion that enables us to prepare for retaliation for a perceived wrongdoing. Aristotle was a very streetwise philosopher. He presented his ideas on emotions in his book *The Art of Rhetoric*, a handbook for orators in which emotions are just one tool they can use in order to manipulate their audience to their own ends. It is only since the 1980s that Aristotle has begun to receive the recognition that he deserves for what many consider to be far-reaching ideas on emotion. His discussion of emotions in *The Art of Rhetoric* is broadly similar to most late twentieth century writing on cognitive aspects of emotion; in this sense he was some 2,000 years ahead of his time – a sobering thought for present-day students of emotion.

If Aristotle was the father of the cognitive approach to emotion, as well as being the pioneer of functionalism, then Charles Darwin was the father of the analysis of physiological or bodily aspects of emotion. Darwin became interested in emotions while carrying out his studies on evolution. He began his studies in 1838 by observing emotional expressions in animals as well as in both adult and infant humans. He was also intrigued by emotional expression in abnormal populations and he recruited the help of the director of a large psychiatric asylum in the north of England so that he might make observations of patients there. Darwin also pioneered cross-cultural research in emotions by sending out a set of printed questionnaires to missionaries and others who could observe people in distant cultures.

Darwin saw emotions as providing good evidence for the continuity between humans and animals. However, given that Darwin pioneered the ideas of fitness and adaptability in his book *The Origin of Species*, it is ironic that he actually viewed emotions as having *no* function at all. He viewed emotional expressions as patterns of behaviour that occurred as a response to stimuli in the environment even 'though they may not ... be of the least use' (Darwin 1859: 28).

Darwin's biological approach to emotions was later taken up by William James (1884, 1890). For James, emotions were no more than the experience of bodily symptoms. He famously argued 'if we fancy some strong emotion, and then try to abstract from our consciousness of it all the feelings of its bodily symptoms, we find we have nothing left behind' (1890: 451). James's ideas and those of the Danish psychologist, Karl Lange, published at almost the same time (Lange 1885), came to influence psychological thinking on emotions for most of the twentieth century, despite the minimal role of any cognitive or meaning component in their presentation. James's influence was so pervasive that in the hundredth anniversary edition of the influential psychological journal, *Psychological Review*, Ellsworth (1994) published a paper entitled 'William James and Emotion: Is a Century of Fame Worth a Century of Misunderstanding?' to illustrate her opinion that the widespread adoption and, more particularly, the misunderstanding, of James's ideas had been something of an impediment to the development of psychological thinking on emotions.

At this point, it would be usual to introduce the name of Sigmund Freud. However, his ideas on emotion were principally driven by an interest in psychopathology and, consequently, they are appropriately reviewed in Chapter 18.

In sum, Aristotle and Darwin between them pioneered research and thinking on functional, cognitive, developmental, social, biological and cross-cultural aspects of emotion. These various ways of looking at emotions still prevail. Being pioneers, however, was about all Aristotle and Darwin had in common with respect to emotions. Their views on what emotions were and how they worked differed radically, and in the next section we consider the questions of what exactly are emotions? How might we define them? How might they be working?

These different aspects of emotion that were introduced and hinted at in the work of great thinkers such as Aristotle and Darwin form something of a blueprint for this chapter. First, we shall examine what the different components of emotion and emotional experience might be. We shall then, in turn, consider emotions from developmental, biological, cognitive, social and cultural perspectives in five separate sections. These sections, rather than representing mutually exclusive takes on the concept of emotion, instead introduce a number of different levels of explanation and description that complement each other and add together to provide an overall view of emotions that exceeds the sum of its parts. Each perspective embraces different points of view and areas of contention as well as considerable agreement. It is the intention behind the chapter to highlight the debates and to allow you, the student, to form your own opinions as to the nature of emotion. Many questions are raised by the work in this area, and an alarming number remain nowhere near to being answered. This is, at once, the pleasure and the frustration of emotion research.

❑ Defining emotion

The reason that there has been so much historical debate concerning the essence of emotions is probably because emotions seem to be made up of multiple components. Emotions obviously involve bodily changes and feelings; however, they also seem to be more than this: they encompass propensities for behaviour, action and social interaction and they provide us with a different way of understanding the world – emotions help us to know if things 'feel right'. Contemporary views of emotion acknowledge their multi-componental makeup. Exactly what the multiple components of emotions are and how they relate to each other, however, are still bones of contention in the research community. For example, Van Brakel (1994) provides 22 contemporary definitions of emotion, all slightly different from each other. Despite this variety, there appears to be a consensus that emotions usually consist of the following four components: first, emotions seem to involve physiological change of some type and most usually some form of emotional expression; second, emotions are associated with readiness to behave, what some authors have called an 'action potential' (Frijda 1986). This may or may not be associated with actual behaviour. Furthermore, the behaviour might sometimes best be conceptualized systemically as the interaction between individual parties in a social situation. Third, emotions arguably involve conscious experience. When we experience an emotion we *feel* something. Finally, emotions have a cognitive or meaning component. They involve a weighing up of events in the world with respect to current concerns. Again, ideas about these concepts of evaluation, interpretation and current concern are couched in models ranging from the individualistic, cognitive to the social.

Let us illustrate these various components of emotion with a famous illustration from William James's (1884) paper, 'What is an Emotion?'. James cites the example of encountering a bear. Imagine you are walking casually through the woods enjoying the sights and sounds of nature. Suddenly, there is a roaring sound, a crashing of undergrowth and a bear emerges into the clearing immediately in front of you. You immediately come to a halt, your heart is pounding, your mouth is dry, your muscles tense and you feel intensely afraid. You remember that it's important, when confronted by bears, to stand your ground and so you stay very still despite your fear. Eventually, after an impressive paw-waving show of aggression, the bear wanders off and you are safe.

In this example, then, the emotion is one of intense fear – terror – when you encounter the bear in the woods. The fear goes hand-in-hand with marked physiological changes; for example, the dryness in the mouth, the tension in the muscles, the racing heart and so on. The fear is also characterized by a readiness to run or to fight – the 'fight or flight' syndrome. This is the **functionality** of fear in this instance. However, although there is this **action readiness**, you don't actually follow that through to the level of behaviour; instead, you stand your ground. Another part of the fear is the feeling. You actually feel extremely afraid. Finally, and most elusively, is the cognitive component. You most likely feel afraid because the bear has been understood at

some level to be threatening to your current concerns such as personal survival. If, instead, you had been a big game hunter looking for your first bear trophy, then your current goals and concerns may have been different. Consequently, successfully encountering your target may have led to emotions of excitement and exhilaration rather than, or more likely as well as, fear.

This componential view of emotion is largely derived from the work of Nico Frijda (1986) which provides an excellent overview of psychological research and theorizing on emotions. Frijda's components are endorsed by numerous other theorists in the field such as Oatley (1992), Stein *et al.* (1994) and Power and Dalgleish (1997). This type of idea is, in principle, compatible with other types of accounts ranging from the psychodynamic to the social. In this section we briefly consider each of these major components of emotion (most of which are revisited in greater detail later in the chapter) before going on to address the question of exactly how many emotions there might be.

Physiological changes allied to emotion

In an interesting piece of research on bodily changes in emotion, Harrer and Harrer (1977) monitored the heart rate of the conductor Herbert von Karajan while he went about his daily business. Herr von Karajan owned his own jet and piloted it himself. When landing his plane at Salzburg airport, the authors found that his heart rate rose as he became slightly anxious due to the difficulty of the manoeuvre. It rose even further as he became more anxious on being told to make an emergency take-off just after landing. An interesting footnote to this research, however, is that in neither situation was Herr von Karajan's heart rate as high as when he was conducting emotional passages of one of his favourite pieces of music - Beethoven's *Leonora Overture No. 3*.

There is little disagreement about the fact that emotions such as anxiety go hand in hand with physiological changes, such as heart rate, in this way. However, a more irksome question is whether bodily changes are *specific* to particular emotions. This was the view of the psychologist, William James (see p. 465), in the latter part of the nineteenth century (James 1890). He suggested that every kind of emotional state could be characterized by a *distinct* physiological pattern. In fact, for James the emotion was nothing more than the feeling of what is going on inside our body. Recent research, though, suggests that although some emotions may be distinguished on the basis of their physiological characteristics, it is clearly not the case that every nuance of emotion is physiologically distinct from every other. This work is considered in more detail in the section on biological aspects of emotion.

Expression of emotion

Work on the expression of emotions was pioneered by Charles Darwin in his book, *The Expression of the Emotions in Man and Animals* (1872). Darwin argued that each emotion is a discrete state with a characteristic and unique expression (see Table 15.1).

Table 15.1 Emotional expressions proposed by Darwin (1872) and the emotions to which they are most closely associated

Expression	Possible emotion
Blushing	Shame, modesty
Body contact	Affection
Clenching fists	Anger
Crying	Sadness
Frowning	Anger, frustration
Laughing	Pleasure
Perspiring, screaming	Pain
Hair standing on end	Fear, anger
Shrugging	Resignation
Sneering	Contempt
Trembling	Fear, anxiety

Source: adapted from Oatley (1992)

Research into the expression of emotion has taken place not only in a developmental framework but also in groups of adult subjects across different cultures. This research is consequently considered in detail in the sections on developmental aspects of emotion and on biological aspects of emotion.

Functionality

Some functional accounts of emotion, such as that of Nico Frijda, see **action readiness** as the *raison d'être* of being in an emotional state. For them, emotions are about being able to deal with unexpected events quickly and effectively. In support of this argument, Frijda *et al.* (1989) carried out a survey of 32 emotions by asking their participants to remember episodes corresponding to those emotions. Each of these episodes was then rated on 29 dimensions of action readiness and the authors

found that they were able to predict the original emotion from the list of 32 from the pattern of action readiness dimensions on 46 per cent of occasions. As Oatley and Jenkins (1996) point out, this percentage would probably have been higher, were it not for the fact that some of the emotion names were synonymous making accuracy difficult; for example, sadness, sorrow and misery. The action readiness dimensions included things such as: wanting to oppose, wanting to approach, wanting to avoid, being inhibited, being paralysed, and so on.

The essence of this type of functionalist argument is that it is the readiness to act or behave in certain ways that is important in defining the emotion, not whether the behaviour actually occurs. It is the feeling that we are ready to punch the traffic warden who has just given us a ticket that helps define our anger, not the fact that all we actually do (it is hoped) is smile apologetically. However, there is also a body of research examining the *actual* behaviour associated with emotions and showing that, within certain limits, it is possible to predict people's emotional state from how they are behaving. In a classic study, Sogon and Masutani (1989) filmed four Japanese actors from behind so that viewers of the films were unable to see their faces. American and Japanese participants watched the films and carried out a forced choice recognition task of the emotions which best corresponded to each scene. Some emotions, notably fear, sadness and disgust, were well recognized by all subjects. Others, however, such as a low bow, which is indicative of fear in Japanese society, were not universally recognized.

Historically, there have been approaches to emotion that focus exclusively on these behavioural components. This idea that emotions are nothing more than behaviour is the essence of the various so-called behaviourist theories of emotion in the literature (e.g. Holland and Skinner 1961; Skinner 1974; Watson 1919). Although certain behaviour patterns are loosely associated with different emotions as we saw in the Sagan and Masutani study, this is somewhat removed from the idea that one can reliably determine an emotion from the pattern of behaviour that is exhibited. For example, as Power and Dalgleish (1997) argue when considering a possible Skinnerian account of their Jamesian example of Susan having a lucky escape from a bear that is trying to attack her:

Susan is defined as being afraid because she is running away and because the running away is an escape from the bear. However, it is difficult to see how we could be sure that Susan was not afraid if she stood and smiled at the bear (indeed, the US Park Service rec-

ommends standing still in such situations) or scratched her nose, or performed any other behaviour. Skinner is forced to argue that Susan's behaviour is only fear behaviour if it occurs in the presence of the correct (fearful) event; that is, in the presence of a bear. However, by what means can we decide that the bear is a fearful event? Skinner must resort to saying that it is a fearful event because it give rise to fear and therein lies the circularity of the Skinnerian theory of emotions.

(Power and Dalgleish 1997: 36–7)

The behaviourists' view is also prominent in some writings in philosophy (e.g. Ryle 1949). For example, Ryle argues 'The bored man finds out that he is bored, if he does find this out, by finding that among other things he glumly says to others and to himself "I am bored" and "How bored I feel"' (1949: 99). So, in this example, according to Ryle we are aware of our own emotional states by observing our own behaviour. Perhaps the final word on this subject should be left to Johnson-Laird (1988) in which he tells a joke about two behaviourists who have just made love and are lying in bed talking to each other. Johnson-Laird suggests: 'One behaviourist said to another: "That was fine for you, but how was it for me?"' (1988: 18).

Other functionalist accounts of emotion focus on the putative social functions that emotions might serve (Arnon-Jones 1986b). For example, guilt may serve the social function of reconciliation between an injured party and a guilty party. More complex views suggest that emotions are functional social interactions and this idea is considered in more detail in the section on social aspects of emotion.

Cognitive components of emotion

A number of cognitive aspects of emotion have been examined by investigators and all fall within the umbrella of the research area of cognition and emotion (see Dalgleish and Power 1998; Power and Dalgleish 1997). These diverse aspects include attention, perceptual and memory performance associated with emotion (see e.g. Wells and Matthews 1994; J.M.G. Williams *et al*. 1997), the meanings associated with emotion, representations of emotional information in the mind (see Christiansson 1992), and the development of emotional cognition (e.g. Stein *et al*. 1993). We return to a number of these aspects at various points in the chapter. Here, however, the discussion is restricted to a brief introduction to the ideas behind the main cognitive theories of emotion; namely, interpretation and appraisal.

The idea of **appraisal** was introduced by Arnold and

Gasson (1954) and refers to the suggestion that events in the world are processed in terms of their significance in relation to the concerns of the individual and that this is an important aspect of emotion. Modern-day approaches to appraisal, and to emotions generally, have two important features. The first feature is the idea that a given event can be evaluated in terms of a number of appraisal features or components such as pleasantness, situational control, importance, predictability, effort required, and so on (Ellsworth and Smith 1988). In this analysis, the combination of appraisal features helps determine which emotion is instigated in a given situation. So, for example, according to Ellsworth and Smith's scheme, happiness would be associated with events appraised as pleasant, low in effort, high in certainty, and high in attention. In contrast, fear might be unpleasant, attention-provoking, uncertain, low in control, important, and unpredictable.

The second feature involves the idea that events are appraised of events in terms of the ongoing goals or concerns of the individual at a given time (e.g. Lazarus 1991; Oatley and Johnson-Laird 1987; Power and Dalgleish 1997; Stein *et al*. 1993). So, for example, Lazarus (1991) argues that the initial appraisal of a given situation occurs with respect to three goal-related dimensions:

- whether or not there is goal relevance
- whether there is goal congruence or incongruence – moving towards a goal causes positive emotions in Lazarus's scheme and moving away causes negative ones
- according to the nature of the ego involvement in the event.

For instance, if the event is appraised as damaging to self-esteem then negative emotions such as anger, fear, and sadness are implicated. The notion of appraisal is covered in more detail later in the chapter when we consider some examples of cognitive theories of emotion, and we shall put off any further discussion until then. Other aspects of cognition are covered in the developmental section and in the section on social aspects of emotion.

Feelings

In Fehr and Russell's (1984) large-scale survey in which they asked people to define what is an emotion, almost universally the subjects included in their definitions the idea that the emotion must somehow be felt or experienced. For most of us, emotions are predominantly about feelings. They may lead us to behave in certain ways, they may be involved with particular functions or interpretations of the environment, but the most overwhelming sense we have of emotions is how they make us feel. For some philosophers and psychologists, this is all that emotions are. According to the philosopher, René Descartes, in his book, *On the Passions of the Soul* (1649), emotions are nothing more than the awareness of changes in the body but the emotions have no functional or causal role to play in those changes. In philosophy, this is known as the 'feeling theory' (Lyons 1980) of emotions and was the fundamental basis of William James's theory referred to above. One major problem with the feeling theory seems to be the lack of any cognitive component. So, bodily changes just happen in response to certain events and emotions are the subjective awareness of those changes. However, it is unclear why bodily changes happen in response to particular events and not others – the differentiating role that cognition performs in later theories of emotions.

Some approaches to emotion focus exclusively on the dimension of experience. These theories fall within what is known as the Humanist tradition in psychology (see Stevens 1990 for a useful introduction). Such conceptualizations of emotion receive little academic support within European psychology and will not be considered in detail here.

Consciousness and emotions

Having underlined the importance of conscious feelings as a component of emotions, it is only right to consider the alternative possibility – that there may be *unconscious* emotional states. This is discussed further in Chapter 18 and it is probably not possible to give a definitive answer to the question of whether there are or are not unconscious emotions. Surprisingly, the view put forward by Freud in *The Unconscious* (1915: 104) was as follows: 'It is surely of the essence of an emotion that we should feel it, i.e. that it should enter consciousness. So for emotions, feelings and affects to be unconscious would be quite out of the question'. However, others do not agree. For example, the philosopher William Lyons (1980) argues that unconscious emotions are distinctly possible. At the moment, the jury is still out but the cases for the defence and prosecution are eloquently put in the section on unconscious emotions in Ekman and Davidson's (1994) *The Nature of Emotion: Fundamental questions*.

Relationship between emotions and moods

So far, we have used the terms emotion, feeling and affect in a fairly loose way. However, in emotion research and theorizing, clear distinctions are often drawn between different types of emotional states and conditions. This is summarized in Table 15.2.

Table 15.2 The time course of various emotion-related phenomena

Phenomenon	Timescale
Expression	Seconds–minutes
Physiological change	Seconds–minutes
Self-reported emotion	Minutes–hours
Mood	Hours–months
Emotional disorder	Weeks–years
Personality trait	Years–lifetime

Source: adapted from Oatley and Jenkins (1996)

So far, when we have talked about emotions we have usually been referring to some combination of expressions, autonomic changes and self-reported emotions; that is, relatively short-term emotional states or episodes. The emotional disorders are considered in Chapter 17 and personality is considered in Chapter 14. Consequently, we shall just consider the concept of moods here. Most people would agree that the term 'mood' refers to a relatively long-term emotional experience over hours, days, or even weeks. Power and Dalgleish (1997) have argued that the difference between moods and emotional episodes is that moods are essentially a background state reflecting an increased likelihood to enter into an emotional episode. Similarly, Frijda (1993a) suggests that the difference between emotion episodes and moods is that the former always refer to a particular object in the world whereas the latter are objectless or 'free floating'. So, for example, during an angry episode we may be angry that somebody stole our parking space. However, when we are in an angry or irritable mood, it is not so clear what we are angry about, if anything at all. In research, mood states are normally measured by checklists or questionnaires and these methodologies are excellently reviewed by Green *et al.* (1993). For the purposes of this chapter, we shall limit our discussion to what Oatley and Jenkins (1996) have classified as 'emotion episodes'. A good discussion of the relationship between episodes and moods can be found in Ekman and Davidson (1994).

ψ Section summary

We have looked at how emotions are defined, and the historical development of these ideas. We have considered the various components of emotion: feelings, physiological change, readiness for action, and cognition and we have previewed their more detailed consideration in later parts of the chapter. Finally, we have considered the relationship between emotions and moods.

1   Are emotions a unitary phenomenon or are they made up of a number of components?

Number and type of emotions

Having examined the question of which components go together to make up what we think of as an emotion, the next question of importance is: exactly how many emotions are there? Furthermore, are all of the different emotions to be considered equivalent or are some emotions more fundamental or basic than others? There have been a number of different answers to these questions and in this section we consider some of them. For example, William James suggested that there are as many emotions as there are words to describe them and that every emotion is characterized by a distinct physiology. These days, most researchers would not place themselves in James's camp and some would even go so far as to argue that there is only a small handful of core emotions. Yet others have suggested that, although there are a small number of core or **basic emotions**, there is a host of **complex emotions** which can be derived from the basic emotions. We begin with a consideration of the arguments for the existence of a core group of basic emotions.

Basic emotions

The idea that some emotions are more fundamental or basic than others dates back to the Greek philosophers and, although, as Ekman et al. (1972) have shown, there is some diversity among the various proponents of the basic emotion approach, most investigators agree on a

central list of six basic emotions: happiness, surprise, fear, sadness, anger and disgust/contempt. What do these researchers mean when they suggest that these emotions are basic? Ekman (e.g. 1992, 1998a) proposes nine characteristics that distinguish basic emotions: distinctive **universals** in antecedent events (i.e. the same things instigate the same emotions across cultures); distinctive universal signals (e.g. facial expressions); distinctive physiology; presence in primates other than humans; coherence among emotional responses; quick onset; brief duration; automatic appraisal; and unbidden occurrence. We shall consider the evidence in support of distinctive physiology for different emotions in the section on biological aspects of emotions and it is beyond the scope of the chapter to look in detail at all of the other of Ekman's nine characteristics. Consequently, we shall consider the idea of distinctive universals in antecedent events and distinctive universal signals to illustrate his line of argument and the counter-arguments of those less enamoured with the idea of basic emotions.

Universals in antecedent events

The gist of the argument that basic emotions can be defined as having universal antecedent events is that if emotions are functional tools that have evolved to deal with common problems of life for humans of all cultures, then one would expect there to be some common elements in the context or antecedent events in which emotions occur, despite major cross-cultural differences due to the influences of social learning. As Ohman (1986) suggests

evolutionary economy has left to environmental influences to inscribe the exact characteristics of dangerous predators . . . learning is critically involved in selecting which stimuli activate the predatory defence system. But this learning is likely to be biologically primed or constrained in the sense that the responses are much more easily attached to some types of stimuli than to others. In other words, it is appropriate to speak about biologically prepared learning. Thus, it is likely to require only minimal input in terms of training, and to result in very persistent responses that are not easily extinguished.

(Ohman 1986: 128–9)

Support for this interaction of nature and nurture was provided by Boucher and Brant (1981). They examined emotional antecedents in a variety of western and non-western cultures. Although the events differed in their specific details, Boucher and Brant found that on an abstract level there was a great deal of universality in antecedent events. For example, the loss of a significant other they found to be 'an antecedent to sadness in many, perhaps all cultures. But who a significant other is or can be will differ from culture to culture' (Boucher 1983: 407). Similar findings have been presented by Klaus Scherer and his colleagues in their study of the antecedents of emotion in western cultures (Scherer *et al.* 1983). A note of warning here though. As Ekman argues

Unfortunately there is little ethological description of the commonalities in the naturally occurring antecedent events for emotions within and across cultures. There is questionnaire and also interview data in which subjects are asked to describe emotional events. However, we do not yet know the extent to which such data resembles what actually occurs during emotion, how much idealisation and stereotyping may occur when subjects coldly describe what they think about their emotional experience.

(Ekman 1998a)

These data on the universality of antecedent events for emotion have led a number of theorists to posit exactly what these events might be for the various basic emotions (e.g. Ekman and Friesen 1975; Lazarus 1991). The exact specifications differ but the general gist is that fear is a function of an appraisal of threat, sadness is a function of an appraisal of sadness, anger is a function of an appraisal of a blocked goal by a recognizable agent, happiness is a function of goal achievement, and disgust is a function of violation of gustatory goals.

Lazarus and colleagues have carried out a number of research studies (e.g. Speisman *et al.* 1964) in support of an appraisal theory of emotions. In one study, subjects were shown various films. One involved Stone Age rituals where adolescent boys had their penises deeply cut. In another film industrial accidents were the theme, and one scene shows an industrial accident in which a circular saw slices a man in the midriff and he dies writhing on the floor. The subjects' cognitive appraisals were manipulated in various conditions; for example, by using an accompanying soundtrack saying, in a denial condition, that the participants were all actors or that the Stone Age ritual was not in fact painful. An intellectualization condition was introduced by, for instance, asking subjects in the ritual film to view the incision from the point of view of an anthropologist. Various psychophysiological measures were taken during the film. The findings indicated that manipulations of cognitive appraisal such as denial and intellectualization reduced emotions in terms both of self-report and physiological measures, compared to a control condition.

Universal signals

There is a wealth of data bearing on the question of whether emotions have universal signals and on what the social interactionist function of these signals might be. Most of this research has concentrated on facial expression and we shall examine some of these data here. The principal research methodology has been to show pictures of facial expressions to observers in different cultures who are then asked to judge which emotion is shown. If, across cultures, the same emotions are labelled with the same terms (in the language system of the culture being studied), the argument is that this is evidence for universality. There have been fewer studies looking at other aspects of facial expression; for example, whether facial behaviour itself is different across cultures. An excellent review of these data is provided in Ekman (1998b) and the issue is hotly debated in a series of review articles in the journal, *Psychological Bulletin* (e.g. Ekman 1994; Russell 1994).

To date there are data from 21 literate regions examining the perception of facial expression of emotion. These comprise Africa, Argentina, Brazil, Chile, China, England, Estonia, Ethiopia, France, Germany, Greece, Italy, Japan, Kirghizistan, Malaysia, Scotland, Sweden, Sumatra (Indonesia), Switzerland, Turkey and the United States. In all of the studies, the observers in each culture were given pictures of a facial expression of emotion and were asked to select an emotion term from a short list of 6–10 terms, translated into their own language. On reviewing these data, Ekman (1998b) reports an extraordinary amount of agreement in terms of emotion recognition across the various cultures. For the emotions of happiness, sadness and disgust, there was majority agreement in every one of the 21 countries. For the emotion of surprise there was agreement by the majority in 20 of the 21 countries, for fear in 19 of the 21, and for anger in 18 of the 21. In those 6 cases in which the majority did not use the same emotion as was chosen in every other country, it was still the case that the most frequent response was the same as was given by the majority in other countries. Ekman argues that evidence against universality would need to have been that the majority of people in a given country judged a certain expression as depicting one emotion whereas people in another country judged it as depicting another emotion. This was not the case in any of the studies reviewed.

There are a number of challenges to Ekman's conclusions, particularly by Russell (1994), who has argued that the large amount of agreement across the data is an artefact of the methodology. He suggests that the use of a forced choice recognition paradigm where the subjects have to choose an emotion from a limited list, rather than say what the expression is in their own words, leads to a falsely elevated sense of agreement across studies. Ekman's reply to this suggestion is that if the words in the forced choice list such as fear, anger, disgust and so on, were genuinely unrelated to the expressions that were shown in the studies, then there would have been widespread disagreement both within and between cultures, which was not the case. However, it is perhaps true that the use of a forced choice methodology hides any smaller disagreements across cultures. Experimental evidence does exist in which subjects were allowed to use their own words. Izard (1971) examined people in Britain, France, Greece and the United States. Similar studies were carried out by Boucher and Carlson (1980) in the United States, Malaysia, and the Temuans (an aboriginal Malaysian group), and Rosenberg and Ekman (1994) in the USA. In all of these studies in which people chose their own words, it turned out that the words were quite similar, but interestingly not identical, to those used in the forced choice recognition studies of the 21 countries.

A more serious challenge to the universality data is the argument that all of the cultures studied had been influenced by western media and therefore the subjects may have learnt that certain expressions went with certain emotions through this channel. In order to address this problem, Ekman actually visited a pre-literate, visually isolated culture in Papua New Guinea – the South Fore – in the mid-1970s. Most of the South Fore have seen few or no outsiders, they were still using stone implements, and had reportedly never seen a photograph, magazine, film or television. The South Fore have no written language so it was not possible to use the same methodology involving lists of emotion words as in the 21 literate cultures. Ekman therefore adopted another methodology in which a translator read the subject a brief story and asked the person to point to the picture that fitted that story. The stories were centred on situations in which emotion was likely to occur for that culture and had been piloted with other members of the culture. The data revealed that the South Fore, who could not have learned expressions from the media, chose the same expressions for each emotion as had the people in the 21 literate cultures (Ekman and Friesen 1971). Similar results were found by the anthropologist Karl Heider in the Dani people of West Irian (reported in Ekman 1972).

Although data such as these are powerful they are not conclusive. These data may be consistent with basic emotion components rather than emotions *per se* (e.g. Scherer 1994). Furthermore, many would argue that liberties are taken with the difficulties of cross-cultural research. For example, Shweder (1994) in discussing Wierzbicka's work (e.g. 1994) states that

the whole world does not speak English; that English words such as happiness, sadness, anger, fear and disgust encode concepts that are 'different from those encoded in the emotion terms of different languages'; that 'in fact there are NO emotion terms which can be matched neatly across language and culture boundaries'; that 'there are NO universal emotion concepts, lexicalized in all the languages of the world'; and that it is all too easy in the translation process to unwittingly assimilate other people's linguistic meanings to an ethnocentric set of analytic categories – the abstract 'emotional' states favored by the English-speaking world.

(Shweder 1994: 33)

Ψ Section summary

We have considered the question of how many emotions there are. We have concentrated on the idea that there may be a set of basic emotions, as proposed by authors such as Ekman. There is widespread agreement that, if there are basic emotions, they probably include anger, fear, disgust, sadness and happiness. We have looked at some of the evidence for basic emotions such as universality of antecedent events and universality of facial expression and we have considered some of the criticisms of this research.

1   Is there overwhelming evidence in favour of the concept of basic emotions?

2   What do we mean by universality? Illustrate with examples.

❏ Development of emotions

From the new-born baby's first cry to the rich and complex emotional life of adults, a vast number of changes occur in the development of the experience, expression and function of the human emotions. So, what develops during emotional development? Are we born with a full set of basic and **complex emotions** with which to do battle with the challenges and difficulties of the world? Or are young babies able to deploy only a small set of core prototypical emotions? Perhaps new-born babies do not have emotions at all in the sense that we defined them earlier but instead possess a number of basic building blocks or components of emotional experience which merge and combine together in set patterns in response to the environment with which they have to interact.

No emotion theorists concerned with the question of what develops during emotional development really endorse the first of the above possibilities, that new-born infants are in possession of the full set of basic and complex emotions that one might find in an adult. However, researchers are divided as to which of the latter two approaches they champion. The first approach – that young children possess a prototypical set of basic emotions – is known as **differential emotions theory** (Izard 1991; Tomkins 1962). The second approach is somewhat more recent and is known as **dynamic systems theory** (e.g. Fogel *et al.* 1992; Lewis 1995). Throughout this section on emotional development we shall return to these two approaches and examine the different predictions and sets of explanations they provide for the data on the various aspects of the ways in which emotions develop from infancy to adulthood.

Problems of researching emotions in young subjects

Such theoretical schism in the field of emotional development is primarily a function of methodological difficulties. When a researcher wishes to understand the emotional experience of adults, the best approach is to ask them what they are feeling and what the components of their feelings might be. There are some problems with this method; for example, a number of components of emotion may be inaccessible to conscious awareness, or the people may fabricate or mislead the interviewer because they are uncomfortable with revealing aspects of their emotional experience. However, despite these drawbacks, this method of self-report provides a large and reasonably clear window into adult emotional life. Such luxury is unavailable to the researcher who is concerned with pre-linguistic infants. Infants are unable to articulate what they are feeling and so researchers in this area have to find other methods to try and pinpoint the emotional life of their subjects. The principal limitation of working with infants who cannot talk is that researchers cannot help but view the emotional life of

their infant subjects through adult eyes. For example, the emotional **expressions** of the infants, the things which lead to those expressions, and the infants' ability to recognize emotional expressions in others are all understood in terms of which expressions go with which emotions in adults. Young children may *look* disgusted when presented with something that tastes unpleasant. However, we are making the assumption that the children *are* disgusted merely on the basis that their facial expression is one that an adult would make when feeling disgusted, and that the object which they are tasting is one that an adult would find unpleasant to taste. We have no guarantee, however, that these children are actually *feeling* disgust or anything that resembles it. With this caveat in mind, we shall begin this section by examining some of the research on the expression of emotions in young infants, the ability of young infants to recognize emotional expression in others, and the factors which normally elicit emotional reactions in young infants.

Development of the expression of emotions

Studies of the emotional expressions of young infants fall into two categories. The first category addresses the question of whether the infants' expressions *per se* can be labelled reliably as pertaining to different emotions. This approach takes no account of the context in which the so-called emotional expression was elicited. The second category of research is more contextualized. The additional constraint that the emotional expression must have occurred in the presence of an appropriate elicitor more frequently than in the presence of an inappropriate elicitor (according to adult criteria) is included.

One of the classic studies from the second category that examined emotional expressions in context was performed by Hiatt *et al.* (1979). They presented 10–12 month old infants with six contextual conditions. The conditions were supposed to elicit the emotions of fear, happiness or surprise. For example, the fear conditions involved being presented with a visual cliff (a set-up where the infant is placed next to a drop, covered over by glass) or the approach of a stranger, while the happiness conditions involved playing peek-a-boo and so on.

The components of the infants' facial expressions were coded using the Ekman and Friesen (1978) coding system (see section on biological aspects of emotion on pp. 479–89).

Hiatt *et al.* found that, for the emotion of happiness, infants produced a facial expression which could be reliably coded as happiness and that they did so in the context of happiness elicitors (e.g. peek-a-boo) more often than in the elicitors for the other emotions. The emotion of fear met these criteria least well. In the context of stimuli intended to elicit fear, the infants produced a wide range of emotional expressions such as fear, surprise and sometimes happiness. These data suggest that only for the emotion of happiness is there good support for the argument that it is a discrete emotion present in young infants. It seems difficult, however, to extend this argument to a range of discrete emotions such as fear and surprise in 10–12 month olds.

Similar findings have been obtained by other researchers looking at emotional expression in young infants in the context of appropriate elicitors. Lewis et al. (1990) tied a piece of string to the arms of their infant subjects. In one condition, pulling the string started a short piece of happy music. In the other condition, pulling the string started the music initially, but subsequently failed to elicit the music. When the music was turned on, the infant subjects reliably showed expressions consistent with feelings of interest and happiness. However, when the string pulling no longer led to the playing of music, the infants exhibited expressions consistent with anger, as might be expected in a frustrating situation, but also fear, sadness and fussing. Again, it may seem that for positive emotions one can make the argument that discrete expressions/emotions are present in very young infants but that this is not the case for negative emotions. One exception appears to be the expression/emotion of disgust which also seems to be reliably elicited in the appropriate context (Steiner 1979).

Once the research constraint that the emotional expression has to be elicited in what adults deem to be the appropriate context is removed, the evidence for discrete emotions in young infants suddenly and unsurprisingly becomes more powerful. Malatesta et al. (1989) showed that, in the first weeks of life, infants smile during rapid eye movement sleep. After the first month, smiles begin to occur when the infants are gently stroked and by 2 months they occur frequently in interaction with the principal caregiver. Clearly then, if we take uncontextualized smiling as an index of happiness, then we can say that it occurs within hours of birth. However, if smiling is merely a reflex to bodily changes such as those that occur during certain patterns of sleep and not a valid indication of any internal emotional state, then we would have to say that clear signs of the emotion of happiness do not emerge until some months into development.

As with the case of purported happiness, Izard and colleagues argue that genuine expressions of fear, anger and sadness can all be seen from very early infancy (e.g. Izard and Malatesta 1987). In contrast, researchers such as Oster et al. (1992) have proposed that what are deemed to be discrete negative emotional expressions in young infants are merely signs of undifferentiated distress. This latter view has also been endorsed by Camras (1992) who carried out a thorough naturalistic study of emotional expression by making frequent video recordings of her daughter, Justine, in the first year of life. Camras did indeed find that Justine exhibited expressions consistent with disgust, fear, distress/pain and anger in the first few months. However, these expressions often did not occur in the expected context. For example, Justine would show a sad face when experiencing a bitter taste.

These two contrasting theoretical positions, that differentiated emotions do exist in the first few months of life versus the proposal that what appear to be differentiated expressions are merely signals of undifferentiated distress, clearly reflect the two theories of emotional development which we referred to at the beginning of this section. Differential emotions theory, as the name suggests, would predict differentiated emotions at the very beginning of infancy, whereas dynamic systems theory would propose that such differentiation would occur later after a set of undifferentiated emotion components had gelled together as a function of person–environment interactions. Both theories are plausible explanations of the data as they stand and crucial tests of the two approaches are difficult to come up with due to the research hurdle discussed above – namely, that we cannot talk to babies about what they are feeling.

Infants' abilities to recognize emotional expression in others

When considering the question of what emotional expressions infants can recognize in those around them, the methodological problem that we cannot talk to young infants is perhaps even more difficult to overcome than in the case of the experience of emotion in infants. How can we know whether infants know or recognize something or not, when they are unable to tell us? The way that researchers have overcome this hurdle traditionally has been to take advantage of the process of habituation. The rationale here is a simple one – that infants will spend more time investigating something novel than something familiar; in other words, they will habituate to and become uninterested in stimuli that they recognize. Field *et al.* (1982) used the habituation method in a famous study with new-born babies: 36-hour-old infants were able to habituate and dishabituate to three expressions made by an adult: happiness, surprise and sadness. They also showed some ability to imitate these expressions; for example, they showed more widening of the mouth and eyes when the adult's expression was one of surprise. These findings were replicated in 10-week-old infants by Haviland and Lelwicka (1987).

One could argue then, on the basis of these data, that very young infants can discriminate reliably among emotions shown by the same adult. However, an equally plausible explanation is that the infants are habituating to some aspect of the facial expression that has nothing to do with emotions. Again, the first of these proposals would be highly consistent with differential emotions theory, whereas the latter proposal is more consistent with dynamic systems theory. Caron *et al.* (1985) shed some light on this issue. They presented their 4–7 month old young infants with pictures of angry and happy faces in which the faces were either revealing the person's teeth or not revealing the person's teeth. Using the habituation method, the results showed that the infants could discriminate between toothy and non-toothy faces, but if both angry and happy emotional expressions involved the revealing of teeth, they were unable to discriminate between them. So, it seems that infants can habituate to differential features of expression that do not necessarily correspond to differential emotions. Further research by the same group (e.g. Caron *et al.* 1988) has examined the generalization of infants' discrimination and perceptual abilities to vocal patterns and to adults other than the principal caregiver.

In summarizing the findings on the expression and the recognition of expression of emotion in pre-linguistic infants, we can draw the following conclusions:

- young infants appear to be able to differentially express pleasure/happiness and distress
- young infants appear to be able to perceive major shifts in the emotional behaviour of their principal caregivers.

Functionally, it seems likely that this is all the pre-linguistic infant needs in order to engage in meaningful emotional communication (Oatley and Jenkins 1996). The question of whether the pre-linguistic infant's emotional life is more differentiated than this, and involves subtle distinctions between sadness, anger, pain and the like, is still open to considerable debate and remains a point of contention between the differential emotion theorists and dynamic systems theorists referred to at the beginning of the section.

Emotion and cause in young children

We have already seen that the context in which emotions occur – what causes or elicits different emotional reactions – is an important factor in understanding the research on emotional expression in young infants. In this section we examine how those causal factors change as the infant develops, and how, in infants who are able to use language, their understanding of the causes of their own emotions begins and changes.

An elegant experiment examining developmental changes in the causation of emotions in young infants was carried out by Scarr and Salapatek (1970). They presented infants from 2 months to 2 years of age with a number of different stimuli all hypothesized to be fearsome. The stimuli were a stranger, a visual cliff, a jack-in-the-box, loud noises, a moving toy dog, and someone wearing a mask. The older the children, the more they showed fearful behaviour to the visual cliff, the stranger, and to somebody wearing a mask. In contrast, fear of loud noises and of unfamiliar toys began around 7 months, peaked at 1 year, and then declined. For children under 7 months of age, none of the stimuli used by Scarr and Salapatek (1970) reliably elicited fearful behaviour or expressions. Similar research with somewhat older children reveals the coming and going of fears of imaginary objects such as ghosts and monsters, fears of bodily injury and physical danger and, in adolescence, social fears (e.g. Bamber 1979; Bauer 1976).

Once children reach 2–3 years of age, the development of their language ability (see Chapters 7 and 9) enables researchers to investigate the complexity of their emotional life more thoroughly. Research on language-aged children indicates that as they become older, children's understanding of the causes of emotion is increasingly a function of their own beliefs, desires and goals, and the beliefs, desires and goals of those around them. For example, Stein and Levine (1989) read 3–6 year olds' stories of various types. In one story a child wanted something and obtained it. In another story the child wanted something but did not get it and in a final story the child did not want something but got it anyway. Essentially then, the stories manipulated the goals of the characters as well as the outcome. The results showed that children as young as 3 were able to predict positive or negative emotional reactions in the characters in the story as a function of whether or not their goals were fulfilled.

Naturalistic evidence in support of this understanding of internal emotional states by young children was provided in a study by Fabes *et al*. (1991) investigating 3, 4 and 5 year olds in a nursery school setting. Again, children as young as 3 were able to account for the emotions of other children with whom they were playing, in terms of the internal states of those children. For example, 'She was happy because she was given her toy back'.

The development of the infants' understanding of their own emotions in terms of internal mental states and, in particular, the emotional life of others, in terms of those same states, is a major building block in the development of the young child's social life and the beginnings of co-operative partnerships with peers and caregivers. These issues are examined in detail in Chapter 10 on social development though we shall look at the socialization of emotion later on in this section. Before that, however, we consider the issues of **temperament** and personality.

Temperament

In the previous section we looked at the development and differentiation of emotional states. However, if we were to take any group of parents and place them in a room together and ask them to talk about the emotional life of their children, discussion would be less about emotional states than about how the children differed from one another in terms of how moody or temperamental they were. Some babies and infants are calm and quiet and get upset only for brief periods. Others seem more volatile; they get upset easily and intensely, and their periods of distress last longer. Some babies engage well and enjoy the company of strangers and other people; others become distressed when people try to engage them or play with them. These individual differences from one baby to another have been referred to as temperament. Temperament has been defined as those aspects of emotion and behaviour that have some form of biological or neurophysiological underpinning; that is, they are constitutional with a degree of heritability (Buss and Plomin 1975; Goldsmith 1993).

Most researchers agree that **temperament** has quite a considerable genetic component, though there is some dispute over exactly how much (Buss and Plomin 1984; Campos *et al*. 1983). Most of the research in this area has involved twin studies using either identical or monozygotic (MZ) twins who share all of their genes, or non-identical, dizygotic (DZ) twins who share half their genes (see Chapter 13 on intelligence for a detailed dis-

cussion of twin studies). Other studies have compared the temperament of natural and adopted siblings with one another. The majority of these studies look at parental ratings of the temperament of the twin pairs and compare them, though some studies have used observers' ratings made in a laboratory.

Research from the three main studies (Goldsmith and Campos 1982; Matheny and Dolan 1975; Matheney *et al*. 1982) has been reviewed in detail by Plomin (1988) and is summarized in Table 15.3.

Table 15.3 Early genetic studies of temperament in twins. In the data columns, the first figure is the amount of concordance in identical (monozygotic) twins and the second figure is concordance in fraternal (dizygotic) twins

Study	Measures	6 month data	2 year data
Matheny and Dolan (1975)	Experimenter ratings of emotionality in playroom		0.66 : 0.30
Matheny *et al.* (1981)	Interviewing parents:		
	hurt feelings		0.37 : 0.13
	temper frequency	0.39 : 0.26	0.41 : 0.15
	irritability	0.45 : 0.29	0.46 : 0.28
	episodes of crying	0.62 : 0.51	0.59 : 0.39
Goldsmith and Campos (1982)	Parental ratings:		
	fear		0.66 : 0.46
	distress to limitation		0.77 : 0.25
	ability to be soothed		0.71 : 0.69

Source: adapted from Plomin (1988)

In Table 15.3, the two right-hand columns present the correlations between the twin pairs on measures of temperament. The first figure in each column contains the correlation between MZ twins and the second contains the correlation between DZ twins. The greater the correlation, the greater the similarity in ratings of temperament for the two twins. The size of the correlation is taken to be a measure of concordance – a reflection of the degree of heritability of the aspect of temperament being measured. As can be seen from the table, the concordance for MZ twins is greater on all measures of temperament than for DZ twins. There is some variation in this (Goldsmith 1993) in that soothability seems to have a smaller genetic component; that is, the difference between MZ concordance and DZ concordance is small, and is less than for ratings of more negative or distress-based emotions.

As well as endeavouring to establish the extent of the heritability or genetic component of individual differences in temperament from one infant to another, researchers have also been concerned to show that temperament is stable over time. The methodology used in these studies is to obtain ratings of temperament of the infants at one time point and then to carry out the study a second time at a later date and examine whether the ratings of temperament at the two time points are strongly related to each other. Numerous studies have been carried out investigating the stability of temperament and these are summarized in Table 15.4.

As is clear from the table, using ratings by parents of emotional behaviour or just using facial expression of infants, it has been shown that some aspects of temperament are extremely stable over periods of up to 10 years. Bad news for parents with grumpy babies!

This raises the important question of what the implications of childhood temperament for the emotional life of the adults they will become might be. A seminal study in this area was carried out by Caspi et al. (1987, 1988). They examined a group of people in their late thirties who had initially been assessed as 8 year olds and classified as either ill-tempered or shy. Caspi et al. discovered that those children who were ill-tempered at age 8 were most likely to become ill-tempered adults. Related to this were a number of other differences in lifestyle from the children who had been shy. Ill-tempered children were less likely to have stayed in school and, as men, had experienced a more erratic work life. Consequently they tended to have a lower occupational status. As women, the ill-tempered girls tended to marry below their social class expectations, were more likely to get divorced, and were less satisfied with the quality of the marital relationship.

In contrast, shy boys, as men, married later, were likely to have children later and were more likely to

Table 15.4 Studies on the stability of measures of temperament

Study	Measures	Time points	Correlation (ns = not significant)
Rothbart (1986)	Parents' ratings	6 and 9 months	
	smiling/laughter		0.48
	fear		0.37
	distress to limitations		0.51
Hyson and Izard (1985)	Facial expression in the strange situation of:	13 and 18 months	
	interest		0.90
	anger		0.61
	total negative		0.90
Malatesta et al. (1989)	Facial expression while playing with mother and after separation:	7 and 22 months	
	anger		0.32
	sadness		0.37
	positive		ns
Chess and Thomas (1990)	Summed rating of easy vs difficult temperament	3 years and adult	0.31
		4 years and adult	0.37
		5 years and adult	0.15
Worobey and Blajda (1989)	Ratings of:	2 and 12 months	
	positive reactivity		0.46
	negative reactivity		0.50

establish a stable career. These data give some flavour of the ways in which individual differences in emotional behaviour and temperament in children filter through to individual differences in adults. However, a word of warning: there are very few studies in this area as the longitudinal nature of the research makes it difficult and expensive to carry out and it is inadvisable to draw too many conclusions on the basis of a single study.

This question of individual differences in temperament in adults obviously bears a close relation to the concept of personality. A detailed discussion of personality and its relationship to temperament and emotion is provided in Chapter 14 and will not be discussed here.

Social aspects of the development of emotion

Research shows that even in young infants, emotions play an important social communicative role between the infant and the caregiver. Field (1994) has argued that the caregiver regulates the infant's emotional **arousal** by reading the infant's signals, keeping in time with them, and adjusting the environment in order to maintain the optimal level of stimulation for the child. Field calls this 'attunement' and suggests that without it, the infant's behaviour can become disorganized and chaotic. The important role of emotions in the regulation of infant–caregiver interactions in this way was examined in an experimental setting by Cohn and Tronick (1983). In this study the mothers and infants sat face to face. In the first condition (called flat **affect**) the mothers looked directly at the infant but spoke in a flat uninteresting monotone and kept their faces expressionless with minimal body movement and no bodily contact. The contrasting condition was three-minute periods of normal behaviour on the part of the mother. The results showed that when the mothers demonstrated flat affect, the infants seemed more wary, made more protest and showed briefer and more infrequent positive expressions. In general they were much more disorganized and were more likely to become upset (see research update, p. 479).

This kind of research shows the importance of emotions as a form of social communication in infants and young children. Another important social role of emotions that develops at an early age is in the development of partnerships to achieve joint goals. Hoffman (1984) has outlined four stages in the development of this process. In the first stage, known as global empathy, children merely pick up signs of distress from others through emotional contagion and feel distressed themselves. In the second stage, known as egocentric empa-

thy, children know that another is in distress but again can react only as if they themselves are in distress. In the third stage, the child begins to develop an understanding that the other's feelings are different from his or her own, and in the final stage true empathy for another person's experiences has developed. It is this ability to gradually appreciate the emotional perspective of other people that allows a developing person to co-operate more and more with his or her peers in the achievement of joint goals. Bowlby (1971) has called this the development of the 'goal-corrected partnership'.

So far we have talked mostly about the use of emotional signals in social relationships. However, there has been an increasing amount of research on the way in which infants and caregivers talk about emotions with each other. Dunn *et al.* (1991) recorded emotional dialogue between mothers and children, and between children and their siblings when the children were 3 years old. Results showed that the more mothers talked to their children about emotions at the age of 3, the more skilled and articulate the children were in discussing and making judgements about emotions displayed by unfamiliar adults when they were aged 6. More specifically, it was the discussion of negative emotions that was most strongly related to an increased ability to conceptualize and recognize emotions in a standardized task.

Such differences in the development of emotions as a function of the mother–infant relationship have been most thoroughly examined in the research on attachment theory (Bowlby 1971, 1973). Bowlby saw attachment as an evolutionarily adapted aspect of the caregiver–child relationship that is activated when the infant experiences a threat of some kind. In attachment research the threat is most usually the interaction with a **strange situation**; most traditionally, a brief separation of child and caregiver followed by an opportunity for them to reunite (Ainsworth *et al.* 1978)

In her research on strange situations, Ainsworth categorized three styles of infant–parent attachment. The first she labelled 'securely attached'. In this style infants are distressed at separation but when their caregivers return they seek them out and can be easily comforted. A second style Ainsworth called 'ambivalently attached'. Here, children again seek out the caregivers upon return after a separation but refuse to be comforted and show considerable angry and resistant behaviour. Ainsworth's third style was 'avoidantly attached'. Avoidant infants make no effort to interact with the caregivers when they return following a separation in the strange situation. Research has shown that each **attachment style** is associated with a specific

Research update

Attachment in children of mothers with psychosis illness

Work carried out at the Bethlem and Maudsley Joint Hospitals in London by Alison Hipwell and her colleagues (Hipwell and Kumar 1997; Hipwell *et al.* 1998) has examined the long-term effects on attachment behaviour of the children of mothers who have experienced a psychotic illness immediately after the child's birth – a postpartum psychosis.

Eighty-two mentally ill mothers (the case group) and matched controls were followed up for one year and observations were made of the mother–infant interaction patterns and of the quality of the mother–infant attachment relationship at the 12 month time point. The results showed that, despite almost no evidence of residual mental illness in the mothers at follow-up, there was evidence of disturbed mother–infant interactions in the case group subjects.

Furthermore, the results revealed that a manic illness in the postpartum period was, perhaps surprisingly, related to a secure mother–infant attachment, whereas a depressive illness was related to an insecure-avoidant attachment.

At present a five-year follow-up of the mothers is being carried out and the research findings are awaited with interest.

pattern of emotionality. Secure infants seem to show a balance of positive and negative emotions. Ambivalent infants, on the other hand, show a predominance of negative emotions and avoidant infants show fewer emotions of all kinds (Goldberg *et al.* 1994; see research update). A detailed discussion of attachment theory and its relevance to emotions is presented in Chapter 10 on social development.

Ψ Section summary

We have looked at the development of emotions. We considered the problems of researching emotions in pre-linguistic infants and we suggested that firm conclusions about the nature of emotions in this age group are not possible. We discussed the development of the expression of emotions in infants and of their ability to recognize emotional expression in others. We then considered the concept of temperament – whether some infants are more temperamental than others and the possible reasons for this. Finally, we described social aspects of the development of emotions, in particular, the idea of attachment styles.

1 What are the methodological limitations of researching emotions in pre-linguistic infants? Illustrate your answer with respect to the development and recognition of emotional expression.

2 What do we mean by temperament? Is this a useful psychological construct?

Biological aspects of emotion

Physiology

Prototypical experiments in the area of physiological changes allied to emotion have been carried out by Ekman and colleagues (e.g. Ekman *et al.* 1983; Levenson *et al.* 1990), who asked their subjects to pose facial expressions corresponding to six different emotions (fear, anger, sadness, happiness, surprise and disgust). The facial expressions were video-recorded and a number of physiological measures were taken (heart rate, skin conductance, hand temperature and forearm muscle tension). Subjects were not informed about which emotions corresponded to which pose and the posing instructions were given in steps, for example, 'Now raise your upper eyelids, now pull the corners of your mouth down', and so on. The results showed that each posed expression matched a specific physiological pattern on the four measures taken. Low heart rate was associated with happiness, disgust and surprise. In contrast, high heart rate was characteristic of sadness, anger and fear. Furthermore, anger was characterized by high skin temperature, relative to fear and sadness which were characterized by low skin temperature.

A similar study was carried out by Stemmler (1989). Stemmler's study was a complicated one involving connecting subjects to a polygraph machine from which eight bodily measures could be derived. The experiment included three real-life emotion induction situations: anger (being given impossible anagrams to solve while being told to shout 'I don't know' louder and louder because the sound equipment was allegedly not working); fear (listening to a terrifying poem accompanied by scary music and then experiencing the lights suddenly going out); and happiness (being told that the experiment had been successful and that there was an increase in the payment for taking part). There were also emotional imagery conditions and control conditions. The results showed that some bodily measures were able to discriminate between fear, anger and happiness. These included skin conductance and head temperature. However, measures which were found to discriminate in other studies, such as those by Ekman and colleagues, did not discriminate emotions in the present experiment. Furthermore, physiological discrimination between emotions was apparent only in the real-life induction condition and not in the imagery condition.

Expression

We saw in the section on defining emotion (pp. 465–70) that Charles Darwin pioneered research on the expression of emotion. A more contemporary version of Darwin's taxonomy has been proposed by Ekman and Friesen (1969), who outlined five classes of non-verbal emotional expression:

- emblems – these are what most of us would call gestures, such as raising two fingers as an insult in the UK
- illustrators – expressions that accompany verbal output and which vary with the degree of intensity of that output, such as waving the arms as you become more excited
- regulators – subtle expressions that are used to adjust the flow of discourse, for example, nodding
- affect displays – for example, smiling
- adapters – these are complicated expressions which exhibit anxiety or discomfort on the part of the person expressing them, for instance, self-touching.

Despite these admirable attempts at a broad taxonomy of emotional expression, since the time of Darwin most researchers have narrowly focused on expressions involving the face – 'affect displays' in the list above. This research has served two principal aims. The first aim has been to attempt to classify different facial expressions as belonging to different emotions. We all know, for example, that a smile is usually linked to happiness. The question is whether such links exist for the range of emotions. The second aim, which we looked at in detail in the section on basic emotions, has been to address the question of whether certain aspects of emotional expression are pan-cultural or universal; that is, are they the same in all cultures, primitive or industrialized?

In order to pursue these aims we need to have good stimulus materials. Research has shown that, with the exception of happiness, it is actually very difficult to accurately recognize spontaneous, dynamic, facial expressions of emotion if all other clues are removed (Wagner *et al.* 1986). However, most research in this area has involved freeze-frames or photographs of highly selected and (usually) clearly posed facial expressions and these prove generally easy to recognize (see Figure 15.1).

In order to classify these various freeze-frame facial expressions as pertaining to one emotion or another, a number of detailed coding systems of facial expression were developed (Ekman and Friesen 1978, 1984; Izard 1979; Izard *et al.* 1983). Izard's systems, MAX and AFEX, are based on the idea that there is a discrete group of basic emotions (see p. 470) and his coding system defines facial features that best discriminate among them. Ekman's systems, the Facial Action Coding System (FACS) and an update, EM-FACS, are aimed at coding specific facial muscle groups, called 'action units', and their visible movements and configurations.

Subjects' ability to recognize accurately these freeze-frame facial expressions is extremely good. Consequently, as we have seen in the section on basic emotions, these stimuli have been extensively used in research on the pan-cultural nature of the expression of emotion and on the relationship between emotional expression, bodily change and emotional context.

Although most work on emotional expression has concentrated on the face, some research has shown that the voice is also an important component in emotional expression (Pittam and Scherer 1993). Again, there is some suggestion that aspects of vocal expression may be universal. For example, van Bezooijen *et al.* (1983) had Dutch subjects say a neutral Dutch phrase in a neutral voice and in voices expressing various different emotions. The audio recordings were then played to Dutch subjects and to subjects in Taiwan and Japan who were not Dutch speakers. The Dutch subjects, as was expected, did significantly better than the others at identifying correctly the neutral and emotional tones. Overall, the sad voice was well recognized by all groups as was the fearful voice; however, happy tones were not recognized well by the eastern listeners (see also case study, p. 482).

Figure 15.1 Posed expressions corresponding to the basic emotions of (1) happiness, (2) anger, (3) disgust, (4) sadness and (5) fear

Research linking the expression of emotion to the actual experience of emotion has been carried out by Kraut and Johnson (1979). They secretly filmed subjects playing or watching sporting events in order to investigate the relationship between aspects of the event that the subject was experiencing and their facial expressions. In one study they examined people playing ten-pin bowling. They found that, for some 1,793 rolls of the ball, the incidence of smiling was unrelated to how well the bowler had done on each roll. In fact, when the bowlers turned to face their friends, there was no difference in the frequency of smiling following a good score or a bad score. The rather confusing literature on the relationship between emotional expression and the experience of emotions is discussed by Cacioppo *et al.* (1993). The bottom line is that it is unclear at the moment whether or not specific expressive changes correspond to the experience of specific emotions.

Ψ Case study

D.R. – The woman who couldn't hear fear

D.R. is a woman in her early fifties who first suffered from epilepsy at the age of 28. After the standard medications failed to help her with the problem, she underwent a series of brain operations involving lesions to the left and right **amygdala** (see section on emotion and the brain). Following the operation D.R. exhibited specific impairments in the processing of the expression of emotion – both facial and vocal.

Prior to her operation, D.R.'s processing of faces was unimpaired. However, after the operation D.R. found it difficult to perform a number of facial processing tasks involving recognition and matching. First, D.R. was asked to identify the emotional expressions in Ekman and Friesen's (1976) series of faces. In this task, a model posing a series of emotional expressions is presented to the subject, who has to select a label that best describes the expression. D.R. was severely impaired on this. The matching task (Gainotti 1989) involves matching a posed emotional expression with one of four other pictures – a target picture and three distracters. Again, D.R. was impaired. Further investigation of D.R.'s performance revealed that she was particularly poor at recognizing and matching facial expressions of fear and to a lesser extent disgust.

D.R. was next asked (Calder *et al.* 1996) to perform an ingenious task in which morphed blends of different emotions were presented to her. These pictures were computer generated and involved blending two pictures of the same person posing different facial expressions such as fear and surprise. A continuum of blends in physically equal steps between different emotions was presented to D.R. The results showed that D.R. was markedly impaired in recognition in the fear, disgust and anger regions of the continua but was unimpaired in the happiness, sadness and surprise regions.

Finally, D.R. was asked to listen to a tape of sentences in which intonation patterns were used to express meaning. D.R. was impaired on tasks involving these sentences. D.R. was then presented with neutral words spoken with an emotional tone of voice and nonverbal sound patterns again with an emotional tone of voice. Various emotions were tested and the results revealed that D.R. was poor at recognition of anger vocalization and even more impaired at the recognition of fear (Scott *et al.* 1997).

The fact that D.R. is impaired on the processing of emotional expressions for particular emotions (fear and anger) across different sensory modalities (visual and auditory) suggests that these emotions might be processed selectively in different parts of the brain. As Scott and colleagues suggest: 'a plausible hypothesis is therefore that impaired recognition of fear and anger after amygdala damage reflects involvement of the amygdala in the appraisal of danger and the emotion of fear' (1997: 256).

Emotion and the brain

Phineas Gage was a site foreman working on the construction of the Rutland and Burlington railway in Vermont in the middle half of the nineteenth century. On 13 September 1848, Gage's workers were about to blast a rock blocking the way of the railway. The traditional method of rock blasting was to drill a hole in the rock and fill it with gunpowder before applying a fuse. Gage took it upon himself to tamp the gunpowder down in its hole with an iron rod some 1.5 metres long and several centimetres in diameter. Unfortunately, the tamping rod must have struck a spark on the rock for there was an explosion and the iron entered Gage's skull just beneath the left eyebrow and exited again from a hole in the top of his head, finally landing some 15–20 metres away (see research update). Remarkably, Gage survived the accident and was attended by the physician, John Harlow, who later wrote up the case (Harlow 1868). Although Gage recovered physically almost completely, his personality underwent fundamental change. In place of the likeable, hardworking, calm and efficient man from before the accident, Gage was now impatient, rude and highly irritable. He was quick to anger and also seemed unable to carry out plans of behaviour, which made him unreliable and unpredictable in the workplace. Gage inevitably lost his job as a foreman and ended up drifting around the United States as a member

Ψ Case study

'We can rebuild him' – a reconstruction of Gage's brain

Hanna Damasio and colleagues (1994) set out to try and reconstruct Phineas Gage's head injury by looking carefully at the point of entry of his skull. They went to the Warren Medical Museum where Gage's skull is housed and carefully photographed it from different angles, measuring the distances between the areas of bone damage and a variety of standardized bone landmarks. By analysing these pictures in tandem with careful descriptions of the wound, they were able to narrow down the range of possible directions that the iron bar had taken as it passed through Gage's brain. The authors then used these sources of information to reconstruct a three-dimensional brain image of Gage's brain using state-of-the-art neuro-imaging technology known as Brainvox (H. Damasio and Frank 1992). A three-dimensional iron rod with the same dimensions as Gage's tamping iron was then built and impaled on the three-dimensional brain which had been constructed, along the various possible trajectories that the computer analysis had generated.

This technique allowed Damasio and her colleagues to confirm earlier assumptions about Gage's brain (Ferrier 1878) that the iron did not touch the brain regions involved in motor function or language, that the damage was more extensive on the left than on the right hemisphere, and on the anterior rather than the posterior sectors of the frontal region of the brain as a whole. This pioneering research allowed Damasio and her colleagues to draw certain conclusions:

It was selective damage in the prefrontal cortices of Phineas Gage's brain that compromised his ability to plan for the future, to conduct himself according to the social rules he previously had learned and to decide on the course of action that ultimately would be most advantageous to his survival.

(A.R. Damasio 1994: 33)

---

of a fairground side-show where he would exhibit himself along with the iron bar that had caused his injury. He died in 1861.

The case of Phineas Gage illustrates one of the three main methods that psychologists have of understanding the relationship between psychological function, in this case the emotions, and brain function. This is known as the lesion method; that is, damage to the brain has either occurred accidentally as in the tragic cases of Gage or other accident victims, or has been inflicted deliberately through surgery in experiments on animals. The second method used to investigate relationships between emotions and the brain employs chemical or electrical stimulation of brain areas and consequent observation of the behavioural changes that such stimulation induces. Finally, and most recently, a series of sophisticated imaging techniques have been used to look at differential activation of different brain regions as a function of changes in emotional experience and/or behaviour (see Figure 15.2).

An excellent illustration of how the established methods of lesion and stimulation can inform each other is provided by considering a pair of pioneering research programmes from the beginning of the twentieth century looking at emotional behaviour in cats: the work of Cannon and Bard on neocortical lesions, and the work of Hess on electrode stimulation of the hypothalamus (see Chapter 2 for a brief introduction to the major brain areas).

Cannon and Bard (e.g. Bard 1928) showed that cats whose neocortices have been surgically removed were apt to make sudden unprovoked and ill-directed attacks on things around them. Cannon (1931) labelled the phenomenon 'sham rage'. Such displays of sham rage prompted Cannon and Bard to suggest that the cortical brain areas that they had removed served to inhibit emotional expression in normal cats.

At around the same time Hess conducted a series of experiments in his laboratory in Zurich in which he implanted electrodes into the hypothalamic region of the brains of cats (see Hess 1950). Hess found that stimulation of one part of the hypothalamus lead to increases in the cats' heart rate, alertness and arousal and that, if such stimulation was prolonged, the cat would become angry and often ferociously attack objects in its surrounding environment. Hess called this the 'affective

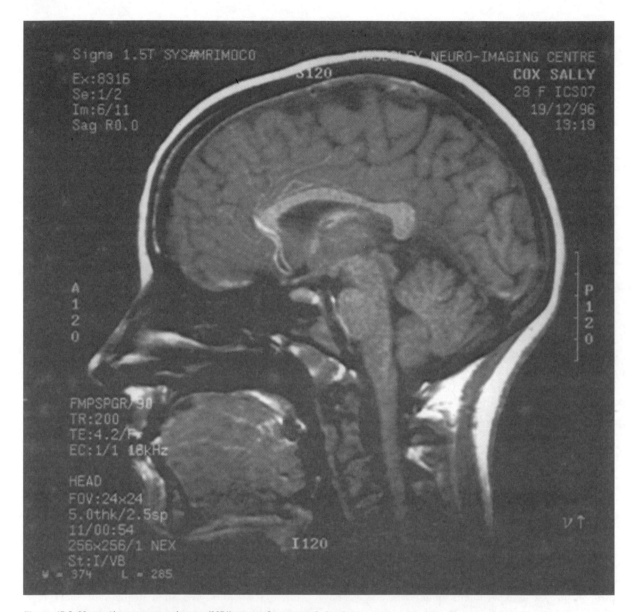

Figure 15.2 Magnetic resonance image (MRI) scan of a woman's brain

defence reaction', and suggested that the region of the hypothalamus that he had been interfering with was devoted to the organization of 'fight or flight' responses. Stimulation of more anterior regions of the hypothalamus lead to slowed heart rate and caused the cats to become calm and drowsy.

Taking the results of these two research programmes together, one obvious conclusion is that basic hypothalamic brain regions are responsible for angry behaviour in cats and that these anger behaviours are inhibited by higher neocortical regions. This rather crude model of brain and emotional functioning had, in fact, already been proposed by the Victorian neurologist, Hughlings-Jackson (1959). Hughlings-Jackson had suggested that the lower levels of the brain are simple reflex pathways controlling reactions to simple stimuli, basic posture, and movement. The next level, he suggested, includes more recently evolved structures that modulate these lowest level functions; it is this level that includes the structures associated with emotion such as the hypothalamus. At the highest and most recently evolved level, Hughlings-Jackson argued, the cortical structures control and modulate all of those levels below them.

Although contemporary conceptualizations of the relationship between the brain and emotions are more sophisticated than Hughlings-Jackson's model, the basic distinction between low level structures concerned with emotional behaviour and emotion production on the one hand and higher level cortical structures concerned with sensory processing and the experience of emotion on the other remains. It is worth noting that this way of thinking bears an uncanny resemblance to Plato's idea that the mind is a battleground between reason and emotion.

Perhaps the greatest advances since the time of Hughlings-Jackson have been in our understanding of how these different layers of anatomical structure function together as part of an emotional network. We now not only know which parts of the brain are concerned with processing emotion but also have the beginnings of an understanding of how they do it. In the next sections we consider the various components in this network in more detail. We begin by looking briefly at neocortical aspects of emotion processing before considering the role of lower brain regions such as the amygdala in the 'computation' of emotion.

Emotion and the neocortex

The brain structures of the neocortex are illustrated in Figure 15.3. The cortical structures of the brain are most heavily involved in the experience and expression of emotions. For both of these aspects of emotion there is consid-

erable **lateralization** of cortical processing. In humans information from the world crosses over to the opposite side of the brain. A good example of this is vision; information falling on the retina of the left eye is passed through the optic nerves and crosses over to the visual cortex on the right side of the brain. This crossover of brain projections is similar for most other functions of the cortex. Therefore, if someone has a stroke (a haemorrhage due to a burst blood vessel which leads to brain damage), on the *right* side of the brain, then that person is likely to lose motor functions in the body on the *left* side. For instance, the person may be selectively paralysed on the left side.

The lateralization of emotional expression information in the brain

There is now a considerable body of evidence to suggest that the right side of the cortex is closely associated with the processing of emotional expression but that the left side of the cortex has little role to play in this aspect of emotional analysis. A simple demonstration of this is illustrated in Figure 15.4 which shows what have come to be known as chimeric faces. From the figure it can be seen that chimeric faces have the up-turned lips of a smile on one side and the down-turned lips of a sad expression on the other. Non-brain-damaged individuals tend to interpret the emotional expression on the chimeric face in terms of the expression on the right side of that face – in other words, in terms of what the left side of their brain is doing. Look at the two faces in Figure 15.4 and decide which face you think is more happy and which face you think is more sad. For most right-handed people, Face A is likely to appear sadder and Face B happier.

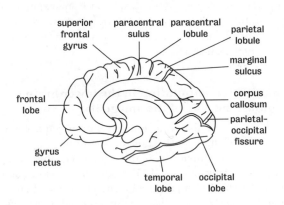

Figure 15.3 Major brain structures of the neocortex

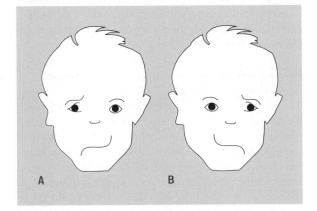

Figure 15.4 Chimeric faces: for most right-handed people, face A looks sadder

Other evidence for the right-sided superiority in emotional expression recognition comes from more sophisticated experimental work. Strauss and Moscovitch (1981) flashed emotionally expressive faces very quickly to the left and right visual fields separately of non-brain-damaged subjects. They found that recognition of emotional expression was better for faces presented to the left visual field (and thus relayed to the right cortex). Further support comes from research on so-called split-brain patients (Gazzaniga 1988). These patients have had a surgical operation to sever the part of the brain known as the corpus collosum which connects the two sides of the cortex. The operation is usually carried out in order to prevent the spread of epileptic discharges from one side of the brain to the other. Split-brain patients are again able to recognize emotionally significant events only when they are portrayed to the right side of the cortex (that is, to the left visual field).

An interesting extension of the work on facial expression was carried out by Etcoff et al. (1992). Three groups of subjects were used: those with left cortical damage; those with right cortical damage; and non-brain-damaged controls. All three groups were presented with people who were either deliberately lying or not lying. The results showed that those subjects with damage to their left cortex were significantly better than the other two groups in detecting lying. The authors explained this by suggesting that attention to language (which is largely a function of left-hand cortical structures) means that the recipient is more likely to be misled by the words used by the subject who is lying. In contrast, subjects with poor language ability (those whose left cortex is damaged) are more likely to pay attention to the subtle emotional facial expression changes – analysed on the intact right side of the brain – and therefore be able to detect more accurately when the stooge in the study is lying or not.

Relationship of the cortex to the experience and expression of emotions

The recognition of facial expression of emotions which we have discussed above seems to be a function of the rear or dorsal areas of the right cortex. In contrast, it is the *frontal* areas of the cortex which are involved in the experience and expression of emotions. In general terms, unlike the case of the recognition of emotion, there appears to be little laterality of emotional expression and experience, with both sides of the frontal cortex being involved. However, when one starts to consider differences between positive and negative emotions then lateral effects do emerge. It appears that at least some mechanisms concerned with the expression and experience of positive emotions are a function of the left cortex, whereas those for negative emotions are a function of the right frontal cortex.

A number of pieces of evidence point towards this conclusion. Patients who have suffered left-sided strokes in the frontal cortex have a high probability of becoming depressed (see Chapter 18), while those with stroke damage to the right frontal region are more likely to exhibit symptoms of mania (Starkstein and Robinson 1991) – a condition characterized by elated mood states. Furthermore, Schiff and Lamon (1994), in a very neat study, asked their subjects to deliberately contract muscles on either the left or the right sides of their face in turn. Contraction of the muscles on the left side of the face tended to induce negative emotions, especially sadness. In contrast, contraction of the muscles on the right side of the face tended to produce positive emotions and sometimes made the subjects assertive.

Finally, the work of Davidson and his colleagues has focused on taking electroencephalogram (EEG) recordings from different sides of the brain while presenting subjects with emotional film material. The subjects watched both positive and negative film clips (Davidson et al. 1990) and while watching the films, the subjects, as expected, made characteristic positive and negative facial expressions as a function of the films' content. The EEG results showed that, while the subjects were making happy expressions, there was a significant average increase in activation in the left frontal region of the cortex as compared to the right, but that this was reversed when subjects were expressing disgust.

In sum, it appears that the cortical brain regions are important in the recognition, experience and expression of emotion with recognition being processed by the right dorsal cortex and experience and expression by the frontal cortical areas.

Emotional computation in the lower brain regions: the role of the amygdala

We saw earlier that emotional reactions require the integrity of the hypothalamus in the brain (e.g. Bard 1928) and we mentioned the very early theory of Hughlings-Jackson (see 1959). On the basis of such work, Papez (1937) proposed a circuit theory of emotion involving the hypothalamus and related structures. MacLean (1949, 1952) named the structures of the

Papez circuit, along with several additional regions including the amygdala, the **limbic system**. The limbic system was viewed by MacLean as a general purpose circuit involved in the mediation of various functions required for the survival of the organism including emotions.

MacLean's writings were highly influential for many years; however, more recently the notion of the limbic system has come under attack in the research community. In tandem with this, there has been a growing realization that much of the emotional processing attributed to the limbic system is in fact a function of the amygdala alone (e.g. LeDoux 1992, 1993, 1996).

The earliest indications of the importance of the amygdala came from the famous work of Klüver and Bucy (1937). They found that, following surgical removal of large parts of the limbic system including the amygdala, monkeys lost their usual fear of humans and normal aggressiveness and instead became docile and lacking in facial expression. Klüver and Bucy's monkeys, however, were also rendered pathologically curious. They examined every object and put anything in their mouths including broken glass and live flames. They also became carnivorous and sexually disinhibited. Together these effects were labelled the Klüver-Bucy Syndrome and it is now known that the Klüver-Bucy Syndrome is a function of removal or damage specifically to the amygdala (Weiskrantz 1956).

So, why does the amygdala cause such major behavioural changes? A current front runner as a theory of amygdala functioning is the work of LeDoux (e.g. 1993, 1996). LeDoux has argued that the amygdala is the central 'emotional computer' for the brain, analysing sensory input for any emotional significance it might have and performing the cognitive functions of appraisal discussed later in the chapter. Certainly the amygdala has all the right brain connections to perform this role. It receives inputs from the regions of the cortex discussed above concerned with visual recognition and auditory recognition. It also has close connections with the hypothalamus which, as we saw from the work of Hess, is known to be concerned with emotional behaviour. Perhaps the most distinctive aspect of LeDoux's theory is his suggestion that the amygdala can compute the emotional consequences of sensory information from two sources, not only sensory information from the visual and auditory cortex, but also sensory information directly via the thalamus. LeDoux argues that the former information is important in detailed processing of the relevance of the emotional material with respect to the ongoing goals and current concerns of the organism. In contrast, sensory information via the thalamic route is a function of emotional learning and is based on the simplest features of stimuli, such as intensity, that have had emotional consequences for the individual in the past. A schematic summary of LeDoux's ideas is presented in Figure 15.5.

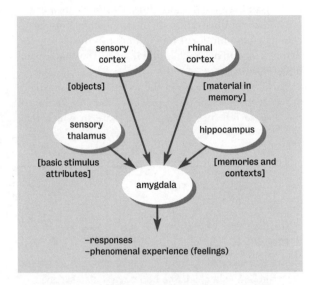

Figure 15.5 Schematic illustration of LeDoux's model

The Klüver-Bucy monkeys, without their amygdalas, would therefore have been unable to 'compute' the emotional implications of their own behaviour in relation to objects in the world and their generation of emotion and emotional behaviour would therefore have been impaired.

Neurochemistry and the emotions

In parallel with research programmes investigating which brain regions are involved in the processing of emotion, there has been a large amount of research on how those brain regions communicate with each other. Following the work of Brazier (1959) on frogs, we now know that such brain communication relies on various chemicals known as **neurochemicals** that fall into three functional families. The first are known as **transmitter substances** released into the synapses of nerve cells (see Chapter 2). The second family are hormones – chemicals carried around the body by the blood to effect organs that are sensitive to them. The final family is known as neuromodulators, many of which are peptides. Currently, we know very little about the operation of peptides. Most of the work has looked at the way they modulate the pain system and many of them bear a striking resemblance to addictive drugs like opium and heroin.

Neurotransmitters are discussed in more detail in Chapter 2. Also, an excellent review of the role of neurotransmitters in emotion is provided in Panksepp (1993) and we shall limit ourselves here to nothing more than an illustration of the importance of neurochemistry in emotional functioning by considering the patients of Oliver Sacks, glorified in the Hollywood film, *Awakenings*.

Sacks (1973) described the experience of survivors of the sleeping sickness, *Encephalitis Lethargica*. Victims of the disease fell into a suspended state in which they would sit without movement or speech for days and years on end. Several remained alive in hospitals for up to 50 years until, in 1969, the drug L-DOPA was discovered. L-DOPA is a precursor (a necessary building block) of the neurotransmitter substance dopamine which is vitally important for a great deal of brain communication. Administration of L-DOPA seemed to restore functioning in the patients with *Encephalitis Lethargica*. Once again they were able to act spontaneously and plan their time and experience a range of emotions. However, the patients did not return to their pre-disease emotional state. They experienced emotions, passions and appetites that were stronger and more disinhibited than before and there are some excellent descriptions of these transformation processes in Sacks's 1973 book (see case study).

Ψ Case study

Asleep for ten years – the case of Magda B.

Mrs B. was born in Austria in 1900 and had emigrated to the USA as a child. She had no serious childhood illnesses and was a high achiever both academically and athleticly at school. In her late teens, while employed as a secretary, she contracted a severe somonolent-opthalmoplegic form of the disease *Encephalitis Lethargica*; after a short period of improvement, she declined markedly until she was seen in the later 1960s and early 1970s by the neurologist Oliver Sacks, who included her in his book, *Awakenings* (1973), later made into a film. Sacks describes Magda B. at the time of her referral as follows:

akinesia was so extreme at this time that she would sit without blinking, or change of facial expression, or any hint of bodily movement, for the greater part of the day. . . . she had been speechless for more than 10 years . . . added to the motor problems were a striking apathy and apparent incapacity for emotional response, and considerable drowsiness and torpor for much of the day.

(Sacks 1973: 61–2)

Sacks started Mrs B. on the 'miracle drug' L-DOPA. After one week, Mrs B. began talking and thence began to show a stable and continuous improvement. As Sacks describes:

Mrs B. became quite talkative, and showed an intelligence, a charm, and a humour, which had been almost totally concealed by her disease. . . . Little by little Mrs B. emerged as a *person*, and as she did so was able to communicate to us in vivid and frightening terms, what an *unperson* she had felt before receiving L-DOPA.

(Sacks 1973: 64)

Mrs B. went on to have an emotional reunion with her family and she experienced very little bitterness about the years that she had lost to her illness. Magda B.'s story has an unusual ending. In July 1971 she had a sudden premonition of her own death and phoned her daughters to tell them to come and visit her that day, as she felt she was going to die in her sleep that night. The family came and Mrs B. assured them that she felt fine. Doctors carried out tests and everything was normal. In the evening Mrs B. went round and soberly said goodbye to all of her friends. That night she indeed went to bed and died.

Ψ Section summary

We have considered the broad area of biological aspects of emotion. We looked at the physiological and expressive changes associated with emotion, then we concentrated on a consideration of emotions and the brain. A historical review of the work of Cannon, Bard and Hughlings-Jackson and their consideration of the interaction of cortical brain regions with lower regions such as the amygdala was followed by a more detailed consideration of cortical involvement in emotions. We looked at recent work by LeDoux on the role of the amygdala as an emotional computer and we touched briefly on brain biochemistry.

1 Describe the development of ideas concerning the role of the amygdala in emotion.

2 Is there good evidence to suggest that particular expressions go with particular emotions?

☐ Cognitive aspects of emotion

In earlier sections of the chapter we examined the argument that cognitive or appraisal processes are a fundamental component of what we think of as an emotion. This view that cognition is an integral part of emotion is predominant in contemporary thinking in psychology. However, it is not the only stance and since the mid-1960s the debate about the relationship between cognition and emotion has been fierce. The clearest illustration of the different opinions is the so-called Lazarus–Zajonc debate. This centred on the primacy of affect versus the primacy of cognition in the instigation of emotion. Zajonc's view (e.g. Zajonc 1980) was that initial processing of stimuli in the world is an assessment of the affective tone or 'feel' of the stimuli – good or bad, safe or threatening and so on. Only subsequently, Zajonc argues, do more sophisticated cognitive interpretation and appraisal processes enter into the equation. In contrast, Lazarus (e.g. Lazarus 1991), as we saw in the section on components of emotion, has argued that Zajonc has confused the concepts of *cognitive* processes and *conscious* processes. Lazarus's line is that Zajonc's so-called affective processes are cognitive also but that they operate automatically and outside of awareness. In a way, the Zajonc–Lazarus debate is largely one of seman-

tics. Which lobby you vote in is really a function of how you define the word 'cognitive'. Should 'cognitive' be a broad, umbrella term that includes fast, acting unconscious processes or should it be restricted to higher-order appraisals and the like. Thirty years of debate in the emotion literature suggest that the answer to this question is by no means straightforward.

So if, as we have suggested, cognitive processes are important in emotion, what is the relationship between this component of emotional experience and others such as physiological arousal? In the early 1960s, one of the seminal studies on cognitive theories of emotion that directly examined this question was carried out by Schachter and Singer (1962). Subjects were told that they were to be injected with a vitamin compound called 'Suproxin' before carrying out a number of tasks. In fact, half of the subjects were injected with adrenaline (an arousal inducing drug) and the other half with a saline placebo. Some of the adrenaline subjects were then informed of the drug's real effects (e.g. increased heart rate), some were misinformed (e.g. told that their feet would feel numb), and some were left ignorant, including all of the placebo group. Each subject was then left in a room with one of two stooges and observed from behind a one-way mirror. In one condition, the stooge behaved in a euphoric way; for example, he played basketball with rolled-up paper. In the other stooge condition, the subject and the stooge were each asked to fill in a lengthy questionnaire that became increasingly personal and asked questions such as 'How many affairs has your mother had?' At this invasion of his privacy, the stooge became more and more angry, finally ripping up the questionnaire and leaving the room.

Schachter and Singer's hypothesis was that emotions are due to a cognitive interpretation of an undifferentiated state of physiological arousal which is common to all emotions in the context of specific situations. Therefore, following injection of an arousal-inducing drug such as adrenaline, those subjects who did not have a convincing explanation of how their bodies were feeling (i.e. the misinformed and ignorant groups) would interpret their arousal emotionally in line with their current circumstances. In other words, in the euphoric stooge condition they should become euphoric and in the angry stooge condition they should become angry.

The results from Schachter and Singer's (1962) study revealed that in the euphoria condition, the adrenaline-misinformed and the adrenaline-ignorant groups were indeed more euphoric than the adrenaline-informed group, as predicted by the hypothesis. However, the placebo group in the euphoria condition were intermediate and did not differ from any of the adrenaline groups on either the self-report or the behavioural measures of euphoria. Furthermore, in the anger condition, there were no significant differences between any of the groups on the self-report measures. Only on the behavioural measure did the adrenaline-ignorant group score significantly higher than the adrenaline-informed and the placebo groups.

Despite the equivocal nature of the results, Schachter and Singer's study achieved pride of place in the list of prototypical studies in psychology and led to the reasonably widespread adoption of the idea that cognition is important in emotion and that it acts so as to interpret undifferentiated physiological arousal. Schachter and Singer called this the **arousal-interpretation theory**. As we have seen in the section on basic emotions, there is now good evidence that different emotions are associated with different physiological arousal patterns in contrast to Schachter and Singer's uniform arousal view. Therefore, emotion 'selection' must have occurred, at least in part, at a pre-physiological stage. However, there is general agreement that emotional experience can be modulated and refined by interpretations of physiological processes and so it seems that there was a germ of truth in Schachter and Singer's work after all (Power and Dalgleish 1997).

If we therefore accept that emotions are not usually a function of cognitive processes operating on physiological arousal, then what might the relationship between the various components of emotion be? As noted earlier in the chapter in the section on components of emotion, the usual answer to this question, in contemporary writing on emotions, is that appraisals act as interpretations of events and that the other components such as physiological arousal, expression, action readiness, feelings and behaviour follow on from this event–appraisal interaction. Earlier we looked at two broad elements of appraisal theories of emotion. The first involved the appraisal of events with respect to the individual's goals in the world. So here, fear might be a response to appraisal of threat to a valued goal such as personal survival. The second aspect was that appraisals are carried out in terms of a number of appraisal themes such as pleasant/unpleasant and that the nature of the eventual emotion was a function of the particular combination of themes involved in the appraisal. In this section, for the purposes of illustration we consider one appraisal theory in detail – that of Oatley and Johnson-Laird (1987). A detailed review of other theories can be found in Power and Dalgleish (1997).

Oatley and Johnson-Laird proposed that the cognitive-emotional system is engaged in pursuing multiple goals and plans for which there is a finite amount of cognitive resources. They argued that, in this kind of arrangement, there have to be mechanisms by which priority can be assigned to a given goal because not all active goals and plans can be pursued at once. They propose that emotions provide a possible mechanism by which such priorities can be assigned or altered.

Oatley and Johnson-Laird's (1987) theory is that each of the five emotions discussed in the section on basic emotions is related to key junctures in goals and plans. So: happiness is linked to progress towards a goal; sadness is linked to the failure or loss of a goal; anger results when a goal or plan is blocked or frustrated; anxiety results when a goal is threatened; and disgust is considered to result from the violation of a gustatory goal.

According to Oatley and Johnson-Laird, the nature of the relationship between junctures in goals and plans and the corresponding emotions is two-fold. When a juncture in a goal or plan is appraised in an emotion-related way in the system, two forms of information are generated. The first is a primitive 'emotion signal' that serves to reconfigure the cognitive system into different patterns for each of the five basic emotions. The emotion signal does not carry any meaning information, according to Oatley and Johnson-Laird, and so the person would find themselves in an emotional state without any awareness of the reason why. In addition, a second, slower process occurs by which meaning information about exactly what was appraised at the juncture of the goal or plan is made available to conscious awareness. The theory proposes that these two processes operate in tandem such that on most occasions we experience an emotional state along with some understanding of what it is about. However, emotion signals, in the theory, have the capacity to occur in the absence of the meaning information, leading to an experience of emotions 'out of the blue' that we do not understand.

One problem with Oatley and Johnson-Laird's theory is that it is unclear how the system 'knows' which emotion signal to generate in a given situation, in the absence of a cognitive or meaning component. This is similar to the criticisms levelled at Zajonc's ideas mentioned earlier about affect in the absence of cognition. Another problem involves trying to define junctures in goals or plans. It is possible that at such junctures we may calmly reflect on things that went wrong on one occasion but get very distressed about them on another occasion; that is, junctures may or may not give rise to emotion. Alternatively, one could define junctures explicitly as those points where emotions are generated. The problem then arises that this type of definition is circular: emotions are those functional states arising from juncturs in plans and junctures are those decision points in plans that give rise to emotion.

Since the early 1990s, a new generation of multi-level theories of emotion has emerged (Johnson and Multhaup 1992; Power and Dalgleish 1997; Teasdale and Barnard 1993). These models propose different levels of the representation of meaning in the cognitive system. This allows the same stimulus to have emotional meaning at one level while simultaneously having cold, factual meaning at another level. This type of set up can help us to account more easily for dissociations in our experience where we can either know something 'with the head' or 'with the heart'. In this section we provide a brief overview of just one of these models – the **SPAARS** approach of Power and Dalgleish – as it is the one that has been most widely applied to different aspects of emotional experience, both normal and abnormal. An excellent review of other multi-level models is provided in Teasdale (1998).

SPAARS stands for Schematic, Propositional, Associative, and Analogical Representational Systems. These are the names of the different levels of representation within the model which lead to different forms of emotional experience (see Figure 15.6). The model is clearly a complicated one and the intention is merely to communicate the gist of it here. The analogical system is concerned entirely with low-level processing of sensory aspects of the environment and can be largely ignored for the present purposes. The first important distinction is between what are called the Propositional system and the Schematic system. Only one of these, the Schematic level, is involved in the generation of emotion, though both are levels of representation of meaning in the world. The Propositional system essentially is the level at which cold facts about the world and the self are stored; for example, that the capital of France is Paris. Cognitive processing at this level is reflected by what we might call emotion-free thinking. By remaining at the Propositional level, we can talk or think dispassionately about the most distressing of subjects. In contrast the Schematic level is where propositional facts are combined with our current goals and plans to form a 'model' of the current situation. If this model incorporates the information that the plans are compromised in some way then the corresponding emotion is generated.

A good example to illustrate the difference between propositional and schematic processing is the subject of

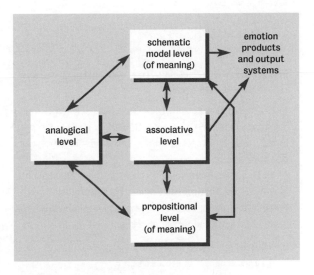

Figure 15.6 Schematic Propositional Associative and Analogical Representational Systems (SPAAR) approach to emotion
Source: adapted from Power and Dalgleish (1997)

giving up smoking (but also see the case study). Hardened smokers seem able to contemplate the evidence about the health and survival risks of their habit quite dispassionately much of the time, even though it involves thinking about things which potentially pose a major threat to survival. Multi-level theories such as the SPAARS model would suggest that these smokers are able to remain at the Propositional level of analysis when thinking about giving up. For this reason, most anti-smoking campaigns force the recipients up to the Schematic level with graphic pictures and descriptions of the possible consequences of smoking. These campaigns are therefore rarely experienced dispassionately but, rather, invoke a range of emotions.

There are many interesting issues to be discussed here, such as why things are sometime processed Propositionally and at other times Schematically but they are outside the scope of this brief overview. A fuller description is provided in Power and Dalgleish (1997). One other point that is worth highlighting, though, is the power that multi-level theories such as SPAARS have for dealing with emotional conflict. The theory predicts that sometimes information at the Propositional level is different from information at the Schematic level. So, for instance, sometimes we can tell ourselves over and over again that we are not at fault about something, that is we can repeatedly process propositional level information of our innocence, while still feeling guilty as a function of our schematic representation of the situation.

ψ   **Case study**

Heineken – a beer with multiple levels of representation

In the 1980s the British television network was showing an advert for the beer – Heineken. The slogan was that, as a drink, '*it reaches the parts other beers cannot reach*'.

In this particular advert, the young poet Wordsworth is wandering around the English Lake District contemplating his next poem. He inarticulately generates several attempts at an opening line:

'I walked about a bit on my own . . .'
'I strode around with nobody else . . .'

and so on. None of these first lines seemed to satisfy the poet. Eventually, he succumbs to his thirst and partakes of his glass of Heineken before orating:

'I wandered lonely as a cloud . . .'

The relevance of the story to emotions is that, at a propositional level, there is no difference between the young Wordsworth's pre-Heineken and post-Heineken attempts at poetry. They both have the same semantic content. However, the post-Heineken version also taps into the schematic level of meaning and includes nuances of feeling and understanding that were not there before (cf. Teasdale and Barnard 1993). Perhaps then, the part that Heineken uniquely reaches is the schematic level of meaning!

So far we have looked at two of the important levels for the generation of emotions in the SPAARS model – the Propositional and the Schematic. The third level, the Associative, essentially reflects the efficiency of the emotional system within SPAARS. The argument is that if the same event is repeatedly processed in the same way at the schematic level, then an associative representation will be formed such that, on future encounters of the same event, the relevant emotion will be *automatically* elicited without the system having to go through the process of building a model out of propositional and goal information. In a way, this is similar to Oatley and Johnson-Laird's (1987) primitive emotions signal except that it does not occur in all situations, only in over-learned ones. An important point to make about the automatization of emotions in this way is that it necessarily reflects the sorts of schematic level models that would have been *built in the past* when the associative level representation was first established. Consequently, although generally efficient and adaptive, Associative level emotional reactions sometimes leave us responding emotionally to situations that, were a Schematic level model to be constructed in the present, would not cause an emotional reaction. A good example of this is spider phobia. Most spider phobias are a result of a nasty encounter with a spider in childhood. The SPAARS analysis of this would be that in childhood a Schematic level analysis of the nasty spider event was laid down as an Associative level representation such that all future encounters of spiders automatically caused fear and distress without the need for resource-consuming Schematic-level processing. As a result, in adulthood, spider phobics feel instantly afraid in the presence of the spider while at the same time being able to say that they know there is nothing to be afraid of.

In this section we have examined two cognitive theories of emotion – the seminal model of Oatley and Johnson-Laird and one of the new generation multi-level theories. There are other forms of cognitive approach to emotion such as spreading activation or network models (e.g. Bower 1981) and social-attribution models (e.g. Weiner 1985). However, these are beyond the scope of the space here and an accessible review is provided in Power and Dalgleish (1997).

The effects of emotion on cognitive processes

So far we have examined the role of cognitive processes such as appraisal in the generation of emotions. However, what about the effects of emotion on cognitive processing? As Marc Lewis's work on dynamic systems theory has indicated, this relationship can involve the interaction of current emotion with subsequent appraisal; that is, any given appraisal is a function of *both* the current cognitive *and* emotional state of the individual (Lewis 1995). However, other research on the effects of emotion on cognition has focused explicitly on how basic cognitive processes such as perception, attention and memory are affected by emotional states.

Research in this area has involved either artificially inducing emotions in subjects or has considered individuals with so-called emotional disorders (see Chapter 18). There is an enormous body of such research on the effects of emotion on cognitive processes and so we shall just consider one or two studies for the purposes of illustration here. A comprehensive review of the material is presented in J.M.G. Williams *et al.* (1997).

The general finding in the literature has been that different emotions are associated with changes in cognitive processes in a way that 'helps out' the emotion as much as possible. So, research has shown that anxious individuals seem especially vigilant for danger or threat (see M.W. Eysenck 1992) whereas sad or depressed individuals selectively remember negative material from the past which may bear on their current loss. In this section we shall investigate two studies that have examined these issues – the work of Mathews and MacLeod (1985) using the modified emotional Stroop task and an experiment by Clark and Teasdale (1982) looking at memory in depression.

MacLeod and Mathews wanted to investigate attentional vigilance for threat in anxious individuals. They therefore adapted the Stroop (1935) task so that subjects were required to name as fast as possible the ink colours that several lists of words were written in. The words were either threatening or neutral. The subjects were specifically asked to ignore what the words said and to just concentrate on the colour of the ink. The hypothesis was that the anxious subjects would involuntarily be distracted by the meaning of the threat words more than they would by the neutral words and consequently their speed at naming the ink colours of the threat words would be slower than for the neutral words. The results strongly supported this prediction. Furthermore, the controls, who were not anxious, named the ink-colours of the threat, but not the neutral, words more quickly than their anxious peers. This kind of study therefore provides support for an involuntary attentional vigilance for threat in individuals who are anxious (see Figure 15.7).

In the study by Clark and Teasdale (1982), depressed individuals were asked to recall happy and sad memories from their past at different times of the day. The reason for using different times was that the patients experienced what is called diurnal variation in their mood so they tended to be depressed more at one time of the day than at another. The results revealed that, at the most depressed part of the day, the subjects recalled more unhappy memories whereas at the least depressed part of the day they recalled more happy memories. This

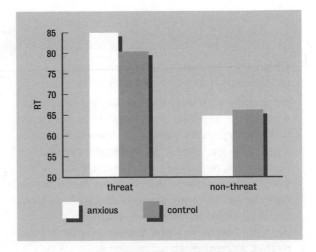

Figure 15.7 Results of the modified Stroop study of Mathews and MacLeod (1985): reaction time (RT) to colour-name threat and non-threat words by the anxious and control subjects is on the y-axis

study indicates that bias towards the recall of negative material is associated with increased depressed mood, an effect known as **mood congruent memory**. Perhaps one explanation of why this might be is that the emotions involved in depression such as sadness are a func-

---

Ψ **Section summary**

We have looked at cognitive aspects of emotion. Researchers have considered cognition–emotion relations in different ways; for instance, they have looked at how cognitive interpretations or appraisals about the world are involved in emotion and they have also considered the effects of emotion on basic cognitive processes such as attention and memory. We considered appraisal components and looked at the appraisal theory of Oatley and Johnson-Laird. We discussed an example of the new generation of multi-level theories of emotion and saw how such theories deal with dissociations in emotion experience. Finally we looked at how emotional states lead to biases in memory and attention processes in favour of relevant emotional information.

1 Discuss two cognitive theories of emotion. What are their similarities and differences?

2 In what ways do emotional states bias cognitive processing?

Research update

Cognitive processing of emotional information in younger subjects

The question of whether children with emotional problems exhibit cognitive processing biases consistent with their emotional concerns has been investigated by a team of researchers at the Institute of Psychiatry in London. They presented children with clinical depression, clinical anxiety, and Post-Traumatic Stress Disorder (PTSD) with a series of cognitive tasks assessing attention, memory and judgement. The stimuli in the task were either trauma-related, threat-related, depression-related or neutral.

The results showed that on attentional tasks such as the emotional Stroop task the children with anxiety selectively attended to threat-related information (Taghavi *et al.* 1997), the children with PTSD selectively attended to trauma-related information (Moradi 1996; Moradi *et al.* 1997) whereas the depressed children showed no attentional bias in their performance (Neshat-Doost *et al.* 1997) relative to controls. In contrast, on memory tasks, only the depressed children exhibited a bias in selectively remembering more depression-related words (Neshat-Doost *et al.* 1997). The other groups performed the same as the controls. Finally, on a judgement task in which subjects were asked to estimate the likelihood that bad things would happen to either themselves or to an unspecified other person, there was no difference in the performance of the anxious, PTSD and control subjects. All of the groups felt that bad things were more likely to happen to other children than to themselves. In contrast, the depressed children were more even-handed in their performance, estimating that bad things were about equally likely to happen to them as to other people (Dalgleish *et al.* 1997c), though this pattern reverted to being the same as in controls in recovered depressed children (Dalgleish *et al.* 1997).

These data show that depression is associated with biases in the cognitive processing of emotional information but only when a substantial memory element is involved. In contrast, anxiety is associated with biases when a substantial attentional component is involved. This reflects the pattern of data in adult subjects described above using similar methodologies (see J.M.G. Williams *et al.* 1997 for a review).

The most plausible explanation for these data is that anxiety is an emotion that requires quick responses to potential threats in the environment and is therefore most likely to be associated with attentional processing biases. In contrast, depressed mood requires reflection of changes in resources following loss and is therefore more likely to be associated with biases in mnemonic processing (Power and Dalgleish 1997).

---

tion of some form of loss. Therefore, it would be advantageous of the system to be able to have easy access to information concerning loss in order to reallocate resources to cope with the change in circumstances (Power and Dalgleish 1997). Most of this research on biased cognitive processing associated with emotion has been carried out in adults. However, the research update considers some 1997 studies on younger subjects.

☐ Social aspects of emotion

We saw in the section on the development of emotions how emotions become socialized through the first years of life and are an essential component of the complex relationship between infants and their caregivers. In this section we consider social aspects of emotion in adults. Over and again in the writings on the social psychology of adult emotions two dimensions seem to recur (e.g. Kemper 1990; Oatley and Jenkins 1996). On the one hand there is the dimension of affection and co-operation between individuals and on the other there is the dimension of aggression, dominance or power reflected in superordinate and subordinate relationships between individuals. These dimensions seem to reflect the need to compete and the need to co-operate in human society (Oatley and Jenkins 1996). Most of the research in this area has been carried out on the dimension of aggression or anger within groups and within relationships. Consequently, we shall concentrate on a consideration of this research in this section and address only briefly the smaller amount of work on affection and co-operation.

Social aspects of anger and aggression

Averill (1982) has written what many would regard as the classic essay on anger. In his book, Averill describes detailed studies in which he distributed diaries to 80 randomly chosen married people and 80 single university students and asked them to record their incidents of anger and annoyance. Averill reported that most subjects (over 60 per cent) reported at least one or two incidents of anger a week and almost 50 per cent of subjects reported an episode of annoyance each day. As Oatley and Jenkins (1996) point out, these are probably underestimates as people tend to forget incidents rather than remember incidents that did not happen. Over 90 per cent of the subjects in the study said that most anger-inducing events, in their experience, were a function of the transgression by others of social rules and social expectations. Anger then appears to be the emotion of social conflict and is an extremely ubiquitous aspect of the human condition.

These social aspects of anger, conflict and aggression have been studied in various ways. In this section we will sample this research and look at one of the famous studies of inter-group conflict carried out by Sherif and Sherif (1953), before moving on to looking at the research on anger and contempt in marriage. Sherif and Sherif invited young boys aged 11–12 to a summer camp in the country in the United States. The boys were culturally homogenous, being white, healthy, and from middle-class backgrounds. Every boy had an IQ of around 100 (see Chapter 13). There were three phases to the study and in this section we shall talk about the third phase, when the 24 boys who were taking part were split into two groups – the 'Bulldogs' and the 'Red Devils'. After a period in which the groups had become established, the investigators arranged a series of competitions between them including football, baseball and so on, with desirable prizes for the winners and no prizes for the losers. Once the competitive element had been set up, the boys in the groups began to make distinctions between 'us' and 'them'. Verbal aggression between the two groups commenced with accusations and name calling. Finally, physical aggression between members of one group and the other began to occur.

Having watched inter-group relations deteriorate between the Bulldogs and the Red Devils, the investigators endeavoured to try to improve relations. Their first attempt involved arranging a shared meal for members of both groups. However, one group arrived before the other and ate most of the food; this eventually led to a fight when the second group turned up.

Eventually, the meal had to be abandoned. In discussing these data, Sherif and Sherif (1953) remarked that each individual in the group seemed to believe himself to possess all the strengths of the group as a whole, being strong, fearless and proud. While within each group there was a great deal of affection (see below) and inter-reliance, between the groups relations could not have been much worse. They emphasized that the deterioration in relations was a function of the introduction of competition and that prior to this point (in phases 1 and 2, see below) conflict between the groups was at a minimum. These issues are discussed further in Chapter 12.

Anger and contempt in marital relationships

Emotions such as anger and experiences that involve conflict and aggression are clearly not confined to inter-group relations but are also to be found in more intimate relationships such as marriage. Perhaps the most famous research programme investigating these issues has been ongoing since the 1960s, under the direction of Gottman and Levenson (1992). Over a period of time Gottman and Levenson asked 73 married couples to come into the laboratory and complete a range of questionnaires. The couples were also filmed and recorded after a period of separation of 8 hours. During this reunion, the couples were asked to discuss three topics: the events of the day; a matter that was a conflict between the two members of the couple; and an agreed pleasant topic. Several days after these discussions, each member of the couple returned to the laboratory individually and was reassessed. In particular, the subjects were asked to remember how they had felt during each moment of the videotaped discussion.

Gottman and Levenson (1992) performed a detailed content analysis of the videotapes. For each turn in the discussion, the speaker was given either a positive or negative rating on the basis of five types of contact, such as assent, humour, complaint, criticism and so on. On the basis of these data, Gottman and Levenson classified their couples into 'regulated' and 'non-regulated' pairs. Regulated couples were those in which both members of the couple exhibited a predominance of neutral or positive features during the discussion. In contrast, non-regulated couples had at least one member whose turns in the discussion were dominated by negative features. For example, the non-regulated couples had a tendency to engage in more conflict, be more defensive, withdraw as listeners, exhibit more anger, exhibit less affection and display less interest and pleasure in the interaction with their partners. Reviewing the research, Gottman and Levenson came up with the magic number of a 5:1 ratio of positive to negative affect as necessary for a successful relationship, based on their longitudinal outcome data. Less than this, as exemplified by the non-regulated couples is, they argued, a step on the road to relationship failure. Interestingly however, it was not so much anger that was the most destructive emotion within the relationship in these studies. According to Gottman (1993b) it was expressions of contempt, frequent complaining, defensiveness, withdrawal, and stubbornness that were the destructive forces.

Another study by Jenkins *et al.* (1989) examined the role of anger in relationships in more detail. They studied 139 families and found that 79 per cent of the women interviewed in their sample felt that, although anger was frequently expressed in conflict within the family relationship, that at least some good often came from such expression. As Oatley and Jenkins (1996) point out, anger can be an expression of individuality and is not necessarily unhealthy for a relationship. In contrast, when partners view each other with contempt, this seems to imply that there is no longer an entitlement to respect or consideration. As Oatley and Jenkins (1996: 313) suggest, 'in evolutionary terms it seems that contempt is the emotion of complete rejection, of unmodulated power, treating the other as a non-person'.

Fortunately, relationships are not always doom, as is illustrated by a discussion of positive emotions in the social domain – the emotions of affection, love and co-operation.

Social aspects of the emotions of co-operation

In the previous section we discussed the seminal research of Sherif and Sherif (1953) on in-groups and out-groups. We talked about the third phase of Sherif and Sherif's study in which two groups of young boys at summer camp were pitted against each other in a series of competitive tasks and we considered how this led to conflict and aggression between members of the different groups. However, the first two phases of Sherif and Sherif's work showed how human hierarchies actually need not involve anger, and can operate on the basis of co-operation and affection between members of a given group.

In the first phase of the study the 24 11–12-year-old male participants were housed together for several days and encouraged to carry out activities on the basis of personal interest and choice. All of the boys quickly made

friends with each other and coalesced into small groups of buddies. In the second phase of the study, the two groups referred to above (the Bulldogs and the Red Devils) were formed. The investigators took great care to separate boys who had become good friends in phase one. Each group now had its own lodgings to sleep in and immediately each group was sent on a separate hike and camp out, which the boys found exhilarating. From that point on, all duties such as cooking, game playing and so on were done in the separate groups and all rewards were issued on a group basis. Each of the two groups quickly developed a culture of its own; a leader emerged and a hierarchy formed based on supportive decision making and co-operation, rather than fighting or threats. Each group developed insignia, established territories, customs and nicknames, and proceeded with its affairs in an harmonious and stable manner. By the end of phase two, the friendships of phase one had largely been replaced and 90 per cent of the friendships were within the group. There were some differences between the groups. The Bulldogs exhibited more solidarity and less interpersonal competition; contrastingly the Red Devils achieved cohesion occasionally by the use of threat or actual physical encounters on the part of the leader. We have already seen what happened in phase three.

The similarity between Sherif and Sherif's accounts of the Bulldogs and Red Devils and research on animal behaviour such as Goodall's (1986) work on chimpanzees is striking. Indeed, the similarities even extend to Sherif and Sherif's third phase of the study where the groups were set up in competition with each other (see p. 495). In the chimpanzees of Gombe, Goodall reports an occasion when a sub-group of chimpanzees broke off from the main group. Eventually violent episodes between the sub-group and the main group began, involving the death of several chimpanzees. This happened despite the fact that all of the chimpanzees had lived relatively harmoniously together in one group on a previous occasion.

It seems then that although conflict and dominance are important factors in the establishment of group hierarchies and leadership arrangements, such community relations can also be established and maintained on the basis of co-operation and affection. These emotions are perhaps even more important in the area of intimate relationships. Clearly there are many types of love and affection. Love can be that of a carer and the cared for, affectionate love between members of a couple, love between friends, familial love, as well as erotic love. The functions of affectionate, caregiving love in a relationship are perhaps obvious. These emotions foster recipro-cal support and encouragement between members of a couple to enable them to stay together and, in evolu-tionary terms, facilitate the rearing of children. The role of erotic love is somewhat more problematic. However, rather cynically, a number of researchers have suggested that forming a lifelong partnership with another human being is such a momentous choice that a somewhat blinding emotional state is necessary in order for that choice to be made (Oatley 1992).

Social aspects of gender and emotion

The idea that women are more emotional and more emotionally expressive than their male counterparts is as old as the hills. Such ideas recur throughout popular culture such as fiction and drama as well as in scientific surveys (e.g. Shields 1986). Such stereotypes of course may become self-fulfilling prophecies and lead to actual differences in behaviour between men and women and vice versa. Research on gender and emotion has tried to uncover what substance there is in these stereotypes by investigating a number of characteristics of emotional life including self descriptions of emotion, the expres-sion of emotion, the ability to decode emotional expres-sion in others, and the use of language in emotional interaction. This literature has been excellently reviewed by Brody and Hall (1993). In their review, Brody and Hall found that the cultural stereotypes mentioned above were consistently borne out by the systematic data collected from a number of research studies. They drew the following strong conclusions:

The evidence indicates that females are superior to males both at recognising feelings in others and at verbally and facially express-ing a wide variety of feelings themselves. Anger and some other outer-directed emotions (e.g., contempt and disgust) sometimes appear as exceptions to this general pattern. Gender differences in such emotions may be situationally, and perhaps culturally, specific.
(Brody and Hall 1993: 457)

Most of the theoretical speculation, at a psychological level rather than a sociological one, as to why such gender differences might exist concerns the role of lan-guage and the onset of the ability to verbalize about emotions across males and females. Stern (1985) has argued that, with the emergence of verbal language, the communication of shared feelings, experiences and meaning begins and the infant is able to communicate and articulate experiences that had previously been pri-vate. Brody (1994) argued that the early verbal language

superiority of females may set up a 'transactional pat-tern' such that parents verbalize about emotions more with their daughters than with their sons. Consequently, females are likely to become more publicly accountable for their emotional states whereas males may tend to deny emotions both to themselves and to others.

Theoretical issues in the social psychology of emotion

At the beginning of this section on social aspects of emotion, we discussed the ideas of Kemper (e.g. Kemper 1990), who argued that people in social situa-tions can be arrayed along two relational dimensions: a status or affection dimension, and a conflict or anger/aggression dimension. Kemper's ideas are an example of a social deterministic theory of emotions. Social determinists interpret the relation of emotions and sociocultural phenomena by conceptualizing emo-tions as authentic, involuntary responses that occur at particular junctures of social discourse. Emotions emerge at a particular point in a situation and allow people to sense the social consequences of the actions occurring in that situation.

A contrasting view to that of the social determinists is that of social constructionism. Social constructionists approach the relationship of emotions and sociocultural phenomena by conceptualizing expression of emotions as a form of intelligent discourse, constructed according to cultural rules so as to maximize the likelihood of desired interpersonal outcomes. As Harré (1986b) warns:

There has been a tendency among both philosophers and psycholo-gists to abstract an entity – call it 'anger', 'love', 'grief' or 'anxiety' – and to try to study it. But what there is are angry people, upset-ting scenes, sentimental episodes, grieving families and funerals, anxious parents pacing at midnight, and so on. There is a concrete world of contexts and activities. We reify and abstract from that concreteness at our peril'.

(Harré 1986b: 4)

In this view, as Heise and O'Brien (1993: 491) point out: 'Displays of emotion are not uncivilised eruptions coming from deep within individual psyches, but rather amount to sophisticated social discourse that is employed to influence others.' This discourse is seen as a function of shared expectations regarding appropriate behavioural repertoires in a given situation. According to the constructivist position, emotions do still involve beliefs, desires and so forth, as outlined in the section on components of emotion, but the thesis is that these elements are shaped and determined by the systems of cultural beliefs and values of a given community. Furthermore, these aspects of emotion are learnt as part of growing and developing in a given culture. Essentially, then, a social constructivist approach is compatible with the cognitive ideas about emotions we have presented earlier, in terms of the basic cognitive architecture and elements needed. Armon-Jones (1986a) makes this point well. She proposes that social constructivist approaches to emotion require 'a theory of mind in which emotions, as instances of psychological states, are defined as cognition based' (Armon-Jones 1986a: 36).

A final view is that of social interactionism, which is essentially a combination of social determinism and social constructionism. In this analysis, emotions spontaneously occur during social interaction and are then judged for suitability according to a set of cultural and ideological standards. The emotions are then managed and tuned in order to maximize the likelihood of culturally and socially acceptable goals. Further discussion of these various theoretical ideas is eloquently presented in Rom Harré's (1986a) edited book *The Social Construction of Emotions*.

Ψ Section summary

We have considered a number of aspects of the social psychology of emotion. We looked principally at two broad dimensions of conflict and co-operation. Research on conflict was examined; principally, Sherif and Sherif's work on boys at summer camp and other work on marital conflict. Sherif and Sherif's work was also considered in relation to the issue of social co-operation. We then looked at social psychological theories of emotion, especially the social constructionist position.

1 Outline the study of Sherif and Sherif (1963). What does this tell us about the social psychology of emotions?

☐ Cultural and cross-cultural aspects of emotion

In the previous section on social psychological theories of emotion, we looked briefly at ideas that emotions are social constructions as a function of the cultural system

we grow up in. This contrasts somewhat with the ideas discussed earlier in the section on basic emotions, where we were concerned with similarities across cultures in various aspects of emotion such as facial expression. The bottom line is that, although there is some evidence that certain aspects of emotion may be universal (that is, they occur across all cultures), beyond these basic components there is a considerable amount of cultural variation in the emotional life of different groups in human society. In this section of the chapter we illustrate this variety by considering the similarities and differences between, first, a non-industrialized society, the Ifaluk, and second, an industrialized, non-western society, the Japanese with western society, as exemplified by European culture.

Such comparisons are contemporary ones. However, another form of comparison is that between present-day culture and past cultures (see Harré and Finlay-Jones 1986) such as the Romantic period in the west, and we saw in the introduction how attitudes to emotion in various societies from the ancient Greeks onward have changed and varied. Before we turn to the Ifaluk, a word of warning is perhaps in order. One can never be objective in cross-cultural research; any analysis of one's own culture and the similarities and differences with other cultures is inevitably culture-bound. As Oatley and Jenkins (1996: 42) put it, 'there is no fixed point on which to stand outside cultural tradition'. This is at once the frustration and the fascination of this area of work.

The Ifaluk

Ifaluk is a tiny Pacific island with a population of approximately 430 people. In the 1980s, Ifaluk was visited by the American psychologist and anthropologist, Catherine Lutz, for nine months. Lutz's experiences are described in her excellent book, *Unnatural Emotions: Everyday sentiments on a Micronesian atoll and their challenge to western theory* (Lutz 1988). Lutz undertook the task of understanding, as far as she could, the emotional life on Ifaluk. She was not attempting to describe what it was like to be an Ifalukian, but was more concerned with the interaction between herself with her westernized emotional approach and the different approach of the Ifaluk. As Lutz herself said, she was 'an American female at a particular point in historical time' (1988: 15).

One of the principal differences between Lutz and the Ifaluk that arose concerned the contrast between notions of the self, which we shall see again in our discussion of Japanese culture. In the west, the self is viewed as what Lewis (1992) has called an **I-self**. The **I-self** is an autonomous personality, the maker of decisions, the source of thought and action, and the focus of emotional experience. In the west, there is a clear sense of separation of the self from other selves. There is a social emphasis on the importance of independence and individuality. In contrast, on Ifaluk the self is more accurately described as a **We-self**, in which connections with other family members and the social group in general are far more important than any sense of autonomy or individuality. In illustration of the difference, Lutz famously recounts an episode from the first few weeks of her stay on Ifaluk in which her autonomous **I-self** and the Ifalukian **We-self** ran up against each other. Lutz was visited by some young women in her hut. Lutz asked them, 'Do you want to come with me to get drinking water?' (1988: 88). This simple question caused the Ifalukians some distress and they looked sad. Lutz had made the mistake of addressing them as you, and thus implying a separation between herself and them, a social *faux pas* on Ifaluk.

One of the most engaging aspects of Lutz's book is her ability to describe the many social mistakes that she made, such as the one above, and use them to illustrate the principal differences between her western, North American social attitudes and those of the Ifaluk, with humility and humour. The book is a rich source of interesting anecdotes and anthropological material and it is not possible to do justice to this in the space available. However, one or two further examples should serve to illustrate the principal finding that emotions on Ifaluk are principally about the mediation of social relationships whereas, although this is also important in a western culture, there is, in addition, the western notion of individualized emotional experience.

Another excellent example of this is the Ifaluk notion of *ker*. Lutz translated this as 'happiness/excitement'. In western society, a great deal of social behaviour is aimed at the achievement of happiness or excitement and, indeed, the right to the pursuit of happiness is enshrined in the US Constitution. In contrast, on Ifaluk, Lutz has suggested that the view is that individuals experiencing *ker* are likely to be too pleased with themselves. They may have a tendency to show off or become rowdy or misbehave. These are all behaviours which the Ifalukians find less than acceptable. The appropriate response to individuals expressing *ker* on Ifaluk is *song*. *Song* is translated as appropriate anger at a violation of social rules and it is a social duty on Ifaluk to express *song* if another

individual is expressing *ker*. The natural response to song should then be one of *metagu* – translated as anxiety about the welfare of the social group.

In fact, anxiety is one of the most important emotions on Ifaluk. However, as illustrated by the example of *metagu*, the anxiety is about social disruption rather than threats to the individual and this provides a clear example of where a social constructivist account of emotions seems particularly apt. This aspect of *metagu* was illustrated in another anecdote by Lutz in which she became afraid when an uninvited man entered her hut in the middle of the night. Lutz's fear was a topic of some intrigue among the Ifaluk as, for them, unsolicited visits by men to women in the night were an acceptable form of social behaviour and, in fact, were seen as the antithesis of fear.

It is tempting to suggest that many of the differences between westernized emotional life and the emotional life on Ifaluk are a function of the non-industrialized, 'primitive' nature of Ifaluk society. However, this is too naive an interpretation and many similar differences can also be found by comparing western society with other advanced non-western societies such as the Japanese.

Emotional climates in Japan and the west

As with the Ifaluk, Japanese culture is viewed as a We-self society. In fact, as Geertz (1975) has pointed out, the individualistic nature of the self in western society is what is unusual in world culture. A good example is the Japanese emotion of *amae* (see Morsbach and Tyler 1986). There is no simple translation of *amae* into English and it is best described as an emotion of interdependence, a feeling derived from the complete acceptance of another person and complete acceptance by that other person. In the west, as Oatley and Jenkins (1996) point out, one is expected to grow out of this kind of emotion. To remain interdependent in this way is perhaps seen as weak in some way. However, other emotions in the west seem more acceptable than in Japan. The general western view is that suppression of emotions is undesirable and even related to health risks (see Pennebaker 1982). In contrast, in Japan many emotional states are highly controlled in certain social situations. For example, anger between Americans who are colleagues is reasonably common. However, in Japan such anger is considered highly inappropriate (Markus and Kitayama 1991).

Although, as we saw in the section on basic emotions earlier, it has been argued that some aspects of emotional processing may be universal across all cultures, it is clear from a consideration of the differences between western, Ifalukian and Japanese emotional climates that the nature and experience of emotions are strongly influenced by cultural ideas as would be anticipated from a social constructivist perspective. Hence the title of Lutz's book, *Unnatural Emotions*; emotions are not a function so much of nature as they are of culture. The exact extent of how much of emotion is universal and how much is socially constructed as a function of culture or whether this is even a meaningful way of examining the issue are difficult and thorny questions and ones that are becoming harder and harder to answer with the pervasive influence of western ideas and ideals on even the remotest of non-industrialized societies.

Ψ **Section summary**

We have looked at some examples of cross-cultural research on emotion. We considered Lutz's work on the island of Ifaluk and compared it to research on Japanese subjects. We discussed the idea that non-western societies, both primitive as in the case of the Ifaluk and advanced as in the case of the Japanese, are we-centred in that the social, pluralistic aspects of social relationships are emphasized. In contrast, western society seems to be more I-centred in that the autonomous, individualistic aspects of social interaction are emphasized.

1 What are the we-self and the I-self? Illustrate your answer with respect to western and non-western societies.

2 What does research on the Ifaluk tell us about the cultural nature of emotions?

Conclusion

Emotions present the interested researcher with a beguiling set of questions to tackle. What exactly are they? Why do we have them? Are they the same for everyone? How do they develop? How is it that they seem to be both mental and physical states? In this chapter we have tried to examine some of these questions and others also, by considering the psychological research on emotions. We examined the claim that emotions are not unitary phenomena, but rather complex combinations of different components: physiological change, readiness for action, cognitive change, and conscious feeling. We considered whether some of the many emotions we experience are more basic or fundamental than others and we looked at the arguments for a core group of emotions of disgust, sadness, anger, fear and happiness.

The various postulated components of emotion are mirrored by different levels of explanation or analysis of emotion phenomena and indeed the section on the components of emotion previewed more detailed consideration of a variety of approaches presented in the rest of the chapter. So, we can look at emotions from a biological standpoint, from a cognitive standpoint, from a social perspective or a cross-cultural perspective and finally from a developmental perspective. These different ways of thinking about emotions are not mutually exclusive but can combine to provide a rich multidisciplinary account of emotional life. The chapter is structured to reflect these different perspectives on emotion with detailed sections on development, biology, cognition, social psychology and cross-cultural psychology. Having read the chapter, you should now have at least a preliminary understanding of the richness and variety of emotion research, and, it is hoped, of the nature of emotions themselves.

Ψ Chapter summary

● Defining emotion

We considered what we mean when we use the term emotion and we saw that psychological ideas about what constitutes an emotion have shifted with the sands of time from the pioneering work of the ancient Greeks to the cognitive and social-constructionist accounts of the late twentieth century. We described the various components that go to make up what might be called emotion. These include feelings, physiological arousal, cognition, and readiness for action. We looked at the relationship between emotions, moods and more enduring characteristics such as personality traits.

● Number and type of emotions

We asked whether all emotions should be considered equal or if some emotions were more basic or fundamental than others, as proposed by researchers such as Ekman. We looked at the evidence for this, including the proposed universality of some emotions such as anger, sadness, disgust and fear across all cultures. We considered some of the problems, both methodological and conceptual, with this work; for example, the fact that in many studies of non-western cultures, western emotion terms had a contaminating influence on the way that data were collected.

● Development of emotions

We focused on a number of aspects of the development of emotions. We looked at how most research on emotions relied on people's self-report, that is, their ability to say how they feel. This poses a problem for understanding emotions in very young children who cannot yet talk; there are various ways that researchers have tried to overcome this hurdle. We described the development of facial expressions of emotion in infants and also their ability to recognize facial expressions in others. Individual differences in the emotionality of infants in terms of temperament were then considered. Social aspects of the development of emotions were discussed; in particular, attachment styles.

● Biological aspects of emotion

Biological aspects of emotion include the physiological and expressive changes associated with emotion but more centrally are concerned with the roles of various brain regions in the perception, generation and experience of emotions. A historical review of the development of our understanding of these brain regions began with the early work of Cannon and his peers and culminated in LeDoux's model of the amygdala as an emotional computer. We looked briefly at aspects of neurochemistry associated with emotion.

● Cognitive aspects of emotion

We described the reciprocal influence of cognition on emotion and emotion on cognition. Various cognitive theories of emotion revolve around the idea that the way we feel about something is determined by the way our cognitive system interprets and analyses it. We considered two cognitive theories of emotion to illustrate this general philosophy: the work of Oatley and Johnson-Laird and the SPAARS model of Power and Dalgleish. We looked at the other side of the coin, that is, how the emotional state that we are in leads us to interpret and process information in a relatively biased fashion.

● Social aspects of emotion

We highlighted a number of topics from the broad domain of social aspects of emotion. We considered the two dimensions of conflict and co-operation by discussing Sherif and Sherif's pioneering work on boys at summer camp alongside work on marital conflict. We touched briefly on the different classes of social theories of emotion and looked at their similarities and differences.

● Cultural and cross-cultural aspects of emotion

We considered emotions from the broadest perspective possible – the cultural and cross-cultural. To illustrate the types of ideas and methodologies in this approach we looked at work on a primitive society, the Ifaluk, and on a non-western industrialized society, the Japanese. Our discussion concentrated on the ideas of individualism as characterized by western society and pluralism as characterized by the Japanese and the Ifaluk. We discussed the implications of these different social dynamics for our thinking about emotion.

Further reading

● Lewis, M. and Haviland, J.M. (eds) (1993) *The Handbook of Emotions*. New York: Guilford Press. An excellent compendium of up-to-the-minute articles on all aspects of emotion by leading researchers in the field.

● Oatley, K. and Jenkins, J.M. (1996) *Understanding Emotions*. Cambridge, MA: Blackwell. An undergraduate text that provides a highly accessible and well-written overview of basic theory and research in emotion.

● Power, M.J. and Dalgleish, T. (1997) *Cognition and Emotion: From order to disorder*. Hove: Psychology Press. A textbook that also presents a set of new theoretical ideas. This book focuses exclusively on cognitive aspects of emotion and includes sections on emotional disorders.

● Dalgleish, T. and Power, M.J. (eds) (1998) *The Handbook of Cognition and Emotion*. Chichester: Wiley. An exhaustive compendium of theory and research in cognition and emotion by leading researchers in the field.

● Frijda, N.H. (1986) *The Emotions*. Cambridge: Cambridge University Press. The seminal psychology text on the emotions. Slightly older than the other books but well worth reading.

● Damasio, A.R. (1994) *Descartes' Error*. New York: Putnam. A readable account of some of the work on emotions and the brain and an accessible summary of Damasio's own work.

● Ellsworth, P.C. (1994) William James and emotion: is a century of fame worth a century of misunderstanding?, *Psychological Review* 101: 222–9. A critical analysis of psychological thinking about emotions over the past 100 years.

● Harré, R. (ed.) (1986) *The Social Construction of Emotions*. Oxford: Blackwell. An excellent edited compendium of chapters outlining the social constructivist approach to emotions and chapters on important cross-cultural research such as work on Ifaluk.

Motivation

Edmund Rolls and Michael Eysenck

KEY CONCEPTS ● hunger and the control of food intake ● thirst ● sexual behaviour ● psychosocial motives ● motivation and performance

☐ Chapter preview

When you have read this chapter, you should be able to

- understand how two examples of motivated behaviour, hunger and thirst, are controlled
- understand the signals that initiate hunger
- describe how rewards are modulated by motivational state, for example, how the reward produced by the sight, smell and taste of food is modulated by hunger
- understand some of the processing in the brain that controls food intake, including how taste processing is interfaced to hunger, and how learning about the reward value of different food occurs
- discuss some of the factors that operate in obesity
- understand the signals that control another example of motivated behaviour, thirst
- describe some of the biological and neural principles that underlie sexual behaviour
- understand some of the major psychosocial motives exhibited by humans
- discuss some of the reasons why there are individual differences in motivation for work
- understand the relationship between motivation and performance, together with some of the factors underlying that relationship

Introduction

The study of motivation is of central importance in psychology. It is concerned with the issue of *why* individuals behave in the ways they do. If someone completely lacked motivation, he or she would simply sit passively and not interact with the environment. A state resembling that is found in catatonic schizophrenics, who remain almost completely immobile for hours at a time. However, the vast majority of people are active and display a wide range of motivated behaviour.

Before proceeding further, we should consider the meaning of the term 'motivation' in more detail. According to Taylor *et al.* (1982: 160), 'Motivation ... is generally conceived of by psychologists in terms of a process, or a series of processes, which somehow starts, steers, sustains and finally stops a goal-directed sequence of behaviour'. Thus, for example, a hungry person may engage in a series of actions designed to achieve the goal of finding food to eat.

How many kinds of motivation are there? According to McDougall (1912), there are numerous instincts or basic motives. He produced a list of these instincts, which included the following: fear, disgust, food-seeking, sex, submissiveness, curiosity, gregariousness, rest, migration, appeal for assistance, acquisitiveness, self-assertiveness, laughter, and parental protectiveness. The value of this long list of instincts may be doubted, but at least it illustrates the fact that there are many different sources of motivation.

The first three sections of this chapter are devoted to hunger, thirst and sex, all of which are of fundamental importance to nearly all species. Much is known of the basic physiological processes involved in hunger, thirst and sexual behaviour. Of course, human beings are not only motivated by hunger, thirst and sex. For example, they have several psychosocial motives, such as the need for affiliation, the need for intimacy, and the need to grow as individuals. Some of these aspects of motivation are discussed in the fourth section of the chapter.

Motivation is also important when it comes to predicting how well different individuals will perform a task. In general terms, we expect high levels of motivation to be associated with better performance than low levels of motivation. However, some theories of motivation predict that very high levels of motivation will produce worse performance than moderate motivational levels. Other theories of motivation focus on individual differences in various dimensions such as need for achievement.

This chapter begins with hunger and thirst. Some of the main questions to be addressed are as follows:

- What motivates us to work for particular rewards such as food when we are hungry, or water when we are thirsty?
- How do these motivational control systems operate to ensure that we eat approximately the correct amount of food to maintain our body weight or to replenish our thirst?
- What factors account for the overeating and obesity which some humans show?

We focus on the control of hunger and thirst, not only because there is considerable evidence about how the brain processes the relevant signals to control these types of motivated behaviour, but also because overeating and obesity lead to significant health risks which make the control of food intake important to understand. After that, some of the biological and neural underpinnings of another type of motivated behaviour, sexual behaviour, are introduced.

We need to start with some definitions. A **reward** is something for which an animal will work. A **punishment** is something that an animal will work to escape or avoid. In order to exclude simple reflex-like behaviour, the concept invoked here by work is to perform an arbitrary form of behaviour (called an **operant response**) in order to obtain the reward or avoid the punishment. An example of an operant response might be pressing a lever in a Skinner box (see p. 87) or putting money in a vending machine to obtain food. Thus, motivated behaviour is present when an animal (including a human) will perform an arbitrary operant response to obtain a reward or to escape from or avoid a punishment. This definition implies that learned responses are important in demonstrating motivated behaviour (see Chapter 3).

Hunger and the control of food intake

Peripheral factors in hunger and satiety

To understand how food intake is controlled, we first consider the functions of the different peripheral factors (i.e. factors outside the brain) such as taste, smell and gastric distension, and the control signals, such as the amount of glucose in the blood. Then we consider how the brain integrates these different signals, learns about which stimuli in the environment provide food, and initiates behaviour to obtain the correct variety and amount of food.

The functions of some different peripheral factors in the control of eating can be revealed with the sham feeding preparation shown in Figure 16.1. In this situation, the animal can taste, smell and eat the food normally, but the food drains from the stomach, so that no distension of the stomach occurs, and nor does any food enter the intestine for absorption. It is found that rats, monkeys and humans will work to obtain food when they are sham feeding. This shows that it is the taste and smell of food which provide the immediate reward for food-motivated behaviour. Consistent with this, humans rate the taste and smell of food as being pleasant when they are hungry.

A second important aspect of sham feeding is that **satiety** (reduction of appetite) does not occur: instead rats and monkeys continue to eat often for more than an hour when they can taste and smell food normally, but food does not accumulate in the stomach, and enter the intestine. We can conclude that taste and smell, and even swallowing food, do not produce satiety. There is an important psychological point here: reward itself does not produce satiety. Instead, the satiety for feeding is produced by food accumulating in the stomach, and entering the intestine. Evidence that gastric distension is an important satiety signal is that if an animal is allowed to eat to normal satiety, and then the food is drained through a **cannula** (tube) from the stomach, then the animal starts eating again immediately (Gibbs *et al.* 1981). Evidence that food entering the intestine can produce satiety is that small infusions of food into the duodenum (the first part of the intestine) decrease sham feeding (Gibbs *et al.* 1981). It is also interesting that food delivered directly into the stomach, or even glucose intravenously, is not very rewarding, in that animals learn only with difficulty to perform a response to obtain an intragastric or intravenous infusion of food (see E.T. Rolls 1999).

These findings are summarized in Table 16.1.

Important conclusions about the control systems for motivated behaviour follow. First, reward and satiety are different processes. Second, reward is produced by

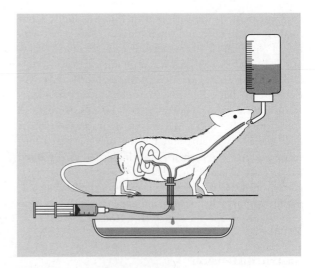

Figure 16.1 Sham feeding preparation

oropharyngeal factors such as the taste and smell of food. Third, satiety is produced by gastric, intestinal and eventually other signals after the food is absorbed from the intestine. Fourth, hunger and satiety signals modulate the reward value of food (in that the taste and smell of food are rewarding when hunger signals are present and satiety signals are not present). In more general and psychological terminology, motivational state modulates the reward or reinforcement value of sensory stimuli. Fifth, given that reward and satiety are produced by different peripheral signals, one function of brain (i.e. central) processes in the control of feeding is to bring together satiety and reward signals in such a way that satiety modulates the reward value of food. One brain process which must be important in understanding the control of food intake is where and how in the brain gastric and other satiety signals are brought together with taste and smell signals of food, to produce a taste/smell reward signal which is modulated by satiety.

Control signals for hunger and satiety

There is a set of different signals, each of which plays a role in determining the level of hunger vs satiety. These signals must all be integrated by the brain. The signals are summarized next, taken to some extent in the order in which they are activated in a meal.

Sensory-specific satiety

If we eat as much of one food as we want, then pleasantness ratings of its taste and smell change from indicating

Table 16.1 Summary of functions of peripheral factors in feeding

	Reinforcement	Satiety
Oropharyngeal factors	Yes	No (though contributes to sensory-specific satiety)
Gastric and intestinal factors	No	Yes

506 Psychology

very pleasant to indicate neutral. Interestingly, other foods may still taste and smell pleasant. Associated with this, if one of the foods not already eaten in a meal is now offered, subjects will eat a reasonable quantity of this food. In this way variety stimulates food intake. An example is that when as much chicken is eaten as is wanted for a meal, its pleasantness ratings decrease to approximately neutral. However, the rating of banana may remain pleasant, and banana may be eaten in a second course even when as much chicken as is wanted has already been eaten. Because this type of satiety is partly specific to the sensory qualities of the food including its taste, smell, texture and appearance, it has been named sensory-specific satiety (B.J. Rolls *et al.* 1981).

Gastric distension

This is one of the signals that is normally necessary for satiety, as shown by the experiment in which gastric drainage of food after a meal leads to the immediate resumption of eating (Gibbs *et al.* 1981). Gastric distension builds up only if the **pyloric sphincter** closes. The pyloric sphincter controls the emptying of the stomach into the next part of the gastro-intestinal tract, the duodenum. The sphincter closes only when food reaches the duodenum, stimulating **chemosensors** and **osmosensors** to regulate the action of the sphincter, by both local neural circuits and by hormones, in what is called the enterogastric loop (see Gibbs *et al.* 1981).

Duodenal chemosensors

The duodenum contains receptors sensitive to the chemical composition of the food draining from the stomach. One set of receptors responds to glucose, and can contribute to satiety via the vagus nerve, which carries signals to the brain. The evidence that the vagus is the pathway is that cutting the vagus nerve (vagotomy) abolishes the satiating effects of glucose infusions into the duodenum. Fats infused into the duodenum can also produce satiety, but in this case the link to the brain may be hormonal (a hormone is a blood-borne signal), for vagotomy does not abolish the satiating effect of fat infusions into the duodenum (see Greenberg *et al.* 1990; Mei 1993).

Glucostatic hypothesis

There are many lines of evidence, summarized next, that one signal that controls appetite is the concentration of

glucose circulating in the plasma: we eat in order to maintain **glucostasis** – constancy of glucose in the internal milieu. More accurately, the actual signal appears to be the utilization of glucose by the body and brain: if the arterial minus the venous concentration is low, indicating that the body is not extracting much glucose from the blood stream, then we feel hungry and eat; and if the utilization measured in this way is high, we feel satiated. Consistent with this correlation between glucose and eating, there is a small decrease in plasma glucose concentration just before the onset of meals in rats, suggesting that the decreasing glucose concentration initiates a meal (Campfield and Smith 1990) (see Figure 16.2). At the end of a meal, plasma glucose concentrations (and insulin, which helps the glucose to be used by cells) rises. A second line of evidence is that injections of insulin which reduce the concentration of glucose in the plasma (by facilitating its entry to cells and storage as fat) provoke food intake. Third, 2-DeoxyGlucose, a competitive inhibitor of glucose metabolism, elicits feeding. Fourth, infusions of glucose and insulin can reduce feeding. Fifth, the brain's monitoring system for glucose availability seems to be in the area postrema in the medulla (part of the brainstem), for infusions there of a competitive inhibitor of glucose, 5-thio-glucose, elicit feeding (Ritter 1986).

It is worth noting that in diabetes (that is, diabetes mellitus), the cells can become insulin resistant, so that in this condition it is difficult to interpret whatever plasma levels of glucose are present in terms of their possible role in hunger and satiety.

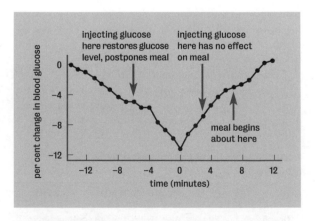

Figure 16.2 The fall in glucose concentration in the plasma that is typically seen in rats before a meal is initiated
Source: after Campfield and Smith (1990)

Research update

Body fat regulation: leptin or OB protein

The signals described so far would be appropriate for regulation on the meal-to-meal timescale, but might not be adequate for the longer-term regulation of body weight, and in particular of body fat. So the search has been on for another signal that might affect appetite based on for example the amount of fat in the body. Research has uncovered a candidate hormone that performs this function. Some of the evidence is as follows (see Campfield *et al.* 1995):

- OB protein or leptin is the hormone encoded by the mouse ob gene (here ob stands for obesity).
- Genetically obese mice that are double recessive for the ob gene, and are hence designated as obob mice, produce no leptin.
- Leptin decreases food intake in wild type (lean) mice (who have genes which are OBOB or OBob so that they produce leptin) and in obob mice (showing that obob mice have receptors sensitive to leptin).

- The satiety effect of leptin can be produced by injections into the brain.
- Leptin does not produce satiety (decrease food intake) in another type of genetically obese mouse designated dbdb. These mice may be obese because they lack the leptin receptor, or mechanisms associated with it.
- Leptin has a long time course: it fluctuates over 24 hours, but not in relation to individual meals. Thus it might be appropriate for the longer-term regulation of appetite.
- Leptin is found in humans.
- Leptin concentration may correlate with body weight/**adiposity**, consistent with the possibility that it is produced by fat cells, and can signal the total amount of body fat.

A hypothesis consistent with these findings is that a hormone, leptin, is produced in proportion to the amount of body fat, and that this is normally one of the signals that controls how much food is eaten.

Conditioned appetite and satiety

If we eat food with much energy (e.g. rich in fat) for a few days, we gradually eat less of it. If we eat food with little energy, we gradually, over days, ingest more of it. This regulation involves learning, learning to associate the sight, taste, smell, texture, etc. of the food with the energy that is released from it in the hours after it is eaten. This form of learning was demonstrated by Booth (1985), who after giving subjects sandwiches with different flavours for lunch for several days, on a test day then offered subjects medium energy sandwiches (so that the subjects could not select on the amount of energy in the food): the subjects ate few of the sandwiches if they had the flavour of the high energy sandwiches eaten previously, and many of the sandwiches if they had the flavour of the low energy sandwiches eaten previously.

The brain control of eating

From clinical evidence it has been known since early in the twentieth century that damage to the base of the brain can influence food intake and body weight. Later it was demonstrated that one critical region is the ventro-

medial hypothalamus, for bilateral lesions here in animals led to hyperphagia and obesity (see Grossman 1967, 1973). Then Anand and Brobeck (1951) discovered that bilateral lesions of the lateral hypothalamus can produce a reduction in feeding and body weight. Evidence of this type led in the 1950s and 1960s to the view that food intake is controlled by two interacting 'centres', a feeding centre in the lateral hypothalamus and a satiety centre in the ventromedial hypothalamus (see Grossman 1967, 1973; Stellar 1954; see also Figure 16.3).

Soon, problems with this evidence for a dual centre hypothesis of the control of food intake appeared. It appears that lesions of the ventromedial hypothalamus act indirectly to increase feeding. These lesions increase the secretion of insulin by the pancreas; this reduces plasma glucose concentration, and then feeding results. This mechanism is demonstrated by the finding that cutting the vagus nerve, which disconnects the brain from the pancreas, prevents ventromedial hypothalamic lesions from causing hypoglycemia, and also prevents the overeating that otherwise occurs after ventromedial hypothalamic lesions. The ventromedial nucleus of the hypothalamus is thus thought of as a region which can

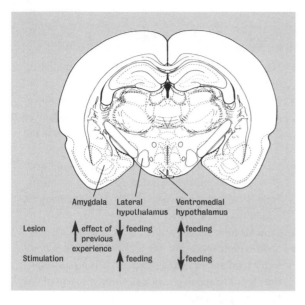

Figure 16.3 Effects of lesions and stimulation of the lateral and ventromedial hypothalamus on eating. A coronal (transverse or vertical) section through the rat brain is shown

influence the secretion of insulin and thus indirectly can influence body weight, but not as a satiety centre.

With respect to the lateral hypothalamus, a contribution to the reduced eating that follows lateral hypothalamic lesions arises from damage to fibre pathways coursing nearby such as the dopaminergic nigro-striatal bundle. Damage to this pathway leads to motor and sensory deficits because it impairs the normal operation of the basal ganglia (striatum and globus pallidus), brain structures involved in the initiation and control of movement (Marshall *et al*. 1974). However, in more recent investigations it has been possible to damage the cells in the lateral hypothalamus without damaging fibres of passage, using locally injected neurotoxins such as ibotenic acid or N-methyl-D-aspartate (NMDA) (see J.M. Clark *et al*. 1991). With these techniques, it has been shown that damage to lateral hypothalamic cells does produce a lasting decrease in food intake and body weight. Moreover, the lesioned rats do not respond normally to experimental interventions which normally cause eating by reducing the availability of glucose (J.M. Clark *et al*. 1991). Thus the more recent lesion evidence does suggest that the lateral hypothalamus is involved in the control of feeding and body weight.

The evidence just described implicates the hypothalamus in the control of food intake and body weight, but does not show what functions important in feeding are being performed by the hypothalamus and by other brain areas. More direct evidence on the neural processing involved in feeding, based on recordings of the activity of single neurons in the hypothalamus and other brain regions, is described next. These other brain systems include systems that perform sensory analysis involved in the control of feeding such as the taste and olfactory pathways; brain systems involved in learning about foods including the amygdala and orbitofrontal cortex; and brain systems involved in the initiation of feeding behaviour such as the striatum. Some of the brain regions and pathways described in the text are shown in Figure 16.4 on a lateral view of the brain of the macaque monkey; some of the connections are shown in Figure 16.5. Some of the findings described have been made in monkeys, because neuronal activity in non-human primates is especially relevant to understanding brain function and its disorders in humans. Full references to the original literature are provided by E.T. Rolls (1994, 1996, 1997, 1999); only key references are provided here.

Neuronal activity in the lateral hypothalamus during feeding

Responses to the sight and taste of food
Some neurons in the lateral hypothalamus respond to the sight and/or taste of food. Some neurons respond only to the sight of food (11.8 per cent), some respond to the taste of food (4.3 per cent), and some of these (2.5 per cent) respond to both the sight and taste of food (E.T. Rolls *et al*. 1980).

Effects of hunger
The responses of these neurons occur to the sight, or to the taste, of food only if the monkey is hungry (see example in Figure 16.6) (Burton *et al*. 1976). Thus neuronal responses which occur to food in the hypothalamus depend on the motivational state of the animal. This provides evidence that these neurons have activity which is closely related to either or both autonomic responses and behavioural responses to the sight and taste of food, which occur to food only if hunger is present. Thus the responses of these neurons reflect the integration of inputs which provide the rewards for eating such as the sight and taste of food, and satiety signals. We will soon see that this convergence occurs one stage of processing before the hypothalamus, in the orbitofrontal cortex. The lateral

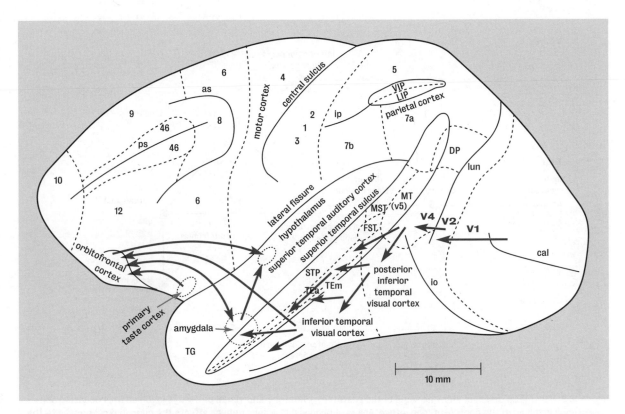

Figure 16.4 Some of the pathways described in the text are shown on this lateral view of the brain of the macaque monkey. VI – primary visual cortex. The stream of visual processing from VI to V2, V4, posterior inferior temporal visual cortex, and anterior inferior temporal visual cortex has among its outputs connections to the amygdala and orbitofrontal cortex. These in turn connect to the hypothalamus and (not shown) to the basal ganglia. The orbitofrontal cortex also contains the secondary taste cortex, which receives from the primary taste cortex, and in addition contains higher order olfactory cortical areas. The numbers and terms such as TEa refer to cytoarchitectonically defined brain areas. as – arcuate salcus; cal – calcarine sulcus; io – inferior occipital sulcus; ip – intraparietal sulcus; ps – principal sulcus in the dorsolaterial prefrontal cortex

hypothalamus probably thus provides a route for the output of structures such as the **orbitofrontal cortex** and amygdala, with the outputs affecting especially autonomic and endocrine functions (see Figure 16.5).

To investigate whether hunger modulates neuronal responses in parts of the visual system through which visual information is likely to reach the hypothalamus, the activity of neurons in the visual inferior temporal cortex has been recorded in the same testing situations. It was found that the neuronal responses here to visual stimuli are not dependent on hunger (E.T. Roll *et al.* 1977). Nor were the responses of an initial sample of neurons in the **amygdala**, which connects the inferior temporal visual cortex to the hypothalamus, found to depend on hunger (E.T. Rolls 1992b; Sanghera *et al.* 19792). However, in the orbitofrontal cortex, which

receives inputs from the inferior temporal visual cortex, and projects into the hypothalamus, neurons with visual responses to food are found, and neuronal responses to food in this region are modulated by hunger. Thus for visual processing, neuronal responsiveness only at late stages of sensory processing and in the hypothalamus has been found to be modulated by hunger. The adaptive value of modulation of sensory processing only at late stages of processing, which occurs also in the taste system of primates, is discussed when food-related taste processing is described on pp. 511–14.

Sensory-specific modulation

If a lateral hypothalamic neuron has ceased to respond to a food on which the monkey has been fed to satiety, then the neuron may still respond to a different food. This

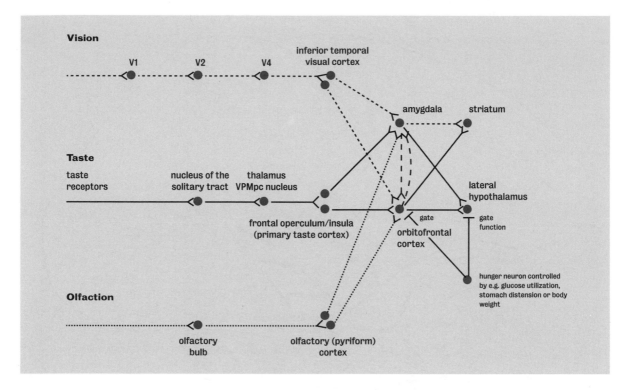

Figure 16.5 Schematic diagram showing some of the gustatory, olfactory and visual pathways involved in processing sensory stimuli involved in the control of food intake. Areas of processing where hunger affects the neuronal responses to the sight, smell or taste of food are indicated by the gate or modulatory function of hunger

occurs for neurons with responses associated with the taste or sight of food (see example in Figure 16.6) (E.T. Rolls *et al*. 1986). Corresponding to this neuronal specificity of the effects of feeding to satiety, the monkey rejected the food on which it had been fed to satiety, but accepted other foods which it had not been fed. Thus sensory-specific satiety is represented in the activity of hypothalamic neurons. We shall soon see that it is produced by the responses of orbitofrontal cortex neurons, which provide inputs to the hypothalamus.

Effects of learning
The responses of these hypothalamic neurons in the primate become associated with the sight of food as a result of learning. This is shown by experiments in which the neurons come to respond to the sight of a previously neutral stimulus, such as a syringe, from which the monkey is fed orally; in which the neurons cease to respond to a stimulus if it is no longer associated with food (in extinction or passive avoidance); and in which the responses of these neurons remain associated with

whichever visual stimulus is associated with food reward in a visual discrimination and its reversals (Mora *et al*. 1976; Wilson and Rolls 1990). This type of learning is important for it allows organisms to respond appropriately to environmental stimuli which previous experience has shown are foods. The brain mechanisms for this type of learning are discussed on pp. 511–14.

Evidence that the responses of these neurons are related to the reward value of food
Given that these lateral hypothalamic neurons respond to food when it is rewarding, that is when the animal will work to obtain food, the responses of these neurons could be part of the mechanism that makes food rewarding to a hungry animal. There is interesting evidence that supports this. It has been found that electrical stimulation of some brain regions is rewarding in that animals including humans will work to obtain electrical stimulation of some sites in the brain (see Olds 1977; E.T. Rolls 1975, 1976, 1979). At some sites, including the lateral hypothalamus, the electrical stimulation appears to pro-

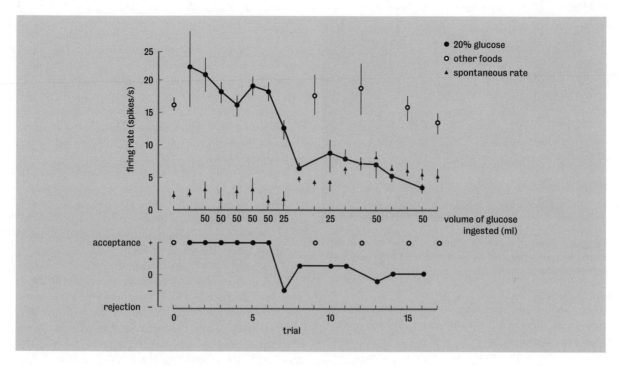

Figure 16.6 The effect of feeding the monkey to satiety with 20 per cent glucose solution on the responses of a hypothalamic neuron to the taste of the glucose (filled circles) and to the taste of other foods (open circles). After the monkey had fed to satiety with glucose, the neuron responded much less to the taste of glucose, but still responded to the other foods. The sateity of the monkey, shown below, was measured by whether he accepted or rejected the glucose
Source: E.T. Rolls *et al.* (1986)

duce reward which is equivalent to food for the hungry animal, in that the animal will work hard to obtain the stimulation if it is hungry, but will work much less for the stimulation if it has been satiated (see Hoebel 1969). It was therefore interesting to discover that some of the neurons normally activated by food when a monkey is hungry are also activated by brain-stimulation reward (E.T. Rolls 1975, 1976; Rolls *et al.* 1980). Thus there is convergence of the effects of natural food reward, and brain-stimulation reward at some brain sites (e.g. the orbitofrontal cortex and amygdala), onto single hypothalamic neurons. It was also found that the monkey would work for small electrical currents through the recording electrode if it was near a region where hypothalamic neurons had been recorded which responded to food, and that this self-stimulation was attenuated by feeding the monkey to satiety (E.T. Rolls *et al.* 1980).

The finding that these lateral hypothalamic neurons are activated by brain-stimulation reward is consistent with the hypothesis that their activity is related to reward produced by food, and not to some other effect of food.

Indeed, this evidence from the convergence of brain-stimulation reward and food reward on to these hypothalamic neurons, and from the self-stimulation found through the recording electrode, suggests that animals work to obtain activation of these neurons by food, and that this is what makes food rewarding. At the same time this accounts for self-stimulation of some brain sites, which is understood as the animal seeking to activate the neurons which he normally seeks to activate by food when he is hungry. This and other evidence (see E.T. Rolls 1975, 1994) indicates that feeding normally occurs in order to obtain the sensory input produced by food which is rewarding if the animal is hungry (see Plate 16.1).

Activity in the taste pathways during feeding

To understand the neural basis of any behaviour, including feeding, it is helpful to be able to trace the underlying information processing in the brain all the way from sensory receptors through central systems involved in functions such as learning, motivation and cognition, to

Plate 16.1 Feeding normally occurs in order to obtain the sensory input produced by food which is rewarding if the animal is hungry

reach finally brain systems involved in the initiation of movement. This helps to show exactly what computations are performed by each stage of neural processing. We therefore now consider how taste signals, which provide one of the rewards for eating, are processed through different stages in the brain, to produce among other effects activation of the lateral hypothalamic neurons described above (for references, see E.T. Rolls 1996, 1997, 1999). These investigations on the **gustatory pathways** have also been able to show where flavour, which is produced by a combination of taste and olfactory inputs, is computed in the primate brain. The gustatory and olfactory pathways, and some of their onward connections, are included in Figure 16.5.

The first synapse in the brain of the taste system is in the rostral part of the nucleus of the solitary tract. It has been shown that neurons in the nucleus of the solitary tract do respond (with quite broad tuning) to taste, and that the responses of these neurons are not influenced by whether the monkey is hungry or satiated.

Moving past the thalamus (see Figure 16.5) to the primary taste cortex, it has been shown that neurons are more sharply tuned to gustatory stimuli than in the nucleus of the solitary tract, with some neurons responding primarily for example to sweet, and much less to salt, bitter or sour stimuli. However, here also, hunger does not influence the magnitude of neuronal responses to gustatory stimuli.

A secondary cortical taste area, in the caudolateral orbitofrontal taste cortex of the primate, has been discovered, and in this area at least some taste neurons are even more sharply tuned to particular taste stimuli (E.T. Rolls *et al.* 1990) (see Figure 16.7). In addition to representations of the 'prototypical' stimuli sweet, salt, bitter and sour, different neurons in this region respond to umami (protein) taste (e.g. glutamate, Baylis and Rolls 1991), and to a wide range of complex foods. In this region, it is found that the responses of taste neurons to the particular food with which a monkey is fed to satiety decrease to zero (E.T. Rolls *et al.* 1989). That is, not only is motivational modulation of taste responses found in this region, but this modulation is sensory-specific (see Figure 16.8).

Thus it appears that the reduced acceptance of food as satiety develops, and the reduction in its pleasantness, are not produced by a reduction in the responses of neurons in the nucleus of the solitary tract or frontal opercular or insular gustatory cortices to gustatory stimuli. In these regions, the neuronal activity could not reflect the pleasantness of the taste of a food, but could instead represent its sensory qualities (what the taste is, its intensity, etc.) independently of motivational state. On the other hand, the responses of the neurons in the orbitofrontal taste area and in the lateral hypothalamus are modulated by

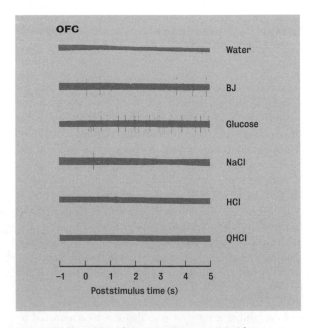

Figure 16.7 Examples of the responses recorded from one caudolateral orbitofrontal taste cortex neuron to the six taste stimuli, water, 20% blackcurrant juice (BJ), 1 M glucose, 1 M NaCl, 0.01 M HCl, and 0.001 M quinine HCl (QHCl)
Source: E.T. Rolls *et al.* (1990)

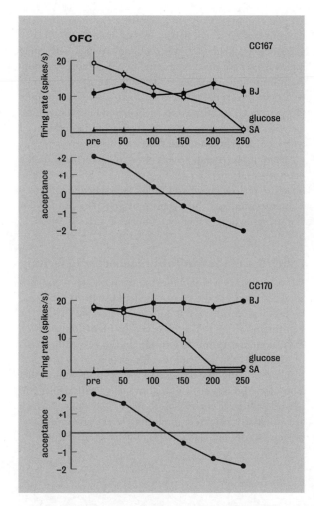

Figure 16.8 The effect of feeding to satiety with glucose solution on the responses of a neuron in the secondary taste cortex to the taste of glucose and of blackcurrant juice (BJ). The spontaneous firing rate is also indicated (SA). Below the neuronal response data for each experiment, the behavioural measure of the acceptance or rejection of the soution on a scale from +2 to −2 (see text) is shown. The solution used to feed to satiety was 20% glucose. The monkey was fed 50 ml of the solution at each stage of the experiment as indicated along the abscissa, until he was satiated as shown by whether he accepted or rejected the solution. Pre – the firing rate of the neuron before the satiety experiment started
Source: after E.T. Rolls *et al.* (1989)

satiety, and it is presumably in areas such as these that neuronal activity may be related to whether a food tastes pleasant, and to whether the human or animal will work to obtain and then eat the food, that is to whether the food is rewarding. Evidence that the activity of neurons in the orbitofrontal cortex does reflect reward includes the evidence that electrical stimulation here produces reward which is like food in that its reward value is attenuated by satiety (Mora *et al.* 1979). One output of these neurons may be to the hypothalamic neurons with food-related responses, for their responses to the sight and/or taste of food show a decrease which is partly specific to a food which has just been eaten to satiety. Another output may be to the ventral and adjoining striatum, which may provide an important link between reward systems and action (see below and Figure 16.5).

These findings illustrate an important principle of brain function, at least in primates: in sensory processing, first a representation of a stimulus is built, and only after that stage is the reward value of the stimulus evaluated. This is the case in several sensory systems. Part of the utility of this design is that it is only after the nature of the stimulus has been decoded that the motivational value of the stimulus can be evaluated. If the decoding to the stimulus level was incomplete, then the motivational value of the stimulus could not be correctly ascribed to it, and mistakes would be made due to inaccurate representation of the stimulus. Moreover, it would not be appropriate to decrease the representation of the stimulus itself as satiety progressed, for then we would not be able to taste the stimulus, or be able to learn about possible sources of sweet taste when we were not hungry. We do not become blind to the sight of a food which we have just eaten to satiety, but it does look less pleasant to us. This emphasizes that the brain mechanisms that represent sensory stimuli are different from those that represent their motivational significance (see Figure 16.5).

This approach also provides evidence on the nature of the mechanisms which underlie sensory-specific satiety. Sensory-specific satiety cannot be largely accounted for by adaptation at the receptor level, in the nucleus of the solitary tract, or in the primary (frontal opercular and insular) gustatory cortices, to the food which has been eaten to satiety, otherwise modulation of neuronal responsiveness should have been apparent in the recordings made in these regions. On the other hand, the findings indicate that sensory-specific satiety is represented in the orbitofrontal taste cortex (E.T. Rolls *et al.* 1989). It could be produced in the orbitofrontal cortex by making it a property of the synapses onto the orbitofrontal neurons that they tend to habituate with a time course of several minutes, and remain at least partly habituated for 1–2 hours, thus producing the characteristic time course of sensory-specific satiety.

This would result in the orbitofrontal cortex neurons having the required response properties. It would then only be necessary for other parts of the brain to use the activity of the orbitofrontal cortex neurons to reflect the reward value of that particular taste.

Convergence between taste and olfactory processing to represent flavour

At some stage in taste processing, it is likely that taste representations are brought together with inputs from different modalities, for example with olfactory inputs to form a representation of flavour. The connections of the taste and olfactory pathways in primates (see Figure 16.5) suggest that this could be in the orbitofrontal cortex.

Consistent with this, E.T. Rolls and Baylis (1994) were able to show that some neurons in the orbitofrontal cortex, 10 per cent of those recorded, responded to both taste and olfactory inputs (see example in Figure 16.9). Some of these multimodal single neurons had corresponding sensitivities in the two modalities, in that they responded best to sweet tastes (e.g. 1 M glucose), and responded more in a visual discrimination task to the visual stimulus which signified sweet fruit juice than to that which signified saline; or responded to sweet taste, and in an olfactory discrimination task to fruit odour. The fact that there were many unimodal neurons in the same region (taste 47 per cent, olfactory 12 per cent, visual

10 per cent) is consistent with the hypothesis that the neurons that represent flavour by responding to both taste and smell are formed in this region by having converging inputs from neurons that respond to either taste or smell.

Interestingly, some neurons (17 per cent) were shown to have convergence between taste and visual inputs (17 per cent), and this convergence could implement the fact that the taste that subjects report can be influenced by the colour of the food that they are tasting.

There is also a high order cortical olfactory area in the orbitofrontal cortex (see Figure 16.5). Some of these olfactory neurons respond to food only when the monkey is hungry, and so they represent the pleasantness or reward value of the smell of food (see E.T. Rolls 1997).

Functions of the orbitofrontal cortex in feeding

We have just seen that the orbitofrontal cortex contains areas that process the taste, smell and sight of food, and respond to food only if hunger is present. Thus the orbitofrontal cortex is involved in identifying which environmental stimuli are foods, and in responding to a food only when an appetite for that food is present. Consistent with this, damage to the orbitofrontal cortex alters food preferences, in that monkeys with damage to the orbitofrontal cortex select and eat substances which are normally rejected, including meat and non-food objects (Baylis and Gaffan 1991; Butter et al. 1969).

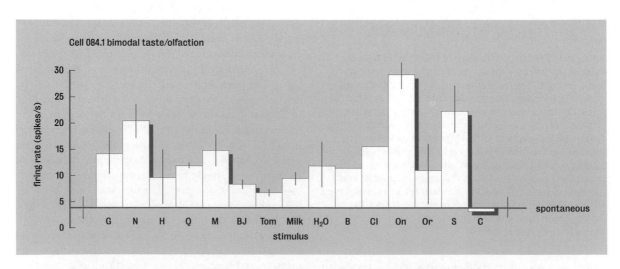

Figure 16.9 The responses of a bimodal neuron recorded in the caudolateral orbitofontal cortex. G – 1M glucose; N – 0.1M NaCl; H – 0.01M HCl; Q – 0.001M Quinine HCl; M – 0.1M monosodium glutamate; BJ – 20% blackcurrant juice; Tom – tomato juice; B – banana odour; Cl – clove oil odour; On – onion odour; Or – orange odour; S – salmon odour; C – control no-odour presentation. The mean responses ± se are shown. The neuron responded best to the tastes of NaCl and monosodium glutamate and to the odours of onion and salmon.

The neurons that respond to the sight of food respond in this way by learning to associate a visual stimulus with its taste. In that the taste is a reinforcer, this is called stimulus–reinforcement association learning. If the visual to taste association is reversed (for example by changing the taste with which a visual stimulus is paired from glucose to salt), then these neurons reverse the visual stimulus to which they respond. The orbitofrontal cortex neurons thus show rapid reversal of visual to taste associations. Consistent with this, lesions of the orbitofrontal cortex impair this type of learning. For example, lesions of the orbitofrontal cortex lead to a failure to correct feeding responses when these become inappropriate. Examples of the situations in which these abnormalities in feeding responses are found include

- extinction, in that feeding responses continue to be made to the previously reinforced stimulus
- reversals of visual discriminations, in that the monkeys make responses to the previously reinforced stimulus or object
- go/no-go tasks, in that responses are made to the stimulus which is not associated with food reward
- passive avoidance, in that feeding responses are made even when they are punished (see E.T. Rolls 1996, 1999).

Thus the orbitofrontal cortex is important not only in representing whether a taste is rewarding, and therefore whether eating should occur, but also in learning about which (visual and olfactory) stimuli are foods (E.T. Rolls 1996).

Functions of the amygdala and temporal visual cortex in feeding

The amygdala has many similar connections to the orbitofrontal cortex, and indeed has many connections to the orbitofrontal cortex (see Figure 16.5). Bilateral damage to the temporal lobes including the amygdala of primates leads to the Klüver-Bucy syndrome, in which lesioned monkeys for example select and place in their mouths non-food as well as food items shown to them, and repeatedly fail to avoid noxious stimuli (Aggleton and Passingham 1982; Baylis and Gaffan 1991; B. Jones and Mishkin 1972; Klüver and Bucy 1939). Rats with lesions in the basolateral amygdala also display altered food selection, in that they ingest relatively novel foods (Borsini and Rolls 1984; E.T. Rolls and B.J. Rolls 1973). The monkeys with temporal lobe damage have a visual

discrimination deficit, in that they are impaired in learning to select one of two objects under which food is found, and thus fail to form correctly an association between the visual stimulus and reinforcement (Gaffan 1992; B. Jones and Mishkin 1972). Gaffan and Harrison (1987) and Gaffan et al. (1988) have shown that the tasks which are impaired by amygdala lesions in monkeys typically involve a cross-modal association from a previously neutral stimulus (such as the sight of an object) to a primary reinforcing stimulus (such as the taste of food), consistent with the hypothesis that the amygdala is involved in learning associations between stimuli and primary reinforcers (see also Gaffan 1992; Gaffan et al. 1989). Further evidence linking the amygdala to reinforcement mechanisms is that monkeys will work in order to obtain electrical stimulation of the amygdala, and that single neurons in the amygdala are activated by brain-stimulation reward of a number of different sites (E.T. Rolls 1975; E.T. Rolls et al. 1980). In recordings from the amygdala in monkeys, it has been shown that single neurons can respond to taste, olfactory and visual stimuli (E.T. Rolls 1992b).

Although the amygdala thus has many properties similar to those of the orbitofrontal cortex, a difference is apparent in the speed of learning. When the pairing of two visual stimuli with two tastes (e.g. sweet and salt) is reversed in a visual discrimination task, orbitofrontal cortex neurons can reverse the visual stimulus to which they respond in as little as one trial (see E.T. Rolls 1996). In contrast, neurons in the amygdala are much more reluctant to reverse their responses (E.T. Rolls 1992b). Put in the context of evolution of the brain, it is the case that the amygdala is present in reptile and bird brains, as well as throughout mammals, whereas the orbitofrontal cortex (together with other parts of the frontal lobe) has developed very greatly in primates. It may be that in primates the orbitofrontal cortex is performing some of the functions of the amygdala, but better, because as a cortical region it is better adapted for learning, especially the rapid learning and relearning or reversal in which the orbitofrontal cortex is implicated (E.T. Rolls 1996).

A remaining issue is now considered. Given that visual stimuli are given 'meaning' in terms of whether they indicate food reward or not in the responses of orbitofrontal cortex and amygdala neurons, putatively as a result of learning in the orbitofrontal cortex and amygdala, is there evidence that this learning is not already present at the preceding stage of visual processing, the inferior temporal visual cortex (see Figure

16.5)? On anatomical grounds such learning is not likely in the inferior temporal cortex, in that although visual inputs reach this region (via the primary visual cortex i.e. V1, then V2 and V4), there are no connections for taste inputs to reach the inferior temporal visual cortex (see Figure 16.5). Recordings made from single neurons in the inferior temporal visual cortex in monkeys showed that these neurons respond to visual stimuli on the basis of physical properties such as shape, colour and texture; do not respond to visual stimuli that are foods differently to those that are non-foods; and do not reverse their responses in the reversal of visual discrimination tasks (E.T. Rolls *et al.* 1977). These findings thus indicate that the responses of neurons in the inferior temporal visual cortex do not reflect the association of visual stimuli with reinforcers such as food. Given these findings and the lesion evidence described above, it is thus likely that the inferior temporal cortex is an input stage for this learning process, which is implemented by neurons showing visual and taste convergence in the orbitofrontal cortex and amygdala.

Functions of the striatum and other parts of the basal ganglia in feeding

We have seen that the orbitofrontal cortex and amygdala are involved in decoding the stimuli that provide the rewards for feeding, and in interfacing these signals to hunger and satiety signals. This process involves a particular type of learning, stimulus–reinforcement association learning, which can be thought of as a type of classical conditioning. We now consider how these brain regions connect to behavioural output systems. One path is via the hypothalamus, which is involved in at least autonomic responses during feeding, and is also implicated in rewarding aspects of food. Another main system particularly for behavioural outputs is the striatum and then on through the rest of the basal ganglia (see Figure 16.5). This route is important as a behavioural output system, in that disruption of striatal function by damage to the nigrostriatal bundle, which depletes the striatum of dopamine, produces **aphagia** (lack of eating) and **adipsia** (lack of drinking), in the context of a general **akinesia** or lack of voluntary movement (Marshall *et al.* 1974; Stricker and Zigmond 1976, 1984; Ungerstedt 1971; see E.T. Rolls and Treves 1998). Damage to this system in humans produces the difficulty in initiating movements in Parkinson's disease. The striatal system may be especially involved in learning the correct behavioural response to make to obtain a particular reward.

This type of learning is called **instrumental learning**.

The ways in which the basal ganglia could operate are considered in more detail elsewhere (E.T. Rolls and Treves 1998). One or two aspects especially relevant to motivational behaviour are introduced here.

Different parts of the striatum receive from different brain systems. A part that receives from the amygdala and orbitofrontal cortex is the ventral striatum (and adjacent part of the head of the caudate nucleus). Damage to the ventral striatum impairs the effects which learned rewards have on behaviour (Everitt and Robbins 1992; Robbins and Everitt 1992). An example of such a learned reward in a primate might be the sight of food. This evidence thus indicate that one route for the amygdala and orbitofrontal cortex to influence behavioural output is via the ventral striatum. Consistent with this, a population of neurons in the ventral striatum was found to respond to visual stimuli of emotional or motivational significance, that is to stimuli which have in common the property that they are positively or negatively reinforcing (G.V. Williams *et al.* 1993). These neurons with reinforcement-related responses represented 13.9 per cent of the neurons recorded in the ventral striatum. The ventral striatum is also involved in types of reward other than food. For example, the self-administration of drugs such as amphetamine in rats depends on the ventral striatum (Everitt 1997; Everitt and Robbins 1992; Robbins and Everitt 1992). The basal ganglia are thus implicated as output systems for many brain regions, including those involved in the initiation of feeding, drinking, and other types of reward (see further E.T. Rolls and Treves 1998).

Obesity

Many different factors can contribute to obesity, and there is only rarely a single cause (see Garrow 1988) though the most common problem tends to be the continuation of normal eating when physical activity decreases as a result of the modern, essentially sedentary lifestyle. Occasionally, hormonal disturbances, such as hyperinsulinemia, can produce overeating and obesity. It is possible that the appetite of some obese people is stimulated by external factors such as the sight and smell of food than in more normal weight individuals (Schachter 1971). In any case, the palatability of food has been increased by cooking and cuisine to be much greater than that with which our ancestors evolved, leading to an imbalance between the enhanced reward now available from **orosensory** control signals relative to the gastrointestinal and post-absorptive satiety signals which control the reward value of sensory input. Another factor is that although animals evolved to produce sensory-specific satiety, which was adaptive in leading animals to eat a variety of foods and thus nutrients, the tremendous variety of modern foods could lead to some overeating, because there will often be new flavours available that have not yet been eaten in a meal. Another contributory factor to obesity may be the fact that human meal times tend to be fixed. Animals normally regulate their food intake by adjusting the inter-meal interval. In particular, the post-meal interval is regulated, with a long interval after a high energy meal, and a short interval after a low energy meal. Quite simple control mechanisms, such as slower gastric emptying, and therefore a feeling of fullness for a long time after an energy-rich meal, may contribute to this. However, with the fixed meal times of humans, this control does not operate normally. A feature of the eating pattern of obese people is that they tend to eat high energy meals, and although slower gastric emptying for high energy meals may contribute to regulation, the compensation is less than perfect. Another feature of the eating pattern of many obese people is that they may eat relatively late in the day, and this is also not adaptive, for the large energy intake must be converted into fat, and

cannot easily by burned off by exercise and heat loss. Regulation of heat loss is in fact one way that animals can compensate for excessive energy intake. They do this by activating brown fat metabolism, which with this special type of fat cell, burns fat to produce heat. (This is part of the mechanism of temperature control in small mammals.) Although brown fat is hardly present in humans, there is nevertheless some mechanism that when activated by the sympathetic nervous system enables metabolism to be increased or reduced, depending on energy intake (see Garrow 1988; Trayhurn 1986). Although stress, by activating this mechanism, can increase energy expenditure, it is also the case that sometimes stress can lead to overeating. Part of the mechanism here seems to be strong general activation produced in the presence of a prominent reward, for rats with a paper clip on their tail show similar overeating and obesity, which in this model of obesity is reduced by antianxiety drugs. Thus the general picture in humans is that compensation for altered energy intake by altering the amount of food eaten is a relatively inefficient and slow process, which can take two weeks to become apparent (see Garrow 1988). Perhaps it is a relatively inefficient process because of the operation in humans of all the other factors just described.

Plate 16.2 Obese people tend to eat high energy meals late at night, which converts energy intake into fat, as it cannot be burnt off by exercise and heat loss

Ψ Section summary

Hunger is signalled by decreases of glucose concentration in the blood plasma. The reward for eating is provided by the taste, smell and sight of food. Satiety is produced by sensory-specific satiety produced by the sight, taste, smell and texture of food; by gastric distension; by the activation by food of duodenal chemosensors; by rises in glucose concentration in the blood plasma, and by high levels of leptin or OB protein. Satiety signals modulate the reward value of the taste, smell and sight of food to control appetite and eating. The lateral hypothalamus contains neurons that are necessary for the normal control of food intake. Neurons in the lateral hypothalamus respond to the sight, taste and smell of food, but only if hunger is present. These neurons thus reflect the reward value of food, by reflecting the integration between the sensory inputs that maintain eating, and satiety signals.

The orbitofrontal cortex contains the secondary taste cortex and the secondary olfactory cortex. In the orbitofrontal cortex, neurons respond to the sight, taste and smell of food, but only if hunger is present. Thus the orbitofrontal cortex, which has outputs to the lateral hypothalamus, is the first stage of processing at which the reward or hedonic aspects of food is represented. The orbitofrontal cortex is the crucial site in the brain for the integration of the sensory inputs activated by food (taste, smell, sight) and satiety signals. The orbitofrontal cortex, and the amygdala, are involved in learning which environmental stimuli are foods, for example in learning which visual stimuli taste of food. The striatum contains neural systems which are important for the initiation of different types of motor and behavioural responses, including feeding. The striatum receives inputs from the orbitofrontal cortex and amygdala, as well as from motor structures of the brain.

The motivation for food is thus controlled by a set of physiological signals such as glucose concentration, gastric distension and body fat; the motivational state sets the reward value of sensory stimulation produced by food.

1 What signals control hunger and satiety?
2 Outline some of the brain processing that affects whether a food is eaten.

❏ Thirst

Thirst is a sensation normally aroused by a lack of water and associated with a desire to drink water. The mechanisms involved in the control of drinking are useful to study, not only because of their medical relevance, but also because the stimuli that lead to drinking can be identified, measured and manipulated, so allowing the basis of a relatively complex, motivated behaviour to be analysed.

Body water is contained within two main compartments. The intracellular water accounts for approximately 40 per cent of body weight, and the extracellular water is approximately 20 per cent of body weight, divided between the blood plasma (the blood without the cells) (5 per cent of body weight) and the interstitial fluid (the fluid between / outside the cells of the body and not in the blood vascular system) (15 per cent of body weight) (see Figure 16.10). After water deprivation, significant depletions of both the cellular and extracellular fluid compartments are found.

Control of normal drinking

In humans, it was found that with free access to water, the **osmotic** and extracellular thresholds for the elicitation of thirst were not normally reached before the humans had water to drink (Phillips *et al.* 1984). Thus in humans, at least when working in an air-conditioned temperature-controlled environment, drinking may anticipate needs. This anticipation is likely to be at least partly based on learning, so that after some time, actual body fluid deficits would be avoided. The humans would learn to initiate drinking based on any stimuli that are associated later with thirst signalled by cellular or extracellular body fluid deficits. In this way, drinking might become conditioned to stimuli such as large meals, salty food, or hot temperatures and dry conditions, or even to time of day. Of course, the primary thirst signals would be important for setting up this learning, but after the learning, the drinking would occur to the conditioned stimuli, and the primary thirst signals would not be activated. One would expect the primary thirst signals to become activated again if conditions changed, an example of which might be moving from sedentary work in an air-conditioned environment to physical work outdoors in a hot country. As a result of the activation of primary thirst signals, new learning would produce appropriate conditioned drinking for the new conditions. Another factor in humans that may lead to pri-

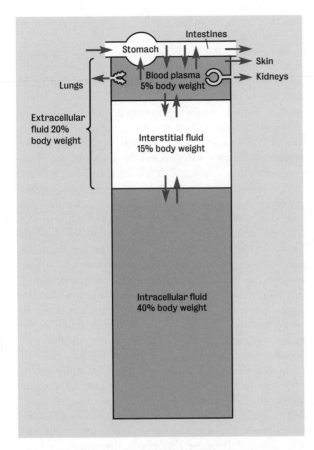

Figure 16.10 Body water compartments. Arrows represent fluid movement
Source: after B.J. Rolls and E.T. Rolls (1982: Figure 2.1)

angiotensin system is less important in humans than in other animals. It is nevertheless important to know about angiotensin in humans, for under some pathological conditions such as congestive heart failure, much angiotensin may be released as part of the body's attempt to compensate for some of the lack of fluid on the arterial side of the circulation (see Fitzsimons 1992). However, to the extent that such pathologically high levels of angiotensin may produce thirst and lead to drinking, this is inappropriate, for it may merely exacerbate the problem. Under these conditions, appropriate clinical care might include monitoring of water and fluid intake, to ensure that it is not excessive.

> ### Ψ Section summary
>
> Drinking can be initiated by depletion of either the cellular or extracellular fluid compartments. Cellular dehydration as a thirst stimulus is indicated by the shrinkage of cells in or near the preoptic area of the brain. Extracellular depletion as a thirst stimulus is indicated by activation of the renin-angiotensin system, and by signals from volume receptors in the low pressure circulation on the venous side of the heart. Angiotensin is sensed by neurons in the subfornical organ, which have connections to a brain region close to the preoptic area. Drinking is maintained or reinforced by oropharyngeal factors such as the taste of water, and it appears that the pleasantness of the taste of water in humans is influenced by the degree of thirst. When water is consumed, the following changes occur in sequence and all contribute to the termination of drinking: oropharyngeal stimulation by water, gastric distension and gut stimulation by water, and finally systemic dilution.
>
> 1   What signals control thirst?

mary body fluid deficit signals being unusual is that there is frequently available a large set of attractive drinks, including soft drinks, tea and coffee.

Another interesting aspect of thirst is that in humans, it was found that infusions of angiotensin did not always elicit drinking (Phillips *et al.* 1985). Moreover, large variations of angiotensin concentrations are found in humans when the person moves for example from lying down to standing up. The reason for this is that the change of posture in humans to standing upright on two legs produces a sudden drop in pressure in the renal arteries (as blood accumulates initially in the lower half of the standing body), and the release of angiotensin (stimulated by the reduced pressure in the renal arteries) produces vasoconstriction, which helps to compensate for the reduced blood pressure. Under these conditions (just standing up), thirst is not necessarily appropriate, and it may therefore be that the renin-

☐ Sexual behaviour

We next consider some of the processes involved in the control of sexual behaviour. Because there have been many advances recently in understanding and theorizing about the different patterns of sexual behaviour and why they have evolved, we consider these advances in sociobiology first. Part of this approach is to consider what biological functions could be implemented by different aspects of sexual behaviour. After considering this, we turn to consider the brain mechanisms that implement sexual behaviour.

An intentional stance is adopted in much writing about sociobiology, and is sometimes used here, but should not be taken literally. It is used just as a shorthand. An example is that it might be said that genes are selfish (Dawkins 1989). But this does not mean at all that genes think about whether to be selfish, and then take the decision. Instead it is just shorthand for a statement along the lines 'genes produce behaviour which operates in the context of natural selection to maximize the number of copies of the gene in the next generations'. Much of the behaviour produced is implicit or unconscious, and when the intentional stance is used as a descriptive tool, it should not be taken to mean that there is usually any explicit or conscious processing involved in the behavioural outcome. Moreover, with respect to humans, even though there may be these underlying biological processes which may influence our behaviour, this does not mean that human behaviour is influenced only by these often implicit or unconscious processes. Indeed, humans with their explicit verbal processing are able to take rational and responsible decisions about what behaviour to produce.

A sociobiological approach to understanding sexual behaviour

Monogamous primates which live in scattered family units, such as the baboon, tend to have small testes. Polygamous primates which live in large groups, such as chimpanzees and monkeys, have larger testes and copulate frequently. This may be as a result of what sociobiologists call *sperm warfare*. This is the idea that a male living in a **polygamous** society and trying to ensure his genes are carried on to the next generation needs to increase his chances of fertilizing a female. In a competitive situation with other males who are all trying to do the same thing he has to copulate with as many females as possible and ejaculate large amounts of sperm to try to ensure that it is his sperm which reaches the egg rather than that of one of the other males. To produce the quantity of sperm necessary for this approach the male needs to have large testes. Conversely, in **monogamous** groups where there is no competition between sperm the male only has to pick a healthy partner, produce enough sperm to fertilize an egg and then stay with the female once the offspring are produced long enough to ensure

that they grow up safely and his genetic investment is protected (Ridley 1993).

So how does this relate to humans? Despite appearing in most cultures or groups to be mainly monogamous, the human male has an intermediate testes and penis size, larger than might be expected in a monogamous species, but which might be explained by some degree of sperm competition. For though humans do usually pair up and appear to be monogamous, they also live in groups or colonies and so it may be useful here to look at other animals which are paired but also live in groups.

A problem with comparing humans with most other primates in this respect is that in most primates (and indeed in most mammals), the main parental investment is by the female (in producing the egg, in carrying the foetus, and in feeding the baby until it can become independent). The male does not have to invest in his children for them to have a reasonable chance of surviving. For this reason, the typical pattern in mammals is that the female is 'choosy' about her sexual partners in order to obtain healthy and fit males, and to complement this the males compete for females. However, in humans, because the children must be reared for a number of years before they become independent, there is an advantage to paternal investment in helping to bring up the children, in that the paternal resources (e.g. food, shelter and protection) can increase the chances of the male's genes surviving into the next generation to reproduce again. Part of the reason why investment by both parents is needed in humans is that because of the large final human brain size, the brain is not fully developed at birth; therefore the infant needs to be looked after, fed, protected, and helped for a considerable period while the infant's brain develops, favouring pair bonding between the parents. A useful comparison can be made with some birds which live in colonies, such as the swallow, but in which the male and the female pair up, and both invest in bringing up the offspring, taking it in turns for example to bring back food to the nest. If tests are made in swallows using DNA techniques for determining paternity, it is found that approximately one-third of a pair's young are not sired by the 'father', the male of the pair (see Ridley 1993). What happens is that the female mates sometimes with other males. She probably does not do this just with a random male either; she may choose an 'attractive' male, in which the signals that attract her are signals that indicate health, strength and fitness. A well-known example is the gaudy tail of the male peacock. One argument is that, given that the tail is a real handicap in life, any male that can survive with such a large tail must be very healthy or fit. Another argument is that if his tail is very attractive indeed, then the female should choose him, because her sons with him would probably be attractive too, and also chosen by females. (This is an example of the use of the intentional stance in the description, when no real propositional thought is likely to occur at all.) In such a social system, for example that of the swallow, the 'wife' needs a reliable 'husband' with whom she mates (so that he thinks the offspring are his, which for the system to be stable they must be sometimes) to help provide resources for 'their' offspring. (Remember that a nest must be built, the eggs must be incubated, and the hungry young must be well fed to help them become fit offspring. Here 'fit' means successfully passing on genes into the next generation – see Dawkins 1986.) But the 'wife' swallow (or at least her genes) also benefits by obtaining as fit genes as possible, by sometimes cheating on her 'husband'. To ensure that her husband does not find out and therefore leave her and stop caring for the young, she 'deceives' the husband by committing her 'adultery' as secretly as possible, perhaps hiding behind a bush to mate with her lover. So the (swallow) wife maximizes care for her children using her husband, and maximizes her genetic potential by finding a lover with fit genes that are likely to be attractive in her sons to other females.

Could anything like this be true in humans? There is some evidence that suggests that factors such as those just described could play a part in human sexual behaviour, though the evidence is far from complete, and it is not clear how important these factors are. One line of evidence for humans already described is the relatively large testis and penis size of men. (The general argument in sociobiology is that a large penis could be adaptive in sperm competition, by possibly displacing other sperm, and by ensuring that the owner's sperm are placed as close as possible to where they have a good chance of reaching an egg.) A second line of evidence is that studies in humans of paternity using modern DNA tests suggest that in fact the wife's partner (e.g. husband) is not the father of about 14 per cent of their children. Although possibly surprising, and the evidence is still incomplete, this has been suggested in a study in Liverpool, in another in the south of England, and in other studies (Baker and Bellis 1995; see Ridley 1993). It is therefore possible that factors which have shaped sexual behaviour in evolution include the advantage for women of choosing a partner to provide reliability, stability, provision of a home, and help with bringing up her children, while at the same time being attracted to

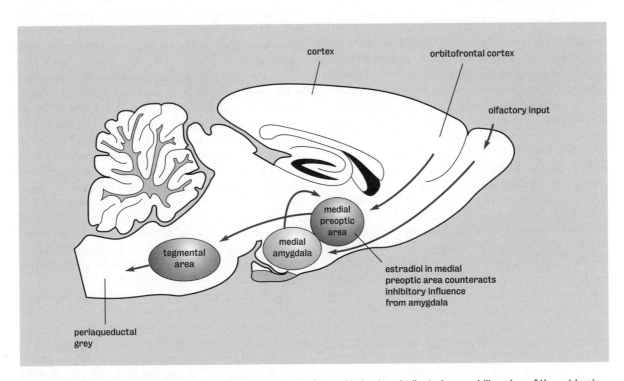

Figure 16.11 Some of the brain regions involved in the control of sexual behaviour indicated on a midline view of the rat brain
Note: this figure is after Carlson (1994: Figure 10.26) but with periaqueductal grey and orbitofrontal cortex added

men who are perhaps successful and powerful, as these might during evolution have indicated a likelihood of producing genetically fit children, especially sons who can themselves potentially have many children. For males, the evolutionary pressure might select for behaviours such as guarding the partner from the attentions of other males, to increase the likelihood that the children in which the male invests are his; and being attracted to other women, including younger women with much child-bearing potential.

Although much of the research on the sociobiological background of human sexual behaviour is quite new, and many of the hypotheses remain to be fully established and accepted, this research does have interesting potential implications for understanding some of the factors that may influence human behaviour (see Baker 1996; Baker and Bellis 1995; Ridley 1993).

Having now outlined some of the functions at play in sexual behaviour we are in a better position to consider the brain processes that implement rewards to produce these different types of behaviour.

Brain regions involved in the control of sexual behaviour

In males, the preoptic area (just in front of the hypothalamus) is involved in the control of sexual behaviour (see Figure 16.11 which shows some of the brain regions discussed). Several types of evidence show this (see Carlson 1994). First, lesions of this region permanently abolish male sexual behaviour. Second, electrical stimulation of the preoptic area can elicit copulatory activity. Third, neuronal and metabolic activity is induced in the preoptic area during copulation. Fourth, small implants of the male hormone testosterone into the preoptic area restore sexual behaviour in castrated rats.

In females, the medial preoptic area is involved in the control of reproductive cycles. It is probably also involved in controlling sexual behaviour directly. The ventromedial nucleus of the hypothalamus (VMH) is involved in some aspects of sexual behaviour, including **lordosis** in rodents; this behaviour can be reinstated in ovariectomized female rats by injections of the female hormones oestradiol and progesterone into the ventromedial nucleus. Outputs from the VMH project to the periaqueductal grey of the midbrain, which is also necessary for female sexual behaviour such as lordosis in rodents (see Carlson 1994). The VMH receives inputs from regions such as the medial amygdala.

The preoptic area receives inputs from the amygdala and orbitofrontal cortex, and thus receives information from the inferior temporal visual cortex (including information about face identity and expression), from the superior temporal auditory association cortex, from the olfactory system, and from the somatosensory system. It is presumably by these neural circuits that the primary rewards relevant to sexual behaviour (such as touch and perhaps smell) and the learned stimuli which act as rewards for sexual behaviour (such as the sight of a partner) reach the preoptic area. It is likely that in the preoptic area the reward value of these sensory stimuli is modulated by hormonal state, consistent with the evidence described above. The neural control of sexual behaviour may thus be organized in an analogous way to the way in which motivational behaviour for food and water is organized. In all three, external sensory stimuli are needed to provide the reward, and the extent to which they do provide reward depends on internal signals, such as plasma glucose concentration for hunger, body fluid concentration for thirst, and hormonal state for sexual behaviour. For sexual behaviour, the internal signal which controls the motivational state, and the reward value of appropriate sensory stimuli, alters relatively slowly, over for example four days in the case of the rat oestrus cycle, and over weeks or even months in the case of many animals which breed only at certain seasons of the year.

The outputs of the preoptic area include connections to the tegmental area in the midbrain, and in this region neurons are found that respond in relation to different aspects of male sexual behaviour (Shimura and Shimokochi 1990). However, it is likely that only some outputs of the orbitofrontal cortex and amygdala which control sexual behaviour, act through the preoptic area. The preoptic area route may be necessary for computationally simple aspects of sexual behaviour such as copulation in males, but the attractive effect of sexual stimuli may survive damage to the medial preoptic area (see Carlson 1994), suggesting that, as for feeding, outputs of the amygdala and orbitofrontal cortex can influence behaviour through the basal ganglia.

Much research remains to be performed to understand the details of the implementation of the rewards underlying sexual behaviour in brain regions such as the amygdala, orbitofrontal cortex, preoptic area, and hypothalamus. An interesting recent result is that the pleasantness of touch is represented in the human orbitofrontal cortex (E.T. Rolls et al. 1997).

Ψ Section summary

Sexual behaviour has been shaped differently in males and females by natural selection, in a way that in different species is related to the relative investment in the offspring by the male and the female. Brain regions important in the control of sexual behaviour include the hypothalamus, preoptic area and amygdala.

1 In what different ways can different aspects of sexual behaviour be considered adaptive?

❑ Psychosocial motives

Hunger, thirst and sex are all basic biological motives which involve identifiable physiological processes. However, humans (and the members of many other species) possess other motives which less obviously depend on specific physiological systems. These motives (which we may term psychosocial motives) include the need for self-esteem, the need for self-actualization, and various social motives (e.g. the need for affiliation). Some of these psychosocial motives are dealt with in this section of the chapter.

Maslow's theory

Abraham Maslow was a prominent advocate of the humanistic approach to psychology (see Chapter 14). This approach focused on major issues in people's lives (e.g. the need for growth; development of the self). Scientific methods were rejected in favour of a reliance on **phenomenology**, or direct descriptions of conscious experience. Maslow (1954, 1968) proposed a five-level hierarchy of needs (see p. 437). At the bottom level, there are the basic physiological survival needs, including hunger, thirst and sex. At the next level up, there are safety needs (e.g. the need for a predictable environment). At the third level, there is the need for love and belonging, and at the fourth level there is the need for esteem (e.g. having the respect of others). At the top level of the hierarchy, there is the need for **self-actualization**, involving discovering and fulfilling one's own potential.

There are *deficiency needs* (which reduce deficiencies or inadequacies) and growth needs (which promote personal growth). Deficiency needs are towards the bottom of the hierarchy, whereas growth needs are towards the top. Individuals are more likely to focus on satisfying growth needs when most of their deficiency needs are largely satisfied. Maslow (1970) estimated that Americans on average satisfy 85 per cent of their physiological needs, 70 per cent of their safety needs, 50 per cent of their belongingness and love needs, 40 per cent of their self-esteem needs and 10 per cent of their self-actualization needs.

Sugarman (1986) identified 12 aspects of the self-actualized person. These aspects were as follows: accurate perception of others; acceptance of self and others; spontaneity; focused on problems outside the self; detached; autonomous and uninfluenced by conformity pressures; appreciation of what is good and beautiful; peak experiences with intense emotional experience; close relationships with a few people; respect for other people; clear moral standards; and creative.

Some support for Maslow's assumption that individuals whose lower-level needs are satisfied will be most likely to pursue higher-level needs was reported by Aronoff (1967). Fishermen in the British West Indies had more interesting jobs than cane cutters, but their pay fluctuated much more, and they were not paid if they were ill. According to Maslow's theory, it should be those whose lower-level needs were met who would choose to become fishermen. As expected, fewer of the fishermen than the cane cutters had high safety needs (25 per cent vs 80 per cent, respectively) or suffered from low self-esteem (20 per cent vs 80 per cent, respectively).

One of the ways in which Maslow (1962) investigated self-actualization was by studying **peak experiences**. These are the rare occasions on which the individual totally accepts the world as it is, and has feelings of wonder and euphoria. Peak experiences were reported most frequently during sexual intercourse or when listening to music, and were more commonly reported by those high in self-actualization.

In sum, Maslow identified important psychosocial motives that had been largely neglected by previous theorists. However, there are four major problems with his theoretical approach. First, his reliance on phenomenology and his rejection of the scientific approach mean that most of his theoretical ideas cannot be tested adequately. As a result, the progress that characterizes most science has been lacking with respect to Maslow's theory of motivation. Second, the notion of self-actualization is poorly defined and difficult to measure. Third, Maslow assumed that the need for self-actualization is based on processes within the individual. In so doing, he de-emphasized the role that society can play in making people more self-actualized via training pro-grammes, cultural norms, and so on. Fourth, when it has proved possible to test Maslow's theoretical ideas, the evidence has not generally provided much support for them (see Arnold *et al.* 1995).

Social motives

Most members of the human species are social crea-tures, spending much of their time interacting with other people. This suggests that we have strong social motives, and that interactions with others can be very rewarding. Psychologists have often argued that there are rather separate social motives leading us to associate with others: the need for intimacy, and the need for affiliation, that is, social contact and interaction with other people. There is some similarity between these two needs, in that satisfying them involves a high level of involvement in social relationships. However, there are some important differences. Those with a high **need for affiliation** are mainly concerned with the desire to have a large number of positive social contacts, whereas those with a **need for intimacy** seek very close per-sonal relationships with others. In general terms, the need for affiliation relates to the number or quantity of social contacts, whereas the need for intimacy relates to quality of relationships with others. These two social motives are discussed in turn below.

Need for affiliation

Most people desire numerous social contacts with others, but there are important individual differences of a trait-like nature in the strength of that desire. Why do people have a need to affiliate or to have social contact with others? According to Hill (1987), there are four main reasons:

- to reduce uncertainty by comparing oneself against other people
- to receive emotional support
- to obtain attention and/or praise from others
- to be stimulated by social interaction

Schachter (1959) carried out a classic study on the need for affiliation. Female students were told that they were going to receive either very mild or painful electric shocks. After that, they were given the choice of waiting by themselves or with other participants before the

shocks were administered. There was a marked differ-ence between the two conditions: 63 per cent of the stu-dents due to receive painful shocks chose to wait with others, compared to only 33 per cent of those expecting mild shocks. The students expecting painful shocks may have chosen to wait with other participants because it was reassuring for them to see how their fellow partici-pants were coping, or because being with other partici-pants provided a distraction from thinking about the future shocks.

The above problem of interpretation led Schachter (1959) to carry out another study in which all of the participants expected painful shocks. As before, the par-ticipants had to choose whether to wait on their own or with other students. However, some of the participants were told that the other students were waiting to see their academic advisers, and were not expecting shocks. The participants chose to wait with other students if these students were due to receive shocks, but on their own if the students were not expecting shocks. Thus, the participants affiliated with others to compare themselves against others in the same situation rather than simply to distract themselves.

Most studies support Schachter (1959), but there are some exceptions. Molleman *et al.* (1986) studied the wish to affiliate among cancer patients. Patients with a very high level of anxiety had less wish to affiliate with others than those with a moderate level of anxiety. The very anxious patients were probably concerned that talking with others would increase their fears rather than decrease them.

One of the ways of assessing the importance of affilia-tion or social contact is to compare individuals who have either a high or a low level of social support from others. It has been argued that social support acts as a kind of buffer against stress. In other words, the adverse effects of stress on physical and psychological well-being are reduced among those enjoying a high level of social support. The evidence is inconsistent, but some findings support the buffering notion. Cohen and Hoberman (1983) measured the effects of stress on physical symp-toms such as insomnia and the number of headaches. Stress had a much greater effect on physical symptoms in those low in social support.

What happens when affiliation (and perhaps intimacy as well) is lacking? Berkman and Syme (1979) carried out a longitudinal study in which the participants were followed up nine years after the study began. Those who had died had been more socially isolated at the start of the study than those who survived, being more likely to be unmarried and having fewer contacts with families and friends. Additional evidence obtained by Berkman and Syme (1979) indicated that these findings did not arise because the socially isolated had less healthy lifestyles or were isolated through disability. Atkins *et al.* (1991) reviewed several further studies in which it was found that socially isolated elderly people were more likely to die from heart disease than elderly people with good social contacts.

Need for intimacy

Nearly everyone has a need for intimacy, but there are enormous individual differences in terms of the strength of that need. McAdams (1988) has studied the need for intimacy as essentially a dimension of personality. He found that those high in the need for intimacy are more trusting and warm in their social relationships than are those who are low in the need for intimacy. McAdams (1985) found that those with a high need for intimacy typically have a fairly small number of friends, but the friends they do have are very close ones.

Knapp and Vangelisti (1992) developed a communication model of the ways in which intimacy develops and later deteriorates. This model consists of ten interaction stages, five of which refer to the build-up of intimacy and five to its deterioration. The first stage is initiating, which is followed by experimenting (e.g. finding points of common ground). Then comes the stage of intensifying, with the level of commitment on both sides increasing and the communication pattern becoming increasingly unique. The next level of intimacy is integrating, when the two people concerned start to share private and public intimacies and to identify themselves to others as a couple. The highest level of intimacy is bonding, in which there is a public declaration that commitments have been made (e.g. engagement or marriage).

Knapp and Vangelisti (1992) identified five interaction stages during the decline of an intimate relationship. These five stages resemble the first five stages in reverse order, but they differ because of the shared knowledge and mutual history now possessed by the couple. The five stages of decline are as follows: differentiating, circumscribing, stagnating, avoiding and terminating. In general terms, the quality and the quantity of communication between the two people decrease, until eventually all communication ceases.

McAdams and Vaillant (1982) obtained measures of the need for intimacy and the need for affiliation in 30-year-old men; 17 years later, their psychosocial adjust-

ment was assessed. Those with a high need for intimacy were significantly better adjusted than those with a low need for intimacy, and they had happier and more stable marriages. However, there was no relationship between need for affiliation and adjustment.

Triandis *et al.* (1988) argued that there are important differences between individualistic and collectivistic cultures in terms of social motives:

> People in individualistic cultures often have greater skills in entering and leaving new social groups. They make 'friends' easily, but by 'friends' they mean nonintimate acquaintances. People in collectivist cultures have fewer skills in making new 'friends' but 'friend' in their case implies a life-long intimate relationship with many obligations . . . people in individualistic cultures are likely to *appear* more sociable, while intimacy is not a readily observable attribute.
> (Triandis *et al.* 1988: 325)

In other words, the need for intimacy is greater in collectivistic cultures, whereas the need for affiliation is greater in individualistic cultures. Evidence consistent with that conclusion was obtained by Hofstede (1980). There was a correlation of +0.46 between cultural individualism and the need for affiliation.

Plate 16.3 People in individualistic cultures have greater skills in entering and leaving new social groups. For people in collectivist cultures, 'friend' implies a lifelong relationship with many obligations

Ψ Section summary

Maslow was a humanistic psychologist who proposed a hierarchy of needs running from basic biological needs at the bottom to growth needs such as self-actualization at the top. His approach was much more comprehensive than most previous approaches. However, it lacked scientific rigour, and many of the concepts he used (e.g. self-actualization) were ill defined. His reliance on phenomenology means that it has proved difficult to apply scientific methods in testing his ideas. The need for affiliation and the need for intimacy are two key social motives. Both needs relate to social contact, but the former focuses more on the quantity of social contacts, whereas the latter focuses more on their quality. There are various reasons why people affiliate with others, including the wish for emotional support and the desire for attention and praise. The need for affiliation is more important in individualistic cultures than in collectivistic ones. Physical health and longevity depend in part on the extent to which the needs for affiliation and for intimacy are met.

1 Explain Maslow's hierarchy of needs. What are the problems in using it as a measure of motivation?

2 What are the various stages of intimacy and affiliation? What are the differences between them and the needs they fulfil?

☐ Motivation and performance

Some people are highly motivated, and will always do their best whether it be a question of writing essays or carrying out some other piece of work. Others prefer a more relaxed style of working, and seem relatively lacking in motivation. There are two key issues in the area of motivation and performance:

- Why are some people more motivated than others?
- What is the relationship between motivation and performance?

In what follows, these two issues will be considered in turn.

Determinants of motivation for work

There are many factors that jointly determine any given individual's motivation for work, including both personal characteristics and the nature of the work situation. However, some of the key factors are rooted in personality. In this section, we consider one very relevant dimension of personality.

Need for achievement

Henry Murray (1938) identified a personality dimension of **need for achievement**, which he defined as the desire 'to accomplish something difficult; to master, manipulate or organise…to overcome obstacles and attain a high standard; to excel one's self' (Murray 1938: 164). Murray assessed the need for achievement by using the Thematic Apperception Test, in which the participants have to tell a story about each of a series of pictures. People who include much imagery relating to achievement and mastery themes in their stories are regarded as higher in need for achievement than those who do not.

McClelland worked with Murray, and went on to develop other, related measures of the need for achievement. He argued that people high in need for achievement should be much more likely than those low in need for achievement to become entrepreneurs. This was investigated in a study by McClelland (1965). Men who had been assessed as high or low in need for achievement 14 years previously were followed up. Of those who were in entrepreneurial positions, 83 per cent had scored high on need for achievement. In contrast, only 21 per cent of those who were not entrepreneurs had been in the high need for achievement group.

Further evidence indicating the importance of need for achievement was discussed by Koestner and McClelland (1990). Societies high in need for achievement tended to have higher levels of productivity than societies that were low in need for achievement. They also discussed several studies in which the participants had to choose the difficulty level of the tasks they were going to perform. Those high in need for achievement tended to prefer moderately difficult tasks, because these tasks presented a challenge. On the other hand, those low in need for achievement tended to prefer very easy or very difficult tasks, presumably because they did not want to expose themselves to real challenge.

In sum, individuals (and even societies) high and low in need for achievement differ in systematic and predictable ways. However, there are three main problems with this approach to motivation. First, the measures that are used to assess need for achievement typically have rather limited reliability and validity. Second, it has been assumed that need for achievement is basically trait-like, that is, it remains fairly consistent over time. This assumption de-emphasizes the role played by situational factors in determining an individual's level of motivation. For example, some students show high need for achievement in their work but not when playing sport, whereas others show the opposite pattern.

Third, need for achievement is a complex construct. Cassidy and Lynn (1989) argued that it consists of six components:

- work ethic (the notion that work is 'good' in itself)
- pursuit of excellence;
- status aspiration (wish to dominate others)
- competitiveness
- acquisitiveness (desire for money)
- mastery (competitiveness against set standards rather than against other people).

Those who are high in need for achievement differ in terms of which components contribute most to that need, and so simply knowing someone's level of need for achievement is not very informative.

Relationship between motivation and performance

Several theorists since the early years of the twentieth century have attempted to account for the relationship between motivation and performance. This has proved difficult, in part because there is no single relationship. Performance often improves as motivation increases from low to moderate, but then either ceases to improve or worsens as the level of motivation becomes high. The classic work in this area was that of Yerkes and Dodson (1908). Subsequent theorists such as Easterbrook (1959), M.W. Eysenck and Calvo (1992) and Locke and Latham (1990) have tried to identify some of the main processes determining the effects of motivation on performance.

Yerkes–Dodson law

Yerkes and Dodson (1908) carried out a study on mice. The level of motivation was manipulated by vary-

ing the intensity of electric shock, and the mice performed a range of tasks of varying difficulty level. The pattern of findings led Yerkes and Dodson (1908) to propose what has come to be known as the Yerkes-Dodson law: there is an inverted-U relationship between the level of motivation or arousal and the level of performance. Thus, performance is best when the level of motivation is moderate. The Yerkes-Dodson law also includes the assumption that the optimal level of motivation or arousal is inversely related to task difficulty (see Figure 16.12).

There is reasonable evidence that the optimal level of motivation or arousal is inversely related to task difficulty (see M.W. Eysenck 1982 for a review). However, the notion that there is an inverted-U relationship between the level of motivation and the level of performance is harder to test. If only three levels of motivation are compared, there are six possible orderings of these three levels with respect to performance. Only two of these six orderings are inconsistent with the Yerkes-Dodson law. Thus, approximately two-thirds of all studies would 'support' the Yerkes-Dodson law even if chance alone were operating!

The Yerkes-Dodson law is descriptive rather than explanatory. It fails to specify why performance is lower when the level of motivation is very low than when it is very high, and why the optimal level of motivation is inversely related to task difficulty. These issues were addressed by Easterbrook (1959), who provided a poten-

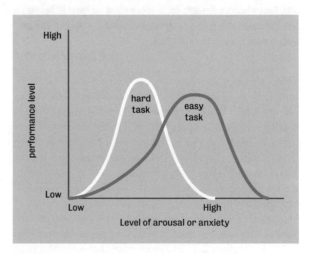

Figure 16.12 The Yerkes–Dodson law, proposed by Yerkes and Dodson (1908)

tial explanation of the various findings. Accordingly, we turn next to a consideration of his hypothesis.

Easterbrook's hypothesis

According to Easterbrook's (1959) hypothesis, high levels of motivation, anxiety or arousal reduce the breadth of attention and increase attentional selectivity. The breadth of attention in terms of the range of cues used reduces as motivation or anxiety increases, which

will reduce the proportion of irrelevant cues employed, and so improve performance. When all irrelevant cues have been excluded, however . . . further reduction in the number of cues employed can only affect relevant cues, and proficiency will fall.

(Easterbrook 1959: 193)

Easterbrook's hypothesis also provides an explanation for the relationship between motivation and task difficulty if we assume that difficult tasks involve the use of more cues than easy tasks.

Easterbrook's hypothesis has been tested by measuring performance on a primary or main task and a secondary task carried out at the same time. According to the hypothesis, high levels of motivation or arousal should have a greater negative effect on secondary than on primary task performance. There is empirical support for this prediction (see M.W. Eysenck 1982 for a review). However, as Eysenck pointed out,

There are nine possible combinations of main-task and subsidiary-task performance, only three of which are clearly incompatible with Easterbrook's hypothesis; in those cases, arousal either has a less detrimental effect or a greater enhancing effect on the subsidiary task than on the main task.

(M.W. Eysenck 1982: 50–1)

Some support for Easterbrook's hypothesis has been obtained using other experimental designs. For example, Koksal (1992) presented his participants with a small or large visual display of 25 dots, with the task being to identify which dot moved on each trial. High levels of anxiety had no effect on performance with the small visual display. However, high anxiety was associated with impaired performance on the large visual display, presumably because of a narrowing of attention.

Easterbrook's hypothesis represents an advance on the Yerkes-Dodson law, but it possesses some limitations. First, Easterbrook (1959) assumed that the effects of motivation, emotionality, arousal, and anxiety on attentional processes and on performance were broadly simi-

lar. However, motivation in the form of financial or other incentives is much less likely than anxiety to produce impaired performance on a secondary task (M.W. Eysenck 1982). Perhaps anxiety reduces attentional capacity, but motivation on its own does not. Second, Easterbrook (1959) assumed that high levels of motivation or arousal produce attentional narrowing in a rather passive and automatic way. It is more plausible to regard attentional narrowing as an active coping response which is used mainly when there is information overload.

Processing efficiency theory

M.W. Eysenck and Calvo (1992) proposed processing efficiency theory, according to which the effects of anxiety on performance are partly motivational and partly emotional. In essence, anxiety creates worry (e.g. about task performance), and this produces positive and negative effects. The positive effects are motivational, as the individual uses extra effort to improve performance and eliminate the worry. The negative effects occur because worry uses some of the resources of the working memory system, thus leaving fewer resources available for task performance.

On the basis of the above assumptions, M.W. Eysenck and Calvo (1992) distinguished between performance effectiveness and processing efficiency. **Performance effectiveness** refers to the quality of task performance, whereas **processing efficiency** refers to the relationship between performance effectiveness and the effort or processing resources applied. The key prediction is that anxiety will typically impair processing efficiency more than performance effectiveness. The reason for this is that worry will impair processing efficiency, but may not reduce performance effectiveness if sufficient extra effort is applied. Seven different types of studies have provided support for processing efficiency theory (see M.W. Eysenck and Calvo 1992 for a review).

The clearest evidence for the theory has come from studies in which those high and low in trait anxiety (a personality dimension relating to susceptibility to anxiety) have comparable levels of performance effectiveness. In these studies, high trait-anxious individuals have typically had significantly lower processing efficiency than the low trait-anxious ones. Consider, for example, a study by MacLeod and Donnellan (1993) with verbal reasoning as the primary task and memory load as the secondary task. There was no effect of trait anxiety on performance of the primary task when the secondary task consisted of maintaining a low memory load. Thus, anxiety did not affect performance effectiveness on the primary task. However, there was a highly significant effect of trait anxiety on performance of the primary task when a high memory load had to be maintained. Presumably the high trait-anxious participants had reduced processing efficiency in the low memory load condition, but compensated for this by extra effort. These attempts at compensation failed when the overall demands became much greater in the high memory load condition.

The processing efficiency theory has proved reasonably successful in accounting for the motivational and emotional effects of anxiety on performance. What is needed in future is to develop more understanding of the precise ways in which extra effort and the use of compensatory strategies can offset the negative effects of worry on performance.

Goal-setting theory

How do motivational processes differ between the human species and other species? One of the most obvious differences is that the goals pursued by other species tend to be short term (e.g. finding food to eat), whereas the goals of humans are often very long term (e.g. obtaining a degree; establishing a career). Humans are much more likely than the members of other species to have long-term goals, because they have a considerably more complex cognitive system. Since the 1950s, several cognitive theories of motivation based on goals have been put forward. Here we will focus on one of the most influential of such theories, the goal-setting theory proposed by Locke (1968) and developed subsequently (e.g. Locke and Latham 1990).

The natural starting point is to address the meaning of the term 'goal'. According to Locke *et al.* (1981: 126), 'A goal is what an individual is trying to accomplish; it is the object or aim of an action. The concept is similar in meaning to the concepts of purpose and intent'.

The main prediction of goal-setting theory is that difficult goals lead to higher levels of performance, particularly when individuals commit themselves to goal achievement. Locke (1968) discussed the evidence from 12 studies involving a variety of tasks including uses for objects, additions, reaction time, and toy construction. There was an overall correlation of +0.78 between goal difficulty and performance.

In subsequent research, goal-setting theory was applied to real-world work settings with reasonable success. For example, Latham and Yukl (1975) carried out a study on workers whose work consisted of cutting and transporting wood. These workers were divided into three types of groups: participative groups; assigned groups; and do-your-best groups. Within each participative group, all of the workers helped to set a specific hard production goal in terms of hundreds of cubic feet of wood per week. Assigned groups were simply given a specific hard goal, and do-your-best groups were told to 'do your best', but were not asked to set a specific goal. The average goal that was set in the participative groups was 8 per cent higher than in the assigned groups, and so it follows from goal-setting theory that work production should have been highest in the participative groups.

The findings obtained by Latham and Yukl (1975) were in line with goal-setting theory. The participative groups averaged 56 cubic feet of wood per hour, which was more than the assigned groups (53 cubic feet) or the do-your-best groups (46 cubic feet). These findings are by no means exceptional. Locke *et al.* (1981) reviewed several studies of work performance, and calculated that goal-setting produced a median 16 per cent improvement in work performance.

The most significant development in goal-setting theory has been the increasing recognition that setting hard goals is most likely to lead to improved performance under certain conditions. Locke *et al.* (1981) identified five such conditions:

- goal commitment
- feedback in the form of information about progress towards the goal
- rewards for attaining the goal
- ability, in that the individual must have the skills required to attain a hard goal
- support, in that workers benefit from encouragement from management.

In sum, there is strong evidence that difficult goal-setting often leads to higher levels of performance than easy goal-setting. It remains extremely influential within work psychology. Indeed, according to Arnold *et al.* (1995: 220), 'by the early 1990s, well over half the research on motivation published in leading academic journals reported tests, extensions or refinements of goal-setting theory'.

In spite of its success, goal-setting theory is limited in various ways. First, most of the experimental and occupational studies of goal-setting theory have focused on goals defined in terms of quantity rather than quality. This is a significant limitation, because for many workers the quality of their work is of more importance than the quantity.

Second, the setting of hard goals sometimes improves performance quantity at the expense of performance quality. For example, Bavelas and Lee (1978) found that the number of objects listed which were 'hard, white and edible' was directly related to goal level. However, the rated quality of the responses in terms of meeting the criteria decreased as goal level increased.

Third, there is increasing evidence that goal setting can be counterproductive when someone is trying to learn how to perform a task. According to Kanfer and Ackerman (1989),

interventions [such as goal-setting] designed to engage motivational processes may impede task learning when presented prior to an understanding of what the task is about. In these instances, cognitive resources necessary for task understanding are diverted towards self-regulatory activities (e.g., self evaluation).

(Kanfer and Ackerman 1989: 687)

Fourth, goal-setting theory is concerned only with motivational forces of which the individual is aware. It is probable that many important aspects of motivation are omitted from consideration as a consequence.

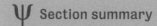

Section summary

Individual differences in motivation for work depend in part on personality factors such as need for achievement. Those high in need for achievement prefer tasks of moderate difficulty rather than easy or hard tasks, they tend to be successful in their work, and they tend to choose challenging jobs (e.g. entrepreneur). It is unwise to focus too much on personality factors, because motivation depends very much on situational factors. The relationship between motivation and performance often takes the form of an inverted-U relationship, and the optimal level of motivation or arousal has been found to vary inversely with task difficulty. Easterbrook (1959) accounted for these findings by assuming that attention narrows progressively as the level of motivation increases. Eysenck and Calvo (1992) argued that anxiety has motivational and emotional effects, with the result that anxiety typically impairs processing efficiency more than performance effectiveness. There is evidence for a direct relationship between the difficulty level of the goals set by individuals and their level of performance. However, this seems to be more the case when the emphasis is on quantity of performance than on quality. The relevance of goal-setting to performance is less clear when someone is learning how to perform a task.

1   List the characteristics of the individual and the society with a high need for achievement.
2   What evidence is there for a relationship between goal-setting and achievement?

Chapter summary

• Hunger and the control of food intake

Reward is produced by factors such as the taste and smell of food, whereas satiety is produced by gastric and intestinal signals. Brain processes bring together satiety and rewards signals, so that satiety affects the reward value of food. In part, we eat to maintain glucostasis. The hypothalamus is implicated in the control of food intake and body weight. The orbitofrontal cortex contains areas that process the taste, smell and sight of food, and respond to food only if hunger is present. The amygdala has many properties resembling those of the orbitofrontal cortex. There are neural systems in the striatum which initiate feeding responses

• Thirst

Water deprivation produces depletion of either the cellular or the extracellular fluid compartments, and this initiates drinking behaviour. Changes in the cellular

Box continued

compartment are more important in producing drinking. Drinking is maintained or reinforced by the taste of water. The termination of drinking is produced by various factors, including oropharyngeal stimulation, gastric distension and gut stimulation by water, and systemic dilution.

- **Sexual behaviour**

Human sexual behaviour is determined only in part by biological processes. From a sociobiological perspective, evolutionary pressures may lead male humans to guard their partner from other males and to be attracted to younger women with child-bearing potential. In females, evolutionary processes may lead them to choose a powerful partner who can provide stability and help with bringing up their children. In males, the preoptic area in front of the hypothalamus is involved in the control of sexual behaviour. In females, the medial preoptic area controls reproductive cycles and probably also controls sexual behaviour.

- **Psychosocial motives**

Maslow proposed a hierarchy of needs, with deficiency needs in the bottom part of the hierarchy and growth needs in the top part. The need for self-actualization was at the apex of the hierarchy. This approach is comprehensive. However, it is vaguely expressed, is based on a rejection of the scientific approach, and de-emphasizes the potentially beneficial role of society in promoting self-actualization. The need for affiliation and the need for intimacy are major social motives.

The former refers mainly to the quantity of social contacts, whereas the latter refers mainly to the quality of personal relationships. People affiliate to reduce uncertainty, to receive emotional support, to obtain stimulation, and to receive attention and praise. Individuals lacking adequate social support are more vulnerable to stress and illness.

- **Motivation and performance**

Individuals differ in their need for achievement. Those high in need for achievement are more likely to choose challenging tasks, to become entrepreneurs, and to succeed in most jobs. However, measures of need for achievement tend to have fairly low reliability and validity. According to the Yerkes-Dodson law, there is an inverted-U relationship between motivation or arousal and performance, and the optimal level of arousal varies inversely with task difficulty. Easterbrook offered an explanation of this law, based on the assumption that increased levels of arousal or motivation cause a progressive narrowing of attention. According to Eysenck and Calvo, anxiety causes worry, which reduces processing efficiency but not necessarily performance effectiveness. According to Locke's goal-setting theory, there is a direct relationship between the difficulty of the goals that are set and the level of performance. This relationship is found most often when there is a high level of goal commitment and feedback on performance is provided. Hard goal setting is generally more effective in improving quantitative aspects of performance than qualitative ones.

Further reading

- Arnold, J., Cooper, C.L. and Robertson, I.T. (eds) (1995) *Work Psychology: Understanding human behaviour in the workplace*, 2nd edn. London: Pitman. Theories and research on motivational factors are discussed in Chapter 11.

- Buunk, B.P. (1996) Affiliation, attraction and close relationships, in M. Hewstone, W. Stroebe and G.M. Stephenson (eds) *Introduction to Social Psychology*, 2nd edn. Oxford: Blackwell. This has good coverage of many aspects of social motivation.

- Carlson, N.R. (1994) *Physiology of Behaviour*, 5th edn. Boston, MA: Allyn and Bacon. A textbook of physiological psychology with good coverage of hunger and thirst.

- Ridley, M. (1993) *The Red Queen: Sex and the evolution of human nature*. Harmondsworth: Penguin. A readable introduction to the sociobiology of sexual behaviour.

- Rolls, E.T. (1999) *The Brain and Emotion*. Oxford: Oxford University Press. A book that covers hunger, thirst, sexual behaviour and emotion, and the underlying brain processing.

- Rolls, E.T. and Treves, A. (1998) *Neural Networks and Brain Function*. Oxford: Oxford University Press. A book for those who want to start to understand how the brain works.

CHAPTER 17

Abnormal psychology

Andrew MacLeod

KEY CONCEPTS ● concepts of abnormality ● explanations of psychological disorder ● depression ● anxiety ● schizophrenia ● personality disorder

❑ Chapter preview

When you have read this chapter, you should be able to

- describe and evaluate the main approaches to defining abnormality and mental disorder, especially the distinction between fact-based and value-based approaches
- outline the three main types of explanations (biological, psychological, social) given for mental disorders
- discuss how biological, psychological and social factors interact
- describe the main symptoms of depression, schizophrenia, anxiety and personality disorder
- discuss the evidence for social, biological and psychological factors in depression, schizophrenia, anxiety and personality disorder

Introduction

Davina is unable to go out of the house because she fears that she might lose control of herself in front of other people, even though nothing like this has happened before. Marianne has increasingly found herself losing interest in everything and unable to find the energy to do even the simplest thing, for which she blames herself, concluding that she must be a useless person. Paul frequently hears voices speaking to him which no one else can hear and which, far from being comforting, tell him how evil he is. Michael appears at first to be a charming man but after a while it becomes clear that he uses people as objects and appears to be incapable of experiencing feelings such as sympathy or guilt. These are just some of the experiences and behaviours that come under the heading of abnormal psychology. Abnormal psychology is not quite what the name would suggest. It is not the study of all human behaviour and experience which is abnormal in the sense of being unusual. Rather, in practice, abnormal psychology is the application of the theories and methods of psychology to the study of what are called **mental disorders**. Mental disorders, also called psychological disorders, are particular types of unusual or, in some cases, not so unusual, human behaviour and experience which over time have come to be seen as belonging together. In fact, abnormal psychology

has been very closely associated with **psychiatry**, the branch of medicine concerned with mental disorders, and so has been dependent on the way psychiatry has defined mental disorder. What are the defining features of mental disorders? The simple answer to this is that there is no clear set of defining features which can encompass all mental disorders. In practice, mental disorders are defined as what appears in classification systems (see box) such as the Diagnostic and Statistical Manual of the American Psychiatric Association (APA 1994) currently in its fourth version (DSM-IV), or the International Classification of Diseases of the World Health Organization (WHO 1992) currently in its tenth version (ICD-10). Nevertheless, there have been various attempts to provide a definition of abnormality and disorder.

❏ Concepts of abnormality

The definition of what is abnormal, and by implication, what is normal, has been the subject of considerable debate. The most obvious, and simplest, answer to this question of what is normal is that normality refers to what the majority of people do or feel or experience. By this definition, any behaviour or experience which lies outside some range that most people fall into is abnormal. This is called the **statistical concept of**

Diagnostic systems: putting people in boxes

Progress in understanding things in the natural world usually begins with a common language and system of classification that everyone can agree upon. Since the mid-1940s, mental health has seen considerable effort put into trying to develop a definitive classification scheme for mental disorders. The aim is to produce clearly defined categories, such as major depression or schizophrenia, that can then form the basis of research and treatment. There are two major classification systems currently in use.

One is the International Statistical Classification of Diseases, Injuries, and Causes of Death (ICD) produced by the World Health Organization and currently in its tenth version (ICD-10). The other system is the Diagnostic and Statistical Manual (DSM) of the American Psychiatric Association, which is currently in

its fourth version (DSM-IV).

These two schemes are designed to be compatible. In practice ICD is used more in Europe whereas DSM is used in North America. Both ICD-10 and DSM-IV list a wide range of disorders and their symptoms that allow clinicians to make a diagnosis on an individual person. One major criticism of such an approach is that it is based on an all-or-nothing categorization; for example, someone is either depressed or not depressed. This fails to recognize that many psychological problems, including depression, might be best thought of as falling on a gradual continuum rather than being all-or-nothing categories. However, in practice it is often helpful to have definite lines rather than a gradual continuum as decisions have to be made about whether or not someone requires treatment. (See also Chapter 18 p. 577–8).

abnormality, because normality is not defined by any absolute sense but by a statistical norm. Most human behaviour or experience will fall into some sort of normal distribution where the majority of people are somewhere in the middle and as one progresses out to either side of this middle ground the number of people will get progressively less. A clear example of this is height, where there is an average height in the population around which most people fall and the further away one gets from that average the fewer the number of people. The appeal of this view is that it is factual and practical. The place where a person falls on a continuum should be simply a matter of ascertaining the facts and can be expressed in terms of standard deviations from the mean.

However, trying to apply this in practice very quickly becomes problematic. First of all, there are deviations from the norm that are either neutral, such as being tall, or that are seen as positive, such as being very intelligent. Neither being tall or being intelligent are seen as disorders so there must be something to disorder other than simply deviation from the norm. One answer is to say that it is deviation from the norm in a negative direction. This then introduces a new dimension to the definition – a dimension of values. How do we decide what is negative?

We have just introduced the fundamental issue in the argument about what is abnormal – can we decide what is abnormal on the basis of facts or is our view of what is abnormal based on some value judgement? Like most debates, the argument has been fuelled by two very opposing views. On the one side is the view that there are clear, objective grounds for deciding on whether some aspect of human behaviour or experience is abnormal in the sense that it can be considered a disorder. By this view, it is simply a matter of ascertaining the facts, and the facts will then dictate whether something is a disorder or not. The opposing view is not so much one view as a cluster of views which all have something in common. This alternative view of abnormality or disorder takes the position that rather than being a matter of facts, deciding someone's experience or behaviour is a disorder is a matter of values. So, someone's behaviour is judged abnormal not because it actually is intrinsically abnormal but rather because it is deemed to be abnormal because of the set of values held by society. A clear example of the influence of values in defining disorder is the disorder of drapaetomania (Wakefield 1992), an illness that afflicted slaves in the southern states of the USA; the main symptom of this was running away from their owner, which was treated by administering a beating!

The facts versus values view of abnormality will be returned to shortly. However, some attempts have been made to give more practical definitions of abnormality for working purposes. Perhaps the most simplistic of these is to view disorder as whatever mental health professionals treat, or the need for treatment. Of course, this is an avoidance of a definition rather than providing a definition. It can maintain only whatever happens to be the status quo at the time. As Kendell (1975) points out, it also provides a hostage to fortune in that it would sanction the treatment of anything and opens the door to various abuses.

A second way of thinking about disorder in a practical way relates to the experience of distress and/or impairment of functioning. In this view, disorder is indicated by distress or disability. This is in practice the definition that many mental health practitioners would adopt. Of course, this definition does not work if level of distress is used in isolation. Someone who is extremely distressed having just heard about the death of his or her family in a car crash would not be thought to be suffering from a disorder. There has to be some judgement of the appropriateness or expectedness of the distress. Of course, this relies on a value judgement about what is normal. There are also some conditions considered to be disorders, such as personality disorder (discussed on pp. 557–61), where the person does not experience distress or disability and yet is judged to have a psychological disorder.

What should be clear by now is that it is extremely difficult to avoid value judgements when deciding someone is psychologically abnormal or disturbed. Does this mean that disorder is just a matter of value judgements or is there any evidence of a factual basis to disorder? In the factual approach, psychological abnormality is thought to be essentially like physical abnormality. Just as we can usually tell whether people have something wrong with their bodies, we can tell whether there is something wrong with their minds. In fact, this is sometimes called the **medical model** because it treats psychological disorder like physical disorder. It is also the view usually held by psychiatrists, who have a medical training.

The medical model

Most people would acknowledge that physical illness involves some factual basis that does not depend on societal values. If psychological disorder could be thought of in a similar way to physical disorder, then that would certainly support the idea that there is a factual basis to defining psychological abnormality or disorder. An early description of the medical approach to psychological disorder can be found in the editorial of the *Journal of Mental Science* from 1958: 'Insanity is purely a disease of the brain. The physician is now the responsible guardian of the lunatic and must ever remain so' (quoted in Pilgrim 1990) Clearly, the language used would not pass current tests of political correctness, or even general acceptability, but similar, more recent claims can be found. This fact-based view takes the position that psychological disorders, like physical disorders, have an underlying biological basis. Samuel Guze, a professor of psychiatry, summed up this approach in his contribution to the debate, an article entitled 'Biological psychiatry: is there any other kind?' (Guze 1989).

Rather than just issue polemical statements, some advocates of a medical approach have seriously tried to assess the validity of thinking of psychological disorder like physical disorder. John Wing, a psychiatrist who was interested in social influences in psychological disorder, pointed out that the medical model had two main criteria (Wing 1978). The first criterion was that symptoms of a particular illness should tend to occur together. So, a person who has one of the symptoms should also tend to have the others, thus supporting the validity of the particular category of illness. The second criterion is that there should be an underlying biological basis for the disorder. These are the criteria that are met by physical illnesses. How well do psychological disorders fit this model?

One of the most studied psychological disorders has been schizophrenia. However, as discussed later, leading authorities in the field of schizophrenia have emphasized different symptoms as being central to the disorder and there is great variability in the symptom pattern of those who have been labelled 'schizophrenic'. Cross-cultural work has found that in the case of depression, although many of the symptoms of depression are found in different cultures, in some cultures there is no overall concept of depression which sees these various symptoms as being manifestations of the same condition (Cochrane 1983). Findings such as these would seem to undermine the medical model applied to mental disorder because if schizophrenia and depression were illnesses then we would expect them to manifest themselves consistently across different cultures. However, it has also been found that if the criteria are made more strict and the application of the criteria are monitored there is more cross-cultural consistency in schizophrenia.

The second criterion, demonstrating an underlying biological basis for disorders, will be examined in detail for different disorders later in the chapter. However, it is worth exploring some of the general issues at this point. Historically, a major impetus for the medical model came through the discovery that general paresis of the insane (GPI) was caused by syphilis. General paresis was the name given to a particular disorder which began with weakness in the limbs and proceeded to eccentricity and delusions of grandeur, ending up in almost total paralysis and finally death. Some of the symptoms of GPI paint the picture of the classical madman. Over the course of the nineteenth century, evidence began to accumulate that GPI had a definite physical basis, until just after the turn of the century it was confirmed that syphilitic infection caused GPI. Effective drug treatments were subsequently developed and GPI eliminated. As well as being of enormous practical importance for sufferers, the discovery had wider implications. If GPI, a form of 'madness', had a biological cause and could respond to drug intervention then perhaps all mental disorders would follow the same pattern. However, it is fair to say that there have been no comparable discoveries of a physical basis for any other mental disorder (Rosenhan and Seligman 1995).

Neurosis and psychosis

There is, in fact, some ambiguity when talking about mental illness as to whether proponents of the medical model are using the term 'illness' literally or metaphorically. One of the clearest exponents of the literal view was Karl Jaspers, a psychiatrist of the Heidelberg School who moved away from psychiatry and devoted the second half of his professional life to philosophy. For Jaspers (1963), mental illness was literally illness. His view was that just as physical illness represents some malfunction of the body, mental illness represented a malfunction of the brain. So, individuals would begin to suffer mental illness when there was some pathological process going on in their brains. However, a very important point Jaspers made was that this view did not include everything that would normally be classified as psychological disorder. His view was based on the distinction between **neurosis** and **psychosis**. It is probably worth taking some time to explain these widely used terms, which are somewhat confusing, particularly as historically they have had different meanings at different times. Neurosis, a word made popular by Freud, is generally used to mean some psychological disturbance that is an extension of common experience, for example, feeling anxious, although it may be more severe and more prolonged. Psychosis is generally used to refer to any psychological disturbance in which there appears to be a break from reality, such as hearing voices that no one else can hear. In fact, as David Healy (1990) has pointed out, these terms have come to take on an opposite meaning to their original meanings. Neurosis was initially used to describe what was thought to be a disorder of the nerves but in the absence of any observable change in the nerves such as inflammation (neuritis). So, neurosis was the name given to a psychological disorder thought to result from physical changes to the nervous system which were nevertheless not detectable. Neurosis has now taken on the opposite meaning where it generally means a psychological disorder that is *not* based on some physical malfunction. So, although someone may be talked about as having a 'nervous breakdown', mental health professionals would be more likely to look for the root of this in social and psychological factors rather than by examining the person's nervous system.

To return to Jaspers, he made a clear distinction between the psychoses, which represented a malfunction of some part of the brain, and the neuroses, which did not. The psychoses were illness and the neuroses were not. The key to understanding whether something was a mental illness was that it would be indicated by uninterpretable experience. That is, where we cannot give an account of a person's experience or behaviour within any of the usual explanations, that probably indicates a mental illness based on some underlying brain malfunction. Major depression, which at that time meant depression with associated physical features such as sleep and appetite disturbance, was an illness and represented, in part, disorders of the sleep and appetite centres of the brain. Minor depression without those more physical features was not a mental illness for Jaspers and would not be explicable in terms of underlying biological processes. Although the physical, or to be more exact, neurological, basis of mental illnesses had not been discovered, Jaspers thought that it would be discovered in the future, in the same way that the physical basis of GPI had eventually been discovered.

Jaspers (1963) and others who have followed him, for example, Kendell (1975), argued that a biological cause of psychological disorders would be discovered but at the same time excluded some psychological disorders from this claim. The distinction between psychological disorders that are illnesses and those that are not has not been universally accepted. For example, no qualitative distinction is made in diagnostic systems between, for example, schizophrenia and anxiety disorders. Psychiatrists and other mental health professionals

concern themselves with what Jaspers would term the neuroses as much as they do with the psychoses. There is also disagreement about how to draw the line between the two categories. The key for Jaspers was behaviour that was not interpretable within normal explanatory bounds. So, someone hearing voices which no one else hears is inexplicable within psychological or social terms and therefore must be the result of neurological dysfunction. Sleep and appetite disturbance must represent disruption to those centres of the brain that control these activities. However, it is clearly a point of debate exactly where explanations run out. As Healy (1990) has pointed out, within a psychoanalytic framework, explanations are more elaborate and provide accounts of unusual behaviour in terms of psychological conflicts. Someone may not be eating because of an unconscious wish to die or may have disturbed sleep as a result of trying to escape from dreams which threaten his or her ego defences.

Whether one chooses to draw a line down the middle of psychological disorders, allocating some to biological and others to psychological or social causes is in some sense not that relevant because no clear organic basis for *any* psychological disorder has been found. The responses to the lack of any replication of the success of GPI in terms of physical causes have been varied. One response is to assert that such causes will be discovered in the future, particularly as technology improves allowing us to access brain processes more readily and accurately. The excitement generated by new techniques which allow more sophisticated brain scanning represents this view.

Disorder as biological disadvantage

A second response to the failure to find any clear brain dysfunction that is reliably associated with any disorder is to redefine the concept of disease or illness. Scadding (1967) suggested that it was misdirected to look for evidence of brain dysfunction for mental disorders because what characterized disorders was not biological dysfunction but biological disadvantage. Unfortunately, Scadding did not actually say what biological disadvantage was but Robert Kendell, in his inaugural lecture to the chair of psychiatry at Edinburgh University, attempted to do just that. On evolutionary grounds, Kendell (1975) suggested that there were two indices of biological disadvantage – reduced fertility and reduced longevity, i.e. living a shorter life and having fewer children. Illness can be defined as anything which produces either or both of these. To the extent that those with psychological disorder show these effects then they can be thought of as suffering from mental illness, just in the same way that other people suffer from physical illness. People with psychotic disorders (mainly schizophrenia) can be shown to produce fewer children and to live shorter lives, although the evidence is not clear for those who have neuroses or personality disorder. Thus, Kendell reached a similar conclusion to Jaspers, although on very different grounds, that there is such a thing as mental illness but that the term should be applied only to certain psychological disorders and not to others. This position is best summed up by his closing remarks (to his inaugural lecture at the University of Edinburgh):

By all means let us insist that schizophrenia is an illness and that we [psychiatrists] are better equipped to understand and treat it than anyone else. But let us not try to do the same for the woes of mankind.

(Kendell 1975: 314)

It almost goes without saying that there are a number of problems for this view. Reduced fertility is not necessarily harmful to an individual, even within Darwinian terms. Some factors reducing fertility no one would call disorder, such as having a celibate vocation or just simply choosing not to have children. Finally, some of the so-called indicators of mental illness may be the result of society's reaction to those who are labelled mentally ill. Is it any surprise that people classified as

---

Ψ Case study

Is homosexuality a disorder?

Up until 1973 the American Psychiatric Association (APA) classified homosexuality as a disorder in its Diagnostic and Statistical Manual (DSM-II). Interestingly, Kendell (1975) also used evidence of homosexuals having fewer children as evidence for his mental disorder and biological disadvantage argument based on the assumption that homosexuality was a mental disorder. After a campaign to remove homosexuality from the list of disorders, particularly from gay activist groups, the APA agreed to recommend to their membership that it should be deleted from DSM-II. The membership voted their agreement. However, the change was strongly contested, with the strongest protest from psychoanalysts for whom homosexuality represented a fixation at a particular stage of psychosexual development. Homosexuality as a disorder was replaced with **ego-dystonic** homosexuality, which referred to someone who experiences unwanted homosexual arousal. A survey carried out in 1977 found that 69 per cent of the APA's members still regarded homosexuality as a psychopathological adaptation rather than variation of normal sexuality (Cornett and Hudson 1985). In the current version of DSM (DSM-IV 1994) ego-dystonic homosexuality has disappeared. DSM-IV does include a category for those who are distressed by their sexual orientation. In theory, this allows for ego-dystonic heterosexuality as well as

homosexuality, although it is not likely to be common. Homosexuality is a good example of the definition of what constitutes mental disorder changing as a result of changes in societal values.

Plate 17.1 Homosexuality is a good example of changing definitions of what constitutes mental disorder as a result in changes in societal values. Up until 1973 the American Psychiatric Association classified homosexuality as a disorder

mentally ill had fewer children and had shorter lives when they were incarcerated in large asylums which were rife with tuberculosis? Kendell acknowledges that these indirect effects should be separated out, although he presents no evidence to support his position with only direct effects.

Value approaches

Value approaches, in contrast to fact-based approaches like the medical model, emphasize the way that society construes a person's behaviour and experience, which in turn depends on society's value system. There are a variety of such stances, all of which represent a critique of the establishment, fact-based, medically oriented approach, from the right-wing libertarian stance of Szasz (1964), an American psychiatrist, to the left-wing Marxist critique of Foucault (1965), a French social theorist. These approaches vary considerably within themselves but all have in common a belief that the idea of psychological disorder is socially constructed rather than reflecting some objective state of affairs.

Perhaps the clearest example of a value-based approach is **labelling theory** (Scheff 1966). The starting point of Labelling Theory is that psychological 'symptoms', such as being depressed or hearing voices, can develop for a variety of reasons and are actually much more common in the population than recorded rates. The initial appearance of these symptoms is called **primary deviance**. However, in some cases these symptoms get labelled as mental illness, not because of any greater severity in those cases but largely because of social position. For people who are low in social status and influence, the symptoms are more likely to attract a label of mental illness and at the same time these people are less able to resist the label being applied to them. Once the label has been applied, it is difficult to get rid of; in fact the person is rewarded for taking on the role that society has allocated to him or her. Crucially, the person then internalizes the label and the role and so takes on the identity that he or she has been allocated. This process is called **secondary deviance**. Psychiatric hospitals are the main place where the new identity and role are learned and psychiatrists are the chief personnel involved in this process. So, in this view there is no such thing as mental illness in any absolute sense but only in the sense that it is created by the process of labelling someone mentally ill, rather like a self-fulfilling prophecy.

A well-known study by Rosenhan (1973) seemed to add weight to this conclusion. Rosenhan (1973) and his collaborators presented themselves to the admitting doctors at general psychiatric hospitals reporting that they had been having auditory **hallucinations** (hearing the words 'thud', 'dull' or 'empty'). They did not report any other symptoms. They managed to get themselves admitted to psychiatric hospital on this basis, mainly diagnosed as schizophrenic. Once admitted, they behaved normally, that is they did not continue to report those symptoms. The average stay was 52 days before discharge and it appears that never at any point were they suspected of pretending. They concluded that even psychiatrists cannot tell the sane from the insane, thus questioning the objective reality of mental illness. There have been many criticisms of this study and its conclusions, for example, the fact that they initially reported auditory hallucinations but without any distress and in the absence of life stress predisposed the psychiatrists to come to the conclusions they did (see Lilienfeld 1995 for a discussion).

Some evidence has supported labelling theory but it is an example of a theory that fitted the practices of a particular time and place. For example, the points made by labelling theory are particularly important when thinking about involuntary admissions to hospital. When Scheff carried out his research in the 1960s in the United States, 90 per cent of all psychiatric hospital admissions were involuntary. However, in replicating Scheff's original study in Britain at a later date, Bean (1979) found that only 18 per cent of patients were involuntarily admitted by psychiatrists on emergency visits to the patients' homes.

What labelling theory and the Rosenhan (1973) study have been useful in highlighting is the importance of the way people are treated when they are labelled mentally ill. However, what labelling theory is unable to account for is why someone begins to show deviant behaviour in the first place. The somewhat unsatisfactory response is that this initial or primary deviance is unimportant relative to the secondary deviance that results from being labelled.

Facts plus values: an integrated approach

Wakefield (1992) has put forward an integrated approach to disorder (psychological and physical), which takes into account both facts and values. For Wakefield disorder is 'harmful dysfunction'. Both conditions – dysfunction and harm – have to be met for something to qualify as a disorder:

Research update

Critique of Wakefield's 'harmful dysfunction'

Lilienfeld and Marino (1995) have provided a critique of Wakefield's account of disorder as harmful dysfunction. In particular, they have criticized the dysfunction element on several grounds. First, they argue that many mental functions are not the direct result of evolutionary pressures selecting what is adaptive. Rather, many mental functions are by-products of adaptations – effectively side-effects. Such functions may be neutral or may become adaptive themselves but they were not initially selected for the function that they serve. Lilienfeld and Marino (1995) give the analogy of bird feathers, which were probably selected for giving warmth, and their flight-giving ability was a by-product. Second, they argue that Wakefield's analysis underestimates the considerable variability across individuals that is produced by processes of natural selection. Nature produces great variability, most of which is adaptive. Finally, they criticize Wakefield's

account of dysfunction because many mental disorders are not so much the result of a function failing to work but the triggering of an adaptive function. For example, many anxiety responses, such as fear of snakes, can be clearly seen to be adaptive. Lilienfeld and Marino (1995) conclude that it is a mistake to try to provide a scientific, factual definition of mental disorder. Instead, they suggest thinking of mental disorder as a psychological concept, one that is in the head rather than in the world, although it clearly relates to entities in the natural world. As such, the concept will have fuzzy boundaries where it is not clear whether something belongs in or out of the category. There will also be examples, such as major depression and schizophrenia, that more clearly belong in the category. Interestingly, Lilienfeld and Marino appear to end up with a similar conclusion to Jaspers and also to Kendell, suggesting that certain phenomena currently called disorders are best thought of as mental disorders whereas others may not be.

---

a disorder exists when the failure of a person's internal mechanisms to perform their function as designed by nature impinges harmfully on the person's well-being as defined by social values and meanings.

(Wakefield 1992: 373)

How successful this approach has been is difficult to say. Wakefield was attempting to find a definition of disorder that could apply equally to psychological and physical disorder. According to Wakefield (1992) we know the function of something by what it does. The function of the heart is to pump blood around the body, and we know that is its function because that is what it does. Leaving aside the circularity of this argument, it is actually much more difficult to think about what the function of psychological mechanisms are than it is to think about what the function of physical mechanisms are. Wakefield (1992: 383) acknowledges this difficulty: 'Discovering what is natural or dysfunctional may be extraordinarily difficult . . . especially with respect to mental mechanisms, about which we are still in a great state of ignorance'. However, this begins to sound like the special pleading of the proponents of the medical model who, not having found any biological basis for

psychological disorders, argue that such a basis will be discovered in the future. Conversely, it is easier to think about the value component of psychological disorders than physical disorders. Why did we stop thinking of drapaetomania or, more recently, homosexuality as disorders? It was not because of the discovery of new 'facts' about their function, as Wakefield suggests, but because of changes to societal values.

ψ Section summary

The definition of abnormality and the related question of what constitutes a disorder are problematic. One approach to the issue has been to emphasize the factual nature of mental as well as physical disorders. This view is most clearly expressed in the medical model, where disorders are seen as arising from some internal biological dysfunction. Saying something is a disorder then becomes a matter of scientific fact, through discovering what the dys-

Box continued

function is. In contrast, critics of this approach have emphasized the role of value judgements in calling something a disorder. According to adherents of the value-based view, we call something a disorder, not because of some factual dysfunction, but because it is something we do not value. It is not difficult to see that values play a role in something being called a disorder; the case of homosexuality is a recent enough example to bring this point home forcefully. The factual aspects to disorder are more problematic because, as we shall see, there have been no clear underlying biological bases shown for any mental disorders. Wakefield (1992) proposed an integrated view that combines both facts and values which views disorder as harmful dysfunction. However, there appear to be problems with the factual, dysfunction element of this view. Lilienfeld and Marino (1995) have suggested that the concept of mental disorder is best thought of as a psychological one rather than being something that exists in nature. This being the case then there would be some disorders that are clearer examples than others, a view that can be found in earlier writers such as Jaspers (1963) and Kendell (1975).

1 What are the main ways in which abnormality has been defined?
2 Are both facts and values important in defining mental disorder?

Explanations of psychological disorder

The alternative to deciding on a definition of disorder and seeing to what extent various disorders fit this definition is to look at what are generally considered to be disorders and to see how those disorders are best explained. We will first review the different types of explanations usually given for psychological disorders then turn to looking at the contribution of these explanations to understanding a number of different psychological disorders. Four specific disorders will be focused on – depression, anxiety, schizophrenia, and personality disorder – as they represent the more common psychological disorders as well as illustrating many of the points that are true of other disorders.

Explanations of psychological disorder fall into three broad categories: biological, psychological and social.

Biological explanations, essentially what has been talked about as the medical model, emphasize the importance of parts of the body, in particular the brain, not functioning as they should. Mental disorders, such as depression, anxiety or schizophrenia, are seen as a direct result of this physical abnormality or dysfunction. The dysfunction is commonly thought to be inherited, which can be shown by genetic studies, or may result from some insult to the system, such as brain damage at birth. Techniques such as brain scanning can, in principle, show which particular parts of the brain are involved in certain disorders. Social explanations emphasize the role of people's experience of what is around them in explaining the cause of mental disorder. In this view, someone might become psychologically disturbed through suffering an unusual amount of bad experiences or through having a lack of support from friends or family to help them through difficult times, or even through having suffered abuse and neglect at an early age. Psychological explanations emphasize the importance of psychological processes which have gone wrong, such as faulty thinking or inappropriate learning in producing the disorder and also maintaining it.

These three types of explanations – biological, social and psychological – are not necessarily mutually exclusive. It is becoming increasingly clear that mental disorders might well result from an interaction of social, psychological and biological factors. Neither is it always clear exactly where to draw the line between the different types of explanations as they are interdependent. For example, psychological problems are related to biological processes in that they depend on biological processes for their occurrence. However, they are not necessarily reducible to faulty biological processes. People walking through the jungle who think they have seen a lion will feel fear. The feeling of fear will have corresponding activity in the brain, probably in the limbic system. However, we would not necessarily want to attribute the cause of the fear to activity of the limbic system. In this case, it would make more sense to say that these people were fearful as a result of thinking that they had seen a lion. The link between psychological and social explanations is also illustrated by this example because the psychological state is about something in the environment. If there was a lion present then the fear would be best explained by the presence of the lion – a social explanation. When social and psychological explanations do not seem able to account for the experience then it may be best accounted for at the biological level. It will become clear that often all three levels interact to produce mental disorder. Perhaps the best known example of an interactive model is the **diathesis-stress model**. In this model, a stressful life event interacts with a pre-existing vulnerability within the person (the diathesis) to produce disorder. The diathesis was originally seen as a biological weak point, but more recently the diathesis-stress approach has been used to understand how life events might interact with psychological vulnerabilities, which will be illustrated in the case of depression.

Ψ Section summary

Explanations of psychological disorder fall into three main categories. Social explanations emphasize the importance of what happens to the person, for example, suffering early abuse or experiencing negative life events. Psychological explanations account for disorders by reference to patterns of faulty thinking or learning. Biological explanations emphasize the importance of abnormal brain processes, which may be genetically transmitted. Increasingly biological, social and psychological factors are seen as interacting in producing psychological disturbance rather than being mutually exclusive.

1　What are the main types of explanations of psychological disorder?
2　Are these explanations mutually exclusive or can they be integrated? Give an example.

❏ Depression

Most people have at some time felt depressed, in the sense of feeling sad or down, or perhaps gloomy, pessimistic or self-blaming. Although such feelings may be common, the term 'depression' actually takes on quite a different meaning when used in the context of abnormal psychology. In this section we will be talking about what is sometimes called clinical depression, in order to make clear that it is something different from the way we use the term in everyday life. In fact, it is a matter of some debate whether clinical depression is something qualitatively distinct from ordinary, everyday depression or whether it is a more extreme form of the same sort of state. One view is that clinical depression is simply a more extreme form of everyday depression, but just that people suffering clinical depression will have more symp-

Plate 17.2 Winston Churchill was said to suffer from clinical depression

toms, experience them more severely and for a longer period of time, and as a result find themselves unable to cope. An alternative view is that clinical depression is qualitatively distinct, particularly when it gets to some of the more physical symptoms such as sleep disturbance. As in many of the debates in psychology it may be that the two views are not contradictory. One possibility is that depression is on a continuum but that when it reaches a certain point it starts to introduce qualitatively different aspects. An analogy would be with water temperature, which is on a continuum but at a certain point water will freeze, thus introducing a qualitatively new dimension. In the case of depression, when it reaches a certain severity it may mean the person is unable to function normally in everyday life, which introduces a new dimension to the problem. At this point someone is likely to be classified as clinically depressed.

Symptoms of depression

The syndrome of clinical depression refers not just to feelings but to a pattern of emotional, cognitive and behavioural characteristics. Table 17.1 shows the main symptoms of depression. The most obvious symptom of depression is depressed mood. Clinically depressed mood has been described as being like falling into a black hole or bottomless pit, drowning, or suffocating.

Table 17.1 Main symptoms of depression

- Depressed mood
- Diminished interest or pleasure
- Negative view of self: self-blaming and feelings of guilt
- Weight loss or weight gain
- Sleep disturbance (difficulty falling asleep, disturbed sleep or early morning wakening)
- Agitation or being slowed down in movement
- Difficulty concentrating
- Thoughts of death or suicide

Other feelings can include feeling irritable, angry or guilty, and depression is often also accompanied by feelings of anxiety (Clark and Watson 1991). There is often a loss of interest in any activities and a desire to be on one's own. Depression is also associated with changes in the way someone thinks. These cognitive changes can be general, like poor concentration and impaired memory or difficulty making decisions. There can also be more mood-congruent changes in thinking, where the depressed person thinks negatively about the world, the self and the future (Beck *et al.* 1979). Thus, those who are depressed will have difficulty recalling positive memories, will attribute blame to themselves when inappropriate, believe other people think more negatively of them than they really do, and feel pessimistic about the future. There are also a number of physical symptoms of depression. Loss of energy is very common; getting out of bed can become a major task. With more severe depression there can be changes in sleep pattern, for example, sleeping too much or waking early in the morning and not being able to get back to sleep. Similarly, appetite can be disrupted, either eating more than usual or less than usual, with accompanying weight gain or weight loss. Finally, suicidal thoughts and behaviour are associated with depression.

There is, in fact, quite a variation in the experience of depression and in response to this over the years different subtypes have been suggested. One of the best known of these distinctions has been between **endogenous depression**, where there was thought not to be an external cause, and **reactive depression** (also called exogenous depression), where the depression is in response to some life event or circumstance. However, these terms are now used more to refer to different symptom patterns, with endogenous depression being characterized by a loss of the ability to experience pleasure (**anhedonia**) as well as some of the more physical symptoms such as appetite and sleep disturbance and slowed down movement (psychomotor retardation). It

has been found that the distinction in terms of what causes the depression was not as clear cut as might be expected. Sufferers of endogenous type depression have been found to have as many preceding negative life experiences as sufferers of reactive type depression (Bebbington and McGuffin 1989) Confusingly, other terms have been used to refer to endogenous-type depression, such as melancholia and retarded depression. One distinction which is currently used in the DSM-IV depends on whether the depression is more minor but longer term (**dysthymia**) or more severe and short lived (**major depression**). Dysthymia and major depression can even occur together, which is called **double depression**. **Manic depression**, or bipolar depression, is where the depression alternates with periods of intense elation accompanied by grandiose ideas, bursts of activity and racing thoughts.

Clinical depression is one of the most common of psychological disorders. In fact, it has been called the 'common cold' of **psychopathology**. Studies have found that the risk of having depression at least once in the course of a lifetime is about 10 per cent (Angst 1992). One of the most consistent findings is that women are about twice as likely as men to experience depression (Nolan-Hoeksema 1987). There are some interesting exceptions to this ratio. The gender difference is not found in children but emerges in adolescence (J.H. Block *et al.* 1991) and is also not found in university students. These exceptions are useful in that they may tell us something about the cause of depression.

Women and depression

Various explanations have been put forward – social, biological and psychological – to account for the difference in depression rates between men and women (Nolan-Hoeksema 1987). Biological explanations are partly based on evidence that times of hormonal fluctuation, such as after giving birth and the menopause, can carry heightened risk for depression. Social explanations have focused on role conflict: pressure on women through being expected to fulfil both traditional and contemporary female roles, lack of varied sources of self-esteem or depression being more consistent with feminine stereotypes. Nolan-Hoeksema (1987) puts forward a psychological explanation which focuses on the way women respond to depressive feelings. She identifies two possible responses to a mildly depressed mood: distraction, usually doing something active to take your mind off it, and rumination, which involves thinking about the mood and trying to understand why you are feeling like that. Distraction is likely to lead to an improvement in mood whereas rumination is likely to intensify and prolong the depressed mood. As women are more likely to ruminate and men more likely to distract, this may account for why women are more likely to suffer depression.

Biological factors

Some of the symptoms of depression, such as sleep and appetite disturbance, seem to suggest directly altered functioning of biological systems. As we have seen earlier, for Jaspers (1963) such symptoms were evidence that depression involving these symptoms was an illness and was the result of some dysfunction of the brain. The view that depression, or at least some depressions, are the result of biological dysfunction is still prominent. Several other lines of evidence support this view. Depression has been observed to occur at times of natural biological changes, such as after childbirth or menopause. In addition, drugs which directly alter brain chemistry have been found to be effective in treating depression.

Neurochemistry

Neurochemical views of depression state that depression is caused by insufficiencies of certain neurochemicals that facilitate transmission between neurons. Attention has focused on the monoamines, a class of neurotransmitters that divide into the catechomamines, including dopamine and noradrenaline (commonly called norepinephrine in the USA) and the indoleamines, including serotonin, also called 5HT. The main biological hypothesis has been the **catecholamine hypothesis** which in particular has emphasized the role of low noradrenergic activity. Lack of noradrenaline activity in areas that are important for motivation and pleasure is thought to result in the symptoms of depression. Support for this view comes from the action of anti-depressant drugs. When a neurotransmitter is released and causes the adjacent cell to fire there is then a process whereby the neurotransmitter is neutralized by enzymes which break it down and it is then taken back into the cell. This self-regulating process means that neurones do not go on firing endlessly once started. Until the 1980s there have been two main types of anti-depressants, both of which act upon noradrenaline activity. Monoamine oxidase inhibitors (MAOIs) act by preventing the activity of the enzymes which break down the monoamines (of which noradrenaline is one), thus prolonging the neuronal

activity. Tricylic anti-depressants also prolong noradrenergic activity but do so by preventing the re-uptake of the neurotransmitter into the cell. Can we conclude from this that depression is caused by a lack of noradrenergic activity? The logically correct answer is 'no'. Making inferences about the cause of a disorder from the way its treatment works is called the **treatment-aetiology fallacy**, which is discussed in Chapter 18. Given that our experience is crucially dependent on the activity of our brains it would be very surprising indeed if depression was not associated with some definable neural activity. However, leaving this philosophical issue aside there are more mundane problems with the catecholamine hypothesis. Importantly, the tricyclic anti-depressants and MAOIs are known to have very wide effects, other than their effects on noradrenaline. It may be that their efficacy in treating depression is due to their impact on transmitters other than noradrenaline.

Since the mid-1980s, it has been suggested that in fact it is the reduced activity of one of the indoleamines, serotonin, which is important in depression. Both the MAOIs and the tricyclic anti-depressants are also known to affect serotonin. However, more specific drugs that do not have the global effects of the traditional anti-depressants have been developed. These drugs, called the selective serotonin re-uptake inhibitors (SSRIs), inhibit the re-uptake of serotonin but have negligible effects on noradrenaline and dopamine. If the SSRIs are effective in alleviating depression then this would suggest that serotonin is the key neurotransmitter and that previous anti-depressants were having their effect through altering serotonin function. One such drug is fluoxetine or, as it is more commonly known, Prozac. In fact, the SSRIs are similarly effective in the treatment of depression as older anti-depressants, but are reported as having fewer of the unpleasant side-effects of anti-depressants such as dry mouth, drowsiness and sweating, making it less unpleasant for patients to take. The SSRIs are also less toxic than other anti-depressants and present less of a risk for overdose.

Genetic factors

Depression, like many psychological features, tends to run in families. However, this does not mean that depression is genetically inherited as obviously families share many aspects other than their genes. There are various methods that are used to try to disentangle the effects of genes and environments in causing disorders, which will be discussed in more detail when considering schizophrenia. These methods include comparing rates in identical (monozygotic, MZ) versus non-identical (dyzygotic, DZ) twins. If rates are higher in MZ twins (who have exactly the same genetic make-up) than in DZ twins (who share only some of their genetic make-up) this would suggest a genetic basis to the disorder. Of course, this argument rests on the assumption that identical twins do not have any more similar environments than non-identical twins, an assumption that may not always be valid. Bertelson *et al.* (1977) in a study carried out in Denmark identified over 100 twin pairs in which at least one of the twins had received a diagnosis of mood disorder (depression or manic-depression). The individual identified with the disorder in such studies is called the **proband**. The question of interest was how many times the twin of the proband also had a similar diagnosis. The extent to which the twin shows the same problem is known as the **concordance rate**, which can vary from zero (no consistency) to one (complete consistency). The concordance rates were higher for MZ twins than they were for DZ twins, but this was much more marked for manic-depression (0.69 for MZ twins and 0.16 for DZ twins) than for unipolar depression (0.54 for MZ twins and 0.24 for DZ twins). The conclusion from this study, and from other similar studies, is that genes play a role in depression, but that this role is much clearer in the case of manic-depression than it is in unipolar depression.

Psychological factors

Psychological theories of depression have tended to rely on the dominant paradigm, or way of looking at things, within general psychology. This is clearly illustrated in the history of the concept of learned helplessness, which started life as a theory based on learning from the environment and was revised to accommodate a more central role for cognitions, thus mirroring the move in general psychology from behaviourism to cognitivism. Based on laboratory studies with dogs as subjects, Martin Seligman and his colleagues noticed that when a dog was faced with a stressor (an electric shock in this case) that it was unable to escape, it showed a state resembling depression. Furthermore, when escape became possible in a later similar situation the dog failed to take the opportunity to escape or took a long time to catch on that it was possible. Seligman (1975) termed this phenomenon 'learned helplessness' and suggested that it provided an analogue to human depression, where individuals faced with a stress that they were unable to do anything about would develop depressed mood, lack motivation and fail to perceive positive pos-

sibilities. However, in 1978 the model was modified to take into account the person's interpretation of the cause of the uncontrollable outcome (Abramson *et al.* 1978). That is, people become depressed not simply when something negative and uncontrollable happens but specifically when they attribute the cause to a feature of themselves (internal) that is relatively permanent (stable) and also has implications for other aspects of their lives (global). An example of such an internal, stable and global attribution would be a student explaining his or her poor exam result as arising from a lack of ability, which is more likely to lead to depression than an attribution of, for example, lack of studying. More recently the theory has undergone another revision, called hopelessness theory, which refines some of the features of the model and applies it to a more specific type of depression (Abramson *et al.* 1989). It is not really clear that this latest revision has added anything to the model.

The most influential approach to understanding how particular ways of thinking are involved in depression is the cognitive model of Aaron Beck. Beck, a psychiatrist initially trained within a psychoanalytic framework, began to be struck by the self-critical and pessimistic thoughts his patients reported, cognitions which often appeared to be a distortion of reality. From this observation Beck developed the idea that depression is as much a disorder of thinking as a disorder of mood. Beck's cognitive model of depression proposes that not only is depression characterized by negative ways of thinking (cognitions), but that these cognitions play a causal role in the disorder rather than simply being a symptom of depression. Furthermore, these cognitions are enduring features of a person and will be a vulnerability factor for future depression, even if the person is not depressed currently.

What is the evidence for Beck's cognitive model of depression? There is plenty of evidence showing that depressed people do think negatively. Those who are depressed are self-critical, pessimistic, and dwell on failures (Gotlib and Hammen 1992). However, the other facets of the model are less well supported. Tests of the causal and vulnerability aspects of the model have essentially used two strategies. The first is to take a sample of people who are not currently depressed, measure their cognitions and follow the sample over a period of time to see if those who show negative cognitions, even though not depressed at the time of assessment, are more likely to become depressed at a later date. The main difficulty of this strategy is the scale of the study that would be required. A large number of people would need to be followed up over a long period of time to ensure that there were enough people who became depressed for the results to be reliable. Related, scaled down versions of this have been adopted where it has been observed whether those who relapse after an episode of depression are those who still have negative cognitions even after they have recovered from the other symptoms.

In fact, despite the scale of the undertaking a prospective study was carried out by Peter Lewinsohn and his colleagues in Oregon in the north-west USA (Lewinsohn *et al.* 1981). Lewinsohn and colleagues recruited almost a thousand volunteers from the community and assessed their levels of depression on two occasions, up to twelve months apart. The subjects' cognitions were also assessed on the first occasion, which included their expectancies of positive and negative events in the future, their perception of control over outcomes in their lives and various irrational beliefs thought to be important in depression. What was of interest for the cognitive model was those people who were not depressed on the first occasion but who had become depressed by the time they were seen at follow-up. Were those people more negative in their thinking at the first occasion, which may have accounted for them becoming depressed during the course of the study? The answer was 'no'. The only group to show more negative cognitions at the outset of the study were those who were already depressed at the outset of the study.

The results of Lewinsohn *et al.* (1981) do not support the cognitive model. What can be concluded is that when people are depressed they think negatively but they don't think negatively *before* they become depressed. Other studies have shown that when people recover from depression, their previously negative thinking – beliefs, attitudes, perceptions and memories – is restored to normal (Barber and DeRubeis 1989). The obvious interpretation is that negative cognitions do not play a causal role in depression but rather represent the way that people think when they are depressed. However, some researchers have argued that the answer is not so simple.

Segal and Shaw (1986) argued that the negative cognitions of those who will later become depressed may lie in a latent state, that is be present but unobservable. Not surprisingly, such a view has come in for criticism as it puts forward an escape clause for any studies which fail to find negative cognitions in those vulnerable to depression (Coyne and Gotlib 1983). John Teasdale (1988) has proposed the differential activation

hypothesis to account for the failure to find negative cognitions in those vulnerable to depression. Teasdale's view is based on the assumption that mild depressed mood is common but transient; the normal course is remission or recovery. However what determines whether such normal fluctuations in mood become severe or persistent to the point of clinical depression is the nature of the cognitions that become accessible while the person is in the mild depressed mood. If, while in a depressed mood, what comes to mind are thoughts of self-blame, defeat, pessimism and hopelessness, that depressed mood is unlikely to take the normal course of recovery but rather will intensify and become more severe, even leading to a state of clinical depression. Thus, cognitions do have a causal role, not necessarily in initiating the depressed mood, that can arise for any number of reasons, but in maintaining and intensifying the depressed mood.

Some support for this view comes from a study by Miranda *et al.* (1990). These researchers capitalized on the fact that people who have previously been depressed but have recovered are vulnerable to becoming depressed again and therefore, even though they are not currently depressed, they should still as a group show signs of cognitive vulnerability. However, if Teasdale's differential activation hypothesis is correct then this should be the case only if they are also in a mildly depressed mood. They found that with people who had never previously been depressed, who were therefore not a vulnerable group, their current level of mood showed little relationship to negative cognitions. In contrast, the previously depressed group did show a relationship such that those who were in a mildly depressed mood did show negative cognitions. This finding supports the idea of certain people who are vulnerable to depression having negative cognitions but those cognitions becoming apparent only when they are brought to the surface by a mildly depressed mood.

Social factors

There has been a substantial amount of research on the social factors involved in depression. In many ways this seems the obvious place to look for the source of depression, as many of our changes in mood do seem to reflect what is going on around us. Is it the case that people who become depressed are those who have suffered the greatest amount of adversity or stress in their lives? Research which has looked at the occurrence of negative life events, for example, loss of job, death of spouse, disability, have found that those who are depressed have suffered more such experiences (Paykel 1979). Most commonly these events involve a loss of something important to the person. The way that most of the research is conducted is to compare the amount of such events experienced in a sample of people who are depressed and those who are not. There are a number of possible methodological problems in this approach. As already pointed out, being in a depressed state affects a person's thinking patterns. Specifically, depression has been shown to increase the accessibility of negative memories relative to positive memories (J.M.G. Williams 1992). Therefore, asking people who are depressed about what has happened to them in the recent past may prove to be unreliable. A second problem of this type of retrospective design is the problem of cause and effect. It may be that unhappy things happen to people at least partly because they are depressed. There is in fact evidence to support this, which will be discussed shortly.

The work of George Brown and his colleagues in London probably represents the most systematic attempt to examine the role of social factors in depression while taking into account the sort of methodo- logical problems outlined. Brown and colleagues (G.W. Brown and Harris 1978) developed a comprehensive interview schedule, the Life Events and Difficulties Schedule (LEDS) to assess what had happened to people in the recent past. They found in their sample of women in London that 89 per cent of those who were depressed had experienced what they called a provoking agent, either a very severely threatening acute event or a major chronic difficulty, in the nine months before the onset of depression. In contrast, of the women in their sample who were not depressed at the time of being interviewed, only 30 per cent had experienced similar events. They also found that the risk of depression was greater if, in addition to having experienced an event or difficulty, the woman also had certain background vulnerability factors, the most important of which was the absence of a partner to confide in.

In a second study (described in G.W. Brown 1989), these researchers, rather than relying just on retrospective reports, interviewed a sample of working-class women on two occasions twelve months apart. They were particularly interested in women who became depressed over the course of the study. Again, a very high percentage of the women who became depressed had suffered a severe event, usually associated with loss and often in the few weeks before the onset of their depression. Again, support from those around was important, particularly at time of the crisis. The important elements of this support seemed to be to have someone to confide in who would provide emotional support and who would not react negatively, for example, with criticism. The importance of support from other people as a protective factor has been reinforced by other research (Cohen and Wills 1985).

George Brown (1989) reported that an important aspect of support consisted of not getting a negative reaction from the person providing the support. It has been suggested that, in fact, the lack of negative aspects of relationships is the most important feature of support: 'the apparent benefits of having support may in large part represent freedom from the deleterious effects of relationships that are conflictual, insecure or otherwise not sustaining' (Coyne and Downey 1991: 413). Some support for this view comes from Weissman (1987). Generally, it is found that the risk for depression is higher in those who are divorced and single than those who are married. However, Weissman (1987) found that although those who were married and able to communicate with their spouse were less at risk than those who were single, separated or divorced, the highest risk was found in those who were married but felt unable to communicate with their spouse. Thus, having a close confiding relationship is valuable but better to have no relationship than to have one which is undermining.

The possibility has already been raised that as well as negative events leading to depression, depression might also lead to experiencing more negative events. Coyne (1976) asked subjects to carry out a 20 minute telephone conversation with a stranger and then make various ratings including their own mood state and their willingness to have further contact with the person they had been speaking to. Subjects who had spoken to a depressed patient felt more depressed and hostile at the end of the conversation than those who had conversed with a non-depressed person. Furthermore, those who had spoken to the depressed patient indicated less desire for further contact with that person. What appeared to mediate this effect was the depressed patients' greater tendency to disclose personal details, such as details of medical operations, marital infidelities and life problems. This finding suggests that being depressed may have consequences for how other people respond and may actually lead to having more negative experiences, such as being rejected by other people. With such a negative cycle it is not difficult to see how depression can be so difficult to get out of.

Interactions between factors

Each of the levels of explanation discussed has something to contribute to understanding the cause of depression. What adds to this explanatory power is when we begin to consider the interaction between factors. It is often assumed, as in the diathesis-stress model, that a disorder will result from some inherent vulnerability, often thought to be biological, encountering an environmental trigger. As a position statement few would disagree that the interaction of factors is important in producing depression, or indeed any other psychological disorder. However, demonstrating which particular vulnerabilities interact with which particular stressors is a much more difficult exercise. One study has demonstrated the interaction between cognitive vulnerability and life events in the production of depression. Segal *et al.* (1992) assessed the extent to which recovered depressed patients endorsed dysfunctional attitudes such as 'My value as a person depends greatly on what others think of me' (dependent) and 'If I fail partly it is as bad as being a complete failure' (self-critical). They followed up the subjects over a period of twelve months, assessing what happened to them in that time. The question of interest was to see if they could identify common features of those who relapsed. What accounted for whether someone relapsed or not was the combination of dysfunctional attitudes and a life event that matched that attitude. Someone who was high in self-criticalness was likely to relapse, but only if that person also experienced a negative event involving failure during the time. This study clearly demonstrates the importance of looking at the interaction of social and cognitive factors in depression.

Ψ Section summary

Depression is a common psychological problem that involves a wide range of symptoms, including cognitive, affective and physical symptoms. Research on depression has concentrated on biological, social and cognitive factors. Support for a biological view of depression comes from research on alterations in neurotransmitters such as noradrenaline and serotonin and, in particular, the effectiveness of medications which alter these neurotransmitters. There is also considerable evidence of social factors being important in depression, such as having poor

Box continued

---

social support and experiencing negative life events. Finally, cognitive theories emphasize the importance of certain ways of thinking in depression. These views are not necessarily mutually exclusive and attempts have been made to show how they may interact.

1 What are the main symptoms of depression?
2 What is the evidence for biological, social and cognitive factors being important in causing depression?

❑ Anxiety

Like feelings of depression, the experience of anxiety is very common indeed. Not only is anxiety common in daily life for a very large number of people, but also anxiety is a common element of many other psychological disorders, such as depression and schizophrenia. Anxiety is a feeling but it is experienced very clearly in the body, for example through tensed muscles, sweating, dry mouth and dizziness. Anxiety also has a cognitive component, usually consisting of thoughts about the likelihood of something unpleasant happening in the future. Various researchers have focused on this future-oriented aspect of anxiety as its defining cognitive feature (e.g. Barlow 1988).

A number of other terms tend to go along with anxiety, such as fear, worry and panic. Fear is the term used to describe an emotional state that is aroused in the face of an immediate danger. It builds up quickly, and is usually intense but short lived. Fear, it has been argued, is related to the flight-or-fight response. In other words it is about preparing us to deal with a dangerous situation that requires some rapid response. Panic is closely related to fear. Barlow has suggested that panic is a fear response triggered at an inappropriate time, what he calls a 'false alarm'; like fear, it tends to be associated with strong bodily sensations. Worry, like anxiety, refers to a more diffuse state that is not focused very specifically on an imminent perceived threat but is focused on a range of negative outcomes some of which may be some way ahead in the future. One way of thinking about worry is that it is the cognitive component of anxiety.

Why is anxiety so common, particularly as it is usually a fairly unpleasant experience? The answer seems to be that anxiety is good for us. This is true in a number of ways. First, anxiety may actually help us to perform better in some situations, as long as it is not too severe. The well-known **Yerkes-Dodson law** states that performance is enhanced with mild levels of anxiety but begins to suffer if the anxiety becomes too great. Second, anxiety acts as a way of alerting us to possible danger and thus enables us to take steps to avoid the very thing that we feel anxious about. Part of being human is being able to make plans and anticipate the future and part of being able to think about the future is the capacity to feel anxious or worried about things that might go wrong or might not work out. An inability to experience anxiety might seem like a good thing but it would be a disadvantage in important ways. Just as the inability to experience pain might lead people into harmful situations so would the inability to experience anxiety.

However, having outlined the usefulness of anxiety there are clearly cases where anxiety can become a problem rather than a help. When anxiety reaches a certain extreme point someone can be said to be suffering from an anxiety disorder. There are, in fact, a variety of ways that anxiety is expressed. As research in anxiety has grown there has been a tendency to denote various types of anxiety disorder, all different from each other although all having in common the inappropriate experience of high levels of anxiety. The main types of anxiety disorders are shown in Table 17.2.

Panic disorder is the tendency to experience panic attacks, involving strong physiological reactions such as palpitations, nausea, sweating and dizziness, accompanied by the thought that one is going to die or go mad or lose control. Having experienced such an attack the person becomes anxious and worried about the possibility of future attacks. The case study on Elizabeth illustrates panic disorder (see p. 549). The phobias all have in common a specific focus for the anxiety. In simple phobia, the focus is a very discrete object, for example, snakes or spiders. In agoraphobia, the fear is rather more diffuse but centres around public places, such as shops.

Table 17.2 Main types of anxiety disorders

- Generalized anxiety disorder
- Simple phobia
- Agoraphobia
- Social phobia
- Panic disorder
- Obsessive-compulsive disorder
- Post-Traumatic Stress Disorder

Social phobics may also avoid public places but whereas for the agoraphobic the anxiety stems from a sense of being separated from things which normally make them feel safe and secure, such as familiar people and surroundings, for the socially anxious individual the anxiety is about being noticed and evaluated negatively by others. Post-Traumatic Stress Disorder is the result of having experienced a traumatizing event and developing a set of specific symptoms as a result, such as having flashbacks about the event which are associated with physiological symptoms of anxiety. Generalized anxiety disorder is the name given to anxiety which does not have any of these very specific elements but nevertheless is a tendency to experience anxiety across a wide range of situations and to experience worry frequently. In obsessive-compulsive disorder (OCD) the sufferer is preoccupied to an unusual and unrealistic degree with danger from a particular source (obsession) and takes steps to minimize this danger (compulsion). A common example would be feelings of contamination which have to be dealt with by compulsive washing. Although these different types of anxiety can be identified, they also quite often overlap, with sufferers experiencing more than one type of anxiety.

Biological factors

Like most psychological disorders anxiety tends to run in families. Torgerson (1988) found that anxiety states were around twice as common in first degree relatives of anxious probands than they were in first degree relatives of a control sample. Some twin studies have been carried out to identify whether there is evidence of a genetic influence in this family factor. Torgerson (1988) found evidence of higher concordance in MZ than DZ twins of panic disorder patients but did not find this for generalized anxiety patients, suggesting that the extent of genetic influence will vary in different anxiety disorders. Kendler et al. (1992) also reported higher concordance rates for panic in MZ than DZ twins and found similar effects for other anxiety disorders – agoraphobia, social phobia and simple phobia. Of course, as discussed earlier, there is the possibility that the MZ twins were treated more similarly than the DZ twins, elevating similarities between them, although Torgerson argues that this could not account for his findings. The evidence from twin studies suggests that there might be a genetic basis to anxiety although it does not appear to be that strong.

Ψ Case study

Panic disorder: 'I thought I was going to die'

Elizabeth was a 44-year-old woman who was referred to a clinical psychologist by her family doctor. She had seen her doctor on a number of occasions complaining of times when she felt that she was going to die and wondering if there was anything wrong with her heart. Elizabeth had first felt these sensations when she was driving in her car one day. She felt hot and began to feel dizzy and faint. She pulled into the side of the road but the feeling just seemed to get worse. She became increasingly aware that her heart was pounding very fast and she began to struggle for breath. The thought started going through her mind that she was going to die, which just made the feelings worse. Somehow she managed to get through it and made her

way home, where she felt much better. There was no obvious reason for her to feel like this, although she had recently been under some strain at work. Her second panic attack happened when she was lying in bed one night and became aware of her heart beating. Her mind immediately went back to the incident in the car and soon she was feeling much worse, thinking that she was about to have a heart attack. Since then, she had become very preoccupied with the possibility of another attack and had also started to avoid driving whenever possible. After a period of treatment with cognitive-behavioural therapy (see Chapter 18), she was much more able to deal with such feelings, recognizing that the way she misinterpreted her bodily sensations was crucial in producing the feelings of panic.

Neurological factors

Certain areas of the brain are implicated in anxiety. Gray (1982) has pieced together various bits of evidence to argue that certain sub-cortical areas, mainly the hippocampus and septal area, are involved in anxiety. Two neurotransmitters are particularly important for the functioning of this system – noradrenaline and serotonin, which carry information from lower brain centres, the locus ceoruleus in the case of noradrenaline and the raphe nuclei in the case of serotonin. Much of the evidence for Gray's theory is based on the effectiveness of drugs that reduce anxiety (anxiolytics). Anxiolytics reduce locus ceoruleus and noradrenergic activity whereas certain drugs that increase locus ceoruleus and noradrenergic activity can induce anxiety (Redmond 1985). Gray calls these brain areas involved in anxiety the behavioural inhibition system (BIS) as one of the main effects of anxiety is to inhibit behaviour.

Many of Gray's conclusions derive from work carried out on animals, mainly rats, and it is therefore also an assumption of this work that anxiety is essentially similar across different species. Applying this model to human anxiety leads to the conclusion that people who are prone to anxiety have a highly reactive BIS. Redmond (1985) has pointed out that differences in noradrenergic locus ceoruleus activity may arise for a

number of reasons. First, there may be genetically influenced differences in the inherited reactivity of this system. Second, repeated exposure to threatening stimuli may alter the sensitivity of this system, making it more prone to activity. Finally, the prolonged experience of anxiety itself may alter the sensitivity of the system. Thus, genetic or environmental influences could lead to a more reactive neural system which causes the experience of anxiety. Redmond (1985) views this system as being like an alarm that goes off to signal danger. One way to think of it is that some people have alarms that trigger more easily, sometimes even in the absence of any real threat. These are the people who will suffer from excessive anxiety.

It is an open question as to how well this sort of account which emphasizes the role of lower brain centres can account for human anxiety. In human anxiety there is typically a marked linguistic aspect, for example, worrying about something. Gray (1982) suggests that there are two routes to anxiety. One is the ascending pathways from the lower brain centres (locus ceoruleus and raphe nuclei) to the septo-hippocampal system; the second is from descending pathways from the cortex, which may be particularly important in humans and reflect the more conscious, verbal aspect of anxiety. However, he has little to say about this second route.

A similar view of accounting for anxiety through the inappropriate activity of fairly primitive neural systems has been given by Rapoport (1988) for obsessive-compulsive disorder. Rapoport suggests that OCD involves activity of the basal ganglia area of the mid-brain. Indirect evidence for this comes for the greater incidence of ticks and movement disorders found in OCD sufferers, and the basal ganglia is known to be involved in controlling movement. More direct evidence comes from brain scanning studies of OCD patients, which have found higher levels of brain activity in the frontal lobes and cingulate pathways which connect to the basal ganglia. Rapoport suggests that OCD represents the inappropriate triggering of neuro-motor programmes which are automatic and stored in the brain. These patterns, such as checking and grooming, have evolved as being important in survival and so are stored in the brain. However, if these patterns are triggered off by inappropriate brain activity in the relevant regions there is no mechanism for shutting them off.

Social factors

Experience of traumatic events in producing anxiety has a long history in psychology, particularly in the formation of phobias. Early behaviourist formulations of anxiety stressed the importance of conditioning experiences which relied on exposure to a negative event in the environment. This early experience becomes internalized through a process of conditioning and so the fear is reproduced in later situations in which the threat is absent. The psychological details of this process will be discussed in the next section but the important point here is the stress on environmental events.

There is evidence that social factors or life experiences do play a role in anxiety. By definition, experience of severely threatening events is a major cause of Post-Traumatic Stress Disorder. But, in other anxiety disorders life events have also been found to be important. Finlay-Jones and Brown (1981) interviewed a sample of women attending their general practice surgery. Some women met criteria for anxiety (general), some met criteria for depression and some met criteria for both. The women who met criteria had experienced significantly more negative life events in the preceding year than those who did not meet criteria for disorder. However, there was also some specificity in that the depressed women had experienced more events involving a loss, whereas the anxious women had experienced the sorts of events that involved a threat, such as a partner threat-

ening to leave them. Those meeting criteria for both depression and anxiety had experienced both types of events. A study by Surtees (1995) supports this finding. Surtees (1995) reports a study that followed up a group of women whose husband either had had a non-fatal heart attack or had died. Onset of psychiatric disorder in both groups was greater than that found in a control group. However, the onset disorder in the group whose husbands had a heart attack was mainly anxiety whereas in the bereaved group the onset disorder was very largely depression. The results are consistent with the view of anxiety as primarily a response to the possibility of something threatening happening in the future, whereas depression is a response to a loss that has already happened.

Psychological factors

As already mentioned, the role of what is learned from experience has long been seen as important in anxiety. Learning theory early on stressed the role of conditioning in the acquisition of fears and phobias. In the well-cited study (Watson and Rayner 1920), Little Albert, an 11-month-old boy, was conditioned to show fear to a tame white rat. After being presented with the rat and showing no fear the experimenter produced a loud, unpleasant noise whenever Albert went to touch the rat. Soon, Albert began to be afraid of the rat. Via **classical conditioning** (see also Chapter 3) Albert had learned to respond to a previously non-threatening object with fear through its having been paired or associated with an unpleasant stimulus (the loud noise). Although this study has since proved to be difficult to replicate, it was influential as a model of how phobias might be acquired.

The type of learning shown by Albert is classical conditioning. A second process of learning, **operant conditioning**, describes how behaviour patterns develop through the consequences of that behaviour. When a particular response is followed by something desirable (reward) the person is more likely to make that response again; when, however, it is followed by an unpleasant outcome (punishment) the response is less likely to happen again. Most importantly in the case of anxiety, the reward can be the avoidance or reduction of something unpleasant. This is called **negative reinforcement**. Negative reinforcement is often confused with punishment but the two are quite different. In punishment, a response is followed by something unpleasant making that response less likely to occur in the future. In negative reinforcement a response is followed by something desirable, making the response more likely to occur again, but the desirable outcome is the reduction or avoidance of something unpleasant. The agoraphobic who every time he or she gets to the door to go out of the house feels anxious and decides not to go out is negatively reinforcing staying in the house because of the feeling of relief that occurs each time. Putting classical and operant conditioning together leads to a nice account of anxiety. Through classical conditioning someone learns to associate a particular situation with a fear or anxiety. Then, in order to avoid those feelings the person avoids the situation thus preventing him or herself from feeling anxious but leaving the learned association in place. Later accounts extended the initial learning stage to include observational learning from others rather than having to experience something directly (Bandura 1969a).

Anxiety and cognition

Learning theory has provided a reasonable account of some of the simpler aspects of anxiety, such as specific phobias, and has also been extremely useful in elucidating the role played by avoidance in maintaining anxiety which has led to effective treatments. However, anxiety is a complex state which involves cognitions about danger as well as automatic learned associations. There is now considerable evidence that cognitions are important in anxiety. Research has focused on a number of aspects of cognition such as attention, interpretation of ambiguity and judgements of risk likelihood. Clinical and anecdotal evidence suggests that anxious individuals are more likely to attend to or notice threatening information in the environment. Reading a newspaper, the attention of the anxious person might well be drawn to the story about the increase in fatal road accidents, even if it is a small story printed in the corner. A clever experiment by Colin MacLeod et al. (1986) set out to examine the evidence for this sort of phenomenon. In their experiment, anxious and non-anxious subjects were presented with two words together, one above the other, on a computer screen. They were asked to read the top word aloud. The words went off the screen and sometimes a dot replaced the space where one of the words had been. Whenever a dot appeared subjects had to press a button as soon as they saw it. How quickly subjects saw the dot gave an indication of where they had been attending on the screen: if they were quick to notice a dot appearing in the location of the top word, it would suggest that their attention had remained on that

spot; if they were quick to notice a dot when it appeared at the lower (supposedly ignored) location, then it would show that their attention had wandered to that location. The results showed that if the dot replaced a negative word, such as 'cancer' or 'useless', the anxious subjects were faster than if it replaced a neutral word. The non-anxious subjects were faster to notice a dot whenever it replaced a neutral word. These results provide support for the idea that in anxious individuals show some preference to attending to or noticing negative information whereas non-anxious individuals show a tendency for the opposite. MacLeod and Mathews (1988) found a similar effect in highly anxious medical students, especially when they were tested in the week before an exam. The generally anxious students, who were also in a higher than usual state of anxiety leading up to the exam, were faster to notice the dot when it replaced words like 're-sit' and 'inferior', showing that they had been attending more to those words than to other neutral words. Interestingly, students who reported that they were not usually anxious showed the opposite effect: as they became more anxious towards the exam they showed more of a tendency to avoid the exam-related words.

Much of what happens to us in real life is ambiguous and needs to be interpreted in some way. It is possible that where there are a number of ways of interpreting something, the anxious person will tend to interpret in a more negative, threatening way. Psychology has a long history of trying to make inferences about a person's mental life from the way he or she interprets ambiguous situations. A well-known example of this is the Rorschach inkblot tests where what people see in an ambiguous inkblot is supposed to reveal something about their mental life. Mathews et al. (1989) carried out an experimental study of interpretation bias in anxiety. They had anxious and non-anxious individuals listen to a tape recording of someone reading a number of words aloud. The words were all homophones. Homophones are words that sound the same but are actually two different words, with different meanings. Of interest for this study is that one of the homophone pair had a negative meaning and the other a neutral meaning. Examples of these homophones are shown in Table 17.3.

All subjects showed a tendency to interpret the spoken word in its negative meaning but this tendency was greater in the anxious patients, thus confirming the impression that anxious individuals interpret ambiguous information in a negative direction.

Table 17.3 Homophones which have a neutral and negative meaning

Die/dye
Slay/sleigh
Foul/fowl
Moan/mown
Groan/grown
Liar/lyre
Bore/boar
Pain/pane
Weak/week
Skull/scull
Tease/teas
Bury/berry
Guilt/gilt
Flu/flew

Interactions between factors

Learning theory accounts of anxiety are based on an interaction of social and psychological factors. Anxiety is seen as resulting from psychological processes of learning operating upon social or environmental events. Cook and Mineka (1989) report an elegant experiment that addressed the issue of whether phobias are learned, i.e. a social-psychological explanation, or innate, i.e. a biological explanation. The most obvious argument against phobias being innate is that not everyone has them. However, against the learning position is the fact that phobias frequently tend to be about certain themes. People experience phobic reactions about spiders and snakes but not guns or knives, which are equally or even more dangerous. In addition, many people suffering from phobias cannot report any particular experience where they acquired the fear. Cook and Mineka (1989) developed an experimental procedure to test the idea that phobias are a combination of learning and innateness. This view is known as 'preparedness' because although learning is important the learning can act only upon certain innate pre-prepared responses. Learning is known to be important in the acquisition of fears because whereas young laboratory-reared monkeys do not show fear of snakes, monkeys in the wild do. Furthermore, if young laboratory-reared monkeys are allowed to observe older monkeys behaving fearfully in the presence of snakes then they will also show fear when confronted with a snake. However, both the simple learning view and the preparedness view are consistent with this finding. Cook and Mineka (1989)

 Research update

Bridging the gap from the laboratory to daily life

One criticism of the research on cognitive processes in anxiety is that it is artificial. For example, presenting people with anxiety-relevant words and observing their reaction does not relate very closely to anything that might happen in daily life. Researchers have tried to bridge the gap between the laboratory and daily life in a number of ways. One study by Lundh and Ost (1996) was concerned with whether anxiety is related to a bias in remembering anxiety-related material. Previous studies have tended to examine this issue by presenting anxious subjects with anxious words and later on testing their memory for these words. Lundh and Ost (1996) did not use words but instead used faces with different expressions. Their subjects were socially anxious individuals, whose main concern is known to centre around disapproval or negative eval-

uation from other people. Thus, faces with an angry or disapproving expression should be particularly salient for socially anxious individuals. Subjects were presented with pictures of faces and were asked to say how critical or accepting the person looked. Five minutes later, subjects were given an unexpected recognition memory test, where they were presented with some of the faces from the earlier phase and some new faces, and they had to say which ones they had seen before. The socially anxious subjects recognized more of the critical than the accepting faces, whereas a control group of non-anxious subjects showed the opposite tendency of recognizing more accepting than critical faces. Clearly, much more needs to be done to make such laboratory experiments more valid in how they relate to real life, but laboratory researchers are at least beginning to make steps in this direction.

showed young, laboratory-reared monkeys film of an adult monkey behaving fearfully, either towards a toy crocodile or towards a toy rabbit (the videos were spliced to produce the fear response to the rabbit). Having been exposed to the films, the young monkeys learned to show fear when faced with a similar toy crocodile but did not show fear when faced with a similar toy rabbit. Thus, it appears that learning is important in the acquisition of fear but only for certain stimuli which are already innately programmed to be feared.

ψ Section summary

Anxiety is not a uniform problem, but, rather, there are a number of different types of anxiety disorder. Research on the causes of anxiety has focused on brain processes (altered levels of noradrenergic activity) and psychological factors such as cognitive processes (e.g. interpretation of ambiguity and attention to threat) and learning processes. Social factors have not been found to be as identified with anxiety as they have with depression. As with depression, interactions between different types of factors offers the best chance of understanding anxiety.

1   What are the main anxiety disorders and what are their symptoms?

2   Does any approach to anxiety (biological, social, cognitive) offer more of an explanation of anxiety than the others?

☐ Schizophrenia

When we think of psychological disorder or 'madness' what probably comes to mind is the picture of someone who is suffering from schizophrenia. The symptoms of schizophrenia are in fact very varied and there is no single symptom or constellation of symptoms that characterizes all those who are suffering from schizophrenia. This has led to a debate about whether this heterogeneity points to the existence of different disorders or to different manifestations of the same disorder, a debate which continues. The symptoms can be roughly divided into two types: positive symptoms and negative symptoms. Positive symptoms, also known as psychotic symptoms, can be thought of as the presence of things

which are not usually part of normal human experience, and negative symptoms as the absence of things which are a usual part of human experience. The main symptoms are shown in Table 17.4.

Thought disorder is reflected in ideas which are often bizarre, such as delusions, as illustrated in the case study of David. The person's thoughts are also difficult to follow because the way the ideas are expressed is often disjointed. Disorders of perception refer mainly to hallucinations, usually hearing voices when no one is speaking. An example of incongruous affect would be laughing inappropriately. The negative symptoms are in some ways like some of the symptoms of depression. The person suffering from schizophrenia will often be uninterested in any activity and will often want to be left alone. Some of the symptoms are shown in the case study of David (see Case study on page 554).

Descriptions of symptoms such as those outlined in the case study have been around for a long time. However, it was only in the late nineteenth century that Emil Kraepelin proposed that some of these symptoms should be thought of as belonging together and constituting a distinct disorder, which he called 'dementia praecox'. Kraepelin called the disorder dementia praecox because he thought that the main characteristics were that the disorder had an early onset (praecox) and invariably ended up with severe intellectual deterioration (dementia). This course of early onset and severe intellectual decline was the disorder's defining feature. The term 'schizophrenia' was coined by a Swiss psychiatrist, Eugene Bleuler, who agreed with much of Kraepelin's description of the symptoms but disagreed with the necessity of an early onset and the inevitability of intellectual decline. As such, dementia praecox was an inappropriate term. For Bleuler, a key defining

Table 17.4 Main symptoms of schizophrenia, divided into positive and negative types

Positive symptoms
- disorders of thought (form and content)
- disorders of perception
- incongruity of affect

Negative symptoms
- lack of responsiveness
- social withdrawal
- lack of motivation

ψ Case study

The rock star who never was

David was a student in his early twenties who was admitted to hospital after becoming increasingly unable to cope. The first signs of a problem had been when he began not handing in work, not turning up to classes and becoming increasingly isolated. When asked, he complained of having no energy and of not being able to concentrate. However, he also had some more bizarre complaints, one of which was that he felt that there was something large in his mouth, probably a stopper of some kind which had been put there. He had also written a love letter to one of his tutors and became convinced that he was going to be punished for this by being castrated. He became increasingly agitated and fearful and so was admitted to the local psychiatric hospital. David was also convinced that he was a rock star. One of the justifications he gave for this was that he had seen himself being interviewed on TV and he could think of no explanation for this other than that he was a rock star. When asked, he also said that he must be a rock star because he hadn't done anything else with his life. He thought that he was being treated to make him forget about being a rock star because it was a stressful occupation and the doctors thought it was not good for him. Upon being admitted to hospital David underwent a programme of treatment which is discussed in Chapter 18.

---

feature was the splitting of associations, reflected in speech that was difficult to follow as it jumped about rather than followed a single train of thought. This gave rise to the term schizophrenia which means split mind. One unfortunate effect of using the term schizophrenia is that it has given rise to much confusion, where it is taken to mean split personality, that is, someone who has two or more personalities, something which has absolutely nothing to do with schizophrenia. There have been further disagreements about what constitute the key symptoms of schizophrenia. Modern diagnostic systems such as DSM-IV encompass the range of symptoms and also emphasize impairment in social or occupational functioning and a long duration (six months or more) in order to qualify for the diagnosis.

Epidemiological studies have estimated that about 1 per cent of the population at some time in their lives will experience schizophrenia. The first occasion, or onset, is typically in adolescence or early adulthood and the rate drops off after about age 35. The actual outcome upon experiencing schizophrenia is highly variable. About 30 per cent make a good recovery, another 30 per cent suffer repeated episodes and the remainder tend to have chronic relapses (Oltmanns and Emery 1995).

Biological factors

Genetics

It has long been observed that schizophrenia tends to run in families. Of course, this does not necessarily point to a genetic basis as families share environments as well as genes. Typically, studies will take a schizophrenia proband and then assess the extent to which other members of the family also suffer from schizophrenia, either by examining hospital records or, preferably, interviewing family members. Gottesman (1991) pooled data from a large number of studies of this kind and found that the closer the genetic link between the family member and the proband, the greater the risk of that family member suffering schizophrenia. For example, second degree relatives of a proband, such as nephews or grandchildren, have about a 5 per cent risk of having schizophrenia; first degree relatives, such as siblings, have a 9 per cent risk. It is the twin data that are the most compelling. Dizygotic twins (who are no more alike genetically than siblings) had a concordance rate (i.e. both suffering) of 17 per cent whereas monozygotic twins (who have identical genetic make-up) had a concordance rate of 48 per cent. Of course, it could be argued that MZ twins, being much more alike than DZ twins, are likely to be treated more similarly and it is therefore not surprising that they show greater concordance. Interestingly, the fact that DZ twins show almost twice the concordance rate of siblings, despite not sharing any more of their genetic make-up, adds some weight to this argument.

In order to further try to disentangle environmental and genetic contributions, studies have focused on children who have been adopted. In the Danish Adoption Study (Kety 1987), the rates of schizophrenia were compared in proband's biological relatives (with whom they shared genes but not environments) and their adopted relatives (with whom they shared environments but not genes). Rates were higher in biological relatives than adopted relatives, strengthening the argument for a genetic rather than an environmental interpretation of the family studies. Although twin studies do point to a genetic influence in schizophrenia, they also point to the limitations of this influence. MZ twins, even where raised together, show a concordance of about 50 per cent leaving half of the variance to be explained. That is, out of every 100 pairs of identical twins, where one of the twin has schizophrenia only half the other of the pair will develop it. A major weakness of the genetic argument has been the failure to find a genetic basis for schizophrenia. Claims have been made to have found the gene or group of genes responsible but these have not been replicated, either by other researchers or even the same researchers carrying out a follow-up study. It is possible that a single gene will be discovered or that schizophrenia will turn out to be a **polygenic disorder**, that is, one which is under the control of a combination of different genes rather than a single gene.

Brain structure

The second main biological thrust in schizophrenia research is to examine directly the brains of schizophrenia sufferers. If there is a direct biological basis to schizophrenia, then in principle there should be some observable difference in brain structure or process. Examining brains is directly dependent on technology. Research which has used static brain imaging techniques, such as CT scans, have sometimes observed enlarged ventricles (cavities filled with cerebrospinal fluid) in the brains of schizophrenia sufferers. Some studies have also found reduced size in limbic structures, which are known to be involved in emotion. More

recently, imaging techniques such as positron emission topography (PET) or regional cerebral blood flow (rCBF) have been developed which enable pictures of the brain to be taken that show activity over a period of time. Using these techniques, people can be asked to carry out certain tasks and activity of brain areas monitored. Some studies have found lower than average activity in areas of the frontal cortex in schizophrenic subjects when performing tasks which normally utilize frontal cortex activity (Weinberger et al. 1986). This would suggest a particular deficit of frontal cortex activity in schizophrenia. However, other research has found deficits in temporal cortex activity as well. Given the inconsistencies of research findings as well as the fact that the frontal and temporal lobes together constitute a very large area of the brain it may be fairer to say that the neurological studies point to diffuse rather than specific structural impairment.

Neurochemistry

The third main biological approach has been to try to understand schizophrenia in terms of neurotransmitter activity. A major factor in driving this research was the success of certain drugs called neuroleptics in reducing the positive symptoms of schizophrenia. An appealing logic is that if certain drugs reduce symptoms by changing particular neurochemical patterns then those neurochemical patterns must form the basis of the symptoms. As discussed earlier, this is an example of the treatment–aetiology fallacy. Nevertheless, the action of the neuroleptics may shed some valuable light on neural processes in schizophrenia. Indirect evidence that neuroleptics work by reducing dopamine activity is provided by the finding that prolonged use of neuroleptics can lead to the sort of motor problems generally associated with Parkinson's disease, such as tremors and rigidity. Parkinson's disease is known to be related to reduced dopamine activity and treatment consists of L-DOPA, a drug which increases dopamine activity. Second, overuse of amphetamines can lead to a psychotic state which closely resembles the positive symptoms of schizophrenia. Amphetamines work by increasing dopamine activity. It is therefore possible that an excess of dopamine is central to, and perhaps even the cause, of schizophrenia. Direct evidence for the dopamine hypothesis using PET scans was found by a US study (Wong et al. 1986) which found that schizophrenic patients had an excess of dopamine (D2) receptors. However, other studies have failed to replicate this finding. More recently, clozapine, a drug which works by blocking a different neurotransmitter, serotonin, has been found to be an effective treatment in otherwise drug-resistant schizophrenic patients. The neurochemical substrate of schizophrenia is likely to involve a complex interaction of neurotransmitter activity rather than any single neurotransmitter.

There has been a vast amount of research on the biological aspects of schizophrenia, from genetic, neurological and neurochemical stances. There are problems with this research, many of them stemming from findings which prove to be unreliable when attempts are made to replicate them. What is clear is that sometimes a biological difference between a group of schizophrenia sufferers and a control group can be found. However, what is equally clear is that these findings are so broad that they are of no value in deciding whether an individual is suffering from schizophrenia or not. Oltmanns and Emery (1995) give the example of a pair of discordant MZ twins, one of whom was found to have ventricles that were five times larger than those of his twin. Unfortunately for the study, the twin with the enlarged ventricles had never had any problem with mental disorder whereas his twin with the smaller ventricles had suffered from schizophrenia for 20 years.

Psychological factors

A number of researchers have questioned the utility or validity of the concept of schizophrenia (e.g. Boyle 1990). One consequence has been to focus on individual symptoms of schizophrenia, such as delusions or hallucinations (Bentall 1990), and to try to understand those particular phenomena rather than schizophrenia as a whole. Since the late 1980s a number of researchers have tried to understand the psychological basis of delusions and hallucinations. It is interesting to note that this is an impossible enterprise according to Jaspers (1963) for whom the definition of a delusion was that it was not explicable in psychological terms. For Jaspers (1963) delusions were the result of organic (brain) disturbance; if they were explicable in psychological terms then they were delusion-like ideas rather than delusions. However, most researchers would now accept that delusions are psychologically meaningful. Maher (1988) has suggested that delusions arise as a result of people trying to make sense of abnormal experiences. Due to a dysfunction of basic perceptual systems, the person experiences perceptual anomalies – highly vivid and intense sensory experiences. These experiences are pro-

duced by a basic biological dysfunction and do not correspond to events happening in the environment. The person then tries to make sense of these anomalous experiences using normal reasoning processes, which often results in delusions as the only way of making sense of the experience. The case of David (discussed in the case study) reasoning he must be a rock star because he had seen himself being interviewed on TV is a good example of Maher's ideas. The delusional beliefs are reinforced by their anxiety-reducing function through reducing uncertainty and confusion. Some delusions are grandiose, where people feel they have a special status or mission, and may function as protection from depressive feelings (Winters and Neale 1983).

Garety and Hemsley (1994) put forward a psychological model of delusions that emphasizes the overreliance on current experience at the expense of past experience. The person prone to delusions will jump to some conclusion on the basis of what is happening at that moment, ignoring all that has happened in the past that would contradict that conclusion. Frith (1987) has emphasized a basic disorder of attention and the information that reaches consciousness. Frith suggested a breakdown of the system that monitors the link between one's action and one's own intentions. Thus, those who are suffering delusions feel that their behaviour is being controlled when in fact what is happening is that they are not picking up on the fact that they themselves are the source of those thoughts and actions. It should be noted that this monitor of the link between intentions and actions normally operates at a preconscious process, that is, the person is not aware of its operation. Like all theories, the test of the usefulness of theories such as Frith's and Garety and Hemsley's is whether they lead to new understanding of the phenomena rather than simply offering a new and sophisticated way of describing the phenomena.

Social factors

The classic study by Faris and Dunham (1939) pointed to the importance of social factors in schizophrenia. Faris and Dunham (1939) looked at the addresses of patients admitted to psychiatric hospitals in Chicago. They found that certain areas where there was high social deprivation were over-represented, and this was especially true for schizophrenic patients. They concluded that social deprivation causes mental disorder. Of course, the other obvious interpretation is that, on the contrary, schizophrenia causes social deprivation.

Plate 17.3 Studies by Faris and Durham (1939) showed the importance of social factors in schizophrenia, with a high incidence of social deprivation among schizophrenic patients

Schizophrenia is a debilitating condition that makes it extremely difficult to function at a high enough level to maintain social position. This latter explanation is known as the **drift hypothesis** because it suggests that schizophrenia produces a downward social drift in those suffering from it. There have been no definitive answers to this issue. It is not difficult to see how a debilitating condition like schizophrenia would have important social consequences. However, it is equally clear that the environment is important in affecting schizophrenia. G.W. Brown and Birley (1968) found that an acute schizophrenic breakdown tended to be associated with the occurrence of preceding life events. Interestingly, these life events could be either positive or negative. In schizophrenia it appears to be the degree of change or disruption caused by the events that is important, rather than that the events are negative.

A second line of research has shown that schizophrenia sufferers are highly sensitive to what is going on in their environment. G.W. Brown et al. (1972) found that although schizophrenia does tend to be a relapsing condition, rates of relapse after discharge from hospital were highly variable and tended to be associated with certain environmental factors. There was a higher rate of relapse in those patients who went back to families where there were a lot of critical comments and hostility directed towards them, combined with a high degree of overinvolvement in their lives by the other family members. This combination of criticism, hostility and overinvolvement was termed **expressed emotion** (EE). The relapse rates in high EE homes was 58 per cent compared with 10 per cent in low EE homes. Reducing the amount of face to face contact with the other household members and maintaining the patient on medication reduced the relapse rates in high EE homes to a similar rate to low EE homes (Vaughn and Leff 1976). There is in fact a long line of research looking into the families of schizophrenia sufferers, some of which has attributed the cause of the schizophrenia to the behaviour of family members. For example, Wynne and Singer (1963) argued that the parents of schizophrenics have abnormal communication patterns which result in the child failing to develop normal ways of thinking and communicating. However, evidence has been unable to clearly establish a causal link between abnormal parental behaviour and the development of schizophrenia. What the EE research shows is that ways of relating to the person are important in the course of the disorder, but they do not show that high EE is the cause of schizophrenia.

Those vulnerable to schizophrenia are clearly overly sensitive to stimulation in their surrounding environment. However, too little social stimulation seems to exacerbate the negative symptoms of schizophrenia, leading to greater social withdrawal, blunting of affect and poverty of speech. It appears that schizophrenia is related to a narrower band of acceptable stimulation than is usual and finding the correct band for each individual is of major importance in therapeutic interventions.

> ### ψ Section summary
>
> Schizophrenia is one of the most debilitating of psychological disorders. Symptoms, such as hallucinations and delusions, represent more of a break from normal experience than do the symptoms of depression or anxiety. For this reason, many have suggested that schizophrenia has a biological basis and is genetically transmitted. However, social factors, such as family style and life events, have also been found to be important factors; more recently research has begun to focus on cognitive aspects of schizophrenia.
>
> 1 Describe the main positive and negative symptoms of schizophrenia.
>
> 2 Is there any evidence that schizophrenia has a biological basis?

❏ Personality disorder

There is a class of psychological disorder where the disorder is seen not so much as something which happens to the person but rather as something more integral to the person. In the case of personality disorders the person's personality is itself considered to be disordered. Furthermore, the disorder is **ego-syntonic** rather than **ego-dystonic**, that is, typically the person does not feel that he or she has a problem.

Personality disorder is also the area of psychopathology where more than any other the influence of societal values can be clearly observed. Not surprisingly, the personality disorders are very controversial. A study by Lewis and Appleby (1988) illustrated the kind of value labelling that is associated with personality disorder. They gave a number of psychiatrists a short vignette description of a person who was suffering some of the symptoms of depression. Some psychiatrists' vignettes included a statement that the person had previously been given a diagnosis of personality disorder, and some did not. On the basis of the vignette the psychiatrist had to make a number of ratings. Those ratings were significantly more unfavourable when the personality disorder label was included: they rated the person as less likely to respond to treatment, said the cause of the problem was more under the person's control, and judged that the person was being manipulative rather than suffering. Not surprisingly given their other judgements, the raters also judged the person to be less deserving of National Health Service resources. This study falls short of showing that personality disorder is constructed by the attitudes of professionals but does indicate a clear negative stereotype that is likely to be harmful therapeutically.

Historically, personality disorder tended to be associated with psychopathy, which is sometimes now called anti-social personality disorder or sociopathic personality disorder in the United States. Now, there are descriptions of a number of personality disorders; the DSM-IV lists ten different types of personality disorder. These types tend to fall into three clusters and are shown in Table 17.5. In fact, with each revision of the DSM, more personality disorders appear, raising the question of whether these are real entities that are being discovered or whether they represent a trend to pathologize behaviour which is deemed unacceptable according to societal values.

Table 17.5 Personality disorders listed in DSM-IV

Cluster A: odd/eccentric type
- paranoid
- schizoid
- schizotypal

Cluster B: dramatic/emotional/erratic type
- anti-social
- borderline
- histrionic
- narcissistic

Cluster C: anxious/fearful type
- avoidant
- dependent
- obsessive-compulsive

Case study

The greatest (undiscovered) researcher in the world

Stephanie was a young researcher who was determined to get ahead in her chosen field of cell biology. She was convinced that she would achieve greatness if only other people would recognize her genius and stop blocking her path. In her view, her superior ability meant that she was not bound by the normal rules, such as giving other people credit for their ideas. She would quite happily pass off work as her own, when in fact it had been the work of other people in her department. Her colleagues were also beginning to suspect her of fabricating research data.

Stephanie's attitude toward her colleagues was dismissive, except for when she wanted them to do something for her, which she regarded as her right rather than a favour. If things did not work out exactly as she wanted she was likely to go into a rage or sulk (very publicly) for days. Only when there was someone very important or high ranking in the organization did she show any concern with making a good impression. Stephanie went through a number of different jobs, each time blaming everyone else for her lack of success in them and for the failure to be recognized as the genius she thought she was, which recognition never materialized.

The detailed features of all the various personality disorders are to be found in textbooks such as Oltmanns and Emery (1995) or Kendall and Hammen (1995). Rather like reading a medical textbook and deciding that we have the symptoms of a major illness, consideration of the symptoms of the personality disorders can make it seem as if everyone must be suffering from a personality disorder. Some of the disorders represent extreme versions of ordinary tendencies. For example, paranoid personality disorder refers to people who are overly suspicious and mistrusting, and those with a narcissistic personality disorder, as illustrated in the case study of Stephanie, have a greatly exaggerated sense of their own importance. However, the diagnosis requires a number of symptoms to occur together and to occur over a long period of time.

How many people can be considered to be suffering from diagnosable personality disorder? Casey and Tyrer (1986) assessed a community sample of urban adults using a structured interview; at the time of being interviewed 13 per cent of the sample met diagnostic criteria for personality disorder. The most common subtype was obsessional personality disorder. Other epidemiological studies have found higher rates in selected groups, for example, between 48 per cent and 65 per cent, mainly of the borderline type, in suicide attempters (Casey 1989). A number of studies have looked at the rates of personality disorders in prisoners, and found very varying rates, between 20 per cent and 70 per cent, mainly of psychopathic disorder , depending on the sample and the diagnostic criteria used (Gunn et al. 1978).

One of the major criticisms of personality disorder is that they are inappropriately treated as categories rather than as dimensions. A categorical approach takes the view that there is a clear dividing line between normal and abnormal: people either meet the criteria for a disorder or they do not. First, as indicated earlier, some of the features of personality disorder appear to be extreme examples of normally distributed characteristics. Second, some critics have argued that the different categories of personality disorders are bad categories. Widiger and Costa (1994) pointed out the high degree of overlap between categories. For example, about half of those meeting criteria for borderline personality disorder also meet criteria for schizotypal personality disorder, or anti-social personality disorder, or histrionic personality disorder. Widiger and colleagues have argued for a dimensional view of the personality disorders where rather than a number of different categories, individuals are rated on a number of personality dimensions. Widiger and Costa (1994)

have shown how the categories can be reduced to the Five Factor model of personality (see Chapter 14). So, for example, paranoid personality disorder would consist of low extraversion/positive affect, low openness and very low agreeableness. Narcissistic personality disorder would comprise high neuroticism/negative affect, high extraversion, very low agreeableness and high conscientiousness.

Psychopathic personality disorder

Although research has been carried out on the different personality disorders, most research relates to the psychopathic personality disorder. There has long been a recognition that there are certain people who lie, steal, cheat, and generally do not conform to the norms that govern society but who seem to differ from ordinary criminals. In the nineteenth century, such people were thought to suffer from a disorder of the will, termed moral insanity (Prichard 1837, cited in Rosenhan and Seligman 1995). The key features of someone suffering from moral insanity was the preservation of normal intellectual functioning in the absence of any adherence to codes of moral decency. The classic description of the psychopathic personality is to be found in Hervey Cleckley's *The Mask of Sanity* (1988), first published in the 1940s. From studying a number of cases, Cleckley outlined 16 criteria. Some of the main criteria are shown in Table 17.6.

Table 17.6 Cleckley's major criteria for psychopathic personality disorder

Superficial charm, intelligence
Unreliability, no sense of responsibility
Untruthfulness and insincerity
Lack of remorse, no sense of shame
Impulsive, poorly planned anti-social behaviour
Lack of life plan
Poor judgement, failure to learn
Pathological egocentricity
No deep, lasting emotions
Lack of insight
No delusions, lack of anxiety

Social factors

Lee Robins (1966) reported a study that looked at both continuity of anti-social behaviour and possible contributors to it. The study located 584 children who had been referred to child guidance clinic up to 30 years earlier and interviewed them as adults. One of the best predictors of anti-social (psychopathic) personality disorder in the adults, usually men, was whether they had exhibited conduct disordered behaviour as children, such as serious theft or aggression or truancy. Thus, there was evidence of continuity across the lifespan. However, there were other factors related to anti-social personality disorder in the adults. Those who showed anti-social personality disorder as adults had poor parental discipline as children, either inconsistent discipline or lack of discipline. They also tended to have a father who showed anti-social behaviour.

Biological factors

Researchers have used twin studies to examine whether there is any evidence for a genetic basis to psychopathic behaviour. In one study of MZ and DZ twins, there was a concordance of 69 per cent for criminality in MZ twins and of 33 per cent in DZ twins. There are two obvious limitations to this study. The first is that, as discussed earlier, MZ twins are likely to share more environmental similarity than DZ twins. The second is that criminality, although it overlaps with psychopathy, cannot be equated with it. Some studies have looked at adopted children and observed whether there is greater concordance in biological relatives than adopted relatives. Cloninger et al. (1982) report data from a study carried out in Sweden comparing rates of criminal behaviour in men as a function of whether their biological and adoptive parents had a history of criminal behaviour. The rates of criminality were lowest in those who did not have a record of criminality in either their biological or adoptive family (3 per cent) and were highest in those who had a record of criminality in both adoptive and biological families (40 per cent). Rates of criminality were 12 per cent in those who had a history in adoptive relatives only and 7 per cent in those who had a history in biological relatives only. These data support the idea of both genetics and environment having a role to play in criminality, and also that genetic and environmental factors can combine to produce a particularly bad outcome. Again these data are on criminality. The exact contribution of genetic and environmental factors to psychopathy, as opposed to criminality, remains open to debate.

Psychological factors

Some of the features of psychopathy, such as an inability to learn from experience or impulsive behaviour that is self-detrimental, suggest a disruption to normal psychological mechanisms. Several psychological accounts have been proposed, such as that psychopaths are insensitive to punishment or that they are oversensitive to reward. This would account for them being unable to change behaviour which has previously been, but is no longer, associated with reward. Newman et al. (1987) compared prisoners who met criteria for psychopathy with those who did not, on their performance on a laboratory task. The task was a computerized game that involved a decreasing likelihood of winning on every trial. After each trial the subjects had to decide whether they wanted to continue or stop. The psychopathic group chose to continue to play longer and as a consequence made less money than the control group. This difference between the groups was eliminated by providing cumulative feedback about the amount won in each of the preceding trials and enforcing a 5-second wait before deciding whether to carry on or stop. It is therefore not the case that psychopaths simply do not care about punishment or non-reward, but they do seem less able to interrupt behaviour previously associated with reward in order to reflect on the fact that is not being rewarding any more.

Interestingly, Levenson (1992) has provided a different angle on psychopathy that views psychopathy as a choice of lifestyle within a particular social context. The key elements of such a philosophy of life are the trivialization of others combined with complete self-regard. As it stands, that description does not represent much more than a restatement of some of the key features of psychopathy. However, what is different is the emphasis on choice and the fact that someone can choose to adopt such a philosophy. As a result of behaving in psychopathic ways the person then may become unable to feel empathy for others. Furthermore, the psychopathic approach to life can be corporate and cultural rather than just individual, and so the person can become psychopathic through living and working in a culture where others' rights are trivialized and one's own goals are elevated to the highest status. Examples of corporate psychopathy would be multinational companies who destroy the environment in pursuit of profit.

Section summary

Personality disorder is a very contentious area in psychopathology, probably because it represents an area where the influence of values becomes more apparent. Increasing numbers of different types of personality disorder have been identified since the mid-1970s, although the most researched personality disorder is psychopathic (or anti-social) personality disorder. Again, social, biological and psychological factors have been examined, although there have also been criticisms of a categorical approach to personality disorder.

1 What are the main criticisms of the concept of personality disorder?

2 What factors might be important in psychopathic personality disorder?

Explanations of psychological disorder revisited

Having discussed four disorders – depression, anxiety, schizophrenia and personality disorder – in some detail it should be clear that psychological disorders have social, psychological and biological dimensions. Two further conclusions can be drawn. First, these different types of explanations are not mutually exclusive, but often interact. For example, an inherited vulnerability to schizophrenia can combine with stressful life events to produce a full-blown episode of schizophrenia, or early experiences can produce a psychological vulnerability to depression. Second, it is not necessarily the case that all psychological disorders have equal contributions from social, psychological and biological sources. Schizophrenia is probably the clearest example of a disorder with biological roots, although the evidence reviewed also showed the important contribution of social and psychological factors. Depression showed a very clear relationship to social factors, such as adverse life events, although these also interact with psychological vulnerabilities and, certainly for manic depression, with genetic vulnerability. Research since the 1970s has demonstrated the importance of cognitive factors such as interpretation of ambiguity or attentional processes, but the source of these psychological factors remains to be discovered. Much also remains to be discovered about personality disorders. This particular disorder more than any illustrates the role that societal values play in defining psychological disorders. The fascination of abnormal psychology is that we know so little and there is so much to know.

Chapter summary

• Concepts of abnormality

The two main approaches to defining mental disorders are fact based, for example the medical model, or value based. Fact-based accounts emphasize the factual nature of psychological disorders whereas value-based views argue that what is considered a disorder is based on societal values. Wakefield (1992) has tried to provide a definition of mental disorder that includes both facts and values.

• Explanations of psychological disorder

There are three main types of explanations given in trying to explain psychological disorders. Social explanations emphasize the importance of the environment, for example, suffering early abuse or experiencing negative life events. Psychological explanations explain psychological disorders mainly by reference to faulty thinking or learning processes. Biological explanations look to abnormal biological processes, such as dysfunctional neurotransmitter activity, to explain psychological disorders. It is often assumed that such biological dysfunctions will be inherited and so genetic studies are important for biological explanations. These explanations are not mutually exclusive; increasingly biological, social and psychological factors are seen as interacting in producing psychological disturbance.

• Depression

Depression is a relatively common psychological disorder which includes changes to mood, thinking and behaviour. Depression is probably best explained as an

Box continued

interaction between social factors, for example, suffering negative life events, and psychological factors, such as negative thinking and having dysfunctional attitudes. However, there is also some evidence of genetic vulnerability to depression, particularly in the case of manic-depressive disorder.

- **Anxiety**

Anxiety disorders are a range of different psychological disorders, including panic disorder and obsessive-compulsive disorder. Explanations which emphasize the importance of individual differences in learning experiences and also differences in attention to, and interpretation of, experiences have been particularly influential.

- **Schizophrenia**

Schizophrenic disorders are a mixture of positive symptoms, such as delusions, and negative symptoms, such as social withdrawal. There is stronger evidence of a genetic basis to schizophrenia than for most other disorders, although this still leaves much unexplained. Social factors, particularly the family environment, are known to have a strong influence on the course of schizophrenia, that is, whether someone relapses or not. Since the mid-1970s, some researchers have also tried to identify psychological factors, although this work is still in its early stages.

- **Personality disorder**

Personality disorder is the disorder that comes closest to societal values. There have been a number of different personality disorders described and categorized. Many personality disorders appear to be extreme versions of normal personality traits. Psychopathic (or anti-social) personality disorder is the most widely studied of the personality disorders and again appears best understood by a combination of social, biological and psychological aspects. The evidence for biological factors is based mainly on research on criminality which makes it only partly relevant for psychopathy.

Further reading

- Bentall, R. (ed.) (1990) *Reconstructing Schizophrenia*. London: Routledge. Chapters provide viewpoints on schizophrenia from different perspectives, all of which are alternatives to the mainstream medical model.

- Davison, G.C. and Neale, J.M. (1997) *Abnormal Psychology*, 7th edn. New York: Wiley. Provides good overall coverage of the area of abnormal psychology.

- Lilienfeld, S.O. (1995) *Seeing Both Sides: Classic controversies in abnormal psychology*. Pacific Grove, CA: Brooks/Cole. Presents both sides as well as an integrated view of 19 different controversies in abnormal psychology.

- Paris, J. (1996) *Social Factors in the Personality Disorders*. Cambridge: Cambridge University Press. An integrated overview of social, psychological and biological factors in the personality disorders.

CHAPTER 18

Therapeutic interventions

Andrew MacLeod

KEY CONCEPTS • approaches to therapy • assessment and diagnosis • do psychological therapies work? • legal and ethical issues in therapy

❏ Chapter preview

When you have read this chapter, you should be able to

- understand and describe the main approaches to therapy (biological, psychodynamic, humanistic, cognitive and behavioural) and how they relate to models of psychological disorders
- describe the main ways in which psychological disorders are assessed, and specifically the role that diagnosis plays in therapy
- understand what is involved in evaluating the effectiveness of therapy and be aware of the main conclusions of research examining therapy effectiveness
- describe the main factors involved in therapy effectiveness and the factors involved in negative effects of therapy
- weigh up and reflect upon some of the ethical issues involved in therapy such as consent, diminished responsibility and confidentiality

Introduction

When most of us think about therapy it probably conjures up an image of two people – a therapist and a client – sitting in a room. The therapist is asking questions, listening and occasionally offering observations; the client is describing his or her problems. Although psychologists do often engage in therapy of this type – individual therapy – it is by no means the only type of therapy that they are involved in. Sometimes couples are seen together, and problems will be discussed in the context of their ongoing relationship, particularly problematic patterns of communication. In family therapy, families are seen together, based on the underlying assumption that problems are often best understood within the context of an overall social system, such as a family, and the interrelationships that exist within that system. Group therapy is where a number of different individuals are brought together with one or, more commonly, two therapists. The group forum provides an opportunity for people to share problems of a similar nature and should provide an opportunity for problems to be expressed in a supportive atmosphere. The idea behind all therapy is to restore or improve someone's level of functioning and well-being. At its simplest form the model is one of problem and remedy: someone has developed a problem and therapy is all about curing that problem and restoring the person to what he or she was like before the problem. However, it will become clear that psychological therapies are often not simply about curing a problem. In fact, one approach to therapy – rehabilitation – is built around the view that some problems are long term; the goal of rehabilitation therapy is to help someone to adapt to their problems and to maximize normal functioning within the context of an ongoing problem.

The focus of this chapter will be on therapies for psychological problems, such as anxiety, depression and schizophrenia. Therapies tend to rely on and inform models of the problems they address, and so the essential features of these models will also be discussed. As well as outlining the various approaches to therapy, the chapter will also discuss the evidence concerning the effectiveness of therapy, before examining some of the wider legal and ethical issues involved in therapy.

❑ Approaches to therapy

There are a great number of different types of psychological therapies. These therapies have things in common as well as distinctive features. The first distinction to be made in differentiating approaches to therapy is between psychotherapy, or talking therapies, and the more physical forms of therapy, mainly drug therapy, but also including psychosurgery and electro-convulsive therapy (ECT). Psychotherapy is 'a social interaction in which a trained professional tries to help another person, the client or patient, behave or feel differently' (Davison and Neale 1996: 528). Within psychotherapies, there is a further distinction that can be made between what are called **insight-oriented therapies** and **action-oriented therapies**. Insight therapies aim at helping the client to understand the basis of his or her behaviour, thinking, and feeling, and hence to understand the underlying nature of the problem. Providing the client with an understanding of the source of the problems is thought to be the key to successful therapeutic change. Action therapies tend to take a different approach, and emphasize a more active, pragmatic approach to changing the person's behaviour and experience. The difference between insight therapies and action therapies will become clear as particular therapies are discussed. Figure 18.1 illustrates some of the different approaches to therapy that will be looked at. It will also become clear that no distinctions are absolute; there is considerable overlap between different types of therapies, but it is probably quite useful to make sense of general approaches to therapy by categorizing them into broad types.

Models are general ways of thinking about the nature of disorders and include beliefs about the aetiology, or cause, of disorders as well as wider assumptions about human nature. Models are useful in abnormal psychology and therapy in that they provide a framework for integrating facts and stimulate research hypotheses. In

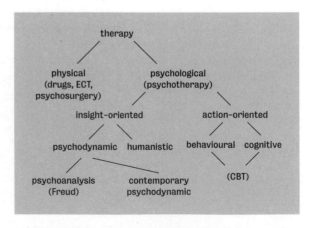

Figure 18.1 Categorization of different approaches to therapy

abnormal psychology models also usually entail prescriptions about therapeutic interventions. However, one common mistake in thinking about the relationship between treatments and models is that if a treatment is successful it must imply that the cause of the disorder was whatever the treatment affected. Although tempting, such a conclusion is not logically warranted, and is called the **treatment-aetiology fallacy**. Perhaps the fallacy can be most clearly seen by the relationship between headaches and aspirin. Taking an aspirin may relieve a headache but that does not mean that the headache was caused by a lack of aspirin. Caution should therefore be exerted, particularly when thinking about the effects of drugs, in drawing conclusions about causes on the basis of treatment.

Models and their associated therapies are sometimes talked about as if they are mutually exclusive. Increasingly, it is being realized that this is not the case. Many disorders can be understood most effectively by integrating various models. As far as therapy goes, the trend towards integration is also apparent. In surveys the majority of therapists have described themselves as **eclectic** (D. Smith 1982), which means using different treatments for clients with different disorders or combining elements of different treatments into the one integrated approach.

Biomedical model and treatment

The biomedical model was discussed in detail in Chapter 17. This model also goes under various other names such as the medical, organic, biological or disease model. The essential element of the model is that psychological problems are symptoms of an underlying biological dysfunction. The biological roots can be varied, for example, brain defects, biochemical imbalance, or even infectious transmission. It is widely assumed that there is often a genetic predisposition that acts in tandem with some triggering agent, such as a stressful life event, to produce the disorder.

The parallel is with physical disorders. So for example, tuberculosis is caused by a combination of the tubercule bacillus and an underlying vulnerability in the individual. This is an example of the **diathesis-stress model**, where some stressor interacts with an underlying vulnerability to produce disorder. As discussed in Chapter 17, the discovery that the cause of general paresis of the insane was syphilitic infection strengthened the belief in the medical model of psychological disorder, giving rise to the hope that other psychological disorders would yield to this type of explanation.

As psychological symptoms are the result of an underlying biological abnormality, the obvious answer is to treat the underlying biological abnormality. Thus, treatment is physical rather than psychological, mainly drug therapy but also including electro-convulsive therapy (ECT) and in extreme cases psychosurgery. The idea of treating psychological problems with some form of physical therapy has been around for some time. One rather bizarre example, described by Scull (1987), is the case of Henry Cotton, the superintendent at the Trenton State Hospital in New Jersey in the early twentieth century. Cotton's view was that the 'insane' were physically sick due to bacteriological invasion, with the main focus of the infection being the teeth. For Cotton 'modern dentistry was "a menace" to the community, producing "wonderful cosmetic work" that did "incalculable damage" by producing "serious systemic disease"' (cited in Scull 1987). Treatment therefore revolved around removal of the patients' teeth. Cotton's staff extracted more than 6,000 teeth in one year. Although the treatment was deemed to be a success, there were nevertheless those who did not seem to benefit and attention turned to the removal of other possible repositories of infection such as the gall bladder, small intestine and stomach. Despite Cotton's claims for an 87 per cent success rate, suspicion and dissatisfaction grew, resulting in the treatment being forcibly discontinued by the authorities. Although it seems bizarre now, the story does capture the enthusiastic optimism of the period for physical treatment of 'insanity'.

Some physical approaches – insulin shock therapy and ECT – rely on giving a 'shock' to the sufferers' system to bring about changes in their psychological state. In the 1930s a Berlin physician, Manfred Sakel, accidentally administered an insulin overdose to one of his diabetic patients, resulting in a coma. The patient also happened to be addicted to morphine but when she came out of the coma her craving for morphine had gone. Sakel soon began giving insulin overdoses to other patients (ethical permission was less strict than it is now!) one of whom also happened to be psychotic. Following the coma this patient appeared to be more rational. In his enthusiasm, Sakel was soon administering insulin overdoses to schizophrenic patients, claiming high rates of success. About the same time in Italy, two physicians, Bini and Cerletti, were interested in the possible therapeutic effects of naturally occurring epileptic seizures. This led them to develop ways of artificially producing such seizures through passing a current through someone's head, and thus ECT was born. Like Sakel, they were soon reporting high success rates with psychotic and depressed patients.

Such forms of therapy are controversial for a number of reasons, not least because of their brutal nature, although ECT is now always administered along with muscle relaxants and under anaesthesia. Insulin therapy stopped being used in the 1950s when anti-psychotic medication became available. ECT continues to be used, mainly for depression which is resistant to other forms of treatment, although its use is banned in some countries. There is a debate about whether ECT is effective and even those who advocate its effectiveness would not claim to know how it works. Finally, there is concern about side-effects such as memory loss, as a result of ECT (Breggin 1991).

Certainly the most invasive of all physical techniques is psychosurgery. Psychosurgery involves destroying parts of the brain thought to be the source of the person's psychological problems. The technique was developed by Egas Moniz, a Portuguese neurologist using a knife to sever nerve fibres to the prefrontal cortex, a technique he called leucotomy, later renamed lobotomy by Freeman and Watts in the United States. The technique gained wide acceptance and was practised on tens of thousands of patients. Like all new therapies, initial reports indicated great success but it became clear that many people did not benefit by a reduction of their psychological distress and those that did benefit also often suffered damaged higher mental function. Lobotomies are still carried out in the 1990s, albeit in small numbers and in very few places.

Psychotropic drugs

By far the most common biological approach to treatment is the use of **psychotropic drugs**, drugs which alter the symptoms of mental disorder. There are three main types of psychotropic drugs: anti-psychotic drugs (which reduce hallucinations and delusions), anti-depressives, and anti-anxiety drugs (anxiolytics). As discussed in Chapter 17, psychotropic drugs can work in a number of ways such as increasing the release of a neurotransmitter, blocking its re-uptake, binding to particular receptors, or altering the number of receptors. The main neurotransmitter systems affected by psychotropic drugs are serotonin (also called 5HT), noradrenaline (also called norepinephrine) and dopamine.

Psychotropic drugs affect symptoms, that is they can raise mood, reduce anxiety, or stop someone hearing voices or experiencing delusions, such as in the case study of David. Sometimes the symptoms themselves are the problem, in which case medication can be effective. However, often other approaches will be needed to either deal with the cause of the problem or to provide an answer that is stable and permanent rather than depending on taking medication which cannot continue indefinitely. Furthermore, psychotropic drugs all have, to a greater or lesser degree, unpleasant side-effects, such as a dry mouth, dizziness and drowsiness. The therapeutic limitations and the side-effects, coupled with the fact that many people do not like the idea of taking

---

ψ Case study

Use of psychotropic medication and rehabilitation in schizophrenia

The case of David was discussed in Chapter 17. To recap, David had started to experience a number of psychotic symptoms, such as a hallucination about something having been inserted into his mouth and the delusion that he was a rock star. Upon admission to hospital, David was treated with chlorpromazine, a major tranquillizer that often reduces the positive symptoms of schizophrenia such as delusions and hallucinations. He responded well to this and, after some time, no longer felt the object in his mouth and described it as having been a hallucination. He was much calmer although he did still believe that he might be a rock star. The drugs had been effective in reducing his positive symptoms but during his time being

treated in hospital he had become increasingly lethargic and apathetic. Typically, he would stay in bed until early afternoon and then just wander back and forth to the hospital shop. He had no interest in any activities, though he described himself as being extremely bored. A programme of active rehabilitation, establishing a manageable routine and regular pattern of work and other activities, was implemented to try to reduce these negative symptoms. After some time of engaging in this programme, David's energy and interest improved sufficiently for him to take on some part-time paid work and shortly afterwards he was discharged from hospital. This particular case highlights the importance of dealing with both the positive and negative symptoms of schizophrenia using a combination of drug therapy and rehabilitation.

drugs, make psychotropic medication useful in some cases but limited as an overall approach to treatment.

Psychological models and therapies

Although there are many different approaches to therapy, as already discussed psychological therapies tend to fall into two broad categories: insight-oriented therapies and action-oriented therapies. Insight therapies, such as psychodynamic and humanistic approaches, place great importance on the person coming to an understanding of his or her problem, which will happen largely through talking. In contrast, action-oriented therapies, such as cognitive therapy and behaviour therapy (now largely merged in cognitive-behaviour therapy or CBT) place less emphasis on insight and more emphasis on changing current behaviour and thinking, which will certainly involve talking about the problem but will also include more active tasks to be carried out by the patient outside the therapy session.

The psychodynamic model

One of the main tenets, and main contributions, of psychoanalysis was to suggest that most psychic life takes place outside of conscious awareness. Many others before and since Freud have stated a similar view but Freud's contribution was to emphasize the dynamic nature of the unconscious. The unconscious was not simply a passive storehouse of memories and knowledge waiting to be used by consciousness if required, but had an active life of its own that carried on outside of conscious awareness. The wishes, impulses memories and so on of the unconscious has a profound influence on daily life. Most conscious experience is influenced by unconscious processes but the person experiencing those processes is unaware of their activity, although their effects will be experienced in one form or another. Essential to the working of unconscious mental life, and what gives it its active nature, is the concept of psychic energy. Freud's view was that psychic energy was like physical energy, in that there was a fixed amount of psychic energy which could not be created or destroyed, only changed in form. This active, dynamic role of the unconscious is what is being referred to when people talk about psychodynamic models or psychodynamic therapy. The term **psychodynamic** covers a range of approaches, not simply the strictly Freudian approach, for which the term **psychoanalytic** is usually

reserved. Psychodynamic approaches can all be seen as being derived from Freud and they certainly all have in common the idea of an active unconscious.

A second main strand of psychodynamic models is the view that early experiences are crucial for how the unconscious develops. Freud posited a series of psychosexual stages that were passed through. How the person progressed through these stages would be a major influence on their later mental life. The various stages were discussed in some detail in Chapter 14, which also discussed how personality can be divided into the **id**, which is the unorganized source of desire, mainly sexual and aggressive, the **superego**, which is an internalized set of rules and ethical standards, and the **ego**, which mediates the relationship between the id and the superego. Conflicts within these systems give rise to psychological disturbance.

Freud's initial view was that sexual energy, if it is blocked, can be transformed into depression, anxiety, obsessions and other psychological problems. However,

Plate 18.1 Freud's contribution to psychoanalysis was to emphasize the dynamic nature of the unconscious. The wishes, impulses and memories of the unconscious had a profound influence on daily life

he later developed a different view in which anxiety was a signal or warning that repressed sexual energy was on the verge of breaking through to consciousness. Anxiety was therefore a signal that the ego needed to be defended against forbidden wishes or impulses. The most obvious way of defending the ego was through the defence mechanism of **repression** – the unconscious but purposeful exclusion of painful or unacceptable thoughts from entering consciousness. Repression is not simply forgetting. The difference between a forgotten memory and a repressed memory is that in the former case the memory is preconscious, that is, below the level of consciousness but potentially available to consciousness, whereas in the latter case it is unconscious. Repression represents an active process whereby material, for example early memories, are kept from reaching consciousness but this active, goal-directed process of repression itself operates at a unconscious level. So individuals using repression would not be aware that they are doing so. Overuse of defence mechanisms such as repression means that conflicts which should have been faced and resolved have been driven underground into the unconscious, but, of course, do not go away.

Freud developed his ideas over many years and during that time and in the years since, there have been many variations on his ideas. Some of these variations were from his contemporaries or followers who disagreed with a particular aspect of his theory. Jung disagreed with Freud's emphasis on the sexual aspect of the unconscious and put forward views that emphasized a more spiritual role for the unconscious. He also advocated a collective unconscious, which consisted of a collection of primitive ideas that are shared across all cultures. Adler similarly disagreed with the view that the unconscious was driven by sexual energy, and advocated a view that put social roles in a more central position. Object relations theorists (e.g. Klein 1932) emphasized the importance of interpersonal rather than intrapersonal forces. The focus in object relations theory is on the way the developing child relates and is related to by important figures around him or her, particularly the mother-figure.

Psychodynamic therapy

Psychodynamic therapy, as in the models described, has two main strands, classical psychoanalysis based on Freud's original ideas, and contemporary psychodynamic therapy, which is not so much one approach as a number of approaches based on adaptations of psycho-

analytic thinking. Psychodynamic therapies have as a goal the aim of uncovering the underlying problems through facilitating the client's insight into the nature of his or her unconscious conflict. Bringing into consciousness the underlying conflict is a difficult endeavour as it requires the bypassing of the defences which over the years have kept the material from consciousness. By definition the client does not know what the unconscious conflicts are and so asking him or her directly will yield little information about them. Therefore, a number of special techniques are utilized to make unconscious thoughts and feelings conscious.

Free association is where the client is encouraged to say whatever comes into his or her mind, without trying to make any sense of it. In this way, it is hoped to gain access to the unconscious through bypassing the usual censoring that is thought to preclude this access. The content of the client's free association will give the therapist clues about the nature of the unconscious conflicts. Dream analysis is also thought to provide an insight into the unconscious as dreams afford the opportunity for the unconscious to bypass the normal defences. Indeed, Freud called dreams 'the royal road to the unconscious' (Freud 1913). According to Freud (1913), dreams have both manifest content, which is the obvious content recalled by the dreamer, and latent content, where the unconscious is expressing itself in a symbolic way that needs to be interpreted by the therapist. So, for example, a patient may report a dream about going on a long journey, which the therapist might interpret as symbolizing a fear or preoccupation with death. The therapist interprets the latent content based not only on simple translation rules but also on his or her knowledge of the individual patient.

As the therapist begins to develop an idea or hypothesis about the nature of the unconscious conflict, he or she will begin to suggest interpretations of the client's behaviour or experiences to the client. It is through **interpretations** that the therapist begins to make the client aware of the conflicts and so it is important to time the interpretations carefully. Sometimes the client may disagree with the interpretation offered by the therapist and this would normally be construed by the therapist as **resistance**. Within a psychoanalytic framework, resistance is therapeutically important because it indicates the client's attempts to prevent exploration or uncovering of the unconscious conflict. Of course, it may be that the client resists the interpretation because it is wrong, not because of a defensive reaction. One of the problems of psychoanalysis is how a disagreement between client and therapist can be resolved, given that every reaction the client makes can be interpreted as a manifestation of his or her problem, even if it is not.

What marks psychodynamic therapies, and psychoanalysis in particular, as being distinct from other therapies is the emphasis that is placed on the relationship between therapist and client. Other therapies may emphasize the importance of a good relationship but for psychodynamic therapies the therapeutic relationship is more fundamental. Within the relationship the therapist can come to be seen by the client as an authority figure, and so can relive some of the thoughts and feelings that were experienced in childhood towards authority figures such as a parent. In this way, some of the unconscious conflicts which stem from this time can be acted out towards, or transferred to, the therapist. This process is known as **transference**. Initially Freud viewed transference as a obstacle in therapy but came to view the re-enactment and working through the transference as an essential element in therapy. **Countertransference** refers to the process where the therapist develops feelings towards the client based on the therapist's unconscious. Countertransference can be an obstacle in therapy as it is important that the therapist does not bring his or her own emotional vulnerabilities to the client. To deal with this, training analysis, where the therapist undergoes analysis as part of the training, is essential in psychoanalytic training. Traditional psychoanalysis is intensive and may last for many years; there is no time limit. Contemporary psychodynamic therapies are shorter and sometimes time-limited.

The influence of psychodynamic theories has been immense. One problem in evaluating the psychodynamic approach is that the sheer comprehensiveness of the theories makes them difficult to test. There have also been criticisms about Freud's change of view when he abandoned the seduction theory, which took at face value the accounts that his patients gave of being sexually interfered with as children, and came to view those accounts as fantasies (Masson 1989). The therapeutic relationship, so crucial to psychodynamic therapy, has also been criticized as one in which all the power resides in the hands of the therapist who can, over a period of time, virtually brainwash the client into accepting the therapist's view of him or herself (Masson 1988). In all therapies there is a danger of abuse of power on the part of the therapist, but it is fair to say that this danger is greater in therapies such as psychoanalysis where there is a greater mystique involved (many of the concepts have to be learned by the client) and where the therapist

is seen as the expert. It is also a considerable act of faith that therapists' own analyses will have freed them from influences and biases due to what they are like as people. It is dangerous to always interpret what goes on in a relationship, including a therapeutic one, in terms of what is going on with the other person and not oneself. Since the 1970s the reality of childhood sexual abuse has become more widely known about and some, like Masson, have argued that Freud's influence has held back progress in this area.

The humanistic model

Like psychodynamic approaches, a humanistic approach stresses the importance of the person coming to an understanding of his or her problems as a precursor to change. However, there are a number of important differences between the two approaches. Unlike psychoanalysis, humanistic approaches emphasize the here-and-now rather than give weight to the importance of past experiences. Humanism also emphasizes the positive aspects of human experience and views individuals as having an innate drive to fulfil their potential. Part of achieving this potential involves exploring and accepting the self, the nature of one's personality, and accepting the needs and responsibilities that go along with this. According to Carl Rogers (1951), one of the main exponents of the humanistic approach, the positive outcome of this process is a person who is open to experience, spontaneous and self-directed rather than simply responds to others. Such individuals, according to Rogers, show **personal authenticity**, that is, they are being truly themselves. As can be seen from this, humanism adopts an optimistic view of human nature, believing that people are inherently good. Rather than being a manifesto for personal selfishness, the authentic person is also able to accept the responsibilities that go along being authentic. Abnormality and psychological problems arise when people do not accept themselves or allow their inherent drive for self-fulfilment to be realized, which is likely to be associated with relating to other people in an inauthentic way.

The other major figure in humanistic thinking in the 1940s and 1950s was Abraham Maslow. Maslow is famous for his description of a hierarchy of human needs. For Maslow, as for Rogers, the fulfilling of needs and potentials was the key to a successful emotional life. These needs could be thought of as a hierarchy, with basic needs such as food, shelter and sex, progressing through safety needs, such as safety from danger, through love and belongingness needs (closeness to and acceptance by others) to esteem needs of recognition and approval. At the top of the hierarchy was **self-actualization**, which is the ability to be one's self at the same time as participating and sharing fully with other people. The hierarchical nature of the various needs indicates that lower level needs must be met before higher level needs are able to be met. When needs are not met, then conflict and psychological problems emerge. (See also Chapter 16).

Humanistic therapy

The most clearly worked out humanistic therapy is Carl Roger's client-centred therapy (Rogers 1951). The therapy is based on the views already outlined, especially the idea that people have an inherent drive to achieve their potential and that the achievement of this potential is the most valuable as well as the most psychologically healthy outcome. Therapy aims to overcome obstacles which have blocked or prevented individuals achieving their potential. Rather than providing interpretations or giving advice, the role of the therapist is to listen and to reflect back to the client in order to clarify what the client has said. The therapist creates an environment that will facilitate the process of self-discovery and change for the client rather than enforcing any of particular view or outlook. Rogers identified three crucial ingredients of the therapist for this process to work successfully. First, therapists must have **genuineness**, which means that they must allow true feelings and thoughts to emerge in the therapy session rather than acting a role towards the client. As can be seen, this makes client-centred therapy quite different from traditional psychoanalysis where it is important that the therapist allows little of his or her own personality into the therapeutic relationship in order for transference to take place. Second, therapists must have empathy. They need to come to understand the client's experience and feel with the client. Finally, the therapist should actively accept and value the client, which Rogers called **unconditional positive regard**. These therapist characteristics overcome defensiveness and allow the expression of the client's problems as well as an exploration of the client's true nature. Rogers *et al.* (1967) found that these three therapist characteristics were associated with positive outcome in therapy whereas clients who had therapists who were low in these characteristics showed deterioration.

The humanistic approach is useful in that it reminds us of the importance of choice, the sense of self, and per-sonal responsibility in human experience. Its influence has been fairly pervasive and has altered the way we think about our lives, emphasizing personal fulfilment rather than duty. However, if taken in a one-sided way this can provide an alibi for self-indulgence, which itself creates problems. As an approach to therapy and to resolving problems it is probably fair to say that the humanistic approach is more relevant to milder problems where the client is verbally intelligent and motivated to change. As an approach to more severe problems within people who are resistant to engage in therapy its value seems very limited. Like psychoanalysis, humanistic therapy has not been at the forefront of scientific research, although Roger's research on the successful ingredients of therapy is a notable exception to this rule. Many of the concepts, such as self-actualization, are vague and difficult to define in clear terms that would make them researchable. We turn now to an approach which, in contrast, is firmly rooted in scientific, academic psychology.

Behavioural model

Behaviour therapy is the clearest example of an action-oriented therapy. Some of the fundamental concepts of the behavioural model have already been outlined when talking about psychological factors in anxiety in Chapter 17. Essentially, the behavioural model sees psychological disorders as arising from previous learning experiences. These learning experiences will often have involved a combination of classical conditioning, for example, where something fairly innocuous comes to be associated with something unpleasant, and operant conditioning, where the problem is maintained as a result of negative reinforcement resulting from avoidance. This analysis is most clearly seen for anxiety disorders, which is largely where it was developed, but has also been applied to other disorders. For example, depression can be viewed as a lack of **positive reinforcement**, either because sufferers have lost their capacity to experience anything as pleasurable or rewarding (**anhedonia**) or because they are in a situation that lacks sources of rewarding experiences.

The behavioural model therefore emphasizes the role of past experience in producing the problem. Current behaviour is thought to be under the control of previous learning experiences. However, as we shall see, behaviour therapy focuses on changing current behaviour rather than uncovering past experiences. Therefore, unlike psychodynamic and humanistic approaches, insight into the problem is not deemed to be that important for the success of therapy. What is important is to change the person's behavioural patterns. The assumption is that once behaviour is changed, then so thoughts and feelings will also change.

The behavioural model of disorders and behaviour therapy was a direct application of behavioural principles from experimental psychology and was closely related to laboratory based studies of learning (conditioning) which were often carried out on rats. As such, behaviour therapy has been more closely connected with scientific methodology, both in elaborating the principles of therapy and in evaluating the success of therapy. As such, behaviour therapists tended to be the most vociferous critics of psychodynamic therapies which rely much less on a scientific bias.

Behaviour therapy

As already discussed, behaviour therapy relies for its rationale on learning theory. The actual techniques used in behaviour therapy are also firmly rooted in learning theory. A main technique, devised by Wolpe (1958), is **systematic desensitization**, which is based on classical conditioning principles and is used in the treatment of anxiety. There are two main elements to systematic desensitization – relaxation and working through an anxiety hierarchy. The rationale behind systematic desensitization is to induce a relaxed response, which is obviously incompatible with feeling anxious, while thinking about or confronting the feared situation. A list of the client's anxiety-provoking scenarios is elicited and each item is ranked from lowest to highest in terms of its anxiety-provoking properties. For example, a spider phobic might have been looking at pictures of spiders at the bottom of the hierarchy and allowing a spider to crawl over her at the top. In **imaginal desensitization** the therapist teaches the person to relax and when in a relaxed state to imagine an item on the hierarchy. Once the client is able to consistently imagine the item and still maintain a relaxed state, the treatment moves onto the next item in the hierarchy, until the final stage is reached. In **in-vivo desensitization**, the exposure to the feared situation is carried out in real life, sometimes with the therapist present or sometimes clients would carry it out on their own. Again, exposure to a particular item in the hierarchy carries on until anxiety is diminished, and the next item of the hierarchy is then embarked upon. The emphasis is on gradual exposure, unlike **flooding**, a technique which was more popular in the early days of behaviourism and which involves a sudden and total exposure to the feared situation. As well as directly experiencing new learning, being able to

observe others is also thought to play a role in developing new behaviours and overcoming problems. This is called **modelling**, where, for example, someone who is snake phobic will be helped to overcome the fear by observing someone else behaving in a non-fearful way towards snakes.

Principles of operant conditioning are also used in behavioural techniques, such as token economies. Token economies, which are mainly used with children or people with learning disabilities, work on the principle that behaviour that is rewarded will be repeated. Individuals are given tokens, sometimes stars are used with children, upon performance of some desired behaviour, such as going to bed on time or eating food using cutlery. Tokens can later be exchanged for something that is rewarding to the person.

The behavioural model and behaviour therapy has been very influential within mainstream psychology. It has been important in providing a firmer foundation upon which to evaluate therapy, in contrast to psychodynamic and humanistic models. However, its precision and emphasis on only considering what is observable is also its great weakness in that it has meant leaving out much of what is important about human experience, such as thoughts and feelings. Indeed, for the more radical behaviourists, experience is by definition unimportant! As such, behaviourism was always going to be limited. Those limits have now been reached.

Cognitive model and cognitive therapies

From the early 1960s, in academic psychology learning theory and behaviourism began to be overtaken by cognitive psychology, which emphasized the importance of internal mental states in determining action. Adherents to a behaviourist approach could do so either on the grounds that other aspects of experience, such as thoughts, were impossible to study because they were not observable (methodological behaviourism) or on the grounds that thoughts had no causal role in behaviour (scientific, or radical, behaviourism). Methodological behaviourism could be agnostic about whether thoughts did play a causal role in behaviour, whereas radical behaviourists, such as Skinner, were convinced that they did not. Either way, it meant that thoughts (cognitions) did not figure in the approach. However, it became increasingly clear that behaviour could not be understood simply in terms of stimulus and response, but needed to accommodate what happened in between stimulus and the response. As a result, psychology began to move on from simply looking at behaviour.

Ψ Case study

Behavioural treatment of obsessive-compulsive disorder

Rachel was referred by her general practitioner as she was experiencing increasingly strong urges, which she was unable to resist, to clean excessively. The problems had started not long after the birth of her first child, when he became ill. Although an allergy was diagnosed and he recovered, she became convinced that his illness was due to her not being hygienic enough. She was spending up to five hours each day in the bath, and was late for her first appointment because it had taken her over three hours to wash up the (very few) breakfast dishes. She was spending vast quantities of money on cleaning materials, but at the same time avoiding whole areas of the house, which were becoming not very clean. If she had to go out of the house or do anything which made her feel contaminated, such as putting out the rubbish, she would compensate by spending even longer cleaning herself. Treatment focused on setting goals, constructing an anxiety hierarchy and using exposure and response prevention, which meant gradually trying to expose herself to what she felt to be contaminating but the same time tolerating the accompanying feelings of anxiety, and allowing them to diminish naturally, rather than reducing them through taking compensatory action like washing. As Rachel became less anxious about a particular activity, she moved on to something slightly more anxiety-provoking. For example, over the course of treatment, time spent washing up in the morning was gradually reduced from 3.5 hours to about 45 minutes, still a long time but a considerable improvement. The advantage of a cognitive-behavioural approach is that Rachel now had the knowledge and the techniques to continue helping herself once contact with the therapist stopped.

As attention turned in academic psychology to what went on inside people's heads – the way they processed information – so researchers and clinicians began to think about conceptualizing psychological disorders in cognitive terms. Ironically, one of the first people to do this was not a psychologist at all, but a psychoanalytically trained psychiatrist in Philadelphia called Aaron Beck.

Beck's cognitive therapy

Beck developed his cognitive approach, initially to depression, when he was struck by how negative the thinking of his depressed patients seemed to be. From this he concluded that depression might be caused by faulty thinking that led the person to negative conclusions about the self, the world, and the future – the **cognitive triad** (Beck *et al.* 1979). An outline of Beck's view of how depression can develop is shown in Figure 18.2. Distortions in thinking are probably learned early in life, possibly through problematic relationships which come to be internalized in the form of dysfunctional schemata. These schemata consist of rules and attitudes, such as 'I must be loved by everyone all of

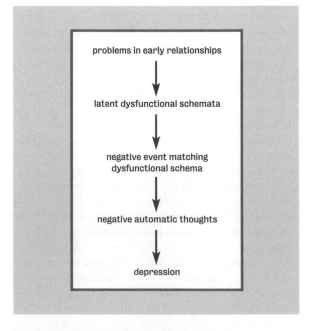

Figure 18.2 Beck's cognitive model of depression
Source: Power and Champion (1992)

the time' and 'I must achieve everything I set out to do or I am worthless'. Dysfunctional schemata may not manifest themselves all the time but nevertheless lie dormant, waiting to be activated. A negative event which matches the schema will activate it, for example, being made redundant for someone who has a dysfunctional schema about his or her worth depending on being successful. This then produces **negative automatic thoughts**, such as 'I'm a worthless person' or 'I will always fail at everything I do' which in turn leads to depression. Beck *et al.* (1979) identified a number of thinking errors, such as **overgeneralization**, where people draw a conclusion about a whole area of their life based on a single incident.

Cognitive therapy aims to restructure the client's thinking. The first step in the therapeutic process is for client and therapist to come to some agreement about the nature of the problem and goals for therapy. Beck *et al.* (1979) called this **collaborative empiricism**. The empiricism aspect of the term refers to the fact that the approach is to treat the client's thoughts as hypotheses

and to test them out. That is, the goal is not to replace negative thoughts with positive thoughts, but rather to devise ways of putting negative thoughts to the test. The underlying assumption, of course, is that most negative thoughts will be shown to have no foundation in reality. Cognitive therapy is collaborative in that the aim is to have an open and relatively equal relationship between therapist and client, with an agenda negotiated from the outset. Sessions will involve the therapist uncovering and challenging the client's thoughts, and will be aided by homework given to the client to carry out between sessions. Commonly, clients will be asked to record their negative thoughts and so learn to identify when they are having them, which is the first step to challenging them. Sometimes, negative thoughts can be tested out in the session using Socratic dialogue, a logical question and answer sequence, and sometimes they can only be tested out by the client carrying out some test or exercise in between sessions. The case study illustrates the type of faulty thinking described by Beck and also some of the key aspects of cognitive therapy.

ψ Case study

Cognitive therapy for depression

Tom was a 34-year-old man who worked as a computer programmer. He was referred for depression and for social anxiety, which centred on thoughts of being negatively evaluated by others around him. As therapy progressed it became clear that underlying these thoughts was a view of himself as a useless person and imagining that other people must think that of him. Part of the therapy consisted in testing out this view of himself when it came up. The following is an excerpt from one session. Note that in cognitive therapy the therapist tries to test out negative thoughts rather than trying simply to replace them with positive thoughts.

Tom   I'm really useless as a person, I'm no good at anything.

Therapist Can you give me an example of something that you are useless at?

Tom   My job, well, not completely but there are parts of the job I'm terrible at.

Therapist What are those?

Tom   Well, programming, seeing solutions to things – I'm not as fast or as creative as others.

Therapist What makes you think that – can you give me an example?

Tom   Well, looking through other people's program I sometimes see things that I wouldn't have thought of doing.

Therapist Is that a big part of your job, I mean, how often would you look through other people's programs?

Tom   Well, every day, I suppose.

Therapist Can you think of specific occasions in the past year when you have had that experience of seeing something that you wouldn't have thought of?

Tom   (after some thought) I can think of probably up to three times. I see what you mean. It doesn't seem evidence that I'm bad at my job at all.

Therapist Do you really think that or are you just saying what you think I'm getting at?

Tom   No, it does seem ridiculous.

Around the same time that Beck was developing his cognitive model of depression, Albert Ellis (1962) was formulating rational-emotive therapy (RET). Like Beck, Ellis viewed psychological disorder as arising from faulty thinking. Rather than emotional problems being the result simply of things that happened in the environment, the way the person understood or interpreted those events was crucial. Ellis's model can be described in three stages, the 'A-B-C' model. Things happening in the environment, or activating events (A) will give rise to emotional consequences (C) but the nature of those consequences will be determined by the person's private belief system (B). To the extent that the person's beliefs consist of irrational assumptions and standards then they are likely to result in emotional disturbance. Particularly problematic are beliefs which contain imperatives such as 'musts', 'oughts', and 'shoulds', what Ellis (1997) called 'musturbatory ideology'. Table 18.1 shows some examples of such irrational beliefs. Therapy is aimed at making the client aware of such beliefs and challenging them through a variety of techniques.

Cognitive models and therapies have been valuable in raising awareness that how people think about their experience is crucially important in how they react emotionally. This has also led to useful therapeutic approaches and techniques aimed at changing thought processes. Some have criticized the cognitive model for not paying enough attention to the realities of people's lives, which may actually be quite grim, and paying too much attention to what is going on inside their heads. What if life is really bad, not just the person's interpretation of it? Although this is sometimes a valid point, it is also a criticism that it is possible to make of most therapies. As it is often not possible for the therapist to change the person's

Table 18.1 Examples of irrational beliefs which play a central role in psychological disturbance

One should be thoroughly competent, adequate and achieving in all possible respects if one is to consider oneself worthwhile.

There is invariably a right, precise and perfect solution to human problems, and it is catastrophic if this perfect solution is not found.

It is a dire necessity for an adult human being to be loved or approved by virtually every significant person in his community.

Source: Ellis (1962)

circumstances the best that can be done is to change how the person reacts to those circumstances.

Comparing insight- and action-oriented therapies

Two broad types of psychological therapies have been talked about: insight-oriented therapies, such as traditional psychoanalysis, modern psychodynamic therapy and humanistic therapies, and action-oriented therapies, such as behaviour therapy and cognitive therapy, more commonly merged as cognitive-behaviour therapy (CBT). These two approaches differ in important ways. For insight therapies the presenting problem is usually a symptom of some underlying problem and therapy aims to uncover the real problem. For action therapies, problems tend to be taken at face value and therapy aims to remove the problem. Insight therapies, certainly psychodynamic therapies, will focus more on the past than action therapies will. Psychodynamic therapies will also use the therapeutic relationship as a focus of therapy, where the client can project feelings onto the therapist, whereas for CBT what is important is that client and therapist have a good collaborative relationship – the relationship itself is not a focus of therapy. Accompanying these practical differences are differences in the intellectual base upon which the therapies rest. Whereas psychodynamic therapies rely on case studies and theoretical writings, action therapies place much more value on scientific principles and empirical data. Some of these differences lead to major problems as we shall see when reviewing the evidence about the success of the different types of therapy.

Historically, the two approaches, psychoanalysis and behaviour therapy, have traditionally been enemies, each decrying the other's methods and rationale. However, since the 1970s there has been considerable rapprochement, with both sides showing an interest in accommodating and integrating elements of the other's practices. Psychodynamically oriented therapists are developing shorter-term therapies which pay more attention to the conscious content that patients report while cognitive-behaviour therapists are paying more attention to the nature of the therapeutic relationship (Rosenhan and Seligman 1995).

Social models and treatments

The approaches to understanding and treating disorders discussed so far are essentially individual approaches. Although the wider world and other people may be seen as playing a role in the development of the problem, the focus is squarely on the individual and therapy aims at changing individuals, either through altering their brain chemistry, uncovering their conflicts, helping them to realize their identity and achieve their potential, alter their behaviour through new learning experiences or restructure their cognitions. Another diverse set of therapies place more emphasize on the social nature of problems and look more to a social dimension to therapy.

Interpersonal psychotherapy (IPT) for depression (Klerman *et al.* 1984) is in some ways an intermediate approach in that it takes as its focus the individual but deals primarily with changing the clients ways of relating to others. IPT is based on the observation that depression often appears to be related either to a lack of fulfilling relationships or to the presence of relationships which are stressful and laden with conflict. A typical course of therapy would last for 15 to 20 weekly sessions. Therapist and client identify areas of relationship problem and work to alter those situations, such as reducing conflicts or improving social and communication skills or adjusting to the loss of a relationship. IPT is a development of the work of interpersonally oriented psychoanalysts such as Harry Stack Sullivan, although the therapy is in many respects more of an action therapy, concentrating on identifying and solving current problems.

Some therapeutic approaches are based on couples or families rather than individuals. Couples therapy, or marital therapy as it used to be known, focuses on problems in the relationship of two people and often focuses on improving communication and breaking vicious cycles that have developed in their relationship. Family therapy, which can be insight-oriented or action-oriented, assumes that individuals who are experiencing problems do not do so in isolation from their interpersonal surroundings. Rather than seeing the problem as being an individual who is depressed or who has an eating disorder, the problem is thought to reflect some dysfunction within the family. An example is Minuchin's (1974) work on anorexia, which emphasized the role of family organization. Minuchin (1974) observed that the families of the anorexic girls referred for therapy were often overly involved and interdependent, what he called **enmeshed families**, rather than encouraging of autonomy of the individual members. The anorexia, usually of a teenage daughter, was seen as a way of asserting independence and autonomy. Often parents would relate to each other only through the children, and part of the treatment would therefore involve helping the parents to re-establish a direct relationship with each other.

Integration of models and treatments

Models and their associated treatments have been talked about so far as alternative conceptualizations and interventions for psychological problems. However, in practice this is often not the case. First, many therapists do not adhere exclusively to one particular approach, being able to change their approach depending on the particular needs of the individual client or integrating aspects of a number of different approaches. As already pointed out, this flexibility of approach, eclecticism, characterizes the work of most therapists. In practice it is difficult to be completely **eclectic** as it is not easy for therapists to have expertise in a wide range of approaches. Some researchers and clinicians have outlined how elements of different approaches could be combined, such as Safran and Segal's (1990) integration of cognitive and interpersonal approaches to depression, which also takes into account the therapeutic relationship as a tool in the therapy. The practice of integrating therapeutic approaches is

---

Ψ Section summary

Psychotherapy, as opposed to biological therapy, aims to change a person's feelings, thoughts and behaviour through a social interaction between therapist and client. Two broad approaches to psychological therapy have been described – insight-oriented therapy and action-oriented therapy. Insight therapies aim to change the person through uncovering the nature of his or her problems, usually by uncovering the source of these problems in the past. Action-oriented therapies are more focused on current rather than past experience and tend to be of shorter duration. Other approaches emphasize the importance of the person's current social situation in the problem and therapy may include partners or other family members. Although different types of therapy have traditionally been seen as rival approaches, increasingly there are attempts to integrate therapies and in practice most therapists do not adhere simply to one approach.

1 What are some of the main ways that insight-oriented and action-oriented therapies differ from each other?
2 Discuss how different therapies relate to underlying models of psychological disorders.

difficult but the future is likely to hold more examples of how different elements of different therapies can be combined to greatest effectiveness.

Assessment and diagnosis

No therapy can take place without the therapist coming to some understanding about the nature of the person's problems. Therefore, therapy is preceded by assessment, which is the process of finding out what the person's problem is, as well as coming to a view about what some of the factors causing the problem might be. In addition, assessment will influence the type of therapy that is given, as some therapies are known to work most effectively for particular disorders. One particular type of assessment is **diagnosis**, where a formal system is used to arrive at a label for the patient's disorder. When we use terms such as schizophrenia, major depression, and generalized anxiety, we are using diagnostic terms.

Assessment

Clinical assessment is affected by the same issues of reliability and validity that run through all psychological assessment and have been discussed extensively in Chapter 21. Assessment is a very broad term, ranging from looking at brain structure to evaluations of ability to function in everyday life. Biological assessment relates to the biomedical model. If psychological disorder arises from dysfunctional physical processes in the brain, it makes sense to look at those processes directly. There have been very significant advances in the ability to scan, or examine directly, brain activity. Computerized axial tomography (CAT) scans produce a two-dimensional picture of a cross-section of the brain, using x-rays techniques which can detect differences in tissue density. In positron emission topography (PET) scans and nuclear magnetic response imaging (NMR) scans a picture of the brain is derived by measures which can assess the metabolic activity of the brain, thus enabling the researcher to form a picture of brain activity at that point in time. As well as such direct measures of brain activity, neuropsychological tests provide more indirect measures which can inform us about brain function. From these neuropsychological tests, inferences can be made about damage or dysfunction to particular brain areas. Finally, psychophysiological measures assess changes in a variety of bodily states that are related to psychological states, such as muscle tension, skin conductance and heart rate.

Psychophysiological measures such as these have been extensively used in the study of anxiety. Although methods of physical assessment such as the ones just outlined can be very useful in certain cases, for example where the therapist may suspect that the patient's problems might be the result of brain damage, most assessment for therapy is psychological in nature.

Clinical interview

The most common form of assessment in therapy is the clinical interview, where, through a series of questions and answers the therapist comes to a formulation of the patient's problem. Different theoretical orientations of the therapist will lead to different questions being asked. For example psychoanalytic therapists will ask about early experiences and because they believe much of what is important is unconscious will not necessarily take the patient's responses at their face value. Cognitive-behaviour therapists will tend to ask more about current experience and also be more likely to take what is said at face value rather than look for underlying meanings in what the patient says. However, as in characterizing therapies, it is easy to present a caricature of assessment, and therapists of all persuasions will assess past as well as current experience and assess *how* something is said as well as *what* is said. Clinical interviews do not usually follow a predetermined course, although attempts have been made to develop structured interviews in order to improve the reliability of diagnoses, which will be discussed shortly. However, in the normal practice of therapy, therapists will not follow a script, preferring to tailor the assessment to the individual patient, which probably has the effect of reducing reliability.

Structured interview schedules have been devised in order to ensure that assessments are more reliable, which is vital for research studies. One commonly used schedule is the Structured Clinical Interview for DSM-III-R (SCID: Spitzer *et al*. 1990). Interviews such as these give the interviewer detailed instructions about criteria on which to make ratings and also when to use follow-up questions establishing duration, frequency and severity of the problem. Such interview schedules can take very varying lengths of time to complete, as a respondent who does not report many symptoms will then not be asked follow-up questions to determine how often he or she experiences the symptom, how severe it is and how long it has been going on.

There are important elements to all clinical interviewing such as the therapist creating an atmosphere of trust where the patient can disclose fairly intimate information. It is also important to show empathy and interest in the patient's description of his or her problems. Techniques such as the therapist reflecting back to the patient what she has said, using the patient's own words, and using what the patient has said as a starting point for asking further questions are valuable. The first meeting between therapist and patient is invariably taken up with assessment, but the process of assessment will continue beyond that and initial formulations will be revised and updated in the light of new information.

Psychological tests

Psychological tests are standardized procedures designed to measures performance on a particular task. Some tests are tied to particular theoretical approaches, for example the Rorschach inkblot test and the Thematic Apperception Test (see Chapter 14) are intended to assess patients' unconscious processes through bypassing their unwillingness or inability to describe their true inner state. Such a goal makes sense if patients do not have direct access to the source of their problems. Such tests are called projective tests because the patient's responses to an ambiguous stimulus such as an inkblot or a picture are open to several interpretations and are thought to allow the patient to project wishes and impulses onto the picture.

In contrast, self-report measures directly ask the respondents to report on their problems. There are many such measures which assess depression, anxiety, schizotypal thoughts, obsessive-compulsive tendencies, and so on. The value of such questionnaires is that they allow the patient to self-assess, that is, they are not open to a great deal of interpretation on the part of the therapist, but simply produce a score reflecting what the patients say about their own experience. The drawback of such open, up-front measures is that it is usually clear what is being asked for and patients may wish to present themselves in a better, or sometimes worse, light than is really the case. Behaviour therapists have, not surprisingly, been interested in measuring behaviour more directly. Such measures are different from self-report measures of behaviour, where the patients report on their own behaviour, for example, how many times they have gone out of the house in the past week. Direct measures might involve the therapist observing the behaviour of the patient within a real-life setting, for example, the amount of times the socially anxious patient makes eye contact in a role-played social situa-

tion. The advantages are that direct measures give direct insight into the patient's behaviour. The drawbacks are that they are sometimes difficult practically and that many psychological problems, for example, negative thoughts in depression, are not observable as they are not necessarily expressed behaviourally.

Diagnosis

The ultimate assessment statement is to provide the patient with a diagnosis. The concept of diagnosis is a medical one, and so is part of the biomedical model of mental disorder, although many adherents of psychological models will also utilize diagnosis. Psychodynamic therapists are unlikely to use formal diagnosis, preferring to formulate the patient's problem within the theoretical framework of psychoanalysis.

Over the history of medicine there has been a growing recognition that different disorders require different treatments. This has partly arisen out of the serendipitous success of different types of treatments for different disorders and also partly out of accurate observation of the clustering together of different sets of symptoms. The result has been the development of classification systems (See also Chapter 17 page 533). Classification systems, as in all scientific endeavours, then aid further understanding of the different entities identified, in this case, disorders. In 1948 the World Health Organization produced the sixth version of the International Statistical Classification of Diseases, Injuries, and Causes of Death (ICD) which was a comprehensive classification of known disorders. The sixth version was the first to include a classification of mental disorders. The aim was to provide consistency across different countries and so provide a solid base for the development of medical science, including psychiatry. However, the aim was immediately sabotaged by the American Psychiatric Association producing its own diagnostic scheme for mental disorders, the Diagnostic and Statistical Manual (DSM) in 1952, due to some disagreements about the classification of mental disorders in ICD. Whereas ICD was just a listing of recognized disorders, DSM was intended to be able to provide enough description of the symptoms to enable an individual to be diagnosed as suffering a particular disorder. DSM was revised extensively in 1969 (DSM-II) and again in 1980 (DSM-III). A smaller revision was made to DSM-III in 1987 (DSM-III-R) and finally DSM-IV appeared in 1994 (APA 1994). Similarly, ICD has undergone revisions and is currently (WHO 1992) in its tenth edition (ICD-10). After some divergence, ICD-10 (mental disorders section) and

DSM-IV are intended to be compatible, although for mental disorders DSM-IV is more commonly used. One of the major changes to DSM over the revisions has been the explicit attempt to make it more descriptive and atheoretical rather than being tied to any theoretical view of disorders. This has led to dissatisfaction within the psychoanalytic community for whom specifying underlying mechanisms is crucial in the formulation of the problem, rather than simply concentrating on manifest symptoms. A second change has been to provide ever more specific descriptions of symptoms and criteria for meeting diagnosis. The aim has been to provide greater reliability and create less room for difference of individual clinical judgement.

Diagnostic and Statistical Manual (DSM)

Since DSM-III on, assessment has been based on five axes. The major axis is Axis 1, which contains the classification of all the different disorders, such as anxiety disorders, mood disorders, schizophrenia, eating disorders and substance-related disorders. On Axis 2 the person is assessed on personality disorder. The remaining axes allow the clinician to specify any medical conditions which are relevant to the psychological disorder, any relevant social and environmental problems, and to assess the patient's current level of functioning. Thus use of DSM-IV provides the opportunity of a very comprehensive assessment of the patient, including making a diagnosis of a particular disorder.

DSM-IV is a system of classification, and one of the objections to any classification is that it results in the loss of valuable information by overemphasizing the similarities between individuals while ignoring important differences. However, a specific criticism of diagnosis is that it is based on an all-or-nothing categorization; someone is either depressed or not. There is no recognition that many psychological problems might be best thought of as a falling on a continuum rather than being made up of discrete, all-or-nothing categories. This is a difficult issue as it is clear that many disorders do fall on a continuum but it is equally clear that it is clinically useful to have some line beyond which people are considered to be suffering from the disorder and in need of help. A final point that should be noted about diagnosis is that it has economic and political ramifications. As Strupp (1996) has pointed out, in the United States having a DSM-IV diagnosis is often the only way to get reimbursed by medical insurance companies for psychotherapy costs. It is not difficult to see the economic pressures on therapists to provide a diagnosis.

Ψ Section summary

Therapy cannot proceed without an assessment of the nature of a person's problem. Many assessment techniques exist, such as brain scanning, psychometric tests, self-report inventories and clinical interviews. One form of interview which is highly structured is a diagnostic interview, which leads to a formal classification of a person's problem according to an exisiting scheme such as DSM-IV. Diagnosis is almost always an oversimplification of a person's problems and ignores the dimensional as opposed to categorical nature of psychological problems, but can nevertheless be useful in suggesting particular types of therapy.

1 What are the main types of assessment procedures and what are their uses?
2 Is diagnosis a valuable tool in understanding psychological problems?

☐ Do psychological therapies work?

Having covered the main approaches to therapy the obvious question is whether therapy works and, if so, does any therapy work better than the others. There is a third question, which is, if therapy does work, exactly how does it work? The next section will attempt to answer these questions.

There has been great debate over the years about whether psychological therapies work. Hans Eysenck, in typically controversial fashion, acted as a catalyst when he published a paper in 1952 claiming to show that there was no reason to believe that psychotherapy (by which he meant insight-oriented therapy) was effective and, even worse, that there was reason to believe that psychoanalysis in particular was harmful. Eysenck's conclusion was based on his analysis of the results of a number of different reports of ratings made by therapists at the end of treatment. These reports were from a number of different countries and from various institutes and summarized the results of over 7,000 patients who had undergone treatment for neurotic disorders (mainly anxiety- and depression-related problems). The therapy involved was either psychoanalysis or eclectic therapy (which would have meant insight therapy at that time). Eysenck's analysis of these data claimed that eclectic therapy had a success rate of 66 per cent and psycho-analysis a success rate of 44 per cent. However, the crux of his argument was that in order to show that psychotherapy was effective it must be shown to have better effects than simply leaving people alone. It is known that many psychological problems do improve if given time, a phenomenon known as **spontaneous remission**. Any effects of therapy therefore need to be compared with spontaneous remission rates. His control groups for spontaneous remission rates were patients discharged from hospitals in New York who had been suffering from neurotic conditions but had been given custodial care only, not any psychotherapy. A second control group was based on records of insurance disability claimants who had been unable to work because of psychological problems. These claimants did not receive psychotherapy but were assessed from time to time by a general practitioner to see whether they were well enough to return to work. Therefore, recovery rates could be deduced. Eysenck's analysis of his control groups led him to conclude that spontaneous remission rates over a period of two years (comparable to treatment length) were 71 per cent, therefore leading him to his conclusions about the effectiveness of psychotherapy.

Not surprisingly, upon publication these conclusions sparked a heated debate. Over the next 20 years or so, there were many criticisms of Eysenck's conclusions, mainly based on the inappropriateness of the control groups and the non-comparability as well as the interpretation of the outcome measures. In 1971 Bergin published a reinterpretation of Eysenck's analysis, based on the same data set but using different criteria for recovery. In his analysis, eclectic therapy showed the same 66 per cent success rate but psychoanalysis showed a 91 per cent success rate, whereas the rates he arrived at for spontaneous remission were only 30 per cent. The comparison between Eysenck's and Bergin's analysis of the data is shown in Figure 18.3. The fact that the same basic data set can give rise to such different conclusions gives some indication of the difficulty in trying to evaluate the effectiveness of therapy.

How to evaluate therapy

The process of evaluating the effectiveness of therapy seems from the outset to be deceptively simple. What is required is a measure taken before and after therapy, and success can be gauged by the degree of change in the measure. The first complication is that there must be a control group in order to control for factors like sponta-

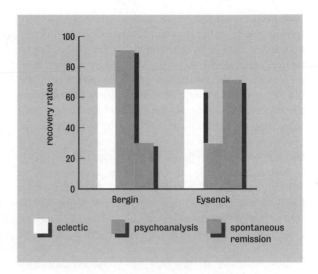

Figure 18.3 Comparison of H.J. Eysenck's and Bergin's analysis of the same outcome data on effectiveness of therapy

neous remission and even effects of repeating a measure. One obvious control group is a sample of people suffering from the same problem or set of problems who do not receive any treatment. Apart from the ethical problems of denying treatment to those who need it there are other problems with this strategy. In trying to see whether a therapy is effective, one of the aims is usually to assess whether it is something about that particular therapy that makes the difference rather than simply the fact of having someone to talk to or who takes an interest in the client's problems. This problem of identifying **specific factors** involved in a therapy's effectiveness, as opposed to non-specific effects, or what are also called **common factors**, is like the **placebo effect** in medical treatments. When evaluating the effectiveness of a drug, there will also be a control group of patients who are given a placebo, something which looks like the drug but does not contain any active ingredients. Neither those who are allocated to the group receiving the drug or those who are allocated to the placebo group know which group they are in, and in a properly conducted trial, neither do those administering the medication know whether they are giving the drug or the placebo. Such a trial is called a **double-blind trial** because neither patients or therapists know who is in the drug group and who is in the placebo group. All patients are aware that the study is taking place, have consented to take part, and know that they will have been randomly allocated either to the drug group or the placebo group. The point of this rather elaborate procedure is to eliminate any effects which are not attributable to the specific effects of the treatment, such as having someone take an interest in your problems or the expectancy of recovery that might arise from knowing you are getting treatment. If the treatment group do better than the placebo group this can then confidently be attributed to the effects of the drug. However, in psychotherapy there is an important difference to chemotherapy. Whereas in chemotherapy the active, specific factors are chemical and the non-specific, common effects are psychological, in psychotherapy both the specific and common effects are psychological. We shall return to this issue, which has been a major issue in psychotherapy research. The typical design of a current treatment trial addressing the effectiveness of psychotherapy is to compare different treatments rather than compare treatment with no treatment, which deals with both the ethical issues and also the problem of non-specific factors.

There are a number of other difficulties in evaluating psychological therapies, such as heterogeneity of patients. Patients, even those with the same diagnosis, often have quite different problems. Therapists, despite being trained in the same therapy, will be very variable in their effectiveness and differ in their preference for particular therapies. There are solutions to these problems such as selecting patients for a particular trial very carefully and using treatment manuals to which therapists have to adhere. However, such steps tend to call into question the generalizability of any findings as it may become quite remote from what happens normally in therapy.

One of the major issues in therapy outcome evaluation is which measure of outcome to use. Hans Strupp (1996), one of the leading figures in psychotherapy research since the early 1970s, points out that there is no clear consensus on what constitutes mental health and gives a number of examples making this point. Is a patient who becomes more assertive but also more abrasive as a result of therapy an example of a good outcome? What about someone who gets a divorce, or someone who changes sexual orientation as opposed to becoming more accepting of it, or an ambitious person who becomes less striving but achieves less? Strupp (1996) has argued that therapy should be evaluated from three perspectives. The first perspective is that of society, including the patient's significant others, and is largely a measure of how much the patient's behaviour has changed. Factors such as behavioural stability, conformity to social norms, and ability to function are likely to be the main influences in this measure. The second factor is the patient's own view, which will largely be a reflection of subjective well-being, how good or bad the patient feels as a result of therapy. The third factor is the judgement of the therapist, independently of the patient's self-report. This judgement will usually be made within some sort of theoretical framework of healthy personality functioning. An example of such a framework would be psychoanalysis where the therapist might judge the outcome of the therapy in terms of the patient's use of defence mechanisms and ego structure. The results of the three dimensions might be quite different, which was part of the problem with Eysenck's (1952) analysis as the controls, at least the insurance claimants, were judged largely from the first vantage point whereas the psychotherapy patients were all judged from the third vantage point. The important point is that all three vantage points are important. However, it is no coincidence that Strupp's (1996) example of the therapist's independent judgement within a theoretical framework is a psychodynamic one. It is much more likely that this type of judgement will be made within a psychodynamic framework. For a cognitive-behavioural therapist, if the patient is functioning well and reports feeling fine then it is unlikely that the therapist would ever make any judgement other than a successful outcome. In other words, the three dimensions are not seen as equally important to all therapies.

Is therapy effective?

For the twenty years or so following Eysenck's (1952) paper there was a great deal of research carried out on the effects of psychotherapy, much of it motivated by a desire to show that psychotherapy was effective. The question was not only does psychotherapy work but also does any therapy work better than any other? The results of this research are quite clear: psychotherapy (which includes both insight and active therapy) is better than no therapy, and there is very little to choose between different types of therapy in terms of their effectiveness. The results were nicely summarized by Luborsky *et al.* (1975) borrowing a quotation from *Alice's Adventures in Wonderland*: '*Everybody* has won, and *all* must have prizes'.

The question was answered even more conclusively by M.L. Smith and Glass (1977) who produced a **meta-analysis** of 475 studies that had been conducted on psychotherapy outcome. Meta-analysis is a statistical technique for aggregating the differences between conditions, where those conditions have been compared in a number of separate, unrelated studies. Obviously, this produces a much more comprehensive test of whether there is a significant difference between conditions than a number of studies in isolation can do. Their conclusion was the same as had previously been reached by researchers reviewing the literature, that is, that therapy was better than no therapy but no one therapy was better than any other. They directly compared action therapies (mainly behaviour therapy up to that point) and insight therapies, and concluded that they were equivalent in their effects. However, controversy followed as Smith and Glass (1977) deliberately reduced the size of the effects of behaviour therapy. The reason given for this was that studies involving behaviour therapy tended to have patients who were less severely disturbed and also employed more reactive measures, measures that were more likely to show change, such as self-reports of behaviour. Smith and Glass (1977) also found that the allegiance of the therapist was important,

with greater effects coming from therapists who adhered to the therapy they were asked to conduct rather than therapists who were asked for the sake of the study to carry out a different therapy. As most research is carried out by action-oriented researchers and therapists, who are more committed to empirical evaluation, then this may have also meant that studies tended to favour action-oriented therapies, thus justifying Smith and Glass's (1977) decision to moderate those effects.

Since the publication of this and other reviews, the question has moved on from whether therapy is effective to the question of how therapy works. In the current edition of the influential *Handbook of Psychotherapy Research* (Bergin and Garfield 1994) Eysenck's study questioning the efficacy of therapy is not even cited (Jacobsen and Christensen 1996). There are exceptions to this change and one interesting exception is the results of a survey produced by the Consumers Union in the United States. A summary of this survey is described in the research update.

 Research update

Therapy: the consumer's view

The Consumers Union is an organization in the United States which carries out independent research into a range of areas and services affecting consumers such as hotels, lawyers, homeowner's insurance, and so on. In 1994 it decided to carry out some research into its subscribers' experiences of therapy. The results of the research were published in 1995 in Consumer Reports and is summarized in Kotkin *et al.* (1996). About 184,000 randomly chosen subscribers were sent the annual survey, some of which asked about experiences of therapy. Of the 6,900 who filled in the section on therapy, over 4,000 had sought professional help over the past three years, and results were based on those people. The most frequently cited problem was depression; other problems included general anxiety, marital or sexual problems, and problems with children or other family members. The main results were the following:

- The vast majority of respondents said that therapy had helped them (42 per cent said it had helped a lot

and 44 per cent said it had helped somewhat; only 1 per cent said it had made things worse).
- There was no difference in helpfulness ratings between different types of therapy.
- Longer-term therapy (greater than six months) was associated with better ratings than short-term therapy (less than six months).
- Psychologists, social workers and psychiatrists performed equally well, all better than marriage counsellors and general practitioners (even after controlling for the type of problem).
- Those who had been prescribed medication rated it as helpful, although for those who were also receiving psychological therapy drugs did not seem to confer any extra advantage.

Clearly, there are many limitations to this study: the sample is not random and therefore may not be representative; the outcome is based on the retrospective reports of the respondents only; and there is no control group. However, as an indication of what goes on in practice, as opposed to what happens in specially designed trials, the report represents a valuable insight.

How is therapy effective?: common factors versus specific factors

The distinction between common factors and specific factors has already been talked about. Common factors are elements such as warmth, acceptance, empathy, and so on that should be common to all therapies, the sort of therapist qualities outlined by Rogers (1951). Specific factors are techniques that are elements of a particular type of therapy, such as thought-catching in cognitive therapy or use of the transference in psychoanalysis. The fact that different therapies seem to have equivalent effects would suggest that common factors rather than specific factors are the key to successful therapy. As already discussed, Rogers's view of what was crucial for therapy to be successful emphasized qualities of the therapist, rather than any specific techniques the therapist might use. Another way to address the question is to ask clients who have benefited from therapy what it was they found most helpful. Sloane *et al*. (1975) found that patients who had benefited from therapy, whether they had undergone behavioural therapy or insight-oriented therapy, gave very similar answers to the question of what was helpful. The main variables identified were the personality of the therapist, the therapist's help in gaining an understanding of their problems, the encouragement given by the therapist to gradually face up to things that they found difficult, and being able to talk to an understanding person. The fact that patients undergoing therapies of different theoretical persuasions emphasized the same set of factors reinforces the belief that common rather than specific factors are what makes therapy effective. Furthermore, the fact that patients undergoing insight-oriented therapy emphasized the value of being helped to gradually face up to difficult things, a key element of behaviour therapy, and those undergoing behaviour therapy placed value on gaining an understanding of problems, the rationale behind insight therapies, suggests that therapists of whatever persuasion were enacting these common factors. It is now widely accepted that common factors play a large part in the therapeutic process. Strupp (1996) concludes that about 85 per cent of the variability in therapy outcomes can be attributed to common factors.

The emphasis placed on common factors raises questions about the role of specific factors and, in particular, calls into question the value of training in psychotherapy, which can be long and costly. If common factors are so important, do people really need to be trained in specific therapeutic techniques? Strupp and Hadley (1979) carried out an interesting study where they took a sample of students who were suffering from mildly neurotic problems and allocated them to either a trained experiential therapist or a college professor. The professors were selected on the basis of being known by students to be good to talk to. The student met with the therapist or the professor twice weekly for a total of about 18 sessions. At the end of this period, both groups were found to be doing better than controls (students with similar problems but who did not receive any specific help) in terms of their emotional well-being, but did not differ from each other. That is, those who had seen the sympathetic college professors were doing as well as those who had seen the trained therapists. It is tempting to conclude that training does not make any difference to therapy effectiveness. However, as Strupp (1996) and others have pointed out, there are reasons why this is not a valid conclusion. First, the college professors were not randomly chosen but were a highly selected group who were known to be able to relate well to students and their concerns, whereas the therapists were not specially selected in this way. In addition, the therapists were not specialists in time-limited therapy, which was what was given, but would have been more used to longer-term therapy. Strupp (1996) suggests that there are important differences between professional therapists and non-professionals. First, training enhances common factors such as warmth, listening skills, and a commitment to the patient's welfare. Second, training equips the therapist to be more able to manage the way that the patient's problems manifest themselves in the therapeutic relationship, for example, hostility, dependence and idealization towards the therapist. A trained therapist is more likely to be able to avoid playing a complementary role to the patient's problems, for example, taking on excessive responsibility for a patient who is overly dependent. Seligman (1996) suggests that trained expertise becomes important when the client's problem is more complicated, there is no treatment manual to be followed, and where clinical judgement needs to be used, for example, in formulating the problem. Finally, training does equip the therapist with technical skills, which, alongside common factors, do make an impact in therapy. Persons and Burns (1985) examined patients' mood change during (cognitive) therapy and found that there were independent contributions to mood change from the therapist's qualities (common factors) and technical interventions from the therapist (specific factors).

There is one other important dimension to evaluating therapy which has not yet been discussed, that is the question of whether any benefits observed at termination of therapy are maintained. Some disorders, for example depression, are known to be recurring disorders. Thus, evaluating the success of any therapy to prevent future relapse may be as important as evaluating its success in producing recovery from the current episode, especially in recurring disorders like depression. Barber and DeRubeis (1989) review evidence which shows that although CBT and drug therapy for depression produce equivalent results in terms of recovery, studies including a follow-up (e.g. one year after the end of treatment) have shown that patients who received CBT were less likely to relapse over the follow-up period. They suggest that CBT works by equipping people with a new set of skills, such as general problem-solving and self-management skills, and also reduces depression about depression. Depression about depression, or secondary depression as it is usually called, is where people become depressed about the fact that they are depressed. Secondary depression can be a major problem in maintaining a depressed state. Effectively, patients learn through cognitive therapy to become their own therapist. Such a set of skills can then be brought into play when the person is under pressure at some vulnerable point in the future, thus preventing relapse. Recipients of CBT are being given a way to deal with their own depressive thoughts as they arise, and, over time, it is hoped that the exercise of these skills will reduce the tendency to have depressive thoughts in the first place.

Hazelrigg et al. (1987) have also put forward a similar argument for family therapy. Family therapy does not appear to produce better results at termination than other types of therapy, even on measures of family functioning, which would be expected to be better after family therapy than after another therapy, such as drug therapy. However, they point out that fewer families return for treatment in family therapy. There are obviously a number of ways of interpreting this finding but they suggest that fewer families return because they have been empowered to deal with their own problems, rather like CBT equipping individuals to deal with their own depressive tendencies.

Deterioration

As we have seen, the evidence is overwhelmingly in favour of therapy being, on average, beneficial. However, can therapy sometimes be harmful? This question of deterioration or, as it is more commonly called, 'negative outcome' has also been examined. M.L. Smith et al. (1980), as part of their large meta-analysis, conclude that there was little evidence of negative effects. However, the actual figure they reported was that in 9 per cent of the studies they looked at, the group receiving therapy had a worse outcome than those not receiving therapy. This 9 per cent seems rather a high figure to be dismissed so easily, especially as it is likely to be an underestimate. In research trials, therapists are usually carefully selected, are motivated to try their hardest, and both patients and therapists are likely to feel some pressure to report a good outcome.

Given that negative outcome clearly exists in some cases, what causes it? If therapist factors are important in recovery then therapist factors seem a likely candidate for patient deterioration. Rachman and Wilson (1980) concluded that there was no evidence of a causal link between therapist activities and patient worsening. However, others have not supported this conclusion. Yalom and Liberman (1971) examined deterioration in patients in group therapy and concluded that groups with authoritarian leaders, who insisted on immediate self-disclosure and emotional expression, were associated with a poor outcome for the patients attending those groups. Thus, although disclosure and emotional expression are generally recognized to be important elements of therapy, it is equally important that they take place voluntarily within the context of a trusting relationship between therapist and patient. Similarly, higher rates of negative outcome have been found in expressive-experiential therapies, which emphasize the importance of experiencing heightened emotional states. In one study (Daldrup et al. 1988), an anger arousing therapy called focused expressive psychotherapy was associated with a 19 per cent deterioration rate in patients with major depression. This is not to say that such therapies cannot be helpful, but the risk of negative outcome is higher, particularly in patients with more severe problems. Sachs (1983) found that negative outcome was associated with therapists who failed to structure sessions properly, who allowed patients to talk about their problems in an unstructured way.

Research has also identified patient factors that are associated with negative outcome, such as having severe problems or having unrealistic expectations about therapy. In a review, Mohr (1995) summarizes the findings showing both the therapist characteristics and patient characteristics that are associated with negative outcome. These characteristics are shown in Table 18.2. Mohr (1995) also highlights the potential negative

Table 18.2 Therapist and patient factors associated with negative outcome in psychotherapy

Therapist factors
- lack of empathy
- underestimation of the severity of the patient's problems
- negative countertransference (i.e. feelings of dislike or rejection for the patient)
- high concentration of transference interpretations
- poor technique
- disagreement with the patient about the therapy process

Patient factors
- diagnosis of borderline personality disorder or obsessive-compulsive disorder
- severe interpersonal difficulties and poor interpersonal functioning
- poor motivation
- expectation that therapy will be easy and painless

Source: Mohr (1995)

Table 18.3 Specific therapies known to be effective for specific problems

Problem	Therapy
Anxieties, fears, phobias and panic	Progressive relaxation Transcendental meditation Systematic desensitization Modelling Cognitive therapy Medication (e.g. Valium, imipramine)
Obsessions and compulsions	Exposure and response prevention Medication (clomipramine)
Depression	Medication (e.g. Prozac) ECT Cognitive therapy Interpersonal psychotherapy
Manic-depression and mania	Medication (lithium)
Schizophrenia	Medication (neuroleptics, e.g. chlorpramazine, haloperidol) Family intervention (education, and communication skills)

Source: Rosenhan and Seligman (1995)

impact of unethical behaviour, such as sexual contact between therapist and patient. Such behaviour is very difficult to estimate reliably but estimates suggest that up to 20 per cent of male therapists and 2 per cent of female therapists have had sexual contact with their patients (Lambert and Bergin 1994).

Clearly, deterioration is likely to involve an interaction between therapist and patient. A patient who has more severe problems or who has poor interpersonal skills or who is poorly motivated is likely to provoke a negative reaction in the therapist, which will feed back to the patient and make the patient even less motivated. A therapist who has poor technique and is overly optimistic is likely to react badly when progress is not as he or she would have hoped, which, in turn, will have a bad effect on the patient's morale and motivation.

Which therapy for which disorder?

On average it appears that no therapy produces better overall results than any other therapy. However, this does not mean that all therapies work equally well for all problems. It is obviously not possible to specify all of the variables involved in outcome but we do know something about the relative efficacy of different treatments for different disorders. Rosenhan and Seligman (1995) discuss some of the findings on selective efficacy and their discussion is summarized in Table 18.3.

Minor levels of anxiety are likely to respond reasonably well to relaxation training and meditative techniques that deal with the physical and mental aspects of anxiety. More severe anxieties, especially agoraphobia and social anxiety, respond well to systematic desensitization and simple phobias are helped by modelling. Cognitive therapy has been found to be particularly effective for the treatment of panic attacks. Certain medications, for example, Valium, have been widely used to reduce feelings of anxiety. However, as with all drug treatments there are often undesirable side-effects as well as the problem of dependency (the symptoms return when the medication is stopped). Obsessions and compulsions have been found to respond to clomipramine, which is actually an effective anti-depressant. However, undesirable side-effects include drowsiness and loss of sexual interest. The problems also return once the drug is stopped. Exposure and response prevention, as was illustrated in the case of Rachel, helps up to two-thirds of OCD sufferers and, crucially, the beneficial effects have been found to persist (Foa and Kozak 1993).

There are many different drug treatments for depression. One of the newest is the selective serotonin re-uptake inhibitors (SSRIs), of which Prozac is an example.

Although drug treatments are effective in alleviating the symptoms of depression, follow-up studies have shown that if the drugs are stopped, relapse and recurrence rates are high. For example although a large-scale trial found that drug treatment, IPT and CBT all produced significant improvements in depression, when followed up to 18 months later relapse rates were highest in those who had received drug treatment (Shea *et al.* 1992). Rosenhan and Seligman (1995) argue that ECT, although controversial, can be effective especially in cases of severe depression. Manic-depression, which is characterized by mood swings from elation to depression, or mania unaccompanied by depressive swings, is best treated by lithium, which stabilizes mood.

The neuroleptic drugs, for example, chlorpromazine and haloperidol, revolutionized the treatment of schizophrenia when they were introduced in the 1950s. However, their effectiveness is largely confined to reducing the positive symptoms of schizophrenia. More socially based interventions, such as family education and therapy to reduce the amount of hostility and criticism that the patient will face, have been found to be effective in preventing relapse (Falloon *et al.* 1985).

As in many other disorders, the most effective form of treatment seems to involve a combination of different therapeutic forms.

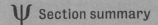

Section summary

There are many issues to be taken into account when trying to decide whether therapy works or not. It is now clear that therapy works, in the sense that therapy is better than no therapy, although there is no clear evidence that one type of therapy is generally superior to another. There is also evidence that in some cases therapy can have a deleterious effect on some people, although these are a minority. One of the reasons that no therapy appears generally superior is the evidence that therapist qualities, such as warmth, imparting a structure to sessions, and helping people to face up to things they find difficult are important factors in a good therapeutic outcome. As no type of therapy will have a monopoly on the best therapists these beneficial effects are likely to be felt in all types of therapy. However, there is accumulating evidence that particular disorders respond better to some therapeutic approaches than to others.

1 What are some of the difficulties inherent in evaluating whether therapy works?

2 Does therapy work and, if so, how?

 ## Research update

A treatment challenge: suicidal behaviour

Suicidal behaviour, either lethal (suicide) or non-lethal (parasuicide), represents a major health problem. The World Health Organization in its *Health for the Year 2000* document has identified halting the rise in suicide rates in Europe as one of its priorities. In the UK the Department of Health has identified suicide as one of its five priority areas, and has set a target of a reduction in suicide by 15 per cent by the year 2000. How effective are interventions in reducing suicidal behaviour? Unfortunately, neither psychological nor biological interventions have been found to have much success in reducing suicidal behaviour. Although interventions have been found to reduce depression and hopelessness and improve social functioning in parasuicides, such interventions have generally not been able to affect the likelihood of

those individuals engaging in further suicidal behaviour (see A.K. MacLeod *et al.* 1992 for a review). One promising intervention which has been developed by Marsha Linehan (1993) at the University of Washington is Dialectical Behaviour Therapy (DBT). Using DBT, it has been possible to demonstrate a reduction in the risk of suicidal behaviour in a group of high risk individuals (those with borderline personality disorder). This therapy is intensive and time-consuming and it is not clear how successfully it will be applied outside of its original setting. However, a number of researchers and clinicians in the UK have now trained in DBT at the University of Washington and trials are currently underway to test its efficacy in settings in the UK. It remains to be seen how effective DBT or other interventions will be in attaining the targets for the year 2000 set by the World Health Organization or the UK Department of Health.

❏ Legal and ethical issues in therapy

Therapy raises a number of ethical issues. As well as some specific issues which will be discussed shortly, there is a wider question about whether psychotherapy itself is ethical. Jeffrey Masson (1989) has argued that because of the inevitable power differential between therapist and client, therapy is inevitably unethical:

the very idea of psychotherapy is wrong. The structure of psychotherapy is such that no matter how kindly a person is, when that person becomes a therapist, he or she is engaged in acts that are bound to diminish the dignity, autonomy, and freedom of the person who comes for help.

(Masson 1989: 24)

Few would take such an extreme position, although it is a useful reminder of the inevitability of a power differential in psychotherapy, even in therapies which try to minimize it. It is certainly better to acknowledge the problem and try to build in safeguards, checks and balances, rather than to pretend that it does not exist.

Considerable attention has been paid to more specific ethical issues in psychotherapy, which also usually have a legal dimension, such as the following:

- Should someone ever be forced to have treatment, or at least be detained involuntarily in a mental hospital?
- Should it be possible to find someone not guilty of a criminal act by virtue of his or her mental state at the time of the act?
- Should therapy be governed by a strict, unbreakable code of confidentiality or are there circumstances where the therapist is obligated to break confidentiality?

Consent and involuntary commitment

In the majority of cases people willingly engage in therapy. However, in some instances, individuals do not feel that they need therapy whereas it is the judgements of others, either friends or family, or mental health professionals, that they do need help. On occasion the issue can become more serious when there is a perceived safety issue. It also makes sense to ask who the potential beneficiary is. As Barlow and Durand (1995: 675) put it: 'are people with mental illness in need of help and protection from society or is society in need of protection from them?' Barlow and Durand (1995) point out that in the USA the pendulum has swung from an emphasis

on protection of rights and freedoms of the individual in the 1960s and 1970s to the greater emphasis on protection of society since the early 1980s, resulting in greater control and restriction on patients.

In the past there have been many instances of people being unjustly committed to mental hospitals against their will, such as husbands committing their wives because of differing views or families committing unmarried daughters who became pregnant. Most countries still do have laws that allow involuntary commitment. Typically, there are three main criteria, not all of which have to occur together:

- the person has a mental illness and is deemed to be in need of treatment
- the person is considered dangerous to himself/herself or to others
- the person is unable to care for himself/herself

In Britain, Section 2 of the Mental Health Act for England and Wales (1983) allows for compulsory admission and detention for up to 28 days on the basis of the patient being thought to suffer from a mental disorder that requires assessment and treatment and/or the detention is necessary for the patient's own health or safety or the protection of others. The order must be supported by an approved social worker and the opinion of two doctors. A further order for compulsory treatment for up to six months (renewable) can be obtained on the basis that the patient requires treatment, that the treatment is likely to be effective, and that the treatment is necessary for the patient's health or safety or the protection of others, and that the treatment cannot be provided without the patient being detained (Section 3). Section 4, which is often converted into a Section 2 order, provides for emergency compulsory admission for 72 hours, based on the recommendation of an approved social worker and one doctor.

There are many problems inherent in trying to define risk, either to oneself or to others. This is very clearly seen in the case of trying to assess suicide risk. Many attempts have been made to identify the factors that put someone at risk for committing suicide (A.K. MacLeod et al. 1992). Despite these efforts, risk prediction is extremely poor, partly because suicide is a relatively rare occurrence and there are great difficulties in predicting uncommon behaviours. The problem is that in drawing up criteria which are associated with suicidal risk there will always be many more people who have the criteria but who turn out not to be at risk than who have the criteria and are at risk. Thus, the cost of identifying people who are genuinely at risk is to incorrectly identify people as being at risk when they are not.

Rosenhan and Seligman (1995) point out that decisions about involuntary commitment should be guided by the 'thank you' test (Stone 1975), which asks the question whether the person, when recovered, would have been grateful for the hospitalization, even in the face of protests at the time.

The insanity defence, or diminished responsibility

One of the earliest cases of the insanity defence was the cause of Daniel M'Naghten who in 1843 attempted to assassinate Robert Peel, the then British Conservative Prime Minister. M'Naghten claimed he was being persecuted by the Conservative Party and was responding to a voice of God instructing him to kill Peel. In fact, he was unsuccessful in his mission but did succeed in killing Peel's secretary, Edward Drummond. The defence argued, successfully, that M'Naghten was suffering from paranoid delusions and could not be held accountable for his actions. Thus, the idea passed into law that people could be found not guilty of a criminal act by reason of them not knowing that what they were doing was wrong due to their mind being disturbed.

The insanity plea divides public opinion. The most publicized case is that of John Hinckley, who tried to assassinate Ronald Reagan when he was President of the United States in 1981. Hinckley's account was that he

was obsessed with the actress Jodie Foster and had thought that by assassinating Reagan she would be impressed and the two of them could somehow live in the White House. Hinckley was judged by a jury to be not guilty by reason of insanity, a judgment which many Americans found difficult to accept. However, it should be noted that being found not guilty by reason of insanity does not mean that the offender gets off free. Typically, those individuals will be sent to a secure psychiatric hospital for an indeterminate time, and in theory could spend longer being detained there than they would if they were sent to prison.

Confidentiality

Clearly, confidentiality should be a fundamental principle of therapy. A principle of confidentiality is essential to fostering the sort of atmosphere in which disclosure can take place and a therapeutic relationship can be built. However, it would be wrong to think that therapy is strictly confidential, in the sense that no third party will have access to any information, or that the therapist will not discuss any details of the case with any other person. An important ingredient of all therapy is peer supervision, where cases are discussed with colleagues. As well as being in the therapist's interests, supervision also benefits the patients by providing more input and greater reflection on their cases. Furthermore, most therapists work for an organization.

Are there any circumstances in which a therapist will disclose details of a case to a third party, outwith the

Ψ Case study

Do therapist responsibilities have a limit?

In some cases, legal judgments have gone further in holding therapists responsible for warning an individual who might be in danger from a patient. Barlow and Durand (1995) describe a tragic case where Prosenjit Poddar, a graduate student at the University of California, became obsessed with a fellow student, Tatiana Tarasoff. He had made advances to Tarasoff, who had shown no interest in him. At the time, he was being seen by therapists at the University Health Centre and had been diagnosed as suffering from

paranoid schizophrenia. At the final therapy session, Poddar hinted at plans to kill Tarasoff and his therapist was concerned enough to inform the campus police. Despite assurances to the police that he would leave her alone, a few weeks later, Poddar shot and stabbed Tarasoff to death. The Tarasoff family successfully sued the university, including the therapists, who were deemed negligent in not warning Tatiana Tarasoff herself of the danger. It was not judged to be sufficient for the therapists to inform the authorities. Clearly, the therapist's role in the area of confidentiality is not an easy one.

organization (apart from the use of clinical material for teaching purposes, which would involve the patient's consent and also the changing of sufficient details to preserve anonymity)? Most countries have laws that place an obligation on therapists to disclose information in certain circumstances. In the UK, there is no general obligation for therapists to disclose information to the authorities, although the therapist may feel morally obligated to do so. The exceptions to this rule are where the information relates to acts of terrorism or to the welfare of children, in which case the therapist is legally obliged to inform the relevant authorities.

Ψ Section summary

There are those who would argue that the whole enterprise of therapy is unethical in that it necessarily represents an imbalance of power between the parties involved. Even those who do not adopt such a strong position would agree that there are important ethical issues in therapy, such as involuntary treatment, diminished responsibility and confidentiality. It is impossible to escape the fact that attitudes towards these issues reflect wider societal values prevalent at the time. For example the balance between protecting society from the individual and allowing indidivual freedom has changed in the recent past. There is no simple answer to ethical issues; they represent ongoing conflicts in the area of therapy.

1   What are the main ethical issues in therapy?
2   Is therapy itself ethical or unethical?

Ψ Chapter summary

● Approaches to therapy

There are a variety of models of psychological problems, each of which has implications for therapy. These models fall into two broad categories, biomedical and psychological. Psychological therapies can be further subdivided into action-oriented and insight-oriented therapies. Action therapies, such as CBT, emphasize the here-and-now and the elimination of problems whereas insight therapies, such as psychoanalysis or contemporary psychodynamic therapies, emphasize the importance of the past and uncovering the source of problems.

● Assessment and diagnosis

Assessment is a major element of the therapeutic process, and relies on a variety of techniques and methods, such as the clinical interview, psychometric tests, brain scanning and projective tests. Diagnosis, providing a formal psychiatric label for a disorder, is also an important element in many therapies.

● Do psychological therapies work?

Evaluating the effectiveness of different psychotherapies is extremely difficult, especially because of the differences in underlying philosophies. However, following a period of debate, there is now overwhelming evidence that psychotherapy works, although it appears that no type of psychotherapy works better overall than any other. Factors shared by all therapies, such as the therapist showing empathy, are known as common factors. These common factors seem to account for most of the effectiveness of therapies. However, some particular disorders are known to respond better to some therapies than to others, such as cognitive therapy for depression and lithium treatment for manic-depression. Some individuals do deteriorate in therapy and this can be the result of patient factors or therapist factors, or, more likely, an interaction between the two.

● Legal and ethical issues in therapy

Therapy poses a number of legal and ethical issues, such as confidentiality, involuntary treatment and diminished responsibility for criminal conduct. Attitudes to these issues are largely determined by societal values at any point in time and so are subject to change.

Further reading

● Lambert, M.J. and Bergin, A.E. (1994) The effectiveness of psychotherapy, in A.E. Bergin and S.L. Garfield (eds) *Handbook of Psychotherapy and Behavioural Change*, 4th edn. New York: Wiley. A very thorough overview of the evidence on the effectiveness of psychotherapy.

● Davison, G.C. and Neale, J.M. (1997) *Abnormal Psychology*, 7th edn. New York: Wiley. Useful coverage of the major therapeutic approaches and their effectiveness.

● Masson, J. (1989) *Against Therapy*. Glasgow: Collins. An interesting critique of the whole enterprise of therapy, arguing that therapy is essentially unethical.

● Vitkus, J. (1996) *Casebook in Abnormal Psychology*, 3rd edn. New York: McGraw-Hill. Nineteen case histories covering the range of psychological problems, including details of therapeutic intervention in each case.

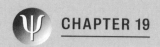

CHAPTER 19

Health psychology and stress

Stan Maes and Thérèse van Elderen

KEY CONCEPTS • what is health psychology? • health behaviour and health promotion • stress, coping and disease

❑ Chapter preview

When you have read this chapter, you should be able to

- describe the area and the reasons for the fast growth of health psychology
- make a distinction between psychological, medical and sociological approaches to health and disease
- understand some of the basic health behaviour models
- give and illustrate basic principles of health promotion
- explain basic approaches to the study of stress and disease
- understand and illustrate with examples an extended stress coping model for chronic disease
- give examples of psychological interventions in chronic disease which differ in aim, level and channel of influence

❏ What is health psychology?

In a way **health psychology** did not, as many people think, originate in North America but in Ancient Greece. According to legend, Zeus, the chief Olympian god, brought the healer Asclepios into the heavens because of his healing skills. Asclepios became a half-god, and had two famous daughters: Hygeia and Panacea. Hygeia, the goddess of health and prevention, taught the Greeks that they could be healthy if they were moderate in all forms of behaviour. Panacea, the other daughter, was known as the goddess of medicine and represented the continuous search for treatment of all illnesses (Lyons and Petrucelli 1978). As health psychology is concerned with the role of behaviour in health and illness, we can think of Hygeia as being the goddess of health psychology.

Matarazzo (1980) has provided a more detailed definition:

Health psychology is the aggregate of the specific educational, scientific and professional contributions of the discipline of psychology to the promotion and maintenance of health, the prevention and treatment of illness, the identification of etiologic and diagnostic correlates of health and illness and related dysfunctions, and the analysis and improvement of the health care system and health policy.

(Matarazzo 1980: 815)

From this perspective, health psychology can be defined as a sub-discipline of psychology which addresses the relationship between psychological processes and behaviour on the one hand and health and illness on the other hand. It should be noted however that health psychologists are more interested in 'normal' everyday-life behaviour and 'normal' psychological processes in relation to health and illness than in psychopathology or abnormal behaviour. From a health psychology perspective, someone who avoids sexual contact after a heart attack out of fear of triggering another one is showing a normal, functional reaction to a dysfunctional situation (the heart attack) rather than an abnormal, phobic reaction.

Rapid growth of health psychology

Health psychology is a rapidly growing sub-discipline of psychology. In 1978 the American Psychological Association (APA) founded a health psychology division, which is now its second largest division. Following the US example many other health psychology groups were formed all over the world, including the health psychology division of the International Association of Applied Psychology, established in 1984. The European Health Psychology Society was founded in 1986; in the late 1990s there are national health psychology groups in many European countries, including Austria, Belgium, Finland, Germany, Hungary, Italy, the Netherlands, Poland, Spain, Switzerland and the United Kingdom. It is important to stress that there were no health psychologists in the mid-1970s. Professionals from very different disciplines with a common interest in matters of health and illness have joined forces to create this relatively new sub-discipline. These disciplines include, among others, physiological psychology, clinical psychology, social psychology, medical psychology, social epidemiology and health education. This may explain important differences between European countries in practical orientation and research (Maes 1992a).

There are many reasons for the rapid growth of health psychology, but the most important is undoubtedly the dramatic shift in causes of death in western countries during the twentieth century. Around 1900 the most important killers in Europe were communicable diseases such as influenza, pneumonia, tuberculosis and diphtheria. After the Second World War, it became clear that **cardiovascular diseases** and **cancer** had become the most important killers. Figure 19.1 lists the most important causes of death in European Community countries in 1992, confirming this picture: more than 80 per cent of **mortality** is attributed to chronic diseases and accidents, implying that death due to communicable diseases has dropped to very low levels. While Figure 19.1 illustrates this dramatic shift, it should be stressed that this is a general picture and that there are important age and gender differences in mortality which are not shown in these data. Accidents and injuries are the most important cause of death among young people, for example, while women live significantly longer than men in western countries.

While micro-organisms play a causal role in communicable diseases, the causes of most of the chronic diseases mentioned in Figure 19.1 are of a very different nature. As can be seen in Table 19.1, the **risk factors** associated with these diseases are to a large extent behavioural or behaviour related. A group of American experts has concluded that as much as 50 per cent of present mortality is due to unhealthy behaviour, about 20 per cent to environmental factors, 20 per cent to human biological factors and 10 per cent to inadequacies in healthcare (Shirrefs 1982). As psychology can be

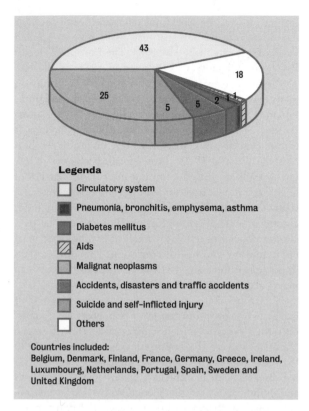

Legenda

☐ Circulatory system

◼ Pneumonia, bronchitis, emphysema, asthma

◻ Diabetes mellitus

▨ Aids

☐ Malignat neoplasms

◼ Accidents, disasters and traffic accidents

◻ Suicide and self-inflicted injury

☐ Others

Countries included:
Belgium, Denmark, Finland, France, Germany, Greece, Ireland, Luxumbourg, Netherlands, Portugal, Spain, Sweden and United Kingdom

Figure 19.1 Causes of death in European countries, 1992
Source: Demographic Statistics (1996); Eurostat (1997)

Table 19.1 Top five causes of death and associated behavioural variables

Rank	Cause	Behavioural correlates
1	Cardiovascular diseases	Smoking, high fat diet, sedentary lifestyle, high sodium diet
2	Cancer	Smoking, high fat/low fibre diet
3	Unintentional injuries	Alcohol use, failure to use seatbelts
4	Chronic obstructive pulmonary diseases	Smoking

Source: adapted from Kaplan et al. (1993)

cessful application of psychological principles and techniques in the field of **compliance** with medical regimen and to various disorders and health problems such as pain, **coronary heart disease** and **diabetes**, has shown that psychologists have the tools to influence health conditions. In addition, modern psychology is characterized by an expertise in research methodology, which puts psychologists in a position to carry out research on disease prevention and evaluation research in healthcare settings. Thus, while health psychologists can contribute to the study and the management of health and disease, their approach is quite different from a traditional medical approach.

Health psychology and medicine: different perspectives on health and disease

The evolution of any science occurs in stages, and the transition from one stage to another is characterized by conflict between old and new ideas. The same applies to the health and medical sciences. Health psychology can be viewed as a typical product of new ideas, which in this case concern the role of behaviour in matters of health and illness. More traditional ideas, however, are characterized by a mind–body dualism. In the traditional view disease is primarily caused by biomedical factors, and psychological or social factors are not seen as contributing substantially to the explanation of the disease process as a whole (Bishop 1994; Engel 1980). This concept of **disease** as deviation from a measurable biological norm still dominates medical thinking and practice. Such a point of view is based on assumptions which no longer seem applicable. The most important of these assumptions is the specificity assumption, which holds that understanding of an illness is more advanced if it

defined as the science of behaviour and behavioural change, it is obvious why psychologists have become increasingly interested in matters of health and illness since the 1950s.

A second reason for the rapid emergence of health psychology was the realization in the 1970s that national health expenditures in western countries were quickly growing out of control. As Figure 19.2 shows, some countries have in the mean time gained more control over these expenditures than others. It is obvious that the United States is still facing very serious problems in this respect. As a consequence of these budgetary problems many countries began to explore possibilities for disease prevention. As **health promotion** may be the most powerful preventive strategy in the western health context, governments are showing increasing support for the involvement of behavioural scientists in disease prevention, and health psychology has indeed made significant contributions in this area since the mid-1970s.

Finally, the third reason for the rapid development of health psychology is closely linked to the development of the discipline of psychology itself. For example, the suc-

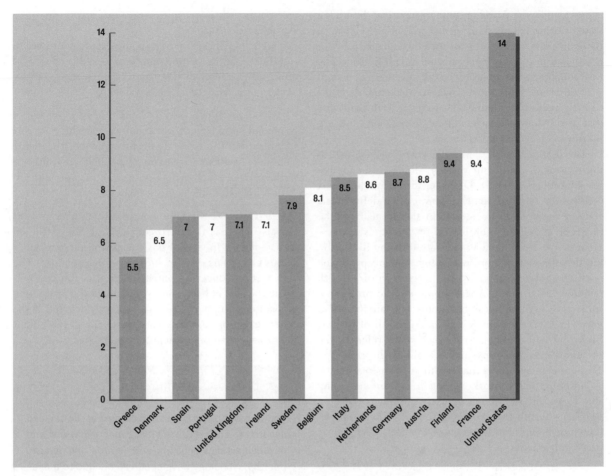

Figure 19.2 Heathcare costs in European countries and the USA, 1992
Source: OESO, *Statistisch Jaarboek* (1996); *CBS and Statistisches Jahrbuch der Schweiz* (1997)

can be defined at more specific biochemical levels. This reductionistic view originated when infectious diseases were still the major causes of death. In the mean time, **mortality** due to infectious diseases has dropped to very low levels, and chronic diseases, which are primarily related to lifestyle, are now the major killers. Nevertheless, many physicians are still of the opinion that all diseases are caused by specific pathogenic agents.

In addition, traditional medicine is more focused on disease than on health. It would be more appropriate to call our healthcare systems 'disease care systems', as their primary aim is to treat or cure people with various diseases rather than to promote health or prevent disease. For example, in the Netherlands, as in other European countries, less than 3 per cent of the national healthcare budget is spent on prevention. Some authors refer to this phenomenon as medicine's passive attitude

towards health, in contradistinction to an active focus on health promotion.

In contrast to medicine, health psychology focuses more on health than on disease. Although health is a central concept of the discipline, the term is not easily definable. Since the mid-1940s, **health** has been defined in many ways, yet mostly in negative terms (e.g. health as the absence of disease, dysfunction, pain, suffering or discomfort). Although such a point of view may seem acceptable at first sight, its consequences are considerable as it implies that one can be considered healthy only if the absence of disease is proven. This comes close to the viewpoint that one is guilty until proven innocent instead of innocent until proven guilty. In other words, a negative definition of health favours a dependent relationship with the healthcare system, which may even endanger health. A good example of a positive definition is provided by the World Health Organization: 'health is a state of complete physical, mental and social wellbeing'. Although this definition was introduced back in 1946, health and disease are rarely treated as holistic concepts. Instead, approaches to health and disease are fragmented over different, scientific disciplines. Medicine has traditionally emphasized physical aspects of health and disease, psychology mental health and disease, and sociology social aspects of health and disease.

The significance of these differences is illustrated in definitions of the terms disease, illness and sickness (Feuerstein *et al.* 1985). **Disease**, the term which best reflects the medical point of view, can be defined as a state of the body characterized by deviations from the norm on measurable biological or somatic variables. **Illness** can be defined as the state of being ill, implying that illness is a more psychological concept, which is closely related to one's own perception of a health problem (e.g. pain). Apart from somatic problems, subjective psychological symptoms (e.g. anxiety) also play a substantial role in the construction of illness. **Sickness** is also a subjective concept as it refers to the social aspects and consequences of health problems. This concept shows us that health consequences, such as not being able to work, staying in bed, and not being able to go out add to a large extent to our perception of others' health problems. Consequently, health problems can be defined in terms of medical, personal or social judgements.

This point of view has important implications. First, it suggests that health and disease can be adequately defined only in terms of a combination of somatic, psychological and social factors. Second, in daily life, different sources of judgement may not always agree: persons who consider themselves ill (I) or not ill (NI), may be considered as having a disease (D) or not (ND) by their medical doctor, and as being sick (S) or not sick (NS) by their social environment. Even this example is a simplification, since medical doctors may disagree, and the social environment of a patient may not behave as one entity (e.g. a patient's partner may react differently from colleagues at work, neighbours or friends). But even if we simplify reality, it is obvious that it is only in situations of full agreement (e.g. I + D + S in a case of terminal cancer; or NI + ND + NS, which is a negative definition of health) that no definitional problems arise. Even if there is only one instance with a different conclusion (e.g. I + ND + S, as in the case of a cleaning woman who complains of low back pain, but is sent back to work by her medical doctor, who cannot find any somatic deviation, while her colleagues are of the opinion that she is not fit to work) this may create quite a problematic situation.

Psychology therefore has a unique approach to health and illness. In line with Krantz *et al.* (1985) one could distinguish three possible relationships which are of particular importance to health psychology:

- psychological processes or behaviour can have direct physiological effects, which influence health
- unhealthy lifestyles may endanger health, while healthy habits may maintain people in good health
- the way in which people perceive and cope with illness influences the course of illness.

The first two relationships concentrate on healthy individuals, whereas the third concerns persons afflicted with an illness. In view of this distinction, the remainder of this chapter is divided into two main sections. The next section concerns contributions of health psychology in the area of health behaviour and health promotion or disease prevention. The final section is devoted to the contribution of health psychology to the development and management of health problems and diseases.

Ψ Section summary

Health psychology is a sub-discipline of psychology devoted to the relationship between behaviour and psychological processes and health and illness. Health psychology developed rapidly due to a dramatic change in causes of death in western countries. While communicable diseases were the main causes of death at the beginning of the twentieth century, cardiovascular diseases, cancer, accidents and chronic respiratory diseases are now the major killers. These causes are strongly associated with unhealthy lifestyles like smoking, unhealthy nutrition, lack of physical exercise, alcohol abuse and various unsafe behaviours. As psychology is the science of behaviour and behavioural change, psychologists are expected to make a contribution to lifestyle changes. Health psychology focuses however more on health and health maintenance than on disease and disease prevention. As such health psychology can complement the efforts of medicine by a more active, health promotive approach. In addition health psychology is more concerned with the perception of health problems and the subjective construction of illness than

Box continued

with more objective biological or social and environmental aspects of health.

1 If a medical doctor were to tell you that there is no need for a discipline like health psychology, what would be your answer if you were a health psychologist?

Health behaviour and health promotion

Relationship between health behaviour and health outcomes

There is considerable evidence of a relationship between **health behaviours** and health or disease outcomes, although the strength of the association is stronger in some cases than in others. For example, smoking is a proven risk factor for cardiovascular diseases, cancer and chronic respiratory diseases. People who engage in regular physical activity are less likely to develop heart disease, **stroke**, chronic pulmonary disease, diabetes and osteoporosis. Unhealthy diet is associated with cancer, cardiovascular disease and diabetes. Excessive body weight increases the risk of cardiovascular disease, especially in combination with other risk factors. Consumption of alcohol is related to various types of accidents and cirrhosis of the liver. Drug use is related to accidents and crime. Stress has been shown to be related to chronic conditions such as high blood pressure, gastrointestinal disease, infectious disease and suicide (World Health Organization (WHO) 1988).

Since it is now common knowledge that health behaviour is related to the onset and progression of various diseases, it may be interesting to know how we acquired this knowledge. In order to demonstrate a causal relationship between specific health behaviours and health and disease outcomes, **prospective studies** are necessary. One well-known study will serve to illustrate the nature of such studies. In a nine-year study, Belloc and Breslow (1972) and Breslow and Enstrom (1980) investigated the relationship between health behaviour and life expectancy in a population of approximately 7,000 adults in Alameda county, California, USA. At the beginning of the study respondents were asked simple questions about their health behaviour, and in the next nine years data on physical health and mortality were collected. It was found that simple daily health behaviours

such as sleeping 7 to 8 hours per 24 hours, eating breakfast regularly, avoiding snacks, maintaining a desirable weight given one's height, moderate or no use of alcohol, regular physical exercise, and not smoking were associated with better health status and a higher average life expectancy. It was calculated that a 45 year old man who engaged in 6 to 7 of these behaviours had a life expectancy of 78 years of age, whereas the life expectancy of a 45 year old man who engaged in 0 to 3 of these behaviours was only 67 years. This means that these simple daily behaviours accounted for a difference of 11 years in average life expectancy. Remarkably, there was a smaller life expectancy difference (7 years) for comparable 45 year old women. One plausible explanation for this sex difference is that women may be hormonally protected from the effects of unhealthy habits.

While a discussion of the separate contribution of every potentially relevant health behaviour would be beyond the scope of this chapter, it is worth mentioning that not all of the health behaviours included in the Alameda study showed equally strong relationships with disease outcomes and mortality. While eating breakfast daily and snacking between meals were weakly related to mortality, smoking was undoubtly the most important predictor of premature death. For this reason smoking serves as a case in point in the next section.

Smoking: a case in point

Yearly about 440,000 Europeans die from smoking. About 90 per cent of those who die from lung cancer are smokers. Smoking is also responsible for about one-quarter of mortality due to coronary heart disease, and for about three-quarters of mortality due to chronic obstructive pulmonary diseases. Smoking is thus undoubtedly the most important preventable cause of death. Percentages of mortality attributable to smoking range from 7–8 per cent in Portugal and Sweden to as high as 21 per cent in Denmark, Ireland and the United Kingdom, as is shown in Figure 19.3.

A number of hypotheses have been formulated about why people start smoking and why they keep smoking. According to Hans Eysenck (1982) personality traits play an important role. Eysenck postulates that extraverted people need more physiological stimulation or excitement than introverted people. The evidence for this hypothesis is however weak (Brannon and Feist 1997). In contrast, what is known as the stimulation hypothesis does seem to hold. Since smoking contains a stimulating drug (nicotine) to which people get addicted, people smoke to maintain their habitual nicotine level and with-

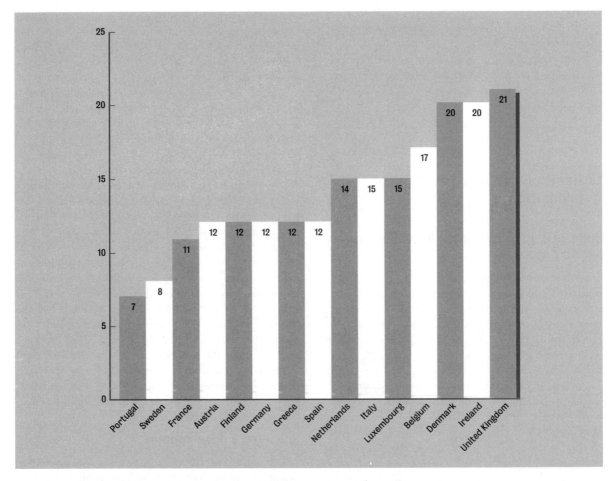

Figure 19.3 Percentage of deaths attributed to smoking in European countries, 1990
Source: Dutch Foundation for Public Health and Smoking

drawal problems occur when they stop or decrease their smoking. This **addiction** hypothesis cannot be the sole explanation for maintaining the habit, however, since use of nicotine chewing gum, which mimics the physiological effects of smoking, is not very effective. A combination of nicotine chewing gum and behavioural therapy shows far better results (30–50 per cent of smokers to whom this intervention is offered remain abstinent in the year after completion of the treatment), which suggests that addiction has not only physiological but also behavioural components (Brannon and Feist 1997). Social learning theory is the source of yet another explanation. According to social learning theory, positive social reinforcement plays an important role in the adoption and

maintenance of a behaviour (Bandura 1977). Numerous studies support this hypothesis, since peer pressure and tolerant parental attitudes towards smoking are the most powerful predictors of the onset of smoking in adolescence; moreover, social factors also seem to play an important role in maintaining or quitting the habit (Leventhal *et al.* 1988).

There is a long tradition in interventions aimed at combating smoking. Two basic types of intervention programmes can be distinguished. The first offers smokers help in quitting the habit; such interventions are called smoking cessation programmes. Other interventions attempt to prevent youngsters from taking up the habit and are called smoking prevention programmes.

Smoking cessation programmes

There is great variety in **smoking cessation programmes**. The techniques used include aversion therapy (e.g. rapid smoking), operant conditioning, **stimulus-control**, **systematic desensitization**, self-monitoring, self-regulation, **modelling** and social skills training. The most successful smoking cessation programmes show a success rate of only about 30 per cent one year after completion of the programme (Chatrou and Borgo 1993; Vinck 1993). If one considers that the delivery of most of these programmes is quite time consuming and expensive (we once calculated that it takes a full-time psychologist a year to help about 150 smokers quit with the average behaviour modification programme), it is obvious why there has been increasing interest in smoking prevention programmes since the 1950s.

Smoking prevention programmes

While some **smoking prevention programmes** are undoubtly moderately effective (Tones and Tilford 1994), the original optimism about the effectiveness of these programmes has decreased over time. The lack of success of some programmes can be attributed to the fact that they were not multimodal (i.e. most programmes did not address physiological, economic, cognitive, social influence, social skill and emotional factors); were offered in a school setting only (rather than reinforcing work done in schools in other settings such as the family, leisure or the media); were offered at one moment in time (rather than being part of a continuous intervention through adolescence); were not targeted to the various developmental stages of the smoking habit and/or were not adopted and delivered by the youngsters themselves (Chatrou and Maes 1993). In addition, as the prevalence of smoking has dropped to low levels in early adolescence, it is more difficult for a smoking prevention programme to yield effects in the late 1990s than it was in the mid-1970s.

Another problematic issue is that few programmes have a sound theoretical base, a problem which limits the effectiveness of interventions aimed at various health behaviours. To illustrate this point, basic models and principles of intervention are described in the next few sections.

Models of health behaviour

The first models: from fear to knowledge

One of the oldest health behaviour models is Miller and Hovland's 'fear-drive model' (Sutton 1982), which was originally based on experimental research with animals. This model postulates that fear or anxiety is the motivating force for 'trial-and-error' behaviour, while fear reduction reinforces the learning of a response which is associated with fear reduction. In other words, if a specific message or stimulus provokes anxiety, the receiver will be motivated to develop behaviour which diminishes this anxiety. Traditional dental education followed this model, as professionals were taught to provoke strong anxiety in people, for example by showing them rotten teeth immediately before teeth cleaning procedures, so that the latter would be reinforced by a reduction in anxiety.

The traditional **fear reduction model** proved to be too simplistic. Janis (1967) postulated that anxiety can lead not only to anxiety reducing behaviour, but also to other forms of behaviour. He proposed an inverted U-shape relationship between anxiety and acceptance of a message, such that moderate levels of anxiety are related to optimal acceptance whereas both high and low levels of anxiety are associated with less acceptance. For example, messages concerning the negative health effects of smoking are more easily accepted by smokers if the message is not too threatening, since smokers would otherwise develop resistance to the message. Although these models seemed to work in certain cases, more recent research has demonstrated that fear appears to have no consistent effect on behaviour change, and is neither necessary nor sufficient to change behaviour (S.E. Taylor 1995).

Another model assumes that people do not know, or do not understand enough about relevant health and risk behaviours and their effects. As a consequence, it is postulated that provision of adequate information will enhance understanding and/or satisfaction and lead to compliance with advice through attitude change (Ley 1982). Unfortunately, most people know the possible effects of risk behaviours, but they are resistent to attitude and behaviour change for many other reasons. For example, almost all smokers in western countries are well informed about the risks of smoking.

Plate 19.1 Although all smokers in western Europe are well informed about the risks of smoking, they are resistant to attitude and behaviour change for many other reasons

Subjective expected utility theory

In reaction to these early models, health behaviour models have become more sophisticated over time. One of the first to bring forward a stronger theory was Edwards (1961), who introduced **subjective expected utility theory**. According to this theory, a person who is confronted with two or more possible actions will choose the one with the greatest subjective expected utility. Subjective expected utility is a function of the expected utility of the outcomes of the action, and the subjective probability that the action will lead to these outcomes. To give one example, a message about exercising to prevent heart disease will be successful according to this theory if it convinces the message recipient that (a) heart disease is a bad thing and (b) exercising will prevent him or her from getting it. Subjective expected utility theory has had a very important influence on more recent models, such as the health belief model, the theory of reasoned action and the theory of planned behaviour, which are described in the next sections.

The health belief model

The health belief model (HBM) (Becker 1974; Janz and Becker 1984) is based on Kurt Lewin's ideas about the attractiveness of certain behaviours. Key concepts in the health belief model are threat perception and behavioural evaluation. Threat perception is dependent on beliefs about personal susceptibility to illness or health breakdown and beliefs about the anticipated severity of the consequences of such illness. Behavioural evaluation concerns beliefs about the benefits or efficacy of a recommended health behaviour, and the costs of or barriers to enacting the behaviour (Sheeran and Abraham 1996). In addition to demographic variables and these psychological characteristics, general health motivation and cues to action are also important concepts in the model (see Figure 19.4). According to the model, a woman will more likely participate in breast cancer screening if she is convinced of her personal susceptibility by the fact that other females in her family have had a mastectomy due to breast cancer (perceived susceptibility and expectation of severe consequences). She will also be more

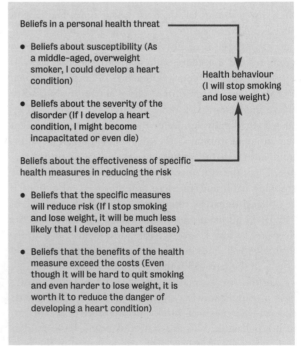

Figure 19.4 The health belief model applied to the health behaviours of giving up smoking and losing weight
Source: Stroebe and Stroebe (1995)

likely to participate if she believes that breast cancer screening is an effective method for detecting cancer and preventing its spread (perceived benefits) and if an opportunity for screening is offered in the neighbourhood where she lives (perceived barriers). Finally, she is more likely to participate if she shows a general health motivation or readiness to be concerned about health matters and if there are triggers or cues to action. Examples of such triggers are advice from family members and mass media messages.

Theory of reasoned action and theory of planned behaviour

The theory of reasoned action (TRA) (Fishbein and Ajzen 1975) assumes that behaviour is a function of behavioural intentions, and that intentions to perform certain behaviours are determined both by attitudes towards performing those behaviours and by subjective norms.

In the theory of reasoned action some changes were made in reaction to the health belief model. Beliefs and attitudes are distinguished, and subjective norms are taken into account. Beliefs about the outcome of a specific behaviour and evaluation of the expected outcome of this behaviour determine the attitude toward this behaviour. A heart patient who thinks 'If I stop smoking, I will probably live longer', and 'I want to get old', is showing a positive attitude towards quitting the habit. Another important component of the model is subjective norms. Normative beliefs and motivation to comply determine the subjective norm. From this point of view, beliefs such as 'My partner wants me to stop smoking' and 'I want to do what my partner asks' lead to a positive subjective norm. Together with a positive attitude, subjective norms predict the behavioural intention, in our example intending to stop smoking. This intention is in turn a significant predictor of the actual behaviour, namely quitting smoking. The assumption that behaviour is a function of intentions, however, limits the applicability or heuristic value of the model to volitional behaviours, that is, to behaviours that are perceived to be under personal control. Therefore, the theory of reasoned action was modified, resulting in the **theory of planned behaviour** (TPB) (Ajzen 1985, 1991).

Inspired by Bandura's work, (1991) added the concept of perceived behavioural control or self-efficacy to the model (Figure 19.5). Control beliefs are important determinants of the perception of behavioural control. The conviction, for example that one is unable to stop smoking, will have a powerful effect on actual quitting. Together with attitudes and subjective norms, perceptions of behavioural control predict intentions, and intentions in turn predict the actual behaviour.

Communication of innovations theory

While the previous models concentrate on the individual or micro level, communication of innovations theory emphasizes changes at the macro level, that is the level of the social system. The theory (Rogers and Shoemaker 1971) is extensively used in studies of the adoption of health-related innovations, and offers a useful tool for describing changes both at the individual level and at higher levels such as organizations, social systems or societies. The innovation-decision process is the process by which an individual (or other decision-making unit) passes from initial knowledge of an innovation, to an attitude towards the innovation, to a decision to adopt or reject the innovation, to implementation of the decision, to confirmation of the decision. The innovation-decision period is the length of time required to pass through the innovation-decision process. This process consists of the five stages mentioned above: knowledge, persuasion, decision, implementation and confirmation.

Based on the period of time needed to adopt an innovation, Rogers and Shoemaker (1971) distinguished various adopter categories. They classified members of a social system on the basis of innovativeness. This classification system can be represented in terms of a bell-shaped (frequency) curve or S-shaped cumulative curve (see Figure 19.6).

The adoption of an innovation follows a normal bell-shaped curve when plotted over time on a frequency basis. This normal distribution represents the number of persons adopting a specific innovation in each time period. Consider for example the number of people buying cars with airbags each year. In the beginning few people will buy cars with airbags, then the majority will follow and finally, the conservative people will also adopt the innovation. The cumulative number of adopters can be represented as an S-shaped curve. Based on the mean and the standard deviation of the bell-curve, five adopter categories can be distinguished. Rogers and Shoemaker (1971) presented a thumbnail sketch of the dominant characteristics of each adopter category:

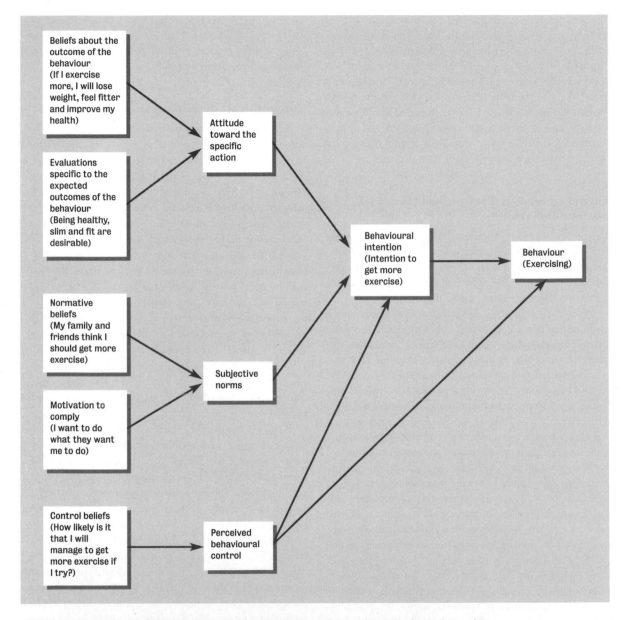

Figure 19.5 The theory of planned behaviour applied to the intention to engage in physical exercise
Source: Stroebe and Stroebe (1995)

- innovators are 'cosmopolites' and venturesome, able to overcome possible negative consequences and mentally and technically capable of trying out the innovation
- early adopters are 'localites' and respectable; the early adopter is a perfect role model for other potential adopters

- the early majority deliberates before taking over the innovation; the motto is 'Be not the last to lay the old aside, nor the first by which the new is tried'
- the late majority is sceptical and cautious; the pressure of earlier adopters is needed to motivate this category
- the laggards are traditional people, backward-looking and suspicious of innovations.

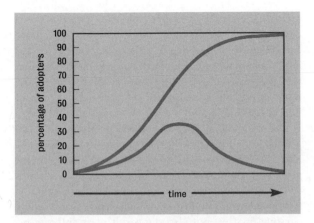

Figure 19.6 The bell-shaped frequency curve and the S-shaped cumulative curve for an adopter distribution
Source: Rogers and Shoemaker (1971)

In addition to adopter categories Rogers and Shoemaker (1971) postulated other variables to be important for the rate of adoption, including characteristics of 'opinion leaders' and 'change agents'.

A critical note

While these models are undoubtedly very popular, they represent only a few examples of current theoretical approaches in health psychology. Other models are described by Conner and Norman (1996) and Tones and Tilford (1994). Models such as the health belief model and the theory of reasoned action or the theory of planned behaviour can be characterized as social cognition models. While they undoubtedly have advantages in the sense that they provide a clear theoretical background for our understanding of health behaviour, they also have limitations. First of all, some researchers seem to regard specific models as religions, to which they must stay faithful. This may lead to repetitive and sterile application of one model to a variety of health behaviours. While these models focus our attention on certain (in this case cognitive) factors and processes, this implies almost by definition that they neglect others (e.g. emotional, volitional, physical, social and environmental). The cognitive or conceptual viewpoint stressed by these models suggests that humans are only rational and that decisions are mainly taken on the basis of perceived advantages and disadvantages of certain actions. Furthermore, the relationship between the model components is almost mathematical and it can be questioned whether humans do in fact act on the basis of such 'cold cognitions'. Another important limitation is that they do not sufficiently emphasize the social setting, which is known to be an important predictor of health behaviour (Stroebe and Stroebe 1995).

Leventhal *et al.* (1985) explained that at least four mechanisms can play an important role in the development and maintenance of health behaviours. These mechanisms are:

- social control, implying that behaviour results from coping with social demands (e.g. in a decision regarding medication compliance: the social power of the medical doctor who prescribes the drug, or the attitude of partners towards drugs and drug-taking)
- emotional or stress control, meaning that behavioural change or opposition to behavioural change can be the consequence of stress regulation (for example, if the prescribed drug produces side-effects which negatively affect someone's well-being, the chance that the person will continue to take them will be lower)
- symptom-based control, implying that symptoms or sensations are interpreted as signs of illness threats, which have strong effects on behaviour (for example, if symptoms disappear, patients may stop taking their medication, and will do the same if the medication seems to be having no effect)
- conceptual control, implying that commitments to specific beliefs control health and risk behaviours (for example, if patients believe they are susceptible to another heart attack and that tablets may prevent them from having one, they are more likely to take them).

One could add to these mechanisms a fifth one:

- self-control, meaning that those who make the decision to change themselves are more likely to maintain the changes (for example, people who are actively involved in a decision concerning medication are more likely to persist in adhering to their medication protocol).

It is quite clear that social cognition models do not address all these control mechanisms to the same extent. In addition, these models undoubtedly provide us with valuable information concerning (cognitive) determinants of health behaviour, but they do not specify how salient cognitions can be changed. In other words they offer a better basis for (partial) understanding health behaviour than for health behaviour change (Conner and Norman 1996).

The communication of innovations theory complements the social cognition models in that it specifies steps in the implementation of a health measure or innovation. While this model thus provides us with the insight that adoption of a health behaviour or measure requires a gradual process of acceptance, there are many other principles and guidelines for health behaviour change, some of which are presented in the case study.

Principles of health behaviour change

There are a number of other psychological approaches, such as operant conditioning, associative learning, cognitive-behavioural theories, and self-management and social learning theories that, together with the above described models, provide a sound basis for an effective and integrative approach to behaviour change. As it is impossible to describe all of these approaches in detail in this chapter, the interested reader is referred to the chapters on the modification of health behaviour in S.E. Taylor (1995).

Lee and Owen (1985) derived principles for the promotion of physical activity from these theories. Maes (1990) stressed the relevance of these general principles for the promotion of a wide range of health behaviours. Before describing these eleven principles, it is important to note that behaviour change is not only a personal matter, but also the result of an interaction

---

Ψ Case study

How to help someone make a health behaviour change

In our quest to help loved ones change unhealthy behaviours, we sometimes become self-righteous. We then become 'warriors against pleasure' to our loved ones and all our brilliant advice falls on deaf ears.

Why do our good intentions go up in smoke? Probably because of the way we communicate our advice. Ask yourself the following questions before offering your words of wisdom:

- Did your friend ask your advice or help?
- Did your friend give any indication of being dissatisfied about something? Is there something that your friend indicated needed a change?
- Are you in a position to offer advice? Are you practising what you preach?
- If you were in need of advice or help, how would you want someone to approach the subject with you?
- How honest can you be? How well do you know your friend's reactions? Can your friend take constructive advice? Is your friend very sensitive or defensive about his or her problem?

After you've asked yourself these questions,

- Go slow. Wait for some suggestion that your friend wants to talk. Don't just meet him or her in class and say, 'Hey, have you thought about getting rid of that weight?'

- If your friend doesn't initiate a conversation about the problem, try to ease into it slowly. You could say, 'Boy, I sure put on weight over the holidays. I really need to start working out to get rid of these extra pounds. I hate to go alone. Would you be interested in going swimming with me sometime this week?'
- If your friend brings up the problem, be supportive. 'I know how hard it is to lose weight. I've struggled with it myself over the years, but have found that such and such works for me. I need to lose some weight myself. Let's work on it together. It'd really help me to have someone help me stay motivated'.
- If your friend is successful in getting started, regularly compliment his or her persistence in sticking to the diet/exercise programme. Don't overdo the compliments, particularly with someone who isn't comfortable with a cheer-leader approach. Treat him or her as you'd normally do. Don't go overboard.
- If your friend has a set-back, say it's okay. Say you understand, but also encourage him or her to get back on track and stay motivated.
- Help your friend stay interested. Try to think of new things to do, new exercise routines, and new eating habits that will make behaviour change a lifestyle rather than an obstacle to be overcome.
- Keep positive and offer support whenever it's asked for. If you are brushed off or if your friend becomes angry, be patient and try another method.

(Adapted from Donatelle and Davis 1996: 25)

between a person and his or her social, political and biological environment. As such, political measures to restructure the environment may be just as important as efforts at an individual level to encourage health-enhancing lifestyles.

Behaviour change occurs in stages

Behaviour change is a dynamic process rather than an event. The process may be characterized in terms of at least three stages:

- the decision to change
- the initial active change
- the maintenance and generalization of the new behaviour

Intervention planners should be aware of these three distinct stages and devise activities that take into account the specific processes linked to each stage. As such, the first stage should focus on the subjects' motivation. Large-scale media campaigns (e.g. smoking, alcohol or weight reduction campaigns) can serve this purpose. In the second stage, skills should be taught (e.g. by offering smoking cessation, weight loss or stress management programmes) and opportunities created to elicit the desired behaviour. In the final stage, self-efficacy should be enhanced, and support and facilities provided to facilitate maintenance of the new behaviour (Prochaska and Di Clemente 1984).

Appropriateness and convenience of settings

The ease and convenience with which health promotive personal actions can be carried out is a strong predictor of their occurrence. It is therefore useful to decentralize facilities and advertise their existence, and to provide possibilities for change at home or at work.

The success of health promotion programmes at the worksite (Fielding and Piserchia 1989) may be partly ascribed to the fact that the facilities necessary for behaviour change are made easily accessible at work for various social groups. The criteria formulated by Chenoweth (1987) for successful health promotion programmes at the worksite may illustrate the value of this criterion. According to Chenoweth, a successful programme will

- have a flexible format
- respect time constraints for participants and providers
- keep equipment and space needs simple
- be easy for the client to administer

- seek ways to integrate health promotion activities as part of company practice
- have appropriate follow-up strategies
- be available for employees on all shifts
- have attractive and informative take-home materials
- include a plan for motivating employees to participate
- be inexpensive or, whenever possible, free to participants.

Setting realistic goals and shaping the process of change

There is evidence that the promotion of a small change towards a new pattern of behaviour is more likely to be effective in producing initial change, as people may become discouraged when the goal of an intervention is very different from their current way of behaving. Apart from this, gradual changes through a series of successful approximations to the target behaviour have proven to be more successful than attempts to change the target behaviour all at once (S.E. Taylor 1995). Asking people who are 20 kilos overweight to lose 2 kilos in the next two weeks is more realistic than asking them to lose 20 kilos in the next six months. Promoting lower level physical activities (e.g. walking) may be a more appropriate way to motivate the sedentary than proposing intense activity (e.g. aerobic fitness training).

Soundness and specificity of instruction

The more specific the aim of a message or intervention, the more likely it is to be effective. Research has consistently demonstrated that health habit change largely depends upon specificity of instructions concerning how, when and where to act (Leventhal 1970). S.E. Taylor (1995) showed that a communication urging the use of a breast self-examination training programme will be more successful in changing behaviour if it includes specific instructions about where and when the programme is to be held and if instructions are provided to scheduling an appointment.

Variety

Although specific interventions and programmes are more effective, they are appropriate only for particular groups under particular circumstances. As such, alternative programmes must be available to ensure behaviour change. To give a few examples: weight reduction can be achieved by means of dieting, fasting, physical exercise, appetite-suppressing drugs or various behaviour modification techniques. Regular physical exercise is achieved in many different ways by different individuals, depending on their social group, gender and so forth. Since there is no such thing as one superior programme from which everyone profits, any programme or intervention should, in principle, focus on a variety of paths to the target behaviour.

Multiple levels

People are influenced by input at many levels, e.g. by mass media, by social reference groups at home, at work, at school and during leisure time, and by one on one interactions. The multiple level principle recommands changes both in individuals and in their immediate environment, stimulated by simultaneous use of various kinds of preventive measures. In other words, restriction of unhealthy behaviours by restructuring the environment or through regulation and legislation, should, whenever possible, accompany the diffusion of strategies for behaviour change. Reducing motor vehicle accidents requires, for example, the use of behavioural strategies to reduce alcohol abuse, but also motor vehicle design (e.g building in a reaction test device to start a car), and new (or better enforcement of existing) legislation and regulations (e.g. restrictions on advertise-

ments for alcohol or increases in the minimal legal age for alcohol consumption).

Use of social networks

The use of existing social networks (e.g. parent and teacher associations, church groups and social clubs) to disseminate information and organize groups and activities is more likely to be effective than attempts to develop new structures and organizations. This is because health behaviour change is more likely to be influenced and maintained by proximal than by distal social influence. The more intense, intimate or similar the individuals, groups or organizations, and the more frequently they interact, the more proximal the social influence (Brannon and Feist 1997).

Choice

If people are of the opinion that they have chosen an activity, or that they themselves have made the decision to change, they are more likely to persist in it. The solid base for this criterion is that self-efficacy expectations are powerful mediators of change and maintenance of change (Bandura 1977). Among the many examples perceived self-efficacy proves to play an important role in dieting, weight control, condom use, uptake and maintenance of physical exercise and resistance to the development of addictive behaviours (Schwarzer and Fuchs 1996).

Plate 19.2 People are influenced by input at many levels, for example by the mass media

Intrinsic value

People are more likely to persist in activities they find enjoyable or interesting. In other words, well-being and health are sometimes conflicting targets, as is the case, for example, with people who stop smoking. In moving towards an important health target, they may experience a significant reduction in well-being. In other words, the principle of intrinsic value specifies that these conflicts should be reduced to a minimum, as they may have serious consequences for the maintenance of the new behaviour. Such reduction can be achieved by presenting new behaviours in an enjoyable manner. The provision of a range of activities, from which people can choose, is already an important step in this direction. In addition to this, it is important to assess the well-being problems people experience when adopting a new behaviour, and to integrate activities in intervention programmes which counteract this reduction in well-being. For the promotion of fitness, this can, for example, be done by providing group games in pleasant settings. In the case of smoking cessation, pleasant physical exercise and the use of stress management techniques may be necessary aspects of an intervention.

Independence

Dependence on any particular place or person reduces the individual's capacities to continue the target behaviour if the situation alters. Individuals should, therefore, be taught skills which will enable them to implement new behaviours relatively independently, to recognize when problems arise, and to seek advice when necessary. Maintenance depends on the capacity to cope with situations or emotional states which may cause relapse. Shiffman (1982) found that ex-smokers who used any sort of active coping response in a relapse-crisis were less likely to relapse than those who used a more passive coping response. There is also evidence that people with strong efficacy expectations with respect to coping with high risk situations are more likely to avoid relapse after weight reduction (S.E. Taylor 1995).

Maintenance of interventions

As stated before, maintenance of initial health behaviour change is a critical issue. However, if we look to the literature, it seems as if many people stick to the naïve belief that single and short interventions will have long-lasting effects. This may be due to the fact that interven-tion projects or programmes are often designed as experiments rather than as a continuous effort to change health behaviour in a population. The consequence of this is that when the experiment stops, the intervention or programme stops. A good example of this is the Belgian Heart Disease Prevention Project, which served to reduce cardiovascular risk factors, **morbidity** and mortality by means of an intervention which focused on behavioural change related to risk factors for coronary heart disease. These favourable effects disappeared four years after discontinuation of the intervention (De Backer *et al.* 1986).

Conclusion

Although the above described principles of health promotion are elementary, it is astonishing how frequently they are violated in health promotion initiatives. These principles have proved to be very helpful in the process of planning and evaluation of such initiatives (Maes *et al.* 1992). In addition, they also have another advantage over sophisticated psychological models and theories: they can be easily explained and understood by non-psychologists (e.g. health educators, medical doctors, policy makers and even self-help groups). As an analytic exercise, the reader is encouraged to read a report of a specific health promotion initiative and to evaluate the initiative with the help of these principles.

Ψ Section summary

Health psychology offers a theoretical base for the understanding and promotion of health behaviour. In this chapter smoking serves as an example in a discussion of the distinction between approaches focusing on determinants of health behaviour, health promotion or primary prevention (smoking prevention programmes) and secondary prevention (smoking cessation programmes). Elementary models of health behaviour are introduced, including the fear reduction model, which states that fear may motivate health behaviour, and more recent social cognition models such as the health belief model, the theory of reasoned action and the theory of planned behaviour. The main components of these latter theories are beliefs about the severity of behavioural consequences, about personal vulnerability and about personal com-

Box continued

petence to carry out the desired behaviour. These cognitive models can be criticized for their neglect of other (emotional, volitional, physical and social) determinants of health behaviour. In an attempt to summarize and integrate existing theories of behavioural change, the following basic principles of health promotion are introduced: behaviour change occurs in stages, settings must be appropriate and convenient, goals must be realistic and achieved gradually, instruction should be sound and specific, a variety of methods should be offered, interventions should be aimed at multiple levels, use of social networks increases the effectiveness, people must be able to make their own choices, activities must have intrinsic value, people must become independent of the initiative and interventions should be maintained over time.

1 Could you describe each of the health behaviour models presented in this section by means of a specific example and make some critical remarks related to these models?

2 Try to provide a description of a specific health promotion project, using the eleven principles described in the text as a basis for discussion.

▢ Stress, coping and disease

Stress and the onset of disease

Many lay persons, patients and health practitioners believe that stress causes illness. On the one hand scientific findings confirm the common notion that stress contributes to the development of many diseases; on the other hand it is now widely acknowledged that diseases can have multiple determinants, including environmental factors, genetic factors and lifestyle. While lay persons, patients and health practitioners tend to overemphasize the causal role of stressful events in illness (see case study), there is accumulating evidence of at least an indirect link between stress and some diseases.

As the example in the case study demonstrates, there is a widely held belief that stress causes illnesses, and that certain life events or **stressors** are interchangeably used with their impact on the individual, that is strain or stress, and their consequences, namely stress reactions. Strictly speaking stress means tension or pressure. The concept of stress was originally used in a technical way

to represent the force that could be applied to a certain material without damage to the material, for example the stress which a bridge must be able to withstand. The medical and behavioural sciences have adopted the term, to denote the perception or experience of tension and tension symptoms by humans.

Contrary to the widely held view that stress always implies distress, stress can also have positive consequences. Many achievements of the welfare state are the result of positive adaptations to stressful events. Every situation that demands adaptation causes stress. The associated tension enables us to adapt to our environment. In the case of positive or favourable adaptation we speak of 'eustress', in contradistinction to 'distress', which results from unfavourable or negative adaptation by an individual who cannot cope adequately with alterations in the environment.

Answering scientific questions about the relationship between stress, health and illness requires a theory of stress. A framework or model is needed in order to define and measure stress in a theoretically grounded and empirically reliable way. Cohen and Kessler (1995) have distinguished three models or accounts of the relationship between stress and illness. These approaches can better be seen as complementary than as competing accounts. Furthermore, the models are linked to three different disciplines: biology, epidemiology, and psychology, respectively.

Biological stress theories

Chronologically the first approach, biological stress theory, focuses on physiological responses. In 1932 Cannon reported on 'the fight-flight response' or emergency reaction. When physical and psychological stimuli threaten an organism, the sympathetic autonomic nervous system is activated, and hormones are released by a part of the brain called the adrenal medulla. These physiological processes enable quick adaptive reactions to environmental demands. In our industrialized western society, however, the mobilization of physical energy to fight or to flight is no longer a functional response. Physical reactions are often inappropriate reactions to threatening situations and continual physiological arousal may result in damage to the body.

Selye (1956) also studied stress from a biological perspective. He postulated the general adaptation syndrome (GAS: see Figure 19.7), a non-specific pattern of physiological reaction by an organism to environmental demands or stressors. The organism reacts with the same

Ψ Case study

Stress and coronary heart disease

There is ample anecdotal evidence of overestimation of the role of environmental factors or stressful events in the onset and progression of illness. In a research programme on the effects of psychoeducational programmes on quality of life and life habits of coronary heart patients a few hundred patients were asked: 'In your view, what factors caused your heart disease?' The great majority of the patients postulated stress as the main cause of their heart disease, followed by smoking and hereditary factors. These patients' part-

ners were more specific and attributed the heart disease to stress at the workplace, probably because partners prefer to view stress as something outside the family and want the patient to stay safely at home in the future (Van Elderen 1991).

Health practitioners in hospitals share this view on the relationship between stress and the manifestation of certain illnesses. When asked to substantiate this view they mention an increase in hospital admissions shortly after large corporate reorganizations in the Netherlands, where many employees lost their jobs.

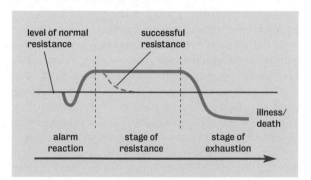

Figure 19.7 The general adaptation syndrome
Source: Selye (1956)

physiological pattern in a given time course, independent of the nature of the environmental demands.

Selye distinguished three different phases in the general adaptation syndrome:

(1) the alarm-phase: initially the organism reacts with a state of a shock. In this shock-phase resistance decreases temporarily. The second part of the alarm-phase, referred to as countershock or rebound, is characterized by increased secretion of a **hormone**, which stimulates the release of substances called glucocorticoids (hydrocortisone, corticosterone and cortisol) by the brain

(2) the resistance- or adaptation-phase: in this phase the organism tries to take action to adjust to the stressor, which is reflected in a state of increased resistance and changes in the level of catecholamines (Gray 1987)

(3) the exhaustion-phase: if the stress-situation continues long enough, the organism enters the exhaustion-phase, in which a lowering of resistance is accompanied by a depletion of physical resources. Selye assumed that continued depletion of resources would lead to greater susceptibility to disease and, finally, to death.

Although the GAS model offered new and useful insights into the relationship between demanding environmental events and adverse health outcomes, many present-day researchers have questioned the non-specificity of the reaction pattern (e.g. Hobfoll 1989). Anxiety, for example, may result in a different physiological reaction pattern than anger.

There has been a recent revival of interest in the biological approach in the area of '**psychoneuroimmunology**'. This area of study is concerned with how psychological processes can affect the immune system (and thus render an individual more vulnerable to diseases) via neurophysiological pathways. There is a great deal of evidence indicating that stress has an effect on the release of catecholamines (epinephrine and norepinephrine) and corticosteroids (e.g. cortisol), which have immunosuppressive effects (Suter 1986). The effect of stress on the activity of natural killer cells has been particularly well documented. Natural killer cells are a special type of leucocytes (white blood cells) that destroy viruses or cancer cells. As a consequence the activity of these cells is a good indicator of the immune respons. In a study by Kiecolt-Glaser *et al.* (1984) blood samples were taken from medical students at two points in time: in the middle of term (for US students a low stress period) and at the start of their final exams (a stressful period). Students were asked whether they were experiencing stressful life events and to what extent they had felt lonely during the past year. On the basis of blood samples, the activity of their natural killer cells was determined. The activity of natural killer cells was significantly lower in the total group of students at the beginning of final exams than in the middle of term. In addition, students who reported a high number of stressful events and high loneliness showed a significantly lower natural killer cell activity at both measurement points than students who reported no or few stressful events and low loneliness. It is an established fact that decreased natural killer cell activity makes an individual more susceptible to diseases. A study by S. Cohen *et al.* (1991) illustrates that, via this pathway, stress can be ultimately responsible for the onset of a disease. These researchers studied the role of stress in susceptibility to colds. Of the 394 subjects included in the study, besides medical and immunological data, a battery of stress measures was taken. Next, subjects were quarantined and administered cold viruses or saline via nasal drops. In the subsequent period they were monitored daily on immunological parameters and clinical symptoms. It was found that cold symptoms were related in a dose-response way to the amount of stress reported by subjects who had been administered the cold virus. This study clearly showed that stress affects the immune system, and that changes in the immunocompetence in turn lead to the onset of infections.

While there is considerable evidence that stress plays a role in the incidence and severity of many other infectious diseases (Herbert and Cohen 1993), there is also growing evidence of a possible link between stress and the progression of some forms of cancer. In a controlled study of cancer patients, Levy *et al.* (1989) reported positive effects of cognitive behavioural intervention on the number and activity of natural killer cells, which have the capacity to attack and kill cancer cells. In the mean time several studies on the effects of psychological interventions in cancer patients have shown positive effects on survival time. To cite the best known example, Spiegel *et al.* (1989) conducted a controlled study of the effects of supportive-expressive group therapy for women with metastatic breast cancer. Within 48 months all control patients had died, while one-third of the treatment group was still alive. Ten years after the study had begun, the group therapy showed a statistically significant effect on survival: women from the treatment group lived an average of 18 months longer.

Although there is as yet no definite answer to the question of how stress affects the progression of cancer, there is undoubtedly enough evidence to hypothesize such a relationship.

Environmental stress theories

The second general model of stress, health and disease utilizes a stimulus-based definition of stress. The focus in this model is on environmental conditions or life events that increase the risk of adverse health outcomes. Holmes and Rahe (1967) were the first to categorize life events according to their impact on the organism, in terms of the extent of adaptation required to cope with the events. They argued that life events could be measured and quantified in terms of life-change units, based on their impact on the health status of the individual. Their 43-item Social Readjustment Rating Scale (SRRS) is based on extensive testing in large populations and summarizes 43 (positive and negative) events, varying from the death of a spouse, to pregnancy, to going on holiday or being fined by a police officer. Every event has a mean value (e.g. death of a spouse has a mean value of 100, pregnancy 40, going on holiday 13 and being fined 11). Respondents are asked to check off which event occurred during the past year. A total score is obtained by adding up the values related to these events.

Using the SRRS, Rahe (1975) studied the relation between stressful life events prior to a six-month cruise and the number of sick-bay visits during the cruise in a population of naval personnel. It turned out that there was a positive relation between life-change units and the number of sick-bay visits. However, most of these studies show only weak relationships between life-change units and the onset of disease (Rahe 1973). In addition, more recent studies have shown that minor life events or 'daily hassles' can also contribute to physiological wear and tear. Concerns about weight, losing things, rising prices of common goods, and demanding household chores are examples of frequently mentioned daily hassles (Kanner *et al.* 1981).

On the one hand the accumulation of daily hassles can show a direct link to symptoms; on the other hand such minor events can serve to mediate the relationship between major life events and illnesses. Weinberger *et al.* (1987) found that major life events caused many daily worries, which in turn had a negative influence on health. Pillow *et al.* (1996) showed that major life events can lead to distress both directly and indirectly via minor stressors.

Psychological stress models

Both the response-oriented biological theories and the stimulus-oriented environmental theories have been criticized for their lack of attention to psychological processes or individual differences in appraisal of environmental demands. In the third, psychological approach, stress is defined as the result of a transaction between the individual and the environment. In attempting to cope with their environment, individuals will experience stress when the demands of the environment exceed their resources. Subsequent emotions and behaviour will depend on both psychological processes involving appraisal of environmental demands and response capabilities. The Lazarus and Folkman (1984) model is the best known and most widely used stress coping model. The basic assumptions of this model are that people who are confronted with a stressor will evaluate this stressor, and that this evaluation determines their emotional or behavioural reactions. Lazarus and Folkman (1984) distinguish two kinds of parallel evaluation or appraisal processes: primary and secondary appraisal.

Primary appraisal involves assessment of the personal meaning of an event, that is whether the event or the stressor has positive, neutral or negative meaning for the individual in terms of potential harm or benefit. In primary appraisal, the individual answers the question 'Am I okay or in trouble?' Positive emotions result if the interpretation is positive (e.g. because the stressor is seen as a challenge), negative emotion if the stressor is seen as a threat to the physical and/or psychological self. Two classes of negative outcome can be distinguished: feelings of anxiety if the stressor is perceived as a threat, and feelings of anger and/or grief if the stressor involves personal damage or loss.

Secondary appraisal, or response to the question, 'What can I do about it?', refers to thoughts through which the person explores his or her coping capacity, that is the capacity to reduce the threat, damage or loss caused by the event.

Coping is defined as any effort to manage or adapt to external or internal demands which have been appraised as negative or challenging. External demands refer to the event itself, internal demands to emotional reactions to the event. This distinction led Lazarus and Folkman to differentiate between problem-focused coping, i.e. responses directed at the external event, and emotion-focused coping, i.e. responses directed at the individual's emotional reactions or internal state. An example of these two different forms of coping can be seen in individuals who engage in problem-focused coping by under-going genetic screening to prevent offspring with hereditary diseases, and emotion-focused coping when they engage in avoidant thinking in an effort to reduce anxiety. Additionally, coping behaviour may vary greatly over time and from person to person. This explains why there are differences in the effectiveness of coping behaviour, and why some persons adapt more quickly and easily to stressors, while others do not. How people cope with stressors will have important psychological, social and physical consequences. Some people will take measures to overcome a problem, others will take refuge in wishful thinking or an unhealthy lifestyle to overcome emotional problems. Depending on other individual factors, some will get ill as a result of dysfunctional or maladaptive coping processes.

The core idea of the transactional models is that it is the appraisal of an event which causes stress, or in other words that intermediate cognitive processes are necessary to explain the relationship between a stressor and health consequences. While Lazarus and Folkman put much emphasis on coping, there are several other variables which may moderate the connection between a stressful event and the development of a disease. The most important of these are described in the next section.

Moderating factors in the relationship between stress and illness

Type A pattern

Two US cardiologists, Rosenman and Friedman (1974), noticed that many of their heart patients shared the same personality characteristics. They defined this constellation of characteristics as the **type A behaviour** pattern, an action-emotion complex or syndrome consisting of vigorous voice and psychomotor mannerisms, hard-driving and time-pressured job involvement, competitiveness, impatience, and easily aroused anger and hostility. Type B behaviour is defined as the relative absence of most of the type A characteristics and behaviours. A structured interview was developed to assess the type A behaviour pattern. Interviewers were instructed to create conditions diagnostic of the presence of type A characteristics. For example, they asked questions in a challenging matter, and hesitated and delayed their questions on purpose to stimulate impatient and hostile reactions. Both the content of the answers and overt manifestations of the behaviour pattern were scored, e.g. explosive, accelerated speech and impatient body movements.

Plate 19.3 Dealers on the floor of the stock exchange displaying type A behaviour patterns. This entails vigorous voice and psychomotor mannerisms, hard-driving and time-pressed job involvement, competitiveness, impatience and easily aroused anger and hostility

In many studies in the 1970s the type A pattern, measured by the structured interview, was found to predict coronary heart disease, even after controlling for other risk factors (e.g. Rosenman *et al*. 1975). More recent studies, however, did not replicate these findings (Dembroski *et al*. 1985). As a consequence, in many subsequent studies a distinction was made between coronary-prone behaviour and type A behaviour. Hostility was postulated to be the most coronary-prone dimension of type A behaviour. Friedman (1992) referred to the search for the truly harmful element in type A behaviour as a 'Search for the Holy Grail', because the focus of the search went from type A to hostility to the expression or suppression of anger. Moreover, research results in this domain are not always consistent. On the one hand there are studies supporting a relationship between the suppression or internalization of anger and health problems; on the other hand some studies suggest that it is the expression or externalization of anger that

is related to the development of health problems (Van Elderen *et al*. 1997).

Perceived control

There is a lot of evidence pointing to the importance of **perceived control** as a moderator of the stress–illness relationship. A study by Langer and Rodin (1976) showed for example that giving people a sense of control may have a powerful impact on health outcomes, including longevity. In this study a group of nursing home residents heard a speech from the nursing home director which stressed the responsibility of the residents for their own life and health. In addition, these residents were given the opportunity to choose a movie night, to express their opinion on how complaints should be handled and to select a plant to care for. A comparison group, with similar levels of health and disability, also heard a speech from the director, but in this case the residents were told that it was the staff who was responsible for their care. In contrast to the first group, the residents in this group were offered a movie night without any choice, were told how complaints would be handled and were given a plant that would be cared for by others. Three weeks after the speech the residents in the first group reported higher levels of well-being and activity. After 18 months the death rate in the first group was one-half of the death rate in the second group: 15 per cent versus 30 per cent.

This study does not stand alone. Similar results were obtained in research based on the Job Demand/Control model (Karasek and Theorell 1990). The basic premise of this model is that psychological strain (fatigue, anxiety, depression) and physical ill-health result from an interaction between job demands and decision latitude or control. It has repeatedly been demonstrated that high job demands in particular produce adverse mental and physical health consequences (including cardiovascular morbidity and mortality) if decision latitude or in other words the control which the workers have over these demands is low.

While these studies show that perceived control moderates the relationship between stress and health outcomes, it is important to realize that there are individual differences in perceived control. This can be illustrated by means of the concepts of locus of control, learned helplessness and self-efficacy.

Locus of control
Locus of control concerns whether control over reinforcements is perceived to lie in oneself or in the envi-

ronment. Some people seem to have an internal locus of control (see also Chapter 14), which means that they believe that what happens to them is mainly the result of their own actions. Others have an external locus of control, which implies that they believe that what happens to them is the result of luck or the action of others. It is clear that people with an internal locus of control will tend to cope in a different way with problems from people with an external locus of control. 'Internals' are in general more active copers, while 'externals' tend to be more passive copers. While one may think that being more active inevitably leads to better health outcomes, the efficacy of active coping strategies is also strongly dependent on situational factors. This may explain why Wallston and Wallston (1984) found only weak relationships between health locus of control and preventive health behaviour. In other words, being active does not guarantee that people will always do the right things from a health point of view.

Learned helplessness

The theory of **learned helplessness** (Seligman 1975) postulates that a person who is continuously confronted with a lack of control in a particular situation will stop trying to influence outcomes not only in that situation, but also in new situations where control is possible. Maier and Seligman (1976) described three types of deficits associated with such learned helplessness: motivational, cognitive and emotional. After experiencing that one's partner, a heart patient, does not stop smoking despite one's utmost efforts to help, one may develop feelings of learned helplessness. In this case one may no longer be motivated to offer help or support, will no longer think about ways to influence the habit and will most probably become pessimistic about future risks. It is not difficult to imagine that giving up completely, or failing to react to a major stressor, may lead to adverse psychological and physical health consequences. However, although research has shown a link between learned helplessness and psychological ill health (especially depression), physical health consequences of learned helplessness have not been adequately demonstrated.

Self-efficacy

Perceived **self-efficacy** refers to beliefs in one's capability to mobilize the motivation, cognitive resources and courses of action needed to meet given situational demands (Bandura 1991). A student who intends to quit smoking but thinks that he or she is not capable of stop-

ping is showing for example low self-efficacy in relation to stopping. Bandura writes:

> It is now widely acknowledged that people's health rests partly in their own hands. To prevent the ravages of disease, they must exercise control over their health habits and the environmental conditions that impair physical well-being.
>
> **(Bandura 1991: 229)**

Perceived self-efficacy can influence our health in two ways. First, beliefs of self-efficacy can have effects on biochemistry and biochemical variables, and as such on the possible onset of disease. Second, they can also influence health promotive behaviours. For example, when occasional smoking by former smokers is explained as the result of personal weakness and not as the result of exposure to smoking colleagues, relapse is more probable (Marlatt and Gordon 1985). It has been demonstrated that high levels of self-efficacy moderate the stress-illness relationship in a beneficial sense. For instance, perceived self-efficacy seems to increase pain tolerance (Bishop 1994).

Social support

The concept of **social support** has been conceptualized in various ways. In the first place type and size of a social network can be differentiated from kinds of social support. Berkman and Syme (1979) found that individuals with many social contacts had a lower mortality rate than individuals with few social contacts, independent of age, gender, health and health behaviour. A stable social network, characterized by living together with a partner, personal friends, or membership of clubs or societies, also has a positive effect on people's well-being (Sheridan and Radmacher 1992). Several kinds of social support can be distinguished, e.g. social support which facilitates understanding of or coping with the stressful event, help in solving problems and emotional support (S.E. Taylor 1995). Another distinction can be made between perceived and actually received social support. In a study by Peters-Golden (1982) women were interviewed about the social support they would expect to receive from their partners if they had breast cancer. Most women considered it self-evident that they would receive such social support. In contrast, women with breast cancer are often very disappointed with the support they receive from their partners.

In addition to direct effects of a stable social network or social support, a 'buffering' effect of social support is often hypothesized. In a meta-analysis of over 100 studies, Leppin and Schwarzer (1990) showed that social support was significantly related to mortality, blood pressure, subjective health status and depression. However, since this study does not provide insight in the nature of the stress–illness relationship it is not clear whether these findings are the result of a direct effect (implying that social support has an effect on health outcomes independent of stressful situations) or of a buffering effect (implying that social support protects people from adverse health consequences in stressful conditions). This buffering or moderating effect has been demonstrated in several individual studies. Kulik and Mahler (1989) found for example that married men recover more quickly from coronary bypass surgery than unmarried men. This **buffering hypothesis** was also confirmed by means of a prospective study by De Longis *et al.* (1988). In this study 75 couples were assessed repeatedly over a six-month period concerning daily hassles, social support, self-esteem and psychological and physical health outcomes. People who reported low self-esteem and low social support showed more illness in response to stress than those who reported high levels of self-esteem and social support. Other studies have also confirmed this hypothesis for other health outcomes such as flare-up of genital herpes and sports injuries, but there are also several studies showing no evidence of a buffering effect (Bishop 1984). Whether social support fulfils this moderating role is probably dependent on characteristics of the stressor, the form of social support (quantitative or qualitative), and the type of health outcome (psychological or physical) which is investigated (Cohen and Wills 1985).

Stress and coping with chronic disease

Van den Berg and Van den Bos (1989) estimated that one-quarter to one-third of the adult population in the Netherlands has a chronic disease, i.e. an illness that is irreversible and which one must live with for weeks, months or years. It is extremely important to recognize that there is no single, universally accepted medical definition of chronic illness, as there are vast differences in the causes, course, changeability and consequences of chronic conditions. The chronic conditions of greatest concern are typically the most prevalent (i.e. afflict large numbers of individuals) and/or are long-lasting, have a major impact on the healthcare system (e.g. many days in hospital and high treatment costs) and produce high rates of mortality. Virtually all of the heart and vessel diseases, most cancers, **asthma** and chronic obstructive pulmonary diseases, diabetes mellitus and rheumatic diseases satisfy the criteria of prevalence, longevity and high cost. Many other chronic

diseases, e.g. Parkinson's disease, multiple sclerosis, epilepsy, migraine, muscle diseases, Crohn's disease, colitis ulcerosa, chronic rhenal insufficiency and psoriasis, also have a substantial impact on quality of life and may be susceptible to psychological intervention, but their lower prevalence and lesser impact on mortality removes them somewhat from the focus of public attention.

The stage model of adaptation to chronic disease

As discussed earlier in this chapter, the relationship between stress and illness has been found to be dependent upon biological, environmental and cognitive processes. In a comparable way these factors influence the progression of most diseases.

As chronic diseases threaten an individual's current and future life perspective, learning to live with or adapt to a chronic disease is not an easy task. This adaptation process may entail a number of different stages. In an attempt to characterize these stages, Morse and Johnson (1991) developed their **illness constellation model**, which postulates four stages in the psychological development of an illness representation:

(1) a stage of uncertainty, during which patients attempt to understand the meaning and the severity of the first symptoms
(2) a stage of disruption, when it becomes obvious that one is affected by a serious disease (because of the disease state or communication of the diagnosis); during this stage the patient experiences a crisis, which is characterized by intense levels of stress and a high degree of dependence on professionals and/or relatives
(3) a stage which can be defined as a strive for recovery of the self, during which patients try to gain control over their illness with the help of their environment by using various forms of coping behaviour
(4) a stage of restoration of well-being, which indicates that the patient has attained a new equilibrium within the environment since he or she has now accepted the illness and its consequences.

This model shows that adaptation to chronic disease is largely dependent on the individual's evaluation of the stressor, the effectiveness of coping behaviour and the social support the patient receives in attempts to gain control over the stressor. It also emphasizes that, despite the images of doom and the realities of disability accompanying the most severe chronic conditions, most patients adapt to chronic disease. Cassileth *et al.* (1984) have shown that most outpatients with diabetes, cancer, rheumatic diseases, renal disease and skin disease do not report higher levels of stress and lower levels of well-being in comparison to comparable healthy subjects, except in the initial and end stages of the disease.

Lazarus and Folkman stress coping model and chronic disease

According to the model of Lazarus and Folkman (1984), which is described on p. 608, patients evaluate their stressor or particular syndrome and this evaluation determines their emotional or behavioural reactions. Since primary appraisal and as such negative interpretations and their effects are often most evident during the initial stages of confrontation with the stressor, it is not surprising that studies report strong emotional reactions of anxiety, depression and anger upon confrontation with the initial signs of or unexpected changes in the features of a **chronic illness**. For example, patients with **myocardial infarction** generally suffer from heightened levels of anxiety during their few first days at the coronary care unit and are said to become depressed shortly afterwards, but for the majority of patients, these increased levels of distress seem to drop quite rapidly during hospitalization or shortly afterwards (Van Elderen 1991). Later on, however, other stressors such as returning to work, sexual intercourse, complications or coronary bypass surgery may once again cause high levels of anxiety or depression. Similarly, immediate reactions to the discovery of having insulin dependent diabetes mellitus may involve grief and mourning and fear of death, which decrease over time, while specific stressors such as states of severe hypoglycemia may be regular sources of anxiety and depression (Pennings-van der Eerden and Visser 1990). Anxiety and depression, to a lesser extent, are characteristic for asthmatic patients, but after a period of adaptation, anxiety tends to be associated with asthmatic attacks (Maes and Schlosser, 1987). Confusion, anxiety, sorrow and grief are typical reactions to the diagnosis of cancer, which are also subject to change over time (Couzijn *et al.* 1990).

Affective changes during the course of an illness may also result from secondary appraisal, or responses to the question, 'What can I do about it?' In the Lazarus and Folkman model, a distinction is made between emotion-focused coping (internal stressor) and problem-focused coping (external stressor). An example of the two dif-ferent forms of coping can be seen in patients with asthma who engage in problem-focused coping by taking medication to suppress oncoming asthmatic attacks, and emotion-focused coping when they engage in relaxation or avoidant thinking in efforts to reduce anxiety.

During secondary appraisal, thoughts and actions directed at both the external and internal stressor may coincide or alternate and give rise to emotional and behavioural consequences. In turn, each response can have complex consequences, i.e. a response may produce effects that require further coping (e.g. a treatment may have 'side-effects' which require additional treatment) in addition to having the intended effect on the disease and/or one's emotions. Additionally, coping behaviour may vary greatly over time and from person to person. This explains why there are differences in the effectiveness of coping behaviour, but also why some patients adapt more quickly and easily to stressors associated with chronic disease, while others do not. How people cope with each aspect of a chronic disease will have important psychological, social and physical consequences.

Limitations of the Lazarus and Folkman stress/coping model

While our understanding of the factors affecting adaptation to chronic disease has expanded as a result of empirical studies using the stress-coping model of Lazarus and Folkman (1984), these studies also highlight a few of the model's limitations.

First, the model is more a frame of reference than a model as it fails to incorporate concepts respecting the common and specific features of a chronic illness that establish goals and criteria for evaluating coping. Thus, although Lazarus and Folkman (1984) state that a stress-coping model should describe person–situation transactions, the situation dimension is poorly represented in this and most other coping models. Indeed, as Perrez and Reicherts (1992) have argued, since Lewin's early attempts, relatively few social-psychological theories have invested effort in describing the psychological situation.

Leventhal *et al.* (1984) have differentiated five sets of attributes of illness threats that appear to describe an individual's representation of the features of a disease threat. These include the identity or label and disease-specific symptoms of the illness, its time line or duration (acute, cyclic, chronic), its causes (genetic, infection, food poisoning, etc.), consequences (fatal, painful, etc.) and its controllability (susceptibility to medical treatment). Second, the model has neglected contextual interactions, i.e. the influence that other life events may have on the coping process. For example, due to the 'psychological' focus of the model, it gives insufficient attention to the importance of social support and other environmental factors on coping and adjustment. The model also ignores the potential direct impact of life events extrinsic to a chronic disease on the chronic condition, i.e. exacerbation of adverse biological effects, in addition to emotional effects on the individual via the appraisal process. For example, research has shown that diabetic patients who have recently experienced stressful life events have more problems with their metabolism (Cox *et al.* 1986).

Finally, by focusing exclusively on the way a stressor shapes coping behaviour, this and other models have overlooked the effects of the individual's life goals and social relationships on the meaning or representation of the disease and the selection of coping procedures. For example, diabetic patients may violate diet regulations because it is more important to them to please their host than to prevent a state of hyperglycemia, or coronary heart patients who are capable of returning to work may stop working because it is more important to them to spend more time with their partners.

These comments led to an elaboration of the stress-coping model (see Figure 19.8), based on Lazarus's (1991) insights, as well as the work of Hobfoll (1988, 1989), Moos (1988), Moos and Schaefer (1993) and S.E Taylor (1991).

An extended model of coping with chronic diseases

Life events

According to the model presented in Figure 19.8 (Maes 1994; Maes *et al.* 1996), other important life events contribute to the appraisal of disease-related events. Severe life events can influence reactions to a chronic disease. For example, patients who are given a diagnosis of rhenal insufficiency will probably evaluate this event in a different way if the diagnosis is given one month after the death of their partner or the loss of their job.

Disease characteristics

Disease characteristics can have a major impact on the appraisal of and thus coping with the event. Research in this domain points to a positive relationship between perceived severity or identity and avoidant or passive forms of coping (Dunkel-Schetter *et al.* 1992). Other authors have found lack of controllability to be related to more avoidant, emotion-focused coping in rheumatic patients, and controllability to active problem-focused coping in patients with diabetes mellitus (Andersson and Ekdahl 1992). Heim *et al.* (1987) found that ambiguity was related to passive forms of emotion-focused coping in women with possible breast cancer and research conducted by Warren *et al.* (1991) showed that there was an association between likelihood of reoccurrence with avoidance and emotion-focused forms of coping in multiple sclerosis patients.

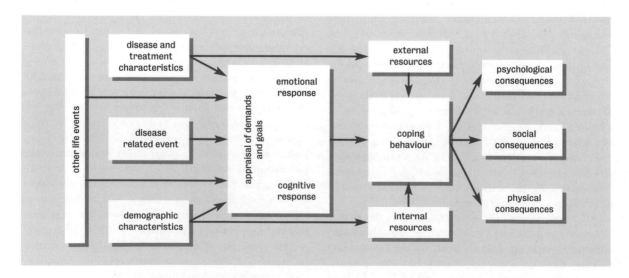

Figure 19.8 Coping with chronic diseases
Source: Maes *et al.* (1996)

Treatment characteristics

Not only characteristics of the disease, but also treatment characteristics contribute to the appraisal of a disease-related event. Many studies indicate that hospital admission, medical examinations, and surgery or other forms of treatment such as chemotherapy, do contribute to changes in the patient's perception and experience of the illness (M. Johnston *et al.* 1990; S.E. Taylor and Aspinwall 1993). It is clear that this is due not only to the stress of undergoing treatment, but also to changes brought about by treatment in perceptions of the above mentioned disease characteristics.

Personal characteristics

Relatively stable personal characteristics such as age, gender, race and social class also contribute to the interpretation of chronic illness and thus influence coping with chronic disease, although many researchers do not take adequate account of these variables. There are not a great many data to support this view, but research indicates that females, the less educated and especially older chronic patients tend to use more avoidant and/or emotion-focused coping (De Ridder and Schreurs 1994).

Appraisal

As mentioned above, the appraisal of an event is determined not only by event characteristics, but also by goals or values, according to expectancy-value theory. Expectancies can be defined as people's degree of confidence of attaining their goals. The more goals a stressor threatens and the more important these goals are, the more stressful the experience will be. As a result, stress can be defined as the result of a demand/goal appraisal.

Actual coping behaviour not only is the result of demand/goal appraisals, but also depends on demand/resources and goal/resources appraisals. According to Hobfoll (1988: 54), resources can be defined as 'those objects, conditions, personal characteristics, or energies that are valued by the individual or that serve as a means for attainment of valued resources'. In our terminology, valued resources are personal goals, and we will refer to resources as internal or external conditions which can be used to cope with demand/goal conflicts.

External resources

External resources include money, time, and distance from professional help, as well as the social support on which a patient can rely. It is an established fact that there is a relationship between social support and adaptation to chronic disease and that there is even a

relationship between social support and disease progression, although this relationship seems to be stronger for some chronic diseases than for others (Leppin and Schwarzer 1990). It is not clear, however, whether social support works as a buffer (influencing appraisals, and thus coping with stressful events) or has a direct effect (suggesting beneficial effects of social relationships irrespective of the experience of stress). Social support may determine how one will cope with a situation. While seeking help can be a coping strategy in itself, (lack of) social support may also affect a patient's ability to cope with the stresses of illness. Manne and Zautra (1989) found that **rheumatoid arthritis** patients with critical, less supportive spouses were more inclined to use maladaptive coping behaviours such as wishful thinking, while patients with supportive spouses reported more problem-focused coping. Effects of coping on social support were demonstrated by Newman (1990) who found that rheumatoid arthritis patients showing the best psychological adjustment tended to cope in an active and expressive way but did not seek support from others, probably because internal resources were already sufficient to solve the problem.

Internal resources

Internal resources include the energy or physical strength a person possesses, together with personality characteristics such as intelligence, trait anxiety, depression, optimism, autonomy, ego-strength, hardiness, locus of control and self-efficacy. Research has shown several personality characteristics to be related to appraisal, coping and adaptation (Carver *et al.* 1989; Moos and Schaefer 1993). In one study, for example, pessimists reported higher levels of hostility and depression on the day before coronary artery bypass surgery, as well as less relief and happiness after surgery, than optimists (Carver *et al.* 1992). Optimistic patients seem to cope in a more active, problem-oriented way, while pessimistic patients tend to show more passive or avoidant forms of coping. However, Carver *et al.* (1989) have pointed out that the impact of personality characteristics on coping is modest. Most of the research on the relationship between personality characteristics and coping is not longitudinal, however, and it could be argued that the existing research results therefore lead to an underestimation of the relationship.

Coping behaviour

In sum, a variety of factors affect coping behaviour. As stated above, it is important to differentiate between coping actions or actual responses to a stressor problem and coping functions that refer to the goals these actions are intended to achieve (Leventhal *et al.* 1993). Only a hierarchical model of coping as proposed by Krohne (1993) can adequately represent these different concepts. At the highest level, individuals display generalized coping intentions, preferences or dispositions (e.g. avoidance of risk, conservation of energy or vigilance). At the intermediate level, there are coping strategies. And the lowest or behavioural level consists of specific coping acts and responses (Krohne 1993). Research on coping with chronic diseases has been conducted on various levels, with little attention to distinctions between these levels. This has led to seemingly inconsistent results. At the higher order level, an important distinction is between problem-focused and emotion-focused coping (Lazarus and Folkman 1984). Other higher order dimensions distinguish between approach and avoidance (Krohne 1993; Roth and Cohen 1986; Suls and Fletcher 1985). The latter concepts, denoted with a variety of labels, have been used since the early 1960s to describe coping in various patient groups. The **approach coping style** refers to a tendency to approach, focus upon or even maximize the significance of the stressful event. The **avoidant coping style** refers to a tendency to avoid, ignore, deny or minimize the significance of the event.

Coping effectiveness
Coping effectiveness refers to the relationship between coping behaviour and outcomes in various domains. Cohen and Lazarus (1983) distinguish three kinds of outcomes: psychological, social and physiological. They state that coping effectiveness is related to the outcome domain, the time frame (short or long term) and the context. On the basis of the existing research literature, one can differentiate between the effects of passive or avoidant (emotion-focused) and more active (problem-focused) coping strategies. Use of passive or active coping strategies has been linked to psychosocial and physical adjustment, including self-management and compliance. Research conducted at this level has produced relatively consistent findings: patients who use avoidant, emotion-focused strategies have more difficulty adjusting to chronic disease than those who use active, problem-focused strategies (Maes *et al.* 1996).

It is important to point out that definitions of adjustment are often too restricted. Most studies operationalize adjustment in terms of psychological outcomes, thus neglecting effects on medical or even social outcomes. Studies should include outcome measures related to

each of these domains because positive effects on psychological adjustment are not necessarily accompanied by beneficial effects in other domains such as work absenteeism, adherence to medical advice or use of medical resources.

Psychological interventions in chronic illness

Figure 19.9 depicts a model (Maes 1994) which attempts to bring structure into the variety of psychological interventions offered to patients suffering from a chronic illness. The model distinguishes between differences in

- intervention aims (restoring or increasing quality of life versus promotion of self-management)
- intervention level (the patient, a group of patients and the larger physical and social environment of the patient)
- intervention channel (direct face-to-face contact between a psychologist and a patient or indirect interventions).

In the next section, the various dimensions of the model will be further discussed.

Aims: quality of life and self-management

All psychological interventions are in principle directed at quality of life or self-management or both.

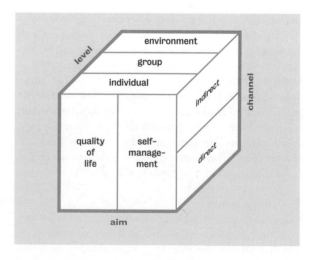

Figure 19.9 A model of psychological intervention in chronic diseases
Source: Maes (1994)

Interventions which focus primarily on **quality of life** aim at increasing the physical, psychological or social well-being of the patient and his or her immediate environment. These interventions are designed to stimulate a process of adaptation to or acceptance of the disease. In other words they are aimed at reducing undesirable psychological and social consequences of the disease and/or medical treatment and to counteract negative changes in life perspective induced by the disease. More specifically these interventions are aimed at reducing stress, pain or problems related to the performance of daily activities (including work, leisure, household activities as well as activities related to social roles within the family). Such interventions include physical training programmes, stress management programmes, social skills training or forms of counselling which can be described as palliative interventions. Various physical training programmes are offered to different groups of patients, including patients with coronary heart diseases, rheumatic diseases, neurological diseases and chronic respiratory diseases. While these programmes may undoubtedly have other important effects, they have only limited or temporary effects on quality of life and well-being (as e.g. a reduction of anxiety and depression) (Maes 1992b; Van den Broek 1995).

Stress management programmes include intervention techniques such as relaxation and **cognitive restructuring**. Research shows the effectiveness of this approach in cancer patients and patients with coronary heart disease (CHD) (D.W. Johnston 1992; S.E. Taylor 1995). There are several studies which show that more elaborate stress management programmes not only may improve quality of life but also can affect the progression of the disease and even mortality in cancer patients and patients with CHD (Frasure-Smith and Prince 1985; Friedman *et al.* 1984; Spiegel *et al.* 1989). Relaxation is also widely recognized as an effective intervention strategy for hypertension (D.W. Johnston 1992). The effectiveness of relaxation is puzzling since there is no easy explanation for why interventions aimed primarily at improving psychosocial outcomes would have effects on physical or disease outcomes. In the past the explanation was sought within psychosomatic medicine: changes at a personality level were thought to influence the course and development of disease. Research since the mid-1940s has proved such hypotheses to be wrong. However, while very few psychologists still believe that personality factors contribute to the onset of asthma or diabetes, some still think that modification of type A behaviour in patients with coronary heart

---

Ψ **Case study**

Effects of self-efficacy

Any painful, chronic illness often leads people to believe that nothing can be done to help them and that their situation is hopeless. Dramatic changes in pain relief can occur, however, if such people can gain some sense of control or efficacy.

At the Stanford Arthritis Center, significant improvement occurred in patients who attended five weekly classes for an hour each time, and were taught relaxation techniques, physical activities and cognitive skills designed to reduce arthritis pain. They were compared with a similar group of patients who did not take the classes.

Although there were no correlations between increased knowledge of relaxation or change in activity and reduction in pain, there was a significant association between greater self-efficacy - which the pro-

gramme participants experienced - and pain relief. In other words, no specific element of the programme accounted for the improvement, but overall the classes gave the patients a better outlook and a greater sense of control, and these were associated with less pain. Increased self-efficacy was correlated not only with less pain but also with a decrease in swollen joints and a decline in depression.

People who believe they can be effective in managing problems, including their own arthritis, have also been reported to experience beneficial effects in their immune systems. In addition to less pain and fewer swollen joints, they have higher levels of suppressor T-cells. Such cells seem to keep the body from producing antibodies against its own tissue - a problem that occurs in auto-immune diseases like rheumatoid arthritis.

(Adapted from Blair 1987: 312)

disease or type C personality characteristics in cancer patients are acceptable forms of intervention. They are most probably not aware that even psychologists who were protagonists of the type A behaviour hypothesis have abandoned their point of view (T.Q. Miller *et al.* 1991) and that a critical review of the research does not support the relationship between onset of cancer and personality factors (Fox 1988).

More recently attention has been focused on the psychophysiological effects of stress on the immune system, which were described above, in the context of biological stress models. The case study may illustrate this mechanism.

Forms of **social skill training** or **assertiveness training** aim at reducing social anxiety and/or at developing alternative behaviours to replace dysfunctional reactions to social anxiety provoking situations (S.E. Taylor 1995). For chronic patients who develop avoidant behaviour or behave in a stigmatized way (e.g. not going to work to hide symptoms of diabetes, avoiding sexual contact out of fear of another myocardial infarction or not going to parties out of fear of an asthma attack) social skills training may be undoubtedly indicated.

Another group of interventions aimed at improving quality of life can be characterized as **palliative interventions**. Palliative interventions are interventions which provide emotional support to the patient in order to reduce stress and encourage acceptance of the chronic condition. These interventions are especially helpful for patients who experience high amounts of stress, e.g. following diagnosis of a chronic illness or in the terminal end stages of a life-threatening disease when the patient is facing death and dying. Although emotional expression and social sharing always play an important role in palliative interventions, the precise nature of the intervention will differ depending on the stage and the consequences of the disease. For this reason these interventions are not necessarily offered by psychologists or even healthcare workers. There is a great deal of literature demonstrating the effects on quality of life outcomes of social support from family and friends as well as other patients, as for example in support groups for patients with cancer or epilepsy (S.E. Taylor 1995).

The other aim of psychological interventions is to increase **self-management** in chronic patients. Living with a chronic disease is a difficult task which frequently requires important lifestyle changes and adherence to medical advice aimed at stabilizing or slowing down the progression of the disease or to reducing undesirable physical consequences and complications. Influencing the progression of the disease or preventing things from getting worse is defined in the literature as **secondary prevention**. Preventing undesirable consequences and complications, e.g. accidents in epileptic patients or gangrene in diabetic patients, is seen as tertiary prevention. Required behavioural changes from a disease management point of view vary from disease to disease, but include changes such as

- taking medication or keeping appointments with healthcare workers for various forms of diagnosis and treatment
- changing unhealthy behaviours like smoking and excessive fat, salt, sugar or alcohol intake
- adopting healthy habits like physical exercise, taking regular meals, maintaining normal body weight, having enough sleep, rest or relaxation
- engaging in a variety of self-management behaviours like monitoring blood sugar, taking sanitary measures at home and at work, avoiding working with machines, driving a car or swimming alone, and maintaining regular exercise for arthritic hands and fingers.

Research has repeatedly demonstrated that about half of chronic patients do not adequately follow medical advice. Some patients even go as far as flushing their medication down the toilet or feeding it to the plants in order to simulate compliant behaviour, as a study of patients suffering from chronic obstructive pulmonary diseases showed (Rand *et al.* 1992). Many healthcare workers seem to be unfamiliar with the reasons for non-adherence. Research has shown that **adherence** to medical advice is not related to personal characteristics such as age, gender, race, religion, educational level, income or personality characteristics. Non-compliance is also not dependent on objective disease characteristics such as severity of the disease or the nature and severity of symptoms. Whether people follow medical advice is instead related to the nature and form of the advice, social support, illness perceptions, comprehension of the advice and the treatment plan, and characteristics of the provider–patient relationship (Brannon and Feist 1997).

In other words faulty communication by health professionals is one of the most important sources of non-adherence. On the other hand, it is the patient, and not the health professional, who is ultimately responsible for adequate management of a chronic disease. From this perspective terms like compliance or adherence are concepts of the past, since they suggest that patients must follow medical advice. There are at least two problems related to such a point of view. First, it suggests that healthcare providers know what is best for the patient under all circumstances. As such, they offer the patient a set of absolute and restrictive general rules, which are not easily applicable in complex everyday life situations. Second, since these rules are the rules of their medical doctor rather than their own, they will not be followed if they conflict with the patients' other life goals. This is the main reason why self-management of a chronic disease is a more defendable intervention target than compliance or adherence.

Many types of self-management techniques have been applied in interventions with chronic patients, including self-monitoring, goal-setting, behavioural contracting, shaping the process of change, self-reinforcement, stimulus-control and modelling (S.E. Taylor 1995).

- **Self-monitoring or self-observation** techniques are used to assess the occurrence, antecedents and consequences of an important target behaviour. It is an established fact that people who keep a record of the number of cigarettes they smoke, the circumstances in which they smoke, and related feelings decrease their smoking.
- **Goal-setting** implies that the patient rather than the healthcare provider defines an achievable goal (e.g. 'I want to lose 2 kilos in the next two weeks').
- **Contracting** means that these personal goals are communicated in the form of a contract to important others and that these others will actively help the patient in achieving this goal and/or providing a desired reinforcer.
- **Shaping** implies that the process of achieving the goal is defined in terms of specific, achievable steps.
- **Self-reinforcement** means that the patient is offered the opportunity to choose a reinforcer when a self-treatment target is reached.
- **Stimulus-control** is important in interventions which attempt to gain control over the antecedents of a target behaviour. Such interventions encourage the patient to eliminate stimuli that could lead to an unwanted behaviour (e.g. no alcohol or cigarettes in the house).
- **Modelling or observational learning** means that the patient can learn an important self-management technique by observing others who have mastered the technique (e.g. monitoring blood sugar, injecting insulin, measuring peak flow or self-administering asthma medication).

Self-management programmes for chronic patients make use of a combination of these and other techniques. At present, there are self-management pro-

grammes for a variety of chronic conditions such as **hypertension**, coronary heart disease, asthma, diabetes, rheumatic diseases and rhenal failure. In a meta-analytic review of asthma patient education, Bauman (1993) came to the conclusion that self-management programmes produce stronger effects on psychological outcomes, compliance and self-management skills than traditional health education programmes, which are characterized by provision of information only. Other meta-analyses of arthritis, cardiac and diabetes education programmes came to comparable conclusions (S. Brown 1992; Hirano *et al.* 1994; P.D. Mullen *et al.* 1992). This illustrates the need for behavioural expertise in the development and implementation of programmes for patients with chronic diseases which goes beyond a traditional didactic approach.

In view of the need for behavioural expertise Arborelius (1996) has developed a comprehensive model for individual health counselling on lifestyle issues. Based on the limited effects of providing information and exhorting people on recommended lifestyle changes, she formulated seven principles for successful strategies in individual health counselling. These strategies are:

- Patient-centredness instead of directing. Patient-centredness can be defined as the physician's intention to start from the patient's situation, from the patient's opinion about what is suitable for the patient, rather than directing the patient towards a previously determined objective.
- The intention to get patients to reflect and decide on their behaviour, in other words encouraging/helping the patient to consider his or her lifestyle.
- To find out the patient's readiness to change. According to the Motivational Interview Model (Priest and Speller 1991; Prochaska *et al.* 1987) individuals can be distinguished in terms of five successive motivational states: there are precontemplators not interested in considering change, contemplators still uncertain about a change, persons in a preparation stage, persons who have already taken action and finally, individuals in a stage of maintenance of the lifestyle alteration.
- To give neutral knowledge instead of judgements. A main principle is to give clear information about the consequences of particular behaviours without suggesting what patients ought to do.
- To focus on the actual behaviour instead of information-giving. Based on Social Learning Theory

(Bandura 1977) attention has to be paid to discussion of the desired behaviour, helping patients to record their behaviour (self-monitoring), facilitating decision-making, and providing feedback about and reinforcement for efforts which have been made.

- Highlighting patients' health beliefs, ideas about health, illness and management. Deci and Ryan (1985) argued that humans have an intrinsic need to be self-determining. Self-determination stimulates internal motivation. G. Williams *et al.* (1991) proposed a three-question approach to promote and support internal motivation to change: (i) What do you understand about the health consequences of (e.g. smoking)? (ii) Are you ready to (quit)? (iii) What would it take for you to (stop smoking)?

- Discussion of advantages and disadvantages compared with information. This enables the patients to display their possible dilemmas and ambivalence about their life habits.

The level of intervention: the individual patient, the group and the larger environment

Clinical psychologists are mostly educated within an intervention paradigm which supports the idea that effective interventions are relatively intensive direct forms of intervention to individual patients, which are targeted at psychological problems. While this approach is certainly valuable in some cases, the disadvantage of such an approach is that it implies doing a lot for a very small group of patients. According to one estimate, there is about one psychologist per 5,000 chronic patients in the Dutch healthcare system. Since the Netherlands is the European country with the highest number of psychologists per capita, psychological expertise for chronic patients is most probably even more scarce in other European countries. Therefore, more indirect forms of intervention at a group and environmental level are clearly called for if health psychologists are to make a significant contribution to the care of chronic patients at a population level. Clinical health psychologists must in other words go for the numbers rather than for the most intensive or personally satisfying form of intervention. In line with this reasoning, there is a trend towards development of programmes for groups of patients and their partners. Most of these interventions are based on cognitive behaviour or social learning theory, and make use of many of the above

mentioned self-management techniques. Such programmes exist in several European countries for patients suffering from diabetes, rheumatic diseases, chronic respiratory diseases and coronary heart disease (Pennings-Van der Eerden and Visser 1990; Taal *et al.* 1992; Van den Broek 1995; Van Elderen *et al.* 1994a).

One such group intervention programme is the Dutch 'heart and health' programme, which has been developed for patients with coronary heart disease (Van Elderen *et al.* 1994a). The programme is offered to groups of about eight patients and their partners during cardiac rehabilitation and consists of eight weekly two-hour sessions and two follow-up sessions. Each session is devoted to a particular topic, selected on the basis of an assessment of the specific needs of the patient, such as the aetiology of arteriosclerosis, lifestyle related to risk factors such as smoking, high serum cholestrol, hypertension, lack of physical exercise and overweight and psychosocial factors such as excessive stress, return to work, resumption of roles within the family in domains such as sexual contact, leisure activities and coping with symptoms. During the first part of each session a member of the rehabilitation team (cardiologist, rehabilitation physician, general practitioner, physiotherapist, nurse, dietician, social worker or psychologist) answers the patients' questions on one of these topics. During the second part of the session patients and partners try, under the supervision of a psychologist, to identify and change irrational beliefs or thoughts which can obstruct important rehabilitation goals. It should be stressed that it is the patient and not the healthcare worker or the psychologist who defines these goals. Apart from positive effects on patient satisfaction, the programme has been shown to have beneficial effects on smoking cessation, changes in diet and use of medical resources (Van Elderen *et al.* 1994a).

Psychologists also frequently underestimate the relevance of interventions on a broader environmental level. Such interventions are sometimes described as **social engineering**, because they are aimed at modifying the home, work or leisure environment of the patient so as to facilitate normal functioning of the patient in everyday life. Psychological expertise at this level is of special importance for some patients, for example those with rheumatic diseases, not only because the screening of these patients' environments requires some psychological expertise, but also because acceptance of environmental changes by patients and their relatives may require psychological guidance (Moos 1988).

The channel: direct versus indirect interventions

As stated in the previous section many psychologists prefer direct interventions, in other words psychological interventions which they deliver themselves, over indirect interventions. Such a preference is however not defensible from a cost-effectiveness point of view. First of all, intensive face-to-face interventions are not the best type of intervention for all patients. Some patients may require less intensive intervention than others. Furthermore, intensive interventions do not necessarily produce superior effects. For example, Bob Lewin and his colleagues (1992) demonstrated that cardiac patients can profit from a manual ('The Heart Manual') given to them upon discharge from the hospital. The manual addresses common misconceptions and stress reactions related to a coronary incident, introduces stress management techniques and suggests appropriate levels of activity and physical exercise for various stages of recovery. Half of a group of 190 coronary heart disease patients received the manual, while the other half (the control group) did not. Both groups received similar medical and psychosocial care. The group which received the manual (the experimental group) reported less anxiety and depression, even one year after discharge. In addition, patients in the experimental group made significantly fewer visits to their general practitioner and were less frequently readmitted to the hospital than patients in the control group.

These results indicate that indirect interventions can have impressive effects. There is however also another advantage associated with indirect interventions. Even if psychologists were superior in the delivery of psychological interventions, it would remain the case that other health professionals, including medical doctors, nurses, physiotherapists and dieticians, are often in a better position to employ them (Swerrison and Foreman 1991). For example, while there is little doubt that psychosocial care should be offered as a component of cardiac rehabilitation, the results of a European survey show important differences in the degree of involvement of psychologists in cardiac rehabilitation in different European countries (Maes 1992b). In the Netherlands and Italy, psychologists are key members of most cardiac rehabilitation teams, but their involvement in cardiac rehabilitation is negligible in Sweden, Finland, Denmark, the United Kingdom and Switzerland. This does not necessarily mean that no psychosocial care is offered to cardiac patients in these countries, but rather that other health professionals (e.g. nurses in the UK) may play a central role in its delivery (Maes 1992b).

Even in countries where psychologists are thought to be fairly well represented in cardiac rehabilitation teams, as in the Netherlands, Italy and Austria, their presence is very modest, at about one full-time psychologist per 500 cardiac rehabilitation patients.

As a consequence health psychologists need to work to assist and empower others in the delivery of psychological interventions to enhance quality of life and self-management behaviours. Such indirect intervention may involve training of health personnel in psychological intervention and communication skills, and psychological consultation with other health professionals. There are many examples of effective intervention designed by psychologists, but delivered by others. One of the most successful is undoubtedly the 'weight watchers' movement, in which trained lay persons offer a weight reduction programme at the local community level. The original programme was designed by Stunkard, an American psychologist. Another example can be found in health education and counselling programmes offered to myocardial infarction patients during and after hospitalization. While many of these programmes have been designed by psychologists, they are typically delivered by nurses and/or social workers, which does not seem to decrease their effectiveness (Van Elderen et al. 1994b). In many other contexts, as in the case of terminally ill patients, regular health personnel will be responsible for standard care, while psychologists may play a more distant advisory role.

In short, indirect interventions may vary from developing materials or self-help courses for patients, to teaching psychological principles and methods to other health professionals, to designing intervention programmes and providing advice and training in face-to-face situations to both professionals and lay persons. Some critics of indirect interventions have argued that they imply 'giving psychology away'. As psychologists, we should instead be proud to have so much to give away.

Ψ Section summary

In this section three different models of the relationship between stress and illness were introduced: biological stress theories, environmental stress theories and psychological stress theories. Modern health psychology has devoted a lot of attention to psychobiological stress theories (for example in the

Box continued

area of psychoneuroimmunology), and to psychological stress theories. The best known psychological or transactional model is Lazarus and Folkman's stress coping model. In this model it is the appraisal of the stressor which causes stress reactions or consequences and not the stressor itself. Perceptions and coping responses are seen as important mediating variables between a stressful event and its potential consequences. Other possible moderators of the stress illness relationship, including type A behaviour, perceived control (locus of control, learned helplessness and self-efficacy) and social support, were introduced and discussed.

To shed light on the process by which an individual adapts to a chronic disease, Morse and Johnson's illness constellation model was presented. This model distinguishes between four consecutive stages of adaptation: a stage of uncertainty, a stage of disruption, a stage of strive for recovery of the self and a stage of restoration of well-being.

Next, an extended model of coping with chronic disease was introduced, based on a critique of Lazarus and Folkman's stress coping model. The most important characteristics of this extended model are its focus on life events and situational characteristics (including disease and treatment characteristics), its recognition of the role of goals in adaptation to a chronic disease, and the importance of internal and external resources for adequate coping behaviour.

Finally, to provide a basis for discussing the diverse psychological interventions which have been offered to patients with chronic diseases, an intervention model was introduced. The main feature of the model is the distinctions it draws among intervention aims (increasing quality of life vs self-management), intervention levels (the patient, a group of patients and the larger social and physical environment) and intervention channels (direct vs indirect interventions). Examples were provided to illustrate the point that a combination of intervention approaches may lead to more powerful and lasting effects.

1   What are the key differences between the three main theories of the stress illness relationship? Which one of these theories do you find most convincing?

2   Describe Lazarus and Folkman's stress coping theory by means of an example and discuss the limitations of this model.

Box continued

3   What factors moderate the stress–illness relationship? Give an example of each moderator. Use examples to describe and explain the extended stress coping model described in this chapter.

4   Apply the intervention model introduced in this chapter to patients suffering from coronary heart disease, cancer, diabetes or rheumatoid arthritis. Try to be as complete as possible, giving examples of all of the features which the model distinguishes.

Conclusion

This chapter provides an introduction to a new and rapidly growing sub-discipline of psychology, which is concerned with the relationship between behaviour and psychological processes on the one hand and health and illness on the other. We hope to have convinced the reader that health psychology can contribute to an understanding of health behaviour and health behaviour change, of the onset and the development of illness and of adaptation to illness.

However, it goes without saying that this chapter provides only a brief introduction to health psychology. Many important issues were left largely or entirely unaddressed, for instance the relationships between age, gender, social class, educational level and race on the one hand and health or disease on the other. The same is true for specific health behaviours (e.g. managing weight, use of alcohol, nutrition, physical exercise, drug abuse, sexual behaviour, safety behaviours) and health promotion settings (e.g. the community at large, work, school, leisure, family and clinical settings). Important skills of health psychologists such as psychological assessment, intervention, research and training of other health professionals were not systematically described. Many other topics have also been omitted or not fully discussed, for instance psychological preparation for surgery, compliance and adherence, pain and pain management, the effect of placebos and medication, various models of health and illness behaviour, communication between health professionals and patients, stress in healthcare professionals and specific interventions for various patient groups (e.g. patients suffering from coronary heart disease, cancer, stroke, rheumatic diseases, diabetes or rhenal insufficiency). We hope however that this appetizer will motivate the reader to further explore the area of health psychology. For this reason suggestions for further reading are provided.

Chapter summary

• What is health psychology?

Health psychology is a sub-discipline of psychology devoted to the relationship between behaviour and psychological processes and health and illness. Health psychology focuses, however, more on health and health maintenance than on disease and disease prevention. As such health psychology can complement the efforts of medicine by a more active, health-promotive approach.

• Health behaviour and health promotion

Health psychology offers a theoretical base for the understanding and promotion of health behaviour. In this chapter elementary models of health behaviour were introduced. Most of these are cognitive models, which can be criticized for their neglect of other (emotional, volitional, physical and social) determinants of health behaviour. In an attempt to summarize and integrate existing theories of behavioural change, basic principles of health promotion were introduced.

• Stress, coping and disease

Three different models of the relationship between stress and illness were introduced: biological stress theories, environmental stress theories and psychological stress theories. To shed light on the process by which an individual adapts to a chronic disease, Morse and Johnson's illness constellation model was presented. This model distinguishes between four consecutive stages of adaptation: a stage of uncertainty, a stage of disruption, a stage of strive for recovery of the self and a stage of restoration of well-being. Next, an extended model of coping with chronic disease was introduced, based on Lazarus and Folkman's stress coping model. Finally, to provide a basis for discussing the diverse psychological interventions which have been offered to patients with chronic diseases, an intervention model was introduced. The main feature of the model is the distinctions it draws among intervention aims, intervention levels and intervention channels.

Further reading

● Taylor, S.E. (1995) *Health Psychology*. New York: McGraw-Hill. The book covers all areas of health psychology with instructive chapters on health behaviour and its modification, stress and coping, and pain and psychological issues in chronic illness.

● Brannon, L and Feist, J. (1997) *Health Psychology*. Pacific Grove, CA: Brooks/Cole. This book is comparable to the previous one, with more emphasis on health behaviours.

● Tones, K. and Tilford, S. (1994) *Health Education: Effectiveness, efficiency and equity*. London: Chapman and Hall. This is probably the best book on the market on health promotion and health education. The book provides, in addition to a sound theoretical basis, many examples of health promotion in different settings.

● Conner, M. and Norman, P. (1996) *Predicting Health Behaviour*. Buckingham: Open University Press. This book offers very instructive chapters by different authors on the most common health behaviour models.

● Broom, A. and Llewelyn, S. (1995) *Health Psychology: Processes and applications*. London: Chapman and Hall. This book is highly recommended for its interesting chapters on psychological aspects of specific health problems and chronic diseases.

CHAPTER 20

Work and organizational psychology

Michael Frese

KEY CONCEPTS • organizational socialization • training • selection • organizational structure • performance • stress and health at work • leadership and management • work and organizational design

☐ Chapter preview

When you have read this chapter, you should be able to

- understand some central work and organizational concepts, such as socialization, training, selection, stress, performance, leadership and work design
- understand the major theories and empirical findings in each area
- be able to critically evaluate the advances made in work and organizational psychology
- understand how practice and science are related in the area of work and organizational psychology

Introduction

There are many reasons for studying work and organizational psychology. First, work and organizational psychology is useful. In my introductory class I often challenge students to name an important societal issue for which work and organizational psychology does not play any role. Usually, we find that work and organizational psychology is involved in nearly all issues ranging from distribution of income, railway or nuclear power plant accidents, environmental problems, the emergence of a leisure time society, to the issue of unemployment in the European Union. As most societal issues have implications for people working, work and organizational psychology has something useful to contribute.

Second, everything that one learns about work and organizational psychology can be applied in everyday life. For example, the section on performance may help you to study or work more efficiently or you could analyse the bar tender in your favourite pub or bar.

Third, a large number of psychologists are employed in this area. Approximately one-third of psychology students will eventually be employed as work and organizational psychologists. In the European Union, there are 30,000 work and organizational psychologists (de Wolff *et al.* 1991). The fastest growing sub-discipline of psychology in terms of both employment and student enrolment in nearly every European country is work and organizational psychology (de Wolff *et al.* 1991).

Fourth, psychology without work and organizational psychology is not complete. Work is composed of actions that use tools systematically and is societally organized. Tools are broadly conceptualized to include not only physical tools (e.g. a hammer) but also mental ones (e.g. a theory). Work in this sense differentiates humans from animals (Dolgin 1985; Schurig 1985). While animals sometimes show instinctive or accidental tool use (e.g. bees or beavers), only humans develop tools systematically and teach tool use to their offspring. Our environment – houses, machines, streets, clothes, food – is a product of human work. Thus, not only do we apply psychology but also the category work needs to be studied in its own right as an area of psychology in general.

Fifth, people regard their work as important. The question 'Imagine that you won a lottery or inherited a large sum of money and could live comfortably for the rest of your life without working, would you continue to work?' is answered 'Yes' by an average of 86 per cent (the British were lowest with 55 per cent and former Yugoslovians were highest with 96 per cent affirmative answers) (MOW 1987: 348). Moreover, people suffer when work is taken away from them. The clearest evidence comes from unemployment research, which shows conclusively that unemployment leads to depression and other forms of ill-health (Frese 1987a; Frese and Mohr 1987; Warr *et al.*1985; see also the case study).

Finally, there is the objective influence of work on people. Work usually comprises the largest proportion of adults' waking hours and thus influences people' s values, ideas, attitudes, personality and actions (see next section).

Ψ Case study

Unemployment

Mr B. is a 56 year old German plumber, who has been unemployed for two years. He describes his psychological state:

In the beginning, there was total despair, not really because of the material situation (I can live on 68 per cent of gross income that I receive as unemployment benefit). But from a psychological point of view . . . not to be useful any more, to be put on a dead end track, this just pulled me down.

He attempted to get work through various means but he would dread the question about his age and then hearing 'Sorry, you are too old for us'. He reports that he could deal with this for six months but then he started to brood and became very depressed. As he describes it: 'Those who are insecure drink and smoke more, they get depressed and nothing is worth it; nothing is fun any longer, going for a walk, and not even sleeping.' He tried to do something about it: he took a French language course at evening school and he has regular times to walk with his dog, which give the days some structure. He describes his work:

Work was really fun; it was hard work, but I was needed. Sometimes, I worked for 14 and even 18 hours, at night, when I cleared a blocked pipe in an apartment house; the tenants were glad then, when I got everything in working order again.

Source: Frese and Mohr (1979)

What do work and organizational psychologists do? A study in Germany found that they were most frequently involved in training, personnel selection and organizational development as well as personnel development (Methner 1990). In Europe, more work and organizational psychologists are employed in industry in comparison to the USA. In the UK and France, work and organizational psychologists work mostly as human factors specialists; in the Netherlands many work and organizational psychologists work as consultants; in the USA a much larger proportion of work and organizational psychologists (36 per cent) are based in universities (Howard 1990).

There are three branches of work and organizational psychology (Roe 1995): work, organizational, and personnel psychology. Work psychology includes stress, training, job design, automation and software ergonomics, performance appraisal and performance improvement programmes, motivation and safety. Organizational psychology covers organizational development, group development and management consulting. Personnel psychology includes career counselling, test construction and selection (Greif and Bamberg 1994; Katzell and Austin 1992; Roe *et al*. 1994; Wilpert 1995).

All these topics cannot be covered in one chapter. Therefore we shall concentrate on those issues that arise when you join an organization and when you work in an organization and perhaps even want to change it. Figure 20.1 describes all the topics. At first you enter the organization after you have been selected and you have selected the organization. Then you are socialized into the job and you are trained. These are the first three topics discussed in this chapter (but arranged in a slightly different order). Of course, you want to know what the organization looks like and want to be able to describe it – this is the next topic. You are supposed to perform in the organization and this may affect your well-being and stress levels. Thus, these are two further topics. Usually you will have a supervisor or manager. You might also want to change the organization; so does work and organizational psychology, which is a science that intervenes so that working conditions and organizational functioning are improved. This is the final topic.

❑ Organizational socialization

People enter different organizations at various stages of their lives. Students enter a university and graduates get

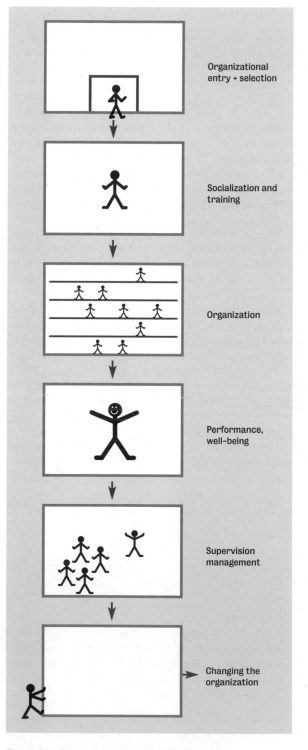

Figure 20.1 Stages in working for an organization

their first job in a company. On entry, the individual attempts to find a place in the organization and the organization changes the person. Why are organizations interested in socializing people? The main reason is that there are demands by the organization that individuals should comply with and issues that are important but which cannot be regulated. An example is customer orientation which is difficult to define because it changes its meaning from situation to situation. One solution is to select the right people but this does not assure customer orientation. Socialization produces a set of similar values, similar behaviours and similar ideas of customer orientation.

Three issues are discussed: phases of organizational socialization, impact of the job on the person, and strength and extent of socialization processes.

Phases of organizational socialization

There are four phases of **organizational socialization**. First, is the phase of **anticipatory socialization**, people develop expectations about the job, e.g. when you develop ideas of what your first job will be like and perhaps you start to practise behaviours which you think will be needed.

Second is arriving and **reality shock**: when entering the organization, one is usually disconcerted (Louis 1980). Wanous (1978) has suggested that companies can reduce reality shock by providing a **realistic job preview**. Most recruiters describe only favourable aspects of the job; **a realistic job preview** presents the negative aspects too (Wanous *et al.* 1992). This helps people to be more committed to the organization and to stay with the organization longer. These positive effects occur because a realistic job preview clarifies the work role, presents the company as honest and caring, and improves information for self-selection (Wanous 1978).

Third is the period of settling in, people become used to how things are done. Everything appears 'natural'. Actually, the problem here is that people are too settled in their ways and are no longer keen to participate in change any longer. The long-term effects are the fourth phase of socialization.

Impact of the job on the person

This issue is of theoretical importance. If people change because of the job, this shows the importance and strength of work as a developmental influence factor.

Frese (1982) argued that socialization can have cognitive effects (e.g. intellectual flexibility), effects on activity (e.g. leisure time activities), role taking and development of values (e.g. commitment) and emotional effects (e.g. stress effects, job satisfaction).

Cognitive effects

Both psychologists and non-experts agree that intelligence does not change much and there is clear evidence that a large part of intelligence is genetically determined (see Chapter 14). If we can show that work changes intelligence, then work is important. Kohn and Schooler (1978) studied the relation between complexity at work and 'intellectual flexibility' in a ten-year period and found a substantial **reciprocal relationship**. Both socialization (impact of work on the person) and selection effects (impact of individuals on jobs) occur. That is, complexity at work leads to higher intellectual flexibility and lack of complexity to lower flexibility. In addition to the socialization, there is also the selection effect: higher intellectual flexibility leads to more complexity at work; thus, intellectually flexible people eventually find more complex jobs. The selection effect is stronger than socialization. Schallberger (1988) confirmed these results by using a traditional IQ measure.

Effects on activity

Ulich and Ulich (1977) argued that there are the following potential relationships between work and leisure activities:

- compensation: people compensate for something in their leisure activities (e.g. they rest more to make up for hard work)
- generalization or spill over: work activities spill over into leisure activities (e.g. those socially more active at work are also more active outside work)
- identity: one does the same thing at work as one does for leisure (e.g. a farmer)
- non-relationship: work does not have anything to do with leisure activities.

Unfortunately, the empirical evidence is not good enough yet, although first results are interesting. Meissner (1971) argued for the generalization effect – the 'long arm of the job'; people with social contacts at work also have more social contacts outside work. Getting more decision latitude in the job resulted in more active leisure-time activities (Karasek 1978). Kohn and Schooler (1982) found that lack of complexity and control in the job leads to higher fatalism.

Role taking and development of values

One interesting finding is that occupational self-direction (being able to decide things at work by oneself and the complexity of work) is related to how authoritarian parents educate their children (Kohn and Schooler 1969). Since authoritarian education reduces children's activity levels, parents' occupation may influence the long-term likelihood of children being active copers.

Values are changed quite easily when a new job demands this. For example, rank-and-file workers who become foremen or forewomen readily change to a more management-oriented position (Lieberman 1956). People who start with a 'green' attitude and who support environmental protection and are against career orientation, become more career oriented (and less 'green') once they have a job in a company (Von Rosenstiel 1989).

Mortimer and Lorence (1979a) carried out a longitudinal study of the development of extrinsic (money, prestige), intrinsic (job content, autonomy, challenge) and social values (liking people). People usually want more of what they already have. People with high incomes would like to have more money, people with social jobs seek more social contacts, and people with high work autonomy want more challenges. People value those things that they are receiving in the job more and more. Thus, job selection and socialization feed upon each other.

Emotional effects

These are quite important at work (Pekrun and Frese 1992); one part of it will be discussed in the section on stress at work.

Strength and extent of socialization processes

Some organizations have strong socialization regimes that attempt to remodel the person. US Marines, religious groups, and fraternities are examples. Successful organizations have a stronger culture (Collins and Porras 1994) which means that they rely on internal promotion and continuing education, use collective and formal socialization strategies, have a mentor system, and sometimes even use debasement to break down individuals' self-pride to replace it by organizational pride (Van

Plate 20.1 Socialization at work can have effects on intellectual flexibility, leisure activities, role taking, the development of values and emotional effects

Maanen and Schein 1979). Many Japanese firms rely on such strong socialization strategies (see pp. 661–2).

The goal of these strong socialization strategies is to ensure a higher degree of compliance and internalization of values. While there is anecdotal evidence that these strategies work (and given that one of the oldest organizations – the Roman Catholic Church – uses them extensively, there is at least some relationship to longevity of the organization), we do not know much about how these strategies interact with personality and what short-term and long-term problems they produce. One drawback of strong socialization is that people lose an innovative and fresh approach and stop trying to change the organization.

ψ Section summary

Organizations attempt to influence people in the workplace. This may be done with an explicit design or by implicit strategies. People change with their work and their roles in an organization. However, there is also an interaction with selection effects: some people stay longer in a certain organization and in a certain job, while others leave or are never selected for this job in the first place

1 Think of how an organization that you belong to has influenced you (this may be the university, a sport association or an enterprise). Try to explain this by relating it to the concepts, theories and empirical findings of organizational socialization.

❑ Training

Importance of training and learning

A standard part of the socialization process is that the newcomer receives some training in the new organization. In principle, much of work and organizational psychology is concerned with increasing the fit between the person and the organization and the job. Socialization and training are two ways of increasing this **fit**. Training is defined as a learning process structured in a systematic fashion to raise the performance level of the employee. Contrast this with the education you are getting at university which is broader, longer and not so task specific. Training and learning on the job occurs, of course, not only at the start of a job but throughout the working life (and will be more and more important in the future). Training is big business. German firms spend about DM26.7 billion (c. US$18 billion) per year on training and development of their personnel, which is more than the total expenditure for all German universities, for example (Weiss 1990). Training is also important for every student because some part of what he or she does in the university is training for future performance. Figure 20.2 gives an overview of issues that are important in training (see also Goldstein 1991; Hacker and Skell 1993; Patrick 1992; Stammers 1996).

Training needs assessment

It is necessary to analyse in a **training needs assessment** the present and future tasks people do to know what people have to learn. In principle all the known methods of task and job analysis can be used: observation, questionnaires, key people consultation, interviews, group discussion, using records, and work samples (that is letting people perform a certain activity and checking what they need to know to perform well).

The training plan: how to do training

European work and organizational psychologists have traditionally done quite a bit of work in this area, most notably from the UK (Patrick 1992) and from Germany (Hacker and Skell 1993; Semmer and Pfäfflin 1978; Volpert 1971). US work and organizational psychologists have also become interested in training (Tannenbaum and Yukl, 1992).

There are, of course, many different training methods – on-the-job training, lectures, simulations, case studies and programmed instruction to name a few. Two influential ones are **behaviour modelling** and **action training**.

Behaviour modelling

This combines role play and behaviour modelling (cf. Bandura's social cognitive theory: Bandura 1986). A model is presented on video or in real life and the

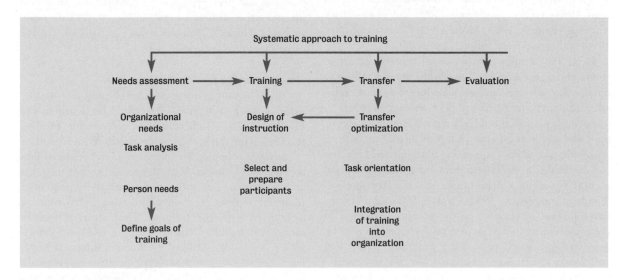

Figure 20.2 Training issues

special behaviours of this model and the rationale for the behaviour are discussed with the trainees. Then the trainees role play the behaviour, receiving feedback from the trainers and fellow trainees. This type of training has proved to be very effective (Burke and Day 1986; Tannenbaum and Yukl 1992). A typical example of behavioural modelling is a study by Latham and Saari (1979). An experimental group of foremen received nine sessions of two hours on various important topics (e.g. motivating poor performers, reducing absenteeism, overcoming resistance to change). A film was shown in each session to provide a model of a supervisor effectively handling the situation. Learning points (principles of good behaviour) were presented (e.g. avoid responding with hostility and defensiveness; ask for and listen openly to the employee's complaints). This was followed by role play, with one supervisor playing the supervisor and another one playing the employee. The trainer gave feedback so that people's confidence was not undermined, by restating negative comments in a positive manner (e.g. 'encourage the hourly employee to talk', not 'you talk too much'). The supervisors of those trained foremen were encouraged to praise them if they showed the desired behaviour. The experimental group was significantly better in all measures of supervisory behaviours at work than the control group.

Action training

Action training follows from action theory (Frese and Zapf 1994; Hacker and Skell 1993) and exploratory learning (Bruner 1966; Greif 1992; Greif and Keller 1990) and includes the following principles.

First, the trainees are supposed to take an active approach and are asked to learn while doing a task (e.g. through role playing). Various studies have found that exploration leads to better performance (E. Smith *et al.* 1997).

Second, people should get a good mental model of the tasks and how to approach it. A mental model is a representation of how something functions and how one can act in this area. The importance of having a good mental model is a prerequisite for effective actions (Gentner and Stevens 1983; Hacker 1992). One trainer developed an 'orientation poster' giving an overview of the hierarchical structure of a software program to be learnt (e.g. a word processing program) (Greif and Janikowski 1987). Another approach is to give heuristic rules (rules of thumb). These heuristics have been shown to be important in training (Volpert *et al.* 1984). A few examples by Skell (1972: 48) for training tool and dye

maker apprentices (non-literal translation by the present author): 'Compare the drawing with the raw material. What do you have to do to achieve the changes demanded by the drawing?', 'Try to eliminate movements that are not necessary; you can do that by thinking about the following questions: can I do different types of actions with the material clamped the same way into the vice? Can I use the clamped item again?'

Third, actions lead not only to feedback but also to errors. Adequate and informative feedback and learning from errors are both emphasized. Feedback has to be given frequently in the beginning but less frequently later on so that people develop their own internal feedback process (Kluger and DeNisi 1996). Action training provides both positive and negative feedback in order to give full information to the trainee. This is in contrast to the behaviouristic learning theory, which argues that there should be only positive feedback (Skinner 1968).

Fourth, an extreme form of negative feedback is error. Errors have a positive function for learning. Error training has been added to the action training approach. Error training has been experimentally researched by comparing one group that received ample opportunity for making errors (essentially by being given tasks too difficult to do) with another group that was given an instruction of how to go through these difficult tasks and therefore could not make any error. The error training group has consistently fared better (Dormann and Frese 1994; Frese *et al.* 1991; Greif 1992). Most of these trainings also presented general heuristics to produce a more positive attitude towards errors (e.g. 'I have made an error. Great!' 'There is always a way to leave the error situation': Frese *et al.* 1991: 83).

Action training for negotiating skills

A typical action training for developing negotiating skills of shop stewards is described by Semmer and Pfäfflin (1978). Each trainer is responsible for five trainees. The trainers provide negative and positive models in a role play. The negative model is played first and is used to discuss with the trainees what mistakes and errors appear. From these mistakes, principles (heuristic rules) of good negotiating behaviour are developed with the trainees. Thereafter, a positive model is shown. Participants then practise these principles in a role play. At first, the trainers interrupt ongoing sequences to give immediate positive and negative feedback (the trainer always gives the positive feedback first so that the trainee's self-esteem is not reduced). The feedback is always explained in functional terms and related to a rudimentary theoretical understanding (mental model) of what a good negotiation looks like (e.g. 'If you say this, then the other person will just get upset, but you do not get what you want; so you should be more specific in your demands'). Initial feedback by the trainer is frequent, but later the other trainees provide more and more feedback.

Transfer

Students know the problem of **transfer** very well and they often complain that their studies are not practical enough. This means that they assume that what they have learnt in the study cannot be used in one's work afterwards. The issue of transferring what has been learnt in the training to the tasks at work is a big problem in training in general. People are using only half of what they have learnt in their job (J.K. Ford *et al.* 1992) and personal and organizational characteristics make it less likely to use new skills in practice (Tziner *et al.* 1991). The challenge for work and organizational psychologists is to bridge the transfer gap. Three general factors are important: first, the similarity of training to work tasks; second, the motivation to use the newly learnt behaviour at work; and third, organizational issues.

Task examples

Task examples should be used in the training process. The theory of **identical elements** (Thorndike 1906) explains that there should be identical elements in the behaviours trained and in the behaviours required at work. However, a trainer may also go too far. If one teaches only the bare minimum of necessary skills, people are not prepared for future tasks that change quite frequently and that often turn out to be more complex than thought originally. People also need some knowledge of the overall context in which tasks are situated (for example, people who do not deal directly with customers outside the organization should know how their work contributes to the finished products for the customers).

Transfer knowledge

Von Papstein and Frese (1988) have suggested that training should increase **transfer knowledge**, which conveys the knowledge acquired in training to the task situation. Transfer knowledge was shown to mediate between performance at the end of the training and the amount of time the knowledge was used six months later (von Papstein and Frese 1988). Transfer knowledge

---

 Research update

Self-management and learning vs performance goals

Self-management techniques were influenced by advances in clinical psychology (Kanfer and Kanfer 1991). Self-management implies that one acquires the skills to deal with difficulties, rewards oneself and increases self-efficacy (Frayne and Latham 1987). A typical study of self-management principles is by E.M. Smith *et al.* (1995), who studied metacognition (with statements like 'I noticed where I made the most mistakes during practice and focused on improving those areas') and self-efficacy (among other variables). They found that metacognition was related to training performance and to self-efficacy and self-efficacy related to transfer performance. Similarly, Martocchio (1994) found that computer efficacy increased knowledge after training. Thus, self-efficacy functions both as a predictor of training performance and as a predictor of transfer performance.

'Learning vs. performance goals' is used to explain differences in how people conceptualize their ability (Dweck and Leggett 1988). It is argued that some people conceptualize their ability as something that grows with learning (**learning orientation**), while others see it as something fixed (**performance orientation**). People with a learning orientation learn from mistakes and challenges. However, if people are performance oriented, a mistake is an example of poor performance and challenges make it unlikely that they succeed. Thus, performance oriented people will be helpless more often and learn less. Martocchio (1994) has manipulated the ability conceptualization (mistake is a reminder that you should work more effectively, versus a mistake is just normal in training) and found that it relates to both computer anxiety and self-efficacy after the training (however, it was not related to knowledge).

is increased if trainees are asked to think of examples on how they can use what they have learnt.

Motivation

Motivation is of particular importance in transfer (Baldwin and Ford 1988; Noe 1986). Numerous issues of motivation have been studied, the most important ones being self-efficacy, relapse prevention, pay-off perceived by the trainee, goals and training or transfer contract. **Self-efficacy** has been shown to be important for transfer. People will use a skill only if they have the expectation that they can actually perform the appropriate behaviour (Tziner *et al*. 1991). **Relapse prevention** focuses on teaching solutions to those situations in which it may prove difficult to use the newly learnt skills (R.D. Marx 1982). Trainees who received a relapse prevention training used their skills more often and were doing their job better (Tziner *et al*. 1991). Trainees develop expectations whether or not it will pay off when they use what they have learnt in training. Often, companies teach one thing and reward a completely different behaviour. For example, trainees learn to be co-operative in a training course, but then they are paid for their individual contribution in a highly competitive environment. In such situations there is no transfer.

A **transfer contract** stipulates when and where the skills learnt in training will be used in practice. Sometimes positive or negative reinforcers will be incorporated (e.g. having to give a high amount of money to the political party that one abhors most in case one does not use the skills within a certain time).

Organizational issues

Organizational issues have been largely ignored in transfer research but are also important (Kozlowski and Salas 1977). We have already alluded to the pay-off situation at work. Another factor is the amount of supervisor support that is given to transfer skills learnt in training. Practice niches and task-oriented advice have been suggested in the human computer literature (Frese and Brodbeck 1989). Since people rarely learn a skill well enough in the training situation, there will always be a need to practise the skill (e.g. a new computer program) under favourable circumstances. As an example of a **practice niche**; a bank clerk learnt a new program to calculate mortgages, and practised it first while answering written requests (instead of in front of the customer). Thus, the customer does not

see all the mistakes the bank clerk makes when using the new program.

Evaluation of training

All training needs to be evaluated, otherwise it can at worst have negative consequences. Moreover, only precise data on how well the training works can lead to improvements. In practice, evaluations are done infrequently, partly because it is inherently difficult to evaluate a training programme and partly because training departments are anxious that negative or null-effects may lead to negative consequences for them. A discussion of **training evaluation** principles is given by Goldstein (1991).

> ### Ψ Section summary
>
> Training works via assessment of training needs, the training design, transfer and evaluation. Two useful and partly overlapping training designs are behaviour modelling and action training. The issue of how to improve transfer from training into doing the tasks at work is particularly important and difficult to do.
> 1 Think of a wordprocessing system that you use and develop a training programme for this system. Use different training procedures and think of psychological reasons for each step in your training programme.

Selection

Selection is a widespread phenomenon. People select their friends, lovers and spouses, groups select their members, and companies select their employees. Of course, to be a member of an organization you have to select one you want to be a member of and the organization has to select you. There are several reasons for paying a lot of attention to selection: the person ought to fit into the organization to be able to work well. One way to increase this fit is to get the 'right' person. Moreover, selecting a 'wrong' person is costly both for the person and for the company. An individual who has trouble doing a job well or who does not fit into a company suffers from this experience. Hunter and Hunter (1984) have calculated that the US federal government could save US$15.6 billion per year when using a high validity selection procedure (cognitive ability) in comparison to a random procedure. The savings are still US$11.6 billion if it uses a high as compared to a low validity test (an example of a low validity test is an unstandardized interview). Finally, people need to get the feeling that they are treated fairly in the selection procedure; discrimination and nepotism should be reduced by an objective selection procedure.

It is sometimes surprising for lay people that any selection instrument is called a psychological test by psychologists. Thus, someone who gazes deeply into another person's eyes is using a psychological test (even though the validity of this test is zero); when personnel managers say a few words and get 'a good (or bad) impression' of somebody, they are using a psychological test (again, one with very poor validity).

Different selection procedures are used in different countries. In the European Union interviews are preferred in nearly every country (cf. overview of Levy-Leboyer 1994). Cognitive (intelligence) and personality tests are not used in Germany but frequently in France, Belgium and the UK. References by the former employee are used in the UK and Belgium but not in Germany and France. Structured interviews are more frequently used in Germany. German firms use assessment centres more frequently, sometimes even for the selection of blue-collar workers. In France and Belgium, there is a higher reliance on graphology. It is unfortunate that graphology is still used because this technique has been shown to be not valid (Rafaeli and Klimoski 1983: 212). Sometimes, graphologists may have a certain hit rate because the handwritten material is autobiographical but *only* because of the autobiographical content (Ben-Shakhar *et al.* 1986: 645).

Whether or not the tests used are good is an important competitive factor, particularly in Europe, which does not have the hire-and-fire mentality of other areas of the world and, therefore, potential employers have to be more careful in the selection process.

Test criteria: reliability and validity

All testing instruments can be judged on whether they show a reliability and validity. **Reliability** means that the same results are obtained every time and that there is little measurement error. An example of an unreliable measure is to use a rubber band to measure head size. Since it is elastic, it is not reliable. Each time it is used, there is a different result. **Validity** is whether the test actually measures what it is required to measure. (See also Chapters 18 and 21).

Reliability

Suppose you want to develop a measure of psychological energy level. How do you know that you have a reliable scale? Obviously, one answer is that you get the same result every time you use the same measure. This is called **test-retest reliability**.

Another reliability measure is to correlate **parallel tests**. Thus, you use two tests which measure the same thing. An easier way to get two tests is to assemble a large number of items and use alternate items for the first and the second test. The correlation between these two tests is then your reliability (corrected for the length of the test, because longer tests are more reliable).

The most frequently used measure of reliability is **internal consistency** or Cronbach's alpha (Cronbach 1951) which is based on the intercorrelations of the items. This is really just a variant of a parallel test, but now every item is taken as a sort of parallel test.

Why should more than one question be used? Psychological energy cannot be directly ascertained. It manifests itself in different situations. Therefore, several questions need to be asked to encompass the full concept of energy level. Moreover, every question carries some truth and some error in it. Errors appear, because individuals may not understand a particular question; they may be unattentive for a short period; they may think of an example when answering a particular question that is not representative of their real energy level (Guion 1965). Errors that appear when answering one item are not necessarily the same ones when answering another item. Thus, the more items there are in a test, the more the errors cancel each other out and the more accurate is the test.

Reliabilities of 0.70 are usually considered necessary to use a test for a study of group differences. However, when making an individual selection decision (taking one person instead of another one), reliabilities of 0.90 and higher are required (Nunnally 1978).

Validity

Even perfect reliability does not ensure validity. If you want to measure the weight of a person but you use a metre rule, you have an instrument that has perfect reliability (for measuring height) but low validity to measure weight. Of course, nobody would do that. However, in psychology we often do not know precisely how to measure a theoretical concept.

Some personnel officers regard the firmness of a handshake as a measure of how energetic a person is. It is necessary to be 'theoretical' here: sometimes it may be possible to infer the energy level of a person from a handshake. But one observation (a one-item test) is never enough. Moreover, people can be trained to give a firm handshake; this is just a superficial motoric response which can be easily changed.

Construct validity

Arguments like this are related to the **construct validity** of a test (Cronbach and Meehl 1955). Construct validation means to derive hypotheses from a theory and to establish empirically that a test behaves in the hypothesized way. One may, for example, argue that high energy people work long hours. Thus, people who score highly on your newly developed energy tests should work longer than people with low scores. Obviously, there are many other potential hypotheses and they have to be tested similarly. One is never finished with construct validation. As Guion (1965: 128) explained: 'Construct validity must be expressed as a judgment, inferred from the weight of research evidence gathered in many independent studies.'

Content validity

Content validity means that a sample of test items is drawn from a universe of items that make up the whole construct; this implies that one has to have a good idea of what belongs to this construct and what does not belong to it. Therefore, one must know the construct and its boundaries well.

Criterion validity

Criterion validity measures the relationship of the test with a criterion. Often, some measure of productivity is taken as a criterion. Productivity is measured by supervisors' assessments, output measures (e.g. number of sales made by insurance people), money earned, career advances, grades in training courses (Landy and Farr 1980). It is not easy to decide on an appropriate criterion. Output would be a good criterion; however, it is not always in the hands of the workers to determine the output (e.g. when machines can run only at a certain maximum speed). Thus, we have to make theoretical (or at least plausible) judgements, whether or not we accept something as a good criterion for a certain test.

Validity generalization

Traditionally, work psychologists have suggested redoing validity studies in each company and with each group of workers (e.g. blue-collar vs white-collar employees, dif-

ferent races). Schmidt and Hunter (1981) argued that this procedure is unnecessary because one can make **validity generalizations** from one context to the next. They showed that differences between companies and different groups of employees were mostly due to methodological reasons (e.g. number of subjects, reduced variance, reliability of the criteria) and not to real differences in the validity data.

Intelligence tests, personality tests, assessment centres and interviews

Intelligence tests

Intelligence tests are frequently used in the Anglo-American world and have been shown to have good correlations with performance criteria. Hunter and Hunter (1984) argued that one of the best predictors of good performance is general intelligence and that this is a good predictor across most jobs with the exception of very simple jobs. They found that the average corrected correlation is 0.53 between cognitive abilities and performance in various jobs (Table 20.1). This correlation is higher with training performance than with performance in the job (after all, intelligence measures how well one learns). Other meta-analyses report smaller average correlations, for example Schmitt *et al.* (1984) reported an uncorrected correlation of 0.25 (Table 20.1). A major reason for these differences is that Hunter and Hunter (1984) used correction formulas (Hunter and Hirsh 1987), while Schmitt *et al.* (1984) did not. (See also Chapter 13).

Table 20.1 Meta-analytic validity coefficients of various selection procedures

Selection procedure	(Corrected) mean validity coefficient
Unstructured interview [a]	0.20
Unstructured interview by board [a]	0.37
Structured interview [b]	0.56
Cognitive ability (e.g. IQ tests) [c]	0.53
Cognitive ability [d]	0.25
Personality [d]	0.15
Work sample [d]	0.41
Assessment centre [d]	0.43

Sources: (a) Wiesner and Cronshaw (1988) (b) Hufcutt and Arthur (1994) (c) Hunter and Hunter (1984) (d) Schmitt *et al.* (1984: here coefficients are lower because they are not corrected)

Research update

Social validity of tests

Schuler (1993) studied the selection process from the applicant's perspective. This led to the concept of **social validity**: is the selection procedure accepted by the applicants? Social validity is influenced by four factors: information, participation, transparency and feedback to the applicants. Information on why certain areas are covered should be given. One of the reasons why assessment centres are preferred in Germany (in spite of their expense) is that they are more accepted than other tests. Despite their low validity, interviews are also accepted more than IQ and personality tests because applicants believe they have more control in the interview. Privacy and fairness are important issues here.

Personality tests

Personality tests show much lower correlations to performance (Table 20.1). Nevertheless, there has been a revival of interest in personality tests. One reason for this relates to new theoretical developments of the performance construct. Motowidlo and Van Scotter (1994) have shown that supervisors actually have two concepts in mind when they think of good performance – task performance and contextual performance (see p. 639). Task performance is doing the tasks well. Contextual performance means that people help each other and the company by doing extraordinary things, by following organizational rules and procedures (Borman and Motowidlo 1993). Contextual performance is a bit better predicted by personality measures than by ability (Van Scotter and Motowidlo 1996).

Assessment centres

Work samples as precursors were developed in Germany (Giese 1924) and the UK and were later applied as **assessment centres** in the USA (Bray *et al.* 1974). An assessment centre looks at people's behaviour when they do tasks thought to be important in their jobs. An example is the leaderless group discussion in which leadership ability, co-operative behaviour and problem-solving skills are observed. One advantage of an assessment centre is that potential supervisors are included in the selection procedure, after they have been trained in observational skills. Assessment centres have good validities (Table 20.1). They attempt to measure job-relevant behaviour directly. Assessment centre results are highly correlated with intelligence, social competence, achievement motivation, dominance and self-confidence (Scholz and Schuler 1993).

Interviews

The most frequently used selection test is the interview. Unfortunately, the unstandardized interview by one interviewer is a poor psychological test. The validity of interviews can be improved relatively easily, by increasing the number of interviewers – two interviewers show a much better validity than one (Wiesner and Cronshaw 1988; see also Table 20.1) – or by structuring questions and answers (Huffcutt and Arthur 1994). Structuring involves asking the same questions in all interviews and standardizing the scoring of the answers.

Ψ Section summary

All selection decisions are based on some kind of test. Tests developed by psychologists usually have a higher reliability and validity. Most selection decisions are based on unstructured interviews which have a poor validity; however, they can be improved by having two interviewers or by structuring the questions and developing a coding key for the answers. Assessment centres and intelligence tests are also valid selection procedures.

1 Develop a few items for a test that measures knowledge in work and organizational psychology. Note some of the difficult decisions you have to make to develop these items.

2 Give these items to a few friends. Observe them and have them think aloud while they work through the items.

☐ Organizational structure

A person entering an organization is confronted with a certain organization. Socialization, training and selection function to increase the **fit** between the individual on the one hand and work and the organization on the other hand. To understand the other side of the fit, we need to examine the **organizational structure** in more detail.

People cannot help being involved in organizations. Students are members of a department, of a university, of some student organization, a state and a recreational association. You probably belong to many more organizations than you think. You should find that you can describe the organization better with the following analysis in mind.

Descriptive dimensions and structure of organizations

When comparing the organizational features of, say, a local sport association and a company, some descriptive dimensions are needed in order to carry out this comparison. Pugh and colleagues (1968) differentiated:

- specialization: the degree of division of labour
- standardization and formalization: the degree to which work is proceduralized and written up
- centralization: the degree to which decisions are made at the top
- configuration: how the organization is structured in terms of organizational charts, with line and staff positions, etc.

Mentally compare a local sport association with a company you know well. You may notice that there are systematic configurations. Your sport association might be a chaotic organization that is mainly dependent upon one leader; if the leader should leave, the association might fall apart (here, specialization and standardization are low, centralization is very high, configuration is simple); the company might be bureaucratic (specialization and standardization are high, centralization might be medium, configuration is complex, with many clearly defined chains of command that one is not allowed to circumvent).

Five types of organizations

An influential configurational approach (Mintzberg 1979) distinguished five types of organizations.

Simple structure

In young, entrepreneurial organizations, **simple structures** prevail. The owner may be authoritarian. Communication is informal and goes across all levels. The sport association discussed above has such a simple structure.

Machine bureaucracy

This is the kind of bureaucratic organization with a high degree of specialization, many routine tasks, formalized procedures, many regulations, low flexibility, and relatively centralized power structure. 'Attempts are made to eliminate all possible uncertainty, so that the bureaucratic machine can run smoothly, without interruption' (Minzberg 1979: 320). The **machine bureaucracy** is usually found in mature organizations; a mass production assembly line is a good example.

Professional bureaucracy

Professionals have internalized standards (e.g. in nursing or medicine). They use fixed procedures but the adherence to them is the result of training and socialization and not of external forces as in the machine bureaucracy. Such structures are often decentralized. The university is a good example of a **professional bureaucracy**. Usually, its structure is inflexible and it is hard to change procedures that are deeply engrained in the profession.

Divisionalized form

It 'relies on the market basis for grouping units' (Mintzberg 1979: 381). Many large corporations have **divisionalized forms** that work independently of each other and that are supposed to react better to market forces. Each division may be rather bureaucratic in itself; however, the divisions overall are not governed bureaucratically; usually the divisions are left to their devices as long as the output (profit) is above a certain standard.

Adhocracy

This has little formalization. **Adhocracies** are often created within larger organizations to make it possible to innovate.

Ideal types

Mintzberg's theory not only describes different types of organization but also posits ideal types: organizations that are more similar to the ideal type should be more effective than organizations that misapply a certain type. So, for example, a young organization working in a dynamic environment should be better off if it uses a simple structure than if it relies on a bureaucratic structure. Unfortunately, the empirical evidence speaks against this hypothesis (Doty *et al.* 1993).

Four types of strategies

A better fit with the data appears for the Miles and Snow (1978) organizational typology, which differentiates four types of strategies to adapt to the environment: the prospector, the analyser, the defender, and the reactor.

Prospector

The prospector adapts to environmental turbulence by scanning the environment for opportunities. Whenever a good market opportunity arises, the prospector quickly takes the chance and develops an appropriate product. To be able to do this, the prospector should have a low level of specialization and formalization and a high degree of decentralization. An example is Richard Branson, whose many business interests include an airline (Virgin Airline), a music retailer and a railway company.

Plate 20.2 Richard Branson is a good example of a personality adapting to environmental turbulence by scanning the environment for opportunities

Defender

'The most notable feature of the Defender's product-market domain is its narrowness and stability' (Miles and Snow 1978: 37). In stable environments, the defender focuses on efficiency, economy of scale, and a mechanistic orientation, leading to bureaucratization.

Analyser

The analyser is in the middle between prospector and defender and has elements of both approaches. The analyser locates and exploits 'new product and market opportunities while simultaneously maintaining a firm base of traditional products and customers' (Miles and Snow 1978: 78). Mass production and product innovation is combined.

Reactor

Finally, there is the reactor, a company that does not have any stability, lacks a clear strategy and therefore reacts only to turbulences in the environment. According to Miles and Snow (1978), this type is not successful, while the three others can all be successful. The empirical support for this theory is quite good (Doty *et al.* 1993; Zahra and Pearce 1990).

Organizational factors leading to success

Companies are naturally interested in knowing which organizational factors lead to success. Therefore, there have been many attempts to look at such factors. One of the most interesting ones has been by Collins and Porras (1994) who compared so-called 'visionary' companies with not so visionary ones (e.g. Hewlett-Packard vs Texas Instruments or General Electric vs Westinghouse). Visionary companies had a strong core ideology, they were driving for progress and they were organizational visionaries.

Examples of core ideologies were technical contributions in the case of Hewlett-Packard. A strong ideology most clearly showed up when these companies were taking heavy losses to defend their core ideology. Moreover, they created very strong cultures which would sometimes repel people ('love it or leave it'). For example, Nordstrom (a visionary company) made sure that every employee started on the sales floor rather than as a manager. The core ideology is also preserved by recruiting top management from within the company.

The drive for progress is accomplished by developing very high goals ('big hairy audacious goals') and a purposeful evolution by trying things out and keeping what works; there is continuous self-improvement and more long-term investments in equipment, in people, and in research and development.

The visionary companies are called clock builders; they were able to develop new organizational solutions; for example, General Electric was the first one to build a systematic Research and Development Unit. The visionary companies had organizational visions that facilitated continuous development even when the founders died or left the company.

These are interesting results; however, there are obvious weaknesses of these kinds of studies (in the case of Collins and Porras the authors know this). The visionary companies were nominated by other managers. Obviously, they selected successful ones. But what about those companies that used the same strategies and died along the way? They might have used the same 'risky' strategies but were just not lucky. Moreover, could it be that some of the assumed causes are just side-products of a high degree of success?

Organizational theorists have become rather sceptical of one-dimensional explanations. People have argued too long for organizational solutions that fit all purposes and environments. Probably a much better answer is: success depends on the environment; this is discussed next.

The contingency approach: organization–environment interactions

The **contingency approach** argues that there is no such thing as an organizational design that is always successful. Rather, there has to be a good fit of the organization to the technology used, to environmental conditions, and to the state of the life cycle that the organization is in.

Woodward (1958) was the first one to point out that British firms had different organizations depending upon their manufacturing technology. Three production systems were differentiated: unit production (which produced only small batches of specialty products, e.g. locomotives), mass production (which manufactured large batches of the same product, e.g. cars on an assembly line) and process production (in which a continuous process would exist, e.g. in a chemical firm). Different technologies were associated with different organizational features. In process control and small batch production, supervisors had fewer people to supervise than in mass production. The number of levels and the proportion of highly qualified employees increased with level of technology (and was highest in process control). Moreover, the better the fit between

the technology and the structure, the better was the performance of the firm.

Three environmental dimensions are important:

- Simple–complex: is it an environment that is easy to understand or not?
- Stable–dynamic: how high is the volatility of the market, how much turbulence is there, and can one predict how the market will develop?
- **Munificence** (generosity)–hostility: is it an easy environment to work in, did the company develop a niche product that 'sells itself' or is it a highly hostile market with many competitors?

These dimensions are often related. For example, the airplane market is complex, unstable and hostile, while the foodstuff market is much less complex and more stable, and usually also less hostile. Some representative results are that a complex environment necessitates a more decentralized structure (Mintzberg 1979). The more dynamic the environment is, the better it is to have a non-bureaucractic and decentralized structure (Burns and Stalker 1961). Finally, the more hostile the environment is, the more organizations tend to centralize their structure (Mintzberg 1979). A good example is trade unions, who had to operate in adversarial environments and became quite centralized.

Organizational culture

Organizations develop certain cultures. They manifest themselves in values and beliefs, in symbols and rituals, in certain habits, and in taking certain things for granted.

One practical implication of **organizational culture** is that it is not easy to 'marry' two organizations. Indeed, mergers and acquisitions often do not work out because the different cultures do not get along (Cartwright and Cooper 1990). A further problem is that people make implicit assumptions of how things are to be done in a company. Again, this leads to conflicts and difficulties when new people enter such an organization. Cultures have a tenacity that goes beyond rationality; thus, it is quite difficult to change a deeply embedded culture in an organization.

Not every culture has the same strength; in some cultures there is a high degree of consensus among the members of the organization, in others there is not. The assumption is that a strong culture will have a stronger influence on the individuals in terms of organizational socialization (Payne 1996).

ψ Section summary

While there have been many attempts to describe the best organizational design, this may be in vain, because success comes about only in the interaction with the environment – the contingency theory of organizations. Organizational culture is a new area of research which looks at what distinguishes one organization from the next and describes which aspects of the organization are taken for granted by its members.

1 How could Ford in the early part of the twentieth century with his strict hierarchical organization and his assembly line actually produce more efficiently than other organizations of his time?

Performance

The concept of performance and its differentiations

When working in an organization, ones **performance** is important. Usually some kind of standard of excellence is applied here. Raising performance is one of the goals of work and organizational psychology (the others are to increase health and to foster the development of employee's personality).

Performance is sometimes used to signify the outcome of behaviour (e.g. 'X has performed well') and sometimes it refers to the action itself. Performance is probably better defined as an action that is relevant to the organization's goals and carries a certain standard of excellence (Campbell *et al.* 1993: 40). Since we equate performance and actions, this section is based on a theory of action (Austin and Vancouver 1996; Frese and Zapf 1994; Hacker 1986).

Actions at work are oriented towards two domains: one is the task domain and the other is the social domain. As already discussed (p. 635), it has significantly advanced our understanding of performance to differentiate between task and contextual performance (Borman and Motowidlo 1993). **Task performanc**e is the more obvious aspect of performance – work is defined by having a certain task to do. The task is usually given to the worker or a group of workers.

The following are issues of **contextual performance** (Borman and Motowidlo 1993):

- upholding the smooth functioning of the organization through conscientiousness and compliance; this is sometimes also called organizational citizenship behaviour (Organ 1988)
- making the social situation conducive to effective task performance; altruism – another factor of organizational citizenship behaviour – is important here
- keeping up and servicing the technical and production equipment; this implies that production methods have to be continually improved, etc.
- keeping up human production capabilities; of particular importance is participation in continuing education
- supporting and defending organizational objectives.

Contextual performance is not usually written into a work contract. Thus, people show contextual performance without formal demands; this implies that some degree of personal initiative is shown by the employee. **Personal initiative** is defined as a behaviour syndrome resulting in an individual' s taking a self-starting, proactive, and persistent approach to work that goes beyond the job description (Frese *et al.* 1996). Initiative is related to problem-focused coping and to getting a job more easily if someone was unemployed before; small-scale entrepreneurs exhibit a higher degree of initiative (Frese 1997) and it is related to objective job effectiveness (Crant 1995).

Analysis of performance

In the following we present an action theory account of performance. Think for a moment of your own performance as a student or an employee. Most certainly, you will recognize that some things you know how to do and you do not have to pay much attention to them; other tasks are more difficult to do and you have to concentrate very strongly. This will be discussed as a hierarchical structure of levels of regulation. Moreover, you develop goals, check and make sense of the environment, you have a certain plan of action and you pay close attention to the results of your actions. They will be discussed under the heading of action process.

Action process

The following steps can be minimally differentiated in the **action process**: goal-setting, orientation, plan development, monitoring of the execution, and feedback (Dörner and Schaub 1994; Frese and Zapf 1994).

Goal-setting

A goal is an 'internally represented desired state' (Austin and Vancouver 1996: 361). Goals can be developed from within the person or through external tasks. An example of the former is wanting to do an assignment particularly well (sometimes the term 'intrinsic goal' is used here). At work, people are usually assigned external tasks. However, we do not usually take over organizationally prescribed goals completely; there is a translation process which actually changes the goals, sometimes quite subtly, sometimes quite strongly – this is the redefinition process (Hacker 1986; Hackman 1970; Staw and Boettger 1990).

Goals have a motivating function. One of the best practices of motivation is to give specific and high goals to people, which leads to higher performance than 'do your best' or easier goals (Locke and Latham 1990).

Goals change; the driving forces for such changes can again be internal as well as external. External reasons are task changes (e.g. because of market or job changes). Internal reasons may be that one wants to increase goal difficulty so that enough challenges are present (McClelland 1987; White 1959).

Orientation

Extensive orientation and the development of an adequate problem representation is often observed in expert task performance. For example, Klemp and McClelland (1986) described 'diagnostic information seeking' as a central characteristic of high performing managers.

Plan development

Plans (or action programmes) are not to be confused with their everyday meaning. Plans comprise everything from an elaborate blueprint, a general idea, to an automatized schema (or frame) for working (G.A. Miller et al. 1960). Gollwitzer (1993) has shown that combining goals (he calls them intentions) with a concrete anticipatory plan (e.g. specifying when and where one will start the action) leads to a much higher goal implementation rate than when one has just a goal but without the appropriate specific plan. Think how often you actually wanted to do something but did not do it. If you had then decided on a specific plan of action, the likelihood of putting the goal to work would have been increased.

There is evidence that high performers plan their actions to a greater extent than average or low performers (Dörner et al. 1983; Early et al. 1987; Klemp and McClelland 1986). However, more important than single acts of planning are general strategies. Hacker

(1986) differentiated between a momentary and a planning strategy (see also Frese and Zapf 1994). The planning strategy can be characterized as a proactive strategy based on a long-term goal-hierarchy. The planning strategy includes preventive actions and active search for task-relevant information. In contrast, the momentary strategy is characterized by mainly reacting to ongoing processes. Research summarized by Hacker (1992) shows that high performers in manufacturing tasks use a planning strategy more often; however, high performers do not necessarily plan everything out in detail but they do some sort of localized planning (Sonnentag 1997).

Monitoring of the execution

The concept of plan already implies execution: it is the bridge between cognition and action (G.A. Miller et al. 1960). Nevertheless, plans are sometimes in a sort of waiting line; therefore, we differentiate a phase called executing. Monitoring of the execution draws heavily on working memory; therefore, omission errors appear here easily, particularly when there are interruptions to one's work.

Feedback

Without feedback individuals would not know where they stand with regard to a goal (Erez 1977; Locke and Latham 1990; G.A Miller et al. 1960). On the other hand, feedback may also divert attention from the task, actually producing negative learning effects (Kluger and DeNisi 1996). An important issue is, whether or not feedback triggers self-relevant thoughts that divert from the task (Kluger and DeNisi 1996; Kuhl 1992).

Some important parameters with regard to feedback are the degree of realism vs self-serving interpretations (Dörner and Schaub 1994) and reactions to the social content of feedback vs performance content (e.g. losing face instead of learning from criticism).

Feedback processing was found to be essential for superior performance. There is evidence from some studies that high performers engage more in feedback processing (Dörner et al. 1983) and seek more negative feedback (Ashford and Tsui 1991).

Hierarchical structure of action: regulation levels

Table 20.2 explains how these steps are related to the **levels of regulation**. Only the concept of hierarchy can explain that a higher level goal (e.g. writing a thesis) actually regulates (affects) lower level behaviours (e.g. typing the word 'behaviour', or using the appropriate muscles to strike a key) (Carver and Scheier 1982;

Table 20.2 A model of levels of regulation

Levels of action regulation	Skill level	Level of flexible action pattern	Conscious level	Heuristic level
Consciousness of regulation	Unconscious; normally no access to consciousness	Access to consciousness possible, but not necessary	Conscious representation necessary	Both conscious and automatic use of heuristics
Goals	Automatic goals	Sub-goals	Goals	Standard meta- and life goals
Action programmes	Blueprints of elementary movement patterns and cognitive routines	Well-known patterns with situational specifications	Conscious complex plans, strategies	Metaplans, heuristics
Feedback/ signals	Stereotype test programmes, unconscious processing of kinaesthetic and proprioceptive feedback signals	Processing of known signals/ feedback	Analysis and synthesis of new information	Abstract (non-object-oriented) checks of logical inconsistencies

Sources: adapted from Hacker (1986); Frese and Zapf (1994)

G.A. Miller *et al.* 1960). The higher levels are conscious, thought oriented and more general, the lower levels are automatic, specific and involve muscle movements. There are three levels of regulation of task-oriented actions and one metacognitive level.

Skill level of regulation

This lowest level of regulation has been variously called skill level (Rasmussen 1982), sensory-motor level of regulation (Hacker 1986), psychomotor (Ackerman 1988) and procedural knowledge (Anderson 1983). It is the lowest level of regulation with highly specific automatized skills, usually involving some motor components. Information on this level is parallel, rapid, effortless, and without apparent limitations. However, it is difficult to modify **automaticity of action** at this level. In order to change these programmes, they have to be lifted to a higher level of regulation, so that some conscious form of (effortful) processing can be applied. An example is to change a certain technique in a sport; usually it is not easy to change it and use a somewhat different technique.

Flexible action patterns

Well-trained schematic action patterns (Norman 1981) dominate here. These ready-made action programmes are available in memory but must be flexibly adjusted to situationally defined parameters. Perceptual processes of action signals are important (Ackerman 1988; Hacker 1986). Rasmussen (1982) uses the concept of rule-based regulation for this level.

Conscious level

This level is concerned with conscious regulation of goal-oriented behaviour. It has been variously called knowledge based (Rasmussen 1982), declarative knowledge (Anderson 1983), controlled (Shiffrin and Schneider 1977), cognitive (Ackerman 1992), intellectual level (Frese and Zapf 1994; Hacker 1986). Conscious processing implies effort (Kahneman 1973), it is slow, it is constrained by limited resources of the central (conscious working memory) processor (Baddeley 1986), and works in a serial mode. Thus, when working on this level, it is slow, difficult and often not very elegant. Just think about learning to ski for the first time.

Metacognitive heuristics

People have some knowledge about how they use their thoughts and strategies (knowledge on cognitive regulation: A.L. Brown 1987). People know how much they will be able to learn and what kinds of strategies they use (Gleitman 1985; Weinert and Kluwe 1987). Further, people have general heuristics, of how they plan, set goals, and process feedback (Frese *et al.* 1987). We assume that these general heuristics can be either conscious or automatic (A.L. Brown 1987; Flavell 1987) and they may be highly generalized or specific. The highest level – the meta-level – is usually not implicated when we receive an outside task and when the task solution is known. This is one reason why we typically do not think about our life goals in our everyday activities. The meta-level will be consulted, however, when things go wrong or when the situation is new. Therefore, when one moves house or when one separates from a love, one thinks of one's life goals more generally.

Automaticity and the levels of regulation

It is not only sensory-motor acts that can be and are routinized and thus become automatic, but also our thoughts and metacognitive strategies. Mental skills may be automatized as well. This also applies to the use of theories. For example, somebody raised in the tradition of the psychoanalytic theory will automatically think about the importance of sexual development of clients when he or she is confronted with a practical problem. This is one reason why theories have a life of their own and it is difficult (and effortful) to change them (even if one becomes convinced that the theory is wrong). The automatic use of the theory gives an impulse to ask certain questions and not other ones, for example in therapy.

Evidence for the differentiation of levels of regulation comes primarily from training studies. Ackerman (1988) has shown that intelligence predicts performance better in the beginning of the training process (when processing is done consciously), perceptual speed is a good predictor in the middle (when processing is on the level of flexible action patterns) and psychomotor predictors are good at the end of the training (when the task is handled routinely).

Relationship between upper and lower level processing

Routines are developed when the environment is redundant and when satisfactory results can be achieved with the routine. Whenever possible, people prefer to regulate their actions on the lower levels because processing on this level is less effortful and the action is smoother. It leaves the higher levels of regulation free from the constraints of the working memory; it also allows people to do other things, for example, while walking one can take delight in nature's beauty or daydream about one's future.

However, routines can also have negative effects. Keeping routines makes people conservative. This goes for thought routines (e.g. using a certain theory and keeping this theory even when there are actually better alternatives available) as well as for sensory-motor routines (e.g. a certain way of skiing or doing one's banking although more efficient alternatives are available). Performance problems ensue, particularly when continuous improvement is necessary, when innovations have to be speedily implemented (e.g. 'not invented here syndrome'), or when team composition is changed quickly (e.g. in project work). In all these cases, there is a tendency to keep conservative routines going even against a certain amount of environmental pressure. On the other hand, routines may also lead to boredom because the higher levels of regulation are underoccupied.

Actions are regulated on a higher level when barriers, opportunities for new goals, or environmental pressures appear.

- Barriers are, for example, errors or problems that are difficult to solve, or a no-go situation. The consequence of moving up the level of regulation is that one is able to think consciously about the problem. This is frustrating because one's plan of action is interrupted (Mandler 1964) but it can also lead to new learning (Frese 1995).
- Opportunities for new goals may appear, if these opportunities are important given a certain latent action tendency or current concern (e.g. when someone cleans the kitchen and notices that a cupboard is not in order and rearranges the contents as well). In such a case the person may focus consciously on the task and decide whether to finish it or to use the opportunity as a trigger of new actions.
- Environmental pressures may be direct pressures by the environment to process something on a higher level. An example is a training situation, in which people are asked to think consciously about how they are doing things.

Most probably, there is some kind of self-reflection when processing one's actions on a higher level. One positive side-effect of this higher level of self-reflection may be a higher innovation rate (West *et al.* 1997).

On the other hand, problems appear when moving up the level of regulation: overload of processing capacity, lower degree of elegance, and sometimes a disruption of the smoothness of actions. Overload is the direct result of having more things to do on the upper levels of regulation (Kahneman 1973). Especially frustrating is the lower degree of performance elegance and smoothness when people are asked to control consciously a routinized action (Kimble and Perlmuter 1970).

Performance appraisal

Whenever we talk about people, we also make judgements of their performance, for example after watching a ballet (it was excellent) or after a dinner (there was incompetent service). **Performance appraisal** is usually a bit more systematic and is often fed back to the employee in an appraisal interview. Grades serve as performance appraisals for students.

The following are important issues of performance appraisal: developing good criteria, appraisal errors, strategies to overcome these errors via training and ratings scales, and the relationships of performance appraisal with performance.

Criterion development for performance appraisal

Performance appraisals should be based on objective and observable criteria, which are related to those results that are under the control of the person to be appraised; the criteria should also be representative to the job. It is difficult to achieve all of these. For example, the output of an automatic tool and dye machine operator can be measured quite objectively. However, this output is not under the control of the worker, who is dependent upon the programmer, the quality requirements, the repair people, the prior shift, the condition of the machine, etc. All these factors contribute to higher or lower output. If one uses the criterion of how diligently the worker works, there are problems with observability, particularly when the managers have to supervise many workers.

Errors in performance appraisal

Social cognition research has shown that we make errors when judging other people. These errors are related to rater and ratee characteristics, different rating procedures (more on this later), the amount of training received by the rater, the type of job, and other background variables (Landy and Farr 1980). The most important appraisal errors are the following:

- The **halo effect** implies that the manager generalizes from one positive or negative characteristic to other ones, e.g. an intelligent person is also seen to be more conscientious (Pulakos *et al.* 1986). Thus, different dimensions of the rating tend to be lumped together.
- The **leniency/severity error** means that some people tend to be generally more positive while

others tend to give more negative ratings. On the whole, leniency errors are more frequent.
- **Central tendency** errors means that raters only use the midpoints of a scale, rather than the extremes (Guion 1965).
- The **similar-to-me-error** (Wexley and Yukl 1977) occurs when managers judge their workers better when they use similar work methods or when their personality characteristics are similar to them.

Training for performance appraisal

Four different training concepts have been used to increase appraisal accuracy (Woehr and Huffcutt 1994).

- In rater error training, the managers are taught the above errors and told to reduce them. There is some controversy over whether this training is useful (summarized by Woehr and Huffcutt 1994).
- In performance dimension training, the raters are taught the performance dimensions in detail, how to keep them apart and how to operationalize them (D.E. Smith 1986).
- In a frame-of-reference training, the trainees are taught to keep the dimensions apart, to discuss and practise on samples of behavioural incidents for each dimension. Thus, common evaluative standards are trained.
- Behavioural observation training distinguishes sharply between observation and evaluation of behaviour. Raters are taught how to observe behaviour and to use appropriate records (note taking, diary, etc.) and not to fall into the trap of immediately judging the ratee.

The frame-of-reference and the behavioural observation trainings generally showed the best effects (Woehr and Huffcutt 1994).

Rating scales to improve appraisal

Several different rating procedures have been developed for performance appraisal. In general, the more behaviourally oriented the rating scales are, the better, for example, the Behaviourally Anchored Rating Scale (BARS) (P.C. Smith and Kendall 1963) and Behavioural Observation Scale (BOS) (Latham and Wexley 1977). Two items of an behavioural observation scale to measure a manager's ability to overcome resistance to change are 'Describes the details of the change to subordinates' and 'Asks the employee for help in making the change work' (Latham and Wexley 1981: 56).

Performance appraisal and performance

It has been assumed up to this point that performance appraisal interviews always have positive consequences on subsequent performance. However, doubts have been raised about this presupposition. Kluger and DeNisi (1996: 254) found little evidence in their **meta-analysis** that feedback interventions (feedback given in addition to the task, as in an appraisal interview) had generally positive effects on performance. The majority of their studies were experimental; thus one cannot generalize from these findings to all appraisal systems. However, these results cast some doubt on the naïve assumption common to most psychological theorizing in this area. Kluger and DeNisi (1996) have provided a comprehensive theory of feedback intervention. Important for our discussion is the fact that whenever the self-system gets involved, feedback can even have negative consequences on performance. You might think that this is true only for negative feedback. If you are told that your class paper is really inferior, you may be less motivated later on. However, this is also true for positive feedback, e.g. getting the feedback that you have done a marvellous job with your paper. Your attention is then diverted to the self and away from the task; you are thinking about yourself, about how great you are, and so on.

Thus, performance appraisal systems are far from trivial and have many inherent problems that need to be taken into account before they can produce positive performance effects.

Action errors: the opposite of good performance?

Action errors are discussed here for three reasons: first, they are often seen as the opposite of good performance. If individuals perform well, they should not make any errors. Second, errors are intrinsically fascinating, partly because they are so frequent. Most probably, you do not even realize how many errors you have made today. Third, errors are the 'building blocks' of positive and negative events in the workplace: errors may lead not only to negative events like accidents and low quality, but also to positive events, such as learning and exploration.

Definition of errors

Errors imply the non-attainment of a goal and they should have been potentially avoidable (Frese and Zapf 1994; Reason 1990). Errors and violations have to be dif-

ferentiated, the latter being a conscious behaviour against some norm. Errors should also be differentiated from faults (e.g. product or machine faults). Since machines do not have goals, they cannot make errors. However, faults may be the result of a designer error.

Concept of error management

Usually, people try to prevent errors from occurring. However, recently, I have become convinced that it is as important to think of **error management**. This term should be distinguished from error handling (Frese 1995). Error handling is a descriptive term and implies any type of response towards an error, while error management is prescriptive. Error management means that error handling is supported with the goals of avoiding negative error consequences, of dealing quickly with error consequences once they occur, and of learning from an error to reduce the future occurrence of this type of error. The issues of error management will now be explained.

Avoiding negative error consequences

One prerequisite of the concept of error management is the differentiation between the error itself and the negative error consequences. People do not break an arm every time they trip over. Tripping is the error, the negative error consequence is to break an arm. The concept of error management argues that the negative error consequences have to be avoided, not the error *per se*. Figure 20.3 explains the differences between error prevention and error management. The strategy of error prevention attempts to reduce the number of faulty actions. Thus, a barrier is erected to prevent a faulty action occurring. The error management strategy is not concerned with a

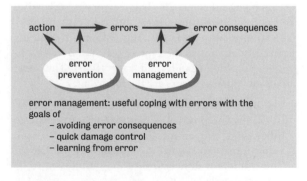

Figure 20.3 Error prevention and error management
Source: adapted from Frese (1995)

specific error but attempts to erect a barrier between the error and the potential negative error consequences. Learning how to fall over without breaking an arm would be an error management approach (as is routinely done when learning a sport like Judo).

Dealing quickly with the negative error consequences once they occur

This aspect of error management works from the assumption that errors have more negative consequences if the person does not detect errors immediately and/or does not correct the error consequences quickly. This is so particularly in dynamic systems, for example organizations which deal with a competitive market (Dörner 1989).

Learning from an error to reduce the future occurrence of this type of error

Error prevention strategies attempt to prevent errors. The concept of error management entails a much more sceptical view of the viability of such an approach. More likely than not, errors will appear but individuals should not repeat the errors that they have made. Therefore, error management implies that people should learn as much as possible from their errors.

Errors and organizational learning

Error training was discussed in the section on training, where it was shown that errors can lead to learning. Prerequisites to learn from errors are that people get good error feedback, are not too upset about an error, and are able to explore (Frese 1995). These principles can also be used in organizational learning. Therefore, a positive or negative error culture will determine organizational learning to some extent. Organizations that are strong on error prevention and sanction errors negatively will probably have the following problems:

- A reduced anticipation of errors: people assume that errors will not really appear but if so, that other people or subsystems will find the error and deal with the error consequences.
- Losing one's ability to cope with errors: if error prevention works, actions to cope with errors are rehearsed less frequently and are, therefore, not available when really needed.
- Errors are not accepted: this leads to concealing errors, less communication about errors and, therefore, less individual and collective learning from them.

Errors and accidents

Up to this point, we have talked about ridding the error concept of some of its negative connotations. Thus, errors may lead to exploration, opportunities to learn and eventually to higher performance. But errors are, of course, also related to accidents and negative events such as inferior quality of products. A good case is the Three Mile Incident that nearly led to disaster (see Reason's account of it in the case study).

Figure 20.4 explains how an accident may occur (Maurino *et al.* 1995). There are organizational processes that lead to working conditions and to defences and barriers against accidents. An active error occurs when there are local conditions (triggers) that mismatch with the working conditions and with the procedures. Usually, there are also organizationally produced latent errors when an accident occurs (because otherwise the safeguards prevent an accident even if individuals make errors). Therefore, organizational defences should be strengthened to avoid accidents. Thus, errors may lead to accidents, but we should remember that an organization that attempts to minimize errors may have its own problems because it is too much focused on error prevention.

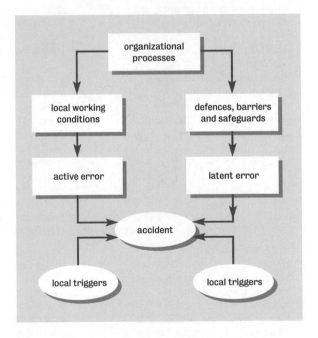

Figure 20.4 How errors lead to accidents
Source: adapted from Maurino *et al.* (1995: 24)

Ψ Case study

Three Mile Island

Chain of events and active errors	Contributing conditions and latent failures
Maintenance crew introduces water into the instrument air system.	Although this error had occurred on two previous occasions, the operating company had not taken steps to prevent its recurrence. (*Management failure*)
Turbine tripped. Feedwater pumps shut down. Emergency feedwater pumps come on automatically, but flow blocked by two closed valves.	The two block valves had been erroneously left in the closed position during maintenance, probably carried out two days prior to the accident sequence. One of the warning lights showing that valves were closed was obscured by a maintenance tag. (*Maintenance failures*)
Rapid rise in core temperature and pressure, causing the reactor to trip. Relief valve (PORV) opens automatically, but then sticks in the open position. The scene is now set for a loss of coolant accident (LOCA) 13 seconds into the emergency.	During an incident at the Davis-Besse plant (another Babcock & Wilcox PWR) in September 1977, the PORV also stuck open. The incident was investigated by Babcock & Wilcox and the US Nuclear Regulatory Commission. However, these analyses were not collated, and the information obtained regarding appropriate operator action was not communicated to the industry at large. (*Regulatory failure*)
Operators fail to recognise that the relief valve is stuck open. Primary cooling system now has hole in it through which radio-active water, under high pressure, pours into the containment area, and thence down into basement.	1 Operators were misled by control panel indications. Following an incident 1 year earlier, an indicator light had been installed. But this merely showed whether or not the valve had been commanded shut: It did not directly reveal valve status. (*Design and management failures*) 2 Operators wrongly assumed that high temperatures at the PORV drain pipe was due to a chronically leaking valve. The pipe temperature normally registered high. (*Management/procedural failures*)
Operators failed to diagnose stuck-open PORV for more than 2 hours. The resulting water loss caused significant damage to the reactor.	1 The control panel was poorly designed with hundreds of alarms that were not organised in a logical fashion. Many key indications were sited on the back wall of the control room. More than 100 alarms were activated with no means of suppressing unimportant ones. Several instruments went off-scale, and the computer printer ran more than 2 hours behind events. (*Design and management failures*) 2 Operator training, consisting largely of lectures and work in the reactor simulator, provided an inadequate basis for coping with real emergencies. Little feedback given to students, and training programme was insufficiently evaluated. (*Training and management failures*)
The crew cut back the high-pressure injection (HPI) of the water into the reactor coolant system, thus reducing the net flow rate from around 1000 gallons/min to about 25 gallons/min. This 'throttling' caused serious core damage.	1 Training emphasised the dangers of flooding the core. But this took no account of the possibility of a concurrent LOCA. (*Training and management failures*) 2 Following the 1977 Davis-Besse incident, the Nuclear Regulatory Commission issued a publication that made no mention of the fact that these operators had interrupted the HPI. The incident appeared under the heading of 'valve malfunction' not 'operator error'. (*Regulatory failure*)

Source: Reason (1990: 251)

Section summary

Performance is one of the most important criteria of psychological interventions at the workplace. Performance falls into two parts: task and contextual performance. Performance can be analysed according to the action process and the levels of regulation. Performance appraisal is the systematic appraisal of employees. Action errors are not just to be seen as negative events, although they can also lead to accidents.

1 Analyse a fellow student's high or low performance in a study task. (You can also observe a bar tender if you prefer.) Ask yourself where the student (or bar tender) is high or low in performance, how the person works on the task, what errors he or she makes, and so on.

2 Think of an error that has happened to you; how can you analyse the error and in which way did you respond? How could error prevention and error management have been supported?

Stress and health at work

Stress

In an organization you are expected to perform well but this may lead to stress. Work is interesting because it can contribute not only to well-being (consider the fact that depressed unemployed people become well again, when they find a job) but also to ill-health. Work and organizational psychologists have, therefore, attempted to understand the issue of stress better. (See also Chapter 19).

Stress at work is a major factor contributing to ill-health, to human suffering, and to productivity loss. Rosch and Pelletier (1989) have estimated the costs of stress at work to be US$150 billion in the USA because of increased absenteeism, diminished productivity, compensation claims, health insurance and medical expenses. About 35 per cent of the European employees said that they were working at high speed, 40 per cent that they were carrying out repetitive tasks, and 27 per cent said that they are working in painful positions; 39 per cent said that they could not change the work speed by themselves (Paoli 1992).

Research has suggested that many different ill-health problems are related to stress, for example, coronary

heart disease, elevated blood pressure, disturbances, depression, etc. (Cooper 1976; Fletcher 1991; Karasek and Theor related diseases, such as musculo-skeleta... also be related to stress at work (Osterholz et al. 1987). Even cancer and the common cold may be related to stress because stress has an effect on the immune system which in turn influences the development of cancer cells and infections (Fletcher 1991; Herbert 1993).

Table 20.3 Stressors at work

Physical stressors
- noise, dirt, heat, vibrations, chemical substances
- danger

Work-related stressors
- time pressure (quantitative overload)
- work too complex (qualitative overload)
- monotony (qualitative underload)
- not enough to do (quantitative underload)
- disruptions (e.g. machine breakdown)

Role in organization
- role ambiguity (unclear role requirements)
- role conflict (conflicts from different role requirements)
- responsibility for people

Career
- overpromotion
- underpromotion
- job insecurity

Social stressors
- poor relations with supervisor, colleagues, subordinates, others (e.g. customers)
- mobbing

Timing of work
- night-work and shift-work
- odd hours or badly designed shift schedules

Specific stressors at work

A list of stressors is presented in Table 20.3. Stress research has always emphasized the fact that there is an interrelationship between the physical and the psychological side of the human. This is also true of physical stressors. For example, noise that people can control has less negative impact than uncontrollable noise (Glass and Singer 1972). Work-related stressors tax the person's capabilities. Role conflicts exist when a secretary has two bosses and role ambiguity means 'uncertainty about

Psychology

Research update

Mobbing or harassment

Harassment (sometimes called **mobbing**) has been discussed in the press. Mobbing implies that individuals at work are bullied and harassed over a long period by several people (usually including the direct superior). Mobbing is directed against an individual and occurs frequently (once a week) and over a long period of time (at least six months) (Leymann 1996). There are clear relationships of mobbing with psychosomatic and psychological disturbances although the causal connection is as yet unclear (Leymann and Gustafsson 1996; Zapf et al. 1996). In Norway 8.6 per cent had been bullied at work in the previous six months and in Sweden 3.5 per cent (Einarsen and Skogstad 1996).

what the occupant of a particular office is supposed to do' (Katz and Kahn 1978: 206). Social stressors are aversive interactions with co-workers and supervisors and harassment (see the research update). Other organizational stressors may be related to career-related stress. Finally, night-work and shift-work are serious stressors.

Resources in the stress process

Up to this point we have just talked about the stressors. From a practical perspective this would mean that one should reduce these stressors. However, this is often not feasible and may sometimes even lead to negative effects (see the case study on p. 652). There is also a paradox from this viewpoint. Managers have stressful jobs. They work long hours and they have to make complex decisions at high speed. Nevertheless, their psychological illness rates or the degree of stress-related diseases are much lower than those of blue-collar workers (Karasek and Theorell 1991; Schaefer and Blohmke 1977).

One answer is that resources play a role. **Resources** are conditions and personal characteristics that can be used to attain goals (Hobfoll 1989; Schönpflug 1985). Internal resources are qualifications and knowledge. External resources are control and social support. Since both internal and external resources of managers are higher, this would explain why there is less ill-health in managers than in blue-collar workers.

Just think of whether or not you can control a stressor. If it is no problem to walk over to your neighbours and ask them to turn the music lower, the music does

not bother you. But if you know that no matter what you do, your neighbours will blast the music into your ears, you may become annoyed (and feel strain).

Thus, instead of a simple relationship between stressors and ill-health, we now have to consider the moderating factor of resources. Figure 20.5 shows that there is a high correlation when control at work is low (that is, stressors produce ill-health for these people) and a low relationship when control is high (that is, these people do not become ill from stressors because they are protected from having a higher level of control).

Control

Control (autonomy or job discretion) involves having an impact on the conditions and activities in correspondence with some higher order goal (Frese 1989; Gardell 1971; Karasek and Theorell 1990). Control is an important variable because it explains why managers have less strain than non-managers although the stressor level of managers is probably higher than those of non-managers.

Control has been shown to be a moderator, both in experimental and (to a lesser extent) in field research. Glass and Singer (1972) showed that noise as a stressor had stronger emotional and performance effects on people when they thought that they could not turn this noise off. Sometimes it is enough to know that one has potential control. Subjects had a button that could turn off a loud noise; they were asked, however, not to use this button (all of them complied). This condition produced less stress than not having a control button (Glass and Singer 1972).

The basic experiment by Seligman (1975) was to shock two groups of animals. One group was able to turn the shock off (e.g. by pressing a bar). Another group of animals received exactly the same amount and

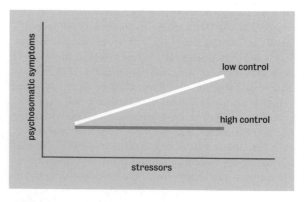

Figure 20.5 The moderating effect of control

time of electric shock as the first group, but the helpless group had no control over the stressor. In a second phase of the experiment, the animals were put in a shuttle box and were shocked again. But this time, all animals could escape the shock by jumping across a barrier. This was no problem for the animals that had experienced control over the stressors: they quickly jumped over the barrier and learned that it was safe on the other side. However, the helpless animals sat in the shuttle box and did not attempt to jump across the barrier. They showed all signs of emotional turmoil, such as defecating, urinating and whimpering. Seligman likened their state to human depression and showed that there was considerable symmetry between learned helplessness in animals and depression in humans.

Gardell (1971), Frankenhaeuser and Gardell (1976) and Karasek (1979) showed the importance of control at work. In each case, ill-health was more frequent if there was little control at work. However, this so-called moderator effect could not be shown reliably in non-experimental field studies (Kasl 1989). Currently there is a debate about what this means: some people argue that this means control is simply not a moderator, others argue otherwise. Most of those studies that failed to find a moderator effect have shown a direct relationship of non-control at work with ill-health (Carayon, 1993; Clegg et al. 1987; Kauppinen-Toropainen et al. 1983; Melamed et al. 1991; Payne and Fletcher 1983; Sonnentag et al. 1994; Spector 1987). Moreover, there are several studies that showed the hypothesized moderator effect (Dwyer and Ganster 1991; Fox et al. 1993; Parkes et al. 1994; Wall et al. 1996). There are three reasons for the difficulties in finding a moderator effect. First, the statistical method (moderated regression analysis) is quite conservative and often does not find the effect, for example, because the sample size is too small (Aiken and West 1991). Second, stressors and non-control at work may be confounded; if the employees have control, they have reduced the stressors in the first place. Thus, people who have high stressors usually also have little control; thus, when one asks them about stressors, they usually report on non-controllable stressors. Finally, affectively charged stress scales or subjectively worded control scales are used. The more subjectively worded items should confound control and strain because people perceive stress situations that are non-controllable as more straining. Better scale development may lead to getting interaction effects more reliably (Wall et al. 1996). For all of these reasons and the fact that there is ample support from the laboratory, it is my contention that we should assume control to act as a moderator with low levels leading to a high relationship of stressors and ill-health and with high levels of control producing no impact of stressors on strain.

Social support

Social support – another resource – is characterized by affective support (i.e. love, liking, respect), confirmation (i.e. confirming the moral and factual 'rightness' of actions and statements) and direct help (aid in work, giving information or money) (Kahn and Antonucci 1980). One prominent hypothesis about the function of social support is the so-called buffer hypothesis (House 1981; LaRocco et al. 1980) whereby social support is supposed to moderate the relationship between stressors and ill-health; high support should protect individuals from the negative effects of stressors. Social support works like sun-cream. If one uses sun-cream, the radiation (the stressor) is still there but it does not affect the skin negatively.

As with control, the **moderator effect** hypothesis (in the sense of the buffer effect) has received confirmation (House and Wells 1978; LaRocco et al. 1980; Norbeck and Tilden 1983; Roos and Cohen 1987; Winnubst et al. 1982), but there have been opposite findings as well (e.g. Ganster et al. 1986; LaRocco and Jones 1978; R.J. Turner 1981). In their overview, Cohen and Wills (1985: 314) argue that buffer effects occur when there is a 'reasonable match between the coping requirements and the available support'. For practical purposes, it makes sense to assume that social support has positive effects at work, although there are some inklings in the literature that also show some negative effects under special circumstances (e.g. when social support undermines self-confidence: cf. Peeters 1994).

Theories of the stress process

The two most influential theories about stress are by Selye and Lazarus.

General adaption syndrome

Selye coined the term 'stress' in 1936. Selye (1976) has described the **general adaptation syndrome** (GAS) as a general response of the organism to every stressor. The first stage of this syndrome is the alarm reaction. In this alarm reaction, the organism is made ready for a flight-or-fight response. Like other animals, humans fear predators. When a predator comes near, the organism has to be prepared for fight or flight. Thus, there is an arousal of the sympathetic arousal system which leads to stronger pumping of blood to increase oxygen transport to the body cells. It also leads to more support for the heart muscles, but less to the stomach and the skin. Further, the blood clots more rapidly, which helps stop bleeding in case of an injury (but it also contributes to a heart attack when the arteries get blocked). Further, many different hormones are excreted, for example catecholamines which have an energizing effect. After this alarm reaction, there is a resistance stage, which is followed by the exhaustion stage if the stressor persists.

Selye rightly observed that in the workplace, there is no opportunity for flight or fight. People cannot attack their boss (fight) or get away (flight). When people are trapped in the stressful situation, the psychophysiological system becomes exhausted in the work environment.

Cognitive stress theory

Selye's theory has one problem: as a purely physiological theory it does not tell us anything about the cognitive processes which play a role, as Lazarus *et al.* (1962) showed. They compared different soundtracks on a film on the initiation rites of Australian Aborigines. This film showed in excruciating detail their Stone Age methods of circumcision. Soundtrack of denial ('it does not hurt that much') and intellectualization ('let's look at how different cultures do their initiation rites') reduced the physiological strain of the subjects considerably.

Figure 20.6 describes Lazarus's cognitive transactional stress theory (Lazarus and Folkman 1984; Lazarus and Launier 1978); its central concept is the appraisal process. External stimuli are appraised on whether they constitute harm or loss, a threat or a challenge. This **primary appraisal of stress** is the phase in which the person finds out whether or not there are stressors. A **secondary appraisal of stress** process looks at coping resources and coping options to deal with these stressors. There are two broad coping strategies: coping with the problem (e.g. 'let me change this situation now') or coping with the emotions (e.g. 'let me relax now'). The appraisal determines the reactions; reactions can be to escape the negative stimulus, to attack it (i.e. do something actively about the negative situation), or to be passive. A form of passivity is just to sit and take the negative situation (as in helplessness). Finally, there is the possibility that the person reappraises the stress situation (possibly in the sense of a defensive reappraisal) and comes to the conclusion that there is no harm or threat in the environment.

Prevention of stress: practical approaches

Stress prevention can be achieved with different sorts of programmes. Figure 20.7 gives an overview. In the USA, stress management programmes are usually directed at the individual. In Europe, there has been more emphasis on job-oriented stress prevention programmes (Cooper and Payne 1992). However, it would

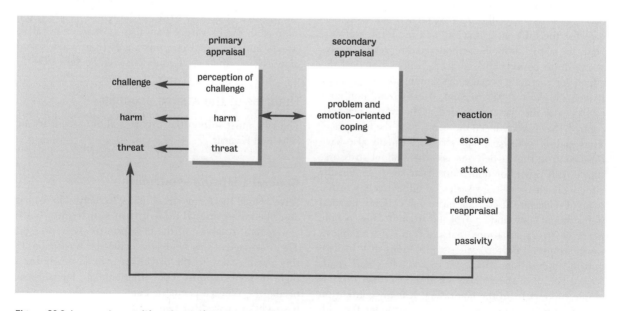

Figure 20.6 Lazarus's cognitive stress theory

	individual	institutional
resources oriented	competence training	increase of control
stressor oriented	reduction of individual stressors	reduction of stressors
stress/stress reaction oriented	relaxation training	rest periods

Figure 20.7 Examples of stress prevention in an organization

not be useful to pit one method against another; the best approach is probably to attempt to reduce the stress problem via several methods.

Figure 20.7 displays institutional and personal approaches and stressor, strain and resource approaches.

Stressor-reduction

Stressors can be reduced by technical and organizational means (e.g. reduction of noise, change of assembly line speed in accordance with the circadian rhythm, reduction of interruptions of work). This institutional stressor reduction approach is useful, although there are a few problems:

- Reducing one stressor and concentrating on just this stressor may actually lead to an increase of other stressors (see the case study on p. 652).
- Reducing stressors may sometimes lead to a reduction of challenges. If there is high qualitative overload, one may be tempted to reduce this overload by decreasing the cognitive demands of this job. Often this is suggested by engineers and leads not only to a reduction of overload but also to a reduction of challenges and resources (see the case study on p. 652).
- Since technological changes are quite frequent, research is too slow to tell us which stressors are particularly problematic and need to be taken care of. For this reason, reduction of stressors should usually be accompanied by an increase in resources.

Increase in resources

Resources in the sense of control (or social support) help individuals to have an influence on how to do their work and to increase or reduce stressors appropriately. Stressors that come about through new technology can best be dealt with when resources are given to influence one's work. Thus, restructuring work by increasing job content and responsibilities often has a stress preventive function as well. However, this should be complemented by improvements in skills because skills are needed to make use of the higher resources.

Strain reduction

Stress management programmes are designed to reduce the perception that something is stressful and to rather appraise something as a challenge. It also attempts to teach a person to increase the quality of one's coping strategies and to attempt to reduce strain (stress immunization or relaxation techniques). In addition, they often attempt to improve diet, to support healthy living (e.g. reducing alcohol and tobacco consumption) and to increase physical exercise (e.g. Neidhardt et al. 1985). Stress immunization works by helping the person to use more rational self-instructions. For example, a person might exaggerate a given stress situation and see catastrophies when something goes wrong (primary appraisal). Alternative self-instructions are then trained (for example, it is not catastrophic if something goes wrong, because it happens to most people from time to time) (Meichenbaum et al. 1975).

The success of any one approach is usually overrated. There are success stories on stress management programmes, however; for example New York Telephone Company's 'wellness' programme saved $2.7 million by decreasing absence and treatment costs (Cooper and Cartwright 1995). A meta-analysis of such programmes found a good effect size of 0.41 (Bamberg and Busch 1996). However, it is quite plausible that negative or zero effects do not find their way into the journals. For this reason, a certain degree of scepticism has to prevail (Murphy 1984). An additional constraint of most stress management programmes is that they presuppose that the employees can actually do something about their stress level (i.e. have at least some measure of control at work). For this reason, stress management programmes are probably less useful for blue-collar workers than for white-collar workers and managers.

Ψ Case study

A case of wrong stress reduction

An instructive historical example for the problems that appear when taking a one-sided approach to dealing with stress at work is the introduction of typing pools in Germany. Central typing pools were introduce partly because they seemed to reduce stress. T. Peters (1974) had found that interruptions to work because of telephone calls, people walking into the office, etc. was the most important stressor for typists and secretaries. A steady state of the pulse rate could be maintained if there were no interruptions. Therefore, he suggested homogenizing work and reducing all potential disruptions. A typing pool seemed ideal for this purpose because it precluded

the boss storming into the office, clients to take care of, and intrusive phone calls.

Unfortunately, typing pools eliminated not only the stressor disruption of work, but also the positive aspects of work. After the 'homogenization' of work, there was no more complexity, challenge and control in the typists' work. Previously, they could do their work according to their own ideas and they had a sense of the importance of their work because of their close association with their boss. After homogenization, their work was given to them by the typing pool supervisor without regard to the variety and content of work. The end-result was that monotony increased and challenges and control at work decreased (Jacobi and Weltz 1981; Saupe and Frese 1981).

Ψ Section summary

Stressors at work can arise from several areas: physical layout and environment, work itself, role, career, social situation and timing. However, a complete picture not only looks at those stressors but also looks at the resources, most notably control and social support. The most important theories are by Selye (this theory is more physiological) and by Lazarus.

1 Think about the job of an operator of an automatic tool and dye machine. What stressors might exist in this job? What can a psychologist do to reduce stressors and strain at work?

❏ Leadership and management

We now go one step further in our travel through the organization: you work in an organization but usually you do not work alone. Unfortunately we cannot discuss group work here due to space constraints. But more likely than not, the most significant person for you is probably your supervisor or manager, who will tell you what kind of work you have to do and will give some

appraisal of how well you doing. Moreover, we know a lot about managers because this occupation has been studied more frequently by work and organizational psychologists than any other one.

Leaders and managers are often conceptually distinguished; leaders are thought to help define the goals of the organization or the group, while managers are those with formal authority who make sure that the organization is functioning well and that people behave in accordance with its goals (House 1995).

Because of their popularity as research topics, there have been numerous theories of **leadership** and **management**. Five issues are (in my opinion) the most important ones and will be discussed here: differences between emergent and effective leaders, behavioural theory of leadership, Fiedler's contingency theory of leadership, charismatic and transformational leadership, and leadership substitute theory.

Differences between emergent and effective leaders

Some kind of leadership occurs in every group of people (whether the leader is a manager or not). Think of a study group that comes together for the first time – some person will emerge as leader. The leader will be most active in the discussion, structure the discussion and suggest when to meet again, etc. However, this emergent leader does not have to be an effective and good leader, who helps to increase the chances of achieving the group's goals and motivating the participants to do their work well. There are many examples of politicians who have emerged but have not been good leaders. Thus, an emergent leader is a leader because people perceive this person to be a leader, but not because this person proves to be effective as a leader.

This differentiation between effectiveness and **emergence of leaders** is important for the debate, whether or not personality traits play a role in leadership. At one point, there was a consensus in work and organizational psychology, based on the reviews by Mann (1959) and Stogdill (1948), that personality factors do not matter in leadership. This conclusion turned out to be wrong in the light of a meta-analysis (Lord *et al.* 1986) which proved that personality measures were indeed important in leadership. However, personality did not predict effectiveness but emergence of leaders (i.e. perceptions by the followers that this person is a leader). Intelligence (corrected r = 0.50), adjustment (r = 0.24), extraversion (0.26), as well as masculinity (0.34), and conservatism (0.22) show appreciable relationships with followers' perception of leadership. Such correlations did not appear for leadership effectiveness. Thus, these personality traits are probably important for the emergence of a leader but not for the effectiveness of leadership.

Behavioural theory of leadership

The Ohio studies (Fleishman 1973) led to a two factor description of leadership behaviour. The first factor is **consideration**, which means that the leader is concerned about the people, emphasizes satisfaction with the job, treats the subordinates as equals, etc. The second factor is **initiation of structure**, which implies that the leader activates, organizes and defines work for the subordinates. Clear work tasks are given without consulting the group. Reviewing the evidence on the leadership behaviour approach, Bass (1990) concluded that consideration increases job satisfaction and initiating structure increases performance.

In contrast to laypeople's opinion, consideration and initiating structure are independent (orthogonal) dimensions; thus, leaders can be high on both, low on both or be high on one and low on the other. It follows that one should attempt to teach leaders to be high on both so that the group is satisfied and shows high performance

(Blake and Mouton 1964).

When you think about this theoretical approach, you will probably see the problem very quickly: managers do not just behave in one way, without regard to the situation. Moreover, in one situation, one strategy may be more successful, in another, the manager should behave differently. Thus, the situation needed to be taken into account as well. This is the core of Fiedler's theory (discussed next).

Fiedler's contingency theory of leadership,

Fiedler (1971) took two factors into account: the person's leadership style and the situation. The person's leadership style was ascertained with a measure of the **least preferred co-worker**. A high score means that leaders say nice things about the co-worker they like least and they are therefore relationship oriented. A low score means that leaders say nasty things about this person which makes them task oriented (Fiedler and Chemers 1984).

With regard to the situation, Fiedler differentiated leader–member relations (how good is the relationship with the subordinates), task structure (how much is the task structured) and position power (the extent to which the leader has power over the subordinate and the subordinate accepts it). These three factors make up the difficulty of the situation because they determine how much control the supervisor has. If the leader–member relations are good, if the tasks are clearly structured, and if the leader has a lot of power, then the leader has a high degree of control.

Figure 20.8 shows the results of Fiedler's theory. The x-axis spans the eight situations. The high control situation is on the left, the low control situation on the right. The dots in the figure are correlations. Thus, this figure is different from others – you actually see the correlation between the least preferred co-worker (LPC) score and the group performance. A low score (e.g. –0.40 as in the first octant) means that those with a high score on the preferred co-workers' scale (they like even the most disliked co-worker) have groups that perform badly. In other words, in this situation it is much better to be task oriented and not relationship oriented. In octant IV, on the other hand, you see a positive correlation of 0.40. This means that being relationship oriented as a leader helps to have a good group performance. Thus, relationship-oriented leadership is better in this situation. If you have a situation in which there are poor relations, an unstructured task, and a weak leader position (octant VIII), the correlation is again negative: the group will perform better if you are task oriented in this situation. Thus, if the situation is very easy, you can be task oriented and even authoritarian because you are accepted anyhow. If the situation is very difficult, task orientation may be necessary to get the group off the ground. In the middle, it is better to be relationship oriented.

Given the complexity of the theory, it is surprising that meta-analyses have been quite positive; there is good evidence for Fiedler's theory to be correct (L.H. Peters *et al.* 1985; Strube and Garcia 1981). Support for the theory is better in laboratory studies, however, than in field studies (L.H. Peters *et al.* 1985).

Nevertheless, there are weak points in this theory (Landy 1989). First, the dependent variable (as displayed in Figure 20.8) is a correlation, which means that we do not really know anything about the absolute level of performance, we just know something about the relationship between leadership style and group performance.

Second, Landy (1989) distrusts the least preferred co-worker scale and questions whether the validity of

this scale has been established well enough.

Third, the characteristics of the situation are not independent of the leadership style. This problem is most obvious for leader–member relations which should be influenced by how the leader behaves.

These criticisms notwithstanding, Fiedler was the first one to develop a theory that took into account situational and leader characteristics at the same time, thus advancing our knowledge considerably.

Charismatic and transformational leadership

Charisma means originally a gift of god and implies that people follow a leader based on their emotions. House and Bass and their co-workers have used the concept of charismatic leadership to understand why some leaders can get the followers to make an extra effort while others do not. Charisma is defined as 'the ability of a leader to exercise diffuse and intense influence over the beliefs, values, behaviour, and performance of others' (House *et al.* 1991: 366). Central features of charismatic

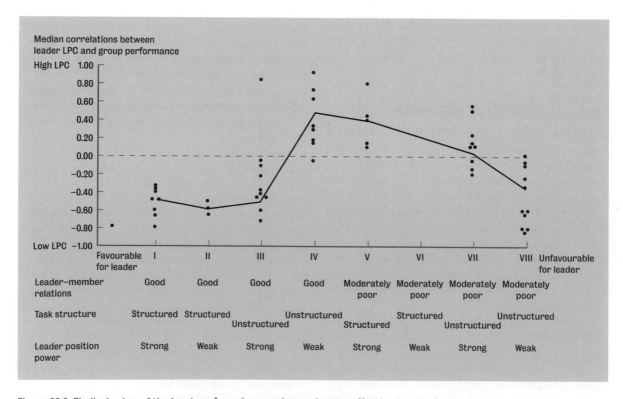

Figure 20.8 Fiedler's view of the least preferred co-worker and group effectiveness performance
Source: Fiedler (1971)

leaders are that they are high in dominance, self-confidence, the need to influence others, and belief in own values. These leaders articulate their goals and visions well which leads to favourable perceptions of the leader in the eyes of their followers. Charismatic leaders have high expectations of their followers' performance. All of this leads to better self-confidence, trust, etc. in the followers which in turn helps to increase performance (House 1977).

The concept of **transformational leadership** is similar to House's theory (Bass 1990), although Bass differentiates between the four factors (the four Is):

- idealized influence: charismatic leadership in the sense of being a model and symbol for the followers
- inspiration: inspiring the subordinates to put in extra effort to achieve the goals of the organization and having high expectations of the followers
- intellectual stimulation: in the sense of creating and encouraging new ideas and making sense of things
- individual consideration: similar to the factor consideration of the Ohio studies.

There are three types of studies that have supported the claim that charismatic leadership enhances productivity. First, it was shown that leaders who are perceived to be charismatic, have higher productivity (Geyer and Speyrer 1997; see research update below), produce higher levels of effort and satisfaction in their followers (House *et al.* 1997).

Second, an experimental study showed that charismatic leaders actually caused higher performance and satisfaction, particularly in groups with low productivity norms (Howell and Frost 1989).

Finally, former US presidents were appraised as to their charisma in several different ways. Moreover, their power, achievement and affiliation motives were coded. It could be shown that several performance indicators (e.g. economic performance, great decisions made, etc.) were related to charisma and power orientation (House *et al.* 1991; Spangler and House 1991).

Thus, charismatic leadership is of high importance; it is also something that can be changed through training (because it was possible to enact it in an experiment, it is also possible to learn to be more enthusiastic and to be inspirational). Charismatic leadership has given the emotional appeal of leaders to their followers its proper place in leadership theory.

However, it is obvious (particularly for this German author) that charismatic leadership can also have negative consequences. Hitler certainly was charismatic.

Howell and House (1995) have, therefore, distinguished between personalized and socialized charismatic leadership. Socialized means that the leadership

(a) is based on egalitarian behaviour, (b) serves collective interests and is not driven by the self-interest of the leader and (c) develops and empowers others. Socialized leaders tend to be altruistic, to work through legitimate established channels and systems of authority when such systems exist, and to be self-controlled and follower-oriented rather than narcissistic.

(Howell and House 1995: 6)

Personalized charisma is the opposite. Thus, one can distinguish psychologically between leaders like Hitler who used personalized charisma and other leaders who show the more helpful socialized charisma.

Leadership substitute theory

Reading some of the management literature gives the impression that managers are the real heroes of organizations and that everybody else in the firm is really quite unimportant. The poet Bertolt Brecht (1935) has aptly suggested that it was not Alexander the Great who conquered India but that it was his soldiers who did it.

To counter this heroization of leadership, it is useful to acknowledge that leadership is often not really that important for high performance. This has been discussed under the topic of **leadership substitute theory**

 Research update

Transformational leadership

Geyer and Speyrer (1997) have looked at transformational leadership and productivity in Austrian banks. In all, they had 1,456 direct reports of 116 branches of 20 banks fill out the questionnaire by Bass and Avolio. Unlike other studies, this study was extremely careful to develop a good measure of productivity. Therefore, they developed a number of categories for banking (such as volume and number of checking accounts) and weighted these by market conditions (because every branch works under different conditions) and developed in this way an objective performance indicator. They showed that transformational leadership was clearly related to such objective indicators. Thus, it pays off for companies to enhance transformational leadership in their companies.

Table 20.4 Specific substitutes and neutralizers: supportive and instrumental leadership

Substitute or neutralizer	Supportive leadership	Instrumental leadership
Subordinate characteristics		
• experience, ability, training		Substitute
• 'professional' orientation	Substitute	Substitute
• indifference toward rewards offered by organization	Neutralizer	Neutralizer
Task characteristics		
• structured, routine, unambiguous task		Substitute
• feedback provided by task		Substitute
• intrinsically satisfying task	Substitute	
Organization characteristics		
• cohesive work group	Substitute	Substitute
• low position power (leader lacks control over organizational rewards)	Neutralizer	Neutralizer
• formalization (explicit plans, goals, areas of responsibility)		Substitute
• inflexibility (rigid, unyielding rules and procedures)		Neutralizer
• leader located apart from subordinates with only limited communication possible	Neutralizer	Neutralizer

Source: Landy (1989) after Kerr and Jermier (1978)

(Kerr and Jermier 1978; Podsakoff *et al.* 1993). Examples are first, leadership in terms of giving direction is not important when the subordinates know how to do things because they have been trained. Second, on the assembly line, much of what the leader does is actually materialized in the line itself, for example, giving a rhythm to work, making sure that there is always enough work around to be done, etc. Third, the relationship with the leader is less important, when the task is intrinsically satisfying (Kerr and Jermier 1978; see also Table 20.4).

While empirical research on the substitute for leadership model was only partially successful in the support of its claims (Podsakoff *et al.* 1993), the notion is useful and should be pursued further. This view will become more important in the future, because there will be less direct contact between a manager and the subordinates in future virtual and lean companies.

We began this section on leadership by describing the importance of leaders; we have appropriately ended with some findings that call the heroization of leadership into question. We already know quite a bit about how to describe and change leaders' behaviours and it is still an area of great interest for work and organizational psychology.

ψ Section summary

There are many theories of leadership and each one seems to cover one particular part. It is important to differentiate between emergent and effective leadership; traits are more important for the emergence of leaders than for the effectiveness of leaders. We have discussed behavioural, contingency and charismatic leadership theories. To avoid the idea that leaders are the only important heroes of organizational success, we have also covered the leadership substitute theory.

1 Write down as many comments, sentences and adjectives that you can think of that describe leaders. Discuss these from the background of the different theories and critically examine where these theories can help you to descibe effective leaders and where they do not.

2 Differentiate between leaders and managers and discuss how you can easily make this differentiation and where it may break down.

❏ Work and organizational design

Organizational development and change

In Figure 20.1, you saw a person trying to move the organization, that is to change it. I am sure that after you have entered an organization, you have thought about the necessity of changing some features of it. It is not enough to describe an organization well, it is also necessary to change it. Thus, for work and organizational psychologists it is necessary to know not only how something works but also how to make it better. An organization functions better if work is done skilfully, if efficiency and effectiveness are high, if there is general well-being and no short- or long-term damage from work, and if employees develop their skills at work (Hacker 1986; Ulich 1991; Warr 1987).

This list suggests that all of the issues discussed so far are relevant for job design. Moreover, the reason why European work and organizational psychologists have traditionally insisted on the unity of work and organizational psychology is that work design can be done only if you have expertise in ergonomics (the study of the interaction of the human with the machine), work design (how work should be designed to decrease strain, maximize knowledge and efficiency), and organizational issues (organizational development and change). In the USA, there has been an unfortunate division between personnel psychologists (testing, training), organizational psychologists, and ergonomics (called human-factor specialists in the USA) that leads to separate developments with little cross-reference to each other's areas.

Historical traditions of work design

There have been a number of grand theories or approaches to work design. Two important ones that originated in the United States are Taylorism and the human relations school.

Taylorism

Frederick W. Taylor (1856–1915), the father of scientific management, started out with the problem of loafing (employees being idle or wasting time). To reduce it, he eventually came up with the following strategies. First, he made the workers' income depending upon their output. Money was the all-important motivator in his management system. Second, he divided up the labour

in various functions. Taylor broke radically with the handicraft tradition of work which was prevalent then. He argued that people could do only one task well. Third, the various functions would be devised by a scientific planning department. In this way, he would work against the rules of thumb that were prevalent in the craftsman tradition. An important method used in planning was **time and motion studies** developed by the psychologist Gilbreth. This helped to cut out superfluous movements. Fourth, work would be supported by exactly planned tools, again arranged by the planning department or by the supervisor. For example, different size shovels were developed for materials with different weights. If you have to shovel iron into a wagon, you need a smaller shovel than if you shovel grain.

Taylor's teachings were highly controversial in his day. Workers usually went on strike when they heard that Taylor was asked to be a consultant in their company. However, for better or for worse, **Taylorism** laid the foundation for modern work with its high division of labour and its detailed planning, with an emphasis on saving seconds. Moreover, Taylor helped to define the role of supervisors (the functional foremen) so that they would become helpful managers who had the task to increase productivity. However, many present-day problems, such as stressful jobs with little control at work and a division of labour that reduces individuals' responsibility for their work and makes them 'cogs in the machine', were also a result of Taylor's teachings.

Human relations

The **human relations school** was developed during the so-called Hawthorne studies (Roethlishberger *et al.* 1956) and sees itself as an important alternative to Taylor's scientific management. The first set of experiments concerned illumination. This was still done within the tradition of Taylor: the engineers wanted to see whether productivity was increased or decreased by illumination. The amazing finding was that productivity went up even when there was very low illumination (in one experiment it was as little as under moonlight). The researchers interpreted this to be due to the good relations between the experimenters and supervisors with the workers. Relations were good because workers received friendly attention during these experiments. Thus, the human relations at work became the focus of further experiments. (See also Chapter 21.)

In a second set of experiments, a kind of human relations supervision was introduced – relaxed, with little Tayloristic discipline. Roethlishberger *et al.*

(1956) thought that the relationship between the workers and the supervisor had improved which led to higher productivity.

In contrast to Taylor, the human relations school was interested in overcoming workers' loafing by developing a common goal and by human touch. Mayo (the popularizer of the human relations school) actually thought that through the human relations idea, trade unions would wither away (Landy 1989).

The Hawthorne studies have been criticized by several scientists. For example Bramel and Friend (1981) maintain that it was actually external pressure and not human relations that led to remarkable improvements of productivity in the one group that was studied most intensively. However, in spite of these criticisms, there is no doubt that human relations play an important role in the workplace.

European alternatives to Taylorism

Taylorism essentially took away responsibility for production from rank-and-file workers and gave it to supervisors and to the planning department. This kind of system had several disadvantages: industrial engineering cannot anticipate all the mishaps that are possible; therefore problems and faults regularly occur even in a well-designed workplace. If workers behaved as Taylor thought, they would simply not care; the result would be extreme quality problems. However, workers do not behave the way Taylor thought. Rather, workers frequently compensate for work design problems and adjust flexibly and intelligently (for example, in one car company that I visited, control tags were marked by the blue-collar workers because otherwise wrong headlights would have been installed). Thus, spontaneous responsibilities were assumed by the blue-collar workers. The paradoxical result is that Tayloristic job design could function only because the workers did not behave as Taylor thought.

However, workers' interventions of this kind are not done systematically, therefore quality problems do arise because of Tayloristically designed jobs. Moreover, the workers do not have an overview of what they are doing. For example, car company workers would sometimes drill too far because they did not know that they could damage the previously installed cables lying on the other side of the metal to be drilled.

Taylor's critics wanted to give responsibility back to the workers. One of the more radical approaches was group work.

Autonomous work groups

The first group work experiment was done by Lang and Hellpach (1922). In this experiment, a whole product – a motor – was produced by a group and the authors argue that productivity and job satisfaction were higher in this group (Lang and Hellpach 1922).

After the Second World War, Trist and Bamforth (1951) showed in a detailed account of coal-mining that a new technology installed without regard to human factors, led to a number of problems; for example, workers did not trust safety precautions done by a prior shift – so there was inefficient double checking (in the previous system, every shift took care of their own safety work). Moreover, people did not co-operate as well as they had done in their old system. People became sick more often and productivity decreased with the new technology. These problems were solved when group production was introduced (Trist *et al.* 1963); group work led to lower rates of absence, fewer accidents and higher efficiency.

Autonomous work groups (sometimes also called semi-autonomous because there is no complete autonomy in companies) were regarded as alternatives to traditional assembly lines and machine operating. The assembly line was dissolved and, for example, a group of three workers produced a motor. The work groups were allowed to make all the necessary decisions: who would work, where, and how long. The supervisors were not supposed to interfere with the functioning of the groups but were supposed to serve as resource persons to help when needed and to train the workers. The group was responsible for the upkeep of their tools and simple repairs. Group leaders were elected by the group (and could be deselected if the group chose to do that). In some experiments, the groups could also decide on their own composition (Gulowsen 1972) and select new members. Pay was determined by how many tasks an individual could do and by how much the group actually produced. There was a weekly or monthly negotiation on how many products the group would produce.

Unfortunately, there are only a few well-controlled studies that look at the effects of autonomous work groups (Cummings *et al.* 1977; Goodman *et al.* 1988; Wall *et al.* 1992). Some of the best controlled studies have been done by Wall, Clegg and colleagues (Wall and Clegg 1981; Wall *et al.* 1986, 1992); by Schmidt and co-workers (Schmidt *et al.*1981a, 1981b), by Cordery (1991), by Antoni (1996) and by Den Hertog (1977). All of them reported positive outcomes of group work, although in Wall *et al.* (1986) and Antoni (1996), not all of the expected results prevailed.

Introduction of group work was also seen as an answer to many problems that beset European companies in the 1960s and 1970s (Den Hertog 1977; Ulich *et al.* 1973):

- a high degree of absenteeism from work
- high fluctuation, particularly in assembly-line work
- difficulty in finding workers willing to take assembly-line jobs because people became more interested to actualize themselves in work than earlier cohorts
- co-ordination problems, e.g. when absenteeism or machine trouble led to standstills at the assembly line
- lack of flexibility
- product quality concerns
- strikes and sabotage by the workers

More comprehensive productivity studies concluded that local productivity improvements may sometimes lead to productivity losses of the whole system. For example, the introduction of central typing pools led to higher productivity if one considered the number of keystrokes typed in a particular typing pool. But at the same time, turnover of mail actually slowed down because of the number of mistakes made by the typists and the lack of co-ordination between the specialists and the typists – thus, the whole system became less efficient (Gaugler *et al.* 1977). (See Case study, page 652).

Introducing semi-autonomous work groups is one of the most powerful interventions to enhance productivity, as shown by a meta-analysis (Guzzo *et al.* 1985, see also Table 20.7, p. 665). Only goal-setting and training were more powerful. Another meta-analysis showed that

productivity (output and quality) was increased but absenteeism and fluctuation were not reduced much (Beekun 1989). Beekun (1989) also showed that the effects of semi-autonomous work groups were lower in the USA than in other countries. This may be related to the higher degree of individualism in the USA in comparison to Europe (Hofstede 1991). The following is a summary of the effects of autonomous work groups:

- more job satisfaction (although in some cases, it decreased after a while)
- increased well-being
- higher work involvement
- absenteeism and fluctuation are reduced only slightly
- more flexibility in production (e.g. when products are changed or new technology is introduced)
- more direct costs (workers receive more money for their higher qualifications) and fewer indirect costs (fewer repair people and supervisors, etc.)
- concomitant technological change made the intervention less successful for reasons yet unknown
- higher product quality and in many cases also higher output
- works much better when pay system is changed accordingly
- works much better if there is a higher degree of autonomy in the groups
- both white-collar as well as blue-collar workers are positively affected
- workers who once participated in these groups did not want to go back to the old production system.

Plate 20.3 Team work and group work often lead to higher efficiency

In spite of public and government support, most autonomous work groups have either disappeared with time or have continued only as isolated experiments. This was true of the work groups introduced in the British coal-mines as well as of many experiments in the automobile industry. Even the Volvo plant in Kalkar — the showcase for this design concept — was recently closed down. There are several complex reasons for this. Many times, the first-line supervisors and middle management sabotaged the autonomous work groups because they did not want to give up power. Sometimes, a change in management led to a change in management style. More autocratic managers have little interest in autonomous groups. In some cases, the trade union was against it (particularly in the USA and to a lesser degree in Germany) because they feared that their traditional strategies of negotiations would be undermined by shopfloor participation. In many cases, management thought that roboterization and increased use of technology would do away with assembly lines more efficiently and were better alternatives than autonomous work groups. Moreover, increased unemployment levels and reduced welfare support reduced fluctuation and made workers more interested in jobs they would not have taken before. Finally, the threat from Japan to industry in the USA and Europe convinced people that one had to look for answers with assembly lines intact (see lean production, p. 661).

However, in the late 1990s there is a revival of group work both in Europe and in the USA (in Asia group work was always done more frequently). The old ideas of autonomous work groups are often taken as a starting point (as in the case of Opel in Germany). There is an attempt to combine the old ideas of humanization of work with the newer ideas of empowerment, lean production and modern technology.

In a way, the history of what happened to autonomous work groups is typical of many ideas developed by work and organizational psychology: an idea is around for a while and it takes many experiments, modifications of these ideas, new challenges from the outside, and newly educated managers until it is really used. The time has to be ripe for a new idea. Self-managed groups are alive and well again and seem to be used more frequently today than ever before although the more recent uses of group work are not exact replicas of older approaches in this area.

Sociotechnical system approach

The **sociotechnical system approach** was developed by Trist and Emery to understand the effects of group work (Alioth 1980; Cherns 1976; Clegg 1979; Emery and Thorsrud 1969; Emery and Trist 1969). The following propositions explain the theory (note that they contradict Taylor's concepts in nearly every point):

- There is a technical and a social side to each job. Neither the technical nor the social side should be optimized without regard to the other; thus, only the complete sociotechnical system should be optimized.
- Systems are conceptualized as open systems. This means that turbulences in the environment also lead to problems in a company's work groups. These problems should be regulated via self-regulation in those groups affected (in traditional firms only the highest management decides and then gives orders to the employees). This allows a more flexible and task oriented reaction to environmental turbulences.
- Work practices should not be specified any more than is necessary so that people can use their own ingenuity in making a product; however, there should be continuous training and search for improved procedures.
- All problems of product and production quality should be dealt with as near to the point of origin as possible (e.g. machine failures or errors).
- The work group should get all the information in order to do the job optimally (e.g. customer complaints should be quickly communicated to the group).
- Self-regulation is best done within the work groups. Everybody should be able to do all the tasks within a group to maximize flexibility.
- Boundaries between groups should be drawn to reduce interference but these boundaries should be permeable to allow sharing of knowledge. This means, for example, that planning of an action, executing it, and quality inspection should not be done in different departments but should be kept in one group.
- Different work groups, different departments within an organization have dynamic interactions with each other. Negative effects on the whole organization may appear if only a part of an organization is optimized (as in the example of a typing pool above).
- The function of supervisors in a self-regulated group should not be to disturb self-regulation but to support it. Thus, the supervisor is a trainer, helps with tips and ideas and communicates with the other departments.

- There is no one 'best way' as described by Taylor. In a complex task, there are several effective ways to do work.
- One should look not only at the short-term but also at the long-term consequences of change. For example, rigid division of labour may have positive consequences in the short term, but may lead to rigid organizations which cannot react flexibly to changing environmental demands.

US alternatives to Taylorism

Job enrichment

The high degree of individualism in the USA has made job enrichment much more popular. In contrast to autonomous groups, **job enrichment** does not leave it up to the group to organize task distribution, but expands the job content for the individual worker. Herzberg put forward the idea of job enrichment (Herzberg 1968; Paul *et al.* 1969). An example for job enrichment is to empower sales representatives to make deals within certain limits without having to ask any-

body. Thus, they can immediately settle claims, can reduce or increase prices and do not have to write reports on every customer call (Paul *et al.* 1969). Introducing job enrichment has been shown to have a major positive impact on productivity (Guzzo 1985).

The most sophisticated theoretical concept (as well as a measurement model) has been put forward by Hackman and Oldham (1975). Figure 20.9 describes this model: it differentiates core job characteristics from critical psychological states. The five core characteristics are skill variety (how many different activities are required), task identity (completing a whole identifiable piece), task significance (important for others), autonomy (independence and job discretion) and feedback from job (information on performance). The critical psychological states are experienced meaningfulness of the work, experienced responsibility for outcomes of the work, and a knowledge of results of the work activities. These in turn are supposed to produce better performance outcomes through higher motivation. A moderating factor is growth need strength. This means that people who have a higher need for self-actualization react more positively to job enrichment.

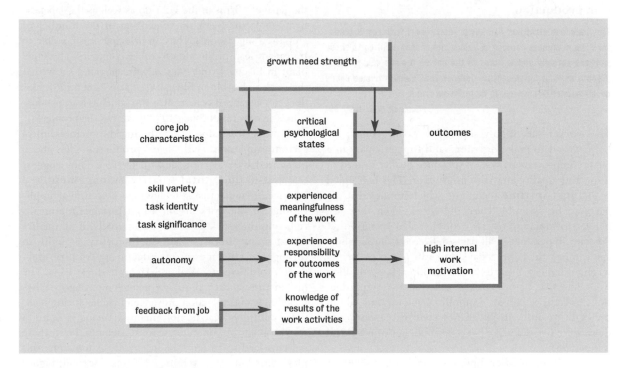

Figure 20.9 Job characteristics model of Hackman and Oldham
Source: Hackman and Oldham (1976: 256)

Hackman and Oldham's model has stirred up some controversies (well described by Ilgen and Hollenbeck 1991). While the details of the model can certainly be called into question, the general motivating function of the core job characteristics has been well substantiated (Berlinger *et al.* 1988).

The Japanese challenge: lean production

Traditional mass production – as in the example of the assembly line for cars – has several implications: workers are seen as variable capital (thus, workers are dismissed if there is not enough work for them and reducing training costs is positive). Efficient use of machinery implies that many parts are produced and put into a storage room to be later assembled with other parts produced later. Thus, stocks are high. An assembly line may not be stopped. Thus, when problems and mistakes occur, the line still has to move on. At the end of the line, skilled workers are then repairing the newly produced cars. This is wasteful because as Womack and Jones (1996) argue, something that can be repaired for $1 at the assembly line may cost $100 at the end of the line and $1000 after delivery of the car.

This mass production system can be contrasted to **lean production**.

The truly lean plant has two key organizational features: it transfers the maximum number of tasks and responsibilities to those workers actually adding value to the car on the line, and it has in place a system for detecting defects that quickly traces every problem, once discovered, to its ultimate cause.

(Womack *et al.* 1990: 99)

The workers are highly skilled, work in groups, are empowered to make decisions and to participate in a quality improvement system, produce quality instead of inspecting quality after the production. This is coupled with a **just-in-time** technique which implies that the parts to be assembled are delivered when they are needed (reducing costs for stocks). For example, at Porsche 20 per cent of all parts delivered from suppliers came more than three days late (30 per cent having wrong numbers of parts) and 10,000 parts per million were defective, before Porsche switched to lean production. In contrast, Toyota's supplies came on time and in the right quantity in 99.96 per cent of the cases and there were five defective parts per million (Womack and Jones 1996).

From an organizational point of view, responsibility is given back to the workers. Rank-and-file workers are trained continuously, quality control and improvement

rests with the workers and they get the necessary information in highly visible form. The assembly line is organized in self-managed teams that trouble-shoot immediately when problems occur. In this sense, lean production shares the theoretical concepts of the sociotechnical system and the job characteristics model of Hackman and Oldham. However, it couples this with a much stronger emphasis on reducing waste through reorganization, on product innovation, and just-in-time techniques (Womack and Jones 1996). Since the shopfloor is supposed to participate in the rationalization process, it is necessary to give guarantees that no worker will be dismissed because of improving production.

Table 20.5 shows the superiority of lean production. Automobile productivity was much higher and number of defects much lower in Japan than in North America and Europe (these figures were assembled in the late 1980s; since then both US and European car manufacturers have done a lot to increase productivity). The size of the repair area was smaller in Japan; the same goes for inventories. Many more people worked in teams and did some job rotation; there were fewer job categories, and training was frequent. However, there were no differences in the degree of automation: lean production is not dependent on new technology. Table 20.5 also shows that the Japanese firms in the USA do as well as the Japanese firms in Japan (with the exception of the number of employee suggestions). Thus, in principle it is possible to transplant lean production to other countries. The Opel plant in Eisenach and Porsche's turnaround show that this is also possible in Europe (see also Taira 1996). This does not mean, of course, that introducing lean production is an easy task (Young 1992 describes the problems).

A modern version of combining the sociotechnical system approach with lean production has been presented by Wall and Jackson (1995). They suggest that just-in-time, **total quality management** and advanced manufacturing technology have similar implications for the work organization. Just-in-time means reducing the stock costs organizationally. Total quality management implies that 'high quality is built in throughout all stages of manufacturing from product design to delivery' (Wall and Jackson 1995: 144). The just-in-time and total quality management approaches make up lean production. Advanced manufacturing technology implies that flexible manufacturing is done in small batches by computer-driven machines. First, these systems lead to an increase in cognitive demands; this may contribute to psychological stress. Second, higher responsibility for production is given to the workers. For example, every interruption of the work flow has serious

Table 20.5 Summary of assembly plant characterics, volume producers, 1989 (averages for plants in each region)

	Japanese in Japan	Japanese in North America	American in North America	All Europe
Performance				
Productivity (hours/vehicle)	16.8	21.2	25.1	36.2
Quality (assembly defects/100 vehicle)	60.0	65.0	82.3	97.0
Layout				
Space (sq. ft/vehicle/year)	5.7	9.1	7.8	7.8
Size of repair area (as % of assembly space)	4.1	4.9	12.9	14.4
Inventories (days for 8 sample parts)	0.2	1.6	2.9	2.0
Workforce				
% of workforce in teams	69.3	71.3	17.3	0.6
Job rotation (0 = none, 4 = frequent)	3.0	2.7	0.9	1.9
Suggestions/employee	61.6	1.4	0.4	0.4
Number of job classes	11.9	8.7	67.1	14.8
Training of new production workers (hours)	380.3	370.0	46.4	173.3
Absenteeism	5.0	4.8	11.7	12.1
Automation				
Welding (% of direct steps)	86.2	85.0	76.2	76.6
Painting (% of direct steps)	54.6	40.7	33.6	38.2
Assembly (% of direct steps)	1.7	1.1	1.2	3.1

Source: Womack *et al.* (1990: 92)

consequences with a just-in-time system; therefore, there are high attentional demands and a high degree of responsibility for the work flow. Similarly under total quality management, the shopfloor workers are supposed to take care of problems immediately and improve production, and thus, have to assume responsibilities. Finally, there is a high interdependency because modern production strategies imply that the links between work teams have to run smoothly. Thus, there has to be good communication between the workers. There are two mechanisms by which modern production processes lead to higher productivity. One mechanism is via higher motivation; here Wall and Jackson agree with Hackman and Oldham. The other mechanism is that a higher degree of knowledge on the production process is developed and used by the workers. The latter implies:

The more general implication is that there are two underlying processes: an initial application of existing knowledge, where the mandate to rectify faults necessarily brings benefits through enabling a quicker response, and a subsequent development of predictive knowledge through learning, which allows fault prevention.

(Wall and Jackson 1995: 160–1)

Human–computer interaction

It may seem surprising to find a short description on human-computer interaction here. As we have seen, lean production was an organizational improvement that did not *per se* depend on new technology. Further, human–computer interaction is often relegated to human factors specialists. But the important point is that change processes are unitary: work and organizational psychologists have to be able to deal with the ergonomic and human factors part of the problems as well as with the organizational ones; this is the essence of the sociotechnical system approach (discussed on pp. 660–1). Fortunately, in Europe, the unitary function of work and organizational psychology still exists.

Human–computer interaction is one part of ergonomics and, since nearly all machines are now computer driven to a certain extent, it is the most important part of ergonomics (for a review see Frese 1987b; Oborne 1987). Table 20.6 presents one aspect, the ergonomic requirements for office work with computers – the so-called dialogue principles (which are based on Dzida *et al.* 1978).

Table 20.6 Standards on Dialogue Design of the International Standards Organization (ISO 9241, Part 10)

Principle	Example
Suitability for the task	One should have to do only a few steps from turning on the computer to being able to work on the task.
Self-descriptiveness	In one text-processing program, a file with name DESIGN was to be loaded. However, this was not possible. The text program needed the name. 'DESIGN.' (with the full stop). No error message explained this.
Controllability	The user is able to ask how much the data bank is being used today to estimate how many different requests can still be answered.
Conformity with user expectations	The user works with a dialogue system with different application programs. In all applications the user can use the same syntax and semantics.
Error tolerance	The system can continue to work in spite of an obvious error or only minimal correction effort is needed.
Suitability for individualization	The program can be adjusted to individual tasks, individual preferences and skills.
Suitability for learning	The system supports learning.

Source: ISO (1995)

Organizational development and its difficulties

Change in any organization means trouble. The following are the main difficulties:

- lack of readiness and motivation for change
- too little power behind the change process
- conflicting interests
- anxieties
- resistance and reactance
- passivity, helplessness and overconformity
- keeping old routines
- double work

We are not able to discuss these issues in detail. Often, there is too little managerial support for a change process (French and Bell 1995). Most frequently, changes lead to conflicting interests, for example, the change process may make one department bigger and more influential in comparison to another one. Conflicts are not a problem *per se*; as a matter of fact, work and organizational psychology has a rather positive view of conflicts because they are necessary for innovations; however, conflicts have to be managed well (De Dreu and Van de Vliert 1997; Greenhalgh 1987).

Whenever changes occur, there is resistance to change (Coch and French 1948; see the case study, p. 665).

A change situation can be a non-control situation which may lead to learned helplessness (Seligman 1975), that is to passivity and overconformity. Change may lead to situations of non-control, because old skills and ideas do not work any more and new skills may be difficult to learn. Moreover, people may have repeatedly learnt that the change situation itself cannot be controlled because management does not allow participation.

Overconformity is a form of helplessness because people do not question the rules and just conform to them without adapting them creatively and without showing initiative. The opposite of helplessness and passivity is a high degree of initiative. Initiative itself is related to how much control individuals have at the workplace; people learn through organizational socialization to approach things actively (Frese *et al.* 1996)

Change means we have to break our old habits which leads to the following problems:

- We fall back into our old habits, particularly under stress and when things have to be done quickly.
- Since the new behaviour has to be regulated consciously, we find it difficult and effortful.
- The new behaviours do not run as smoothly as our old habits.
- We make more errors in our new behaviours than in our old habits.
- There is a feeling of reactance when we cannot apply our old habits any longer with the concomitant feeling of frustration and negative emotions.

Comparing different interventions at the workplace

Organizational change interventions are frequently unsuccessful (Porras and Robertson 1992), but companies have to change to adjust to new demands by the market, by technological development, by society, and by employees. Therefore, it is an important question

Case study

Resistance to change

Coch and French (1948) observed that many employees were less productive after a new technology was introduced than before. There was also aggression towards management. To reduce this resistance, they suggested participation in decision-making. Three groups were formed:

- direct participation in the decisions of how to introduce a new technology
- indirect participation with elected representatives talking to management about how to introduce the new technology

- no participation (which was similar to how changes are 'normally' introduced in companies).

The group without participation showed resistance to change; after 30 days they were still 12 per cent below the work rate they had achieved before. There was aggression, lack of co-operation, and high absenteeism. The group with indirect participation was much more co-operative. After 14 days they had reached their normal work rate again; after 30 days, their productivity was 10 per cent higher than before. The group with direct participation showed the best results. They reached the same work rate as before after 5 days and they were 14 per cent more productive after 30 days.

---

which change concepts are more successful than others. Two meta-analyses help us to answer this question. In one, the effects of organizational development interventions on satisfaction are described (Neumann et al. 1989) and the other one looks at productivity of the workers (Guzzo et al. 1985). Tables 20.7 and 20.8 describe their results. Table 20.7 (Neumann) presents correlations and Table 20.8 (Guzzo) shows effect sizes. The correlations have to be read as relationships whereby a correlation of 0.30 is sizeable. Effect sizes have to be read as differences between the intervention

group and the non-intervention group. An effect size of 0.40 is sizeable.

Tables 20.7 and 20.8 suggest that some methods work better on attitudes while others produce better productivity enhancement. The most effective methods to increase productivity are **goal-setting** (that is giving high and concrete goals to the employees), sociotechnical improvements (which is a mixed bag of several procedures including autonomous work groups to improve the technological and social demands at work) and increasing qualifications (training). Financial incentives also have an effect size above 0.50; however, its variance is very high which means that in many cases

Table 20.7 Corrected correlations of interventions and satisfaction and other attitudes combined

	Correlation
Specific human process interventions	
• laboratory training	0.567
• participation	0.254
• goal-setting/management by objectives	0.436
• realistic job preview	0.204
• survey feedback	0.324
• team building	0.579
Sociotechnical interventions	
• job enlargement	0.219
• job enrichment	0.183
• flexible working hours	0.239

Source: adapted from Neumann et al. (1989)

Table 20.8 Corrected effect size for intervention programmes on productivity factors

	Effect size
All programmes	0.44
Training	0.78
Appraisal and feedback	0.35
Management by objectives	0.12
Goal-setting	0.75
Financial incentives	0.57
Word redesign	0.42
Supervisor methods	0.13
Work rescheduling	0.21
Sociotechnical	0.62

Source: adapted from Guzzo et al. (1985)

it works very well but in other cases it may lead to negative effects (Guzzo *et al.* 1985). Also note that changing supervisory techniques (e.g. increasing participation in decision-making) alone does not have a large effect on performance.

Job satisfaction is increased by laboratory training and team-building techniques, which are similar; trainees discuss how decisions are made in the group, how they feel in the group, and which problems should be solved by the group. Job enrichment and sociotechnical interventions are effective for productivity improvements but not so effective for increasing job satisfaction. Note, however, that goal-setting is one of the best intervention strategies both for job satisfaction and productivity enhancement.

The most important message of these two meta-analyses is that organizational development methods derived from psychology are effective in most circumstances (possibly with the exception of financial incentives, which sometimes lead to productivity losses). Thus, if one uses organizational development techniques, the effects may not always be very high but they are most likely not negative. This stands in contrast to other interventions (e.g. purely technical or Tayloristic ones) which have been shown to decrease output in many cases.

Ψ Section summary

Work and organizational psychology cannot be content with just describing a job. It should also be able to suggest how to change jobs so that people can work better, with better results and with an increased well-being. It is possible to differentiate Tayloristic, human relations, sociotechnical, job enrichment and lean production perspectives, although there is clearly some overlap among them. Regardless from which perspective workplaces are changed, there are certain difficulties. The most important ones are anxiety, resistance, helplessness, breaking old routines, and lack of personal and institutional power to back up the change process.

1 Think of a job you know well. Can you change the workplace to make it more efficient and/or increase well-being? Attempt to change the job from each perspective described.

2 What do you have to do in the change process so as to make the change more effective?

Ψ Chapter summary

• Organizational socialization

Socialization means that the organization has an impact on the person working in it; sometimes this is intended (e.g. when changing values), sometimes not (e.g. when reducing intelligence).

• Training

Training works via assessment of training needs, the training design, transfer and evaluation. Two training designs are behaviour modelling and action training.

• Selection

Selection is done with tests which have a certain reliability and validity. Interviews can be improved by having two interviewers or structured interviews. Assessment centres and intelligence tests are also valid selection procedures

• Organizational structure

The organizational structure can be described in different ways; some of the more prominent configurations are simple structure, machine bureaucracy, professional bureaucracy, divisionalized form, adhocracy, prospector, defender, analyser and reactor. There are many attempts to understand the relationship of the organizational structure with business success. It seems most likely that interactions with the environment are crucial.

• Performance

Performance falls into two parts: task and contextual performance. Performance can be analysed according to the action process and the levels of regulation. Performance appraisal is the systematic appraisal of employees. Action errors are not just to

Box continued

be seen as negative events, although they may lead to accidents.

● **Stress and health at work**

Stressors at work interact with lack of resources to bring about ill-health. The most important theories are by Selye and Lazarus.

● **Leadership and management**

It is important to distinguish between emergent and effective leadership. There are various theories of effective leadership: behavioural, contingency, and charismatic leadership.

● **Work and organizational design**

Job and organizational design can be done from a Tayloristic, human relations, sociotechnical, job enrichment, or lean production perspective. Change processes always lead to some difficulties in the way.

Further reading

● *Work and Personality* (special issue editor: Nicholson, N.) *Applied Psychology: An International Review* (1996, vol. 45, issue 3). A good overview of organizational socialization is given in this issue of the journal.

● Patrick, J. (1992) *Training: Research and practice.* London: Academic. Consult this for details on training.

● Smith, M. and Robertson, I. (1993) *Systematic Personnel Selection.* London: Macmillan. A good account of issues in selection.

● Mintzberg, H. (1979) *The Structuring of Organizations.* Englewood Cliffs, NJ: Prentice Hall. A classic reading on organizational structure.

● Warr, P.B. (1987) *Work, Unemployment, and Mental Health.* Oxford: Oxford University Press. Gives an overview on well-being.

● Karasek, R.A. and Theorell, T. (1990) *Healthy Work: Stress, productivity, and the reconstruction of working life.* New York: Basic Books. The authors use their well-known demand-control model to explain stress at work.

● Bass, B.M. (1990) *Bass and Stogdill's Handbook of Leadership*, 3rd edn. New York: Free Press. The most authoritative book on leadership.

● Wall, T.D. and Jackson, P.S. (1995) New manufacturing initiatives and shopfloor job design, in A. Howard (ed.) *The Changing Nature of Work.* San Francisco, CA: Jossey-Bass. A good introduction to modern systems of job design.

● Ilgen, D.R. and Hollenbeck, J.R. (1991) The structure of work: job design and roles, in M.D. Dunnette and L.M. Hough (eds) *Handbook of Industrial and Organizational Psychology.* Palo Alto, CA: Consulting Psychologists Press. A more in-depth discussion of all the theoretical and empirical problems of job design can be taken from this chapter.

● French, W.L. and Bell, C.H., Jr (1995) *Organization Development*, 5th edn. Englewood Cliffs, NJ: Prentice Hall. A very good and easily readable introduction to organizational development.

CHAPTER 21

Research methods

Hugh Coolican

KEY CONCEPTS • science and psychology • general problems in research with people • methods of psychological researchers • studies using correlations and group comparisons • interviews • questionnaires and surveys • observation • significance testing • sampling • qualitative approaches in psychology

❏ Chapter preview

When you have read this chapter, you should be able to

- understand the difference between common sense and psychological theory development and testing
- understand what is meant by a scientific approach to data gathering and theory testing in psychology
- identify well-known potential problems involved in the investigation of people's behaviour and mental processes
- distinguish between assessments of the reliability and validity of a research measure or finding
- understand the difference between experimental and non-experimental approaches to psychological research
- identify various forms of experimental design and possible flaws in these
- recognize the nature of several common non-experimental research designs and outline their strengths and weaknesses
- understand and apply the concept of significance in the assessment of differences and correlations demonstrated in research data
- distinguish between the nature of quantitative and qualitative data
- outline and evaluate the various commonly used arguments for and against the use of qualitative data-gathering methods
- evaluate the use of conventional scientific methodology in psychological research

Introduction

Throughout this book you will read about the results of psychologists' research efforts. You will have read something like 'Craik and Tulving (1975) found that...' and the findings will have been used to support a particular theory or model. In each case this means that the researchers will have passed through the following steps:

- consider problems with existing *theory* and/or ways to support/extend it
- develop specific *hypotheses* to test or aims to achieve
- create good *design* to test the hypotheses or realize the aims
- purchase and prepare all necessary *materials*
- train experimenters, interviewers, assessors and observers where necessary
- select a *sample* of people who will participate in the research
- carry out the research *procedures*
- collate and analyse *results*
- consider carefully the *implications of the results* for the original hypotheses or aims
- write up a detailed *report*
- submit this report to one or more academic journals
- have work accepted for publication

This is a long and arduous process. As a student of psychology you will almost certainly experience some of the steps above in order to gain an insight into how psychological knowledge is generated. In particular, the italicized terms above will be important when writing up a report of your practical work. Many psychology students find their research methods course difficult or uninteresting. This is a bit like getting fed up with road works (which are intended to make your journey safe); perhaps a better analogy is that of getting fed up with car maintenance when it is the car which takes you on interesting and useful journeys. The outcomes one reads about in psychology wouldn't have occurred without someone doing the research.

The good thing about a methods course is that this is the time when you get to *do* psychology rather than simply read about it. *Doing* psychology ought to be interesting, if not downright fun, even if the subsequent report writing can take some time and effort. It is where you can set out to test an interesting proposal and get a result which either tells you that the original idea might have something to it *or* that you need a far more elaborate and careful research study to test out what, at first, seemed a simple idea, or that the idea was too vaguely expressed or just plain nonsense. Table 21.1 lists some ideas which could be investigated in an introductory psychology course.

We ought to be able to check out all these and many other ideas. In order to do so, and have our audience take us seriously when we report our findings, we need to become familiar with a toolbox and become competent to use research tools. The basic aim of research is to gather **empirical** evidence to support or challenge a theoretical idea. Many situations which call for the use

---

Ψ Case study

How honest are we?

Stuart Miller reported in the *Guardian* on a study conducted for the *Reader's Digest* magazine in which 10 wallets, each containing £30 and identification, were dropped in each of 8 towns and cities in the UK. The numbers of people either keeping or returning the wallets were as follows:

	Returned	Kept
Glasgow	8	2
Leamington Spa/Warwick	8	2
Basildon	7	3
London	7	3

	Returned	Kept
Pontefract	7	3
Liverpool	6	4
Exeter	5	5
Cardiff	4	6

Adapted from *Guardian*, 17 June 1996

Miller says: 'Residents of Glasgow and Leamington Spa/Warwick emerged as Britain's most honest citizens, each handing in eight out of 10 wallets'. 'The author of the original article, Jack Crossley (1996), claims: 'Medium size towns were slightly more honest than cities', and shows that the respective totals returned were 27 and 25.

Table 21.1 Some hypotheses to test in psychology practical work

- Does knowledge of a person's sex affect judgements about how appropriate certain jobs are for them?
- Does knowledge of a defendant's ethnic origin make a difference when people are asked to judge what sentence is appropriate for a crime?
- Are people's anxiety levels at all related to their level of self-esteem?
- Is it true that men are more likely than women to strike a match towards their body?
- Are people more likely to agree with a silly statement when other people also agree with it in their presence?
- Does a person's mood affect their recall for events?

of psychological research methods appear in the press regularly. If you were asked to accept the outcomes in the research described in the case study on honesty, what questions might you raise about the way the research was conducted that might cast some doubt on the validity of the results?

The writers in the case study go well beyond what has been established as fact. A sample of ten can hardly give us confidence in a statement about the entire population of each city. In addition, were the different samples of ten people equivalent? Were the wallets dropped in exactly the same kinds of environment? At the same time of day? This gives rise to a debate about how far the gathered evidence supports the background theory – geographical differences in honesty. This is the heart of much of the reasoning in psychological science.

Science and psychology

For more than a century now, what has distinguished psychology from, say, philosophy or the hunch-based claims of 'common sense', has been the psychologists' emphasis on support of theory with research evidence. The world of psychological investigation has attempted, to a great extent, to follow the pattern of research in the natural sciences. Here, scientists put forward ideas (theories, hypotheses, speculations) about their area of interest in the world and attempt to support these with real-world findings. It is a place where others may dispute the validity or the implications of what these theories claim to be the case, *not* just to be awkward but because the whole research body is interested in finding out what human psychological and social life really is

about and in avoiding the acceptance of merely subjective, 'armchair common-sense' or even bigoted theories about human nature, behaviour and experience.

Methods, models and approaches

It is a pity that one cannot simply say, at this point, 'here are the methods used in psychological research'. However, over the decades, specific methods have become inextricably bound up with certain overall approaches. The behaviourist and cognitive paradigms have created a great emphasis on the **experiment** and **hypothesis** testing within psychological research. The influence of psychometrics on the study of individual differences has generated an extreme emphasis on **quantification** of psychological variables and the **psychometric test**. On the other hand, developmental psychology has often employed **longitudinal** and **cross-sectional research**, social psychology has leant more heavily on the survey and certain forms of **observational technique**. Applied psychology has more recently created a seam of **field research** methodology, including the analysis of **quasi-experimental designs** and has also been influential, in recent years, in promoting the use of more **qualitative approaches** to data gathering and analysis.

To a large extent, psychological research has incorporated most of its methods within the conventional scientific hypothesis testing approach. Since this is a textbook reviewing both the contemporary scene *and* the general development of psychology as science, it will be the main focus of this chapter and much of the research cited within this book. However, since the mid-1980s there has been a growth in the development of more exploratory and qualitative approaches; this chapter will therefore integrate these where possible and at other times address them directly as contrasts.

The hypothetico–deductive paradigm

A major model of science which has dominated the development of psychology as a research-based discipline has been the hypothetico-deductive paradigm, which adheres to the logic that underlies the following argument:

- if 2-week-old babies seek varied visual stimulation they should spend more time looking at the more complex of a pair of visual stimuli
- babies *do* spend more time looking at the more complex visual stimulus
- therefore the theory that they prefer visual variety is supported.

There are two important things to notice here, first that what is studied is carefully defined and second that researchers do not claim to have 'proven a theory true'.

Positivism – defining variables

Scientific psychology has borrowed from the nineteenth-century philosophical school of positivism which held the belief that things could not be scientifically studied unless a method of measuring them precisely could be specified. (This is known as the hypothetico-deductive method.) This has had the benefit of ridding the discipline of some unworkable concepts such as 'instinct', often invoked to 'explain', retrospectively, why people succeeded in life or survived against adversity. Newspapers used this non-explanation in reporting the survival of a lone round-the-world yachtsman under his capsized boat for five days in the Antarctic. Either these terms were abandoned or researchers were forced to state exactly what they meant in terms of measurement procedures – what we shall discuss as **operational definitions** later on. For now note that 'visual variety' is pinned down specifically and measurably as the difference between complex and simple patterns.

Scientific theories are not 'proven true' – but must be falsifiable

In everyday life it is often easy to slip into accepting a non-logical conclusion from an apparently logical argument. Take for example the argument of a prosecuting lawyer:

(1) If the defendant had committed the murder his shoe print would appear in the mud outside the house.
(2) His shoe print does appear outside the house.
(3) Therefore he committed the crime.

Point 3 is not a logical conclusion since there are several possible explanations for shoeprints at a murder scene, other than that their owner is the murderer, just as there are several possible explanations for fewer wallets being returned in Cardiff than Glasgow, other than the far-fetched and sweeping theory that Cardiff people are, in general, less honest than Glaswegians. What we do, when we query evidence, is to say, in effect, 'Well, I can see that your evidence supports what you claim to be true but it also supports other theories'.

For the visual variety theory too we do not say it is 'proved'. However, the more that the gathered evidence for one theory 'hangs together' and remains relatively undisputed, the longer the theory holds its position in competition with other theories. Popper (1959) argued for this view of science and that any good theory should be at least falsifiable – that is, it may be true but there must be some conceivable way to attempt to demonstrate its falsity. For instance, someone might claim that life is all a dream. We might counter with evidence, such as pinching, hitting or comparison of ourselves when 'awake' with people who certainly are dreaming or at least in REM (rapid eye movement) sleep. If the theory holder refutes all this evidence on the grounds that the experience of all such events is still part of a dream (begging the question of how a waking state could then be defined at all) it is a

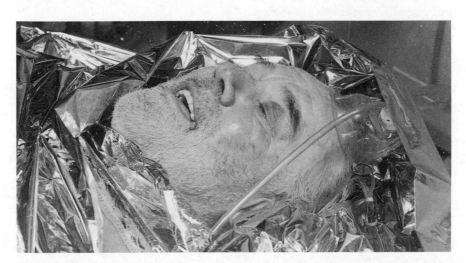

Plate 21.1 The concept of the 'survival instinct' was used to explain how Tony Bullimore survived under his capsized boat for five days in the Antarctic

useless theory since it cannot be tested in any way – it is in the 'interesting but silly' category of theories.

'Normal science'

It is important to note that the issues discussed here, including Popper's arguments, apply to *all* science, not just psychology. Kuhn (1972), in an extremely influential book *The Structure of Scientific Revolutions*, argued that all science evolved through various **paradigm** stages. In the 'pre-science' stage a world-view might be based on superstition, received wisdom or non-empirical argument. From this stage there evolves a 'paradigm' which is a near-universally accepted world-view of the particular science's subject matter, incorporating both the overall theoretical approach and a set of relatively well-agreed 'rules' for the conduct of research. After some time this stage of 'normal science' is undermined by a combination of contrary views, too many unexplained phenomena, theoretical contradictions and alternative methods for investigation. A 'paradigm shift' then occurs and, if a new view takes a dominant role, there is a return to 'normal science' under the new paradigm. Classic examples would be the evolutionary perspective in biology, or the Newtonian and then Einsteinian models in physics.

Kuhn argued that psychology was in a pre-paradigmatic stage with no one theoretical approach in ascendance. Others have argued that psychology has left superstition and non-empirical method behind in the nineteenth century and progressed through several paradigms – structuralist, behaviourist and cognitive; others argue that several paradigms now coexist making psychology either *still* pre-paradigmatic or currently in a stage of rather complex shift (see Gross 1996; Valentine 1992).

Competing theories

A picture which emerges from both Popper's and Kuhn's discussions is that of theories competing for position as the best explanation so far of all observed phenomena in the field of interest. Their views apply to all science including, for instance, astronomy, where there is heated dispute about the theory of the 'big bang' origin of the universe. In these long-standing physical sciences, as in psychology, one finds the same use of language. Theories are 'supported' not finally proven true. Further evidence can certainly damage a theory, leading to its eventual rejection, but positive results simply lend their support (see Figure 21.1).

The process of hypothesis testing

All science involves initial observation and the gathering of data. These data must be organized, sorted, categorized and inspected for patterns. This is the early part of scientific investigation. When a new disease is under investigation, such as the problems in the UK with BSE (bovine spongiform encephalopathy) and CJD (Creutzfeldt-Jakob disease), researchers study areas, rates, foodstuffs, offspring and every conceivable link, searching for some connection. However, researchers do not look at data with complete naïveté. It is difficult for a human to look at any gathered data without some prior 'schema' or crude theory of *why* they should hang together, *what* lies behind them. In scientific terms this involves outlining a theory – an explanation for observed patterns. Whether we are doing psychology, hearing a court case or grappling with an everyday problem, the logic of hypothesis-testing proceeds, once theory is articulated, as shown in Figure 21.1.

If we do not obtain support for a theory, then possible reasons are

- the theory is plain wrong
- the theory is incorrectly formulated
- the research design was faulty (so X might happen with a better design)
- the results were incorrectly analysed (again, X might be so)

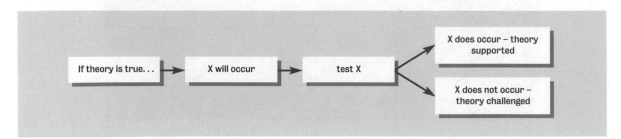

Figure 21.1 Supporting and challenging theories

The steps in the production of evidence for a theory can be listed as in Table 21.2 and illustrated by the testing of Freud's famous theory of child socialization, avoiding for now the observations which led Freud to his ideas. Table 21.2 develops a hypothesis and study which was actually carried out by Hall and van der Castle in 1965 and produced positive support for the theory. However, the questionable point in the design of this research is tucked away as part of step 3 in the lower half of Table 21.2: the definition of aggressive content which included such events as losing parts of one's body, being hit, and so on. Males may dream of these events more often because, for whatever reason, they are more physically aggressive, and not necessarily because they have suppressed desires for their mothers.

When *do* psychologists prove theories true?

The short answer is – never. When a theory is 'proven true' it is no longer a theory. Because we have reached a more sophisticated level of explanation and have developed more complex and subtle technology, it is no longer a theory that air is composed of hydrogen and oxygen – it amounts to a fact. But a couple of centuries ago the theory was supported by experiments such as that water rises from a saucer into an upturned tumbler under which a candle is burning: the water must take the place of whatever is burned from the air. In psychological science, there are a very large number of theories most of which compete with others to explain phenomena and to produce supportive research evidence.

Ψ Section summary

Psychology goes beyond common sense and employs empirical evidence in arguing for the validity of its claims about human experience. Psychology researchers traditionally accepted a somewhat positivistic, scientific model in which theories are proposed and hypotheses are developed which logically follow from the theory. The hypotheses are tested using thorough research designs, employing operationally defined variables, and often, but not exclusively, gathering quantitative data. If predicted outcomes are achieved a theory is supported not 'proven'. Greater support tends to produce a more universally accepted theory but competition between theories is part of the nature of scientific evolution.

1. A friend argues that if there exists a human instinct for altruism then people across the world would often help others for no reward. Since this *does* happen (after all, there are newspaper stories every day) there must be such an instinct. How would you advise her to reassess the logic of her proof?
2. Try to create a research design for each of the research questions in Table 21.1. In each case be careful to define the variables (e.g. 'anxiety', 'self-esteem') so that they can be measured and precisely compared. Decide also on the exact procedure for testing the proposed hypothesis.

Table 21.2 Steps in the logic of the hypothetico-deductive method

1. Make observation(s)
2. Formalize observations into patterns
3. Create a plausible theory
4. Make a precise hypothesis which follows logically from the theory
5. Test the hypothesis
6a Predicted outcome (from hypothesis) supports the theory
6b Contrary outcome (to hypothesis)
   - contradicts the theory, or
   - fails to support the theory, or
   - may be explained by poor research design

Steps in testing Freud's Oedipal theory
1. Males suppress an Oedipal love for their mother but this would be symbolized unconsciously in their dreams
2. Males will report more 'castration anxiety' (symbolized as aggression) in their dream contents than do females
3. Record dream content for sample of males and females; have independent assessors count occurrences of predefined aggressive incidents
4. Males report more aggression – theory supported
5. Males report same aggression as, or less than, females – theory weakened (or faulty research design)

❏ General problems in research with people

Some problems are so general and pervasive in research with people that we shall introduce these now before moving on to specific methods so that we can refer to them as we go along. Some of the problems are often discussed only with respect to a particular method yet they can apply almost completely across the board. Some solutions to these problems can be specific to the method used and so, whereas you may find few answers to problems in this section, you will find answers as each method is dealt with further on. In fact, what are 'problems' in some types of research are seen as advantages in other circumstances.

Bias from participants

Participant reactivity: the Hawthorne effect

In the late 1920s an extensive series of studies, forming an early foundation of industrial and work psychology as a research subject, commenced at the Hawthorne electrical plant in Chicago and carried on into the 1930s (Roethlisberger and Dixon 1939; see also Hollway 1991). One of the early and surprising findings, an apparent blessing for management, was that whatever changes were made to the working conditions of a small group of selected workers, such as the amount of lighting, rest pauses, drinks, wages, length of the working day and even returning to the original working conditions, the workers' productivity improved. It appeared that, rather than the manipula-

tion of any of the variables, it was the very experience of being under experimental investigation which was responsible for the increases in output observed. In general, this is the problem of participant **reactivity** – effects produced because people know they are being studied – though it has also become commonly known as the **Hawthorne effect**.

Any measure of participant behaviour which might suffer from this effect is known as a 'reactive measure' and 'reactivity' refers to the consequent changes in behaviour. Few studies can escape this possible weakness. Those that do must keep participants unaware that they are being studied. Possible designs for achieving this are **naturalistic** and **participant observation**, where the role of the observer is completely disguised from the people observed. The traffic calming case study avoids reactivity while drivers are being observed but could suffer from various effects (discussed below) once the questionnaires are sent out.

Social desirability

An aspect of reactivity can be people's desire to present a public image of social respectability. There is a strong chance that drivers in the the traffic calming case study would wish to appear socially responsible and claim not to drink and drive. All research which obtains 'self-

Ψ Case study

A fictitious flawed field study on driver behaviour

Imagine that some rather naïve researchers set up the following study into the effects of introducing speed cameras along a stretch of road in a residential area used by many drivers as a short cut. Before the measures are introduced, the researchers observe vehicles on weekdays between 10 and 11 a.m. and between 3 and 4 p.m. because the road is less busy at these times and it is therefore easier to jot down all licence plates and speeds of cars using the road. They note the speed of each vehicle and then send out a questionnaire to all the owners of the vehicles, traced by their registration plate numbers. The questionnaire covers several items about regular driving habits, whether the driver tends to stay within speed limits, whether they drink and drive and so on. A second sample of drivers, contacted

after introduction of the cameras, is dealt with in the same way, but is also sent a further questionnaire concerning the effect of the calming measures on their driving along the specific stretch of road.

The main aim of the research is to show that, although the two samples of drivers are relatively comparable there is, nevertheless, a significant reduction in speed along the stretch of road . A further aim, tackled with the follow-up questionnaire to the second driver sample, is to establish the extent to which drivers report that the measures affected their driving along the stretch of road.

You might like to pause at this point and make a list of all the factors possibly present in this research project which could affect results leading to an unsafe assumption that the measures either do or do not work.

report' information from participants can suffer from the problem of participant deceit. 'Looking good', though, may not be a matter of lying, but of a more subtle, perhaps relatively 'unconscious', set of processes which protect people's self-image.

Even where information is not sought from participants but where they are asked to perform a task, such as rating a fictitious rape defendant, or even adjusting a visual illusion, participants may wish to appear 'good' and will perhaps conceal their sexism or try harder than usual to be 'right' (see p. 675).

Observer effects

When people know their behaviour is being assessed, as did the Hawthorne workers, it is highly likely that a reactive effect will occur. Zegoib et al. (1975) found that mothers were more patient, warm and involved with their children in the presence of observers and Brody et al. (1984) found that siblings teased, threatened and quarrelled with each other less. Reduction of such effects can be achieved by the ethically problematic approach of hiding a camera, or by observers familiarizing themselves with the family for a while before genuine recording takes place

Drivers in the traffic-calming case study would not know they were being observed, unless the researchers wore bright yellow coats! There is an *ethical* issue of consent, but this can be dealt with by including with the questionnaires an offer to remove data from the research study.

Demand characteristics

The second sample, like most participants in psychology investigations, would be interested in what the study is all about. People try to guess research aims and Orne (1962) argued that this is part of their natural response to the research situation. He showed that, so long as people knew they were participating in a formal experiment, they were prepared to perform hundreds of numerical additions of random numbers for several hours, without question, even when, in one experimental version, they were asked to tear up each page of additions once they had completed it!

Orne and Scheibe (1964) asked an experimental group in a sensory deprivation study to sign a form releasing the researcher from liability for harm to the participant. They were also shown a panic button they

could use if they could not tolerate the deprivation conditions (four hours sitting alone in a room – there was no serious deprivation). A control group did not sign the form and were not shown the panic button. Experimental participants showed more extreme reactions to the deprivation conditions than did the control group, even though conditions for both groups were identical, apart from form signing and the panic button.

In defining **demand characteristics**, Orne stated:

The totality of cues that convey an experimental hypothesis to the subject become significant determinants of the subject's behaviour. We have labelled the sum total of such cues as the 'demand characteristics of the experimental situation'.

(Orne 1962: 779)

Orne's major point was that, contrary to the view of psychological participants as non-reactive, passive responders to stimuli – a view particularly associated with early behaviourist research – we should view participants as cognitively active, enquiring human beings, even within our research context. They are trying, as we all do most of the time, to make sense of their immediate environment and its novelties. Here, in an unfamiliar experimental situation, there are various 'cues' available to help participants work out what is going on and what is expected of them.

Although introduced as a critique of experiments, Orne's demand characteristics can be said to have potential effect in *any* research where participants are aware of being researched. Titled the 'social psychology of the social psychology experiment', Orne's critique argues that the research context is a social situation where the usual norms of human interaction are in operation, albeit often in a strange situation for the participant.

Placebo effects and participant expectancy

In some experiments the cues to understanding the research aims are not subtle. If an experimenter gives participants a drink containing a chemical, then asks them, after exposure to a violent film, about feelings of excitation, they might conclude they should feel more excited because of the drug. They might then 'find' more of the normal feelings we all have and report these as exceptional. This is a **placebo effect** – an effect solely from knowing one has received a treatment – and it can be exposed by having one **placebo group** in such an experiment receive a drink but no chemical.

*Pleasing the experimenter/researcher –
evaluation apprehension*

Participants may well be working out what is expected of them but this does not necessarily entail that they will do their best or attempt to present their best self-image. However, there is evidence that volunteers for research studies tend to have a positive view towards science and its possible beneficial effects for society (Ora 1965). Up to the 1980s a vast majority of research participants in experimental psychology were students, mostly of psychology, and, since the research was mostly carried out in the psychology departments of their own universities or colleges, it would not be surprising if most participants therefore wished to help the researcher! Although contemporary studies tend to be broader based and look further afield to more appropriate participant groups, Sears (1986) coded almost all 1985 research reports in four of the United States' most prestigious and mainstream journals, finding that 74 per cent of studies still used undergraduate students, mostly of psychology. Many researchers report that their participants are particularly interested in how well they did and whether the research is likely to 'work'. This need to be seen to do well, perhaps more conscious than the social desirability effect, can also be generally termed 'evaluation apprehension' – the effect on behaviour of knowing that it is to be evaluated, and caring about that fact.

'Yeah saying' – response acquiescence

Closely related to the last point is the phenomenon of **response acquiesence set**. A 'set' is an induced tendency to respond in one direction and acquiescence (agreement) seems psychologically easier than disagreement with a relative stranger (the research interviewer). As we shall see, in questionnaires or psychometric tests, a common technique used to detect response set is to include diametrically opposite items where answering 'yes' to both would be a self-contradiction. For instance, the drivers in the case study might have been given the statement 'I drive slightly faster than average' at one point in the questionnaire, and 'I always keep well within speed limits' at another point. Acquiescence is a particularly important phenomenon to bear in mind in work with children where the effect is particularly pronounced.

Bias in researchers and research designs

Pygmalion effects: effects on participants of experimenter/researcher expectancy

Some classic work in the mid-1960s (see case study) appeared to substantiate the often suspected phenomenon of the self-fulfilling prophecy – that if we 'label' people, then others may react to the label and 'see' characteristics that aren't actually there or respond so that the labelled people do, in fact, develop those characteristics.

Since Rosenthal and Fode (1963) used their students in their rat experiment, one can possibly imagine that pressures to conform or to obtain good grades could be at play here. Similarly, researchers could possibly be affected by threats to research degrees or funding. The extreme importance of such a threat to validity in psy-

---

Ψ Case study

Seeing what you want to see

Rosenthal and Fode (1963) randomly allocated rats to two groups of student experimenters and told one group that their rats were bred from a 'bright' maze-learning strain while the others were told their rats were from a 'dull' strain. Even though there could have been no difference between the two rat groups, the experimenters reported significantly better maze learning for the 'bright' group.

In a report with the enchanting title *Pygmalion in the Classroom*, Rosenthal and Jacobsen (1968) reported that they had arranged for teachers to overhear information about some of their children (actually selected at random). The children were said to be late developers, likely to make academic gains in their later school years. When tested a year later these children had indeed made significant gains compared with non-selected children, suggesting that teachers had responded to the information by somehow, probably unknowingly, offering them greater attention and encouragement.

chological research prompted many attempted replications of the Rosenthal studies but with many failures. However, Seaver (1973) elegantly showed that where the same school teacher had taught both an older and younger sibling, the two were closer together academically than were similarly aged sibling pairs taught by different teachers. There are also a few relatively contemporary findings in keeping with the original hypothesis (e.g. Eden 1990).

Single and double blinds

A solution to the problem of participant expectancy is to use a placebo condition and/or a single blind procedure where participants do not know, in general, which condition they are in nor (usually) the rationale for the hypothesis being tested. To tackle researcher expectancy effects at the same time a double blind procedure can be employed in which neither participant, nor the data gatherer, know which condition the participant is in. This could happen where, for instance, a third person allocates participants to conditions on a random basis, measures out the dose of caffeine (or placebo) and then passes the participant on for experimental testing. Something akin to this occurred in a study by Langer and Rodin (1976) where a researcher gave two different sorts of talk and instruction to two groups of elderly nursing home residents, one talk emphasizing personal control and responsibility. Neither the staffing nurses, nor the assistant who interviewed and rated residents, knew who had been given which talk.

Halo effects

Halo effects occur when an assessor's overall positive or negative evaluation of a person affects their assessment of other specific traits. One of the drivers in our fictitious study may have started out with very polite remarks. A positively impressed researcher, assessing this questionnaire, might rate an otherwise ambiguous response as showing courtesy.

Contrast effects

Observers may tend to use themselves as a frame of reference in assessing personality. The tendency is to rate people different from oneself as even further away than they actually are, and people similar to oneself as more similar to oneself than they actually are (Murray 1938). A rater in our driver study who is a very courteous driver might see the respondent just mentioned as more courteous than is actually the case.

Contemporary and local history effects

Our drivers' behaviour might also be confounded by a 'contemporary history' effect if, during the course of the study, there had been a national advertising campaign designed to reduce traffic speeds. A 'local history' effect is one which affects one group but not another. Suppose researchers were interested in the effectiveness of an anti-bullying initiative at a certain school. They might select a class and compare this with a comparable class in another school before and after six months of the programme. It is possible that the comparison group might experience a local tragic bullying incident in their area, sensitizing them to bullying issues and possibly obscuring any effects of the programme.

Confounding variables

A **confounding variable** is either one which causes a misinterpreted difference to appear, or one which hides a real difference, such as when Test B is really harder than Test A but, by poor sample selection, brighter children have taken Test B. Shortly we shall see that, even in a well-controlled experiment, it is often very difficult to rule out all variables, other than the one we are interested in, as causing an effect. In field studies, especially non-experimental ones, it is impossible ever to conclude that a single variable must be the cause of an effect. There are always several possible confounding variables and much of the effort and creativity in designing subsequent research often goes into attempts to eliminate possible confounding variables as an explanation. The influence of a confounding variable is depicted in Figure 21.3 (p. 681). Table 21.3 suggests possible solutions to various research problems.

Reliability

If we are to use the results of research as evidence in the support of theory we must be sure that any result is not just a one-off coincidence. For instance, consider the wallet study outlined on p. 669. If we were to have any faith at all in the claim that Glaswegians were more honest than Liverpudlians, the least we would expect would be to see the same result repeated, preferably with larger numbers. If a **replication** of a research study produces similar results we can talk of the effect being **reliable**. Exact replications of research studies are near impossible. Even if we use the same participants we cannot truly claim them to be 'the same' as in the original study: we have changed them by asking them to participate in that original study.

Table 21.3 Possible solutions to various research problems

Problem	Possible solutions
Reactivity effects • participant expectancy • hypothesis guessing • pleasing the experimenter, etc.	Deception: participants do not know the hypothesis or are misled about it Placebo/single blind: participants do not know the condition they are in Naturalistic observation: participants do not know they are being studied
Social desirability	Deception about aims Include a 'lie scale' Reword questionnaire items
Response acquiescence	Balance items: ask questions in both directions Make questions concrete
Researcher bias	Double blind procedure keeps assessor unaware of the origin of material for assessment
Inter-rater or observer reliability	Correlate ratings: where correlations are low either eliminate rater or provide further training and standardization; use adjustment factor where deviations are consistent
Contrast and halo effects	Further training of raters and standardization of procedures
Observer effects	Familiarize participants to observation setting Observe covertly (and request permission later) Naturalistic observation

Replications

Most 'replications' are near repeats of an original study. In some cases the replication is conducted with the specific intention of demonstrating that a finding was limited to the specific type of sample used and not to samples from other populations. Other studies demonstrate that measures used were weak or inadequate, or that the effect is limited to a specific research design or or to a narrower definition of the variables than expressed in the original study. Whenever a repeat study does not support original findings, we talk of a 'failure to replicate'. There are many studies whose results continue to feature prominently in basic psychology textbooks and courses, even though there have been quite serious failures to replicate. This is often because the 'paradigm' they introduced or topic they tackled was so important, thus generating a large amount of research impetus and critical debate.

Inter-rater reliability

In various parts of this chapter we shall need to question the reliability of people who assess participants' responses in psychological research studies. Typically 'raters' are asked to employ a scale (say 1 = 'harsh parenting' to 10 = 'warm parenting'), having received

training and examples, to quantify data produced by participants. These could be, for example, interview answers, essays, letters to a fictitious friend, behaviour towards their child while playing, responses to a projective test (see p. 699) or drawings.

In order to check that raters are adequately trained for scoring, or in order to check that their rating has been reliable after the trials, scores of different raters can be compared using **correlation** (see p. 687). This comparison process is known as a test of **inter-rater** or **inter-observer reliability**.

Internal and external validity

A basic requirement of any research study is that its outcomes or results can be trusted as valid. In a simple sense we mean are they correct? Do they reflect reality in some way? Can we assume that we observed a genuine effect on people or obtained genuine accounts from people?

Internal validity largely concerns whether an effect found reflects a genuine cause–effect link. In the driver behaviour study described on p. 674, it is possible that any apparent speed reduction is not related to the calming measures but could be caused by errors in statistical calculation or use of test, differences between the samples taken (e.g. slower drivers in the second sample) or by demand characteristics.

External validity concerns the possible generalization of a found effect to or across:

- **populations**: can we generalize to a larger population similar to that from which the samples come or across populations represented in the samples? Will the driver behaviour study generalize to rush hour drivers?
- **locations** (often known as **ecological validity**): can we generalize from the researched situation to similar or somewhat different situations? Will the driver research generalize to other towns or to cities?
- **constructs**: to what extent is the effect limited to the specific measures of variables used? Can we assume this effect would occur with different calming measures, with a different questionnaire measure?

Figure 21.2 illustrates the concepts of internal and external validity.

Ecological and population validity

A common knee-jerk reaction in the evaluation of research studies, especially experiments, is to claim that a result is weak since it does not generalize to real life. As we shall see when evaluating the experimental method, there is an argument for conducting well-controlled studies which sacrifice much of their generalizability in favour of strong internal validity. As Leary (1995) points out, science tends to generalize the conse-

quences of theory rather than the results of individual experiments. The latter are used to check the theory thoroughly. If we know the theory is supported in rigorous testing we can begin, tentatively, to explore its possible practical applications.

However, the extent to which the results of a study do generalize to other geographical situations, especially from laboratory to real life, has become known as a study's ecological validity. This does not mean that every study which is 'naturalistic' has 'greater ecological validity' as is often claimed. These concepts of validity were largely introduced by Campbell and Stanley (1966) and are thoroughly discussed in Cook and Campbell's *Quasi-experimentation* (1979) where the distinctions are rather more complex, overlapping and subtle than the now common usage of 'internal validity' and 'external validity'.

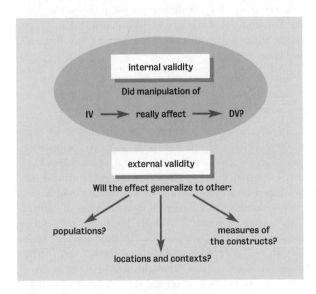

Figure 21.2 Internal and external validity

Ψ Section summary

Psychological researchers have come across many problems associated with the various designs for investigation which can be employed. Some are general, possibly occurring in most research designs, and these are dealt with above. The problems can be seen as aspects of how participants approach and behave in research situations, or as aspects of the designs themselves and the ways in which researchers, as fallible human information gatherers and interpreters, conduct their investigations. All studies and particular measures may be analysed for their reliability (consistency in several respects) and their validity (whether an effect is really what it appears to be and its extent of application). Replication is highly desirable in order to check reliability and validity.

1 Without referring to the text, run through the driver research described on p. 674 again, listing all the weaknesses you can see, but now identifying them where possible with the typical research problems and weaknesses which have been described in the section just covered.

2 Refer to a research study you have covered in theory recently and with a friend/colleague discuss what factors would be threats to the study's *internal validity* (what apart from the independent variable, could have caused an apparent effect?) and which would threaten *external validity* (in what ways won't its effect generalize?).

❏ Methods of psychological researchers

Getting down to method: defining variables

'Survival instinct' was dismissed earlier as a 'non-explanation'. If individuals live through a disaster which should have killed them, such as a shipwreck, people tend to 'explain' this amazing feat by assuring us that the survivor had a 'strong instinct for survival'. Psychologists early in the twentieth century pointed out that such 'explanations' were circular and retrospective. What and where is this 'instinct'? How would we recognize that someone possessed it *before* a tragedy? The 'easy thinker' tends to get impatient and claim 'He *must* have the instinct. How else would he have survived where others would die?' Research psychologists argue that we need independent evidence. Psychological variables must be carefully defined in measurable terms if we are to test theoretical predictions.

Not all psychologists would go along with this principle, especially many qualitative researchers (see p. 720), but most operate according to the general notion that we must somehow account for what it is we are investigating in terms that others can both understand and utilize in order to repeat or extend our investigations. **Variables** are phenomena which can change in value, such as abilities and personality characteristics. One important reason for defining variables accurately when conducting research is that we wish to agree on effects and to avoid misunderstandings such as 'Ah! You mean *that* kind of "conformity" – no wonder you don't get the effects I did.'

Operational definitions

Suppose someone makes the common-sense claim that 'nurses generally have a very caring nature'. It is usually fairly easy to imagine how we would go about testing this notion in terms of the groups (**samples**) we would need to select for investigation. We would need a group of nurses and a group of non-nurses, perhaps selected so that they are roughly equivalent in everything (e.g. age, sex, education, income and so on) except their occupation. The hard part is almost always the definition of what we shall count as 'caring'. People who make such claims know pretty well what they mean but find it extremely difficult to see how such a quality of human personality could be measured. In this area psychologists

have developed various ways to measure, or at least assess, such traits. We could create a questionnaire, conduct an interview, make direct observations of nurses' behaviour, ask them to keep a diary. Obviously, there cannot be one final universally accepted measure of 'caring': the concept is too culture bound and socially flexible for that (compared with the universal acceptance of a 'metre' as a measure of length). What psychologists and other scientists do, in communicating their method of measurement, is to declare an operational definition of their variable. What this means is that the variable is defined in terms of the operations taken to measure it. Hence, in one study the measure may be a questionnaire and in another a set of observations. Inevitably such measures differ, but what is essential in any study involving testing of a claim about measured variables is that an operational definition is provided by the researcher.

Constructs

Many of the variables studied or proposed by psychologists are constructs. Typically, a questionnaire designed to measure, say, computer anxiety is produced and contains, say, 40 items. Using a statistical procedure known as factor analysis, the interrelationships between all items are investigated and it might be found that the questionnaire seems to measure three or four distinct 'factors'. The statistical programme obviously cannot name or otherwise identify these factors other than as statistical entities and it is the interpretation of the researcher which gives them some form of possible reality. The computer anxiety questionnaire, for instance, might apparently measure several factors, not just one, and these might be

- fear of technical equipment in general
- fear of computer control
- dislike of technical activity.

Some psychological constructs are intended to be close to the everyday meaning of the term used, for instance, 'intelligence', 'anxiety' or 'authoritarianism'. However, many constructs are created through research and may not figure at all in everyday speech about roughly psychological issues. An example might be 'locus of control' – the extent to which individuals' life events are seen by those individuals to be controlled by their own efforts or by external forces beyond their control. Even further from 'common sense' thought would be several of Freud's concepts concerning unconscious thought processes. Though Freud himself did not provide operational definitions or quantitative support for their reality, many psychologists have attempted to do so using scientific methods (see e.g. Fisher and Greenberg 1978).

The experiment: determining cause and effect

People use the term 'experiment' very often and very loosely compared with its strict meaning. The reason why people debate what is and isn't an experiment is that, properly used in an appropriate context, it is the most powerful method for indicating a causal relationship between events. A simple non-psychological example can start us off, while also demonstrating that, like many other methods concepts, the experiment is used in our everyday thinking about events, though not as strictly as in scientific research.

Suppose a friend tells you that one of your favourite houseplants is a type that thrives on a little drop of lemon juice every week. (I'm sure there's no such plant!) To establish your claim that the friend must be talking nonsense you might select two plants, equal in health and size, place both on the same windowsill and give only one of them the weekly drop of lemon juice. You would both then observe any consequent differences between the plants with great interest. We will not bother with the exact outcome here but we can concentrate on the procedure. The basic experimental principle here is that one variable was altered while all others were controlled. You were wise to ensure that the two plants started out relatively equal. The variation of only one factor (lemon juice) is central. You would also be wise to spend the same time in front of each plant, otherwise someone could argue that the extra breath given to the experimental plant (as with the argument over talking to plants) might confound the study and be the true causal variable (see Figure 21.3).

With all other variables controlled, the manipulation of just one variable is assumed to be the cause of any consequent change in another variable. John Stuart Mill (1874) referred to this logical approach as the 'method of difference'. Let us now look at the way this principle of change in one variable is applied in psychological research.

One could start with a simple design used by E. E. Jones *et al.* (1968) which investigated the effect of first or later impressions. Here participants observed a person trying to solve multiple choice problems. In both conditions of the experiment the person solved 15 out of the 30 questions but in one condition these correct

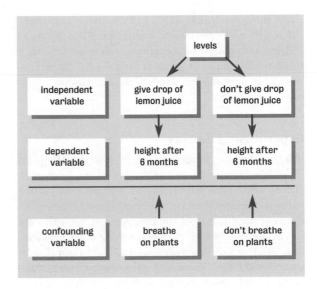

Figure 21.3 Independent, dependent and confounding variables

answers were bunched near the beginning of the trials whereas in the other condition they were bunched near the end. Participants in the first condition apparently gained a more favourable impression of the person's problem-solving skills since they reported that he got an average of 20.6 problems correct, while the second group reported only 12.5 correct. Yet both groups actually observed him solving exactly the same number of problems overall.

Independent variable and dependent variable

In experimental terminology, the variable which is manipulated by the experimenter is known as the **independent variable**. In the Jones *et al.* example this would be the position of the solved problems – early or late. The variable which is measured and is assumed to be affected by the independent variable is known as the **dependent variable** – its variation is assumed to be dependent upon the variation of the independent variable (see Figure 21.3).

Each independent variable has two or more 'levels'. In a simple experiment, these are the conditions you choose to use in your experiment – for instance, two sets of memorizing instruction or the early or late solving conditions in the Jones study. The levels of some independent variables can be chosen from a scale which is continuous. For example, we might vary the amount of caffeine we give to participants and then observe the effect this has on their ability to throw darts accurately. We might use conditions of 5 mg, 20 mg and 50 mg of caffeine and, of course, a condition where no caffeine is taken at all. Other independent variables are discontinuous or categorical – for instance, the two types of memorizing instruction.

Experimental designs

Imagine you have a group of, say, 40 willing participants and you wish to conduct a replication of the Jones *et al.* (1968) study. How might you decide to use your participants in the conditions of the experiment? Remember the two conditions (of the independent variable) are solving more problems early and solving more problems later on. You have one very important and central decision to make first. You could either have all 40 participants observe both the early and late problem solving, or have one group (of 20) observe the early solving condition and the rest observe the late problem solving. These two basic forms of design have names, though researchers vary in the terminology they tend to use, partly dependent upon the research context. Various almost equivalent names are given in Table 21.4; in this chapter, we shall use the term 'repeated measures' (sometimes written as 'repeat measures') and 'independent samples'.

Repeat measures design

Where we can test all our experimental conditions on the same people we have one of the strongest designs in experimental work. Differences cannot be attributed to differences between the people in the various conditions. Here, we can compare how each person's performance alters as a result of the change in conditions.

Very often one of the conditions in a repeated measures design is a control condition which gives us a baseline measure of how a person performs with no special

Table 21.4 Terminology for basic experimental designs

Description of experimental design	
Each participant takes part in all conditions	**Different group of participants for each condition**
repeat(ed) measures	Independent samples
within subjects	independent groups
within groups	between subjects
	between groups

circumstances applied. For instance, in the caffeine example there would be a measure of performance with no caffeine at all.

Problems with designs
In order to establish the internal validity of their research, experimenters attempt to control as many confounding variables as they can, choosing a design which gives a fairly clear demonstration of the effect of an independent variable on a dependent variable. However, things are rarely that simple; each experimental design has its drawbacks in terms of the intrusion of alternative explanations of observed effects.

Repeated measures and order effects: counterbalancing and randomization
The repeated measures design presents a rather obvious problem. The participants in the Jones *et al.* (1968) experiment would already have formed their impression of the problem solver when they come to the second condition. There seems to be no other way out of this problem of 'order effect' than to shift to the second type of design and have two separate groups. However, in other sorts of experiments this may not be the only solution. Consider, for example, an experiment in which the two conditions are threading a needle in front of an audience and without an audience. Here we can ask half our participants to perform with an audience, then without, and ask the other half to perform the conditions in the reverse order. We counterbalance the order of conditions. This way any differences caused by the order in which participants took the conditions ought to cancel each other out and the remaining difference between the two conditions can be more reliably attributed to the manipulation of the independent variable. An alternative approach, where participants experience several trials in any one condition, is to randomize the order of presentation of stimuli under the two conditions of the independent variable. For instance, in an experiment where participants are to see words in upper case and words in lower case, for later recall, these can be randomly mixed in the presentation list and participants asked to recall any items they can. The number correctly recalled from each level of the independent variable can be separated out in the analysis.

Separate groups for each condition
In some studies it seems rather pointless to have participants experience both conditions. An example would be where participants are asked to choose a prison term for either a man or a woman who have committed the same

crime. There are two main ways in which we might form two separate groups: matched pairs design and independent samples design.

Matched pairs design

What we might do here is to substitute a pair of scores from the same person for a pair of scores, one from each of two similar people. How similar depends upon the criteria we use for matching. In a memory experiment looking into differences resulting from two types of instruction for recall, for instance, we might match participants on their initial recall ability under normal conditions. We would rank all participants on recall ability and then allocate them alternately to one condition, then the other. The matching test might be given a week earlier in order that it does not interfere with the experimental procedures. We could, of course, match for age, sex, educational background, social class, income, political attitude and a host of other variables. In practice this would require far too many participants and, in any case, we need match only those variables relevant to the experimental design. The important point about this design then is that we achieve pairs of matched scores and, for this reason, the design can be blocked together with the repeat measures design as a 'related design', where final pairs of scores are related to each other (see Figure 21.4).

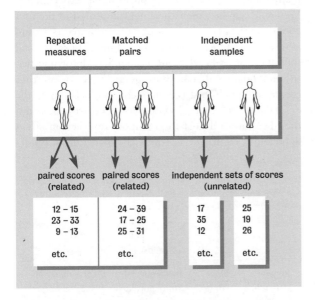

Figure 21.4 Related and unrelated experimental designs

Independent samples design – using a control group

On many occasions the matching procedure is impracticable and researchers rely on being able to detect differences between conditions using entirely separate groups of people in each condition. The two samples will be drawn from one 'pool' of people in as unbiased a manner as possible. The resulting data form two groups of unrelated scores. The design is known as an 'unrelated design' for this reason (see Figure 21.4).

Independent samples designs often include use of a control group with which to compare an experimental group. This is the role of the houseplant which does not receive lemon juice (p. 680). A control group must experience everything the experimental group does, in exactly the same way as far as is possible, but excluding the one independent variable under examination.

Independent samples and participant variables: random allocation to conditions

Suppose that we conduct the Jones et al. (1968) study using two separate groups of participants, one for each condition. Any difference we subsequently find between the two groups could be caused by differences in the type of people in each group. For instance, the group seeing the problems solved early might just happen to contain more people who tend to form early impressions, rather than there being a general tendency for people to form such impressions. The main way in which we can guard against this threat to internal validity is to use **random allocation** of participants to groups – we ensure each participant has an equal chance of being in any condition. This way we can be as sure as possible that there is not some selection bias in our allocation of participants. The individual differences between participants, that is, will still be there but, if we always follow this procedure, the differences will be randomly spread across conditions.

True and quasi-experiments

This random allocation of participants to conditions is a hallmark of the 'true' experiment where independent samples are being used. Where this is not possible, the study may be referred to as a quasi-experiment. Such experiments are discussed by Cook and Campbell (1979) and Campbell and Stanley (1966). They include examples where one can only obtain a specific group for each condition. Cook and Campbell's objective was to help broaden the use of traditional experimental procedures for use by field researchers where it is rarely possible to allocate participants at random or to maintain complete control over the relevant independent variable. Included as quasi-experiments would be the following designs.

Equivalent groups are tested

A school may be asked to operate an experimental road safety campaign and a school is selected with which to compare outcomes in traffic awareness over one term. The second 'control' school would be selected as being equivalent in terms of overall numbers, sex and ethnic group composition, age range, local socio-economic circumstances, academic performance and so on.

Events are recorded after 'natural' manipulation of a variable

Cook and Campbell (1979) cite Ross *et al.* (1973) who demonstrated that serious accidents declined more during drinking hours after the introduction of the breathalyzer to the UK in 1967 because drivers were drinking less. They produced archival data (see p. 711) to weaken alternative interpretations that people, in general, were drinking less, that people were driving less or that drunken drivers were just driving more carefully. The research by Seaver (1973) (see p. 676) neatly exploits natural comparisons and would qualify as a quasi-experiment, with same teacher/different teacher as the independent variable and difference in academic attainment as a dependent variable.

More complex experimental designs

Psychological experiments are rarely as simple as the two condition designs outlined above. A large number of experiments fall into the following two categories:

- more than two experimental conditions
- more than one independent variable

As an example of an experiment with more than two conditions consider the classic 'levels of processing' experiments (e.g. Craik and Tulving 1975). In one of these, M.W. Eysenck (1974) asked participants to deal with a list of words in one of five ways: counting letters in the word, finding a rhyming word, finding an appropriate accompanying adjective, forming a vivid image and, finally, just to 'memorize' the list. Only the last group knew they would be asked later to attempt recall of the words in their list. Somewhat contrary to 'common sense', the imagery group correctly recalled the greatest number of words with the 'intentional' group second. Other experiments which use several

conditions are those where the researcher sees a need to use a control group (e.g. no caffeine) and a placebo group, in addition to the main conditions of the independent variable.

Still more complex are 'factorial design' experiments which manipulate more than one independent variable simultaneously. For instance Gordon *et al.* (1988) asked students to read about a crime and then decide upon an appropriate sentence for the fictitious guilty defendant. One independent variable (known as a 'factor' in these designs) was the defendant's race. Values of the independent variable are known as 'levels' – in this case the defendant being described as 'black' or 'white'. The other independent variable was the type of crime committed, and this had the levels of 'embezzlement' or 'burglary'. Hence, each student participated in just one of the four possible 'treatments' outlined in Table 21.5.

The theory concerned internal and external attributions for actions. An external attribution is made when a reason for a person's action is found in the external environment rather than in an enduring trait of the person themselves. Prior research had shown that burglary is seen as a (stereo-)typical crime for black people whereas embezzlement is seen as typically a white crime. Research also showed that internal attributions lead to harsher sentences (since the crime was more the person's fault and less a result of any environmental factors such as poor education or enticement).

Technically this is a more sophisticated approach than conducting two isolated but simpler experiments. We could conduct the experiment indicated in the first row of Table 21.5. Two groups of participants would allocate a sentence, one for the crime of burglary and the other for embezzlement, having been informed that the defendant is black. Subsequently we, or another researcher, might test the same conditions but with the defendant described as white. However, we would not then be able to detect the complex interaction effect depicted in Figure 21.5, where the direction of differ-

Table 21.5 Information given to participants in four groups formed from crossing one independent variable (race of defendant) with a second (type of crime)

		Type of crime	
		Burglary	Embezzlement
Race of defendant	Black	Black burglar	Black embezzler
	White	White burglar	White embezzler

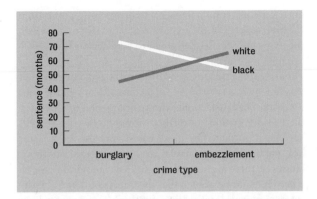

Figure 21.5 Months of sentence given, by defendant race and type of crime
Source: data from Gordon *et al.* (1988)

ence across one factor alters for different values of the other factor, because the two sets of participants were not drawn from the same overall 'pool' and allocated at random to the four groups. The two sets of participants in the two separate experiments are drawn at different times and in different ways so it is harder to make direct comparisons.

From Figure 21.5 we can see that, as predicted, whereas black defendants were given harsher sentences for burglary than white defendants, the latter received harsher sentences for embezzlement than black defendants.

Evaluation of experimental method

Isolating cause and effect
The main strength of the experiment is its claim to be able, under the strictest conditions, to identify the direction within a causal relationship. For instance, those given more violent television viewing subsequently produce higher levels of aggression. Other studies may show a relationship between aggression and the viewing of violent television but one cannot tell whether viewing causes the aggression or whether aggressive people are simply more likely to choose violent television. Of course the experimental 'demonstration' of cause and effect can be challenged – variation in television viewing may not directly cause increased aggression. However, in well-controlled conditions and with strong effects, the direction of events, though perhaps not precise causes, may be established.

Artificiality
However, it is often difficult to see how some results obtained in the artificial conditions and rarefied social atmosphere of a laboratory experiment can easily be applied to normal human life. Sears's (1986) research (see p. 675) showed that 78 per cent of the 1985 studies surveyed used a laboratory setting and 67 per cent of these also used undergraduates. Given these narrow participant populations, both the ecological and population validity of many experimental studies might be weak. In addition, many aspects of human experience cannot sensibly or ethically be tested by experiment. Some examples are

- effects of social deprivation on children's language development
- possible causal links between housing conditions and criminal behaviour
- relationship between emotional disorders and parental style in infancy

However, it might be said that the experiment's artificiality is its strength. When people claim that a weakness of an experiment was the artificialty of its surroundings, they are often missing an essential feature of experimental methods. In scientific investigation it is often necessary to create artificial circumstances in order to isolate a hypothesized effect. In physics, for instance, it has been productive to accelerate sub-atomic particles in a highly artificial atmosphere in order to understand the nature of matter. Such conditions would not be found naturally in a manner which could be controlled and carefully measured. At a far more basic level, as most school children are aware, it was necessary to create a vacuum in order to demonstrate that objects (such as a feather and a piece of coal) fall at a uniform rate in the absence of air resistance and atmospheric conditions. In the UK, the *Guardian* newspaper (18 October 1996) carried an article concerning the use of a virus on mice genetically engineered to develop human tumours. The virus apparently plays a role in correcting the effects of a gene which, when it goes wrong, permits the multiplication of abnormal cells. The completely artificial conditions of the research nevertheless provide extremely valuable and potentially life-saving information.

The experiment, then, may produce results from a highly artificial setting, but this does not logically entail that such results cannot be used in the development of theory or in the development of useful applications which further our understanding and ability to deal effectively with human problems. Leary (1995) argues

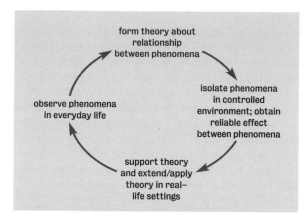

Figure 21.6 Relationship between theory, controlled research environment and real-life settings

that, in psychology, we usually do not wish to generalize the results of our study but the theory which produced the hypothesis for testing. Stanovich (1992) argues that the complaint 'But it's not real life' is not a valid criticism of experimental research (see Figure 21.6).

Field research and field experiments
Many psychological studies are carried out 'in the field', – that is, in natural surroundings, usually the study of people in their normal place of work or recreation. In a field experiment, for instance, children can be randomly allocated to experimental or control group, a 'treatment' can be applied (for instance, watching violent or educational cartoons) and a dependent variable assessed (aggressive responses to a questionnaire; observation of aggression in play). However, the field experiment naturally entails that more uncontrolled variables can 'contaminate' or confound the validity of any apparent effects. Nevertheless, a decision can be made that the loss of artificiality compensates for the increased lack of control. Many of the studies using the 'non-experimental' methods described in this chapter have been carried out in the field.

Mundane and experimental realism
A useful distinction made by Carlsmith *et al.* (1976) is that between those experiments which more closely approximate to everyday real life – those with 'mundane realism' and those which, though quite artificial, nevertheless engage the participant's full attention and produce as natural a response as is possible because they are so compelling in their effects. This latter category – with 'experimental realism' – may be artificial but they pro-

duce valuable results from participants fully committed to those aspects of the experimental environment which the experimenter wished them to take seriously.

Where experimental weaknesses are least critical
Psychology is a very broad subject area. Many of the contemporary dissatisfactions with experimental methods (or the broader critique of qualitative methods – see p. 720) have been produced by those whose interests lie in areas not particularly amenable to experimental method. However, there are several areas of psychological research where it could be argued that the effects of demand characteristics, social desirability, artificiality of surroundings and equipment, and so on, are minimal if not trivial. Where psychologists investigate cognitive systems (for instance, the effects of letter font or size on word recognition speeds) or the link between, say, stimuli input and physiological response, it is less likely (though not impossible) that the social aspects of the experimental situation will have a significant effect on observed behaviour. However, the pure experiment is often quite inappropriate in the investigation of phenomena which are of interest to the social, developmental or applied psychologist.

Multiple methods
The experiment can be seen as a method to be used in conjunction with others in order to obtain the fullest possible picture of a phenomenon. An experimental result will tell us that a certain independent variable produces differences in behaviour but usually not why. From Asch's studies (1955) we know that the number of people responding publicly in a group affects the likelihood of obtaining agreement with an obviously wrong answer by an unsuspecting participant. However, we do not know exactly why. Speculation produces more hypotheses to test but far more efficient than speculation is the interviewing of participants after their experience of the experiment. The information Asch obtained here is highly revealing and immediately leads to further interesting hypotheses for investigation.

Many elaborate studies in the applied field involve experiments, interviews and observations all used to triangulate information for the fullest possible perspective on a research topic. A less well known fact about the Hawthorne studies is that they included interviews with over 20,000 employees in all, with what started out as a fixed questionnaire. However, as the studies progressed, the Hawthorne researchers shifted to an interview approach which was more suited to obtain the '"emotional significance" of experience in a way which was not predetermined by the interviewer' (Hollway 1991: 81). Since the studies also involved a good deal of naturalistic observation work on employees in their workplace, the overall set of approaches was likely to reveal a mass of interconnected and complementary data unavailable from a narrow experimental perspective.

> ## Ψ Section summary
>
> In order to make their work publicly verifiable and to gain agreement on the validity of demonstrated effects, researchers carefully outline the theoretical constructs they are employing in argument and **operationally define** the variables they investigate in testing consequent hypotheses. Operational definitions limit constructs to the processes used to measure them. A major controlled form of investigation has been the experiment, which manipulates one or more independent variables in order to measure subsequent effects on one or more dependent variables. Various experimental designs incur several major design problems which, if they cannot be controlled for, may necessitate the use of an alternative design. Quasi-experiments lack the complete control of the true experiment but are much used in fieldwork where conditions may not be ideal. They nevertheless involve a good deal of control in order to facilitate unambiguous analysis of results. Various criticisms of the experiment can be answered either by the quasi-experiment or more complex designs, or by employing a non-experimental method.
>
> 1 Discuss and decide whether each of the research examples below is a true experiment, a quasi-experiment or not an experiment at all.
>
> (a) A researcher studies the effects of an experimental health maintenance programme at a local clinic where a control group is formed from among patients who have not signed up for the programme. Measures are taken of health improvements and attitude to illness after six months.
>
> (b) A researcher identifies 20 authoritarian and 20 democratic style leaders and investigates differences in the time taken for their teams to solve a complex problem.
>
> **Box continued**

> (c) A group of participants is randomly allocated to two conditions under which they perform arithmetic operations – alone and with an audience watching their performance.
>
> 2 In each of the examples above identify the independent variable, the dependent variable and the design of the study (e.g. independent samples, repeated measures), whether it is an experiment or not.

☐ Studies using correlations and group comparisons

We have said that it would not be ethically possible to investigate experimentally the relationship between social deprivation and children's language development. We cannot manipulate social deprivation, control all other variables and observe a consequent effect on language. Sadly, however, the natural social environment has, in a sense, already performed the manipulation for us. We can certainly investigate the existing relationship between these two variables, so long as we define them precisely. We can look at differences between, say, impoverished and enriched groups, or, better still, we can look at the correlation between the two variables across a wide range of the socio-economic scale.

Correlation studies

A correlation statistic is based on the extent to which two variables co-vary, that is, the extent to which they vary in the same manner or direction. It is likely that, measured day by day, the more anxious a person is, the more cigarettes that person will smoke (a particular problem for those highly optimistic smokers who think they can do themselves some good by cutting down rather than stopping altogether). The relationship may not be perfect but we may observe a trend. Correlation is a way of assessing this trend. If we assess each person's current anxiety level using a questionnaire such as Spielberger's State Anxiety Test (Spielberger *et al.* 1983) and pair this with the number of cigarettes they smoke we might obtain the fictitious data depicted in the table and scattergram shown in Figure 21.7.

Correlations are calculated and reported on a scale from −1 through 0 to +1. The very strong relationship

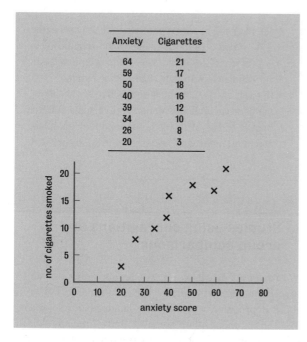

Anxiety	Cigarettes
64	21
59	17
50	18
40	16
39	12
34	10
26	8
20	3

Figure 21.7 Fictitious correlational data – daily anxiety level and number of cigarettes smoked

Table 21.6 Consumption of red wine and brown sauce by housing area

	Red wine*	Brown sauce*
High-status non-family areas	207	58
Affluent suburban housing	156	48
Better-off retirement areas	138	87
Modern family housing, higher incomes	112	62
Agricultural areas	97	129
Mixed inner metropolitan areas	95	87
Older housing of intermediate status	82	92
Better-off council estates	59	155
Poorer council estates	53	143
Older terrace housing	52	124
Poorest council estates	38	217

Note: *number of families with frequent use/population average
Source: Ford (1988) cited in Argyle (1994)

depicted in Figure 21.17 has a positive correlation of 0.94, very close to 1 indeed. Some relationships are inverse or negative: as one variable in each pair increases so the other decreases, as would the relationship between reading ability and errors made in reading. Have a look at the data in Table 21.6, which show a fairly strong negative correlation between consumption of red wine and brown sauce!

Cause, effect and correlations

This relationship between brown sauce and red wine consumption neatly demonstrates why assumptions very commonly made about correlations are in fact false. You would probably laugh at the notion that drinking red wine tends to cause people to eat less brown sauce (or the reverse). The two are most certainly linked through social causes – something to do with the attitudes, lifestyles and customs of people in differing social strata. But neither of the two is a direct cause of variation in the other. However, people readily accept that a correlation between level of education and salary at age 30 is evidence that better education leads to more successful jobs. In fact, it is possible that those receiving better education will earn more at 25 irrespective of their educational career. The relationship may be partly between

parental socio-economic status, opportunities and expectations, with education only a part of the equation. A correlation between the amount and quality of talk by parents and the quality of their children's speech by age 3 does not 'prove' or even necessarily support the idea that parental speech caused the child's speech to be at the level it is. Possibly, children who are going to speak well have qualities which are more likely to stimulate parental speech. Possibly the link is one of genetic inheritance. In certain cases it seems more reasonable to assume a causal direction: one assumes that variation in temperature causes people to wear more or fewer clothes rather than the other way around. However, in many cases this assumption may seem reasonable from experience and common sense, yet may need serious questioning and further research and analysis. For instance, data support a moderately strong relationship between the use of physical punishment by parents and subsequent aggression in their offspring. This could be because punishment causes aggression, or because aggressive children attract more punishment, or because the two are indirectly linked. A similar ambiguity exists around the demonstrated relationship between higher levels of aggression and greater watching of violent television.

Approaching cause with correlations
One way to provide more substantial support for a direction in the relationship between viewing TV violence and aggression is to compare several correlations across time in what is known as a 'cross-lagged' design. Lefkowitz *et al.* (1977) interviewed parents of 8–9 year olds to obtain a value for the amount of violent TV each child watched.

Aggression scores were obtained through peer (classmate) assessment. Findings showed a significant correlation between boys' violent TV viewing and aggression. This is the regular finding. However, the researchers also followed up with the same measures ten years later. They found

- aggression at 9 correlated 0.38 with aggression at 19
- violent TV viewing at 9 correlated 0.31 with aggression at 19 – almost the same value as for aggression at 9
- violent TV viewing at 9 did *not* correlate (0.05) with violent TV viewing at 19

The really interesting result was that for girls, assessed in the same ways, there were no correlations at all except for aggression at 9 and aggression at 19 (0.47).

This evidence appears to support more strongly the theory that television viewing has an effect on aggression, rather than aggression prompting viewing, since early aggression did not result in later violent viewing whereas early violent viewing remained related to later aggression. Also, as shown for girls as well, early aggression seems relatively stable across growth. All the correlations are small but they were significant. In general, where a correlation is reported as a research result, it is implicit that the correlation was significant, whereas 'did not correlate' implies that there would be a figure (not zero) but it would be too small to count as significant (see p. 712).

Group comparisons

Longitudinal studies

The research into television and aggression described above (Lefkowitz et al. 1977) is a good example of a longitudinal study – one which is carried out on the same group of participants over a substantial period of time with the intention of looking at relatively long-term effects of earlier conditions. This need not be on children. It could involve the long-term follow-up of patients and their adherence to a health regime, or of clients who have received some form of psychological therapy, or even of tragedy survivors.

Problems include a particular danger of 'participant attrition' (see p. 719), the sheer length of the study and possible 'contemporary history effects', such as military conscription being introduced during Lefkowitz's study.

Cross-sectional studies

A solution to the time factor in longitudinal studies can be the use of a cross-sectional study where several groups of participants are studied simultaneously and the groups represent people at different stages of development or

from different social groups (e.g. classes, ethnic groups). Many studies generated by Kohlberg's (1969) theory of moral development have used cross-sectional approaches, though a substantial number have also been longitudinal. An example of a cross-sectional study is that of Meilman (1979). The study used an interview technique developed by Marcia (1966) to assess an individual's changes in identity through adolescence as originally postulated by Erikson. Results for the development of 'identity achievement' in males of 12, 15, 18, 21 and 24 years of age found that the development of a stable identity did not occur until after 24 years old for almost half of the participants studied, if it occurred at all.

> ## Ψ Section summary
>
> Correlation is a measure of the strength of relationship between two variables – the extent to which variation in one is associated with or can be 'explained by' variation in the other. The relationship can be positive or inverse; one variable tends either to increase or decrease as the other increases. Unlike the true experiment, a correlation cannot logically indicate the direction of cause and effect. However, several complex ways of using correlations can serve as strong support for causal hypotheses.
>
> Group comparison designs (often but not exclusively employing correlational statistics) can be longitudinal (groups studied across a substantial time frame) or cross-sectional (comparison of several sub-groups).
>
> 1 Decide which of the following hypothetical relationships are *positive correlations* and which are *negative correlations*:
>   (a) The higher a person's anxiety score the more they will perspire.
>   (b) The higher a person's aggression score the fewer correct answers they produce in a test.
>   (c) The older you get the worse your memory becomes.
>   (d) The older you get the better your driving performance becomes.
>   (e) The older you get the less you pay for car insurance.
>   (f) The older you get the fewer car accidents you have.
>
> **Box continued**

(g) Increasing temperature causes people to spend more money on drinks.
2 Describe two designs for a study which would assess language development in Welsh bi-lingual children from age 2 to age 7. The two studies should be
(a) Cross-sectional
(b) Longitudinal

Interviews

One way of getting information from people is, of course, to talk to them. Where this occurs face to face, by telephone, or by electronic communication such as e-mail, we are, to some extent, engaging in a form of interview. Although telephone techniques are now much more common than previously, it is found that they produce a much lower agreement to be interviewed than does a face-to-face request. The response rates for e-mail and similar media have yet to be established. A weakness with these indirect techniques is that they lack one of the special advantages which the face-to-face interview possesses over impersonal questionnaires. This is that the interviewer can observe all the non-verbal information which accompanies speech in normal interpersonal interaction. This information may help the interviewer realize when a point is misunderstood, sensitive or especially important and worth following up. This advantage of the interview is at a minimum where the session is highly structured but, as with observation, within contemporary psychology, there is a range of techniques from structured – highly constrained and predetermined – to non-directive, with the interviewee talking freely (see Figure 21.8).

Structure

Interviews, then, can be more or less structured (see Figure 21.8). The most highly structured interviews would contain identical questions for all interviewees and a closed scale for responding, such as the Likert scale (see p. 698). Effects occurring from variation in the social interaction between interviewer and interviewee might be seen as 'nuisance variables'. However, standardization of the preliminary introduction and of the response scale would be expected to minimize these problems. This kind of assessment is not at all closely related to common lan-

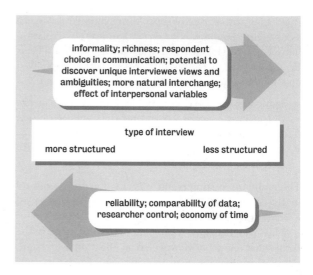

Figure 21.8 Features of more and less structured interview styles

guage use of the term 'interviewing' where we would normally find open questions, the interviewee's full point of view and the interviewer following up interesting but unpredicted avenues of thought.

Non-directive interview

Usually, an interviewer has a specific research question in mind and has a fairly specific set of questions prepared. However, within psychology there is sometimes a role for what is termed the 'non-directive' interview. Although many psychologists would associate this method specifically with Carl Rogers and the practice of client centred therapy, the technique was developed before his work (see case study). The main principle of this form of interview is to constrain the interviewee as little as possible with few predetermined boundaries, permitting the interviewee free rein in exposing their thoughts and following up associations and stream of consciousness in order to produce the most interesting and relevant data. (See also Chapters 14 and 18).

Though the therapeutic version of this interview is almost entirely non-directive, or interviewee led, a more researcher-led version is known as the 'focused interview' (Merton et al. 1956). Here, although the actual interview process is relatively unstructured and interviewee-led, concentrating on their subjective experience, the researcher has previously developed and will cover a range of issues and research questions.

Case study

Non-directive interviewing at the Hawthorne plant

The 'non-directive' interview figured prominently in the Hawthorne studies described earlier, and was used in the discovery of what Hollway (1991) terms the 'sentimental worker'. Structured questionnaires were not eliciting the information needed to determine which sorts of incentive really had effects and were welcomed by the workforce. It was felt that the aim of obtaining genuine views could be achieved only by having each interviewee feel that their thoughts were welcomed, valued, utilized and completely confidential. The 'rules' for interviewers in this research are summarized below and according to Hollway 'would do justice to a [contemporary] counselling training course'. The theory behind the approach was basically psychoanalytic and still required interviewers (who might need several years to become fully skilled) to consider what the worker did *not* say and the effect of the interviewee's sentiments on the interviewer.

The Hawthorne interview technique, according to Hollway, produced two significant things:

- valuable information that was not available from the experimental procedures in use, such as those which produced the perplexing 'Hawthorne effect'
- changes in workers' attitudes and the recognition that these attitudes (including, for instance, those of 'job satisfaction') were important factors intervening between worker and job; this model was later incorporated into what became known as the 'human relations' approach to work and industrial psychology.

Rules to guide non-directive interviewers at the Hawthorne works studies

The interviewer should listen to the speaker in a patient and friendly, but intelligently critical manner, should not display any kind of authority, nor give advice or moral admonition, nor argue with the speaker. The interviewer should talk or ask questions only to help the person talk, relieve fears affecting the interview relationship, give praise for reporting of thoughts and feelings, to include a missed topic and to discuss implicit assumptions.

Source: adapted from Hollway (1991)

Semi-structured interview

The **semi-structured interview** is far more common within mainstream psychological research and is particulaly popular with, but not exclusive to, those taking a qualitative approach to their research. It uses open questions, not necessarily posed in a prescribed order, yet there is an agreed framework covered within each interview. The interviewee experiences a relatively natural conversation. However, the interaction, co-ordinated by an experienced interviewer, rises above the level of superficial chat, obtaining similar sorts of information from each interviewee, but in a way which permits their unique perspectives and attitudes to emerge as clearly and fully as possible.

Quantification of semi-structured interview data can be achieved by training assessors to grade the data on some form of rating scale, or by use of content analysis, where, for instance, interviews with parents might be analysed by identifying themes or terms and providing some frequency counts of their occurrence under differing circumstances or across differing interviewee groups. Trained assessors might rate the interview content for evidence of certain traits. However, many researchers using this approach argue that quantification would waste a large amount of useful and rich detail. Quantitative analysis, in this context, might well play only a supplementary role.

This sort of interview has to balance two possibly conflicting aims: that of obtaining full, rich and genuine accounts from each interviewee, and that of asking only a certain range of questions within a well-prescribed research topic area. J.A. Smith (1995) produced a useful guide to semi-structured interviewing incorporating many of the points made below about interviewing in general but including a very useful guide to analysis of data and subsequent report writing.

Structured interview

Structured interview: open questions

Many interview schedules are highly structured in that the same questions are given to each interviewee in exactly the same order and, as far as is possible, with exactly the same wording. However, the answers required are 'open', that is, the interviewee can reply in ordinary language at any length; there is no fixed response scale. This approach attempts to recognize the value of permitting interviewees to voice their opinion or attitude in their own words in a natural, spontaneous manner. It avoids the frustration felt by interviewees who do not wish to reply with a categorical 'yes' or 'no', or even with a '[strongly] agree' when they agree in some ways with a statement but also have definite reservations about it. However, it also incorporates the general aim of quantification, usually through some form of rating scale employed by trained assessors who are often 'blind' to the research hypothesis or to the particular origin of the interview data (e.g. 'blind' to the sex of the interviewee if this is a variable of interest in the hypotheses).

Structured interview: closed questions

In this approach the interviewer reads out the items and notes down the respondent's responses. An advantage of this is that all questions will be completed. The interviewer cannot respond to unique interviewee interpretations of the questions but it is possible to correct misconceptions or explain unusual terms. Otherwise, it is here, in particular, that the social context of the interview should have minimal effect, through its influence might still not be negligible.

As can be seen from Table 21.7 the strengths of the structured approach are that we can at least be relatively sure we have comparable data on the same questions. If an identical answering format has been employed we can certainly make quantitative comparisons but, of course, we can never be sure that each interviewee has interpreted each question in the same way. This is where the semi-structured approach has an advantage in that the interviewer can check for understanding and can discover quite unpredicted answers to unusual interpretations of the same question. To the qualitative researcher this variation in understood meaning might be seen as a useful research finding, whereas to the structured user it might be seen as an unwanted source of 'error' in subsequent statistical analysis. As Smith puts it:

you may need to ask yourself how engaged the respondent is. Are you really entering the personal/social life world of the participant or are you forcing him or her, perhaps reluctantly, to enter yours?

(J.A. Smith 1996: 15)

Table 21.7 Products, strengths and weaknesses of types of interview technique

	Likely product	Strengths	Weaknesses
Non-directive	Interviewee problems and self-reflection	Rich, authentic data; benefits to interviewee; illuminative Information; genuine	Difficulties of comparison; weak reliability checks
Semi-structured	Interviewee's unique and full views rather than superficial attitudes; answers, though, are to a set of questions prepared by the interviewer	Rich, authentic, genuine and illuminative data which can be pooled'; quantification is possible if desired; interview process flexible and adaptable to responses obtained; relaxed interviewee and possibly more personal information to follow up	Difficulties in comparison across interviewees; fairly weak reliability checks; effects from interpersonal differences – within and across interviews; problem of personal interpretation
Structured	Interview schedule predetermines data obtained; open questions allow for individual variation in responses; closed questions (e.g. 'yes/no') produce only frequencies	High reliability; comparison across participants; result can be used in quantitative hypothesis test; no desired response likely to be missed; open answers can be rated or categorized	Limited data – not spontaneously constructed 'accounts'; similar scores may hide quite different intended meanings; ambiguous points cannot be checked; more stressful experience of 'assessment'

The social context

Even the strictly controlled interview takes place in a social setting and the usual norms of human interaction occur, whether the interviewer takes account of these or not. Unless the interviewees are carefully and honestly briefed about the genuine reasons behind the research, there may still be an effect from demand characteristics (a term often applied only to the experimental context). Interviewees may well be attempting to discover or at least ponder upon what might be the reasoning or requirement behind the questions. They may well also try to please by giving what they perceive to be the sought after responses. Certainly, social desirability can play a strong role and it would take a very tactful, persistent and experienced interviewer to get the 'honest truth' from every interviewee on the more sensitive issues which can be covered by interview research. Very few people will reveal what they consider to be their worst characteristics and behaviour to a relative stranger in a somewhat formal situation.

In the less structured forms of interview there is of course more scope for variation according to the individual chemistry of the particular personality combinations in any one interview session. However, the aims of this sort of interview are also usually more transparent with the interviewer giving a fairly clear indication as to what the research is about and what will be done with the data. Hence there may be a trade-off between the enquiring participant, unable to see the deeper purpose but relatively little affected by the interviewer's personality, and the open, 'free' interview in which there is far greater opportunity for unique interpersonal interaction to produce a great deal of valuable information, or very little.

Preparing the interview

Preparation for interview research involves creating an interview schedule which is the set of questions to be used along with instructions to interviewers about the order of questions, instructions and extra information to interviewees, probes, prompts, and so on. As with questionnaires, the form of questions used in an interview is crucial in order to avoid the gathering of quite inadequate data.

Poor questions

In all but the completely structured interview, a major difference from questionnaire administration is that at least some questions must be created on the spot, as part of normal conversation. Here, the particular personality and speaking habits of the interviewer are central and it will be far easier to slip into producing some of the forms of questions to be avoided (see examples listed on p. 700). For instance, if the interviewee grimaces when mentioning a particular department at work it may be tempting to use the leading question 'Tell me why you don't like X department' rather than 'Tell me how you feel about X department?' It will be harder to avoid emotive terms and relatively easy to present a complex or even an unanswerable question. 'Do you think . . . ' questions may well elicit only a monosyllabic 'yes' or 'no'. It is possible to fire out two or three questions at once, leaving the interviewee confused, for instance 'Tell me about that; was it interesting? Did you feel important when it happened?' One essential feature of interview preparation then is to pilot in as realistic a manner as possible – give the interview schedule a trail run but do not use a close partner or friend.

'Why' questions

Why questions are notorious for producing a very wide set of possible answer types. Consider the possible answers to '. . . and why do you think your father used physical punishment?'

- because he was a cruel beast
- because I was naughty
- because he knew no better; it's the way he was brought up
- well – who doesn't?
- he thought it was quick, simple and less mentally cruel than other approaches

If the last answer was the type sought then better to refine the question to something like 'and why do you think your father chose physical punishment over other types of discipline?'

Probes and prompts

Piloting will also help in deciding what 'probes' work best for the particular interviewer and what 'prompts' to include. 'Probes' are the sort of thing we say when trying to get someone to produce a little more on a topic you suspect they have more to say about. These might be, for instance:

'I wonder if you could elaborate a little more on [your father's attitude to punishment]'

'Hmmmm . . . . I'm really interested in that point, do go on.'

'Prompts', more common in structured interviews, are predetermined sub-questions or items. Here is an example of a main question plus probes from Mussen and Distler (1960) in an interview schedule on parental practice in child discipline:

'How often do you spank X?' [Probes: (1) How about your husband? How often does he spank him? (2) For instance, how often has X been spanked in the last two weeks?]

(Fisher and Greenberg 1978)

Notice that, if the main question had not been preceded by establishing that spanking was indeed a practice in the household then it would be a clear example of a leading question of the 'when did you stop beating your wife?' variety (see p. 700).

Whereas probes must be natural, not too demanding and created spontaneously as the need arises, prompts are given to every interviewee unless they happen to come up with the appropriate answers themselves.

Conducting the interview

Listening skills

One might think 'Surely listening is just hearing. There can't be a way to do it'. However, what is referred to is more the evidence of the way in which the interviewee experiences being listened to. To be avoided, for example, are trivializing ('Ah yes I know that but . . .') or hijacking ('I know. We had the same problem. You wouldn't believe . . .').

Sensitivity to the interviewee

Even in the most structured interview situation, the interviewer needs to be able to put the interviewee at ease and to create the most comfortable atmosphere possible, especially where issues themselves are sensitive. Only experience can make the interviewer able to tackle sensitive issues with tact yet obtain relatively

Table 21.8 Strengths and weaknesses of interview recording methods

Method	Strengths	Weaknesses
Interviewer completes structured answer sheet	no items are missed; completely comparable with data from other interviewees	little initiative from interviewee; passive role
Notes taken at the time	little information should be lost or forgotten; information can be checked with interviewee at the time	disrupts normal conversation; can be too cryptic for later translation; interviewee may feel inhibited by detailed recording of comments; gets 'cues' from energetic note writing
Notes taken later on	conversation can be natural; interviewee not inhibited by seeing information recorded	loss of information; data recorded through memory bias (M. Smith (1986) found that interviewers forgot around half of the given information at the point the interview is over)
Notes by third person	natural conversation; interviewer can concentrate on questions; reliability enhanced; notes can be checked with interviewer later; comparison of different interpretations possible	greater inhibition from interviewee in the presence of two people; confidentiality and anonymity depends on two people; interviewee sees comments recorded in detail and gets 'cues'
Audio or video recording	freedom to converse naturally and concentrate on questions; data publicly available; reliability can be checked in several ways across several researchers; video provides non-verbal cues to meaning; interview can be part of wider observational study or technique	danger of malfunction – all data are lost; recording instrument may inhibit some participants; ethical issues if recording undisclosed; transcription time consuming – ratio of 1 to 10 between interview and transcription times; video produces even greater inhibition

genuine and otherwise well-guarded thoughts and feelings. The interviewer needs to keep several guiding principles in mind during the entire interview procedure:

- remain non-judgemental: any other behaviour will, at the very least, produce non-comparability across interviews and, at worst, create an unethically negative experience for the interviewee; whatever their views, participants have the right to be respected and valued
- monitor comfort of the interviewee, for ethical reasons if no other
- give appropriate feedback to indicate satisfactory progress, clarify and summarize; change topic; indicate the approach of sensitive issues
- keep interviewee informed as fully as possible, through introduction and debriefing
- enjoy the process: this is not just to make the session more pleasant for the interviewee (though it helps) but to recognize that the interviewee's presence and contribution are valued.

Recording the interview data

There are several ways to record the interview process and a list of methods and their strengths and weaknesses are is given in Table 21.8.

Transcription

Note that the estimated ratio of time between running the interview and transcribing the data is 1 to 10 (Pidgeon and Henwood 1996) or even 1 to 20 (Potter 1996). Hence, a half-hour interview might take five hours or more to transcribe into written text. There are also several ways to transcribe recorded speech from those methods which record every last hesitation, cough, pause and murmur, as recommended by Potter (1996) for discourse analysis work, to those in which the main gist is retained or only statements that make grammatical sense in isolation. Methods of transcription are themselves another 'filter' through which researchers impose a theoretical framework upon the raw data they have gathered (see Ochs 1979). For the most commonly used detailed system see Jefferson (1985) and for a very useful contemporary introduction to transcription issues and types see O'Connell and Kowal (1993).

Analysing interview data

As with observation studies, methods of analysing interview data vary along a scale from quantitative to qualitative largely dependent upon the particular researcher's outlook and research philosophy. Several possible options are listed in Table 21.9.

Table 21.9 Methods for analysis of interview content

Method of analysis	Comment
obtain overall questionnaire/scale score	possible where interviewer completed structured questionnaire during the interview; can move straight to hypothesis testing
frequency count/coding of certain terms/themes/ concepts occurring in the interview content	part of content analysis of open-ended answers; inter-rater reliability check is possible
rate interview content according to detailed rating system with explicit criteria	used on open-ended questions; requires extensive rater training; inter-rater reliability check is possible
qualitative analysis (use of coding procedure)	e.g. thematic analysis, grounded theory, conversation analysis techniques, discourse analysis

Ψ Section summary

Interview designs range in the extent of structure, with consequent advantages and disadvantages in each case. The loosely structured approach tends to give richer and more realistic data while the structured approach tends toward comparability and quantification. Social interaction variables have greater potential to confound findings in this design than in most others. The form of interview questions needs to avoid common pitfalls in order to produce valid and unambiguous responses. The interviewer needs to develop certain skills and to consider carefully the strengths and weaknesses of various recording methods in terms of reliability, validity, completeness and potential for analysis of data obtained.

Box continued

1   Design a semi-structured interview schedule using open-ended questions which will investigate people's memory of their feelings and reactions on hearing about the death of Diana, Princess of Wales, in 1997. In particular, the aim is to study the nature, detail and vividness of flashbulb memories of the event – how exactly do people recall what they were doing when they first heard the news? To what extent is their memory of the scene now affected by having repeated the story several times among friends, if at all, and so on? You should predict answers and devise appropriate prompts to be used where fuller answers may be withheld. Remember to debrief fully each interviewee should you put the schedule into action.

2   Discuss ways in which data from structured and semi-structured interviews can be assessed for reliability and validity.

Questionnaires and surveys

Survey questionnaires

Surveys usually involve asking many people several questions about themselves: what they do, how they think, where they go, what they tend to buy, and so on. You have probably been stopped in the street at some time in your life (if you were alert you may have looked the other way and hurried on!). You would have been taken through a set of questions by, for instance, a market research assistant; it is not only psychologists who use the survey method. The questionnaire used in a street survey is basically a **self-report** method for obtaining useful information from the public. However, it is unlikely that such a survey would use a psychological test or scale. Whereas some surveys (especially the street type) use only information gathering questions, other research, including some types of surveys, employs some attempted measure of people's personality characteristics, abilities and attitudes.

A warning when developing a psychological measure for a student project

The type of question asked on a questionnaire is crucial in terms of later data analysis. Careful decisions about

statistical analysis must be made before any data are collected, otherwise you may end up with useless data. Have a look at the sorry tale in the case study.

Psychological tests or scales

For the general public, one issue that has perhaps caused apprehension or even distrust of the psychological profession has been that of psychological testing, that is, attempted measures of people's psychological characteristics using tests and scales. It is interesting however, that, quite often, those people who shudder at the mention of psychological measurement will also not hesitate to make quantitative comparisons between people in their everyday conversations. A parent, for instance, will have no trouble at all describing a child in this manner:

'Kevin is very anxious but also very caring and protective towards others. He's quite socially inept and still has trouble with eye contact when he talks. He reads about three years beyond his age.'

Obvious or not, Kevin *is* being compared with others here. How do we know Kevin is 'very caring'? He must do caring things more often than other children do, otherwise there's no comparison to be made.

The nomothetic approach

Psychologists who take a **nomothetic** approach believe that it is possible to objectify and operationalize those statements which most people make in their everyday assessments of other people. The basic 'psychometric' model is that variables such as 'aggression', 'social skill', 'anxiety' or 'extraversion' are entities of some sort which can be assessed in people, using a measure to separate individuals in much the same way as does a measure of height or strength.

The measures which have been developed are referred to as 'scales' or 'tests' or even as 'instruments', the last term indicating a strict scientific approach to test creation. The scales are a particular kind of questionnaire, often containing, as we shall see, no questions at all! The scale is seen as a measurement tool, taking its place in psychological science on a level with the barometers, thermometers and micrometers of physical science. However, partly because people are such variable entities, psychology has had nowhere near the success of 'parent' sciences in obtaining agreement on the accuracy and appropriateness of human psychological measuring instruments, despite the development of a large literature on testing techniques, pitfalls and analysis. For this

ψ Case study

Look before you leap: how not to get the measure you wanted in a research project

A student was replicating a study on stranger vs acquaintance rape. Participants read one or other of two versions of a rape incident, identical except that in one the attacker was a person known to the victim. In the original study participants were asked to rate the responsibility of both the man and woman, on a 1–11 scale, with the worrying but predictable consequence that the woman was seen as slightly but significantly more responsible in the acquaintance incident, especially by men.

For the responsibility measure, the student asked:

Who was responsible?

woman ☐   man ☐   both ☐

Sadly, the degree of subtlety required to show that groups might differ in assessing responsibility will now disappear, because respondents are asked to choose one category rather than make a rating assessment. It is highly likely that all but the most extreme sexist would choose 'man' rather than 'woman' in the forced choice format given, whereas more might have given a higher responsibility rating for the acquaintance compared with the stranger and this was the subtle difference that the project was attempting to demonstrate. In the latter case a more subtle statistical test can be employed. The student in this particular story decided to go back and test all the participants again, using the more subtle measure.

---

reason, and for more philosophical ones, some psychologists find tests an inadequate method for investigating people. However, most psychological researchers, while recognizing that there are serious limitations in the use of scales and tests, will employ them as a handy diagnostic or research tool and will often incorporate them into research studies which also exploit a variety of other data gathering methods, such as interview or observation techniques.

An idiographic approach: repertory grids

Theorists who do not agree with the notion of common measurable personality traits, those who treat the individual holistically in possessing indivisible and unique characteristics, are said to take an **idiographic** approach. One very popular approach to idiographic study of personality has been the use of the 'repertory grid' technique. This is not so much a measure of personality as a measure of our own individual concepts of personality. The technique asks individuals to compare three known people at a time who could be friends, people who occupy various work roles, people in three different occupations or similar. In each comparison the individual is asked how any two might differ from the third. Successive comparisons of this sort generate the individual's set of most predominant personality concepts.

The approach is used quite often in applied areas such as management training and clinical psychology, where it is more of a useful tool in creating change (a part of 'action research') than it is a generator of generalizable quantitative data. An important feature is that participants are centrally involved in the research process, in keeping with the principles of many qualitative researchers. An example is Brown and Detoy's (1988) report of their training work with new and experienced managers, seeking managers' concepts of managing, summarized in Banyard and Grayson (1996).

What do psychological tests measure?

Table 21.10 lists examples of types of test available to psychological researchers. Notice that, as Kline (1993) points out, the 'aptitude' tests are really ability tests, or at least there is overlap, but the idea is to use aptitude tests in some sort of prediction of how an individual is likely to develop with a certain competence or skill. Attitude and personality also overlap. For instance, Kline categorizes the various measures of authoritarianism as attitude measures but it could be argued that this general orientation (along with 'dogmatism' or 'locus of control') is a lasting personality characteristic. There is also similar overlap between tests of motivation and personality. In fact some have argued (e.g. Heim 1970) that intelligence is a part of overall personality and that any

Table 21.10 What psychological tests can attempt to measure

Type of test	What it attempts to measure	Example
Ability	what you can do, mentally or physically	general intelligence (e.g. British Ability Scales: Elliot *et al.* 1983); verbal ability; physical tests are often termed 'tests of motor ability'
Aptitude	your potential level of development of a particular competence	logical ability (as indicator of likely computer programming ability)
Achievement	what you have done so far; knowledge level	a class test; exam
Personality	what you are like (e.g. anxiety) anxiety 'state' is what you are like now anxiety 'trait' is what you are normally or generally like	test of extraversion-introversion (e.g. EPQ: H.J. Eysenck and S.B.G. Eysenck 1975) general personality inventory (e.g. PPQ: Kline and Lapham 1990)
Attitude	your 'stance' (belief, feelings, behaviour) towards a particular issue or object	position on physical punishment; level of racial prejudice (e.g. Right–Wing Authoritarianism scale: Altemeyer 1981)
Motivation	your 'drive' in a particular context	effort to achieve in your career (e.g. Occupational Personality Questionnaire 1990)

such splitting of characteristics is misleading. For our present purposes it is worth noting that the various divisions are partly a result of differing 'schools' of thought tackling the various issues, using their favoured methods, and partly a matter of commercial interest, where certain tests were developed which were easier to use in a mass testing context, such as the general IQ tests and assessments used for occupational selection.

How do psychological tests measure?

Most psychological tests have fixed response formats. That is, participants are asked simply to choose one from two or more possible responses – the simplest being 'yes/no'. In a general intelligence test there will often be a set of possible answers to choose the best answer from – a 'multiple choice' approach. Table 21.11 illustrates examples of test items.

Categorical items

Items like the last example in Table 21.11, typical of the type of questions found in general information gathering surveys, generate what are known as categorical data. That is, we do not get a score of any sort for each person tested. We know only that they fall into the category which they tick. Therefore, we cannot correlate this information, for instance, with, say, age or educa-

tional achievement, where we need to compare an individual score on these variables with a single score on the questionnaire. This is a trap which often catches the naïve student researcher (see case study on p. 696).

Non-exclusive categories

It is thoughtful to include an 'other' category and useful to ask for specification. Here, respondents are not frustrated by being unable to state their favourite but less well known newspaper, and the resultant information, in some items, might throw up a category which should have been included or at least is very interesting.

Overlapping categories

It is also fairly easy to confuse respondents by having one response category overlap another. For instance:

	0	1–10	10–20	(etc.)	....
How many cigarettes do you smoke per day:					

Where does the 10 a day smoker place the tick?

Projective items

Projective items are psychoanalytically based and would form part of a similar set in a personality questionnaire or diagnostic instrument such as those men-

Table 21.11 Types of test or scale item

Open/open ended	Tell me how anxious you feel right now.
Open/single response	The capital of Italy is ___
Multiple choice	1 Are you an anxious person? yes/no 2 Choose which of the following is a correct spelling: A develop B conceive C accommodate D likely <div align="right">(select the most appropriate or correct answer)</div>
Bi-polar rating	Please mark where you would place yourself on the following scale: optimistic - - - - - - - - - - - - - - - - - pessimistic

Likert-type	1 Boxing is a barbaric sport
	    strongly agree agree undecided disagree strongly disagree
	
	2 I find it very hard to get up early in the morning
	    very like me like me undecided unlike me very unlike me

Ordering	Below are five possible reasons for coming to college. Please use the numbers 1 to 5, in the right-hand column, to put the reasons into rank order of importance for you. (1) would be the most important reason. <div align="right">Rank no.</div>To get a good qualification\ To enjoy the social life Because I felt my parents/family wanted me to come To delay starting to earn a living in a full time job Because I enjoy education and learning
Projection	Thematic apperception test (TAT): participant is shown a picture and asked to say what they see in it Rorschach ink blots: participant is shown an abstract, symmetrical design and asked to say what they see in it or what it reminds them of
Performance items	Child has to recall 5 digits Child/adult has to arrange coloured blocks to match a given pattern (as in the British Ability Scales: Elliot *et al.* 1983)
Categorical (survey-type) information	Which newspaper do you read on a regular basis? (please tick) 1 *The Times* ☐ 6 *Sun* ☐ 2 *Guardian* ☐ 7 *Mirror* ☐ 3 *The Independent* ☐ 8 *Star* ☐ 4 *Daily Mail* ☐ 9 Other ☐ 5 *Express* ☐ please specify ....

tioned in Table 21.11. Quite rigid scoring systems have been devised for the open-ended responses produced but raters need intensive training in the particular philosophy of the test, which is that the 'manifest' (presented) content can be symbolically disguised clues to 'latent' material concerning the respondent's underlying personality characteristics or unconscious conflicts.

Attitude scales

The Likert type item in Table 21.11 would form one of a similar set in an attitude scale designed to measure a habitual pattern of responding or 'stance' towards an issue, person, event or similar. Some of the more global and overarching attitude scales could also be seen as personality tests to some extent. Even at a more local level, scales designed to measure 'computer anxiety', for instance, which is a personality characteristic, have been found to contain factors which tap attitudes to computers (rather than anxiety as such).

Constructing a Likert-type attitude scale

There are several types of attitude scale and too many to present here (for details see Coolican 1994; Kline 1993). However, since the reader may well be involved, on a psychology course, in developing the most popular kind – a Likert scale – we shall concentrate on this type of measure.

The response scale

The typical Likert response scale is shown in the Likert type items in Table 21.11. If we wish people who are very much in favour of boxing to be indicated by a high score then we would let 'strongly agree' on 'Boxing is a barbaric sport' score 1 and 'strongly disagree' score 5. It is always best to think this through clearly before doing any scoring and to use the system which is most mentally comfortable; we may want anti-boxing people to have a high score but this is harder to conceive. The direction of the scoring system is arbitrary though it must remain consistent. Kline (1993) suggests that the best self-assessment scale has an odd number of points, preferable seven, is graphic, and has verbal descriptions as 'anchors'. Kline argues for a middle point, even though some participants will very often opt out by remaining indecisive. He feels it is annoying for participants to be forced to choose and that, if items are salient to the lives of participants, they will take up a non-neutral position. Evidence from Guilford (1956) showed

that reliability increases markedly as a scale is given more points, reaching a maximum at seven and gradually levelling out from there on. 'Anchors' are 'verbal designations' and tell participants what the scale point means; preferably all points should be labelled, as is the case with the Likert items but not the 'bi-polar' rating scale shown in Table 21.11. However, the bi-polar scale is graphic and this is apparently an advantage.

Types of items

The items of a Likert-type scale are all statements rather than questions. In constructing a scale you need to generate a number of items which are things people might say about the attitude object; brainstorming with learner colleagues is a useful way to start. There are a number of points to be borne in mind when developing the first pilot set of around 40 to 50 items (which will be reduced after item analysis – see p. 702). The points concern avoiding several sources of bias and the achievement of good reliability and validity. The reader might like to refer to these concepts on pp. 701–2 before proceeding further.

First, items are intended to discriminate between at least two groups, those who are fundamentally for (e.g.) boxing and those who are against it. However, life is never that clear cut. Many people are generally in favour of boxing but have reservations about certain aspects, especially recent deaths in the ring. Others are basically against it but are willing to leave those who want to be involved to get on with hitting each other. Items should, therefore, discriminate along the whole of the assumed dimension of the attitude. We wish to avoid items which will not discriminate among people with differing attitudes. The following are non-discriminating:

1	Boxers earn a lot of money	Factual – who would disagree?
2	All boxing promoters should be jailed for life	Extreme – who will agree?
3	Boxing involves a certain amount of aggression	Bland and true – most would agree

Items should also be unambiguous:

4	Boxing should not be encouraged in mixed schools	Does 'mixed' mean by sex or by ethnicity or by ability?

Items should be possible to answer:

5	Boxing is safer now than it was twenty years ago	Who is experienced or old enough to know?

Items should not be leading:

6 Wouldn't you agree that boxing is about causing an injury?

Note this is a question not a statement; this is also an emotive item and may have unwanted knock-on effects on the rest of the respondents' answers or attitude towards completing the questionnaire for you

Items should not be too complex or double-barrelled:

7 Boxing should be banned and the organizers made to pay compensation

Asks participants to agree to two things at once

Avoiding acquiescence set

A favoured way to deal with acquiescence set is to have half the items with positive content, so agreement with the statement indicates a favourable position towards the attitude object (see Item 5). The other items require a negative response to indicate a favourable attitude (see Items 6 or 7). In scoring the scale, one set of items, either the positive or the negative ones, will need to be reversed (1 becomes 5, 2 becomes 4, etc.) in order to maintain consistency such that the person opposed to boxing obtains a low overall score. If 1 = 'strongly agree', as in Table 21.11, then we would reverse the scores on positive items like (5) (since the person is agreeing with a pro-boxing item and should be given a high score for this item) and we would keep the original score on items like (7).

The idea here is that the acquiescent respondent will have to think more carefully before answering since, assuming they have some position on the issue, it will be harder for them to agree with a negative item from their point of view. If the respondent is completely acquiescent then agreement will overcome true belief. Such a person's score would then fall pretty well in the middle of the range (the opposite direction of scores would cancel each other out) and they would therefore be unlikely to affect results in a serious way – but such pathological acquiescence must be extremely rare.

Guilford (1959) pointed out that items are more likely to suffer from acquiescence if they are ambiguous, vague or general. Many people would probably agree with 'I like art' but this could be recast as several more specific items like: 'I visited an art gallery at least once last year' where agreement can be assumed to indicate enjoyment.

It is worth noting that reversing positive items often loses the sense of the original. Whereas an obsessive person might agree with the statement 'I enjoy keeping things tidy', its reverse ('I do not enjoy keeping things tidy') does not imply that a person who agrees with this description is necessarily *untidy*.

Avoiding social desirability

It is always going to be difficult to avoid the effect of people presenting an acceptable public image on an attitude scale. In a full personality questionnaire it is going to be necessary to ask about characteristics which most people would not like to admit to possessing. There are several ways to rewrite items so that undesirable qualities might still be agreed with, perhaps in a rather indirect way. Kline (1993) suggests using a proverb where we wish to measure, for instance, 'meanness'. Probably very few people would agree that they were 'mean' but they may well agree, even strongly, with a statement like 'waste not, want not; this should be imprinted on children's minds'.

Another method of checking for social desirability bias is to include a few items which form a 'lie' sub-scale. This consists of items that extremely few people could answer in one direction without being a virtual angel. Eysenck's Personality Inventory (EPI: H.J. Eysenck and S.B.G Eysenck 1965), for instance, contains such 'lie' items as 'Have you ever been late for an appointment or work?' and 'Are all your habits good and desirable ones?' Answering in the angelic direction ('no' for the first and 'yes' for the second) on too many such items results in rejection from the study; the person may not have been lying but the result is considered unreliable. Chapter 14 raises the possibility that social desirability scores may reflect an underlying dimension of personality.

Diagnostic value of items

It is not necessary for every item to have intuitive 'face' value in assessing part of the quality being measured. An example is the 'meanness' item above. Items can have 'diagnostic' value in that, for whatever unknown reason, they do turn out to contribute to reliability or validity overall. It may be, for instance, that higher scores on boxing attitude tend to be related to some extent with the item 'I have participated quite a lot in sport'.

Organizing the items

To start organizing we should have developed a set of say 40 or 50 moderately positive and negative items which fit the criteria outlined above. Whereas items in an ability test would normally run from easy to hard, in an attitude scale, to avoid further acquiescence bias, it would be usual to arrange the items randomly.

Developing the scale

Steps to be followed now would be:

- pilot the initial items on a large sample representative of the intended population
- reverse appropriate items, score and find the total on all items for each participant
- conduct a reliability analysis (see Table 21.12)
- if not enough items remain, or if content or balance of positive and negative is now spoilt, add more items and repeat whole procedure so far
- when the test is reliable, conduct a validity test (see below)

Reliability and validity of psychological scale measures

Reliability

Any measure of anything needs to be reliable, else we wouldn't be able to trust it. It is no use if I buy an instrument to measure the charge of batteries and find that it gives me different readings for the same battery. This is a bit like the problems of reliability concerning psychological tests. The issue is one of consistency and there are several ways of measuring and dealing with what are known as internal and external reliability:

- **External reliability** is relatively simple to assess and refers to the tendency for the test to produce the same results with the same respondents on different occasions.
- **Internal reliability** refers to the extent to which the test is internally consistent. That is, to what extent does people's scoring in strength and direction on certain items compare with their scoring on other items in the test? In a sense, to what extent do the items show up contradictions? There are several ways of detecting the level of item comparability:
  - Split-half reliability calculates the correlation between two halves of a test where the items have been divided either into odds and evens or randomly.
  - Cronbach's alpha, in a sense, is an estimate of the average split-half reliability that would be found if the split-half procedure were carried out on all possible divisions of the items. In fact, its definition is that it is the correlation that would be found with an equivalent test, though this sounds

Table 21.12 Three methods for checking an initial item pool for reliability

1 Find the respondents with the top and bottom 25 per cent of total scores. For each item find the mean scored on that item by the top 25 per cent and by the bottom 25 per cent. The difference between means is the item's discriminative power (DP). Take items with the greatest DP.
2 For each item correlate the score of each participant on that item with their overall score. Items with the highest correlations show the greatest consistency with what participants scored overall.
3 Using a statistic package such as SPSS™, calculate Cronbach's α (see P. 702) for all the scale items except item 1. Then calculate α without item 2, without item 3 and so on. (In SPSS this is done instantly by checking a box entitled 'scale if item deleted'). Take out the item which would produce the greatest α if it were deleted from the scale. Then repeat the whole procedure on the remaining items, gradually reducing items and increasing reliability.

somewhat metaphysical. It is calculated from a simple formula involving the standard deviations of all total scores and scores on each item (see Rust and Golombok 1992).

- Item analysis, which investigates the level of discrimination of items (see Table 21.12) can be used in an attempt to improve overall reliability.

Validity

Along with expecting consistency from measuring instruments we also tend to desire appropriateness. In keeping with the earlier example, we expect a battery charge measure to assess charge and not, say, leakage or polarity. Likewise we expect psychological tests to assess the characteristic after which they are named. An anxiety measure should assess anxiety and not, say, liveliness. Here we hit a rather central and enormously important philosophical debating area within psychology. Can we assess such phenomena? How could we ever know we are measuring, say, 'authoritarianism' or 'political conservatism'? Are these real entities in the same way that we assume electrical charge or temperature are, or are they social constructions forever changing in the eye of the specific beholder? Whatever the questions and answers in that debate, there is nevertheless a long tradition of checking psychological measures for validity in the following ways:

- face validity: Does the measure hold clear relevance, especially in the view of the test-taker?
- content validity: Does the test contain breadth and depth which is appropriate as assessed by experts in the field?
- criterion validity: Is there some external criterion by which the test could be validated? Does it show differences between groups predicted to differ, e.g. smokers and non-smokers on a health attitude test? Does it agree with another, perhaps older, test of the same variable?
- construct validity: Does it tend to confirm hypotheses that follow from the theory surrounding and producing the test?

Standardization of tests

In order to create reliable and valid instruments of measurement which can be used across a population, scale constructors must try the test out on a large, **representative sample** of the intended target group (say, 4 to 7 year olds for a test of early self-esteem) and develop norms. These are simply cut-off points on the scale for different percentages of the population. The mean should divide the population in half and it will be useful to know what score is that which only 5 per cent or 10 per cent of children exceed and so on. If the test produces a non-symmetrical distribution, or differences between groups which are unacceptable (for instance, it would be odd to produce a prototype test of teenage morality on which young offenders scored higher than non-offenders), then the test constructors might conduct further reliability and validity tests in order to achieve a result in keeping with their theoretical predictions and measurement criteria.

ψ Section summary

Psychological tests or scales ('measures' in general) which attempt to assess human characteristics, particularly psychometric tests, tend to be based on a nomothetic assumption of a linear, bipolar dimension. Tests measure various characteristics (mostly intellectual, personality or attitude factors) for various research, welfare or organizational purposes. The vast majority of measures use a self-report approach and employ fixed response items,

Box continued

---

but open answers may be rated according to a scale which coders are trained to use. In general, scale items should discriminate among respondents, and should avoid formats (e.g. complexity or ambiguity) which will weaken or devalue the analysis of results. Questionnaires are subject to influence by several social variables, in particular, acquiescence and social desirability. Reliability and validity are particularly important in the area of test and scale construction and can be assessed in several ways. In order to become general measuring 'instruments', tests need to be standardized on large representative samples.

1 If possible get hold of any one volume of a mainstream psychology research journal (e.g. *British Journal of Psychology, Child Development*), go through each article and make a list of the measurement scales that have been mentioned or used in the report. In each case decide:

   (a) whether the measure is a 'mental test', a self-report measure or some other measure (such as a projective assessment)

   (b) exactly what psychological characteristic the measure attempts to assess

   (c) how you might get to use the measure if you wished to

2 Discuss ways in which psychological tests might be of benefit to society and also discuss technical and theoretical problems in their use.

❑ Observation

All scientists must make direct observations of the natural environment in order to investigate. Observations have often produced dramatic solutions to theoretical problems. Archimedes watched his bath water rise as his body displaced it and he cracked the problem of how to determine the volume of an awkwardly shaped object; Newton observed an apple fall and made a breakthrough in his theory of attraction between physical bodies. Or so we are told. There are no such dramatic stories in psychology but direct links have been proposed between the observations of ethologists, who generally study animals in their natural habitat, and theories of human behaviour such as those concerning infant attachment, aggressive instincts and even mating behaviour. The most famous of these ethologists would probably be Lorenz and Tinbergen, though Watson, strongly associated with laboratory conditioning experiments, was led to some of his ideas about association learning (as an explanation of the apparent 'intelligence' of animals) from naturalistic observation studies of the sooty tern.

In a sense, all humans are 'people watchers', but observation as a technique must rise above the use of common sense to produce data which can be trusted to possess a certain degree of validity and generality. What can observation tell us that other methods might not? Table 21.13 lists its advantages and disadvantages.

Although we always have to observe in order to gather data, the term 'observation', used in the description of a psychological study, usually means that, at the very least, observations are made of participants' freely chosen behaviour or speech over a specific period or when specific events occur.

Studies employing observation can vary from the experiment, in which one variable is assessed through observation, to studies in which researchers observe several people's behaviour in a natural setting over a very considerable period – even up to a year or more. An example of the former would be Bandura's studies (described e.g. pp. 455–9) where strictly guided observation was used to assess aggression in well-controlled

Table 21.13 Particular advantages and disadvantages of observation as a research method

Advantages	Disadvantages
does not rely on participant recall	behaviour is seen through the observer's perspective – selection and distortion
does not involve distortion through interaction with interviewer (except in participant observation)	reactivity if disclosed
can observe what the participant cannot – because events are too familiar to them	some (private; rare) events not open to observation
can research those who cannot answer questions – young children, animals	often costly and time-consuming
full, rich data source	problem of analysing qualitative data if treated quantitatively

experiments. Rosenhan's now famous study (1973) of psychiatric diagnosis and treatment of pseudo-patients reporting minimal symptoms would be an example of the latter approach. Once admitted to hospital, the research confederates in Rosenhan's study agreed to stay, observing staff behaviour among other things, until discharged through normal procedures. In one case this meant a stay of 52 days. A mixture of both quantitative and qualitative records were kept through note-taking and diary keeping. An interesting aspect of the method used in this study was the fact that the note-taking behaviour itself was, in at least one case, noted by staff as 'excessive'!

Observational studies vary in design along the four major dimensions shown in Figure 21.9.

Setting: contrived or natural

The psychologist's 'laboratory' is often not at all what the common use of this term would suggest. A 'laboratory' setting can include a meeting room, comfortable discussion room, playroom or any other kind of organized or simulated setting. The term 'laboratory' simply refers to the fact that the participant must come to the researcher's premises rather than being observed in 'naturalistic' circumstances. In the latter case participants are observed at work, at home or even in the street – wherever they would have been if the study had not taken place, and the study is one of naturalistic observation. Some contexts are hard to categorize. Bakeman and Brownlee (1980), for instance, set up a 'day camp' lasting three weeks for children taking part in a wider longitudinal study. This was in order to observe them each day in a 'natural' play environment.

It can always be argued that a natural setting would be more likely to produce natural behaviour but, as with the argument over artificiality of the experiment, there are times when the ecological difference can have only a faint effect, if any. A new-born baby is less likely to be bothered about familiarity of setting than a 3 year old, for instance. In the Bakeman and Brownlee study, the setting was naturalistic for the children – many children go to such day camps – but the environment was contrived by the researchers at their workplace. There are times when a researcher is prepared to sacrifice the advantages of observing behaviour in a natural context for the sake of gaining strict control over experimental variables, as in Bandura's case. It is also true, however, that much is lost in the laboratory. It is not hard to imagine that quite the mildest of young boys, given an adult to copy and a Bobo doll to hit (see p. 456), might assume that this is what the experimenter must want — and what fun anyway — whereas the same child, embedded in the social rules and taboos of family and playground, may not be tempted at all into aggressive mimicry.

Structure

Quantitative studies

Structured methods are used to produce quantitative data. The target of observation might be children's play patterns, their aggressive behaviour, or the interactions between sexes or between leaders and followers. The behaviour of the children may be categorized by coders, using an observation grid or checklist, or scored along some form of rating scale. This scoring may be carried out as the behaviour occurs or it may be recorded and analysed later. The strengths and weaknesses of either approach are similar to those for quantifying interview data and are listed in Table 21.13. What is important about structured approaches is that they employ a predetermined framework for recording observations and observers usually require training in the use of the system. Controlled observation, using a structured data gathering system, is often termed **systematic observation**. Such studies will be concerned with as high a degree of inter-observer reliability (see p. 678) as is possible.

Qualitative, ethological and ethnographic studies

At quite a different level from these sorts of study are those which do not predetermine their observation categories and leave the research process open so that a wide variety of data can be gathered for subsequent analysis. Very many of the studies at this level are 'participant observation' studies and in these more qualitative approaches, method and data analysis merge to some extent, so that there is not a clear divide between the processes of data gathering and data analysis. Early findings are considered, interpreted to some extent then acted upon in the form of further data gathering, often with a change of method or emphasis. Typically, the researcher lives or works in the observed setting, which could be a wo1rkplace, leisure or interest organization, street gang, family group or similar. The main possible levels of observer participation are listed in Figure 21.9.

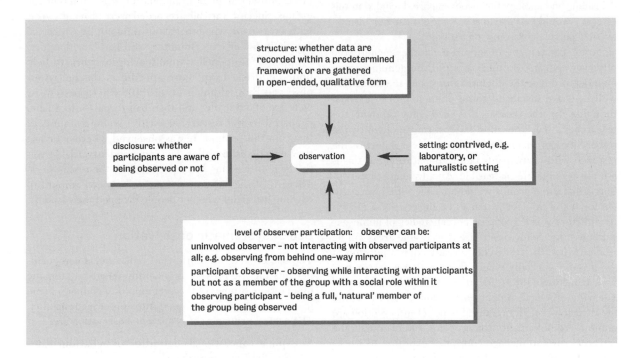

Figure 21.9 Dimensions of observational studies

Qualitative observational studies typically gather a huge amount of mainly qualitative field data; Rachel (1996) talks of 'reams of paper, miles of tape and stacks of photographs'. Observational data like these are usually coded and organized but not further quantified. The aim of the study is usually to give an account of 'life as it really is' in the observed context, and to extract meanings.

Disclosure

Though 'observer effects' are clearly avoided where people are not aware of being observed, such designs raise the ethical issue of informed consent to being a participant in a psychological study. It is difficult to draw a line indicating where the principle of informed consent has been breached. At one extreme it seems clear that observation of patterns of interaction in a shopping mall, where people are publicly going about their everyday business, do not require the consent of every person observed before collective data can be published. At the other extreme we have the person brought to a research institution and covertly filmed while performing a task. Roughly speaking though, wherever a researcher has intervened in the lives of ordinary citizens, and made some formal observations of consequent behaviour, it appears that consent to publish findings would be required, along with a thorough debriefing and apology for inconvenience. Included in this category would be Piliavin *et al.*'s (1969) use of a 'drunk' or 'sick' person 'collapsing' on a train.

Some participant observation studies, where the observer appears to others as a full and genuine group member, produce the dilemma that group members may well *not* have disclosed some of their more personal thoughts to the researcher, had they known the researcher's true role. Besides ensuring anonymity, the researcher can share the proposed public report of the research with participants before publication but this is not always possible or feasible. An advantage of deception is that some groups would not otherwise be accessible for research – for instance, Festinger *et al.*'s (1956) 'end-of-the-world' group or covert studies of homosexual behaviour. Some otherwise inaccessible areas can be studied when the researcher already holds a position in the group, especially where this position is an occupation. Holdaway (1983), for instance, used his position as a serving officer to report on the police culture within the British force. Here, ethical issues of intervention are minimal, confidentiality is a problem, and of course, the researcher has to manage continued exposure to workmates after disclosure of the research role!

A workable solution to the consent issue has been used by Ickes *et al.* (1990) and involves the observation of interaction between two innocent participants who believe they are waiting for the start of an experiment. Their interpersonal behaviour and conversation are recorded automatically but no one gets to see or hear any of the data until the participants have been debriefed and asked whether they would consent. If not, the tapes are destroyed in their presence.

Observing different sized units of behaviour

At the sharp end of contrived-structured studies there is only a narrow gap between 'observation' and mechanical recording. For instance, an observer might count the number of times a baby's head turns to the left but so might a sensor placed in the baby's pillow. (The sensor, though, would not notice greater vigour for some stimuli compared with others.) Precise and unambiguous recording of human behaviour has occurred, for instance, in Argyle's (1975) studies of interpersonal interaction where one key piece of coded behaviour has been amount and length of eye gaze or eye contact.

In a natural setting too, variables to be recorded can be very specifically defined. Green and Schneider (1974) observed altruism in children from different age groups. Specific variables recorded were sharing sweets with a classmate who otherwise would not have received any; helping an experimenter who had 'accidentally' dropped some pencils; volunteering to work to help poor children. Even more specific is the behaviour observed by Cialdini *et al.* (1990), where passers-by were handed a leaflet and then had to pass into a lane, prepared by the researchers with varying amounts of litter on the ground. It was observed whether or not they dropped the leaflet. The independent variable was the level of existing litter prepared by the researchers. There was a significant association between amount of existing litter and whether people dropped their leaflet.

Use of systematic observation

The use of strict definitions of behavioural categories permits the use of what is generally termed systematic observation. Studies of this sort employ a coding scheme in an attempt to achieve good inter-observer reliability. The central principles of systematic observation are:

- explicit (operational) definition of behaviour categories before data analysis

- training of data gatherers to reach agreement (observer reliability) on the same sequences of behaviour
- systematic and representative sampling of behaviour

In this approach specific hypotheses can be tested, each referring to a precise relationship between operationalized variables. However, Bakeman and Gottman (1986) point out that systematic observation studies need not start out with predefined codes and categories, nor even with known hypotheses to test. Initial stages of an observational research programme can be descriptive, with a focus on categories, and hypotheses emerging only after a search for order among gathered data. 'The wonderful thing about observational research is that it maximizes the possibility of being surprised' (Bakeman and Gottman 1986: 17).

Coding

An early example of a coding system is that of Parten (1932) who investigated the level of children's social interaction during play and established a classic view that play became more 'social' with increasing age. After several weeks of preliminary observation, Parten produced codes for clearly defined categories of play which were used in the rest of the study period. Part of the coding system is shown in Table 21.14. Once observers have been trained to use the scheme reliably, all they

need do, as they observe an individual child, is to note down the code number of the child's behaviour at the point of observation. In Parten's study the code recorded was that associated with the dominant play mode for the one minute per day, over an average of 70 days, when each child in the study was observed. The 'weights' permit conversion of the frequencies recorded to a scale of measurement, with a high score representing more socially oriented play.

Sequential analysis

Parten appeared to show that children moved through to more social stages of play as they grew older. However, in a fuller empirical test of this idea, P.K. Smith (1978) showed that children did not typically move through a transitory stage of parallel play on the way from alone play to group play. This was achieved using a much longer time frame and recording dominant play modes for each five weeks.

Bakeman and Gottman (1986) argue that important information is lost by simply observing what a child is doing at particular moments and summing the resulting frequencies. They emphasize an approach termed 'sequential analysis' in which the number of times a child is in a state of play is not as important as the nature and direction of transitions from one stage to another, some of which appear to be far more common. Bakeman and Brownlee (1980) had observers, unaware

Table 21.14 Parten's (1932) categories of play defined for systematic observation (extracts)

Code			Weight
3	Solitary independent play	The child plays alone and independently with toys that are different from those used by the children within speaking distance and makes no effort to get close to other children. He pursues his own activity without reference to what others are doing.*	−1
4	Parallel activity	The child plays independently, but the activity he chooses naturally brings him among other children. He plays with toys that are like those which the children around are using, but he plays with the toy as he sees fit, and does not try to influence or modify the activity of the children near him. He plays *beside* rather than *with* the other children. There is no attempt to control the coming or going of children in the group.	1
6	Co-operative or organized supplementary play	The child plays in a group that is organized for the purpose of making some material product, or of striving to attain some competitive goal, or of dramatizing situations of adult and group life, or of playing formal games. There is a marked sense of belonging or not belonging to the group. The control of the group situation is in the hands of one or two of the the members who direct the activity of the others. The goal . . . necessitates a division of labour.	3

Note: * As was common practice at the time, the writer uses the generic form of 'he/his' to represent both male and female children
Source: Parten (1932)

of the research hypothesis, categorize play states in each 15 seconds of play. They then claimed that the transition from parallel to group forms of play was more a matter of seconds than it was of years, in that parallel play was very often a precursor of some form of group play even for the 2½ to 3½ year olds they studied.

Developing a coding system

Systematic observation must be preceded by the development of a coding system. This stage requires painstaking attention to detail and can become very frustrating. However, the effort invested in the scheme is well worth the pay-off in terms of a clear path to analysis. It should not be the case that, having obtained data, the researcher is left with a difficult problem to solve about how to analyse them. In a systematic study, the final coding system which is used to categorize behaviour as it takes place, or as it is viewed in recorded form, should already determine how the data are to be analysed in general terms. If no permanent recording is made and the coding system is weak – too crude or omits important categories – then nothing can be done at the stage of analysis to save the situation.

For instance, to give a rather simple and obvious example, suppose it has been decided, in a study of disruptive classroom behaviour, to record the number of times each pupil leaves their seat during a session. It may be that by the end of data collection it becomes obvious that number of times out of seat will not necessarily discriminate between disruptive and non-disruptive pupils whereas time out of seat might well have done. It is now too late to record that information and a return visit may not be permitted.

Generally, when developing a coding system, it is best to work down a level from the behaviour of interest in the research question. For instance, if 'aggressive behaviour' is to be a category on which participants or groups are compared, then it is best to ask 'What sorts of action count as aggressive?' We might list, among other things:

- raising an arm (threatening a blow)
- hitting in fun
- hitting to obtain goal
- hitting as retaliation
- hitting with no obvious provocation or cause
- shouting
- swearing
- throwing an object (as part of a game)

The initial stage of developing a coding system will usually start out at a qualitative level of data collection. The researcher requiring a coding system for aggression in pre-school children, apart from studying the schemes used in past research studies, will need to observe children and can write a narrative account of what goes on, talk into a recording device and study video recordings in order to determine the sorts of behaviour patterns which occur. Later, these early observations will be refined into patterns and categories that can be recognized, after description and training, by any capable observer or coder, who would use a grid, part of which might appear like Table 21.15.

Behaviour sampling

Using this grid, observers would take an observation at the time intervals shown and tick the box(es) applying to that time and the child's behaviour at that moment or, say, during the next 15 seconds. This is known as time sampling. Event sampling occurs where specific events are sampled on a random or systematic basis. For instance, an organizational researcher might select a series of staff meetings to attend either from a calendar of meetings or from among a random selection of departments.

Table 21.15 Possible part of observation check sheet for child aggression in play

Child A	verbal insult	verbal threat	shouts	hits in fun	hits to obtain goal	hits to retaliate	hits (no cause)	throws	. . .	. . .
11.00										
11.05										
11.10										
11.15										
11.20										
. . .										

Problems with structured observation

The main problem with structured observation, certainly as seen from the qualitative researcher's eyes, is that, once the coding scheme has been set up and full observation initiated, only behaviour falling into the predefined categories can be obtained. Nothing new or novel can be included in the main body of findings. In addition, the producers of the behaviour have no say in its interpretation; this is done entirely by the coders and research report writer. We do not discover the meaning of events from the acting participants' point of view. Further problems are more simply technical. What if observer reliability turns out low? Do we trust the observations, abandon or start again, thereby wasting most of the original effort? Some of these points might appear to be answered by the use of participant observation.

Participant observation

The general criterion for a study being termed 'participant observation' is that the researcher somehow participates in the group which is the subject of investigation, as did Festinger in the end-of-the-world group (Festinger *et al.* 1956) and Rosenhan (1973) in the psychiatric ward. Observers in these two studies did make a lot of notes on what actually happened in front of them but 'participant observation' is actually a somewhat misleading title for this type of research in that the means of data generation in many studies is hardly 'observation'. Data gathered may include informal interview recordings, notes of events memorized from earlier in the day, reports of informal conversations, notes on other members' interactions and comments, printed matter, photographs, overall interpretations of 'atmosphere' and so on. Of the 250 odd studies reported in major publications since 1990 which mention the use of participant observation, the vast majority mention a combination of methods, many using in-depth interviews and some using survey questionnaires. An interesting finding is that an unexpectedly high number come from the applied, caring fields, in particular journals focusing on disability research.

Advantages of the method

The advantage of the observer being among the observed people is that little of relevance is missed; the researcher can discover and share the perspective of the group members and be fairly sure that genuine meanings

are recorded. The distortions and omissions of the structured interview, questionnaire or distant observation study are largely avoided. Participant observation studies, such as that described in part by Rachel (1996), use a conscious philosophy not to impose structure before data are gathered, for reasons already described. Rachel's ethnographic investigation attempted to track radical organizational change in a computer systems design office, focusing on the interrelationships between a 'Systems' team and a 'Change Management' team. She sums up tidily the role division inherent in any such participant study as follows:

The skill then becomes that of finding a way to . . . maintain oneself as a member of an academic community while opening oneself up to the possibilities that would follow from belonging to the community that one wants to study.

(Rachel 1996: 115)

A constructivist perspective

In many contemporary participant observation studies it is recognized that the researcher's presence is interactive and effective on the behaviour and perceptions of those around them. It is also argued that whatever is reported of the researcher's experience is a construction not 'the facts' as any observer might see them. This admission or claim about knowledge in general anticipates the positivist objection that, in such an open and flexible approach, there are problems of interpretation and reliability. It is difficult to see how another person could share the live perceptions of the observer, though, of course, they could help the observer organize and analyse the qualitative data produced at a later date, and serve as a check on unfettered speculation beyond the data available.

Problems with participant observation

The problem that uninformed group members might disclose information unwittingly was mentioned above as a disadvantage of disguised participant research. A further problem is the effect on the social science image of feelings of 'betrayal' upon the researcher's disclosure of his or her true role. Full participant observers are far more likely than other researchers to have a real effect on people's lives, particularly if the group is small. The researcher is also more likely to become completely immersed in the life of the group and therefore find it difficult to report on an impartial basis.

Data-gathering devices

At a more technical level, the more involved the researcher is with the real life of the group, the less opportunity there is for unhindered recording of data. Participant observers can create subterfuge for recording 'live' observations, such as:

- taking a formal role (e.g. secretary) in the group so that writing (at meetings for instance) is not a noteworthy occurrence
- using a little deception: Whyte (1984) told his street gang he was writing a book about the area
- relying on memory and writing up at the first opportunity; in a residential setting this could mean a long gap between observation and recording

Given M. Smith's (1988) finding (mentioned in Table 21.8) this last point is serious since many researchers undertaking on-site observation do rely on a certain lag between events and recordings.

Case studies

Each participant observation study is an example of **case study** research and this is not another method or technique but an overall approach to research. It involves the intensive study of one individual, group or organisation in their own natural environment, usually by a multiplicity of methods. Mostly, such studies generate qualitative data. An extremely powerful and influential argument was put forward by Bromley (1986: ix) who held that the case study is the 'bedrock of scientific investigation'. His argument is partly that, if you trace back any new development in science, you will find an intense and multifaceted study of a single phenomenon at the start of the history of that concept and its subsequent research (see Figure 21.10). This is a rather broad and philosophical debate which could have figured in the discussion of the nature of scientific research in general. However, what will be presented here is simply a guide to some classic case studies and the main features of the approach.

Despite the 'emergence' of qualitative methods and the accompanying philosophy of in-depth study, mainstream psychology already includes many case studies, some classic examples of which appear in the box. Although some are embedded in the traditional research paradigm, and some may employ quantitative data, they may all be seen as individual case studies with their major focus on qualitative data.

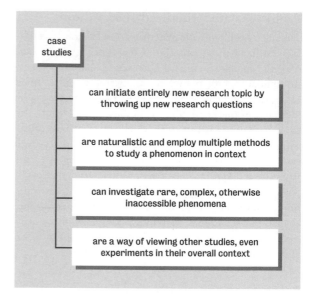

Figure 21.10 Features of case studies

An example of a case study which is often not seen as such would be that by Watson and Rayner (1920) where, infamously, 9-month-old 'Little Albert' was classically conditioned to develop a phobia towards a white rat. The great interest here is not particularly the number of trials and time taken to 'condition' Albert, though this was carefully recorded. It is in the record of *how* Albert responded, to what he responded and the complete catalogue of the case. These data, in qualitative form, comprise the main body of the research report. The study even makes use of multiple methods, in that it is written up as an experiment, yet there are detailed diary notes which consist of precise observations of Albert's reactions (Watson would have welcomed a film camera!) and at least one interview with Albert's mother. The complementary study by M.C. Jones (1924) on 'Little Peter' who was 'counterconditioned' out of a similar (but naturally occurring) phobia towards a rabbit, is equally rich as a qualitative account as well as being an 'experiment' on a single child.

Case studies have the usual strengths of qualitative research in that they gather data as accessible meaningful information, in large amounts, in depth and mostly directly from the person studied, or people concerned with them, in their own terms. They have the weakness that cases cannot be repeated and generalized from but that is not the purpose of conducting them. They may serve to counter a prevalent view — for instance, the

Some classic examples of case study research

Thigpen and Cleckley (1954)
Studied the multiple (three) personalities who emerged in psychotherapy with a psychiatric patient – serious 'Eve White' unaware of vivacious 'Eve Black', who scorned her, and balanced 'Jane', aware of both the others. The case is important because it details a case of a type about which many in the profession were sceptical (and still are, since almost all cases occur only in the USA: Aldridge-Morris 1989). The methods used include the therapeutic interviews in addition to psychological tests and EEG measures on the patient's brain waves patterns.

Gregory and Wallace (1963)
Produced a case study of SB – a patient who received a corneal graft to restore his sight at the age of 52. The story of his gradual recognition of objects familiar by touch is unique and fascinating, forcing rethinking of various assumptions about perceptual learning.

Luria (1968)
Studied a unique case of enormous memory capacity in Sherishevsky, a Russian journalist. Although many of the data comprise the journalist's amazing feats with recall of word and number lists over as long a period as 30 years, there is also a wealth of qualitative detail in Luria's work describing how Sherishevsky developed and maintained his techniques.

Koluchová (1976)
Studied the harrowing effects of severe deprivation on two identical twins, found at age 5, who made immense gains in the following two years. Similar cases reported

in Clarke and Clarke (1976) add weight to the argument that even serious deprivation does not necessarily have irreversible effects on development as 'critical period' theories would argue. The unique counter-example is extremely valuable.

Freud
All of Freud's evidence is qualitative and emergent from case study work, though he used only one overall method.

Festinger et al. (1956)
Participated as a disguised researcher and observed what occurred in a group who believed the world would end on a certain night. A good example of real and unique social events not amenable to research in any other way.

Rosenhan (1973)
Although the 'pseudo-patients' did keep quantitative records, such as number of contacts from nurses, doctors, and so on, they also kept diaries and these, when analysed, contain highly illuminative comments from patients and staff (see pp. 703–4).

Haney, Banks and Zimbardo (1973)
A role play simulation in which students played the parts of prisoners and guards in a highly realistic setting, including initial arrest and processing by real local police. Had to be ended after five days when planned to last two weeks. Produced wealth of insights recorded as qualitative data.

Clarke and Clarke examples in the case study. They may also serve to stimulate a great deal of further research in a variety of different ways.

Diary studies

Diary studies usually require participants to keep records of their behaviour, thoughts or emotions, or a similar record of people they are with constantly, very often their children. The approach can, like other observational techniques, vary from the highly structured to the relatively open ended. A mother might be trained to record specified incidents in her child's behaviour on a pre-structured sheet or to keep more qualitative notes on specified events. The latter approach was used by Zahn-Wexler et al. (1979) who asked mothers to record

- the reactions of her 1½–2½ year old child to the distress of other children
- her own reactions if her child had been the cause of that distress

This study showed that mothers of less compassionate children tended to punish with some form of physical reaction (hitting or moving away) whereas more compassionate children had mothers who tended to explain (forcefully) why the harm-doing was wrong, emphasizing the other child's feelings.

Some diary studies are referred to as 'participant observation' studies, not because the researcher is present but because the participants do the observing – of their children, for instance, or of their own behaviour. An example is Peterson *et al.* (1995) who asked mothers to log events where their child suffered injury (including minor cuts and bruises) and the sorts of advice and guidance for the future given by the mother as a consequence.

Archival data

A secondary form of observation is to obtain records of people's behaviour or characteristics through archives, that is, publicly available data on say, purchasing, types of dwelling, crime records, suicide rates, health visits and so on. Seaver's (1973) research (see p. 676) is a good example. Here, 'participants' were not required to do anything and no intervention occurred. Seaver simply used existing data on the pupils to establish support for a theoretical prediction of greater academic similarity between siblings taught by the same teacher.

A rich source of archival data can be the contents of popular magazines and these were used effectively by Etaugh (1980) and Etaugh *et al.* (1992) to map attitudes to non-maternal childcare in the USA over the period 1956 to 1977 and again from 1977 to 1990. The researchers conducted a content analysis of the magazine's contents, scoring authors' statements according to how positive or negative they were. They found that statements tended to increase in positive content up to 1977, but since then they have discovered a gradual increase in negative comment. They believe this trend tends to reflect the publishing of scientific research over the period, and a gradual disillusionment with earlier optimistic claims about the lack of negative effects from non-maternal childcare.

Ψ Section summary

Observational techniques can be used in a controlled setting or in the natural habitat of those observed, often termed naturalistic observation. The technique may be more or less structured, the former tending to generate quantitative data. Awareness of being observed has the potential to alter behaviour artificially. The researcher needs to consider the level of detail of observation, and also the importance of sequences of behaviour and of representative sampling. Systematic observation permits operational definitions and coding of behaviour for quantitative analysis and direct comparison with other similar studies. Some critics of structured approaches argue that we can only ever present a subjective construction of what we observe. An approach often used as an alternative is that of participant observation in which the observer is an interacting member of the group observed, though there are consequent problems of influence on data interpretation and of recording data in general.

Case studies involve in-depth study on one person or group, often using a variety of techniques but usually a combination of interviews and observations. In addition researchers may make use of diaries, either in their observation of others or as a means for participants to record their own experiences and behaviour. Archival data can be loosely considered observational and consist of publicly available records of human behaviour and statistics.

1   List and discuss the relative merits of and problems with naturalistic, unstructured observation and do the same for a structured, laboratory observation research design.

2   Preferably with a colleague, devise a system for observing the frequency with which males and females turn their bodies *towards* or *away from* another person when they have to make a close pass (e.g. through a narrow doorway or corridor). If possible set up a situation where you can carry out your observation, but be sure to create no intrusion or inconvenience to others. If possible, analyse your data using a *chi-squared* test of significance. Discuss the problems you encountered during observation with the criteria you had originally devised for counting a pass as 'towards' or 'away'.

☐ Significance testing

Wherever a research result has been reported in this book, for instance 'the experimental group recalled more words than the control group', you can be sure that the result has been tested and found 'significant'. This means it is just too unlikely that we could have drawn two groups so different at random from the same population: it is not a fortunate coincidence. To investigate this further let me attempt a little bit of telepathy. I thought very hard about a certain number when I wrote this page and I hope that, somehow, the image of the number has stayed with the page. In order for you to receive the image you need to think of a number according to the following rules:

- the number is between 1 and 50
- the number has two digits
- the two digits are not both the same (so 15 would count but 11 would not)
- the number doesn't begin or end evenly

Try hard to think of the number now. The number I actually thought of is printed at the foot of the next page.

This may have worked for you, perhaps not, but, if you belong to a class studying psychology, you should check with them and find out how many received my number. Let me just report that in a class I held recently, four out of ten students reported the number. Now is that good evidence of telepathic powers ... or just a coincidence?

This is really the heart of the problem of significance testing. We want some criterion by which to decide when an outcome is so unusual, were it merely a chance happening, that we would in fact reject the notion that it *is* coincidental (Figure 21.11).

Some coincidences mean a lot to us but, from the view of a cool-headed observer, they are no less likely to occur than many other chance happenings. For instance, we meet an old friend quite by chance in a marketplace and say 'Well that's amazing! I was only thinking about you the other day. What are you doing here?' We need to ask (if we're cool-headed and not bothered about losing the romance attached to enjoyable coincidences):

- How often do you think of that friend anyway?
- How many old friends could this have happened with?
- Just how remote or unlikely is the spot you've met them in?

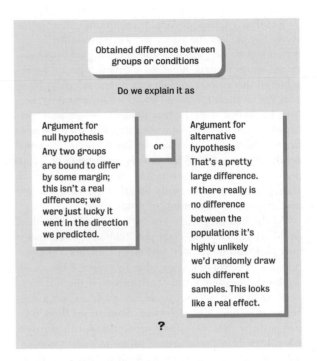

Figure 21.11 The significance dilemma

Probability

First of all let us tackle one of the problems we have here – that of calculating some value for probability of events occurring. We cannot do that for the meeting-a-friend coincidence because there are just too many unknowns and too many interacting variables. There are simple situations where we know our chances. For instance, where the job is to select the queen from among three cards, mixed up by a street gambler, we know our chances of being correct and winning some money are one in three. In probability terms this is written as a fraction '$\frac{1}{3}$' or as a decimal '0.33'. The reason we know this is that we employ, perhaps not too consciously, a general equation for calculating probability where we know the necessary quantities:

$$\text{Probability} = p = \frac{\text{number of events that count}}{\text{total possible number of events}}$$

Used for throwing two dice, the probability of a 2 and a 3 is $\frac{2}{36}$ (0.06) since the 2 (or the 3) can come up on either of the two dice. That is, there are just two ways that 2 and 3 can be a result, out of the 36 possible results.

Returning to my students then, the situation is relatively simple. At the time, we were investigating the notions of theory and hypothesis testing and we knew there were several possible explanations of how I achieved the 'success' of four out of ten, telepathy being only one of these (perhaps I could see their writing, perhaps I colluded with the four students beforehand, perhaps I simply guessed and was lucky). However, we must first establish whether or not we should count the actual result as 'successful'. What was the probability of it happening if I was only guessing? In social science research terms, we can say precisely whether the result would have counted as 'significant' or not.

As the box on parapsychology shows, each student could select from only eight possibilities. It's easy to see now that, had there been just eight students, then getting one 'hit' would be just what to expect if they were randomly guessing. From ten students, if the test were performed over and over again, we might expect a little better than one 'hit' each time. Sometimes there'd be two perhaps even three, but *four*, on the specific occasion when I tried the performance, seems to make 'guessing' quite an unlikely explanation. What in fact is the likelihood that four students would *guess* my number?

If ten students are each selecting one of eight numbers, there are just:

$8 \times 8 \times 8 \times 8 \times 8 \times 8 \times 8 \times 8 \times 8 \times 8 = 1{,}073{,}741{,}824$ possible outcomes!

This figure goes on the bottom of the probability equation. On top go the number of ways we can arrange the outcomes so that any four students choose the same number while the rest choose any of the remaining numbers. You'll have to trust my calculation for that but I make the number 55,050,240. So the likelihood of four students out of ten choosing my number by chance alone was:

$$\frac{55050240}{1073741824} = 0.051$$

This means there was about a one in twenty chance that four students would choose my number. But remember, I had to choose the number in the first place. I would not normally enter a class to perform a trick, designed for the specific purpose of education, of illuminating a tricky concept, if I knew I had only a one in twenty chance of success! Hence, probably there *is* something going on here and the box explains just what. You can try this trick on a fairly large group (say twenty or more) and be pretty confident of a good outcome.

The null hypothesis

In the telepathy example it was found necessary to find some sort of baseline against which to compare the apparently unusual or unexpected outcome in the classroom. We chose to compare what actually happened

---

Parapsychology, telepathy, or just faith in numbers?

If we ask people to select a number where:

- the number is between 1 and 50
- the number has two digits
- the two digits are not both the same (so 15 would count but 11 would not)
- the number doesn't begin or end evenly

then only eight numbers: **13 15 17 19 31 35 37 39** are possible.

When stage 'telepathists' or magicians perform the trick they often add a certain embellishment. Typically they would try to 'send', write down the sent number, then screw that paper up because 'I wasn't concentrating properly there. Let's start again . . .' The number they would then 'send' and write down would be 37. After finding that perhaps 40% of the audience had thought of

37 they would reveal that their imperfect 'send' used the number 35. Why? Of the eight possible numbers it has been found that 37, then 35, are the most popular. (Perhaps you, as reader, thought of 35 rather than 37?) Notice that 15 is really ruled out since it was used as an example when giving the rules. You can increase your chances of success by giving a further example for the second rule ('e.g. 31 rather than 9'). Notice too that in giving the first improperly 'sent' number the telepathist immediately doubles the possible number of results that would fit the hypothesis that they have telepathic power – that is if the audience are gullible enough to accept this bit of cheating. Funnily enough, this little digression is rarely questioned when discussing the result with classes. Anyway, people like to be entertained!

Number transmitted was 37

with what would have been expected to happen if all students were selecting their number on a random basis. This notion of comparing a special sample with what could be expected as a random sample is what forms the basis of significance testing. In all significance testing the 'baseline' takes the form of the null hypothesis – it is the hypothesis of no difference, no effect or random variation only. If someone wishes to claim that a found difference is real, and not just coincidence, we say, in effect, 'well, if you want to dismiss the idea of mere coincidence let's find the probability of that event occurring as mere coincidence'. Suppose the found difference is that a sample of nurses have higher stress levels than a sample of clerical workers. Is this a reflection of a real difference in the two populations or is the difference just the product of random sampling differences – we just happened to obtain some rather stressed nurses in our sample? The null hypothesis takes this latter view and claims statistically that the two population means are in fact equal. An implication of this is that any differences found between samples drawn from these two populations are a result of the sampling strategy or of inconsistency in the procedure used with each group.

Significance: comparing results with the null hypothesis

Suppose your tutor comes into the room with a box full of raffle tickets numbered 1 to 100, verified by you and your class colleagues and all fully shuffled about. The tutor writes down a number on the board and then asks you to put your hand into the box, blindfolded, and pull out any ticket. Lo and behold you select the very number which is on the board. Only a tutor who is also a very good magician would attempt this trick since, *if* the selection is truly random, he or she would get a successful 'hit' only once in every 100 classes! Notice this big emphasized '*if*'. We will use it several times in what follows. The reason we are impressed in this case is that we know that *if* the null hypothesis is true – that the selection was random – the probability of obtaining the result was $1/100$ or $p = 0.01$.

The probability value calculated in simple significance tests is

the probability of obtaining the tested result IF the null hypothesis is true

and a low probability indicates significance itself in social science research. Notice that the logic of the argument is first to assume that the null hypothesis is true, then to calculate the probability of the result occurring *if* it is

true, then to reject the null hypothesis if this probability is small enough. It just remains to decide what would be 'small enough'. α ('alpha') is the symbol used to represent the level of probability at which we decide to reject or accept our null hypothesis.

Setting a level of alpha (α)

In most psychological research (indeed, in most social science) the set level at which we reject or accept a null hypothesis is:

$\alpha = 0.05$

If we are testing a difference between two data sets, what this means is that,

when the probability of the difference occurring falls below $p = 0.05$, *if* the null hypothesis is true, we reject that null hypothesis.

The null hypothesis will usually be that the data were drawn at random from similar or identical populations. If we calculate the probability of our difference happening, *if* this null hypothesis is true, and find p is under 0.05, we would usually reject the null hypothesis.

For example, and returning now to psychological cases, suppose psychologists believe a child is particularly advanced for their age in reading. The child is given a reading test for which we know the population mean and distribution – see Figure 21.12. We find the child's reading score is well above the mean but we want to know whether it is *significantly* above the mean. To do this we argue from the null hypothesis that the child's score was taken at random from the normal population and then calculate the probability of finding a score so high if this is true. Let's say the data are as shown in Table 21.16.

Usually we do not know the population mean and we have *groups* of scores to compare, rather than just one child's. In those very common cases in research work we need to use an inferential statistical test to calculate the probability that found differences between groups

Table 21.16 Testing a score for significance

1	population mean for individual children on the reading test	= 50
2	child's score is	= 68
3	probability of obtaining a score as high as 68 drawing at random from the normal population of reading scores	= 0.02
4	0.02 is less than the set α of 0.05	
5	hence we reject the *null hypothesis* that the child's score is randomly drawn from the normal population	

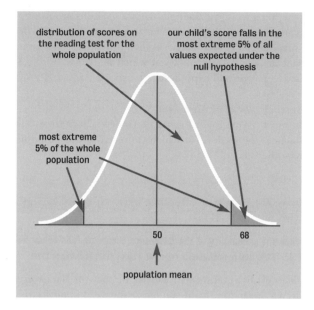

distribution of scores on the reading test for the whole population

our child's score falls in the most extreme 5% of all values expected under the null hypothesis

most extreme 5% of the whole population

50   68

population mean

Figure 21.12 Testing a score for significance

would occur under the null hypothesis. Significance testing is likely to be an important part of your psychology course and there are many texts which might be recommended, for instance Clegg (1982); Coolican (1994, 1996: methods *and* statistics); Greene and d'Oliveira (1982); Howell (1992: more advanced).

All you need to be assured of here, however, is that there are procedures for calculating this kind of probability and that, where the calculated probability for an outcome falls below 0.05, if the null hypothesis were true, we reject the null hypothesis and assume we have a genuine effect.

From this point on we depart from the statistics and set about interpreting what the effect might be. For instance, in the case of the 'telepathy' demonstration, we accept that the students' choice was not completely random. What, then, were the forces at work creating the effect? As I said earlier, there are the possibilities that I primed several students, that I could see what they were writing, that my observable behaviour somehow gave away the number I was thinking of (this assumes they wish to 'please the experimenter') or, as is the case, I exploited known facts about number preferences. It is obvious that the statistical test tells us nothing about reasons *why* an effect occurred. All it does is to tell us that the difference found was a relatively unlikely one.

Type I and type II errors and the role of replication

But not *that* unlikely! The conventional level of 0.05 is quite generous. It means, for instance, that a clinic claiming to be able to help couples have a baby of their preferred sex would need to be successful only nine times in ten trials to have obtained a 'significant' result. Alternatively, if you manipulated twenty completely arbitrary independent variables, for no good reason whatsoever (such as the effect of eating asparagus on dart throwing accuracy), you would expect to get one 'significant' result. That is, every now and then, using an alpha as high as 0.05, researchers will reject a null hypothesis when it is correct, simply because they have obtained that odd coincidence. This is known as making a type 1 error. Of course, it could also be that an effect is rather weak and our testing procedures fail to distinguish what happened from what would be expected to happen under the null hypothesis. This typically happens where samples are too small. Here we would fail to reject the null hypothesis when it is false; we fail to detect a real effect and this is known as making a type 2 error.

A guard against type 1 error is, of course, to have other researchers replicate the investigation, in as identical a manner as is possible, and to see whether they obtain similar results. Partial replication may also reveal effects which were missed as a type 2 error, though this would often include altering the sample size or subtly altering the values or qualities of the independent variables.

Where there is a need to be particularly careful in accepting results as significant, α might be set at 0.01. This might occur where the result would be contrary to previous well-established findings, where health and safety are dependent upon the results (medical trials) or where the researcher is unlikely to be able to replicate the study (e.g. a rare natural circumstance).

Retaining the null hypothesis

If we fail to obtain a significant result must we accept the null hypothesis as the correct state of affairs? What if we have made a type 2 error? Researchers do not 'accept' a null hypothesis as the truth when they retain it. They simply accept that it remains unchallenged. A null hypothesis is often only an idealized concept. Who could believe that the population of nurses have an absolutely identical mean stress score to that of the population of all clerical workers? The aim of most research studies is to gain support for the **alternative hypothesis** (that there *is* a meaningful population difference or correlation) by demonstrating how unlikely results were to occur if the null hypothesis is true. The likelihood of avoiding type 2 error is known as the 'power' of the statistical procedures employed and this power depends directly upon sample size if all else (alpha and the research design) is held constant.

Ψ Section summary

Good theories clearly predict differences or relationships between variables. When any two samples are taken and tested on the variables, random fluctuations will occur even where there is no real underlying difference. Significance testing is a procedure for deciding whether a found difference is to be taken, at least temporarily, as a reflection of a real difference or as explicable by mere random variation. The theoretical null hypothesis claims no difference at all between variables for the population. A statistical significance test gives the probability of a found difference occurring at random if the null hypothesis is in fact true. Where this probability is below 0.05, differences are termed 'significant' and the alternative hypothesis is accepted as supporting the tested theory. If p is greater than 0.05 the null hypothesis is provisionally retained. Replication guards against type 1 errors – those that occur when a null hypothesis is wrongly retained – and type II errors, where the null hypothesis is wrongly retained. Significance may sometimes be claimed at a probability of 0.01 where researchers need to be very sure of their results.

1 Write out the exact null hypothesis for the three research scenarios listed as questions a, b and c on p. 686–7.

2 What is wrong with the following statements?
   (a) The mean recall score for students who had taken coffee was significantly higher than the mean recall score for students who had not taken coffee ($p<0.5$). Therefore, coffee improves recall.
   (b) The mean recall score for students who had taken coffee was significantly higher than the mean recall score for students who had not taken coffee ($p<0.1$).
   (c) Females did not score significantly higher than males on the reading test. Therefore the null hypothesis that male and female reading skills are equal is true.

☐ Sampling

The sample used in a research investigation is of crucial importance. However, in many student practical reports it is the section paid perhaps the least attention, yet the sample used is central to notions of psychology as a science. Where the sample taken is an 'opportunity sample', as is the case with a very large number of research studies, the characteristics of the sample may well have a lot to do with explaining some of the features of the data obtained. On the other hand, the student researcher should not become overanxious when it is found that a research sample cannot possibly be representative of, or randomly selected from, a wide population. A large proportion of UK and US studies have used undergraduate students as their participants – probably more than 75 per cent (Valentine 1992).

Samples and populations

In psychological research the term population does not always refer to a geographical population such as that of a country. It refers theoretically to all members of a category and here are some possible populations of interest to researchers:

- all female computer programmers
- all possible scores obtainable on a standard 60 angle Muller-Lyer illusion with specified dimensions
- all pupils at Trotsbury Upper School
- all science students at Trotsbury College whose fees are paid by their local council

Note that some populations are infinite and are not necessarily, or even usually, composed of people. The scores on the Muller-Lyer illusion can be obtained from anyone – perhaps the same person many times and not necessarily everyone in the population whatever that might be (the college, the county). Others are quite finite and manageable, such as all pupils at a certain school. To talk of all computer programmers or nurses as a finite population, though, is again rather hypothetical since it would take forever to track every last one down and, by the time this was done, others would have left and joined the profession no doubt. Very often, we take a sample because we cannot feasibly measure a certain characteristic in all members of a population. Where an entire population *is* measured or assessed this group is referred to as a cohort. Data are collected from almost every member of the country's population during a census.

A sample is a group selected from among the members of a population. Unless every person were identical to every other person (in which case samples of one would always be adequate) we know that where we take a sample from a population, it will never perfectly represent the population. However, what we usually want is to be able to make some sort of generalization about the population as a whole, using our sample as representative of it.

Generalization may not be crucial

In some circumstances, particularly within more qualitative forms of research, we may not require our sample to be closely representative of any larger population. What might be required instead is a sample of experts or a sample who will give the fullest picture and most salient detail on the topic under research. For instance, to obtain a fuller understanding of the perspectives of war veterans, a researcher might interview those with a unique experience and those who can recall details particularly well. A random sample in this case is not necessary, might be hard to contact and might indeed provide only superficial accounts.

Samples and generalization

An example of invalid generalization

Not so long ago some students carried out a mini-project designed only to give them the experience of constructing a questionnaire and discovering the consequent problems. When they presented their results to the rest of the class they confidently claimed to have shown that northerners (in the UK) were less racist than southerners. This was based on several reactions to questions about stereotyping in popular jokes and on two samples – eight participants from the north of the UK and six from the south, the latter being spread from Cornwall in the south-west to London in the east.

Fortunately the class receiving the presentation were quick to point out that the conclusion was based on extremely flimsy evidence. Even if we take only those old enough to understand the issue, the students were generalizing from a sample of six to more than 15 million of England's 47 million people.

Although the assumptions here were clearly unfounded the effects of other assumptions, based on

equally flimsy evidence, are sometimes harder to dispel. In the wallet study (p. 669) the samples used are similarly minimal. The comparison made about honesty, between Cardiff and Glasgow for instance, is based on ten people from each city, whereas those cities each contain around half a million people. Though this research was not reported in a serious academic journal it was discussed in the national press.

Sampling bias and sampling error

The projects just described use samples where it would be easy for results to be affected by certain types of people entering the samples. Just one racist in the former, or two dishonest rogues in the latter will substantially affect the results and therefore any generalizations made from them. Earlier we discussed 'selection bias' of participants into conditions. Here, for a whole sample, we talk of **sampling bias**, a disproportionate representation of certain characteristics or types of people in our overall 'pool' of people selected for research. When you considered the driver behaviour research, you might have noted that observations taken at 3–4 p.m. would catch the school run while both times avoid rush hour, evenings and weekends. Clearly some groups of drivers are excluded from the research.

A newspaper report compared the performance of 1,000 British adults with similar samples from several other countries on twelve mental arithmetic problems. The British sample came out worst. This news might prompt you to investigate the performance of students at your college on these problems. You cannot test them all, but a good sample should give you a reasonable estimate. However, if you went to the canteen at 10.30 and this happened to be the time when all the maths students were free, you might happen to acquire a large number of maths students in your sample. The mean score on the problems could then be well above the real mean for all students and your estimate from this biased sample would be inflated. Your investigation would suffer from **sampling error**, a difference between sample statistics and the same values for the whole population.

Taking unbiased samples

Unbiased samples are required for two major reasons:

- We are testing a hypothesis. Where we do not have a statistic (such as the mean or standard deviation)

Plate 21.2 A sampling bias occurs when driver behaviour is observed between 3 and 4 p.m., as this would catch the school run and avoid rush hour. This would clearly exclude some groups of drivers

for a whole population we may use sample statistics to estimate these values. The true values of these statistics, for the whole population, are known as population parameters. Testing for significant differences entails assumptions about population parameters estimated from samples so these samples must be unbiased.

- We are attempting to establish population scores on some measure (say, a reading ability test) for a general category of people (say, all 7 year olds).

It is important to note that most sampling worries are for these statistical reasons, not because we want to be able to generalize directly from observed behaviour to the world outside the testing situation (see the arguments from Leary on p. 685).

Avoiding sampling bias in practice

There are several techniques employed for attempting to ensure that samples drawn are as unbiased as is possible.

What size sample?

Where we aim to make estimates of underlying populations, the rule is 'the larger the better'. There will be less error in taking the mean of a large sample to be an accurate estimate of the population mean than if we take a smaller sample. We can demonstrate with a simple concrete example of estimating the mean salary of people on a particular housing estate (see Figure 21.13). Let us suppose the top three wage earners receive £500, £490 and £480 per week. The next set of wages is a group of five people each earning £450 per week. The overall mean for the estate, however, is £250. As Figure 21.13 shows, if we sample from this population taking only three people at a time it is possible to obtain a sample containing just the top three wage earners and derive a mean of £490 for the estate – quite a distorted estimate of the population mean. If, however, we take samples of eight, this outcome is not possible and the highest mean we could possibly obtain is £465 (having selected the top eight cases). For $N = 15$ the highest sample mean would be £357. As our chosen size of sample grows larger so the limits of how wrong we could be grow narrower until, of course, we get perfect accuracy by selecting the entire population.

If you were to take samples of thirty, many times over, from the residents of this housing estate, and if you were to plot the value of the sample mean each time, you would obtain a distribution looking something like the blue line in Figure 21.14. On the other hand, if you did this with samples of eight, your distribution would look more like that shown by the white line. When you conduct significance tests the calculations depend upon estimates of sampling error. As Figure 21.14 shows, *far*

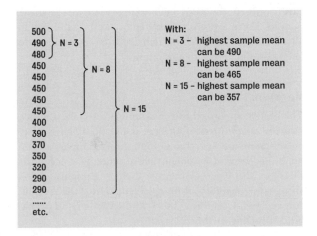

Figure 21.13 Means of different size samples of salaries

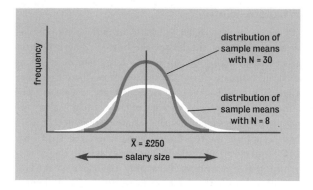

Figure 21.14 Likely distributions of sample means for different size samples

more error can occur when using small samples, since it is possible to obtain means much further away from the true mean compared with the use of larger samples.

It is impossible to say what is the ideal or minimum sample size in any research study. We need to know various parameters of the proposed design. As a rough guide though, if your experimental design is extremely tight, and there is little room for the influence of randomly acting extraneous variables, it is possible to use about ten participants in each condition, but this really is a minimum for the ideal, strictly controlled design. In the average project investigating, for instance, male–female differences on some attitude or personality characteristic, you would be well advised to look for samples of at least thirty, if not more.

Avoiding bias in limited samples

Although larger samples will always give us a fairer picture of a population attitude or characteristic we can rarely afford the time and expense to assess many people. There are several strategies, well established in social science research, which are used in attempts to keep sampling error to a minimum.

Random samples

The best way to avoid bias in sampling is to take a simple random sample from the target population. This is a circular statement since the definition of a simple random sample is just that it contains no selection bias. It follows therefore that every element in the target population has an equal probability of being selected into the sample. Any technique achieving this is known as an equal probability sampling method ('epsem').

Random is not haphazard or 'just anyone'

Many students write that their sample was 'randomly selected'. In fact, research samples are very rarely selected at random. To do so is extremely difficult, even from a captive population such as the members of a college. Methods for doing this would involve having a complete list of *all* students at the college; do part-time evening students count, or those currently enrolled but on a long period of absence? Next a method must be chosen which selects from this list completely at random. A lottery approach is adequate though a more likely approach is to have a computer extract the names.

Problems now would be first, successfully contacting the person with each name produced and second, obtaining permission from each person contacted. In a longer-term study **participant attrition** (losing participants) can have a biasing effect on results since those who remain may differ in some way from those departed. Cox *et al.* (1977), for instance, found that children with severe adjustment problems tended to be over-represented among drop-outs from research on adjustment.

Systematic (random) samples

A slightly easier 'systematic' method is to select every *n*th person (say every fifth) on the list. If this number *n* is itself initially selected at random then the method is still 'epsem'.

Stratified sampling

If the year contains major, minor and elective students a researcher might decide to take samples from within these groups according to the proportion within each group. So, let's say 15 majors, 10 minors and 5 electives because there are 150, 100 and 50 of these respectively in the whole population. Again, if these samples are taken at random within the sub-groups the technique is epsem.

It is not possible to take every conceivable stratum into account in a stratified sampling approach. What strata to concentrate on will depend very much upon the nature of the study. Being a major or a minor will probably be irrelevant in a study of student attitudes to course fees, whereas the establishment of norms for an 8 year old reading test certainly should take at least gender, ethnicity and socio-economic status into account and perhaps a lot more.

Cluster sampling

A course year of, say, 300 psychology students might be divided into fifteen seminar groups. It might be argued that each of these is relatively representative of the whole year. A researcher might randomly select three of these in order to generate views on the course and this is still an epsem. Very often however, clusters are not chosen randomly and are not equally representative.

Non-probability sampling: convenience/ opportunity/haphazard samples

The sort of sample most often used in or by psychology practical classes is best described as 'haphazard' ('we went to the canteen and just picked anybody'), 'opportunity' ('we used the class members') or 'convenience' ('we used friends and acquaintances') with no great distinction between the last two. Psychological research is very often performed on volunteers and these are very often psychology students! We know that volunteers may differ in psychological make-up from the norm. One should be up-front about this. What is essential, in reporting practical work, is that the sampling procedure *is* described. Everyone knows it is extremely hard to get balanced samples and virtually impossible to obtain random ones. However, an attempt can be made and those attempts carefully reported.

Ψ Section summary

In statistical terms a population is a theoretical and often infinite set of possible scores from which samples are taken. When, as in survey work, an actual population of people is referred to it is important to specify exactly which population is the subject of the research investigation. It is also important to describe exactly what sampling procedure was employed since results may not be generalized easily from unrepresentative samples and such samples will also invalidate statistical tests of significance. Sampling bias is therefore a source of confounding. Researchers usually try to obtain representative samples and a popular method of avoiding bias is to use an equal probability sampling method where every target population member has an exactly

Box continued

equal probability of being selected. Such an ideal is difficult to achieve in practice and several other methods for obtaining equal probability samples, or at least fairly representative samples, are available.

1 When might a random sample probably not be a representative sample and how could a sample be representative, even though it is not drawn completely at random?

2 Explain exactly why sampling bias is a problem to research psychologists, giving several reasons and offering some ways to avoid such biases.

❏ Qualitative approaches in psychology

There has been growing debate since the 1970s, but particularly prominent in the 1990s, about the extent to which psychological research, in using quantification and the hypothetico-deductive approach, has mimicked the natural sciences to the detriment of furthering knowledge. As we shall see, psychology uses the experiment, the laboratory, quantification of variables and the language of natural science. Some would argue that the discipline was mere superstition and mystical conjecture until it did so, and that it could not have amassed the wealth of theory, findings and respectability that it has, without the objectivity and common communication of a classical scientific approach.

Others now argue that the emphasis on positivism, quantification and a rigid hypothesis-testing framework has seriously limited the developments which psychology can make in producing realistic theory and findings applicable to everyday human experience. There is no single qualitative position. Tesch (1990) listed 26 identifiable varieties, some of these now quite opposed to one another. However, there is general common agreement among these theorists about things that are fundamentally wrong with what they sometimes term the 'old paradigm' – relative to the 'new paradigm' approaches – the latter term made popular by Reason and Rowan (1981). Although this *is* a crude division, in this chapter we shall use the term **qualitative approach** to represent an emphasis on qualitative data collection and a rejection of what we shall term the **conventional (scientific) paradigm**.

Quantitative and qualitative data

The initial form of raw data gathered by psychologists is very often qualitative rather than quantitative (see Table 21.17). Data can be, for instance, answers to interview questions, a list of words recalled in a memory experiment, solutions to problems, videotaped sequences of behaviour, field notes, choices on a questionnaire and so on. The distinctive moment comes when a decision is made on what to do with the gathered data. In quantitative research the method of quantification and analysis would usually be clear well before data gathering is started. Usually the aim is to demonstrate predicted relationships among data, and therefore data are passed through a kind of numerical 'filter' (Figure 21.15) in order to provide hypothesis-testing evidence. The qualitative researcher would argue that it is at this point that most meaningful information is lost, leaving behind only a fragment of what is most useful and interesting about human experience and relationships.

Numbers and words

Here is an illuminative statement from the first page of a popular text on qualitative data analysis:

words, especially organized into incidents or stories, have a concrete, vivid meaningful flavor that often proves far more convincing to a reader ... than pages of summarized numbers.

(Miles and Huberman 1994: 1)

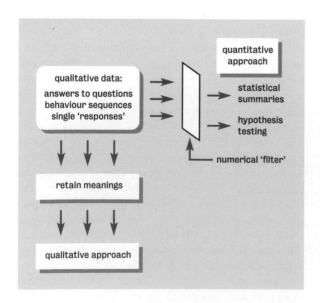

Figure 21.15 Data and quantitative or qualitative approaches

This, for the quantitative researcher, is often just the problem. A colourful convincing story might well have strong effect, even when it is far from the truth. Statistics play a strong role in counter-arguments. Take for instance the very colourful and, unfortunately, often very convincing speeches of racist politicians. When a 'panic' is caused, as it periodically is, about the numbers and nature of UK 'immigrants' (often a euphemism for 'black people'), it is very important indeed to make cool reference to figures: in the UK just 5 per cent of the population is black, 70 per cent of immigrants are white and black people make significantly less proportional claim on welfare services and council housing.

Principles not practice

The use of qualitative data in psychological research is not new. There will be many studies described in this book which report a good deal of qualitative information (see box on p. 710). However, the qualitative–quantitative issue is not mainly about which data are appropriate for which sort of research study. Deep ideological disagreements entail that quantitative and qualitative approaches do not always coexist comfortably: see Table 21.18, especially the fourth point. The debate can be highly charged and emotive. Whereas standard research methods textbooks rarely start by justifying the position they rest upon (the hypothetico-deductive method and some level of positivism), the increasing number of qualitative methods texts, even if they carry some 'how to do it' content, are mostly heavy with polemical argument against the 'old paradigm' and in justification of the use of non-numerical data collection and analysis. Table 21.19 summarizes the contrasting principles. Let us now review the main arguments against the conventional paradigm.

Arguments against the conventional scientific paradigm

The need for numbers camouflages richness of meaning

To test a hypothesis about people's attitudes to physical punishment we apply a measurement 'scale' and each respondent eventually receives a single number score on that scale. These scores are then tested for differences, correlated or otherwise numerically summarized. However, a number along a singular dimension cannot represent the depth and variety of people's feelings. The quantitative researcher would argue that preparatory

Table 21.17 Quantitative and qualitative data

Quantitative data	numerical data such as	<ul><li>time in seconds</li><li>score on a psychology test</li><li>number of people dropping litter</li><li>number of times baby turns head to right</li></ul>
Qualitative data	non-numerical data, mostly in the form of meanings	<ul><li>what people say</li><li>pictorial e.g. graffiti</li><li>content of stories, songs, myths</li><li>uncategorized, unedited recordings of behaviour</li></ul>

Table 21.18 Positions in the qualitative–quantitative debate

- **No qualitative data**
  Extreme positivists who argue that there *is* an absolute truth, all psychological variables can be measured and that what cannot be measured is awaiting discovery or not worthy of or susceptible to scientific investigation. Without quantitative measures we can have no grounds for assessing the validity of findings.

- **Qualitative data convert to quantitative data**
  Qualitative data can and must be quantified before analysis using methods such as content analysis which codes and categorizes data so they can be dealt with at a frequency level or better (if rated).

- **Qualitative data can support quantitative findings**
  Initial interviews produce ideas for stricter measures; interviews and observations provide qualitative ideas to expand and amplify basic quantitative findings. Examples of these processes are found in the Asch (1956) and Milgram (1963) studies: interviews tell us *why* people conformed or obeyed (quantitative data tell us how many and how often); but also, interviews give us ideas for fresh testing – what would happen if we made the initial conformity study decision private? What if we move the 'victim' closer to the participant?

- **Qualitative and quantitative methods – equal but different**
  Some argue that use of method simply depends upon the type of research question – a position termed 'technical' by Bryman (1988) and the position supported by Watts (1992), but not by many qualitative researchers. This idea was also expressed by Strauss and Corbin (1990) who advocate the grounded theory approach. Whereas Strauss and Corbin feel the value of quantitative method is limited, there is an opposite tendency of the traditional paradigm to accept qualitative data and methods only as a substitute for a thorough experimental approach where the latter is ('unfortunately') not possible (Henwood and Pidgeon 1996). Most qualitative researchers will include statistical data where it might be appropriate. Few obsessively avoid them. But there is more than just a 'technical' issue involved in the choice of a qualitative approach. Many qualitative researchers make their decision on ideological grounds, moved by the arguments listed above.

- **Qualitative methods only**
  This is the other extreme on the dimension - the more political and ideological position; it can be held on the basis that resort to 'enemy weapons' leads to corruption; or the objectors just have no time for numbers. Feminist researchers, in particular, have argued that positivism and the hypothetico-deductive method are inherently sexist – 'masculinist' or 'masculine science' - promoting a power-subject relationship, unhealthy distancing from the object of study and a consequent distorted view of one version of reality (Tavris 1993; Ussher 1992).

research should canvass all possible views which are then encompassed by the final questionnaire. However, qualitative researchers argue that each person's view is rich and unique and that numbers are a huge reduction from this richness of meaning.

Sterile theory

It is argued (e.g. Henwood and Pigeon 1995) that, because the conventional model expects each research project to test precise hypotheses derived from background theory, the result is plenty of very precise but

Table 21.19 Contrasting principles of quantitative and qualitative approaches

Quantitative	Qualitative
hypothetico–deductive method – research study tests hypothesis to support theory	inductive analysis – open-ended data gathering and analysis; patterns emerge *from* data; theories developed (and tested) *during* research study
reductionism – we can identify 'factors' of human psychological characteristics	holism – person can be treated only as a whole, otherwise essential meaning is lost
positivism – psychological variables exist and can be measured, though 'instruments', as yet, may be crude or non-existent	constructivism; relativism – it is unrealistic to attempt the measurement of such 'variables' as self-esteem since the concept is constructed in social interaction; it has no independent existence
knowledge – facts gained from the world	knowledge – social construction
significance testing - decides whether 'effect' becomes accepted as real/useful	data gathering and analysis not separated but are parts of a cyclical process
research on 'subjects' who are a sample from the population; they are not experts and could not contribute to the research design; they enter when this is carefully set up	research with participants – the participant is part of the entire research social context; they broaden the knowledge base and contribute to theory; they can even collaborate in research design
structure and control – elimination of extraneous variables	flexibility – look for all possible contributory information
numbers – numerical quantities representing variables and in principle separable from all other variables	human meanings in social contexts – analysis keeps data close to their meaning as produced by the original source
laboratory or somewhat controlled environment – general emphasis on this although field studies and naturalistic observation are common	naturalistic – behaviour observed out of social context is meaningless
reliability – tests (see p. 678)	reliability – no overall qualitative agreement. An example from Mason (1966) is that the data gathering should be 'thorough, careful, honest and accurate' though 'correct' is rejected as a 'quantitative term'
validity – tests (see p. 678)	validity (see box p. 727)

exceedingly narrow research results with only a very 'thin' relationship to the original idea. New and exploratory theory making is thus inhibited. As an example, consider the rather broad theory that people actively seek information which is useful, rather than simply exposing themselves to information they agree with and avoiding 'dissonant' information. Cited as evidence for this by Secord and Backman (1974) is a study by Maccoby *et al.* (1961) in which it was shown that women were more likely to accept and read an offered pamphlet on toilet training if they had children in the appropriate age bracket! The need for testable hypotheses, it is argued, leads to such obvious and trivial results. A counter-argument is that many studies with apparently 'obvious' outcomes (Milgram 1963 is a clear example) produce completely counter-intuitive and surprising results.

Predetermined structure determines results and theory

If we decide what we are going to ask or observe, before we have gained information about what people actually think and believe, then we are superimposing existing theory on any possible outcome from the research. A highly structured coding and categorizing system loses sight of the wholeness of the individual, their flow of behaviour or the full impact and context of freely produced speech.

Social context of research

There is a long critique of the experimental situation based on the argument that the psychology laboratory situation, though presented as coolly scientific, is nevertheless a social interaction between thinking people. Variables such as participant expectancy, non-naïveté, social desirability and hypothesis guessing have been seen as 'nuisance variables' in the past, getting between the researcher and 'fact'. However, they are the inevitable consequence of asking someone to do something special for you. The term 'demand characteristics' refers to the participant's basically human characteristic of thinking about their environment, questioning and constantly trying to make sense of the world.

Role of the researcher

The scientific model requires that the investigator remains cool, distant from the 'subject matter', emotionally uninvolved and objective, lest emotional feeling overcomes pure reason. However, is this the most effective way of knowing people? The 'scientific' relationship models specific roles in society generally, namely those of powerful expert and naïve subject, and this was precisely what Milgram (1963) exploited so successfully in his famous studies. The word 'subject' is indeed commonly used (for human equally as for rat) and signifies the passive, reactive model of humans which the qualitative researcher claims is unrealistic. The British Psychological Society currently advocates use of the term 'participant' to indicate involvement in the research process.

Reductionism (vs holism)

In traditional laboratory research, people, mostly parts of them (e.g. their memory, intelligence or self-esteem), are isolated from their social context; their powers to plan and act as normal are severely limited yet results are used to make broad generalizations about the same psychological process (e.g. memory; group formation; bystander intervention) outside the experimental laboratory. Qualitative approaches tend to treat the individual as an integrated whole (a 'holistic' approach) within a social context.

Superficial information

Reducing variables to the precisely measurable often has the effect of making research variables a pallid, thin representation of their real-world counterparts. Consider, for instance, the Brown-Peterson (see Peterson and Peterson 1959) technique where participants are asked to look at three letters (a meaningless 'trigram'), then count backwards in threes for a certain period (to prevent rehearsal) and to repeat this procedure many times over. This bears virtually no relationship at all to everyday memory events. True, the artificiality of the experimental laboratory can be strongly argued for (see p. 685) but even a traditional (and influential) cognitive researcher, Ulric Neisser, was driven to say:

The results of a hundred years of the psychological study of memory are somewhat discouraging. We have established firm empirical generalisations but most of them are so obvious that every ten-year old knows them anyway. . . . If X is an interesting or socially significant aspect of memory, then psychologists have hardly ever studied X.

(Neisser 1978: 4–5)

Mystique and language of science

It is argued that treating psychology as a science creates a mystique and a language of control (terms such as 'contamination', 'control of variables', 'experimental manipulation' and so on). Reports are dense, 'treatment' of human 'subjects' sounds mechanical, and terms used seem purposely designed to avoid their everyday equivalents which mean exactly the same thing. 'Non-systematic subject mortality', for instance, means 'people haphazardly leaving a study'. It has to be said though, that the unwary learner, looking to conduct some form of qualitative research project, will encounter an equally baffling set of obscure, complex terms and concepts as an introduction to most of the variety of qualitative alternatives being discussed in the literature in contemporary psychological debate.

The naturalistic fallacy

What is known as a relativist or constructionist view of knowledge argues that 'facts' are just not 'out there' for us to 'gather' or 'uncover'. On this view, a person's attitude to hanging just does not pre-exist as, might say, a piece of coal. An attitude is a dynamic construct, constantly in flux and, as it were, 'reconstructed' each time the issue is broached, depending upon the social context. We need only question how we express our views on a deeply felt issue dependent upon the people we are with. We can commiserate and strengthen our view, or 'soften' our view under pressure from opponents or with those whom we wish to 'convert'. Either way, is there a pre-existing concrete, fixed 'view' just waiting to be measured by a research psychologist?

Research update

Some contemporary forms of qualitative approach

Grounded theory

See Glaser and Strauss (1967: original theory) and Strauss and Corbin (1990) for a 'hands on' approach. The strategy is imported from sociology. It advocates research with no prior commitment to expectations. Theory 'emerges' from repeated sampling of qualitative data from 'local' circumstances in their social context, i.e. people are consulted in their everyday world, as interacting within it, and 'grand' theories are de-emphasized. Data stay close to participants' phenomenological accounts (how *they* see it). Researcher attempts to extract and (co-) construct participants' meanings.

Action research

An old term now revived (Lewin 1946). See Elliott (1980) for work in schools. Research necessarily impacts on participants' normal lives but action research recognizes this up front and is used where some form of social change is envisaged. The basic idea is to effect social change at a modest level and observe consequent changes, often in the search for effective change procedures or techniques. It is very much tied to applied psychological work (e.g. that of educational, industrial or health psychologists). The techniques employed might be quite conventional (questionnaire survey, semi-structured interview). The context is commonly participative (participants are engaged in the design and execution of research), collaborative (psychologist is seen as a consultant; participants do their own research) or evaluation research (testing the effectiveness of social change programmes).

Ethnography

See Hammersley and Atkinson (1993). An approach used more extensively within anthropology and sociology. It concentrates on field research of and within the lifestyle of the social group of interest, for example, football 'hooligans' (Marsh *et al.* 1978), football fans, women at work, a drug 'sub-culture', a small and identifiable ethnic group, people with a particular 'identity' – tragedy survivors, or cults, such as the Moonies (see Barker 1984).

The approach is multi-method and is strongly associated with intensive participant observation. The

account and data interpretation should be a faithful representation of the ways in which people make sense of and explain their everyday world. It recognizes the effect of the researcher's role and attempts to understand this. it also recognizes that no researcher can claim prior neutrality to gender, race and class.

Feminist research

As with all the above approaches, any method might be employed but feminist principles relate closely to those of most qualitative approaches. The early approach concentrated on the exposure of male bias in theory and research – 'neutral' measures which favour males, unchallenged 'natural' assumptions about women, omission of a female perspective in supposedly 'neutral' psychological models and, of course, disparity between men and women in the psychological profession, as elsewhere. A later contrast was a kind of 'separatist' position where women reject 'masculine' science, and construct their own psychology and methods. A tension here has occurred in the recognition that female experience is not universal and that there are cross-categories such as race and class. The distinction is now less clear with several 'relativist' or 'post-modern' positions emerging. However, in general research tends to be action-oriented with interventions aimed at some measure of increased awareness and, ultimately, a world free of male, or perhaps any, oppression.

Discourse analysis

See Edwards and Potter (1992) for a readily accessible account or Potter (1996). Believes that discourse constructs our social world. Focuses on what people *do* with their talk and the social actions performed with speech. Emphasizes particularly the 'stake' which people have in a conversation and which they construct to deal with issues such as accountability, responsibility, blame. Socially, people create an 'interpretive repertoire', a sort of mutual 'common sense' version of the world which works and serves a purpose for them (e.g. racist formulations). When people 'memorize' we do not then have items which we can use as evidence for inner cognitive processes – as the cognitive psychologist would claim - we have a 'version' of reality serving a social purpose.

Leaving it open-ended?

The quantitative–qualitative debate is a fascinating one to watch. It is a 'live' debate, by which I mean, if you read current psychology textbooks, pick up the publications through which psychologists communicate (such as *The Psychologist*, the regular bulletin of the British Psychological Society) or if you were able to listen in on everyday conversations and meetings in psychology departments, it would not be long before you came across the issues (see the research update). Academics debate the criteria for marking qualitative assignments or perhaps resist having the issues raised on their courses. Currently the examining boards for pre-degree psychology are beginning to include qualitative methods or data as terms on their syllabuses. There is a current mini-boom in texts on qualitative methods and approaches.

It is rather early to predict whether the development of an emphasis on qualitative approaches constitutes anything like a Kuhnian 'paradigm threat' or 'revolution', as some enthusiastic devotees have often claimed, but there is much talk of a 'crisis' in psychology on the qualitative side (see J.A. Smith *et al.* 1995b).

Qualitative methods are not a 'soft option'

One point is worth making very strongly – a qualitative approach is not a 'soft option' for the student who does not care for statistics. The point just made was that much of the reading around qualitative issues can be heavy going. A further point is that there is a lot of it about and there is a wide variation in method and argument. On a practical level, the prospective qualitative researcher must recognize that most qualitative data gathering or creation takes place over a relatively lengthy period. Having said this, it is also true that a qualitative approach will always be satisfying in that the final analysis will deal with a rich data set comprising full thoughts and accounts, the reality of people's lives. In some circumstances it would appear to be the only approach possible (see p. 710). The difficulty is in developing skills of analysis which rise above everyday 'common sense' or well-executed journalism.

Achieving validity in qualitative research

Obviously researchers worry, when they reject in principle the relative security of statistical analysis, that others will not accept their accounts and interpretations. Qualitative researchers believe very strongly that their methods present a more valid, more realistic, even more dignified approach to studying people. Nevertheless they have realized that not all 'anti-positivists' (for want of a better collective term) see 'truth' or 'valid account' in at all the same philosophical way. They realize too that the more powerful conventional paradigm has prominence and its members will need convincing of the authenticity of data not presented in the form of significance testing or other mathematical analysis. This is certainly true when a researcher makes the following sort of comment

I felt it was right to trust my new intuitions, while being unable in any empiricist way to point to exact 'proof' in field notes that my ideas were sound.

(Okely 1994: 32)

a comment which, apart from apparently conflating 'empiricist' with 'empirical', demonstrates a misunderstanding of the role of 'proof' in science.

In fact, there has been much debate on the pressing problems of establishing validity and reliability across the disparate 'schools' of qualitative research (see Mason 1996: ch. 7; J.A. Smith 1996). The following are a set of criteria which occur most frequently in several writings on the issue of achieving validity in qualitative research:

- trustworthiness and genuineness – of data sources, author's methods and writing
- triangulation –assess from various points of view or with a variety of methods
- respondent validation – check that the people investigated recognize the interpretations in the final report (though some writers say this is not realistic where participants are unfamiliar with the discipline)
- peer agreement – with interpretations
- independent audit – Yin (1989) suggests others should be able to follow the trail of data to the same conclusion
- internal coherence – internal consistency of the data*
- reflexivity – does the researcher self-reflect upon data collection biases and reasoning processes which lead to interpretations (see Woolgar 1988)?

*Note that, in questionnaire construction, 'internal consistency' defines *internal reliability* rather than validity.

Ψ Section summary

Qualitative data have been gathered for many years in psychological research but the term 'qualitative approach' now usually carries with it some implication of dissatisfaction with a purely quantitative approach. Qualitative researchers have produced a strong critique of the conventional, mainly quantitative, scientific hypothesis-testing paradigm, though there is a wide range of differing methodological and philosophical views among qualitative researchers themselves. Central to the critique are the views that quantitative analysis ignores or trivializes a rich source of individual meanings; hypothesis testing inhibits the generation of new theory; the scientific model of the natural sciences is inappropriate for the study of human social interaction, treating 'subjects' as non-reactive responders, and individual constructions of behaviour as 'fact'; the laboratory experiment in particular creates artificial phenomena through a pseudo-technical mystique and a power relationship between researcher and researched. The main concerns about qualitative approaches have been the apparent loss of systematic rigour, comparability of data and checks on reliability of findings. The debate on qualitative approaches is one of the most vigorous and cutting edge issues in present-day psychological research.

1 Make a list of the reasons why the conventional quantitative psychological research approach has received criticism in recent years. For each criticism try to create the argument which a quantitative researcher might produce in defence.

2 Weigh up the advantages and disadvantages of using a participant observation approach to the study of stress within an organization compared with the use of a questionnaire approach. What strengths does each method have and what problems?

Ψ Chapter summary

● Science and psychology

For the most part psychological research follows the conventional scientific method of data collection and hypothesis testing, though there are several well-voiced contemporary objections to this approach, generally gathered under the heading of 'qualitative approaches'.

● General problems in research with people

There are several threats to internal and external validity in conducting psychological research, in particular in designing strictly controlled experiments. Sources of error and bias can come from participants' expectations, concerns and their attempts to understand what is going on in the social context of an experimental study, particularly in the laboratory.

● Methods of psychological researchers

Studies in the field, as opposed to in the laboratory, suffer from less control over extraneous variables but are more closely related to natural and realistic human behaviour in an everyday setting. There are various experimental designs, concerning the allocation of participants to conditions, and each has certain weaknesses and compensating strengths.

● Studies using correlations and group comparisons

Correlation is a measure of the relationship between two variables and can be positive or inverse. Group comparisons can be longitudinal or cross-sectional.

● Interviews and observation

Interviews and observation can vary from being strictly controlled and tightly structured (suffering from some artificiality and limits on possible data col-lection) to being more flexible and open to a rich data set (but suffering from reduced reliability and validity in some senses).

● Questionnaires and surveys

Questionnaires and surveys are largely quantitative approaches and certain types are seen by psychometrists as measurement instruments requiring a systematic and intensive cycle of adjustment in order to achieve good reliability, validity and standardization.

● Significance testing

A statistical significance test gives the probability of a found difference between two variables occurring at random if the null hypothesis is true.

● Sampling

Sampling is central to the aims of a research study and needs careful attention. Very few studies can be representative of a wide population. The target population needs to be borne in mind and the sampling method used should always be clearly communicated, so that limits of generalization can be appreciated.

● Qualitative approaches in psychology

Qualitative researchers generally reject the rigidity and narrowness in variable terms of quantitative methods, preferring to gather data which keep human meanings in social contexts. They criticize the researcher–participant relationship, and the formality of laboratory experiments on the grounds that they produce quite distorted and unrepresentative behaviour. They tend to stay close to meanings provided by research participants and to analyse in terms of themes, accounts and emergent theories. To some extent the two approaches can complement one another but there are also ideological difference in some debates.

Further reading

● Breakwell, G.M., Hammond, S. and Fife-Schaw, C. (1995) *Research Methods in Psychology*. London: Sage. Separate chapters from experts in their field on many aspects of modern psychological research approaches. Doesn't include statistics but covers concepts of significance testing.

● Clegg, F. (1982) *Simple Statistics*. Cambridge: Cambridge University Press. A long-standing friendly approach to the statistical methods used in analysis of psychological data, written by an author who admits she struggled with statistics as taught by mathematical experts. She resolved to produce an accessible text and succeeded.

● Coolican, H. (1994) *Research Methods and Statistics in Psychology*, 2nd edn. London: Hodder and Stoughton. Comprehensive coverage of a broad range of quantitative and qualitative methods, along with a user-friendly, hands-on guide to most statistical techniques taught in the first two years of most undergraduate courses.

● Richardson, J.T.E. (ed.) (1996) *Handbook of Qualitative Research Methods for Psychology and the Social Sciences*. Leicester: BPS Books. A set of edited chapters covering the qualitative–quantitative debate, and the critique of mainstream, 'old paradigm' research methods, written by mainly UK-based authors.

● Robson, C. (1993) *Real World Research*. Oxford: Blackwell. Covers well what its title suggests. Describes methods for field research and includes coverage of the more mainstream qualitative methods used in contemporary social and applied psychological research, along with conventional experimental designs, interviewing, questionnaires and observations.

● Smith, J.A., Harré, R. and Langenhove, L.V. (1995) *Rethinking Methods in Psychology*. London: Sage. Excellent and accessible edited articles on the current state of play in the qualitative–quantitative debate, and the critique of mainstream, 'old paradigm' research methods.

Glossary

AAI: see Adult Attachment Interview

accommodation: a cue to depth based on the changing curvature of the eye

achromatopsia: blindness just for colour

acquiescence response set: tendency to respond 'yes' to questionnaire items regardless of their content; also known as **response acquiescence set**

acquired dyslexia: impaired reading ability in adults caused by brain damage

acquired immune deficiency syndrome: see **Aids**

action-oriented therapies: therapies which emphasize the learning and application of skills

action potential: a rapid pulse of electricity in a neuron; this constitutes the means of communication of information within neurons

action process: an action unfolds via setting goals, orienting in the environment, developing plans, monitoring the execution of the action and receiving feedback

action readiness: a concept introduced by Frijda (1986) as the central functional aspect of **emotions**; it refers to the role of emotions in preparing the system to act in some way

action training: a training technique based on active individuals, developing an idea (**mental model**) of the action to be learnt and feedback

activity theory: the view that **health** and life satisfaction are maintained through continuing social activity and involvement in old age, and that any decrease tends to be brought about by societal discrimination

acuity: a measure of the ability to resolve fine detail

adaptation: a decrease in response of a **neuron** following a period of continuous stimulation

addiction: dependence on a drug to the extent that stopping causes withdrawal symptoms

adherence: the degree to which an individual follows health or illness related advice

adhocracy: organization without a set of rules developed when needed

adiposity: fatness

adipsia: lack of drinking

adolescence: transition from childhood to adulthood; the teenage years; see **puberty**

adolescent growth spurt: the sudden acceleration in height and weight gain around **puberty**, after a period of steady physical growth through middle childhood, and before levelling off toward adult height

Adult Attachment Interview (AAI): an assessment of how adults represent their own experiences of being parented; see **internal working models**

affect: the state of mental feeling, ranging from positive (e.g. elation) to negative (e.g. **depression**); a generic term used to include **emotions**, **moods** and emotional dispositions

affordance: in Gibson's theory, directly perceivable uses of an object

afterimages: visual sensations persisting after exposure to a visual stimulus

ageism: discrimination against older people; negative stereotypes of elderly people and the ageing process

agonist: a chemical added to the body, which attaches to **receptors** and mimics the action of a natural **transmitter**

agrammatism: a condition found in brain-damaged patients, in which there is poor sentence construction and omission of function words and word endings

Aids (acquired immune deficiency syndrome): infectious disease caused by the human immunodeficiency virus (HIV) which attacks the immune system

akinesia: lack of voluntary movement

algorithmic methods: specific procedures (e.g. those used in mathematics) which are guaranteed to produce correct solutions if applied properly; see **heuristic methods**

alternative hypothesis: **hypothesis** which a researcher sets out to support, usually claiming a difference or correlation between **variables**; see **null hypothesis**

amnesia: a condition in which there is severe impairment of long-term memory (especially for **declarative knowledge**) but with little or no effect on short-term memory; see **anterograde amnesia** and **retrograde amnesia**

amygdala: an almond-shaped part of the **limbic system** of the brain, implicated in **emotions** since the early twentieth century

anal retentive character: a type of adult **personality** characterized by meanness, orderliness and stubbornness

anal stage: a stage of psychosexual development centred on the anal region, lasting between 18 and 36 months of age

analytical introspection: a method of **self-report** in which individuals focus on specified aspects of their personal experience

anarthria: a condition in which the systems controlling the speech musculature are damaged but most language abilities remain intact

anhedonia: a loss of the ability to feel pleasure

anomia: a condition found in brain-damaged patients in which there is impaired naming of objects and pictures of objects

ANS: see **autonomic nervous system**

antagonist: a chemical added to the body, which attaches to **receptors** and opposes the action of a natural **transmitter**

anterograde amnesia: impaired ability to store and remember information presented after the onset of **amnesia**; see **retrograde amnesia**

anticipatory socialization: a phase of developing expectations about the job

aphagia: lack of eating

aphasia: a condition found in brain-damaged patients in which there is impaired speech production

appraisal: the evaluation of an event according to a number of dimensions; cognitive theories of **emotion** argue that the pattern of appraisal determines which emotion is produced by the event

approach coping style: a tendency to approach, focus upon or even maximize the significance of a stressful event

arousal: a state of being physiologically alert; it involves the activation of the sympathetic nervous system, the body prepared for action

arousal-interpretation theory: an idea proposed by Schachter and Singer (1962) that **emotions** are the result of cognitive interpretations of undifferentiated physiological arousal

arthritis: inflammation of a joint; joints of the body are found at the knees, wrists, elbows, fingers, toes, hips and shoulders; symptoms of chronic arthritis are pain, swelling and deformity in one or more joints; see **rheumatoid arthritis**

assertive training: programmes which offer people help in appropriately standing up for themselves

assessment centre: a selection procedure that is based on observing people's behaviour in tasks thought to be important in their future jobs

associative activity: children interact together at an activity, doing similar things

asthma: a chronic respiratory disorder characterized by intermittent breathing difficulties caused by a spasm of the muscles of the bronchial tube in response to irritants such as an infection, allergy, cold air or cigarette smoke

attachment: preferential approach or proximity-maintaining behaviour to certain person(s)

attachment style: a classification of the patterns of interaction between children and their caregivers into secure, avoiding or ambivalent on the basis of their performance on Ainsworth's **strange situation** test

attention: generally used to refer to the selection of certain stimuli rather than others for further processing; see **divided attention** and **focused attention**

attitude: a favourable or unfavourable stable orientation towards an object

attitude object: entities towards which one can respond positively or negatively

autokinetic effect: a perceptual illusion whereby the light appears to move about erratically in the absence of a stable reference point

automatic processes: processes which are fast, do not use processing capacity, are not accessible to conscious awareness, and are unavoidable

automaticity of actions: very little conscious attention needed to do an action

autonomic nervous system (ANS): that part of the nervous system that is responsible for effecting action on the internal environment of the body; it does so via muscles (e.g. heart muscle) and through glands (e.g. salivary glands)

autonomous work group: the work group is allowed to make all necessary decisions on who does which work, where and how long

availability heuristic: a rule of thumb in which judgements about the frequencies of various events are determined by the ease with which relevant examples can be accessed in memory

avoidant coping style: a tendency to avoid, ignore, deny or minimize the significance of a threatful event

axon: a part of a **neuron** consisting of a long extension

base-rate information: the numbers of people or events in the **population** being considered who fall into various categories

basic cognitive interview: an approach to questioning eyewitnesses based on the findings from memory research (e.g. **encoding specificity principle**); see **enhanced cognitive interview**

basic emotions: a small set of core or fundamental **emotions**; most researchers agree that the list includes happiness, sadness, anger, fear and disgust; see **complex emotion**

basic level category: the intermediate level category which is of more general usefulness than the more abstract higher level category or the more specific lower level category

behaviour genetics: the study of genetic influences on behaviour, characteristically by twin and adoption studies

behaviour modelling: a specific training technique based on presenting a model and role play

behaviour therapy: an approach to clinical treatment based on the conditioning principles contained within **behaviourism**

behavioural compliance: acting in the ways expected by others, though not consistent with one's **attitudes** or beliefs; see **compliance**

behaviourism: an approach to psychology which emphasized the importance of studying behaviour in an objective fashion

belief bias: the tendency in syllogistic reasoning to accept believable conclusions and to reject unbelievable conclusions regardless of their actual validity

belonging: a condition in which a person feels part of a socially harmonious community

binocular cues: cues to depth which require the use of both eyes; see **monocular cues**

biomedical model: the viewpoint that disease is primarily caused and determined by biological factors and bodily processes

bipolar depression: see **manic depression**

blindsight: vision without conscious awareness

blood pressure: the force of the blood in the vessels

bottom-up processing: processing of a stimulus which is determined entirely by aspects of the stimulus itself; see **top-down processing**

buffering hypothesis: this hypothesis focuses on psychological **variables** which act as a 'buffer' to protect people against the negative consequences of **stress**

bullying: persistent aggressive behaviour carried out by one child, or a **group**, usually repeated against a particular victim who cannot retaliate effectively

cancer: malignant tumour; a group of diseases characterized by the uncontrolled growth of abnormal cells

cannula: a tube

cardiac rehabilitation: intervention programme designed to restore the patient's level of functioning before the cardiac incident (from a physical, psychological, social and economical point of view) and to prevent progression of the cardiac disease

cardiovascular diseases: diseases of the heart and blood vessels

case study: study of one particular individual, event or organization, usually in some depth

castration anxiety: fear in boys that their father will cut off their penis

catecholamine hypothesis: the idea that depression is the result of reduced activity of certain neurotransmitters of the catecholamine family

categorical clustering: the tendency to recall categorized word lists category by category

categorical perception: allocating slightly different sounds in speech to the same **phoneme**

category prototype: the attributes and characteristics definitive or diagnostic of a social category, see **self-stereotyping**

caudal: towards the tail of an animal; see **rostral**

causal attributions: the process by which one attributes an event or an effect to particular causes

causal explanation: an explanation in terms of the here-and-now events that immediately precede behaviour

causal schema: an implicit theory of how certain causes are likely to interact to produce a specific result

central nervous system (CNS): the brain and spinal cord; see **peripheral nervous system**

central tendency: using only the middle and not the extremes of an **appraisal** instrument

cerebral cortex: the brain's outer layer

charisma: originally meant a gift of god; the ability of a leader to exercise diffuse and intense influence over the beliefs, values, behaviour and performance of others

chemoreceptor: a **receptor** that is sensitive to the presence of a particular chemical and plays a role in the initiation of taste and smell

chemosensors: **receptors** for chemical signals such as glucose concentration

chronic illness: long continued illness, mostly irreversible

chunks: meaningful units of information

classical conditioning: the learning of an association between a stimulus and a rewarding or punishing **unconditioned stimulus**; e.g. learning an association between the sight and taste of food or other biologically significant stimuli; sometimes called Pavlovian conditioning; see **operant conditioning**

client-centred therapy: a form of therapy developed by Carl Rogers, in which the therapist is very encouraging so as to promote the personal development of the client

CNS: see **central nervous system**

cognitive behaviour therapy: intervention strategy based on learning theory to change cognitions and related behav-

iours which are associated with a deviant target behaviour (in this context the target behaviour can be smoking, alcohol abuse, food intake, reckless driving, etc.)

cognitive dissonance: when someone simultaneously holds two cognitions (e.g. beliefs or **attitudes**) that are psychologically inconsistent; a theory based on the assumption that individuals strive to achieve consistency within their cognititons

cognitive neuropsychology: an approach to understanding human cognition based on the study of the patterns of impairment shown by brain-damaged patients

cognitive restructuring: modifying cognitions (e.g. by monitoring **self-talk**) which play a mediating role between the **stressor** and stress reactions

cognitive science: the approach to studying human cognition based on computer simulations

cognitive therapy: a form of clinical treatment based on altering irrational thoughts and beliefs

cognitive triad: in Beck's cognitive model, it refers to the depressed person's negative outlook on the world, the self and the future

cohort: a group of people who share a common trait or experience, such as being the same age

collaborative empiricism: in cognitive therapy, it refers to the process of therapist and client agreeing goals and testing out ideas

collective action: where a **group** member engages in collective action any time that he or she is acting as a representative of the group and the action is directed at improving the conditions of the entire group; see **group-mind theory**

colour contrast: a perceptual effect in which the perceived differences in colour of two adjacent objects are exaggerated

common factors: factors potentially shared by all therapies, such as patient expectations and therapist qualities

comparative fit: a principle of **self-categorization** theory which refers to the match between category and the comparative properties of the stimuli; see **normative fit**

complex emotion: an **emotion** which is an elaboration of a **basic emotion**, often involving the self or social/interpersonal components

compliance: the individual behaves in line with **group** obligations to attain a favourable reaction from its agents, either for approval and reward, or to avoid punishment; in a **health** context, adherence to medical advice; see **behavioural compliance** and **obedience**

conceptually driven processes: processes started by the individual rather than by external stimuli; see **data-driven processes**

concordance: the extent to which individuals correspond in a characteristic (e.g. **intelligence** or proneness to depression)

concordance rate: the co-occurrence of the same psychiatric diagnoses or traits within pairs of twins

conditioned immune suppressive effect: a suppression of activity in the immune system caused by being in the presence of stimuli that have earlier been associated with its suppression

conditioned response (CR): response produced only after learning has taken place, e.g. salivating to a tone can only occur after conditioning has taken place; see **unconditioned response** (UR)

conditioned stimulus (CS): stimulus which produces only a weak **orienting response** (OR) at first, but by means of its association with an **unconditioned stimulus** (US) it gradually comes to produce a **conditioned response** (CR)

conditions of worth: the conditions that need to be fulfiled for an individual to experience positive self-regard

confidentiality: the notion that no information about individual participants in a study should be revealed publicly

conformity: a process whereby an individual behaves in accordance with the norms and expectations of others

confounding variable: variable affecting the **dependent variable** and which varies with the **independent variable** such that effects of the independent variable are erroneously assumed to exist or are camouflaged; see **internal validity**

connectionism: an approach to language involving computer-based modelling

conscience: the part of the **superego** which is acquired through the use of punishment; see **ego-ideal**

conscious: in **psychoanalysis**, it consists of the information which is currently the focus of attention; see **defence mechanisms**

consensual validity: a form of **validity** in which **self-report** scores are correlated with ratings

conservation: conservation problems are designed to test children's understanding of the principle of invariance of a particular quantity, i.e. that the quantity changes only if it is added to or subtracted from

consideration: a factor in the Ohio theory of leadership, concerned about people's welfare

construct: internal factor (e.g. **self-esteem**) assumed to explain variations in observed behavioural phenomena

construct validity: a form of **validity** involving testing the predictions of some theory

constructionism: a perspective that questions the taken-for-granted ways in which we make sense of our world and selves; these ways are seen as having been built up through sociohistorically specific linguistic interactions

constructionist: deriving from the assumption that reality is socially constructed

content analysis: analysis of **qualitative data** (often oral or written meanings) by identifying categories and counting frequencies of occurrence

content validity: a **sample** is drawn from a universe of items

contextual performance: things done outside the technical core, e.g. helping another worker

contingency approach: argues that an organization or a **leadership** style is successful depending upon environmental features

contingent responsiveness: a response contingent on the other person's behaviour

control: one special resource which means to have an impact on the conditions and activities in correspondence with some higher order goal

control condition or **controlled group**: condition or group providing a baseline measure against which effects of the **independent variable** are assessed by comparing performance here with that in an experimental condition or experimental group

control theory: a body of theory that describes how control systems function, involving feedback

conventional (scientific) paradigm: see **paradigm**

convergence: a cue to depth based on the fact that the eyes turn inwards more when focusing on a nearly object

co-operative activity: when children interact together in complementary ways, e.g. one child gets blocks out of a box and hands them to another child, who builds a tower; see **parallel activity**

co-operative group work: a system of organizing classroom work in which children must co-operate to achieve a common goal

coping: efforts to deal with stressful situations or events

coronary heart disease: heart diseases which are caused by the narrowing of the coronary arteries

correlation: extent to which variation in one variable is linked to variation in a second variable, see **factor analysis**

correspondent inference: a theory concerned with how we make judgements about people's underlying traits, beliefs or attitudes from their observed behaviour

countertransference: in **psychoanalysis** the feelings of the analyst for the patient that stem from the analyst's unconscious conflicts; see **transference**

CR: see **conditioned response**

cranial nerve: one of the nerves that convey information between the brain and the head outside the brain

creativity: it is revealed by unusual or insightful problem solutions which are of real value; see **originality**

criterion validity: measures the relationship of a test with a criterion, usually performance

cross-sectional study: a research design in which subjects are studied at one point in time; study of **groups** representing strata of a **population**

cross-situational consistency: similar behaviour demonstrated across a number of different situations

CS: see **conditioned stimulus**

cue-dependent forgetting: forgetting of information stored in long-term memory based on inadequate retrieval cues: see **trace-dependent forgetting**

cultural tools: term introduced by Vygotsky (1978, 1981) for new systems which have been invented to enhance human intellectual prowess, for example, literacy, number systems, geometry, algebra, computers, systems of measurement, computers, navigational systems and dictionaries (and perhaps even psychology textbooks)

data-driven processes: processes determined entirely by external stimuli; see **conceptually driven processes**

debriefing: the notion that participants in a study should be given full information about it afterwards

declarative knowledge: knowledge stored in long-term memory which is concerned with **episodic memory** or with **semantic memory**; see **procedural knowledge**

deductive reasoning: a form of logical reasoning in which certain conclusions follow logically from initial assumptions; see **inductive reasoning**

defence mechanisms: in **psychoanalysis**, ways of keeping unacceptable thoughts and feelings out of the **conscious**

demand characteristics: cues which participates might interpret in order to assess the purpose and expectations of a research study

denial: a **defence mechanism** which involves refusing to accept that a very threatening event has occurred

dependent variable: a **variable** apparently affected by an **independent variable**; see **experiment depersonalization**: a change in the level of inclusiveness of the **self-concept**; individuals' tendency to define themselves less as differing individuals and more as members of a particular social category

depression: see **dysthymia**

developmental stages: developmental theorists who claim that there are qualitative changes in children's intellectual abilities usually argue that children go through a sequence of step like stages; Piaget's theory is the clearest example of a stage theory

diabetes (mellitus): a disease in which sugar is inadequately utilized by the body due to lack of insulin

diagnosis: determining the nature of a disorder by relating the person's problems to an existing classification system

diathesis-stress model: the view that psychological disorder arises when someone who is predisposed towards disorder encounters **stress**

differential emotions theory: a model of **emotion** proposed by Izard in which a set of discrete emotions with specific neurophysiological concomitants exist

direct aggression: this is done face-to-face, e.g. hitting or taunting someone; see **indirect aggression**

disease: a state of the body characterized by deviations from the norm on measurable biological or somatic **variables**

disengagement theory: the view that old age involves a natural withdrawal from social activities and societal obligations

displacement: a **defence mechanism** which involves shifting impulses away from a threatening object to a non-threatening one

dissociative identity disorder: the possession of two or more relatively independent personalities, one of which is in control at any given time

distortion: in Roger's approach, inaccurate perception of reality when there is a discrepancy between actual experiences and self-perceptions of those experiences

divided attention: **attention** spread across two or more stimulus inputs; see **focused attention**

divisionalized form: divisons that govern themselves

dizygotic twins: fraternal twins produced from two fertilized ova; see **monozygotic twins**

dominance: getting one's one way or influencing others in interpersonal encounters

double-blind study: a study in which participant and researcher are 'blind' to the treatment being given to the participant; a third person knows which participants receive which treatment

double-blind trial: process to reduce bias in assessing therapy outcome, where neither the therapist nor the patient know whether the patient is receiving the active treatment

double depression: the occurrence of an episode of major depression within an individual who has ongoing minor depression (**dysthymia**)

double dissociation: it is shown when one patient performs well on one task and at an impaired level on another task, and another patient shows the opposite pattern

drift hypothesis: the idea that those suffering from a major disorder such as schizophrenia will be unable to maintain the social position of their families of origin

drug therapy: a form of treatment for mental illness based on the administration of drugs

dualism: theory that there is a fundamental separation between a physical body and a non-physical mind

dynamic systems theory: an approach to emotional development that suggests that **emotions** consist of components that become organized together as a function of interaction with the environment and other people.

dysthymia: long lasting but not severe depression; see **double depression**

echoic store: a memory store specialized for holding auditory information for no more than about 2 or 3 seconds

eclectic: the employing of concepts and methods for a variety of therapeutic approaches rather than from a single approach

ecological validity: extent to which effects observed in one environment (e.g. laboratory) are transferable to other environments (e.g. real world); sometimes called location

efficacy expectations: beliefs that the individual can produce certain outcomes

ego: within Freud's theory, the rational mind which is largely conscious; see **id** and **superego**

ego-dystonic: experience that is felt to be not part of one's self; see **ego-syntonic**

ego-ideal: the part of the **superego** which is acquired through the use of reward; see **conscience**

ego-syntonic: experience that is consistent with a one's view of oneself; see **ego-dystonic**

elaborative rehearsal: rehearsal which involves processing at a more semantic or deep level; see **maintenance rehearsal**

Electra complex: according to Freud, the tendency of young girls to develop a strong sexual attraction for their father; see **Oedipus complex**

emergence (of leaders): which person turns out to be the leader of a **group**

emergent property: a property that emerges as a result of the interactions between component parts and is not evident in the performance of a component on its own

emotion: a felt state most normally instigated by an event of importance to the individual, typically understood to include conscious feeling, physiological change, meaning **appraisal**, and a readiness for action; see **action readiness** and **mood**

empirical: based on observation of events in the world

empirical research: research which gathers **qualitative data** or **quantitative data** through some form of numerical or verbal recording

empirical validity: a form of **validity** in which test scores are compared against some relevant external criterion

empiricism: the belief that the only valid knowledge is that which is derived from observation and experiment

encoding specificity principle: the notion that memory performance depends on the overlap between the information available at retrieval and the information stored in memory; see **basic cognitive interview**

endocrine system: system of the ductless glands (thyroid, parathyroid, adrenal, pituitary, thymus, ovaries and testicles) which secrete directly hormones into the blood stream

endogenous depression: initially used to refer to depression without an external cause, though latterly to refer to depression with more physical features, such as sleep and appetite disturbance

enhanced cognitive interview: a larger and improved version of the **basic cognitive interview**

enmeshed families: families where no member is allowed to have an identity independent from the others

episodic memory: long-term memory for autobiographical information and for personal experiences; see **declarative knowledge** and **semantic memory**

epistemology: the philosophy of science or theory of knowledge; the study of the status of particular types of knowledge and methods of obtaining it

error management: the opposite of error prevention; it means that error handling is supported with the goals of avoiding negative error consequences, of dealing quickly with error consequences, and of learning from an error

ethical research: see **right to withdraw** and **voluntary informed consent**

ethnic identity: an awareness of which racial, national, linguistic or religious group one belongs to

ethnocentrism: display of ingroup bias (preference for the **group** to which one belongs) and inter-group discrimination (the display of hostility or unfair practices towards a group to which one does not belong)

evocative interaction: the extent to which the behaviour of others is influenced by our own behaviour

evolutionary psychology: according to this approach, human social behaviour is determined in large part by biological factors and by the goal of gene survival

excitatory synapse: a **synapse** in which activity in one **neuron** increases the chances of action potentials arising in a second neuron; see **inhibitory synapse**

expectancies: in Rogers's theory, the perceived probabilities of rewards and punishments following on certain actions; see **locus of control**

experiment: research design in which all **variables** except an **independent variable** are controlled and held constant while consequent variation in a **dependent variable** is measured; control includes use of equivalent samples produced by **random allocation**; see **quasi-experiment**

experimental cognitive psychology: the approach to studying human cognition based on laboratory research

experimental condition or **experimental group**: see **control condition**

explicit memory: memory performance enhanced by past experience in the presence of conscious recollection of that past experience; see **implicit memory**

expressed emotion (EE): in the schizophrenia literature, it refers to the amount of criticalness and overprotection directed towards the patient, usually by the patient's family

expression: a Darwinian term for the changes of face, voice and posture associated with **emotion**

external attribution: the attribution of an effect to a cause that resides in the environment; see **internal attribution**

external reliability: extent to which a measure produces similar results on similar occasions, with the **same** participants; see **internal reliability**

external validity: extent to which a demonstrated research effect can be generalized to other populations or contexts, or across different measures of the variables investigated; see **internal validity**

extraversion: a **personality** trait relating to sociability and impulsiveness

extrinsic context: context present at learning which has no direct impact on the meaning of the to-be-learned material; see **intrinsic context**

extrinsic motivation: motivation which is produced by the external

factor analysis: a complex statistical technique based on **correlation** used to calculate the number and nature of factors within a test

false belief tasks: currently the most commonly used method of testing children's theory of mind; in these tasks a scene is enacted and the child sees that one of the protagonists has incomplete and therefore incorrect information about what has happened; the child knows more than the protagonist and the question is whether the child can work out that the protagonist should have a false belief and what this belief should be

false memory syndrome: cases in which it is supposed that allegations of sexual abuse arise from memory distortion and even indoctrination

fear reduction model: model stating that people will more easily adopt a behaviour if this behaviour is presented as a measure against a fear-arousing situation or communication

feature detection: the extraction of a particular feature in sensory information as a result of processing

field experiment, field research or **field study**: carried out in the natural environment of the participants; the **independent variable** is manipulated and there is **random allocation** of participants in a field experiment; see **quasi-experiment**

figure-ground organization: the organization of visual perception into a central object (the figure) and its blurred surroundings (the ground)

fistula: an opening

fit (of person and job): fit is increased by socialization, training, selection and job design

fixation: the attachment of basic energy or **libido** on to one of the stages of psychosexual development, produced by problems or excessive gratification, see **regression**

flooding: behaviour therapy technique in which people are exposed to their fears while experiencing high levels of anxiety

focused attention: **attention** to one stimulus input at the expense of any others; see **divided attention**

free association: psychoanalytic technique in which the patient is encouraged to give free rein to his or her thoughts without any monitoring or censoring

free recall: a memory test in which the words or other information can be recalled in any order

frequency coding: within a given neuron the frequency of action potentials generated by an event conveys ('codes') information on that event

function: the contribution of behaviour to genetic perpetuation

functional age: an individual's actual capacities, irrespective of chronological age

functional explanation: an explanation in terms of how behaviour arose in evolution and contributed to the success of the animal exhibiting it

functional fixedness: the tendency to perceive objects as having only a limited range of functions or uses on the basis of past experience

functionality: a term broadly interpretable as the adaptive utility of a given psychological (or otherwise) process

Garcia effect: see **taste-aversion learning**

GAS: see **general adaptation syndrome**

gate theory: a theory suggesting that in the spinal cord at the point where nociceptive neurons synapse with **T-cells** there is, in effect, a gate; the gate can be in an open or closed state

gender identity: the awareness that one is a boy or a girl

general adaptation syndrome (GAS): according to Selye, a general response of the organism to a **stressor** with the stages alarm reaction, resistance and exhaustion

genes: structures that act to code for the production of proteins in the body and hence for the form that the body will take

genital character: according to Freud, it involves being mature and well adjusted, and being able to love and to be loved

genital stage: a stage of sexual development in which the focus is on the genitals and on sexual pleasure with another person; it starts at about the time of **puberty**

genotype: an individual's genetic potential; see **phenotype**

genotype-environment interaction: the extent to which a person's **genotype** helps select or create his or her own rearing and living environment

genuineness: in person-centred therapy, it describes the ability of therapists to allow their true inner feelings to be known to the client

glucostasis: maintenance of constancy of glucose levels within the body (e.g. reflected in the glucose concentration in the plasma)

goal-directed behaviour: behaviour which is not in response to a presently existing situation but can be understood as directed to a goal not yet attained

goal-setting: a motivational method to increase production by giving high and specific goals to workers

grandmother cell: theory that we have a specific **neuron** for the perception of each object is generally summed up in this expression, meaning that we would have a neuron specific to a particular grandmother

grapheme: the set of units in a writing system that represent the same sound (**phoneme**); thus *f* in fin, *ph* in phantom and *gh* in laugh are members of one grapheme

grapheme–phoneme correspondence rules: rules of language which convert spellings into sounds; see **phoneme**

group: a group exists when two or more people define themselves as members of it and when its existence is recognized by at least one other (R. Brown 1988)

group-mind theory: theory that individuals revert to a primitive unconscious state in crowd situations, thereby accounting for why **collective action** is so barbaric

group polarization: this describes the extreme shift in the perceptions, **attitudes** and behaviours of a **group** along an evaluative or descriptive scale (e.g. attitudes become more or less risky) that occurs after a discussion

groupthink: the uniformity and dogmatism displayed by a **group** where members display a total adherence to group norms and expectations and refuse to contemplate alternative ways of thinking and doing things

gustatory pathways: taste pathways through the brain

hallucination: sensory experience without external stimuli causing that experience

halo effect: an appraisal error due to generalization from one positive or negative characteristic to other ones

harassment: see **mobbing**

Hawthorne effect: effect produced when behaviour alters only because it is the subject of investigation; named after Hawthorne electrical plant in Chicago, where studies in the 1920s were influential in work and organizational psychology

health: a state of complete physical, mental and social well-being (WHO 1946); see **illness**

health behaviour: behaviour which enhances or maintains **health** from an objective or subjective point of view

health promotion: any action or measure which enhances or maintains (control over) **health**

health psychology: a subdiscipline of psychology which focuses on the relationship between behaviour and psychological processes on the one hand and **health**, **illness** and the healthcare system on the other hand

hedonic relevance: an attributional bias concerning the effect that the particular behaviour has on the perceiver; see **personalism**

helplessness: the belief that one has lost control over taxing demands; see **learned helplessness**

heritability: the degree to which a difference between two individuals is due to a genetic difference; the ratio of genetically caused variation to total variation (environmental and genetic) in a **population**

heuristic methods: rules of thumb or educated guesses used with complex problems; see **algorithmic methods**

hierarchy of needs: Maslow's five levels of needs, ranging from basic physiological needs to **self-actualization**

hindsight bias: the tendency to be wise after the event

HIV: see **Aids**

homeostasis: the tendency of certain **variables** in biological systems (e.g. human body temperature) to remain within close limits; see **non-regulatory behaviour**

hormone: a chemical that is released by glands into the blood stream at one site and effects action at a distant site

hostile aggression: distress or harm is inferred to be the primary intent of the act; see **instrumental aggression**

human relations school: emphasizes the relations between supervisor and employees

hyperphagia: overeating

hypertension: pathological elevation of blood pressure in the arteries; risk factor for cardiovascular diseases

hypothesis: testing a hypothesis is attempting to obtain support for a prediction from a theoretical explanation (hypothesis); since minor differences always occur between equivalent **samples** in identical conditions, the actual difference is compared with what might be expected if the **null hypothesis** is true; if the probability of the obtained sample difference is very low, the difference is **significant** and the **alternative hypothesis** is conditionally accepted; the effect then awaits **replication**

hypothesis testing: see **hypothesis**

hypothetical construct: see **construct**

I-self: a model of the self, characteristic of western culture, in which the self is experienced as independent and autonomous; see **we-self**

iconic store: a memory store specialized for holding visual information for approximately 500 milliseconds

id: within Freud's theory, sexual and aggressive instincts which are largely unconscious; see **ego** and **superego**

ideal self: the set of characteristics that an individual would most like to possess; see **Q-sort method**

identical elements: according to Thorndike, only identical behaviour elements are transferred from training to practice

identification: in boys, the resolution of the **Oedipus complex** by incorporating many of the values and standards of the father; a similar process with the same-sexed parent occurs in girls

identity crisis: Erikson's **normative crisis** of adolescence, in which young people must decide their identity in areas such as occupation, religion and sexual behaviour

identity status: Marcia's way of measuring achievement of identity in Erikson's model

identity theory: theory that brain events and mental events are identical but are to be understood in two different explanatory languages

idiographic: view that each **personality** is unique in the quality of characteristics and not just their numerical combination

ill-defined problems: problems in which the initial and goal states and the available operators are not clear; see **well-defined problems**

illness: a state of being ill, which also includes one's own perception of a health problem; see **health**

illness constellation model: a stage model of adaptation to chronic disease, distinguishing a stage of uncertainty, a state of disruption, a stage of recovery of the self and a state of restoration of well-being

illusion: where the world *appears* to be different from the way it can be shown to be by a more objective measure

imaginal desensitization: behavioural treatment approach which allows for gradual toleration in the imagination of previously feared stimuli; see **in-vivo desensitization** and **systematic desensitization**

immunity: the body's resistance to invading organisms

implicit memory: memory performance enhanced by past experience in the absence of conscious recollection of that past experience; see **explicit memory**

in-vivo desensitization: similar to imaginal desensitization but requires real-life exposure to whatever is feared; see **systematic desensitization**

independent variable: a **variable** manipulated by the researcher in an **experiment**; see **dependent variable**

indirect aggression: done via a third party, for example persuading others not to play with someone, or spreading nasty stories about someone; also called relational aggression; see **direct aggression**

inductive reasoning: a non-logical form of reasoning in which some conclusion follows probably, but not certainly, from the available evidence; see **deductive reasoning**

inferential statistical test: procedure which makes estimates of **population** values or probabilities using **quantitative data** from **samples**, in order to decide if the results are statistically significant

informational influence: influence to accept information obtained from another as evidence of reality

informed consent: see **voluntary informed consent**

inhibitory synapse: a **synapse** in which activity in one **neuron** decreases the chances of action potentials arising in a second neuron; see **excitatory synapse**

initiation of structure: a factor in the Ohio theory of **leadership** implying that the leader activates, organizes and defines work for the subordinates

insecure attachment: in the **strange situation**, the child will show some ambivalence to, or avoidance of, the **attachment** figure, or may show a disorganized response; see **secure attachment**

insight: a sudden restructuring of a problem which usually leads to the correct solution

insight-oriented therapies: therapies which stress the therapeutic importance of the patient gaining an understanding of the nature of his or her problem

inspection-time task: a method of assessing **intelligence** based on the speed with which simple perceptual decisions can be made

instrumental aggression: distress or harm is not inferred to be the primary intent of the act; see **hostile aggression**

instrumental conditioning: see **operant conditioning**

instrumental learning: learning of a behavioural response in order to obtain a reward or to escape from or avoid a punishment; see **response-outcome (R-O) association**

instrumental response: a voluntary response used as an instrument to obtain a desired event or to escape from an aversive event; also known as **operant response**

intellectual realism and visual realism: Luquet (1927) introduced these terms to describe two different types of drawings, intellectually realistic drawings depict features of the object which could not all be seen at once (e.g. all four wheels on a car or all six sides of a cube); visually realistic drawings, in contrast, portray only features which the artist/observer can see at one time from a particular position

intellectualization: a **defence mechanism** involving thinking about threatening information in ways which remove the emotion from it

intelligence: purposeful mental activity relating to adaptation to the environment and to shaping the environment

intelligence quotient (IQ): a global measure of intellectual ability

inter-group analysis: explaining a phenomenon in terms of **group** relationships

inter-groups behaviour: behaviour involving interaction between two or more **groups**

inter-individual analysis: explaining a phenomenon in terms of processes of the interaction and relationship between individuals

inter-observer reliability and **inter-rater reliability**: extent to which two or more raters' or observers' ratings or codings are in agreement; a check on consistency between raters or observers

internal attribution: the attribution of an effect to an attribute or a characteristic of the actor; see **external attribution**

internal consistency: the degree to which the items measure the same **construct**

internal reliability: extent to which responses to similar items in scale are answered consistently by the *same* person; see **external reliability**

Internal validity: extent to which a demonstrated research effect can be assumed to be authentic and not a result of recording error, statistical error or **confounding variable**; see **external validility**

internal working models of relationships: internalized representations of generalized relationship experiences which can be assessed in middle childhood (e.g. by the **Separation Anxiety Test**) and through to adulthood (by the **Adult Attachment Interview**)

internalization: a process whereby an individual takes on the attributes and characteristics of another as his or her own

interpersonal behaviour: behaviour involving interaction between two or more individuals

interpretation: psychoanalytic technique where the analyst conveys his or her views to the patient about the nature of the patient's problem

interview: research study where data are gathered mainly through interviewing participants; data may be treated qualitatively or rated on scales

intra-group behaviour: behaviour involving interaction between **group** members

intra-individual analysis: explaining a phenomenon in terms of factors within an individual

intrinsic context: context present at learning which has a direct impact on the meaning of the to-be-learned material; see **extrinsic context**

intrinsic motivation: motivation based on feelings of self-determination

introjection: in Rogers's approach, a way in which the values of others are incorporated by children

introspection: observation and examination of one's own thought processes

involuntary movement: a movement which is not based upon a conscious intention to act but is the automatic consequence of presenting a stimulus

IQ: see **intelligence quotient**

isomorphism: the notion that there is a close correspondence between organized perceptual processes and organized processes in the brain

jargon aphasia: a condition caused by brain damage in which speech contains wrong words and made-up words

JIT: see **just-in-time**

job enrichment: a job design to combine various job elements into a wider job with a bigger scope of actions and with more important decisions to be made

just-in-time (JIT): means to reduce the stock costs organizationally by delivering spare parts when needed and producing on demand; see **lean production**

labelling theory: the view that **mental disorders** are largely the product of other people applying that label to an individual

latency stage: a stage of psychosexual development in which there is a relative lack of sexual interest; it lasts from about the age of 6 until **puberty**

lateral inhibition: inhibition from one location to another, e.g. across the retina from one location to another

lateralization: referring to the distribution of psychological functions to one side of the brain or the other

law of Prägnanz: the notion that perceptual organization is as simple as possible

leadership: to have a vision and define the goals of an organization

leadership substitute theory: some issues at work make it less important to have a leader to give direction and support

lean production: Japanese (Toyota) system of job design which combines **just-in-time** and **total quality management**

learned helplessness: theory which postulates that a person who is continuously confronted with a lack of control in a particular situation will stop trying to influence outcomes not only in that situation, but also in new situations where control is possible; see **helplessness**

learning orientation: to be interested in learning and to take mistakes as an indication that one can still learn; see **performance orientation**

least preferred co-worker: a factor in Fiedler's contingency model of **leadership**; a high score means that the leader is relationship oriented, a low score, task oriented

leniency/severity error: systematically giving too positive or too negative **appraisals**

levels of analysis: see **intra-individual analysis, inter-individual analysis** and **inter-group analysis**

levels of regulation: a hierarchical structure of levels that control actions (from meta-level, via conscious, via action patterns, to automatic skills)

libido: the sexual instinct or motivational force contained within the **id**; see **fixation**

lifespan perspective: seeing development as a lifelong process, from conception to death

limbic system: a circuit in the brain that includes the **amygdala** and which is thought to be especially important in **emotions**

linear perspective: a cue to depth provided by the fact that parallel lines pointing away from us look closer together as they approach the horizon

local history effect: a phenomenon that affects one **group** being studied but not another group **location**; see **ecological validity**

locus of control: a **personality** dimension, which can be internal or external; internals (people with internal locus of control) believe that attainment of desired outcomes is mainly due to their own doing; externals believe that desired outcomes are mainly dependent on luck or the power of others; see **expectancies**

longitudinal research and **longitudinal study**: research design in which a group of subjects is studied over an extended period of time; see **prospective study**

lordosis: position adopted by a female to accept a male

machine bureaucracy: high specialization, many routine tasks, many formalized rules and regulations

magnetic resonance imaging (MRI): a technique that detects the presence of structural abnormalities in the brain and spinal cord; see **positron emission tomography**

magno system: a part of the visual system which is particularly tuned for changes in the image

maintenance rehearsal: verbal rehearsal based on repeating analyses already performed; see **elaborative rehearsal**

management: use of formal authority to make sure that the organization is functioning well

manic depression: also known as bipolar depression; characterized by extreme mood swings from mania to depression

means-ends analysis: a key aspect of problem solving, in which the individual tries to reduce the difference between the current state of a problem and the goal state

medical model: an approach to the understanding and treatment that views psychological disorder as being like physical disorder

mental disorders: also called psychological disorders; the general term used to cover all types of psychological disturbance

mental model: a representation of complex information (e.g. that contained in the premises of a reasoning problem); it may be in the form of visual imagery; see **action training**

meta-analysis: a quantitative method of comparing many different therapy outcome studies through standardizing their results, so that one can look at the overall effect size

meta-contrast ratio: the extent that the subjectively perceived difference between people is less than the difference between them and other people psychologically present in a setting

metarepresentation: something represents something else (e.g. a banana represents a telephone)

microgenetic studies: the same children are seen by experimenters repeatedly over a short period in the hope that developmental changes in their behaviour will take place during this period and that it will be possible to study these changes directly

microspectrophotometry: a technique in which the amount of light absorbed at different wavelengths by individual cones within the eye is measured

midlife crisis: from Levinson's description, a stage in which adults may feel dissatisfied, trapped between the generations, perhaps embark on an intense affair or abruptly seek out a new career direction

mind-body problem: a philosophical problem of understanding how mental events and physical (bodily) events can relate to each other

minimal group: a laboratory **group**, devoid of context and without history or future or the possibility for interaction

minority influence: the process by means of which a minority **group** influences a majority group

misapplied size-constancy theory: an explanation of many visual illusions based on the notion that the processes using apparent distance to calculate apparent size with three-dimensional objects are misapplied to two-dimensional drawings

mobbing: also known as harassment; an individual is bullied and harassed at work over a long period by several people

modelling: learning by observing and imitating the behaviour of others

moderator effect: the moderator **variable** changes the relationship between two other variables, e.g. there is little **stressor**–ill health relationship in high social support, while there is a high relationship under low social support

modularity: the notion that cognitive processing involves a number of relatively separate or independent processors or modules

modus ponens: a rule of inference in which the premises 'If A, then B' and 'A is true' produce the valid conclusion 'B is true'; see **modus tollens**

modus tollens: a rule of inference in which the premises 'If A, then B' and 'B is false' produce the valid conclusion 'A is false', see **modus ponens**

monocular cues: cues to depth which require the use of only one eye; see **binocular cues**

monogamous: with one sexual partner; *see* **polygamous**

monozygotic twins: identical twins produced from a single fertilized ovum; see **dizygotic twins**

mood: an emotional state or a disposition to enter an emotional state that lasts for hours, days or even weeks; often thought to be objectless or free-floating; see **emotion**

mood congruent memory: a memory bias to retrieve emotional material when the person is in the same **mood** state as the material refers to

mood-state-dependent memory: a phenomenon in which memory is better when the **mood** state at learning and at memory are similar than when they are dissimilar

moral reasoning: how someone thinks or reasons about moral issues

morbidity: disease rate; see **mortality**

mortality: death rate; see **morbidity**

motion parallax: one of the **monocular cues** to depth; based on the movement of an object's image across the retina

motor neuron: a neuron that activates a muscle

munificence: an easy and benign environment for an organization

mutation: a change in the genetic contribution made by a male or female relative to the precursor cell

myocardial infarction: heart attack caused by a clot in a coronary vessel

naturalistic observation: observation of individuals in their natural habitat

need for achievement: a **personality** dimension relating to the motivation to excel at work and to overcome challenges at work

need for affiliation: the need to have numerous social contacts and positive interactions with others; often regarded as a **personality** dimension

need for intimacy: the need to have very close relationships with a small number of other people; often regarded as a **personality** dimension

negative automatic thoughts: in Beck's cognitive model, the name given to depressing thoughts that occur effortlessly

negative feedback: a system in which deviations from a value create a tendency to return to that value

negative reinforcement: strengthening of a response as a result of the response reducing an unpleasant psychological state; reinforcement resulting from the removal, not the presentation, of the reinforcer; see **positive reinforcement**

nerve: a collection of axons in the **peripheral nervous system** rather like wires that make up a cable

neural: adjective to refer to **neurons** and systems of neurons

neurochemicals: general term for chemical substances that operate in the brain and nervous system such as neurotransmitters

neuromuscular junction: a particular type of **synapse**, which forms the junction between a motor neuron and a muscle

neuron: a cell of the nervous system

neuronal: adjective to refer to **neurons** and systems of neurons

neurosis: term used broadly to refer to psychological disorders, such as anxiety and minor depression, that do not involve a break from reality; see **psychosis**

neuroticism: a **personality** trait relating to feelings of tension, anxiety and depression

nociceptive neuron: a **neuron** whose tip is sensitive to tissue damage and which generates action potentials in response to such damage

nomothetic: view that **personality** characteristics occur along dimensions which cen be measured in principle

non-invariance problem: a difficulty in speech perception caused by the fact that any given **phoneme** is pronounced differently in different contexts

non-regulatory behaviour: behaviour (e.g. feeding or drinking) that cannot be understood as serving the **homeostasis** of the body

non-shared family environment: the particular rearing environment each child has, not shared with siblings

normative crisis: in Erikson's stage model, the important crisis at that stage (**identity crisis**), for most people, and which should be dealt with successfully if healthy development is to continue

normative fit: a principle of **self-categorization** theory which refers to the match between category and the content properties of the stimuli; the extent to which specific instances of a category match our normative beliefs about the social meanings of the social category; see **comparative fit**

normative influence: influence to conform to the positive expectations of another person or a **group**

null hypothesis: **hypothesis** which a researcher sets out to dismiss, usually claiming that no difference or **correlation** exists between **variables**; see **alternative hypothesis**

obedience: a display of **compliance** with the demands and orders of authority without question or challenge

obesity: excessive fatness or corpulence

object recognition: the processes involved in identifying objects in the environment

oblique factors: **personality** factors which correlate with each other; see **orthogonal factors**

observational (design, observational study and **observational technique**: involves direct recording of behaviour, mechanically, by structured coding or note taking; observer may or may not participate in the observed **group**; see **participant observation**

observational learning: learning which occurs from observing the behaviour of a model rather than by performing actions oneself; see **vicarious reinforcement**

occupational psychology: a branch of applied psychology focusing on individuals in the workplace

Oedipus complex: according to Freud, the tendency of young boys to desire their mother combined with antagonism towards their father; see **Electra complex** and **identification**

olfactory receptor: a **receptor** that initiates the process of smell

operant conditioning: a type of learning when an individual's behavioural responses become more or less frequent as a consequence of **reinforcement**; sometimes called instrumental conditioning; see **classical conditioning**

operant response: an arbitrary response or behaviour performed in order to obtain a reward or escape from or avoid a punishment; also known as **instrumental response**

operational definition: defining a **variable**, psychological phenomenon or **construct** in terms of the procedures employed to measure it

opioid: a particular class of substance, the members of which have similar effects; includes certain chemicals produced naturally by the body such as enkephalins and those taken into the body such as morphine and heroin

opponent-process coding: a system of coding in which two sensory qualities are coded by a given neuron by means of two different directions of response, e.g. an increase in firing above the spontaneous level might indicate the presence of green light and a suppression to below this level might indicate a red light

optic aphasia: a condition caused by brain damage in which the patient has great problems in recognizing familiar objects from vision in spite of the fact that many visual processes remain intact

optic flow patterns: the apparent movement of the visual environment away from the point to which the observer is moving

OR: see **orienting response**

oral aggressive character: a type of adult **personality** characterized by aggression and dominance

oral receptive character: a type of adult **personality** characterized by dependency and trustingness

oral stage: a stage of psychosexual development centred on the mouth; it lasts from birth until about 18 months of age

orbitofrontal cortex: the cortex above the orbits of the eyes; it is part of the prefrontal cortex, which is the part of the frontal lobes in front of the motor cortex (area 4) and the premotor cortex (area 6)

organizational culture: a set of common values and beliefs, symbols, rituals and habits, taken for granted in an organization

organizational psychology: a branch of applied psychology focusing on group and structural factors in the workplace

organizational socialization: the effects of work on the person

organizational structure: relationship of the components of an organization

orienting response (OR): Pavlov called this the 'what is that' reflex; it consists of paying attention to a new, and neutral, stimulus; see **conditioned stimulus**

originality: tendency to produce unusual solutions to problems; see **creativity**

oropharyngeal: the oral cavity and pharynx

orosensory: the sensory systems concerned with the oral cavity, including taste, smell and the texture of what is in the mouth

orthogonal factors: **personality** factors which do not correlate with each other; see **oblique factors**

osmosensors: receptors for osmotic signals

osmosis: the passage of solvent (e.g. water) across a semipermeable membrane (e.g. a cell wall) caused by differences in the concentration of solutes such as sodium chloride (salt) across the membrane; e.g. if the concentration of the body fluids is stronger outside the cells because of eating salty food, then water will be drawn out of the cells to equilibrate the concentrations of salt inside and outside the cell; cell shrinkage will occur; this is a stimulus for thirst

osteoporosis: a disease characterized by low bone mass and deterioration of bone tissue

outcome expectancies: expectations concerning the likelihood of **reward** following successful performance

outcome value: the perceived value of the **reward** that will be received for successful performance

overgeneralization: the tendency to draw general conclusions on the basis of single instances; one of Beck's thinking errors in depression

palliative interventions: interventions designed to increase quality of life by providing emotional support, especially when the person cannot be cured, as in terminal care

paradigm: a commonly accepted explanatory framework within which a majority of contemporary research is presented

parallel activity: when children play near each other with the same materials, but do not interact much; see **co-operative activity**

parallel tests: the **correlation** of two tests

participant attrition: losing participants from a long-term study, which can have a biasing effect on results

participant observation: the observer participants in the social behaviour of the observed group in order to record information on several individuals or the whole group; see **observational design**

parvo system: a part of the visual system which is specialized for the analysis of the details of the world, a process that can take time and involve exploiting differences in colour

Pavlovian conditioning: see **classical conditioning**

peptides: a collection of amino acids that affects the function of the brain or other parts of the body

perceived control: the belief that one's internal or personal resources permit to influence a situation or outcome in a desired way

perception: processes by which environmental information is transformed into experiences of objects, sounds, and so on; see **sensation**

perceptual segregation: the identification of the objects within the visual field

perceptual span: the total field of view, extending about three letters to the left of the fixation point and fifteen letters to the right during reading

performance: refers to actions done for the organization that has hired the person with a certain standard of excellence

performance appraisal: more or less systematic evaluation of how well an employee does his or her job

performance effectiveness: the quality of task performance; see **processing efficiency**

performance orientation: to show how well one is able to do things and to take mistakes as an indication of failure; see **learning orientation**

peripheral nervous system: the nervous system outside the **central nervous system**

personal authenticity: a way of living that shows an awareness and care for self and others

personal identity: that part of one's self that makes one a unique individual

personal initiative: self-starting and proactive behaviour

personalism: an attributable bias referring to the perceiver's belief that the actor behaved in a way that had an affect on the perceiver and that the actor intended to benefit or harm the perceiver; see **hedonic relevance**

personality: consistent individual differences at the emotional and motivational levels

phallic character: according to Freud, a **personality** type consisting of vanity, impulsiveness and self-assuredness

phallic stage: a stage of psychosexual development centred on the genitals; it lasts between 3 and 6 years of age

phantom limb pain: pain that is perceived to arise in a limb that does not exist

phenomenology: an approach based on direct descriptions of conscious experience

phenotype: an individual's observable physical and psychological characteristics, based on the **genotype** and on environmental factors

pheromone: an airborne chemical that plays a role in communication between animals of the same species, e.g. as a mating signal

philosophy: a discipline involving the search for knowledge or wisdom

phoneme: the smallest unit of sound that can affect the meaning of a word; individual alphabetic letters generally represent phonemes; see **categorical perception** and **grapheme**

phonemic restoration effect: a phenomenon in speech perception, in which a missing **phoneme** is perceived because of **top-down processes** initiated by the context

phonological dyslexia: a condition produced by brain damage in which unfamiliar words and non-words are hard to pronounce

phonological loop: part of the working memory system which consists of a passive store concerned with speech perception and an articulatory control process

physical abuse: the intentional, non-accidental use of force on the part of the parent or other caretaker interacting with a child in his or her care aimed at hurting, injuring or destroying that child

place code: the basilar membrane is caused to move back and forth at a particular location; this location depends upon the frequency of the vibrations, a relationship that is termed a place code

placebo: an inactive substance or dummy treatment given to a **control group** to compare its effects with those of a real drug or treatment (from the latin word meaning 'I shall please')

placebo condition: condition where administration of the **independent variable** is simulated, but the investigated factor of the independent variable is absent, to exclude expectation effects produced by the independent variable, e.g. giving participants coffee without caffeine, when the effects of caffeine in coffee are being investigated

placebo effect: if a procedure (e.g. injecting morphine) has an effect by known physiological means (e.g. acting on specific receptors), then a procedure that shares common features with this but lacks the specific component (e.g. injection of a neutral substance) can sometimes have a similar effect; it describes change that takes place, particularly in chemotherapy, which is attributable to patient expectations rather active therapeutic ingredients

placebo group: participants in an **experiment** who are given a **placebo**

plasticity: the concept that connections between **neurons** are not fixed but can be modified as a function of development and learning

play hierarchy: a scheme for coding children's activities, based on social participation and level of play

polygamous: with many sexual partners; see **monogamous**

polygenic disorder: disorder that is controlled by the interaction of a number of **genes** rather than one single gene

population: all members of a nominated group, from which a **sample** is taken to investigate proposed effects; in an **inferential statistical test**, the population is often a hypothetical set of all scores that could be obtained by repeatedly testing samples

population coding: information carried by means of the population of **neurons** that is activated by a stimulus

positive distinctiveness: the striving of a **group** for distinctiveness or evaluative superiority relative to another group; the striving of an individual to achieve positive **self-esteem**

positive reinforcement: when a reinforcer with rewarding properties is presented, thereby increasing the probability that the response will occur more frequently in the future; see **negative reinforcement**

positivism: Comte's philosophy of science, holding that only phenomena which can be observed and measured are legitimate subjects of scientific study

positron emission tomography (PET): a technique whereby researchers can gain a profile of the activity of neurons in different regions of the brain; see **magnetic resonance imaging**

practice niche: a safe situation at work where employees can practise what they have learnt

preconscious: stored thoughts and information which can easily be brought into the **conscious**

prejudice: preconception based on insufficient information; a negative attitude towards a category of people, especially minority groups

primacy effect: the tendency for the early items in a list to be recalled better than the items from the middle of the list; see **recency effect**

primary appraisal: perception of an event; see **secondary appraisal**

primary appraisal of stress: according to Lazarus, it is an evaluation that there is a **stressor** in the environment; see **secondary appraisal of stress**

primary deviance: in **labelling theory**, this refers to the initial deviant behaviour of the individual; see **secondary deviance**

primary memory: information remaining in consciousness after it has been presented; the psychological present; see **secondary memory**

primary prevention (of disease): measures to prevent, eliminate or reduce risk factors for disease before manifestation of the disease; see **secondary prevention**

primary visual system: system consisting of ganglion cells which make synaptic contact in a region of the thalamus, termed the lateral geniculate nucleus (LGN); the axons of LGN cells together constitute the optic tract; the LGN axons terminate in the visual cortex; see **secondary visual system**

principles before skills: term used by Gelman and Gallistel (1978) to describe their theoretical position about young children's understanding of number; these authors claimed that children understand the basic principles of number long before they can count proficiently

proactive interaction: the extent to which individuals choose the situations in which they find themselves

proactive interference: disrupted performance in which what was learned previously interferes with subsequent learning; see **retroactive interference**

proband: in behavioural genetics research, this refers to the family member who has a disorder

procedural knowledge: information stored in long-term memory based on knowing how to perform certain actions (e.g. skilled motor performance); see **declarative knowledge**

processing efficiency: the relationship between **performance effectiveness** and the amount of effort exerted

productive language: language output, usually in the form of speech or writing; see **receptive language**

professional bureaucracy: based on professionals with a high degree of training and socialization

projection: a **defence mechanism** in which the individual's undesirable characteristics are attributed to others

prosocial behaviour: helping someone else, for example by sharing something, or comforting someone who is hurt or distressed

prosodic cues: cues to syntactic structure contained in speech, e.g. intonation, timing and stress

prospective study: a **longitudinal study** in which a large group of subjects is followed over time in order to investigate cause – effect relationships, such as the relationship between a risk factor and disease outcomes

prototype: a set of characteristic features of a category

psychiatry: branch of medicine dealing with **mental disorders**; psychiatrists all have a general medical training

psychoanalysis: an approach to psychology introduced by Freud which consists of theories of emotional development and a form of therapy for **mental disorders**

psychoanalytic: term used specifically to refer to the Freudian approach

psychodynamic: describes any approach to therapy that emphasizes the role of unconscious conflicts and early experience

psychological disorders: see **mental disorders**

psychometric test: carefully constructed and **standardized** measures of psychological characteristics, typically **personality** and **intelligence** scales

psychoneuroimmunology: a multidisciplinary area concerned with the interactions among psychological processes, the brain and the immune system

psychopathology: field concerned with the nature of **mental disorders**

psychophysics: the use of scientific methods to establish some of the relationships between the mental and physical realms

psychosis: refers to a severe **mental disorder** where the person is out of touch with reality; see **neurosis**

psychosocial moratorium: according to Erikson, a time in which society allows or sanctions young people to try out different beliefs, whether sexual, religious or political, without undue pressure

psychoticism: a **personality** trait relating to coldness, aggression and an absence of caring

psychotropic drugs: drugs which alter symptoms of **mental disorder**

puberty: the stage of reaching reproductive maturity; see **adolescent growth spurt**

punishment: something an animal will work to escape or avoid; reducing the probability of an **instrumental response** by pairing it with an aversive event, see **reinforcement**

pyloric sphincter: controls the release of food from the stomach to the duodenum

Q-sort method: a technique used by Rogers to assess the **self-concept** and the **ideal self**

qualitative approach: tends to reject the traditional pre-eminence of statistical data in psychological research and emphasizes analysis of meanings; quantification is thought to minimize distinctive information unnessarily; see **quantitative approach**

qualitative data: non-numerical data, typically verbal, but can include pictorial and other symbolic material; see **quantitative data**

quality of life: subjective concept of wellness, based on a perceived difference between the actual state and a desired state of life

quantitative approach: traditional dominance in psychological research has been criticized for trivializing information; see **qualitative approach**

quantitative data: data in numerical form used to summarize common characteristics and phenomena; required for **inferential statistical tests** and **significance testing**; see **qualitative data**

quasi-experiment: the researcher may not have complete control over an **independent variable** (its variation may occur naturally) and/or may not be able to allocate participants randomly; see **experiment** and **field experiment**

R-O association: see **response-outcome (R-O) association**

racial prejudice: negative evaluation of individuals as a consequence of their being in a certain racial or ethnic group

random allocation: a pool of participants is allocated to experimental conditions; each participant has an equal chance of being in any condition

random sample: **sample** where every member of the target **population** had an equal probability of being included; see **representative sample**

random selection: selection directly from a **population** with no attempt to select from sub-groups on a proportional basis; see **sampling bias**

rationalization: used by Bartlett to refer to the tendency for errors in story recall to conform to the participants' cultural expectations

reaction formation: a **defence mechanism** in which people behave in a way which is the opposite of their unconscious thoughts and feelings

reactive depression: initially used to describe depression in response to environmental changes but a largely discarded term

reactive interaction: individual differences in behaviour in a situation deriving from differences in the interpretation of the situation

reactive measure: behavioural measure that is susceptible to **reactivity** effects

reactivity: tendency of participants to react to the context of the research, to attempt to guess the research aims and to assess what kind of performance is desired

realistic conflict: goal incompatibility or negative interdependence between **groups** (i.e. win–lose scenario)

realistic job preview: presents not only positive but also negative aspects of job

reality principle: this is used by the **ego** and involves taking account of the external consequences of behaviour

reality shock: this happens when someone is confronted with a new job

recency effect: the tendency for the last items in a list to be recalled better than those in the middle of the list; see **primacy effect**

receptive field: the receptive field of a **neuron** is that area of sensory surface which, when stimulated, will influence the activity of the neuron in question

receptive language: language comprehension based on listening to speech or reading a text; see **productive language**

receptor: a structure to which a chemical attaches itself (e.g. a **transmitter** attaches to a receptor at a **synapse**) also a **neuron** sensitive to a stimulus in the external environment

reciprocal determinism: the notion that environmental factors, internal factors and behaviour all influence one another

reciprocal relationship: both socialization and selection effects occurring

reductionism: a process of explanation which appeals to events at a lower level, e.g. social problems might be explained in terms of individual psychology and psychology explained in terms of biology

referential informational influence: a process of influence whereby individuals ascribe to themselves a social category and internalize the attributes and characteristics prototypical of that category

reflex: an automatic reaction to a stimulus

regression: moving back to an earlier psychosexual stage, produced by stressful conditions in adulthood; see **fixation**

regressions: eye movements during reading which backtrack through the text

regulatory behaviour: behaviour that serves to regulate the internal environment of the body, e.g. drinking following a period of water deprivation

reinforcement: increasing the probability of an **instrumental response** either by pairing it with an appetitive event (**positive reinforcement**) or with the omission of an aversive event (**negative reinforcement**); see **punishment**

reinforcement value: the extent to which one reinforcer is preferred to another when the probability of obtaining each reinforcer is the same

relapse prevention: preventing a person from falling back into old routines instead of the newly learnt ones

relational aggression: see **indirect aggression**

relative accessibility: relative ease of recall of categories we have in out minds

reliability: the extent to which a test provides consistent and replicable measurement; see **external reliability** and **internal reliability**

repetition-priming effects: facilitated performance when stimuli are processed for the second or subsequent time compared to the first occasion

replication: an attempt to repeat an earlier study precisely, in order to check the **validity** of the original findings

representative sample: selected group for research who are largely representative of the **population** under investi-

gation; sub-groups of the population are represents in similar proportions in the **sample**; see **random sample**

representativeness heuristic: a rule of thumb involving the assumption that representative or typical members of any given category occur more often than non-representative ones

repression: forgetting in which anxiety-related information is prevented from gaining access to consciousness

resistance: in **psychoanalysis** the patient's tendency to unconsciously repel any material that will threaten the **ego**

resonance: in Gibson's theory, the process by which invariant information is 'picked up' from the visual environment

resources: conditions and personal characteristics used to attain goals; they are moderators of the stress process

response acquiescence set: tendency to answer positively to questionnaire items, irrespective of content; a negative effect is also possible; also known as **acquiescence response set**

response-outcome (R-O) association: association between the mental representation of two events, with the first event being an **instrumental response** and the second event being the outcome that this response produces; these associations are presumably responsible for **instrumental learning**

retroactive interference: disrupted performance in which what was learned previously is interfered with by subsequent learning; see **proactive interference**

retrograde amnesia: impaired ability to remember events occurring before the onset of **amnesia**; see **anterograde amnesia**

reversibility: Piaget's best known theoretical tenet; Piaget argued that the fundamental underlying change during the so-called concrete operations period was in the development of reversible thought processes, which involve contemplating a change in the environment and working out, simultaneously, what would happen if the change was reversed

reward: something for which an animal will work; it is associated with successful performance, see **Skinner box**

rheumatoid arthritis: the most serious form of **arthritis**

right to withdraw: an aspect of ethical research in which participants are told they may abandon the experiment at any time without providing a reason

risk factor: a factor (personal or environmental characteristic) which is associated with the onset and the development of a disease

rostral: towards the head or front end of an animal; see **caudal**

rough-and-tumble play: friendly play-fighting with a partner

S-R association: see **stimulus-response association**

S-S association: see **stimulus-stimulus association**

saccades: rapid eye movements lasting for about 15 milliseconds

saccadic eye movements: sudden and jerky movements of the eyes

sample: selection of items or people from a **population**; see **random sample** and **representative sample**

sampling bias and **selection bias**: sampling which is affected by a systematic factor causing the sample not to be a **random selection** from the **population**, e.g. selecting from students present rather than from all on the class list

sampling error: a (hypothetical) measure of the extent to which a **sample** statistic differs from the true value for the **population**

satiety: the reduction of appetite

savings method: a way of assessing memory based on the greater speed of relearning than of original learning

scaffolding: providing the right response to whatever the infant or child does, and timing responses appropriately to mesh in with the infant's timing

schedule-induced polydipsia: excessive drinking by animals that receive small pellets of food at intervals

schema: a cognitive structure that represents organized knowledge about a given concept, object or event that influences the processing of information relevant to that stimulus; see **self-schemata**

secondary appraisal: the evaluation of one's coping abilities when facing an event; see **primary appraisal**

secondary appraisal of stress: according to Lazarus, it estimates which coping strategies can be used to deal with a **stressor**; differentiation of problem oriented coping and emotion focused coping; see **primary appraisal of stress**

secondary deviance: in **labelling theory**, this describes the exacerbation of symptoms in an individual as a result of being labelled mentally ill; see **primary deviance**

secondary memory: information which is stored in memory, but is not currently in consciousness; the psychological past; see **primary memory**

secondary prevention (of disease): measures to stop or slow down the progression of a disease; see **primary prevention**

secondary visual system: a system consisting of ganglion cells which make synaptic connections in the superior colliculi; see **primary visual system**

secure attachment: in the **strange situation**, the child is reassured by the **attachment** figure; see **insecure attachment**

segmentation problem: the difficulty in speech perception of identifying individual words from the almost constant auditory stream produced by normal speech

selection bias: see **sampling bias**

self-actualization: the need to discover and to fulfil one's own potential; see **hierarchy of needs**

self-categorization: cognitive-perceptual process involving the classification of oneself as part of one social category rather than another

self-concept: in Rogers's approach, the conscious thoughts and beliefs about the self; the recognition by the infant that he or she exists as a person, separate from other people; see **Q-sort method**

self-efficacy: people's beliefs that they have the ability to cope with a given situation and produce the desired outcomes

self-esteem: how one describes or evaluates oneself

self-management: these techniques are oriented towards managing one's own person

self-management interventions: these are designed to increase the patient's control over a disease.

self-monitoring: assessment of frequency, antecedents and consequences of a target behaviour

self-report measure: measure of a human characteristic (typically a **psychometric test**) obtained by respondents reporting their own behaviour, often in a questionnaire

self-schemata: cognitive structures that represent generalizations about the self and influence the processing of information about the self which is contained in the individual's social experience; see **schema**

self-socialization: the idea that children attend to and imitate same-sex models, and follow sex-appropriate activities, because they realize that this is what a child of their own sex usually does

self-stereotyping: cognitive-perceptual process involving the internalization of the **catagory prototype**

self-talk: internal monologues

semantic memory: long-term memory for knowledge of the world in the form of a mental thesaurus; see **episodic memory**

semi-structured interview: method where the interviewer has a set schedule of items to cover and information to obtain, but where question order or wording is not entirely predetermined

sensation: the basic, uninterpreted information presented to the sense organs; see **perception**

sensory homunculus: a mapping of the body on to the somatosensory cortex according to the correspondence of body region to responsive neurons

sensory neuron: a **neuron** involved in the process of detection of information and conveying it towards the **central nervous system**

sensory receptor: neuron or part of a neuron which serves the role of detecting sensory information

sensory transduction: the process of transformation between external energy and a pattern of activity within a sensory **receptor**, e.g. a nociceptive **neuron** transduces between tissue damage and action potentials

Separation Anxiety Test: an assessment of **internal working models** in childhood, through asking children to respond to photographs of separation experiences

set-point: the command to a negative feedback system (e.g. the setting on the dial of a thermostat)

sex-role stereotypes: beliefs about what is most appropriate for one sex or the other

sexual abuse: the involvement of dependent, sexually immature children and adolescents in sexual activities that they do not fully comprehend, to which they are unable to give informed consent or that violate the social taboos of family roles

shaping: reinforcement of progressive steps toward a target behaviour (e.g. rewarding obese people for every kilo of weight lost)

shared family environment: the aspects of the family environment common to all siblings

sickness: a subjective concept which refers to the social aspects or consequences of health problems

significance testing: when **inferential statistical testing** has found differences or **correlations**, a test of statistical significance will determine if they reflect real **population** variations; see **hypothesis**

similar-to-me-error: positive **appraisal** when the person is similar to the appraiser

simple random sample: see **random sample**

simple structure: no elaborate system of rules

skeletal muscles: muscles responsible for performing work on the external world

Skinner box: apparatus in which a rat presses a lever or a pigeon pecks a key to obtain a **reward**

smoking cessation programmes: programmes which offer people help in giving up smoking.

smoking prevention programmes: programmes which attempt to keep people from taking up smoking

social categorization: cognitive-perceptual process involving the classification of social phenomena into meaningful categories; categorizing people as belonging to different **groups**

social cohesion: the degree to which members of **groups** are attracted to each as exemplars of a social category, i.e. social as opposed to interpersonal attraction

social cohesion theory: this argues that a collection of individuals will form a **group** (either spontaneously or deliberately) to the extent that they have needs capable of mutual satisfaction as a result of their association; group formation and maintenance arise out of inter-individual interaction via which individual needs are fulfiled

social comparison: a cognitive-perceptual process by means of which one individual (or **group**) benchmarks themselves against another individual (or group)

social comparison processes: processes involved in the comparison of an individual's own beliefs, behaviour and emotions with those others in order to evaluate their correctness and adequacy

social desirability: tendency to behave in accordance with typical positive norms; 'looking good' in public behaviour; this can obscure more realistic reactions to research stimuli

social desirability response set: tendency to give socially desirable responses on questionnaires when these responses are not accurate

social engineering: social or behavioural change through legislation or restructuring of the environment

social identity: a person's sense of who he or she is at a **group** as opposed to individual level of analysis

social influence: the process by means of which one party shapes the **attitudes** and/or behaviours of another

social skill training: programmes which offer people help in the acquisition of social skills

social support: a resource characterized by affective support, confirmation and direct help; tangible and intangible esteem, help or care that one receives or perceives to receive from others

social validity: how much is selection procedure accepted by applicants

sociogram: pictorial representation of social structure in a group

sociometric status: a categorization of children as popular, controversial, rejected, neglected or average, according to whether they are high or low on positive and negative nominations

sociometry: a picture of the social structure in a group, derived from observation or interview

sociotechnical system approach: emphasizes that there should be joint optimization of the technical and a social side to each job within an open system's perspective

solitary tract: the taste pathway in the brain where it is close to the first synapse of the taste pathways in the brain, which is in the nucleus of the solitary tract

somatic nervous system: that part of the nervous system that is responsible for effecting action on the world via the skeletal muscles, doing work such as lifting weights or moving the legs as in running

somatosensory neuron: a **neuron** that is sensitive to tactile stimulation at the skin

SPAARS: a multi-level theory of **emotions** proposed by Power and Dalgleish (1997)

species-specific behaviour or **species-typical behaviour**: for a particular species, a behaviour that is shown by all members of the **population**

specific factors: aspects of a therapeutic approach that are unique and not shared by other therapies

spectrogram: a visible record of sound frequencies over time

spontaneous remission: the rate at which psychological disorders will improve without any therapeutic intervention

standardized test: a test which has been administered to large and representative **samples**, so that the **significance** of any individual's score can be assessed

statistical concept of abnormality: the view that abnormality and **mental disorders** can be defined by the extent to which the individual deviates from the population norm

stereopsis: a cue to depth based on the disparity or discrepancy in the retinal images of the two eyes

stereotypy: a repetitive, apparently pointless behaviour

stimulus-control interventions: interventions designed to eliminate or substitute stimuli that evoke undesired reactions

stimulus-response association (S-R association): the association between an environmental stimulus and a response; the response can either be a conditioned response or an **instrumental response**

stimulus-stimulus association (S-S association): an association between the mental representations of two stimuli, S1 and S2; these stimuli can either be a **conditioned stimulus** and an **unconditioned stimulus** in a Pavlovian situation, or can be a cause and an effect in a casual learning situation, or a predictor and an outcome in predictive learning, or just mere neutral stimuli such as a light and a tone, as, for example, in sensory preconditioning

story grammar: the notion that stories have an underlying hierarchical structure which can be described in terms of themes, plots, settings, and so on

strange situation: test developed the Ainsworth to examine the pattern of reactions when infants are separated from and then reunited with their caregivers; used to classify infants into different **attachment styles**; see **insecure attachment** and **secure attachment**

street mathematics: term introduced by Nunes *et al.* (1993) to describe the fact that children actively involved in the informal economy (in Brazil) often make impressive mathematical calculations in informal situations but fail to take advantage of their mathematical knowledge at school

stress: a condition in which normally effective **defence mechanisms** are stretched to beyond their range of operating effectively

stress management: programme in which people learn to deal with **stress** by influencing appraisal processes, coping strategies and stress reactions

stressors: condition in the environment that tends to evoke **stress**

stroke: a sudden severe attack, e.g. when the brain is damaged by disrupted blood supply

subjective expected utility theory: theory stating that people will more likely adopt a target behaviour if they believe that this behaviour may prevent them from getting into an undesired state (e.g. a disease) to which they think they are vulnerable

sublimation: according to Freud, the channelling of sexual forces into the attainment of productive and creative goals

superego: within Freud's theory, it incorporates society's values and standards; it consists of the **conscience** and the **ego-ideal**; see **ego** and **id**

suppression: conscious blocking of anxiety-related or threatening information from awareness

surface dyslexia: a condition produced by brain damage in which it is very difficult to pronounce irregular words correctly

survey: research that involves questioning a relatively large number of people, usually using questionnaires and **interviews**

symbolic interactionism: refers to a group of theories developed around the idea that (1) people act towards things on the basis of the meaning they attach to them, (2) these meanings are a product of social interaction and (3) these meanings are continuously changing through the way people interpret the signs they encounter in their everyday lives

synapse: the junction between (1) a **neuron** and (2) either another neuron or a muscle

syndrome: a set of symptoms which are often found together

systematic desensitization: a technique by which a subject, who is in a state of deep muscle relaxation, is exposed gradually to increasing intensity levels of a fear-arousing stimulus in order to acquire control over the stimulus; the hierarchy of anxiety-arousing situations are both imagined and real; this behaviour therapy encompasses both **imaginal desensitization** and **in-vivo desensitization**

systematic observation: technique where observers use a standardized procedure to code behaviour as it occurs

T-cell: a **neuron** that transmits information on tissue damage from the spinal cord to the brain, the information derives from nociceptive neurons synapsing in the spinal cord

task performance: refers to fulfilling the officially described tasks

taste-aversion learning: the modification of a taste from evoking acceptance to evoking rejection as a result of exposure to the taste being followed by nausea

taste bud: a small organ on the tongue, each of which is made up of **receptors** for chemicals

Taylorism: a method of work design with money as motivator, high division of labour, centralized work structuring and specialized tools

temperament: that aspect of behaviour and **affect** that is constitutional, shows stability over time, and has some genetic component; characteristics of behaviour, such as prevalent **mood** or response to new situations, which tend to distinguish individuals and to be persistent through development

template: a miniature copy of a pattern stored in long-term memory

test-retest reliability: the **correlation** of one test over time

theory of mind: term currently used in studies of children's ability to work out what other people know, believe and feel, even when the other people's mental state, knowledge, beliefs and feelings are different from the child's

threshold: the minimum level of physical intensity that can be detected

time and motion studies: observing, filming or videotaping behaviour at work to cut out superfluous movements or to determine the optimal movements; often used to develop a pay standard

tonotopic representation: at the auditory cortex particular **neurons** are responsive to particular frequencies, corresponding to particular basilar membrane locations, known as tonotopic representation

top-down processing: processing which is influenced by context, stored knowledge, expectations, and so on; see **bottom-up processing**

topographical map: a mapping in which spatial relationships are preserved, e.g. when the response properties of **neurons** in the visual cortex are examined there is an orderly relationship between the retina and the cortex, adjacent regions of retina are associated with adjacent neurons in the visual cortex

total quality management (TQM): usually a team-based job design which emphasizes continuous improvement of quality and feedback; see **lean production**

TQM: see **total quality management**

trace-dependent forgetting: forgetting due to the loss of the relevant memory trace; see **cue-dependent forgetting**

training evaluation: checking the success of training

training needs assessment: checks what the person and the organization need in terms of future skills and competencies

transfer: using behaviours in work that were learnt in training

transfer contract: it stipulates when and where the skills learnt in training will be used in practice

transfer knowledge: the knowledge needed to **transfer**

transference: in **psychoanalysis** the feelings that the patient develops towards the analyst which are assumed to represent the patient's unconscious conflicts; see **countertransference**

transformational leadership: followers transcend their self-interest for the good of the organization; according to Bass it consists of idealized influence, inspiration, intellectual stimulation and individual consideration

transmitter: a chemical that is released at one neuron and influences either a neuron or muscle cell with which the neuron is in contact

transmitter substance: chemical secreted by nerve cells for the purpose of communication with other nerve cells, e.g. acetylcholine, noradrenaline, serotonin and dopamine.

treatment aetiology fallacy: the logical error whereby the success of a particular treatment is taken to indicate the cause of the disorder

trial-and-error learning: a slow form of learning based on the correct response occurring after apparently random behaviour

tripartite model of attitude: a model of **attitude** comprising three components, i.e. cognitive, affective and behavioural responses toward an object; see **unidimensional model of attitude**

type A behaviour: an action-emotion complex or **syndrome** consisting of vigorous voice and psychomotor mannerisms, hard-driving and time-pressured job involvement, competitiveness, impatience and easily aroused anger and hostility

unconditional positive regard: acceptance and respect given to someone regardless of how that person behaves; used by therapists within Rogers's approach to therapy

unconditioned response (UR): a response (e.g. salivation) which is produced by the **unconditioned stimulus** (e.g. food) without any prior learning or conditions in all members of the same species; see **conditional response**

unconditioned stimulus (US): according to Pavlov, a stimulus which is biologically significant (e.g. food or a painful stimulus) in that it elicits an **unconditioned response**; that is, a stimulus that, in the absence of any prior learning or any prior conditions, produces the same response (UR) in all members of the same animal species; see **conditioned stimulus**

unconscious: in **psychoanalysis**, it consists of thoughts which are very hard or impossible to bring into the **conscious**

unidimensional model of attitude: a model of **attitude** as a general and stable evaluative orientation towards a person, object or issue; see **tripartite model of attitude**

universals: things shared by all human beings

UR: see **unconditoned response**

US: see **unconditoned stimulus**

validity: the extent to which a test measures what it claims to be measuring; see **external validity**

validity generalization: one validity coefficient applies to various settings and groups of people

variable: a phenomenon (e.g. psychological characteristics or behaviour) whose value (established by **operational definition**) varies and can be measured; see **dependent variable** and **independent variable**

vicarious reinforcement: the notion that the effects of **observational learning** depend on whether the model is rewarded or punished

visual agnosia: a condition caused by brain damage in which there are great problems with recognizing common objects from vision in spite of the fact that many visual processes are intact

visual constancies: the tendency for the perceived size, colour, shape, and so on of objects to remain the same in spite of large variations in the retinal image

visual realism: see **intellectual realism**

voluntary informed consent: a key aspect of ethical research, based on the notion that participants in a study should agree voluntarily to take part after having been fully informed of the nature of the study and what will be required of them

voluntary movement: a movement that is initiated with a conscious intention or goal

we-self: concept of the self, characteristic of eastern culture, in which the self is experienced as dependent on other members of the society rather than autonomous; see **I-self**

well-defined problems: problems in which the initial state, the goal state and the permissible operators are all clearly specified; see **ill-defined problems**

word superiority effect: the finding that people can decide faster whether or not a letter was in a letter string when the string forms a word

Yerkes-Dodson Law: the principle that general performance is better at moderate degrees of anxiety than it is at high or low degrees of anxiety

zone of proximal development (ZPD): the term introduced by Vygotsky (1978) to describe the time between children learning to perform a new skill with the help of a more experienced person and the time when they can manage it by themselves

References

Aboud, F. (1988) *Children and Prejudice*. Oxford: Blackwell.

Abrams, D. (1984) Social identity, self-awareness, and intergroup behaviour. Unpublished doctoral thesis, University of Kent, Canterbury.

Abrams, D. and Hogg, M. (1990) *Social Identity Theory: Constructive and critical advances*. Hemel Hempstead: Harvester Wheatsheaf.

Abramson, L.Y., Seligman, M.E.P. and Teasdale, J.D. (1978) Learned helplessness in humans: critique and reformulation. *Journal of Abnormal Psychology* 87: 49–74.

Abramson, L.Y., Metalsky, G.I. and Alloy, L.B. (1989) Hopelessness depression: a theory-based subtype of depression. *Psychological Review* 96: 358–72.

Ackerman, P.L. (1988) Determinants of individual differences during skill acquisition: cognitive abilities and information processing. *Journal of Experimental Psychology: General* 117: 288–318.

Ackerman, P.L. (1992) Predicting individual differences in complex skill acquisition: dynamics of ability determinants. *Journal of Applied Psychology* 77: 598–614.

Adams, C.D. (1982) Variations in the sensitivity of instrumental responding to reinforcer devaluation. *Quarterly Journal of Experimental Psychology* 34B: 77–98.

Adams, C.D. and Dickinson, A. (1981) Instrumental responding following reinforcer devaluation. *Quarterly Journal of Experimental Psychology* 33B: 109–22.

Aggleton, J.P. and Passingham, R.E. (1982) An assessment of the reinforcing properties of foods after amygdaloid lesions in rhesus monkeys. *Journal of Comparative and Physiological Psychology* 96: 71–7.

Aiken, L.S. and West, S.G. (1991) *Multiple Regression: Testing and interpreting interactions*. Newbury Park, CA: Sage.

Ainsworth, M.D.S., Blehar, M.C., Walters, E. and Wall, S. (1978) *Patterns of Attachment: A psychological study of the strange situation*. Hillsdale, NJ: Lawrence Erlbaum.

Ajzen, I. (1985) From intentions to actions: a theory of planned behaviour, in J. Kuhl and J. Beckmann (eds) *Action-Control: From cognition to behavior*. Heidelberg: Springer-Verlag.

Ajzen, I. (1988) *Attitudes, Personality and Behavior*. Chicago: Dorsey.

Ajzen, I. (1991) The theory of planned behavior. *Organizational Behavior and Human Decision Processes* 50: 179–211.

Ajzen, I. and Fishbein, M. (1977) Attitude–behavior relations: a theoretical analysis and review of empirical research. *Psychological Bulletin* 84: 888–918.

Ajzen, I. and Madden, T.J. (1986) Prediction of goal-directed behavior: attitudes, intentions and perceived behavioral control. *Journal of Experimental Social Psychology* 22: 453–74.

Ajzen, I., Dalto, C.A. and Blyth, D.P. (1979) Consistency and bias in the attribution of attitudes. *Journal of Personality and Social Psychology* 37: 1871–6.

Ajzen, I., Timko, C. and White, J.B. (1982) Self-monitoring and the attitude–behavior relation. *Journal of Personality and Social Psychology* 42: 426–35.

Alba, J.W. and Hasher, L. (1983) Is memory schematic? *Psychological Bulletin* 93: 203–31.

Aldrich, H.E. (1982) The origins and persistence of social networks: a comment, in P.V. Marsden and N. Lin (eds) *Social Structure and Network Analysis*. Beverly Hills, CA: Sage.

Aldridge-Morris, R. (1989) *Multiple Personality: An exercise in deception*. Hove: Lawrence Erlbaum.

Alexander, C.N. and Wiley, M.G. (1981) Situated activity and identity formation, in M. Resenberg and R.H. Turner (eds) *Social Psychology: Sociological perspectives*. New York: Basic Books.

Alioth, A. (1980) *Entwicklung und Einführung alternativer Arbeitsformen*. Bern: Huber.

Allan, L.G. and Jenkins, H.M. (1983) The effect of representations of binary variables on judgment of influence. *Learning and Motivation* 14: 381–405.

Allbritton, D.W., McKoon, G. and Ratcliff, R. (1996) Reliability of prosodic cues for resolving syntactic ambiguity. *Journal of Experimental Psychology: Learning, Memory, and Cognition* 22: 714–35.

Allen, V.L. and Wilder, D.A. (1979) Group categorisation and attribution of belief similarity. *Small Group Behaviour* 19: 73–80.

Alloy, L.B. and Abramson, L.Y. (1979) Judgment of contingency in depressed and nondepressed students: sadder but wiser? *Journal of Experimental Psychology: General* 108: 441–85.

Allport, D.A. (1993) Attention and control: have we been asking the wrong questions? A critical review of twenty-five years, in D.E. Meyer and S.M. Kornblum (eds) *Attention and Performance*, vol. 14. London: MIT Press.

Allport, D.A., Antonis, B. and Reynolds, P. (1972) On the division of attention: a disproof of the single channel hypothesis. *Quarterly Journal of Experimental Psychology* 24: 225–35.

Allport, G.W. (1924) *Social Psychology*. New York: Houghton Mifflin.

Allport, G.W. (1935) Attitudes, in C.M. Murchison (ed.) *Handbook of Social Psychology*. Worcester, MA: Clark University Press.

Allport, G.W. and Odbert, H.S. (1936) Trait-names: a psycho-lexical study. *Psychological Monographs* 47: 211.

Altemeyer, B. (1981) *Right-Wing Authoritarianism*. Winnipeg: University of Manitoba Press.

American Psychiatric Association (1994) *Diagnostic and Statistical Manual of Mental Disorders*. 4th edn. Washington, DC: American Psychiatric Association.

American Psychological Association (1991) Draft of APA Ethics Code. *APA Monitor* 22: 30–5.

Anand, B.K. and Brobeck, J.R. (1951) Localization of a feeding center in the hypothalamus of the rat. *Proceedings of the Society for Experimental Biology and Medicine* 77: 323–24.

Anderson, J.R. (1983) *The Architecture of Cognition*. Cambridge, MA: Harvard University Press.

Anderson, J.R. (1993) *Rules of the Mind*. Hillsdale, NJ: Lawrence Erlbaum.

Anderson, J.R. and Bower, G.H. (1972) Recognition and retrieval processes in free recall. *Psychological Review* 79: 97–123.

Anderson, J.R., Greeno, J.G., Kline, P.J. and Neves, D.M. (1981) Acquisition of problem solving skill, in J.R. Anderson (ed.) *Cognitive Skills and their Acquisition*. Hillsdale, NJ: Lawrence Erlbaum.

Anderson, M. (1992) *Intelligence and Development*. Oxford: Blackwell.

Andersson, S.I. and Ekdahl C. (1992) Self-appraisal and coping in out-patients with chronic disease. *Scandinavian Journal of Psychology* 33: 289–300.

Angst, J. (1992) Epidemiology of depression. 2nd International Symposium on Moclobemide: RIMA (Reversible Inhibitor of Monamine Oxidase Type A): A new concept in the treatment of depression. *Psychopharmacology* 106 (suppl.): 71–4.

Annau, Z. and Kamin, L.J. (1961) The conditioned emotional response as a function of intensity of the US. *Journal of Comparative and Physiological Psychology* 54: 428–32.

Antell, S.E. and Keating, D.P. (1983) Perception of numerical invariance in neonates. *Child Development* 54: 695–701.

Antoni, C. (1996) *Teilautonome Arbeitsgruppen*. Weinheim: Psychologie Verlags Union.

Arborelius, E. (1996) Using doctor–patient communication to affect patients' lifestyles: theoretical and practical implications. *Psychology and Health* 11: 845–55.

Arcediano, F., Ortega, N. and Matute, H. (1996) A behavioural preparation for the study of human Pavlovian conditioning. *Quarterly Journal of Experimental Psychology* 49B: 270–83.

Archer, J. and Lloyd, B. (1986) *Sex and Gender*. Cambridge: Cambridge University Press.

Argyle, M. (1984) *Bodily Communication*, 2nd edn. London: Methuen.

Argyle, M. (1994) *The Psychology of Social Class*. London: Routledge.

Aristotle (1991) *The Art of Rhetoric*. Harmondsworth: Penguin.

Armon-Jones, C. (1986a) The thesis of constructivism, in R. Harré (ed.) *The Social Construction of Emotions*. Blackwell: Oxford.

Armon-Jones, C. (1986b) The social function of emotions, in R. Harré (ed.) *The Social Construction of Emotions*. Oxford: Blackwell.

Arnett, J. (1992) Reckless behavior in adolescence: a developmental perspective. *Developmental Review* 12: 339–73.

Arnold, J., Cooper, C.L. amd Robertson, I.T. (1995) *Work Psychology: Understanding human behaviour in the workplace*, 2nd edn. London: Pitman.

Arnold, M.B. and Gasson, J.A. (1954) Feelings and emotions as dynamic factors in personality integration, in M.B. Arnold and S.J. Gasson (eds) *The Human Person*. New York: Ronald.

Aronoff, J. (1967) *Psychological Needs and Cultural Systems: A case study*. Princeton, NJ: Van Nostrand.

Asch, S.E. (1952) *Social Psychology*. Englewood Cliffs, NJ: Prentice Hall.

Asch, S.E. (1955) Opinions and social pressure. *Scientific American* 193: 31–5.

Asch, S.E. (1956) Studies of independence and conformity: a minority of one against a unanimous majority. *Psychological Monographs* 70(9).

Ashcraft, M.H. (1994) *Human Memory and Cognition*, 2nd edn. New York: HarperCollins.

Ashford, S.J. and Tsui, A.S. (1991) Self-regulation for managerial effectiveness: the role of active feedback seeking. *Academy of Management Journal* 34(2): 251–80.

Atkins, C.J., Kaplan, R.M. and Toshiman, M.T. (1991) Close relationships in the epidemiology of cardiovascular disease, in W.H. Jones and D. Perlman (eds) *Advances in Personal Relationships*, vol. 3. London: Jessica Kingsley.

Atkinson, R.C. and Shiffrin, R.M. (1968) Human memory: a proposed system and its control processes, in K.W. Spence and J.T. Spence (eds) *The Psychology of Learning and Motivation*, vol. 2. London: Academic Press.

Atkinson, R.L., Atkinson, R.C., Smith, E.E. and Bem, D.J. (1993). *Introduction to Psychology*, 11th edn. New York: Harcourt Brace.

Atrens, D.M. (1984) Self-stimulation and psychotropic drugs: a methodological and conceptual critique, in N.W. Bond (ed.) *Animal Models in Psychopathology*. Academic Press.

Austin, J T. and Vancouver, J.B. (1996) Goal constructs in psychology: structure, process, and content. *Psychological Bulletin* 120: 338–75.

Averill, J. R. (1982) *Anger and Aggression. An essay on emotion*. New York: Springer.

Avis, J. and Harris, P.L. (1991) Belief-desire reasoning among Baka children: evidence for a universal conception of mind. *Child Development* 62: 460–7.

Axsom, D. and Cooper, J. (1981) Cognitive dissonance and psychotherapy: the role of effort justification in inducing weight loss. *Journal of Experimental Social Psychology* 21: 149–60.

Azjen, I. (1985) From intentions to actions: a theory of planned behaviour, in J. Kuhland and J. Beckman (eds) *Action-Control: From cognitions to behavior*. Heidelberg: Springer.

Azjen, I. (1991) The theory of planned behavior. *Organizational Behavior and Human Decision Processes* 50: 179–211.

Baars, B.J. (1988) *A Cognitive Theory of Consciousness*. Cambridge: Cambridge University Press.

Baars, B.J. (1997) Consciousness versus attention, perception, and working memory. *Consciousness and Cognition* 6: 363–71.

Back, K.W. (1951) Influence through social communication. *Journal of Abnormal and Social Psychology* 46: 9–23.

Baddeley, A.D. (1982) Domains of recollection. *Psychological Review* 89: 708–29.

Baddeley, A.D. (1984) Neuropsychological evidence and the semantic/episodic distinction. *Behavioral and Brain Sciences* 7: 238–9.

Baddeley, A.D. (1986) *Working Memory*. Oxford: Oxford University Press.

Baddeley, A.D. (1990) *Human Memory: Theory and practice*. Hove: Lawrence Erlbaum.

Baddeley, A.D. and Hitch, G.J. (1974) Working memory, in G.H. Bower (ed.) *The Psychology of Learning and Motivation*, vol. 8. London: Academic Press.

Baddeley, A.D. and Hitch, G. (1977) Recency re-examined, in S. Dornic (ed.) *Attention and performance*, vol. 6. Hillsdale, NJ: Lawrence Erlbaum.

Baddeley, A.D. and Lewis, V.J. (1981) Inner active processes in reading: the inner voice, the inner ear and the inner eye, in A.M. Lesgold and C.A. Perfetti (eds) *Interactive Processes in Reading*. Hillsdale, NJ: Lawrence Erlbaum.

Baddeley, A.D. and Warrington, E.K. (1970). Amnesia and the distinction between long- and short-term memory. *Journal of Verbal Learning and Verbal Behavior* 9: 176–89.

Baddeley, A.D. and Wilson, B. (1985) Phonological coding and short-term memory in patients without speech. *Journal of Memory and Language* 24: 490–502.

Baddeley, A.D., Thomson, N. and Buchanan, M. (1975) Word length and the structure of short-term memory. *Journal of Verbal Learning and Verbal Behavior* 14: 575–89.

Bahrick, H.P. (1970) Two-phase model for prompted recall. *Psychological Review* 77: 215–22.

Baillargeon, R. (1986) Representing the existence and the location of hidden objects in 6 and 8 month old infants. *Cognition* 23: 21–52.

Baillargeon, R., Spelke, S. and Wasserman, S. (1985) Object permanence in five-month-old infants. *Cognition* 20: 191–208.

Bakan, D. (1966) *The Duality of Existence: Isolation and communion in western man*. Boston, MA: Beacon Press.

Bakeman, R. and Brownlee, J.R. (1980) The strategic use of parallel play: a sequential analysis. *Child Development* 51: 873–8.

Bakeman, R. and Gottman, J.M. (1986) *Observing Interaction: An introduction to sequential analysis*. Cambridge: Cambridge University Press.

Baker, A.G. and Mackintosh, N.J. (1977) Excitatory and inhibitory conditioning following uncorrelated presentations of CS and US. *Animal Learning and Behavior* 5: 315–19.

Baker, A.G. and Mercier, P. (1989) Attention, retrospective processing, and cognitive representations, in S.B. Klein and R.R. Mowrer (eds) *Contemporary Learning Theories: Pavlovian conditioning and the status of traditional learning theory*. Hillsdale, NJ: Lawrence Erlbaum.

Baker, R. (1996) *Sperm Wars*. London: Fourth Estate.

Baker, R. and Bellis, M. (1995) *Human Sperm Competition: Copulation, competition and infidelity*. London: Chapman and Hall.

Balch, P. and Ross, A.W. (1975) Predicting success in weight reduction as a function of locus of control: a unidimensional and multidimensional approach. *Journal of Consulting and Clinical Psychology* 43: 119.

Baldwin, T.T. and Ford, J.K. (1988) Transfer of training: a review and directions for future research. *Personnel Psychology* 41: 63–105.

Balleine, B. and Job, R.F.S. (1991) Reconsideration of the role of competing responses in demonstrations of the interference effect (learned helplessness). *Journal of Experimental Psychology: Animal Behavior Processes* 17: 270–80.

Bamber, J.H. (1979) *The Fears of Adolescence*. London: Academic Press.

Bamberg, E. and Busch, C. (1996) Betriebliche Gesundheitsförderung durch Streßmanagementtraining: Eine Metaanalyse (quasi-)experimenteller Studien. *Zeitschrift für Arbeits- und Organisationspsychologie* 40: 127–37.

Bandura, A. (1965) Influence of models' reinforcement contingencies on the acquisition of imitative responses. *Journal of Personality and Social Psychology* 1: 589–95.

Bandura, A. (1969a) *Principles of Behaviour Modification*. New York: Rinehart and Winston.

Bandura, A. (1969b) Social learning theory of identificatory processes, in D.A. Goslin (ed.) *Handbook of Socialization Theory and Research*. Chicago: Rand McNally.

Bandura, A. (1977a) Self-efficacy: toward a unifying theory of behavioural change. *Psychological Review* 84: 191–215.

Bandura, A. (1977b) *Social Learning Theory*. Englewood Cliffs, NJ: Prentice Hall.

Bandura, A. (1986) *Social Foundations of Thought and Action: A social cognitive theory*. Englewood Cliffs, NJ: Prentice Hall.

Bandura, A. (1991) Self-Efficacy mechanism in physiological activation and health-promoting behavior, in J. Madden IV (ed.) *Neurobiology of Learning, Emotion and Affect*. New York: Raven Press.

Bandura, A. and Kupers, C.J. (1964) The transmission of patterns of self-reinforcement through modeling. *Journal of Abnormal and Social Psychology* 69: 1–9.

Bandura, A., Ross, D. and Ross, S.A. (1963) Imitation of film-mediated aggressive models. *Journal of Abnormal and Social Psychology* 66: 3–11.

Banyard, P. and Grayson, A. (1996) *Introducing Psychological Research*. London: Macmillan.

Barber, J.P. and DeRubeis, R.J. (1989) On second thought: where the action is in cognitive therapy for depression. *Cognitive Therapy and Research* 13: 441–57.

Barclay, J.R., Bransford, J.D., Franks, J.J., McCarrell, N.S. and Nitsch, K.E. (1974) Comprehension and semantic flexibility. *Journal of Verbal Learning and Verbal Behavior* 13: 471–81.

Bard, P. (1928) A diencephalic mechanism for the expression of rage with special reference to the sypathetic nervous system. *Americal Journal of Physiology* 84: 490–513.

Bargh, J.A. (1982) Attention and automaticity in the processing self-relevant information. *Journal of Personality and Social Psychology* 43: 425–36.

Barker, E. (1984) *The Making of a Moonie: Choice or brainwashing?* Oxford: Blackwell.

Barlow, D.H. (1988) *Anxiety and its Disorders: The nature and treatment of anxiety and panic*. New York: Guilford Press.

Barlow, D.H. and Durand, V. (1995) *Abnormal Psychology*. Pacific Grove, CA: Brooks Cole.

Barnick, M.R. and Mount, M.K. (1991) The Big Five personality dimensions: a meta-analysis. *Personnel Psychology* 44: 1–26.

Barratt, M. and Lyons, E. (1997) Self-Categorisation theory and European identities. Unpublished paper, Social Psychology European Research Institute, University of Surrey.

Barrett, P.T. and Eysenck, H.J. (1992) Brain electrical potentials and intelligence, in A. Gale and M.W. Eysenck (eds) *Handbook of Individual Differences: Biological perspectives*. Chichester: Wiley.

Barrett, P.T. and Kline, P. (1982) An item and radial parcel analysis of the 16PF questionnaire. *Personality and Individual Differences* 3: 259–70.

Barry, H. III, Bacon, M.K. and Child, I.L. (1957) A cross-cultural survey of some sex differences in socialization. *Journal of Abnormal and Social Psychology* 55: 327–32.

Barsalou, L.W. (1982) Context-independent and context-dependent information in concepts. *Memory and Cognition* 10: 82–93.

Barsalou, L.W. (1983) Ad hoc categories. *Memory and Cognition* 11: 211–27.

Barsalou, L.W. (1989) Intra-concept similarity and its implications for inter-concept similarity, in S. Vosniadou and A. Ortony (eds) *Similarity and Analogical Reasoning*. Cambridge: Cambridge University Press.

Bartlett, F.C. (1932) *Remembering: A study in experimental and social psychology*. Cambridge: Cambridge University Press.

Bartoshuk, L.M. and Beauchamp, G.K. (1994) Chemical senses. *Annual Review of Psychology* 45: 419–49.

Bartsch, R., and Judd, C. (1993) Majority–minority status and perceived ingroup variability revisited. *European Journal of Social Psychology* 23: 471–85.

Bass, B.M. (1990) *Bass and Stogdill's Handbook of Leadership*, 3rd edn. New York: Free Press.

Battersby, W.S., Teuber, H.L. and Bender, M.B. (1953) Problem-solving behaviour in men with frontal or occipital brain injuries. *Journal of Psychology* 35: 329–51.

Bauer, D.H. (1976) An exploratory study of developmental changes in children's fear. *Journal of Child Psychology and Psychiatry* 17: 69–74.

Bauman, A. (1993) Effects of asthma patient education upon psychological and behavioural outcomes, in S. Maes, H. Leventhal and M. Johnston (eds) *International Review of Health Psychology 2*. Chichester: Wiley.

Baumrind, D. (1993) The average expectable environment is not good enough: a response to Scarr. *Child Development* 64: 1299–317.

Bavelas, J. and Lee, E.S. (1978) Effects of goal level on performance: a trade-off of quantity and quality. *Canadian Journal of Psychology* 32: 219–40.

Baylis, L.L. and Gaffan, D. (1991) Amygdalectomy and ventromedial prefrontal ablation produce similar deficits in food choice and in simple object discrimination learning for an unseen reward. *Experimental Brain Research* 86: 617–22.

Baylis, L.L. and Rolls, E.T. (1991) Responses of neurons in the primate taste cortex to glutamate. *Physiology and Behavior* 49: 973–9.

Beale, D.A. and Manstead, A.S.R. (1991) Predicting mothers' intentions to limit frequency of infants' sugar intake: testing the theory of planned behaviour. *Journal of Applied Social Psychology* 21: 409–31.

Bean, P. (1979) Psychiatrists' assessments of mental illness. *British Journal of Psychiatry* 135: 122–8.

Beauchamp, A.J., Gluck, J.P., Fouty, H.E. and Lewis, M.H. (1991) Associative processes in differentially reared rhesus monkeys (Macaca mulatta): blocking. *Developmental Psychobiology* 24: 175–89.

Beauvois, M.-F. (1982) Optic aphasia: a process of interaction between vision and language. *Philosophical Transactions of the Royal Society of London*, Series B 298: 35–47.

Beauvois, M.-F. and Derousne, J. (1979) Phonological alexia: three dissociations. *Journal of Neurology, Neurosurgery and Psychiatry* 42: 1115–24.

Beauvois, M.-F. and Derousne, J. (1981) Lexical or orthographic agraphia. *Brain* 104: 21–49.

Bebbington, P.E. and McGuffin, P. (1989) Interactive models of depression: the evidence, in K. Herbst and E. Paykel (eds) *Depression: An integrative approach*. Oxford: Heinemann.

Beck, A.T., Rush, A.J., Shaw, B.F. and Emery, G. (1979) *Cognitive Therapy of Depression*. New York: Guilford Press.

Becker, M.H. (1974) *The Health Belief Model and Personal Health Behavior*. San Fransico, CA: Society for Public Health Education.

Beekun, R.A. (1989) Assessing the effectiveness of sociotechnical interventions: antidode or fad? *Human Relations* 42: 877–97.

Belloc, N.B. and Breslow, L. (1972) Relationship of physical health status and health practices. *Preventive Medicine* 1: 409–21.

Belsky, J. (1984) The determinants of parenting: a process model. *Child Development* 55: 83–96.

Belsky, J. (1988) Infant day care and socioemotional development: the United States. *Journal of Child Psychology and Psychiatry* 29: 397–406.

Ben-Shakhar, G., Bar-Hillel, M., Bilu, Y., Ben-Abba, E. and Flug, A. (1986) Can graphology predict occupational success? Two empirical studies and some methodological ruminations. *Journal of Applied Psychology* 71(4): 645–53.

Bentall, R.P. (1990) The syndromes and symptoms of psychosis, in R. Bentall (ed.) *Reconstructing Schizophrenia*. London: Routledge

Bentler, P.M. and Speckart, G. (1979) Models of attitude–behavior relations. *Psychological Review* 86: 452–64.

Berdondini, L. and Smith, P.K. (1995) Cohesion and power in the families of children involved in bully/victim problems at school: an Italian replication. *Journal of Family Therapy* 18: 99–102.

Berger, B. and Kellner, H. (1973) *The Homeless mind: Modernization and consciousness*. Harmondsworth: Penguin.

Berger, P.L. and Luckman, T. (1966) *The Social Construction of Reality*. London: Allen Lane.

Bergin, A.E (1971) The evaluation of therapeutic outcomes, in A.E. Bergin and S.L. Garfield (eds) *Handbook of Psychotherapy and Behavioural Change*. New York: Wiley.

Bergin, A.E. and Garfield, S.L. (1994) *Handbook of Psychotherapy and Behavioural Change*, 4th edn. New York: Wiley.

Berkman, L.F. and Syme, S.L. (1979) Social networks, host resistance and mortality: a nine year follow-up of Alameda county residents. *American Journal of Epidemiology* 109: 186–204.

Berkowitz, L. (1964) Aggressive cues in aggressive behavior and hostility catharsis. *Psychological Review* 71: 104–22.

Berkun, M.M., Bialek, H.M., Kern, R.P. and Yagi, K. (1962) Experimental studies of psychological stress in man. *Psychological Monographs* 76: 15.

Berlinger, L.R., Glick, W.H. and Rodgers, R.C. (1988) Job enrichment and performance improvement, in J.P. Campbell and R.J. Campbell (eds) *Productivity in Organizations*. San Francisco, CA: Jossey-Bass.

Berndt, T.J. (1979) Developmental changes in conformity to peers and parents. *Developmental Psychology* 15: 608–16.

Bernstein, I.L. (1978) Learned taste aversions in children receiving chemotherapy. *Science* 200: 1302–3.

Bernstein, I.L. (1991) Aversion conditioning in response to cancer and cancer treatment. *Clinical Psychology Review* 11: 185–91.

Berridge, K.C. (1995) Food reward: brain substrates of wanting and liking. *Neuroscience and Biobehavioural Reviews* 20: 1–25.

Berridge, K.C. and Robinson, T.E. (1997) The role of dopamine in reward: hedonics, learning, and incentive salience after 6-hydroxydopamine lesions. *Brain Research Reviews* (submitted).

Berridge, K.C. and Valenstein, E.S. (1991) What psychological process mediates feeding evoked by electrical stimulation of the lateral hypothalamus? *Behavioural Neuroscience* 105: 3–14.

Berridge, K.C., Venier, I.L. and Robinson, T.E. (1989) Taste reactivity analysis of 6-hydroxydopamine-induced aphagia: implications for arousal and anhedonia hypotheses of dopamine function. *Behavioural Neuroscience* 103: 36–45.

Bertelson, A., Harvald, B. and Hauge, M. (1977) A Danish twin study of manic-depressive disorders. *British Journal of Psychiatry* 130: 330–51.

Best, D.L., Williams, J.E., Cloud, L.M., Davis, S.W., Robertson, L.S., Edwards, J.R., Giles, H. and Fowles, J. (1977) Development of sex-trait stereotypes among young children in the United States, England and Ireland. *Child Development* 48: 1375–84.

Best, P.J., Best, M.R. and Henggeler, S. (1977) The contribution of environmental noningestive cues in conditioning with aversive internal consequences, in L.M. Barker, M.R. Best and M. Domjan (eds) *Learning Mechanisms in Food Selection*. Waco, TX: Baylor University Press.

Beutler, L.E., Cargo, M. and Arizmendi, T.G. (1986) Therapist variables in psychotherapy process and outcome, in S.L. Garfield and A.E. Bergin (eds) *Handbook of Psychotherapy and Behaviour Change*, 3rd edn. Chichester: Wiley.

Biederman, I. (1987) Recognition-by-components: a theory of human image understanding. *Psychological Review* 94: 115–47.

Biederman, I. (1990) Higher-level vision, in D.N. Osherson, S. Kossyln, and J. Hollerbach (eds) *An Invitation to Cognitive Science: Visual cognition and action*. Cambridge, MA: MIT Press.

Biederman, I., Ju, G. and Clapper, J. (1985) The perception of partial objects. Unpublished manuscript, State University of New York at Buffalo.

Bigelow, B.J. and La Gaipa, J.J. (1980) The development of friendship values and choice, in H.C. Foot, A.J. Chapman and J.R. Smith (eds) *Friendship and Social Relations in Children*. Chichester: Wiley.

Billig, M. (1991) *Ideologies and Opinions*. London: Sage.

Billig, M. and Tajfel, H. (1973) Social categorisation and similarity in intergroup behaviour. *European Journal of Social Psychology* 3: 27–52

Birch, H.G. (1945) The relationship of previous experience to insightful problem solving. *Journal of Comparative Psychology* 38: 267–383.

Birren, J.E. (1969) The concept of functional age. *Human Development* 12: 214–15.

Bishop, G.D. (1994) *Health Psychology, Integrating Body and Mind*. Boston, MA: Allyn and Bacon.

Bjorkqvist, K., Lagerspetz, K.M.J. and Kaukainen, A. (1992) Do girls manipulate and boys fight? Developmental trends in regard to direct and indirect aggression. *Aggressive Behavior* 18: 117–27.

Blackburn, J.R., Pfaus, J.G. and Phillips, A.G. (1992) Dopamine functions in appetitive and defensive behaviours. *Progress in Neurobiology* 39: 247–79.

Blair, J. (1987) *Who Gets Sick*. Houston, TX: Peak Press.

Blake, R.R. and Mouton, J.S. (1964) *The Managerial Grid*. Houston, TX: Gulf.

Blake, R. Helson, H. and Mouton, J.S. (1957) The generality of conformity of factual anchorage, difficulty of task and amount of social pressure. *Journal of Personality* 23(3): 48–58.

Blanz, M., Mummendey, A. and Otten, S. (1995) Perceptions of relative group size and group status: on intergroup discrimination in negative evaluations. *European Journal of Social Psychology* 25: 231–47.

Blinkhorn, S. and Johnson, C. (1990) The insignificance of personality. *Nature* 348: 671–2.

Block, J. (1995) A contrarian view of the five-factor approach to personality description. *Psychological Bulletin* 117: 187–215.

Block, J.H., Gjerde, P.F. and Block, J.H. (1991) Personality antecedents of depressive tendencies in 18 year olds: a prospective study. *Journal of Personality and Social Psychology* 60: 726–38.

Block, N. (1995) How heritability misleads about race. *Cognition* 56: 99–128.

Blum, J.E., Jarvik, L F. and Clark, E.T. (1970) Rate of change on selective tests of intelligence: a twenty-year longitudinal study. *Journal of Gerontology* 25: 171–6.

Blumer, H. (1937) Social psychology, in E.P. Schmidt (ed.) *Man and Society*. New York: Prentice Hall.

Boakes, R.A. (1984) *From Darwin to Behaviourism: Psychology and the minds of animals*. Cambridge: Cambridge University Press.

Boakes, R.A., Westbrook, R.F., Elliot, M. and Swinbourne, A.L. (1997) Context dependency of conditioned aversions to water and sweet tastes. *Journal of Experimental Psychology: Animal Behavior Processes* 23: 56–67.

Bock, K. and Levelt, W. (1994). Language production: grammatical encoding, in M.A. Gernsbacher (ed.) *Handbook of Psycholinguistics*. London: Academic Press.

Bolles, R.C. (1970) Species-specific defense reactions and avoidance learning. *Psychological Review* 77: 32–48.

Bolton, N. (1972) *The Psychology of Thinking*. London: Methuen.

Booth, D.A. (1985) Food-conditioned eating preferences and aversions with interoceptive elements: learned appetites and satieties. *Annals of the New York Academy of Sciences* 443: 22–37.

Borman, W.C. and Motowidlo, S.J. (1993) Expanding the criterion domain to include elements of contextual performance, in N. Schmitt and W.C. Borman (eds) *Personnel Selection in Organizations*. San Francisco, CA: Jossey-Bass.

Borsini, F. and Rolls, E.T. (1984) Role of noradrenaline and serotonin in the basolateral region of the amygdala in food preferences and learned taste aversions in the rat. *Physiology and Behavior* 33: 37–43.

Boucher, J.D. (1983) Antecedents to emotions across cultures, in J.W. Berry and S.H. Irvine (eds) *Human Assessment and Culture Factors*. New York: Plenum.

Boucher, J.D. and Brant, M.E. (1981) Judgment of emotion: American and Malay antecedents. *Journal of Cross-Cultural Psychology* 12: 272–83.

Boucher, J.D. and Carlson, G.E. (1980). Recognition of facial expression in three cultures. *Journal of Cross-Cultural Psychology* 11: 263–80.

Boulton, M.J. and Smith, P.K. (1994) Bully/victim problems in middle school children: stability, self-perceived competence, peer perceptions and peer acceptance. *British Journal of Developmental Psychology* 12: 315–29.

Bouton, M.E. (1993) Context, time, and memory retrieval in the interference paradigms of Pavlovian learning. *Psychological Bulletin* 114: 80–99.

Bovard, E.W. (1948) Social norms and the individual. *Journal of Abnormal and Social Psychology* 43: 1–8.

Bovard, E.W. (1951) Group structure and perception. *Journal of Abnormal and Social Psychology* 46: 398–405.

Bovard, E.W. (1985) Brain mechanisms in effects of social support on viability, in R.B. Williams (ed.) *Perspectives on Behavioral Medicine*, vol. 2. Orlando, FL: Academic Press.

Bower, G.H. (1981) Mood and memory. *American Psychologist* 36: 129–48.

Bower, G.H., Black, J.B. and Turner, T.J. (1979) Scripts in memory for text. *Cognitive Psychology* 11: 177–220.

Bower, T.G.R. (1964) Discrimination of depth in premotor infants. *Psychonomic Science* 1: 368.

Bower, T.G.R. (1971) Objects in the world of the infant. *Scientific American* 225: 30–8.

Bower, T.G.R. (1982) *Development in Infancy*, 2nd edn. New York: W.H. Freeman.

Bowers, K. (1973) Situationism in psychology: an analysis and a critique. *Psychological Review* 80: 307–36.

Bowlby, J. (1953) *Child Care and the Growth of Love.* Harmondsworth: Penguin.

Bowlby, J. (1971) *Attachment and Loss, Vol. 1. Attachment.* London: Hogarth.

Bowlby, J. (1973) *Attachment and Loss, Vol. 2. Separation: Anxiety and anger.* London: Hogarth.

Boyanoswky, E.O. and Allen, V.L. (1973) Ingroup norms and self-identity as determinants of discriminatory behaviour. *Journal of Personality and Social Psychology* 25: 408–18.

Boyle, M. (1990) The non-discovery of schizophrenia, in R. Bentall (ed.) *Reconstructing Schizophrenia.* London: Routledge.

Braine, M.D.S. (1978) On the relationship between the natural logic of reasoning and standard logic. *Psychological Review* 85: 1–21.

Braine, M.D.S. and O'Brien, D.P. (1991) A theory of If: a lexical entry, reasoning program and pragmatic principles. *Psychological Review* 98: 182–203.

Braine, M.D.S., Reiser, B.J. and Rumain, B. (1984) Some empirical justification for a theory of natural propositional logic, in G.H. Bower (ed.) *The Psychology of Learning and Motivation*, vol. 18. New York: Academic Press.

Bramel, D. and Friend, R. Jr (1981) Hawthorne, the myth of the docile worker, and class bias in psychology. *American Psychologist* 36: 867–78.

Brannon, L. and Feist, J. (1997) *Health Psychology: An introduction to behavior and health.* Pacific Grove, CA: Brooks/Cole.

Branscombe, N., Wann, D., Noel, J. and Coleman, J. (1993) Ingroup or outgroup extremity: importance of the threatened social identity. *Personality and Social Psychology Bulletin* 19: 381–8.

Bransford, J.D. (1979) *Human Cognition: Learning, understanding and remembering.* Belmont, CA: Wadsworth.

Bransford, J.D. and Johnson, M.K. (1972) Contextual prerequisites for understanding: some investigations of comprehension and recall. *Journal of Verbal Learning and Verbal Behavior* 11: 717–26.

Bransford, J.D., Barclay, J.R. and Franks, J.J. (1972) Sentence memory: a constructive versus interpretive approach. *Cognitive Psychology* 3: 193–209.

Bransford, J.D., Franks, J.J., Morris, C.D. and Stein, B.S. (1979) Some general constraints on learning and memory research, in L.S. Cermak and F.I.M. Craik (eds) *Levels of Processing in Human Memory.* Hillsdale, NJ: Lawrence Erlbaum.

Bray, D.W., Campbell, R.J. and Grant, D.L. (1974) *Formative Years in Business: A long term AT and T study of managerial lives.* New York: Wiley.

Brazier, M.A.B. (1959) The historical development of neurophysiology, in *Handbook of Physiology*, section 1, vol. 1. Bethseda, MD: American Physiological Association.

Breakwell, G. (1986) *Coping with Threatened Identities.* London: Methuen.

Breakwell, G. (1992a) Processes of self-evaluation: efficacy and estrangement, in G.M. Breakwell (ed.) *Social Psychology of Identity and the Self-concept.* London: Academic Press.

Breakwell, G. (ed.) (1992b) *Social Psychology of Identity and the Self-concept.* London: Academic Press.

Breakwell, G. (1993) Integrating paradigms: methodological implications, in G. Breakwell and D. Cantor (eds) *Empirical Approaches to Social Representations.* Oxford: Clarendon Press.

Breakwell, G. and Fife-Schaw, C. (1992) Sexual activities and preferences in a United Kingdom sample of 16 to 20-year-olds. *Archives of Sexual Behavior* 21: 271–93.

Breakwell, G., Millward, L. and Fife-Schaw, C. (1994) Commitment to safer sex as a predictor of condom use amongst 16–20 year olds. *Journal of Social and Applied Psychology* 24(3): 189–217.

Brecht, B. (1935) Svendborger Gedichte, in B. Brecht (ed.) *Gesammelte Werke.* Frankfurt: Suhrkamp.

Breggin, P. (1991) *Toxic Psychiatry.* New York: St Martin's Press.

Breslow, L. and Enstrom, J.E. (1980) Persistence of health habits and their relationship to mortality. *Preventive Medicine* 9: 469–83.

Bretherton, I. and Waters, E. (eds) (1985) *Growing points of attachment theory and research. Monographs of the Society for Research in Child Development* 50: 1–2.

Brettencourt, B.A., Brewer, M.B., Croak, M. and Miller, N. (1992) Cooperation and the reduction of intergroup bias: the role of reward structure and social orientation. *Journal of Experimental Social Psychology* 28: 301–19.

Brewer, M.B. (1979) Ingroup bias in the minimal intergroup situation: a cognitive-motivational analysis. *Psychological Bulletin* 86(2): 307–24.

Brewer, M.B. and Kramer, R.M. (1985) The psychology of intergroup attitudes and behaviour. *Annual Review of Psychology* 36: 219–43.

Brewer, M.B. and Silver, M. (1978) Ingroup bias as a function of task characteristics. *European Journal of Social Psychology* 8: 393–400.

Brewin, C.R. (1988) *Cognitive Foundations of Clinical Psychology.* London: Lawrence Erlbaum.

Brim, O.G. and Wheeler, S. (1971) *Socialisation after Childhood: Two essays*. New York: Wiley.

British Psychological Society (1990). Ethical principles for conducting research with human participants. *The Psychologist* 3: 270–2.

Britton, B.K., Muth, K.D. and Glynn, S.M. (1986) Effects of text organisation on memory: test of a cognitive effect hypothesis with limited exposure time. *Discourse Processes* 9: 475–87.

Broadbent, D.E. (1958) *Perception and Communication*. Oxford: Pergamon.

Broadhead, R.S. (1980) Multiple identities and the process of their articulation: the case of medical students and their private lives. *Studies in Symbolic Interaction* 3: 171–91.

Brody, G.H., Stoneman, Z. and Wheatley, P. (1984) Peer interaction in the presence and absence of observers. *Child Development* 55: 1425–8.

Brody, L.R. (1994) On understanding gender differences in the expression of emotion: gender roles, socialization and language, in S. Ablon, D. Brown, E. Khantzian and J. Mack (eds) *Human Feelings: Explorations in affect development and meaning*. New York: Analytic Press.

Brody, L.R. and Hall, J.A. (1993) Gender and emotion, in M. Lewis and J.M. Haviland (eds) *Handbook of Emotions*. New York: Guilford Press.

Brogden, W.J. (1939) Sensory pre-conditioning. *Journal of Experimental Psychology* 25: 323–32.

Bromley, D.B. (1986) *The Case Study Method in Psychology and Related Disiplines*. Chichester: Wiley.

Bronson, G. (1974) The postnatal growth of visual capacity. *Child Development* 45: 873–90.

Brown, A.L. (1987) Metacognition, action control, self-regulation, and others, still more mysterious mechanisms, in F.W. Weinert and R.H. Kluwe (eds) *Metacognition, Motivation, and Understanding*. Hillsdale, NJ: Lawrence Erlbaum.

Brown, B.B., Mory, M.S. and Kinney, D. (1994) Casting adolescent crowds in a relational perspective: caricature, channnel, and context, in R. Montemayor, G.R. Adams and T.P. Gullotta (eds) *Personal Relationships during Adolescence*. London: Sage.

Brown, C.A. and Detoy, C.J. (1988) A comparison of the personal constructs of management in new and experienced managers, in F. Fransella and L. Thomas (eds) *Experimenting with Personal Construct Psychology*. London: Routledge and Kegan Paul.

Brown, G.W. (1989) Depression: a radical social perspective, in K. Herbst and E.S. Paykel (eds) *Depression: An integrative approach*. Oxford: Heinemann Medical.

Brown, G.W. and Birley, J.L.T. (1968) Crisis and life change and the onset of schizophrenia. *Journal of Health and Social Behaviour* 9: 203–14.

Brown, G.W. and Harris, T.O. (1978) *Social Origins of Depression: A study of psychiatric disorder in women*. London: Tavistock.

Brown, G.W., Birley, J.L.T. and Wing, J.K. (1972) Influences of family life on the course of schizophrenic disorders: a replication. *British Journal of Psychiatry* 121: 241–58.

Brown, R. (1984) The role of similarity in intergroup relations, in H. Tajfel (ed.) *The Social Dimension: European developments in social psychology*, vol. 2. Cambridge: Cambridge University Press.

Brown, R. (1988) *Group Processes: Dynamics within and between groups*. Oxford: Blackwell.

Brown, R. (1995) *Prejudice: Its social psychology*. Oxford: Blackwell.

Brown, R. (1996) Intergroup relations, in M. Hewstone, W. Stroebe and G.M. Stephenson (eds) *Introduction to Social Psychology*, 2nd edn. Oxford: Blackwell.

Brown, R. and Ross, G.F. (1982) The battle for acceptance: an investigation into the dynamics of intergroup behaviour, in H. Tajfel (ed.) *Social Identity and Intergroup Relations*. Cambrige: Cambridge University Press.

Brown, R. and Turner, J.C. (1981) Interpersonal and inter-group behaviour, in J.C. Turner and H. Giles (eds) *Intergroup Behaviour*. Oxford: Blackwell.

Brown, R. and Williams, J. (1984) Group identification: the same thing to all people? *Human Relations* 37: 547–64.

Brown, R., Hinkle, S., Ely, P., Fox-Cardamone, L., Maras, P. and Taylor, L. (1992) Recognising group diversity: individualist/collectivist and autonomous/relational social orientations and their implications for intergroup processes. *British Journal of Social Psychology* 31: 327–42.

Brown, R.J. and Millward, L.J. (1993) Perceptions of group homogeneity during group formation and change. *Social Cognition* 11: 126–49.

Brown, R.J. and Smith, A. (1987) Perceptions of minority groups: the case of women in academia. *European Journal of Social Psychology* 19: 61–75.

Brown, R.J. and Wade, G. (1987) Superordinate goals and intergroup behaviour: the effect of role ambiguity and status on intergroup attitudes on task performance. *European Journal of Social Psychology* 17: 131–42.

Brown, R.J., Condor, S., Mathews, A., Wade, G. and Williams, J.A. (1986) Explaining intergroup differentiation in an industrial organization. *Journal of Occupational Psychology* 59: 273–86.

Brown, S. (1992) Meta-analysis of diabetes patient education research: variations in intervention effects across studies. *Research in Nursing and Health* 15: 409–19.

Browne, K. (1989) The naturalistic control of family violence and child abuse, in J. Archer and K. Browne (eds) *Human Aggression: Naturalistic approaches*. London: Routledge.

Bruce, V. and Green, P.R. (1990) *Visual Perception: Physiology, psychology, and ecology*, 2nd edn. Hove: Lawrence Erlbaum.

Bruce, V., Green, P.R. and Georgeson, M.A. (1996) *Visual Perception: Physiology, psychology, and ecology*, 3rd edn. Hove: Psychology Press.

Bruner, J.S. (1966) *Toward a theory of instruction*. Cambridge: Harvard University Press.

Bruner, J.S., Postman, L. and Rodrigues, J. (1951) Expectations and the perception of colour. *American Journal of Psychology* 64: 216–27.

Bruno, N. and Cutting, J.E. (1988) Mini-modularity and the perception of layout. *Journal of Experimental Psychology: General* 117: 161–70.

Bryant, P.E. (1974) *Perception and Understanding in Young Children*. London: Methuen.

Bryant, P.E. and Bradley, L. (1985) *Children's Reading Problems*. Oxford: Blackwell.

Bryant, P.E. and Trabasso, T. (1971) Transitive inferences and memory in young children. *Nature* 232: 456–8.

Bryant, P.E., Bradley, L., MacLean, M. and Crossland, J. (1989) Nursery rhymes, phonological skills and reading. *Journal of Child Language* 16: 407–28.

Bryant, P.E., MacLean, M., Bradley, L.L. and Crossland, J. (1990) Rhyme, alliteration, phoneme detection and learning to read. *Developmental Psychology* 26: 429–38.

Bryman, A. (1988) *Quantity and Quality in Social Research*. London: Unwin Hyman.

Bub, D., Cancelliere, A. and Kertesz, A. (1985) Whole-word and analytic translation of spelling to sound in a nonsemantic reader, in K.E. Patterson and M. Coltheart (eds) *Surface Dyslexia: Neuropsychological and cognitive studies of phonological reading*. Hove: Lawrence Erlbaum.

Bub, D., Black, S., Hampson, E. and Kertesz, A. (1988) Semantic encoding of pictures and words: some neuropsychological observations. *Cognitive Neuropsychology* 5: 27–66.

Bühler, C. and Massarik, F. (eds) (1968) *The Course of Human Development*. New York: Springer.

Bullock, M. and Gelman, R. (1979) Preschool children's assumptions about cause and effect. *Child Development* 50: 89–96.

Bullough, V.L. (1981) Age at menarche: a misunderstanding. *Science* 213: 365–6.

Burger, J.M. (1993) *Personality*, 3rd. edn. Pacific Grove, CA: Brooks/Cole.

Burke, M.J. and Day, R.R. (1986) A cumulative study of the effectiveness of managerial training. *Journal of Applied Psychology* 71: 232–45.

Burkitt, I. (1991) *Social Selves: Theories of the social formation of personality*. London: Sage.

Burman, E. (1994) *Deconstructing Developmental Psychology*. London: Routledge.

Burns, R.B. (1982) *The Self-Concept: Theory, measurement, development and behaviour*. London: Longman.

Burns, T. and Stalker, C.M. (1961) *The Management of Innovation*. London: Tavistock.

Burnstein, E. and Vinokur, A. (1973) Testing two classes of theories about group induced shifts in individual choice. *Journal of Experimental Social Psychology* 9: 123–37.

Burnstein, E. and Vinokur, A. (1977) Persuasive argumentation and social comparison as determinants of attitude polarisation. *Journal of Experimental Social Psychology* 13: 315–32.

Burt, C. (1955) The evidence for the concept of intelligence. *British Journal of Educational Psychology* 25: 158–77.

Burton, M.J., Rolls, E.T. and Mora, F. (1976) Effects of hunger on the responses of neurons in the lateral hypothalamus to the sight and taste of food. *Experimental Neurology* 51: 668–77.

Buss, A.H. (1983) Social rewards and personality. *Journal of Personality and Social Psychology* 44(3): 53–6.

Buss, A.H. (1989) Personality as traits. *American Psychologist* 44: 1378–88.

Buss, A.H. and Plomin, R.A. (1975) *A Temperament Theory of Personality Development*. New York: Wiley.

Buss, D.M., Larsen, R.J., Weston, D. and Semmelroth, J. (1992) Sex differences in jealousy: evolution, physiology and psychology. *Psychological Science* 3: 251–5.

Butter, C.M., McDonald, J.A. and Snyder, D.R. (1969) Orality, preference behavior, and reinforcement value of non-food objects in monkeys with orbital frontal lesions. *Science* 164: 1306–7.

Butters, N. and Cermak, L.S. (1980) *Alcoholic Korsakoff's syndrome: An information-processing approach*. London: Academic Press.

Buunk, B.P., Angleitner, A., Oubaid, V. and Buss, D.M. (1996) Sex differences in jealousy in evolutionary and cultural perspective: tests from the Netherlands, Germany and the United States. *Psychological Science* 7: 359–63.

Byrne, R.M.J. and Johnson-Laird, P.N. (1990) Models and deductive reasoning, in K.J. Gilhooly, M.T. Keane, R. Logie and G. Erdos (eds) *Lines of Thinking: Reflections on the psychology of thought*, vol. 1. Chichester: Wiley.

Cacioppo, J.T., Petty, R.E. and Sidera, J.A. (1982) The effects of a salient self-schema on the evaluation of proattitudinal editorieas: top-down versus bottom-up message processing. *Journal of Experimental Social Psychology* 18: 324–38.

Cacioppo, J.T., Klein, D.J., Berntson, G.C. and Hatfield, E. (1993) The psychophysiology of emotion, in M. Lewis and J.M. Haviland (eds) *Handbook of Emotions*. New York: Guilford Press.

Caddick, B. (1982) Perceived illegitimacy and intergroup relations, in H. Tajfel (ed.) *Social Identity and Intergroup Relations*. Cambridge: Cambridge University Press.

Calder, A.J., Young, A.W., Rowland, D., Perrett, D.I., Hodges, J. and Etcoff, N.L. (1996) Facial emotion recognition after bilateral amygdala damage: differentially severe impairment of fear. *Cognitive Neuropsychology* 13: 699–745.

Campbell, D.T. (1968) Stereotypes and the perception of group differences. *American Psychologist* 22(10): 817–29.

Campbell, D.T. and Stanley, J.C. (1966) *Experimental and Quasi-experimental Designs for Research*. Chicago: Rand McNally.

Campbell, J. and Tesser, A. (1986) Conformity and attention to the stimulus: some temporal and contextual dynamics. *Journal of Personality and Social Psychology* 51: 315–24.

Campbell, J.D. and Fairey, P.J. (1985) Effects of self-esteem, hypothetical explanations, and verbalizations of expectancies on future performance. *Journal of Personality and Social Psychology* 48: 1097–111.

Campbell, J.P., McCloy, R.A., Oppler, S. and Sager, C.E. (1993) A theory of performance, in N. Schmitt, W.C. Borman *et al.* (eds) *Personnel Selection in Organizations*. San Francisco, CA: Jossey-Bass.

Campfield, L.A. and Smith, F.J. (1990) Systemic factors in the control of food intake, in E.M. Stricker (ed.) *Handbook of Behavioral Neurobiology*, vol. 10. New York: Plenum.

Campfield, L.A., Smith, F.J., Guisez, Y., Devos, R. and Burn, P. (1995) Recombinant mouse OB protein: evidence for a peripheral signal linking adiposity and central neural networks. *Science* 269: 546–9.

Campos, J.J., Barrett, K.C., Lamb, M.E., Goldsmith, H.H. and Sternberg, C. (1983) Socioemotional development, in M.M. Haith and J.J. Campos (eds) *Handbook of Child Psychology*. New York: Wiley.

Camras, L.A. (1992) Expressive development and basic emotions. *Cognition and Emotion* 6: 269–83.

Cannon, W.B. (1931) Again the James-Lange and the thalamic theories of emotion. *Psychological Review* 38: 281–95.

Cannon, W.B. (1932) *The Wisdom of the Body*. New York: Norton.

Cantor, N. and Mischel, W. (1979) Prototypes in person perception. *Advances in Experimental Social Psychology* 12: 3–52.

Capron, C. and Duyne, M. (1989) Assessment of effects of socio-economic status on IQ in a full cross-fostering study. *Nature* 340: 552–4.

Carayon, P. (1993) A longitudinal test of Karasek's job strain model among office workers. *Work and Stress* 7: 299–314.

Carlsmith, J., Ellsworth, P. and Aronson, E. (1976) *Methods of Research in Social Psychology*. Reading, MA: Addison-Wesley.

Carlson, N.R. (1994) *Physiology of Behaviour*. Boston, MA: Allyn and Bacon.

Caron, A.J., Caron, R.F. and MacLean, D.J. (1988) Infant discrimination of naturalistic emotional expressions: the role of face and voice. *Child Development* 59: 604–16.

Caron, R.F., Caron, A.J. and Myers, R.S. (1985) Do infants see facial expressions in static faces? *Child Development* 56: 1552–60.

Carroll, J.B. (1986) Factor analytic investigations of cognitive abilities, in S.E. Newstead, S.H. Irvine and P.I. Dan (eds) *Human Assessment: Cognition and motivation*. Nyhoff: Dordrecht.

Cartwright, D. (1968) The nature of group cohesiveness, in D. Cartwright and A. Zander (eds) *Group Dynamics: Research and theory*. London: Tavistock.

Cartwright, D.S. (1956) Self-consistency as a factor affecting immediate recall. *Journal of Abnormal and Social Psychology* 52: 212–18.

Cartwright, D.S. (1979) *Theories and Models of Personality*. Dubuque, IA: Brown.

Cartwright, S. and Cooper, C.L. (1990) The impact of mergers and acquisitions on people at work: existing research and issues. *British Journal of Management* 1: 65–76.

Carver, C.S. and Scheier, M.F. (1982) Control theory: a useful conceptual framework for personality-social, clinical, and health psychology. *Psychological Bulletin* 92: 111–35.

Carver, C.S., Scheier, M.F. and Weintraub, J.K. (1989) Assessing coping strategies: a theoretically based approach. *Journal of Personality and Social Psychology* 56: 267–83.

Carver, C.S., Scheier, M.F. and Pozo C. (1992) Conceptualizing the process of coping with health problems, in S. Friedman (ed.) *Hostility, Coping and Health*. Washington, DC: American Psychological Association.

Caryl, P.G. (1991) Evoked potentials, inspection time, and intelligence. *The Psychologist* 4: 537–41.

Case, R. (1992) *The Mind's Staircase: Exploring the conceptual underpinnings of children's thought and knowledge*. Hillsdale, NJ: Lawrence Erlbaum.

Casey, P.R. (1989) Suicide intent and personality disorder. *Acta Psychiatrica Scandinavica* 79: 290–5.

Casey, P.R. and Tyrer, P.J. (1986) Personality, functioning, and symptomatology. *Journal of Psychiatric Research* 20: 363–74.

Caspi, A., Elder, G.H. and Bem, D.J. (1987) Moving against the world: life course patterns of explosive children. *Developmental Psychology* 23: 308–13.

Caspi, A., Elder, G.H. and Bem, D.J. (1988) Moving against the world: life course patterns of shy children. *Developmental Psychology* 24: 824–31.

Casscells, W., Schoenberger, A. and Graboys, T.B. (1978) Interpretation by physicians of clinical laboratory results. *New England Journal of Medicine* 299: 999–1001.

Cassidy, T. and Lynn, R. (1989) A multifactorial approach to achievement motivation: the development of a comprehensive measure. *Journal of Occupational Psychology* 62: 301–12.

Cassileth, B.R., Lusk, E.J., Strouse, T.B., Miller, D.S., Brown, L.L., Cross, P.A. and Tenaglia, A.N. (1984) Psychosocial status in chronic illness. *New England Journal of Medicine* 311: 506–11.

Cattell, R.B. (1943) The description of personality: basic traits resolved into clusters. *Journal of Abnormal and Social Psychology* 38: 476–506.

Cattell, R.B. (1945) The description of personality: principal findings in a factor analysis. *American Journal of Psychology* 58: 69–90.

Cattell, R.B. (1963) Theory of fluid and crystallised intelligence: a critical experiment. *Journal of Educational Psychology* 54: 1–22.

Ceci, S.J. and Liker, J.K. (1986) A day at the races: a study of IQ, expertise, and cognitive complexity. *Journal of Experimental Psychology: General* 115: 255–66.

Cermak, L.S., Talbot, N., Chandler, K. and Wolbarst, L.R. (1985) The perceptual priming phenomenon in amnesia. *Neuropsychologia* 23: 615–22.

Chaiken, S. and Stangor, C. (1987) Attitudes and attitude change. *Annual Review of Psychology* 38: 575–630.

Chandler, M., Fritz, A.S. and Hala, S. (1989) Small scale deceit: deception as a marker of 2, 3 and 4 year olds' early theories of mind. *Child Development* 60: 1263–77.

Chapman, G.B. (1991) Trial order affects cue interaction in contingency judgment. *Journal of Experimental Psychology: Learning, Memory, and Cognition* 17: 837–54.

Chapman, G.B. and Robbins, S.J. (1990) Cue interaction in human contingency judgment. *Memory and Cognition* 18: 537–45.

Chapman, L.J. and Chapman, J.P. (1969) Illusory correlation as an obstacle to the use of valid psychodiagnostic signs. *Journal of Abnormal Psychology* 74: 271–80.

Charness, N. (1991) Expertise in chess: the balance between knowledge and search, in A. Ericsson and J. Smith (eds) *Toward a General Theory of Expertise*. Cambridge: Cambridge University Press.

Chase J. (1995) Stability, permeability and mutability: defining the boundaries of social change. Unpublished paper.

Chase, W.G. and Simon, H.A. (1973) Perception in chess. *Cognitive Psychology* 4: 55–81.

Chatrou, M. and Borgo, S. (1993) Smoking and health, in L. Sibilia and S. Borgo (eds) *Health Psychology in Cardiovascular Health and Disease*. Rome: CNR.

Chatrou, M. and Maes, S. (1993) Prevention of smoking in adolescents, in L. Sibilia and S. Borgo (eds) *Health Psychology in Cardiovascular Health and Disease*. Rome: CNR.

Chen, H., Yates, B.T. and McGinnies, E. (1988) Effects of involvement on observers' estimates of consensus, distinctiveness, and consistency. *Personality and Social Psychology Bulletin* 14: 468–78.

Cheng, P. (1985) Restructuring versus automaticity: alternative accounts of skills acquisition. *Psychological Review* 92: 414–23.

Cheng, P. and Holyoak, J.J. (1985) Pragmatic reasoning schemas. *Cognitive Psychology* 17: 391–416.

Chenoweth, D.H. (1987) *Planning Health Promotion at the Worksite*. Indianapolis, IN: Benchmark Press.

Cherns, A. (1976) The principles of sociotechnical design. *Human Relations* 29: 783–92.

Cherry, E.C. (1953) Some experiments on the recognition of speech with one and two ears. *Journal of the Acoustical Society of America* 25: 975–9.

Chess, S. and Thomas, A. (1990) Continuities and discontinuities in temperament, in L. Robins and M. Rutter (eds) *Straight and Devious Pathways from Childhood to Adulthood*. Cambridge: Cambridge University Press.

Child, I.L. (1968) Personality in culture, in E.F. Borgatta and W.W. Lambert (eds) *Handbook of Personality Theory and Research*. Chicago: Rand McNally.

Christensen-Szalanski, J.J.J. and Bushyhead, J.B. (1981) Physicians' use of probabilistic information in a real clinical setting. *Journal of Experimental Psychology: Human Perception and Performance* 7: 928–35.

Christianson, S-A. (ed.) (1992) *The Handbook of Emotion and Memory: Research and theory*. Hillsdale, NJ: Lawrence Erlbaum.

Cialdini, R. (1988) *Influence: Science and practice*. Glenview, IL: Scott, Foresman/Little Brown.

Cialdini, R., Reno, R.R. and Kallgren, C.A. (1990) A focus theory of normative conduct: recycling the concept of norms to reduce litter in public places. *Journal of Personality and Social Psychology* 58: 1015–20.

Cialdini, R., Green, B. and Rusch, A. (1992) When tactical pronouncements of change become real change: the case of reciprocal persuasion. *Journal of Personality and Social Psychology* 63: 30–40.

Cicerone, C.M. and Nerger, J.L. (1989) The relative number of long-wavelength-sensitive to middle-wavelength- sensitive cones in the human fovea centralis. *Vision Research* 29: 115–28.

Cinnirella, M. (1997) Towards a European identity: interactions between the national and the European social identities. *British Journal of Social Psychology* 36(1): 19–31.

Claridge, G.S. (1986) Eysenck's contribution to the psychology of personality, in S. Modgil and C. Modgil (eds) *Hans Eysenck: Consensus and controversy*. Philadelphia PA: Falmer.

Clark, A.B. (1897) The child's attitudes towards perspective problems, in E. Barnes (ed.) *Studies in Education*. Stanford, CA: Stanford University Press.

Clark, A.H., Wyon, S.M. and Richards, M.P.M. (1969) Free-play in nursery school children. *Journal of Child Psychology and Psychiatry* 10: 205–16.

Clark, D.M. and Teasdale, J.D. (1982) Diurnal variation in clinical depression and accessibility of memories of positive and negative experiences. *Journal of Abnormal Psychology* 91: 87–95.

Clark, H.H. (1994) Discourse in production, in M.A. Gernsbacher (ed.) *Handbook of Psycholinguistics*. London: Academic Press.

Clark, H.H. and Carlson, T.B. (1981) Context for comprehension, in J. Long and A. Baddeley (eds) *Attention and Performance*, vol. 9. Hillsdale, NJ: Lawrence Erlbaum.

Clark, H.H. and Haviland, S.E. (1977) Comprehension and the given-new contract, in R.O. Freedle (ed.) *Discourse Processes: Advances in research and theory*, Vol. 1. Norwood, NJ: Ablex.

Clark, J.M., Clark, A.J.M., Bartle, A. and Winn, P. (1991) The regulation of feeding and drinking in rats with lesions of the lateral hypothalamus made by N-methyl-D-aspartate. *Neuroscience* 45: 631–40.

Clark, K. and Clark, M. (1947) Racial identification and preference in negro children, in T. Newcomb and E. Hartley (eds) *Readings in Social Psychology*. New York: Holt, Rinehart and Winston.

Clark, L.A. and Watson, D. (1991) Tripartite model of anxiety and depression: psychometric evidence and taxonomic implications. *Journal of Abnormal Psychology* 100: 316–36.

Clark, R. (1990) Minority influence: the role of argument refutation of the majority position and social support for the minority. *European Journal of Social Psychology* 20: 489–97.

Clark, R. (1995) On being excommunicated from the European view of minority influence: a reply to Perez *et al*. *European Journal of Social Psychology* 25: 711–14.

Clarke, A.M. and Clarke, A.D.B. (1976) *Early Experience: Myth and evidence*. London: Open Books.

Cleckley, H. (1988) *The Mask of Sanity*, 5th edn. St Louis, MO: Mosby.

Clegg, C. (1979) The process of job redesign: signposts from a theoretical orphanage? *Human Relations* 12: 999–1022.

Clegg, C., Wall, T. and Kemp, N. (1987) Women on the assembly-line: a comparison of main and interactive explanations of job satisfaction, absence and mental health. *Journal of Occupational Psychology* 60: 273–87.

Clegg, F. (1982) *Simple Statistics*. Cambridge: Cambridge University Press.

Cloninger, C.R., Sigvardsson, S., Bohman, M. and von Knorring, A.L. (1982) Predispositions to petty criminality in Swedish adoptees, II, Cross-fostering analysis of gene–environment interaction. *Archives of General Psychiatry* 39: 1242–49.

Coch, L. and French, J.R.P. (1948) Overcoming resistance to change. *Human Relations* 19: 39–56.

Cochrane, R. (1983) *The Social Creation of Mental Illness*. Harlow: Longman.

Codol, J.P. (1986) Estimation et expression de la sessemblance et de la difference entre pairs. *Année Psychologique* 86: 527–50.

Cohen, C. (1981) Person categories and social perception: testing some boundaries of the processing effects of prior knowledge. *Journal of Personality and Social Psychology* 40: 441–52.

Cohen, F. and Lazarus, R. (1983) Coping and adaptation in health and illness, in D. Mechanic (ed.) *Handbook of Health, Illness and Social Adaptation*. New York: Free Press.

Cohen, N.J. (1984) Preserved learning capacity in amnesia: evidence for multiple memory systems, in L.R. Squire and N. Butters (eds) *Neuropsychology of Memory*. New York: Guilford Press.

Cohen, N.J. and Squire, L.R. (1980) Preserved learning and retention of pattern-analysing skill in amnesia using perceptual learning. *Cortex* 17: 273–8.

Cohen, S. and Hoberman, H.M. (1983) Positive events and social supports as buffers of life change stress. *Journal of Applied Social Psychology* 13: 99–125.

Cohen, S. and Kessler, R.C. (1995) Strategies for measuring stress in studies of psychiatric and physical disorders, in S. Cohen, R.C. Kessler and L.G. Gordon (eds) *Measuring Stress: A guide for health and social scientists*. New York: Oxford University Press.

Cohen, S. and Wills, T.A. (1985) Stress, social support, and the buffering hypothesis. *Psychological Bulletin* 98: 310–57.

Cohen, S., Tyrell, D.A.J. and Smith, A.P. (1991) Psychological stress and susceptibility to the common cold. *New England Journal of Medicine* 325: 606–12.

Cohn, J.F. and Tronick, E.Z. (1983) Three-month-old infants' reaction to simulated maternal depression. *Child Development* 54: 185–93.

Coie, J.D. and Dodge, K.A. (1983) Continuities and changes in children's social status: a five-year longitudinal study. *Merrill-Palmer Quarterly* 29: 261–82.

Colby, A., Kohlberg, L., Gibbs, J. and Lieberman, M. (1983) A longitudinal study of moral judgement. *Monographs of the Society for Research in Child Development* 48: 1–2.

Cole, M. (1985) The zone of proximal development: where culture and cognition create each other, in J.V. Wertsch (ed.) *Culture, Communication and Cognition*. Cambridge: Cambridge University Press.

Cole, M. (1996) *Cultural Psychology: A once and future discipline*. Cambridge, MA: Bellknap Press.

Coleman, J.C. (1980) *The Nature of Adolescence*, 2nd edn. London: Methuen.

Coleman, J.C. and Hendry, L.C. (1990) *The Nature of Adolescence* (2nd edn). London: Routledge.

Coles, M. and White, C. (1985) *Strategies for Studying*. London: Collins Educational.

Collaer, M.L. and Hines, M. (1995) Human behavioral sex differences: a role for gonadal hormones during early development? *Psychological Bulletin* 118: 55–107.

Collins, A.M. and Loftus, E.F. (1975) A spreading-activation theory of semantic processing. *Psychological Review* 82: 407–28.

Collins, A.M. and Quillian, M.R. (1969) Retrieval time from semantic memory. *Journal of Verbal Learning and Verbal Behavior* 8: 240–8.

Collins, J.C. and Porras, J.I. (1994) *Built to Last: Successful habits of visionary companies*. New York: HarperCollins.

Colman, A.M. (1988) *What is Psychology? The inside story*. London: Hutchinson.

Coltheart, M., Besner, D., Jonasson, J.T. and Davelaar, E. (1979) Phonological encoding in the lexical decision task. *Quarterly Journal of Experimental Psychology* 31: 489–507.

Coltheart, M., Curtis, B., Atkins, P. and Haller, M. (1993) Models of reading aloud: dual-route and parallel-distributed-processing approaches. *Psychological Review* 100: 589–608.

Colwill, R.M. and Rescorla, R.A. (1985) Postconditioning devaluation of a reinforcer affects instrumental responding. *Journal of Experimental Psychology: Animal Behavior Processes* 11: 120–32.

Colwill, R.M. and Rescorla, R.A. (1986) Associative structures underlying instrumental learning, in G.H. Bower (ed.) *The Psychology of Learning and Motivation*, vol. 20. San Diego, CA: Academic Press.

Condor, S. (1986) Sex role beliefs and 'traditional women': feminist and intergroup perspectives, in S. Wilkinson (ed.) *Feminist Social Psychology*. Milton Keynes: Open University Press.

Condor, S., Brown, R. and Williams, J. (1987) Social identification and intergroup behaviour. *Journal of Social Affairs* 3: 99–317.

Conley, J.J. (1984) Longitudinal consistency of adult personality: self-reported psychological characteristics across 45 years. *Journal of Personality and Social Psychology* 47: 1325–33.

Conner, M. and Norman, P. (1996) *Predicting Health Behaviour*. Buckingham: Open University Press.

Connine, C.M., Blasko, P.J. and Titone, D. (1993) Do the beginnings of spoken words have a special status in auditory word recognition? *Journal of Memory and Language* 32: 193–210.

Conrad, C. (1972) Cognitive economy in semantic memory. *Journal of Experimental Psychology* 92: 148–54.

Cook, M. and Mineka, S. (1989) Observational conditioning of fear to fear-relevant versus fear-irrelevant stimuli in Rhesus monkeys. *Journal of Abnormal Psychology* 98: 448–59.

Cook, T.D. and Campbell, D.T. (1979) *Quasi-Experimentation: Design and analysis issues for field settings*. Chicago: Rand McNally.

Cooley, C.H. (1902) *Human Nature and Social Order*. New York: Schroken.

Coolican, H. (1994) *Research Methods and Statistics in Psychology*, 2nd edn. London: Hodder and Stoughton.

Coolican, H. (1996) *Introduction to Research Methods and Statistics in Psychology*, 2nd edn. London: Hodder and Stoughton.

Cooper, C.L. and Cartwright, S. (1995) Workplace stress: the primary approach, in O. Svane and C. Johansen (eds) *Work and Health: Scientific basis of progress in the working environment*. Luxembourg: European Commission.

Cooper, C.L. and Marshall, J. (1976) Occupational sources of stress: a review of the literature relating to coronary heart disease and mental ill health. *Journal of Occupational Psychology* 49: 11–28.

Cooper, C.L. and Payne, R.L. (1992) International perspectives on research into work, well-being, and stress management, in J.C. Quick, L.R. Murphy and J.J.J. Hurrell (eds) *Stress and Well-being at Work*. Washington, DC: American Psychological Association.

Cooper, J.J. and Nicol, C.J. (1993) The 'coping' hypothesis of stereotypic behaviour: a reply to Rushen. *Animal Behaviour* 45: 616–18.

Cooper, R.G. (1984) Early number development: discovering number space with addition and subtraction, in C. Sophian (ed.) *The Origins of Cognitive Skill*. Hillsdale, NJ: Lawrence Erlbaum.

Cordery, J.L. (1991) Attitudinal and behavioural effects of autonomous group working: a longitudinal field study. *Academy of Management Journal* 34: 464–76.

Coren, S., Ward, L.M. and Enns, J.T. (1994) *Sensation and Perception*. Fort Worth, TX: Harcourt Brace.

Cornett, C.W. and Hudson, R.A. (1985) Psychoanalytic theory and affirmation of gay lifestyle. *Journal of Homosexuality* 12: 97–108.

Coslett, H.B. (1991) Read but not write 'idea': evidence for a third reading mechanism. *Brain and Language* 40: 425–43.

Cosmides, L. (1989) The logic of social exchange: has natural selection shaped how humans reason? *Cognition* 31: 187–276.

Cosmides, L. and Tooby, J. (1996) Are humans good intuitive statisticians after all? Rethinking some conclusions from the literature on judgement under uncertainty. *Cognition* 58: 1–73.

Cote, J.E. and Levine, C. (1988) A critical examination of the ego identity status paradigm. *Developmental Review* 8: 147–84.

Cotton, J. (1935) Normal 'visual hearing'. *Science* 82: 592–3.

Couzijn, A.L., Ros, W.G.J. and Winnubst, J.A.M. (1990) Cancer, in A.A. Kaptein, H.M. van der Ploeg, B. Garssen and R. Beunderman (eds) *Behavioural Medicine*. New York: Wiley.

Cowan, N. (1993) Activation, attention, and short-term memory. *Memory and Cognition* 21: 162–7.

Cowie, H. and Sharp, S. (1996) *Peer Counselling in Schools: A time to listen*. London: David Fulton.

Cowie, H., Smith, P.K., Boulton, M. and Laver, R. (1994) *Cooperative Group Work in the Multi-ethnic Classroom*. London: David Fulton.

Cox, A., Rutter, M., Yule, B. and Quinton, D. (1977) Bias resulting from missing information. *British Journal of Preventative Medicine* 31: 131–6.

Cox, D.J., Gonder-Frederick, L., Phol, S. and Pennebaker, J.W. (1986) Diabetes, in K.A. Holroyd and T.L. Creer (eds) *Self-Management and Chronic Disease*. Orlando, FL: Academic Press.

Cox, M.V. (1993) *Children's Drawings of the Human Figure*. Hove: Lawrence Erlbaum.

Cox, M.V. (1997) *Drawings of People by the Under-5s*. London: Falmer.

Coyle, A. (1995) Discourse analysis, in G.M. Breakwell, S. Hammond and C. Fife-Schaw (eds) *Research Methods in Psychology*. London: Sage.

Coyle, A., Millward, L.J. and Wilson, S. (1998) *Psychology for Health Professionals*. London: Macmillan.

Coyne, J.C. (1976) Depression and the response of others. *Journal of Abnormal Psychology* 85: 186–93.

Coyne, J.C. and Downey, G. (1991) Social factors and psychopathology. *Annual Review of Psychology* 43: 401–25

Coyne, J.C. and Gotlib, I.H. (1983) The role of cognition in depression: a critical reappraisal. *Psychological Bulletin* 94: 472–505

Craik, F.I.M. (1973) A 'levels of analysis' view of memory, in P. Pliner, L. Krames and T.M. Alloway (eds) *Communication and Affect: Language and thought*. London: Academic Press.

Craik, F.I.M. and Lockhart, R.S. (1972) Levels of processing: a framework for memory research. *Journal of Verbal Learning and Verbal Behavior* 11: 671–84.

Craik, F.I.M. and Tulving, E. (1975) Depth of processing and the retention of words in episodic memory. *Journal of Experimental Psychology: General* 104: 268–94.

Crain, S. and Steedman, M.J. (1985) On not being led up the garden path: the use of context by the psychological parser, in D. Dowty, L. Karttunen and A. Zwicky (eds) *Natural Language Parsing*. Cambridge: Cambridge University Press.

Crant, J.M. (1995) The proactive personality scale and objective job performance among real estate agents. *Journal of Applied Psychology* 80: 532–7.

Creed, F. (1993) Stress and psychosomatic disorders, in L. Goldberger and S. Breznitz (eds) *Handbook of Stress, Theoretical and Clinical Aspects*. New York: Free Press.

Crick, N.R. and Dodge, K. (1994) A review and reformulation of social-information processing mechanisms in children's social adjustment. *Psychological Bulletin* 115: 74–101.

Crick, N.R. and Grotpeter, J.K. (1995) Relational aggression, gender, and social-psychological adjustment. *Child Development* 66: 710–22.

Crittenden, P. (1988) Distorted patterns of relationship in maltreating families: the role of internal representation models. *Journal of Reproductive and Infant Psychology* 6: 183–99.

Crocker, J. and Luhtanen, R. (1990) Collective self-esteem and ingroup bias. *Journal of Personality and Social Psychology* 58: 60–7.

Crocker, J. and Schwartz, I. (1985) Prejudice and ingroup favouritism in a minimal intergroup situation. *Personality and Social Psychology Bulletin* 11(4): 372–86.

Croker, J., Thompson, L.L., McGraw, K.M. and Ingerman, C. (1987) Downward comparison, prejudice and evaluations of others: effects of self-esteem and threat. *Journal of Personality and Social Psychology* 52: 907–16.

Crocker, J., Blaine, B. and Luhtanen, R. (1993) Prejudice, intergroup behaviour and self-esteem: enhancement and protection motives, in M. Hogg and D. Abrams (eds) *Group Motivation: Social psychological perspectives*. London: Harvester Wheatsheaf.

Cronbach, L.J. (1951) Coefficient alpha and the internal structure of tests. *Psychometrika* 16: 297–334.

Cronbach, L.J. and Meehl, P.E. (1955) Construct validity in psychological tests. *Psychological Bulletin* 52: 281–302.

Crosby, F. (1976) A model of egotistical relative deprivation. *Psychological Review* 83: 85–113.

Crosby F. (1982) *Relative Deprivation and Working Women*. New York: Oxford University Press.

Crossley, J. (1996) How honest are we? *Readers' Digest* July.

Crowder, R.G. (1993) Short-term memory: where do we stand? *Memory and Cognition* 21: 142–45.

Cumberbatch, G. (1991) Is television violence harmful?, in R. Cochrane and D. Carroll (eds) *Psychology and Social Issues*. London: Falmer.

Cumming, E. and Henry, W.E. (1961) *Growing Old*. New York: Basic Books.

Cummings, E.M., Iannotti, R.J. and Zahn-Waxler, C. (1989) Aggression between peers in early childhood: individual continuity and developmental change. *Child Development* 60: 887–95.

Cummings, T.G., Molloy, E.S. and Glen, R.A. (1977) Methodological critique of 58 selected work experiments. *Human Relations* 30: 675–708.

Cummins, D. (1992) Role of analogical reasoning in induction of problem categories. *Journal of Experimental Psychology: Learning, Memory, and Cognition* 18: 1103–24.

Cunningham, J.D. and Kelley, H.H. (1975) Causal attributions for interpersonal events of varying magnitude. *Journal of Personality* 43: 74–93.

Curran, T. and Schacter, D.L. (1997) Implicit memory: what must theories of amnesia explain? *Memory* 5: 37–47.

Cushman, P. (1990) Why the self is empty: toward a historically situated psychology. *American Psychologist* 44(5): 599–611.

Daldrup, R.J., Beutler, L.E., Engle, D. and Greenberg, L.S. (1988) *Focused Expressive Psychotherapy*. New York: Guilford Press.

Dalgleish, T. and Power, M.J. (1998) *The Handbook of Cognition and Emotion*. Chichester: Wiley.

Dalgleish, T., Neshat-Doost, H., Taghavi, R., Moradi, A., Yule, W., Canterbury, R. and Vostanis, P. (1997a) Information processing in recovered depressed children and adolescents. Manuscript submitted for publication.

Dalgleish, T., Taghavi, R., Neshat-Doost, H., Moradi, A., Yule, W. and Canterbury, R. (1997b) Information processing in clinically depressed and anxious children and adolescents. *Journal of Child Psychology and Psychiatry* 38: 535–41.

Dalgleish, T., Neshat-Doost, H., Taghavi, R., Moradi, A., Yule, W. and Canterbury, R. (1997c) The judgement of risk in children and adolescents with PTSD. Manuscript submitted for publication.

Daly, M. and Wilson, M. (1996) Violence against stepchildren. *Current Directions in Psychological Science* 5: 77–81.

Damasio, A.R. (1994) *Descartes' Error: Emotion, reason and the human brain*. New York: Putnam.

Damasio, H. and Frank, R. (1992) Three dimensional *in vivo* mapping of brain lesions in humans. *Archives of Neurology* 49: 137–43.

Damasio, H., Grabowski, T., Frank, R., Galaburda, A.M. and Damasio, A.R. (1994) The return of Phineas Gage: the skull of a famous patient yields clues about the brain. *Science* 264: 1102–5.

Dannemiller, J.L. (1989) Computational approaches to colour constancy: adaptive and ontogenetic considerations. *Psychological Review* 96: 255–66.

Dantzer, R. (1986) Behavioural, physiological and functional aspects of stereotyped behaviour: a review and a reinterpretation. *Journal of Animal Science* 62: 1776–86.

Darley, J.M. and Latané, B. (1968) Bystander intervention in emergencies: diffusion of responsibility, *Journal of Personality and Social Psychology* 8: 377–83.

Dartnall, H.J.A., Bowmaker, J.K., and Mollon, J.D. (1983) Human visual pigments: microspectrophotometric results from the eyes of seven persons. *Proceedings of the Royal Society of London* Series B 220: 115–30.

Darwin, C. (1872) *Expression of the Emotions in Man and Animals*. London: Murray.

Darwin, C.J., Turvey, M.T. and Crowder, R.G. (1972) An auditory analogue of the Sperling partial report procedure: evidence for brief auditory storage. *Cognitive Psychology* 3: 255–67.

Das Gupta, P. and Bryant, P.E. (1989) Young children's causal inferences. *Child Development* 60: 1138–46.

Davey, A. (1983) *Learning to be Prejudiced: Growing up in multiethnic Britain*. London: Edward Arnold.

Davidson, A.R. and Jaccard, J.J. (1979) Variables that moderate the attitude–behavior relation: results of a longitudinal survey. *Journal of Personality and Social Psychology* 37: 1364–76.

Davidson, R.J., Ekman, P., Saron, C.D., Senulis, J.A. and Friesen, W.V. (1990) Approach-withdrawal and cerebral asymmetry: emotional expression and brain physiology I. *Journal of Personality and Social Psychology* 58: 330–41.

Davies, D.R. and Parasuraman, R. (1982) *The Psychology of Vigilance*. London: Academic Press.

Davis, A.M. (1984) Noncanonical orientation without occlusion: children's drawings of transparent objects. *Journal of Experimental Child Psychology* 37: 451–62.

Davis, A.M. (1986) The canonical bias: young children's drawings of familiar objects, in N.H. Freeman and M.V. Cox (eds) *Visual Order: The nature and development of pictorial representation*. Cambridge University Press.

Davis, F. (1975) Professional socialisation as subjective experience: the process of doctrinal conversion among student nurses, in C. Cox and A. Mead (eds) *A Sociology of Medical Practice*. London: Collier-Macmillan.

Davis, P. (1987) Repression and the inaccessibility of affective memories. *Journal of Personality and Social Psychology* 53: 585–93.

Davison, G.C. and Neale, J.M. (1996) *Abnormal Psychology*, revised 6th edn. New York: Wiley.

Davison, G.C. and Neale, J.M. (1986) *Abnormal Psychology: An experimental clinical approach*, 4th edn. Chichester: Wiley.

Dawkins, R. (1986) *The Blind Watchmaker*. Harlow: Longman.

Dawkins, R. (1989) *The Selfish Gene*, 2nd edn. Oxford: Oxford University Press.

Day, C., Calderhead, J. and Denicolo, P. (eds) (1993) *Research on Teacher Thinking*. London: Falmer Press.

De Backer, G., Kornitzer, M., Dramaix, M. and Kittel, F. (1986) The Belgian Heart Disease Prevention Project: 10 years follow-up. *European Heart Journal Abstract Supplement* 1(51): 27.

De Dreu, C.K.W. and Van de Vliert, E. (eds) (1997) *Benefits of Conflicts in Groups and Organizations*. London: Sage.

De Groot, A.D. (1966) Perception and memory versus thought, in B. Kleinmuntz (ed.) *Problem Solving*. New York: Wiley.

De Longis, A., Folkman, S. and Lazarus, R.S. (1988) The impact of daily stress on health and mood: psychological and social resources as mediators. *Journal of Personality and Social Psychology* 54: 486–95.

De Ridder, D.T.D. and Schreurs, K.M.G. (1994) *Coping en Sociale Steun van Chronisch Zieken* (Coping and Social Support in Patients with Chronic Diseases). Report for the Dutch Commission for Chronic Diseases. Utrecht: Section of Clinical and Health Psychology.

De Wolff, C.J., Dachler, H.P., Hosking, D., Hurley, J. and Toplis, J. (1991) An invitation to construct a policy for the European Work and Organizational Psychologist. *European Work and Organizational Psychologist*, 1: 1–8.

Deaux. K (1992) Personalising identity and socialising self, in G.M. Breakwell (ed.) *Social Psychology of Identity and the Self-concept*. London: Academic Press

Deci, E.L. (1971) Effects of externally mediated rewards on intrinsic motivation. *Journal of Personality and Social Psychology* 18: 105–15.

Deci, E.L. (1975) *Intrinsic Motivation*. New York: Plenum.

Deci, E.L. and Ryan, R.M. (1985) *Intrinsic Motivation and Self-determination in Human Behaviour*. New York: Plenum.

DeFreur, M.L. and Westie, F.R. (1958) Verbal attitudes and overt acts: an experiment on the salience of attitudes. *American Sociological Review*, 23: 667–73.

Dell, G.S. (1986) A spreading-activation theory of retrieval in sentence production. *Psychological Review* 93: 283–321.

Dell, G.S. and O'Seaghdha, P.G. (1991) Mediated and convergent lexical priming in language production: a comment on Levelt *et al*. (1991) *Psychological Review* 98: 604–14.

Dembroski, T.M., MacDougall, J.M., Williams, R.B., Haney, T.L. and Blumenthal, J.A. (1985) Components of Type A, hostility, and anger-in; relationship to angiographic findings. *Psychosomatic Medicine* 47(3): 219–33.

Den Hertog, F.J. (1977) *Werkstrukturering*. Alphen a/d Rijn, Netherlands: Samson.

Denniston, J.C., Miller, R.R. and Matute, H. (1996) Biological significance as a determinant of cue competition. *Psychological Science* 7: 325–31.

Denzin, N.K. and Lincoln, Y.S. (eds) (1994) *Handbook of Qualitative Research*. London: Sage.

Derakshan, N. and Eysenck, M.W. (1998) Interpretive biases for one's own behaviour in high-anxious individuals and repressors. *Journal of Personality and Social Psychology*.

Descartes, R. (1911/1649) *On the Passions of the Soul*, in E.L. Haldane and G.R. Ross (eds) *The Philosophical Works of Descartes*. New York: Dover.

Deschamps, J.C. and Brown, R.J. (1983) Superordinate goals and intergroup conflict. *British Journal of Social Psychology* 22: 189–95.

Deschamps, J.C. and Doise, W. (1978) Crossed category membership in intergroup relations, in H. Tajfel (ed.) *Differentiation between Social Groups*. London: Academic Press.

Deutsch, M. (1949) A theory of cooperation and competition. *Human Relations* 2: 129–52.

Deutsch, M. and Gerard, H. (1955) A study of normative and informational influences upon individual judgement. *Journal of Abnormal and Social Psychology* 51: 629–36.

DeValois, R.L. and DeValois, K.K. (1975) Neural coding of colour, in E.C. Carterette and M.P. Friedman (eds) *Handbook of Perception*, vol. 5. New York: Academic Press.

DeValois, R.L. and DeValois, K.K. (1988) *Spatial Vision*. New York: Oxford University Press.

Devine-Wright, P. and Lyons, E. (1997) Remembering pasts and representing places: the construction of national identities in Ireland. *Journal of Environmental Psychology*, 17: 33–45.

Dickinson, A. (1980) *Contemporary Animal Learning Theory*. Cambridge: Cambridge University Press.

Dickinson, A. (1989) Expectancy theory in animal conditioning, in S.B. Klein and R.R. Mowrer (eds) *Contemporary Learning Theories: Pavlovian conditioning and the status of traditional learning theory*. Hillsdale, NJ: Lawrence Erlbaum.

Dickinson, A. and Balleine, B. (1992) Actions and responses: the dual psychology of behaviour, in N. Eilan, R.A. McCarthy and M.W. Brewer (eds) *Problems in the Philosophy and Psychology of Spatial Representation*. Oxford: Blackwell.

Dickinson, A. and Balleine, B. (1994) Motivational control of goal-directed action. *Animal Learning and Behavior* 22: 1–18.

Dickinson, A. and Burke, J. (1996) Within-compound associations mediate the retrospective revaluation of causality judgements. *Quarterly Journal of Experimental Psychology* 49B: 60–80.

Dickinson, A. and Shanks, D.R. (1995) Instrumental action and causal representation, in D. Sperber, D. Premack and A.J. Premack (eds) *Causal Cognition: A multidisciplinary debate*. Oxford: Clarendon Press.

DiClemente, C.C., Prochaska, J.O. and Gilbertini, M. (1985) Self-efficacy and the stages of self-change of smoking. *Cognitive Therapy and Research* 9: 181–200.

Diehl, M. (1988) Social identity and minimal groups: the effects of interpersonal and intergroup attitudinal similarity on intergroup discrimination. *British Journal of Social Psychology* 27: 289–300.

Diehl, M. (1989) The minimal group paradigm: theoretical explanations and empirical findings, in W. Stroebe and M. Hewstone (eds) *European Review of Social Psychology*, vol. 1. Chichester: Wiley.

Digman, J.M. and Takemoto-Chock, N.K. (1981) Factors in the natural language of personality: re-analysis, comparison, and interpretation of six major studies. *Multivariate Behavioral Research* 16: 149–70.

Dion, K.L. (1973) Cohesiveness as a determinant of ingroup/outgroup bias. *Journal of Personality and Social Psychology* 28: 163–71.

Dittes, J.E. and Kelley, H.H. (1955) Effects of different conditions of acceptance upon conformity to group actions. *Journal of Abnormal and Social Psychology* 53(1): 100–7.

DiVesta, F.J. (1959) *Susceptibility to Pressures toward Uniformity of Behaviour in Social Situations: A study of task, motivational and personal factors in comformity behaviour*. Washington, DC: Syracuse University.

Dodd, J. and Castellucci, V.F. (1991) Smell and taste: the chemical senses, in E.R. Kandel, J.H. Schwartz and T.M. Jessell (eds) *Principles of Neural Science*. New York: Elsevier.

Dodge, K.A., Schlundt, D.C., Shocken, I. and Delugach, J.D. (1983) Social competence and children's sociometric status: the role of peer group entry strategies. *Merrill-Palmer Quarterly* 29: 309–36.

Dodge, K.A., Pettit, G.S., McClaskey, C.L. and Brown, M.M. (1986) Social competence in children. *Monographs of the Society for Research in Child Development* 51: 2.

Doise, W. (1978) *Groups and Individuals: Explanations in Social Psychology*. Cambridge: Cambridge University Press.

Doise, W. (1993) Debating social representations, in G.M. Breakwell and D.V. Canter (eds) *Empirical Approaches to Social Representations*. Oxford: Oxford University Press.

Doise, W. (1997) Organising social psychological explanations, in G. McGarty and S.A. Haslam (eds) *The Message of Social Psychology*. Oxford: Blackwell.

Doise, W., Deschamps, J.C. and Meyer, G. (1978) The accentualtion of intracategory similarities, in H. Tajfel (ed.) *Differentiation between Social Groups*. London: Academic Press.

Dolen, L.S. and Bearison, D.J. (1982) Social interaction and social cognition in aging. *Human Development* 25: 430–42.

Dolgin, K.G. (1985) An action-theory perspective of the tool-using capacities of chimpanzees and human infants, in M. Frese and J. Sabini (eds) *Goal Directed Behaviour: The concept of action in psychology*. Hillsdale, NJ: Lawrence Erlbaum.

Dollard, J., Doob, L.W., Miller, N., Mower, O.H. and Sears, R.R. (1939) *Frustration and Aggression*. New Haven, CT: Yale University Press.

Domjan, M. and Burkhard, B. (1998) *The Principles of Learning and Behavior*, 5th edn. Pacific Grove, CA: Brooks-Cole.

Doms, M. and Van Avermaet, E. (1985) Majority influence, minority influence and conversion behaviour: a replication. *Journal of Experimental Social Psychology* 16: 283–92.

Donaldson, M. (1978) *Children's Minds*. London: Fontana.

Donatelle, R.J. and Davis, L.G. (1996) *Access to Health*. Boston, MA: Allyn and Bacon.

Dooling, D.J. and Christiaansen, R.E. (1977) Episodic and semantic aspects of memory for prose. *Journal of Experimental Psychology: Human Learning and Memory* 3: 428–36.

Dormann, T. and Frese, M. (1994) Error training: replication and the function of exploratory behaviour. *International Journal of Human–Computer Interaction* 6(4): 365–72.

Dörner, D. (1989) *Die Logik des Mißlingens: Strategisches Denken in komplexen Situationen*. Reinbek b. Hamburg: Rowohlt.

Dörner, D. and Schaub, H. (1994) Errors in planning and decision-making and the nature of human information processing. *Applied Psychology: An International Review* 43: 433–54.

Dörner, D., Kreuzig, H.W., Reither, F. and Stäudel, T. (1983) *Lohhausen: Vom Umgang mit Unbestimmtheit und Komplexität*. Bern: Huber.

Dosher, B.A. and Corbett, A.T. (1982) Instrument inferences and verb schemata. *Memory and Cognition* 10: 531–9.

Doty, D.H., Glick, W.H. and Huber, G.P. (1993) Fit, equifinality, and organizational effectiveness: a test of two configurational theories. *Academy of Management Journal* 36: 1196–250.

Dovidio, J., Mann, J. and Gaertner, S. (1989) Resistance to affirmative action: the implications of aversive racism, in F. Blanchard and F. Crosby (eds) *Affirmative Action in Perspective*. New York: Springer.

Downing, J. (1958) Cohesiveness, perception and values. *Human Relations* 11: 157–66.

Drever, J. (1964) *A Dictionary of Psychology*. Harmondsworth: Penguin.

Drevets, W.C., Price, J.L., Simpson, J.R., Todd, R.D., Reich, T., Vannier, M. and Raichle, M.E. (1997) Subgenual prefrontal cortex abnormalities in mood disorders. *Nature* 386: 824–7.

Duck, S.W. (1977) *The Study of Acquaintance*. Farnborough: Gower.

Dumont, L. (1970) The individual as an impediment to sociological comparison and Indian history, in L. Dumont (ed.) *Religion, Politics and History in India: Collected papers in Indian sociology*. Paris/The Hague: Mouton.

Duncan, J. (1979) Divided attention: the whole is more than the sum of its parts. *Journal of Experimental Psychology: Human Perception and Performance* 5: 216–28.

Duncan, J. and Humphreys, G.W. (1989) A resemblance theory of visual search. *Psychological Review* 96: 433–58.

Duncker, K. (1945) On problem solving. *Psychological Monographs* 58 (270).

Dunkel-Schetter, C., Feinstein, L., Taylor, S.E. and Falke, R. (1992) Patterns of coping with cancer and their correlates. *Health Psychology* 11: 79–87.

Dunn, J. (1995) Studying relationships and social understanding, in P. Barnes (ed.) *Personal, Social and Emotional Development of Children*. Oxford: Blackwell and Open University.

Dunn, J. and Kendrick, C. (1982) *Siblings: Love, envy and understanding*. Oxford: Blackwell.

Dunn, J., Brown, J. and Beardsall, L. (1991) Family talk about feeling states and children's later understanding of others' emotions. *Developmental Psychology* 27(3): 448–55.

Duval, S. and Wicklund, R.A. (1972) *A Theory of Objective Self-Awareness*. New York: Academic Press.

Dweck, C.S. and Leggett, E.L. (1988) A social-cognitive approach to motivation and personality. *Psychological Review* 95: 256–73.

Dwyer, D.J. and Ganster, D.C. (1991) The effects of job demands and control on employee attendance and satisfaction. *Journal of Organizational Behavior* 11: 293–307.

Dzida, W., Herda, S. and Itzfeldt, W.-D. (1978) User-perceived quality of interactive systems. *IEEE Transactions on Software Engineering* 4(4): 270–6.

Eagly, A.H. and Chaiken, S. (1993) *The Psychology of Attitudes*. San Diego, CA: Harcourt Brace Jovanovich.

Eagly, A., Ashnore, R., Makhijani, M. and Longo, L. (1991) 'What is beautiful is good, but . . .': a meta-analytic review of research on the physical attractiveness stereotype. *Psychological Bulletin* 110: 109–28.

Early, P.C., Wojnaroski, P. and Prest, W. (1987) Task planning and energy expended: exploration of how goals influence performance. *Journal of Applied Psychology* 72: 107–14.

Easterbrook, J.A. (1959) The effect of emotion on cue utilization and the organization of behaviour. *Psychological Review* 66: 183–201.

Ebbinghaus, H. (1885/1913) *Uber das Gedächtnis*. Leipzig: Dunker (translated by H. Ruyer and C.E. Bussenius (1913) Memory. New York: Teacher College, Columbus University).

Eccles, J. (1991) *Evolution of the Brain: Creation of the self*. London: Routledge.

Echabe, A.E. and Castro, J.G. (1996) Images of immigrants: a study of xenophobia and permeability of intergroup boundaries. *European Journal of Social Psychology* 26: 341–52.

Eden, D. (1990) Pygmalion without interpersonal contrast effects: whole groups gain from raising manager expectations. *Journal of Applied Psychology* 75(4): 394–8.

Edwards, D. and Potter, J. (1992) *Discursive Psychology*. London: Sage.

Edwards, W. (1961) Behavioral decision theory. *Annual Review of Psychology* 12: 473–98.

Egan, V. (1994) Intelligence, inspection time and cognitive strategies. *British Journal of Psychology* 85: 305–16.

Eibl-Eibesfeldt, I. (1989) *Human Ethology*. New York: Aldine de Gruyter.

Einarsen, S. and Skogstad. A. (1996) Prevalence and risk groups of bullying and harassment at work. *European Journal of Work and Organizational Psychology* 5(2): 185–202.

Eiser, J.R. (1980) *Cognitive Social Psychology*. London: McGraw-Hill.

Eiser, J.R. (1985) *The Expression of Attitude*. New York: Springer-Verlag.

Eiser, J.R. and van der Pligt, J. (1984a) Attitudes in social context, in H. Tajfel (ed.) *The Social Dimension: European developments in social psychology*, vol. 2. Cambridge: Cambridge University Press.

Eiser, J.R., and van der Pligt, J. (1984b) Attitudinal and social factors in adolescent smoking: in search of peer group influence. *Journal of Applied Social Psychology* 14(4): 348–63.

Eiser, J.R. and van der Pligt, J. (1988) *Attitudes and Decisions*. London: Routledge.

Ekman, P. (1972) Universals and cultural differences in facial expressions of emotion, in J. Cole (ed.) *Nebraska Symposium on Motivation (1971)*. Lincoln, NB: University of Nebraska Press.

Ekman, P. (1992) Are there basic emotions? *Psychological Review* 99(3): 550–3.

Ekman, P. (1994) Strong evidence for universals in facial expression: a reply to Russell's mistaken critique. *Psychological Bulletin* 115: 268–87.

Ekman, P. (1998a) Basic emotions, in T. Dalgleish and M.J. Power (eds) *The Handbook of Cognition and Emotion*. Chichester: Wiley.

Ekman, P. (1998b) Facial expression, in T. Dalgleish and M.J. Power (eds) *The Handbook of Cognition and Emotion*. Chichester: Wiley.

Ekman, P. and Davidson, R.J. (1994) *The Nature of Emotion: Fundamental questions*. New York: Oxford University Press.

Ekman, P. and Friesen, W. V. (1969) The repertoire of non-verbal behavior: categories, origins, usage and coding. *Semiotica* 1: 49–98.

Ekman, P. and Friesen, W.V. (1971) Constants across cultures in the face and emotion. *Journal of Personality and Social Psychology* 17: 124–9.

Ekman, P. and Friesen, W.V. (1975) *Pictures of Facial Affect*. Palo Alto, CA: Consulting Psychologists Press.

Ekman, P. and Friesen, W.V. (1978) *Facial Action Coding System: A technique for the measurement of facial movement*. Palo Alto, CA: Consulting Psychologists Press.

Ekman, P. and Friesen, W.V. (1984) *Emotion Facial Action Coding System* (EM-FACS). Obtainable from Paul Ekman, University of California, San Francisco.

Ekman, P., Friesen, W.V. and Ellsworth, P. (1972) *Emotion in the Human Face: Guidelines for research and an integration of findings*. New York: Pergamon.

Ekman, P., Levenson, R.W. and Friesen, W.V. (1983) Autonomic nervous system activity distinguishes among emotions. *Science* 221: 1208–10.

Elias, N. (1978) *The History of Manners: The civilizing process*, vol. 1. Oxford: Blackwell.

Elias, N. (1982) *State Formation and Civilization: The civilizing process*, vol. 2. Oxford: Blackwell.

Elkind, D. (1967) Egocentrism in adolescence. *Child Development* 38: 1025–34.

Ellemers, N., Van Knippenberg, A., de Vries, N. and Wilke, H. (1986) Social identification and permeability of group boundaries. *European Journal of Social Psychology* 18: 497–513.

Ellemers, N., Van Knippenberg, A. and Wilke, H. (1990) The influence of group boundaries and stability of group status on strategies of individual mobility and social change. *British Journal of Social Psychology* 29: 233–46.

Ellemers, N., Wilke, H. and Van Knippenberg, A. (1993) Effects of legitimacy of low group or individual status as individual and collective status-enhancement strategies. *Journal of Personality and Social Psychology* 64: 766–78.

Ellinwood, E.H. and Escalante, O. (1970) Chronic amphetamine effect on the olfactory forebrain. *Biological Psychiatry* 2: 189–203.

Ellinwood, E.H. and Kilbey, M.M. (1975) Amphetamine stereotypy: the influence of environmental factors and pre-potent behavioural patterns on its topography and development. *Biological Psychiatry* 10: 3–16.

Elliot, C., Murray, D.J. and Pearson, L.S. (1983) *British Ability Scales Revised*. Windsor: National Foundation for Educational Research.

Elliott, J. (1980) Action research in schools: some guidelines. *Classroom Action Research Network Bulletin 4*. Norwich: University of East Anglia.

Ellis, A. (1962) *Reason and Emotion in Psychotherapy*. Secaucus, NJ: Prentice Hall.

Ellis, A. (1977) The basic clinical theory of rational emotive therapy, in A. Ellis and G. Grieger (eds) *Handbook of Rational Emotive Therapy*. New York: Springer.

Ellis, A.W. and Young, A.W. (1988) *Human Cognitive Neuropsychology*. Hove: Lawrence Erlbaum.

Ellis, A.W., Miller, D. and Sin, G. (1983) Wernicke's aphasia and normal language processing: a case study in cognitive neuropsychology. *Cognition* 15: 111–44.

Ellsworth, P.C. (1994) William James and emotion: is a century of fame worth a century of misunderstanding? *Psychological Review* 101: 222–9.

Ellsworth, P.C. and Smith, C.A. (1988) From appraisal to emotion: differences among unpleasant feelings. *Motivation and Emotion* 12: 271–302.

Elman, J. and McClelland, J. (1988) Cognitive penetration of the mechanisms of perception: compensation for coarticulation of lexically restored phonemes. *Journal of Memory and Language* 27: 143–65.

Elman, J.L., Bates, E.A., Johnson, M.J., Karmiloff-Smith, A., Parisi, D. and Plunkett, K. (1996) *Rethinking Innateness: A connectionist perspective on development*. Cambridge, MA: MIT Press.

Emerson, E. and Howard, D. (1992) Schedule-induced stereotypy. *Research in Developmental Disabilities* 13: 335–61.

Emery, F.E. and Thorsrud, E. (1969) *Form and Content in Industrial Democracy*. London: Tavistock.

Emery, F.E. and Trist, E.L. (1969) Socio-technical systems, in F.E. Emery (ed.) *Systems Thinking*. Harmondsworth: Penguin.

Endler, N.S. and Edwards, J. (1978) Person by treatment interactions in personality research, in L.A. Pervin and M. Lewis (eds) *Perspectives in Interactional Psychology*. New York: Plenum.

Engel, G.L. (1977) The need for a new medical model: a challenge for biomedicine. *Science* 196: 129–36.

Engel, G.L. (1980) The clinical application of the biopsychosocial model. *American Journal of Psychiatry* 137: 535–44.

Epstein, S. (1977) Traits are alive and well, in D. Magnusson and N.S. Endler (eds) *Personality at the Crossroads: Current issues in interactional psychology*. Hillsdale, NJ: Lawrence Erlbaum.

Erez, M. (1977) Feedback: a necessary condition for the goal setting–performance relationship. *Journal of Applied Psychology* 62: 624–27.

Eriksen, C.W. (1990) Attentional search of the visual field, in D. Brogan (ed.) *Visual Search*. London: Taylor and Francis.

Erikson, E. (1950) *Childhood and Society*. New York: W.W. Norton.

Erikson, E. (1968) *Identity, Youth and Crisis*. London: Faber.

Erlenmeyer-Kimling, L. and Jarvik, L.F. (1963) Genetics and intelligence: a review. *Science* 142: 1477–79.

Eslinger, P.J. and Damasio, A.R. (1985) Severe disturbance of higher cognition after bilateral frontal lobe ablation: patient EVR. *Neurology* 35: 1731–41.

Estes, W.K. and Skinner, B.F. (1941) Some quantitative properties of anxiety. *Journal of Experimental Psychology* 29: 390–400.

Etaugh, C. (1980) Effects of non-maternal care on children: research evidence and popular views. *American Psychologist* 35: 309–19.

Etaugh, C., Carlson, P. and Williams, B. (1992) Changing attitudes towards day care and maternal employment as portrayed in women's magazines: 1977–1990, paper presented at the meeting of the 25th International Congress of Psychology. Brussels, July.

Etcoff, N.L., Ekman, P., Frank, M., Magee, J. and Torreano, L. (1992) Detecting deception: do aphasics have an advantage?, paper presented at *Conference of International Society for Research on Emotions*, Carnegie Mellon University, Pittsburgh, PA, August.

Ettenberg, A. (1982) Behavioural effects of neuroleptics: performance deficits, reward deficits or both. *Behavioral and Brain Sciences* 5: 56–7.

Evans, J.St.B.T., Barston, J.L. and Pollard, P. (1983) On the conflict between logic and belief in syllogistic reasoning. *Memory and Cognition* 11: 295–306.

Evans, J.St.B.T., Newstead, S.E. and Byrne, R.M.J. (1993) *Human Reasoning: The psychology of deduction*. Hove: Lawrence Erlbaum.

Evans, J.St.B.T., Over, D.E. and Manktelow, K.I. (1994) Reasoning, decision making and rationality, in P.N. Johnson-Laird and E. Shafir (eds) *Reasoning and Decision Making*. Oxford: Blackwell.

Evans, J.St.B.T., Clibbens, J. and Rood, B. (1995) Bias in conditional inference: implications for mental models and mental logic. *Quarterly Journal of Experimental Psychology* 48A: 644–70.

Everitt, B. (1997) Craving cocaine cues: cognitive neuroscience meets drug addiction research. *Trends in Cognitive Sciences* 1: 1–2.

Everitt, B.J. and Robbins, T.W. (1992) Amygdala-ventral striatal interactions and reward-related processes, in J.P. Aggleton (ed.) *The Amygdala*. Chichester: Wiley.

Exline, R.V. (1957) Group climate as a factor in the relevance and accuracy of social perception. *Journal of Abnormal and Social Psychology* 55: 382–8.

Eysenck, H.J. (1944) Types of personality – a factorial study of 700 neurotic soldiers. *Journal of Mental Science* 90: 851–61.

Eysenck, H.J. (1952) The effects of psychotherapy: an evaluation. *Journal of Consulting Psychology* 16: 319–24.

Eysenck, H.J. (1956) The inheritance of introversion–extraversion. *Acta Psychologica* 12: 95–110.

Eysenck, H.J. (1967) *The Biological Basis of Personality*. Springfield, IL: C.C. Thomas.

Eysenck, H.J. (1978) Superfactors P, E, and N in a comprehensive factor space. *Multivariate Behavioral Research* 13: 475–82.

Eysenck, H.J. (1982) *Personality, Genetics and Behaviour*. New York: Praeger.

Eysenck, H.J. and Barrett, P. (1985) Psychophysiology and the measurement of intelligence, in C.R. Reynolds and V. Willson (eds) *Methodological and Statistical Advances in the Study of Individual Differences*. New York: Plenum.

Eysenck, H.J. and Eysenck, M.W. (1985) *Personality and Individual Differences*. New York: Plenum.

Eysenck, H.J. and Eysenck, M.W. (1989) *Mindwatching: Why we behave the way we do*. London: Prion.

Eysenck, H.J. and Eysenck, S.B.G. (1965, reprinted 1973) *Eysenck Personality Inventory*. London: University of London Press.

Eysenck, H.J. and Eysenck, S.B.G. (1975) *Manual of the Eysenck Personality Questionnaire*. London: Hodder and Stoughton.

Eysenck, H.J. and Kamin, L. (1981) *The Intelligence Controversy: H.J. Eysenck vs. Leon Kamin*. New York: Wiley.

Eysenck, H.J. and Prell, D.B. (1951) The inheritance of neuroticism: an experimental study. *Journal of Mental Science* 97: 441–65.

Eysenck, M.W. (1974) Age differences in incidental learning. *Developmental Psychology* 10: 936–41.

Eysenck, M.W. (1978) Verbal remembering, in B.M. Foss (ed.) *Psychology Survey, No. 1*. London: Allen and Unwin.

Eysenck, M.W. (1982) *Attention and Arousal: Cognition and performance*. Berlin: Springer.

Eysenck, M.W. (1988) Individual differences, arousal, and monotonous work, in J.P. Leonard (ed.) *Vigilance: Methods, models, and regulation*. Frankfurt: Peter Lang.

Eysenck, M.W. (1990) *Happiness: Facts and myths*. Hove: Lawrence Erlbaum.

Eysenck, M.W. (1992) *Anxiety: The cognitive perspective*. Hope: Lawrence Erlbaum.

Eysenck, M.W. (1994a) *Individual Differences: Normal and abnormal*. Hove: Lawrence Erlbaum.

Eysenck, M.W. (1994b) *Perspectives on Psychology*. Hove: Lawrence Erlbaum.

Eysenck, M.W. (1997) *Anxiety and cognition: A unified theory*. Hove: Psychology Press.

Eysenck, M.W. and Calvo, M.G. (1992) Anxiety and performance: the processing efficiency theory. *Cognition and Emotion* 6: 409–34.

Eysenck, M.W. and Keane, M.T. (1995) *Cognitive Psychology: A student's handbook*, 3rd edn. Hove: Lawrence Erlbaum.

Eysenck, M.W., Mogg, K., May, J., Richards, A. and Mathews, A. (1991) Bias in interpretation of ambiguous sentences related to threat in anxiety. *Journal of Abnormal Psychology* 100: 144–50.

Fabes, R.A., Eisenberg, N., Nyman, M. and Michealieu, Q. (1991) Young children's appraisals of others' spontaneous emotional reactions. *Developmental Psychology* 27: 858–66.

Fahrenberg, J. (1992) Psychophysiology of neuroticism and anxiety, in A. Gale and M.W. Eysenck (eds) *Handbook of Individual Differences: Biological perspectives*. Chichester: Wiley.

Falbo, T. and Polit, D.F. (1986) Quantitative review of the only child literature: research evidence and theory development. *Psychological Bulletin* 100: 176–89.

Falk, J.L. (1961) Production of polydipsia in normal rats by an intermittent food schedule. *Science* 133: 195–6.

Falk, J.L. (1967) Control of schedule-induced polydipsia: type, size and spacing of meals. *Journal of the Experimental Analysis of Behaviour* 10: 199–206.

Falk, J.L. (1969) Conditions producing psychogenic polydipsia in animals. *Annals of the New York Academy of Sciences* 157: 569–93.

Falk, J.L. (1971) The nature and determinants of adjunctive behaviour. *Physiology and Behaviour* 6: 577–88.

Falk, J.L., Dews, P.B. and Schuster, C.R. (1983) Commonalities in the environmental control of behaviour. in P.K. Levison, D.R. Gerstein and D.R. Maloff (eds) *Commonalities in Substance Abuse and Habitual Behaviour*. Lexington, MA: Lexington Books.

Falloon, I.R.H., Boyd, J.L., McGill, C.W., Williamson, M., Razani, J., Moss, H.B., Gilderman, A.M. and Simpson, G.M. (1985) Family management in the prevention of morbidity of schizophrenia. *Archives of General Psychiatry* 42: 887–96.

Farah, M.J. (1989) The neuropsychology of mental imagery, in F. Boller and J. Grafman (eds) *Handbook of Neuropsychology*, vol. 2. Amsterdam: Elsevier.

Faris, R.E.L. and Dunham, H.W. (1939) *Mental Disorders in Urban Areas: An ecological study of schizophrenia and other psychoses*. Chicago: University of Chicago Press.

Farr, R. (1996) *The Roots of Modern Social Psychology*. Oxford: Blackwell.

Farrell, C. (1978) *My Mother Said*. London: Routledge and Kegan Paul.

Farrington, D.P. (1990) Childhood aggression and adult violence: early precursors and later-life outcomes, in D.J. Pepler and K.H. Rubin (eds) *The Development and Treatment of Childhood Aggression*. Hillsdale, NJ: Lawrence Erlbaum.

Fazio, R.H. (1989) On the power and functionality of attitudes: the role of attitude accessibility, in A.R. Pratkanis, S.J. Breckler and A.G. Greenwald (eds) *Attitude Structure and Function*. Hillsdale, NJ: Lawrence Erlbaum.

Fazio, R.H. (1990) Multiple processes by which attitudes guide behavior: the MODE model as an integrative framework, in M.P. Zanna (ed.) *Advances in Experimental Social Psychology*, vol. 13. San Diego, CA: Academic Press.

Fazio, R.H. and Zanna, M.P. (1981) Direct experience and attitude–behavior consistency, in L. Berkowitz (ed.) *Advances in Experimental Social Psychology*, vol 14. New York: Academic Press.

Fazio, R.H., Chen, J., McDonel, E.C. and Sherman, S.J. (1982) Attitude accessibility, attitude–behavior consistency and the strength of the object–evaluation association. *Journal of Experimental Social Psychology* 18, 339–57.

Fazio, R.H., Sanbonmatsu, D.M., Powell, M.C. and Kardes, F.R. (1986) On the automatic activation of attitudes. *Journal of Personality and Social Psychology* 50: 229–38.

Fechner, G.T. (1860) *Elemente der Psychophysik*. Berlin: Springer.

Fehr, B. and Russell, J.A. (1984) Concept of emotion viewed from a prototype perspective. *Journal of Experimental Psychology: General* 113: 464–86.

Feldman, N. and Ruble, D. (1981) Social comparison strategies: dimensions offered and options taken. *Personality and Social Psychology Bulletin* 7(1): 11–16.

Ferguson, T.J. and Wells, G.L. (1980) Priming of mediators in causal attribution. *Journal of Personality and Social Psychology* 38: 461–70.

Ferri, E. (1984) *Stepchildren: A national study*. London: NFER/Nelson.

Ferrier, D. (1878) The Goulstonian Lectures on the localisation of cerebral disease. *British Medical Journal* 1: 399–447.

Ferster, C.B. and Skinner, B.F. (1957) *Schedules of Reinforcement*. New York: Appleton-Century-Crofts.

Festinger, L. (1950) Informal social communication. *Psychological Review* 57: 271–82.

Festinger, L. (1954) A theory of social comparison processes. *Human Relations* 7: 117–40.

Festinger, L. (1957) *Theory of Cognitive Dissonance*. Stanford, CA: Stanford University Press.

Festinger, L. and Carlsmith, J. (1959) Cognitive consequences of forced compliance. *Journal of Abnormal and Social Psychology* 58: 203–10.

Festinger, L., Schacter, S. and Back, K. (1951) *Social Pressures in Informal Groups*. London: Tavistock.

Festinger, L., Riecken, H.W. and Schachter, S. (1956) *When Prophecy Fails*. Minneapolis, MN: University of Minneapolis Press.

Feuerstein, M., Labbe, E.E. and Kuczmierczyk, A.R. (1985) *Health Psychology: A psychobiological perspective*. New York: Plenum.

Fiedler, F.E. (1971) *Leadership*. New York: General Learning Press.

Fiedler, F.E. and Chemers, M.M. (1984) *Improving Leadership Effectiveness: The leader match concept*. New York: Wiley.

Fiedler, K. (1982) Causal schemata: review and criticism of research on a popular construct. *Journal of Personality and Social Psychology* 42: 1001–13.

Fiedler, K. (1988) The dependence of the conjunction fallacy on subtle linguistic factors. *Psychological Research* 50: 123–9.

Field, T. (1994) The effects of mother's physical and emotional unavailability on emotion regulation, in N.A. Fox (ed.) *The Development of Emotion Regulation. Monographs of the Society for Child Development* 59 (2–3, serial no. 240): 208–27.

Field, T.M., Woodson, R., Greenberg, R. and Cohen, D. (1982) Discrimination and imitation of facial expressions by neonates. *Science* 218: 179–81.

Fielder, F. (1954) Assumed similarity measures as predictors of team effectiveness. *Journal of Abnormal and Social Psychology* 49: 381–8.

Fielding, J.E. and Piserchia, P.V. (1989) Frequency of worksite health promotion activities. *American Journal of Public Health* 79: 16–20.

Filshie, J. and Morrison, P.J. (1988) Acupuncture for chronic pain: a review. *Palliative Care* 2: 1–14.

Finkelstein, N.W. and Haskins, R. (1983) Kindergarten children prefer same-color peers. *Child Development* 54: 502–8.

Finlay-Jones, R. and Brown, G.W. (1981) Types of stressful life event and the onset of anxiety and depressive disorders. *Psychological Medicine* 11: 803–15.

Fischhoff, B. (1977) Perceived informativeness of facts. *Journal of Experimental Psychology: Human Perception and Performance* 3: 349–58.

Fischhoff, B. and Beyth, R. (1975) 'I knew it would happen' – Remembered probabilities of once-future things. *Organizational Behaviour and Human Performance* 13: 1–16.

Fischler, I., Rundus, D. and Atkinson, R.C. (1970) Effects of overt rehearsal procedures on free recall. *Psychonomic Science* 19: 249–50.

Fishbein, M. and Ajzen, I. (1975) *Belief, Attitude, Intention and Behavior: An introduction to theory and research*. Reading, MA: Addison-Wesley.

Fisher, J.D. and Fisher, W.A. (1992) Changing AIDS-risk behavior. *Psychological Bulletin*, 111: 455–74.

Fisher, R.P., Geiselman, R.E., Raymond, D.S., Jurkevich, L.M. and Warhaftig, M.L. (1987) Enhancing enhanced eyewitness memory: Refining the cognitive interview. *Journal of Police Science and Administration* 15: 291–7.

Fisher, R.P., Geiselman, R.E. and Amador, M. (1990) A field test of the cognitive interview: enhancing the recollections of actual victims and witnesses of crime. *Journal of Applied Psychology* 74: 722–7.

Fisher, S. and Greenberg, R.P. (eds) (1978) *The Scientific Evaluation of Freud's Theories and Therapy*. Hassocks, Sussex: Harvester Press.

Fiske, S.T. and Dyer, L.M. (1985) Structure and development of social schemata: evidence from positive and negative transfer effects. *Journal of Personality and Social Psychology*, 48: 839–52.

Fiske, S.T. and Linville, P.W. (1980) What does the schema concept buy us? *Personality and Social Psychology Bulletin*, 6, 543–57.

Fiske, S.T. and Neuberg, S.L. (1990) A continuum of impression formation, from category-based to individuating processes: influences of information and motivation on attention and interpretation, in M.P. Zanna (ed.) *Advances in Experimental Social Psychology*, vol. 23. New York: Academic Press.

Fiske, S.T. and Taylor, S.E. (1991) *Social Cognition*, 2nd ed. New York: McGraw-Hill.

Fitzsimons, J.T. (1992) Physiology and pathophysiology of thirst and sodium appetite, in D.W. Seldin and G. Giebisch (eds) *The Kidney: Physiology and pathophysiology*, 2nd edn. New York: Raven.

Flavell, J. (1963) *The Developmental Psychology of Jean Piaget*. Princeton, NJ: Van Nostrand.

Flavell, J.H. (1987) Assumptions on the concept metacognition and on the development of metacognitions, in F.E. Weinert and R.H. Kluwe (eds) *Metacognition, Motivation, and Understanding* Hillsdale, NJ: Lawrence Erlbaum.

Fleishman, E.A. (1973) Twenty years of consideration and structure, in E.A. Fleishman and J.G. Hunt (eds) *Current Developments in the Study of Leadership*. Carbondale, IL: Southern Illinois University Press.

Fleming, J. and Watts, W. (1980) The dimensionality of self-esteem: some results of a college sample. *Journal of Personality and Social Psychology* 39(5): 921–9.

Fletcher, C. (1991) Candidate's reactions to assessment centres and their outcomes: a longitudinal study. *Journal of Occupational Psychology* 64(2): 117–28.

Fletcher, G.J.O. and Ward, C. (1988) Attribution theory and processes: a cross-cultural perspective, in M.H. Bond (ed.) *The Cross-Cultural Challenge to Social Psychology*. Newbury Park, CA: Sage.

Floderus-Myrhed, B., Pedersen, N. and Rasmuson, S. (1980) Assessment of heritability for personality based on a short form of the Eysenck Personality Inventory. *Behavior Genetics* 10: 153–62.

Foa, E. and Kozak, M. (1993) Obsessive-compulsive disorder: long term outcome of psychological treatment, in M. Mavissakalian and R. Prien (eds) *Long Term Treatments of Anxiety Disorders*. Washington DC: American Psychiatric Press.

Fodor, J.A. and Pylyshyn, Z.W. (1981) How direct is visual perception? Some reflections on Gibson's 'ecological approach'. *Cognition* 9: 139–96.

Fogel, A., Nwokah, E., Dedo, J.Y., Messinger, D., Dickson, K.L., Matusov, E. and Holt, S.A. (1992) Social process theory of emotions: a dynamic systems approach. *Social Development* 2: 122–42.

Fonagy, P. (1994) The theory and practice of resilience. *Journal of Child Psychology and Psychiatry* 35: 231–57.

Fonagy, P., Steele, H., Steele, M. and Holder, J. (1997) Attachment and theory of mind: overlapping constructs?, in

G. Forrest (ed.) *Bonding and Attachment: Current issues in research and practice*. Occasional Papers no. 14. London: Association for Child Psychology and Psychiatry.

Ford, D.H. and Urban, H.B. (1963) *Systems of Psychotherapy: A comparative study*. New York: Wiley.

Ford, J.K., Quinones, M.A., Sego, D.J. and Sorra, J.S. (1992) Factors affecting the opportunity to perform trained tasks on the job. *Personnel Psychology* 45: 511–27.

Ford, M. (1995) Two modes of mental representation and problem solution in syllogistic reasoning. *Cognition* 54: 1–71.

Ford, R. (1988) The problem with socio-economics. Paper presented at a conference on *The Challenges Currently Facing Research*, London International Business Communications Ltd.

Foucault, M. (1965) *Madness and Civilisation*. New York: Pantheon.

Fox, B.H. (1988) Psychogenic factors in cancer, especially its incidence, in S. Maes, C.D. Spielberger, P.B. Defares and I.G. Sarason (eds) *Topics in Health Psychology*. Chichester: Wiley.

Fox, E. (1993) Allocation of visual attention and anxiety. *Cognition and Emotion* 7: 207–15.

Fox, M.L., Dwyer, D.J. and Ganster, D.C. (1993) Effects of stressful job demands and control on physiological and attitudinal outcomes in a hospital setting. *Academy of Management Journal* 36: 289–318.

Frank, M.G. and Gilovich, T. (1989) Effect of memory perspective on retrospective causal attributions. *Journal of Personality and Social Psychology* 57: 399–403.

Frankenhaeuser, M. and Gardell, B. (1976) Underload and overload in working life: outline of a multidisciplinary approach. *Journal of Human Stress* 35–46.

Frasure-Smith, N. and Prince, R. (1985) The Ischemic Heart Disease Life Stress Monitoring Program: impact on mortality. *Psychosomatic Medicine* 47: 431–45.

Frauenfelder, U.H., Segui, J. and Dijkstra, T. (1990) Lexical effects in phonemic processing: facilitatory or inhibitory? *Journal of Experimental Psychology: Human Perception and Performance* 16: 77–91.

Frayne, C. and Latham, G. (1987) Application of social learning theory to employee self-management of attendance. *Journal of Applied Psychology* 72: 387–92.

Frazier, L. and Rayner, K. (1982) Making and correcting errors during sentence comprehension: eye movements in the analysis of structurally ambiguous sentences. *Cognitive Psychology* 14: 178–210.

Freeman, N.H. and Janikoun, R. (1972) Intellectual realism in children's drawing of a familiar object with distinctive features. *Child Development* 43: 1116–21.

Freeman, N.H., Eiser, D. and Sayers, T. (1977) Children's strategies in producing three-dimensional relationships. *Journal of Experimental Child Psychology* 23: 305–14.

French, J. and Raven, B. (1959) The bases of social power, in D. Cartwright (ed.) *Studies in Social Power*. Ann Arbor, MI: University of Michigan.

French, W.L. and Bell, C.H. (1995) *Organizational Development*, 5th edn. Englewood Cliffs, NJ: Prentice Hall.

Frese, M. (1982) Occupational socialization and psychological development: an underemphasized research perspective in industrial psychology. *Journal of Occupational Psychology* 55: 209–24.

Frese, M. (1987a) Alleviating depression in the unemployed. *Social Science Medicine* 25: 213–15.

Frese, M. (1987b) The industrial and organizational psychology of human–computer interaction in the office, in C.L. Cooper and I.T. Robertson (eds) *International Review of Industrial and Organizational Psychology*. London: Wiley.

Frese, M. (1989) Theoretical models of control and health, in S.L. Sauter, J.J. Hurrell and C.L. Cooper (eds) *Job Control and Worker Health*. Chichester: Wiley.

Frese, M. (1995) Error management in training: conceptual and empirical results, in C. Zucchermaglio, S. Bagnara and S.U. Stucky (eds) *Organizational Learning and Technological Change*. Berlin: Springer.

Frese, M. and Brodbeck, F. (1989) *Computer in Büro und Verwaltung: Psychologisches Wissen für die Praxis*. Heidelberg: Springer.

Frese, M. and Mohr, G. (1979) Soziale Massnahmen für Arbeitslose: Überlegungen im Rahmen einer psychologischen Untersuchung. *Psychosozial* 2(1): 22–35.

Frese, M. and Mohr, G. (1987) Prolonged unemployment and depression in older workers: a longitudinal study of intervening variables. *Social Science and Medicine* 25: 173–8.

Frese, M. and Zapf, D. (1994) Action as the core of work psychology: a German approach, in H.C. Triandis, M.D. Dunnette, and L. Hough (eds) *Handbook of Industrial and Organizational Psychology*. Palo Alto, CA: Consulting Psychologists Press.

Frese, M., Stewart, J. and Hannover, B. (1987) Goal-orientation and planfulness: action styles as personality concepts. *Journal of Personality and Social Psychology* 52: 1182–94.

Frese, M., Brodbeck, F.C., Heinbokel, T., Mooser, C., Schleiffenbaum, E. and Thiemann, P. (1991) Errors in training computer skills: on the positive function of errors. *Human–Computer Interaction* 6: 77–93.

Frese, M., Kring, W., Soose, A. and Zempel, J. (1996) Personal initiative at work: differences between East and West Germany. *Academy of Management Journal* 39(1): 37–63.

Frese, M., Fay, D., Hilburger, T., Leng, K. and Tag, A. (1987) The concept of personal initiative: operationalization, reliability and validity in two German samples. *Journal of Occupational and Organization Psychology* 70: 139–61.

Freud, S. (1913) *The Interpretation of Dreams*, trans. A.A. Brill. London: Allen and Unwin.

Freud, S. (1915) Repression, in *Freud's Collected Papers*, vol. 4. London: Hogarth.

Freud, S. (1915/1949) The unconscious, in J. Strachey (ed. and trans.) *The Standard Edition of the Complete Psychological Works of Sigmund Freud*, vol. 14. London: Hogarth.

Freud, S. (1938) Three contributions to a theory of sex, in *The Basic Writings of Sigmund Freud*. New York: Modern Library.

Frey, D. and Gaska, A. (1993) Die Theorie der kognitiven Dissonanz, in D. Frey and M. Irle (eds) *Theorien der Sozialpsychologie*, vol. 1. Bern: Huber.

Frey, D., Stahlberg, D. and Gollwitzer, P.M. (1993) Einstellung und Verhalten: die Theorie des überlegten Handelns und die Theorie des geplanten Verhaltens, in D. Frey and M. Irle (eds) *Theorien der Sozialpsychologie*, vol. 1. Bern: Huber.

Friedman, A. (1979) Framing pictures: the role of knowledge in automatised encoding and memory for gist. *Journal of Experimental Psychology: General* 108: 316–55.

Friedman, H.S. (1992) Understanding hostility, coping, and health, in H.S. Friedman (ed.) *Hostility, Coping, and Health*. Washington, DC: American Psychological Association.

Friedman, M., Thoresen, C., Gill, J., Powell, L., Ulmer, D., Thompson, L., Price, V., Rabin, D., Breall, W., Dixon, T., Levy, R. and Bourg, E. (1984) Alteration of type A behavior and reduction in cardiac recurrences in post-myocardial infarction patients. *American Heart Journal* 108: 237–48.

Friedson, E. (1975) The future of professionalization, in M. Stacey, M. Reid, C. Health and R. Dingwall (eds) *Health and the Division of Labour*. London: Croom Helm.

Frijda, N.H. (1986) *The Emotions*. Cambridge: Cambridge University Press.

Frijda, N.H. (1993a) Moods, emotion episodes, and emotions, in M. Lewis and J.M. Haviland (eds) *Handbook of Emotions*. New York: Guilford Press.

Frijda, N.H. (1993b) Appraisal and beyond: the issue of cognitive determinants of emotion. *Cognition and Emotion* 7: 225–387.

Frijda, N.H., Kuipers, P. and ter Schure, E. (1989) Relations among emotion, appraisal, and emotional action readiness. *Journal of Personality and Social Psychology* 57: 212–28.

Frith, C.D. (1987) The positive and negative symptoms of schizophrenia reflect impairments in the perception and initiation of action. *Psychological Medicine* 17: 631–48.

Fruzzetti, A.E., Toland, K., Teller, S.A. and Loftus, E.F. (1992) Memory and eyewitness testimony, in M. Gruneberg and P. Morris (eds) *Aspects of Memory: The practical aspects*. London: Routledge.

Fry, G.A., Bridgman, C.S. and Ellerbrock, V.J. (1949) The effect of atmospheric scattering on binocular depth perception. *American Journal of Optometry* 26: 9–15.

Funnell, E. and Sheridan, J. (1992) Categories of knowledge? Unfamiliar aspects of living and non-living things. *Cognitive Neuropsychology* 9: 135–53.

Furman, W., Rahe, D.F. and Hartup, W.W. (1979) Rehabilitation of socially withdrawn preschool children through mixed-age and same-age socialization. *Child Development* 50: 915–22.

Furnham, A. (1981) Personality and activity preference. *British Journal of Social and Clinical Psychology* 20: 57–68.

Fuson, K. and Kwon, Y. (1992a) Korean children's understanding of multidigit addition and subtraction. *Child Development* 63: 491–506.

Fuson, K. and Kwon, Y. (1992b) Learning addition and subtraction: effects of number words and other cultural tools, in J. Bideaud, C. Meljac and J.-P. Fischer (eds) *Pathways to Number*. Hillsdale, NJ: Lawrence Erlbaum.

Gaertner, S., Mann, J., Dovidio, J., Murrell, A. and Pomare, M. (1990) How does cooperation reduce intergroup bias? *Journal of Personality and Social Psychology* 59(4): 692–704.

Gaffan, D. (1992) Amygdala and the memory of reward, in J.P. Aggleton (ed.) *The Amygdala*. New York: Wiley-Liss.

Gaffan, D. and Harrison, S. (1987) Amygdalectomy and disconnection in visual learning for auditory secondary reinforcement by monkeys. *Journal of Neuroscience* 7: 2285–92.

Gaffan, D., Gaffan, E.A. and Harrison, S. (1989) Visual-visual associative learning and reward-association learning in monkeys: the role for the amygdala. *Journal of Neuroscience* 9: 558–64.

Gaffan, E.A., Gaffan, D. and Harrison, S. (1988) Disconnection of the amygdala from visual association cortex impairs visual reward-association learning in monkeys. *Journal of Neuroscience* 8: 3144–50.

Gainotti, G. (1989) The meaning of emotional disturbance resulting from unilateral brain injury, in G. Gainotti and C. Caltagirone (eds) *Emotions and the Dual Brain*. Berlin: Springer-Verlag.

Gale, A. (1983) Electroencephalographic studies of extraversion–introversion: a case study in the psychophysiology of individual differences. *Personality and Individual Differences* 4: 371–80.

Galton, F. (1883) *Inquiry into Human Faculty and its Development*. London: Macmillan.

Ganster, D.C., Fusilier, M.R. and Mayes, B.T. (1986) Role of social support in the experience of stress at work. *Journal of Applied Psychology* 71:102–10.

Garcia, J. (1989) Food for Tolman: cognition and cathexis in concert, in T. Archer and L-G. Nilsson (eds) *Aversion, Avoidance and Anxiety: Perspectives on aversively motivated behaviour*. Hillsdale, NJ: Lawrence Erlbaum.

Garcia, J. and Koelling, R.A. (1966) Relation of cue to consequence in avoidance learning. *Psychonomic Science* 4: 123–4.

Gardell, B. (1971) Alienation and mental health in the modern industrial environment, in L. Levi (ed.) *Society, Stress, and Disease, vol. 1, The psychosocial environment and psychosomatic diseases*. London: Oxford University Press.

Gardner, H. (1983) *Frames of Mind: The theory of multiple intelligences*. New York: Basic Books.

Gardner, H. (1993) *Creating Minds: The anatomy of creativity as seen through Freud, Einstein Picasso, Stravinsky, Eliot, Graham, and Gandhi*. New York: Basic Books.

Garety, P.A. and Hemsley, D. (1994) *Delusions: Investigations into the psychology of delusional reasoning*. Oxford: Oxford University Press.

Garland, H., Hardy, A. and Stephenson, L. (1975) Information search as affected by attribution type and response category. *Personality and Social Psychology Bulletin* 4: 612–15.

Garnham, A. (1993) A number of questions about a question of number. *Behavioral and Brain Sciences* 16: 350–1.

Garnham, A., Oakhill, J. and Johnson-Laird, P. N. (1982) Referential continuity and the coherence of discourse. *Cognition* 11: 29–46.

Garrett, M.F. (1975) The analysis of sentence production, in G.H. Bower (ed.) *The Psychology of Learning and Motivation*, vol. 9. San Diego, CA: Academic Press.

Garrett, M.F. (1976) Syntactic processes in sentence production, in R.J. Wales and E. Walker (eds) *New Approaches to Language Mechanisms*. Amsterdam: North-Holland.

Garrow, J. S. (1988) *Obesity and Related Diseases*. Edinburgh: Churchill Livingstone.

Gaugler, E., Kolb, M. and Ling, B. (1977) *Humanisierung der Arbeitswelt und Produktivität*, 2nd edn. Ludwigshafen: Friedrich Kiehl.

Gauld, A. and Stephenson, G.M. (1967) Some experiments relating to Bartlett's theory of remembering. *British Journal of Psychology* 58: 39–50.

Gazzaniga, M.S. (1988) Brain modularity: towards a philosophy of conscious experience, in A.J. Marcel and E. Bisiach (eds) *Consciousness in Contemporary Science*. Oxford: Oxford University Press.

Geertz, C. (1975) On the nature of anthropological understanding. *American Scientist* 63: 47–53.

Geis, M. and Zwicky, A.M. (1971) On invited inferences. *Linguistic Inquiry* 2: 561–6.

Geiselman, R.E., Fisher, R.P., MacKinnon, D.P. and Holland, H.L. (1985) Eyewitness memory enhancement in police interview: cognitive retrieval mnemonics versus hypnosis. *Journal of Applied Psychology* 70: 401–12.

Gelb, I.J. (1963) *A Study of Writing*. Chicago: University of Chicago Press.

Gelman, R. and Gallistel, C.R. (1978) *The Child's Understanding of Number*. Cambridge, MA: Harvard University Press.

Gelman, R. and Meck, E. (1983) Preschoolers' counting: principles before skill. *Cognition* 13: 343–60.

Gelman, R., Bullock, M. and Meck, M.E. (1980) Preschoolers' understanding of simple object transformations. *Child Development* 51: 691–9.

Genta, M.L., Menesini, E., Fonzi, A., Costabile, A. and Smith, P.K. (1996) Bullies and victims in schools in central and southern Italy. *European Journal of Psychology of Education* 11: 97–110.

Gentner, D.R. and Stevens, A.L. (1983) *Mental Models*. Hillsdale, NJ: Lawrence Erlbaum.

Gentner, D., Rattermann, M.J. and Forbus, K.D. (1992) The role of similarity in transfer. *Cognitive Psychology* 25: 431–67.

Gergely, G., Nadasdy, Z., Csibra, G. and Biro, S. (1996) Taking the intentional stance at 12 months of age. *Cognition* 56: 165–93.

Gergen, K. (1971a) Social psychology as history. *Journal of Personality and Social Psychology* 26(2): 309–20.

Gergen, K.J. (1971b) *The Concept of Self*. New York: Holt, Rinehart and Winston.

Gergen, K.J. (1985) Social pragmatics and the origins of psychological discourse, in K.J. Gergen and K.E. Davis (eds) *The Social Construction of the Person*. New York: Springer-Verlag.

Gergen, K.J. (1989) Warranting voice and the elaboration of the self, in J. Shotter and K.J. Gergen (eds) *Texts of Identity*. London: Sage.

Geyer, A.L.J. and Speyrer, J.M. (1997) Transformational leadership and objective performance in banks. *Applied Psychology: An International Review* 46.

Gibbons, F.X. (1978) Sexual standards and reactions to pornography: enhancing behavioral consistency through self-focused attention. *Journal of Personality and Social Psychology* 36: 976–87.

Gibbs, J., Maddison, S.P. and Rolls, E. T. (1981) The satiety role of the small intestine in sham feeding rhesus monkeys. *Journal of Comparative and Physiological Psychology* 95: 1003–15.

Gibbs, R.W. (1986) What makes some indirect speech acts conventional? *Journal of Memory and Language* 25: 181–96.

Gibson, J.J. (1950) *The Perception of the Visual World*. Boston, MA: Houghton Mifflin.

Gibson, J.J. (1966) *The Senses Considered as Perceptual Systems*. Boston, MA: Houghton Mifflin.

Gibson, J.J. (1979) *The Ecological Approach to Visual Perception*. Boston, MA: Houghton Mifflin.

Gick, M.L. and Holyoak, K.J. (1980) Analogical problem solving. *Cognitive Psychology* 12: 306–55.

Giese, F. (1924) Die Arbeitsprobe in der Psychodiagnostik. *Zeitschrift für Angewandte Psychologie* 23: 3–4.

Gigerenzer, G. and Hug, K. (1992) Domain specific reasoning: social contracts, cheating and perspective change. *Cognition* 43: 127–71.

Gil, D. (1970) *Violence against Children*. Cambridge, MA: Harvard University Press.

Gilhooly, K.J. (1995) *Thinking: Directed, undirected and creative*, 3rd edn. London: Academic Press.

Gilligan, C. and Attanucci, J. (1988) Two moral orientations: gender differences and similarities. *Merrill-Palmer Quarterly* 34: 223–37.

Glanzer, M. and Cunitz, A.R. (1966) Two storage mechanisms in free recall. *Journal of Verbal Learning and Verbal Behavior* 5: 351–60.

Glaser, B.G. and Strauss, A.L. (1967) *The Discovery of Grounded Theory: Strategies for qualitative research*. Chicago: Aldine.

Glass, D.C. and Singer, J.E. (1972) *Urban Stress: Experiments on noise and social stressors*. New York: Academic Press.

Gleitman, H. (1985) Some trends in the study of cognition, in S. Koch and D.E. Leary (eds) *A Century of Psychology as Science: Retrospections and assessments*. New York: McGraw-Hill.

Gleitman, H. (1986) *Psychology*, 2nd edn. London: Norton.

Glenberg, A.M., Smith, S.M. and Green, C. (1977) Type I rehearsal: maintenance and more. *Journal of Verbal Learning and Verbal Behavior* 16: 339–52.

Gluck, M.A. and Bower, G.H. (1988) From conditioning to category learning. *Journal of Experimental Psychology: General* 117: 227–47.

Glushko, R.J. (1979) The organisation and activation of orthographic knowledge in reading aloud. *Journal of Experimental Psychology: Human Perception and Performance* 5: 674–91.

Godden, D.R. and Baddeley, A.D. (1975) Context-dependent memory in two natural environments: on land and under water. *British Journal of Psychology* 66: 325–31.

Godden, D.R. and Baddeley, A.D. (1980) When does context influence recognition memory? *British Journal of Psychology* 71: 99–104.

Goetz, J.P. and LeCompte, M.D. (1984) *Ethnography and Qualitative Design in Educational Research*. Orlando, FL: Academic Press.

Gold, R. (1987) *The Description of Cognitive Development: Three Piagetian themes*. Oxford: Clarendon Press.

Goldberg, L.R. (1990) An alternative 'Description of personality': the Big-Five factor structure. *Journal of Personality and Social Psychology* 59: 1216–29.

Goldberg, L.R. (1993) The structure of pheonotypic personality traits. *American Psychologist* 48: 26–34.

Goldberg, S., MacKay, S. and Rochester, M. (1994) Affect, attachment, and maternal responsiveness. *Infant Behaviour and Development* 17: 335–9.

Golding, E. (1981) The effect of unilateral brain lesion on reasoning. *Cortex* 17: 31–40.

Goldsmith, H.H. (1993) Temperament: variability in developing emotion systems, in M. Lewis and J.M. Haviland (eds) *Handbook of Emotions*. New York: Guilford Press.

Goldsmith, H.H. and Campos, J.J. (1982) Genetic differences on individual differences in emotionality. *Infant Behaviour and Development* 5: 99–115.

Goldstein, I.L. (1991) Training in organizations, in M.D. Dunnette and L. Hough (eds) *Handbook of Industrial and Organizational Psychology*. Palo Alto, CA: Consulting Psychologists Press.

Gollwitzer, P.M. (1993) Goal achievement: the role of intentions, in W. Stroebe and M. Hewstone (eds) *European Review of Social Psychology*, Chichester: Wiley.

Golumbok, S. and Fivush, R. (1994) *Gender Development*. Cambridge: Cambridge University Press.

Gomulicki, B.R. (1956) Recall as an abstractive process. *Acta Psychologica* 12: 77–94.

Goodacre, D. (1951) The use of a sociometric test as a predictor of combat unit effectiveness. *Sociometry* 14: 148–52.

Goodall, J. (1986) *The Chimpanzees of Gombe: Patterns of behavior*. Cambridge, MA: Harvard University Press.

Goodman, P.S., Devadas, R. and Hughson, T.L.G. (1988) Groups and productivity: analyzing the effectiveness of self-managing teams, in J.P. Campbell and R.J. Campbell (eds) *Productivity in organizations*. San Francisco, CA: Jossey-Bass.

Goodnow, J.J. (1977) *Children's Drawings*. London: Open Books.

Gopnik, A. and Astington, J.W. (1988) Children's understanding of representational change and its relation to the understanding of false belief and the appearance–reality distinction. *Child Development* 59: 26–37.

Gopnik, A. and Meltzoff, A. (1986) Relations between semantic and cognitive development in the one word stage: the specificity hypothesis. *Child Development* 57: 1040–53.

Gopnik, A. and Meltzoff, A. (1992) Categorization and naming: basic level sorting in 18-month-olds and its relation to language. *Child Development* 63: 1091–103.

Gopnik, A. and Meltzoff, A. (1997) *Words, Thoughts and Theories*. Cambridge, Mass: MIT Press.

Gordon, C. (1976) Development of evaluated role identities. *Annual Review of Sociology*, 2: 405–33.

Gordon, I.E. (1989) *Theories of Visual Perception*. Chichester: Wiley.

Gordon, R., Bindrim, T., McNicholas, M. and Walden, T. (1988) Perceptions of blue-collar and white-collar crime: the effect of defendant race on simulated juror decisions. *Journal of Social Psychology* 128(2): 191–7.

Gorsuch, R.L. and Ottberg, J. (1983) Moral obligation and attitudes: their relation to behavioral intentions. *Journal of Personality and Social Psychology* 44: 1025–8.

Goswami, U. and Bryant, P. (1990) *Phonological Skills and Learning to Read*. London: Lawrence Erlbaum.

Gotlib, I.H. and Hammen, C.L. (1992) *Psychological Aspects of Depression: Toward a cognitive-interpersonal integration*. Chichester: Wiley.

Gottesman, I.I. (1991) *Schizophrenia Genesis*. New York: W.H. Freeman.

Gottmann, J.M. (1993a) *Why Marriages Succeed or Fail*. New York: Simon and Schuster.

Gottmann, J.M. (1993b) The roles of conflict engagement, escalation, and avoidance in marital interaction: a longitudinal view of five types of couples. *Journal of Consulting and Clinical Psychology* 61: 6–15.

Gottmann, J.M. and Levenson, R.W. (1992) Marital processes predictive of later dissolution: behavior, physiology and health. *Journal of Personality and Social Psychology* 63: 221–33.

Gough, H.G., Lazzari, R. and Fioravanti, M. (1978) Self versus ideal self: a comparison of five adjective check list indices. *Journal of Consulting and Clinical Psychology* 46: 1085–91.

Gould, R. and Sigall, H. (1977) The effects of empathy and outcome on attribution: an examination of the divergent-perspectives hypothesis. *Journal of Experimental Social Psychology* 13: 480–91.

Graesser, A.C., Singer, M. and Trabasso, T. (1994) Constructing inferences during narrative text comprehension. *Psychological Review* 101: 371–95.

Graf, P. and Schachter, D.L. (1985) Implicit and explicit memory for new associations in normal and amnesic subjects. *Journal of Experimental Psychology: Learning, Memory*, and Cognition 11: 501–18.

Graf, P., Squire, L.R. and Mandler, G. (1984) The information that amnesic patients do not forget. *Journal of Experimental Psychology: Learning, Memory, and Cognition* 10: 164–78.

Granberg, D. (1987) Candidate preference, membership group, and estimates of voting behavior. *Social Cognition* 5: 323–35.

Granberg, D. and Holmberg, S. (1990) The intention–behaviour relationship among US and Swedish voters. *Social Psychological Quarterly* 53: 44–54.

Gray, J. (1971) The mind–brain identity theory as a scientific hypothesis. *Philosophical Quarterly* 21: 247–54.

Gray, J. (1982) *The Neuropsychology of Anxiety*. Cambridge: Cambridge University Press,

Gray, J.A. (1987) *The Psychology of Fear and Stress*, 2nd edn. Cambridge: Cambridge University Press.

Gray, J.A. and Wedderburn, A.A. (1960) Grouping strategies with simultaneous stimuli. *Quarterly Journal of Experimental Psychology* 12: 180–4.

Green, D.P., Goldman, S.L. and Salovey, P. (1993) Measurement error masks bipolarity in affect ratings. *Journal of Personality and Social Psychology* 64: 1029–41.

Green, F.P. and Schneider, F.W. (1974) Age differences in the behavior of boys on three measures of altruism. *Child Development* 45: 248–51.

Greenberg, D., Smith, G.P. and Gibbs, J. (1990) Intraduodenal infusions of fat elicit satiety in the sham feeding rat. *American Journal of Physiology* 259: R110–R118.

Greene, J. and D'Oliveira, M. (1982) *Learning to Use Statistical Tests in Psychology*. Milton Keynes: Open University Press.

Greenhalgh, L. (1987) Interpersonal conflicts in organizations, in C.L. Cooper and I.T. Robertson (eds) *International Review of Industrial and Organizational Psychology 1987*. Chichester: Wiley.

Greeno, J.G. (1974) Hobbits and orcs: acquisition of a sequential concept. *Cognitive Psychology* 6: 270–92.

Gregory, R.L. (1970) *The Intelligent Eye*. New York: McGraw-Hill.

Gregory, R.L. (1973) *Eye and Brain*. London: Weidenfeld and Nicolson.

Gregory, R.L. (1980) Perceptions as hypotheses. *Philosophical Transactions of the Royal Society of London* Series B 290: 181–97.

Gregory, R.L. and Wallace, J.G. (1963) *Recovery from Early Blindness*. Cambridge: Heffer.

Greif, S. (1992) Computer systems as learning environments, in J. Valsiner and H.G. Voss (eds) *The Structure of Learning Processes*. Norwood, NJ: Ablex.

Greif, S. and Bamberg, E. (eds) (1994) *Die Arbeits- und Organisationspsychologie*. Goettingen: Hogrefe.

Greif, S. and Janikowski, A. (1987) Aktives Lernen durch systematische Fehlerexploration oder programmiertes Lernen durch Tutorials? *Zeitschrift für Arbeits- und Organistionspsychologie* 31: 94–9.

Greif, S. and Keller, H. (1990) Innovation and the design of work and learning environments: the concept of exploration in human–computer interaction, in M.A. West and J.L. Farr (eds) *Innovation and Creativity at Work*. New York: Wiley.

Grice, H.P. (1967) Logic and conversation, in P. Cole and J.L. Morgan (eds) *Studies in Syntax*, vol. 3. New York: Seminar Press.

Griffin, C. (1995) Feminism, social psychology and qualitative research. *The Psychologist*, 8: 119–21.

Griffiths, J. and Luker, K. (1994) Intra-professional research in district nursing in whose interests? *Journal of Advanced Nursing* 20(b): 1038–45.

Griggs, R.A. and Cox, J.R. (1982) The elusive thematic-material effect in Wason's selection task. *British Journal of Psychology* 73: 407–20.

Griggs, R.A. and Cox, J.R. (1983) The effects of problem content and negation on Wason's selection task. *Quarterly Journal of Experimental Psychology* 35A: 519–33.

Gross, E. (1954) Primary functions of the small group. *American Journal of Sociology* 57: 546–64.

Gross, R.D. (1992) *Psychology: The science of mind and behaviour*, 2nd edn. London: Hodder and Stoughton.

Gross, R.D. (1996) *Psychology: The science of mind and behaviour*, 3rd edn. London: Hodder and Stoughton.

Grossman, S.P. (1967) *A Textbook of Physiological Psychology*. New York: Wiley.

Grossman, S.P. (1973) *Essentials of Physiological Psychology*. New York: Wiley.

Grundy, E. (1994) Live old, live well. *MRC News* autumn 22–5.

Guilford, J.P. (1934) Introversion–extroversion. *Psychological Bulletin* 31: 331–54.

Guilford, J.P. (1936) Unitary traits of personality and factor theory. *American Journal of Psychology* 48: 673–80.

Guilford, J.P. (1956) *Psychometric Methods*. New York: McGraw-Hill.

Guilford, J.P. (1959) *Personality*. New York: McGraw-Hill.

Guilford, J. P. (1967) *The Nature of Human Intelligence*. New York: McGraw-Hill.

Guilford, J.P. (1982) Cognitive psychology's ambiguities: some suggested remedies. *Psychological Review* 89: 48–59.

Guilford, J.P. and Guilford, R.B. (1936) Personality factors S, E. and M, and their measurement. *Journal of Psychology* 2: 109–27.

Guion, R.M. (1965) *Personnel Testing*. New York: McGraw-Hill.

Guitton, D., Buchtel, H.A. and Douglas, R.M. (1985) Frontal lobe lesions in man cause difficulties in suppressing reflexive glances and in generating goal-directed saccades. *Experimental Brain Research* 58: 455–72.

Gulowsen, J. (1972) A measure of work-group autonomy, in L.E. Davis and J.C. Taylor (eds) *Design of jobs*. Harmondsworth: Penguin.

Gunn, J., Robertson, G., Dell, S. *et al.* (1978) *Psychiatric Aspects of Imprisonment*. London: Academic Press.

Guze, S.B. (1989) Biological psychiatry: is there any other kind? *Psychological Medicine* 19: 15–23.

Guzzo, R.A., Jette, R.D. and Katzell, R.A. (1985) The effects of psychologically based intervention programs on work productivity: a meta-analysis. *Personnel Psychology* 38: 275–91.

Hacker, W. (1986) *Arbeitspsychologie*. Bern: Huber.

Hacker, W. (1992) *Expertenkönnen: Erkennen und Vermitteln*. Göttingen: Hogrefe.

Hacker, W. and Skell, W. (1993) *Lernen in der Arbeit*. Berlin: Bundesinstitut für Berufsausbildung.

Hackman, J.R. (1970) Tasks and task performance in research on stress, in J.E. McGrath (ed.) *Social and Psychological Factors in Stress*. New York: Holt, Rinehart and Winston.

Hackman, J.R. and Oldham, G.R. (1975) Development of the job diagnostic survey. *Journal of Applied Psychology* 60: 259–70.

Hackman, J.R. and Oldham, G.R. (1976) Motivation through the design of work: test of a theory. *Organizational Behavior and Human Design Process* 16: 256.

Haight, W.L. and Miller, P.J. (1993) *Pretending at Home: Early development in a sociocultural context*. Albany, NY: State University of New York Press.

Halff, H.M., Ortony, A. and Anderson, R.C. (1976) A context-sensitive representation of word meanings. *Memory and Cognition* 4: 378–83.

Halford, G.S. (1993) *Children's Understanding: The development of mental models*. Hillsdale, NJ: Lawrence Erlbaum.

Hall, C.S. and Van de Castle, R.L. (1966) *The Content Analysis of Dreams*. New York: Appleton-Century-Crofts.

Hammerl, M. (1993) Blocking observed in human instrumental conditioning. *Learning and Motivation* 24: 73–87.

Hammersley, M. and Atkinson, P. (1993) *Ethnography: Principles in practice*. London: Routledge.

Hampson, S.E. (1988) *The Construction of Personality: An introduction*, 2nd edn. London: Routledge.

Hampton, J.A. (1981) An investigation of the nature of abstract concepts. *Memory and Cognition* 9: 149–56.

Haney, C., Banks, W.C. and Zimbardo, P.G. (1973) A study of prisoners and guards in a simulated prison. *Naval Research Review* 30: 4–17.

Hare, A. (1962) *Handbook of Small Group Research*. New York: Free Press.

Harley, T. A. (1995) *The Psychology of Language: From data to theory*. Hove: Lawrence Erlbaum.

Harlow, J.M. (1868) Recovery from the passage of an iron bar through the head, reprinted in *History of Psychiatry* (1993) 4: 274–81.

Harmon-Jones, E., Greenberg, J., Solomon, S. and Simon, L. (1996) The effects of mortality salience on intergroup bias between minimal groups. *European Journal of Social Psychology* 26: 677–81.

Harré, R. (1983) *Personal Being: A theory for individual psychology*. Oxford: Blackwell.

Harré, R. (1985) The language game of self-ascription: a note, in K.J. Gergen and K.E. Davis (eds) *The Social Construction of the Person*. New York: Springer-Verlag.

Harré, R (ed) (1986a) *The Social Construction of Emotions*. Oxford: Blackwell.

Harré, R. (1986b) An outline of the social constructionist viewpoint, in R. Harré (ed.) *The Social Construction of Emotions*. Oxford: Blackwell.

Harré, R. (1986c) Emotion across times: I accidie and melancholy in the psychological context, in R. Harré (ed.) *The Social Construction of Emotions*. Oxford: Blackwell.

Harré, R. and Finlay-Jones, R. (1986) An outline of emotion talk across times, in R. Harré (ed.) *The Social Construction of Emotions*. Oxford: Blackwell.

Harré, R. and Gillett, G. (1994) *The Discursive Mind*. London: Sage.

Harré, R. and Secord, P.F. (1972) *The Explanation of Social Behaviour*. Oxford: Blackwell.

Harrer, G. and Harrer, H. (1977) Music, emotion, and autonomic function, in M. Critchley and R.A. Henson (eds) *Music and the Brain*. London: Heinemann.

Harstone, M. and Augustinos, M. (1995) The minimal group paradigm: categorisation into two versus three groups. *European Journal of Social Psychology* 25: 179–93.

Harte, J.L., Eifert, G.H. and Smith, R. (1995) The effects of running and meditation on beta-endorphin, corticotrophin-releasing hormone and cortisol in plasma, and on mood. *Biological Psychology* 40: 251–65.

Hartup, W.W. (1996) The company they keep: friendships and their developmental significance. *Child Development* 67: 1–13.

Harvey, L.O., Roberts, J.O. and Gervais, M.J. (1983) The spatial frequency basis of internal representations, in H.-G. Geissler, H.F.J.M. Buffart, E.L.J. Leeuwenberg and V. Sarris (eds) *Modern Issues in Perception*. Rotterdam: North-Holland.

Haslam, S.A. and Oakes, P. (1995) How context-independent is the outgroup homogeneity effect? A response to Bartsch and Judd. *European Journal of Social Psychology* 25: 468–75.

Haslam, S.A. and Turner, J. (1992) Context-dependent variation in social stereotyping 2: The relationship between frame of reference, self-categorisation and accentuation. *European Journal of Social Psychology* 22: 251–77.

Haslam, S.A., Turner, J.C., Oakes, P.J., McGarty, C. and Hayes, B.K. (1992) Context-dependent variation in social stereotyping 1: The effects of intergroup relations as mediated by social change and frame of reference. *European Journal of Social Psychology*, 22: 3–20.

Haslam, S.A., Oakes, P., Turner, J. and McGarty, C. (1995) Social identity, self-categorisation, and the perceived homogeneity of ingroups and outgroups: the interaction between social motivation and cognition, in R. Sorrento and E. Higgins (eds) *Handbook of Motivation and Cognition*, vol.3. New York: Guilford Press.

Haviland, J. and Lelwicka, M. (1987) The induced affect response: 10-week old infants' responses to three emotional expressions. *Developmental Psychology* 23: 97–104.

Haxy, J.V., Grady, C.L., Horwitz, B., Ungerleider, L.G., Mishkin, M., Carson, R.E., Herscovitch, P., Schapiro, M.B. and Rapoport, S.I. (1991) Dissociation of object and spatial visual processing pathways in human extrastriate cortex. *Proceedings of the National Academy of Sciences of the USA* 88: 1621–25.

Hayes, N. (1991) Social identity, social representations and organisational culture. Unpublished PhD thesis, CNAA/Huddersfield.

Hayes, N. (1993) *Principles of Social Psychology*. Hove: Lawrence Erlbaum.

Hayvren, M. and Hymel, S. (1984) Ethical issues in sociometric testing: impact of sociometric measures on interaction behavior. *Developmental Psychology* 20: 844–9.

Hazelrigg, M.D., Cooper, H.M. and Borduin, C.M. (1987) Evaluating the effectiveness of family therapies: an integrative review and analysis. *Psychological Bulletin* 101: 428–42.

Healy, D. (1990) *The Suspended Revolution: Psychiatry and psychotherapy re-examined*. London: Faber and Faber.

Hearnshaw, L.S. (1987) *The Shaping of Modern Psychology: An historical introduction*. London: Routledge and Kegan Paul.

Hebden, J. (1986) Adopting an organization's culture: the socialization of graduate trainees. *Organizational Dynamics* 54–72.

Heider, F. (1944) Social perception and phenomenal causality. *Psychological Review* 51: 358–78.

Heider, F. (1946) Attitudes and cognitive organization. *Journal of Psychology* 21: 107–12.

Heider, F. (1958) *The Psychology of Interpersonal Relations*. New York: Wiley.

Heim, A. (1970) *Intelligence and Personality: Their assessment and relationship*. Harmondsworth: Penguin.

Heim, A., Augusting, K., Blaser, A. and Burki, C. (1987) Coping with breast cancer: a longitudinal perspective study. *Psychotherapy and Psychosomatics* 48: 44–59.

Heindel, W.C., Butters, N. and Salmon, D.P. (1988) Impaired learning of a motor skill in patients with Huntingdon's disease. *Behavioural Neuroscience* 102: 141–7.

Heise, D.R. and O'Brien, J. (1993) Emotion expression in groups, in M. Lewis and J.M. Haviland (eds) *Handbook of Emotions*. New York: Guilford Press.

Heiss, J. (1981) Social roles, in M. Rosenberg and R.H. Turner (eds) *Social Psychology: Sociological Perspectives*. New York: Basic Books.

Heller, J.I. (1979) Cognitive processing in verbal analogy solution. Unpublished PhD thesis, Pittsburgh, PA.

Hendrickson, D.E. and Hendrickson, A.E. (1980) The biological basis of individual differences in intelligence. *Personality and Individual Differences* 1: 3–33.

Hendrickson, D.E. and Hendrickson, A.E. (1982) The biological basis of intelligence, in H.J. Eysenck (ed.) *A Model for Intelligence*. New York: Springer-Verlag.

Henningfield, J.E., Johnson, R.E. and Jasinski, D.I. (1987) Clinical procedures for the assessment of abuse potential, in M.A. Bozarth (ed.) *Methods of Assessing the Reinforcing Properties of Abused Drugs*. New York: Springer-Verlag.

Henriques, J., Hollway, W., Urwin, C., Venn, C. and Walkerdine, V. (1984) *Changing the Subject: Psychology, social regulation and subjectivity*. London and New York: Methuen.

Hensley, T. and Griffin, G. (1986) Victims of groupthink: the Kent State University Board of Trustees and the 1977 gymnasium controversy. *Journal of Conflict Resolution* 30: 497–531.

Henwood, K. and Pidgeon, N. (1995) Grounded theory and psychological research. *The Psychologist* 8: 115–18.

Herbert, T.B. (1993) Stress and immunity in humans: a meta-analytic review. *Psychosomatic Medicine* 55: 364–79.

Herbert, T.B. and Cohen, S. (1993) Stress and illness, in V.S. Ramachandran (ed.) *Encyclopedia of Human Behavior*, vol. 4. San Diego, CA: Academic Press.

Hering, E. (1890) Beitrag zur Lehre vom Simultankontrast. *Zeitschrift für Psychologie under Physiologie der Sinnesorgane* 1: 18–28.

Herman, S. (1977) *Jewish Identity: A socio-psychological perspective*, vol. 48, Sage Library of Social Research. London: Sage.

Herrnstein, R.J. (1966) Superstition: a corollary of the principles of operant conditioning, in W.K. Honig (ed.) *Operant Behavior: Areas of research and application*. New York: Appleton.

Herrnstein, R.J. and deVilliers, P.A. (1980) Fish as a natural category for people and pigeons, in G.H. Bower (ed.) *The Psychology of Learning and Motivation*, vol. 14. San Diego, CA: Academic Press.

Hertz-Lazarowitz, R., Feitelson, D., Zahavi, S. and Hartup, W.W. (1981) Social interaction and social organisation of Israeli five-to-seven-year olds. *International Journal of Behavioral Development* 4: 143–55.

Herzberg, F. (1968) One more time: how do you motivate employees? *Harvard Business Review* 46: 53–62.

Hess, W.R. (1950/1981) Function and neural regulation of internal organs, in K. Akert (ed.) *Biological Order and Brain Organization: Selected works of W.R. Hess*. Berlin: Springer-Verlag.

Hetherington, E.M. (1989) Coping with family transitions: winners, losers and survivors. *Child Development* 60: 1–14.

Hewstone, M. (1990) The ultimate attribution error: a review of the literature on intergroup causal attribution. *European Journal of Social Psychology* 20: 311–35.

Hewstone, M. and Brown, R. (1986) *Contact and Conflict in Intergroup Encounters*. London: Blackwell.

Hewstone, M. and Fincham, F. (1996) Attribution theory and research: basic issues and applications, in M. Hewstone, W. Stroebe and G.M. Stephenson (eds) *Introduction to Social Psychology*, 2nd edn. Oxford: Blackwell.

Hewstone, M. Fincham, F. and Jaspars, J. (1981) Social categorisation and similarity in intergroup behaviour: a replication with penalties. *European Journal of Social Psychology* 11: 101–7.

Hiatt, S., Campos, J.J. and Emde, R.N. (1979) Facial patterning and infant facial expression: happiness, surprise and fear. *Child Development* 50: 1020–35.

Hill, C.A. (1987) Affiliation motivation: people who need people but in different ways. *Journal of Personality and Social Psychology* 52: 1008–18.

Hinkle, S. and Brown, R. (1990) Intergroup comparisons and social identity: some links and lacunae, in D. Abrams and M. Hogg (eds) *Social Identity Theory: Constructive and critical advances*. Hemel Hempstead: Harvester Wheatsheaf.

Hinkle, S., Taylor, L. and Fox-Cardimone, D. (1989) Intragroup identification and intergroup differentiation: a multi-component approach. *British Journal of Social Psychology* 28: 305–17.

Hipwell, A.E. and Kumar, R. (1997) The impact of post-partum affective psychosis on the child, in L. Murray and P.J. Cooper (eds) *Postpartum Depression and Child Development*. New York: Guilford Press.

Hipwell, A.E., Goossens, F.A., Melhuish, E.C. and Kumar, R. (1998) Severe maternal psychopathology, 'joint' hospitalisation and infant–mother attachment. *Development and Psychopathology*.

Hirano, P.C., Laurant, D.D. and Lorig, K. (1994) Arthritis patient education studies 1991: a review of the literature. *Patient Education and Counseling* 24: 9–54.

Hiroto, D.S. and Seligman, M.E.P. (1975) Generality of learned helplessness in man. *Journal of Personality and Social Psychology* 31: 311–27.

Hirst, W., Spelke, E.S., Reaves, C.C., Caharack, G. and Neisser, U. (1980) Dividing attention without alternation or automaticity. *Journal of Experimental Psychology: General* 109: 98–117.

Hitch, G.J. and Baddeley, A.D. (1976) Verbal reasoning and working memory. *Quarterly Journal of Experimental Psychology* 28: 603–21.

Hobfoll, S. (1988) *The Ecology of Stress*. New York: Hemisphere.

Hobfoll, S. (1989) Conservation of resources: a new attempt at conceptualizing stress. *American Psychologist* 44: 513–24.

Hockett, C. (1955) Manual of Phonology, Publications in Anthropology and Linguistics no. 11. Bloomington IN: Indiana University.

Hockey, G.R.J., Davies, S. and Gray, M.M. (1972) Forgetting as a function of sleep at different times of day. *Quarterly Journal of Experimental Psychology* 24: 386–93.

Hodge, M.H. and Otani, H. (1996) Beyond category sorting and pleasantness rating: inducing relational and item-specific processing. *Memory and Cognition* 24: 110–15.

Hodges, J. and Tizard, J. (1989) Social and family relationships of ex-institutional adolescents. *Journal of Child Psychology and Psychiatry* 30: 77–98.

Hoebel, B.G. (1969) Feeding and self-stimulation. *Annals of the New York Academy of Sciences* 157: 757–78.

Hoffman, D.C. and Beninger, R.J. (1986) Feeding behaviour in rats is differentially affected by pimozide treatment depending on prior experience. *Pharmacology, Biochemistry and Behaviour* 24: 259–62.

Hoffman, D.D. and Richards, W.A. (1984) Parts of recognition. *Cognition* 18: 65–96.

Hoffman, M.L. (1984) Interaction of affect and cognition in empathy, in C. Izard, J. Kagan and R. Zajonc (eds) *Emotions, Cognition and Behaviour*. New York: Cambridge University Press.

Hofling, C.K., Brotzman, E. Dairymple, S., Graves, N. and Pierce, C.M. (1966) An experimental study in nurse–physician relationships. *Journal of Mental and Nervous Diseases* 143: 171–80.

Hofstede, C. (1980) *Culture's Consequences: International differences in work-related values*. Beverly Hills, CA: Sage.

Hofstede, G. (1991) *Cultures and Organizations*. London: McGraw-Hill.

Hogg, M. (1987) Social identity and group cohesiveness, in J.C. Turner, M.A. Hogg, P.J. Oakes, S.D. Reicher and M.J. Wetherall, *Rediscovering the Social Group: A self-categorisation theory*. Oxford: Blackwell.

Hogg, M. (1992) *The Social Psychology of Group Cohesiveness: From attraction to social identity*. London: Harvester Wheatsheaf.

Hogg, M. (1993) Group cohesiveness: a critical review and some new directions. *European Review of Social Psychology* 4: 85–111.

Hogg, M.A and Abrams, D. (1988) *Social Identifications: A social psychology of intergroup relations and group processes*. London: Routledge.

Hogg, M. and Hardie, E. (1991) Social attraction, personal attraction and self-categorisation: a field study. *Personality and Social Psychology Bulletin* 17: 175–80.

Hogg, M. and Hardie, E. (1992) Prototypicality, conformity and depersonalised attraction: a self-categorisation analysis of group cohesiveness. *British Journal of Social Psychology* 31: 41–56.

Hogg, M. and McGarty, C. (1991) Self-categorisation and social identity, in D. Abrams, and M. Hogg (eds) *Social Identity Theory: Constructive and critical advances*. New York: Harvester Wheatsheaf.

Hogg, M. and Turner, J. (1985a) Interpersonal attraction, social identification and psychological group formation. *European Journal of Social Psychology* 15: 51–66.

Hogg, M. and Turner, J. (1985b) When liking begets solidarity: an experiment on the role of interpersonal attraction in psychological group formation. *British Journal of Social Psychology* 24: 267–81.

Hogg, M. and Turner, J. (1987) Intergroup behaviour, self-stereotyping and the salience of social categories. *British Journal of Social Psychology* 26: 325–40.

Hogg, M., Turner, J. and Davidson, B. (1990) Polarised norms and social frames of reference: a test of the self-categorisation theory of group polarisation. *Basic and Applied Social Psychology* 11: 77–100.

Hogg, M., Hardie, E. and Bailey, N. (1991) Depersonalised perception: a self-categorisation analysis of group cohesiveness. Unpublished manuscript, University of Queensland.

Hogg, M., Hardie, E. and Reynolds, K. (1992) Prototypical similarity, self-categorization and depersonalised attraction: a perspective on group cohesiveness. Unpublished manuscript, University of Queensland.

Hogg, M., Hardie, E. and Reynolds, K. (1995) Prototypical similarity, self-categorisation, and depersonalised attraction: a perspective on group cohesiveness. *European Journal of Social Psychology* 25: 159–77.

Holdaway, S. (1983) *Inside the British Police: A force at work*. Oxford: Blackwell.

Holding, D.H. and Reynolds, J.R. (1982) Recall or evaluation of chess positions as determinants of chess skill. *Memory and Cognition* 10: 237–42.

Holland, J.G. and Skinner, B.F. (1961) *The analysis of Behaviour: A program for self-instruction*. New York: McGraw-Hill.

Holland, J.H., Holyoak, K.F., Nisbett, R.E. and Thagard, P.R. (1986) *Induction*. Cambridge, MA: MIT Press.

Hollon, S.D. (1996) The efficacy and effectiveness of psychotherapy relative to medications. *American Psychologist* 51: 1025–30

Hollway, W. (1989) *Subjectivity and Method in Psychology: Gender, meaning and science*. London: Sage

Hollway, W. (1991) *Work Psychology and Organizational Behaviour*. London: Sage.

Holmes, D.S. (1990) The evidence for repression: an examination of sixty years of research, in J. Singer (ed.) *Repression and Dissociation: Implications for personality theory, psychopathology, and health*. Chicago: University of Chicago Press.

Holmes, T.H. and Rahe, R.H. (1967) The social readjustment rating scale. *Journal of Psychosomatic Research* 11: 213–18.

Holzner, B. and Roberts, R. (1980) *Identity and Authority: A problem analysis of processes of identification and authorization*. Oxford: Blackwell.

Homans, G. (1950) *The Human Group*. New York: Harcourt Brace Jovanovich.

Homans, G. (1968) *The Human Group*. London: Routledge and Kegan Paul.

Horn, J.L. and Knapp, J.R. (1973) On the subjective character of the empirical base of Guilford's structure-of-intellect model. *Psychological Bulletin* 80: 33–43.

Horn, J.M. (1983) The Texas Adoption Project: adopted children and their intellectual resemblance to biological and adoptive parents. *Child Development* 54: 268–75.

Horowitz, M., and Rabbie, J. (1982) Individuality and membership in the intergroup system, in H. Tajfel (ed.) *Social Identity and Intergroup Relations*. Cambridge: Cambridge University Press.

Hough, L.M., Eaton, N.K., Dunnette, M.D., Kamp, J.D. and McCloy, R.A. (1990) Criterion-related validities of personality constructs and the effect of response distortion on those validities. *Journal of Applied Psychology* 75: 581–95.

House, J.S. (1981) *Work Stress and Social Support*. London: Addison-Wesley.

House, J.S. and Wells, J.A. (1978) Occupational stress, social support and health, in A. McLean, G. Black and M. Colligan (eds) *Reducing Occupational Stress: Proceedings of a conference*. Cincinnati, OH: National Institute for Occupational Safety and Health.

House, J.S., Landis, K.R. and Umberson, D. (1988) Social relationships and health. *Science* 241: 540–5.

House, R.J. (1977) A 1976 theory of charismatic leadership, in J.G. Hunt and L.L. Larson (eds) *Leadership: The cutting edge*. Carbondale, IL: Southern Illinois University Press.

House, R.J. (1995) Leadership, in N. Nicholson (ed.) *Encyclopedic Dictionary of Organizational Behaviour*. Oxford: Blackwell.

House, R.J., Spangler, W.D. and Woycke, J. (1991) Personality and charisma in the U.S. Presidency: a psychological theory of leader effectiveness. *Administrative Science Quarterly* 36: 364–96.

Howard, A. (1990) *The Multiple Facets of Industrial-organizational Psychology: Membership survey results*. USA: Society for Industrial and Organizational Psychology.

Howarth, E. and Browne, J.A. (1971) An item-factor-analysis of the 16PF. *Personality* 2: 117–39.

Howe, M.J.A. (1990a) Does intelligence exist? *The Psychologist* 3: 490–93.

Howe, M.J.A. (1990b) Useful word but obsolete construct. *The Psychologist* 3: 498–9.

Howell, D.C. (1992) *Statistical Methods for Psychology*. Boston, MA: PWS-Kent.

Howell, J.M. and Frost, P.J. (1989) A laboratory study of charismatic leadership. *Organizational Behavior and Human Decision Processes* 43: 243–69.

Howell, J.M. and House, R.J. (1995) *Socialized and Personalized Charisma: A theory of the bright and dark sides of leadership*. Western Business School, University of Western Ontario, Canada.

Howes, C. and Matheson, C.C. (1992) Sequences in the development of competent play with peers: social and pretend play. *Developmental Psychology* 28: 961–74.

Hubel, D.H. and Wiesel, T.N. (1962) Receptive fields, binocular interaction and functional architecture in the cat's visual cortex. *Journal of Physiology* 160: 106–54.

Huesmann, L.R., Eron, L.D., Lefkowitz, M.M. and Walder, L.O. (1984) Stability of aggression over time and generations. *Developmental Psychology* 20: 1120–34.

Huffcutt, A.I. and Arthur, W.J. (1994) Hunter and Hunter (1984) revisited: interview validity for entry-level jobs. *Journal of Applied Psychology* 79: 184–90.

Hughlings-Jackson, J. (1959) *Selected Writings of John Hughlings-Jackson*, ed. J. Taylor. New York: Basic Books.

Huici, C., Ros, M., Cano, I., Hopkins, N., Emler, N. and Carmona, M. (1997) Comparative identity and evaluation of socio-political change: perceptions of the European Community as a function of the salience of regional identities. *European Journal of Social Psychology* 27: 97–113.

Hull, C.L. (1943) *Principles of Behavior*, New York: Appleton.

Humphrey, G. (1951) *Thinking: An introduction to its experimental psychology*. London: Methuen.

Humphreys, G.W. and Bruce, V. (1989) *Visual Cognition: Computational experimental and neuropsychological perspectives*. Hove: Lawrence Erlbaum.

Humphreys, G.W. and Riddoch, M.J. (1984) Routes to object constancy: implications from neurological impairments of object constancy. *Quarterly Journal of Experimental Psychology* 36A: 385–415.

Humphreys, G.W. and Riddoch, M.J. (1987) *To See But Not to See: A case study of visual agnosia*. Hove: Lawrence Erlbaum.

Hunt, M. (1987) The process of translating research findings into nursing practice. *Journal of Advanced Nursing* 12: 101–10.

Hunter, J.E. and Hirsh, H.R. (1987) Applications of meta-analysis, in C.L. Cooper and I.T. Robertson (eds) *International Review of Industrial and Organizational Psychology 1987*. Chichester: Wiley.

Hunter, J.E. and Hunter, R.F. (1984) Validity and utility of alternative predictors of job performance. *Psychological Bulletin* 96: 72–98.

Hunter, J., Platow, M. Howard, M. and Singer, M. (1996) Social identity and intergroup evaluative bias: realistic categories and domain specific self-esteem in a conflict setting. *European Journal of Social Psychology* 26: 631–47.

Hurvich, L.M. (1981) *Colour Vision*. Sunderland, MA: Sinauer.

Hyde, T.S. and Jenkins, J.J. (1973) Recall for words as a function of semantic, graphic, and syntactic orienting tasks. *Journal of Verbal Learning and Verbal Behavior* 12: 471–80.

Hyman, H. and Singer, E. (eds) (1968) *Readings in Reference Group Theory and Research*. New York: Free Press.

Hyson, M.C. and Izard, C.E. (1985) Continuities and changes in emotion expressions during brief separation at 13 and 18 months. *Developmental Psychology* 21: 1165–70.

Ibbotson, A. and Bryant, P.E. (1976) The perpendicular error and the vertical effect in children's drawing. *Perception* 5: 319–26.

Ickes, W., Bissonnette, V., Garcia, S. and Stinson, L.L. (1990) Implementing and using the dyadic interaction paradigm, in C. Hendrick and M.S. Clark (eds) *Research Methods in Personality and Social Psychology*. Newbury Park, CA: Sage.

Ikemoto, S. and Panksepp, J. (1994) The relationship between self-stimulation and sniffing in rats: does a common brain system mediate these behaviours? *Behavioural Brain Research* 61: 143–62.

Ilgen, D.R. and Hollenbeck, J.R. (1991) The structure of work: job design and roles, in M.D. Dunnette and L.M. Hough (eds) *Handbook of Industrial and Organizational Psychology*. Palo Alto, CA: Consulting Psychologists Press.

Inhelder, B. and Piaget, J. (1958) *The Growth of Logical Thinking from Childhood to Adolescence*. New York: Basic books.

Inhelder, B. and Piaget, J. (1964) *The Early Growth of Logic in the Child*. London: Routledge and Kegan Paul.

Isenberg, D. (1986) Group polarisation: a critical review and meta-analysis. *Journal of Personality and Social Psychology* 50: 1141–51.

Islam, M. and Hewstone, M. (1993) Dimensions of contact as predictors of intergroup anxiety, perceived outgroup variability and outgroup attitude: an integrative model. *Personality and Social Psychology Bulletin* 64, 700–10.

ISO (International Standardization Organization) (1995) *ISO 9241–10: Ergonomic Requirements for Office Work with Visual Display Units, part 10*. Brussels: European Committee for Norming.

Ittelson, W.H. (1951) Size as a cue to distance: static localisation. *American Journal of Psychology* 64: 54–67.

Ittelson, W.H. (1952) *The Ames Demonstrations in Perception*. New York: Hafner.

Izard, C.E. (1971) *The Face of Emotion*. New York: Appleton-Century-Crofts.

Izard, C.E. (1979) *The Maximally Discriminative Facial Movement Coding System (MAX)*. Newark, DE: University of Delaware, Office of Instructional Technology.

Izard, C.E. (1991) *The Psychology of Emotions*. New York: Plenum.

Izard, C.E. and Malatesta, C.Z. (1987) Perspectives on emotional development I: differential emotions theory of early emotional development, in J.D. Osofsky (ed) *Handbook of Infant Development*. New York: Wiley.

Izard, C.E., Dougherty, L.M. and Hembree, E.A. (1983) *A System for Identifying Affect Expressions by Holistic Judgments (AFFEX)*. Newark, DE: University of Delaware, Office of Instructional Technology.

Jacobi, U. and Weltz, F. (1981) Zum Problem der Beanspruchung beim Maschinenschreiben, in M. Frese (ed.) *Stress im Büro*. Bern: Huber.

Jacobsen, N.S. and Christensen, A. (1996) Studying the effectiveness of psychotherapy: how well can clinical trials do the job? *American Psychologist* 51: 1031–89.

Jacoby, L.L. (1983) Remembering the data: analysing interactive processing in reading. *Journal of Verbal Learning and Verbal Behavior* 22: 485–508.

Jacoby, L.L., Toth, J.P. and Yonelinas, A.P. (1993) Separating conscious and unconscious influences of memory: measuring recollection. *Journal of Experimental Psychology: General* 122: 139–54.

James, W. (1884) What is an emotion? *Mind* 9: 188–205.

James, W. (1890) *Principles of Psychology*, 2 vols. New York: Holt, Reinehart and Winston.

James, W. (1912) Does 'consciousness' exist?, in W. James, *Essays in Radical Empiricism*. London: Longmans.

Janis, I.L. (1967) Effects of fear arousal on attitude change: recent developments in theory and experimental research, in L. Berkowitz (ed.) *Advances in Experimental Social Psychology*, vol. 3. New York: Academic Press.

Janis, I.L. (1972) *Groupthink: Psychological studies of foreign policy decisions and fiascos*, 2nd edn. Boston, MA: Houghton Mifflin.

Janis, I.L., and King, B. (1954) The influence of role playing on opinion change. *Journal of Abnormal and Social Psychology* 49: 211–18.

Janz, N.K. and Becker, M.H. (1984) The Health Belief Model: a decade later. *Health Education Quarterly* 11: 1–47.

Jarrold, C., Carruthers, P., Smith, P.K. and Boucher, J. (1994) Pretend play: is it metarepresentational? *Mind and Language* 9: 665–8.

Jaspers, K. (1963) *General Psychopathology*, trans. J. Hoenig and M.W. Hamilton. Manchester: Manchester University Press.

Jefferson, G. (1985) An exercise in the transcription of and analysis of laughter, in T. van Dijk (ed.) *Handbook of Discourse Analysis*, vol. 3. London: Academic Press.

Jenkins, J.G. and Dallenbach, K.M. (1924) Obliviscence during sleep and waking. *American Journal of Psychology* 35: 605–12.

Jenkins, J.M., Smith, M.A. and Graham, P. (1989) Coping with parental quarrels. *Journal of the American Academy of Child and Adolescent Psychiatry* 27: 182–9.

Jensen, A.R. (1969) How much can we boost IQ and scholastic achievement? *Harvard Educational Review* 39: 1–123.

Jersild, A.T. and Markey, F.V. (1935) Conflicts between preschool children. *Child Development Monographs 21*. New York: Teachers College, Columbia University.

Johnsgard, K.W. (1989) *The Exercise Prescription for Depression and Anxiety*. New York: Plenum.

Johnson, M.H. (1990) Cortical maturation and the development of visual attention in early infancy. *Journal of Cognitive Neuroscience* 2: 81–95.

Johnson, M.H. (1995) The inhibition of automatic saccades in early infancy. *Developmental Psychobiology* 28: 281–91.

Johnson, M.K. and Multhaup, K.S. (eds) (1992) *Emotion and MEM*. Hillsdale, NJ: Lawrence Erlbaum.

Johnson-Laird, P.N. (1983) *Mental Models*. Cambridge: Cambridge University Press.

Johnson-Laird, P.N. (1988) *The Computer and the Mind: An introduction to cognitive science*. London: Fontana.

Johnson-Laird, P.N. and Byrne, R.M.J. (1991) *Deduction*. Hove: Lawrence Erlbaum.

Johnston, D.W. (1992) The management of stress in the prevention of coronary heart disease, in S. Maes, H. Leventhal and M. Johnston (eds) *International Review of Health Psychology 1*. Chichester: Wiley.

Johnston, M., Weinman, J. and Marteau, T.M. (1990) Health psychology in hospital settings, in A.A. Kaptein, H.M. van der Ploeg, B. Garssen, P.J.G. Schreurs and R. Beunderman (eds) *Behavioural Medicine*. New York: Wiley.

Johnston, W.A. and Dark, V.J. (1986) Selective attention. *Annual Review of Psychology* 37: 43–75.

Johnston, W.A. and Heinz, S.P. (1978) Flexibility and capacity demands of attention. *Journal of Experimental Psychology: General* 107: 420–35.

Johnston, W.A. and Heinz, S.P. (1979) Depth of non-target processing in an attention task. *Journal of Experimental Psychology* 5: 168–75.

Jolicoeur, P., Gluck, M.A. and Kosslyn, S.M. (1984) Pictures and names: making the connection. *Cognitive Psychology* 16: 243–25.

Jones, B. and Mishkin, M. (1972) Limbic lesions and the problem of stimulus-reinforcement associations. *Experimental Neurology* 36: 362–77.

Jones, E.E. and Davis, K.E. (1965) From acts to dispositions: the attribution process in person perception, in L. Berkowitz (ed.) *Advances in Experimental Social Psychology*, vol. 2. New York: Academic Press.

Jones, E.E. and Gerard, H. (1967) *Foundations of Social Psychology*. New York: Wiley.

Jones, E.E. and Harris, V.A. (1967) The attribution of attitudes. *Journal of Experimental Social Psychology* 3: 1–24.

Jones, E.E. and Nisbett, R.E. (1972) The actor and the observer: divergent perceptions of the causes of behavior. in E.E. Jones, D.E. Kanouse, H.H. Kelley, R.E. Nisbett, S. Valins and B. Weiner (eds) *Attribution: Perceiving the causes of behaviour*. Morristown, NJ: General Learning Press.

Jones, E.E., Rock, L., Shaver, K.G., Goethals, G.R. and Wand, L.M. (1968) Patterns of performance and ability attribution: an unexpected primacy effect. *Journal of Personality and Social Psychology* 10: 317–40.

Jones, G.V. (1982) Tests of the dual-mechanism theory of recall. *Acta Psychologica* 50: 61–72.

Jones, M.C. (1924) The elimination of children's fears. *Journal of Experimental Psychology* 7: 382–90.

Judd, C.H. (1908) The relation of special training and general intelligence. *Educational Review* 36: 42–88.

Judd, C. and Bartsch, R. (1995) Cats, dogs and the OH effect: a reply to Simon and to Haslam and Oakes. *European Journal of Social Psychology* 25: 477–80.

Judd, C. and Park, B. (1988) Out-group homogeneity: judgements of variability at the individual and group levels. *Journal of Personality and Social Psychology* 54: 778–8.

Just, M.A., Carpenter, P.A. and Woolley, J.D. (1982) Paradigms and processes in reading comprehension. *Journal of Experimental Psychology: General* 111: 228–38.

Kahn, R.L. and Antonucci, T. (1980) Convoys over the life course: attachment, roles and social support, in P.B. Baltes and O. Brim (eds) *Life Span Development and Behaviour*. Boston, MA: Lexington Press.

Kahneman, D. (1973) *Attention and Effort*. Englewood Cliffs, NJ: Prentice Hall.

Kahneman, D. and Tversky, A. (1971) Subjective probability: a judgement of representativeness. *Cognitive Psychology* 3: 430–54.

Kahneman, D. and Tversky, A. (1973) On the psychology of prediction. *Psychological Review* 80: 237–51.

Kamin, L.J. (1968) 'Attention-like' processes in classical conditioning, in M.R. Jones (ed.) *Miami Symposium on the Prediction of Behavior: Aversive stimulation*. Miami, FL: University of Miami Press.

Kanfer, R. and Ackerman, P.L. (1989) Motivation and cognitive abilities: an integrative/aptitude-treatment interaction approach to skill acquisition. *Journal of Applied Psychology* 74: 657–90.

Kanfer, R. and Kanfer, F.H. (1991) Goals and self regulation: applications of theory to work settings. *Advances in Motivation and Achievement* 7: 287–326.

Kaniza, G. (1976) Subjective contours. *Scientific American* 234: 48–52.

Kanner, A.D., Coyne, J.C., Schaefer, C. and Lazarus, R.S. (1981) Comparison of two modes of stress measurement: daily hassles and uplifts versus major life events. *Journal of Behavioral Medicine* 4: 1–39.

Kaplan, H. (1982) Prevalence of self-esteem motive, in M. Rosenberg and H. Kaplan (eds) *Self-Concept in Social Psychology*. London: Collier-Macmillan.

Kaplan, R.M., Sallis, J.F. and Patterson, T.L. (1993) *Health and Human Behaviour*. New York: McGraw-Hill.

Karasek, R.A. (1978) *Job Socialization: A longitudinal study of work, political and leisure activity*. Stockholm: Swedish Institute for Social Research.

Karasek, R.A. (1979) Job demands, job decision latitude and mental strain: implications for job redesign. *Administrative Science Quarterly* 24: 385–408.

Karasek, R.A. and Theorell, T. (1990) *Healthy Work: Stress, productivity, and the reconstruction of working life*. New York: Basic Books.

Kardes, F.R., Sanbonmatsu, D.M., Voss, R.T. and Fazio, R.H. (1986) Self-monitoring and attitude accessibility. *Personality and Social Psychology Bulletin*, 12: 468–74.

Karmiloff-Smith, A. (1992) *Beyond Modularity: A developmental perspective on cognitive science*. Cambridge, Mass: MIT Press.

Karniol, R. (1978) Children's use of intention cues in evaluating behavior. *Psychological Bulletin* 85: 76–85.

Kashima, Y. and Triandis, H.C. (1986) The self-serving bias in attributions as a coping strategy *Journal of Cross-Cultural Psychology* 17: 83–97.

Kasl, S.V. (1989) An epidemiological perspective on the role of control in health, in S.L. Sauter, J.J. Hurrell and C.C. Cooper (eds) *Job Control and Worker Health*. Chichester: Wiley.

Kassin, S.M. and Pryor, J.B. (1985) The development of attribution processes, in J. Pryor and J. Day (eds) *The Development of Social Cognition*. New York: Springer-Verlag.

Kassin, S.M., Ellsworth, P.C. and Smith, U.L. (1989) The 'general acceptance' of psychological research on eyewitness testimony. *American Psychologist* 44: 1089–98.

Katz, D. (1960) The functional approach to the study of attitudes. *Public Opinion Quarterly* 24: 163–204.

Katz, D. (1967) The functional approach to the study of attitude, in M. Fishbein (ed.) *Readings in Attitude Theory and Measurement*. New York: Wiley.

Katz, D. and Kahn, R.L. (1978) *Social Psychology of Organizations*, 2nd edn. New York: Wiley.

Katz, P. and Zigler, E. (1967) Self-image disparity: a developmental approach. *Journal of Personality and Social Psychology* 5: 186–95.

Katzell, R.A. and Austin, J.T. (1992) From then to now: the development of industrial-organizational psychology in the United States. *Journal of Applied Psychology* 77(6): 803–36.

Kaul, T.J. and Bednar, R.L. (1986) Experiential group research: results, questions, and suggestions, in S.L. Garfield and A.E. Bergin (eds) *Handbook of Psychotherapy and Behaviour Change*, 3rd edn. Chichester: Wiley.

Kauppinen-Toropainen, K., Kandolin, I. and Mutanen, P. (1983) Job dissatisfaction and work-related exhaustion in male and female work. *Journal of Organizational Behavior* 9: 217–40.

Kavolis, V. (ed.) (1984) *Designs of Selfhood*. London: Associated University Press.

Kay, J. and Ellis, A.W. (1987) A cognitive neuropsychological case study of anomia: implications for psychological models of word retrieval. *Brain* 110: 613–29.

Kaye, K. (1984) *The Mental and Social Life of Babies*. London: Methuen.

Kazdin, A.E. and Bootzin, R.R. (1972) The token economy: an evaluative review. *Journal of Applied Behavioral Analysis* Monographs 1: 5(3).

Keane, M. (1987) On retrieving analogues when solving problems. *Quarterly Journal of Experimental Psychology* 39A: 29–41.

Keane, M.T. and Gilhooly, K.J. (eds) (1992) *Advances in Thinking Research*. London: Harvester Wheatsheaf.

Keehn, J.D., Coulson, G.E. and Klieb, J. (1976) Effects of haloperidol on schedule-induced polydipsia. *Journal of the Experimental Analysis of Behaviour* 25: 105–12.

Kelley, H. (1952) Two functions of reference groups, in G. Swanson, T. Newcomb and E. Hartley (eds) *Readings in Social Psychology*, 2nd edn. New York: Holt, Rinehart and Winston.

Kelley, H.H. (1967) Attribution theory in social psychology, in D. Levine (ed.) *Nebraska Symposium on Motivation*, vol. 15. Lincoln NB: University of Nebraska Press.

Kelley, H.H. (1972) Causal schema and the attribution process, in E.E. Jones, D.E. Kanouse, H.H. Kelley, R.E. Nisbett, S. Valins and B. Weiner (eds) *Attribution: Perceiving the causes of behaviour*. Morristown, NJ: General Learning Press.

Kelley, H.H. and Michela, A (1980) Attribution theory and research. *Annual Review of Psychology* 31: 457–501.

Kelly, C. (1988) Inter-group differentiation in a political context. *British Journal of Social Psychology* 27: 319–32.

Kelly, C. (1989) Political identity and perceived intragroup homogeneity. *British Journal of Social Psychology* 28: 239–50.

Kelly, C. (1993) Group identification, intergroup perceptions and collective action in W. Stroebe and M. Hewstone. (eds) *European Review of Social Psychology*, vol. 4. Chichester: Wiley.

Kelly, C. and Breinlinger, S. (1996) *The Social Psychology of Collective Action: Identity, injustice and gender*. London: Taylor and Francis.

Kelman, H. (1958) Compliance, identification and internalisation: three processes of opinion change. *Journal of Conflict Resolution* 2: 51–60.

Kelman, H. (1974) The place of Jewish identity in the development of personal identity. *Colloqium on Jewish Education and Jewish Identity* 10–11.

Kempe, C.H. (1980) Incest and other forms of sexual abuse, in C.H. Kempe and R.E. Helfer (eds) *The Battered Child*, 3rd edn. Chicago: Chicago University Press.

Kemper, T.D. (1990) Social relations and emotions: a structural approach, in T.D. Kemper (ed.) *Research Agendas in the Sociology of Emotions*. Albany, NY: State University of New York Press.

Kendall, P.C. and Hammen, C. (1995) *Abnormal Psychology*. Boston, MA: Houghton Mifflin.

Kendell, R.E. (1975) The concept of disease and its implications for psychiatry. *British Journal of Psychiatry* 127: 305–15.

Kendler, K.S., Neale, M.C., Kessler, R.C., Heath, A.C. and Eaves, L.J. (1992) The genetic epidemiology of phobias in women: the interrelationship of agoraphobia, social phobia, situational phobia, and simple phobia. *Archives of General Psychiatry* 49: 273–81.

Kennes, D., Ödberg, F.O., Bouquet, Y. and De Rycke, P.H. (1988) Changes in naloxone and haloperidol effects during the development of captivity-induced jumping stereotypy in bank voles. *European Journal of Pharmacology* 153:19–24.

Kenrich, D. T. and Stringfield, D. O. (1980) Personality traits and the eye of the beholder: crossing some traditional philosophical boundaries in the search for consistency in all of the people. *Psychological Review* 87: 88–104.

Kerr, S. and Jermier, J.M. (1978) Substitutes for leadership: their meaning and measurement. *Organizational Behaviour and Human Performance* 22: 375–403.

Kety, S.S. (1987) The significance of genetic factors in the aetiology of schizophrenia: result from the national study of adoptees in Denmark. *Journal of Psychiatric Research* 21: 423–9.

Keysar, B. (1989) On the functional equivalence of literal and metaphorical interpretations of discourse. *Journal of Memory and Language* 28: 375–85.

Kiecolt-Glaser, J.K., Garner, W., Speicher, C., Penn, G.M., Holliday, J. and Glaser, R. (1984) Psychosocial modifiers of immunocompetence in medical students. *Psychosomatic Medicine* 46: 7–14.

Kieser, C. and Pallak, M. (1975) Minority influence: the effect of majority reactionaries and defectors, and minority and majority compromisers, upon majority opinion and a traction. *European Journal of Social Psychology* 5: 237–56.

Kiesler, C.A. and Kiesler, S. (1969) *Conformity*. Reading, MA: Addison-Wesley.

Killeen, P. (1975) On the temporal control of behaviour. *Psychological Review* 82: 89–115.

Killeen, R.R. (1981) Learning as causal inference, in M.L. Commons and J.A. Nevins (eds) *Quantitative Analyses of Behavior*, vol. 1: *Discriminative properties of reinforcement schedules*. Cambridge, MA: Ballinger.

Kimble, G.A. and Perlmuter, L.C. (1970) The problem of volition. *Psychological Review* 77: 361–84.

Kinchla, R.A. (1992) Attention, in M.R. Rosenzweig and L.W. Porter (eds) *Annual Review of Psychology*, vol. 43. Palo Alto, CA: Annual Reviews.

Kinchla, R.A. and Wolfe, J.M. (1979) The order of visual processing: 'Top-down', 'bottom-up', or 'middle-out'. *Perception and Psychophysics* 25: 225–31.

Kintsch, W. (1988) The role of knowledge in discourse comprehension: a construction-integration model. *Psychological Review* 95: 163–82.

Kintsch, W. (1992) A cognitive architecture for comprehension, in H.L. Pick, P. van den Broek and D.C. Knill (eds) *Cognition: Conceptual and methodological issues*. Washington, DC: American Psychological Association.

Kintsch, W. (1994) The psychology of discourse processing, in M.A. Gernsbacher (ed.) *Handbook of Psycholinguistics*. London: Academic Press.

Kintsch, W. and Keenan, J.M. (1973) Reading rate and retention as a function of content variables. *Journal of Verbal Learning and Verbal Behavior* 14: 196–214.

Kintsch, W., Welsch, D., Schmalhofer, F. and Zimny, S. (1990) Sentence memory: a theoretical analysis. *Journal of Memory and Language* 29: 133–59.

Kitzinger, C. (1989) Deconstructing sex differences. *British Psychological Society: Psychology of Women Section Newsletter* 4: 9–17.

Kitzinger, C. (1992) The individuated self concept: a critical analysis of social-constructionist writing on individualism, in G.M. Breakwell (ed.) *Social Psychology of Identity and Self-concept*. London: Academic Press.

Klein, M. (1932) *The Psychoanalysis of Children*. London: Hogarth.

Klein, S.B., Loftus, J. and Kihlstrom, J.F. (1996) Self-knowledge of an amnesic patient: toward a neuropsychology of personality and social psychology. *Journal of Experimental Psychology: General* 125: 250–60.

Klemp, G.O. and McClelland, D.C. (1986) What characterizes intelligent functioning among senior managers, in R.J. Sternberg and R.K. Wagner (eds) *Practical Intelligence: Nature and origins of competence in the everyday world*. Cambridge: Cambridge University Press.

Klerman, G.L., Weissman, M.M., Rounsaville, B.J. and Chevron, E.S. (1984) *Interpersonal Psychotherapy of Depression*. New York: Basic Books.

Kline, P. (1981) *Fact and Fantasy in Freudian Theory*. London: Methuen.

Kline, P. (1991) *Intelligence: The psychometric view*. London: Routledge.

Kline, P. (1993) *The Handbook of Psychological Testing*. London: Routledge.

Kline, P. and Lapham, S. (1990) *Manual to the PPQ*. London: Psychometric Systems.

Kline, P. and Storey, R. (1977) A factor analytic study of the anal character. *British Journal of Social and Clinical Psychology* 16: 317–28.

Kluger, A.N. and DeNisi, A. (1996) The effects of feedback interventions on performance: a historical review, a meta-analysis and a preliminary feedback intervention theory. *Psychological Bulletin* 119: 254–84.

Klüver, H. and Bucy, P.C. (1937) 'Psychic blindness' and other symptoms following bilateral temporal lobectomy. *American Journal of Physiology* 119: 352–3.

Klüver, H. and Bucy, P.C. (1939) Preliminary analysis of functions of the temporal lobes in monkeys. *Archives of Neurology and Psychiatry* 42: 979–1000.

Knapp, M.L. and Vangelisti, A. (1992) *Interpersonal Communication and Human Relationships*, 2nd edn. Boston, MA: Allyn and Bacon.

Knowles, E.S. and Brickner, M. (1981) Social cohesion effects on spatial cohesion. *Personality and Social Psychology Bulletin* 7: 309–13.

Koehler, J.J. (1996) The base rate fallacy reconsidered: descriptive, normative, and methodological challenges. *Behavioral and Brain Sciences* 19: 1–53.

Koestner, R. and McClelland, D.C. (1990) Perspectives on competence motivation, in L.A. Pervin (ed.) *Handbook of Personality: Theory and research*. New York: Guilford Press.

Koffka, K. (1935) *Principles of Gestalt Psychology*. New York: Harcourt Brace.

Kogan, N. and Wallach, M (1964) *Risk Taking: A study in cognition and personality*. New York: Holt, Rinehart and Winston.

Kohlberg, L. (1969) Stages and sequence: the cognitive-developmental approach to socialization, in D.A. Goslin (ed.) *Handbook of Socialization Theory and Research*. Chicago: Rand McNally.

Kohlberg, L. (1969) *Stages in the Development of Moral Thought and Action*. New York: Holt, Rinehart and Winston.

Köhler, W. (1925) *The Mentality of Apes*. New York: Harcourt Brace and World.

Kohn, M.L. and Schooler, C. (1969) Class, occupation and orientation. *American Sociological Review* 34: 659–78.

Kohn, M.L. and Schooler, C. (1978) The reciprocal effects of the substantive complexity of work and intellectual flexibility: a longitudinal assessment. *American Journal of Sociology* 84: 24–52.

Kohn, M.L. and Schooler, C. (1982) Job conditions and personality: a longitudinal assessment of their reciprocal effects. *American Journal of Sociology* 87: 1257–86.

Kohn, S.E. and Friedman, R.B. (1986) Word-meaning deafness: a phonogical-sematic dissociation. *Cognitive Neuropsychology* 3: 291–308.

Koksal, F. (1992) Anxiety and narrowing of visual attention. Unpublished manuscript, Bogazici University, Istanbul, Turkey.

Koluchová, J. (1976) Severe deprivation in twins: a case study, in A.M. Clarke and A.D.B. Clarke (eds) *Early Experience: Myth and evidence*. London: Open Books.

Koob, G.F. (1982) The dopamine anhedonia hypothesis: a pharmacolgical phrenology. *The Behavioral and Brain Sciences* 5: 63–4.

Korn, J.H., Davis, R. and Davis, S.F. (1991) Historians' and chairpersons' judgements of eminence among psychologists. *American Psychologist* 46: 789–92.

Korsakoff, S.S. (1889) Uber eine besondere Form psychischer Storing, kombiniert mit multiplen Neuritis. *Archiv für Psychiatrie und Nervenkrankheiten* 21: 669–704.

Kothandapani, V. (1971) Validation of feeling, belief and intention to act as three components of attitude and their contribution to prediction of contraceptive behavior. *Journal of Personality and Social Psychology* 19: 321–33.

Kotkin, M., Daviet, C. and Gurin, J. (1996) The Consumer Reports mental health survey. *American Psychologist* 51: 1080–82.

Kozlowski, L.T., Wilkinson, A., Skinner, W., Kent, C., Franklin, T. and Pope, M. (1989) Comparing tobacco cigarette dependence with other drug dependencies. *Journal of the American Medical Association* 261: 898–901.

Kozlowski, S.W.J. and Salas, E. (1997) A multilevel organizational systems approach for the implementation and transfer of training, in J.K. Ford (ed.) *Improving Training Effectiveness in Work Organizations*. Hillsdale, NJ: Lawrence Erlbaum.

Kramer, M. (1974) *Reality Shock:Why nurses leave nursing*. Saint Louis, MO: CV Mosby.

Krantz, D.S., Grunberg, N.E. and Baum, A. (1985) Health psychology. *Annual Review of Psychology* 36: 349–83.

Kranzler, J.K. and Jensen, A.R. (1989) Inspection time and intelligence: a meta-analysis. *Intelligence* 13: 329–47.

Kraus, S.J. (1995) Attitudes and the prediction of behavior: a meta-analysis of the empirical literature. *Personality and Social Psychology Bulletin*, 21: 58–75.

Krause, M.S. (1964) An analysis of Carl Rogers' theory of personality. *Genetic Psychology Monographs* 69: 49–99.

Kraut, R.E. and Johnston, R. (1979) Social and emotional messages of smiling: an ethological approach. *Journal of Personality and Social Psychology* 37: 1539–53.

Krohne, H.W. (1993) Attention and avoidance: two central strategies in coping with aversiveness, in H.W. Krohne (ed.) *Attention and Avoidance*. Seattle, WA: Hogrefe.

Kruglanski, A.W. (1977) The place of naive contents in a theory of attribution: relections on Calder's and Zuckerman's critiques of the endogeous–exogenous partition. *Personality and Social Psychology Bulletin*, 3: 592–605.

Kruglanski, A. (1990) Motivations for judging and knowing: implications for causal attribution, in T. Higgins and R. Sorrentino (eds) *Handbook of Motivation and Cognition: Foundations of social behaviour*, vol. 2. New York: Guilford Press.

Kruglanski, A. and Mackie, M. (1996) Majority and minority influence: a judgemental process analysis. *European Journal of Social Psychology* 26: 229–61.

Kruglanski, A. W., Alon, S. and Lewis, T. (1972) Retrospective misattribution and task enjoyment. *Journal of Experimental Social Psychology* 8: 493–501.

Kruglanski, A.W., Hamel, I.Z., Maides, S.A. and Schwartz, J.M. (1978) Attribution theory as a special case of lay epistemology, in J.H. Harvey, W. Ickes and R.F. Kidd (eds) *New Directions in Attribution Research*. Hillsdale, NJ: Lawrence Erlbaum.

Kruschke, J.K. (1992) ALCOVE: an exemplar-based connectionist model of category learning. *Psychological Review* 99: 22–44.

Kuhl, J. (1992) A theory of self-regulation: action vs. state orientation, self-discrimination, and some applications. *Applied Psychology:An International Review* 41: 97–129.

Kuhn, D., Nash, S.C. and Bruken, L. (1978) Sex role concepts of two-and-three-year-olds. *Child Development* 49: 445–51.

Kuhn, D., Amsel, E. and O'Loughlin, M. (1988) *The Development of Scientific Thinking*. New York: Academic Press.

Kuhn, T.S. (1972) *The Structure of Scientific Revolutions*. Chicago: University of Chicago Press.

Kulik, J.A. (1983) Confirmatory attribution and the perpetuation of social beliefs. *Journal of Personality and Social Psychology* 44: 1171–81.

Kulik, J.A. and Mahler, H.I.M. (1989) Social support and recovery from surgery. *Health Psychology* 8: 221–38.

Kunnapas, T. M. (1968) Distance perception as a function of available visual cues. *Journal of Experimental Psychology* 77: 523–29.

La Pierre (1934) Attitude versus actions. *Social Forces* 13: 230–7.

LaBerge, D. (1983) Spatial extent of attention to letters and words. *Journal of Experimental Psychology: Human Perception and Performance* 9: 71–379.

Ladd, G.W. (1983) Social networks of popular, average and rejected children in school settings. *Merrill-Palmer Quarterly* 29: 283–307.

Lalonde, R. and Silverman, R. (1994) Behavioural preferences in response to social injustice: the effects of group permeability and social identity salience. *Journal of Personality and Social Psychology* 66(1): 78–85.

Lalonde, R., Moghaddam, F. and Taylor, D. (1987) The process of group differentiation in dynamic intergroup setting. *Journal of Social Psychology* 127(3): 273–87.

Lamb, M.E. (1981) The development of father–infant relationships, in M.E. Lamb (ed.) *The Role of the Father in Child Development*, 2nd edn. New York: Wiley.

Lamb, M.E. (1987) Introduction: the emergent American father, in M.E. Lamb (ed.) *The Father's Role: Cross-cultural perspectives*. Hillsdale, NJ: Lawrence Erlbaum.

Lambert, M.J. and Bergin, A.E. (1994) The effectiveness of psychotherapy, in A.E. Bergin and S.L. Garfield (eds) *Handbook of Psychotherapy and Behavioural Change*, 4th edn. New York: Wiley.

Lamm, H. and Myers, D. (1976) Machiavellianism, discussion time and group shift. *Social Behaviour and Personality* 4(1): 41–8.

Lamm, H. and Myers, D. (1978) Group induced polarisation of attitudes and behaviour, in L. Berkowitz (ed.) *Advances in Experimental Social Psychology*, vol. 1 New York: Academic Press.

Lancaster, S. and Foddy, M. (1988) Self-Extensions: a conceptualisation. *Journal for the Theory of Social Behaviour* 18(1): 77–94.

Landers, D. and Luschen, G. (1974) Team performance outcome and the cohesiveness of competitive coacting groups. *International Review of Sports Psychology* 9: 57–71.

Landy, F.J. (1989) *Psychology of Work Behaviour*. Pacific Grove, CA: Brooks/Cole.

Landy, F.J. and Farr, J.R. (1980) Performance rating. *Psychological Bulletin* 87: 72–107.

Lang, R. and Hellpach, W. (1922) *Gruppenfabrikation*. Berlin: Verlag von Julius Springer.

Lange, C. (1885/1922) The emotions, in E. Dunlap (ed.) *The Emotions*. Baltimore, MD: Williams and Wilkins.

Langer, E.J. (1975) The illusion of control. *Journal of Personality and Social Psychology* 32: 311–28.

Langer, E.J. and Rodin, J. (1976) The effects of choice and enhanced personal responsibility for the aged: a field experiment in an institutional setting. *Journal of Personality and Social Psychology* 34: 191–8.

LaRocco, J.M. and Jones, A.P. (1978) Co-worker and leader support as moderators of stress-strain relationships in work situations. *Journal of Applied Psychology* 63: 629–34.

LaRocco, J.M., House, J.S. and French, J.R.P. (1980) Social support, occupational stress and health. *Journal of Health and Social Behaviour* 21: 202–18.

Lashley, K.S., Chow, K.L. and Semmes, J. (1951) An examination of the electrical field theory of cerebral integration. *Psychological Review* 58: 123–36.

Latane, B. and Wolfe, S. (1981) The social impact of majorities and minorities. *Psychological Review* 88: 438–53.

Latham, G.P. and Saari, L.M. (1979) Application of social-learning theory to training supervisors through behavioural modelling. *Journal of Applied Psychology* 64: 239–46.

Latham, G.P. and Wexley, K.N. (1977) Behavioural observation scales for performance appraisal purposes. *Personnel Psychology* 35: 677–86.

Latham, G.P. and Yukl, G.A. (1975) Assigned versus participative goal setting with educated and uneducated woods workers. *Journal of Applied Psychology* 60: 299–302.

Latto, R. (1995) The brain of the beholder, in R. Gregory, J. Harris, P. Heard and D. Rose (eds) *The Artful Eye*. Oxford: Oxford University Press.

Laursen, B. and Collins, W.A. (1994) Interpersonal conflict during adolescence. *Psychological Bulletin* 115: 197–209.

Lazarus, R.S. (1991a) *Emotion and Adaptation*. New York: Oxford University Press.

Lazarus, R.S. (1991b) Progress on a cognitive-motivational-relational theory of emotion. *American Psychologist* 46(8): 819–34.

Lazarus, R.S. and Folkman, S. (1984) *Stress Appraisal and Coping*. New York: Springer.

Lazarus, R.S. and Launier, R. (1978) Stress-related transactions between person and environment, in A.L. Pervin and M. Lewis (eds) *Perspectives in Interactional Psychology*. New York: Plenum.

Lazarus, R.S., Speisman, J.C., Mordkoff, A.M. and Davison, L.A. (1962) A laboratory study of psychological stress produced by a motion picture film. *Psychological Monographs* 76: 34, 553.

Le Bon, G. (1895, trans. 1947) *The Crowd: A study of the popular mind*. London: Ernest Benn.

Leary, M.R. (1995) *Introduction to Behavioral Research Methods*, 2nd edn. Pacific Grove, CA: Brooks/Cole.

LeDoux, J.E. (1992) Brain mechanisms of emotion and emotional learning. *Current Opinions in Neurobiology* 2: 191–8.

LeDoux, J.E. (1993) Emotional networks in the brain, in M. Lewis and J.M. Haviland (eds) *Handbook of Emotions*. New York: Guilford Press.

LeDoux, J.E. (1994) Emotion, memory and the brain. *Scientific American* 270: 32–9.

LeDoux, J.E. (1995) In search of an emotional system in the brain: leaping from fear to emotion and consciousness, in M.S. Gazzaniga (ed.) *The Cognitive Neurosciences*. Cambridge: MIT Press.

LeDoux, J.E. (1996) *The Emotional Brain: The mysterious underpinnings of emotional life*. New York: Simon and Schuster.

LeDuc, P.A. and Mittleman, G. (1995) Schizophrenia and psychostimulant abuse: a review and re-analysis of clinical evidence. *Psychopharmacology* 121: 407–27.

Lee, C. and Owen, N. (1985) Behaviourally-based principles as guidelines for health promotion. *Community Health Studies* 9(2): 131–8.

Lefkowitz, M.M., Eron, L.D., Walder, L.O. and Huesmann, L.R. (1977) *Growing Up To Be Violent*. Oxford: Pergamon.

Legrenzi, P., Girotto, V. and Johnson-Laird, P.N. (1994) Focusing in reasoning and decision making. *Cognition* 49: 37–66.

Leibowitz, H., Brislin, R., Perlmutter, L. and Hennessy, R. (1969) Ponzo perspective illusions as a manifestation of space perception. *Science* 166: 1174–76.

Lemyre, L. and Smith, P.M. (1985) Intergroup discrimination and self-esteem in the minimal group paradigm. *Journal of Personality and Social Psychology* 49: 660–70.

Leppin, A. and Schwarzer, R. (1990) Social support and physical health: an updated meta-analysis, in L.R. Schmidt, P. Schwenkmezger, J. Weinman and S. Maes (eds) *Theoretical and Applied Aspects of Health Psychology*. Chur: Harwood.

Leslie, A.M. (1987) Pretence and representation: the origins of 'theory of mind'. *Psychological Review* 94: 412–26.

Leslie, A.M. (1994) ToMM, ToBY and Agency: core architecture and domain specificity, in L.A. Hirschfield and S.A. Gelman (eds) *Mapping the Mind*. New York: Cambridge University Press.

Leslie, A.M. and Keeble, S. (1987) Do six-month olds perceive causality? *Cognition* 25: 265–88.

Levelt, W.J.M., Schriefers, H., Vorberg, D., Meyer, A.S., Pechmann, T. and Havinga, J. (1991) The time course of lexical access in speech production: a study of picture naming. *Psychological Review* 98: 122–42.

Levenson, M.R. (1992) Rethinking psychopathy. *Theory and Psychology* 2: 51–71.

Levenson, R.W., Ekman, P. and Friesen, W.V. (1990) Voluntary facial action generates emotion-specific autonomic nervous-system activity. *Psychophysiology* 27: 363–84.

Leventhal, E.A., Suls, J. and Leventhal, H. (1993) Hierarchical analysis of coping: evidence from life-span studies, in H.W. Krohne (ed.) *Attention and Avoidance*. Seattle, WA: Hogrefe.

Leventhal, H. (1970) Findings and theory in the study of fear communications, in L. Berkowitz (ed.) *Advances in Experimental Social Psychology*, vol 5. New York: Academic Press.

Leventhal, H., Nerenz, D.R. and Steele, D.J. (1984) Illness representations and coping with illness threats, in A. Baum et al. (eds) *Handbook of Psychology and Health*. Hillsdale, NJ: Lawrence Erlbaum.

Leventhal, H., Prohaska, T.R. and Hirschmann, R.S. (1985) Preventive health behaviour across the life-span, in J. Rosen and L. Solomon (eds) *Prevention in Health Psychology*. New York: New York University Press.

Leventhal, H., Fleming, R. and Glynn, K. (1988) A cognitive-developmental approach to smoking intervention, in S. Maes, C.D. Spielberger, P.B. Defares and I.G. Sarason (eds) *Topics in Health Psychology*. New York: Wiley.

Lever, J. (1978) Sex differences in the complexity of children's play and games. *American Sociological Review* 43: 471–83.

Levine, R. and Campbell, D. (1972) *Ethnocentrism: Theories of conflict, ethnic attitudes and group behaviour*. New York: Wiley.

Levinson, D.J. (1978) *The Seasons of a Man's Life*. New York: Knopf.

Levinson, D.J. (1990) A theory of life structure development in adulthood, in C.N. Alexander and E.J. Langer (eds) *Higher States of Human Development*. New York: Oxford University Press.

Levy, S.M., Herberman, R.B., Simons, A., Whiteside, T., Lee, J., Mc Donald, R. and Beadle, M.C., (1989) Persistently low natural killer cell activity in normal adults: immunological, hormonal and mood correlates. *Natural Immunity and Cell Growth Regulation* 8: 173–86.

Levy-Leboyer, C. (1994) Selection and assessment in Europe, in H.C. Triandis, M.D. Dunnette and L. Hough (eds) *Handbook of Industrial and Organizational Psychology*. Palo Alto, CA: Consulting Psychologists Press.

Lewin, B., Robertson, I.H., Cay, E.L., Irving, J.B. and Campbell, M. (1992) A self-help post MI rehabilitation package – the heart manual. Effects on psychological adjustment, hospitalisation and GP consultation. *Lancet* 339: 1036–40.

Lewin, K. (1943) Psychology and the process of group living. *Journal of Social Psychology* 17: 119–29.

Lewin, K (1946) Action research and minority problems. *Journal of Social Issues* 2: 34 6.

Lewin, K (1948) *Resolving Social Conflicts*. New York: Harper.

Lewinsohn, P.M., Steinmetz, J.L., Larson, D.W. and Franklin, J. (1981) Depression-related cognitions: antecedents or consequences? *Journal of Abnormal Psychology* 90: 213–19.

Lewis, C. and Osborne, A. (1990) Three-year olds' problems with false belief: conceptual deficit or linguistic artifact? *Child Development* 61: 1514–19.

Lewis, G. and Appleby, L. (1988) Personality disorder: the patients psychiatrists dislike. *British Journal of Psychiatry* 153: 44–9.

Lewis, M. (1992) *Shame: The exposed self*. New York: Free Press.

Lewis, M. (1995) Cognition-emotion feedback and the self-organization of developmental paths. *Human Development* 38: 71–102.

Lewis, M. and Brooks-Gunn, J. (1979) *Social Cognition and the Acquisition of Self*. New York: Plenum.

Lewis, M., Young, G., Brooks, J. and Michalson, L. (1975) The beginning of friendship, in M. Lewis and L. Rosenblum (eds) *Friendship and Peer Relations*. New York: Wiley.

Lewis, M.H., Baumeister, A.A. and Mailman, R.B. (1987) A neurobiological alternative to the perceptual reinforcement hypothesis of stereotyped behaviour: a commentary on 'self-stimulatory behaviour and perceptual reinforcement'. *Journal of Applied Behaviour Analysis* 20: 253–8.

Lewis, M., Alessandri, S.M. and Sullivan, M.W. (1990) Violation of expectancy, loss of control and anger expressions in young infants. *Developmental Psychology* 26: 745–51.

Ley, Ph. (1982) Satisfaction, compliance and communication. *British Journal of Clinical Psychology* 21: 241–54.

Leyens, J.P. and Codol, J.P. (1988) Social cognition, in M. Hewstone, W. Stroebe, J.P. Codol and G.M. Stephenson (eds) *Introduction to Social Psychology: A European perspective*. Oxford: Blackwell.

Leyens, J.P. and Dardenne, B. (1996) Basic concepts and approaches in social cognition, in M. Hewstone, W. Stroebe and G.M. Stephenson (eds) *Introduction to Social Psychology*. Oxford: Blackwell.

Leyens, J.P., Yzerbyt, V.Y. and Schadron, G. (1994) *Stereotypes and Social Cognition*. London: Sage.

Leymann, H. (1996) The content and development of mobbing at work. *European Journal of Work and Organizational Psychology* 5: 165–84.

Leymann, H. and Gustafsson, A. (1996) Mobbing and the development of post-traumatic stress disorders. *European Journal of Work and Organizational Psychology* 5: 251–76.

Liberman, A.M., Harris, K.S., Hoffman, H.S. and Griffith, B.C. (1957) The discrimination of speech sounds within and across phoneme boundaries. *Journal of Experimental Psychology* 54: 358–68.

Liberman, A.M., Cooper, F.S., Shankweiler, D.S. and Studdert-Kennedy, M. (1967) Perception of the speech code. *Psychological Review* 74: 431–61.

Liberman, N. and Klar, Y. (1996) Hypothesis testing in Wason's selection task: social exchange cheating detection or task understanding. *Cognition* 58: 127–56.

Lichtenstein, S., Slovic, P., Fischhoff, B., Layman, M. and Combs, J. (1978) Judged frequency of lethal events. *Journal of Experimental Psychology: Human Learning and Memory* 4: 551–78.

Lieberman, D.A. (1990) *Learning. Behavior and Cognition*. Belmont, CA: Wadsworth.

Lieberman, S. (1956) The effects of changes in roles on the attitudes of role occupants. *Human Relations* 9: 383–402.

Lienert, G.A. (1977) Über Werner Trxel: Internationalität oder Provinzialismus, zur Frage: Sollten Psychologen Englisch produzieren? *Psychologische Beiträge* 19: 487–92.

Light, D. (1979) Uncertainty and control in professional training. *Journal of Health and Social Behaviour* 20: 310–22.

Light, P. and McIntosh, E. (1980) Depth relationships in children's drawings. *Journal of Experimental Child Psychology* 30: 79–87.

Light, P. and Simmons, B. (1983) The effects of a communication task upon representation of depth relationships in young children's drawings. *Journal of Experimental Child Psychology* 35: 81–92.

Light, P.H., Buckingham, N. and Robbins, A.H. (1979) The conservation task as an interactional setting. *British Journal of Educational Psychology* 49: 304–10.

Lilienfeld, S.O. (1995) *Seeing Both Sides: classic controversies in abnormal psychology*. Pacific Grove, CA: Brookes/Cole.

Lilienfeld, S.O. and Marino, L. (1995) Mental disorder as a roschian concept: a critique of Wakefield's 'harmful dysfunction' analysis. *Journal of Abnormal Psychology* 104: 411–20.

Lillard, A.S. (1993) Pretend play skills and the child's theory of mind. *Child Development* 64: 348–71.

Lindeman, M. and Sundvik, L. (1995) Evaluative bias and self-enhancement among gender groups. *European Journal of Social Psychology* 25: 269–80.

Linebarger, M.C., Schwartz, M.F. and Saffran, E.M. (1983) Sensitivity to grammatical structure in so-called agrammatic aphasics. *Cognition* 13: 361–92.

Linehan, M.M. (1993) *Cognitive-Behavioural Treatment of Borderline Personality Disorder*. New York: Guildford Press.

Linville, P. and Carlston, D. (1994) Social cognition of the self, in P.G. Devine, D.L. Hamilton and T.M. Ostrom (eds) *Social Cognition: Impact on social psychology*. New York: Springer-Verlag.

Linville, P. and Jones, E. (1980) Polarized appraisals of out-group members. *Journal of Personality and Social Psychology* 38: 689–703.

Linville, P., Salovey, P. and Fischer, D. (1986) Stereotyping and perceived distributions of social characteristics: an application to ingroup–outgroup perception, in J. Dovidio and

S. Gaertner (eds) *Prejudice, Discrimination and Racism*. Orlando, FL: Academic Press.

Linville, P., Fischer, F. and Salovey, P. (1989) Perceived distributions of the characteristics of in-group and out-group members: empirical evidence and a computer simulation. *Journal of Personality and Social Psychology* 57: 165–88.

Livingstone, M. and Hubel, D. (1995) Through the eyes of monkeys and men, in R. Gregory, J. Harris, P. Heard and D. Rose (eds) *The Artful Eye*. Oxford: Oxford University Press.

Ljungberg, T., Apicella, P. and Schultz, W. (1992) Responses of monkey dopamine neurons during learning of behavioural reactions. *Journal of Neurophysiology* 67: 145–63.

Locke, E.A. (1968) Toward a theory of task motivation and incentives. *Organizational Behavior and Human Performance* 3: 157–89.

Locke, E.A. and Latham, G.P. (1990) *A Theory of Goal Setting and Task Performance*. Englewood Cliffs, NJ: Prentice Hall.

Locke, E.A., Shaw, K.N., Saari, L.M. and Latham, G.P. (1981) Goal setting and task performance: 1969–1980. *Psychological Bulletin* 90: 125–52.

Locksley, A., Oritz, V. and Hepburn, C. (1980) Social categorisation and discriminatory behaviour: extinguishing the minimal group intergroup discrimination effect. *Journal of Personality and Social Psychology* 39: 773–83.

Loehlin, J.C. and Nichols, R.C. (1976) *Heredity, Environment, and Personality*. Austin, TX: University of Texas Press.

Loehlin, J.C., Lindzey, G. and Spuhler, J.N. (1975) *Race Differences in Intelligence*. San Francisco, WA: Freeman.

Loehlin, J.C., Horn, J.M. and Willerman, L. (1989) Modelling IQ change: evidence from the Texas Adoption Project. *Child Development* 60: 993–1004.

Loftus, E.F. (1979) *Eyewitness Testimony*. Cambridge, MA: Harvard University Press.

Loftus, E.F. (1991) Made in memory: distortions in recollection after misleading information, in G.H. Bower (ed.) *The Psychology of Learning and Motivation*, vol. 27. New York: Academic Press.

Loftus, E.F. (1993) The reality of repressed memories. *American Psychologist* 48: 518–37.

Loftus, E.F. and Burns, H.J. (1982) Mental shock can produce retrograde amnesia. *Memory and Cognition* 10: 318–23.

Loftus, E.F. and Palmer, J.C. (1974) Reconstruction of automobile destruction: an example of the interaction between language and memory. *Journal of Verbal Learning and Verbal Behavior* 13: 585–9.

Logan, R.D. (1987) Historical change in prevailing sense of self, in K. Yardley and T. Honess (eds) *Self and Identity: Psychosocial perspectives*. Chichester: Wiley.

Logie, R.H. (1986) Visuo-spatial processes in working memory. *Quarterly Journal of Experimental Psychology* 38A: 229–47.

Logvinenko, A.D. and Belopolskii, V.I. (1994) Convergence as a cue for distance. *Perception* 23: 207–17.

LoLordo, V.M., Jacobs, W.J. and Foree, D.D. (1982) Failure to block control by a relevant stimulus. *Animal Learning and Behavior* 10: 183–93.

Long, K.M., Spears, R. and Manstead, A.S. (1994) The influence of personal and collective self-esteem on strategies of social differentiation. *British Journal of Social Psychology* 33: 313–29.

Longoni, A.M., Richardson, J.T.E. and Aiello, A. (1993) Articulatory rehearsal and phonological storage in working memory. *Memory and Cognition* 21: 11–22.

Lord, R.G., De Vader, C.L. and Alliger, G.M. (1986) A meta-analysis of the relation between personality traits and leadership perceptions: an application of validity generalization procedures. *Journal of Applied Psychology* 71: 402–10.

Lorenzi-Cioldi, F. (1988) *Individus dominants et groupes domines*. Grenoble: Presses Universitaires.

Lorenzi-Cioldi, F. (1991) Self-stereotyping and self-enhancement in gender groups. *European Journal of Social Psychology* 21: 267–78.

Lorenzi-Cioldi, F. (1993) They all look alike, but so do we . . . sometimes: perceptions of ingroup and outgroup homogeneity as a function of sex and context. *British Journal of Social Psychology* 32(2): 111–24.

Lott, A. and Lott, B. (1961) Group cohesiveness, communication level and conformity. *Journal of Abnormal and Social Psychology* 62: 408–12.

Lott, A. and Lott, B. (1965) Group cohesiveness as interpersonal attraction. *Psychological Bulletin* 64: 259–309.

Louis, M. (1980) Surprise and sensemaking: what newcomers experience in entering unfamiliar organizational settings. *Administrative Science Quarterly* 25: 226–51.

Loy, I., Alvarez, R., Rey, V. and López, M. (1993) Context–US associations rather than occasion-setting in taste aversion learning. *Learning and Motivation* 24: 55–72.

Luborsky, L., Singer, B. and Luborsky, L. (1975) Comparative studies of psychotherapies. *Archives of General Psychiatry* 32: 995–1008.

Lubow, R.E. and Moore, A.U. (1959) Latent inhibition: the effect of nonreinforced preexposure to the conditioned stimulus. *Journal of Comparative and Physiological Psychology* 52: 415–19.

Luchins, A.S. (1942) Mechanisation in problem solving: the effect of Einstellung. *Psychological Monographs* 54 (248).

Lueck, C.J., Zeki, S., Friston, K.J., Deiber, M.-P., Cope, P., Cunningham, V.J., Lammertsma, A.A., Kennard, C. and Frackowiak, R.S.J. (1989) The colour centre in the cerebral cortex of man. *Nature* 340: 386–9.

Lui, J., Campbell, S. and Condie, H. (1995) Ethnocentrism in dating preferences for an American sample: the ingroup bias in social context. *European Journal of Social Psychology* 25: 111–15.

Lundh, L.G. and Ost, L.G. (1996) Recognition bias for critical faces in social phobics. *Behaviour Research and Therapy* 34: 787–94

Luquet, G.H. (1927) *Le Dessin enfantin*. Paris: Alcan.

Luria, A.R. (1968) *The Mind of a Mnemonist*. New York: Basic Books

Luria, A.R. (1973) *The Working Brain: An introduction to neuropsychology*. Harmondsworth: Penguin.

Lutz, C.A. (1988) *Unnatural Emotions: Everyday sentiments on a Micronesian atoll and their challenge to western theory*. Chicago: University of Chicago Press.

Lyons, A.S. and Petrucelli, R.J. (1978) *Medicine: An illustrated history*. New York: H.N. Abrams.

Lyons, E. and Sotirakopolous, K. (1991) Images of European countries. *British Psychological Society Social Psychology Section Annual Conference*. University of Surrey, September.

Lyons, W. (1980) *Emotion*. Cambridge: Cambridge University Press.

Maass, A., and Clark, R. (1984) Hidden impact of minorities: fifteen years of minority influence research. *Psychological Bulletin* 95: 428–50.

Maccoby, E.E. and Jacklin, C.N. (1974) *The Psychology of Sex Differences*. Stanford, CA: Stanford University Press.

Maccoby, E.E., Maccoby, N., Romney, A.K. and Adams, J.S. (1961) Social reinforcement in attitude change. *Journal of Abnormal and Social Psychology* 63: 109–15.

Macfarlane Smith, I. (1964) *Spatial Ability*. London: University of London Press.

MacKay, D. (1987) Divided brains – divided minds, in C. Blakemore and S. Greenfield (eds) *Mindwaves: Thoughts on intelligence, identity and consciousness*. Oxford: Blackwell.

Mackintosh, N.J. (1975) A theory of attention: variations in the associability of stimuli with reinforcement. *Psychological Review* 82: 276–98.

Mackintosh, N.J. (1977) Conditioning as the perception of causal relations, in R.E. Buttes and J. Hintikka (eds) *Foundational Problems in the Special Sciences*. Dordrecht: Reidel.

Mackintosh, N.J. (1983) *Conditioning and Associative Learning*. Oxford: Oxford University Press.

Mackintosh, N.J. (1986) The biology of intelligence? *British Journal of Psychology* 77: 1–18.

Mackworth, N.H. (1950) Researches in the measurement of human performance. *Medical Research Council Special Report Series* 268.

MacLean, M., Bryant, P.E. and Bradley, L. (1987) Rhymes, nursery rhymes and reading in early childhood. *Merrill-Palmer Quarterly* 33: 255–82.

MacLean, P.D. (1949) Psychosomatic disease and the 'visceral brain': recent developments bearing on the Papez theory of emotion. *Psychosomatic Medicine* 11: 338–53.

MacLean, P.D. (1952) Some psychiatric implications of physiological studies on frontotemporal of limbic system (visceral brain). *Electroencephalography and Clinical Neurophysiology* 4: 407–18.

MacLeod, A.K., Williams, J.M.G. and Linehan, M.M. (1992) New developments in the understanding and treatment of suicidal behaviour. *Behavioural Psychotherapy* 20: 93–128.

MacLeod, C. and Donnellan, A.M. (1993) Individual differences in anxiety and the restriction of working memory capacity. *Personality and Individual Differences* 15: 163–73.

MacLeod, C. and Mathews, A. (1988) Anxiety and the allocation of attention to threat. *Quarterly Journal of Experimental Psychology* 40A: 653–70.

MacLeod, C., Mathews, A. and Tata, P. (1986) Attentional bias in emotional disorders. *Journal of Abnormal Psychology* 95: 15–20.

MacNeilage, P.F. (1972) Speech physiology, in J.H. Gilbert (ed.) *Speech and Cortical Functioning*. New York: Academic Press.

MacWinney, B., Leinbach, J., Taraban, R. and McDonald, J. (1989) Language learning: cues or rules? *Journal of Memory and Language* 28: 255–77.

Maddux, J.E. (1991) Self-efficacy, in C.R. Snyder and D.R. Forsyth (eds) *Handbook of Social and Clinical Psychology*. Oxford: Pergamon.

Madison, P. (1956) Freud's repression concept: a survey and attempted clarification. *International Journal of Psychoanalysis* 37: 75–81.

Maes, S. (1990) Theories and principles of health behaviour change, in P. Drenth, J. Sergeant and R. Takens (eds) *European Perspectives in Psychology*, vol. 2. Chichester: Wiley.

Maes, S. (1992a) Psychological research on life-styles and health in Europe, in J.A.M. Winnubst and S. Maes (eds) *Life-styles, Stress and Health*. Leiden: DSWO Press.

Maes, S. (1992b) Psychosocial aspects of cardiac rehabilitation in Europe. *British Journal of Clinical Psychology* 31: 473–83.

Maes, S. (1994) Chronische Ziekte (chronic diseases). *Handboek Klinische Psychologie*. Houten: Bohn, Stafleu, Van Loghum.

Maes, S. and Schlösser, M. (1987) The role of cognition and coping in health behaviour outcomes of asthmatic patients. *Current Psychological Research and Reviews* 6: 79–90.

Maes, S., Kittel, F., Scholten, H. and Verhoeven, C. (1992) Effects of a comprehensive wellness health project at the worksite. *Safety Science* 15: 351–66.

Maes, S., Leventhal, H. and De Ridder, D. (1996) Coping with chronic disease, in M. Zeidner and N. Endler (eds) *Handbook of Coping*. New York: Wiley.

Magnusson, D., Stattin, H. and Allen, V.L. (1985) Biological maturation and social development: a longitudinal study of some adjustment processes from mid-adolescence to adulthood. *Journal of Youth and Adolescence* 14: 267–83.

Maher, B.A. (1988) Anomalous experience and delusional thinking: the logic of explanations, in T.F. Oltmanns and B.A. Maher (eds) *Delusional Beliefs*. New York: Wiley.

Maier, N.R.F. (1931) Reasoning in humans II: the solution of a problem and its appearance in consciousness. *Journal of Comparative Psychology* 12: 181–94.

Maier, S.F. and Seligman, M.E.P. (1976) Learned helplessness: theory and evidence. *Journal of Experimental Psychology: General* 105: 3–46.

Maier, S.F., Watkins, L.R. and Fleshner, M. (1994) Psychoneuroimmunology. *American Psychologist* 49: 1004–17.

Main, M. (1991) Metacognitive knowledge, metacognitive monitoring, and singular (coherent) vs. multiple (incoherent) model of attachment: findings and directions for future research, in C. Murray Parkes, J. Stevenson-Hinde and P. Marris (eds) *Attachment Across the Life Cycle*. London: Routledge.

Main, M. and Goldwyn, R. (1984) Predicting rejection of her infant from mother's representation of her own experience: implications for the abused-abusing inter-generational cycle. *Child Abuse and Neglect* 8: 203–17.

Major, B. and Forcey, B. (1985) Social comparisons and pay evaluations: references. *Journal of Experimental and Social Psychology* 21: 393–405.

Makin, P., Cooper, C. and Cox, C. (1989) *Managing People at Work*. Leicester: British Psychological Society.

Malatesta, C.Z., Culver, C., Tesman, J.R. and Shepard, B (1989) *The Development of Emotion Expression during the First Two Years of Life, Monographs of the Society for Research in Child Development* 54 (1–2, serial no. 219): 1–103.

Malik, N. and Furman, W. (1993) Problems in children's peer relations: what can the clinician do? *Journal of Child Psychology and Psychiatry* 34: 1303–26.

Mandler, G. (1964) Interruption of behaviour, in D. Levine (ed.) *Nebraska Symposium on Motivation*. Lincoln, NB: University of Nebraska Press.

Mandler, G. (1967) Organisation in memory, in K.W. Spence and J.T. Spence (eds) *The Psychology of Learning and Motivation*, vol. 1. New York: Academic Press.

Mann, R.D. (1959) A review of the relationships between personality and performance in small groups. *Psychological Bulletin* 56: 241–70.

Manne, S. and Zautra, A.J. (1989) Spouse criticism and support: their association with coping and psychological adjustment among women with rheumatoid arthritis. *Journal of Personality and Social Psychology* 56(4): 608–17.

Manstead, A.S. (1996) Attitudes and behaviour, in G.R. Semin and K. Fiedler (eds) *Applied Social Psychology*. London: Sage.

Maracek, J. and Metee, D.R. (1972) Avoidance of continued success as a function of self-esteem, level of esteem-certainty and responsibility for success. *Journal of Personality and Social Psychology* 22: 98–107.

Marcia, J. (1966) Development and validation of ego-identity status. *Journal of Personality and Social Psychology* 3: 551–8.

Marcia, J. (1980) Identity in adolescence, in J. Adelson (ed.) *Handbook of Adolescent Psychology*. New York: Wiley.

Marcus, S.L. and Rips, L.J. (1979) Conditional reasoning. *Journal of Verbal Learning and Verbal Behavior* 18: 199–233.

Marcus-Newhall, A., Miller, N., Holtz, R. and Brewer, M. (1993) Cross-cutting category membership with role assignment: a means of reducing intergroup bias. *British Journal of Social Psychology* 32(2): 125–46.

Mark, V.H. and Ervin, F. (1970) *Violence and the Brain*. New York: Harper and Row.

Markman, A.B. (1989) LMS rules and the inverse base-rate effect: comment on Gluck and Bower (1988). *Journal of Experimental Psychology: General* 118: 417–21.

Markou, A. and Koob, G.F. (1991) Postcocaine anhedonia: an animal model of cocaine withdrawal. *Neuropsychopharmacology* 4: 17–26.

Marks, G. and Miller, N. (1985) The effect of certainty on consensus judgments. *Personality and Social Psychology Bulletin*, 2: 165–77.

Marks, G. and Miller, N. (1987) Ten years of research on the false consensus effect: an empirical and theoretical view. *Psychological Bulletin* 102: 72–90.

Markus, H. (1977) Self-schemata and processing information about the self. *Journal of Personality and Social Psychology*, 35, 63–78.

Markus, H. and Kitayama, S. (1991) Culture and the self: implications for cognition, emotion and motivation. *Psychological Review*, 98: 224–53.

Markus, H. and Zajonc, R. (1985) The cognitive perspective in social psychology, in G. Lindzey and E. Aronson (eds) *Handbook of Social Psychology*, vol. 1. New York: Random House.

Markus, H., Crane, M., Bernstein, S. and Siladi, M. (1982) Self-schemas and gender. *Journal of Personality and Social Psychology*, 42: 38–50.

Marlatt, G.A. and Gordon, J.R. (1985) *Relapse Prevention*. New York: Guilford Press.

Marques, J., Yzerbyt, V. and Leyens, J. (1988) The 'black sheep effect': extremity of judgements towards ingroup members as a function of group identification. *European Journal of Social Psychology* 18: 1–16.

Marr, D. (1982) *Vision: A computational investigation into the human representation and processing of visual information*. San Francisco, CA: W.H. Freeman.

Marr, D. and Nishihara, K. (1978) Representation and recognition of the spatial organisation of three-dimensional shapes. *Philosophical Transactions of the Royal Society* (London) B200: 269–94.

Marr, D. and Poggio, T. (1976) Cooperation computation of stereo disparity. *Science* 194: 283–7.

Marsh, P., Rosser, E. and Harré, R. (1978) *The Rules of Disorder*. London: Routledge.

Marshall, J.C. and Newcombe, F. (1973) Patterns of paralexia: a psycholinguistic approach. *Journal of Psycholinguistic Research* 2: 175–99.

Marshall, J.F., Richardson, J.S. and Teitelbaum, P. (1974) Nigrostriatal bundle damage and the lateral hypothalamic syndrome. *Journal of Comparative and Physiological Psychology* 87: 808–30.

Marslen-Wilson, W.D. (1990) Activation, competition, and frequency in lexical access, in G.T.M. Altmann (ed.) *Cognitive Models of Speech Processing: Psycholinguistics and computational perspectives*. Cambridge, MA: MIT Press.

Marslen-Wilson, W.D. and Tyler, L.K. (1980) The temporal structure of spoken language understanding. *Cognition* 8: 1–71.

Martin, F. and Murray, K. (1983) The end of the road: residential disposals in the Scottish children's hearing system. *Journal of Adolescence* 6(3): 211–27.

Martin, G.N. (1996) Olfactory remediation: current evidence and possible applications. *Social Science and Medicine* 43: 63–70.

Martin, H. and Greenstein, T. (1983) Individual differences in status generalisation: effects of need for social approval, anticipated interpersonal contact and instrumental task abilities. *Journal of Personality and Social Psychology* 45(3): 641–62.

Martin, I. and Levey, A.B. (1991) Blocking observed in human eyelid conditioning. *Quarterly Journal of Experimental Psychology* 43B: 233–56.

Martin, R. (1995) Majority and minority influence using the after image paradigm: a replication with an unambiguous blue slide. *European Journal of Social Psychology* 25: 373–81.

Martocchio, J.J. (1994) Effects of concepts of ability on anxiety, self-efficacy, and learning in training. *Journal of Applied Psychology* 79(6): 819–25.

Martone, M., Butters, N., Payne, M., Becker, J.T. and Sax, D.S. (1984) Dissociations between skill learning and verbal recognition in amnesia and dementia. *Archives of Neurology* 41: 965–70.

Marx, R.D. (1982) Relapse prevention for managerial training: a model for maintenance of behaviour change. *Academy of Management Review* 7: 433–41.

Maslow, A. (1954) *Motivation and Personality*. New York: Harper.

Maslow, A. (1962) *Toward a Psychology of Being*. Princeton, NJ: Van Nostrand.

Maslow, A. (1968) *Toward a Psychology of Being*, 2nd edn. New York: Van Nostrand.

Maslow, A. (1970) *Motivation and Personality*, 2nd edn. New York: Harper and Row.

Mason, J. (1996) *Qualitative Researching*. London: Sage.

Masson, J. (1989) *Against Therapy*. Glasgow: Collins.

Matarazzo, J.D. (1980) Behavioral health and behavioral medicine: frontiers of a new health psychology. *American Psychologist* 35: 807–17.

Matheny, A.P. and Dolan, A.B. (1975) Persons, situations, and time: a genetic view of behavioural change in children. *Journal of Personality and Social Psychology* 14: 224–34.

Matheny, A.P., Wilson, R.S., Dolan, A.B. and Krantz, J.Z. (1981) Behavior contrasts in twinships: stability and patterns of differences in childhood. *Child Development* 52: 579–88.

Mathews, A. and MacLeod, C. (1985) Selective processing of threat cues in anxiety states. *Behaviour Research and Therapy* 23: 563–69.

Mathews, A., Richards, A. and Eysenck, M. (1989) Interpretation of homophones related to threat in anxiety states. *Journal of Abnormal Psychology* 98: 31–4.

Matute, H. (1994) Learned helplessness and superstitious behavior as opposite effects of uncontrollable reinforcement in humans. *Learning and Motivation* 25: 216–32.

Matute, H. (1995) Human reactions to uncontrollable outcomes: further evidence for superstitions rather than helplessness. *Quarterly Journal of Experimental Psychology* 48B: 142–57.

Matute, H. (1996) Illusion of control: detecting response-outcome independence in analytic but not in naturalistic conditions. *Psychological Science* 7: 289–3.

Matute, H., Arcediano, F. and Miller, R.R. (1996) Test question modulates cue competition between causes and between effects. *Journal of Experimental Psychology: Learning, Memory, and Cognition* 22: 182–96.

Maurino, D.E., Reason, J., Johnston, N. and Lee, R.B. (1995) *Beyond Aviation Human Factors*. Aldershot, Hants: Ashgate.

Mayer, R.E. (1990) Problem solving, in M.W. Eysenck (ed.) *The Blackwell Dictionary of Cognitive Psychology*. Oxford: Blackwell.

Mayes, A.R. and Downes, J.J. (1997) What do theories of the functional deficit(s) underlying amnesia have to explain? *Memory* 5: 3–36.

McAdams, D.P. (1985) Motivation and friendship, in S. Duck and D. Perlman (eds) *Understanding Personal Relationships: An interdisciplinary approach*. Beverly Hills, CA: Sage.

McAdams, D.P. (1988) Personal needs and personal relationships, in S. Duck (ed.) *Handbook of Personal Relationships: Theory, research, and interventions*. New York: Wiley.

McAdams, D.P. and Vaillant, G.E. (1982) Intimacy motivation and psychosocial adaptation: a longitudinal study. *Journal of Personality Assessment* 46: 586–93.

McArthur, L.Z. (1972) The how and what of why: some determinants and consequences of causal attributions. *Journal of Personality and Social Psychology* 22: 171–93.

McArthur, L.Z. (1976) The lesser influence of consensus than distinctiveness information on causal attributions: a test of the person–thing hypothesis. *Journal of Personality and Social Psychology* 33: 733–42.

McArthur, L.Z. and Post, D.L. (1977) Figural emphasis and person perception. *Journal of Experimental Social Psychology* 13: 520–35.

McBride, P. (1994) *Study Skills for Success*. Cambridge: Hobsons.

McClelland, D.C. (1965) Achievement and entrepreneurship: a longitudinal study. *Journal of Personality and Social Psychology* 1: 389–92.

McClelland, D.C. (1987) *Human Motivation*. Cambridge: Cambridge University Press.

McClelland, J.L. (1995) A connectionist perspective on knowledge and development, in T. Simon and G. Halford (eds) *Developing Cognitive Competence: New approaches to process modeling*. Hillsdale, NJ: Lawrence Erlbaum.

McClelland, J.L. and Elman, J.L. (1986) The TRACE model of speech perception. *Cognitive Psychology* 18: 1–86.

McClelland, J.L. and Rumelhart, D.E. (1981) An interactive activation model of context effects in letter perception 1: An account of basic findings. *Psychological Review* 88: 375–407.

McCloskey, M.E. and Glucksberg, S. (1978) Natural categories: Well defined or fuzzy sets? *Memory and Cognition* 6: 462–72.

McCrae, R.R. (1982) Consensual validation of personality traits: evidence from self-ratings and ratings. *Journal of Personality and Social Psychology* 43: 293–303.

McCrae, R.R. and Costa, P.T. (1985) Updating Norman's 'adequate taxonomy': intelligence and personality dimensions in natural language and in questionnaires. *Journal of Personality and Social Psychology* 49: 710–21.

McDougall, W. (1908) *Introduction to Social Psychology*. London: Methuen.

McDougall, W. (1912) *Psychology: The study of behaviour*. London: Williams and Norgate.

McDougall, W. (1921) *The Group Mind*. Cambridge: Cambridge University Press.

McFarland, C. and Ross, M. (1982) The impact of causal attributions on affective reactions to success and failure. *Journal of Personality and Social Psychology* 43: 937–46.

McGarrigle, J. and Donaldson, M. (1974) Conservation accidents. *Cognition* 3: 341–50.

McGarty, G. and Haslam, S.A. (eds) (1997) *The Message of Social Psychology*. Oxford: Blackwell.

McGrath, J. (1962) The influence of positive interpersonal relations on adjustment and effectiveness in rifle teams. *Journal of Abnormal and Social Psychology* 65: 363–75.

McGraw, M.B. (1943) *The Neuromuscular Maturation of the Human Infant*. New York: Columbia University Press.

McGue, M., Bouchard, T.J., Iacono, W.G. and Lykken, D.T. (1993) Behavioural genetics of cognitive ability: a life-span perspective, in R. Plomin and G.E. McClearn (eds) *Nature, Nurture and Psychology*. Washington, DC: American Psychological Association.

McGuire, W.J. (1985) Attitudes and attutude change, in G. Lindzey and E. Aronson (eds) *Handbook of Social Psychology*, 3rd edn. New York: Random House.

McGurk, H. and MacDonald, J. (1976) Hearing lips and seeing voices. *Nature* 264: 746–8.

McGurk, H., Caplan, M., Hennessy, E. and Moss, P. (1993) Controversy, theory and social context in contemporary day care research. *Journal of Child Psychology and Psychiatry* 34: 3–23.

McKoon, G. and Ratcliff, R. (1992) Inference during reading. *Psychological Review* 99: 440–66.

McLeod, P. (1977) A dual task response modality effect: support for the multiprocessor models of attention. *Quarterly Journal of Experimental Psychology* 29: 651–67.

Mead, G.H. (1913) The social self, in A.J. Reck (ed.) *Selected Writings: George Herbert Mead*. Chicago: Chicago University Press.

Mead, G.H. (1934) *Mind, Self, and Society*. Chicago: University of Chicago Press.

Mei, N. (1993) Gastrointestinal chemoreception and its behavioural role, in D.A. Booth (ed.) *The Neurophysiology of Ingestion*. Manchester: Manchester University Press.

Meichenbaum, D., Turk, D. and Burstein, S. (1975) The nature of coping with stress, in I. Sarason and C.D. Spielberger (eds) *Stress and Anxiety*, New York: Wiley.

Meilman, P.W. (1979) Cross-sectional age changes in ego identity status during adolescence. *Developmental Psychology* 15: 230–1.

Meins, E. and Russell, J. (1996) Security and symbolic play: the relation between security of attachment and executive capacity. *British Journal of Developmental Psychology* 15: 63–76.

Meisch, R.A. and Carroll, M.E. (1987) Oral drug self-administration: drugs as reinforcers, in M.A. Bozarth (ed.) *Methods of Assessing the Reinforcing Properties of Abused Drugs*. New York: Springer-Verlag.

Meissner, M. (1971) The long arm of the job: a study of work and leisure. *Industrial Relations* 10: 239–60.

Melamed, S., Kushnir, T. and Meir, E.I. (1991) Attenuating the impact of job demands: additive and interactive effects of perceived control and social support. *Journal of Vocational Behavior* 39: 40–53.

Meltzoff, A.N. (1985) Immediate and deferred imitation in 14- and 24-month old infants. *Child Development* 56: 62–72.

Meltzoff, A.N. (1988a) Imitation of televised models by infants. *Child Development* 59: 1221–9.

Meltzoff, A.N. (1988b) Infant imitation after a 1-week delay: long term memory for novel acts and multiple stimuli. *Developmental Psychology* 24: 470–6.

Meltzoff, A.N. (1988c) Infant imitation and memory: 9-month olds in immediate and deferred tests. *Child Development* 59: 217–25.

Melzack, R. (1993) Pain: past, present and future. *Canadian Journal of Experimental Psychology* 47: 615–29.

Melzack, R. and Wall, P. (1984) *The Challenge of Pain*. Harmondsworth: Penguin.

Mercier, P. (1996) Computer simulations of the Rescorla-Wagner and Pearce-Hall models of conditioning and contingency judgment. *Behavior Research Methods, Instruments, and Computers* 28: 55–60.

Merton, L. (1960) The search for professional status: sources, costs and consequences. *American Journal of Nursing* 60(5): 662–4.

Merton, R.K., Fiske, M. and Kendall, P.L. (1956) *The Focused Interview*. Glencoe, IL: Free Press.

Metcalfe, J. (1986) Feeling of knowing in memory and problem solving. *Journal of Experimental Psychology: Learning Memory and Cognition* 12: 288–94.

Metcalfe, J. (ed.) (1992) *Degeneration, Damage and Disorder* (Book 6 of Open University course SD206 Biology, Brain and Behaviour). Milton Keynes: Open University Educational Enterprises.

Methner, H. (1990) Stand und Perspektiven der Arbeits-, Betriebs-, und Organisationspsychologie. *Report Psychologie* 1: 33–6.

Meyer, D.E. and Schvaneveldt, R.W. (1971) Facilitation in recognising pairs of words: evidence of a dependence between retrieval operations. *Journal of Experimental Psychology* 90: 227–34.

Michie, S. (1984) Why preschoolers are reluctant to count spontaneously. *British Journal of Developmental Psychology* 2: 347–58.

Miles, M.B. and Huberman, A.M. (1994) *Qualitative Data Analysis*, 2nd edn. London: Sage.

Miles, R.E. and Snow, C.C. (1978) *Organization Strategy, Structure, and Process*. New York: McGraw-Hill.

Milgram, S. (1963) Behavioral study of obedience. *Journal of Abnormal Psychology* 67: 371–8.

Milgram, S. (1974) *Obedience to Authority: An experimental view*. New York: Harper and Row.

Mill, J.S. (1874) *A System of Logic*. New York: Harper.

Millar, A.G. and Tesser, A. (1989) The effects of affective-cognitive consistency and thought on the attitude–behavior relation. *Journal of Experimental Social Psychology* 25: 189–202.

Miller, A.G., Jones, E.E. and Hinkle, S. (1981) A robust attribution error in the personality domain. *Journal of Experimental Psychology* 17: 587–600.

Miller, D.T. and Ross, M. (1975) Self-serving biases in the attribution of causality: fact or fiction? *Psychological Bulletin* 82: 213–25.

Miller, G.A. (1956) The magic number seven, plus or minus two: some limits on our capacity for processing of information. *Psychological Review* 63: 81–93.

Miller, G.A., Galanter, E. and Pribram, K.H. (1960) *Plans and the Structure of Behaviour*. London: Holt.

Miller, J.G. (1984) Culture and the development of everyday social explanation. *Journal of Personality and Social Psychology* 46: 961–78.

Miller, K.F. and Stigler, J.W. (1987) Counting in Chinese: cultural variation in a basic skill. *Cognitive Development* 2: 279–305.

Miller, R.R. and Matute, H. (1996) Biological significance in forward and backward blocking: resolution of a discrepancy between animal conditioning and human causal judgment. *Journal of Experimental Psychology: General* 125: 370–86.

Miller, R.R. and Matzel, L.D. (1988) The comparator hypothesis: a response rule for the expression of associations, in G.H. Bower (ed) *The Psychology of Learning and Motivation*, vol. 22. San Diego, CA: Academic Press.

Miller, R.R., Hallam, S.C. and Grahame, N.J. (1990) inflation of comparator stimuli following CS training. *Animal Learning and Behavior* 18: 434–43.

Miller, R.R., Barnet, R.C. and Grahame, N.J. (1995) Assessment of the Rescorla-Wagner model. *Psychological Bulletin* 118: 363–86.

Miller, S. (1985) Nurses making a power play. *British Medical Journal* 118(4): 1123–5.

Miller, T.Q., Turner, C.W., Tindale, S.R., Posavac, E.J. and Dugoni, B.L. (1991) Reasons for the trend toward null findings in research on type A Behaviour. *Psychological Bulletin* 110 (3): 469–85.

Millward, L. (1991) Social identity processes in nursing. Unpublished doctoral thesis, University of Kent, Canterbury.

Millward, L.J. (1995) Contextualising social identity in considerations of what it means to be a nurse. *European Journal of Social Psychology* 25: 303–24.

Milner, D. (1983) *Children and Race: Ten years on*. London: Ward Lock Educational.

Mintzberg, H. (1979) *The Structuring of Organizations*. Englewood Cliffs, NJ: Prentice Hall.

Minuchin, S. (1974) *Families and Family Therapy*. Cambridge, MA: Harvard University Press.

Miranda, J., Persons, J.B. and Nix Byers, C. (1990) Endorsement of dysfunctional beliefs depends on current mood state. *Journal of Abnormal Psychology* 99: 237–41.

Mirenowicz, J. and Schultz, W. (1996) Preferential activation of midbrain dopamine neurons by appetitive rather than aversive stimuli. *Nature* 379: 449–51.

Mischel, W. (1968) *Personality and Assessment*. London: Wiley.

Mitchell, D. (1994) Sentence parsing, in M.A. Gernsbacher (ed.) *Handbook of Psycholinguistics*. London: Academic Press.

Mitchell, P. (1997) *Introduction to Theory of Mind*. London: Edward Arnold.

Mittleman, G., Castaneda, E., Robinson, T.E. and Valenstein, E.S. (1986) The propensity for nonregulatory ingestive behaviour is related to differences in dopamine systems: behavioural and biochemical evidence. *Behavioural Neuroscience* 100: 213–20.

Mittleman, G., Rosner, L. and Schaub, C.L. (1994) Polydipsia and dopamine: behavioural effects of dopamine D1 and D2 receptor agonists and antagonists. *Journal of Pharmacology and Experimental Therapeutics* 271: 638–50.

Miura, I.T., Kim, C.C., Chang, C.-M. and Okamoto, Y. (1988) Effects of language characteristics on children's cognitive representation of number: cross-national comparisons. *Child Development* 59: 1445–50.

Miura, I.T., Okamoto, Y., Kim, C.C., Chang, C.-M., Steere, M. and Fayol, M. (1994) Comparisons of children's cognitive representation of number: China, France, Japan, Korea, Sweden and the United States. *International Journal of Behavioural Development* 17: 401–11.

Miyake, A., Carpenter, P.A. and Just, M.A. (1994) A capacity approach to syntactic comprehension disorders: making normal adults perform like aphasic patients. *Cognitive Neuropsychology* 11: 671–717.

Moghadden, F., and Perreault, S. (1992) Individual and collective strategies among minority group members. *Journal of Social Psychology* 132(3): 343–57.

Moghadden, F. and Stringer, P. (1988) Outgroup similarity and intergroup bias. *Journal of Social Psychology* 128(1): 105–15.

Mohr, D.C. (1995) Negative outcome in psychotherapy: a critical review. *Clinical Psychology: Science and Practice* 2: 1–27.

Molleman, E., Pruyn, J. and van Knippenberg, A. (1986) Social comparison processes among cancer patients. *British Journal of Social Psychology* 25: 1–13.

Møller, H. (1985) Voice change in human biological development. *Journal of Interdisciplinary History* 16: 239–53.

Møller, H. (1987) The accelerated development of youth: beard growth as a biological marker. *Comparative Study of Society and History* 29: 748–62.

Monson, T.C. and Snyder, M. (1977) Actors, observers, and the attribution process: toward a reconceptualisation. *Journal of Experimental Social Psychology*, 13: 89–111.

Monteil, J-M. and Michinov, N. (1996) Study of some determinants of social comparison strategies using a new methodological tool: towards a dynamic approach. *European Journal of Social Psychology* 26: 981–99.

Monti-Bloch, L., Jennings-White, C., Dolberg, D.S. and Berlinger, D.L. (1994) The human vomeronasal system. *Psychoneuroendocrinology* 19: 5–7.

Moore, C. and Frye, D. (1986) The effect of the experimenter's intention on the child's understanding of conservation. *Cognition* 22: 283–98.

Moos, R.H. (1988) Life stressors and coping resources influence health and well-being. *Psychological Assessment* 4: 133–58.

Moos, R.H. and Schaefer, J.A. (1993) Coping resources and processes: current concepts and measures, in L. Goldberger and S. Breznitz (eds) *Handbook of Stress*. New York: Free Press.

Mora, F., Rolls, E.T. and Burton, M.J. (1976) Modulation during learning of the responses of neurons in the hypothalamus to the sight of food. *Experimental Neurology* 53: 508–19.

Mora, F., Avrith, D.B., Phillips, A.G. and Rolls, E.T. (1979) Effects of satiety on self-stimulation of the orbitofrontal cortex in the monkey. *Neuroscience Letters* 13: 141–5.

Moradi, A. (1996) The processing of emotional in information in children and adolescents with PTSD. Unpublished doctoral dissertation, University of London.

Moradi, A., Neshat-Doost, H., Taghavi, R., Yule, W. and Dalgleish, T. (1997) Performance of children of adults with PTSD on the Stroop colour-naming task. Manuscript submitted for publication.

Morais, J., Cary, L., Alegria, J. and Bertelson, P. (1979) Does awareness of speech as a sequence of phones arise spontaneously? *Cognition* 7: 323–31.

Morais, J., Bertelson, P., Cary, L. and Alegria, J. (1986) Literacy training and speech segmentation. *Cognition* 24: 45–64.

Morais, J., Alegria, J. and Content, A. (1987) The relationship between segmental analysis and alphabetic literacy. *Cahiers de Psychologie Cognitive* 7: 415–38.

Moreland, R. (1985) Doctors and medical practice, in R. Scase (ed.) *Sociological Approaches to Health and Medicine: Social analysis*. London: Croom Helm.

Moreland, R. and Levine, J. (1982) Socialisation in small groups: temporal changes in individual/group relations, in L. Berkowitz (ed.) *Advances in Experimental Social Psychology*. London: Academic Press.

Moreland, R. and Levine, J. (1993) Group socialisation: the role of commitment, in M. Hogg and D. Abrams (eds) *Group Motivation: Social psychological perspectives*. London: Harvester Wheatsheaf.

Morgan, W.P. (1981) Psychological benefits of physical activity, in F.J. Nagle and H.J. Montoye (eds) *Exercise in Health and Disease*. Springfield, IL: C.C. Thomas.

Morris, C.D., Bransford, J.D. and Franks, J.J. (1977) Levels of processing versus transfer appropriate processing. *Journal of Verbal Learning and Verbal Behavior* 16: 519–33.

Morris, P.E. (1979) Strategies for learning and recall, in M.M. Gruneberg and P.E. Morris (eds) *Applied Problems in Memory*. London: Academic Press.

Morsbach, H. and Tyler, W.J. (1986) A Japanese emotion: Amae, in R. Harré (ed.) *The Social Construction of Emotions*. Oxford: Blackwell.

Morse, J.M. and Johnson, J.L. (1991) Towards a theory of illness: the illness constellation model, in J.M. Morse and J.L. Johnson (eds) *The Illness Experience*. London: Sage.

Mortimer, J.T. and Lorence, J. (1979a) Occupational experience and the self-concept: a longitudinal study. *Social Psychology Quarterly* 42: 307–23.

Mortimer, J.T. and Lorence, J. (1979b) Work experience and occupational value socialization: a longitudinal study. *American Journal of Sociology* 84: 1361–85.

Morton, J. and Johnson, M.H. (1991) CONSPEC and CON-LERN: a two-process theory of infant face recognition. *Psychological Review* 98: 164–81.

Morton, J. and Patterson, K.E. (1980) A new attempt at an interpretation, or, an attempt at a new interpretation, in M. Coltheart, K.E. Patterson, and J.C. Marshall (eds) *Deep Dyslexia*. London: Routledge and Kegan Paul.

Moscovici, S. (1972) Society and theory in social psychology, in J. Israel and H. Tajfel (eds) *The Context of Social Psychology: A critical assessment*. London: Academic Press.

Moscovici, S. (ed.) (1973) *Introduction à la psychologie sociale*. Paris: Presses Universitaires de France.

Moscovici, S. (1976a) *Social Influence and Social Change*. London: Academic Press.

Moscovici, S. (1976b) *La Psychoanalyse: son image et son public*. Paris: Presses Universitaires de France.

Moscovici, S. (1980) Towards a theory of conversion behaviour, in L. Berkowitz (ed.) *Advances in Experimental Social Psychology*. London: Academic Press.

Moscovici, S. (1984) The phenomenon of social representations, in R. Farr and S. Moscovici (eds) *Social Representations*. Cambridge: Cambridge University Press.

Moscovici, S. and Hewstone, M. (1983) Social representations and social explanation: from the 'naive' to 'amateur' scientist, in M. Hewstone (ed.) *Attribution Theory: Social and functional extensions*. Oxford: Blackwell.

Moscovici, S. and Personnaz, B. (1990) Studies in social influence V: minority influence and conversion behaviour in a perceptual task. *Journal of Experimental Social Psychology* 16: 270–82.

Moscovici, S. and Zavalloni, M. (1969) The group as a polariser of attitudes. *Journal of Personality and Social Psychology* 12: 125–35.

Moscovici, S., Lage, E. and Naffrechoux, M. (1969) Influence of a consistent minority on the response of a majority in a colour perception task. *Sociometry* 32: 365–80.

Moscovici, S., Mucchi Faina, A. and Maass, A. (1994) *Minority Influence*. Chicago: Nelson Hall.

Moscovitch, M. (1995) Models of consciousness and memory, in M.S. Gazzaniga (ed.) *The Cognitive Neurosciences*. Cambridge: MIT Press.

Moss, H.E. and Marslen-Wilson, W.D. (1993) Access to word meanings during spoken language comprehension: effects of sentential semantic context. *Journal of Experimental Psychology: Learning, Memory, and Cognition* 19: 1254–76.

Motowidlo, S.J. and Van Scotter, J.R. (1994) Evidence that task performance should be distinguished from contextual performance. *Journal of Applied Psychology* 79: 475–80.

MOW (International Research Team) (1987) *The Meaning of Working*. London: Academic Press.

Mucchi-Faina, A., Maass, A. and Volpato, C. (1991) Social influence: the role of originality. *European Journal of Social Psychology* 21: 183–97.

Mueller, E. and Brenner, J. (1977) The origins of social skills and interaction among playgroup toddlers. *Child Development* 48: 854–61.

Muff, J. (1982) *Socialisation, Sexism and Stereotyping: Women's issues in nursing*. St Louis, MO: C.V. Mosby.

Mugny, G. and Papastamou, S. (1980) When rigidity does not fail: individualization and psychologization as resistances to the diffusion of minority innovations. *European Journal of Social Psychology* 10: 43–62.

Mugny, G. and Papastamou, S. (1982) Minority influence and psychosocial identity. *European Journal of Social Psychology* 12: 379–94.

Mugny, G. and Perez, J. (1989) L'influence sociale comme processus de changement. *Hermes* 6: 227–36.

Mugny, G., and Perez, J. (1991) *The Social Psychology of Minority Influence*. Cambridge: Cambridge University Press.

Mullen, B., Atkins, J.L., Champion, D.S., Edwards, C., Hardy, D., Story, J.E. and Vanderklok, M. (1985) The false consensus effect: a meta-analysis of 115 hypothesis tests. *Journal of Experimental Social Psychology* 21: 262–83.

Mullen, B., Brown, R. and Smith, C. (1992) Ingroup bias as a function of salience, relevance and status: an integration. *European Journal of Social Psychology*, 22: 103–22.

Mullen, P.D., Mains, D.A. and Velez, R. (1992) A meta-analysis of controlled trials of cardiac patient education. *Patient Education and Counseling* 19: 143–62.

Mummendey, A. (1995) Positive distinctiveness and social discrimination: an old couple living in divorce. *European Journal of Social Psychology* 25: 657–70.

Mummendey, A. (1997) Aggressive behaviour, in M. Hewstone, W. Stroebe and G.M. Stephenson (eds) *Introduction to Social Psychology*. Oxford: Blackwell.

Mummendey, A. and Schreiber, J. (1984) Different just means better: some obvious and hidden pathways to ingroup favouritism. *British Journal of Social Psychology* 23: 363–8.

Mummendey, A., Simon, B., Dietz, C., Grunert, M., Haeger, G., Lettgen, S. and Schaferhoff, S. (1992) Categorisation is not enough: intergroup discrimination in negative outcome allocations. *Journal of Experimental Social Psychology* 28: 125–44.

Murphy, G. and Kovach, J.K. (1972) *Historical Introduction to Modern Psychology*. London: Routledge and Kegan Paul.

Murphy, L.R. (1984) Occupational stress management. *Journal of Occupational Psychology* 57: 1–15.

Murray, H.A. (1938) *Explorations in Personality*. New York: Oxford University Press.

Mussen, P. and Distler, L. (1960) Child-rearing antecedents of masculine identification in kindergarten boys. *Child Development* 31: 89–100.

Mussen, P. and Rutherford, E. (1963) Parent–child relations and parental personality in relation to young children's sex-role preferences. *Child Development* 34: 589–607.

Myers, D. (1978) Polarising effects of social comparison. *Journal of Experimental Social Psychology* 14: 554–63.

Myers, D. (1982) Polarising effects of social interaction, in H. Brandstatter, J. Davis and G. Stocker-Kreichgauer (eds) *Group Decision Making*. New York: Academic Press.

Myers, D. (1993) *Social Psychology*, 4 edn. New York: McGraw Hill Inc.

Myers, L.B. and Brewin, C.R. (1994) Recall of early experiences and the repressive coping style. *Journal of Abnormal Psychology* 103: 288–92.

Navon, D. (1977) Forest before trees: the precedence of global features in visual perception. *Cognitive Psychology* 9: 353–83.

Neely, J.H. (1977) Semantic priming and retrieval from semantic memory: roles of inhibitionless spreading activation and limited-capacity attention. *Journal of Experimental Psychology: General* 106: 226–54.

Neidhardt, E.J., Weinstein, M.S. and Conry, R.F. (1985) *Managing stress*. North Vancouver: International Self-Council.

Neill, D. (1982) Problems of concept and vocabulary in the anhedonia hypothesis. *Behavioral and Brain Sciences* 5: 70.

Neisser, U. (1964) Visual search. *Scientific American* 210: 94–102.

Neisser, U. (1967) *Cognitive Psychology*. New York: Appleton-Century-Crofts.

Neisser, U. (1976) *Cognition and Reality*. San Francisco, CA: W.H. Freeman.

Neisser, U. (1978) Memory: what are the important questions?, in M.M. Gruneberg, P.E. Morris and R.N. Sykes (eds) *Practical Aspects of Memory*. London: Academic Press.

Neisser, U. and Becklen, P. (1975) Selective looking: attending to visually superimposed events. *Cognitive Psychology* 7: 480–94.

Nelson, D.L., Reed, V.S. and McEvoy, C.L. (1977) Learning to order pictures and words: a model of sensory and semantic encoding. *Journal of Experimental Psychology: Human Learning and Memory* 3: 485–97.

Nemeth, C. (1982) Stability of fact position and influence, in H. Brandstatter, J. Davis and G. Stocker-Kreichgauer (eds) *Group Decision Making*. New York: Academic Press.

Nemeth, C. (1986) Differential contributions of majority and minority influence. *Psychological Review* 93: 23–32.

Nemeth, C. and Wachtler, J. (1983) Creative problem solving as a result of majority versus minority influence. *European Journal of Social Psychology* 13: 45–55.

Nemeth, C., Swedlund, M. and Kanki, B. (1974) Patterning of the minorities responses and their influence on the majority. *European Journal of Social Psychology* 4(1): 53–64.

Nemeth, C., Mayseless, O., Sherman, J. and Brown, Y. (1990) Exposure to dissent and recall of information. *Journal of Personality and Social Psychology* 58: 429–37.

Neshat-Doost, H., Taghavi, R., Moradi, A., Yule, W. and Dalgleish, T. (1997) Memory for self-referent emotional material in clinically depressed children and adolescents. Manuscript submitted for publication.

Neshat-Doost, H., Taghavi, R., Moradi, A., Yule, W. and Dalgleish, T. (1998) The performance of clinically depressed children and adolescents on the modified Stroop paradigm. *Personality and Individual Differences*.

Neugarten, B.L., Havighurst, R.J. and Tobin, S.S. (1968) Personality and patterns of aging, in B.L. Neugarten (ed.) *Middle Age and Aging*. Chicago: University of Chicago Press.

Neumann, G.A., Edwards, J.E. and Raju, N.S. (1989) Organizational development interventions: a meta-analysis of their effets on satisfaction and other attitudes. *Personnel Psychology* 42: 461–89.

Newcomb, A. and Bagwell, C. (1995) Children's friendship relations: a meta-analytic review. *Psychological Bulletin* 117: 306–47.

Newcomb, T. (1953) An approach to the study of communicative acts. *Psychological Review* 60: 393–404.

Newcomb, T.M., Koenig, K., Flacks, R. and Warwick, D. (1967) *Persistence and Change: Bennington College and its students after 25 years*. New York: Wiley.

Newell, A. and Simon, H.A. (1972) *Human Problem Solving*. Englewood Cliffs, NJ: Prentice Hall.

Newman, J.P., Patterson, C.M. and Kosson, D.S. (1987) Response perseveration in psychopaths. *Journal of Abnormal Psychology* 96: 145–8.

Newman, S. (1990) Coping with chronic illness, in P. Bennet, J. Weinman and P. Spurgeon (eds) *Current Developments in Health Psychology*. Chur: Harwood.

Newstead, S.E., Pollard, P., Evans, J.St.B.T. and Allen, J.L. (1992) The source of belief bias effects in syllogistic reasoning. *Cognition* 45: 257–84.

Nicholson, N. (1987) Work role transitions: processes and outcomes. *Journal of Occupational Psychology* 60:160–177.

Nicholson, N. (1996) Towards a new agenda for work and personality: traits, self-identity, 'strong' interactionism, and change. *Applied Psychology: An International Review* 45(3): 189–205.

Niendenthal, P., Cantor, N. and Kihlstrom, J. (1985) Prototype matching: a strategy for social decision making. *Journal of Personality and Social Psychology* 48(3): 575–84.

Nimoy, L. (1995) *I am Spock*. London: Random House.

Nisbett, R.E. and Ross, L. (1980) *Human Inference: Strategies and shortcomings of social judgment*. Englewood Cliffs, NJ: Prentice Hall.

Nisbett, R.E. and Wilson, T.D. (1977) Telling more than we can know: verbal reports on mental processes. *Psychological Review* 84: 231–59.

Nissen, M., Ross, J., Willingham, D., Mackenzie, T. and Schachter, D. (1988) Memory and amnesia in a patient with multiple personality disorder. *Brain and Cognition* 8: 117–34.

Noe, R.A. (1986) Trainees' attributes: neglected influences on training effectiveness. *Academy of Management Review* 11: 736–49.

Nolan-Hoeksema, S. (1987) Sex differences in unipolar depression: evidence and theory. *Journal of Abnormal Psychology* 101: 259–82.

Norbeck, J.S. and Tilden, V.P. (1983) Life stress, social support and emotional disequilibrium in complications of pregnancy. *Journal of Health and Social Behaviour* 24: 30–45.

Norman, D.A. (1981) Categorization of action slips. *Psychological Review* 88: 1–15.

Norman, D.A. and Shallice, T. (1980) Attention to action: willed and automatic control of behaviour, *CHIP Document no. 99*. Centre for Human Information Processing, University of California, San Diego, La Jolla.

Norman, D.A. and Shallice, T. (1986) Attention to action: willed and automatic control of behaviour, in R.J. Davidson, G.E. Schwartz, and D. Shapiro (eds) *The Design of Everyday Things*. New York: Doubleday.

Norman, W.T. (1963) Toward an adequate taxonomy of personality attributes: replicated factor structure in peer nomination personality ratings. *Journal of Abnormal and Social Psychology* 66: 574–83.

Nunes, T. (1995) Mathematical and scientific thinking, in V. Lee and P. das Gupta (eds): *Children's Cognitive and Language Development*. Milton Keynes: Open University Press.

Nunes, T. and Bryant, P. (1996) *Children Doing Mathematics*. Oxford: Blackwell.

Nunes, T., Schliemann, A.-L. and Carraher, D. (1993) *Street Mathematics and School Mathematics*. New York: Cambridge University Press.

Nunnally, J.C. (1978) *Psychometric Theory*, 2nd edn. New York: McGraw-Hill.

Oaker, G. and Brown, R. (1986) Intergroup relations in a hospital setting: a further test of social identity theory. *Human Relations* 39(8): 767–78.

Oakes, P. (1987) The salience of social categories, in J. Turner, M. Hogg, P. Oakes, S. Reicher and M. Wetherall (eds) *Rediscovering the Social Group*. Oxford: Blackwell.

Oakes, P. and Turner, J.C. (1980) Social categorisation and intergroup behaviour: does minimal intergroup discrimination make social identity more positive? *European Journal of Social Psychology* 10: 295–301.

Oakes, P., Turner, J.C. and Haslam, S.A. (1991) Perceiving people as group members: the role of fit in the salience of social categorisation. *British Journal of Social Psychology* 30: 125–44.

Oakes, P.J. Haslam, S.A. and Turner, J.C. (1994) *Stereotyping and Social Reality*. Oxford: Blackwell.

Oaksford, M. (1997) Thinking and the rational analysis of human reasoning. *The Psychologist* 10: 257–60.

Oatley, K. (1992) *Best Laid Schemes: The psychology of emotions*. New York: Cambridge University Press.

Oatley, K. and Jenkins, J.M. (1996) *Understanding Emotions*. Cambridge, MA: Blackwell.

Oatley, K. and Johnson-Laird, P.N. (1987) Towards a cognitive theory of emotions. *Cognition and Emotion* 1: 29–50.

Oborne, D.J. (1987) *Ergonomics at Work*, 2nd edn. Chichester, Wiley.

O'Brien, E.J., Shank, D.M., Myers, J.L. and Rayner, K. (1988) Elaborative inferences during reading: do they occur on-line? *Journal of Experimental Psychology: Learning, Memory, and Cognition* 14: 410–20.

O'Brien, M.T. (1993) Multiple sclerosis: the relationship among self-esteem, social support, and coping behaviour. *Applied Nursing Research* 6(2): 54–63.

Occupational Personality Questionnaire (1990) London: Saville and Holdsworth.

Ochs, E. (1979) Transcription as theory, in E. Ochs and B.B. Schieffelin (eds) *Developmental Pragmatics*. New York: Academic Press.

O'Connell, D.C. and Kowal, S. (1993) The recent history of transcription methods for spoken discourse. Paper presented at the Sixth International Congress on the *History of the Language Sciences*, Georgetown University, Washington, DC, August.

O'Connor, R.D. (1972) Relative efficacy of modeling, shaping and the combined procedures for modification or social withdrawal. *Journal of Abnormal Psychology* 79: 327–34.

Oden, S. and Asher, S.R. (1977) Coaching children in social skills for friendship making. *Child Development* 48: 495–506.

O'Donohue, W. (ed.) (1998) *Learning and Behavior Therapy*. Boston, MA: Allyn and Bacon.

Ogden, J. (1996) *Health Psychology: A textbook*. Buckingham: Open University Press.

Ohlsson, S. (1992) Information processing explanations of insight and related phenomena, in M.T. Keane and K.J. Gilhooly (eds) *Advances in the Psychology of Thinking*. London: Harvester Wheatsheaf.

Ohman, A. (1986) Face the beast and fear the face: animal and social fears as prototypes for evolutionary analyses of emotion. *Psychophysiology* 23: 123–45.

Okely, J. (1994) Thinking through fieldwork, in A. Bryman and R.G. Burgess (eds) *Analyzing Qualitative Data*. London: Routledge.

Olds, J. (1958) Self-stimulation of the brain. *Science* 127: 315–24.

Olds, J. (1977) *Drives and Reinforcements: Behavioral studies of hypothalamic functions*. New York: Raven Press.

Olson, D.R. (1970) Language and thought: aspects of a cognitive theory of semantics. *Psychological Review* 77: 257–73.

Olson, D.R. (1994) *The World on Paper*. Cambridge: Cambridge University Press.

Olson, D.R. (1996) Literate mentalities: literacy, consciousness of language, and modes of thought, in D.R. Olson and N. Torrance, *Modes of Thought: Explorations in culture and cognition*. Cambridge: Cambridge University Press.

Olson, J.M., Ellis, R.J. and Zanna, M.P. (1983) Validating objective versus subjective judgments: interest in social comparison and consistency information. *Personality and Social Psychology Bulletin*, 9: 427–36.

Oltmanns, T.F. and Emery, R.E. (1995) *Abnormal Psychology*. Englewood Cliffs, NJ: Prentice Hall.

Olweus, D. (1993) *Bullying at School: What we know and what we can do*. Oxford: Blackwell.

Ora, J.P. (1965) Characteristics of the volunteer for psychological investigations. *Office of Naval Research Contract* 2149(03) technical report 27.

O'Regan, K. and Levy-Schoen, A. (1987) Eye-movement strategy and tactics in word recognition and reading, in M. Coltheart (ed.) *Attention and Performance*, vol. 12. Hove: Lawrence Erlbaum.

Organ, D. (1988) *Organizational Citizenship Behaviour: The good soldier syndrome*. Lexington, MA: Lexington Books.

Orne, M.T. (1962) On the social psychology of the psychology experiment: with particular reference to demand characteristics and their implications. *American Psychologist* 17: 776–83.

Orne, M.T. and Scheibe, K.E. (1964) The contribution of non-deprivation factors in the production of sensory deprivation effects: the psychology of the 'panic button'. *Journal of Abnormal and Social Psychology* 68: 3–12.

Orr, E., Assor, P. and Cairns, D. (1996) Social representations and group membership: shared and diffusion of parental ideal in three Israeli settings. *European Journal of Social Psychology* 26: 703–26.

Oster, H., Hegley, D. and Nagel, L. (1992) Adult judgments and fine-grained analysis of infant facial epxressions: testing the validity of a priori coding formulas. *Developmental Psychology* 28: 1115–31.

Ostergaard, A.L. (1994) Dissociations between word priming effects in normal subjects and patients with memory disorders: multiple memory systems or retrieval. *Quarterly Journal of Experimental Psychology* 47A: 331–64.

Osterholz, U., Karmaus, W., Hullmann, B. and Ritz, B. (eds) (1987) *Work-Related Musculo-Skeletal Disorders*. Bremerhafen: Wirtschaftsverlag NW.

Oudejans, R.R.D., Michaels, C.F., Bakker, F.C. and Dolne, M.A. (1996) The relevance of action in perceiving affordances: perception of catchableness of fly balls. *Journal of Experimental Psychology: Human Perception and Performance* 22: 879–891.

Overmier, J.B. and Seligman, M.E.P. (1967) Effects of inescapable shock upon subsequent escape and avoidance learning. *Journal of Comparative and Physiological Psychology* 63: 28–33.

Paez, D. and Gonzalez, J. (1993) A southerner's response to an insular critique: where to find the social and how to understand the use of clusters in our studies on social representations. *Papers on Social Representation* 2(1): 11–25.

Paicheler, G. (1976) Norms and attitude change 1: polarisation and styles of behaviour. *European Journal of Social Psychology* 6: 405–27.

Paikoff, R.L. and Brooks-Gunn, J. (1991) Do parent–child relationships change during puberty? *Psychological Bulletin* 110: 47–66.

Paillard, J. (1987) Cognitive versus sensorimotor encoding of spatial information, in P. Ellen and C. Thinus-Blanc (eds) *Cognitive Processes and Spatial Orientation in Animal and Man*, vol. 2: *Neurophysiology and developmental aspects*. Dordrecht: Martinus Nijhoff.

Paivio, A. (1971) *Imagery and Verbal Processes*. New York: Holt, Rinehart and Winston.

Paivio, A. (1979) Psychological processes in the comprehension of metaphor, in A. Ortony (ed.) *Metaphor and Thought*. New York: Cambridge University Press.

Palmer, S.E. (1975) The effects of contextual scenes on the identification of objects. *Memory and Cognition* 3: 519–26.

Paludi, M.A. (1992) *The Psychology of Women*. Dubuque, IA: Wm. C. Brown.

Panksepp, J. (1982) The pleasure in brain substrates of foraging. *Behavioral and Brain Sciences* 5: 71–2.

Panksepp, J. (1993) Neurochemical control of moods and emotions: amino acids to neuropeptides, in M Lewis and J. M. Haviland (eds) *Handbook of Emotions*. New York: Guilford Press.

Paoli, P. (1992) *First European Survey on the Work Environment 1991–1992*. Luxembourg: Office for Official Publications of the European Communities.

Papez, J.W. (1937) A proposed mechanism of emotion. *Archives of Neurology and Psychiatry* 38: 725–43.

Park, B. and Rothbart, M. (1982) Perception of outgroup homogeneity and levels of social categorisation: memory for the subordinate attributes of ingroup and outgroup members. *Journal of Personality and Social Psychology* 42: 1031–68.

Parke, R.D. and Tinsley, B.J. (1987) Family interaction in infancy, in J.D. Osofsky (ed.) *Handbook of Infant Development*, 2nd edn. New York: Wiley.

Parker, I. (1989) Discourse and power, in J. Shotter and K. Gergen (eds) *Texts of Identity*. London: Sage.

Parker, J.G. and Asher, S.R. (1987) Peer relations and later personal adjustment: are low-accepted children at risk? *Psychological Bulletin* 102: 357–89.

Parkes, K.R., Mendham, C.A. and Rabenau, C.V. (1994) Social support and the demand-discretion model of job stress: tests of additive and interactive effects in two samples. *Journal of Vocational Behavior* 44: 91–113.

Parkin, A.J. (1990) Recent advances in the neuropsychology of memory, in J. Hunter and J. Weinman (eds) *Mechanisms of Memory: Clinical and neurochemical contributions*. London: Harwood.

Parkin, A.J. (1993) *Memory: Phenomena, experiment and theory*. Oxford: Blackwell.

Parkin, A.J. and Leng, N.R.C. (1993) *Neuropsychology of the Amnesic Syndrome*. Hove: Lawrence Erlbaum.

Parkinson, B. (1995) *Ideas and Realities of Emotion*. London: Routledge.

Parten, M.B. (1932) Social participation among preschool children. *Journal of Abnormal and Social Psychology* 27: 243–69.

Patrick, J. (1992) *Training: Research and practice*. London: Academic Press.

Patterson, G.R., DeBaryshe, B.D. and Ramsey, E. (1989) A developmental perspective on antisocial behavior. *American Psychologist* 44: 329–35.

Patterson, K.E. (1982) The relation between reading and phonological coding: further neuropsychological observations, in A.W. Ellis (ed.) *Normality and Pathology in Cognitive Functions*. London: Academic Press.

Paul, W.J.J., Robertson, K.B. and Herzberg, F. (1969) Job enrichment pays off. *Harvard Business Review* 47: 61–78.

Pavlov, I.P. (1927) *Conditioned Reflexes*. London: Clarendon Press.

Paykel, E.S. (1979) Recent life events in the development of depressive disorders: implications for the effects of stress, in R.A. Depue (ed.) *The Psychobiology of the Depressive Disorders*. New York: Academic Press.

Payne, R. (1996) The characteristics of organizations, in P. Warr (ed.) *Psychology at Work*. Harmmondsworth: Penguin.

Payne, R. and Fletcher, B. (1983) Job demands, supports, and constraints as predictors of psychological strain among schoolteachers. *Journal of Vocational Behavior* 22: 136–47.

Pearce, J.M. and Hall, G. (1978) Overshadowing the instrumental conditioning of a lever-press response by a more valid predictor of the reinforcer. *Journal of Experimental Psychology: Animal Behavior Processes* 4: 356–67.

Pearce, J.M. and Hall, G. (1980) A model for Pavlovian learning: variations in the effectiveness of conditioned but not of unconditioned stimuli. *Psychological Review* 87: 532–52.

Pears, R. and Bryant, P. (1990) Transitive inferences by young children about spatial position. *British Journal of Psychology* 81: 497–510.

Pedersen, N.L., Friberg, L., Floderus-Myrhed, B., McClearn, G.E. and Plomin, R. (1984) Swedish early separated twins: identification and characterisation. *Acta Geneticae Medicae et Gemellologiae* 33: 243–54.

Pedersen, N.L., Plomin, R., McClearn, G.E. and Friberg, L. (1988) Neuroticism, extraversion, and related traits in adult twins reared apart and reared together. *Journal of Personality and Social Psychology* 55: 950–57.

Peeters, M. (1994) *Supportive Interactions and Stressful Events at Work: An event-recording approach*. Nijmegen: Druk Quickprint.

Pekrun, R. and Frese, M. (1992) Emotions at work and achievement, in C.L. Cooper and I.T. Robertson (eds) *International Review of Industrial and Organizational Psychology 1992*. Chichester: Wiley.

Pellegrini, A.D. (1994) The rough play of adolescent boys of differing sociometric status. *International Journal of Behavioral Development* 17: 525–40.

Pellegrini, A.D. and Smith, P.K. (1998) Physical activity play: the nature and function of a neglected aspect of play. *Child Development*.

Pennebaker, J.W. (1982) *The Psychology of Physical Symptoms*. New York: Springer-Verlag.

Pennings-Van der Eerden, L. and Visser, A.Ph. (1990) Diabetes mellitus, in A.A. Kaptein, H.M. van der Ploeg, B. Garssen, P.J.G. Schreurs and R. Beunderman (eds) *Behavioural Medicine*. New York: Wiley.

Pepitone, A. (1981) Lessons from the history of social psychology. *American Psychologist*, 36: 972–85.

Pepitone, A. and Reichling, G. (1955) Group cohesiveness and the expression of hostility. *Human Relations* 8: 327–37.

Pepper, R. (1977) Professionalism, training and work: a study of nursing in a general hospital. Unpublished doctoral thesis, University of Kent, Canterbury.

Perez, J., Papastamou, S. and Mugny, G. (1995) Zietgeist and minority influence – where is the causality? A comment on Clark (1990). *European Journal of Social Psychology* 25: 703–10.

Perfect, T.J. and Hollins, T.S. (1996) Predictive feeling of knowing judgements and postdictive confidence judgements in eyewitness memory and general knowledge. *Applied Cognitive Psychology* 10: 371–82.

Perner, J. and Mansbridge, D.G. (1983) Developmental differences in encoding length series. *Child Development* 54: 710–19.

Perner, J., Leekam, S. and Wimmer, H. (1987) Three-year olds' difficulty with false belief: the case for a conceptual deficit. *British Journal of Developmental Psychology* 5: 127–37.

Perrett, D., Benson, P.J., Hietanen, J.K., Oram, M.W. and Dittrich, C. (1995) When is a face not a face?, in R. Gregory, J. Harris, P. Heard and D. Rose (eds) *The Artful Eye*. Oxford: Oxford University Press.

Perrez, M. and Reicherts M. (1992) *Stress Coping and Health*. Seatttle, WA: Hogrefe and Huber.

Perry, G. (1982) Autonomy of RNs. *Nursing Success Today* 3(9): 23–4.

Personnaz, B. (1981) Study in social influence using the spectrometer method: dynamics of the phenomena of conversion and covertness in perceptual responses. *European Journal of Social Psychology* 11: 431–8.

Persons, J.B. and Burns, D.D. (1985) Mechanisms of action of cognitive therapy: the relative contributions of technical and interpersonal interventions. *Cognitive Therapy and Research* 9: 539–51.

Pervin, L.A. (1993) *Personality: Theory and research*, 6th edn. Chichester: Wiley.

Pervin, L.A. (1996) *The Science of Personality*. New York: Wiley.

Peters, L.H., Hartke, D.D. and Pohlmann, J.T. (1985) Fiedler's contingency theory of leadership: an application of the meta-analysis procedures of Schmidt and Hunter. *Psychological Bulletin* 97: 274–85.

Peters, T. (1974) Mentale Beanspruchungen von Büroangestellten in Schreibdienst und bei Vorzimmertätigkeiten. *Zentralblat für Arbeitsmedizin und Arbeitsschutz* 24: 197–207.

Peters-Golden, H. (1982) Breast cancer: varied perceptions of social support in the illness experience. *Social Science and Medicine* 16: 483–91.

Peterson, C. (1980) Memory and the 'dispositional shift'. *Social Psychology Quarterly*, 43: 372–80.

Peterson, L.R. and Peterson, M.J. (1959) Short-term retention of individual items. *Journal of Experimental Psychology* 58: 193–8.

Peterson, L., Bartelstone, J., Kern, T. and Gillies, R. (1995) Parents' socialization of children's injury prevention: descriptions and some initial parameters. *Child Development* 66(1): 224–35.

Petta, G. and Walker, I. (1992) Relative deprivation and ethnic identity. *British Journal of Social Psychology* 31(4): 285–93.

Pettigrew, T. (1979) The ultimate attribution error: extending Allport's cognitive analysis of prejudice. *Journal of Personality and Social Psychology* 53: 621–35.

Pettigrew, T. and Meertons, R. (1995) Subtle and blatant prejudice in western Europe. *European Journal of Social Psychology* 25: 57–75.

Petty, R. and Cacioppo, J. (1981) *Attitudes and Persuasion: Classic and contemporary approaches*. Dubuque, IA: Wm C. Brown.

Phillips, P., Rolls, B.J., Ledingham, J. and Morton, J. (1984) Body fluid changes, thirst and drinking in man during free access to water. *Physiology and Behavior* 33: 357–63.

Phillips, P., Rolls, B.J., Ledingham, J., Morton, J. and Forsling, M. (1985) Angiotensin-II induced thirst and vasopressin release in man. *Clinical Science* 68: 669–74.

Phillips, W.A., Hobbs, S.B. and Pratt, F.R. (1978) Intellectual realism in children's drawings of cubes. *Cognition* 6: 15–33.

Phoenix, A., Woollett, A. and Lloyd, E. (1991) *Motherhood: Meanings, practices and ideologies*. London: Sage.

Piaget, J. (1921) Une forme verbale de la comparaison chez l'enfant. *Archives de Psychologie* 18: 141–72.

Piaget, J. (1932) *The Moral Judgement of the Child*. London: Paul, Trench, Trubner.

Piaget, J. (1952a) *The Child's Conception of Number*. London: Routledge and Kegan Paul.

Piaget, J. (1952b) *The Origins of Intelligence*. London: Routledge and Kegan Paul.

Piaget, J. (1953) How children form mathematical concepts. *Scientific American*.

Piaget, J. (1954) *The Construction of Reality in the Child*. London: Routledge and Kegan Paul.

Piaget, J. (1970) *The Child's Conception of Movement and Speed*. London: Routledge and Kegan Paul.

Piaget, J. and Garcia, R. (1987) *Vers un logique des significations*. Geneva: Muironde.

Piaget, J. and Inhelder, B. (1963) *The Child's Conception of Space*. London: Routledge and Kegan Paul.

Piaget, J. and Inhelder, B. (1974) *The Child's Construction of Quantities*. London: Routledge and Kegan Paul.

Piaget, J. and Inhelder, B. (1975) *The Origin of the Idea of Chance in Children*. London: Routledge and Kegan Paul.

Piaget, J., Inhelder, B. and Szeminska, A. (1960) *The Child's Conception of Geometry*. London: Routledge and Kegan Paul.

Pichevin, M. and Nurtig, M-C. (1996) Describing men describing women: sex membership salience and numerical distinctiveness. *European Journal of Social Psychology* 26: 513–22.

Pidgeon, N. and Henwood, K. (1996) Grounded theory: practical implementation, in J.T.E. Richardson (ed.) *Handbook of Qualitative Research Methods for Psychology and the Social Sciences*. Leicester: British Psychological Society.

Pilgrim, D. (1990) Competing histories of madness, in R. Bentall (ed) *Reconstructing Schizophrenia*. London: Routledge.

Piliavin, I.M., Rodin, J. and Piliavin, J.A. (1969) Good samaritanism: an underground phenomenon? *Journal of Personality and Social Psychology* 13: 289–99.

Pillow, D.R., Zautra, A.J. and Sandler, I. (1996) Major life events and minor stressors: identifying mediational links in the stress process. *Journal of Personality and Social Psychology* 70: 381–94.

Pirolli, P.L. and Anderson, J.R. (1985) The role of learning from examples in the acquisition of recursive programming skill. *Canadian Journal of Psychology* 39: 240–72.

Pittam, J. and Scherer, K.R. (1993) Vocal expression and communication of emotion, in M. Lewis and J.M. Haviland (eds) *Handbook of Emotion*. New York: Guilford Press.

Plato (375 BC/1955) *The Republic*. Harmondsworth: Penguin.

Plomin, R. (1988a) The nature and nurture of cognitive abilities, in R.J. Sternberg (ed.) *Advances in the Psychology of Human Intelligence*, vol. 4. Hillsdale, NJ: Lawrence Erlbaum.

Plomin, R. (1988b) *Development, Genetics and Psychology*. Hillsdale, NJ: Lawrence Erlbaum.

Plomin, R. (1990) *Nature and Nurture*. Pacific Grove, CA: Brooks/Cole.

Plomin, R. (1994) Genetic research and identification of environmental influences. *Journal of Child Psychology and Psychiatry* 35: 817–34.

Plomin, R. and Daniels, D. (1987) Why are children in the same family so different from each other? *Behavioral and Brain Sciences* 10: 1–16.

Plomin, R., DeFries, J.C., McClearn, G.E. and Rutter, M. (1997) *Behavioral Genetics*, 3rd edn. Basingstoke: Macmillan Press.

Plunkett, K., Karmiloff-Smith, A., Bates, E., Elman, J.L. and Johnson, M.H. (1997) Connectionism and developmental psychology. *Journal of Child Psychology and Psychiatry* 38: 53–80.

Podsakoff, P.M., Niehoff, B.P., MacKenzie, S.B. and Williams, M.L. (1993) Do substitutes for leadership really substitute for leadership? An empirical examination of Kerr and Jermier's situational leadership model. *Organizational Behavior and Human Decision Processes* 54: 1–44.

Pollack, I. and Pickett, J.M. (1964) Intelligibility of excerpts from fluent speech: auditory vs. structural context. *Journal of Verbal Learning and Verbal Behavior* 3: 79–84.

Pollack, J.M. (1979) Obsessive-compulsive personality: a review. *Psychological Review* 86: 225–41.

Popper, KR. (1959) *The Logic of Scientific Discovery*. London: Hutchinson.

Popper, K.R. (1968) *The Logic of Scientific Discovery*. London: Hutchinson.

Porras, J.L. and Robertson, P.J. (1992) Organizational development: theory, practice and research, in M.D. Dunnette and L.M. Hough (eds) *Handbook of Industrial and Organizational Psychology*. Palo Alto, CA: Consulting Psychologists Press.

Posner, M.I. and Petersen, S.E. (1990) The attention system of the human brain. *Annual Review of Neuroscience* 13: 25–42.

Potter, J. (1996) Discourse analysis and constructionist approaches: theoretical background, in J.T.E. Richardson (ed.) *Handbook of Qualitative Research Methods for Psychology and the Social Sciences*. Leicester: British Psychological Society.

Potter, J. and Wetherell, M. (1987) *Discourse and Social Psychology: Beyond attitudes and behaviour*. London: Sage.

Potter, J., Stringer, P. and Wetherell, M. (1984) *Social Texts and Context: Literature and social psychology*. London: Routledge and Kegan Paul.

Power, M.J. and Champion, L.A. (1992) An overview of models and treatments, in L.A. Champion and M.J. Power (eds) *Adult Psychological Problems*. London: Falmer.

Power, M.J. and Dalgleish, T. (1997) *Cognition and Emotion: From order to disorder*. Hove: Lawrence Erlbaum.

Pratt, F. (1985) A perspective on traditional artistic practices, in N.H. Freeman and M.V. Cox (eds) *Visual Order: The nature and development of pictorial representation*. Cambridge: Cambridge University Press.

Pratt, M.W. and Norris, J.E. (1994) *The Social Psychology of Aging*. Oxford: Blackwell.

Prichard, J.C. (1837) *Treatise on Insanity and Other Disorders Affecting the Mind*. Philadelphia, PA: Haswell, Barrington and Haswell.

Priest, V. and Speller, V. (1991) *The Risk Factor Management Manual*. Oxford: Radcliffe Medical Press.

Prinzmetal, W. and Lyon, C.E. (1996) The word-detection effect: sophisticated guessing or perceptual enhancement? *Memory and Cognition* 24: 331–41.

Prochaska, J.O. and DiClemente, C.C. (1984) *The Transtheoretical Approach: Crossing traditional boundaries of therapy*. Homewood, IL: Dow Jones/Irwin.

Prochaska, J., DiClemente, C. and Verdi, M. (1987) *Understanding Yourself as a Smoker*. East Greenwich, RI: Mancini.

Pugh, D.S., Hickson, D.J., Hinings, C.R. and Turner, C. (1968) Dimensions of organization structure. *Administrative Science Quarterly* 13: 65–105.

Pulakos, E.D., Schmitt, N. and Ostroff, C. (1986) A warning about the use of a standard deviation across dimensions within ratees to measure halo. *Journal of Applied Psychology* 71: 29–32.

Purkhardt, S. (1993) *Transforming Social Representations: A social psychology of common sense and science.* London: Routledge.

Quattrone, G.A. and Jones, E. (1980) The perception of variability within in-groups and out-groups: Implications for the laws of small numbers. *Journal of Personality and Social Psychology* 38: 141–52.

Quay, L.C. (1971) Language, dialect, reinforcement, and the intelligence test performance of Negro children. *Child Development* 42: 5–15.

Rabbie, J.M. and Horowitz, M. (1969) Arousal of ingroup and outgroup bias by chance win or loss. *Journal of Personality and Social Psychology* 13: 269–77.

Rabbie, J.M. and Horowitz, M. (1988) Categories versus groups as explanatory concepts in intergroup relations. *European Journal of Social Psychology* 18: 117–83.

Rabbie, J. and Wilkens, G. (1971) Intergroup competition and its effects on intra-group and inter-group relations. *European Journal of Social Psychology* 1(2): 215–34.

Rabbie, J.M., Schot, J.C. and Visser, L. (1989) Social identity theory: a conceptual and empirical critique from the perspective of a behavioural interaction model. *European Journal of Social Psychology* 19: 171–202.

Rachel, J. (1996) Ethnography: practical implementation, in J.T.E. Richardson (ed.) *Handbook of Qualitative Research Methods for Psychology and the Social Sciences.* Leicester: British Psychological Society.

Rachman, S.J. and Wilson, G.T. (1980) *The Effects of Psychological Therapy,* 2nd enlarged edn. New York: Pergamon.

Radin, N., Oyserman, D. and Benn, R. (1991) Grandfathers, teen mothers and children under two, in P.K. Smith (ed.) *The Psychology of Grandparenthood: An international perspective.* London: Routledge.

Rafaeli, A. and Klimoski, R.J. (1983) Predicting sales success through handwriting analysis: an evaluation of the effects of training and handwriting sample content. *Journal of Applied Psychology* 68(2): 212–17.

Rahe, R.H. (1973) Life change and subsequent illness reports, in E.K.E. Gunderson and R.H. Rahe (eds) *Life Stress and Illness.* Springfield, IL: C.C. Thomas.

Rahe, R.H. (1975) Life changes and near-future illness reports, in L. Levi (ed.) *Emotions: Their parameters and measurement.* New York: Raven Press.

Rand, R.S., Wise, R.A. and Nides, M. (1992) MDI adherence in a clinical trial. *American Review of Respiratory Diseases* 146: 1559–64.

Randich, A. and LoLordo, V.M. (1979) Associative and non-associative theories of the UCS preexposure phenomenon: implications for Pavlovian conditioning. *Psychological Bulletin* 86: 523–48.

Rank, S. and Jacobson, C. (1977) Hospital nurses' compliance with medication overdose orders: a failure to replicate. *Journal of Health and Social Behaviour* 18: 188–93.

Rapoport, J.L. (1988) The biology of obsessions and compulsions. *Scientific American* March: 63–9.

Rasmussen, J. (1982) Human errors: a taxonomy for describing human malfunction in industrial installations. *Journal of Occupational Accidents* 311–33.

Raven, B. and Kruglanski, A. (1970) Conflict and power, in P. Swingle (ed.) *The Structure of Conflict.* New York: Academic Press.

Rayner, K. and Pollatsek, A. (1989) *The Psychology of Reading.* London: Prentice Hall.

Rayner, K. and Sereno, S.C. (1994) Eye movements in reading: psycholinguistic studies, in M.A. Gernsbacher (ed.) *Handbook of Psycholinguistics.* New York: Academic Press.

Rayner, K., Carlson, M. and Frazier, L. (1983) The interaction of syntax and semantics during sentence processing: eye movements in the analysis of semantically biased sentences. *Journal of Verbal Learning and Verbal Behavior* 22: 358–74.

Rayner, K., Sereno, S.C. and Raney, G.E. (1996) Eye movement control in reading: a comparison of two types of models. *Journal of Experimental Psychology: Human Perception and Performance* 22: 1188–200.

Read, C., Zhang, Y., Nie, H. and Ding, B. (1986) The ability to manipulate speech sounds depends on knowing alphabetic spelling. *Cognition* 24: 31–44.

Reason, J. (1979) Actions not as planned: the price of automatization, in G. Underwood and R. Stevens (eds) *Aspects of Consciousness,* vol. 1, *Psychological Issues.* London: Academic Press.

Reason, J. (1984) Lapses of attention in everyday life, in R. Parasuraman and D.R. Davies (eds) *Varieties of Attention.* Orlando, FL: Academic Press.

Reason, J. (1990) *Human Error.* New York: Cambridge University Press.

Reason, P. and Rowan, J. (eds) (1981) *Human Enquiry: A sourcebook in new paradigm research.* Chichester: Wiley.

Redmond, D.E. (1985) Neurochemical basis for anxiety and anxiety disorders: evidence from drugs which decrease human fear or anxiety, in A.H. Tuma and J.D. Maser (eds) *Anxiety and the Anxiety Disorders.* Hillsdale, NJ: Lawrence Erlbaum.

Reeder, G.D. and Fulks, J.L. (1980) When actions speak louder than words: implicational schemata and the attribution of ability. *Journal of Experimental Social Psychology,* 16: 33–46.

Regan, D.T and Fazio, R.H. (1977) On the consistency between attitudes and behavior: look to the method of attitude formation. *Journal of Experimental Social Psychology* 13: 28–45.

Reicher, G. M. (1969) Perceptual recognition as a function of meaningfulness of stimulus material. *Journal of Experimental Psychology* 81: 274–80.

Reicher, S. (1984) Social influence in a crowd: an explanation of the limits of crowd action in terms of a social identity model. *European Journal of Social Psychology* 14: 1–21.

Reicher, S. (1987) Crowd behaviour as social action, in J. Turner, M. Hogg, P. Oakes, S. Reicher, S., and M. Wetherell (eds) *Rediscovering the Social Group.* Oxford: Blackwell.

Reicher, S. (1993) On the construction of social categories: from collective action to rhetoric and back again, in B. Gonazalez (ed.) *Psicologia Cultural*. Seville: Eudema.

Reicher, S. (1996) The battle of Westminster: developing the social identity model of crowd behaviour in order to deal with the initiation and development of collective conflict. *European Journal of Social Psychology* 26: 115–34.

Reicher, S. and Hopkins, N. (1996) Self category constructions in political rhetoric: an analysis of Thatcher's and Kinnock's speeches concerning the British miner's strike (1984–1985). *European Journal of Social Psychology* 26: 353–71.

Reitman, J.S. (1974) Without surreptitious rehearsal, information in short-term memory decays. *Journal of Verbal Learning and Verbal Behavior* 13: 365–77.

Renzulli, J.S. and Delcourt, M.A. (1986) The legacy and logic of research on the identification of gifted persons. *Gifted Child Quarterly* 30: 20–3.

Rescorla, R.A. (1968) Probability of shock in the presence and absence of CS in fear conditioning. *Journal of Comparative and Physiological Psychology* 66: 1–5.

Rescorla, R.A. (1969) Pavlovian conditioned inhibition. *Psychological Bulletin* 72: 77–94.

Rescorla, R.A. (1988) Pavlovian conditioning: it's not what you think it is. *American Psychologist* 43: 151–60.

Rescorla, R.A. (1996) Preservation of Pavlovian associations through extinction. *Quarterly Journal of Experimental Psychology* 49B: 245–58.

Rescorla, R.A. and Wagner, A.R. (1972) A theory of Pavlovian conditioning: variations in the effectiveness of reinforcement and nonreinforcement, in A.H. Black and W.F. Prokasy (eds) *Classical Conditioning II: Current research and theory*. New York: Appleton.

Restle, F. (1979) Coding theory of the perception of motion configuration. *Psychological Review* 86: 1–24.

Richard, R., van der Pligt, J. and de Vries, N. (1995) Anticipated affective reactions and prevention of AIDS. *British Journal of Social Psychology* 34(1): 9–22.

Richards, M. (1994) The international year of the family: family research. *The Psychologist* 8: 17–24.

Richardson, J.T.E. (ed.) (1996) *Handbook of Qualitative Research Methods for Psychology and the Social Sciences*. Leicester: British Psychological Society.

Riddoch, M.J. and Humphreys, G.W. (1987) Visual object processing in aphasia: a case of semantic access agnosia. *Cognitive Neuropsychology* 4: 131–85.

Ridley, M. (1993) *The Red Queen: Sex and the evolution of human nature*. Harmondsworth: Penguin.

Riley, A.L. and Wetherington, C.L. (1987) The differential effects of naloxone hydrochloride on the acquisition and maintenance of schedule-induced polydipsia. *Pharmacology, Biochemistry and Behaviour* 26: 677–81.

Riley, A.L. and Wetherington, C.L. (1989) Is the rat a small furry human? (An analysis of an animal model of human alcoholism), in S.B. Klein and R.R. Mowrer (eds) *Contemporary Learning Theories: Instrumental conditioning theory and the impact of biological constraints on learning*. Hillsdale, NJ: Lawrence Erlbaum.

Rips, L.J., Shoben, E.J. and Smith, E.E. (1973) Semantic distance and the verification of semantic relations. *Journal of Verbal Learning and Verbal Behaviour* 12: 1–20.

Rist, J.M. (1969) *Stoic Philosophy*. Cambridge: Cambridge University Press.

Ritter, S. (1986) Glucoprivation and the glucoprivic control of food intake, in R.C. Ritter, S. Ritter and C.D. Barnes (eds) *Feeding Behavior: Neural and humoral controls*. New York: Academic Press.

Rizley, R.C. and Rescorla, R.A. (1972) Associations in higher order conditioning and sensory preconditioning. *Journal of Comparative and Physiological Psychology* 81: 1–11.

Rizzo, M., Nawrot, M., Blake, R. and Damasio, A. (1992) A human visual disorder resembling Area V4 dysfunction in the monkey. *Neurology* 42: 1175–80.

Robbins, T.W. (1975) Relationship between reward-enhancing and stereotypical effects of psychomotor stimulant drugs. *Nature* 264: 57–9.

Robbins, T.W. and Everitt, B.J. (1992) Functions of dopamine in the dorsal and ventral striatum. *Seminars in the Neurosciences* 4: 119–28.

Robbins, T.W. and Koob, G.F. (1980) Selective disruption of displacement behaviour by lesions of the mesolimbic dopamine system. *Nature* 285: 409–12.

Robbins, T.W., Roberts, D.C.S. and Koob, G.F. (1983) Effects of d-amphetamine and apomorphine upon operant behaviour and schedule-induced licking in rats with 6-hydroxydopamine-induced lesions of the nucleus accumbens. *Journal of Pharmacology and Experimental Therapeutics* 224: 662–73.

Robbins, T.W., Anderson, E.J., Barker, D.R., Bradley, A.C., Fearnyhough, C., Henson, R. and Hudson, S.R. (1996) Working memory in chess. *Memory and Cognition*. 24: 83–93.

Robertson, R. (1980) Aspects of identity and authority in sociological theory, in R. Robertson and B. Holzner (eds) *Identity and Authority: Explorations in the theory of society*. New York: St Martin's Press

Robins, L.N. (1966) *Deviant Children Grown Up: A sociological and psychological study of sociopathic personality*. Baltimore, MA: Williams and Wilkins.

Robinson, J. and Strong, P. (1987) *Nursing Policy Studies I: Professional nursing advice after Griffiths. An interim report*. University of Warwick: Nursing Policy Studies Unit.

Robinson, T.E. and Berridge, K.C. (1993) The neural basis of drug craving: an incentive-sensitization theory of addiction. *Brain Research Reviews* 18: 247–91.

Robinson, W.P. (1996) *Social Groups and Identities*. London: Butterworth Heinemann.

Rodrigo, T., Chamizo, V.D., McLaren, I.P.L. and Mackintosh, N.J. (1997) Blocking in the spatial domain. *Journal of Experimental Psychology: Animal Behavior Processes* 23: 110–18.

Roe, R.A. (1995) *Work and Organizational Psychology at the Cross-Roads: A European view*. WORC Paper 95.07.016/4. Tilburg: Work and Organization Research Centre.

Roe, R.A., Coetsier, P., Levy-Leboyer, C., Peiro, J.M. and Wilpert, B. (1994) The teaching of work and organizational psychology in Europe: towards the development of a reference model. *European Work and Organizational Psychologist* 4: 355–66.

Roediger, H.L. (1990) Implicit memory: retention without remembering. *American Psychologist* 45: 1043–56.

Roethlisberger, F.J. and Dickson, W.J. (1939) *Management and the Workers*. Cambridge, MA: Harvard University Press.

Roethlisberger, F.J., Dickson, W.J. and Wright, H. (1956) *Management and the Worker*. Cambridge, MA: Harvard University Press.

Rogers, B.J. and Collett, T.S. (1989) The appearance of surfaces specified by motion parallax and binocular disparity. *Quarterly Journal of Experimental Psychology* 41A: 697–717.

Rogers, B.J. and Graham, M.E. (1979) Motion parallax as an independent cue for depth perception. *Perception* 8: 125–34.

Rogers, C.R. (1947) The case of Mary Jane Tildon, in W.U. Snyder (ed.) *Casebook of Non-Directive Counseling*. Cambridge, MA: Houghton Mifflin.

Rogers, C.R. (1951) *Client-Centred Therapy: Its current practice, implications and theory*. Boston; MA: Houghton Mifflin.

Rogers, C.R. (1959) A theory of therapy, personality, and interpersonal relationships, as developed in the client-centred framework, in S. Koch (ed.) *Psychology: A study of a science*, vol. 3. New York: McGraw-Hill.

Rogers, C.R. (1961) *On Becoming a Person: A therapist's view of psychotherapy*. Boston; MA: Houghton Mifflin.

Rogers, C.R., Gendlin, E.T., Keisler, D.J. and Truax, C.B. (1967) *The Therapeutic Relationship and its Impact: A study of psychotherapy with schizophrenics*. Madison, WI: University of Wisconsin Press.

Rogers, E.M. and Shoemaker, F.F. (1971) *Communication of Innovations*. New York: Free Press.

Rolls, B.J. and Rolls, E.T. (1982) *Thirst*. Cambridge: Cambridge University Press.

Rolls, B.J., Rowe, E.A., Rolls, E.T., Kingston, B., Megson, A. and Gunary, R. (1981) Variety in a meal enhances food intake in man. *Physiology and Behavior* 26: 215–21.

Rolls, E.T. (1975) *The Brain and Reward*. Oxford: Pergamon.

Rolls, E.T. (1976) The neurophysiological basis of brain-stimulation reward, in A. Wauquier and E.T. Rolls (eds) *Brain-stimulation Reward*. Amsterdam: North-Holland.

Rolls, E.T. (1979) Effects of electrical stimulation of the brain on behavior, in K. Connolly (ed.) *Psychology Surveys*, vol. 2. Hemel Hempstead: Allen and Unwin.

Rolls, E.T. (1992a) Neurophysiological mechanisms underlying face processing within and beyond the temporal cortical visual areas. *Philosophical Transactions of the Royal Society* 335: 11–21.

Rolls, E.T. (1992b) Neurophysiology and functions of the primate amygdala, in J. P. Aggleton (ed.) *The Amygdala*. New York: Wiley-Liss.

Rolls, E.T. (1994) Neural processing related to feeding in primates, in C.R. Legg and D.A. Booth (eds) *Appetite: Neural and behavioural bases*. Oxford: Oxford University Press.

Rolls, E.T. (1996) The orbitofrontal cortex. *Philosophical Transactions of the Royal Society* B351: 1433–44.

Rolls, E.T. (1997) Taste and olfactory processing in the brain. *Critical Reviews in Neurobiology* 11: 263–87.

Rolls, E. T. (1999) *The Brain and Emotion*. Oxford: Oxford University Press.

Rolls, E.T. and Baylis, L.L. (1994) Gustatory, olfactory and visual convergence within the primate orbitofrontal cortex. *Journal of Neuroscience* 14: 5437–52.

Rolls, E.T. and Rolls, B.J. (1973) Altered food preferences after lesions in the basolateral region of the amygdala in the rat. *Journal of Comparative and Physiological Psychology* 83: 248–59.

Rolls, E.T. and Rolls, B.J. (1982) Brain mechanisms involved in feeding, in L.M. Barker (ed.) *Psychobiology of Human Food Selection*. Westport, CT: AVI Publishing.

Rolls, E.T. and Treves, A. (1998) *Neural Networks and Brain Function*. Oxford: Oxford University Press.

Rolls, E.T., Judge, S.J. and Sanghera, M.K. (1977) Activity of neurons in the inferotemporal cortex of the alert monkey. *Brain Research* 130: 229–38.

Rolls, E.T., Burton, M.J. and Mora, F. (1980) Neurophysiological analysis of brain-stimulation reward in the monkey. *Brain Research* 194: 339–57.

Rolls, E.T., Murzi, E., Yaxley, S., Thorpe, S.J. and Simpson, S.J. (1986) Sensory-specific satiety: food-specific reduction in responsiveness of ventral forebrain neurons after feeding in the monkey. *Brain Research* 368: 79–86.

Rolls, E.T., Sienkiewicz, Z.J. and Yaxley, S. (1989) Hunger modulates the responses to gustatory stimuli of single neurons in the caudolateral orbitofrontal cortex of the macaque monkey. *European Journal of Neuroscience* 1: 53–60.

Rolls, E.T., Yaxley, S. and Sienkiewicz, Z.J. (1990) Gustatory responses of single neurons in the orbitofrontal cortex of the macaque monkey. *Journal of Neurophysiology* 64: 1055–66.

Rolls, E.T., Francis, S., Bowtell, R., Browning, D., Clare, S., Smith, E. and McGlone, F. (1997) Pleasant touch activates the orbitofrontal cortex. *Neuroimage* 5: S17.

Roos, P.E. and Cohen, L.H. (1987) Sex roles and social support as moderators of life stress adjustment. *Journal of Personality and Social Psychology* 52: 576–85.

Rorer, L.G. and Widiger, T.A. (1983) Personality structure and assessment. *Annual Review of Psychology* 34: 431–63.

Ros, M., Cano, I. and Huici, C. (1987) Language and intergroup perception in Spain. *Journal of Language and Social Psychology* 6 (3–4): 243–259.

Rosch, E. (1978) Principles of categorisation, in E. Rosch and B. Lloyd (eds) *Cognition and Categorisation*. Hillsdale, NJ: Lawrence Erlbaum.

Rosch, E. and Mervis, C.B. (1975) Family resemblances: studies in the internal structure of categories. *Cognitive Psychology* 7: 573–605.

Rosch, E., Mervis, C.B., Gray, W.D., Johnson, D.M. and Boyes-Braem, P. (1976) Basic objects in natural categories. *Cognitive Psychology* 8: 382–439.

Rosch, P.J. and Pelletier, K.R. (1989) Designing worksite stress-management programs, in L.R. Murphy and T.F. Schoenborn (eds) *Stress Management in Work Settings*. New York: Praeger.

Rose, D. (1995) A portrait of the brain, in R. Gregory, J. Harris, P. Heard and D. Rose (eds) *The Artful Eye*. Oxford: Oxford University Press.

Rose, S. and Blank, M. (1974) The potency of context in children's cognition: an illustration through conservation. *Child Development* 45: 499–502.

Rosellini, R.A. and Lashley, R.L. (1982) The opponent-process theory of motivation VIII: quantitative and qualitative manipulations of food both modulate adjunctive behaviour. *Learning and Motivation* 13: 222–39.

Rosenberg, E.L. and Ekman, P. (1994) Coherence between expressive and experiential systems in emotion. *Cognition and Emotion* 8: 201–29.

Rosenberg, M. (1979) *Conceiving the Self*. New York: Basic Books.

Rosenberg, M. (1986) *Conceiving the Self*. Malabar, FL: Kreiger.

Rosenberg, M.J. and Hovland, C.I. (1960) Cognitive, affective and behavioural components of attitudes, in C.I. Hovland and M.J. Rosenberg (eds) *Attitude Organization and Change: An analysis of consistency among attitude components*. New Haven, CT: Yale University Press.

Rosenhan, D.L. (1973) On being sane in insane places. *Science* 179: 250–8.

Rosenhan, D.L. and Seligman, M.E.P. (1995) *Abnormal Psychology*, 3rd edn. New York: Norton.

Rosenman, R.H. and Friedman, M. (1974) Neurogenic factors in pathogenesis of coronary heart disease. *Medical Clinics of North America* 58: 269–79.

Rosenman, R.H., Brand, R.J., Jenkins, C.D., Friedman, M., Straus, R. and Wurm, M. (1975) Coronary heart disease in the Western Collaborative Group Study: final follow-up experience of $8\frac{1}{2}$ years. *Journal of the American Medical Association* 233: 872–7.

Rosenthal, R. and Fode, K. (1963) The effects of experimenter bias on the performance of the albino rat. *Behavioral Science* 8: 183–9.

Rosenthal, R. and Jacobson, L. (1968) *Pygmalion in the Classroom*. New York: Holt.

Rosenzweig, M.R., Leiman, A.L. and Breedlove, S.M. (1996) *Biological Psychology*. Sunderland, MA: Sinauer.

Ross, H.L., Campbell, D.T. and Glass, G.V. (1973) Determining the social effects of a legal reform: the British 'breathalyser' crackdown of 1967. *American Behavioral Scientist* 13: 493–509.

Ross, L. (1977) The intuitive psychologist and his shortcomings: distortions in the attribution process, in L. Berkowitz (ed.) *Advances in Experimental Social Psychology*, vol. 10. New York: Academic Press.

Ross, L., Amabile, T.M. and Steinmetz, J.L. (1977a) Social roles, social control and biases in social-perception processes. *Journal of Personality and Social Psychology* 35: 485–94.

Ross, L., Greene, D. and House, P. (1977b) The 'false consensus effect': an egocentric bias in social perception and attribution processes. *Journal of Experimental and Social Psychology* 13: 279–301.

Rossi, A.S. and Rossi, P.H. (1990) *Of Human Bonding*. New York: Aldine de Gruyter.

Roth, I. (1986) An introduction to object perception, in I. Roth and J.P. Frisby (eds) *Perception and Representation: A cognitive approach*. Milton Keynes: Open University Press.

Roth, S. and Cohen, L.J. (1986) Approach, avoidance and coping with stress. *American Psychologist* 41: 813–19.

Rothbart, M.K. (1986) Longitudinal observation of infant temperament. *Developmental Psychology* 22: 356–65.

Rotter, J.B. (1954) *Social Learning and Clinical Psychology*. New York: Prentice Hall.

Rotter, J.B. (1966) Generalised expectancies for internal versus external control of reinforcement. *Psychological Monographs* 80(609).

Roy, D.F. (1991) Improving recall by eye-witnesses through the cognitive interview: practical applications and implications for the police service. *The Psychologist* 4: 398–400.

Rubin, K.H., Watson, K.S. and Jambor, T.W. (1978) Free-play behaviors in preschool and kindergarten children. *Child Development* 49: 534–6.

Ruble, D.N. and Stangor, C. (1986) Stalking the elusive schema: insights from developmental and social-psychological analyses of gender schemas. *Social Cognition* 4: 227–61.

Rumelhart, D.E. (1975) Notes on a schema for stories, in D.G. Bobrow and A.M. Collins (eds) *Representation and Understanding: Studies in cognitive science*. New York: Academic Press.

Runciman, W. (1966) *Relative Deprivation and Social Justice*. London: Routledge and Kegan Paul.

Rundus, D. and Atkinson, R.C. (1970) Rehearsal processes in free recall, a procedure for direct observation. *Journal of Verbal Learning and Verbal Behavior* 9: 99–105.

Russell, J. (1994) Is there universal recognition of emotion from facial expression? A review of the cross-cultural studies. *Psychological Bulletin* 115: 102–41.

Rust, J. and Golombok, S. (1989) *Modern Psychometrics: The science of psychological assessment*. London: Routledge.

Rutter, M., Graham, P., Chadwick, O. and Yule, W. (1976) Adolescent turmoil: fact or fiction? *Journal of Child Psychology and Psychiatry* 17: 35–56.

Ryan, C. and Judd, C. (1992) False consensus and outgroup homogeneity: a methodological note on their relationship. *British Journal of Social Psychology* 34: 269–83.

Rybowiak, V., Garst, H., Frse, M. and Batinic, B. (1998) Error Orientation Questionnaire (EOQ): reliability, validity, and different language equivalence. *Journal of Organizational Behavior*.

Ryckman, R.M. (1993) *Theories of Personality*, 5th edn. Pacific Grove, CA: Brooks/Cole.

Rylander, G. (1939) Personality changes after operations on the frontal lobes. *Acta Psychiatrica Neurologica* (supplement no. 30).

Ryle, G. (1949) *The Concept of Mind*. London: Hutchinson.

Sachdev, I. and Bourhis, R. (1984) Minimal majorities and minorities. *European Journal of Social Psychology* 14: 35–52.

Sachdev, I. and Bourhis, R. (1985) Social categorisation and power differentials in group relations. *European Journal of Social Psychology* 15: 413–34.

Sachdev, I. and Bourhis, R. (1987) Status differentials and intergroup behaviour. *European Journal of Social Psychology* 17: 277–93.

Sachs, J.S. (1983) Negative factors in brief psychotherapy: an empirical assessment. *Journal of Consulting and Clinical Psychology* 51: 557–64.

Sacks, O. (1973) *Awakenings*. London: Duckworth.

Saffran, E.M., Schwartz, M.F. and Marin, O.S.M. (1980) The word order problem in agrammatism, II, Production. *Brain and Language* 10: 249–62.

Safran, J.D. and Segal, Z.V. (1990) *Interpersonal Processes in Cognitive Therapy*. New York: Basic Books.

Salamone, J.D. (1988) Dopaminergic involvement in activational aspects of motivation: effects of haloperidol on schedule-induced activity, feeding and foraging in rats. *Psychobiology* 16: 196–206.

Sampson, E. (1983) Deconstructing psychology's subject. *Journal of Mind and Behaviour* 4: 135–64.

Sampson, E. (1988) The debate on individualism: indigenous psychologies of the individual and societal functioning. *American Psychologist* 43: 15–22.

Sampson, E.E. (1993) *Celebrating the Other*. Hemel Hempstead: Harvester Wheatsheaf.

Samuel, A.G. (1981) Phonemic restoration: insights from a new methodology. *Journal of Experimental Psychology: General* 110: 474–94.

Sanders, G. and Baron, R. (1977) Is social comparison irrelevant for producing choice shifts? *Journal of Experimental Social Psychology* 13: 303–14.

Sanghera, M.K., Rolls, E.T. and Roper-Hall, A. (1979) Visual responses of neurons in the dorsolateral amygdala of the alert monkey. *Experimental Neurology* 63: 610–26.

Sapolsky, R.M. (1994) *Why Zebras Don't Get Ulcers*. New York: W.H. Freeman.

Sarason, I.G., Smith, R.E. and Diener, E. (1975) Personality research: components of variance attributable to the person and the situation. *Journal of Personality and Social Psychology* 32: 199–204.

Sarraga, E. (1993) The abuse of children, in R. Dallos and E. McLaughlin (eds) *Social Problems and the Family*. London: Sage.

Saupe, R. and Frese, M. (1981) Faktoren für das Erleben und die Bewältigung von Stress im Schreibdienst, in M. Frese (ed.) *Stress im Büro*. Bern: Huber.

Savage-Rumbaugh, E.S., McDonald, K., Sevcik, R.A., Hopkins, W.D. and Rupert, E. (1986) Spontaneous symbol acquisition and communicative use by pgymy chimpanzees (*Pan paniscus*). *Journal of Experimental Psychology: General* 115: 211–35.

Saxe, G. (1979) A developmental analysis of notational counting. *Child Development* 48: 1512–20.

Saxe, G. (1991) *Culture and Cognitive Development: Studies in mathematical understanding*. Hillsdale, NJ: Lawrence Erlbaum.

Saxe, G.. and Posner, J.K. (1983) The development of numerical cognition: cross-cultural perspectives, in H. Ginsburg (ed.) *The Development of Mathematical Thinking*. New York: Academic Press.

Scadding, J.G. (1967) Diagnosis: the clinician and the computer. *Lancet* 2: 877–82.

Scarr, S. (1992) Developmental theories for the 1990s: development and individual differences. *Child Development* 63: 1–19.

Scarr, S. and Salapatek, P. (1970) Patterns of fear development during infancy. *Merrill-Palmer Quarterly* 16: 53–90.

Schachter, S. (1959) *The Psychology of Affiliation*. Palo Alto, CA: Stanford University Press.

Schachter, S. (1971) Importance of cognitive control in obesity. *American Psychologist* 26: 129–44.

Schachter, S. and Singer, J.E. (1962) Cognitive, social, and physiological determinants of emotional state. *Psychological Review* 69: 379–99.

Schacter, D.L. (1987) Implicit memory: history and current status. *Journal of Experimental Psychology: Learning, Memory, and Cognition* 13: 501–18.

Schacter, S., Ellertson, N. McBride, N. and Gregory, D. (1951) An experimental study of cohesiveness and productivity. *Human Relations* 4: 229–38.

Schaefer, H. and Blohmke, M. (1977) *Herzkrank durch psychosozialen Stress*. Heidelberg: Huethig.

Schäfer, M. and Smith, P.K. (1996) Teachers' perceptions of play fighting and real fighting in primary school. *Educational Research* 38: 173–81.

Schallberger, U. (1988) Berufsausbildung und Intelligenzentwicklung (vocational training and the development of intelligence), in K. Huafeli, U. Kraft and U. Schallberger (eds) *Berufsausbildung und Persönlichkeitsentwicklung: Eine Längsschnittuntersuchung*. Bern: Huber.

Schank, R.C. (1976) *Conceptual Information Processing*. Amsterdam: North-Holland.

Schank, R.C. (1978) Predictive understanding, in R.N. Campbell and P.T. Smith (eds) *Recent Advances in the Psychology of Language: Formal and experimental approaches*. New York: Plenum.

Scheff, T.J. (1966) *Being Mentally Ill: A sociological theory*. Chicago: Aldine

Scherer, K.R. (1994) Toward a concept of 'modal emotions', in P. Ekman and R.J. Davidson (eds) *The Nature of Emotion: Fundamental questions*. Oxford: Oxford University Press.

Scherer, K.R., Summerfield, W.B. and Wallbott, H.G. (1983) Cross-national research on antecedents and components of emotion: a progress report. *Social Science Information* 22: 355–85.

Schiff, B.B. and Lamon, M. (1989) Inducing emotion by unilateral contraction of facial muscles: a new look at hemispheric specialization and the experience of emotion. *Neuropsychologia* 27: 923–35.

Schiff, B.B. and Lamon, M. (1994) Inducing emotion by unilateral contraction of hand muscles. *Cortex* 30: 247–54.

Schiller, P.H. (1985) A model for the generation of visually guided saccadic eye movements, in D. Rose and V.G. Dobson (eds) *Models of the Visual Cortex*. Chichester: Wiley.

Schlegel, R.P. (1975) Multidimensional measurement of attitude towards smoking marijuana. *Canadian Journal of Behavioral Science* 7: 387–96.

Schlegel, R.P. and DiTecco, D. (1982) Attitudinal structures and the attitude–behavior relation, in M.P. Zanna, E.T. Higgins and C.P. Herman (eds) *Consistency in Social Behavior: The Ontario Symposium*, vol. 2. Hillsdale, NJ: Lawrence Erlbaum.

Schlenker, B. (1982) Translating actions into attitudes: an identity-analytic approach to the explanation of social conduct. *Advances in Experimental Social Psychology* 15: 193–247.

Schlenker, B.R. and Leary, M.R. (1982) Audiences' reactions to self-enhancing, self-denigrating and accurate self-presentations. *Journal of Experimental Social Psychology* 18: 89–104.

Schlenker, B.R., Weigold, M.F. and Hallam, J.R. (1990) Self-serving attributions in social context: effects of self-esteem and social pressure. *Journal of Personality and Social Psychology* 58: 855–63.

Schmidt, F.L. and Hunter, J.E. (1981) Employment testing: old theories and new research findings. *American Psychologist* 36: 1128–37.

Schmidt, K.-H., Kleinbeck, U. and Rutenfranz, J. (1981a) Arbeitspsychologische Effekte von Änderungen des Arbeitsinhaltes bei Montagetätigkeiten. *Zeitschrift für Arbeitswissenschaft* 35: 162–7.

Schmidt, K.-H., Schweisfurth, W., Kleinbeck, U. and Rutenfranz, J. (1981b) Einige arbeitspsychologische Ergebnisse zur Wirkung von Arbeitsinhaltsveränderungen bei Teilefertigungstätigkeiten. *Zeitschrift für Arbeitswissenschaft* 35: 101–7.

Schmitt, N., Gooding, R.Z., Noe, R.A. and Kirsch, M. (1984) Meta-analyses of validity studies published between 1964 and 1982 and the investigation of study characteristics. *Personnel Psychology* 37: 407–22.

Schneider, G.E. (1969) Two visual systems. *Science* 163: 895–902.

Schneider, W. and Shiffrin, R.M. (1977) Controlled and automatic human information processing I: detection, search, and attention. *Psychological Review* 84: 1–66.

Schofield, M. (1965) *The Sexual Behaviour of Young People*. London: Longman.

Scholz, G. and Schuler, H. (1993) Das nomologische Netzwerk des Assessment Centres: Eine Metaanalyse. *Zeitschrift für Arbeits- und Organisationspsychologie* 37: 73–85.

Schönpflug, W. (1985) Goal directed behaviour as a source of stress: psychological origins and consequences of inefficiency, in M. Frese and J. Sabini (eds) *Goal Directed Behaviour: The concept of action in psychology*. Hillsdale, NJ: Lawrence Erlbaum.

Schuler, H. (1993) Social validity of selection situations: a concept and some empirical results, in H. Schuler, J.L. Farr and M. Smith (eds) *Personnel Selection and Assessment: Individual and organizational perspectives*. Hillsdale, NJ: Lawrence Erlbaum.

Schultz, T.R. and Mendelson, N.R. (1975) The use of covariation as a principle of causal analysis. *Child Development* 46: 394–9.

Schultz, W., Apicella, P. and Ljungberg, T. (1993) Responses of monkey dopamine neurons to reward and conditioned stimuli during successive steps of learning a delayed response task. *Journal of Neuroscience* 13: 900–13.

Schultz, W., Dayan, P. and Montague, P.R. (1997) A neural substrate of prediction and reward. *Science* 275: 1593–9.

Schuman, H. (1983) Survey research and the fundamental attribution error. *Personality and Social Psychology Bulletin*, 9: 103.

Schurig, V. (1985) Stages in the development of tool behavior in the chimpanzee (Pan troglodytes), in M. Frese and J. Sabini (eds) *Goal Directed Behavior: The concept of action in psychology*. Hillsdale, NJ: Lawrence Erlbaum.

Schwartz, S.H. and Tessler, R.C. (1972) A test of a model for reducing measured attitude-behavior discrepancies. *Journal of Personality and Social Psychology* 24: 225–36.

Schwarzer, R. (1992) Self-efficacy in the adoption and maintenance of health behaviours: theoretical approaches and a new model, in R. Schwarzer (ed.) *Self-efficacy: Thought control of action*. Washington, DC: Hemisphere.

Schwarzer, R. and Fuchs, R. (1996) Self-efficacy and health behaviours, in M. Conner and P. Norman (eds) *Predicting Health Behaviour*. Buckingham: Open University Press.

Scott, S.K., Young, A.W., Calder, A.J., Hellawell, D.J., Aggleton, J.P. and Johnson, M. (1997) Impaired auditory recognition of fear and anger following bilateral amygdala lesions. *Nature* 385: 254–7.

Scull, A. (1987) Desperate remedies: a Gothic tale of madness and modern medicine. *Psychological Medicine* 17: 561–77.

Searle, J.R. (1979) Metaphor, in A. Ortony (ed.) *Metaphor and Thought*. Cambridge: Cambridge University Press.

Sears, D. (1986) College sophomores in the laboratory: influences of a narrow database on social psychology's view of human nature. *Journal of Personality and Social Psychology* 51: 515–30.

Seaver, W.B. (1973) The effects of naturally induced teacher expectancies. *Journal of Personality and Social Psychology* 28: 333–42.

Secord, P. (1959) Stereotyping and favourableness in the perception of Negro faces. *Journal of Abnormal and Social Psychology* 59: 309–21.

Secord, P., Bevan, W. and Katz, B. (1956) Perceptual accentuation and the Negro stereotype. *Journal of Abnormal and Social Psychology* 53: 78–83.

Seligman, M.E.P. (1975) *Helplessness: On depression, development, and death*. San Francisco; CA: W.H. Freeman.

Seligman, M.E.P. (1996) The effectiveness of psychotherapy: the Consumer Reports study. *American Psychologist* 50: 965–74.

Seligman, M.E.P. and Maier, S.F. (1967) Failure to escape traumatic shock. *Journal of Experimental Psychology* 74: 1–9.

Selye, H. (1956) *The Stress of Life*. New York: McGraw-Hill.

Selye, H. (1976) *Stress in Health and Disease*. Boston, MA: Butterworths.

Semin, G.R. (1997) The relevance of language for social psychology, in C. McGarty and S.A. Haslam (eds) *The Message of Social Psychology*. Oxford: Blackwell.

Semin, G.R. and Fiedler, K. (1991) The Linguistic Category Model, its bases, application and range, in W. Stroebe and M. Hewstone (eds) *European Review of Social Psychology*, vol. 2. Chichester: Wiley.

Semmer, N. and Pfäfflin, M. (1978) *Interaktionstraining*. Weinheim: Beltz.

Seneca (1963) On anger, in J.W. Basore (trans.), *Moral Essays*. Cambridge, MA: Harvard University Press.

Sentis, K.P. and Burnstein, E. (1979) Remembering schema consistent information: effects of a balance schema on recognition memory. *Journal of Personality and Social Psychology*, 37: 2200–11.

Setterland, M. and Niendenthal, P. (1993) Who am I? Why am I here? Self-esteem, self-clarity, and prototype matching. *Journal of Personality and Social Psychology* 65(4): 769–80 .

Shaffer, D.R. (1993) *Developmental Psychology: Childhood and adolescence* 3rd edn. Pacific Grove, CA: Brooks/Cole.

Shallice, T. (1972) Dual functions of consciousness. *Psychological Review* 79: 383–93.

Shallice, T. (1991) From neuropsychology to mental structure. *Behavioral and Brain Sciences* 14: 429–39.

Shallice, T. and Warrington, E.K. (1970) Independent functioning of verbal memory stores: a neuropsychological study. *Quarterly Journal of Experimental Psychology* 22: 261–73.

Shanks, D.R. (1985) Forward and backward blocking in human contingency judgment. *Quarterly Journal of Experimental Psychology* 37B: 1–21.

Shanks, D.R. (1987) Acquisition functions in contingency judgment. *Learning and Motivation* 18: 147–66.

Shanks, D.R. (1995) *The Psychology of Associative Learning*. Cambridge: Cambridge University Press.

Shanks, D.R. and Dickinson, A. (1987) Associative accounts of causality judgment, in G.H. Bower (ed.) *The Psychology of Learning and Motivation*, vol. 21. San Diego, CA: Academic Press.

Shanks, D.R. and Dickinson, A. (1991) Instrumental judgment and performance under variations in action-outcome contingency and contiguity. *Memory and Cognition* 19: 353–60.

Shavitt, S. (1990) The role of attitude objects in attitude functions. *Journal of Experimental Social Psychology* 26: 124–48.

Shavitt, S. and Fazio, R.H. (1991) Effects of attribute salience on the consistency between attitudes and behavior predictions. *Personality and Social Psychology Bulletin* 17: 507–16.

Shaw, M. (1976) *Group Dynamics*. New York: McGraw-Hill.

Shea, M.T., Elkin, I., Imber, S.D., Sotsky, S.M., Watkins, J.T., Collins, J.F., Pilkonis, P.A., Beckham, E., Glass, D.R., Dolan, R.T. and Parloff, M.B. (1992) Course of depressive symptoms over follow-up: findings from the National Institute of Mental Health Treatment of Depression Collaborative Research Program. *Archives of General Psychiatry* 49: 782–7.

Sheeran, P. and Abraham, C. (1996) The Health Belief Model, in M. Conner and P. Norman (eds) *Predicting Health Behaviour*. Buckingham: Open University Press.

Sheppard, B.H., Hartwick, J. and Warshaw, P.R. (1988) The theory of reasoned action: a meta-analysis of past research with recommendations for modifications and future research. *Journal of Consumer Research* 15: 325–43.

Sheridan, C.H. and Radmacher, S.A. (1992) *Health Psychology: Challenging the biomedical model*. New York: Wiley.

Sherif, M. (1935) *The Psychology of Social Norms*. New York: Harper and Row.

Sherif, M. (1966a) *Group Conflict and Cooperation*. London: Routledge.

Sherif, M. (1966b) *In Common Predicament: Social psychology of intergroup conflict and cooperation*. Boston, MA: Houghton Mifflin.

Sherif, M. and Sherif, C. (1953a) *Groups in Harmony and Tension*. New York: Harper and Row.

Sherif, M. and Sherif, C. (1953b) *Social Psychology*. London: Harper and Row.

Sherif, M., White, B. and Harvey, O. (1955) Status in experimentally produced groups. *American Journal of Sociology* 60: 370–9.

Sherif, M., Harvey, O., White, B., Hood, W.R., and Sherif, C. (1961) *Intergroup Conflict and Cooperation: The Robbers Cave Experiment*. Norman, OK: University of Oklahoma Press.

Sherlock, B. and Morris, R. (1967) The evolution of the professional: a paradigm. *Sociological Inquiry* 37: 27–46.

Sherman, S.J., Presson, C.C. and Chassin, L. (1984) Mechanisms underlying the false consensus effect: the special role of threats to the self. *Personality and Social Psychology Bulletin* 10: 127–38.

Shields, J. (1962) *Monozygotic Twins Brought Up Apart and Brought Up Together*. London: Oxford University Press.

Shields, S.A. (1986) Are women 'emotional'?, in C. Tavris (ed.) *Everywoman's Emotional Well Being*. New York: Doubleday.

Shiffman, S.M. (1982) Relapse following smoking cessation: a situational analysis. *Journal of Consulting and Clinical Psychology* 50: 71–86.

Shiffrin, R.M. (1993) Short-term memory: a brief commentary. *Memory and Cognition* 21: 193–7.

Shiffrin, R.M. and Schneider, W. (1977) Controlled and automatic human information processing II: perceptual learning, automatic attending, and a general theory. *Psychological Review* 84: 127–90.

Shimura, T. and Shimokochi, M. (1990) Involvement of the lateral mesencephalic tegmentum in copulatory behavior of male rats: neuron activity if freely moving animals. *Neuroscience Research* 9: 173–83.

Shipley, R.H. (1981) Maintenance of smoking cessation: effect of follow-up letters, smoking motivation, muscle tension, and locus of control. *Journal of Consulting and Clinical Psychology* 49: 982–4.

Shirrefs, J.H. (1982) *Community Health: Contemporary perspectives*. Englewood Cliffs, NJ: Prentice Hall.

Shotter, J. (1975) *Images of Man in Psychological Research*. London: Methuen.

Shotter, J. (1984) *Social Accountability and Selfhood*. Oxford: Blackwell.

Shrauger, J.S. (1975) Responses to evaluation as a function of initial self-perceptions. *Psychological Bulletin* 82: 581–96.

Shultz, T.R., Schmidt, W.C., Buckingham, D. and Mareschal, D. (1995) Modeling cognitive competence with a generative connectionist algorithm, in T. Simon and G. Halford (eds) *Developing Cognitive Competence: New Approaches to competence modeling*. Hillsdale, NJ: Lawrence Erlbaum.

Shuren, J.E., Brott, T.G., Schefft, B.K. and Houston, W. (1996) Preserved colour imagery in an achromatopsic. *Neuropsychologia* 34: 485–9.

Shuval, J. and Adler, I. (1980) The role of models in professional socialisation. *Social Science and Medicine* 14: 5–14.

Shweder, R.A. (1994) 'You're not sick, you're just in love': emotion as an interpretative system, in P. Ekman and

R.J. Davidson (eds) *The Nature of Emotion: Fundamental questions*. Oxford: Oxford University Press.

Sidanius, J. (1993) The psychology of group conflict and the dynamics of oppression: a social dominance perspective, in W. McGuire and S. Iyengar (eds) *Current Approaches to Political Psychology*. Durham, NC: Duke University Press.

Siegel, S. (1983) Classical conditioning, drug tolerance, and drug dependence, in Y. Israel, F.B. Glaser, H. Kalant, R.E. Popham, W. Schmidt and R.G. Smart (eds) *Research Advances in Alcohol and Drug Problems*, vol. 7. New York: Plenum.

Siegel, S. (1984) Pavlovian conditioning and heroin overdose: reports by overdose victims. *Bulletin of the Psychonomic Society* 22: 428–30.

Siegel, S., Hinson, R.E., Krank, M.D. and McCully, J. (1982) Heroin 'overdose' death: contribution of drug-associated environmental cues. *Science* 216: 436–37.

Siegel, S., Krank, M.D. and Hinson, R.E. (1987) Anticipation of pharmacological and nonpharmacological events: classical conditioning and addictive behaviour. *Journal of Drug Issues* 17: 83–110.

Siegler, R.S. (1996) *Emerging Minds*. New York: Oxford University Press.

Siegler, R.S. and Jenkins, E. (1989) *How Children Discover New Strategies*. Hillsdale, NJ: Lawrence Erlbaum.

Siegler, R.S. and Liebert, R.M. (1974) Effects of contiguity, regularity and age on children's causal inferences. *Developmental Psychology* 10: 574–9.

Silverman, D. (1993) *Interpreting Qualitative Data: Methods for analysing talk, text and interaction*. London: Sage.

Silverstein, C. (1972) Behaviour modification and the gay community. Paper presented at the annual convention of the Association for Advancement of Behaviour Therapy, New York.

Simmons, J.V. (1981) *Project Sea Hunt: A report on prototype, development and tests*, technical report 746. San Diego, CA: Naval Ocean System Center.

Simon, B. (1992a) The perception of in-group and out-group homogeneity: reintroducing the intergroup context, in W. Stroebe and M. Hewstone (eds) *European Review of Social Psychology*, vol. 3. Chichester: Wiley

Simon, B. (1992b) Intragroup differentiation in terms of in-group and out-group attributes. *European Journal of Social Psychology* 22: 407–13.

Simon, B. and Brown, R. (1987) Perceived intra-group homogeneity in minority–majority contexts. *Journal of Personality and Social Psychology* 53(4): 703–11.

Simon, B. and Pettigrew, T.F. (1990) Social identity and perceived group homogeneity. *European Journal of Social Psychology* 20: 269–86.

Simon, H.A. (1974) How big is a chunk? *Science* 183: 482–8.

Simon, H.A. (1981) *Entscheidungsverhalten in Organisationen. Eine Untersuchung von Entscheidungsprozessen in Management und Verwaltung*. Landsberg am Lech: Verlag Moderne Industrie W. Dummer.

Simpson, C.H. (1967) Patterns of socialization into the professions: the case study of student nurses. *Sociological Inquiry* 37: 47–54.

Simpson, G.B. (1994) Context and the processing of ambiguous words, in M.A. Gernsbacher (ed.) *Handbook of Psycholinguistic Research*. San Diego, CA: Academic Press.

Singer, J.L. and Kolligian, J. Jr. (1987) Developments in the study of private experience. *Annual Review of Psychology* 38: 533–74.

Sizemore, C.C. and Pittillo, E.S. (1977) *I'm Eve*. Garden City, NY: Doubleday.

Skell, W. (1972) Analyse von Denkleistungen bei der Planung und praktischen Durchführung von Produktionsarbeiten in der Berufsausbildung, in W. Skell (ed.) *Psychologische Analysen von Denkleistungen in der Produktion*. Berlin: VEB Deutscher Verlag der Wissenschaften.

Skevington, S. and Baker, D. (eds) (1989) *The Social Identity of Women*. London: Sage.

Skinner, B.F. (1948) Superstition in the pigeon. *Journal of Experimental Psychology* 38: 168–72.

Skinner, B.F. (1953) *Science and Human Behavior*. New York: Macmillan.

Skinner, B.F. (1968) *The Technology of Teaching*. New York: Meredith Corporation.

Skinner, B.F. (1974) *About Behaviourism*. New York: Alfred A. Knopf.

Skinner, E.A. (1985) Action, control judgments, and the structure of control experience. *Psychological Review* 92: 39–58.

Slamecka, N.J. (1966) Differentiation versus unlearning of verbal associations. *Journal of Experimental Psychology* 71: 822–8.

Sloane, R.B., Staples, F.R., Cristol, A.H., Yorkston, N.J. and Whipple, K. (1975) *Psychotherapy versus Behaviour Therapy*. Cambridge, MA: Harvard University Press.

Slovic, P. and Fischhoff, B. (1977) On the psychology of experimental surprises. *Journal of Experimental Psychology: Human Perception and Performance* 3: 544–51.

Sluckin, A.M. (1981) *Growing Up in the Playground: The social development of children*. London: Routledge and Kegan Paul.

Sluckin, A.M. and Smith, P.K. (1977) Two approaches to the concept of dominance in preschool children. *Child Development* 48: 917–23.

Small, R., Brown, S. and Lumley, J. (1994) Missing voices: what women say and do about depression after childbirth. *Journal of Reproductive and Infant Psychology* 12: 89–103.

Small, S.A., Zeldin, R.S. and Savin-Williams, R.C. (1983) In search of personality traits: a multi-method analysis of naturally occurring prosocial and dominance behaviour. *Journal of Personality* 51: 1–16.

Smetana, J.G. and Adler, N.E. (1980) Fishbein's value × expectancy model: an examination of some assumptions. *Personality and Social Psychology Bulletin* 6: 89–96.

Smilansky, S. (1968) *The Effects of Sociodramatic Play on Disadvantaged Preschool Children*. New York: Wiley.

Smith, D. (1982) Trends in counselling and psychotherapy. *American Psychologist* 37: 802–9.

Smith, D.A. and Graesser, A.C. (1981) Memory for actions in scripted activities as a function of typicality, retention interval, and retrieval task. *Memory and Cognition* 9: 550–9.

Smith, D.E. (1986) Training programs for performance appraisal: a review. *Academy of Management Review* 11(1): 22–40.

Smith, E.M., Ford, J.K., Weissbein, D.A. and Gully, S.M. (1995) The effects of goal orientation, metacognition, and practice strategies on learning and transfer, in *Tenth Annual Conference of the Society for Industrial and Organizational Psychology*, Orlando, FL.

Smith, E.M. Ford, J.K. and Kozlowski, S.W. (1997) Building adaptive expertise: implications for training design strategies, in M.A. Quinones and A. Ehrenstein (eds) *Training for a Rapidly Changing Workplace*. Washington, DC: American Psychological Association.

Smith, J. (1981) Self and experience in Maori culture, in P. Heelas and A. Lock (eds) *Indigenous Psychologies*. London: Academic Press.

Smith, J.A. (1995) Semi-structured interviewing and qualitative analysis, in J.A. Smith, R. Harré, and L. Van Langenhove (eds) *Rethinking Methods in Psychology*. London: Sage.

Smith, J.A. (1996) Evolving issues for qualitative psychology, in J.T.E. Richardson (ed.) *Handbook of Qualitative Research Methods for Psychology and the Social Sciences*. Leicester: British Psychological Society.

Smith, J.A., Harré, R. and Van Langenhove, L. (eds) (1995) *Rethinking Methods in Psychology*. London: Sage.

Smith, M. (1986) Selection: where are the best prophets? *Personnel Management* December: 1963.

Smith, M. and Robertson, I. (1993) *Systematic Personnel Selection*. London: Macmillan.

Smith, M.L. and Glass, G.V. (1977) Meta-analysis of psychotherapy outcome studies. *American Psychologist* 32: 752–60.

Smith, M.L., Glass, G.V. and Miller, T.I (1980) *The Benefits of Psychotherapy*. Baltimore, MD: Johns Hopkins University Press.

Smith, P C. and Kendall, L.M. (1963) Retranslation of expectations: an approach to the construction of unambiguous anchors for rating scales. *Journal of Applied Psychology* 47: 149–55.

Smith, P.K. (1978) A longitudinal study of social participation in pre-school children: solitary and parallel play re-examined. *Developmental Psychology* 14: 517–23.

Smith, P.K. (1983) Human sociobiology, in J. Nicholson and B. Foss (eds) *Psychology Survey no. 4*. Leicester: British Psychological Society.

Smith, P.K. (1991) Introduction: the nature of grandparenthood, in P.K. Smith (ed.) *The Psychology of Grandparenthood: An international perspective*. London: Routledge.

Smith, P.K. and Sharp, S. (eds) (1994) *School Bullying: Insights and perspectives*. London: Routledge.

Smyth, M. and Scholey, K. (1994) Interference in immediate spatial memory. *Memory and Cognition* 22: 1–13.

Snarey, J.R. (1983) Cross-cultural universality of social-moral development: a critical review of Kohlbergian research. *Psychological Bulletin* 97: 202–32.

Snyder, M. (1974) Self-monitoring of expressive behavior. *Journal of Personality and Social Psychology* 30: 526–37.

Snyder, M. and Swann, W.B. Jr (1976) When actions reflect attitudes: the politics of impression management *Journal of Personality and Social Psychology* 34: 1034–42.

Snyder, M. and Tanke, E.D. (1976) Behavior and attitude: some people are more consistent than others. *Journal of Personality*, 44: 501–17.

Sodian, B., Taylor, C., Harris, P. and Perner, J. (1991) Early deception and the child's theory of mind: false trails and genuine markers. *Child Development* 62: 468–83.

Sogon, S. and Masutani, M. (1989) Identification of emotion from body movements. *Psychological Reports* 65: 35–46.

Solomon, P.R. and Crider, A. (1982) Attention, dopamine and schizophrenia. *Behavioral and Brain Sciences* 5: 75–6.

Solyom, L., Turnbull, I.M. and Wilensky, M. (1987) A case of self-inflicted leucotomy. *British Journal of Psychiatry* 151: 855–7.

Sonnentag, S. (1997) *Expertise in Professional Software Design: A process study*. University of Amsterdam.

Sonnentag, S., Brodbeck, F.C., Heinbokel, T. and Stolte, W. (1994) Stressor–burnout relationship in software development teams. *Journal of Occupational and Organizational Psychology* 67: 327–41.

Sophian, C. (1988) Limitations on preschool children's knowledge about counting: using counting to compare two sets. *Developmental Psychology* 24: 634–40.

Spangler, W.D. and House, R.J. (1991) Presidential effectiveness and the leadership motive profile. *Journal of Personality and Social Psychology* 60: 439–55.

Spearman, C.E. (1904) General intelligence, objectively determined and measured. *American Journal of Psychology* 15: 201–93.

Spearman, C.E. (1923) *The Nature of 'Intelligence' and the Principles of Cognition*. London: Macmillan.

Spearman, C.E. (1927) *The Abilities of Man: Their nature and measurement*. London: Macmillan.

Spears, R., van der Pligt, J. and Eiser, J.R. (1986) Generalizing the illusory correlation effect in social perception. *Journal of Personality and Social Psychology* 51: 1127–34.

Spears, R., Oakes, P.J., Ellemers, N. and Haslam, S.A. (1997) *The Social Psychology of Stereotyping and Group Life*. Oxford: Blackwell.

Spector, P.E. (1987) Interactive effects of perceived control and job stressors on affective reactions and health outcomes for clerical workers. *Work and Stress* 1: 155–62.

Speier, C. and Frese, M. (1997) Generalized self-efficacy as mediator and moderator between control and complexity at work and personal initiative: a longitudinal field study in East Germany. *Human Performance* 10(2): 171–92.

Speisman, J.C., Lazarus, R.S., Mordkoff, A.M. and Davison, L.A. (1964) Experimental reduction of stress based on ego-defence theory. *Journal of Abnormal Psychology* 68: 367–80.

Spelke, E.S., Hirst, W.C. and Neisser, U. (1976) Skills of divided attention. *Cognition* 4: 215–30.

Speller, G., Lyons, E. and Twigger-Ross, C. (1996) Self-evaluation processes and representation of social change in a mining community: imposed relocation of Arkwright. XI European Association of Experimental Social Psychology General Meeting, Gmunden.

Sperling, G. (1960) The information available in brief visual presentations. *Psychological Monographs* 74 (498): 1–29.

Sperry, R. (1967) The great cerebral commissure, in J.L. McGaugh, N.M. Weinberger and R.E. Whalen (eds) *The Biological Bases of Behaviour*. San Francisco, CA: W.H. Freeman (reprinted from *Scientific American* January 1964).

Spiegel, D., Bloom, J.R., Kraemer, H.C. and Gottheil, E. (1989) Effect of psychosocial treatment on survival of patients with metastatic breast cancer. *Lancet* 2: 888–91.

Spielberger, C.D., Gorsuch, R. and Lushene, R. (1970) *The State-Trait Anxiety Inventory (STAI) Form X*. Palo Alto, CA: Consulting Psychologists Press.

Spielberger, C.D., Gorsuch, R.L. and Lushene, R.E. (1983) *Manual for the State-Trait Anxiety Inventory*. Palo Alto, CA: Consulting Psychologists Press.

Spini, D. and Doise, W. (1998) Organising principles of involvement towards human rights. *European Journal of Social Psychology*.

Spinillo, A. and Bryant, P. (1991) Children's proportional judgements: the importance of 'half'. *Child Development* 62: 427–40.

Spitzer, R.L., Williams, J.B.W., Gibbon, M. and First, M.B. (1990) *Structured Clinical Interview for DSM-III-R*. Washington, DC: American Psychiatric Press.

Squire, L.R., Knowlton, B. and Musen, G. (1993) The structure and organisation of memory. *Annual Review of Psychology* 44: 453–95.

Srinas, K. and Roediger, H.L. (1990) Classifying implicit memory tests: category association and anagram solution. *Journal of Memory and Language* 29: 389–412.

Staddon, J.E.R. and Simmelhag, V.L. (1971) The 'superstition' experiment: a reexamination of its implications for the principles of adaptive behavior. *Psychological Review* 78: 3–43.

Stammers, R. (1996) Training and acquisition of knowledge and skill, in P. Warr (ed.) *Psychology at Work*. Harmondsworth: Penguin.

Stangor, C. and McMillan, D. (1992) Memory for expectancy-congruent and expectancy-incongruent information: a review of the social and developmental literatures. *Psychological Bulletin* 111: 42–61.

Stanovich, K.E. (1992) *How to Think Straight about Psychology*. Chicago: Scott, Foresman.

Staples, R. and Smith, J.W. (1954) Attitudes of grandmothers and mothers toward child rearing practices. *Child Development* 25: 91–7.

Starkey, P. and Cooper, R. (1980) Perception of numbers by human infants. *Science* 210: 1033–34.

Starkey, P., Spelke, E. and Gelman, R. (1983) Detection of intermodal numerical correspondences by human infants. *Science* 222: 179.

Starkey, P., Spelke, E.S. and Gelman, R. (1990) Numerical abstraction by human infants. *Cognition* 36: 97–128.

Starkstein, S.E. and Robinson, R.G. (1991) The role of the frontal lobes in affective disorder following stroke, in H.S. Levin, H.M. Eisenberg and A.L. Benton (eds) *Frontal Lobe Function and Dysfunction*. New York: Oxford University Press.

Staw, B.M. and Boettger, R.D. (1990) Task revision: a neglected form of work performance. *Academy of Management Journal* 33: 534–59.

Steel, C. and Liu, T. (1983) Dissonance processes as self-affirmation. *Journal of Personality and Social Psychology* 45: 5–19.

Stein, N.L. and Levine, L.J. (1989) The causal organization of emotional knowledge. *Cognition and Emotion* 3: 343–78.

Stein, N.L., Trabasso, T. and Liwag, M. (1993) The representation and organization of emotional experience: unfolding the emotion episode, in M. Lewis and J.M. Haviland (eds) *Handbook of Emotions*. New York: Guilford Press.

Stein, N.L., Trabasso, T. and Liwag, M. (1994) The Rashomon phenomenon: personal frames and future-oriented appraisals in memory for emotional events, in M.M. Haith, J.B. Benson, R.J. Roberts and B.F. Pennington (eds) *Future Oriented Processes*. Chicago: University of Chicago Press.

Steinberg, L. (1987) Impact of puberty on family relations: effects of pubertal status and pubertal timing. *Developmental Psychology* 23: 451–60.

Steiner, J.E. (1979) Human facial expressions in response to taste and smell stimulation, in H. Reese and L.P. Lipsitt (eds) *Advances in Child development and Behavior*. New York: Academic Press.

Steiner, S.S., Beer, B. and Shaffer, M.M. (1969) Escape from self-produced rates of brain stimulation. *Science* 163: 90–1.

Stelling, J. and Butcher, R. (1973) Vocabularies of realism in professional socialisation. *Social Science and Medicine* 7: 661–75.

Stemberger, J.P. (1982) The nature of segments in the lexicon: evidence from speech errors. *Lingua* 56: 235–9.

Stemmler, D.G. (1989) The autonomic differentiation of emotions revisited: convergent and discriminant validation. *Psychophysiology* 26: 617–32.

Stern, D. (1985) *The Interpersonal World of the Infant*. New York: Basic Books.

Sternberg, R.J. (1977) *Intelligence, Information Processing, and Analogical Reasoning: The componential analysis of human abilities*. Hillsdale, NJ: Lawrence Erlbaum.

Sternberg, R.J. (1985) *Beyond IQ: A triarchic theory of human intelligence*. Cambridge: Cambridge University Press.

Sternberg, R.J. (1988) *The Triarchic Mind*. New York: Viking.

Sternberg, R.J. (1995) *In Search of the Human Mind*. Orlando, FL: Harcourt Brace.

Sternberg, R.J. and Davidson, J.E. (1982) The mind of the puzzler. *Psychology Today* 16: 37–44.

Sternberg, R.J. and Frensch, P. A. (1990) Intelligence and cognition, in M.W. Eysenck (ed.) *Cognitive Psychology: An international review*. Chichester: Wiley.

Sternberg, R.J. and Lubart, T.I. (1991) An investment theory of creativity and its development. *Human Development* 34: 1–31.

Stevens, R (1990) Humanistic psychology, in I. Roth (ed.) *Introduction to Psychology*, vol. 2. Hove: Lawrence Erlbaum.

Stogdill, R.M. (1948) Personal factors associated with leadership: a survey of the literature. *Journal of Psychology* 25: 35–71.

Stone, A.A. (1975) *Mental Health and Law: A system in transition*. Rockville, MD: National Institute of Mental Health, Center for Studies of Crime and Delinquency.

Stoner, J. (1961) A Comparison of individual and group decisions involving risk. Unpublished Masters thesis, School of Industrial Management, Massachusetts Institute of Technology.

Storms, M.D. (1973) Videotape and the attribution process: reversing actors' and observers' points of view. *Journal of Personality and Social Psychology* 27: 165–75.

Stratton, G.M. (1897) Vision without inversion of the retinal image. *Psychological Review* 4: 341–60.

Strauss, A.L. and Corbin, J. (1990) *Basics of Qualitative Research: Grounded theory procedures and techniques*. Newbury Park, CA: Sage.

Strauss, E. and Moscovitch, M. (1981) Perceptions of facial expressions. *Brain and Language* 13: 308–32.

Strauss, M.S. and Curtis, L.E. (1981) Infant perception of number. *Child Development* 52: 1146–52.

Strauss, M.S. and Curtis, L.E. (1984) Development of numerical concepts in infancy, in C. Sophian *The Origins of Cognitive Skill*. Hillsdale, NJ: Lawrence Erlbaum.

Stricker, E.M. and Zigmond, M.J. (1976) Recovery of function after damage to central catecholamine-containing neurons: a neurochemical model for the lateral hypothalamic syndrome. *Progress in Psychobiology and Physiological Psychology* 6: 121–88.

Stricker, E.M. and Zigmond, M.J. (1984) Brain monoamines and the central control of food intake. *International Journal of Obesity* 8 (suppl. 1): 39–50.

Strickland, B.R. (1979) Internal–external expectancies and cardiovascular functioning, in L.C. Perlmuter and R.A. Monty (eds) *Choice and Perceived Control*. Hillsdale, NJ: Lawrence Erlbaum.

Stroebe, W. and Stroebe, M. (1995) *Social Psychology and Health*. Buckingham: Open University Press.

Stroop, J.R. (1935) Studies of interference in serial verbal reaction. *Journal of Experimental Psychology* 18: 643–62.

Strube, M.J. and Garcia, J.E. (1981) A meta-analytic investigation of Fiedler's contingency model of leadership effectiveness. *Psychological Bulletin* 90: 307–21.

Strupp, H.H. (1996) The tripartite model and the Consumer Reports study. *American Psychologist* 51: 1017–24.

Strupp, H.H. and Hadley, S.W. (1979) Specific versus nonspecific factors in psychotherapy: a controlled study of outcome. *Archives of General Psychiatry* 36: 1125–36.

Stryker, S. (1980) *Symbolic Interactionism: A social structural version*. Menlo Park, CA: Benjamin/Cummings.

Stryker, S. (1987) Identity theory: developments and extensions, in K. Yardley and T. Honess (eds) *Self and Identity: Psychosocial perspectives*. Chichester: Wiley.

Stryker, S. (1997) 'In the beginning there is society': lessons from a sociological social psychology, in C. McGarty and S. A. Haslam (eds) *The Message of Social Psychology*. Oxford: Blackwell.

Sugarman, L. (1986) *Life-Span Development*. London: Methuen.

Sullivan, L. (1976) Selective attention and secondary message analysis: a reconsideration of Broadbent's filter model of selective attention. *Quarterly Journal of Experimental Psychology* 28: 167–78.

Suls, J. and Fletcher B. (1985) The relative efficacy of avoidant and non-avoidant coping strategies: a meta-analysis. *Health Psychology* 4: 249–88.

Suls, J. and Miller, R. (1977) *Social Comparison Processes: Theoretical and empirical perspectives*. Washington, DC: Hemisphere.

Sumner, W. (1906) *Folkways*. New York: Ginne.

Surber, C.F. (1981) Effects of information reliability in predicting task performance using ability and effort. *Journal of Personality and Social Psychology* 40: 977–89.

Surtees, P.G. (1995) In the shadow of adversity: the evolution and resolution of anxiety and depressive disorder. *British Journal of Psychiatry* 166: 583–94.

Suter, S. (1986) *Health Psychophysiology*. Hillsdale, NJ: Lawrence Erlbaum.

Sutton, S.R. (1982) Fear-arousing communications: a critical examination of theory and research, in J.R. Eiser (ed.) *Social Psychology and Behavioural Medicine*. New York: Wiley.

Sweeney, P.D. and Moreland, R.L. (1980) Self-schemas and the perseverance of beliefs about the self. Paper presented at the American Psychological Association annual meetings, Montreal.

Swerrison, H. and Foreman, P. (1991) Training health professionals in health psychology, in M.A. Jansen and J. Weinman (eds) *The International Development of Health Psychology*. Chur: Harwood.

Szasz, T. (1964) *The Myth of Mental Illness*. New York: Harper and Row.

Taal, E., Seydel, E.F. and Rasker, J.J. (1992) Reumatologie (rheumatology), in A.A. Kaptein, B. Garssen, Ph. Rumke and H.J. Sluiter (eds) *Medische Psychologie in het Ziekenhuis*. Houten: Bohn Stafley Van Loghum.

Taghavi, R., Moradi, A., Neshat-Doost, H., Yule, W. and Dalgleish, T. (1997) Performance on the emotional Stroop task in anxious children and adolescents. Manuscript submitted for publication.

Taira, K. (1996) Compatibility of human resource management, industrial relations, and engineering under mass production and lean production: an exploration. *Applied Psychology: An International Review* 45: 97–117.

Tajfel, H. (1959) Quantitative judgement in social perception. *British Journal of Social Psychology* 50: 16–29.

Tajfel, H. (1969) Cognitive aspects of prejudice. *Journal of Social Issues* 25: 79–97.

Tajfel, H. (1972a) Experiments in a vacuum, in J. Israel and H. Tajfel (eds) *The Context of Social Psychology: A critical assessment*. London: Academic Press.

Tajfel, H. (1972b) La categorisation sociale, in S. Moscovici (ed.) *Introduction à la psychologie sociale*. Paris: Larousse.

Tajfel, H. (ed.) (1978) *Differentiation between Social Groups: Studies in the social psychology of intergroup relations*. London: Academic Press.

Tajfel, H. (1981) *Human Groups and Social Categories: Studies in social psychology*. Cambridge: Cambridge University Press.

Tajfel, H. and Turner, J. (1979) An integrative theory of intergroup conflict, in W. Austin and S. Worchel (eds) *The Social*

Psychology of Intergroup Relations. Monterey, CA: Brooks/Cole.

Tajfel, H. and Turner, J. (1986) The social identity theory of intergroup behaviour, in S. Worchel and W. Austin (eds) *Psychology of Intergroup Relations.* Chicago: Nelson-Hall.

Tajfel, H. and Wilkes, A. (1963) Classification and quantitative judgement. *British Journal of Psychology* 54: 101–14.

Tajfel, H., Sheikh, A. and Gardner, R. (1964) Content of stereotypes and the inference of similarity between members of stereotypes groups. *Acta Psychologica* 22: 191–201.

Tajfel, H., Billig, M.G., Bundy, R.P. and Flament, C. (1971) Social categorization and intergroup behaviour. *European Journal of Social Psychology*, 1: 149–78.

Tanaka, J.W. and Taylor, M. (1991) Object categories and expertise: is the basic level in the eye of the beholder? *Cognitive Psychology* 23: 457–82.

Tanford, S. and Penrod, S. (1984) Social influence model: a formal integration of research on minority and majority influence processes. *Psychological Bulletin* 95: 189–225.

Tannenbaum, S.I. and Yukl, G. (1992) Training and development in work organizations. *Annual Review of Psychology* 43: 399–441.

Taraban, R. and McClelland, J.L. (1988) Constituent attachment and thematic role assignment in sentence processing: influences of content-based expectations. *Journal of Memory and Language* 27: 597–632.

Tarpy, R.M. (1997) *Contemporary Learning Theory and Research.* New York: McGraw-Hill.

Tassoni, C.J. (1995) The least mean squares network with information coding: a model of cue learning. *Journal of Experimental Psychology: Learning, Memory, and Cognition* 21: 193–204.

Tavris, C. (1993) The mismeasure of woman. *Feminism and Psychology* 3(2): 149–68.

Taylor, A., Sluckin, W., Davies, D.R., Reason, J.T., Thomson, R. and Colman, A.M. (1982) *Introducing Psychology*, 2nd edn. Harmondsworth: Penguin.

Taylor, G.R. (1972) *Rethink: A paraprimitive solution.* London: Secker and Warburg.

Taylor, I. and Taylor, M.M. (1990) *Psycholinguistics: Learning and using language.* Englewood Cliffs, NJ: Prentice Hall.

Taylor, S.E. (1995) *Health Psychology.* New York: McGraw-Hill.

Taylor, S.E. and Aspinwall, L.G. (1993) Coping with chronic illness, in L. Goldberger and S. Breznitz (eds) *Handbook of Stress: Theoretical and clinical aspects.* New York: Free Press.

Taylor, S.E. and Crocker, J. (1981) Schematic bases of social information processing, in E.T. Higgins, C.P. Hemran and M.P. Zanna (eds) *Social Cognition: The Ontario symposium*, vol. 1. Hillsdale, NJ: Lawrence Erlbaum.

Taylor, S.E. and Fiske, S.T. (1978) Salience, attention and attribution: top of the head phenomena, in L. Berkowitz (ed.) *Advances in Experimental Social Psychology*, vol. 11. New York: Academic Press.

Teasdale, J.D. (1988) Cognitive vulnerability to persistent depression. *Cognition and Emotion* 2: 247–74.

Teasdale, J. (1998) Multi-level theories of cognition-emotion relations, in T. Dalgleish and M. Power (eds) *The Handbook of Cognition and Emotion.* Chichester: Wiley.

Teasdale, J. and Barnard, P. (1993) *Affect, Cognition and Change.* Hove: Lawrence Erlbaum.

Terman, L.M. (1917) The intelligence quotient of Francis Galton in childhood. *American Journal of Psychology* 28: 206–14.

Terrace, H.S. (1979) *Nim.* New York: Alfred A. Knopf.

Tesch, R. (1990) *Qualitative Research: Analysis types and software tools.* Basingstoke: Falmer.

Tesser, A., Campbell, J. and Smith, M. (1983) Friendship choice and performance: self-evaluation maintenance in children. *Journal of Personality and Social Psychology* 46: 561–74.

Tetlock, P.E. and Manstead, A.S.R. (1985) Impression management versus intrapsychic explanations in social psychology: a useful dicotomy? *Psychological Review* 92: 59–77.

Thigpen, C.H. and Cleckley, H. (1954) A case of multiple personality. *Journal of Abnormal and Social Psychology* 49: 135–51.

Thomas, A. and Chess, S. (1977) *Temperament and Development.* New York: Brunner/Mazel.

Thomas, J.C. (1974) An analysis of behaviour in the hobbits-orcs problem. *Cognitive Psychology* 6: 257–69.

Thomson, D.M. and Tulving, E. (1970) Associative encoding and retrieval: weak and strong cues. *Journal of Experimental Psychology* 86: 255–62.

Thomson, R. (1968) *The Pelican History of Psychology.* Harmondsworth: Penguin.

Thorndike, E.L. (1898) Animal intelligence: an experimental study of the associative processes in animals. *Psychological Review Monograph Supplements* 2 (8).

Thorndike, E.L. (1906) *Principles of Teaching.* New York: A.G. Seiler.

Thorndike, E.L. (1911) *Animal Intelligence: Experimental studies.* New York: Macmillan.

Thorndyke, P.W. (1977) Cognitive structures in comprehension and memory of narrative discourse. *Cognitive Psychology* 9: 77–110.

Thurstone, L.L. (1938) *Primary Mental Abilities.* Chicago: University of Chicago Press.

Tinsley, B.J. and Parke, R.D. (1984) Grandparents as support and socialization agents, in M. Lewis (ed.) *Beyond the Dyad.* New York: Plenum.

Tipper, S.P. and Driver, J. (1988) Negative priming between pictures and words: evidence for semantic analysis of ignored stimuli. *Memory and Cognition* 16: 64–70.

Tizard, B., Cooperman, O., Joseph, A. and Tizard, J. (1972) Environmental effects on language development: a study of young children in long-stay residential nurseries. *Child Development* 43: 337–58.

Toates, F. (1971) The effect of pretraining on schedule induced polydipsia. *Psychonomic Science* 23: 219–20.

Toates, F. (1995) *Stress: Conceptual and biological aspects.* Chichester: Wiley.

Toates, F. (1997) The interaction of cognitive and stimulus-response processes in the control of behaviour. *Neuroscience and Biobehavioural Reviews.*

Tolman, E.C. (1932) *Purposive Behavior in Animals and Men.* New York: Appleton-Century-Crofts.

Tolman, E.C. (1948) Cognitive maps in rats and men. *Psychological Review* 55: 189–208.

Tolman, E.C. and Brunswik, E. (1935) The organism and the causal texture of the environment. *Psychological Review* 42: 43–77.

Tolman, E.C. and Gleitman, H. (1949) Studies in learning and motivation I. Equal reinforcements in both end-boxes, followed by shock in one end-box. *Journal of Experimental Psychology* 39: 810–19.

Tomie, A. (1996) Locating reward cue at response manipulandum (CAM) induces symptoms of drug abuse. *Neuroscience and Biobehavioural Reviews* 20: 505–35.

Tomkins, S.S. (1962) *Affect, Imagery, Consciousness, vol. 1, The positive affects*. New York: Springer.

Tones, K. and Tilford, S. (1994) *Health Education: Effectiveness, efficiency and equity*. London: Chapman Hall.

Torgerson, S. (1988) Genetics, in C.G. Last and M. Hersen (eds) *Handbook of Anxiety Disorders*. New York: Pergamon.

Traindis, M., Brislin, R. and Hui, C. (1988) Cross-cultural training across the individualism–collectivism divide. *International Journal of Intercultural Relations* 12(3): 269–89.

Trayhurn, P. (1986) Brown adipose tissue and energy balance, in P. Trayhurn and D.G. Nicholls (eds) *Brown Adipose Tissue*. London: Edward Arnold.

Treisman, A.M. (1964) Verbal cues, language, and meaning in selective attention. *American Journal of Psychology* 77: 206–19.

Treisman, A.M. (1988) Features and objects: the fourteenth Bartlett memorial lecture. *Quarterly Journal of Experimental Psychology* 40A: 201–37.

Treisman, A.M. and Gelade, G. (1980) A feature integration theory of attention. *Cognitive Psychology* 12: 97–136.

Treisman, A.M. and Sato, S. (1990) Conjunction search revisited. *Journal of Experimental Psychology: Human Perception and Performance* 16: 459–78.

Treisman, A.M. and Schmidt, H. (1982) Illusory conjunctions in the perception of objects. *Cognitive Psychology* 14: 107–41.

Tremblay-Leveau, H. and Nadel, J. (1996) Exclusion in triads: can it serve 'metacommunicative' knowledge in 11- and 23-month-old children? *British Journal of Developmental Psychology* 14: 145–58.

Trevarthan, C.B. (1968) Two mechanisms of vision in primates. *Psychologische Forschung* 31: 299–337.

Trevarthen, C. (1977) Descriptive analyses of infant communicative behaviour, in H.R. Schaffer (ed.) *Studies in Mother–Infant Interaction*. London: Academic Press.

Triandis, H.C., Botempo, R., Villareal, M.J., Asai, M. and Lucca, N. (1988) Individualism and collectivism: cross-cultural perspectives on self-ingroup relationships. *Journal of Personality and Social Psychology* 54: 323–33.

Trist, E.L. and Bamforth, K.W. (1951) Some social and psychological consequences of the long-wall method of goal getting. *Human Relations* 4: 3–38.

Trist, E., Higgin, G., Murray, H. and Pollack, A. (1963) *Organizational Choice*. London: Tavistock.

Trowill, J.A., Panksepp, J. and Gandelman, R. (1969) An incentive model of rewarding brain stimulation. *Psychological Review* 76: 264–81.

Truax, C.B. and Mitchell, K.M. (1971) Research on certain therapist interpersonal skills in relation to process and outcome, in A.E. Bergin and S.L. Garfield (eds) *Handbook of Psychotherapy and Behaviour Change*. Chichester: Wiley.

Tuan, Y.F. (1982) *Segmented Worlds and Self: Group life and individual consciousness*. Minneapolis, MN: University of Minnesota Press.

Tulving, E. (1972) Episodic and semantic memory, in E. Tulving and W. Donaldson (eds) *Organisation of Memory*. London: Academic Press.

Tulving, E. (1974) Cue-dependent forgetting. *American Scientist* 62: 74–82.

Tulving, E. (1979) Relation between encoding specificity and levels of processing, in L.S. Cermak and F.I.M. Craik (eds) *Levels of Processing in Human Memory*. Hillsdale, NJ: Lawrence Erlbaum.

Tulving, E. (1989a) Memory: performance, knowledge and experience. *European Journal of Cognitive Psychology* 1: 3–26.

Tulving, E. (1989b) Remembering and knowing the past. *American Scientist* 77: 361–7.

Tulving, E. and Flexser, A.J. (1992) On the nature of the Tulving-Wiseman function. *Psychological Review* 99: 543–6.

Tulving, E. and Pearlstone, Z. (1966) Availability versus accessibility of information in memory for words. *Journal of Verbal Learning and Verbal Behavior* 5: 381–91.

Tulving, E. and Psotka, J. (1971) Retroactive inhibition in free recall: inaccessibility of information available in the memory store. *Journal of Experimental Psychology* 87: 1–8.

Tulving, E. and Schacter, D.L. (1990) Priming and human memory. *Science* 247: 301–6.

Tulving, E. and Thomson, D.M. (1973) Encoding specificity and retrieval processes in episodic memory. *Psychological Review* 80: 352–73.

Tulving, E., Mandler, G. and Baumal, R. (1964) Interaction of two sources of information in tachistoscopic word recognition. *Canadian Journal of Psychology* 18: 62–71.

Tulving, E., Schacter, D.L. and Stark, H.A. (1982) Priming effects in word-fragment completion are independent of recognition memory. *Journal of Experimental Psychology: Learning, Memory, and Cognition* 17: 595–617.

Turner, J. (1975) Social comparison and social identity: some prospects for group behaviour. *European Journal of Social Psychology* 5: 5–34.

Turner, J. (1978) Social categorisation and social discrimination in the minimal group paradigm, in H. Tajfel (ed.) *Differentiation between Social Groups*. London: Academic Press.

Turner, J. (1980) Fairness or discrimination in intergroup behaviour: a reply to Branthwaite, Doyle and Lightbown. *European Journal of Social Psychology* 10: 131–47.

Turner, J.C. (1982a) The experimental social psychology of intergroup behaviour, in J. Turner and H. Giles (eds) *Intergroup Behaviour*. Oxford: Blackwell.

Turner, J.C. (1982b) Towards a cognitive redefinition of the social group. In H. Tajfel (ed.) *Social identity and Intergroup Relations*. Cambridge: Cambridge University Press.

Turner, J.C. (1985) Social categorisation and the self-concept: a socio-cognitive theory of group behaviour, in E.J. Lawler (ed.) *Advances in Group Processes*, vol. 2. Greenwich, CT: JAI Press.

Turner, J. (1991) *Social Influence*. Milton Keynes: Open University Press.

Turner, J. (1996) Henri Tajfel: an introduction, in W. Robinson (ed.) *A Festchrift for Henri Tajfel*. Oxford: Butterworth Heinemann.

Turner, J. and Bourhis, R. (1996) Social identity, interdependence and social groups: a reply, in W.P. Robinson (ed.) *Social Groups and Identities*. London: Butterworth Heinemann

Turner, J. and Giles, H. (eds) (1983) *Intergroup Behaviour*. Oxford: Blackwell.

Turner, J. and Oakes, P. (1986) The significance of the social identity concept for social psychology with reference to individualism, interactionism and social influence. *British Journal of Social Psychology* 25: 237–52.

Turner, J. and Spriggs, D. (1982) Social categorisation, intergroup behaviour and self-esteem: a replication. Unpublished document, Tajfel Collection, University of Kent, Canterbury.

Turner, J., Sachder, I. and Hogg, M. (1983) Social categorization, interpersonal attraction and group formation. *British Journal of Social Psychology* 22: 227–39.

Turner, J., Hogg, M., Turner, P., and Smith, P. (1984) Failure and defeat as determinants of group cohesiveness. *British Journal of Social Psychology* 13: 97–111.

Turner, J., Hogg, M., Oakes, P., Reicher, S. and Wetherell, M. (1987) *Rediscovering the Social Group: A self-categorisation theory*. Oxford: Blackwell.

Turner, P. (1991) Relations between attachment, gender, and behavior with peers in preschool. *Child Development* 62: 1475–88.

Turner, R.J. (1981) Social support as a contingency in psychological well-being. *Journal of Health and Social Behaviour* 22: 357–67.

Tversky, A. and Kahneman, D. (1973) Availability: a heuristic for judging frequency and probability. *Cognitive Psychology* 5: 207–32.

Tversky, A. and Kahneman, D. (1980) Causal schemas in judgements under uncertainty, in M. Fishbein (ed.) *Progress in Social Psychology*. Hillsdale, NJ: Lawrence Erlbaum.

Tversky, A. and Kahneman, D. (1983) Extensional versus intuitive reasoning: the conjunction fallacy in probability judgement. *Psychological Review* 90: 293–315.

Tweney, R.D., Doherty, M.E., Worner, W.J., Pliske, D.B., Mynatt, C.R., Gross, K.A. and Arkkelin, D.L. (1980) Strategies for rule discovery in an inference task. *Quarterly Journal of Experimental Psychology* 32: 109–23.

Twigger-Ross, C.L. and Uzzell, D. (1996) Place and identity processes. *Journal of Environmental Psychology* 16: 205–20.

Twigger-Ross, C.L., Bonauito, M. and Breakwell, G.M. (1998) Identity theories and environmental psychology, in M. Bonnes and T. Lee (eds) *Environmental Psychology and Psychological Theories*. London: Sage.

Tyszkowa, M. (1991) The role of grandparents in the development of grandchildren as perceived by adolescents and young adults in Poland, in P.K. Smith (ed.) *The Psychology of Grandparenthood: An international perspective*. London: Routledge.

Tziner, A., Haccoun, R. R. and Kadish, A. (1991) Personal and situational characteristics influencing the effectiveness of transfer of training improvement strategies. *Journal of Occupational Psychology* 64: 167–77.

Ucros, C.G. (1989) Mood state-dependent memory: a meta-analysis. *Cognition and Emotion* 3: 139–67.

Ulich, E. (1983) Alternative Arbeitsstrukturen – dargestellt am Beispiel der Automobilindustrie. *Zeitschrift für Arbeits- und Organisationspsychologie* 2: 70–8.

Ulich, E. (1991) *Arbeitspsychologie*. Stuttgart: Poeschel.

Ulich, E. and Ulich, H. (1977) Über einige Zusammenhänge zwischen Arbeitsgestaltung und Freizeitverhalten, in T. Leuenberger and K.H. Ruffman (eds) *Bürokratie*. Bern: Lang.

Ulich, E., Groskurth, P. and Bruggemann, A. (1973) *Neue Formen der Arbeitsgestaltung. Möglichkeiten und Probleme einer Verbesserung der Qualität des Arbeitslebens*. Frankfurt: Europ. Verlagsanstalt.

Underwood, B.J. and Postman, L. (1960) Extra-experimental sources of interference in forgetting. *Psychological Review* 67: 73–95.

Unger, R (1985) Epistomological consistency and its scientific implications. *American Psychologist* 40: 1413–14.

Unger, R. (1988) Psychological, feminist and personal epistemology, in M. Gergen (ed.) *Feminist Thought and the Structure of Knowledge*. New York: New York University Press.

Ungerstedt, U. (1971) Adipsia and aphagia after 6-hydroxy-dopamine induced degeneration of the nigrostriatal dopamine system. *Acta Physiologia Scandinavica* 81 (suppl. 367): 95–122.

Ussher, J.M. (1992) Science sexing psychology: positivistic science and gender bias in clinical psychology, in J. Ussher and P. Nicolson (eds) *Gender Issues in Clinical Psychology*. London: Routledge.

Uzzell, D. (1995) Ethnographic and action research, in G.M. Breakwell, S. Hammond and C. Fife-Schaw (eds) *Research Methods in Psychology*. London: Sage.

Valenstein, E.S. (1969) Behaviour elicited by hypothalamic stimulation. *Brain, Behaviour and Evolution* 2: 295–316.

Valenstein, E.S. (1973) *Brain Control*. New York: Wiley.

Valenstein, E.S., Cox, V.C. and Kakolewski, J.W. (1970) Reexamination of the role of the hypothalamus in motivation. *Psychological Review* 77: 16–31.

Valentine, E.R. (1992) *Conceptual Issues in Psychology*, 2nd edn. London: Routledge.

Vallbo, A.B. (1995) Single-afferent neurons and somatic sensation in humans, in M.S. Gazzaniga (ed.) *The Cognitive Neurosciences*. Cambridge: MIT Press.

Van Avermaet, E. (1996) Social influence in small groups, in M. Hewstone, W. Stroebe and G.M. Stephenson (eds) *Introduction to Social Psychology*. Oxford: Blackwell.

Van Bezooijen, R. (1984) *The Characteristics and Recognizability of Vocal Expression of Emotions*. Dordrecht: Foris.

Van Brakel, J. (1994) Emotions: a cross-cultural perspective on forms of life, in W.M. Wentworth and J. Ryan (eds) *Social Perspectives on Emotion*, vol. 2. Greenwich, CT: JAI Press.

Van den Berg, J. and Van den Bos, G.A.M. (1989) Het (meten van het) voorkomen van chronische aandoeningen

1974–1987 (prevalence of chronic diseases 1974–1987) *Maandbericht Gezondheid* (CBS) 3: 4–21.

Van den Broek, A. (1995) *Patient Education and Chronic Obstructive Pulmonary Disease,* Health Psychology Series no. 1. Leiden: Leiden University.

Van der Pligt, J. (1984) Attributions, false consensus and valance: two field studies. *Journal of Personality and Social Psychology* 46: 57–68.

Van der Pligt, J. and Eiser, J.R. (1984) Dimensional salience, judgment and attitudes, in J.R. Eiser (ed.) *Attitudinal Judgement.* NewYork: Springer-Verlag.

Van der Pligt, J., Ester, P. and van der Linden, J. (1983) Attitude extremity, consensus and diagnosticity. *European Journal of Social Psychology* 13: 437–9.

Van der Veer, R. and Valsiner, J. (1991) *Understanding Vygotsky.* Oxford: Blackwell.

Van Elderen, T. (1991) *Health Education in Cardiac Rehabilitation.* Leiden: DSWO Press.

Van Elderen, T., Maes, S., Seegers G., Kragten, H. and Relik-van Wely, L. (1994a) Effects of a post-hospitalization group health education programme for patients with coronary heart disease. *Psychology and Health* 9: 317–30.

Van Elderen, T., Maes, S. and Van den Broek, Y. (1994b) Effects of a health education programme with telephone follow-up during cardiac rehabilitation. *British Journal of Clinical Psychology* 33: 367–78.

Van Elderen, T., Maes S., Van der Kamp, L. and Komproe Y. (1997) The development of an anger expression and control scale. *British Journal of Health Psychology* 2: 269–81.

Van Hamme, L.J. and Wasserman, E.A. (1994) Cue competition in causality judgments: the role of nonpresentation of compound stimulus elements. *Learning and Motivation* 25: 127–51.

Van IJzendoorn, M. (1995) Adult attachment representations. *Psychological Bulletin* 117: 387–403.

Van Knippenberg, Ad. and Van Oers, H. (1984) Social identity and equity concerns in intergroup perception. *British Journal of Social Psychology* 23: 351–61.

Van Maanan, J. (1976) Breaking in: socialisation to work, in R. Dubin (ed.) *Handbook of Work, Organization and Society.* Chicago: Rand McNally.

Van Maanen, J. and Schein, E.H. (1979) Toward a theory of organizational socialization. *Research in Organizational Behaviour* 1: 209–64.

Van Oudenhoven, J.P., Groenewoud, J.T. and Hewstone, M. (1996) Cooperation, ethnic salience and generalization of interethnic attitudes. *European Journal of Social Psychology* 26: 649–61.

Van Scotter, J.R. and Motowidlo, S.J. (1996) Interpersonal facilitation and job dedication as separate facets of contextual performance. *Journal of Applied Psychology* 81: 525–31.

Vaughn, B.E. and Langlois, J.H. (1983) Physical attractiveness as a correlate of peer status and social competence in preschool children. *Developmental Psychology* 19: 561–7.

Vaughn, C.E. and Leff, J.P. (1976) The influence of family and social factors on the course of schizophrenic and depressed neurotic patients. *British Journal of Psychiatry* 129: 125–37.

Verkuyten, M. (1997) Intergroup evaluation and self-esteem motivation: self-enhancement and self-protection. *European Journal of Social Psychology* 27: 115–19.

Verkuyten, M., Masson, K. and Eiffers, H. (1995) Racial categorisation and preference among older children in The Netherlands. *European Journal of Social Psychology* 25: 637–56.

Vernon, P.E. (1971) *The Structure of Human Abilities.* London: Methuen.

Verrey, L. (1888) Hémiachromatopsie droite absolue – conservation partielle de la perception lumineuse et des formes – Ancien kyste hémorrhagique de la partie inférieure du lobe occipital gauche. *Archives d'Ophthalmplogie* 8: 289–301.

Vinck, J. (1993) Self-management in smoking cessation, in L. Sibilia and S. Borgo (eds) *Health Psychology in Cardiovascular Health and Disease.* Rome: CNR.

Vinokur, A., Burnstein, E., Sechrest, L. and Wortman, P. (1985) Group decision making by experts: field study of panels evaluating medical technologies. *Journal of Personality and Social Psychology* 49: 70–84.

Volkow, N.D., Wang, G.-J., Fischman, M.W., Foltin, R.W., Fowler, J.S., Abumrad, N.N., Vitkun, S., Logan, J., Gatley, S.J., Pappas, N., Hitzemann, R. and Shea, C.E. (1997) Relationship between subjective effects of cocaine and dopamine transporter occupancy. *Nature* 386: 827–30.

Volpert, W. (1971) *Sensumotorisches Lernen.* Frankfurt: Limpert; Fachbuchhandlung für Psychologie.

Volpert, W., Frommann, R. and Munzert, J. (1984) Die Wirkung heuristischer Regeln im Lernprozeß. *Zeitschrift für Arbeitswissenschaft* 38: 235–40.

Von Papstein, P. and Frese, M. (1988) Transferring skills from training to the actual work situation: the role of task application knowledge, action styles and job decision latitude, in E. Soloway, D. Frye and S.B. Sheppard (eds) *CHI'88 Conference Proceedings: Human Factors in Computing Systems.* Washington, DC: Association for Computing Machinery.

Von Rosenstiel, L. (1989) Selektions- und Sozialisationseffekte beim Übergang vom Bildungs- ins Beschäftigungssystem. *Zeitschrift für Arbeits- und Organisationspsychologie* 33(1): 21–32.

Vosniadou, S. and Brewer, W.F. (1992) Mental models of the earth: a study of conceptual change in childhood. *Cognitive Psychology* 24: 535–85.

Vygotsky, L.S. (1978) *Mind in Society.* Cambridge, MA: Harvard University Press.

Vygotsky, L.S. (1981) The genesis of higher mental functions, in J.V. Wertsch (ed.) *The Concept of Activity in Soviet Psychology.* Amonk, NY: Sharpe.

Vygotsky, L.S. (1986) *Thought and Language.* Cambridge, MA: MIT Press.

Wagner, A.R. (1981) SOP: a model of automatic memory processing in animal behavior, in N.E. Spear and R.R. Miller (eds) *Information Processing in Animals: Memory mechanisms.* Hillsdale, NJ: Lawrence Erlbaum.

Wagner, D. (1995) Gender differences in reward preferences: a status based account. *Small Group Research* 261(3): 353–71.

Wagner, H.L., MacDonald, C.J. and Manstead, A.S.R. (1986) Communication of individual emotions by spontaneous facial expressions. *Journal of Personality and Social Psychology* 50: 737–43.

Wagner, R.K. and Sternberg, R.J. (1986) Tacit knowledge and intelligence in the everyday world, in R.J. Sternberg and R.K. Wagner (eds) *Practical Intelligence: Nature and origins of competence in the everyday world*. New York: Cambridge University Press.

Wakefield, J.A., Yom, B.H.L., Bradley, P.E., Doughtie, E.B., Cox, J.A. and Kraft, I.A. (1974) Eysenck's personality dimensions: a model for the MMPI. *British Journal of Social and Clinical Psychology* 13: 413–20.

Wakefield, J.C. (1992) The concept of mental disorder: on the boundary between biological facts and social values. *American Psychologist* 47: 373–88.

Walker, I. and Pettigrew, T. (1984) Relative deprivation theory: an overview and conceptual critique. *British Journal of Social Psychology* 23: 301–10.

Wall, P.D. (1993) Pain and the placebo response, in G.R. Bock and J. Marsh (eds) *Experimental and Theoretical Studies of Consciousness*, Ciba Foundation Symposium 174. Chichester: Wiley.

Wall, T.D. and Clegg, C.W. (1981) A longitudinal study of group work redesign. *Journal of Occupational Psychology* 2: 31–49.

Wall, T.D. and Jackson, P.S. (1995) New manufacturing initiatives and shopfloor job design, in A. Howard (ed.) *The Changing Nature of Work*. San Francisco, CA: Jossey-Bass.

Wall, T.D., Kemp, N.J., Jackson, P.R. and Clegg, C.W. (1986) Outcomes of autonomous workgroups: a long-term field experiment. *Academy of Management Journal* 29: 280–304.

Wall, T.D., Jackson, P.R. and Davids, K. (1992) Operator work design and robotics system performance: a serendipitous field study. *Journal of Applied Psychology* 77: 353–62.

Wall, T.D., Jackson, P.R., Mullarkey, S. and Parker, S. (1996) The demands-control model of job strain: a more specific test. *Journal of Occupational and Organizational Psychology* 69(2): 153–66.

Wallerstein, J.S., Corbin, S.B. and Lewis, J.M. (1988) Children of divorce: a 10-year study, in E.M. Hetherington and J.P. Arasteh (eds) *Impact of Divorce, Single Parenting and Stepparenting on Children*. Hillsdale, NJ: Lawrence Erlbaum.

Wallston, B.S. and Wallston, K.A. (1984) Social psychological models of health behaviour: an examination and integration, in A. Baum, S.E. Taylor and J.E. Singer (eds) *Handbook of Psychology and Health* vol. 4. Hillsdale, NJ: Lawrence Erlbaum.

Walters, J. and Gardner, H. (1986) The crystallizing experience: discovering an intellectual gift, in R.J. Sternberg and J.E. Davidson (eds) *Conceptions of Giftedness*. New York: Cambridge University Press.

Wanous, J.P. (1978) Realistic job preview: can a procedure to reduce turnover also influence the relationship between abilities and performance? *Personnel Psychology* 31: 251.

Wanous, J.P., Poland, T.D., Premack, S.L. and Davis, K.S. (1992) The effects of met expectations on newcomer attitudes and behaviours: a review and meta-analysis. *Journal of Applied Psychology* 77: 288–97.

Warr, P.B. (1987) *Work Unemployment and Mental Health*. Oxford: Oxford University Press.

Warr, P., Banks, M. and Ullah, P. (1985) The experience of unemployment among black and white urban teenagers. *British Journal of Psychology* 76: 75–87.

Warren, R.M. and Warren, R.P. (1970) Auditory illusions and confusions. *Scientific American* 223: 30–6.

Warren, S., Warren, K. and Cockerill, R. (1991) Emotional stress and coping in multiple sclerosis exacerbations. *Journal of Psychosomatic Research* 35: 37–47.

Warrington, E.K. and McCarthy, R. (1983) Category specific access dysphasia. *Brain* 106: 859–78.

Warrington, E.K. and McCarthy, R. (1987) Categories of knowledge: further fractionation and an attempted integration. *Brain* 110: 1273–96.

Warrington, E.K. and Shallice, T. (1984) Category-specific semantic impairments. *Brain* 107: 829–54.

Wason, P.C. (1960) On the failure to eliminate hypotheses in a conceptual task. *Quarterly Journal of Experimental Psychology* 12: 129–40.

Wason, P.C. (1968) Reasoning about a rule. *Quarterly Journal of Experimental Psychology* 20: 273–81.

Wason, P.C. and Shapiro, D. (1971) Natural and contrived experience in reasoning problems. *Quarterly Journal of Experimental Psychology* 23: 63–71.

Wasserman, E.A. (1990a) Attribution of causality to common and distinctive elements of compound stimuli. *Psychological Science* 1: 298–302.

Wasserman, E.A. (1990b) Detecting response–outcome relations: toward an understanding of the causal texture of the environment, in G.H. Bower (ed.) *The Psychology of Learning and Motivation*, vol. 26. San Diego, CA: Academic Press.

Wasserman, E.A., DeVolder, C.L. and Coppage, D.J. (1992) Non-similarity-based conceptualization in pigeons via secondary or mediated generalization. *Psychological Science* 3: 374–9.

Waterman, A.S. (1988) Identity status theory and Erikson's theory: communalities and differences. *Developmental Review* 8: 185–208.

Watkins, M.J. (1973) When is recall spectacularly higher than recognition? *Journal of Experimental Psychology* 102: 161, 163.

Watkins, M.J., Peynircioglu, Z.F. and Brems, D.J. (1984) Pictorial rehearsal. *Memory and Cognition* 12: 553–7.

Watson, D. (1982) The actor and the observer: how are their perceptions of causality divergent? *Psychological Bulletin* 92: 682–700.

Watson, J.B. (1919) *Psychology from the Standpoint of a Behaviourist*. Philadelphia, PA: Lippincott.

Watson, J.B. (1924a) *Behaviourism*. New York: Norton.

Watson, J.B. (1924b) *Psychology from the Standpoint of a Behaviourist*, 2nd edn. Philadelphia, PA: Lippincott.

Watson, J.B. (1930) *Behaviorism*. Chicago: University of Chicago Press.

Watson, J.B. and Rayner, R. (1920) Conditioned emotional reactions. *Journal of Experimental Psychology* 3: 1–14.

Watts, F.N. (1992) Is psychology falling apart? *The Psychologist* 5: 489–94.

Wayner, M.J. (1970) Motor control functions of the lateral hypothalamus and adjunctive behaviour. *Physiology and Behaviour* 5: 1399–1425.

Weary, G. (1980) Examination of affect and egotism as mediators of bias in causal attributions. *Journal of Personality and Social Psychology* 38: 348–57.

Weber, E.H. (1834) *De pulsu resorptione auditu et tactu*. Leipzig: Koehler.

Weigel, R.H. and Newman, L.S. (1976) Increasing attitude–behavior correspondence by broadening the scope of the behavioral measure. *Journal of Personality and Social Psychology* 33: 793–802.

Weinberger, D.A. (1990) The construct validity of the repressive coping style, in J.L. Singer (ed.) *Repression and Dissociation: Implications for personality theory, psychopathology and health*. Chicago: University of Chicago Press.

Weinberger, D.A., Schwartz, G.E. and Davidson, J.R. (1979) Low-anxious, high-anxious, and repressive coping styles: psychometric patterns and behavioural and physiological responses to stress. *Journal of Abnormal Psychology* 88: 369–80.

Weinberger, D.A., Berman, K.F. and Zec, R.F. (1986) Physiologic dysfunction of dorsolateral prefrontal cortex in schizophrenia, I, Regional cerebral blood flow evidence. *Archives of General Psychiatry* 43: 114–24.

Weinberger, M., Hiner, S.L. and Tierney, W.M. (1987) In support of hassles as a measure of stress in predicting health outcomes. *Journal of Behavioral Medicine* 10: 19–32.

Weiner, B. (1985) An attributional theory of achievement motivation and emotion. *Psychological Review* 92: 548–73.

Weiner, B., Frieze, I.H., Kukla, A., Reed, L., Rest, S. and Rosenbaum, R.M. (1971) *Perceiving the Causes of Success and Failure*. Morristown, NJ: General Learning Press.

Weiner, B., Frieze, I., Kukla, A., Reed, L., Rest, S. and Rosenbaum, R.M. (1972) Perceiving the causes of success and failure, in E.E. Jones, D.E. Kanouse, H.H. Kelley, R.E. Nisbett, S. Valins and B. Weiner (eds) *Attribution: Perceiving the causes of behavior*. Morristown, NJ: General Learning Press.

Weinert, F.E. and Kluwe, R.H. (1987) *Metacognition, Motivation, and Understanding*. Hillsdale, NJ: Lawrence Erlbaum.

Weinman, J. (1994) Health psychology, in A.M. Colman (ed.) *Companion Encyclopaedia of Psychology*, vol. 2. London: Routledge.

Weiskrantz, L. (1956) Behavioral changes associated with ablation of the amygdaloid complex in monkeys. *Journal of Comparative and Physiological Psychology* 49: 381–91.

Weiskrantz, L. (1986) *Blindsight: A case study and implications*. Oxford: Clarendon Press.

Weiss, H. (1977) Subordinate imitation of supervisor behaviour: the role of modelling in organizational socialisation. *Organizational Behaviour and Human Performance* 19: 89–105.

Weiss, R. (1990) *Die 26-Mrd-Investition. Kosten und Strukturen betrieblicher Weiterbildung*. Cologne: Deutscher Instituts Verlag.

Weissman, M.M. (1987) Advances in psychiatric epidemiology: rates and risks for depression. *American Journal of Public Health* 77: 445–51.

Weist, R.M. (1972) The role of rehearsal: recopy or reconstruct? *Journal of Verbal Learning and Verbal Behavior* 11: 440–45.

Wells, A. and Matthews, G. (1994) *Attention and Emotion: A clinical perspective*. Hove: Lawrence Erlbaum.

Wells, L. and Marwell, G. (1976) *Self-esteem: Its conceptualisation and measurement*. London: Sage.

Wertheimer, M. (1923) Principles of perceptual organisation, in D.C. Beardslee and M. Wertheimer (eds) *Readings in Perception*. Princeton, NJ: Van Nostrand.

Wertsch, J.V. and Stone, C.A. (1985) The concept of internalisation in Vygotsky's account of the genesis of higher mental functions, in J.V. Wertsch (ed.) *Culture, Communication and Cognition*. Cambridge: Cambridge University Press.

Wertsch, J.V. and Tulviste, P. (1992) L.S. Vygotsky and contemporary developmental psychology. *Developmental Psychology* 28: 548–57.

West, M.A. and Nicholson, N. (1989) The outcomes of job change. *Journal of Vocational Behaviour* 34(3): 335–49.

West, M.A., Garrod, S. and Carletta, J. (1997) Dynamic self-reliance: an important concept for work, in C.L. Cooper and S.E. Jackson (eds) *Creating Tomorrow's Organizations*. Chichester: Wiley.

Wetherell, M. (1987) Social identity and group polarisation, in J. Turner, M. Hogg, P. Oakes, S. Reicher and M. Wetherell, *Rediscovering the Social Group: A self-categorisation theory*. Oxford: Blackwell.

Wetzel, C.G. and Walton, M.D. (1985) Developing biased social judgments: the false-consensus effect. *Journal of Personality and Social Psychology*, 41: 56–62.

Wexley, K.N. and Yukl, G.A. (1977) *Organizational Behaviour and Personnel Psychology*. Homewood, IL: Richard D. Irvin.

Wheatstone, C. (1838) Contributions to the physiology of vision 1: on some remarkable and hitherto unobserved phenomena of binocular vision. *Philosophical Transactions of the Royal Society of London* 128: 371–94.

Wheeler, M.A., Stuss, D.T. and Tulving, E. (1997) Toward a theory of episodic memory: the frontal lobes and autonoetic consciousness. *Psychological Bulletin* 121: 331–54.

White, P.A. (1988) Causal processing: origins and development. *Psychological Bulletin* 104: 36–52.

White, P.A. and Younger, D.P. (1988) Differences in the ascription of transient internal states to self and other. *Journal of Experimental Social Psychology* 24: 292–309.

White, R. (1959) Motivation reconsidered: the concept of competence. *Psychological Review* 66: 267–333.

Whyte, W.F. (1984) *Learning from the Field: A guide from experience*. London: Sage.

Wickens, C.D. (1984) Processing resources in attention, in R. Parasuraman and D.R. Davies (eds) *Varieties of Attention*. London: Academic Press.

Wicker, A.W. (1969) Attitude versus action: the relationship of verbal and overt behavioral responses to attitude objects. *Journal of Social Issues* 25: 41–78.

Wicker, A.W. (1971) An examination of the 'other-variables' explanations of attitude–behavior inconsistency. *Journal of Personality and Social Psychology* 19: 18–30.

Wicklund, R.A. (1974) *Freedom and Reactance*. Hillsdale, NJ: Lawrence Erlbaum.

Wicklund, R.A. (1975) Objective self-awareness, in L. Berkowitz (ed.) *Advances in Experimental Social Psychology*, vol. 8. New York: Academic Press.

Widdicombe, S. (1988) Dimensions of adolescent identity. *European Journal of Social Psychology* 18: 471–83.

Widdicombe, S. and Wooffitt, R. (1995) *The Language of Youth Subcultures: Social identity in action*. New York: Harvester Wheatsheaf.

Widiger, T.A. and Costa, P.T. jr (1994) Personality and personality disorders. *Journal of Abnormal Psychology* 103: 78–91.

Wierzbicka, A. (1994) Language of emotions, in J. Russell, J-M. Fernandez-Dols, A.S.R. Manstead and J. Wellenkamp (eds) *Everyday Concepts of Emotion*, NATO ASI series D, vol. 81. Dordrecht: Kluver.

Wiesner, W.H. and Cronshaw, S.F. (1988) A meta-analytic investigation of the impct of interview format and degree of structure on the validity of the employment interview. *Journal of Occupational and Organizational Psychology* 61: 275–90.

Wilkins, L. and Richter, C.P. (1940) A great craving for salt by a child with cortico-adrenal insufficiency. *Journal of the American Medical Association* 114: 866–8.

Wilkinson, D.A. and Carlen, P.L. (1982) Chronic organic brain syndromes associated with alcoholism: neuropsychological and other aspects, in Y. Israel, S. Jones and N.J. Cohen (eds) *Research Advances in Alcohol and Drug Problems*, vol. 6. New York: Plenum.

Wilkinson, S. (1989) The impact of feminist research: issues of legitimacy. *Philosophical Psychology* 2(3): 261–9.

Willats, J. (1977) How children learn to draw realistic pictures. *Quarterly Journal of Experimental Psychology* 29: 367–82.

Williams, G., Deci, E., Ryan, R. and Freedman, Z. (1991) Self-determination and attrition from a weight loss program. *Clinical Research* 32(2): 633–7.

Williams, G.V., Rolls, E.T., Leonard, C.M. and Stern, C. (1993) Neuronal responses in the ventral striatum of the behaving monkey. *Behavioural Brain Research* 55: 243–52.

Williams, J. (1984) Gender and intergroup behaviour: towards an integration. *British Journal of Social Psychology* 23: 311–411.

Williams, J.M.G. (1992) Autobiographical memory and emotional disorders, in S.A. Christianson (ed.) *The Handbook of Emotion and Memory: Research and theory*. Hillsdale, NJ: Lawrence Erlbaum

Williams, J.M.G., Watts, F.N., MacLeod, C. and Mathews, A. (1997) *Cognitive Psychology and Emotional Disorders*. Chichester: Wiley.

Williams, L.M. (1992) Adult memories of childhood abuse: preliminary findings from a longitudinal study. *The Advisor* 5: 19–20.

Williams, R. (1989) *The Trusting Heart*. New York: Times Books.

Williams, R.B. (1991) A relook at personality types and coronary heart disease. *Progress in Cardiology* 4: 91–7.

Wilpert, B. (1995) Organizational behavior. *Annual Review of Psychology* 46: 59–90.

Wilson, F.A.W. and Rolls, E.T. (1990) Neuronal responses related to reinforcement in the primate basal forebrain. *Brain Research* 502: 213–31.

Wimmer, H. and Perner, J. (1983) Beliefs about beliefs: representation and constraining function of wrong beliefs in young children's undestanding of deception. *Cognition* 13: 103–28.

Wing, J.K. (1978) Reasoning about Madness. Oxford: Oxford University Press.

Winnubst, J.A.M., Marcelissen, F.H.G. and Kleber, R.J. (1982) Effects of social support in the stressor-strain relationship: a Dutch sample. *Social Science and Medicine* 16: 1–17.

Winters, K.C. and Neale, J.M. (1983) Delusions and delusional thinking: a review of the literature. *Clinical Psychology Review* 3: 227–53.

Wise, R.A. (1982) Neuroleptics and operant behaviour: the anhedonia hypothesis. *Behavioral and Brain Sciences* 5: 39–87.

Wiseman, S. and Tulving, E. (1976) Encoding specificity: relations between recall superiority and recognition failure. *Journal of Experimental Psychology: Human Learning and Memory* 2: 349–61.

Wittgenstein, L. (1958) *Philosophical Investigations,* 2nd edn. Oxford: Blackwell.

Wittig, M. (1981) One is not born a woman, in S.L. Hoagland and J. Penelope (eds) *For Lesbians Only: A separatist anthology*. London: Onlywomen Press.

Woehr, D.J. and Huffcutt, A.I. (1994) Rater training for performance appraisal: a quantitative review. *Journal of Occupational and Organizational Psychology* 67(3): 189–206.

Wolffgramm, J. and Heyne, A. (1995) From controlled drug intake to loss of control: the irreversible development of drug addiction in the rat. *Behavioural Brain Research* 70: 77–94.

Wolpe, J. (1958) *Psychotherapy by Reciprocal Inhibition*. New York: Pergamon.

Womack, J.P. and Jones, D.T. (1996) *Lean Thinking: Banish waste and create wealth in your corporation*. New York: Simon and Schuster.

Womack, J.P., Jones, D.T. and Roos, D. (1990) *The Machine that Changed the World*. New York: Rawson.

Wong, D.F., Wagner, H.N., Tune, L.E. *et al.* (1986) Positron emission tomography reveals elevated D2 receptors in drug naive schizophrenics. *Science* 234: 1558–63.

Wood, N. and Cowan, N. (1995) The cocktail party phenomenon revisited: attention and memory in the classic selective listening procedure of Cherry (1953). *Journal of Experimental Psychology: General* 124: 243–62.

Wood, N., Lundgren, S., Quellette, J.A. Buscerne, S. and Blackstone, T. (1994) Minority influence: a meta-analytic review of social influence processes. *Psychological Bulletin* 115: 325–45.

Wood, R.E., Mento, A.J. and Locke, E.A. (1987) Task complexity as a moderator of goal effects: a meta-analysis. *Journal of Applied Psychology* 72: 416–25.

Woodward, J. (1958) *Management and Technology*. London: Her Majesty's Stationery Office.

Woodworth, R.S. and Schlosberg, H. (1954) *Experimental Psychology*, 2nd edn. New York: Holt, Rinehart and Winston.

Wooffitt, R. (1992) *Telling Tales of the Unexpected: The organization of factual discourse*. Hemel Hempstead: Harvester Wheatsheaf.

Woolgar, S. (1988) *Knowledge and Reflexivity*. London: Sage.

Worchel, S., Coutant-Sassic, D. and Grossman, M. (1992) A developmental approach to group dynamics: a model and illlustrative research, in S. Worchel, W. Wood and J.A. Simpson (eds) *Group Process and Group Productivity*. Newbury Park, CA: Sage.

World Health Organization (WHO) (1988) *Health Promotion for Working Populations*, technical report 765. Geneva: WHO.

World Health Organization (1992) *The ICD-10 Classification of Mental and Behavioural Disorders: Clinical descriptions and diagnostic guidelines* Edinburgh: Churchill Livingstone.

World Health Organization (1993) *Weekly Epidemiological Record* 68: 9–10.

Worobey, J. and Blajda, V.M. (1989) Temperament ratings at 2 weeks, 2 months, and 1 year: differential stability of activity and emotionality. *Developmental Psychology* 25: 257–63.

Wortman, C.B. (1975) Some determinants of perceived control. *Journal of Personality and Social Psychology* 31: 282–94.

Wright, J.C. (1962) Consistency and complexity of response sequences as a function of schedules of noncontingent reward. *Journal of Experimental Psychology* 63: 601–9.

Wright, S., Taylor, D. and Moghadden, F. (1990) Responding to membership in a disadvantaged group: from acceptance to collective protest. *Journal of Personality and Social Psychology* 58: 994–1003.

Wynn, K. (1992) Addition and subtraction by human infants. *Nature* 358: 749–50.

Wynne, L.C. and Singer, M.T. (1963) Thought disorder and family relations of schizophrenics, II, A classification of forms of thinking *Archives of General Psychiatry* 9: 199–206

Yalom, I.D. and Lieberman, M.A. (1971) A study of encounter group casualties. *Archives of General Psychiatry* 25: 16–30.

Yeni-Komshian, G.H. (1993) Speech perception, in J.B. Gleason and N.B. Ratner (eds) *Psycholinguistics*. Orlando, FL: Harcourt Brace.

Yerkes, R.M. and Dodson, J.D. (1908) The relation of strength of stimulus to rapidity of habit formation. *Journal of Comparative and Neurological Psychology* 18: 459–82.

Yin, R. (1989) *Case Study Research: Design and methods*, revised edn. Newbury Park, CA: Sage.

Yoburn, B.C. and Glusman, M. (1982) Effects of chronic D-amphetamine on the maintenance and acquisition of schedule-induced polydipsia in rats. *Physiology and Behaviour* 28: 807–18.

Young, S.M. (1992) A framework for successful adoption and performance of Japanese manufacturing practices in the United States. *Academy of Management Review* 17: 677–700.

Yzerbyt, V., Leyens, J-P. and Bellour, F. (1995) The ingroup overexclusion effect: identity concerns in decisions about group membership. *European Journal of Social Psychology* 25: 1–15.

Zahn-Waxler, C. and Radke-Yarrow, M. (1982) The development of altruism: alternative research strategies, in N. Eisenberg (ed.) *The Development of Prosocial Behavior*. New York: Academic Press.

Zahn-Wexler, C., Radke-Yarrow, M. and King, R.A. (1979) Child rearing and children's prosocial initiations toward victims of distress. *Child Development* 50: 319–30.

Zahra, S.A. and Pearce II, J.A. (1990) Research evidence on the Miles-Snow typology. *Journal of Management* 16: 751–68.

Zaitchik, D. (1990) When representations conflict with reality: the preschoolers' problem with false beliefs and 'false' photographs. *Cognition* 35: 41–68.

Zajonc, R.B. (1980) Feeling and thinking: preferences need no inferences. *American Psychologist* 34.

Zanna, M. and Cooper, J. (1974) Dissonance and the attribution process, in J. Harvey, W. Ickes and R. Kidd (eds) *New Directions in Attribution Research*, vol. 1. Hillsdale, NJ: Lawrence Erlbaum.

Zanna, M.P. and Rempel, J.K. (1988) Attitudes: A new look at an old concept, in D. Bat-tal and A.W. Kruglanski (eds) *The Social Psychology of Knowledge*. Cambridge: Cambridge University Press.

Zanna, M.P., Olson, J.M. and Fazio, R.H. (1980) Attitude–behavior consistency: an individual differences perspective. *Journal of Personality and Social Psychology* 38: 432–40.

Zapf, D., Knorz, C. and Kulla, M. (1996) On the relationship between mobbing factors, and job content, the social work environment and health outcomes. *European Journal of Work and Organizational Psychology* 5: 215–37.

Zaragoza, M.S. and McCloskey, M. (1989) Misleading postevent information and the memory impairment hypothesis: comment on Belli and reply to Tversky and Tuchin. *Journal of Experimental Psychology: General* 118: 92–9.

Zechmeister, E.B. and Nyberg, S.E. (1982) *Human Memory: An introduction to research and theory*. Monterey, CA: Brooks/Cole.

Zegoib, L.E., Arnold, S. and Forehand, R. (1975) An examination of observer effects in parent–child interactions. *Child Development* 46: 509–12.

Zeki, S. (1992) The visual image in mind and brain. *Scientific American* 267: 43–50.

Zeki, S. (1993) *A Vision of the Brain*. Oxford: Blackwell.

Zimbardo, P. (1971) The psychological power and pathology of imprisonment, cited in D. Myers (1993) *Social Psychology*, 4th edn. New York: McGraw-Hill.

Zimbardo, P. (1972) The Stanford Prison Experiment, cited in D. Myers (1993) *Social Psychology*, 4th edn. New York: McGraw-Hill.

Zubin, J., Eron, L.D. and Shumer, F. (1965) *An Experimental Approach to Projective Techniques*. New York: Wiley.

Zuckerman, M. (1978) Use of consensus information in prediction of behaviour. *Journal of Experimental Social Psychology*. 14: 163–71.

Zuckerman, M. (1979) Attribution of success and failure revisited, or the motivational bias is alive and well in attribution theory. *Journal of Personality* 47: 245–87.

Zuckerman, M. (1987) All parents are environmentalists until they have their second child. *Behavioral and Brain Sciences* 10: 42–3.

Zuckerman, M. (1989) Personality in the third dimension: a psychobiological approach. *Personality and Individual Differences*: 10: 391–418.

Zurcher, L.A. (1983) *Social Roles*. Beverly Hills, CA: Sage.

Index